W9-BXX-501

# West's Law School Advisory Board

**JESSE H. CHOPER**
Professor of Law,
University of California, Berkeley

**DAVID P. CURRIE**
Professor of Law, University of Chicago

**YALE KAMISAR**
Professor of Law, University of San Diego
Professor of Law, University of Michigan

**MARY KAY KANE**
Professor of Law, Chancellor and Dean Emeritus,
University of California,
Hastings College of the Law

**LARRY D. KRAMER**
Dean and Professor of Law, Stanford Law School

**WAYNE R. LaFAVE**
Professor of Law, University of Illinois

**JONATHAN R. MACEY**
Professor of Law, Yale Law School

**ARTHUR R. MILLER**
Professor of Law, Harvard University

**GRANT S. NELSON**
Professor of Law,
University of California, Los Angeles

**JAMES J. WHITE**
Professor of Law, University of Michigan

# FORCED MIGRATION
## LAW AND POLICY

By

### David A. Martin
*Warner-Booker Distinguished Professor*
*of International Law*
*University of Virginia*

### T. Alexander Aleinikoff
*Dean and Professor of Law*
*Georgetown University Law Center*
*Executive Vice President for Law Center Affairs*
*Georgetown University*

### Hiroshi Motomura
*Kenan Distinguished Professor of Law*
*Associate Dean for Faculty Affairs*
*University of North Carolina School of Law*

### Maryellen Fullerton
*Professor of Law*
*Brooklyn Law School*

**AMERICAN CASEBOOK SERIES®**

**THOMSON**

**WEST**

Mat #40641934

Thomson/West have created this publication to provide you with accurate and authoritative information concerning the subject matter covered. However, this publication was not necessarily prepared by persons licensed to practice law in a particular jurisdiction. Thomson/West are not engaged in rendering legal or other professional advice, and this publication is not a substitute for the advice of an attorney. If you require legal or other expert advice, you should seek the services of a competent attorney or other professional.

*American Casebook Series* and West Group are trademarks registered in the U.S. Patent and Trademark Office.

© 2007 Thomson/West
    610 Opperman Drive
    P.O. Box 64526
    St. Paul, MN 55164–0526
    1–800–328–9352

**ISBN–13:** 978–0–314–14610–6

TEXT IS PRINTED ON 10% POST
CONSUMER RECYCLED PAPER

*To Joan Fitzpatrick and Arthur Helton, whose dedicated and thoughtful work helped define the field of refugee law and whose insight and humanity we continue to miss.*

---

*To Cyndy*

*— DAM*

*To Rachel*

*— TAA*

*To Linda and Amy*

*— HM*

*To my husband, Tom Roberts, who has been a constant source of support. To my mother, Eleanor McDonnell Fullerton, who has encouraged me daily. To my children, Owen, Cullen, and Eleanor, whose lives have been uprooted by my work.*

*— MEF*

\*

# Preface

How do governments and the international community respond to forced migration? How should they? The last half-century has witnessed a sustained effort to build a legal framework, at both the international and domestic level, requiring protection for forced migrants. This stands in stark contrast to the past, when their reception in other countries was largely a matter of discretionary government decision. Nonetheless, the legal system that has evolved—particularly its best-known component, commonly called refugee law or the law of political asylum—falls far short of covering the field. Ad hoc government reactions, entailing hard policy choices anchored in the particularized situation, will continue to play an important role and must be included in any study of forced migrants. The legal framework is also far from static. The legislators, judges, administrators, diplomats, and advocates who shape and refine that law act on the basis of their own visions of policy and of the ethical or moral obligations we have toward the displaced.

In this book we describe the overall phenomenon of forced migration and examine the range of legal responses to the plight of uprooted people. We treat "forced migration" rather than simply "refugee movements" because, as Chapter One will develop in more detail, it is important to be aware of the full range of human displacements in order to assess the law's contributions and shortcomings. In addition, legal definitions or instinctive understandings of the term *refugee* themselves can distort comprehension or bias actors toward certain kinds of responses. The term is evocative and often energizing—much good has come of calls to meet the needs of refugees—but it can shrink the horizons of both analysis and solution.

Our book provides basic materials for a semester-long exploration of these issues. The materials reflect a range of different perspectives, from the anguish of the individuals who have been uprooted (most chapters begin with a first-person narrative) to the dilemmas of government officials coping with large numbers, sometimes in an unreceptive political environment sparked by worries about fraud or misuse of a humanitarian benefit. Other voices—judges, scholars, and journalists—have weighed in on forced migration, and we include many of their viewpoints.

Because so much of the law is based on widely ratified international treaties, refugee protection affords an excellent arena for comparative exploration. We have included cases from Europe, Canada, Australia, New Zealand, and Hong Kong, which sometimes take sharply different approaches from the United States and from each other. We have noted the expansion of protection in the European Union, which has established "subsidiary protection" for certain forced migrants who do not satisfy the requirements for refugee status. We have also pointed out European Union directives seeking to harmonize standards regarding asylum seekers. In addition, we have drawn attention to other sources of protection for forced migrants, such as the European Human Rights Convention and the Convention against Torture, and we make regular use of materials from the Office of the United Nations High Commissioner for Refugees (UNHCR), the chief international agency dealing with forced migrants.

The primary focus of this book, however, is on U.S. practice, procedure, and doctrine. U.S. courts frequently review applications for political asylum, called by one panel "this most sensitive of human claims in the international community." *Reyes-Arias v. INS*, 866 F.2d 500, 504 (D.C.Cir. 1989). Since that characterization was penned nearly two decades ago, the U.S. protection system has witnessed a massive growth in legal subtlety and complexity—as well as volume. Not only has the Immigration and Nationality Act been amended and burdened with additional detail, especially regarding exclusions from asylum and the related remedy called withholding of removal based on criminal behavior or untimely application, but a whole new basis for protection, the Convention Against Torture, has been added to the traditional law of political asylum. Meanwhile, the number of applications has gone up considerably, and the administrative system for dealing with them has evolved, both to cope with the added numbers and to provide more professional and better informed decisions. Roughly a fifth of the current caseload of the federal courts of appeals now consists of immigration cases—a massive increase from even five years ago—and a high percentage of those are based on asylum or related protection claims. Courts thus issue thousands of decisions in asylum cases each year, well over a hundred of them officially reported annually. In this environment the case law has become far more elaborate and fine-grained, treating in detail legal issues barely glimpsed in the 1980s. In addition, applicants increasingly base their claims on forms of threatened harm, such as domestic violence or female genital cutting, rarely invoked twenty years ago. These developments have led to frequent inter-circuit conflicts, providing much grist for debate over the law and its underlying purposes and philosophies.

Refugee protection has long constituted an important component of any basic course on U.S. immigration law. Each of us began approaching these issues, for pedagogical purposes, in exactly such a setting, and three of us (Aleinikoff, Martin, and Motomura) have been involved for years in producing an immigration casebook. *Immigration and Citizenship: Process and Policy* (Thomson/West, 5th ed. 2003). The refugee chapter grew steadily, becoming the longest chapter in the book's fifth edition. Today many users of that book have time to provide only a minimal introduction to refugee protection in the basic course, and many instructors now offer refugee law as an advanced law school course. The continued proliferation of refugee cases and elaboration of the doctrine are likely to increase that curricular momentum. The time had come for a new approach, and this book, focusing only on forced migration, is the result. It draws on the refugee chapter in the earlier volume, but we have reorganized and expanded it considerably. The book is designed for use in a three-hour law school course, and with judicious paring it can be readily used for a two-hour course or as the foundation for a seminar. We expect that it will be used in conjunction with its Statutory Supplement, *Immigration and Nationality Laws of the United States: Selected Statutes, Regulations and Forms* (Thomson/West), updated every year or two. That volume also contains the text of the key treaties considered in this volume. And we hope that this casebook might also prove useful to practitioners and policy makers.

The three immigration casebook authors have welcomed the addition of another author to our ranks. Maryellen Fullerton brought to the task a considerable range of experience doing comparative study of refugee issues in Europe (including stints as a Fulbright Scholar and a German Marshall Fund Fellow), plus a fresh and insightful eye to the task of turning the old chapter into a full-fledged casebook. We are pleased that she will remain part of the team for the next edition of the immigration casebook as well.

**Acknowledgments**. Our work on this book has benefited greatly from interactions with faculty colleagues, immigration lawyers, government officials, and UNHCR officers over the last 20-plus years. We could not begin to recall and capture here a full statement of our indebtedness, but we hope that the many people who have enriched our understanding will recognize some measure of their contribution here and know of our warm appreciation. We thank Carol Lehman in particular for reading and commenting on early drafts of several chapters. Research, cite-checking, and manuscript preparation and review were provided by Katy Duryea, Dhiraj Joseph, Thomas Wintner, and Sue DeMasters at Virginia, Soraya Kelly, Sunil Varghese, and Frank Walsh at Georgetown, Heather Crews at North Carolina, and Joshua Kleiman, Brian Barbour, Joel Borenstein, Susan Cameron, Allie Cheatham, Edward DeBarbieri, Janora Hawkins, Adam Ketcher, Lauren Kosseff, Alida Lasker, Noah Rosen, Jessica Segall, Caitlin Shannon, Zona Sharfman, Benjamin Stockman, and Eric Welsh at Brooklyn. We are deeply grateful for their contributions. We also acknowledge with gratitude the research support provided by the University of Virginia School of Law, the Georgetown University Law Center, the University of North Carolina School of Law, and Brooklyn Law School. Responsibility for any errors rests with the authors alone. We welcome suggestions and corrections from any of the book's users.

DAVID MARTIN
ALEX ALEINIKOFF
HIROSHI MOTOMURA
MARYELLEN FULLERTON

January 2007

*

# Technical Matters

## Editing Style

In editing cases and other materials reprinted here, we have marked textual deletions with triple asterisks, but we have often omitted simple citations to cases or other authorities without any printed indication. Similarly, we have deleted footnotes from reprinted materials without signaling the omission. Where we chose to retain a footnote, however, we have maintained the original numbering. Our own footnotes appearing in the midst of reprinted materials are marked with alphabetical superscripts; they also end with the notation "—eds." When we drop footnotes to text that we wrote ourselves, we have used the ordinary numerical designations.

## INA Citations

How to cite the sections of the Immigration and Nationality Act (INA) has posed an ongoing problem for teachers and writers in this field. Most court decisions refer to INA provisions by means of the numbers employed in Title 8 of the U.S. Code, where the Act is codified. This is understandable, even though the system used to translate Act numbers into U.S. Code numbers strikes us as eccentric and unpredictable. But specialists in the field almost religiously employ the INA section numbers and are not always familiar with references to the U.S. Code enumeration. Moreover, the administrative framework for regulations and certain other manuals and instructions is closely linked to the numbering scheme of the original Act. For example, the regulations of the Department of Homeland Security implementing the asylum provision, § 208 of the INA, appear in Part 208 of 8 C.F.R., while the equivalent asylum-related regulations of the Executive Office for Immigration Review (in the Department of Justice) appear in Part 1208.

For these reasons, we have decided to follow the practice used in our related casebook, *Immigration and Citizenship: Process and Policy.* We use the section numbers of the Act consistently throughout this book, to the exclusion of the U.S. Code numbers. This means that we have excised references to the Act using the U.S. Code numbering system from all cases and materials, and substituted direct INA section references, without expressly indicating where such substitutions have occurred. Readers who must know the corresponding U.S. Code number will find a conversion chart in the opening pages of our Statutory Supplement, *Immi-*

*gration and Nationality Laws of the United States: Selected Statutes, Regulations, and Forms.*

## Citations and Abbreviations

Most citations in the book conform generally to *A Uniform System of Citation,* customarily used by law journals, but without giving full names of authors. For a few items that are cited frequently, however, we have abbreviated even further. Abbreviations that appear frequently, either in our material or in cases, are also set forth below.

**1996 Act**      Illegal Immigration Reform and Immigrant Responsibility Act of 1996, Pub.L. 104–208, Div.C., 110 Stat. 3009–546. Also sometimes referred to as IIRIRA.

**AG**      Attorney General, the Cabinet officer who heads the Department of Justice.

**BIA**      Board of Immigration Appeals, a component of the Executive Office for Immigration Review.

**CBP**      Bureau of Customs and Border Protection, Department of Homeland Security. Created in 2003, this bureau houses border inspection functions and the Border Patrol.

**DHS**      Department of Homeland Security. Created by a 2003 reorganization spurred by the September 11 terrorist attacks, this department inherited most of the functions formerly carried out by the Immigration and Naturalization Service. Those functions are distributed among three DHS bureaus: CBP, ICE, and USCIS.

**EOIR**      Executive Office for Immigration Review. This unit of the Department of Justice houses both the Board of Immigration Appeals and the corps of immigration judges.

**FY**      Fiscal year.

**ICE**      Bureau of Immigration and Customs Enforcement, Department of Homeland Security. Created in 2003, this bureau houses interior enforcement functions transferred from the former Immigration and Naturalization Service, including investigations, detention and removal, and the trial attorneys who represent the government in immigration court.

**IIRIRA**      Illegal Immigration Reform and Immigrant Responsibility Act of 1996, Pub.L. 104–208, Div.C., 110 Stat. 3009–546. We will ordinarily refer to it as the 1996 Act, but some cases and other authorities use this abbreviation.

**IJ**   Immigration judge. The corps of immigration judges is a component of the Executive Office for Immigration Review.

**INA**   The Immigration and Nationality Act, passed in 1952 as Pub.L. 82–414, 66 Stat. 163, as a comprehensive codification replacing earlier immigration and nationality laws, and frequently amended since then. The Act itself is codified, according to an idiosyncratic numbering scheme, in Title 8 of the United States Code; a conversion chart, showing corresponding section numbers, appears in our statutory supplement. In this book we cite by INA section number, not U.S.C. section number, to the current amended statute.

**INS**   Immigration and Naturalization Service. Until 2003, as a component of the Department of Justice, INS was the lead federal agency on immigration policy and operations. In 2003, INS was abolished and its functions were transferred to three separate units of the new Department of Homeland Security (*see* CBP, ICE, USCIS).

**Interp.Rel.**   Interpreter Releases. A leading reporting service on administrative, legislative and judicial developments in the immigration field, published weekly by Thomson/West.

**IOM**   The Intergovernmental Organization for Migration (based in Geneva, Switzerland).

**NGO**   Nongovernmental organization.

**OPE**   Overseas processing entity. A nongovernmental or intergovernmental organization under contract with the Department of State to interview persons who may be eligible for U.S. refugee resettlement and to prepare the case file for a screening interview by a DHS officer.

**ORR**   Office of Refugee Resettlement, Department of Health and Human Services.

**PD**   Presidential Determination. The annual document that sets forth the level of refugee admissions for the coming year.

**PRM**   Bureau of Population, Refugees and Migration, Department of State.

**TPS**   Temporary protected status.

**UNHCR**   United Nations High Commissioner for Refugees.

**USCIS**   Bureau of Citizenship and Immigration Services, Department of Homeland Security. Created in 2003, this bureau houses the principal services and adjudications functions inherited from the Immigration and Naturalization Service, including asylum officers and the refugee corps. Sometimes also referred to as CIS.

**Volag**          Voluntary agency (the term often applied to the nongovernmental organizations that assist in refugee processing and resettlement).

# Acknowledgements

The authors wish to express their thanks to copyright holders and authors for permission to reprint excerpts from the following materials:

Aleinikoff, T. Alexander, From "Refugee Law" to the "Law of Coerced Migration," 9 American University International Law Review 25 (2003-2004). Reprinted by permission.

Aleinikoff, T. Alexander, Social Group, in Refugee Protection in International Law: UNHCR's Global Consultations on International Protection (E. Feller, V. Turk, F. Nicholson, eds., 2003). Copyright © 2003 UNHCR. Reprinted by permission of UNHCR.

Aleinikoff, T. Alexander, The Meaning of Persecution in United States Asylum Law, 3 International Journal of Refugee Law 5 (1991). Reprinted by permission.

Bernstein, Nina, Chased From Island by Volcano and From U.S. by Homeland Security, The New York Times, March 2, 2005. Copyright © 2005 by The New York Times Co. Reprinted by permission.

Bernstein, Nina, New York's Immigration Courts Lurch Under a Growing Burden, The New York Times, Oct. 8, 2006. Copyright © 2006 by The New York Times Co. Reprinted by permission.

Chen, Gregory, Unseen, Unheard, Unaided: Urban Refugees in Dar Es Salaam, Tanzania, Refugee Reports, Oct. 2004. Reprinted by permission.

Cohen, Roberta, The Guiding Principles on Internal Displacement: An Innovation in International Standard Setting, Global Governance (2004). Reprinted by permission of the publisher.

Doctors Without Borders/Médecins Sans Frontières (MSF), Who is a Refugee, http://www.refugeecamp.org/learnmore/whoisarefugee/intuma.htm. Reprinted by permission.

Doornbos, Nienke, On Being Heard in Asylum Cases: Evidentiary Assessment Through Asylum Interviews, in Proof, Evidentiary Assessment and Credibility in Asylum Procedures (2005). Copyright © 2005 by Martinus Nijhoff Publishers. Reprinted by permission of the publisher.

Fallows, James, No Hard Feelings?, The Atlantic Monthly, Dec. 1988. Reprinted by permission of the author.

Fitzpatrick, Joan & Bonoan, Rafael, Cessation of Refugee Protection, in Refugee Protection in International Law: UNHCR's Global Consultations on International Protection (E. Feller, V. Turk, F. Nicholson, eds., 2003). Copyright © 2003 UNHCR. Reprinted by permission of UNHCR.

Fullerton, Maryellen, A Comparative Look at Refugee Status Based on Persecution due to Membership in a Particular Social Group, 26 Cornell International Law Journal 505 (1993). Reprinted by permission.

Fullerton, Maryellen, The International and National Protection of Refugees, Guide to International Human Rights Practice (2004). Reprinted by permission of the publisher.

Goodwin-Gill, Guy, UNHCR and Internal Displacement: Stepping Into a Legal and Political Minefield, World Refugee Survey 2000. Reprinted by permission of the U.S. Committee for Refugees & Immigrants.

Haines, Rodger, Gender-Related Persecution, in Refugee Protection in International Law: UNHCR's Global Consultations on International Protection (E. Feller, V. Turk, F. Nicholson, eds., 2003). Copyright © 2003 UNHCR. Reprinted by permission of UNHCR.

Hathaway, James C., Forward: The Casual Nexus in International Refugee Law, 23 Michigan Journal of International Law 207 (2002). Reprinted by permission.

Hathaway, James C., The Rights of Refugees Under International Law (2005). Copyright © James C. Hathaway 2005. Reprinted with the permission of Cambridge University Press.

Hathaway, James C. & Neve, R. Alexander, Making International Refugee Law Relevant Again: A Proposal for Collectivized and Solution-Oriented Protection, 10 Harvard Human Rights Journal 115 (1997). First published in the Harvard Human Rights Journal. Reprinted by permission.

Helton, Arthur C., Political Asylum Under the 1980 Refugee Act: An Unfulfilled Promise, 17 University of Michigan Journal of Law Reform 243 (1984). Reprinted by permission of the publisher.

Human Rights First, In Liberty's Shadow: U.S. Detention of Asylum Seekers in Era of Homeland Security (2004). Reprinted by permission of Human Rights First.

Kälin, Walter, Troubled Communications: Cross-Cultural Misunderstandings in the Asylum Hearing, 20 International Migration Review 230 (1986). Reprinted by permission of the Center for Migration Studies.

Kirtley, William, The Tampa Incident: The Legality of Ruddock v. Vardalis Under International Law and the Implications of Australia's New Asylum Policy, 41 Columbia Journal of Transnational Law 251 (2002). Reprinted by permission.

Kismaric, Carole, Forced Out: The Agony of the Refugee in Our Time (1989). Copyright © 1989 Human Rights Watch. Reprinted by permission.

Legomsky, Stephen H., Secondary Refugee Movements and the Return of Asylum Seekers to Third Countries: The Meaning of Effective Protection, 15 International Journal of Refugee Law 567 (2003). Copyright © 2003. Reprinted by permission of the Oxford University Press.

Lipka, Sara, Unsettled in America, The Chronicle of Higher Education, Aug. 11, 2006. Copyright © 2006, The Chronicle of Higher Education. Reprinted with permission.

Loughna, Sean, What is Forced Migration?, Forced Migration Online, www.forcedmigration.org/whatisfm.htm, Refugee Studies Centre, University of Oxford, United Kingdom. Reprinted with permission.

Macklin, Audrey, Truth or Consequences: Credibility Determinations in the Refugee Context, International Association of Refugee Law Judges, Oct. 14-16, 1998, Ottowa, Canada. Reprinted by permission.

Malett, Shoshanna, Affirmative Asylum Claims from China Based on Coercive Family Planning, Immigration Briefings (June 2006). Copyright © 2006 by Thomson/West. Reprinted by permission of the publisher.

Martin, David A., Reforming Asylum Adjudication: On Navigating the Coast of Bohemia, 138 University of Pennsylvania Law Review 1247 (1990). Reprinted by permission.

Martin, David A., The Refugee Concept: On Definitions, Politics, and the Careful Use of a Scarce Resource, Refugee Policy: Canada and the United States (H. Adelman ed. 1981). Reprinted by permission from the Centre for Refugee Studies, York University and the Center for Migration Studies of New York, Inc.

Martin, David A., The United States Refugee Admissions Program: Reforms for a New Era of Refugee Resettlement (Washington, DC: Migration Policy Institute), 2005. Reprinted with permission from David Martin. The Migration Policy Institute (MPI) is an independent, nonpartisan, nonprofit think tank in Washington, DC, dedicated to the study of the movement of people worldwide.

Martin, Susan, Schoenholtz, Andrew & Meyers, Deborah, Temporary Protection: Towards a New Regional and Domestic Framework, 12 Georgetown Immigration Law Journal 543 (1998). Reprinted by permission.

Mathew, Penelope, Australian Refugee Protection in the Wake of the Tampa, 96 American Journal of International Law 661 (July 2002). Reproduced with permission from © The American Society of International Law.

Ndege, Yvonne, Investigation: Harrowing Tale I Learnt to Tell as a Bogus 'Refugee', The Independent (London), Jan. 13, 2000. Copyright © 2000 by The Independent. Reprinted by permission.

Nelson, Jonathan R., Shaking the Pillars: An Asylum Applicant Shakes Loose Some Unusual Relief, 83 Interpreter Releases 1 (2006). Reproduced with permission from the author.

Noll, Gregor, Asylum Claims and the Translation of Culture into Politics, 41 Texas International Law Journal 491 (2006). Reprinted by permission.

Noll, Gregor, Introduction: Re-Mapping Evidentiary Assessment in Asylum Procedures, in Proof, Evidentiary Assessment and Credibility in Asylum Procedures (2005). Copyright © 2005 by Martinus Nijhoff Publishers. Reprinted by permission of the publisher.

Pierre, Robert E. & Farhi, Paul, "Refugee": A Word of Trouble, The Washington Post, Sept. 7, 2005. Reprinted by permission.

Refugees, Rebels, and the Quest for Justice, Lawyers Committee for Human Rights (now Human Rights First) (2002). Reprinted by permission of Human Rights First.

Schuck, Peter H., Refugee Burden-Sharing: A Modest Proposal, 22 Yale Journal of International Law 243 (1997). Reprinted by permission.

Shacknove, Andrew, Who is a Refugee?, 95 Ethics 274 (1985). Copyright © 1985 by University of Chicago Press. Reprinted by permission.

Steinberg, Don, His Living Nightmare, The Philadelphia Inquirer, Aug. 4, 2006. Used with permission of The Philadelphia Inquirer Copyright © 2006. All rights reserved.

U.S. Committee for Refugees & Immigrants, Statement of William Majak Deng, Sudan, World Refugee Survey 2001. Reprinted by permission of the U.S. Committee for Refugees & Immigrants.

Walzer, Michael, Spheres of Justice: A Defense of Pluralism and Equality (1983). Copyright © 1983 by Basic Books, Inc. Reprinted by permission of Basic Books, a member of Perseus Books Group.

Weis, Paul, Recent Developments in the Law of Territorial Jurisdiction, 1 Human Rights Journal 378 (1968). Copyright © A. Pedone. Reprinted by permission.

Wines, Michael, Several Squatters Die As Zimbabwe Police Destroy Camp, The New York Times, July 1, 2005. Copyright © 2005 by The New York Times Co. Reprinted by permission.

Zolberg, Aristide R., Suhrke, Astri & Aguayo, Sergio, Escape From Violence: Conflict and the Refugee Crisis in the Developing World (1989). Copyright © 1992 by Oxford University Press, Inc. Reprinted by permission.

# Summary of Contents

# Table of Contents

# Table of Cases

The principal cases are in bold type. Cases cited or discussed in the text are in roman type. References are to pages. Cases cited in principal cases and within other quoted materials are not included.

*

# Table of Statutes, Rules, and Regulations

# Table of Authorities

### Books, Articles, and Government Reports

## Treaties and Conventions

\*

# FORCED MIGRATION

## LAW AND POLICY

\*

# Chapter One

# FORCED MIGRATION: CONCEPT, HISTORY, AND INSTITUTIONS

*I stand here * * * as a voice of all those who have been displaced from their homeland for a variety of reasons.*

*No one leaves their home willingly or gladly. When people leave en masse the place of their birth, the place where they live, it means there is something very deeply wrong with the circumstances in that country. We should never take lightly these flights of refugees fleeing across borders. They are a sign, they are a symptom, they are proof that something is very wrong somewhere on the international scene. When the moment comes to leave your home, it is a painful moment.*

*My parents had a choice to stay behind and risk the deportations that they already witnessed and that, indeed, were to follow in Latvia after the war, year after year, until 1949. They had to choose whether to risk being put into cattle cars after having awakened in the middle of the night and shipped off to Siberia, or to just walk out of their homes with what they could carry in their two hands. They walked off into the unknown, but with a hope of freedom possibly awaiting them, with a hope of saving their lives, and with a choice at least that was theirs to make, little as it was at the time. It can be a costly choice.*

*Three weeks and three days after my family left the shores of Latvia, my little sister died. We buried her by the roadside, we were never able to return or put a flower on her grave. And I like to think that I stand here today as a survivor who speaks for all those millions across the world today who do not have a voice, who cannot be heard, but who are also human beings, who also suffer, who also have their hopes, their dreams and their aspirations. Most of all, they dream of a normal life.*

*I remember as a child throughout the hunger, the fear, the cold, the unknown, each day wondering where we would lay our head to rest the next evening. I had to think of that line I had*

1

*heard in church about the birds having their nests and the foxes their dens and burrows, but where is a child of man to lay down his or her head. It is a painful condition not to know where you are going to lay your head, to look at the lights shining in distant windows, to think of people living their normal lives, sleeping in their own beds, eating at their own table, living under their own roofs. And later when you come to refugee camps—and some people spend decades and much of their lives in refugee camps—you are living outside of space and of time, you have no roots, you have no past, you don't know whether you have a future. You have no rights, you have no voice, you have nowhere to participate in, you are not a citizen, you have no papers, sometimes you haven't even got your name, and you have to pinch yourself to reassure yourself that yes, I am alive. I am me, I am a human being, I am a person. Do I count in this world? I don't know, I'll wait until tomorrow. \* \* \**

*It is up to the governments sitting here, represented by you, ladies and gentlemen holding high office in your countries. Their fate lies in your hands. \* \* \* They are out there waiting on your decisions, on your actions, on your creativity, on your ability to find a way of extending that helpful hand which can make the difference between life and death, between having a future and having none. \* \* \**

*I thank here all those who throughout the decades of my life have extended a helpful hand to their fellow man, near or far, with large help or small. Big interventions and projects, small gifts from very ordinary people, very plain people, used clothes from their homes and from their backs, thank you to all of you. I have worn those worn clothes. I have survived because somebody sent a parcel when we were starving. Thank you to all of those who have helped in the past and who are helping today \* \* \*.*

— Vaira Vike–Freiberga,
President of Latvia[1]

This is a book about forced migration and the law's response to it. Both domestic and international law have developed over the past 60 years in ways that reflect an effort to learn from the searing experience of persecution during World War II and its aftermath, as mentioned in President Vike–Freiberga's remarks. A major step toward better protection of the displaced was taken in the adoption of the most important single legal instrument in the field, the 1951 Convention relating to the Status of Refugees, whose 50th anniversary afforded the occasion for her speech. Other international instruments and, quite significantly, a network of domestic laws, regulations, and practices have also woven a somewhat wider safety net. They constitute a major humanitarian

---

**1.** Address to the Ministerial Meeting of States Parties to the 1951 Convention Re-  lating to the Status of Refugees, Geneva, December 12, 2001.

achievement. But the continued existence of significant ground not covered by precise or wholly effective legal obligations is revealed by Vike–Freiberga's exhortations to the assembled world leaders. She urged them to shape their ongoing policies—which would include diplomacy, economic sanctions, military deployments, humanitarian assistance, development aid, and other resource commitments—so as to relieve the privations of so many of today's refugees and to restore for them a life of dignity and contribution, either in the asylum state or back at home. Law, including the burgeoning field of international human rights, has staked out important protective ground since World War II and its revelation of the Nazi regime's atrocities, but legal innovation has not sufficed, either to prevent forced migration or to assure international protection and assistance when it occurs.

This book will explore the legal terrain, but against the wider backdrop of policy. We will devote considerable time to the 1951 Convention and its 1967 Protocol, with their central obligation of *nonrefoulement* (or non-return to the country where persecution is threatened). Convention relating to the Status of Refugees, *done* July 28, 1951, 189 U.N.T.S. 137 (adhered to by 143 States as of March 2006); Protocol relating to the Status of Refugees, *done* January 31, 1967, 19 U.S.T. 6223, T.I.A.S. No. 6577, 606 U.N.T.S. 267. We will also consider other international treaties, particularly the Convention Against Torture (CAT), as well as the development of customary international law in this field. Convention Against Torture and Other Cruel, Inhuman or Degrading Treatment or Punishment (CAT), *done* 10 December 1984, 1468 U.N.T.S. 85. We will focus in detail on the domestic law of the United States, which implements these treaties and sometimes expands on them through statute and regulation, although we will also take a comparative approach at various points. Because most other countries have likewise built their protection networks on the foundation of the Convention and Protocol, as well as the CAT, the variations one can find in their practices and case law are both illuminating and thought-provoking. We will also see how the deceptively simple formulations of some of the key provisions, especially the definition of *refugee*, have given rise to a rich, complex, and much-disputed body of doctrine, as administrators and judges have tried to turn general concepts into manageable dividing lines.

For the law in this field needs dividing lines. Governments and the publics to which they respond insist on a general framework whereby international migration is controlled and normally subject to deliberate decisions by the polity as to who should be admitted and on what terms.[2]

---

**2.** We will also pay more limited attention to forced migration that does not cross international borders. In that setting some of the concerns are similar, as local residents may resist and resent the arrival of outsiders, even if they are nominally fellow citizens. But often the legal concerns are different, having more to do with reinforcing the national government's obligation to fulfill its normal protection responsibilities (the domain of human rights law), or authorizing or guaranteeing access to the persons in need by international players (humanitarian organizations, UN agencies, peacekeeping troops, other outside intervention).

Given this deeply rooted commitment, refugee treaties and legislation can be seen as marking out privileges available to a subset of qualified migrants, owing to their particular suffering or danger—privileges that trump the normal law of migration control. In the modern world, the ability to relocate—or to legalize a relocation that has already taken place—can be an extremely valuable commodity. The law we will consider is based on determinations about when those normal controls or default rules should be relaxed. Such determinations in turn are based on important and contested value judgments—about the exact type and degree of past suffering or future threat that justifies a departure from the default rules, the extent to which generous protection provisions are subject to manipulation or fraud, whether some such misuse is a reasonable price to pay to assure protection for those who really merit it, and whether the chronic needs of the globe's forced migrants should stimulate a rethinking of the default rules themselves.

In addition to spurring the development of refugee protections, revulsion at the Nazi regime's horrors also impelled the development, halting at first and gradually more robust, of international human rights law. This book will not cover that rich subject in any detail, but it is useful to keep it in mind as part of the background, for one might regard it as providing a more direct way of responding to the existence of persecution or severe deprivation. Modern human rights law departed from classical international law's notion that a sovereign nation's treatment of its own citizens was none of the world's business. Sovereignty was no longer seen as a license for rulers to mistreat or exploit. International human rights law developed standards meant to protect individuals against the gravest threats to personal security—arbitrary imprisonment, summary execution, torture—and also to safeguard a wider array of civil and political rights, as well as economic, social and cultural rights. The very existence of forced migration reflects a failure of the home state to live up to those primary obligations. The law governing forced migration therefore deals in the second best—making up for those primary shortfalls in meeting the rights of individuals in their home state. As it happens, however, at least when refugees flee to relatively stable countries with highly developed legal systems, the secondary body of doctrine often seems to claim center stage in the legal arena. This is to a large degree understandable. In confronting badly ruled or failing states, lawyers find few footholds in international or domestic institutions to leverage their legal skills toward punishing violators or securing direct solutions. But in the more stable regimes to which a troubled country's citizens migrate, a single lawyer can gain tangible results by skillfully presenting an asylum claim on behalf of her clients. Nonetheless, government officials in receiving countries, feeling themselves constrained to say no to many refugee claims, may resent being charged with violating human rights through undue strictness, when they know that the real authors of any underlying human rights problems—the rulers of the home country—escape effective legal scrutiny.

The Nazi concentration camp, Auschwitz, Poland, 1988. (Photo: © David A. Martin)

Several background issues or themes thread through these materials, and the reader or instructor using them can choose which to highlight at various points in the exploration. What types of threats should result in protection? How should those threats be measured and what sorts of procedures or systems are best equipped to judge them? When is migration truly "forced"? Is the application of that label simply shorthand for the speaker's conclusion that a particular kind of migration justifies or demands overriding the normal border controls? If so, what deeper understandings underlie that conclusion? What reasons impel governments or host populations to resist migration, and which among them, if any, are legitimate or reasonable? To what extent or under what circumstances should they yield in the presence of needy migrants? What other global responses to forced migration, besides international relocation, are available and when and how should they be deployed? What inherent institutional limitations should be taken into account in shaping the law of protection? Are there circumstances, for example, when individualized assessment of risks in the country of origin is either too imprecise, too expensive, or too slow? What effect should institutional or political limitations have on the use of legal mechanisms to respond to asylum seekers? When, in other words, does *law* provide the optimal framework for response, and when do more flexible or less categorical *policy* initiatives instead maximize beneficial outcomes—or at least minimize harms?

## SECTION A. WHAT IS FORCED MIGRATION?

Much of this book will focus on a subset of forced migrants, those who cross an international border for reasons bound up in some way with political developments. Nonetheless, it is useful to begin by sketching a far broader map of forced migration, so as to gain some perspective on the magnitude of the phenomenon and to locate the legal questions on which we focus within a broader frame.

Over the centuries millions have been forced to leave their homes. Natural disasters have uprooted whole communities. War, conscription, political upheaval have all impelled migration. In dire economic conditions people move in order to survive. Further, economic development intended to strengthen a larger community or a particular sector of society has sometimes both directly and indirectly displaced many others. Smaller scale economic changes—loss of a job, the closure of a plant—have also caused uprooting. Feuds, personal as well as political, have triggered flight. Criminal activity has targeted others and caused them to flee to safety.

Some impelled to leave their homes have moved to the next neighborhood or the next town or province; others have moved to another continent. Many factors have an impact on their destination: funds, health, geography, language, immigration laws or legal restrictions on internal movement, border patrols, the location of ethnic communities or friends or families, political systems, luck. Often multiple legal systems have played a role in a single person's path: the national law of the country that allowed (or forbade) her to depart, the laws of any other countries she entered, the international law affecting the rights of people involuntarily moved from the places they reside. Different legal issues are raised depending on the reasons for the flight and the path the migrant follows.

## 1. WHY ARE THEY FORCED TO MIGRATE?

People leave their homes for many different reasons, and scholars have written about multiple aspects of the journeys that migrants have made. Recent scholarship has begun to examine the phenomenon of forced migration itself. The following reading outlines three different forced migration scenarios and describes multiple categories of forced migrants.

## WHAT IS FORCED MIGRATION?

Forced Migration Online, <http://www.forcedmigration.org/whatisfm.htm> (last visited Sept. 18, 2006).

TYPES OF FORCED MIGRATION

### 1. *Conflict-induced displacement*

People who are forced to flee their homes for one or more of the following reasons and where the state authorities are unable or unwilling to protect them: armed conflict including civil war; generalized violence; and persecution on the grounds of nationality, race, religion, political opinion or social group.

Refugees from Kosovo wait at Blace to cross into Macedonia,
March 1999. (Photo: © Roger Le Moyne, UNHCR).

A large proportion of these displaced people will flee across international borders in search of refuge. Some of them may seek asylum under
international law, whereas others may prefer to remain anonymous,
perhaps fearing that they may not be granted asylum and will be
returned to the country from whence they fled. Since the end of the Cold
War, there has been an escalation in the number of armed conflicts
around the world. Many of these more recent conflicts have been
internal conflicts based on national, ethnic or religious separatist struggles. There has been a large increase in the number of refugees during
this period as displacement has increasingly become a strategic tactic
often used by all sides in the conflict. Since the end of the Cold War
there has also been an even more dramatic increase in the number of
internally displaced persons (IDPs), who currently far outnumber the
world's refugee population. At the end of 2001, both types combined
comprised some 36 million people worldwide.

## 2. Development-induced displacement

These are people who are compelled to move as a result of policies and projects implemented to supposedly enhance "development". Examples of this include large-scale infrastructure projects such as dams, roads, ports, airports; urban clearance initiatives; mining and deforestation; and the introduction of conservation parks/reserves and biosphere projects.

Affected people usually remain within the borders of their home country. Although some are resettled, evidence clearly shows that very few of them are adequately compensated. While there are guidelines on restoration for affected populations produced by some major donors to these types of projects, such as the World Bank, there continues to be inadequate access to compensation. This tends to be the responsibility of host governments, and interventions from outside are often deemed inappropriate.

This is undoubtedly the largest global cause of displacement, although it often takes place with little recognition, support or assistance from outside the affected population. It disproportionately affects indigenous and ethnic minorities, and the urban or rural poor. It has been estimated that during the 1990s some 90 to 100 million people around the world were displaced as a result of infrastructural development projects. It has also been reported that on average 10 million people a year are displaced by dam projects alone.

## 3. Disaster-induced displacement

This category includes people displaced as a result of natural disasters (floods, volcanoes, landslides, earthquakes), environmental change (deforestation, desertification, land degradation, global warming) and human-made disasters (industrial accidents, radioactivity). Clearly, there is a good deal of overlap between these different types of disaster-induced displacement. For example, the impact of floods and landslides can be greatly exacerbated by deforestation and agricultural activities.

Estimating trends and global figures on people displaced by disaster is even more disputed and problematic than for the other two categories. A 1995 report claimed that there were at least 25 million environmental refugees. Several international organizations provide assistance to those affected by disasters, including the International Federation of the Red Cross and Red Crescent Societies, and the World Food Programme. * * *

TYPES OF FORCED MIGRANTS

There are also various terms which have been adopted to describe groups affected by forced migration. The meaning of some of these terms is not always self-evident: they are sometimes misleading and are not necessarily mutually exclusive. Given below are brief descriptions of the main terms used by those describing and working with forced migrants.

## Refugees

The term 'refugee' has a long history of usage to describe certain groups in broad and non-specific terms. However, there is a legal definition of a refugee, which is enshrined in the 1951 United Nations Convention Relating to the Status of Refugees. Article 1 of the Convention defines a refugee as a person residing outside his or her country of nationality, who is unable or unwilling to return because of a 'well-founded fear of persecution on account of race, religion, nationality, membership in a political social group, or political opinion'. Some 150 of the world's 200 or so states have undertaken to protect refugees and not return them to a country where they may be persecuted, by signing the 1951 Refugee Convention and/or its 1967 Protocol.

Those recognized as refugees are better off than other forced migrants, as they have a clear legal status and are afforded the protection of the United Nations High Commissioner for Refugees (UNHCR). UNHCR has a budget of over 800 million [US dollars] and a presence in some 100 countries. The vast majority of refugees are in the world's poorest countries in Asia and Africa. * * *

## Asylum seekers

Asylum seekers are people who have moved across international borders in search of protection under the 1951 Refugee Convention, but whose claim for refugee status has not yet been determined. Annual asylum claims in Western Europe, Australia, Canada and the USA combined rose from some 90,400 in 1983 to 323,050 in 1988 and then peaked at 828,645 in 1992. Applications fell sharply by the mid–1990s but began to steadily rise again towards the end of the decade.

As the numbers of asylum seekers have risen, there has been increasing skepticism raised by politicians and the media, particularly in western states, about the credibility of the claims of many asylum seekers. They have been labeled 'economic refugees' and 'bogus asylum seekers'. Asylum migration is clearly a result of mixed motivations. Most asylum seekers do not come from the world's poorest states, however many do come from failed or failing states enduring civil war and with high degrees of human rights abuses and, not surprisingly, significant levels of poverty. However, the number of people who are seeking asylum in western states comprises a small fraction of the total number displaced around the world.

## Internally displaced persons

The most widely used definition of internally displaced persons (IDPs) is one presented in a 1992 report of the secretary-general of the UN, which identifies them as 'persons who have been forced to flee their homes suddenly or unexpectedly in large numbers, as a result of armed conflict, internal strife, systematic violations of human rights or natural or man-made disasters, and who are within the territory of their own country.'

Sometimes referred to as 'internal refugees', these people are in similar need of protection and assistance as refugees but do not have the same legal and institutional support as those who have managed to cross an international border. There is no specifically-mandated body to provide assistance to IDPs, as there is with refugees. Although they are guaranteed certain basic rights under international humanitarian law (the Geneva Conventions), ensuring these rights are secured is often the responsibility of authorities which were responsible for their displacement in the first place, or ones that are unable or unwilling to do so. * * *

### Development displacees

People who are compelled to move as a result of policies and projects implemented to supposedly enhance "development'. These include large-scale infrastructure projects * * * [and the displaced generally] remain within the borders of their country. People displaced in this way are sometimes also referred to as 'oustees', 'involuntarily displaced' or 'involuntarily resettled'. * * *

### Environmental and disaster displacees

Sometimes referred to 'environmental refugees' or 'disaster refugees', in fact most of those displaced by environmental factors or disasters do not leave the borders of their homeland. * * *

### Smuggled people

Smuggled migrants are moved illegally for profit. They are partners, however unequal, in a commercial transaction. This is not to say that the practice [lacks] substantial exploitation and danger. People who think they are being smuggled may run the risk of actually being trafficked (see below). And even if they are not, their personal safety and well-being on their journey and after arrival are not necessarily the smugglers' top priority. Smuggled migrants may include those who have been forcibly displaced as well as those who have left their homeland in search of better economic and social opportunities. The motivations are often mixed. As the borders to favoured destination countries have become increasingly strengthened to resist the entry of asylum seekers, migrants of all kinds have increasingly drawn upon the services of smugglers.

### Trafficked people

These are people who are moved by deception or coercion for the purposes of exploitation. The profit in trafficking people comes not from their movement, but from the sale of their sexual services or labour in the country of destination. The trafficked person may be physically prevented from leaving, or be bound by debt or threat of violence to themselves or their family in their country of origin. Like smuggling, by its very clandestine nature, figures on the number of people being trafficked are extremely difficult to obtain.

--------

## Notes and Questions

1. Although the definitions in the excerpt above can be useful, it is important to realize that others may use different terminology or suggest other conceptual frameworks. For example, some scholarship refers to those displaced by development projects as forced resettlers and other writings use terms such as development-induced displaced persons (DIDPs), project affected persons (PAPs), or oustees. Vigorous debates have arisen about the vocabulary and its tendency to depersonalize and objectify the human beings involved. These debates raise complex philosophical, political, legal, and social issues. A sample of scholarly commentary can be found in Malkki, *Speechless Emissaries: Refugees, Humanitarianism, and Dehistoricization*, 11 Cultural Anthropology 377 (1996); Lumsden, *Broken Lives? Reflections on the Anthropology of Exile & Repair*, 18 Refuge 30 (1999); and Barbara Harrell–Bond, The Experience of Refugees As Recipients of Aid, Perspectives on the Experience of Forced Migration 136–68 (1999). (Because smuggled and trafficked persons are at the periphery of the category of forced migrants, we will give these groups little attention in the remainder of this book.)

2. The excerpt above from *Forced Migration Online* provides a variety of statistics or estimates on various populations. Updated statistics on some of those categories appear in the next section of this book.

3. As we introduce new concepts and ideas, you may wish to apply them to familiar situations within our own society. Clearly, the Atlantic slave trade, which brought more than 10 million captured and enslaved Africans to the Americas, constituted forced migration. The mass removals of native Americans from their ancestral lands was another indisputable forced migration. What about other instances? Were those African–Americans who left the segregated south in the early and mid–20th century for better jobs and social conditions in the cities of the north and west forced migrants? What about those displaced by Hurricane Katrina? By natural disasters on a less extensive scale? What about a person who loses a job in Michigan, cannot find new work locally, and therefore moves to California? What if there are other local jobs he could have had, but the pay was seen as too low? Do residents of battered women's shelters qualify as forced migrants? What about individuals relocated through witness protection programs? All of these individuals left their homes under circumstances that reflect less than a fully voluntary choice; many may have been in peril. Are they all forced migrants? If not, how can we tell what this term means? What legal consequences are seen to follow? Should legal consequences provide the basis for working back to affix the label?

4. Often, as the *Forced Migration Online* reading suggests, the term *refugee* is seen as a favorable appellation that helps stimulate outside response in the form of material assistance or permission to relocate. But consider the following:

Tyrone McKnight sleeps in a shelter [in Baton Rouge, Louisiana]. His meals come from the kindness of strangers. It's safe to call him homeless, because his house is under water.

What he doesn't want you to call him, or the thousands of other New Orleans residents plucked from floodwater [of Hurricane Katrina], is this word: refugees.

"The image I have in my mind is people in a Third World country, the babies in Africa that have all the flies and are starving to death," he says, while sitting outside Baton Rouge's convention center, where 5,000 displaced residents are being housed. "That's not me. I'm a law-abiding citizen who's working every day and paying taxes."

Which label to use when describing evacuees might seem trivial when thousands may be dead, thousands are missing, and a major city and its environs have been ravaged.

Katrina evacuees from New Orleans find temporary shelter at the Houston Astrodome, September 2005 (Photo: © FEMA/Andrea Booher).

But at shelters in Louisiana and Texas, workers and volunteers have heard loud and clear from those living there that the government, the media and everyone else should call them something other than refugees.

"We ain't refugees. I'm a citizen," insists Annette Ellis, also sheltered at the convention center with her two children. * * *

So why is the term such a dirty word to some?

"It makes us feel like we're less than everyone else," says Paulette Jolla, a New Orleans resident at the Bethany shelter who spoke to [President] Bush.

The debate pains Lavinia Limon, president and chief executive of the U.S. Committee for Refugees and Immigrants. The millions of refugees who have resettled here from countries including Cuba, Cambodia, Somalia, Kosovo and Ethiopia are courageous and daring people who stood for something, she says. They settle in communities, set up businesses and become citizens of the United States.

"Being a refugee should not be a pejorative term," Limon says.

Still, she says, the people displaced by Katrina can rightly protest the label. "Legally, refugees are people suffering from persecution based on race, ethnicity and religion under U.S. and international law," she says. "These are displaced Americans. They are not people without a country."

Pierre & Farhi, *'Refugee': A Word of Trouble*, Wash. Post, Sept. 7, 2005. What concepts of migration, assistance, and rights underlie this terminological dispute?

## 2.  HOW MANY FORCED MIGRANTS ARE THERE?

People are forced—or pressed, impelled, coerced, induced—to leave their homes for many reasons or combinations of reasons: oppressive governments, political upheaval, civil war, conscription, natural disaster, economic conditions, development projects. No one knows how many have been caused to move against their will. Some estimate that over 100 million have been displaced by dams and other massive structural changes that often accompany development, that more than 25 million have been forced from their homes by environmental disasters, and that close to 40 million have been compelled by conflict to leave their communities. *See* Roberta Cohen, *Lecture: Exodus Within Borders: The Global Crisis of Internal Displacement*, UNHCR, Sofia, Bulgaria (June 4, 2001), *available at* <http://www.unhcr.bg/lecture/roberta_cohen.htm>; Ethan Goffman, *Environmental Refugees: How Many, How Bad?*, <http://www.csa.com/discoveryguides/refugee/review2.php> (June 2006); What Is Forced Migration, *supra*.

Although millions are forced into migrating, with millions of individual destinies, the data on world-wide migration are far from comprehensive. Statistical measures of forced migration are also affected by disputes over exactly which persons count as refugees, IDPs, or other specific categories, and by political agendas that can cause various

**Figure 1.1**

### Refugees, Asylum Seekers, and Others of Concern to UNHCR—End 2005 (Total: 20.8 million)

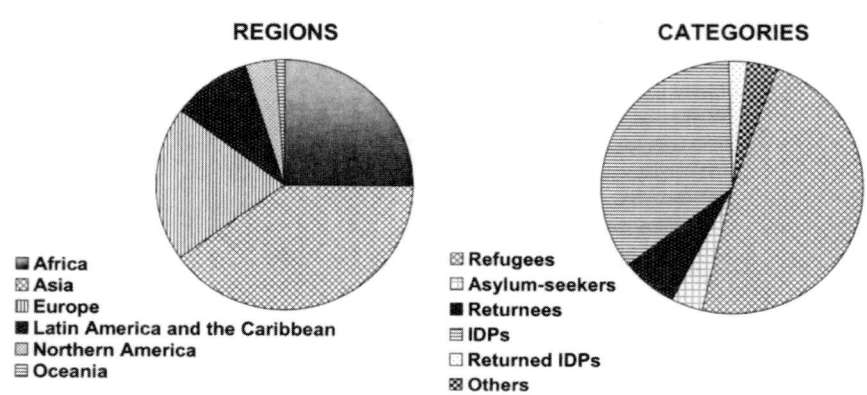

REGIONS

- Africa
- Asia
- Europe
- Latin America and the Caribbean
- Northern America
- Oceania

CATEGORIES

- Refugees
- Asylum-seekers
- Returnees
- IDPs
- Returned IDPs
- Others

Source: UNHCR, The Refugee Story in Statistics, <http://www.unhcr.org/cgi-bin/texis/vtx/statistics>

players either to exaggerate or downplay the numbers. The most consistent figures, albeit with their own acknowledged limitations, are provided by the Office of the UN High Commissioner for Refugees, which counts not only recognized refugees but also that subset of internally displaced persons and other migrants who are "of concern" to the office. The totals include each year several hundred thousands who recently returned to their home country or (if an IDP) to their home area but whose welfare remains within the Office's responsibilities. The chart in Figure 1.1, prepared by UNHCR, along with the following tables, provides information on that portion of the world's forced migrants. These data do not include people forced to leave their homes by natural disaster or development projects. Thus, UNHCR's total of 20.8 million for 2005 does not include the more than one million displaced by the December 2004 tsunami in Indonesia, Sri Lanka, Thailand, Somalia, and other countries, nor the one million people forced to relocate by the Three Gorges Dam project in China.

## Table 1.1

## UNHCR Statistics on the Displaced, 2000–2005

(numbers in millions)

| Year (end) | Refugees | Asylum Seekers | IDPs | Total* |
|---|---|---|---|---|
| 2000 | 12.1 | 0.9 | 6.0 | 21.8 |
| 2001 | 12.0 | 0.9 | 5.0 | 19.8 |
| 2002 | 10.6 | 0.9 | 4.6 | 20.7 |
| 2003 | 9.7 | 0.9 | 4.2 | 17.0 |
| 2004 | 9.6 | 0.8 | 5.4 | 19.5 |
| 2005 | 8.4 | 0.8 | 6.6 | 20.8 |

* Total includes returned refugees and IDPs, and various others still of concern to UNHCR, not separately enumerated in earlier columns.

Source: UNHCR Statistical Yearbooks 2001–2004, UNHCR Global Refugee Trends 2005.

The refugee population (as UNHCR defines that term for its statistics, essentially in accordance with the 1951 Convention) declined considerably during the 1990s. It had been as high as 17.8 million in 1992. UNHCR Statistical Yearbook 2001, Annex A3. Asylum applications in industrialized countries (principally Europe, Australia, New Zealand, Canada, and the United States—a large subset of the asylum seeker total in Table 1.1) also have declined considerably from the numbers discussed in the essay from *Forced Migration Online* above. Table 1.2 shows the statistics on new claims filed in those countries in recent years, as reported by UNHCR.

## Table 1.2

## Asylum Seekers in Industrialized Countries, 2001–2005

| 2001 | 655,150 |
|---|---|
| 2002 | 628,660 |
| 2003 | 508,060 |
| 2004 | 394,540 |
| 2005 | 336,060 |

Source: UNHCR, Asylum Levels and Trends in Industrialized Countries, 2005, Table 1.

## 3.   WHERE DO FORCED MIGRANTS GO?

Figure 1.1 shows that the forced migrants of concern to the United Nations High Commissioner for Refugees remain largely in Asia and Africa. Most do not leave their region of origin. Indeed, if one includes the large and poorly tracked contingent forced to move by development and disaster, it is probably true that most do not leave their country of origin. It is only a small fraction who leave both their homeland and their native region to seek or obtain assistance and protection in other parts of the world, though that is the group that often attracts the most attention from politicians and journalists.

Because most forced migrants are not monitored or counted, comprehensive information about the accommodations they locate and their sources of food and income is lacking, particularly because it appears that most forced migrants do not rely on government or international agencies to provide food and shelter. Nonetheless, the readings below describe the primary situations in which forced migrants find themselves.

### a. *Informal Arrangements and Integration*

Vietnamese refugees in Thailand. (Photo © IDRC/Robert Charbonneau)

A large proportion of forced migrants move from their homes to other locations in their own countries or in neighboring lands and become informally integrated into the society and economy there. These individuals are largely invisible in statistical records. They rely on their own resources, and on the assistance of family, neighbors, and friends. The story below reports on one project that supports informal entrepreneurial efforts by refugees.

## GREGORY CHEN, UNSEEN, UNHEARD, UNAIDED: URBAN REFUGEES IN DAR ES SALAAM, TANZANIA
Refugee Reports, October 2004, pp. 13–14.

The words ''Tailoring Mart'' invite visitors into the small storefront shop in Dar es Salaam (Dar) where Thierry Noel Mageni and other refugees have launched an initiative to support urban refugees' efforts to earn a living while also serving to local Tanzanians. A woman in a blue outfit steps inside the shop and asks to see the dress she had ordered. By supplying her own fabric and design, she saved 15,000 Tanzanian shillings, about $14. The smile on her face signals a happy customer.

\* \* \*

As of August 2004, the mart had trained 15 women; ten work in regular shifts of four. They rent the space from a Tanzanian man for $30 a month. "He knows we are foreigners, but not that we are refugees," said Mr. Mageni, revealing his concern that their refugee status is a liability in the city.

As the founder * * * Mr. Mageni is constantly on the move organizing meetings within the community. Originally from the Democratic Republic of Congo, he fled from conflict in the eastern Kivu region to Uganda in 1996. UNHCR granted him refugee status, but two years later he was transferred to a refugee camp in Tanzania where he found life unbearable: "Our freedom was denied. We were kept like cattle, like cows on a farm. We were denied the right to work or to show what we were capable of." After eight months, Mr. Mageni left for Dar. "Here we must work and live clandestinely but we are earning something which allows us to survive."

* * *

Many urban refugees are much worse off and survive only by begging or on charity. One man, a four-year resident of Dar, said he received about $30 from his church when he first arrived. He tried teaching French to Tanzanians and foreign visitors but his illegal urban status made it hard for him to collect his fees: 10 of 14 students, he said, owed him for up to six months of lessons but were unwilling to pay—as an illegal resident of Dar, he could not complain to the police. Now he survives on money from church or acquaintances. "Our lives are hopeless and meaningless," he says, "I need to contribute to my community but the laws are so strict that businesses won't hire me and my own teaching effort has failed."

Of ten refugees gathered in the tailoring shop, most agree that women have more success in establishing these small business efforts. They offer different explanations: one thinks women are targeted less than men by the immigration authorities and thus can engage in street vending more easily; another says that more women have learned Kiswahili through frequent local contact in the markets; yet another says he prefers to look for activities that generate greater income rather than street vending which [has] limited potential. Of course, more potentially lucrative activities or business ventures pose more risk.

---

First asylum countries, those neighboring states to which international forced migrants first flee, often shelter strikingly large numbers of noncitizens who have been uprooted from their homes. For example, for a period in the late 1970s, Thailand received up to 50,000 Vietnamese per month, in addition to people fleeing Cambodia and Laos. During the mid–1990s hundreds of thousands of Rwandans fled into the Democratic Republic of Congo. Iran and Pakistan each sheltered more than one million refugees from Afghanistan as late as 2004. UNHCR, 2004 Global

Refugee Trends (2005). Frequently, first asylum countries have few resources to offer forced migrants, who try to eke out a living in the local economy.

Villages and agricultural lands often attract forced migrants, as displaced individuals may move in with relatives or fellow clan members (who could be citizens of a different country, depending on how national boundaries were drawn) and as displaced families sometimes find unoccupied land on which to live. For millennia, however, urban centers have been a major magnet for both voluntary and involuntary migrants. For example, researchers report that more than 200 million people have migrated from rural to urban areas in China during the past two decades. Shuguang Zhang & Chengri Ding, Greater China's Transformation Changes: Urbanization and Government Policy (Lincoln Institute of Land Policy 2002). On the other side of the globe, Colombia has 2.5 million internally displaced people (currently the globe's highest total), most of whom have sought refuge in urban centers from the decades-long violent conflict in the countryside. Bogota alone is home to 400,000 displaced persons. US Committee for Refugees, World Refugee Survey 2003, at 244.

These relocations, even when they involve only a country's own nationals, often trigger reaction, which may engender further hardship. A recent news article captures the scene of many left homeless by the destruction of squatter camps in Zimbabwe in 2005.

## MICHAEL WINES, SEVERAL SQUATTERS DIE AS ZIMBABWE POLICE DESTROY CAMP

The New York Times, July 1, 2005.

The Zimbabwe police finished demolishing a squatter camp outside Harare that once had at least 10,000 residents. * * * After three days of work, the police destroyed and burned the remains of the Porta Farm settlement. * * * Mr. Mugabe's government established the camp more than a decade ago for homeless peasants who had migrated to the city seeking work.

* * * [T]he mass evictions * * * have left as many as half a million people homeless* * * * [S]tate-controlled radio quoted [Mr. Mugabe] that the demolitions were "a long-cherished desire in order to clean the cities" of illegal settlers and traders that the government has said have bred crime and filth.

Human rights groups call the evictions an effort to rout the urban poor who supported Zimbabwe's democratic opposition in parliamentary elections in March, and to disperse people who might be tempted to lead protests against the government as Zimbabwe's economic collapse reaches new depths. * * *

Vast numbers of those made homeless by the demolition have been put up in tent camps outside Harare. But far more, ousted by evictions around the nation, have been forced to move to desperate rural areas or to sleep in the open.

---

### b.  Camps in the Developing World

Bengali refugees at Salt Lake Camp near Calcutta, India, 1971. (Photo: © UNHCR)

Although the majority of forced migrants remain in the regions where they originate and devise their own strategies for obtaining shelter and food, many also live in camps. The first-person account below conveys the chaos of flight and the dangers of camp life.

> *I left Liberia when the rebels came at breakfast and killed my uncle. They shot him in the mouth. I was living with my aunt and my cousins. We all ran away. There were others: mothers, babies, little children, pregnant woman. We gathered up some clothes, some food and money, and we walked for two days until we came to the Sierra Leone border. We kept meeting rebels, who frightened us with their guns and talk, but they let us pass. At the border, though, they took everything.*
>
> *Once across the border, we came to a town where we stopped. The people there were very kind. They said that they liked Liberians because they were so friendly. They fed us and we stayed jammed together in thatched mud huts. After a month, we decided to go on to the refugee camp—actually five small camps. Once there, they gave us some heavy plastic for tents. We looked for big sticks to make a frame and erected a two-bedroom tent for my aunt, my six cousins and myself.*
>
> *We stayed in the camp for two years. It was hard. We cooked on fires that we made outside our tents. There was a law that we couldn't go into the bush, so we sold some of our food ration to buy firewood. We slept on the ground—on a tarp or wooden slats—because there were no beds. People were always getting sick. Water was a problem. There was only one hand pump for*

*the camp and that was turned on only for a short period each day. People got impatient and started drinking water from other places and they got cholera. The clinics were crowded and sometimes you had to wait a whole day before you were seen to. Also there was a terrible bathroom system. The latrine was crowded and dirty, and you always had to wait.*

*When I was in the camp, I went to school. The refugees set up a school system. They also arranged for concerts and for soccer games. They established a church. We were busy. I had lots of friends. Sometimes we went swimming.*

*Eventually, war started in Sierra Leone. We didn't know what to do. We didn't know anybody there. Everyone went to the UN office and started to cry because there was nowhere to run anymore. * * * They took us to the town of Boardwaterside where there was a school campus with three buildings, but again it was too crowded and my cousins and I slept on the sand.*

*After a few months, we decided to try to go home again. Once there, however, the fighting started again. This time we ran to Guinea. It was more difficult because Guinea is French-speaking and we didn't know the language. Again, it took us about two days of walking to reach there. A rebel leader that we met helped my cousins and I to cross the border.*

*There were no refugee camps in Guinea, but one of my cousins met a friend in the village who gave us a room in her house. The Red Cross gave us food and money. * * ***

*On Christmas Day 1997, we were kicked out of the house where we were staying because the people suspected us of being rebels. However, around that time, my aunt began to send us money and we were able to rent our own place. * * ***

— Intuma, refugee from
Liberia[3]

As this account emphasizes, circumstances may change and people may move into and out of camps multiple times. Some pass through a camp or a series of camps before striking out on their own. For others the sequence is reversed. And for others the receiving state may quickly usher them into a camp and require them to remain, perhaps for years, until some other durable solution is achieved.

Millions of forced migrants live in camps in the developing world. The International Committee of the Red Cross, the Office of the UN High Commissioner for Refugees (UNHCR), and a host of international NGOs (nongovernmental organizations) are often deeply involved in helping to manage or service particular camps, either during an emer-

**3.** RefugeeCamp.org, Who is a Refugee?, <www.refugeecamp.org/learnmore/ whoisarefugee> (last visited Sept. 18, 2006).

gency phase in the early stages of the outflow or for longer-term residency. Some of the organizations specialize in certain tasks, such as water or sanitation systems, health services and clinics, tracing of relatives, or education. The level of tolerance or support from the host government generally determines the quality of life in a camp, though that can also be importantly influenced by the level of resources and skilled personnel provided by the international community, as well as the involvement and initiative of the displaced population itself. Camps can range from squalid and frightening to reasonably secure—with schools, clinics, and some measure of gainful economic activity for the residents. Some camps have only plastic sheeting or tents to provide shelter, while the housing in other camps ranges from one-room structures made of sticks, mud, and dung to multi-story concrete buildings.

Camps also vary in permanence, and some camps have existed for more than 50 years. More than two million Palestinians live in camps; many have been there for multiple decades. Hundreds of thousands of Africans and Asians have spent generations in camps: Somalis in Kenya, Sudanese in Ethiopia, Kenya, and Yemen, Eritreans in Sudan, Afghans (still) in Iran and Pakistan, Myanmarese (Burmese) in Thailand, Malaysia, and Bangladesh. Recently, refugee advocates have focused attention on the "warehousing" of refugees—practices that keep large populations in stifling or minimally adequate camps or separate settlements for many years. *See, e.g.*, U.S. Committee for Refugees, World Refugee Survey 2004: Warehousing Issue. In these situations many basic human rights are not observed. For example, access to education, employment, and medical care is often limited. Infringement on individual liberty and privacy is frequently severe. Psychological difficulties are exacerbated. Table 1.3, derived from a chart prepared by the US Committee for Refugees, indicates that over seven million people have lived in refugee camps for ten years or more.

Camps also vary in terms of the legal status ascribed to the inhabitants. Cross-border migrants recognized as refugees generally fare better than those the host state treats only as illegal migrants or, at best, as asylum seekers, but this is not always the case. Another significant distinction is that between refugees and internally displaced persons (IDPs), because the latter, at least formally, are citizens of the country where they are housed. In some circumstances citizenship status could be advantageous, but at other times, when the governing regime cares little about the particular group of forced migrants, such status may simply complicate the access of the international community as it tries to provide assistance or protection. If a needy group consists only of IDPs, that fact can also prevent the use of funds or institutions designated specifically for refugees. Such rigid distinctions have assumed a reduced significance in recent years, however, as the world community has come to see advantages in selectively expanding to IDPs the use of institutions, organizations, and skills developed primarily in connection with

## Table 1.3

## Refugees in Long-term Camps

| Years Since Situation Began | Population | Host Country | Number |
|---|---|---|---|
| 57 | Palestinians | Gaza, West Bank, & Lebanon | 1,942,600 |
| 38 | Palestinians | Egypt, Jordan, & Saudi Arabia | 455,200 |
| 37 | Eritreans | Sudan & Ethiopia | 207,600 |
| 32 | Filipinos | Malaysia | 66,800 |
| 30 | Angolans | Congo–Kinshasa, Zambia, et al. | 206,300 |
| 30 | Sahrawi | Algeria | 90,000 |
| 26 | Afghans | Iran & Pakistan | 2,027,000 |
| 26 | Iraqis | Iran | 54,000 |
| 26 | Palestinians | Kuwait | 13,500 |
| 22 | Sudanese | Uganda, Kenya, Ethiopia, et al. | 409,300 |
| 22 | Sri Lankans | India | 73,700 |
| 21 | Myanmarese | Thailand | 150,000 |
| 17 | Somalis | Kenya, Yemen, South Africa, et al. | 279,500 |
| 17 | Myanmarese Chin | India | 49,600 |
| 16 | Liberians | Sierra Leone, Guinea, Ghana, et al. | 198,500 |
| 16 | Tibetans | Nepal | 23,000 |
| 16 | Myanmarese Chin | Malaysia | 15,000 |
| 15 | Ugandans | Congo–Kinshasa | 19,000 |
| 14 | Myanmarese Rohingya | Bangladesh | 150,000 |
| 14 | Bhutanese Lhotsampa | Nepal | 107,300 |
| 14 | Afghans | India & Russian Federation | 129,400 |
| 14 | Georgians | Russian Federation | 14,000 |
| 12 | Burundians | Tanzania & Congo–Kinshasa | 412,700 |
| 12 | Myanmarese Rohingya | Malaysia | 12,000 |
| 9 | Rwandans | Congo–Kinshasa | 42,400 |
| 9 | Congolese (Kinshasa) | Tanzania, Congo–Brazzaville, et al. | 305,000 |
| 9 | Myanmarese | Thailand | 320,900 |
| 7 | Congolese (Kinshasa) | Burundi & Zambia | 92,900 |
| TOTAL | 7,893,400 (7,132,200 for 10 years or more) | | |

Source: U.S. Committee for Refugees, Warehoused Refugee Populations (as of December 31, 2005), World Refugee Survey 2006, at 7.

traditional cross-border refugee crises. UNHCR, in particular, has been given greater latitude since 1990 in helping IDPs, though this new role has triggered controversy, because some believe it dilutes the office's historic mission and risks entangling it in intractable political struggles. See Chapter Eleven, Section C, below.

As the map shown in Figure 1.2 indicates, camps are often established on both sides of a political boundary. Thus, it is easy to imagine that different members of the same family fleeing the same crisis might end up as refugees or as internally displaced persons, depending on their flight path and the camp that allowed them to stay.

## Figure 1.2

### Refugee and IDP Camps Housing Forced Migrants from the Darfur Region of the Sudan

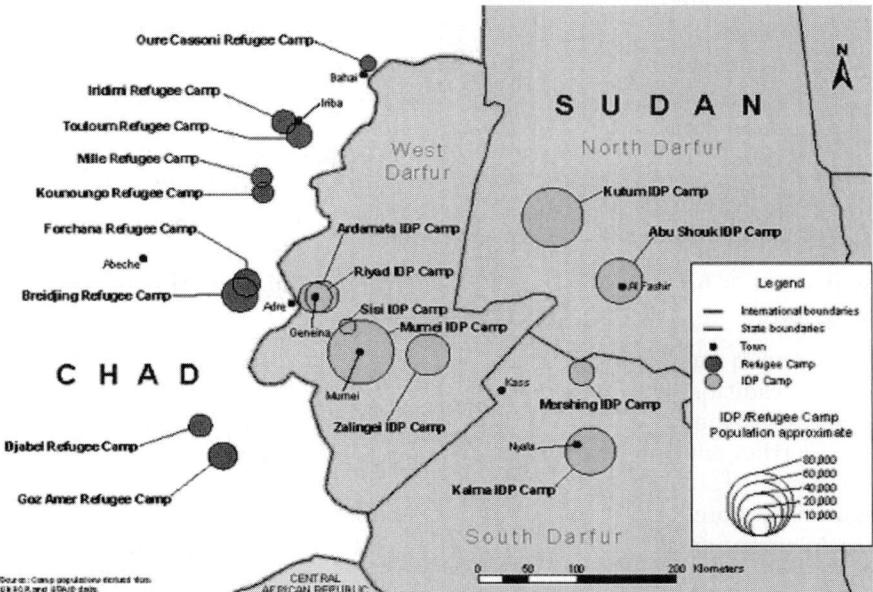

Source: US AID Sudan, <http://www.usaid.gov/locations/sub-saharan_africa/sudan/images/satellite/campsmap.gif> (last visited Sept. 18, 2006).

### c. *Resettlement in Stable States*

Camps for forced migrants, almost by definition, are meant to be temporary—even though they may in fact wind up enduring for decades. In contrast, it is common in refugee discourse to speak of three "durable solutions" to refugee situations: voluntary repatriation, resettlement, and local integration. We have already spoken of the last, local integration, which can take place either informally or with more organized international support and assistance—although the term implies a degree of acceptance and permanence in the haven state that amounts to far more than simply being able to survive outside a camp.

Resettlement is a classic durable solution, receiving considerable attention from journalists and scholars, even though as a practical matter it has been made available only to a small fraction of forced migrants. *See* Table 1.4. Resettlement normally entails a move to a distant and reasonably stable, prosperous nation after a period spent in a first-asylum camp or settlement near the source country, though some forced migrants are screened and selected for resettlement while still within the country of origin. The United States has traditionally conceived of its own role in solving refugee crises primarily as a supplier of resettlement opportunities, particularly during the years of the Cold War. It offered resettlement to persons who managed to escape the

Soviet bloc (and less commonly, other tyrannical regimes), generally after an interview in a transit center in Austria or elsewhere near the European dividing line. The U.S. State Department later adapted this model to respond to persons in refugee camps in Southeast Asia in the years following the Vietnam war. That exodus produced the high point of global resettlement, as over 1.5 million Vietnamese, Cambodians, and Laotians were allowed to move to distant countries from 1975 to 2000. As compared with spontaneous cross-border movements by asylum seekers (or indeed with most internal displacement), the process of resettlement clearly allows receiving states to be selective and to hold their response to a numerical level they choose in advance. The United States has regularly insisted on a detailed screening interview conducted by its own officers before a person or family is included in the resettlement program.

Canada and Australia, which, like the United States, consider themselves traditional countries of immigration, have also had fairly expansive resettlement programs. But few other countries participate regularly in resettlement. Table 1.4 shows UNHCR statistics for resettlement in 2004, and Table 1.5 has comprehensive totals for the past decade. It should be noted, however, that some of the states that offer only a few resettlement spaces make up for the limited quantity by offering to take hard-to-resettle cases, such as refugees with serious and expensive medical conditions. Some of the resettlement states also delegate the task of selection to UNHCR, according to agreed selection criteria and numerical targets.

## Table 1.4

## Countries of Resettlement for Refugees, 2004

| Country | Total |
|---------|-------|
| United States | 52,868 |
| Australia | 15,967 |
| Canada | 10,521 |
| Sweden | 1,801 |
| Norway | 842 |
| New Zealand | 825 |
| Finland | 735 |
| Denmark | 508 |
| Netherlands | 323 |
| United Kingdom | 150 |
| Ireland | 63 |
| Chile | 26 |
| Mexico | 11 |

Source: UNHCR, Refugees by Numbers (2005 edition).

## Table 1.5

## Resettlement Arrivals in Industrialized Countries, 1995–2004

| Country | Total |
|---|---|
| United States | 654,495 |
| Canada | 109,265 |
| Australia | 106,267 |
| Norway | 15,229 |
| Sweden | 12,816 |
| New Zealand | 7,541 |
| Denmark | 6,567 |
| Finland | 6,319 |
| Netherlands | 2,767 |
| Ireland | 1,264 |
| Japan | 1,004 |
| United Kingdom | 240 |
| Iceland | 194 |
| Total | 923,968 |

Source: 2004 UNHCR Statistical Yearbook, Table B14.

### d. *Return to the Country or Place of Origin*

The third classic durable solution is voluntary repatriation, and in fact conditions often do eventually change so that the displaced can return home. The war ends or the oppressive regime is ousted. The international community, particularly through the UNHCR, is often involved in the return, and may provide assistance and monitoring for several months or years to help assure successful reestablishment.

The past 15 years have witnessed a sizeable reduction in the number of refugees as counted by UNHCR, from 17.8 million in 1992 to 8.4 million in 2005, owing primarily to significant voluntary repatriation. Table 1.6 shows UNHCR data for repatriations by region over the past 10 years, a total of 13 million refugees repatriated. Table 1.7 provides greater detail on repatriations that took place in 2004. Comparable data on IDPs who have found it possible to go home are not available, but UNHCR now does maintain a statistic on IDPs who had been assisted by UNHCR (a subset of the full IDP population) and who returned to their place of origin within the stated year. UNHCR reported 241,000 such IDP returnees for 2001; 1,146,000 for 2002; 233,000 for 2003; 146,000 for 2004; and 519,000 for 2005. UNHCR Statistical Yearbook, Table I.1 (for 2001–04); UNHCR, 2005 Global Refugee Trends, Table 1 (for 2005).

"Voluntary" repatriation, of course, like "forced" migration, is a question of degree. Host states can provide a number of incentives or pressures, particularly by reducing the services or liberties in camps, to help encourage a return home. And official return data often do not capture the full picture, as informal returns may occur daily, even when a significant level of danger persists.

### Table 1.6

### Voluntary Repatriation of Refugees, by Region of Origin, 1995–2004 (in thousands)

| | |
|---|---|
| Africa | 5,470.1 |
| Asia | 5,830.1 |
| Europe | 1,695.3 |
| Latin America and the Caribbean | 29.8 |
| North America | 0 |
| Various/unknown | 16.5 |
| **Total** | **13,041.8** |

Source: UNHCR, 2004 Statistical Yearbook, Table B6.

### Table 1.7

### Top Ten Voluntary Repatriation Movements in 2004, by Destination

| To (country of origin) | From (main countries of asylum) | Total |
|---|---|---|
| Afghanistan | Iran / Pakistan | 940,500 |
| Iraq | Various / Iran / Lebanon | 194,000 |
| Burundi | Tanzania / D.R. Congo | 90,300 |
| Angola | Zambia / D.R. Congo / Namibia / Congo | 90,200 |
| Liberia | Guinea / Côte d'Ivoire / Sierra Leone / Ghana / Nigeria | 56,900 |
| Sierra Leone | Liberia / Guinea | 26,300 |
| Somalia | Ethiopia / Djibouti | 18,100 |
| Rwanda | D.R. Congo / Uganda | 14,100 |
| D.R. Congo | Burundi / Central African Republic | 13,800 |
| Sri Lanka | India | 10,000 |

Source: UNHCR, Refugees by Numbers (2005 edition)

## 4. THINKING ABOUT FORCED MIGRATION AND THE LAW

Much of the academic writing has focused on those forced migrants who reach stable, wealthier countries and on the laws that have developed to protect refugees and asylum seekers. The article that follows argues that legal scholars should examine the phenomenon of forced migration in broader compass, in order to be able to understand and respond to the fundamental human rights issues at stake when people are coerced to leave their homes.

## T. ALEXANDER ALEINIKOFF, FROM "REFUGEE LAW" TO THE "LAW OF COERCED MIGRATION"

9 Am. U. J. Int'l L. & Pol'y 25–28 (1993–1994).

Increasingly, conferences, law journals, law school classes, and clinics are devoted to "refugee law," evidencing the apparent arrival of a new sub-specialty in legal scholarship and practice. Is "refugee law" the appropriate label for this field of inquiry?

\* \* \*

The international "refugee" model starts with a person outside his or her state of origin. This notion, of course, represents the traditional (and now out-dated) view that international law could offer protection only to someone beyond the territorial borders—and therefore outside the "sovereignty" of his or her home country. But it is not at all clear what distinguishes classic refugees from persons who have fled to safety within their country, a group of people usually described as the "internally displaced." Nor is the distinction clear—at least in human rights terms—between those two categories of persons and those who, unable to flee serious harm, suffer at home.

Our field of scholarly inquiry should start with the phenomena scholars wish to describe and analyze. Scholars should seek to provide theoretical justifications for such inquiry that are not simply based on the happenstance of a particular international Convention that mentions "refugees" in its title.

\* \* \*

Under [a] coerced migration model, the key idea is flight from harm. As such, it should embrace the internally displaced as well as border crossers. This model also recognizes that there are reasons for flight that merit protection beyond [persecution,] including civil wars, natural disasters, and general social disorder. It is not easy to see, for example, why a person fleeing bullets in a civil war situation is not entitled to some kind of protection and some kind of consideration in our scholarly inquiries. Thus, the coerced migration model \* \* \* goes beyond the Convention "refugee" definition, and therefore, beyond current conceptualization of the "refugee law" field.

\* \* \*

[T]he coerced migration model recognizes and directly addresses the multifaceted nature of the phenomena under investigation. It identifies loss of community as the fundamental harm. The solution, therefore, is conceptualized not simply as protection, but rather as restoration of community either through return (when conditions permit) or the creation of community elsewhere. In this way, the coerced migration approach offers support for resettlement policies not easily encompassed within the human rights model. Furthermore, a coerced migration perspective brings into focus the diverse forms of relief currently provided to involuntary migrants* * *: asylum, withholding of deportation, extended voluntary departure, deferred enforced departure, temporary protected status, parole, and safe haven. These provisions and policies exist not simply to satisfy the legal mind's craving for categories, but because the U.S. legal system appropriately recognizes the numerous causes of involuntary flight and the need for forms of relief crafted to meet the human complexity—a complexity the definition and status of "refugee" do not adequately capture.

There are advantages to refocusing scholarship on coerced migration. First, scholars currently devote an extraordinary amount of effort to exegeses of the definition of "refugee" and the "on account of" grounds. Of course, much of this scholarship remains important work to the extent it aids courts, adjudicators, and lawyers in the understanding and application of the terms one finds in our law. The cost for such narrow attention, however, is the under-investigation of other more flexible forms of relief. * * * Refugee status is a privileged category vis-a-vis other classes of coerced migrants. By focusing our attention on helping a small number of the world's involuntarily displaced obtain this potent form of relief, we miss opportunities to propose and analyze policies that might benefit millions more.

Second, the privileging of the status of refugee tends to depreciate the legitimate claims for relief of other coerced migrants, whose attempts to flee serious harm are frequently referred to as "irregular movements" or "mass flows." Everyday language reflects these differences: the term "displaced person" invokes less urgency, less of a sense of concern, than "refugee."

I propose that we level the field of analysis by understanding the phenomenon under investigation as the involuntary migration of persons from their homes and by asking what form of relief—temporary protection, resettlement, parole, safe haven—best responds to the humanitarian interests at stake. From this perspective, "refugeehood" would no longer exist as the shining status, the ultimate goal, casting shadows on other policies protecting groups designated for "illegal migrants." It would, rather, be one (very important) measure among many creative and flexible policies for accomplishing the goal that motivates most scholars in the field: the alleviation of the human misery of coerced migration.

\* \* \*

# SECTION B: THE LAW APPLICABLE TO FORCED MIGRANTS

## 1. HISTORICAL OVERVIEW

The labels applied to forced migrants have varied, as have their recognition by the prevailing legal regime and the terms used to describe any form of protection that might be given. The excerpts below describe in broad stroke the evolution of concepts, terminology, and protections from ancient times up to the early stages of the current regime.

## UNHCR, THE STATE OF THE WORLD'S REFUGEES: THE CHALLENGE OF PROTECTION

P. 33 (1993).

### THE ORIGINS OF ASYLUM

The concept of asylum has been in existence for at least 3,500 years and is found, in one form or another, in the texts and traditions of many different ancient societies. In the middle of the second millennium BC, as entities resembling modern states with clearly defined borders began to develop across the Near East, several treaties were concluded between rulers which included provisions for the protection of international fugitives. For example, a Hittite king drew up a treaty with the ruler of a different country, in which he declared "Concerning a refugee, I affirm on oath the following: when a refugee comes from your land into mine he will not be returned to you. To return a refugee from the land of the Hittites is not right." In the 14th century BC, another Hittite king, Urhi–Teshup, who had been deposed by his uncle, was given refuge by the Egyptian pharaoh, Rameses II.

In the 7th century BC, an Assyrian king, Assurbanipal, referred to a refugee from the land of Elam "who has seized my royal feet"—meaning that he had requested and been granted asylum.

In Ancient Greece, numerous internal religious sanctuaries were established. However, the idea of external asylum also existed. Herodotus cites the case of a Phrygian, Adrastus, who fled to Sardis in Lydia (now Turkey) after accidentally killing his brother. He presented himself at the palace of Croesus, who welcomed him and told him he could stay as long as he wished. Asylum also features in Ancient Greek drama: in Sophocles's tragedy *Oedipus at Colonus* the Athenian king, Theseus, gives a compassionate reception to the exiled Oedipus.

In AD 8, the Roman poet Ovid was banished by the Emperor Augustus to Tomis on the Black Sea (now Constanta in Romania), on the extreme edge of the Empire. As he records in *Tristia* (Sorrows), the Tomitans received him warmly. Although he continued to perceive them as "barbarians", Ovid was touched by their hospitality, learned their language—Getic—and remained among them until his death in AD 17.

The Old Testament Book of Numbers shows God instructing Moses to designate six cities as places of refuge, "both for the children of Israel, and for the stranger, and for the sojourner among them" (35:9–15). In the New Testament, St. Matthew's Gospel portrays the infant Christ and his family as refugees fleeing into Egypt. Christian sanctuaries were first recognized under Roman law in the 4th century AD, and their physical scope was gradually extended. In the 6th century, the Emperor Justinian—anticipating modern asylum laws—limited the privilege to people not guilty of serious crimes.

During the early years of Islam, the Prophet Mohammed and his followers were forced to take refuge from those who felt threatened by the growing power of the new faith. The Hijra, his flight from Mecca to Medina in AD 622, marks the beginning of the Islamic era according to the religious calendar. The Koran spells out the importance of the notion of asylum in Islam: "Those who have believed and have chosen exile and have fought for the Faith, and those who have granted them help and asylum, these are the true believers" (8:74).

From early times, asylum had both political and humanitarian dimensions. The ancient practice of granting internal sanctuary—often on a temporary rather than permanent basis—in holy places reflected respect for the deity and the Church, while the grant of asylum by kings, republics and free cities was a manifestation of sovereignty. As the power of the monarchy grew, the right to grant asylum increasingly became the prerogative of the state and the inviolability of internal asylum in holy places declined correspondingly. In the 16th century, for example, King Henry VIII of England abolished many religious sanctuaries and nominated seven "cities of refuge" in their stead.

The revocation of the Edict of Nantes in 1685, which forced 250,000 French Protestants (the Huguenots) to flee their country, marked the beginning of the modern tradition of asylum in Europe. It caused the Marquis of Brandenburg to issue the Edict of Potsdam allowing the settlement of Huguenots in his territory. After the French Revolution, the category of refugees fleeing political rather than religious persecution began to gain prominence. Although the first recorded use of the term "the Right of Asylum" occurred as early as 1725, asylum continued to be viewed more as a prerogative of the Sovereign than as an individual right to protection until the early years of the 20th century.

## PAUL WEIS, RECENT DEVELOPMENTS IN THE LAW OF TERRITORIAL ASYLUM
### 1 Human Rights J. 378, 378–80 (1968).

The term "right of asylum" is in current use, but it is not always clear in what sense it is employed. In traditional international law, the right of asylum is considered as the right of the State to grant asylum in the exercise of its territorial supremacy. In the context of human rights, the term has normally been used from the aspect of the individual, i.e. as the right of the individual to asylum. We find here the first reason for conflicting views: the loose use of the term "right of asylum" leads to confusion, as it depends on the outlook of the author and the context whether the term is used in the sense of the right of States to grant asylum or the right of the individual to receive and to be granted asylum.

This conflict became apparent when the Universal Declaration of Human Rights was drafted. The text of article 14, paragraph 1, of the

Declaration as drafted by the United Nations Commission on Human Rights in 1947 read "Everyone has the right to seek and to be granted asylum". This formulation was, however, not considered acceptable by a number of States on the ground that it implied an individual right to asylum. The final version of Article 14, paragraph 1, of the Declaration as adopted by the General Assembly in 1948 does not employ the words "to be granted" and reads: "Everyone has the right to seek and to enjoy in other countries asylum from persecution". This phraseology was called by Professor Lauterpacht "artificial to the point of flippancy" as it recognizes a right to seek but not a right to be granted asylum.

The second ambiguity arises from the term "asylum" itself. The Greek "asylou" means a place which may not be violated, i.e., a sanctuary. Originally a religious institution under which persons fleeing from prosecution or persecution could find shelter in sacred places considered inviolable, the term was later received into secular law and thereafter into international law. Views on the meaning of the term "asylum" as a legal concept in international law differ, but we may accept for present purposes the authoritative definition given by the Institute of International Law when it considered the question of asylum at its Bath Session in 1950, i.e. "Asylum is the protection which a State grants on its territory or in some other place under the control of certain of its organs, to a person who comes to seek it." This definition includes, of course, both territorial or internal asylum and diplomatic or extraterritorial asylum. We are concerned here only with the former.

In any effort to appraise the present position of the law relating to asylum, account must also be taken of historical developments. In earlier times, when passports, visas and rigid frontier controls were still largely unknown, the crossing of frontiers did not present serious problems to fugitives. Asylum consisted in the refusal by the State in which the fugitive found himself of a request for surrender by the State from which the fugitive had fled. The question of asylum arose—and this is the context in which it is dealt with in most of the leading textbooks on international law—mainly in connection with extradition. Up to the eighteenth century "asylum" was, in fact, granted to fugitives from justice who had committed common crimes. In the eighteenth, and more particularly in the nineteenth century, the principle that persons wanted for serious common crimes should be surrendered to other States upon request, became gradually accepted. Conversely, asylum came to be granted to an increasing degree, to political offenders. Thus, the modern law of extradition is characterized by the admissibility of the extradition of common criminals and the exclusion of extradition in the case of political offenders.

The Belgian Extradition Law of 1833 and the Franco–Swiss Treaty of 1831 were the first to embody the principle that political offenders should not be extradited. This principle has since been incorporated in the extradition laws of the majority of countries and in most extradition treaties. * * * It is, however, well known that the question of the meaning to be given to the term "political offence" has given rise to considerable difficulty due to the existence of so-called relative political offences ("délits complexes"), i.e. offences of common law committed with a political motive or for a political purpose. The practice of States and the decisions of courts as regards the interpretation of the term "political offence" varies greatly. * * *

In the twentieth century the problem of asylum, while still arising frequently in connection with extradition, has largely become one of admission. Our century has seen the mass movement of persons who have fled their country on account of oppression for political, racial, or religious reasons. It has been called "the century of the homeless man". Persons seeking asylum are not so much political offenders as victims of political oppression, particularly refugees from monolithic regimes. Recent legal history reflects this development. The law of asylum is not only concerned with the question of extradition but also with the problem of admission of refugees from persecution and their protection once they have received refuge.

* * *

## Note: Diplomatic Asylum

Weis refers to diplomatic asylum, a practice that affords certain threatened persons (usually members of a political elite endangered by a sudden change of government) shelter in a diplomatic mission, ordinarily followed by an agreed safe–conduct pass that will permit their departure to the territory of the asylum country. *See generally The Asylum Case*, 1950 I.C.J. 266. Most countries formally reject this custom, but it has found fairly wide acceptance in Latin America, perhaps because of frequent changes of government there during the twentieth century. The United States has long disavowed diplomatic asylum, *see* Department of State, Public Notice 351, 37 Fed.Reg. 3447 (1972), but U.S. policy does allow for short–term harborage in embassy facilities under some circumstances—for example, to protect persons pursued by an angry mob. *See* 2 A. Grahl–Madsen, The Status of Refugees in International Law 6 (1972) (commenting on this practice of "temporary refuge").

The stated rejection of diplomatic asylum sometimes presents difficult practical problems in implementation, once asylum–seekers (seeking haven against the host government rather than mob violence) have managed to enter diplomatic facilities. Though there is no legal requirement for sheltering them, at times the likely domestic political consequences of expulsion have resulted in lengthy stays. One celebrated case involved Cardinal Jozsef Mindszenty, a Hungarian prelate who opposed the Communist takeover of Hungary after World War II. He was jailed and subjected to a show trial in 1948, then briefly freed during the 1956 uprising. As the uprising was failing, he appeared at the U.S. chancery in Budapest and was allowed to enter. He remained for 15 years, until the Vatican negotiated acceptable terms for his departure to Rome. In the late 1970s a family of Pentecostals remained in the American embassy in Moscow for several years before arrangements were finally concluded to move them to the United States. *See generally* Nash, *Contemporary Practice of the United States Relating to*

*International Law: Diplomatic Asylum*, 75 Am.J.Int'l L. 142 (1981); Note, *Diplomatic Asylum in the United States and Latin America: A Comparative Analysis*, 13 Brooklyn J.Int'l L. 111 (1987). In recent years over 100 North Koreans have attempted to enter diplomatic facilities in China and Russia, seeking to win asylum in the country whose embassy was involved (usually South Korea's). *See* Brooke, *North Korean at U.S. Consulate in Russia Tests New Rules,* N.Y. Times, Nov. 10, 2004.

———————

In early twentieth-century Europe, the Balkan Wars led to forced migration of large populations of Greeks, Bulgarians, and Turks. The Russian Revolution at the end of World War I triggered successive waves of refugees. These displacements and expulsions were a familiar phenomenon, but government responses to forced migrants had begun to change. This, in turn, led to international efforts to assist and protect individuals forced from their homes.

## MARYELLEN FULLERTON, THE INTERNATIONAL AND NATIONAL PROTECTION OF REFUGEES
### Guide to International Human Rights Practice 246–47 (4th ed. 2004).

\* \* \*

Although \* \* \* refugees are an age-old phenomenon, societal responses to refugees during the past century have differed substantially from those in earlier times. Before the emergence of industrialized societies and the rise of the welfare state, rulers often welcomed refugees into their realm, anticipating that artisans would benefit the society they joined while others seeking refuge would increase the taxpayer rolls and enlarge the pool of those who could be conscripted for military service. There was no corresponding public duty to care for refugees from another land. Private charity might sustain refugees for a short time, but quasi-permanent government-supported refugee camps were unknown. Refugees became self-supporting fairly quickly or perished.

During the nineteenth and twentieth centuries, governments grew more wary of refugees. The growth of "nation-states" and the strengthening of national identities led to the view that refugees and other outsiders threatened a society's security and cultural cohesion by introducing disease, subversive ideas, and foreign traditions. Simultaneously, post-Enlightenment societies gradually assumed greater responsibility for the poor but did not want to see their numbers swelled by large groups of outsiders. The ironic result was that, as governmental obligations to assist the helpless and indigent became a fundamental tenet of society, states began to impose extremely restrictive conditions on those who sought to enter the national territory. This tension between generosity towards those at home and wariness of those from abroad still persists and, in many ways, characterizes the responses of developed nations to the millions of refugees in the world today.

\* \* \*

The disintegration of the Turkish, Russian, and Austro–Hungarian empires in the early twentieth century emphasized the international scope of refugee movements. Millions of refugees fled in all directions. International organizations dedicated to refugee assistance were created; with them came attempts to define legally who is a refugee. Early definitions tended to describe refugees in terms of their nationality, implicitly recognizing that political events had triggered the flight of certain groups of people.

\* \* \*

## Questions

Why did the central issues concerning forced migration change focus around the early part of the twentieth century, toward questions of admission and away from issues of forced return for persons specifically sought by the sovereign of the country of origin? What is the significance of Weis's reference to "monolithic regimes"?

## 2. THE EVOLUTION OF INTERNATIONAL INSTITUTIONS

Fullerton notes the beginnings of international efforts to provide assistance to refugees, which took shape as the international community was emerging from the turmoil of World War I. What follows is a brief sketch of the successive efforts to deal with forced migration at the international level.

### a. *League of Nations*

The League of Nations, established in 1920, soon began efforts to assist refugees. Fridtjof Nansen, a famous polar explorer and humanitarian who had initially mounted efforts to assure the repatriation of war prisoners, was appointed as the first High Commissioner for Refugees in 1921. His office assisted many groups displaced by World War I, the Russian revolution, and the demise of the Ottoman empire. Nansen's efforts focused on providing assistance to refugees, seeking resettlement opportunities for them, and issuing identity papers that came to be known as "Nansen passports." That documentary innovation proved quite useful in helping displaced people to move abroad, get settled, and seek employment. *See* UNHCR, The State of the World's Refugees: Fifty Years of Humanitarian Action 15 (2000).

During these years, a series of arrangements and treaties provided a framework for international assistance and protection for certain forced migrants. This early international regime generally defined refugees in terms of specific political crises. Thus, international protection extended only to those who belonged to certain national groups and who no longer enjoyed the protection of their national government. A sample of treaty definitions from the 1920s and 1930s indicates this approach and gives some sense of its limits.

Arrangement relating to the Issue of Identity Certificates to Russian and Armenian Refugees, signed May 12, 1926, 89 L.N.T.S. 47:

> Any person of Russian origin who does not enjoy or who no longer enjoys the protection of the Government of the Union of Soviet Socialist Republics and who has not acquired another nationality.

> Any person of Armenian origin formerly a subject of the Ottoman Empire who does not enjoy or who no longer enjoys the protection of the Government of the Turkish Republic and who has not acquired another nationality.

Arrangement Concerning the Extension to Other Categories of Refugees of Certain Measures Taken in Favour of Russian and Armenian Refugees, signed June 30, 1928, 89 L.N.T.S. 63:

> Any person of Assyrian or Assyro–Chaldaean origin, and also by assimilation any person of Syrian or Kurdish origin, who does not enjoy or who no longer enjoys the protection of the State to which he previously belonged and who has not acquired or does not possess another nationality.

> Any person of Turkish origin, previously a subject of the Ottoman Empire, who under the terms of the Protocol of Lausanne of July 24, 1923, does not enjoy or no longer enjoys the protection of the Turkish Republic and who has not acquired another nationality.

Convention Concerning the Status of Refugees Coming from Germany, Art. I, signed February 10, 1938, 192 L.N.T.S. 59:

> Persons possessing or having possessed German nationality and not possessing any other nationality who are proved not to enjoy, in law or in fact, the protection of the German Government[; or] [s]tateless persons not covered by previous Conventions or Agreements who have left German territory after being established therein and who are proved not to enjoy, in law or in fact, the protection of the German Government. * * * Persons who leave Germany for reasons of purely personal convenience are not included in this definition.

The earlier arrangements primarily provided a legal framework for the efforts of the League of Nations and its High Commissioner to provide assistance and documentation, and contained only recommendations addressed to states parties for the treatment of refugees, rather than clear legal requirements. A 1933 treaty contained more extensive obligations for states with regard to persons covered by the earlier arrangements, including a broad *nonrefoulement* provision that also barred expulsion at the frontier. But only eight states adhered to the treaty, and many of these entered reservations to key provisions. Convention relating to the International Status of Refugees, signed Oct. 28, 1933, 159 L.N.T.S. 199. The drafters of the 1938 treaty on refugees from

Germany therefore scaled back the extent of obligations that states would undertake under that instrument, but it still attracted only three adherents. *See* Beck, *Britain and the 1933 Refugee Convention: National or State Sovereignty?*, 11 Int'l J. Refugee L. 597, 600 (1999).

#### b.  *UNRRA and the International Refugee Organization*

Although the efforts of the 1930s proved bitterly insufficient in the face of the oppression committed by fascist regimes, World War II itself triggered more extensive activity. The allies created the UN Relief and Rehabilitation Administration in 1943, and it remained in operation until 1947. UNRRA had a broad mandate for assistance and rebuilding, but was not created primarily as a refugee agency. All who had been displaced by the war came within its competency. After the war UNRRA focused on repatriating the displaced, but this task became increasingly controversial as the Cold War deepened and significant numbers of persons resisted return to either the USSR, a wartime ally, or countries that had come under Soviet control.

Under pressure led by the United States, UNRRA's mandate was brought to an end and a new temporary specialized agency, the International Refugee Organization, came into being in 1947. As a concession to the Soviets, the IRO retained responsibility to assist repatriation, but a General Assembly resolution creating the Organization also stated that "no refugees or displaced persons who have finally and definitely, in complete freedom, and after receiving full knowledge of the facts, including adequate information from the governments of their countries of origin, expressed valid objections to returning to their countries of origin * * * shall be compelled to return * * *." G.A. Res. 8(1) (Feb. 12, 1946), U.N. GAOR, 1st Sess., UN Doc. A/64 at 12 (July 1, 1946). *See* UNHCR, The State of the World's Refugees: Fifty Years of Humanitarian Action 14–18 (2000). In the end, only about 10 percent of those assisted by the IRO chose to repatriate. The IRO had responsibility for determining the refugee status of individuals according to an extensive new definition, and for considering the validity of objections to return. The IRO Constitution (its founding treaty) counted among valid objections "persecution, or fear, based on reasonable grounds, of persecution because of race, religion, nationality or political opinions, provided these opinions are not in conflict with the principles of the United Nations." It also specifically authorized the IRO to create "some special system of semi-judicial machinery" to carry out its decisionmaking duties. Constitution of the International Refugee Organization, Annex I, done Dec. 15, 1946, 18 U.N.T.S. 3.

The IRO assisted displaced persons, which it defined to include primarily people forced to leave their countries by Nazi, fascist or quisling regimes to "undertake forced labour or who were deported for racial, religious or political reasons." In addition, the IRO Constitution defined several categories of refugees:

•  victims of the Nazi, fascist, quisling or similar regimes

- Spanish Republicans and other victims of the Falangist regime in Spain
- persons considered refugees before World War II for reasons of race, religion, nationality or political opinion
- Jewish or stateless residents of Germany or Austria who had been detained there or had been forced to flee, but had subsequently been returned to those countries
- unaccompanied children, aged 16 or younger, outside their homeland who were orphans or whose parents had disappeared.

A comprehensive account appears in Louise Holborn, The IRO: A Specialized Agency of the UN (1956).

### c.  United Nations Relief and Works Agency for Palestine Refugees

After the end of World War I the British government administered Palestine under a League of Nations mandate. This continued until 1948. When the state of Israel was proclaimed in that year, war broke out, and more than 700,000 Palestinians took refuge in Jordan, Lebanon, Syria, the West Bank, and the Gaza Strip. In response to this crisis, the UN General Assembly created the United Nations Relief and Works Agency (UNRWA—wholly distinct from UNRRA, which had ceased to exist by that time), an agency dedicated to providing relief to the Palestinian refugees.

UNRWA defines Palestinian refugees as those people, and their descendants, who lived in Palestine two years prior to the 1948 hostilities, and who lost their homes and livelihoods as a consequence of the conflict. Almost three million Palestinians are currently registered with the agency, which operates in Jordan, Lebanon, Syria, Gaza and the West Bank. It has responsibility for extensive assistance programs, but no mandate to engage in legal protection and hence no real role in the ongoing refinement of the international law governing refugees. *See* Lex Takkenberg, The Status of Palestinian Refugees in International Law (1998).

### d.  United Nations High Commissioner for Refugees

Members of the United Nations had envisioned the International Refugee Organization as a temporary response to the refugees created by World War II. It would repatriate those that it could, seek resettlement for the rest, and then close its doors. There was significant disagreement about whether the United Nations should thereafter play a role in responding to future refugee crises, as well as about how extensive such a role might be. The UN General Assembly eventually chose a compromise approach; it established the Office of the United Nations High Commissioner for Refugees (UNHCR) for an initial three-year period, beginning in 1951. *See* UNHCR, An Introduction to the International Protection of Refugees 6–7 (1992). The Office's mandate has been regularly extended ever since, in three- to five-year increments. The instrument creating the office and defining its responsibilities foreshadowed the definition of "refugee" that would be included in the 1951 Convention a year later (with some variations). Its central provision gave UNHCR the responsibility to deal with persons outside their country of origin "owing to a well-founded fear of being persecuted for reasons of race, religion, nationality or political opinion." Statute of the Office of the United Nations High Commissioner for Refugees, para. 6(A)(ii), UNGA Res. 428(V) (Dec. 14, 1950). Later General Assembly Resolutions, however, have often expanded the mandate and authority of the Office, usually to cover specific additional populations.

UNHCR was originally intended to be a modest agency, shouldering minimal operational responsibilities and dealing largely with governments—while governments in turn would take on the main work of assisting refugees. But within a few years the world realized that retaining operational responsibilities in a global organization would prove quite useful. *See* Martin, *Refugees and Migration,* in 1 United Nations Legal Order 391, 401–07 (O. Schachter & C. Joyner eds. 1995). On the history, *see* Gil Loescher, The UNHCR and World Politics: A Perilous Path (2001); Louise Holborn, Refugees: A Problem of our Time: The Work of the United Nations High Commissioner for Refugees, 1951–1972 (1975).

Today, the UNHCR has a staff of more than 6,000, working in over 100 countries, and an annual budget of roughly one billion dollars. Very little of that resource pool derives from the mandatory dues paid by UN members as part of the regular UN budget. Because nearly all of UNHCR's operations are funded by voluntary national contributions, the High Commissioner must also serve as a major fundraiser. Recent years have seen painful budget shortfalls. The UNHCR maintains a highly useful website, <www.unhcr.org>, that can be used to access information about movements of refugees and displaced persons, assistance and protection efforts, source country conditions, statistical data, and much more.

## 3.  THE CONVENTION AND PROTOCOL RELATING TO THE STATUS OF REFUGEES

### a.  *The 1951 Convention*

### i.  **Overview and the Definition**

Six months after the UNHCR came into existence, the United Nations convened a Conference of Plenipotentiaries in Geneva to consider the formulation and adoption of a treaty concerning refugees. The 1951 Convention Relating to the Status of Refugees resulted. 189 U.N.T.S. 137, signed July 28, 1951. This treaty and the abundant national law it has spawned will occupy a great deal of our attention in this book. The centerpiece of the Convention's definition of "refugee," Article 1(A)(2), provides:

For the purposes of the present Convention, the term "refugee" shall apply to any person who \* \* \* [a]s a result of events occurring before 1 January 1951 and owing to well-founded fear of being persecuted for reasons of race, religion, nationality, membership of a particular social group or political opinion, is outside the country of his nationality and is unable or, owing to such fear, is unwilling to avail himself of the protection of that country \* \* \*.

The Convention thus limited the category of refugees to those who have crossed an international border and who have a well-founded fear of persecution for any of the five specified reasons (often called the *nexus* requirement): race, religion, nationality, membership in a particular social group, and political opinion. Moreover, as in the UNHCR Statute, refugees are principally defined by individual characteristics and experiences, not by fixed ethnic, geographic, historical, or political background—an approach that characterized many earlier instruments. These elements of the definition have had enduring significance.

The caution of the drafters, however, some of whom explicitly mentioned concerns about writing a "blank cheque" opening up immeasurable obligations into the distant future, is apparent in the dateline provision (which was eventually altered, as we will discuss below). *See* Martin, *Refugees and Migration, supra,* at 416–17. Under the Convention, a person could be a refugee only if outside his or her home country because of events that occurred before 1951—in principle, a finite group of beneficiaries. States were allowed a further option for narrowing their exposure. They could declare at the time of ratification that they would apply the treaty only to refugees displaced by events occurring in Europe. Art. 1(B).

Both these restrictions also reflect the connection of the treaty to the deepening Cold War. The major European displacements before 1951 derived from the turmoil of World War II, as well as the resistance of thousands of the displaced toward returning to countries that had come under Soviet domination, either during the war or as a result of the USSR's maneuvering in central and eastern Europe through the late 1940s. Indeed, Soviet bloc countries remained estranged from the Convention and the work of the UNHCR. They often charged that the concern over refugees in the post-war era was a ploy meant to hamper their own rebuilding efforts.

In separate provisions, the 1951 Convention expressly included coverage of those who had satisfied the refugee definition in the international agreements from the 1920s, 1930s, and 1940s, although those definitions ordinarily had not required refugees to demonstrate a fear of persecution. Art. 1(A)(1). It also explicitly excluded those receiving protection or assistance from United Nations agencies other than UNHCR. Art. 1(D). This provision has had enduring impact with regard to UNRWA, and it still serves to exclude most Palestinians from the coverage of the 1951 Convention. Finally, the treaty barred those guilty of war crimes, crimes against humanity, and other serious crimes from its major protections. Art. 1(F); *see also* Art. 33(2).

### ii. Status and Rights

It is important to note, however, that most of the Convention is not about defining refugees, but instead, as the treaty's title implies, specifies standards for the legal status, rights, and treatment of persons who are refugees and are present in the territory of a treaty party. *See* James C. Hathaway, The Rights of Refugees under International Law 1–14 (2006). The prominence of these status questions in 1951 might seem puzzling to American observers, but should be understood in the context of the continental European civil law tradition observed by most of the states involved in shaping the Convention. Those countries generally based the rights of aliens present in their territory on reciprocity with the country of nationality, or (as with civil status questions such as the requirements and rights pertaining to marriage or divorce) on the law of the country of that person's nationality. For obvious reasons, this approach appeared unfair to refugees who had left regimes that treated both citizens and aliens badly. The detailed gradations of rights set forth in the 1951 Convention alleviated this legal problem.

You may wish to look through the treaty text at this point, to see for yourself the major preoccupations of the drafters. Especially significant are documentary provisions that reflect the heritage of the Nansen passport. Under the Convention, haven states, not UNHCR, are to issue the identity documents, and, for certain refugees, the state must include a pledge to accept the refugee's return at the end of his travels. *See* Arts. 27 & 28, and the Schedule and Annex at the end of the Convention.

Note that some of the specific rights listed in the Convention are available to all refugees physically present, but a host of others are limited to those "lawfully in" the country, or to those "lawfully staying in" the country. The right to engage in employment, broad access to the housing market, and the right to public assistance or social security, for example, apply only to refugees lawfully staying in the country—i.e., those who have received some type of durable residence rights. Merely proving that one meets the refugee definition does not give a refugee any entitlement to lawful residence. This is why older legal texts often emphasize that the 1951 Convention does not provide for asylum.[4] States retain discretion under the Convention to bestow or withhold both lawful status and residence rights. Nonetheless, the Convention does extend to virtually all refugees present, lawfully or not, those rights that are probably the most basic, particularly the *nonrefoulement* provision of

---

**4.** The UN General Assembly adopted a declaration in 1967 calling for a highly qualified right of asylum. Declaration on Territorial Asylum, GA Res. 2312 (XXII) (Dec. 14, 1967). And the UN convened a conference in Geneva in 1977 to draft a treaty on territorial asylum. When its early work seemed likely instead to erode some of the provisions in the 1951 Convention, the conference was quietly adjourned. *See* Weis, *Draft United Nations Convention on Territorial Asylum*, 50 Brit. Y.B. Int'l L. 151 (1980).

Article 33. Professor Goodwin–Gill summarized the outlook that animated the drafters:

> The 1951 Convention was originally intended to establish, confirm or clarify the legal status of a known population of the displaced. This met the needs of the time, and most provisions focus on assimilation, or are premised on lawful residence or tolerated presence. There is nothing on asylum, on admission, or on resettlement.

Goodwin–Gill, *The Future of International Refugee Law,* Refugees, Oct. 1988, at 28.

In the early years, however, many industrialized states did adopt domestic legal provisions that essentially awarded full residence to those who proved that they met the definition—provided they are not disqualified, for example because of past crimes. In such a system, those who obtain the full range of rights based on their refugee status are usually said to have been awarded *asylum*, though this term does not appear in the treaty.

### iii.  Obsolescence of the Convention Dateline and the Adoption of the Protocol

By the early 1960s the numbers of refugees from Asia and Africa were rising significantly. Many had fled across international boundaries to escape persecution, but their flight was impelled by events outside of Europe that had occurred after 1951. The 1951 Convention was therefore inapplicable. A change in the treaty was clearly desirable, but many diplomats worried that states would resist anything but minor, finite additions to its scope. UNHCR, however, took the lead to draft a Protocol that cut to the core of the problem by eliminating the dateline altogether. In an unusually speedy treaty procedure, the UN General Assembly approved the text and transmitted it to states for their accession. Within a few months the treaty had enough parties to enter into force. 1967 Protocol Relating to the Status of Refugees, done January 31, 1967, 19 U.S.T. 6223, T.I.A.S. No. 6577, 606 U.N.T.S. 267. The Protocol also eliminated the option of confining a state's obligations to refugees from Europe (though states that had already adopted such a restriction could continue it even while accepting the new instrument). With the Protocol, the refugee definition became truly universal. The Protocol did not, however, expand the refugee definition to cover fears of harm not related to persecution. As of March 2006, 140 states are parties to both the Convention and Protocol, three are parties only to the Convention and three others, including the United States, are parties only to the Protocol (which incorporates by reference all the operative provisions of the underlying Convention).

### Notes and Questions

1.  What allowed an individual to qualify as a refugee under the treaties of the 1920s and 1930s? How would they be likely to prove their qualifications? What sources of proof could they use?

2. Under the 1920s treaties, what role did threats of persecution play, either as a matter of individual qualification or as a justification for the international community's concern for these forced migrants? Did individuals have to prove a need for protection? Would the 1920s treaties concerning refugees protect both victims of persecution and persons who might have engaged in persecution?

3. Why did the international community during the covered period extend the protection that it was willing to provide only to those who had crossed international borders?

4. Scholars such as James Hathaway have criticized what they see as the Western bias of the 1951 Convention, because it gives "priority in protection matters to persons whose flight was motivated by pro-Western political values." It emphasizes persecution based on five factors under which "East bloc practice has been problematic. Western vulnerability in the area of respect for human rights, in contrast, centres more on the guarantee of socio-economic human rights than on respect for civil and political rights. * * * [But] persons denied even such basic rights as food, health care, or education are excluded from the international refugee regime (unless that deprivation stems from civil or political status)." J. Hathaway, The Law of Refugee Status 6–8 (1991). What do you make of this criticism? Does this simply reflect another round in the debate between universal values and cultural relativism? If so, does that support or undermine the criticism? How would you craft a refugee treaty to cover the omitted rights of which Hathaway speaks? What practical constraints might such a treaty confront? Are consequentialist concerns about numbers a legitimate basis for shaping refugee doctrine?

## 4. EVOLVING NORMS

### a. *Regional Practices and Legal Instruments*

### i. Europe

The 1951 Convention has played a key role in the treatment of refugees in Europe, and its provisions have been widely incorporated into national legislation. But since at least the 1960s, many European states concluded that the Convention might not address all those who should not be required to return to their countries of origin. In fact, the cases of American opponents of the Vietnam war who had fled to Europe to escape conscription often served as the catalyst causing countries to consider wider categories. The details concerning these *de facto*, B-status, or humanitarian refugee categories varied from state to state, but generally the beneficiaries were allowed to remain and were provided some type of legal status, despite their inability to show the requisite fear of persecution.

In later years, additional legal protection developed based on the provisions of the European Convention for the Protection of Human Rights and Fundamental Freedoms, done Nov. 4, 1950, 213 U.N.T.S. 222, E.T.S. 5. The drafters of the original treaty specifically decided not to include any provisions on refugee status, asylum, or *nonrefoulement*.

But Article 3 of the Convention states: "No one shall be subjected to torture or to inhuman or degrading treatment or punishment." In case-law developments that took full shape in the 1990s, Article 3 was interpreted to forbid a state to return an individual to a country where "the individual would face a real risk of being subjected to treatment contrary to Article 3 if removed." *Chahal v. United Kingdom*, 1996–V Eur. Ct. H.R. 1831 (1996) Thus, asylum seekers in any of the 46 states that have acceded to the European Human Rights Convention can rely on Article 3 in challenging their deportation or removal from the country. The Convention establishes a European Court of Human Rights to which individuals can submit complaints after exhausting local remedies.

It has become common in Europe to speak of these additional bases for protection (going beyond the requirements of the 1951 Convention) as "subsidiary protection." The Council of the European Union, after years of detailed consideration, adopted a Directive meant to set minimum standards for subsidiary protection, including the definition of a set of "core benefits," but considerable variation still exists among European states. Council Directive 2004/83/EC, 2004 O.J. (L304) 12 (EC). Chapter Eleven will consider some of these developments in greater detail.

### ii. Africa

By 1969, Africa had experienced over a decade of decolonization, the advent of wars of liberation, and, in many locations, violent ethnic strife or dictatorial repression. The Organization of African Unity (OAU, which changed its name to the African Union in 2002) faced mass movements of people in many corners of the continent. Many African countries were strikingly receptive, often allowing local integration or operating reasonably well-run camps, sometimes with the assistance of international donors. But the OAU considered it useful to promulgate a treaty to guide national and regional response, and specifically to take into account a wider range of forced migration than did the 1951 Convention. The OAU Convention Governing the Specific Aspects of Refugee Problems in Africa, done Sept. 10, 1969, 1001 U.N.T.S. 45, defined its coverage to include both the 1951 Convention definition, as expanded by the Protocol, and the following (Art. I(2)):

> The term "refugee" shall also apply to every person who, owing to external aggression, occupation, foreign domination or events seriously disturbing public order in either part of the whole of his country of origin or nationality, is compelled to leave his place of habitual residence in order to seek refuge in another place outside his country of origin or nationality.

Article II, titled "Asylum," contains a broad *nonrefoulement* provision and also contains a pledge that member states shall use their "best endeavours consistent with their respective legislations to receive refugees and to secure [their] settlement."

### iii. Western Hemisphere

In 1969 the Organization of American States (OAS) adopted the text of the American Convention on Human Rights, done Nov. 22, 1969, 1144 U.N.T.S. 123, which sets forth an extensive list of rights and also establishes an Inter–American Court of Human Rights. It entered into force in 1978, but not all OAS member states are parties to the treaty. (The United States has signed but not ratified.) Among its specific provisions are rights of asylum and *nonrefoulement* (Art. 22(7) and (8)), but their scope does not differ significantly from the coverage of the 1951 Convention. During the 1980s, however, Latin America experienced significant repression, political instability, and civil war that drove many thousands from their homes. Response was needed, but many of these people did not fit the traditional refugee definition. Early in the decade, experts from ten Western Hemisphere countries met in Colombia and adopted the Cartagena Declaration on Refugees. It urged a wide range of improvements in the treatment of refugees, but also contained the following:

> [I]n view of the experience gained from the massive flows of refugees in the Central American area, it is necessary to consider enlarging the concept of a refugee[.] * * * Hence the definition or concept of a refugee to be recommended for use in the region * * * [should include] persons who have fled their country because their lives, safety or freedom have been threatened by generalized violence, foreign aggression, internal conflicts, massive violation of human rights or other circumstances which have seriously disturbed public order.

This description obviously has close parallels to the OAU Convention, but the OAS has never incorporated this language in a treaty. Nonetheless, the Inter–American Commission on Human Rights endorsed the declaration, and later the General Assembly of the OAS adopted a formal resolution noting the work of the experts and resolving "[t]o underscore the importance of the Declaration of Cartagena on Refugees and recommend to the member states that they apply that Declaration in dealing with the refugees in their territory." Legal Status of Asylees, Refugees, and Displaced Persons in the American Hemisphere, AG/RES 774 /XV–0/85 (Dec. 9, 1985).

Thus, government representatives in the Western Hemisphere, Africa, and Europe have recognized the need for a broader conception of protection than that enunciated in the 1951 Convention. Nonetheless, the formulations vary, and the extent to which some of these developments embody international legal obligations as opposed to recommended practices is often contested.

### b. Convention Against Torture

The Convention Against Torture and Other Cruel, Inhuman or Degrading Treatment or Punishment (CAT), done 10 December 1984, 1468 U.N.T.S. 85, came into force in 1987. As of May 2006, 141 states are parties, including the United States. Its central provisions are meant to prevent or punish acts of torture, as defined in the treaty, committed within the territory of states parties. The treaty specifically calls for education and training of that country's own law enforcement and military personnel and other public officials, for investigation and prosecution of alleged torture, and for full compensation of victims of torture. One article of the CAT, however, does provide a special *nonrefoulement* protection. Article 3 bars expulsion, return, or extradition of a person to another state "where there are substantial grounds for believing that he would be in danger of being subjected to torture." This protection applies no matter what might be the precise reason for the torturer's actions. That is, the applicant for protection need not show that he risks torture on the basis of any of the five grounds listed in the 1951 Convention: race, religion, nationality, membership of a particular social group, or political opinion. Moreover, because the CAT has no exclusion clauses, its *nonrefoulement* provision applies to everyone: law-abiding citizens, convicted felons, and even accused or proven terrorists. We will examine the scope of the Convention Against Torture in more detail in Chapter Seven, where we will survey the circumstances in which its protection overlaps that provided by other legal instruments.

### Notes and Questions

1.   None of the refugee instruments discussed in subsection 4a above applies its expanded legal obligations to persons who have not crossed an international boundary. Why might this limitation be more surprising in the OAU Refugee Convention, which came into effect in 1974, and the Cartagena Declaration, adopted in 1984, than in the 1951 Convention?

2.   In contrast to the refugee agreements, the Convention Against Torture makes no explicit reference limiting its *nonrefoulement* protection to those who previously crossed a territorial border. Why not? Although there is no requirement in CAT of extraterritorial presence, many who formally seek protection under CAT do so from a country other than their homeland. What practical reasons explain this phenomenon?

### Exercise

We will devote much of this book to interpreting and applying refugee definitions and other standards governing protection, but it is useful at this point to test out a few practical applications. Which of the following situations would be covered by (i) the definition in the 1951 Convention, and its Protocol, (ii) the protection derived from Article 3 of the European Convention on Human Rights, (iii) the OAU Convention, (iv) protection derived from the Cartagena Declaration, (v) Article 3 of the Convention Against Torture?

1.  Civil war in Fredonia pits a leftist insurgency against an autocratic government dominated by a few wealthy families that have traditionally controlled the political life of the country. Both sides are heavily armed and frequently employ indiscriminate bombardment or shelling of areas held by their opponents. Thousands of civilians flee the destruction, some going to the capital city, while others cross the river into a neighboring country.

2.  The divisions in a civil war in Ruritania generally follow ethnic lines, and both sides have engaged in "ethnic cleansing" in areas they control. Reports of atrocities are plentiful. Classical military battles are also heavy at times, causing extensive damage to cities and towns. Internal relocation is matched by the volume of flight to neighboring countries.

3.  A radical group inspired by Mao Tse Tung and Pol Pot takes over the government of Stanistan and implements a rigid "back to the land" program that forces city-dwellers to leave their jobs and join work teams in the countryside. Food is equitably shared among the team members, but years of economic mismanagement and poor harvests have resulted in widespread hunger and malnutrition. Stanistan's borders are heavily guarded, but thousands manage to escape. Those who are caught are punished severely for breaking the law. Reportedly some have been tortured, and others have been stoned to death.

4.  For decades the rural economy of Altiplano has been controlled by a few large landowners who maintain close control over the impoverished farmers who work those lands. A prolonged drought has brought widespread hunger. Rural workers desperate to feed their families are leaving in increasing numbers, going to urban areas in Altiplano and also to neighboring countries.

5.   A category 5 hurricane left over 300,000 people homeless in Isthmia, devastating farms and businesses. Disaster experts say that reconstruction will require five to ten years. Meantime the population of the affected area has dispersed throughout the region, many living in squalor in shantytowns.

6.   Government in Elbonia has essentially ceased to exist. Various regions are loosely under the control of warlords and armed gangs, but many of the gangs themselves are barely organized. Heavily armed young men, often high on drugs, go out on patrol and extract food and money from people they encounter. Shootings and beatings are common, and worse mistreatment has also been reported. Most of the population now survives through subsistence farming, and many have fled.

### c.  *Principles On Internally Displaced Persons*

The 1951 Convention, the 1967 Protocol, the OAU refugee definition, and the Cartagena Declaration all concentrate on those forced migrants who crossed an international border when they fled their homes. During the past two decades attention has begun to focus on large numbers of people who have not crossed a border, but have been forced from their homes by persecution, civil war, or generalized violence. In a sense, they have sought asylum within their own country. Known as internally displaced persons, these individuals and families were far more numerous than refugees by the mid-1990s. Many of them share the same characteristics as refugees—other than the border crossing—and have the same need for protection as refugees. And yet for decades they were often considered beyond the scope of concern of the international community. Figure 1.3 gives an idea of their numbers and location.

Relief organizations, who were increasingly assisting the internally displaced, found that they lacked clear rules for their actions. Institutional responsibility within the UN was also dispersed among a variety of agencies, missing the clear focus that UNHCR's role often brought to refugee crises. And in particular, demands increased for international access to internally oppressed populations, even over the objection of the national government. In part, this change reflected the end of the Cold War and the reflexive superpower support that abusive regimes had earlier counted on to deflect international concern. The UN pressed the Khartoum government in 1989 to accept Operation Lifeline Sudan and allow international aid to reach the displaced in both government- and rebel-held territory. After the Gulf War of 1991, the UN Security Council used its maximum powers under Chapter VII of the UN Charter to create a security zone in the north of Iraq and to insist on humanitarian access. Similar UN resolutions called for "unimpeded access" to IDPs in Somalia, Bosnia, Rwanda, and East Timor, sometimes authorizing the

## Figure 1.3

## Map of the Internally Displaced, October 2006

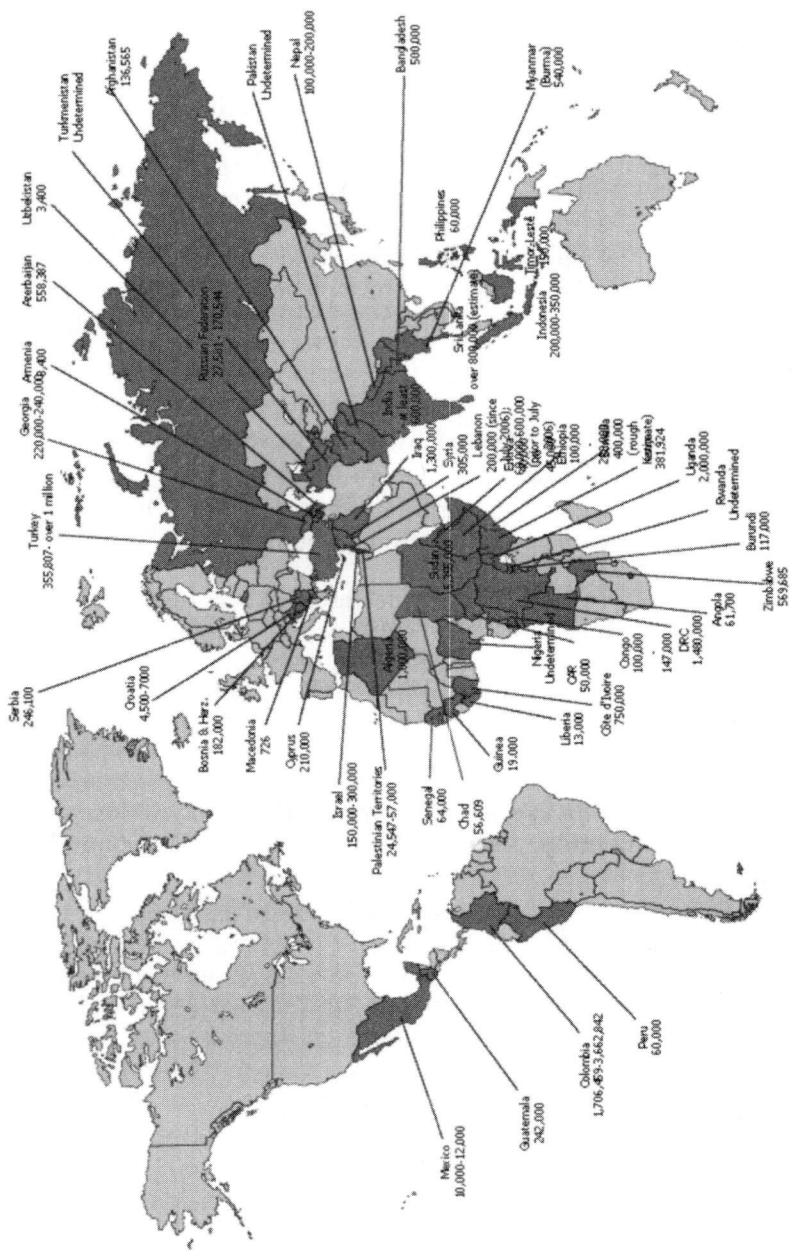

Source: Internal Displacement Monitoring Centre (iDMC), Internally Displaced People Worldwide, <http://www.internal-displacement.org/8025708F004CE90B/http WorldMap?ReadForm & count=1000> (Sept. 2006).

use of force to enforce this mandate. *See* Cohen, *The Guiding Principles on Internal Displacement: An Innovation in International Standard Setting*, 10 Global Governance 459 (2004).

Feeling the need for a better legal framework to address internal displacement, the United Nations appointed a Special Rapporteur, Francis M. Deng, to investigate the situation. Deng prepared a massive report. UN Economic & Social Council [ECOSOC], Commission on Human Rights, *Comprehensive Study on the Human Rights Issues Related to Internally Displaced Persons*, UN Doc. E/CN.4/1993/35 (1993). Though some had hoped for a new treaty, others thought that path either unrealistic or too time-consuming. Deng recommended instead a set of guiding international law principles regarding the treatment of those who are internally displaced. A set was published in 1998. ECOSOC, Commission on Human Rights, *Guiding Principles on Internal Displacement,* UN Doc. E/CN.4/1998/53/Add.2 (1998). Many of the principles simply pulled together legal provisions already applicable (as under international human rights and humanitarian law), but restated in a way that highlighted their relevance to IDPs. Other principles reflected genuine innovation, meant to address gaps in the law that the report had identified. The principles employ the following definition:

> Persons who have been forced or obliged to flee or to leave their homes or places of habitual residence, in particular as a result of, or in order to avoid the effects of, armed conflict, situations of generalized violence, violations of human rights or natural or human-made disasters, and who have not crossed an internationally recognized state border.

The UN General Assembly and the UN Commission on Human Rights adopted resolutions essentially endorsing the Guiding Principles, and many states have referred to and relied on them in responding to the needs of the internally displaced. *See* UNHCR, State of the World's Refugees: Human Displacement in the New Millennium 165 & n. 16 (2006). We will consider some of these developments in greater detail in Chapter Eleven.

### Notes and Questions

1.  Roberta Cohen (*supra,* 10 Global Governance at 466) has written:

> If there can be said to be a philosophical foundation behind the principles, it is the concept of sovereignty as a form of responsibility, developed by Deng and other scholars. Besides positing primary responsibility for the welfare and safety of IDPs with their govern-

ments, the concept also considers it an obligation of the international community to provide humanitarian assistance and protection to IDPs when the governments concerned are unable to fulfill their responsibilities. In such an instance, governments are supposed to request and accept outside offers of aid. If they refuse or deliberately obstruct access and put large numbers of persons at risk, the international community, under this concept, has a right—and even a responsibility—to step in and assert its concern.

What do you make of this foundation for the principles? Does it have wider applicability to refugee crises more generally, providing a basis for the world community to go to the source and address the root causes of cross-border flight by intervention within the country of origin? Is this a realistic stance in a world of sovereign states? In what ways is it vulnerable to manipulation to serve other political agendas?

2.   The definition in the Principles includes those uprooted by natural disasters but excludes those forced to move by economic hardship. Both these decisions touched off controversy. What considerations justify the approach taken? Are they compelling?

3.   Throughout the 1990s, particularly in connection with the breakup of Yugoslavia, the UN General Assembly authorized specific operational involvement of UNHCR with certain internally displaced populations. This departure from UNHCR's traditional approach sparked controversy. The High Commissioner at the time, Sadako Ogata, embraced this role and argued that the world community should do more to help enforce a "right to remain." Ogata, Statement to the Commission on Human Rights, Geneva (March 3, 1993), *available at* <http://www.unhcr.org/cgi-bin/texis/vtx/admin/opendoc.htm?tbl=ADMIN & id=3ae68fad1c>. Ambassador Richard C. Holbrooke, U.S. Representative to the United Nations, and a key player in negotiating the agreements that ended the fighting in Yugoslavia, strongly voiced the belief that refugees and internally displaced persons should receive equal treatment from an expanded UNHCR, in a speech to the U.N. Security Council on January 13, 2000.

Many leading scholars who also had considerable practical experience with UNHCR objected. Professor Guy Goodwin–Gill argued that routinely extending UNHCR's involvement to IDPs would dilute the protection given to refugees, immerse the Office in political controversies it had largely avoided in the past, and deeply compromise its institutional autonomy. Guy Goodwin–Gill, *UNHCR and Internal Displacement: Stepping into a Legal and Political Minefield*, 2000 World Refugee Survey 26–31. (We will revisit this debate in Chapter Eleven.) Professor James Hathaway sharply criticized the emphasis on a right to remain, arguing that it distorted UNHCR's priorities and was used to force people to stay in insecure situations.

It is meaningless as a 'new' right because if already-recognized rights, like freedom from cruel or inhuman treatment, were in fact respected, the 'right to remain' would be redundant. There is no need whatsoever to articulate as a right something which is merely a consequentialist concern flowing from the inadequate enforcement of matters already clearly within the ambit of human rights law. * * * We must not be shy to validate the palliative, the protective, the stop-gap role of refugee law. There is nothing shameful about addressing the human consequences of harm. Whatever movement is made toward more effectively ending or attenuating human rights abuse in-country should *never* be at the expense of the human beings' one truly autonomous remedy: flight when circumstances become unbearable.

Hathaway, *New Directions to Avoid Hard Problems: the Distortion of the Palliative Role of Refugee Protection,* 8 J. Refugee Studies 289, 293–294 (1995). *See also* Frelick, *Down the Rabbit Hole: The Strange Logic of the Internal Flight Alternative,* World Refugee Survey 1999, at 22.

4.   For further discussions of international efforts to establish a firmer legal foundation for assistance to the internally displaced, *see, e.g.,* Walter Kälin, Guiding Principles on Internal Displacement: Annotations (2000); R. Cohen & F. Deng, Masses in Flight: The Global Crises of Internal Displacement (1998); Plender, *The Legal Basis of International Jurisdiction to Act with Regard to the Internally Displaced,* 6 Int'l J.Ref.L. 345 (1994).

## SECTION C.   WHO SHOULD BE CONSIDERED A REFUGEE?

As the discussion of IDPs indicates, many critics have challenged the premises and the scope of the 1951 Convention definition. The excerpts below provide an introduction to some of the moral and political criticisms and responses that have engaged the academic community.

### ANDREW SHACKNOVE, WHO IS A REFUGEE?
95 Ethics 274–84 (1985).

\* \* \*

The predominant, generation-old [legal] conception advanced by international instruments, municipal statutes, and scholarly treatises identifies the refugee as, in essence, a person who has crossed an international frontier because of a well-founded fear of persecution. * * *

A proper conception of refugeehood is an important matter. * * * An overly narrow conception of "refugee" will contribute to the denial of international protection to countless people in dire circumstances whose claim to assistance is impeccable. Ironically, for many persons on the brink of disaster, refugee status is a privileged position. In contrast to other destitute people, the refugee is eligible for many forms of international assistance, including material relief, asylum, and permanent resettlement. Conversely, an overly inclusive conception is also morally suspect and will, in addition, financially exhaust relief programs and impune the credibility of the refugee's privileged position among host populations, whose support is crucial for the viability of international assistance programs.

Whether states and international agencies are obligated to assist refugees is a crucial, but separate, issue from the one at hand. * * * If obligations do exist, then the persons described here have the strongest claims to such assistance. Frequently, states reason in reverse from their fear that they will be forced to shoulder the burden of assisting refugees unilaterally to a narrow conception of refugeehood which limits the number of claimants. In so doing they are attempting to resolve what is in fact a procedural and institutional problem by a legalistic sleight of hand. * * *

My contention is that neither persecution nor alienage captures what is essential about refugeehood. Persecution is a sufficient, but not a necessary, condition for the severing of the normal social bond. It accounts for the absence of state protection under tyrannical conditions where a government is predatory but says nothing about the opposite, chaotic, extreme where a government (or society) has, for all practical purposes, ceased to exist. Persecution is but one manifestation of a broader phenomenon: the absence of state protection of the citizen's basic needs. It is this absence of state protection which constitutes the full and complete negation of society and the basis of refugeehood. The same reasoning which justifies the persecutee's claim to refugeehood justifies the claims of persons deprived of all other basic needs as well.

Similarly, alienage is an unnecessary condition for establishing refugee status. It, too, is a subset of a broader category: the physical access of the international community to the unprotected person.[8] The refugee need not necessarily cross an international frontier to gain such access. Thus I shall argue that refugees are, in essence, persons whose basic needs are unprotected by their country of origin, who have no remaining recourse other than to seek international restitution of their needs, and who are so situated that international assistance is possible. Because this alternative conception of refugeehood accounts more comprehensively than does the current notion for the dual extremes of tyranny and chaos which threaten the normal, minimal bonds of society, it has a stronger claim to moral validity. Moreover, it accounts more exactly for those persons who are in fact taxing asylum states and furthering erosion of minimum order in Lebanon, El Salvador, and elsewhere throughout the world.

### REFUGEES AND THE MINIMAL SOCIAL BOND

* * * I take as my point of departure the assumption that morally (if not in fact) a normal, minimal bond of trust, loyalty, protection and

---

**8.** By "access" I mean, literally, the ability of states or international agencies to supply the requisite material or diplomatic assistance unimpeded by the government of the country of origin, insurrectionists, invading nation, or other powers.

assistance has always existed between virtually every human being and some larger collectivity—be it clan, feudal manor, or modern state—and that the refugee is spawned when these minimal bonds are ruptured. * * *

A political commonwealth is formed on the premise that people experience a generalized condition of insecurity when outside the protective confines of society. People wish to reduce their vulnerability to a variety of threats, including the violent acts of others, resource scarcity, and natural disasters. * * *

In refugee policy circles, basic threats to the individual are usually divided into three categories: persecution, vital (economic) subsistence, and natural calamities. Refugeehood is said to result only from acts of persecution. I shall look in turn at each of these three categories of deprivation and argue that, for purposes of defining "refugee," the distinction between them is neither bright nor clear, that all of them can equally violate the citizen's irreducible rationale for entering society, and that each may constitute a sufficient condition for refugeehood.

* * * To be minimally legitimate and tolerable, the commonwealth must reduce the citizen's vulnerability to others, all others. The sovereign is thus required to provide a minimally mild environment free from the dual extremes of tyranny and chaos, both of which are rife with violence.

Persecution is, therefore, just one manifestation of the absence of physical security. The sovereign must, at least, protect the citizen from foreign invasion and the "injuries of one another," which include civil war, genocide, terrorism, torture, and kidnapping, whether perpetrated by state agents or others. Beneath this threshold there is no state, and the bonds which constitute the normal basis of citizenship dissolve. Hence, persecution is a sufficient, but not a necessary, basis for a justified claim to refugeehood. If persecution establishes a valid claim to refugee status, then other threats to physical security do as well.[12]

When determining who is, or is not, entitled to refugee status, natural disasters, such as floods and droughts, are usually dismissed as the bases for justified claims. Unlike the violent acts one person perpetrates against another, such disasters are not considered "political" events. They are, supposedly, sources of vulnerability beyond social control which therefore impose no obligation on a government to secure a remedy. The bonds uniting citizen and state are said to endure even when the infrastructure or harvest of a region is obliterated. For even an ideally just state cannot save us from earthquakes, hurricanes, or eventual death. * * * But, as writers such as Lofchie, Sen, and Shue have demonstrated, "natural disasters" are frequently complicated by human

**12.** The argument for a right to revolution that Locke develops in his *Second Treatise* also justifies a right to refugeehood. Citizens are at liberty either to prevent tyranny or to escape it. Whether the citizen mobilizes opposition to an unjust regime or simply quits society is strictly a prudential calculation. See John Locke, *The Second Treatise of Government* (Indianapolis: Bobbs Merrill Co., 1952), pp. 119–39.

actions. The devastation of a flood or a supposedly natural famine can be minimized or exacerbated by social policies and institutions. * * *

To the extent that a life-threatening situation occurs because of human actions rather than natural causes, the state has left unfulfilled its basic duty to protect the citizen from the actions of others. All other human rights are meaningless when starvation results from the neglect or malice of the local regime.* * *

Threats to vital subsistence are subject to the same logic. To the extent that such threats to the survival of the citizen are due to human actions, they, like security threats and supposed "natural" calamities, create legitimate claims for state protection.* * *

* * * In situations where subsistence is threatened because of inadequacies in technology [for processing resources], infrastructure [for facilitating commerce], or [methods of] distribution—all factors within human control—the state has failed to perform its basic duty to protect its citizens from the actions of others. When subsistence is in fact threatened by one or another of these conditions, a justifiable claim to refugeehood results.

### REFUGEES AND BASIC NEEDS

In exchange for their allegiance, citizens can minimally expect that their government will guarantee physical security, vital subsistence, and liberty of political participation and physical movement. No reasonable person would be satisfied with less. Beneath this threshold the social compact has no meaning. Thus, refugees must be persons whose home state has failed to secure their basic needs. There is no justification for granting refugee status to individuals who do not suffer from the absence of one or more of these needs. Nor is there reason for denying refugee status to those who do. Moreover, because all these needs are equally essential for survival, the violation of each constitutes an equally valid claim to refugeehood.

For many concerned with refugee affairs, raising the standard of basic needs is a frightening specter. Perhaps the criterion of persecution is too narrow, but, they would argue, a conception of refugeehood tied to basic needs is surely too broad. Half the world will become bona fide refugees overnight, refugee programs will be indistinguishable from development programs, and the international machinery which now protects thousands of people will become so overburdened that all stand to lose. These arguments must be taken seriously because the international regime for attending to the needs of refugees is fragile and can be shattered as much by premature cosmopolitanism as by enduring primordial sentiments. * * * Are all persons deprived of their basic needs refugees?

The answer, in short, is no. An unmet basic need is a necessary, but insufficient, condition for refugeehood: all refugees have been deprived of one or more of their basic needs, though not all persons so deprived are refugees. What separates these two groups of equally destitute persons is their differing positions vis-à-vis the international community. Most individuals deprived of their basic needs are prevented by their government (or other forces) from seeking international assistance. To the contrary, a refugee is, in essence, a person whose government fails to protect his basic needs, who has no remaining recourse than to seek international restitution of these needs, and who is so situated that international assistance is possible.

Thus it is not a matter of entitlements that distinguishes refugees from all other persons whose basic needs are unmet by their home government but a matter of dissimilar objective conditions. Refugees, unlike all others deprived of their basic needs, have a well-founded fear that recourse to their own government is futile and are, in addition, within reach of the international community.

At this point, the time-honored criterion of alienage falters. * * * The origins of this criterion stem from the positivistic legal norm which asserts that states have equal, inviolable sovereign integrity and that the intervention in the internal affairs of one state will reduce stability for all. The corollary * * * is that a victim could only become an international ward when beyond the reach of the oppressive home government. * * * Conceptually, however, refugeehood is unrelated to migration. It is exclusively a political relation between the citizen and the state, not a territorial relation between a countryman and his homeland. Refugeehood is one form of unprotected statelessness.* * * [W]hat is essential for refugee status, distinguishing refugees from all other similarly deprived persons, is either the willingness of the home state to allow them access to international assistance or its inability to prevent such aid from being administered.

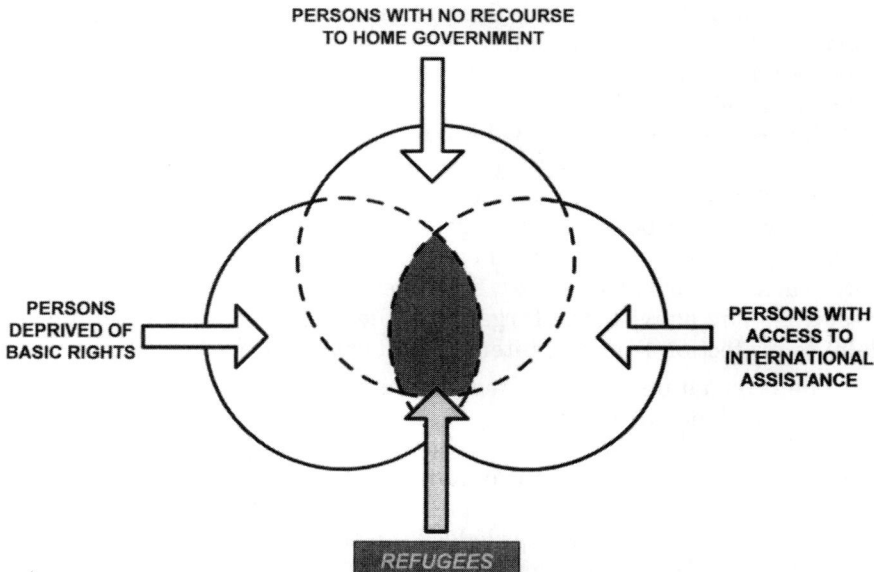

PERSONS WITH NO RECOURSE
TO HOME GOVERNMENT

PERSONS
DEPRIVED OF
BASIC RIGHTS

PERSONS WITH
ACCESS TO
INTERNATIONAL
ASSISTANCE

REFUGEES

Refugee status should only be granted to persons whose government fails to protect their basic needs, who have no remaining recourse other than to seek international restitution of these needs, and who are so situated that international assistance is possible. To the extent that refugee status is refused to these worthy claimants, or granted to others whose basic needs are not in jeopardy, the legitimacy of the policy is compromised.

---

Shacknove argues that refugee status should be unrelated to migration. Rather, it should be assigned to those whose governments fail to protect their basic needs. The authors of the next reading challenge the 1951 Convention from a different perspective. They assert that those who face the risk of life-threatening violence, both physical and structural, should have the greatest claims to international protection.

## ARISTIDE R. ZOLBERG, ASTRI SUHRKE, SERGIO AGUAYO, ESCAPE FROM VIOLENCE: CONFLICT AND THE REFUGEE CRISIS IN THE DEVELOPING WORLD
### Pp. 269–72 (1989).

Our analysis of contemporary refugee movements [has] delineated three sociological types of refugees: (1) the activist, (2) the target, and (3) the victim. * * * [T]he classic activists are dissenters and rebels whose actions contribute to the conflict that eventually forces them to flee. The targeted refugees are individuals who, through membership in a particular group, are singled out for violent action. And the victims are randomly caught in the cross fire or are exposed to generalized social violence. What all three have in common is fear of immediate violence—violence resulting from conflict between state and civil society, between opposing armies, or conflict among ethnic groups or class formations that the state is unable or unwilling to control. Whether the individuals are activists or passive bystanders simply caught in the conflict is immaterial from the point of view of their immediate security. Their need clearly could be the same regardless of the cause, and has demonstrably been so in many of the cases analyzed. It follows that in a historical and normative sense, the three types of refugees are equally deserving. The activist, the target, and the victim have an equally valid claim to protection from the international community.

The international refugee regime has to some extent recognized the moral equivalence of the three types. The U.N. Convention's definition accommodates the first two but has no provision for the victim. On the other hand, victims were in practice recognized as refugees in the European experience, both in earlier centuries and after World War II. The victims were also acknowledged in the institutional response to Third World refugees through the expanded mandate of the UNHCR in the 1960s and the general practices of first asylum countries in Asia,

Africa, and Latin America. Legal codes in Africa and Latin America were also adjusted to allow for mere "victims" (in the 1969 OAU convention and the 1984 Cartagena Declaration). The UNHCR introduced the notion of "victims of violence" in the mid–1980s to plead for asylum seekers in other regions.

From this perspective, the restrictive tendencies evident in North American and West European asylum practices in the 1980s, toward a narrow interpretation of the convention's criterion of persecution as the basis for refugee status, are highly questionable and have been deplored by UNHCR officials. To deny "mere victims" the opportunity to escape from violence is not only morally untenable but runs counter to broader historical trends. It is also open to charges of discrimination on racial and political grounds, as the restrictive tendencies have been most clearly evident with respect to spontaneous asylum seekers of non-European origin who come from noncommunist states.

* * *

An optimal policy would start from the explicit premise of moral equivalence among all three refugee types; the administration of protection and services should also be formal and explicit rather than leaving the beneficiary to an uncertain or semilegal status. Equally important, however, is the need to limit the number of prospective beneficiaries. It will be recalled that with the development toward a universal definition of refugees in the 1930s, it was stressed that some "exact definitions" were necessary to prevent the number of refugees from multiplying *ad infinitum*. Half a century later the point has, if anything, become more self-evident. Because it represents a privileged form of migration, refugee status can be given to only a limited number of people. The question then arises whether the concept of violence lends itself to discriminating interpretations that permit setting priorities.

We submit that it can and that the central ranking principle must be the immediacy and degree of life-threatening violence. Those most exposed must be given preferential access to protection, which becomes the most basic of rights. Farther along in the queue, relief could be given as far as resources and political will permit. More specifically, this would mean that priority be given to individuals or groups who find themselves in extremely threatening situations: civilians in battle areas, likely targets of death squads and pogroms, political prisoners under threat of torture, members of rebel or dissident groups on "wanted" lists, and the like. Proscription on cultural expressions such as lack of freedom of religion would come much farther down on the list, except when it is associated with life-threatening forms of violence.

Situations in which the economic prerequisites for sustaining life have suddenly been removed equally constitute life-threatening violence, and such victims need protection. This definition would include the poverty-stricken masses of the developing world, the victims of structural violence who are systematically pressed toward starvation levels, and the victims of drought and famine, with or without the compounded effect of warfare. It may be objected that such a definitional basis of refugee is totally unrealistic; in particular, the resource-rich countries of the North would not want to relieve famine or massive poverty in the South by means of a large-scale relocation of people.

The objection seems unfounded. Most victims of famine and starvation who today cross international borders remain in neighboring countries, where their claims to life-sustaining support generally are recognized by the international relief or refugee regime. Groups accused of being economic refugees who have claimed asylum in the industrialized countries are not the ones who are most economically destitute and would hardly be admitted as victims of violence even if economically based violence were included in the definition[.] * * *

The rule must be that victims of economic, that is, structural, violence must be helped first in their own country. Observance of the *in situ* clause, * * * is necessary to prevent neighboring and often poor developing countries from becoming overloaded by an influx of desperately poor people seeking relief and not to encourage an international restructuring of populations that in an age of nation-states is politically unacceptable.

* * *

In an earlier chapter, *id.* at 33, Zolberg, Suhrke, and Aguayo discuss the *"in situ* clause," based on a distinction borrowed from Michael Walzer, in these terms:

> [T]he key issue from the perspective of concerned humanitarians is not only whether the movement is involuntary and essentially political but also whether the immediate, intense suffering of the victims can be relieved by helping them in their own country—through policies of their own government or combined with favorable external initiatives—or if relief is possible only by enabling them to move abroad—that is, by providing them with a refuge. * * * [This approach makes it possible, for example,] to distinguish refugees from persons who move as a consequence of a natural disaster. Most victims of malnutrition and slow starvation in the developing world should not be considered as refugees because most of them can be assisted *in situ* in their own countries.

In contrast, David Martin constructs an approach to these issues based on the pragmatic observation that asylum, or a right to relocate in a foreign country, is a politically scarce resource.

## DAVID A. MARTIN, THE REFUGEE CONCEPT: ON DEFINITIONS, POLITICS, AND THE CAREFUL USE OF A SCARCE RESOURCE

Refugee Policy: Canada and the United States (H. Adelman ed. 1991).
Pp. 30–51.

Contemporary commentary on refugee law, in both Canada and the United States, tends to be harshly critical of the reigning refugee definition, derived from the 1951 United Nations Convention Relating to the Status of Refugees. Especially objectionable, say many of the writers, is the dichotomy between political refugees on the one hand, who can claim a host of legal protections, and economic migrants or displaced persons on the other, who cannot. This dichotomy is said to be overly European—appropriate, perhaps, to the circumstances confronting the world in 1951 when the UN Convention was drafted, but insufficiently sensitive to what is really happening on our planet today. It is particularly inept, so runs this line of criticism, at addressing the travails of the developing world, the source of most of today's fifteen million refugees.

The tide of criticism is powerful. I intend, perhaps inadvisedly, to swim against it. For I have become convinced that the Convention definition, understood narrowly but appropriately, may offer the best way to make sense of the precarious legal institution of political asylum in those haven countries where the rule of law enjoys sufficient strength and independence to draw a fairly sharp distinction between law and politics. My argument requires both a careful appreciation of the exact purposes of a definition in this context and an effort to maximize achievement of these purposes in the light of the political constraints confronting refugee protection. * * *

### ASYLUM AS AN ENTITLEMENT

* * * Most of the detailed entitlements [in the 1951 Convention], it turns out, are available only to refugees "lawfully in" or "lawfully staying in" the host country. Nations retain complete discretion regarding the legalization of such aliens' status[.] * * * Merely proving that you are a refugee under the treaty definition, as arduous as that process can be, does not mean you achieve the requisite lawful status.

This is why the 1951 Convention is not a treaty about asylum and why, as refugee-law writings frequently repeat, there is no individual right of asylum in international law. The Convention is, as the title advertises, a treaty about the status of refugees—and primarily about the status of those refugees that the state has chosen, in its discretion, to treat as lawfully present. * * *

* * * Although the treaties do not pronounce a fully operative legal right of asylum—asylum in the sense of an indefinite right to stay, accompanied by a range of other rights that will facilitate a reasonably normal life in the new land—they do firmly establish protection against

return to the persecuting state, even for those who are present illegally: the famous obligation of *nonrefoulement* of Article 33. This was no mean achievement.

More important, behold the significant edifice that has been constructed on this modest foundation, at least in most of those states that are parties to the treaties and have highly developed legal systems. It turns out in practice that the *nonrefoulement* obligation has been virtually transformed into * * * a de facto right of asylum, in the stronger sense given above [involving all the entitlements spelled out in the Convention], for those who manage to establish physical presence in an asylum country and prove that they meet the refugee definition.

* * *[Of course, to] a major extent governments are simply bowing to necessity when they act in this fashion. Although Article 33 prevents return only to the home country and usually poses no obstacles to sending the individual to some other state, in practice, wealthy Western countries almost never find other nations volunteering to take refugees off their hands. * * * [The treaty would still permit the host country to warehouse refugees in a camp.] Nevertheless, these Western countries, because of their own human rights traditions, find it politically unthinkable to keep these individuals—recognized refugees—in such enforced idleness and detention. The domestic political climate simply would not tolerate such an approach.

In reality, then, and with very limited exceptions (having primarily to do with criminal misbehaviour), an asylum-seeker in these Western countries who proves that he or she is a refugee will have established a right to asylum. The political reality is that those who prove entitlement to *nonrefoulement* wind up also with an entitlement to asylum in the stronger sense. A legal obligation under Article 33, of what seems to be exceedingly modest proportions, thus becomes the centrepiece for important *political* consequences that do lead to highly significant protections. * * * Those protections attach for those who, first, establish physical presence, and, second, show that they meet the refugee definition.

The reader whose cynicism is undiminished may immediately focus on the enumerated qualifications. * * * That is, states that wish to minimize their exposure will try, first, to block the establishment of a claimant's physical presence on their national territory, and, second, to tighten the procedural and substantive requirements for satisfying the refugee definition.

Both these restrictionist processes are indeed under way, and I will have more to say about them later, for denial of access should be seen as much more disturbing than certain forms of tightening of the requirements. * * * [But for now we should simply recognize that restrictive pressures seek an outlet. Then,] armed with that recognition, we must learn how to shape our legal doctrine to sustain the political conditions that keep [the de facto entitlement to asylum] vital.

ASYLUM AS A SCARCE RESOURCE

If asylum is an entitlement, it carries its own special fragility, for it easily generates backlash when the press of claimants increases. * * * [A]sylum must respond to two different impulses, largely but somewhat paradoxically shared by much of the public in Western nations since World War II. On the one hand, they—we—genuinely wish to provide haven for the persecuted. On the other hand, we still value the reassurance that comes from reasonable control over the entry of aliens. When the number of asylum-seekers increases sharply, the ability to control appears increasingly threatened, at least in the absence of a convincing demonstration that the increase came from a real outbreak of implacable persecution—that is, evidence that most of the new arrivals are "true refugees".

This negative public reaction is compounded when asylum adjudication systems turn out to be as dismayingly ineffective as most Western systems have proved to be over the past decade. The systems take inordinately long to reach a final decision, and even then they rarely seem capable of deporting those ruled ineligible for asylum. This failure increases the backlash, for it then becomes apparent, sometimes in a vividly public way, that resettlement rights are not being reserved only for those who show the kind of special threat that clearly justifies an exception from the usual rigors of the immigration laws. Moreover, that very ineffectiveness compounds the reaction in another way, because it probably magnifies the attractiveness of the asylum option for people in distant countries facing a variety of political, economic, and personal troubles. * * *

Ironically, the fact that asylum has become an entitlement compounds the sense of threat to immigration control. An entitlement, in contrast to a discretionary bestowal of political grace, holds a unique immunity to the measures for deliberate decisions concerning intake that are available, at least in theory, in other subfields of immigration law. * * *

* * * [A] claim to refugee status trumps most of the other criteria for control, and for good reason, when applied to the truly threatened, but for reasons that appear decreasingly convincing when the radius of the definitional circle is expanded. We did not have to confront this built-in tension so baldly in earlier times, largely because physical distances and the cost of travel provided natural limitations on the numbers who might seek extra-regional asylum, but now that improved communication and transport have radically shrunk the globe, we cannot escape it. * * *

As the past decade has proven, asylum is a scarce resource. This might seem an odd claim to make in a volume focusing on the United States and Canada, two of the globe's wealthiest societies, and certainly among those with the greatest reserves of available land. Asylum's scarcity is political, however, not physical. The negative public reaction is not based on a sense that these societies are unable to absorb 150,000 or so needy people, newly arrived on North American soil; it is based instead on the fear that the intake will not remain at those levels. Asylum as an entitlement undermines confidence in immigration controls, at least when the numbers increase, because it lacks ready conceptual assurance that the entitlement will remain within reasonable limits. The actions of Western governments in recent years, building harsher deterrents and stronger barriers to arrival, afford support for this claim. We can talk ourselves hoarse in condemning these trends and exhorting greater generosity, but we might better expend our energies in accepting certain political limits and searching instead for ways to make the most of the scarce, but potent, legal resource we have at our disposal.

That will have to mean that asylum is available, as an entitlement rather than as an act of optional political grace, only to a relatively modest number of persons.* * *

* * * Nearly all countries seem joined in a parallel effort to narrow the standards and thereby minimize the loss of control that the asylum entitlement otherwise presages. In doing so, however, some very bad doctrine has emerged. Though narrowing may be politically necessary, not all forms of narrowing are appropriate. The task is to preserve as much as possible of the core purposes of asylum without overtaxing the system. This in turn requires a further exploration of these core purposes.

A Defence of the UN Definition: Relocation
and the Primacy of the Political

\* \* \*

The asylum system is not some kind of administrative referendum judging relative need or degree of elicited sympathy in * * * abstract terms. It is instead a system for assigning a very particular sort of scarce resource, a resource that is only one of many possible ways to respond to need or to compassionate claims. And what, stripped to its barest essentials, is that resource? It is an entitlement to relocation—or better, an entitlement to continue one's relocation indefinitely—in a foreign country.

\* \* \*

Relocation is not indispensable in responding to need in the realm of economic and social rights. As elemental and brutal as the need for food and shelter can be, it plainly can be met in situ, sometimes by provision of urgent relief supplies, sometimes by broader aid meant to improve general economic and social conditions. Urgent relief resources sent by outsiders are usually welcomed by the government in control of the territory. If not, then that resistance almost always bespeaks an element of political oppression that probably should itself bring the deprivation within the classic contours of the UN definition, as traditionally understood. Similar observations apply to earthquake and other natural disaster victims; in any event, the source of their needs tends to be of shorter duration than the socio-economic deprivations mentioned earlier.

Civil war poses more complex issues. Depending on the extent and intensity of the fighting, civilians' greatest need often is precisely for relocation. * * *

If justification [for their exclusion from the definition] is to be found, it must derive from a rough generalization about the need for *foreign* relocation, or at least foreign relocation as a matter of entitlement, as opposed to relocation elsewhere within the home country. Civil wars do usually have limited fronts, and civilians may flee to safer zones. Life may be extremely hard for them in these circumstances, having lost, at least for a time, their homes and perhaps all means of providing for their own livelihood, but the privations that result are of a kind that can be met, at least in principle, by urgent relief assistance provided from outside. Beyond this, where foreign flight is indispensable (as when the fighting cuts off access to other regions of the home country, or when no region is safe), such an option has usually been made available, as a matter of temporary political grace, in adjacent countries, again usually accompanied by substantial relief efforts mounted by the international community. The exclusion of such persons from the Convention definition then perhaps reflects a rough judgment that an entitlement system is not indispensable for affording such shelter in these circumstances, particularly because the need for such haven is more reliably temporary.

Contrast these situations with that faced by an "activist" targeted for political persecution, to use the first of the categories helpfully developed by Zolberg, Suhrke, and Aguayo [reprinted, *supra*]. The government recognizes that the activist is a political opponent and is bent on defeating both the individual and the cause. To effect this defeat, the government is likely to visit serious sanctions on the activist: jailing, beatings, perhaps even torture and death. Because of the nature of the government's political objectives, nothing we can send from outside addresses the individual's need. The case is the same with those Zolberg and his colleagues call "targets", that is, the racial, ethnic, or religious minorities singled out for violent government abuse because of that characteristic. Their plight is not addressed by material assistance or emergency relief crews sent from outside; it can be effectively relieved only by relocation outside the national borders.

In tacit recognition of this fact, the Western world has, haltingly and with many conceptual missteps, developed a system—today's asylum system—that provides relocation as an entitlement to individuals facing precisely these sorts of implacable *political* threats. The modern asylum system says, in effect, that it is too much to expect an ordinary mortal to return home in these particular kinds of threatening circumstances, facing dangers that cannot be propitiated in any other fashion, precisely because of their targeted political character.

* * *

ASYLUM AS PART OF AN INTEGRATED HUMAN RIGHTS STRATEGY

* * * [A]nother angle [of approach] * * * reveals more about the basic purposes of the asylum entitlement. * * *

If the home society is beset by serious human rights problems, it is not immediately apparent why individual escapes provide a response that is superior to changes that would benefit the whole community in the home country. That is, those who leave are, to some extent, turning their backs on continuing the struggle for a communal answer to the human rights abuses and instead simply seeking, through relocation, an improvement in their individual human rights situation. This is a perfectly natural and understandable human response, but whether it should be institutionally encouraged is more doubtful. An ambitious asylum system, one with low threshold qualifications and hence a wider circle of beneficiaries, unintentionally promotes such individual solutions[.] * * *

* * * [This insight] brings us back to our starting point. We should help point people toward struggling for community solutions, unless the danger at home is so great that it is too much to ask them to remain or return. The asylum standard thus must not be interpreted to require heroism of those to whom it denies shelter.[a] Return is too much to ask when the home government has targeted the individual (or a group to which he or she belongs) for severe mistreatment, for persecution. It is not too much to ask if the risk is less severe or less focused. Staying put in those circumstances is simply what we, too—ordinary, unheroic citizens—should expect of ourselves if our nations were beset by the same kinds of human rights abuses.

* * * This may mean that [those who stay home] have to keep their heads down until circumstances are more propitious or until the heroic actions, even martyrdom, of the bravest among their number create opportunities for radical changes. Having witnessed the dramatic and surprising changes of this past year in many parts of the globe, we should not underestimate the importance of such support from people of modest fortitude, who previously showed few signs of willingness or ability to work for human rights.

CONCLUSION

Refugee law, taken to extremes, ironically can demean those it means to benefit. Its focus is solely on haven, on sheltering people who fear their governments—as though governments never had anything to fear from the people. * * * With its "exilic bias" * * * ambitious refugee law tends to treat people as history's pawns, never its players: as objects always on the receiving end of home government action, not as subjects capable of acting in their own right.

A narrower political standard, of the kind I advocate here, respects this capacity in those persons. * * * [It] also husbands the limited

---

**a.** Relocated sentence—eds.

political reserves that keep asylum vital in the haven countries for those who are in greatest jeopardy.

———————

## Notes and Questions

1.  Why does Shacknove frame his inquiry as an exposition of "refugee-hood," rather than simply as an exploration of moral obligations falling upon the international community, to which such labels might be irrelevant? Can an analyst really separate a mapping of the concept from the underlying moral or political purposes the concept is meant to serve? Also consider his footnote 12. Why do most modern observers focus on how persecution may give rise to a right to asylum or international protection and assistance rather than (as did John Locke) to a right to revolution against the persecutor? Should the choice between those two courses of action simply be a prudential one, as that footnote states? Whose prudential calculations count—only the individual's or also those of the potential haven country or the international community more generally?

2.  The readings take differing approaches toward economic deprivation as a basis for refugee-type protections. Under what circumstances should severe economic conditions result in mandated protection in a foreign country under Martin's approach? Under Shacknove's? Under Zolberg, Suhrke, and Aguayo's? When does the *"in situ* clause" the latter authors discuss take effect and justify a proposed haven state's rejection of the asylum seekers' claims? What if international relief in place is possible, but has not materialized? What if relief is possible but only if the world community would deploy military force? (Shacknove wrote before the UN Security Council began in earnest in the early 1990s to use—selectively—its broadest military authorities under Chapter VII of the UN Charter for humanitarian purposes.)

3.  Most of the time the safe haven provided to "victims" (as the word is used by Zolberg, Suhrke, and Aguayo) outside the borders of their countries of origin has resulted from ad hoc political efforts undertaken by the receiving states and international organizations, although, as noted in Section C4 of this Chapter, an increasing number of countries have expanded legal provisions to cover some such persons. (We will discuss these developments in greater detail in connection with our examination of other forms of protection in Chapter Eleven, *infra.*) Receiving states, however, have often resisted efforts to characterize such practices as legally required. They prefer to speak of them as desirable measures that may be taken when conditions permit—including conditions having to do with the overall numbers and relative burdens imposed by the asylum seekers. Are such consequentialist concerns appropriate considerations for these purposes? List the advantages and disadvantages of incorporating protections for the victims of war and civil strife in a binding legal regime, as opposed to leaving them to future political response. If a binding legal regime of this type appears advantageous, what legislative standards would you recommend?

4.  There exists a rich and growing literature on the philosophical and legal conceptions of "refugee." For a very selective sampling *see, e.g.,* H.

Adelman, Canada and the Indochinese Refugees 4–16 (1982); J. Hathaway, The Law of Refugee Status (1991); J. Carlier, et al., Who is a Refugee? (1997); F. Nicholson & P. Twomey, eds., Refugee Rights and Realities: Evolving Concepts and Regimes 13–150 (1999); B.S. Chimni, ed., International Refugee Law: A Reader (2000); C. Boswell, The Ethics of Refugee Policy (2005); Note, *Political Legitimacy in the Law of Political Asylum,* 99 Harv.L.Rev. 450, 459–64 (1985); Singer & Singer, *The Ethics of Refugee Policy,* in Open Borders? Closed Societies?: The Ethical and Political Issues 111 (M. Gibney ed. 1988); Hathaway, *A Reconsideration of the Underlying Premise of Refugee Law,* 31 Harv.Int'l L.J. 129 (1990); Carens, *The Philosopher and the Policymaker: Two Perspectives on the Ethics of Immigration with Special Attention to the Problem of Restricting Asylum,* in Immigration Admissions: The Search for Workable Policies in Germany and the United States 3 (K. Hailbronner et al. eds. 1997); Nathwani, *The Purpose of Asylum,* 12 Int'l J. Refugee L. 354 (2000); Carens, *Who Should Get In? The Ethics of Immigration Admissions,* 17 Ethics & Int'l Aff. 95 (2003); Price, *Persecution Complex: Justifying Asylum Law's Preference for Persecuted People,* 47 Harv. J. Int'l L. 413 (2006).

# Chapter Two

## PROTECTION IN THE UNITED STATES: *NONREFOULEMENT* AND ASYLUM

---

*I realized my days of freedom were numbered and that I would have to act immediately. I learned by word of mouth that, with a great deal of money, it would be possible to be smuggled to a safe harbor and escape my fate in Iran. I thought I could go the United States, where I have two sisters with permanent resident status. The prevailing wisdom in Iran, however, was that Canada was a better prospect for political asylum. I had been told that without valid travel documents, the U.S. authorities would send me back to Iran immediately. I therefore took out a substantial amount of my savings and set out to find my way to Canada.*

*[For $10,000 I was smuggled into Pakistan, and then with false documents I made my way to Bombay.] Although I was not happy resorting to forged documents, I knew there was no other way to escape. * * * When I asked [a smuggler in Bombay, Mehdi,] for a ticket and documents to get to Canada, Mehdi discouraged me, saying I had a greater chance of being arrested at a stopover on a Canadian flight than I did if I went to the United States. He asked if I knew anyone in the U.S. Hearing about my two sisters, Mehdi told me I should telephone them and have them meet me at the airport with a lawyer, who could vouch for me and help me in my asylum application. He assured me that because I had relatives there, my application would most likely be approved. Moreover, he noted my arrival could coincide with Christmas, and that everyone in New York is especially nice at that time.*

*I bought a ticket to New York and a passport from Mehdi which had originally been issued to an Afghan woman whose photo and date of birth had been obliterated and my own substituted. This passport cost me $1,800. I called my sisters to* *arrange for them to meet my flight. Though I was unable to reach them, I realized I had to leave the country anyway.*

*\* \* \* Mehdi had instructed me to destroy my travel papers after leaving London [where the plane had a stopover]. I did so. I hid in the lavatory when arrival cards were distributed and collected, so my undocumented passage went unnoticed.*

*When the plane landed in New York on December 26, I disembarked last. I saw a few Indians and a Bangladeshi ahead of me being questioned. I realized I, too, would be questioned. I approached an immigration officer, and he soon discovered I had no documents. He sent for a Persian-speaking Swissair employee who translated for me. I was asked where I was from and who had sent me. Again, following Mehdi's instructions, I said I didn't know. Two Air India employees came to search my bags for documents. I was fingerprinted and asked to sign a form.*

—Mohammed Reza Noori,
Iranian businessman,
detained in New York[1]

Chapter One surveyed the global framework of protection for forced migrants. In this chapter, we will look at the protection afforded by a national system, namely that of the United States. We will first explore the protections afforded by the 1951 Convention, both *nonrefoulement* and asylum, as well as rights for those lawfully admitted. Next we will sketch how U.S. law implements (and occasionally expands) the 1951 Convention's protections. The chapter closes with an overview of the U.S. procedures for obtaining protection and some trends and statistics that shed light on the operation of the U.S. protection system as a whole.

## SECTION A.   1951 CONVENTION PROTECTIONS FOR FORCED MIGRANTS

Hoping for a "safe harbor," Mohammed Reza Noori considered his prospects for obtaining "political asylum" in either Canada or the United States. What did he mean and what protection did he envision? He no doubt hoped that he would not be sent back to Iran. What else? Did he expect to remain permanently in the United States? Did he expect to be able to find work, to live where he chose, to have his family join him, to send his children to school, to own property, to join political organizations, to vote?

As noted in Chapter One, the 1951 Convention Relating to the Status of Refugees, despite all its limitations, has remained the fundamental legal framework for protecting a subset of forced migrants. The 1951 Convention defines as refugees those who are outside of their

---

**1.** C. Kismaric, Forced Out: The Agony of the Refugee in Our Time 144–47 (1989).

country and cannot return to it "owing to a well founded fear of being persecuted for reasons of race, religion, nationality, membership of a particular social group or political opinion." But what does the 1951 Convention guarantee to those who fall within its scope?

Hungarian refugees in Burgenland, Austria, 1956. (Photo: © Christian Brandstätter Verlag, Vienna)

Essentially, the Convention provides two guarantees: (1) no refugee may be returned to a land where her life or freedom would be threatened, and (2) those refugees who have been *lawfully admitted* to the receiving state are guaranteed equal treatment in exercising enumerated civil and political rights. When the 1951 Convention came into force, European countries faced millions of displaced persons who had been uprooted by the Second World War and were unlikely to leave their new country of residence. As a consequence, states focused on measures to integrate lawfully admitted refugees into their population; the bulk of the 1951 Convention addresses refugees and their right to education, employment, housing, public relief, social security, access to courts, and so on. There was no great concern about removing refugees or denying them admission, a topic addressed toward the end of the Convention's text. In today's world, however, this is the major focus, to which we now turn.

## 1. *NONREFOULEMENT*

Article 33 of the Convention prohibits states from turning away refugees if they would be returned to countries in which they are likely to face persecution:

> No Contracting State shall expel or return (*"refouler"*) a refugee in any manner whatsoever to the frontiers of territories where his life or freedom would be threatened on account of his race, religion, nationality, membership of a particular social group or political opinion.

This protection against *refoulement* (the French term often used to refer to the return of refugees to persecution) is the modern-day linchpin of refugee protection. Technically, Article 33 only mandates non-return; it does not require states to provide work authorization or residence permits to those who fall within its ambit. Indeed, it does not even require states to allow the individuals to remain—they can be sent away to any other state so long as they are not returned to a state where their life or freedom would be threatened. In practice, though, most states resist acceptance of needy noncitizens, so they are unlikely to accept a person that a sister state is trying to send away. Consequently, most states realize that they will not be able to expel a noncitizen who satisfies the *nonrefoulement* criteria, and states tend to give these individuals some legal status that allows them to remain and earn a living.

Before turning from *nonrefoulement* to the more extensive protection granted to lawfully admitted refugees, we should note that the concept of *nonrefoulement* is not limited to the 1951 Refugee Convention or, even, to refugees. During the past fifty years this obligation has become firmly established in customary international law in circumstances involving persecution, torture, and massive human rights abuses. *See* Guy S. Goodwin–Gill, The Refugee in International Law 203–04 (2d ed. 1996). Furthermore, multiple instruments, including the 1949 Geneva Convention Concerning the Protection of Civilians in War (Art.4, Fourth Convention, 12 Aug. 1949), the 1950 European Convention on Human Rights, the 1969 American Convention on Human Rights (OAS Official Records, OEA/Ser.K/XVI/1.1), the 1981 African Charter of Human and Peoples' Rights (1001 UNTS 45), and the 1984 Convention Against Torture, all specify a prohibition against *refoulement*.

## 2.  REFUGEE STATUS OR ASYLUM

Under the terms of the 1951 Convention, state parties guarantee extensive legal protection to lawfully admitted refugees, but nothing in the Convention requires states to admit refugees. Shocking as this is to many who assume that a treaty defining refugees must require states to protect refugees who arrive at their borders, it is understandable when one remembers that the European powers that formulated the Convention in 1951 faced a settled refugee population that needed a framework for integration.

Although the 1951 Convention does not impose a duty on states to admit and grant significant protection to refugees who appear on their territory without legal authorization, most industrialized states have imposed this duty on themselves via national legislation. In general, states have adopted the 1951 Convention refugee definition as the lodestar: those who satisfy it, whether lawfully admitted or not, are entitled to stay. They are granted refugee status, often called Convention status or asylum. Because the 1951 Convention itself does not require states to admit refugees, national legislation varies as each state determines the exact circumstances under which it will allow the otherwise unauthorized individuals to enter and remain. Nonetheless, the core requirements are those set forth in the refugee definition in the 1951 Convention.

## SECTION B.  PROTECTION UNDER UNITED STATES LAW

When Mohammed Reza Noori arrived in New York, he landed in a nation whose legal practice has developed elaborate distinctions in the types of protection afforded to refugees, in particular the distinction between *nonrefoulement* and asylum, a status that includes all the rights enumerated by the 1951 Convention. The relatively brief refugee definition plays a role in both *nonrefoulement* and asylum in the United States, and it has spawned surprisingly complex doctrinal questions. The Board of Immigration Appeals (BIA) and the courts are creating a voluminous body of case law analyzing specific legal questions, sometimes reaching strikingly diverse conclusions. These cases also present unique fact-finding and fact-marshaling challenges, to both litigators and adjudicators, leaving ample room for controversy about whether political considerations have intruded on the decisions. We will first outline the development of *nonrefoulement* and asylum in the United States, which we will follow with an overview of the procedural system that has developed in order to evaluate refugee claims.

## 1.  NONREFOULEMENT IN THE UNITED STATES

### a.  *Post–World War II*

In 1950, Congress adopted a provision exempting noncitizens from deportation "to any country in which the Attorney General shall find that such alien would be subjected to physical persecution." Internal Security Act of 1950, Ch. 1024, § 23, 64 Stat. 987, 1010. Early court decisions ostensibly imposed onerous factfinding responsibilities on the Attorney General under this provision. *See, e.g., Sang Ryup Park v. Barber,* 107 F.Supp. 605 (N.D. Cal. 1952); *Harisiades v. Shaughnessy,* 187 F.2d 137, 142 (2d Cir. 1951), *affirmed on other grounds,* 342 U.S. 580, 72 S.Ct. 512, 96 L.Ed. 586 (1952). As a result, Congress rewrote the provision when it drafted the Immigration and Nationality Act (INA) in 1952. (The INA, though heavily amended over the last 50 years, remains the basic, comprehensive statute containing provisions governing U.S. immigration and citizenship, including protection provisions.) Section 243(h) of that Act authorized the Attorney General, *in his discretion,* to withhold deportation of an alien within the United States who was subject to physical persecution in his country of nationality. Since then, *nonrefoulement* protection has ordinarily been known in U.S. law as "withholding of deportation," or more recently, "withholding of removal."

In 1958, the Supreme Court construed this provision rather rigidly, holding in *Leng May Ma v. Barber,* 357 U.S. 185, 78 S.Ct. 1072, 2 L.Ed.2d 1246 (1958), that withholding under § 243(h) was available only to noncitizens who had entered the United States and were in deportation proceedings. But eventually administrative practice developed ways to afford parallel protection to noncitizens who had been initially encountered at the border and therefore were in exclusion proceedings. These provisions were administered for many years under the strong influence of Cold War assumptions. Successful claimants were, in overwhelming proportions, refugees from Communist countries, although the statutes were never thus restricted.

In 1968, the United States became a party to the 1967 Protocol relating to the Status of Refugees, and so became derivatively bound by all of the important substantive provisions of the 1951 Convention relating to the Status of Refugees. Congress enacted no changes in the statutory provisions governing withholding deportation at that time, because the Departments of State and Justice had assured the Senate, while it was considering ratification, that the Protocol could be implemented without requiring any changes in the immigration laws. It is questionable, however, whether the Senators fully appreciated that accepting the treaty transformed some discretionary provisions of § 243(h) into firm legal obligations.

Moreover, the executive branch's testimony had merely stated that the treaty could be implemented under existing *statutes.* It did not promise that the earlier administrative criteria for the exercise of discretion could remain unchanged once the treaty became law. Nor did it promise the opposite; it was simply silent on this crucial question.

### b. *Refugee Act of 1980*

By enacting the Refugee Act of 1980, Congress brought the United States into line with the obligations flowing from the substantive provisions of the 1951 Refugee Convention. Specifically, the Refugee Act of 1980 amended § 243(h) of the INA, the provision that since 1952 had given the Attorney General discretion to withhold the deportation of noncitizens subject to persecution. Congress made this provision mandatory, and, overruling *Leng May Ma*, Congress also made it expressly applicable to all noncitizens. Later, in 1996, Congress renumbered this section as § 241(b)(3), but without major substantive changes, and it formally labeled the remedy "restriction on removal." Nevertheless, it is still commonly called by the old name: "withholding."[2]

Under current U.S. law, removal must be withheld in the following circumstances:

> [T]he Attorney General may not remove an alien to a country if * * * the alien's life or freedom would be threatened * * * because of the alien's race, religion, nationality, membership in a particular social group, or political opinion.

INA § 241(b)(3).

As you can see, this language closely tracks the *nonrefoulement* provision of the 1951 Convention, Article 33. Congress enumerated certain exceptions to this mandatory obligation, § 241(b)(3)(B), which serve generally to disqualify spies, dangerous criminals, and persons who participated in the persecution of others. Although Article 33 itself contains exceptions for security dangers and certain dangerous criminals, the statutory exclusions are not identical to those listed in Article 33, which raises the question whether U.S. legislation violates the treaty. The 1980 Congress intended to avoid any such result, and the legislative history of the Refugee Act states explicitly that the exceptions are to be construed consistently with exceptions to the Protocol's protections. *See* Articles 1(F) and 33(2) of the 1951 Convention. But the wording of § 241(b)(3)(B)(i), disqualifying those who have "ordered, incited, assisted or otherwise participated in" persecution of others, is extraordinarily broad. Whether this or other statutory exclusions correspond to any provisions in the Convention will be explored in Chapter Six.

Persons granted only withholding of removal—and not the more ample protections that come with asylum, to be considered below—usually remain in the United States because third countries will allow them to enter only under exceptional circumstances. Persons granted withholding generally receive work authorization, 8 C.F.R. § 274a.12(a)(10), and can access some public assistance, but unlike asylees they may not bring in members of their immediate families. Nor does the law make any provision for eventual adjustment of status to lawful permanent resident, although they are not precluded from such adjustment if they otherwise qualify, such as through marriage or employment.

---

**2.** Many cases in this book arose before the 1996 amendments and therefore refer to withholding by reference to INA § 243(h). We have not changed the numbering in those older cases as reprinted here.

Most of the U.S. practice concerning *nonrefoulement* developed in the refugee context, but the *nonrefoulement* concept is not so limited. A closely related protection derives from the Convention Against Torture and Other Cruel, Inhuman, or Degrading Treatment or Punishment (CAT), *adopted* Dec. 10, 1984, G.A. Res. 39/46, U.N. GAOR, 39th Sess., Supp. No. 51, U.N. Doc. A/39/51 (1985), *entered into force*, June 26, 1987. Article 3 bars return of a person to a state "where there are substantial grounds for believing that he would be in danger of being subjected to torture." The United States became a party to the treaty in 1994 and fully implemented this specific *nonrefoulement* protection by regulations adopted in 1999. We will consider CAT protection in detail in Chapter Seven.

### c. On the Relationship Between International and U.S. Law

From the foregoing explanation of *nonrefoulement* in U.S. law—and the explanation of asylum that comes next—it is clear that U.S. law mirrors international law. This raises, in turn, the question of the relationship between the two when individuals seek protection in the United States. To what extent may they invoke international law directly? Or must they rely exclusively on U.S. law?

Two basic principles are important to note here. First, a treaty—for example, the 1951 Convention or the 1967 Protocol—operates as a law that is enforceable in U.S. courts only if it is "self-executing." U.S. courts have generally found treaties of this type to be non-self-executing. Congress often implements non-self-executing treaties through legislation meant to ensure compliance (like the 1980 Refugee Act), but courts ordinarily then consider themselves to be enforcing the statute rather than the treaty itself. The second principle—which may mitigate the effects of the first—is a canon of statutory interpretation established by the U.S. Supreme Court in *Murray v. The Schooner Charming Betsy*, 6 U.S. (2 Cranch) 64, 117–18, 2 L.Ed. 208 (1804). According to the *Charming Betsy* canon, "an act of Congress ought never to be construed to violate the law of nations if any other possible construction remains." Of course, the application of this canon requires a court to determine what international law requires in any given situation.

### 2.   ASYLUM

Until 1980 the word "asylum" had never appeared in the immigration laws of the United States. Nonetheless, from the very beginning of federal immigration laws, Congress has recognized that special exemptions may be necessary for otherwise inadmissible or deportable noncitizens who have become political enemies of the government in the nation to which they would be sent. In 1875, when Congress first provided that convicts would be excludable, it exempted persons who had been convicted of political offenses. Similar exemptions appeared with regularity in later laws. *See, e.g.,* Act of March 3, 1875, Ch. 141, § 5, 18 Stat. 477; Act of August 3, 1882, Ch. 376, § 4, 22 Stat. 214; Act of March 3, 1891, Ch.

551, § 1, 26 Stat. 1084; Act of Feb. 20, 1907, Ch. 1134, § 2, 34 Stat. 898, 899; Immigration Act of 1917, Ch. 29, § 3, 39 Stat. 874, 877.

### a.  Post–World War II

There was little systematic attention in the United States to providing asylum to refugees prior to the end of World War II. Indeed, much of the impetus for new American and international efforts after the war derived from a recognition that pre-war efforts, especially on behalf of Jewish refugees, had been shamefully inadequate. *See generally* J. Simpson, The Refugee Problem (1939); D. Wyman, Paper Walls: America and the Refugee Crisis, 1938–1941 (1968); H. Feingold, The Politics of Rescue: The Roosevelt Administration and The Holocaust, 1938–1945 (1970). For the next three decades, most legislative attention was focused on the overseas refugee situation, and statutes mainly provided for bringing forced migrants from distant locations as part of a deliberate U.S. program. (This part of U.S. refugee protection will be examined closely in Chapter Ten.) Nonetheless, the statutory evolution helps us understand the role of asylum in U.S. law.

By directive in 1945, President Truman ordered priority use of regular immigration quota numbers for the admission of some of the millions of displaced persons left stranded by World War II. In 1948, Congress passed the first significant refugee legislation in American history in order to meet the same problem. The Displaced Persons Act of 1948, Ch. 647, 62 Stat. 1009, provided a temporary program that eventually admitted roughly 400,000 people from the categories specified in the legislation.

When the Soviet Union put down the Hungarian revolution in 1956, its action sent hundreds of thousands across the borders, mainly to Austria, and generated pressure for a quick United States response. The Eisenhower Administration responded by bringing 30,000 Hungarian refugees to the United States. There was no applicable refugee admission or asylum provision, so the government relied on an administrative procedure known as "parole" to bring refugees to safety in the United States. The same approach was employed after Fidel Castro came to power in Cuba, as thousands of Cubans sought refuge in the United States. The Hungarian and Cuban crises disabused Americans of any notion that refugee problems would disappear once World War II's displaced persons had all found new homes. Some permanent provision for refugee programs, available to meet new crises, would have to be made.

The landmark 1965 immigration legislation, which abolished the national origins quota system (adopted in the 1920s to favor Northern and Western European immigration), provided the occasion for major changes. In addition to establishing more neutral preference categories (based on family ties and employment needs) for noncitizens seeking regular immigration to the United States, Congress adopted a new seventh preference designed to be a permanent provision for overseas refugee resettlement programs. It made available a certain percentage of admissions for refugees, but the only refugees who qualified were those who had "fled" persecution in a "Communist or Communist-dominated country" or a "country within the general area of the Middle East." Immigration and Nationality Act Amendments of 1965, Pub. L. No. 89–236, § 3, 79 Stat. 911, 913, amending § 203(a)(7) of the INA.

Though the 1965 legislative scheme created a framework for admitting certain refugees who were overseas; it contained no provisions concerning refugees who arrived in the United States on their own. The withholding provision, INA § 243(h), afforded basic protection, but gave no solid immigration status to its beneficiaries. Regulations and administrative guidance clarified some parts of the treatment, but left many details unaddressed. More significant changes in the regulations on these subjects came in the wake of the Kudirka incident in 1970. A Lithuanian seaman named Simas Kudirka managed to escape from a Soviet vessel onto a U.S. Coast Guard cutter, the *Vigilant*, tied alongside in U.S. territorial waters for a discussion of fishing rights. After a series of miscalculations and missed communications, the Coast Guard allowed Soviet authorities to board the cutter and forcibly return Kudirka to the Soviet ship. *See* Mann, *Asylum Denied: The Vigilant Incident*, 62 U.S. Naval War College Int'l L. Stud. 598 (1980); Goldie, *Legal Aspects of the Refusal of Asylum by U.S. Coast Guard on 23 November 1970, id.* at 626. The resulting public outcry led to a thorough review of U.S. asylum provisions and then to the issuance of improved guidelines and administrative regulations by several agencies. The regulations issued by the Immigration and Naturalization Service (INS) in 1974 were the first to spell out in detail the procedures to be used by persons already in the United States asking for refugee protection.[3] Litigation in succeeding years, much of it involving asylum seekers from Haiti, brought additional changes. *See* Martin, *Reforming Asylum Adjudication: On Navigating the Coast of Bohemia*, 138 U. Pa. L. Rev. 1247, 1294–98 (1990).

### b.   The Refugee Act of 1980

By 1980 the controversy over the provisions for asylum and their implementation was mounting, but Congress did not use the occasion of the Refugee Act to undertake a thorough review of these arrangements. The flow of refugees from Indochina was at its peak and Congressional attention was preoccupied with reforming the overseas refugee admissions programs, which we will examine in more detail in Chapter Ten. Nevertheless, the Act made a few important improvements respecting

---

**3.** Until 2003, INS was the principal agency with responsibility for administering and enforcing the immigration laws. As a unit of the Department of Justice, it was the principal delegate of authorities placed by statute in the Attorney General. The Board of Immigration Appeals, which was never part of INS, was also within the Department of Justice and wielded some of the Attorney General's immigration authorities. In 2003, INS was abolished and most of its authorities and staff were transferred to the Department of Homeland Security (DHS). The BIA and the immigration judges remain with Justice, as the major components of that Department's Executive Office of Immigration Review (EOIR).

asylum. In the past, successful applicants who proved the required degree of threatened persecution in the homeland were protected against involuntary return by INA § 243(h), the withholding provision, but there had been no immigration status clearly available to reflect that decision and clarify the beneficiary's right to stay indefinitely.

Cuban refugees during the Mariel boatlift, 1980. (Photo: U.S. Coast Guard)

The 1980 Refugee Act cured this problem by adding a new § 208 to the INA that specifically establishes "asylum" status, also often called "asylee" status. This status can be provided, in the discretion of the Attorney General, to applicants in the United States who show that they meet the statutory definition of refugee—that is, who have a well-founded fear of persecution on account of one of the five specified grounds if returned to their home countries.

In addition to the contrast between the discretionary nature of asylum and the mandatory nature of *nonrefoulement*, note that the asylum requirement of a "well-founded fear" differs from the analogous *nonrefoulement* requirement that the individual's "life or freedom would be threatened." As Chapter Three will explore, the Supreme Court ruled in the 1980s that this difference in language signified a difference in the risk level that the asylum seeker must prove. Withholding requires that persecution is "more likely than not," whereas the "well-founded fear" standard for asylum is easier to meet.

"Asylum" status differs in important respects from "refugee" status, which is the label given to those who have entered as part of the overseas programs. For example, the asylum provisions of the INA (§§ 208 and 209(b)) place greater emphasis on continuing review of conditions in the asylee's home country. Asylum may be terminated if circumstances change abroad so that the threat of persecution is ended. In contrast, refugee status carries no equivalent vulnerability. *See* INA §§ 207(c)(4), 208(c)(2), 209(a), 209(b)(3).

The Refugee Act provides asylees a routine mechanism for adjusting to lawful permanent resident status after one year in the United States. INA § 209(b). In its initial form, this section expressly limited the number of asylee adjustments each year. This limitation eventually caused massive backlogs and was finally deleted from the statute in 2005. When it was in force, it was a ceiling on asylee *adjustments* only; there was never an annual limit on the number of initial grants of asylum.

## SECTION C. U.S. PROCEDURES FOR SEEKING PROTECTION

### 1. APPLICATIONS FOR PROTECTION

Applicants can apply simultaneously for both *nonrefoulement* and asylum in the United States. The applications follow three different paths, depending on whether the applicant is currently in removal proceedings, and if so, in what type of proceeding. The two most important paths are usually called affirmative applications and defensive applications, to be described below. The third applies to most applicants at ports of entry, and to some narrow classes of applicants who are entrants without inspection. They must first clear the preliminary hurdle of "credible fear" screening during the expedited removal procedure, as discussed in Chapter Nine.

Under regulations collected at 8 C.F.R. Part 208, a noncitizen applies for protection under either INA § 208 or § 241(b)(3) (as well as under the Convention Against Torture) by filing Form I–589. This form asks why the applicant is seeking protection and what he or she thinks would happen upon return to the home country. The form requires the applicant to provide other information that may throw further light on the claim, such as past activities and organizational affiliations, current whereabouts and condition of family members, and the circumstances of departure and travel to the United States. Many applicants also provide additional material, sometimes quite voluminous, including affidavits, news accounts, or human rights reports, including those from nongovernmental organizations like Amnesty International or Human Rights Watch.

The statute requires that applicants be advised of the privilege of being represented by counsel, that they be provided with a list of available pro bono representatives, that absent exceptional circumstances the initial interview or hearing shall take place within 45 days of filing and the final adjudication (by the immigration judge) shall be completed within 180 days. INA § 208(d). Also, the applicant must be advised that knowingly filing a frivolous application makes him "permanently ineligible for any benefits under this Act." INA § 208(d)(6). The statute also states that asylum may not be granted until the applicant's identity is fully checked against law enforcement and national security databases. INA § 208(d)(5)(A)(I). As a result, an applicant approved by an asylum officer or immigration judge may receive only a preliminary grant of asylum, and in such cases the applicant may have to wait weeks or months for completion of fingerprint and name checks before delivery of the final documents, including work authorization. *See generally* Kerwin, *The Use and Misuse of "National Security" Rationale in Crafting U.S. Refugee and Immigration Policies*, 17 Int'l J. Ref. L. 749 (2005).

### a. Affirmative Applications

Applicants who are not currently in removal proceedings may file an affirmative application by mailing the I–589 to a regional service center (RSC), which is now part of the United States Citizenship and Immigration Services (USCIS) within the Department of Homeland Security. (In recent years a strong majority of applications have begun as affirmative claims.) The RSC staff checks that the application is complete and, if so, schedules the individual for an interview with an officer, which is to be carried out in a "nonadversarial manner." 8 C.F.R. § 208.9. A specialized corps of full-time professional asylum officers, required by regulation to "receive special training in international human rights law, nonadversarial interview techniques, and other relevant national and international refugee laws and principles," 8 C.F.R. § 208.1(b), receives the application and interviews the applicant.

Asylum officers are currently based in eight asylum offices located in cities throughout the country that have high concentrations of asylum applicants, and they ride circuit to hear claims at other places. Asylum officers make their decisions on the basis of the application form, the information presented during the interview, and possibly other information from the State Department or "other credible sources, such as international organizations, private voluntary agencies, news organizations, or academic institutions." 8 C.F.R. § 208.12(a). They are supported by their own central Resource Information Center, *see id.* § 208.1(b), which makes wide-ranging information about country conditions and legal developments available to the officers on-line. For revealing commentary by the head of the Asylum Office from its creation in 1990 until 1994, see Beyer, *Affirmative Asylum Adjudication in the United States*, 6 Geo. Immig. L.J. 253 (1992); Beyer, *Establishing the United States Asylum Officer Corps: A First Report*, 4 Int'l J. Refugee L. 455 (1992).

Asylum officers grant meritorious cases, which initially ran between 15 and 30 percent of affirmative filings, but in recent years have twice exceeded 40 percent. They do not deny the other cases; instead asylum officers refer them to immigration court, with minimal paperwork that does not have to explain in detail the reasons for the referral. *See* 8 C.F.R. § 208.14(b). At the same time, this system places emphasis on promptly serving referred applicants with a notice to appear, thus placing them swiftly into removal proceedings in immigration court, *see id.* § 208.14(b)(2).

### b. Defensive Applications

If removal proceedings are already underway, the applicant can apply for asylum or withholding only by presenting a defensive application that is heard exclusively by the immigration judge. 8 C.F.R. § 208.2(b). Typically the noncitizen makes known at master calendar (the first appearance in immigration court) her wish to seek asylum (or withholding of removal) as a form of relief from removal, and the judge then grants a specified period of time for completion of the I–589, to be filed with the immigration court. The matter is then heard in the more formal setting of the immigration court, with examination and cross-examination by the noncitizen's counsel (if she has one) and the DHS trial attorney.

Sometimes, the applicant is ordered removed from the United States, and only then applies for asylum, perhaps because the applicant did not have counsel until after the issuance of a removal order. In such cases, the asylum claim can only be raised by means of a motion to reopen filed with the immigration judge or BIA, depending on which forum last heard the matter. A motion to reopen is sometimes the first motion that a newly retained attorney files in a case. Many of the decisions that you will read in this book arose from motions to reopen.

As a general matter, motions to reopen are used to offer previously unavailable, material evidence. INA § 240(c)(6) and 8 C.F.R. § 1003.2 govern. The motion "must reasonably explain the failure to request asylum prior to the completion of the proceedings." 8 C.F.R. § 208.4(b)(3)(ii), (4). The motion also must show prima facie eligibility for the relief sought. In cases where the ultimate grant of relief is discretionary, the decisionmaker may deny the motion to reopen if it decides that that even if these first two requirements were met, the application would still be denied in the exercise of discretion. *See INS v. Abudu*, 485 U.S. 94, 104–07, 108 S.Ct. 904, 99 L.Ed.2d 90 (1988). Generally, only one motion to reopen may be filed, and it must be filed within 90 days of entry of a final removal order. The statute sets out several exceptions to the 90–day deadline, and case law recognizes others.

### c. *Applications in Expedited Removal Proceedings*

Under the expedited removal procedures, INA § 235(b)(1), noncitizens arriving at the port of entry or brought to the United States after interdiction at sea (plus specified classes of entrants without inspection who have been in the country for less than two years) are subject to removal on the order of an immigration officer, not an immigration judge, if found inadmissible under INA § 212(a)(6)(C) or (7) (for having false or inadequate documents or for other fraud or misrepresentation, even at an unrelated time in the past). Those among this group who express a fear of return or ask for asylum are referred to an asylum officer who interviews them (no sooner than 48 hours later) to determine whether they have a "credible fear of persecution," defined in INA § 235(b)(1)(B)(v) as a "significant possibility * * * that the alien could establish eligibility for asylum." If found to have a credible fear, their claims are heard on the merits as defensive asylum claims, based upon a full hearing in immigration court.

Those not found to have a credible fear are ordered removed. They may request that an immigration judge review this negative determination. Within seven days at the latest, and within 24 hours if practicable, an immigration judge considers the asylum officer's report and conducts a review in person, by video, or by telephone. INA § 235(b)(1)(B)(iii)(III). Judicial review of the immigration judge's decisions is available only in limited circumstances. INA §§ 242(a)(2)(A), 242(e). In practice, over 90 percent of those referred to an asylum officer are found to have a credible fear, but sharp controversy remains over several features of expedited removal, to be considered in Chapter Nine.

### d. Work Authorization

Prior to 1995, regulations authorized permission to work to all asylum seekers whose applications were not deemed "frivolous." 8 C.F.R. § 208.7(a)(1995). In effect, almost everyone who filed an asylum claim received employment authorization. Many argued that the easy acquisition of work authorization created an incentive to file asylum applications, whether or not there were grounds to support asylum. In 1995, new regulations postponed the issuance of work authorization until at least 180 days had elapsed—unless asylum is granted before then. They also provided that no authorization would issue if the application had been denied by an immigration judge within that time period. Asylum applications thereafter decreased significantly. These constraints are now written into the statute. INA § 208(d)(2). The government aim is to complete the asylum proceeding within the 180–day period. Delays requested by the asylum seeker do not count in accumulating the 180 days. *See generally* Martin, *Making Asylum Policy: The 1994 Reforms*, 70 Wash. L. Rev. 725, 733–37, 753–54 (1995).

### 2. IMMIGRATION COURT

Immigration judges provide the initial evaluation of all the defensive applications for asylum and withholding, and they provide a second review of affirmative applications referred by asylum officers. In the latter situation, the immigration judge receives the pre-existing I–589, with its attachments, from the asylum officer, along with copies of the charging document. Applicants of course can supplement their claims in immigration court and put on additional witnesses, but the use of the original application form in both settings is meant to enhance efficiency and save time. Immigration judges consider referred cases in much the same fashion as defensive claims, granting some asylum claims and giving rejected applicants a full statement of reasons as part of the decision in the case.

Under the statute, a proceeding to remove a noncitizen ordinarily must be conducted by an immigration judge. *See* INA §§ 101(b)(4); § 240(a)(1). Throughout much of our history, immigration judges (initially called hearing examiners) were simply experienced or senior immigration officers, designated to hold such hearings as part of a range of responsibilities to administer and enforce the immigration laws. Gradually, however, the immigration judges have acquired a degree of independence from the enforcement arms of the federal government. This evolution began with the INS' practice, starting in 1956, of assigning trial attorneys to appear for the government in immigration court. This freed the presiding officer for a more passive, judge-like decisionmaking role.

The separation of judges from prosecutors took a further step in 1983, when new regulations took immigration judges out of the INS and put them in a new unit—the Executive Office for Immigration Review (EOIR). The BIA, always independent of INS, became another component of EOIR, which was likewise in the Department of Justice but directly accountable to the Deputy or the Associate Attorney General rather than to anyone in the INS. For more on the evolution of the immigration judge corps and the BIA, with citations to further sources, see T. A. Aleinikoff, D. Martin, and H. Motomura, Immigration and Citizenship: Process and Policy 248–55 (5th ed. 2003).

The creation of EOIR enhanced the independence and neutrality of immigration judges. EOIR also made efforts to cast a wider net in its recruitment, with a special effort to reach outside the ranks of INS lawyers. Critics still maintained (as critics do today) that an enforcement mentality pervaded all immigration–related agencies, and argued that the structural separation was inadequate because immigration judges and the BIA, like the INS, remained ultimately answerable to the Attorney General. Many critics called for EOIR to become a wholly independent adjudication agency.

Congress responded, to some degree, to this line of criticism when it adopted the Homeland Security Act in 2002, which established the Department of Homeland Security. When DHS absorbed virtually all INS functions, EOIR remained in the Department of Justice and thus not answerable to the Secretary of Homeland Security, who is now the cabinet officer primarily responsible for immigration enforcement. Whether this kind of separation fully satisfies the criticism seems debatable, since the Attorney General of course remains a leading law enforcement officer.

The immigration judge corps has grown dramatically over the past two decades. In fiscal year 1992, there were about 85 immigration judges, who received 110,000 deportation and exclusion cases. By fiscal year 2005, there were over 200 immigration judges, and they received almost 325,000 removal cases. They issued almost 265,000 decisions (obviously many were summary dispositions that did not require full hearings on the merits) and registered almost 50,000 "other dispositions," which can include the administrative closure of a case because the noncitizen obtains a different form of relief, death of the respondent, or withdrawal of an application for admission. *See* 2005 EOIR Statistical Yearbook, at C4, D1.

The major portion of an immigration judge's time is spent with removal proceedings. This includes a variety of matters that extend well beyond adjudication of asylum, withholding, and other forms of protection from conditions in a noncitizen's home country. For example, an immigration judge might also decide whether a noncitizen is covered by one of the grounds of inadmissibility or deportability, or pass upon a wide variety of waivers and other forms of discretionary relief that may be available to noncitizens who concede removability. When considering such matters, the immigration judge often exercises the discretion the statute lodges in the Attorney General. We will see in Chapter Three that asylum is one of these forms of relief that involves the exercise of discretion. Immigration judges also preside over bond redetermination proceedings for detained noncitizens—essentially an expedited appeal of the terms of release that are set initially by the enforcement agencies.

Removal proceedings are typically conducted in two stages: the master calendar hearing and the individual merits hearing. The master calendar hearing is similar to a civil calendar call or a criminal arraignment. It serves to determine if an individual merits hearing is even required, and in many cases it is not. For example, the respondent may admit the government's allegations and waive any relief except voluntary departure. But if the respondent seeks asylum or other complex forms of relief, the immigration judge will set an individual merits hearing for a future date.

### 3. BOARD OF IMMIGRATION APPEALS

The immigration judge's decision on either a defensive asylum claim or a referred claim is appealable to the Board of Immigration Appeals (BIA), an administrative appeals tribunal that is part of the Executive Office for Immigration Review in the Department of Justice. *See* 8 C.F.R. § 1003.1(b). The Board has never been recognized by statute; it is entirely a creature of the Attorney General's regulations, and the Attorney General appoints its members.

BIA decisions are subject to further review within the Department of Justice, although such review is infrequently invoked. They may be "referred" to the Attorney General for a final authoritative decision, either before or after an initial ruling by the BIA, in three circumstances (none at the noncitizen's behest): when the Attorney General so directs; when the Chairman or a majority of the BIA decides that the case should be referred; or when the Secretary of Homeland Security requests referral. *See* 8 C.F.R. § 1003.1(h).

The BIA hands down a large volume of appellate decisions each month. Only a small fraction are designated as precedent decisions for inclusion in the official reports. *See* 8 C.F.R. §§ 103.3(c), 1003.1(i). BIA decisions are available on the EOIR website, <http://www.usdoj.gov/eoir>, which also provides other useful information, including statistical reports and practice manuals, as well as easy access to local immigration court rules. By regulation, interpretation of statute and regulation included in published precedent decisions are binding on all other agencies. *See* INA § 103(a) ("determination and ruling by the Attorney

General with respect to all questions of law shall be controlling"). A BIA decision that is reversed by a federal court of appeals remains binding agency precedent outside that circuit unless and until the agency acquiesces in the reversal nationwide.

Originally, the BIA had five permanent members who heard all cases *en banc*, although only a tiny proportion with oral argument. But because of increasing caseload pressures, the Attorney General gradually expanded the BIA until it reached 23 members in 2002. *See* 8 C.F.R. § 3.1(a)(1) (2002). It came to decide most cases in three-member panels. Even these changes did not keep pace with a caseload that grew steadily. The BIA heard 3630 cases in 1983, 8204 cases in 1987, 12,774 cases in 1992, 30,000 cases in 1997, and over 34,000 cases in 2002. Executive Office for Immigration Review, U.S. Dep't of Justice FY 2003, Statistical Yearbook, at S2 (2004); Executive Office for Immigration Review U.S. Dep't of Justice, Statistical Yearbook 2001, at E1 (2002).

Case completions lagged far behind receipts, and a daunting backlog developed. The BIA responded in 1999 with new streamlining regulations that allowed a single BIA member, rather than a panel, to dispose of a limited range of cases. In some circumstances a single member could issue an affirmance, without opinion, of the appealed decision, if he or she found "that the result reached in the decision under review was correct; that any errors in the decision under review were harmless or nonmaterial." The immigration judge's opinion then became the final agency determination for purposes of any further appeals. *See* 64 Fed. Reg. 56135 (1999).

In 2002, further regulations made disposition of appeals by a single member of the Board the norm. *See* 67 Fed. Reg. 54878–905 (2002). A case will go to a three-member panel only if it falls into one of six categories that cover only a minority of appeals. *See* 8 C.F.R. § 1003.1(e)(6). Single members may affirm with or without opinion, and may also dispose of appeals on procedural grounds. About one-third of BIA appeals are now resolved by affirmance without opinion. The regulations also impose presumptive time limits on BIA decisions and require greater deference to an immigration judge's factual findings. 8 C.F.R. § 1003.1(d)(3). *See* Gallagher, *Practice and Procedure Before the Board of Immigration Appeals,: An Update,* 03–2 Imm. Briefings (2003).

Finally, the 2002 regulations reduced the size of the BIA to 11 members. Some critics contended that the reduction was adopted at least in part to permit the Attorney General to remove the BIA's more liberal members. Others charged that the pressure for completions, coupled with the high-volume clearance rate, prevents a proper consideration of appeals by noncitizens and undermines what had been an admirable record of Board professionalism and independence. *See* Lichtblau & Getter, *Seeking Speedier Deportations, Ashcroft Plans Judicial Reforms,* Los Angeles Times, Feb. 7, 2002, at A24; Getter & Peterson, *Speedier Rate of Deportation Rulings Assailed, id.,* Jan. 5, 2003, at A1.

Though the 2002 regulations largely eliminated a massive BIA case backlog, one byproduct has been a surge in immigration appeals to the federal courts. Not only are there many more BIA decisions, but the rate of appeal to the courts rose from about 10 percent to 25 percent. Some critics attribute the higher appeal rate to unhappiness with the new BIA procedures, including the greater use of affirmances without opinion. Many federal judges have expressed grave concern about the burgeoning immigration caseload, which in the Ninth Circuit went from 8 percent to 48 percent of the court's docket between 2002 and 2005. Some judges have been highly critical of the quality of BIA and IJ decisions, and of the appellate advocacy offered by both the private bar and the government in the face of the new pressures. *See* Motomura, *Immigration Law and Federal Court Jurisdiction Through the Lens of Habeas Corpus*, 91 Cornell L. Rev. 459, 473–75 (2006); Moore & Simmons, *Immigrant Pleas Crushing Federal Courts*, Los Angeles Times, May 2, 2005; Perrotta, *Immigration Appeals Surge in Second Circuit*, N.Y. L.J., Nov. 4, 2004; Executive Office for Immigration Review, *BIA Restructuring and Streamlining Procedures* (Fact Sheet, Dec. 8, 2004 (revised)). The criticism helped trigger a systematic DOJ review of immigration court and BIA practices, ordered by Attorney General Gonzales in January 2006. In August of that year, he announced 22 reforms based on the review, including returning the Board to 15 members.

### 4. JUDICIAL REVIEW

#### a. *Basic Structure of Review*

If the BIA rules against the claim, judicial review may be available as part of the review of the removal order. (DHS is not authorized to appeal to the courts; its only recourse if it is dissatisfied with a BIA decision is to invoke referral to the Attorney General, as described above.) The current structure of court review is found in INA § 242. As a general rule, a noncitizen may appeal a removal order to the federal court of appeals. INA § 242(b) sets out the procedural requirements with regard to deadlines for filing, venue, and service.

Section 242 limits the role of the courts in several ways, first by appearing to eliminate judicial review in broad categories of cases. Any final removal order against a noncitizen deportable under most of the crime-related deportation grounds (except for a single crime of moral turpitude) "shall not be subject to review by any court." INA § 242(a)(2)(C). However, the jurisdiction-limiting provisions found anywhere in the INA generally do not preclude judicial review of "constitutional questions or questions of law." INA § 242(a)(2)(D). Also barred is review of major categories of discretionary decisions: concerning certain waivers, relief from removal, and discretionary adjustment to permanent resident status. In addition, a catch-all provision bars review of any other decisions or actions that are specified to be in the discretion of the Attorney General, but judicial review of asylum decisions is expressly allowed. INA § 242(a)(2)(B). And § 242 generally consolidates judicial review by deferring it until government action is reduced to a final removal order against an individual noncitizen. *See* § 242(b)(9), (f), (g); Motomura, *Judicial Review in Immigration Cases after* AADC: *Lessons from Civil Procedure,* 14 Geo. Immigr. L.J. 385 (2000).

### b.  Review Standards

How much will courts defer to determinations by immigration judges or the BIA? For factual determinations, INA § 242(b)(4)(B) provides that "the administrative findings of fact are conclusive unless any reasonable adjudicator would be compelled to conclude to the contrary." This standard comes from the following language in the U.S. Supreme Court's 1992 decision in *INS v. Elias–Zacarias*, 502 U.S. 478, 112 S.Ct. 812, 117 L.Ed.2d 38 (1992) (other aspects of which we will consider in Chapter Four), which held:

> The BIA's determination that Elias–Zacarias was not eligible for asylum . . . can be reversed only if the evidence presented by Elias–Zacarias was such that a reasonable factfinder would have to conclude that the requisite fear of persecution existed.

502 U.S. at 481. What about court review of discretionary decisions? According to INA § 242(b)(4)(D), the Attorney General's discretionary judgment in asylum cases "shall be conclusive unless manifestly contrary to the law and an abuse of discretion."

The Supreme Court also reinforced the message of deference to the administrative process for deciding on asylum claims when it issued a quick and unanimous per curiam reversal of a Ninth Circuit decision in *INS v. Ventura*, 537 U.S. 12, 123 S.Ct. 353, 154 L.Ed.2d 272 (2002). The appeals court had reversed the BIA's ruling against asylum, finding that the evidence compelled a conclusion that the persecution was on account of imputed political opinion. (The Supreme Court did not address this part of the ruling.) But the Ninth Circuit then refused to remand for consideration of another issue that the Board had not found it necessary to reach. On that issue—whether country conditions had changed—the Ninth Circuit ruled that the evidence in the record would compel a conclusion that no such relevant change had occurred. The Supreme Court found it clearly erroneous to refuse to remand to the BIA. Under basic principles of administrative law; the BIA should first be allowed to apply its expertise to the question of changed country conditions.

### c.  Agency Deference

The Supreme Court decision in *Chevron U.S.A., Inc. v. Natural Resources Defense Council*, 467 U.S. 837, 104 S.Ct. 2778, 81 L.Ed.2d 694 (1984), has had a major impact in defining the respective roles of agencies and courts in implementing regulatory statutes, including the statutes governing *nonrefoulement* and asylum. *Chevron* set forth the two-step process for reviewing an agency's construction of a statute that it administers:

First, always, is the question whether Congress has directly spoken to the precise question at issue. If the intent of Congress is clear, that is the end of the matter; for the court, as well as the agency, must give effect to the unambiguously expressed intent of Congress. If, however, the court determines Congress has not directly addressed the precise question at issue, the court does not simply impose its own construction of the statute, as would be necessary in the absence of an administrative interpretation. Rather, if the statute is silent or ambiguous, the question for the court is whether the agency's answer is based on a permissible construction of the statute.

467 U.S. at 842–43, 104 S.Ct. at 2781–82.

The Supreme Court limited *Chevron* in *United States v. Mead Corp.*, 533 U.S. 218, 121 S.Ct. 2164, 150 L.Ed.2d 292 (2001). The Court ruled that "administrative implementation of a particular statutory provision qualifies for *Chevron* deference when it appears that Congress delegated authority to the agency generally to make rules carrying the force of law, and that the agency interpretation claiming deference was promulgated in the exercise of that authority." 533 U.S. at 226–27. The opinion suggests that interpretations embodied in notice-and-comment rulemaking and adjudications in a "relatively formal administrative procedure" would ordinarily meet this test. Less formal statements of the agency's interpretation, like the Customs Service ruling letter at issue in that case, are entitled only to a lower level of deference under *Skidmore v. Swift & Co.*, 323 U.S. 134, 139–40, 65 S.Ct. 161, 89 L.Ed. 124 (1944). Under *Skidmore*, the "fair measure of deference" varies with the circumstances, and courts should look "to the degree of the agency's care, its consistency, formality, and relative expertness, and to the persuasiveness of the agency's position." *Mead*, 533 U.S. at 228.

### Notes

1.  INA § 208(a)(2)(B) requires asylum applicants to demonstrate "by clear and convincing evidence that the application has been filed within 1 year after the date of the alien's arrival in the United States." There are exceptions for "changed conditions which materially affect the applicant's eligibility for asylum or extraordinary circumstances relating to the delay in filing the application." The regulations spell out the standards to be used in applying these exceptions. 8 C.F.R. § 208.4(a)(4) and (5). *See, e.g.,* Schrag & Pistone, *The New Asylum Rule: Not Yet a Model of Fair Procedure,* 11 Geo. Immigr. L.J. 267, 271–78 (1997). (Chapter Six more fully discusses the one-year deadline.) INA § 208(a)(2)(C) bars asylum applications by persons previously denied asylum, subject to exceptions. INA § 208(a)(3) bars judicial review of any determination of the Attorney General under the exclusions from asylum eligibility set out in § 208(a)(2) (including the one-year filing deadline).

Withholding of removal under § 241(b)(3) is not subject to a filing deadline—a highly important difference. The earliest versions of the legislation imposed the time limit on both forms of persecution-based relief. For a revealing account of the efforts by advocates to defeat the most draconian asylum proposals in 1996, see P.G. Schrag, A Well-Founded Fear: The Congressional Battle to Save Political Asylum in America (2000).

2.  Information about asylum applications is supposed to remain confidential, both to protect family members and friends still in the home country, and to help assure that the mere fact of filing for asylum will not add in any measure to the risks that might be faced by the applicant. In earlier years the stated policy of confidentiality was implemented unevenly, prompting some courts to express concern about the use of names and identifying information in public administrative and judicial proceedings. *See, e.g., Perez–Alvarez v. INS,* 857 F.2d 23, 24 (1st Cir. 1988). The regulations now contain provisions meant to provide better assurance of confidentiality, 8 C.F.R. § 208.6, and the BIA now usually excises the names from published decisions in asylum cases, referring to the noncitizen only by initials.

3.  For useful general treatments of U.S. asylum law and procedure, see D. Anker, Law of Asylum in the United States (3d ed. 1999 & Supp. 2002); R. Germain, AILA's Asylum Primer: A Practical Guide to U.S. Law and Procedure (4th ed. 2005); D. Martin, Asylum Case Law Sourcebook (6th ed. 2006).

## SECTION D.   TRENDS AND STATISTICS

INS received asylum applications in the 1970s at a rate of between 1900 and 5800 per year. *See* 1986 INS Statistical Yearbook, Table 27 (1987). Shortly after the adoption of the Refugee Act, however, the fledgling asylum provisions in the statute were sorely tested by an unexpected combination of geopolitical developments. The Mariel boatlift brought approximately 125,000 asylum seekers from Cuba in the spring and summer of 1980, at a time when several thousand Haitian applications were being received. The Shah's fall in Iran also resulted in thousands of applications from Iranians in the United States during 1980 and 1981, and the ouster of the Nicaraguan dictator Somoza by the Sandinistas led to a similar receipt of Nicaraguan applications. *See* Meissner, *Reflections on the Refugee Act of 1980,* in The New Asylum Seekers: Refugee Law in the 1980s, at 57, 60–63 (D. Martin ed. 1988). As a result, INS developed a backlog of cases that exceeded 170,000, and only by a major priority effort in 1983 and 1984 was that backlog cleared.

Substantial questions were raised about the fairness of that clearance process, however, particularly as it applied to Central American asylum seekers, *see id.* at 63–64, and about other aspects of the treatment of Central Americans. INS ultimately agreed in 1991 to a settlement of the so-called *ABC* case, a massive class action lawsuit involving over 250,000 Guatemalans and Salvadorans. The settlement provided for reconsideration of class members' claims by the then-new INS asylum officer corps. *American Baptist Churches (ABC) v. Thornburgh,* 760 F.Supp. 796 (N.D. Cal. 1991). Readjudication proceeded slowly and with inadequate resources, however, and Congress eventually adopted special legislation in 1997 that is now leading to permanent resident status for most of the ABC class members, but not through a grant of asylum. (See the discussion of the legislation known as NACARA in Chapter Eleven.)

For a few years after the 1984 backlog clearance, the application rate appeared to stabilize, at around 20,000–25,000 annually. This was considerably higher than the experience of the 1970s, but after the 1980 peak, it appeared a politically manageable level. Beginning in 1988, however, a strong upward trend began, mostly involving nationals of Nicaragua, El Salvador, Guatemala and Honduras. *See* 1993 INS Statistical Yearbook 77. The reasons are not clear, but some of the increase may be a delayed effect of the Immigration Reform and Control Act of 1986 (IRCA). By most counts, several hundred thousand people from those Central American nations were living in the United States in undocumented status before 1986, and most probably encountered little difficulty in securing work, thereby enjoying a kind of de facto asylum. After 1986, IRCA's employer sanctions provisions made it more difficult for them and for later arrivals, from a region then torn by civil war, to continue such an existence without papers. Asylum came to be recognized as one way to obtain such papers, at least temporarily, because the regulations at the time mandated issuance of employment authorization to noncitizens who filed a nonfrivolous asylum application. *See* Martin, *The End of De Facto Asylum: Toward a Humane and Realistic Response to Refugee Challenges*, 18 Calif. W. Int'l L.J. 161 (1987–88). After procedural reforms in 1994, the trends reversed and the number of new applications declined significantly for several years, before rising and then again declining starting in FY 2000.

Table 2.1 shows the trends in applications, including the backlogs that fed the clamor for streamlining and reform in the mid–1990s as well as the effects of the 1994 reforms, including increased grant rates. The applications received include both new cases and reopened cases, including through 1996 a very sizeable number of reopened *ABC* cases, which may mask some of the progress in the mid-1990s. A single case may include a principal applicant and family members, so the number of asylum seekers exceeds the number of cases.

Table 2.1 includes only cases filed with INS/USCIS—that is, affirmative asylum applications. Table 2.2 shows data for cases filed with the immigration judges—defensive applications.

Until 2001, EOIR did not maintain statistics that would permit one to distinguish referred cases that began before an asylum officer from purely defensive cases filed for the first time in immigration court. Therefore many cases in Table 2.2 would also have appeared in Table 2.1 as a referred or denied case before INS/USCIS.

Starting in 2001, EOIR statistics distinguish between affirmative filings and cases that began defensively in immigration court. This avoids double-counting of affirmative cases, and thus yields a more accurate picture of grant rates for asylum and for protection in general (*i.e.,* adding in grants of withholding and protection under the Convention Against Torture). Table 2.3 sets out these figures for the years 2001–2005.[4]

## Table 2.1

### Asylum Cases Filed With the INS/USCIS, FY 1984–2005

| Fiscal year | Cases pending start of FY | Cases filed | Cases completed | Cases adjudicated | Grant rate for cases decided |
|---|---|---|---|---|---|
| 1981–1985 | | 161,872 | 124,142 | 99,090 | 25% |
| 1986–1990 | | 281,048 | 310,071 | 99,688 | 24% |
| 1991–1995 | | 593,609 | 205,161 | 137,307 | 23% |
| 1996–2000 | | 326,699 | 410,072 | 227,725 | 28% |
| 2001 | 328,820 | 62,871 | 67,627 | 46,927 | 43% |
| 2002 | 323,251 | 63,021 | 81,875 | 52,215 | 36% |
| 2003 | 303,810 | 46,015 | 86,775 | 39,107 | 29% |
| 2004 | 262,106 | 32,682 | 108,223 | 31,582 | 32% |
| 2005 | 184,643 | 29,752 | 115,881 | 23,457 | 41% |

Sources: 2004 USCIS Statistical Yearbook 51, Table 16; Refugee Reports, Feb. 28, 2006, at 12.

## Table 2.2

### Asylum Cases Filed With Immigration Judges, FY 1995–2005

| Fiscal year | Cases pending start of FY | Cases filed | Cases granted | Cases denied | Grant rate for cases decided |
|---|---|---|---|---|---|
| 1995 | 15,016 | 48,163 | 2,483 | 14,164 | 15% |
| 1996 | 33,408 | 69,828 | 4,001 | 22,466 | 15% |
| 1997 | 46,447 | 84,904 | 6,551 | 21,661 | 23% |
| 1998 | 62,700 | 71,729 | 7,252 | 20,116 | 26% |
| 1999 | 68,542 | 54,916 | 8,355 | 18,169 | 31% |
| 2000 | 59,110 | 51,967 | 8,905 | 16,020 | 36% |
| 2001 | 55,720 | 61,939 | 7,956 | 15,031 | 35% |
| 2002 | n/a | 74,627 | 8,660 | 18,389 | 32% |
| 2003 | 89,288 | 66,931 | 10,908 | 22,415 | 33% |
| 2004 | 72,745 | 56,609 | 10,839 | 20,867 | 34% |
| 2005 | 79,057 | 50,753 | 10,164 | 19,166 | 35% |

Sources: U.S. Dept. of Justice, Executive Office for Immigration Review, Asylum Statistics, Fiscal Year 1997–2005. Available online at: http://www.usdoj.gov/eoir/efoia/foiafreq.htm; Refugee Reports, Feb. 28, 2006, at 12; Refugee Reports, Dec. 31, 1995 at 13; id., Dec. 31, 1996 at 13.

**4.** "Cases completed" in Table 2.1 includes applications approved, denied, or referred, plus other sorts of closures (*e.g.,* the applicant dies, obtains LPR status another way, or fails to show for the interview and the lack of a current address or other deficiency prevents the initiation of removal proceedings). The grant rate is a percentage of the "cases adjudicated," *i.e.,* granted, denied, or referred, without reference to other sorts of closures. Pending cases do not balance with applications received minus cases closed because of changes in how reopened cases are counted. Similarly, such case completions and failure to pursue filed cases explain the difference between "Cases filed," and "Cases granted" plus "Cases denied," in Table 2.2.

## Table 2.3

## Asylum Cases Filed With the INS/USCIS and Immigration Judges, FY 2001–2005

| Fiscal year | USCIS | IJ— defensive only | total asylum cases received | % asylum granted of total cases received | % asylum granted of total cases adjudicated | % protection granted of total cases received | % protection granted of total cases adjudicated |
|---|---|---|---|---|---|---|---|
| 2001 | 64,731 | 18,099 | 82,830 | 37% | 53% | 40% | 58% |
| 2002 | 64,644 | 19,465 | 84,109 | 36% | 47% | 40% | 51% |
| 2003 | 46,945 | 19,789 | 66,734 | 38% | 47% | 44% | 54% |
| 2004 | 34,170 | 17,788 | 51,958 | 45% | 53% | 52% | 62% |
| 2005 | 32,899 | 15,551 | 48,450 | 45% | 52% | 52% | 60% |
| total 2001– 2005 | 239,589 | 90,692 | 330.281 | 40% | 50% | 45% | 56% |

Sources: USCIS Asylum Division and EOIR Statistical Yearbooks for FY 2001–2005.

Table 2.4 shows the leading source countries for applications received by the INS and USCIS in selected years. Note the changes over the years. Do any of the listed countries surprise you? Do any omissions surprise you?

## Table 2.4

## Asylum Applications Filed With INS/USCIS, Selected Years

## Leading Source Countries

FY 1990

| Rank | Country | Number of cases filed | Approval rate for cases decided |
|---|---|---|---|
| 1. | El Salvador | 22,271 | 2.5% |
| 2. | Nicaragua | 18,304 | 16.2% |
| 3. | Guatemala | 12,234 | 1.4% |
| 4. | Cuba | 3,925 | 29.0% |
| 5. | Romania | 1,593 | 54.9% |
| 6. | Liberia | 1,572 | n/a |
| 7. | Iran | 1,550 | 42.7% |
| 8. | Ethiopia | 1,532 | 59.2% |
| 9. | China | 1,287 | 91.1% |
| 10. | Honduras | 1,097 | 1.1% |
| 11. | Soviet Union | 1,043 | 82.4% |
| 12. | Poland | 731 | 4.2% |
| 13. | Lebanon | 573 | 32.5% |
| 14. | Bulgaria | 531 | n/a |
| 15. | Panama | 452 | n/a |

Sources: 1990 INS Statistical Yearbook; Refugee Reports, Dec. 21, 1990, at 12.

FY 1995

| Rank | Country | Number of cases filed | Approval rate for cases decided |
|------|---------|----------------------|---------------------------------|
| 1.   | El Salvador | 72,230 | 3.4% |
| 2.   | Guatemala | 22,913 | 7.1% |
| 3.   | Mexico | 9,304 | 1.3% |
| 4.   | China | 4,915 | 12.1% |
| 5.   | India | 3,209 | 35.4% |
| 6.   | Honduras | 3,093 | 5.8% |
| 7.   | Haiti | 2,820 | 28.9% |
| 8.   | Pakistan | 2,352 | 20.0% |
| 9.   | Nicaragua | 1,993 | 15.5% |
| 10.  | Bangladesh | 1,863 | 18.0% |
| 11.  | Peru | 1,404 | 21.9% |
| 12.  | Cuba | 1,292 | 62.9% |
| 13.  | Philippines | 979 | 3.2% |
| 14.  | Ethiopia | 892 | 59.5% |
| 15.  | Russia | 857 | 37.7% |

Source: Refugee Reports, Dec. 31, 1995, at 12.

FY 2000

| Rank | Country | Number of cases filed | Approval rate for cases decided |
|------|---------|----------------------|---------------------------------|
| 1.   | China | 6,476 | 54.8% |
| 2.   | Haiti | 4,683 | 22.2% |
| 3.   | Mexico | 3,936 | 7.9% |
| 4.   | Colombia | 2,747 | 67.8% |
| 5.   | El Salvador | 2,686 | 12.4% |
| 6.   | Somalia | 2,415 | 74.1% |
| 7.   | Guatemala | 2,084 | 20.1% |
| 8.   | India | 1,615 | 49.6% |
| 9.   | Ethiopia | 1,507 | 79% |
| 10.  | Liberia | 1,082 | 58.5% |
| 11.  | Russia | 946 | 50.7% |
| 12.  | Iran | 934 | 70.5% |
| 13.  | Mauritania | 847 | 25.8% |
| 14.  | Yugoslavia | 749 | 62.1% |
| 15.  | Burma | 630 | 74.0% |

Source: Refugee Reports, Dec. 2000, at 6.

FY 2001

| Rank | Country | Number of cases filed | Approval rate for cases decided |
|------|---------|----------------------|--------------------------------|
| 1. | Mexico | 9,178 | 6.8% |
| 2. | China | 8,760 | 63.9% |
| 3. | Colombia | 7,280 | 62.5% |
| 4. | Haiti | 5,068 | 35.9% |
| 5. | India | 2,125 | 56.9% |
| 6. | El Salvador | 2,063 | 16.0% |
| 7. | Guatemala | 1,990 | 18.4% |
| 8. | Somalia | 1,853 | 81.1% |
| 9. | Ethiopia | 1,526 | 73.4% |
| 10. | Burma | 1,418 | 88.8% |
| 11. | Liberia | 1,369 | 60.0% |
| 12. | Mauritania | 1,120 | 19.4% |
| 13. | Iran | 988 | 75.5% |
| 14. | Russia | 926 | 58.2% |
| 15. | Yugoslavia | 769 | 51.6% |

Source: Refugee Reports, Dec. 31, 2001, at 6.

FY 2002

| Rank | Country | Number of cases filed | Approval rate for cases decided |
|------|---------|----------------------|--------------------------------|
| 1. | China | 11,115 | 59.7% |
| 2. | Mexico | 9,298 | 6.8% |
| 3. | Colombia | 8,115 | 45.1% |
| 4. | Haiti | 4,009 | 35.9% |
| 5. | India | 2,012 | 54.0% |
| 6. | Guatemala | 1,886 | 24.0% |
| 7. | Indonesia | 1,631 | 29.9% |
| 8. | Ethiopia | 1,331 | 75.1% |
| 9. | El Salvador | 1,249 | 10.6% |
| 10. | Mauritania | 1,131 | 18.7% |
| 11. | Russia | 939 | 49.5% |
| 12. | Iran | 935 | 67.0% |
| 13. | Liberia | 841 | 56.8% |
| 14. | Egypt | 628 | 43.7% |
| 15. | Somalia | 591 | 63.7% |

Source: Refugee Reports, Dec. 31, 2002, at 6.

FY 2003

| Rank | Country | Number of cases filed | Approval rate for cases decided |
|------|---------|-----------------------|---------------------------------|
| 1. | China | 5,297 | 59.7% |
| 2. | Colombia | 4,757 | 36.1% |
| 3. | Mexico | 4,111 | 0.9% |
| 4. | Haiti | 3,530 | 32.4% |
| 5. | Indonesia | 2,856 | 6.7% |
| 6. | Guatemala | 2,837 | 8.7% |
| 7. | India | 1,485 | 34.3% |
| 8. | El Salvador | 929 | 7.8% |
| 9. | Ethiopia | 915 | 58.9% |
| 10. | Mauritania | 793 | 6.3% |
| 11. | Russia | 792 | 33.4% |
| 12. | Liberia | 612 | 54.8% |
| 13. | Pakistan | 573 | 37.1% |
| 14. | Iran | 535 | 48.0% |
| 15. | Egypt | 417 | 35.7% |

Source: Refugee Reports, Dec. 31, 2003, at 6.

FY 2004

| Rank | Country | Number of cases filed | Approval rate for cases decided |
|------|---------|-----------------------|---------------------------------|
| 1. | Haiti | 3,543 | 35% |
| 2. | China | 2,839 | 25% |
| 3. | Colombia | 2,452 | 45% |
| 4. | Venezuela | 1,418 | 45% |
| 5. | Cameroon | 1,189 | 42% |
| 6. | Ethiopia | 968 | 60% |
| 7. | Brazil | 774 | 33% |
| 8. | Guatemala | 703 | 10% |
| 9. | Guinea | 660 | 21% |
| 10. | Russia | 657 | 30% |
| 11. | Armenia | 612 | 30% |
| 12. | Indonesia | 487 | 10% |
| 13. | Togo | 472 | 49% |
| 14. | Albania | 468 | 23% |
| 15. | Mauritania | 446 | 12% |

Source: 2004 USCIS Statistical Yearbook 55–60, table 18.

FY 2005

| Rank | Country | Number of cases filed | Approval rate for cases decided |
|------|---------|----------------------|--------------------------------|
| 1. | Haiti | 4121 | 42% |
| 2. | China | 3682 | 41% |
| 3. | Colombia | 1570 | 46% |
| 4. | Mexico | 1247 | 5% |
| 5. | Venezuela | 1146 | 44% |
| 6. | Ethiopia | 707 | 58% |
| 7. | Cameroon | 651 | 47% |
| 8. | Guinea | 602 | 19% |
| 9. | Russia | 587 | 33% |
| 10. | Guatemala | 559 | 11% |
| 11. | Armenia | 484 | 26% |
| 12. | Togo | 409 | 42% |
| 13. | Nepal | 387 | 45% |
| 14. | Indonesia | 372 | 15% |
| 15. | Cote D'Ivore | 326 | 21% |

Source: USCIS Asylum Division.

FY 2006 (preliminary)

| Rank | Country | Number of cases filed | Approval rate for cases decided |
|------|---------|----------------------|--------------------------------|
| 1. | China | 5,128 | 33% |
| 2. | Haiti | 3,372 | 39% |
| 3. | Columbia | 1,421 | 64% |
| 4. | Mexico | 1,302 | 7% |
| 5. | Ethiopia | 892 | 55% |
| 6. | Venezuela | 865 | 51% |
| 7. | Indonesia | 783 | 47% |
| 8. | Guatemala | 566 | 11% |
| 9. | Cameroon | 558 | 44% |
| 10. | Russia | 551 | 39% |
| 11. | Nepal | 451 | 44% |
| 12. | Guinea | 448 | 21% |
| 13. | Armenia | 387 | 34% |
| 14. | El Salvador | 338 | 9% |
| 15. | Egypt | 331 | 37% |

Source: USCIS Asylum Division.

# Chapter Three

# PERSECUTION

---

*My last days in the Soviet Union remain a chaotic blur in my mind's eye. I never slept more than two or three hours out of the twenty-four. Throughout all the years of refusal, I had always promised myself, and had persuaded Lucia to promise, that if our permission ever came, we would not risk waiting an extra hour. We had suffered so much anguish on behalf of friends who delayed—it was only too easy to be trapped again in the interval when one was no longer a Soviet citizen but was still within Soviet borders. Whoever it was among the top party officials that had authorized our release might fall from power— these changes occurred all the time. An overnight switch in policy toward the emigrants, a change in relations with the United States, or a mere remark made by an American congressman at which the Soviets took offense, could reverse our situation without warning. When the gate to freedom opened, we would make a run for it. We wouldn't stay one minute beyond the interval that would be required to pack our most essential belongings and fulfill all the legal and financial demands made by the government of people leaving the country.*

*I couldn't possibly sort out in my memory the details of those frantic days and nights. I had to cope with an unbelievable amount of red tape. I had often accompanied friends who were leaving Russia on their races through Moscow from bureau to department, from ministry to embassy, from bank to customs, where the emigrants had to fill out forms, obtain affidavits, make any number of payments (both legal and bribes); seek officials' signatures, countersignatures, seals, and stamps; produce the enormous sheaf of documents a Soviet citizen has to accumulate—but not until my own permission came did I know what it was like to spend so many of my waking hours performing this staggering number of final duties.*

*I wonder if any slave ever felt as happy buying his own person from his owner as I felt in the savings bank, paying out 800 rubles for our exit visas: two small documents, printed on flimsy yellow paper. (The price for Jewish souls had gone way up since the start of the emigration: the authorities hadn't originally realized that not just a trickle, but tens of thousands of people would want to leave the country, and that a very profitable business could be made of this exodus.)*

—Mark Ya Azbel, refusenik,
USSR[1]

## SECTION A. WHAT IS PERSECUTION?

The concept of persecution is central to the 1951 Convention and to protection under U.S. law through the Immigration and Nationality Act. Both of these laws protect only those forced migrants who have been "persecuted" or who have a well-founded fear of "persecution," but neither law defines this key concept.

The Ninth Circuit has offered this definition of persecution:

> Although the term "persecution" is not defined in the Act, we have explained it as "the infliction of suffering or harm upon those who differ (in race, religion or political opinion) in a way regarded as offensive." We have cautioned that "persecution is an extreme concept that does not include every sort of treatment our society regards as offensive." Discrimination on the basis of race or religion, as morally reprehensible as it may be, does not ordinarily amount to "persecution" within the meaning of the Act. *See Bastanipour v. INS*, 980 F.2d 1129, 1133 (7th Cir. 1992) (distinguishing persecution "from mere discrimination or harassment"). The Board has held that discrimination can, in extraordinary cases, be so severe and pervasive as to constitute "persecution" within the meaning of the Act. In a case such as the one before us, however, where private discrimination is neither condoned by the state nor the prevailing social norm, it clearly does not amount to "persecution" within the meaning of the Act.

*Ghaly v. INS*, 58 F.3d 1425, 1431 (9th Cir. 1995).

A more succinct definition comes from Judge Posner in *Osaghae v. INS*, 942 F.2d 1160, 1163 (7th Cir. 1991): " 'Persecution' means, in immigration law, punishment for political, religious, or other reasons that our country does not recognize as legitimate."

The task in this chapter is to identify a workable notion of when this country is prepared to declare another nation's punishments (or other

---

**1.** C. Kismaric, Forced Out: The Agony of the Refugee in Our Time 82–85 (1989). (Refusenik is a term that came into use during the Cold War to refer to individuals in the Soviet Union, typically but not always Jews, who were refused permission to leave by the government—eds.)

harms) such that the legal system should provide protection. Some cases are easy, but a great many fall at the margin and present surprisingly difficult issues. When does application of a uniform national policy constitute persecution? When does prosecution under the criminal law become persecution? Can there be persecution without an intent to harm? Does persecution imply action by state officials or does it apply to nongovernmental officials acting singly or in groups? To what extent do these questions turn ultimately on deciding whether another nation's punishments are in some sense illegitimate? If so, how can adjudicators develop standards for judging legitimacy?

## 1. UNIFORM NATIONAL POLICY

We will begin exploring the meaning of "persecution" when the government of the country of origin applies criminal or other procedurally regular sanctions in pursuit of a policy aim it deems legitimate, or indeed vital. If the asylum state does not share that view, it may have to pass judgment on the validity of the underlying policy. Ask yourself if it is possible to devise an approach that does not require value choices about the substantive rightness of the underlying policy—*e.g.*, an approach that focuses only on procedural defects in implementation. Or is there anything wrong with the asylum state imposing its values, at least in this limited sense, on the policy choices of the other state?

"It Is Better to Have One Child Only." (Photo: © David Clark)

The first case, *Matter of Chang,* deals with an issue, sanctions imposed pursuant to a coercive population control policy, that has drawn considerable political attention in recent years and eventually resulted in a statutory change.

## MATTER OF CHANG

Board of Immigration Appeals, 1989.
20 I & N Dec. 38.

[The immigration judge found the respondent deportable and denied his applications for asylum and withholding of deportation. The respondent appealed.]

* * * [T]he respondent, a 33-year-old native and citizen of the People's Republic of China, made the following assertions. In his application for asylum, the respondent indicated that he was an anti-Communist who fled his homeland "because of Communist domination of China"; that he did not base his asylum claim on conditions in China that affected his freedom more than the rest of the country's population; and that neither he nor any member of his immediate family had "ever been mistreated by the authorities of his home country." His asylum application did not reference any claim to asylum based on his country's population control measures and he did not allege any mistreatment arising from such policies.

At his deportation hearing, the respondent testified that he was afraid of persecution in China; that people there were "mobilized" and "forced to do the bidding of the government"; that he and his wife were not given any work to do; that he and his wife were forced to flee from their commune because they had two children and did not agree to stop having more children; and, that they disagreed with China's family planning policies because "in the countryside, especially in the farming areas, we need more children." He indicated that the "government" wanted him to go to a clinic to be sterilized, that he thought the operation would "harm" his body, that he did not want to be sterilized, and that if he returned to China he would be forced to submit to the operation. He testified that his wife was supposed to go to the clinic but did not do so because she was ill. He testified that he did not know what would have happened if his wife had gone to the clinic. He further testified that he did not mention his opposition to China's birth control policies on his asylum application because "nobody had asked [him]" and because he was not very "conversant" in expressing himself and did not understand English.

On appeal, the respondent, through counsel, states that the facts of the case are that he and his wife were ordered by their commune to submit to sterilization operations after the birth of their second child, that his wife was able to "postpone" the operation due to illness, but that he fled China because he had no choice other than to submit to the surgery.

In conjunction with the appeal, the respondent also submitted a letter from the Library of Congress dated November 23, 1987, transmitting to the Immigration and Naturalization Service a report entitled "Population Control in the People's Republic of China." The report was apparently requested by the Service in connection with another matter. According to the report, the People's Republic of China ("PRC") has no national law on population control per se. The constitution provides that the state shall carry out family planning to control the size of the population and that spouses have the duty to carry out family planning. The Marriage Law of 1980 sets minimum marriage ages and places responsibility for birth control on both partners. The provinces and the cities governed directly by the state have enacted their own regulations on population control, but the population control program is guided by a joint directive of the Chinese Communist Party and the state entitled "On the Further Implementation of Family Planning Work" of February 1982. The policy provides that state cadres and urban residents are allowed one child per couple, with exceptions when special permission is granted. In rural areas generally the one-child rule is applied, except that where there are special difficulties, such as the birth of a handicapped child who cannot work, application to have a second child can be made. In no case is a third birth to be permitted. The rules are more leniently applied to families of non-Han ethnic minority groups. Late in 1985, it was announced that the one-child rule would be relaxed, and that in some areas a second child would be permitted if the first was a girl and in other special circumstances. The mechanics of the implementation of the program are by and large locally determined. Economic sanctions, peer pressure, and propaganda are used to insure compliance. Single child families receive health and educational benefits for the child. Couples who continue pregnancies which are not allowed may suffer the suspension of wages, fines, loss of seniority for promotion, and so forth. Couples are urged to undergo birth control operations (sterilization). Wages are sometimes paid during a rest period after sterilization, and cash rewards have been used to encourage sterilization. The Chinese Government has consistently denied supporting any use of force to obtain compliance with birth quotas. The transmittal letter forwarding the report states that punishment in the form of a sterilization operation is not provided for in Chinese law, though local officials may have used the one-child campaign to carry out a private vendetta.

Counsel also relies on the 1985 and 1987 [U.S. State Department] Country Reports on Human Rights Practices, Joint Committee of the Senate and the House of Representatives, 99th Congress, 2d Session (1986), and 100th Congress, 2d Session (1988) ("Country Reports"), respectively. The 1985 Country Report on the PRC indicates that "[r]eported instances of family planning malpractice occur mostly in rural areas, where local officials have sometimes translated the policy into rigid quotas. Chinese authorities say they take measures against local officials who violate the Government's policy in this regard, but there have been few reports of punishment of such offenders." 1985 Country Reports at 741. According to the 1987 report, provinces are allowed to make their own regulations regarding implementation of the one-child policy as long as overall birthrates match the state-imposed goals. In the past, local officials coerced significant numbers of women into having abortions. In 1987 the Chinese Government stressed repeatedly that it does not condone forced abortions or sterilizations. Chinese authorities have said that they take measures against local officials who violate the Government's policy. Despite central government efforts to prevent the imposition of rigid quotas, local government officials and peers reportedly continue to exert pressure on some persons seeking to have second children. Economic pressure on families with more than two children can be severe and can include loss of party membership, loss of job, difficulty in purchasing state-supplied seed, fertilizer, and fuel and other sanctions. 1987 Country Reports at 666.

\* \* \*

The respondent's position on appeal is that he has a well-founded fear of persecution based on the likelihood he would face mandatory sterilization, that he has a reasonable fear of persecution as a member of a "particular social group" (namely, persons who actually oppose the government policy of "one child per family"), and that he is eligible for withholding of deportation under section 243(h) of the Act because he has demonstrated a clear probability of being sterilized if returned to China.

We do not find that the "one couple, one child" policy of the Chinese Government is on its face persecutive. China has adopted a policy whose stated objective is to discourage births through economic incentives, economic sanctions, peer pressure, education, availability of sterilization and other birth control measures, and use of propaganda. Chinese policymakers are faced with the difficulty of providing for China's vast population in good years and in bad. The Government is concerned not only with the ability of its citizens to survive, but also with their housing, education, medical services, and the other benefits of life that persons in many other societies take for granted. For China to fail to take steps to prevent births might well mean that many millions of people would be condemned to, at best, the most marginal existence. The record reflects that China was in fact encouraged by world opinion to take measures to control its population.

There is no evidence that the goal of China's policy is other than as stated, or that it is a subterfuge for persecuting any portion of the Chinese citizenry on account of one of the reasons enumerated in section 101(a)(42)(A) of the Act. The policy does not prevent couples from having children but strives to limit the size of the family. It appears that exceptions are made so that couples facing certain hardships may have another child. The policy applies to everyone but expressly protects, and indeed is more leniently applied to, minority (non-Han) peoples within China. It appears to impose stricter requirements on Party members (state cadres) than on some non-Party members. The Chinese Government has stated that it does not condone forced sterilizations and that its policy is to take action against local officials who violate this policy.

The population problem arising in China poses a profound dilemma. We cannot find that implementation of the "one couple, one child" policy in and of itself, even to the extent that involuntary sterilizations may occur, is persecution or creates a well-founded fear of persecution "on account of race, religion, nationality, membership in a particular social group, or political opinion." This is not to say that such a policy could not be implemented in such a way as to individuals or categories of persons so as to be persecution on account of a ground protected by the Act. To the extent, however, that such a policy is solely tied to controlling population, rather than as a guise for acting against people for reasons protected by the Act, we cannot find that persons who do not wish to have the policy applied to them are victims of persecution or have a well-founded fear of persecution within the present scope of the Act.

Thus, an asylum claim based solely on the fact that the applicant is subject to this policy must fail. An individual claiming asylum for reasons related to this policy must establish, based on additional facts present in his case, that the application of the policy to him was in fact persecutive or that he had a well-founded fear that it would be persecutive on account of one of the five reasons enumerated in section 101(a)(42)(A). For example, this might include evidence that the policy was being selectively applied against members of particular religious groups or was in fact being used to punish individuals for their political opinions. This does not mean that all who show that they opposed the policy, but were subjected to it anyway, have demonstrated that they are being "punished" for their opinions. Rather, there must be evidence that the governmental action arises for a reason other than general population control (*e.g.,* evidence of disparate, more severe treatment for those who publicly oppose the policy). Finally, if the applicant claims that the punishment occurred at the hands of local officials, he must normally show that redress from higher officials was unavailable or that he has a well-founded fear that it would be unavailable.

We note that the respondent has not shown that mandatory sterilization is or was authorized under regulations or programs in effect in Fukien province, whence he came, or that forced sterilization has in fact occurred in his locality. The Country Report for 1987 reflects that 48.8% of the births in China in 1986 were second, third, or later births, which indicates that millions of persons in China were allowed or chose to have more than one child in that year. It also is support for the Chinese claim that the one-child policy is not routinely enforced by mandatory sterilization and abortion. The sole evidence at the hearing regarding this respondent's claim was his asylum application itself and his testimony. His testimony was simply not sufficiently detailed to provide a plausible and coherent account of the basis of his asylum claim and was contradicted by other information in the record. His asylum application undermines his testimony as it disclaims any mistreatment by the Government and does not refer to any fear stemming from China's population control measures. However, even if we accept the characterization of the evidence as set forth by the respondent on appeal (*i.e.,* that he and his wife wished to have more than two children and he would be forced to undergo mandatory sterilization if returned to China), we would not find that evidence sufficient in itself to support a well-founded fear of persecution on account of a reason enumerated in section 101(a)(42)(a) of the Act. The respondent has not asserted or established that he was treated differently from other Chinese with respect to application of the "one couple, one child" policy, or that its application in his case was in reality a guise to achieve a governmental goal other than general population control.

Such a showing cannot be made by arguing that there is a "particular social group" made up of those persons who "actually" oppose the policy of "one couple, one child," and that the evidence that this "group" is persecuted is simply the fact that the policy is applied to them despite their opposition to it. If a law or policy is not inherently persecutive (as would be, for example, a law enacted to punish individuals because of their religious beliefs), one cannot demonstrate that it is a persecutive measure simply with evidence that it is applied to all persons, including those who do not agree with it. This is true even where questions of conscience or religion may be involved. In the United States, there are numerous cases upholding the imposition of religiously neutral laws against persons whose religious beliefs conflicted with them. *See, e.g., United States v. Lee*, 455 U.S. 252 (1982) (imposition of Social Security taxes against Amish persons whose religious beliefs forbade payment of the taxes or receipt of the benefits did not interfere with the free exercise of their religion); *United States v. Merkt*, 794 F.2d 950, 954–57 (5th Cir. 1986), *cert. denied*, 480 U.S. 946 (1987) (conviction for illegally transporting noncitizens not barred by first amendment although defendants contended they were religiously motivated in conducting "sanctuary" activities), and cases cited therein.

The respondent submits that the freedom to have children is an absolute right under the 14th amendment to the United States Constitution and, for that reason, countries that abridge this right must be found to be engaging in acts of persecution. The resolution of the constitutional issues that could arise if the population problems underlying the implementation of the "one couple, one child" policy in China were to occur in the United States is a matter of speculation that it is hoped this country need never address. However, the fact that a citizen of another country may not enjoy the same constitutional protections as a citizen of the United States does not mean that he is therefore persecuted on account of one of the five grounds enumerated in section 101(a)(42)(A) of the Act.

The respondent points out that Congress has chosen to provide financial aid only to countries that employ voluntary family planning techniques. It has prohibited the use of such aid to coerce or provide any financial incentive to any person to undergo sterilization, or for the performance of involuntary sterilizations as a method of family planning, or for biomedical research relating to methods of performing abortions or involuntary sterilization as a means of family planning. However, the fact that Congress may strongly disapprove of a foreign country's policy does not mean that Congress has found that the policy involves "persecution on account of race, religion, nationality, membership in a particular social group or political opinion."

* * * [E]ven if involuntary sterilization was demonstrated to be a violation of internationally recognized human rights, that fact in itself would not establish that an individual subjected to such an act was a victim of persecution "on account of race, religion, nationality, membership in a particular social group, or political opinion." We are satisfied that if an individual demonstrated a well-founded fear that such an act would occur "on account of" a reason protected by the Act, the "refugee" definition in section 101(a)(42) of the Act would be met.

The issue before us is not whether China's population control policies, in whole or in part, should be encouraged or discouraged to the fullest extent possible by the United States and the world community. The issue is whether the respondent demonstrates persecution or a well-founded fear of persecution on account of race, religion, nationality, membership in a particular social group, or political opinion simply with evidence that he and his wife desire to have more than two children and that, because of China's population control measures, he may be subjected to mandatory sterilization. Where there is no evidence that the application of the policy is a subterfuge for some other persecutive purpose, we do not find that he demonstrates eligibility for asylum by this evidence alone. Whether these policies are such that the immigration laws should be amended to provide temporary or permanent relief from deportation to all individuals who face the possibility of forced sterilization as part of a country's population control program is a matter for Congress to resolve legislatively.

On the record before us we find that the respondent's claims are insufficient to establish that he has a well-founded fear of persecution on account of one of the five grounds enumerated in section 101(a)(42)(A) of the Act. * * *

* * *

## Notes and Questions

1. *Chang* can be evaluated in two separate lights. First, there was evidence, as described by the BIA, that the Chinese population control policy is enforced only through "[e]conomic sanctions, peer pressure, and propaganda." *Chang* indicates that these kinds of economic sanctions and pressure alone do not amount to persecution. Do you agree? In *Borca v. INS*, 77 F.3d 210, 215 (7th Cir. 1996), the BIA ruled that economic persecution results in refugee status only when "the persecution is so severe as to deprive an applicant of all means of earning their living." Applying this doctrine, it found that the Romanian asylum applicant was not eligible for asylum, even though she had been fired from her job as a radiologist and apparently denied a license for any other government job except farm laborer. The Seventh Circuit reversed, applying a standard derived from *Kovac v. INS*, 407 F.2d 102, 107 (9th Cir. 1969): "deliberate imposition of substantial economic disadvantage for reasons of race, religion or political

opinion" would suffice to justify political asylum. More recently, the Seventh Circuit applied *Borca* to hold that the evidence in a case involving a Mormon in Ukraine might compel a finding of persecution on account of religion. The court explained, "the government prevented her from continuing her education in the Ph.D. physics program, denied her permission to live in Kiev and reduced her to working in menial jobs that required no education, training or acuity." *Koval v. Gonzales*, 418 F.3d 798, 805–06 (7th Cir. 2005). Do *Borca* and *Koval* go too far? At what point do economic sanctions rise to the level of persecution?

2.  The BIA in *Chang* also considers the case on an assumption that more serious consequences await the applicant, including his forced sterilization or his wife's forced abortion. Even so, it appears unwilling to find that these consequences amount to persecution on account of one of the five reasons stated in the definition. Such sanctions could constitute persecution in some settings, but apparently not if they are applied to virtually all in the population who fail to go along with the national policy. Persecution, in this conception, apparently requires some sort of invidious discrimination. Do you agree? Consider how the definition would apply to people who escaped Cambodia under Pol Pot, whose Khmer Rouge, in power from 1975 to 1979, attempted to purge their country of all Western influence, and who killed over a million of their countrymen in the process (often in quite indiscriminate fashion). Should the need for a showing of invidious discrimination be reduced if the threatened harm is regarded as especially severe?

3.  Did the BIA consider the scope of potential immigration from the most populous country in the world? Would any such attention to practical consequences and political limitations be a legitimate factor to consider in shaping the law of *nonrefoulement* and asylum?

4.  The BIA's 1989 decision in *Chang* was followed several months later by the Tiananmen Square massacre in Beijing. The first President Bush, among other steps in response, ordered "enhanced consideration" of asylum claims based on forced abortion or coerced sterilization. 66 Interp. Rel. 1331 (1989). Later, in 1994, the Department of Justice decided to provide a form of administrative relief, separate from asylum, for persons subjected in the past to, or now in danger of, forced abortion or involuntary sterilization. The relief consisted of a stay of deportation with work authorization. 71 Interp. Rel. 1066–70 (1994).

Although all the federal courts of appeals that dealt with PRC population control cases sustained denials of asylum based on the *Chang* approach, *see, e.g., Chen v. INS,* 95 F.3d 801 (9th Cir. 1996); *Di v. Moscato,* 66 F.3d 315 (4th Cir. 1995); *Zheng v. INS,* 44 F.3d 379 (5th Cir. 1995), Congress stepped in to overrule *Chang* and supersede the administrative relief protection established in 1994. The legislation reflected a tension between humanitarian response and concern about numbers. The 1996 Act amended § 101(a)(42) by adding a third sentence to the definition of "refugee":

> For purposes of determinations under this Act, a person who has been forced to abort a pregnancy or to undergo involuntary sterilization, or who has been persecuted for failure or refusal to undergo such a procedure or for other resistance to a coercive population control program, shall be deemed to have been persecuted on

account of political opinion, and a person who has a well founded fear that he or she will be forced to undergo such a procedure or subject to persecution for such failure, refusal, or resistance shall be deemed to have a well founded fear of persecution on account of political opinion.

At the same time, a new § 207(a)(5) placed a ceiling of 1,000 per year on the number of persons who could be granted either asylum or overseas refugee admission based on this new provision. It was not clear what Congress intended for any excess cases (perhaps a sign that the ceiling addressed political rather than policy objectives). Eventually the agencies applying this section decided that those found to qualify but covered by the ceiling would receive only "conditional" grants of asylum. This would become a full grant when a space was available under the quota. Within a decade a backlog developed of close to 9,000 conditional grants; Congress repealed the ceiling in 2005. *See Full Asylum Benefits for FY2004 Available for Certain Conditional Grant Beneficiaries*, 10 Bender's Immigr. Bull. 100 (2005); Pub. L. 109–13, 119 Stat. 231, 305, Div. B, § 101(g)(2).

Neither the 1996 nor 2005 amendments addressed withholding under § 241(b)(3). When the BIA faced this issue in *In re X–P–T–*, 21 I & N Dec. 634 (BIA 1996), it ruled that the 1996 amendment superseded *Chang* and applies in withholding cases as well (for which there was no ceiling).

5.   In his treatise, The Law of Refugee Status, James Hathaway asks why the drafters of the 1951 Convention chose the term "persecution":

> It is generally acknowledged that the drafters of the Convention intentionally left the meaning of "persecution" undefined because they realized the impossibility of enumerating in advance all of the forms of maltreatment which might legitimately entitle persons to benefit from the protection of a foreign state. Bits and pieces of insight into the intended meaning of "persecution" can nonetheless be gleaned from the Convention's drafting history.

> First, the drafters clearly viewed persecution as a sufficiently inclusive concept to capture the spectrum of phenomena which had induced involuntary migration during and immediately after the Second World War, ranging from the deprivation of life and liberty inflicted by the Nazis, to the ideological conformism imposed by the communist states. From the beginning, there was no monolithic or absolute conceptual standard of wrongfulness, the implication being that a variety of measures in disregard of human dignity might constitute persecution. * * *

> Second, the intention of the drafters was not to protect persons against any and all forms of even serious harm, but was rather to restrict refugee recognition to situations in which there was a risk of a type of injury that would be inconsistent with the basic duty of protection owed by a state to its own population. * * *

> These basic tenets—a liberal sense of the types of past or anticipated harm which might warrant protection abroad, and a fundamental preoccupation to identify forms of harm demonstrative

of breach by a state of its basic obligations of protection—are of continuing relevance today. * * *

Drawing on these basic precepts, persecution may be defined as the sustained or systemic violation of basic human rights demonstrative of a failure of state protection.

James Hathaway, The Law of Refugee Status 102–05 (1991).

6. Rodger Haines, a New Zealand refugee law expert and member of that country's Refugee Status Appeals Authority, puts his view succinctly:

Persecution is the construct of two separate but essential elements, namely risk of serious harm and failure of state protection.

Haines, *Gender-related persecution*, in Refugee Protection in International Law 319, 329–30 (E. Feller, V. Türk, & F. Nicholson, eds. 2003).

7. Suppose that Adam faces no direct harm to himself that would count as persecution, but that his daughter, Berta, would be persecuted. Should the law regard Adam as being persecuted by virtue of persecution of a close relative? Does it depend on the nature of the persecution that Berta would suffer? Does it depend on the intent of the persecutor? On other factors? Does it make a difference if Adam left without Berta, who remains back in the country of origin?

8. The full framework for determining whether U.S. law will protect an individual requires not only that he or she be faced with "persecution," but also that any such persecution be "on account of race, religion, nationality, membership of a particular social group or political opinion." Each of these five grounds is a term of art, as is the phrase "on account of," which requires a certain type of nexus among the persecutor, the individual being persecuted, and the reason for the persecution. This chapter focuses on "persecution" and defers to Chapter Four the meaning of "on account of race, religion, nationality, membership of a particular social group or political opinion."

As the preceding notes also suggest, the lines between these issues—(1) "persecution," (2) the five grounds, and (3) "on account of"—are often blurred in practical application. Many cases implicate more than one of these issues, and it is not always possible to tease them neatly apart. For example, the BIA's conclusion that the case did not involve persecution was based in part on the absence of a "particular social group" to which *Chang* belonged. (We defer full consideration of the definition of "particular social group" to Chapter Four.) As you work through the material in this chapter and Chapter Four, we urge you to remain aware of the interaction among these three issues, and to think holistically about the phrase "persecution on account of race, religion, nationality, membership in a particular social group, or political opinion."

## 2. INTENT TO HARM

Judge Posner's *Osaghae* definition of persecution, reprinted at the beginning of this section, describes persecution as "punishment for political, religious or other reasons that our country does not recognize as legitimate." And according to a leading BIA decision, "the term 'persecution' means the infliction of suffering or harm in order to punish an individual for possessing a particular belief or characteristic the persecutor seeks to overcome.'' *Matter of Acosta,* 19 I & N Dec. 211, 234 (BIA 1985). The concept of punishment implies a subjective intent on the part of the alleged persecutor to impose on the victim something the persecutor views as harmful. Is that kind of subjective intent essential to defining persecution for *nonrefoulement* and asylum? The court in the next case addresses this question.

## PITCHERSKAIA v. INS

United States Court of Appeals, Ninth Circuit, 1997.
118 F.3d 641.

BETTY FLETCHER, CIRCUIT JUDGE.

\* \* \*

Alla Pitcherskaia is a 35 year old native and citizen of Russia. She entered the United States as a visitor for pleasure on March 22, 1992, with authorization to remain for six months. On June 2, 1992, she applied for asylum on the basis that she feared persecution on account of her own and her father's anti-Communist political opinions. After a complete interview, the Immigration and Naturalization Service Asylum Office found that she was credible and that she had suffered past persecution. However, it found that she failed to establish a well-founded fear of future persecution and denied her application. She was placed in deportation proceedings for overstaying her visa.

Pitcherskaia renewed her request for asylum and withholding of deportation \* \* \*. In this application, she claimed an additional basis for granting her petition—that she was persecuted and feared future persecution on account of her political opinions in support of lesbian and gay civil rights in Russia, and on account of her membership in a particular social group: Russian lesbians.[1] She also requested voluntary departure.

\* \* \*

Pitcherskaia's father was an artist and political dissident. As a result of his antigovernment activities, he was arrested and imprisoned numerous times during Pitcherskaia's childhood until 1972 when he died in prison. Pitcherskaia testified that, because of her father's anticommunist activities, she has been under the control and surveillance of the police for her entire life.

Pitcherskaia was first arrested by the militia in 1980, when she was eighteen years old. She was charged with the crime of "hooliganism" and detained for fifteen days because she protested her former school director's beating of a gay friend. At the time of this arrest, the director was unaware Pitcherskaia was herself a lesbian.

---

**1.** Pitcherskaia alleges that she did not include a claim for persecution on account of her lesbianism and her political activism for lesbian and gay rights in her original application because she did not know that it was a possible ground for an asylum claim.

In 1981, Pitcherskaia was arrested again, imprisoned for fifteen days, and beaten for participating in an illegal demonstration demanding the release of the leader of a lesbian youth organization which she belonged to. Pitcherskaia claims that, at the time of this arrest, the Russian militia warned her not to continue to associate with other women in the organization and threatened her with involuntary psychiatric confinement if she continued "to see women."

Over the next two years Pitcherskaia claims that she was detained by the militia for short periods, interrogated, and on occasion beaten. On several occasions she was pressed to identify gay and lesbian friends. In May 1983, she was again arrested, charged with "hooliganism," and detained for ten days. Pitcherskaia maintains that the sole reason for her arrest was the arresting officer's knowledge of her sexual identity and political opinions.

In 1985 or 1986, Pitcherskaia's ex-girlfriend was forcibly sent to a psychiatric institution for over four months, during which time she was subjected to electric shock treatment and other so-called "therapies" in an effort to change her sexual orientation. Pitcherskaia testified that while she was visiting this woman at the psychiatric institution, she was grabbed by the militia, forcibly taken to a doctor's office and questioned about her sexual orientation. She was permitted to leave only after she provided a false address outside the jurisdiction of the clinic. Although she denied being a lesbian, the clinic registered her as a "suspected lesbian" and told her she must undergo treatment at her local clinic every six months. When she failed to show up for these outpatient sessions, she received a "Demand for Appearance." She testified that if she failed to comply, the militia would threaten her with forced institutionalization and forcibly take her from her home to the sessions.

Pitcherskaia testified that she attended eight of these "therapy" sessions. During these sessions, Pitcherskaia continued to deny that she was a lesbian. However, she was officially diagnosed with "slow-going schizophrenia," a catchall phrase often used in Russia to "diagnose" homosexuals. The psychiatrist prescribed sedative drugs, which Pitcherskaia never took. On one occasion, the psychiatrist tried to hypnotize her.

On two separate occasions, in 1990 and 1991, Pitcherskaia was arrested while in the homes of gay friends and taken to prison overnight. She received several "Demands for Appearance" when the militia sought to interrogate her about her sexual orientation and political activities. In 1991, she was interrogated about her activities with a gay and lesbian political organization—the "Union of Coming Out"—that had been denied legal recognition by the government.

Since her arrival in the United States, Pitcherskaia has received two more "Demands for Appearance" from the militia that were delivered at her mother's residence. Since she did not respond to the two recent

Demands, Pitcherskaia fears that the militia will carry out their previous threats and forcibly institutionalize her if she returns to Russia.

\* \* \*

\* \* \* The BIA majority concluded that Pitcherskaia had not been persecuted because, although she had been subjected to involuntary psychiatric treatments, the militia and psychiatric institutions intended to "cure" her, not to punish her, and thus their actions did not constitute "persecution" within the meaning of the Act. The BIA majority also concluded that recent political and social changes in the former Soviet Union make it unlikely that she would be "subject to psychiatric treatment with persecutory intent upon [her] return to the present-day Russia." \* \* \*

\* \* \*

Pitcherskaia claims, *inter alia,* that the BIA applied an erroneous legal standard by insisting that intent to punish is a necessary element of "persecution." The meaning of "persecution" under section 101(a)(42)(A) of the Act, is a legal question reviewed *de novo.* However, the BIA's interpretations are generally entitled to deference. [*Fisher v. INS,* 79 F.3d 955, 961 (9th Cir.1996) (en banc)] (citing *Chevron U.S.A. v. Natural Resources Defense Council,* 467 U.S. 837, 104 S.Ct. 2778, 81 L.Ed.2d 694 (1984)). Because the Act does not define "persecution," we defer to the Board's interpretation unless it is "arbitrary, capricious, or manifestly contrary to the statute." *Id.* The Board is also bound by our prior decisions interpreting the Act.

\* \* \*

The majority of the Board required that Pitcherskaia prove that the Russian authorities intended to harm or punish her. While acknowledging that forced institutionalization, electroshock treatments, and drug injections could constitute persecution, the BIA majority concluded that because here the "[i]nvoluntary treatment and confinement [were] intended to treat or cure the supposed illness, not to punish," Pitcherskaia had not been persecuted nor did she have a well-founded fear of persecution. For the following reasons we conclude that in requiring Pitcherskaia to prove intent to harm or punish as an element of persecution, the BIA majority erred.

Although many asylum cases "involve[ ] actors who had a subjective intent to punish their victims ... this subjective 'punitive' or 'malignant' intent is not required for harm to constitute persecution." *In re Fauziya Kasinga,* Int. Dec. 3278 at 12 (BIA June 13, 1996) (en banc) (designated as precedent by the BIA). Neither the Supreme Court nor this court has construed the Act as imposing a requirement that the alien prove that her persecutor was motivated by a desire to punish or inflict harm.

We have defined "persecution" as "the infliction of suffering or harm upon those who differ ... in a way regarded as offensive." This definition of persecution is objective, in that it turns not on the subjective intent of the persecutor but rather on what a reasonable person would deem "offensive." That the persecutor inflicts the suffering or harm in an attempt to elicit information, for his own sadistic pleasure, to "cure" his victim, or to "save his soul" is irrelevant. Persecution by any other name remains persecution.

\* \* \*

Although we have held that unreasonably severe punishment can constitute "persecution," "punishment" is neither a mandatory nor a sufficient aspect of persecution. \* \* \* [The court quoted from Webster's New Collegiate Dictionary.] Hence, punishment implies that the perpetrator believes the victim has committed a crime or some wrong; whereas persecution simply requires that the perpetrator cause the victim suffering or harm. To the extent that *Acosta* and *Mogharrabi* [19 I & N Dec. 439 (BIA 1987), reprinted later in this chapter, p. 154] require an alien to prove the persecutor harbored a subjective intent to punish, we reject their holdings.

\* \* \*

The fact that a persecutor believes the harm he is inflicting is "good for" his victim does not make it any less painful to the victim, or, indeed, remove the conduct from the statutory definition of persecution. The [BIA's] requirement that an alien prove that her persecutor's subjective intent was punitive is unwarranted. Human rights laws cannot be sidestepped by simply couching actions that torture mentally or physically in benevolent terms such as "curing" or "treating" the victims.

\* \* \*

Petition for review granted. Reversed and remanded.

### Notes and Questions

1. Judge Fletcher states that "persecution simply requires that the perpetrator cause the victim suffering or harm," but the actions of most surgeons would fit this description. What other characteristics are required before the act is adjudged to be persecution? Is it a matter of the consent or resistance of the "victim"? Consider then civil commitment of one who truly is schizophrenic and dangerous to himself or others. What other factors must be considered in analyzing persecution?

2. *Pitcherskaia* cites the BIA's opinion in *Matter of Kasinga*, 21 I & N Dec. 357 (BIA en banc, 1996), which Chapter Five will consider in depth. The *Kasinga* case concerned the practice of female genital cutting in Togo. The BIA described the practice as follows

> According to the applicant's testimony, the FGM [female genital mutilation] practiced by her tribe, the Tchamba–Kunsuntu, is of an extreme type involving cutting the genitalia with knives, extensive bleeding, and a 40–day recovery period. The background materials confirm that the FGM practiced in some African countries, such as Togo, is of an extreme nature causing permanent damage, and not just a minor form of genital ritual.

The record material establishes that FGM in its extreme forms is a practice in which portions of the female genitalia are cut away. In some cases, the vagina is sutured partially closed. This practice clearly inflicts harm or suffering upon the girl or woman who undergoes it.

FGM is extremely painful and at least temporarily incapacitating. It permanently disfigures the female genitalia. FGM exposes the girl or woman to the risk of serious, potentially life-threatening complications. These include, among others, bleeding, infection, urine retention, stress, shock, psychological trauma, and damage to the urethra and anus. It can result in permanent loss of genital sensation and can adversely affect sexual and erotic functions.

21 I & N Dec. at 361.

As gruesome as this description of FGM may be, others argue that it is a cultural rite of passage which generally occurs with the intent to admit the young woman into full membership in the community, not with the intent to punish her. Anthropologist Richard Shweder has written:

In those cases of female genital alteration with which I am most familiar (I have lived and taught in Kenya, where the practice is routine for some ethnic groups), the adolescent girls who undergo the ritual initiation look forward to it. It is an ordeal and it can be painful (especially if done "naturally" without anesthesia), but it is viewed as a test of courage. It is an event organized and controlled by women, who have their own view of the aesthetics of the body—a different view from ours about what is civilized, dignified, and beautiful. The girl's parents are not trying to be cruel to their daughter—African parents love their children too. No one is raped or tortured. There is a celebration surrounding the event.

Shweder, *What About "Female Genital Mutilation"? And Why Understanding Culture Matters in the First Place*, 129 Daedalus 209, 222 (2000). The BIA ruled in *Kasinga* that the practice constitutes persecution even if those performing the rite have benign intent.

How would you compare the intent behind China's population policy, which is arguably benign in a different, more general sense? Or is the real explanation for the outcome in *Pitcherskaia* the court's suspicion that the intent behind her "treatment" was not so benign after all?

3. *Pitcherskaia* acknowledges the deference that the BIA generally receives under *Chevron U.S.A., Inc. v. Natural Resources Defense Council*, 467 U.S. 837, 104 S.Ct. 2778, 81 L.Ed.2d 694 (1984), discussed in Chapter Two, p. 86, but the court then concludes that the BIA's reading of the statute was wrong. Consider the Supreme Court's explanation in *Chevron* of the reasons for deference:

"The power of an administrative agency to administer a congressionally created ... program necessarily requires the formulation of policy and the making of rules to fill any gap left, implicitly or explicitly, by Congress." *Morton v. Ruiz*, 415 U.S. 199, 231, 94 S.Ct. 1055, 1072, 39 L.Ed.2d 270 (1974). If Congress has explicitly left a gap for the agency to fill, there is an express delegation of authority to the agency to elucidate a specific provision of the statute by regulation. Such legislative regulations are given controlling weight unless they are arbitrary, capricious, or manifestly contrary to the statute. Sometimes the legislative delegation to an agency on a particular question is implicit rather than explicit. In such a case, a court may not substitute its own construction of a statutory provision for a reasonable interpretation made by the administrator of an agency.

467 U.S. at 842–44, 104 S.Ct. at 2781–83. *See generally* Schuck & Elliott, *To the* Chevron *Station: An Empirical Study of Federal Administrative Law,* 1990 Duke L.J. 984; Schuck & Wang, *Continuity and Change: Patterns of Immigration Litigation in the Courts, 1979–1990,* 45 Stan. L. Rev. 115, 169–72 (1992).

*Chevron* deference may also be defended on additional grounds. First, the agency works with the statute on a daily basis and is likely to have a better understanding of the operational implications of a narrow or broad construction of a particular provision. Second, the agency may have aided in the drafting of the statute and therefore may have greater insight than the courts into the intent of the language chosen and the purposes of the statutory provision. Finally, deference to agency interpretation may create greater uniformity in application of the statute than would be achieved under different opinions among courts of appeals.

Should the court in *Pitcherskaia* have accorded more judicial deference to the BIA's decision? What counterarguments against agency deference on matters of statutory interpretation should be considered, particularly in the immigration context? Does the *Chevron* approach give too much authority to agency administrators?

### 3.  PROSECUTION VERSUS PERSECUTION

The *Chang* case examined the enforcement of a national policy via "economic sanctions, peer pressure, and propaganda." States often enforce uniform national policies via the criminal law. Putting aside for the moment issues of uneven enforcement of the law, when does the application of criminal sanctions constitute persecution? In the case excerpted below this question arises in the politically charged setting of a coup attempt, but you should consider the implications of the court's reasoning on a broader array of conduct that states have criminalized. What if, for example, a state criminalized distribution of contraceptive drugs and devices? Barred all private ownership of firearms? Banned any use of languages other than the national language in all public settings?

## DWOMOH v. SAVA

United States District Court for the Southern District of New York, 1988.
696 F.Supp. 970.

Wood, District Judge.

* * * The petitioner, Nana Asante Dwomoh, is a thirty-one year old Ghanaian soldier who escaped from Ussher Fort Prison in Ghana on

December 22, 1986. Mr. Dwomoh had joined the Ghanaian Army in 1974, at the age of eighteen, and for the next eleven years he had pursued his military career, attaining the rank of Sergeant. However, by 1985, disturbed by worsening political conditions (including summary execution of eight generals and several judges, among others) and the threatened execution of a political prisoner who was a friend of his, he agreed to participate in resistance activities that included efforts to free his friend from prison and to support a coup against the military government.

On November 6, 1985, the morning before the coup was to take place, a Ghanaian military patrol picked up Mr. Dwomoh and beat him in an unsuccessful attempt to obtain a confession. After being arrested, beaten several times, and imprisoned by the Ghanaian military government for more than one year, without access to counsel, family or friends, Mr. Dwomoh escaped from the prison where he was held in Ghana and fled to the United States.

The Ghanaian military regime had seized power from a democratically-elected government in 1981, and has since prohibited all peaceful means of political change and expression, while simultaneously denying due process protections to those who seek political change through more forceful means. There is every indication that, if returned to Ghana, Mr. Dwomoh will again be physically abused and possibly may be executed.

In a split decision, a majority of the BIA held that an individual such as Mr. Dwomoh cannot qualify for protection as a refugee under United States law on the basis of any of the facts recited here, including his resistance activities, which the BIA condemned as "treason."

* * * In the BIA's view, Mr. Dwomoh cannot qualify for refugee status because, unlike those who merely *express* political *views,* he participated in an unsuccessful *coup d'etat* (Mr. Dwomoh "is a fugitive from justice who faces prosecution for his role in an unsuccessful coup d'etat").

* * *

The BIA takes the position that a person can qualify for refugee status if he faces prosecution for openly *espousing* anti-government views, but that he cannot so qualify if he faces prosecution for *acting* on those views, where his action takes the form of a politically motivated attempt to overthrow the government by violent means. Without considering the fact that in totalitarian governments a person may have only one chance to express or act upon anti-government views, and that the only means of effecting political change may be to overthrow the government, the BIA compared Ghana to the United States and stated that both countries have the right to enforce their laws against treason and insurrection, even by imposition of the death penalty. On the question of whether the beatings and one year's detention of Mr. Dwomoh without permitting him contact with the outside world constitute "persecution on account of . . . political opinion" within the Congressional definition, the BIA stated, " . . . he was subjected to mistreatment due to his refusal to provide information about the attempted *coup d'etat,* not because of any political view he may hold." In determining whether the punishment petitioner faced and faces is persecution on account of political opinion, the BIA relied both on its view that governments have the right to enforce laws against treason, and a statement in a publication of the United Nations High Commissioner for Refugees that persons fleeing from punishment for common law offenses are not normally refugees.

\* \* \*

In evaluating the nature of the crime with which Mr. Dwomoh is charged and the punishment he may face, the BIA noted American laws against treason and insurrection. The *UNHCR Handbook* notes that in evaluating the laws and punishments of other countries, it is often useful to compare those laws to national legislation; in this case, however, the comparison was inapt. The United States has procedures whereby citizens can change their form of government peaceably. In Ghana, where no such procedures exist,[11] a coup may be the only means by which political change can be effected. In addition, while it is true that the United States has laws against treason, and punishes violators of those laws severely, United States law also provides due process protections. No United States citizen is punished for treason without a formal charge, and the opportunity for a full trial and appeal. Mr. Dwomoh has no such protections; he might be executed without ever having been charged, no less tried. \* \* \*

An accurate assessment of the political conditions existing in the particular country at the time the political crime is committed is central to the determination of whether prosecution for a political crime constitutes persecution under the guidelines set forth by the UNHCR. It may be that as a general rule prosecution for an attempt to overthrow a lawfully constituted government does not constitute persecution. However, the UNHCR does not view that general rule as applicable in countries where a coup is the only means through which a change in the political regime can be effected. \* \* \*

\* \* \*

The BIA held that because Mr. Dwomoh had not expressed political opinions critical of the Ghanaian regime prior to the coup attempt, "he is not facing prosecution for his political views but rather for the . . . act of trying to overthrow the Government of Ghana." In so doing, the BIA ignored the reality that in certain countries individuals who express opposition to the government are jailed, and in certain of those countries, an attempted coup is the only way to change the government. In

---

**11.** According to the United States State Department:

> The PNDC under Chairman Rawlings exercises total executive, legislative, judicial, and administrative power

in Ghana (PNDC Law 42). There are no elections to governing organs and no current procedure by which citizens can freely and peacefully change their laws, officials, or form of government.

such a country, a person desirous of changing the government would be ill advised to express his opposition publicly before attempting a coup. In that context, his political expression is embodied in his political act.

\* \* \*

Accordingly, the decision of the BIA is hereby reversed; the case is remanded to the BIA for any additional findings of fact made necessary by this Opinion \* \* \*.

So ordered.

## Notes and Questions

1. The court in *Dwomoh* mentions both the absence of procedures for peaceful change of government and the lack of due process protections in any trial of coup plotters. But presumably coup plotters would still be punished in authoritarian states with better judicial procedures. Is the second element therefore essential to the ruling? Or should coup plotters be entitled to protection based only on a showing that the home state lacks effective and meaningfully contested elections? How much of a real option must the voters enjoy before *Dwomoh* ceases to apply? After all, even Ceausescu's Romania held elections. How should one judge the validity of the election process?

2. In *Chanco v. INS*, 82 F.3d 298, 302 (9th Cir. 1996), the court held that because "diverse political views are tolerated in the Philippines, and Chanco could have expressed his political opinion without resort to a violent attempt to overthrow the democratically elected government," the military discipline and criminal prosecution faced by a Philippine coup participant did not constitute persecution on account of political opinion but rather "on account of his illegal action."

3. Under *Dwomoh,* should a participant in the failed 1991 coup staged by old-line Communists against Soviet President Mikhail Gorbachev be considered eligible for asylum, assuming the plotter managed to escape to the United States? Should asylum in coup plotter cases depend on the adjudicator's assessment of the plotter's own attitude toward democracy or protection of the rights of opponents? Should such factors be relevant to granting protection by way of *nonrefoulement* or asylum? How does the reasoning in *Chanco*, described in note 2 above, affect your answer to these questions?

4. Is *Dwomoh consistent with Chang*? In the context of granting *nonrefoulement* or asylum in the United States, how is a government's objective of staying in power in the face of armed opposition different from a government's objective of controlling the size of its population? Is it possible to distinguish the two objectives without comparing their legitimacy? If a legitimacy assessment is unavoidable, is that troubling?

5. In *Matter of Izatula,* 20 I & N Dec. 149 (BIA 1990), the Board cited the court decision in *Dwomoh* with approval. The immigration judge had ruled that the applicant, a national of Afghanistan, would merely be subject to prosecution, not persecution, for his assistance to the *mujahedin* rebels in that country and his resistance to conscription into the Afghan army. The

Board disagreed. Quoting a State Department human rights country report on Afghanistan, it found that "Afghanistan is a totalitarian state," and "[c]itizens have neither the right nor the ability peacefully to change their government." It went on to rule: "there is no basis in the record to conclude that any punishment imposed by the Afghan Government would be a legitimate exercise of sovereign authority." *Id.* at 154. Therefore Izatula was awarded asylum.

Two members concurred specially, on the ground that the threatened punishment was disproportionate to Izatula's offenses, in view of the routine torture meted out in Afghan prisons. Board member Vacca then criticized the grounds relied on by the majority:

> In effect, the majority finds that the Afghan government is illegitimate and therefore incapable of imposing a lawful punishment. * * * [T]he majority wades in dangerous waters when it presumes to make judgments as to the legitimacy of sovereign nations by scrutinizing their political systems. Clearly the President of the United States has constitutional authority to formulate and conduct foreign policy[.] * * * To hold that some governments may create laws affecting crimes, adjudicate criminal cases and impose punishments upon offending citizens and other governments may not[,] depending upon the nature of their political systems[,] is patently absurd. The right of all nations to recruit soldiers and maintain armies to protect themselves from enemies within or without their borders is recognized as fundamental in international law. This sovereign right is not limited to countries whose internal political structures are democratic.

*Id.* at 155–56. Which position, majority or concurrence, makes more sense? Is it possible to excise judgments about the legitimacy of those exercising sovereign rights from the asylum adjudication process? For useful discussions of *Izatula*, see Blum, *License to Kill: Asylum Law and the Principle of Legitimate Governmental Authority to "Investigate Its Enemies,"* 28 Willamette L. Rev. 719, 746–48 (1992); Note, *Refugee Determinations: A Consolidation of Approaches to Actions by Nongovernmental Forces,* 33 Va. J. Int'l L. 927 (1993).

Though assistance to the *mujahedin* rebels in Afghanistan was a key aspect of *Izatula*, equally important was the applicant's resistance to conscription. Because the prosecution/persecution issue often arises in the context of military conscription, keep *Izatula* in mind as you read the materials on conscription later in this chapter.

### 4. PERSECUTION BY NONGOVERNMENTAL ACTORS

U.S. law has readily accepted that harm or threats from non-state actors can give rise to a valid basis for asylum. *See* Moore, *From Nation State to Failed State: International Protection from Human Rights Abuses by Non-State Agents,* 31 Colum. Human Rights L. Rev. 81, 106–109 (1999); Newland, *Managing International Migration: Tracking the Emergence of a New International Regime,* 3 UCLA J. Int'l L. & For. Aff. 637, 644 (1999). As the Ninth Circuit explained in *McMullen v. INS,* 658 F.2d 1312, 1315 n. 2 (9th Cir. 1981), "persecution within the meaning of

§ 243(h) includes persecution by non-governmental groups * * * where it is shown that the government of the proposed country of deportation is unwilling or unable to control that group." The BIA agrees. *See, e.g., Matter of O–Z– and I–Z–,* 22 I & N Dec. 23 (BIA 1998) (affirming asylum grant to a Ukrainian Jew who had been beaten and threatened by an anti-Semitic ultranationalist group).

Ascertaining when a government is unable or unwilling to control a persecuting group is a more complicated question than it might initially seem. In all countries, violent crime occurs to a greater or lesser degree, despite control efforts by the government. No one can be completely guaranteed protection against some such criminal activity. If a threatened violent crime has a political cast to it, must the potential harm be considered persecution of a kind that might give rise to a valid asylum claim? In *Matter of O–Z– and I–Z–, supra,* the BIA emphasized the fact "that the respondent reported at least three of the incidents to the police, who took no action beyond writing a report" before finding that the nongovernmental acts were sufficiently condoned by the government to justify a grant of asylum. On the other hand, in *Matter of V–T–S–,* 21 I & N Dec. 792 (BIA 1997), the Board refused to grant asylum to a person who had been threatened with kidnapping by insurgent forces in the Philippines. In dictum, the BIA noted that the applicant had failed to show a sufficient government default to make the kidnapping a sound basis for asylum, in part because the government had mounted major efforts against the perpetrators when the applicant's siblings had been kidnapped.

In *Singh v. INS,* 94 F.3d 1353 (9th Cir. 1996), the asylum applicant was an ethnic Indian citizen of Fiji. The population of the island is about evenly divided between ethnic Fijians and Indo–Fijians, and there has been considerable ethnic strife there, including two coups. Singh and his family had been threatened and assaulted by groups of ethnic Fijians. Reversing a denial of asylum and remanding the case, the court addressed the nongovernmental persecution issue as follows:

> The INS * * * contends that Singh is not eligible for asylum because there is no evidence that the persecution suffered by Singh and his family was committed by an "organized or quasi-governmental group." We disagree with the INS's legal premise. Persecution meted out by groups that the government is unable or unwilling to control constitutes persecution under the Act. Non-governmental groups need not file articles of incorporation before they can be capable of persecution.

> In this case, Singh testified that he reported each assault and threat to the police and that, although Singh identified his assailants by name, the police failed to respond to any of his crime reports. This failure by the authorities to protect Singh and his family clearly indicates that the police either could not or would not control the ethnic Fijians who threatened Singh and his family.

The record shows that the government has encouraged and condoned the discrimination, harassment, and violence by ethnic Fijians against Indo–Fijians. The interim government adopted a new constitution which institutionalizes discrimination against non-ethnic Fijians and guarantees ethnic Fijians political control of the government. Finally, we note that the police department, which does little to protect Indo–Fijians, is composed primarily of ethnic Fijians. * * *

94 F.3d at 1360.

More recently, Attorney General John Ashcroft explicitly agreed with this doctrine in a case that he decided on referral from the BIA:

There can be no doubt that the terrorist activities of the armed Islamist groups in Algeria during the 1990s constituted "persecution . . . on account of . . . religion . . . or political opinion." It is well established that nongovernmental actors, such as terrorists, insurgents, guerrilla organizations, or other militant opposition groups, can be guilty of "persecution" within the meaning of the Immigration and Nationality Act.

*Matter of A–H–*, 23 I & N Dec. 774, 783–84 (AG 2005). In this case, the doctrine was significant in an unusual way. Because the applicant, as a nongovernmental actor, had inflicted persecution on his armed group's opponents in Algeria, he was barred from withholding of removal. We will study *Matter of A–H–* later in this chapter when we consider discretion to grant or deny asylum.

The view that harm inflicted by nongovernmental actors can qualify as persecution has not been universal. Some countries in Europe, notably France and Germany, had ruled that the Convention definition is limited to persecution by state officials. The new EU Qualifications Directive has modified their interpretation. Persecution by non-state actors whom international organizations and government officials cannot or will not control can give rise to both refugee status and subsidiary protection. Art. 6, Council Directive 2004/83/EC of 29 April 2004 (OJ L 304.12) (hereinafter cited as Qualifications Directive).

## 5.  INTERNAL FLIGHT

In civil war situations there may be substantial portions of territory where no fighting is occurring. If these areas are secure, is it appropriate to require asylum seekers fleeing persecution in a contested area to seek safety within their homeland?

In *Matter of Fuentes*, 19 I & N Dec. 658 (BIA 1988), the Board of Immigration Appeals rejected an asylum claim based on harm that might be inflicted on him by leftist insurgents in El Salvador on account of his association with the Government of El Salvador. In one passage, the Board suggested that the applicant could avoid the risk of harm by moving to another part of El Salvador, rather than returning to his hometown.

Even if one assumes the respondent's claim in this respect has been otherwise demonstrated, however, we do not find an asylum claim based on nongovernmental action adequately established where the evidence the respondent presents is directed to so local an area of his country of nationality. Although the respondent expressed a general fear of returning to El Salvador, his specific evidence focuses on the danger he would face if he returned to his hometown, where he is known by guerrillas and the conflict is still ongoing. The record in fact indicates that the respondent resided in San Salvador for 2 years prior to his departure from El Salvador and only visited his mother on weekends at his hometown when he had permission.

19 I & N Dec. at 663. Similarly, the Board ruled in *Matter of C–A–L–*, 21 I & N Dec. 754 (BIA 1997), that the applicant "must do more than show a well-founded fear of persecution in a particular place within a country. He must show that a threat of persecution exists for him country-wide." *See also Etugh v. INS*, 921 F.2d 36, 39 (3d Cir. 1990) (ineligible for asylum because the scope of alleged persecution is "not national"); *Quintanilla–Ticas v. INS*, 783 F.2d 955, 957 (9th Cir. 1986) (deportation to home country does not require return to home town where the threat existed).

This "internal flight alternative" doctrine, or internal protection alternative, raises thorny questions about fact-finding and burdens of proof. It also raises a basic policy question: should the potential availability of protection in the country of origin disqualify someone who faces persecution from asylum and withholding in the United States?

Several court decisions have held that where the applicant establishes persecution by the government of the country which he has fled, then the U.S. government, if it opposes the asylum application, has the burden of proof to show that the applicant could avoid the risk of harm through internal flight. *See, e.g., Singh v. Moschorak*, 53 F.3d 1031, 1034 (9th Cir. 1995) (Sikh from the Punjab region of India); *Abdel–Masieh v. United States INS*, 73 F.3d 579, 585–87 (5th Cir. 1996) (Christian from the Sudan). One can argue that the presumption should depend on whether parts of the territory are outside the national government's control, as well as on the character of the national government. For example, the level of efficiency in pursuing persons deemed by local officials to be an enemy varies greatly between, say, the former East German regime and the government of as vast a state as India.

Amendments to the asylum regulations in 2000 clarified the internal flight doctrine and answered some of the questions posed above by providing that the applicant lacks a well-founded fear if he or she

> could avoid persecution by relocating to another part of the applicant's country of nationality * * *, if under all the circumstances it would be reasonable to expect the applicant to do so.

8 C.F.R. § 208.13(b)(2).

In deciding on the reasonableness of relocation, the regulations specify that "adjudicators should consider, among other things, whether the applicant would face other serious harm in the place of suggested relocation; any ongoing civil strife within the country; administrative, economic, or judicial infrastructure; geographical limitations; and social and cultural constraints, such as age, gender, health, and social and familial ties. These factors may or may not be relevant, depending on all the circumstances of the case, and are not necessarily determinative of whether it would be reasonable for the applicant to relocate."

If the persecutor is the government, or the applicant has been persecuted in the past, the regulations establish a presumption that internal relocation is not reasonable—essentially that the persecution is nationwide in scope—unless DHS rebuts that presumption by a preponderance of the evidence. 8 C.F.R. § 208.13(b)(3). If there is no proof of past persecution, the applicant bears the burden of establishing that a reasonable possibility of harm exists throughout the country of origin. Similar amendments were made to the regulation governing withholding of removal under INA § 241(b)(3). 8 C.F.R. § 208.16(b)(1).

### A Comparative Perspective

Many other legal systems have also struggled with the relevance of possible alternatives in an asylum seeker's homeland and of the standards that should be used to assess the safety and accessibility of potential relocation sites. The European Union has addressed this issue in its recent legislation on individuals in need of international protection.

> As part of the assessment of the application for international protection, Member States may determine that an applicant is not in need of international protection if in a part of the country of origin there is no well-founded fear of being persecuted or no real risk of suffering serious harm and the applicant can reasonably be expected to stay in that part of the country.
>
> In examining whether a part of the country of origin is in accordance with paragraph 1, Member States shall at the time of taking the decision on the application have regard to the general circumstances prevailing in that part of the country and to the personal circumstances of the applicant.

Art. 8, Qualifications Directive, *supra*.

In early 2006 the highest court in the United Kingdom, the House of Lords, sitting as Britain's highest court, examined four consolidated appeals challenging the government's denial of refugee status based on the finding that protection was potentially available in another part of the asylum seeker's homeland. The opinions were lengthy, surveying relevant decisions that had been entered by courts in New Zealand, Australia, and Canada, and quoting at length from prior opinions. Some of the opinions analyzed the text of the 1951 Convention, scholarly commentary, policy considerations, and UNHCR Guidelines in attempting to determine when internal relocation is reasonable. All opinions expressed agreement with the conclusion in the opinion excerpted at length here, that one of the appeals would be dismissed and the other three sustained.

## JANUZI v. SECRETARY OF STATE FOR THE HOME DEPARTMENT

[2006] UKHL 5.

LORD BINGHAM OF CORNHILL:

My Lords,

2.    * * * Mr Januzi, an Albanian Kosovar, was the victim of ethnic cleansing at Serb hands at his home in Mitrovica in Kosovo. He fled to this country and claimed asylum. This claim was refused on the ground that he could reasonably be expected to relocate to Pristina. He claims, largely for medical reasons associated with his experience of persecution, that it would be unduly harsh to expect him to do so. Messrs Hamid, Gaafar and Mohammed were black Africans living in Darfur in western Sudan. Hamid and Gaafar were the victims of persecution by marauding Arab bands, which the Government encouraged or connived at and did not restrain. Mohammed, it has been found, would suffer such persecution were he to return to Darfur, whence (like Hamid and Gaafar) he fled. They all claimed asylum on arriving here. In each case, recognition as a refugee has been denied on the ground that the appellant could reasonably (and without undue harshness) be expected to relocate to Khartoum. They all fear that they might be the victims of adverse discriminatory treatment, even persecution, in Khartoum, and they contend that relocation there would be unreasonable and unduly harsh.

* * *

5.    The definition of "refugee" * * * has three qualifying conditions. The first is, clearly in my opinion, a causative condition which governs all that follows: "owing to well-founded fear of being persecuted for reasons of race ... political opinion". The second, indispensable, condition, satisfied by all these appellants, is that the person should be "outside the country of his nationality". The third condition contains an alternative: the person must either be "unable ... to avail himself of the protection" of the country of his nationality, or he must be "unwilling", owing to fear of being persecuted for a Convention reason, "to avail himself of the protection" of the country of his nationality.

* * *

7.    The Refugee Convention does not expressly address the situation at issue * * * where, within the country of his nationality, a person has a well-founded fear of persecution at place A, where he lived, but not at place B, where (it is said) he could reasonably be expected to relocate. But the situation may fairly be said to be covered by the causative

condition to which reference has been made: for if a person is outside the country of his nationality because he has chosen to leave that country and seek asylum in a foreign country, rather than move to a place of relocation within his own country where he would have no well-founded fear of persecution, where the protection of his country would be available to him and where he could reasonably be expected to relocate, it can properly be said that he is not outside the country of his nationality owing to a well-founded fear of being persecuted for a Convention reason. Although described by a number of different names [internal flight alternative (IFA), internal protection alternative—eds.] this relocation alternative has now been recognised for a number of years * * *

> The fear of being persecuted need not always extend to the whole territory of the refugee's country of nationality. Thus in ethnic clashes or in cases of grave disturbances involving civil war conditions, persecution of a specific ethnic or national group may occur in only one party of the country. In such situations, a person will not be excluded from refugee status merely because he could have sought refuge in another part of the same country, if under all the circumstances it would not have been reasonable to expect him to do so. [quoting UNHCR Handbook, ¶ 91]

The corollary of this proposition, as is accepted, is that a person will be excluded from refugee status if under all the circumstances it would be reasonable to expect him to seek refuge in another part of the same country.

8. This reasonableness test of internal relocation was readily and widely accepted. * * * But the parties are sharply divided on how the test should be applied, and in particular on whether a person can reasonably be expected to relocate when the level of civil, political and socio-economic human rights in the place of relocation is poor. * * *

9. * * * In *Refugee Appeal No 71684/99* [2000] INLR 165, the Refugee Status Appeals Authority of New Zealand, while acknowledging in para 57 "that no uniform and ascertainable standard of rights for refugees has emerged on which States parties to the Refugee Convention are agreed", carried the Court of Appeal's approach a further step. Having made reference to some of the rights which member states bind themselves to extend to those accepted as refugees, they continued in paras 60–61:

> [60]   . . . The view we have taken is that the appropriate minimal standard of effective protection for the purposes of Art 1A(2) of the Refugee Convention is the standard of human rights set by the Refugee Convention itself, ie, the rights owed by State parties to persons who are refugees.

> [61]   In essence, our reasoning is as follows. Because under New Zealand law the issue of internal protection does not arise unless and until a determination is made that the refugee

claimant holds a well-founded fear of persecution for a Convention reason, the inquiry into internal protection is really an inquiry into whether a person who satisfies the Refugee Convention and who is prima facie a refugee—at least in relation to an identified part of the country of origin—should lose that status by the application of the internal protection principle. There is considerable force to the logic that that putative refugee status should only be lost if the individual can access in his or her own country of origin the same level of protection that he or she would be entitled to under the Refugee Convention in one of the State parties to the Convention. Clearly some State parties will accord to refugees a greater range of human rights and freedoms than the minimal standards prescribed by the Refugee Convention. Other States will barely be able to satisfy the Convention standards. But the Refugee Convention itself sets the minimum standard of human rights which the international community has agreed should be accorded to individuals who meet the Refugee Convention. The "loss" of refugee status by the application of the internal protection principle should only occur where, in the site of the internal protection, this minimum standard is met.

10.   * * *[There is] a similar line of authority in Australia. * * * In *Al-Amidi v Minister for Immigration & Multicultural Affairs* [2000] FCA 1081; (2000) 177 ALR 506, 510, [the Federal Court of Australia] stressed * * * that "there must be satisfaction of the basic norms of civil, political and socio-economic human rights in that relocation".

* * *

12.   Canadian authority reveals a somewhat different approach. In *Thirunavukkarasu v Minister of Employment and Immigration*, [109 D.L.R. (4th) 682], it was held at pp 687–688, using the expression "IFA" to mean what I have called the "relocation alternative":

Thus, IFA must be sought, if it is not unreasonable to do so, in the circumstances of the individual claimant. This test is a flexible one, that takes into account the particular situation of the claimant and the particular country involved. This is an objective test and the onus of proof rests on the claimant on this issue, just as it does with all the other aspects of a refugee claim. Consequently, if there is a safe haven for claimants in their own country, where they would be free of persecution, they are expected to avail themselves of it unless they can show that it is objectively unreasonable for them to do so.

Let me elaborate. It is not a question of whether in normal times the refugee claimant would, on balance, choose to move to a different, safer part of the country after balancing the pros and cons of such a move to see if it is reasonable. Nor is it a matter of whether the other, safer part of the country is more or less appealing to the claimant than a new country. Rather, the question is whether, given the persecution in the claimant's part of the country, it is objectively reasonable to expect him or her to seek safety in a different part of that country before seeking a haven in Canada or elsewhere. Stated another way for clarity, the question to be answered is, would it be unduly harsh to expect this person, who is being persecuted in one part of his country, to move to another less hostile part of the country before seeking refugee status abroad?

An IFA cannot be speculative or theoretical only, it must be a realistic, attainable option. Essentially, this means that the alternative place of safety must be realistically accessible to the claimant. Any barriers to getting there should be reasonably surmountable. The claimant cannot be required to encounter great physical danger or to undergo undue hardship in travelling there or in staying there. For example, claimants should not be required to cross battle lines where fighting is going on at great risk to their lives in order to reach a place of safety. Similarly, claimants should not be compelled to hide out in an isolated region of their country, like a cave in the mountains, or in a desert or a jungle, if those are the only areas of internal safety available. But neither is it enough for refugee claimants to say that they do not like the weather in a safe area, or that they have no friends or relatives there, or that they may not be able to find suitable work there. If it is objectively reasonable in these latter cases to live in these places, without fear of persecution, then IFA exists and the claimant is not a refugee.

In conclusion, it is not a matter of a claimant's convenience or the attractiveness of the IFA, but whether one should be expected to make do in that location, before travelling half-way around the world to seek a safe haven in another country. Thus, the objective standard of reasonableness which I have suggested for an IFA is the one that best conforms to the definition of "Convention refugee". That definition requires claimants to be unable or unwilling by reason of fear of persecution to claim the protection of their home country in any part of that country. The prerequisites of that definition can only be met if it is not reasonable for the claimant to seek and obtain safety from persecution elsewhere in the country.

In *Ranganathan v Canada (Minister of Citizenship and Immigration)* [2001] 2 FC 164, the Federal Court of Appeal (per Létourneau JA, with the assent of his colleagues) said, with reference to *Thirunavukkarasu*:

We read the decision of Linden JA for this Court as setting up a very high threshold for the unreasonableness test. It requires nothing less than the existence of conditions which would jeopardize the life and safety of a claimant in travelling or temporarily relocating to a safe area. In addition, it requires actual and concrete evidence of such conditions. The absence of relatives in a safe place, whether taken alone or in conjunction with other factors, can only amount to such condition if it meets that threshold, that is to say if it establishes that, as a result, a claimant's life or safety would be jeopardized. This is in sharp contrast with undue hardship resulting from loss of employment, loss of status, reduction in quality of life, loss of aspirations, loss of beloved ones and frustration of one's wishes and expectations.

There are at least two reasons why it is important not to lower that threshold. First, as this Court said in *Thirunavukkarasu*, the definition of refugee under the Convention "requires claimants to be unable or unwilling by reason of fear of persecution to claim the protection of their home country in any part of that country". Put another way, what makes a person a refugee under the Convention is his fear of persecution by his home country in any part of that country. To expand and lower the standard for assessing reasonableness of the IFA is to fundamentally denature the definition of refugee: one becomes a refugee who has no fear of persecution and who would be better off in Canada physically, economically and emotionally than in a safe place in his own country.

Second, it creates confusion by blurring the distinction between refugee claims and humanitarian and compassionate applications.[a] These are two procedures governed by different objectives and considerations . . .

13. In England and Wales, the Court of Appeal in *E and another v Secretary of State for the Home Department* [2003] EWCA 1032, [2004] QB 531 declined to adopt what may, without disrespect, be called the Hathaway/New Zealand rule. It was argued for the appellants in that case (see para 16 of the judgment of the court given by Lord Phillips of Worth Matravers MR) that

the "unduly harsh" test is the means of determining whether an asylum seeker is *"unable to avail himself of the protection of"* the country of his nationality. The *protection* in question is not simply protection against persecution. It is a level of protection that secures, for the person relocating, those benefits which member states have agreed to secure for refugees under articles 2 to 30 of the Refugee Convention.

[T]he court said

23. Relocation in a safe haven will not provide an alternative to seeking refuge outside the country of nationality if, albeit

---

**a.** Under Canadian law, "humanitarian and compassionate applications" may be filed by noncitizens who are in Canada without lawful immigration status but who would, if they returned to their home countries to apply for a visa to immigrate to Canada, would face hardship that is unusual, excessive, or undeserved and the result of circumstances beyond their control. Approval of the application confers permanent resident status.—eds.

that there is no risk of persecution in the safe haven, other factors exist which make it unreasonable to expect the person fearing persecution to take refuge there. Living conditions in the safe haven may be attendant with dangers or vicissitudes which pose a threat which is as great or greater than the risk of persecution in the place of habitual residence. One cannot reasonably expect a city dweller to go to live in a desert in order to escape the risk of persecution. Where the safe haven is not a viable or realistic alternative to the place where persecution is feared, one can properly say that a refugee who has fled to another country is "outside the country of his nationality by reason of a well-founded fear of persecution".

24. If this approach is adopted to the possibility of internal relocation, the nature of the test of whether an asylum seeker could reasonably have been expected to have moved to a safe haven is clear. It involves a comparison between the conditions prevailing in the place of habitual residence and those which prevail in the safe haven, having regard to the impact that they will have on a person with the characteristics of the asylum seeker. What the test will not involve is a comparison between the conditions prevailing in the safe haven and those prevailing in the country in which asylum is sought.

\* \* \*

38. \* \* \* The failure to provide (as opposed to a discriminatory denial of) the "basic norms of civil, political, and socio-economic human rights" does not constitute persecution under the Refugee Convention. An asylum seeker who has no well-founded fear of persecution but has left his home country because he does not there enjoy those rights, will not be entitled to refugee status. When considering whether it is reasonable for an asylum seeker to relocate in a safe haven, in the sole context of considering whether he enjoys refugee status, we cannot see how the fact that he will not there enjoy the basic norms of civil, political and socio-economic human rights will normally be relevant. If that is the position in the safe haven, it is likely to be the position throughout the country. In such circumstances it will be a neutral factor when considering whether it is reasonable for him to move from the place where persecution is feared to the safe haven. States may choose to permit to remain, rather than to send home, those whose countries do not afford these rights. If they do so, it seems to us that the reason should be recognised as humanity or, if it be the case, the obligations of the Human Rights Convention and not the obligations of the Refugee Convention.

\* \* \*

67. It seems to us important that the consideration of immigration applications and appeals should distinguish clearly between (1) the right to refugee status under the Refugee Convention, (2) the right to remain by reason of rights under the Human Rights Convention and (3) considerations which may be relevant to the grant of leave to remain for humanitarian reasons. So far as the first is concerned, we consider that consideration of the reasonableness of internal relocation should focus on the consequences to the asylum seeker of settling in the place of relocation instead of his previous home. The comparison between the asylum seeker's situation in this country and what it will be in the place of relocation is not relevant for this purpose, though it may be very relevant when considering the impact of the Human Rights Convention or the requirements of humanity.

\* \* \*

20. I would accordingly reject the appellants' challenge to the authority of *E* and dismiss all four appeals so far as they rest on that ground. It is, however, important, given the immense significance of the decisions they have to make, that decision-makers should have some guidance on the approach to reasonableness and undue harshness in this context. Valuable guidance is found in the UNHCR *Guidelines on International Protection* of 23 July 2003. In paragraph 7 II(a) the reasonableness analysis is approached by asking "Can the claimant, in the context of the country concerned, lead a relatively normal life without facing undue hardship?" and the comment is made: "If not, it would not be reasonable to expect the person to move there". In development of this analysis the guidelines address respect for human rights in paragraph 28:

*Respect for human rights*

Where respect for basic human rights standards, including in particular non-derogable rights, is clearly problematic, the proposed area cannot be considered a reasonable alternative. This does not mean that the deprivation of any civil, political or socio-economic human right in the proposed area will disqualify it from being an internal flight or relocation alternative. Rather, it requires, from a practical perspective, an assessment of whether the rights that will not be respected or protected are fundamental to the individual, such that the deprivation of those rights would be sufficiently harmful to render the area an unreasonable alternative.

They then address economic survival in paragraphs 29–30:

*Economic survival*

The socio-economic conditions in the proposed area will be relevant in this part of the analysis. If the situation is such that the claimant will be unable to earn a living or to access accommodation, or where medical care cannot be provided or is clearly inadequate, the area may not be a reasonable alternative. It would be unreasonable, including from a human rights perspective, to expect a person to relocate to face economic destitution or existence below at least an adequate level of subsistence. At the other end of the spectrum, a simple lowering of living standards or worsening of economic status may not be sufficient to reject a proposed area as unreasonable. Conditions in the area must be such that a relatively normal life can be led in the context of the country concerned. If, for instance, an individual would be without family links and unable to benefit from an informal social safety net, relocation may not be reasonable, unless the person would otherwise be able to sustain a relatively normal life at more than just a minimum subsistence level.

> If the person would be denied access to land, resources and protection in the proposed area because he or she does not belong to the dominant clan, tribe, ethnic, religious and/or cultural group, relocation there would not be reasonable. For example, in many parts of Africa, Asia and elsewhere, common ethnic, tribal, religious and/or cultural factors enable access to land, resources and protection. In such situations, it would not be reasonable to expect someone who does not belong to the dominant group, to take up residence there. A person should also not be required to relocate to areas, such as the slums of an urban area, where they would be required to live in conditions of severe hardship.

These guidelines are, I think, helpful, concentrating attention as they do on the standards prevailing generally in the country of nationality. * * *

* * *

21. [The appellants argue] that internal relocation is never an available option where persecution is by the authorities of the country of nationality* * *

There can, however, be no absolute rule and it is, in my opinion, preferable to avoid the language of presumption. The decision-maker, taking account of all relevant circumstances pertaining to the claimant and his country of origin, must decide whether it is reasonable to expect the claimant to relocate or whether it would be unduly harsh to expect him to do so. The source of the persecution giving rise to the claimant's well-founded fear in his place of ordinary domicile may be agents of the state authorised or directed by the state to persecute; or they may be agents of the state whose persecution is connived at or tolerated by the state, or not restrained by the state; or the persecution may be by those who are not agents of the state, but whom the state does not or cannot control. These sources of persecution may, of course, overlap, and it may on the facts be hard to identify the source of the persecution complained of or feared. * * * The more closely the persecution in question is linked to the state, and the greater the control of the state over those acting or purporting to act on its behalf, the more likely (other things being equal) that a victim of persecution in one place will be similarly vulnerable in another place within the state. The converse may also be true. All must depend on a fair assessment of the relevant facts.

*Disposal*

22. Applying the principles outlined in this opinion, and for reasons more fully given by Lord Hope, I would dismiss Mr Januzi's appeal. I would allow the appeals of Messrs Hamid, Gaafar and Mohammed, and remit their cases to the Asylum and Immigration Tribunal.

## Notes and Questions

1. The doctrine of internal flight alternatives implies that if both San Salvador and San Diego are reasonably safe refuges for a Salvadoran at risk, he should choose the former because it is in his own country. Is this too much to ask of one who already had to flee familiar territory? On the other hand, given that the individual has already chosen to leave his hometown, should this doctrine be seen as a sensible way to preserve the politically limited asylum resource for those who truly need it? The asylum seeker would have to uproot in either case.

2. A noted scholar whose work on this topic was discussed both by the U.K., Canadian, Australian, and New Zealand courts states:

> The logic of the internal protection principle must, however, be recognized to flow from the absence of a need for asylum abroad. It should be restricted in its application to persons who can *genuinely access* domestic protection, and for whom the reality of protection is *meaningful*. In situations where, for example, financial, logistical, or other barriers prevent the claimant from reaching internal safety; where the quality of internal protection fails to meet basic norms of civil, political, and socio-economic human rights; or where internal safety is otherwise illusory or unpredictable, state accountability for the harm is established and refugee status is appropriately recognized.

J. Hathaway, The Law of Refugee Status 134 (1991).

Few states would disagree with Hathaway's formulation in the abstract, but applying this standard generates sharp differences of opinion, as the *Januzi* opinion shows. Elsewhere, Hathaway stresses that the proposed site of internal protection must afford the asylum seeker (1) true safety from the reach of his persecutor, (2) no risk of additional persecution or even generalized serious harm, and (3) "the assimilation of the asylum seeker with others in the site of internal protection for purposes of access to, for example, employment, public welfare, and education." Hathaway, *International Refugee Law: The Michigan Guidelines on the Internal Protection Alternative*, 21 Mich. J. Int'l L. 131 (1999).

Compare this passage, quoted by Lord Bingham in *Januzi*:

When considering whether it is reasonable for an asylum seeker to relocate in a safe haven, in the sole context of considering whether he enjoys refugee status, we cannot see how the fact that he will not there enjoy the basic norms of civil, political and socio-economic human rights will normally be relevant.

*E and another v. Secretary of State for the Home Department* [2003] EWCA 1032, [2004] QB 531, ¶ 38.

3.   For the UNHCR's guidelines on internal flight, see *Guidelines on International Protection: Internal Flight or Relocation Alternative within the Context of Article 1A(2) of the 1951 Convention and/or 1967 Protocol Relating to the Status of Refugees*, 15 Int'l J. Refugee L. 875 (2003). For additional views, see Marx, *The Criteria of Applying the "Internal Flight Alternative" Test in National Refugee Status Determination Procedures,* 14 Int'l J. Refugee L. 179 (2002); Kelley, Internal Flight/Relocation/Protection Alternative: Is It Reasonable? 14 Int'l J. Refugee L. 4 (2002); Frelick, *Down the Rabbit Hole: The Strange Logic of the Internal Flight Alternative,* in U.S. Committee for Refugees, World Refugee Survey 1999, at 27.

---

### Exercise

Meridian is a Eurasian country torn by ethnic conflict between the Muslim Kosars and the Christian Lamperts. When the Kosar militia began shelling the town of Dorvar, the Becks, who are ethnic Lamperts, fled the city on foot, taking only minimal personal effects. Their business and home were destroyed and all their remaining personal property was stolen. Dorvar remains under the control of Kosar forces.

Under recently adopted peace accords, about 49 percent of Meridian has been placed under Lampert control, but Dorvar is outside this area. The Becks do not want to return to Meridian, not even to the Lampert-controlled area. They say they fear that Kosar militia may enter Lampert-controlled territory to attack ethnic Lamperts, but there is no evidence that this has actually occurred. They also say that if forced to relocate, they would have great difficulty finding employment, and the destruction of their business and loss of all their possessions means they would have no means of supporting themselves.

Mr. and Mrs. Beck are now 65 and 55 years old, respectively. Their family members have all been killed or have also fled Meridian.

Assume that the Becks have established a well-founded of persecution if they return to their hometown of Dorvar. Should their asylum application be denied because they could relocate to the Lampert-held part of Meridian?

## 6. MILITARY CONSCRIPTION

Many nations require military service. Some recognize exemptions for those conscientiously opposed to military service, but the exemptions take many forms, and some nations allow none. In cases involving conscription, one frequently articulated rationale for denying *nonrefoulement* or asylum is that governments have a legitimate interest in enforcing national policy regarding conscription through the criminal process. In response, many applicants assert that enforcement of the military service laws amounts to persecution based on political opinion. Others rely on religious grounds for conscientious objection, while still others base their applications on both of these grounds. Here again, the issue of what is "persecution" is hard to separate neatly from the issue of what is "on account of race, religion, nationality, membership in a particular social group, or political opinion."

New recruits in Sierra Leone. (Photo: © Robert Grossman)

The three opinions excerpted below, all arising at different stages of the same case, wrestle with question of when punishment for noncompliance with these laws should be considered persecution, thus supporting a grant of asylum to those who resist military service.

## MATTER OF A–G–

Board of Immigration Appeals, 1987.
19 I & N Dec. 502.

\* \* \* [T]he immigration judge denied the motion to reopen [to apply for asylum]. The respondent appealed. \* \* \*

The respondent is a 30-year-old native and citizen of El Salvador. He entered the United States in March 1982 without having been inspected.

He reported that he left El Salvador because he did not want to serve in the army on account of its violent record, but he feared he would be tortured and possibly killed as a sympathizer of the opposition if he refused to serve. He stated that one cousin, a former soldier, was killed in about 1981 by the army when he participated in an anti-government demonstration and that another cousin was drafted by the guerrillas and killed by them around 1980 after he killed a supervisor. A relative of his common-law wife was an officer in the guerrilla army. This man was killed in about 1980. The respondent himself was recruited by a friend to be an *oreja*, or spy, for the government, but he declined. A member of the civilian patrol allegedly threatened him but was executed himself shortly thereafter. The respondent also reported that he was beaten up by soldiers at a roadblock in 1981 and again in 1982. The brother of the respondent's brother-in-law was killed after the respondent had left El Salvador, apparently by a so-called death squad, for providing food to some guerrillas.

The respondent submitted a brief in support of his motion along with numerous reports and newspaper articles regarding the violations of human rights in El Salvador in the period 1980 through 1985 and a new Form I–589 (Request for Asylum in the United States). The respondent has also invoked the Geneva Conventions and Protocols and customary international law in support of his claim that he should not be deported to a country at war.

A motion to reopen will not be granted unless it states new and material facts and is supported by evidentiary material. A prima facie case of eligibility for the relief sought must be established before a motion to reopen will be granted. An application to reopen is addressed to the sound discretion of the Attorney General. * * *

* * *

The issue before us is whether the respondent has made a prima facie case of at least a well-founded fear of persecution for one of the listed reasons, if he returns to El Salvador. The respondent submitted a considerable body of evidence to the immigration judge on remand, all of a general nature. The respondent argues that he will refuse to serve in the "terrorist" military and that his refusal is based on his political beliefs. He then contends that he would likely suffer severe penalties including death at the hands of the death squads for his refusal, because he would be suspected of anti-government sympathies. He also argues that it would be against his moral values to serve in an army which has engaged in violations of human rights. He alleges that the immigration judge failed to consider his argument that he was not obliged at all to serve in an army which violates human rights. He argues that his position is similar to that of the alien granted asylum in *Matter of Salim,* 18 I & N Dec. 311 (BIA 1982), in that his claim is more than a mere refusal to serve in his country's military.

* * *

We hold to the long-accepted position that it is not persecution for a country to require military service of its citizens. Exceptions to this rule may be recognized in those rare cases where a disproportionately severe punishment would result on account of one of the five grounds enumerated in section 101(a)(42)(A) of the Act, or where the alien would necessarily be required to engage in inhuman conduct as a result of military service required by the government. *See* Office of the United Nations High Commissioner for Refugees, *The Handbook on Procedures and Criteria for Determining Refugee Status Under the 1951 Convention and the 1967 Protocol Relating to the Status of Refugees* 39–41 (Geneva, 1979). We conclude that the respondent has not brought forward evidence that his refusal to serve would result in disproportionately severe punishment for an impermissible reason or that the activity in which he might be involved has been condemned by the international community as contrary to the basic rules of human conduct.

The respondent contends that his refusal to serve is a valid political opinion and a moral conviction which is supported by international law. He asserts that the actions of the Salvadoran Army violate international law and have been condemned by the international community. Although incidents involving the Salvadoran Army have been reported, which undoubtedly involve the violation of the rights of noncombatants and international law, there is no evidence that these incidents represent the policy of the Salvadoran Government or that the respondent would be required to engage in such actions as a member of the armed forces. The statements of opinion of Americas Watch to the contrary in the record may indeed be the belief of those who represent that organization. Such statements of opinion of private unofficial bodies do not constitute evidence of condemnation by recognized international governmental bodies, which would be necessary at a minimum for us to accept this argument. For an example of a statement of opinion of a recognized international governmental body, see the resolution concerning the status of persons refusing service in military or police forces used to enforce apartheid. G.A. Res. 33/165, 33 U.N. GAOR Supp. (No. 45) at 154, U.N. Doc. A/33/45 (1979). Thus, the Government of El Salvador has the same right as other governments to require military service and to enforce that requirement with reasonable penalties. The case of the claimant in *Matter of Salim, supra,* [a national of Afghanistan] is distinguishable from that of the respondent because the former was refusing to serve, not in an army controlled by his own government, but in one which was "under Soviet command."

\* \* \*

Accordingly, the appeal will be dismissed.

---

*Matter of A–G–* then went on appeal to a three-judge panel of the U.S. Court of Appeals for the Fourth Circuit, which issued the following decision.

# M.A. A26851062 v. INS (M.A. I)

United States Court of Appeals, Fourth Circuit, 1988.
858 F.2d 210.

WINTER, CHIEF JUDGE.

\* \* \*

\* \* \* The only issue before the immigration judge was whether M.A. had presented a prima facie case for political asylum so as to warrant reopening his deportation proceedings to prove his eligibility therefor. The Immigration Judge found that he had not. M.A. appealed, and the Board affirmed. \* \* \*

\* \* \*

Failure to serve in the military may also be the expression of a political opinion, subjecting the evader to the same punishment as any other draft evader. When this occurs, the applicant should ordinarily be denied refugee status because the draft is generally recognized as lawful. There is, however, an exception to this general rule:

> There are, however, also cases where the necessity to perform military service may be the sole ground for a claim to refugee status, i.e. when a person can show that the performance of military service would have required his participation in military action contrary to his genuine political, religious or moral convictions, or to valid reasons of conscience.

> Not every conviction, genuine though it may be, will constitute a sufficient reason for claiming refugee status after desertion or draft-evasion. It is not enough for a person to be in disagreement with his government regarding the political justification for a particular military action. Where, however, the type of military action, with which an individual does not wish to be associated, is condemned by the international community as contrary to basic rules of human conduct, punishment for desertion or draft-evasion could, in the light of all other requirements of the definition, in itself be regarded as persecution.

[*UNHCR*] *Handbook* ¶¶ 170–71. It is the possibility that an unwilling conscriptee may be associated with the commission of atrocities which places him in a different predicament from that of a conscriptee who merely disagrees with the political justification of a conflict.

\* \* \*

We think that the Board has made the petitioner's burden unduly harsh. An applicant for political asylum should not be required to prove that he would be compelled to commit atrocities. It is unlikely that such a standard could ever be met. Paragraph 171 of the *Handbook* focuses instead on the *association* with certain types of military action as the relevant inquiry. Whether an individual will be associated with condemned conduct will depend largely on how widespread it has become, and it follows that the likelihood that an individual would be forced to participate in atrocities increases as the atrocities become more widespread. We therefore think that the appropriate inquiry is to consider the pervasiveness of atrocities. We think also that petitioner has presented sufficient evidence from a wide variety of sources to show that atrocities committed against the civilian population by the military are frequent and widespread.

We also decline to adopt the Board's requirement that there be proof that the acts of atrocity with which M.A. does not want to be associated are the policies of the Salvadoran government. It is sufficient that M.A. show that the Salvadoran government is unwilling or unable to control the offending group, here, the armed forces. * * *

Similarly, we do not think that M.A. must wait for international bodies such as the United Nations to condemn officially the atrocities committed by a nation's military in order to be eligible for political asylum. Paragraph 171 of the *Handbook* shelters those individuals who do not wish to be associated with military action "condemned by the international community as contrary to basic rules of human conduct...." These basic rules are well documented and readily available to guide the Board in discerning what types of actions are considered unacceptable by the world community. [The court cited and discussed the Geneva Conventions of 1949].

* * *

To summarize: we think that M.A. has presented sufficient evidence to demonstrate that he could be singled out for persecution for his failure to serve in the military. He has shown that failure to serve results in an individual being labeled subversive. He has presented evidence to show that those whom the military designates subversive are often executed, and sometimes tortured. He has at least two relatives who were summarily executed shortly after demonstrating their opposition to government and military policies. He has established a prima facie case of a well-founded fear of persecution, and he should be given the opportunity to prove his case.

Reversed and remanded.

[The concurring opinion of CIRCUIT JUDGE MURNAGHAN is omitted.]

———————

The government next petitioned for rehearing en banc. The full court of appeals vacated the panel's ruling and issued the following decision.

# M.A. v. INS (M.A. II)

United States Court of Appeals, Fourth Circuit (en banc) 1990.
899 F.2d 304.

WILKINSON, CIRCUIT JUDGE.

\* \* \*

We must address at the outset the standard that governs our review of the Board's decision to deny M.A.'s motion to reopen his deportation proceedings. We hold that Board denials of motions to reopen for failure to establish a prima facie case of eligibility for asylum are to be reviewed under an abuse of discretion standard.

\* \* \*

The Board did not abuse its discretion in denying M.A.'s motion to reopen for failure to establish prima facie eligibility for political asylum. It properly focused upon the fact that, at bottom, M.A. was a draft resister who claimed that his justified refusal to serve in the Salvadoran military would result in his persecution. International law and Board precedent are very clear that a sovereign nation enjoys the right to enforce its laws of conscription, and that penalties for evasion are not considered persecution.

\* \* \*

M.A. claims that the military in which he might be forced to serve has committed acts that are contrary to the basic rules of human conduct. The Board was within its discretion in rejecting this claim based on M.A.'s failure to present cognizable evidence that the alleged atrocities he wanted to avoid were perpetrated as a result of the policies of the Salvadoran military or government. Misconduct by renegade military units is almost inevitable during times of war, especially revolutionary war, and a country as torn as El Salvador will predictably spawn more than its share of poignant incidents. Without a requirement that the violence be connected with official governmental policy, however, *any* male alien of draft age from just about any country experiencing civil strife could establish a well-founded fear of persecution. The Refugee Act does not reach this broadly.

M.A. did, of course, bring forth evidence from prominent private organizations such as Amnesty International and Americas Watch. These organizations have condemned the Salvadoran military and security forces for committing violent acts against all sectors of Salvadoran society. They report that the Salvadoran military engages in "extrajudicial execution on noncombatant civilians, individual death squad-style killings, 'disappearances,' arbitrary detention and torture." Moreover, they contend that the military violence is carried out pursuant to a deliberate policy of the Salvadoran government designed to further that government's political interests.

\* \* \*

[But a] standard of asylum eligibility based solely on pronouncements of private organizations or the news media is problematic almost to the point of being non-justiciable. * * * Although we do not wish to disparage the work of private investigative bodies in exposing inhumane practices, these organizations may have their own agendas and concerns, and their condemnations are virtually omnipresent. Taken alone, they do not suffice to overturn the Board's judgment in M.A.'s case.

It is, of course, the role of private organizations and news reports to energize the political branches. But that is quite a different thing from requiring the courts in each instance to evaluate independently the accusations of private organizations to determine whether they set forth conditions adequate to overturn the Board's discretionary judgment. This responsibility would require us to make immigration decisions based on our own implicit approval or disapproval of U.S. foreign policy and the acts of other nations. Courts could be put in the position of ruling, as a matter of law, that a government whose actions have not been condemned by international governmental bodies engages in persecution against its citizens. * * * Such a role for the courts would transform the political asylum process from a method of individual sanctuary left largely to the political branches into a vehicle for foreign policy debates in the courts.

[The dissenting opinion of Senior Circuit Judge Winter is omitted.]

## Notes and Questions

1. Judge Winter's vigorous dissent in the en banc *M.A.* opinion *(M.A. II)* restated many of the points in his panel opinion, questioning in particular the deferential review standard employed. "It is precisely the politicization of the asylum process that troubles me, and suggests that heightened deference to the Board is unwarranted." 899 F.2d at 319. Judge Winter also defended reliance on reports of private human rights organizations, against the majority's concern that such action would invade foreign policy reserved to the political branches. "Even if such reliance constituted in some way an indirect condemnation of the government in question, the Congress has explicitly empowered the federal judiciary to review and, if necessary, to correct INS determinations of the asylum standard." *Id.*, at 323.

2. The asylum applicant in *M.A.* is a "selective conscientious objector," to use the terminology often applied in the United States during the Vietnam War. That is, he did not claim to be opposed to war in any form, but only to the particular uses of military force employed by the Salvadoran military at the time. U.S. conscription laws have usually allowed Americans who conscientiously oppose all war to avoid military service, subject to an obligation to perform alternative noncombatant service, while denying that option to selective objectors. How do selective conscientious objectors fare under the doctrine prescribed in paras. 170–171 of the UNHCR Handbook, quoted in the excerpt from the initial panel's decision in *M.A. v. INS*? Did the panel accurately apply that doctrine? Did the en banc majority? For a thorough discussion of conscientious objection as a basis for asylum, see Bailliet, *Assessing Jus Ad Bellum and Jus in Bello Within the Refugee*

*Status Determination Process: Contemplations on Conscientious Objectors Seeking Asylum*, 20 Geo. Immigr. L.J. 337 (2006); Note, *Asylum for Unrecognized Conscientious Objectors: Is There a Right not to Fight?*, 31 Va. J. Int'l L. 447 (1991).

---

Compare the stages of the *A–G–/M–A–* case with the next decision.

## TAGAGA v. INS

United States Court of Appeals, Ninth Circuit, 2000.
228 F.3d 1030.

REINHARDT, CIRCUIT JUDGE.

\* \* \*

We consider Aminisitai Tagaga's asylum application against the backdrop of racially based political discrimination in Fiji, a country which has a bare majority of ethnic Fijians, the remainder of the population being composed largely of ethnic Indians. The Alliance Party governed Fiji from the time the country gained independence from Great Britain in 1970 until 1987. In April 1987 the Indian-dominated Labour Party defeated the Alliance Party in an open and free election. One month later, Major General Sitiveni Rabuka led a military coup to overthrow the new government. Rabuka further consolidated power through a second coup that year. According to the U.S. State Department, the "stated purpose of the 1987 military coups was to ensure the political supremacy of the indigenous Fijian people." U.S. Dep't of State, *Country Reports on Human Rights Practices for 1993* 635 (1994). During these coups the military regime arbitrarily arrested and detained Indo–Fijians, and it subsequently encouraged and condoned discrimination, harassment, and violence by ethnic Fijians against Indo–Fijians. In 1990 the regime implemented a new constitution ensuring political dominance by ethnic Fijians. In 1992 Rabuka's political party won electoral control of the Parliament, and he became prime minister.

Tagaga is an ethnic Fijian. As a career military officer, he had earned the rank of major and held a high-level position in the Army's engineering corps. Through his work Tagaga established strong ties with the Indian community of Fiji, and beginning in 1985 he became an active supporter of the Indian-dominated Labour Party. He frequently attended Labour Party meetings and eventually became responsible for providing security at these meetings. Tagaga believed strongly that Indo–Fijians deserved to be treated equally and have the same legal rights as others living in Fiji.

Following the first coup in May 1987, military personnel were ordered to cease contact with the Indian community. Tagaga did not do so. As he testified at the asylum hearing: "My relationship with the Indian community was too strong to have the ties broken." He continued to attend Labour Party meetings, even though he knew that undercover military intelligence agents also attended and had identified him. Military personnel warned Tagaga that if he did not discontinue his relations with the Indian community, he would face arrest and court-martial.

By the time of the second coup in 1987, Tagaga began to refuse orders from his superiors directing him to arrest and detain Indo–Fijians whom the military regime perceived as threats to its power. Tagaga "didn't want to see the Indian population suffer anymore." He even gave information to the Indian community regarding future planned arrests. On September 7, 1987, Tagaga was summoned to appear before a military court, and two weeks later he was prosecuted for disobedience of military orders, breach of discipline, insubordination, and conduct unbecoming an officer. At the court-martial, Tagaga expressed his political opinion that the coup was illegitimate and that the government should be democratic. The military court revoked his military privileges and sentenced him to six months house arrest.

In February 1988 Tagaga was ostensibly reinstated as a major, but denied privileges and authority commensurate with that rank. In July 1989 he was transferred to serve in the Fijian division of the United Nations peacekeeping forces in Lebanon. Tagaga believed that military officials transferred him in order to separate him from the Indian community in Fiji and also to punish him by separating him from his family and subjecting him to the division's notoriously poor living conditions.

In June 1990 a lieutenant colonel and close friend of Tagaga arrived in Lebanon. He informed Tagaga that military officials had in fact sent Tagaga to Lebanon for the purposes of separation and punishment; that he remained under constant surveillance; and that he would face arrest and treason charges if he returned to Fiji. This lieutenant colonel, Tagaga's commanding officer, advised him to leave the army and not return to Fiji. A second lieutenant colonel confirmed this information for Tagaga.

Tagaga decided to seek asylum in the United States. He went to the American Embassy in Israel and obtained visas for himself and his family. He returned to Fiji without reporting to military headquarters, gathered his family, and fled to the United States. He entered this country in September 1990 under a visitor's visa that authorized him to stay until September 6, 1991. Six months prior to the expiration of his visa, he filed an application for asylum with the Immigration and Naturalization Service (INS). An asylum officer denied Tagaga's application, and the INS commenced deportation proceedings in October 1992. An immigration judge (IJ) heard Tagaga's renewed application for asylum and withholding of deportation in January 1995. In support of this application, Tagaga submitted letters from four Fijian military officers stating that he was sent to Lebanon for punishment and that his life and freedom would be in danger if he returned to Fiji.

While stating that she was "extremely sympathetic to the situation of Mr. Tagaga" as it was "apparent he has very democratic beliefs and does not agree with the tact [sic] the current Fijian government has taken against the Indians and other minorities in Fiji," the IJ concluded that Tagaga had failed to establish a well-founded fear of persecution and rejected his application. The BIA affirmed. Tagaga petitioned this court for review of the BIA's decision.

\* \* \*

We hold that a reasonable factfinder would be compelled to conclude that Tagaga had a well-founded fear of future persecution, and that he also has met the higher burden for withholding of deportation. Tagaga established a substantial likelihood that he would be tried for treason if he returned to Fiji. \* \* \*

While the BIA acknowledged that Tagaga "may indeed face a court martial" on his return, it concluded that the reason was his "abrupt departure from the army and his apparent AWOL status." Such status, it remarked, is "unrelated to a statutorily protected ground." This view of Tagaga's predicament is completely contrary to all of the facts in the record. The record is undisputed that Tagaga did not abandon his successful military career and flee his homeland because he was tired of the work or wanted a change in lifestyle. Rather, the uncontroverted facts establish that Tagaga, having already served a six-month sentence imposed by the military regime, fled Fiji because he feared that the regime would prosecute him for treason for, among other reasons, his refusal to participate in the regime's persecution of Indo–Fijians.

The INS argues that we should consider the sentence Tagaga served in 1987 and 1988 "disproportionately lenient" because Tagaga admits to having disobeyed his orders. It is well established, however, that a government may not legitimately punish an official for refusing to carry out an inhumane order. See *Barraza Rivera v. INS*, 913 F.2d 1443, 1451 (9th Cir. 1990) (holding that punishment for "refusing to comply with military orders ... because they violate standards of human decency" can itself amount to persecution). This is a corollary of the universally recognized principle that obedience to superior orders does not relieve an official from responsibility for humanitarian law or human rights violations [citing the Nuremberg trials and a case decided by the International Criminal Tribunal for the Former Yugoslavia]. Indeed, had Tagaga, following orders, directly participated in the persecution of Indo–Fijians, he would be ineligible for asylum under INA § 208(b)(2)(A)(i). Tagaga adhered to higher principles of law by refusing to arrest Indo–Fijians and warning others of planned arrests. For this conduct, his punishment of six months confinement was not "disproportionately lenient." To the contrary, it was excessive, because it was unlawful.

\* \* \*

Because Tagaga faces a well-founded fear of persecution on account of a statutorily protected ground, he and his family are eligible for asylum. We reverse and remand for the Attorney General to exercise her discretion in that respect. We also conclude, for the reasons stated above, that Tagaga has demonstrated that "it is more likely than not that [he] would be subject to persecution in the country to which he would be returned." *Cardoza–Fonseca,* 480 U.S. at 423, 107 S.Ct. 1207. He is therefore entitled to withholding of deportation.

\* \* \*

### Notes and Questions

1. Can *Tagaga* and *M.A. II* be reconciled? Is the difference the existence of specific orders that had directed the asylum seeker to carry out an act of persecution? That is, M.A. had not served in the military, whereas Tagaga had been specifically ordered to commit an act that would have been a human rights violation, and possibly a war crime or crime against humanity. In *Barraza–Rivera*, mentioned in *Tagaga*, the applicant had also refused a specific order. *Cf. Ramos–Vasquez v. INS*, 57 F.3d 857, 861–64 (9th Cir. 1995), where the asylum applicant had deserted from the Honduran army after he had been punished for refusing to execute deserters. The court found that punishment for a deserter in these circumstances could be considered persecution. Should individual orders always be required? What about a person who fled before being conscripted into service in the Khmer Rouge forces of Pol Pot, which ultimately killed one million Cambodians? The army of Afghanistan's Taliban? The army of Iraq under Saddam Hussein? The South African army before *apartheid* was abolished? The army of the Sudanese central government, fighting rebellion in the non-Muslim south or in Darfur? The Russian army for service in the rebellious province of Chechnya?

2. What if anything makes military service (whether in the context of conscription or of following a superior officer's orders) different from the sort of government policy at issue in *Chang*? After all, governments have armed forces, and even if they have no conscription, they impose discipline within the ranks. And what if anything makes military discipline different from the general governmental interest in self-preservation by prosecuting anyone, civilian or military, who might try to overthrow it?

## SECTION B.   LEVEL OF RISK

Besides exploring the meaning of persecution, many cases have examined another fundamental question: what *degree of threat or level of risk* in the homeland must an applicant prove before being found to meet the threshold qualification for protection under U.S. law? Both INA § 208, the asylum provision, and § 241(b)(3), providing for withholding, point toward similar kinds of protection for what might initially seem to be the same group of persons threatened with persecution in their homelands. But the statutory texts are not identical; here are the crucial differences:

<u>Asylum</u> (INA § 208(b))

The Attorney General *may* grant asylum to an alien * * * if the * * * alien is a refugee * * *

<u>Refugee</u> (INA 101(a)(42))

[A]ny person * * * who has a *well-founded fear* of *persecution* on account of race, religion, nationality, membership in a particular social group, or political opinion.

<u>Withholding</u> (INA § 241(b)(3))

[T]he Attorney General may not remove an alien to a country if the Attorney General decides that the alien's *life or freedom would be threatened* in that country because of the alien's race, religion, nationality, membership in a particular social group, or political opinion.

The meaning of these texts, and the interrelation of these statutory provisions, was the subject of major debate for many years. Ultimately, they provided the occasion for the first Supreme Court decisions to consider the Refugee Act of 1980, *INS v. Stevic,* 467 U.S. 407, 104 S.Ct. 2489, 81 L.Ed.2d 321 (1984), and *INS v. Cardoza–Fonseca,* 480 U.S. 421, 107 S.Ct. 1207, 94 L.Ed.2d 434 (1987).

## 1. DISTINGUISHING *NONREFOULEMENT* FROM ASYLUM

The Supreme Court elaborated on the relationship between the two sections in two cases that arose against the following background. Since the 1950s the BIA had required applicants for relief under § 243(h) (then the principal, and for a time the only, avenue for asylum-type relief available under the INA) to demonstrate a "clear probability of persecution" before their applications would be granted. (INA § 243(h) has since been renumbered; it is now INA § 241(b)(3).) This standard was initially established as a criterion governing the exercise of the discretion given to the Attorney General by the original wording of § 243(h). When such protection became, in effect, mandatory after U.S. accession to the UN Protocol in 1968—for persons meeting the standards of Article 33 of the Convention—litigants claimed that the Board was required to relax that criterion and apply instead the "well-founded fear of persecution" test. The Board disagreed. In *Matter of Dunar,* 14 I & N Dec. 310 (BIA 1973), it determined that the treaty worked no change in the governing standards, and it continued to employ the "clear probability" language.

Not long after the Refugee Act was passed in 1980, litigants renewed the argument. The courts of appeals reached disparate results, and the Supreme Court granted certiorari to resolve the split. The Supreme Court's ultimate approach in *INS v. Stevic,* in 1984, came as something of a surprise, because litigants had assumed that the same standard would govern both asylum and withholding. The contest as they pursued it was whether that standard should be "well-founded fear of persecution" or "clear probability of persecution." Justice Stevens, writing for a unanimous Court, laid considerable stress on a fact the parties had given little notice: in the somewhat unusual procedural posture of the *Stevic* case, the applicant was seeking only withholding, not asylum under § 208. Therefore the only issue considered to be properly before the Court was the standard that should govern under § 243(h).

## INS v. STEVIC

Supreme Court of the United States, 1984.
467 U.S. 407, 104 S.Ct. 2489, 81 L.Ed.2d 321.

JUSTICE STEVENS delivered the opinion of the Court.

\* \* \*

Respondent, a Yugoslavian citizen, entered the United States in 1976 to visit his sister, then a permanent resident alien residing in Chicago. Petitioner, the Immigration and Naturalization Service (INS), instituted deportation proceedings against respondent when he overstayed his 6–week period of admission. Respondent admitted that he was deportable and agreed to depart voluntarily by February 1977. In January 1977, however, respondent married a United States citizen who obtained approval of a visa petition on his behalf. Shortly thereafter, respondent's wife died in an automobile accident. The approval of respondent's visa petition was automatically revoked, and petitioner ordered respondent to surrender for deportation to Yugoslavia.

\* \* \*

After receiving notice to surrender for deportation in February 1981, respondent filed his second motion to reopen. He again sought relief pursuant to § 243(h) \* \* \*.

\* \* \*

\* \* \* The Board of Immigration Appeals held that respondent had not shown that the additional evidence was unavailable at the time his first motion had been filed and, further, that he had still failed to submit prima facie evidence that "there is a clear probability of persecution" directed at respondent individually. \* \* \*

\* \* \*

The United States Court of Appeals for the Second Circuit reversed and remanded for a plenary hearing under a different standard of proof. Specifically, it held that respondent no longer had the burden of showing "a clear probability of persecution," but instead could avoid deportation by demonstrating a "well-founded fear of persecution." The latter language is contained in a definition of the term "refugee" adopted by a United Nations Protocol to which the United States has adhered since 1968. The Court of Appeals held that the Refugee Act of 1980 changed the standard of proof that an alien must satisfy to obtain relief under § 243(h), concluding that Congress intended to abandon the "clear probability of persecution" standard and substitute the "well-founded fear of persecution" language of the Protocol as the standard. \* \* \*

\* \* \*

Initially, we do not think there is any serious dispute regarding the meaning of the clear-probability standard under the § 243(h) case law.

The question under that standard is whether it is more likely than not that the alien would be subject to persecution. The argument of the parties on this point is whether the well-founded-fear standard is the same as the clear-probability standard as just defined, or whether it is more generous to the alien.

\* \* \*

For purposes of our analysis, we may assume, as the Court of Appeals concluded, that the well-founded-fear standard is more generous than the clear-probability-of-persecution standard because we can identify no basis in the legislative history for applying that standard in § 243(h) proceedings or any legislative intent to alter the pre-existing practice.

The principal motivation for the enactment of the Refugee Act of 1980 was a desire to revise and regularize the procedures governing the admission of refugees into the United States. The primary substantive change Congress intended to make under the Refugee Act, and indeed in our view the only substantive change even relevant to this case, was to eliminate the piecemeal approach to admission of refugees previously existing under § 203(a)(7) and § 212(d)(5) of the Immigration and Nationality Act,[a] and § 108 of the regulations, and to establish a systematic scheme for admission and resettlement of refugees. \* \* \* The Congress distinguished between discretionary grants of refugee admission or asylum and the entitlement to a withholding of deportation if the § 243(h) standard was met.

\* \* \*

The Court of Appeals' decision rests on the mistaken premise that every alien who qualifies as a "refugee" under the statutory definition is also entitled to a withholding of deportation under § 243(h). We find no support for this conclusion in either the language of § 243(h), the structure of the amended Act, or the legislative history.

\* \* \* [The governing standard for withholding of deportation, the only issue before the Court,] requires that an application be supported by evidence establishing that it is more likely than not that the alien would be subject to persecution on one of the specified grounds. This standard is a familiar one to immigration authorities and reviewing courts, and Congress did not intend to alter it in 1980. \* \* \*

\* \* \*

The judgment of the Court of Appeals is reversed, and the cause is remanded for further proceedings consistent with this opinion.

---

**a.** These are references to refugee admissions under the statutory provisions governing parole and seventh preference, respectively, as explained in Chapter Two, at pp. 75–76.—eds.

Predictably, litigation resumed immediately after *Stevic*, this time carefully targeting the asylum issue under INA § 208 that the Supreme Court had avoided. Again the courts of appeals reached disparate results, but the BIA adhered to its position "that the standards for asylum and withholding of deportation are not meaningfully different and, in practical application, converge." *Matter of Acosta,* 19 I & N Dec. 211, 219 (BIA 1985). The Supreme Court returned to these questions in 1987.

## INS v. CARDOZA–FONSECA

Supreme Court of the United States, 1987
480 U.S. 421, 107 S.Ct. 1207, 94 L.Ed.2d 434.

JUSTICE STEVENS delivered the opinion of the Court.

\* \* \*

Respondent is a 38-year-old Nicaraguan citizen who entered the United States in 1979 as a visitor. After she remained in the United States longer than permitted, and failed to take advantage of the Immigration and Naturalization Service's (INS) offer of voluntary departure, the INS commenced deportation proceedings against her. Respondent conceded that she was in the country illegally, but requested withholding of deportation pursuant to § 243(h) and asylum as a refugee pursuant to § 208(a).

To support her request under § 243(h), respondent attempted to show that if she were returned to Nicaragua her "life or freedom would be threatened" on account of her political views; to support her request under § 208(a), she attempted to show that she had a "well-founded fear of persecution" upon her return. The evidence supporting both claims related primarily to the activities of respondent's brother who had been tortured and imprisoned because of his political activities in Nicaragua. Both respondent and her brother testified that they believed the Sandinistas knew that the two of them had fled Nicaragua together and that even though she had not been active politically herself, she would be interrogated about her brother's whereabouts and activities. Respondent also testified that because of her brother's status, her own political opposition to the Sandinistas would be brought to that government's attention. Based on these facts, respondent claimed that she would be tortured if forced to return.

The Immigration Judge applied the same standard in evaluating respondent's claim for withholding of deportation under § 243(h) as he did in evaluating her application for asylum under § 208(a). He found that she had not established "a clear probability of persecution" and therefore was not entitled to either form of relief. * * *

In the Court of Appeals for the Ninth Circuit, respondent did not challenge the BIA's decision that she was not entitled to withholding of deportation under § 243(h), but argued that she was eligible for consideration for asylum under § 208(a), and contended that the Immigration Judge and BIA erred in applying the "more likely than not" standard of proof from § 243(h) to her § 208(a) asylum claim. Instead, she asserted, they should have applied the "well-founded fear" standard, which she considered to be more generous. The court agreed. * * *

* * *

Under [§ 208(a)], eligibility for asylum depends entirely on the Attorney General's determination that an alien is a "refugee," as that term is defined in § 101(a)(42), which was also added to the Act in 1980. [The Court then quotes the text of INA § 101(a)(42)(A).] Thus, the "persecution or well-founded fear of persecution" standard governs the Attorney General's determination whether an alien is eligible for asylum.[5]

In addition to establishing a statutory asylum process, the 1980 Act amended the withholding of deportation provision, § 243(h). Prior to 1968, the Attorney General had discretion whether to grant withholding of deportation to aliens under § 243(h). In 1968, however, the United States agreed to comply with the substantive provisions of Articles 2 through 34 of the 1951 United Nations Convention Relating to the Status of Refugees. Article 33.1 of the Convention, which is the counterpart of § 243(h) of our statute, imposed a mandatory duty on contracting States not to return an alien to a country where his "life or freedom would be threatened" on account of one of the enumerated reasons. Thus, although § 243(h) itself did not constrain the Attorney General's discretion after 1968, presumably he honored the dictates of the United

**5.** It is important to note that the Attorney General is *not required* to grant asylum to everyone who meets the definition of refugee. Instead, a finding that an alien is a refugee does no more than establish that "the alien *may* be granted asylum *in the discretion of the Attorney General*." § 208(a) [1987 version] (emphasis added).

Nations Convention.[8] In any event, the 1980 Act removed the Attorney General's discretion in § 243(h) proceedings.

In *Stevic* we considered it significant that in enacting the 1980 Act Congress did not amend the standard of eligibility for relief under § 243(h). While the terms "refugee" and hence "well-founded fear" were made an integral part of the § 208(a) procedure, they continued to play no part in § 243(h). * * *

* * *

[T]he language Congress used to describe the two standards conveys very different meanings. The "would be threatened" language of § 243(h) has no subjective component, but instead requires the alien to establish by objective evidence that it is more likely than not that he or she will be subject to persecution upon deportation.[10] *See Stevic.* In contrast, the reference to "fear" in the § 208(a) standard obviously makes the eligibility determination turn to some extent on the subjective mental state of the alien. "The linguistic difference between the words 'well-founded fear' and 'clear probability' may be as striking as that between a subjective and an objective frame of reference.... We simply cannot conclude that the standards are identical." *Guevara Flores v. INS,* 786 F.2d 1242, 1250 (C.A.5 1986) [*cert. denied,* 480 U.S. 930, 107 S.Ct. 1565, 94 L.Ed.2d 757 (1987)].

That the fear must be "well-founded" does not alter the obvious focus on the individual's subjective beliefs, nor does it transform the standard into a "more likely than not" one. One can certainly have a well-founded fear of an event happening when there is less than a 50% chance of the occurrence taking place. As one leading authority has pointed out:

> Let us ... presume that it is known that in the applicant's country of origin every tenth adult male person is either put to death or sent to some remote labor camp ... In such a case it would be only too apparent that anyone who has managed to escape from the country in question will have "well-founded fear of being persecuted" upon his eventual return.

1 A. Grahl–Madsen, The Status of Refugees in International Law 180 (1966).

This ordinary and obvious meaning of the phrase is not to be lightly discounted. * * *

* * *

**8.** While the Protocol constrained the Attorney General with respect to § 243(h) between 1968 and 1980, the Protocol does not require the granting of asylum to anyone, and hence does not subject the Attorney General to a similar constraint with respect to his discretion under § 208(a).

**10.** "The section literally provides for withholding of deportation only if the alien's life or freedom 'would' be threatened in the country to which he would be deported; it does not require withholding if the alien 'might' or 'could' be subject to persecution." *Stevic,* 467 U.S., at 422.

In *Stevic,* we dealt with the issue of withholding of deportation, or *nonrefoulement,* under § 243(h). This provision corresponds to Article 33.1 of the Convention. Significantly though, Article 33.1 does not extend this right to everyone who meets the definition of "refugee." Rather, it provides that "[n]o Contracting State shall expel or return ('refouler') a *refugee* in any manner whatsoever to the frontiers of territories *where his life or freedom would be threatened* on account of his race, religion, nationality, membership of a particular social group or political opinion." Thus, Article 33.1 requires that an applicant satisfy two burdens: first, that he or she be a "refugee," *i.e.,* prove at least a "well-founded fear of persecution"; second, that the "refugee" show that his or her life or freedom "would be threatened" if deported. Section 243(h)'s imposition of a "would be threatened" requirement is entirely consistent with the United States' obligations under the Protocol.

Section 208(a), by contrast, is a discretionary mechanism which gives the Attorney General the *authority* to grant the broader relief of asylum to refugees. As such, it does not correspond to Article 33 of the Convention, but instead corresponds to Article 34. That Article provides that the contracting States "shall as far as possible facilitate the assimilation and naturalization of refugees. . . ." Like § 208(a), the provision is precatory; it does not require the implementing authority actually to grant asylum to all those who are eligible. Also like § 208(a), an alien must only show that he or she is a "refugee" to establish eligibility for relief. No further showing that he or she "would be" persecuted is required.

Thus, as made binding on the United States through the Protocol, Article 34 provides for a precatory, or discretionary, benefit for the entire class of persons who qualify as "refugees," whereas Article 33.1 provides an entitlement for the subcategory that "would be threatened" with persecution upon their return. * * *

\* \* \*

* * * INS repeatedly argues that the structure of the Act dictates a decision in its favor, since it is anomalous for § 208(a), which affords greater benefits than § 243(h), to have a less stringent standard of eligibility. This argument sorely fails because it does not take into account the fact that an alien who satisfies the applicable standard under § 208(a) does not have a *right* to remain in the United States; he or she is simply *eligible* for asylum, if the Attorney General, in his discretion, chooses to grant it. An alien satisfying § 243(h)'s stricter standard, in contrast, is automatically entitled to withholding of deportation. In *Matter of Salim,* 18 I. & N. Dec. 311 (1982), for example, the Board held that the alien was eligible for both asylum and withholding of deportation, but granted him the more limited remedy only, exercising its discretion to deny him asylum. We do not consider it at all anomalous that out of the entire class of "refugees," those who can show a clear probability of persecution are *entitled* to mandatory suspension of deportation and *eligible* for discretionary asylum, while those who can only

show a well-founded fear of persecution are not *entitled* to anything, but are *eligible* for the discretionary relief of asylum.

\* \* \*

This vesting of discretion in the Attorney General is quite typical in the immigration area, *see, e.g., INS v. Jong Ha Wang,* 450 U.S. 139, 101 S.Ct. 1027, 67 L.Ed.2d 123 (1981). If anything is anomalous, it is that the Government now asks us to restrict its discretion to a narrow class of aliens. Congress has assigned to the Attorney General and his delegates the task of making these hard individualized decisions; although Congress could have crafted a narrower definition, it chose to authorize the Attorney General to determine which, if any, eligible refugees should be denied asylum.

\* \* \*

The question whether Congress intended the two standards to be identical is a pure question of statutory construction for the courts to decide. Employing traditional tools of statutory construction, we have concluded that Congress did not intend the two standards to be identical. In *Chevron U.S.A. Inc. v. Natural Resources Defense Council, Inc.,* 467 U.S. 837, 104 S.Ct. 2778, 81 L.Ed.2d 694 (1984), we explained:

> The judiciary is the final authority on issues of statutory construction and must reject administrative constructions which are contrary to clear congressional intent. [Citing cases.] If a court, employing traditional tools of statutory construction, ascertains that Congress had an intention on the precise question at issue, that intention is the law and must be given effect.

*Id.,* at 843, n.9, 104 S.Ct., at 2782, n.9 (citations omitted).

The narrow legal question whether the two standards are the same is, of course, quite different from the question of interpretation that arises in each case in which the agency is required to apply either or both standards to a particular set of facts. There is obviously some ambiguity in a term like "well-founded fear" which can only be given concrete meaning through a process of case-by-case adjudication. In that process of filling " 'any gap left, implicitly or explicitly, by Congress,' " the courts must respect the interpretation of the agency to which Congress has delegated the responsibility for administering the statutory program. *See Chevron, supra,* at 843, 104 S.Ct. at 2781–82, quoting *Morton v. Ruiz,* 415 U.S. 199, 231, 94 S.Ct. 1055, 1072, 39 L.Ed.2d 270 (1974). But our task today is much narrower, and is well within the province of the judiciary. We do not attempt to set forth a detailed description of how the "well-founded fear" test should be applied.[31]

---

**31.** How "meaningful" the differences between the two standards may be is a question that cannot be fully decided in the abstract, but the fact that Congress has prescribed two different standards in the same Act certainly implies that it intended them to have significantly different meanings. \* \* \*

Instead, we merely hold that the Immigration Judge and the BIA were incorrect in holding that the two standards are identical.

\* \* \*

Deportation is always a harsh measure; it is all the more replete with danger when the alien makes a claim that he or she will be subject to death or persecution if forced to return to his or her home country. In enacting the Refugee Act of 1980 Congress sought to "give the United States sufficient flexibility to respond to situations involving political or religious dissidents and detainees throughout the world." Our holding today increases that flexibility by rejecting the Government's contention that the Attorney General may not even consider granting asylum to one who fails to satisfy the strict § 243(h) standard. Whether or not a "refugee" is eventually granted asylum is a matter which Congress has left for the Attorney General to decide. But it is clear that Congress did not intend to restrict eligibility for that relief to those who could prove that it is more likely than not that they will be persecuted if deported.

The judgment of the Court of Appeals is affirmed.

[The concurring opinion of JUSTICE BLACKMUN is omitted.]

JUSTICE POWELL, with whom THE CHIEF JUSTICE and JUSTICE WHITE join, dissenting.

\* \* \*

The Court's opinion seems to assume that the BIA has adopted a rigorous mathematical approach to asylum cases, requiring aliens to demonstrate an objectively quantifiable risk of persecution in their homeland that is more than 50%. The Court then argues that such a position is inconsistent with the language and history of the Act. But this has never been the BIA's position. \* \* \*

\* \* \*

[T]he BIA does not contend that both the "well-founded fear" standard and the "clear probability" standard require proof of a 51% chance that the alien will suffer persecution if he is returned to his homeland. The BIA plainly eschews analysis resting on mathematical probabilities. Rather, the BIA has adopted a four-part test requiring proof of facts that demonstrate a realistic likelihood of persecution actually occurring. The heart of the *Acosta* decision [19 I & N Dec. 211, 219 (BIA 1985)] is the BIA's empirical conclusion, based on its experience in adjudicating asylum applications, that if the facts establish such a basis for an alien's fear, it rarely will make a difference whether the judge asks if persecution is "likely" to occur or "more likely than not" to occur. If the alien can establish such a basis, he normally will be eligible for relief under either standard.

\* \* \*

In reaching [its] conclusion, the Court gives short shrift to the words "well-founded," that clearly require some objective basis for the alien's fear. The critical question presented by this case is whether the objective basis required for a fear of persecution to be "well-founded" differs *in practice* from the objective basis required for there to be a "clear probability" of persecution. Because both standards necessarily contemplate some objective basis, I cannot agree with the Court's implicit conclusion that the statute resolves this question on its face. In my view, the character of evidence sufficient to meet these two standards is a question best answered by an entity familiar with the types of evidence and issues that arise in such cases. * * *

* * *

Common sense and human experience support the BIA's conclusion. Governments rarely persecute people by the numbers. It is highly unlikely that the evidence presented at an asylum or withholding of deportation hearing will demonstrate the mathematically specific risk of persecution posited by the Court's hypothetical. Taking account of the types of evidence normally available in asylum cases, the BIA has chosen to make a *qualitative* evaluation of "realistic likelihoods." As I read the *Acosta* opinion, an individual who fled his country to avoid mass executions might be eligible for both withholding of deportation *and* asylum, whether or not he presented evidence of the numerical reach of the persecution. * * *

* * *

### Notes and Questions

1.  The *Cardoza–Fonseca* majority is convinced, *Chevron* notwithstanding, that the plain meaning of the two sections mandates a differential standard of proof for §§ 208 and 243(h). It emphasizes that the language of § 243(h) is "would," not " 'might' or 'could' be subject to persecution" (footnote 10, quoting *Stevic*). But this juxtaposition of the language is not fully responsive to the actual wording. The withholding provision extends its protection to noncitizens whose "life or freedom would be *threatened*" on the specified grounds, not "would be taken away." Consider the Court's own example of an individual facing return to a country where the government is killing or jailing every tenth adult male. Assuming that the asylum seeker is a male, obviously he has a well-founded fear of persecution on return. But how does the plain language apply here? Would we say that this man's life or freedom would be *threatened* on return?

2.  Which opinion, the majority or the dissent, is more persuasive on the question of whether the Court should defer under *Chevron* to the BIA's reading of the statute?

3.  The Court in *Cardoza–Fonseca* writes: "That the fear must be 'well-founded' does not alter the obvious focus on the individual's subjective beliefs." (Other parts of the opinion, however, lay greater stress on objective risks.) The UNHCR's *Handbook on Procedures and Criteria for Determining Refugee Status*, (Office of the United Nations High Commissioner for Refugees, *Handbook on Procedures and Criteria for Determining Refugee Status* 12, 14 (2d ed. 1988; UN Sales No. HCR/IP/4/Eng.Rev. 1)), goes somewhat

further, placing a relatively strong emphasis on the subjective component of the definition in its advice on how to determine refugee status. The Handbook states:

> The term "well-founded fear" * * * contains a subjective and an objective element, and in determining whether well-founded fear exists, both elements must be taken into consideration. * * * The subjective character of fear of persecution requires an evaluation of the opinions and feelings of the person concerned. It is also in the light of such opinions and feelings that any actual or anticipated measures against him must necessarily be viewed. Due to variations in the psychological make-up of individuals and in the circumstances of each case, interpretations of what amounts to persecution are bound to vary.

Is this a sound way to administer the asylum provisions of the immigration laws? Did Congress intend that asylum officers and immigration judges expend adjudication resources on close inquiry into the psychological make-up of individual applicants? Should equivalent showings of objective risk lead to equal results, whatever the varying states of mind of the claimants? In his treatise on the refugee definition, Hathaway argues that attention to subjective fears "is neither historically defensible nor practically meaningful." Examining the drafting history, he concludes:

> While the word "fear" may imply a form of emotional response, it may also be used to signal an anticipatory appraisal of risk. That is, a person may fear a particular event in the sense that she apprehends that it may occur, yet she may or may not * * * stand in trepidation of it actually taking place. * * * [T]he term "fear" was employed to mandate a forward-looking assessment of risk, not to require an examination of the emotional reaction of the claimant.

J. Hathaway, The Law of Refugee Status 65–66 (1991).

4. Apparently the Supreme Court countenances returning a recognized "refugee" to her country of origin, provided that she falls short of the standard for § 243(h). Is this sound policy? Is it what Congress had in mind? Would the drafters of the UN treaties have intended to permit such a result? Isn't Article 33's protection against *refoulement* the *raison d'être* for an international scheme of refugee protection? Or are there other policy objectives that might account for the distinction the Court draws? More fundamentally, does it make sense to have two different forms of protection, with two different levels of risk required for protection under U.S. law? Look closely at the exact context in which the "life or freedom" language is used in the Convention (in Articles 31 and 33) for other indications of why the treaty drafters might have used a somewhat different verbal formula.

5. Recall from Chapter Two that according to the *Charming Betsy* canon (see p. 74), courts should interpret statutes to avoid violations of international law. What decides the content of international law? What role, for example, does the UNHCR Handbook play in any such inquiry? Not quite addressing this exact question, the Supreme Court in *Cardoza–Fonseca* explained in a footnote in a part of the decision not excerpted here:

We do not suggest, of course, that the explanation in the U.N. Handbook has the force of law or in any way binds the INS with reference to the asylum provisions of § 208(a). Indeed, the Handbook itself disclaims such force, explaining that "the determination of refugee status under the 1951 Convention and the 1967 Protocol ... is incumbent upon the Contracting State in whose territory the refugee finds himself." Office of the United Nations High Commissioner for Refugees, Handbook on Procedures and Criteria for Determining Refugee Status 1 (ii) (Geneva, 1979).

Nonetheless, the Handbook provides significant guidance in construing the Protocol, to which Congress sought to conform. It has been widely considered useful in giving content to the obligations that the Protocol establishes.

*INS v. Cardoza–Fonseca*, 480 U.S. at 439 n.22. *See also INS v. Aguirre–Aguirre*, 526 U.S. 415, 427, 119 S.Ct. 1439, 143 L.Ed.2d 590 (1999) (rejecting the interpretation suggested in the Handbook).

## 2. RESPONSES TO *CARDOZA–FONSECA*

The Board of Immigration Appeals moved quickly to conform its practice to *Cardoza–Fonseca*. It took note of the Supreme Court's direction that the standards for asylum and withholding are "significantly different." 480 U.S., at 448 n.31, 107 S.Ct. at 1222 n. 31. It then surveyed the efforts of earlier lower court decisions to describe that difference.

### MATTER OF MOGHARRABI

Board of Immigration Appeals, 1987.
19 I & N Dec. 439.

\* \* \*

The respondents, husband and wife, are both natives and citizens of Iran. Both respondents were admitted to the United States as nonimmigrant students on or about September 8, 1978. The female respondent's status was subsequently changed to that of a spouse of a nonimmigrant student. The respondents were authorized to remain in this country until February 27, 1982, but they remained beyond that time. Orders to Show Cause and Notice of Hearing (Form I–221) were issued against them on August 28, 1984, charging them with deportability as overstays under section 241(a)(2) of the Immigration and Nationality Act. At a joint deportation hearing begun on November 5, 1984, and concluded on July 2, 1985, the respondents conceded their deportability. The only issues at the hearing, and the only issues on appeal, concern the male respondent's application for asylum and withholding of deportation.

\* \* \*

It is clear that to a large degree the meaning of "well-founded fear" can in fact only be determined in the contexts of individual cases. Whatever words may be used in a definition, the approach must still be to assess each case independently on its particular merits. Nevertheless, we think that some guidance can be provided, and would be helpful. We do not attempt a definitive statement on the meaning of well-founded fear but rather are setting forth a starting point for use in an ongoing effort to formulate a workable and useful definition of the standard in question.

\* \* \*

We agree with and adopt the general approach set forth by the Fifth Circuit; that is, that an applicant for asylum has established a well-founded fear if he shows that a reasonable person in his circumstances would fear persecution. As noted by the Second Circuit, this "reasonable person standard appropriately captures the various formulations that have been advanced to explain the well-founded fear test." It is a standard that provides a "common sense" framework for analyzing whether claims of persecution are well-founded. Moreover, a reasonable person may well fear persecution even where its likelihood is significantly less than clearly probable.

\* \* \*

Where the country at issue in an asylum case has a history of persecuting people in circumstances similar to the asylum applicant's, careful consideration should be given to that fact in assessing the applicant's claims. A well-founded fear, in other words, can be based on what has happened to others who are similarly situated. The situation of each person, however, must be assessed on its own merits.

We note that although our decision in *Matter of Acosta* [19 I & N Dec. 211 (BIA 1985)] has been effectively overruled by *INS v. Cardoza–Fonseca,* insofar as *Acosta* held that the well-founded fear standard and the clear probability standard may be equated, much of our decision remains intact, and good law. Indeed, we still find in *Acosta* some guidance regarding the meaning of a well-founded fear. In *Acosta,* we set forth four elements which an applicant for asylum must show in order to establish a well-founded fear of persecution. What we required was that the evidence establish that

> (1) the alien possesses a belief or characteristic a persecutor seeks to overcome in others by means of punishment of some sort; (2) the persecutor is already aware, or could easily become aware, that the alien possesses this belief or characteristic; (3) the persecutor has the capability of punishing the alien; and (4) the persecutor has the inclination to punish the alien.

*Matter of Acosta, supra,* at 226.

In our view, these requirements, for the most part, survive the Supreme Court's decision in *Cardoza–Fonseca,* and are still useful guidelines in assessing an asylum application. However, we have determined that one small but significant change in these requirements should be made in view of the Court's ruling. The second requirement should be changed by omitting the word "easily." Thus, it is enough for the applicant to show that the persecutor could become aware that the applicant possesses the belief or characteristic in question. The omission of the word "easily" lightens the applicant's burden of proof and moves the requirements as a whole into line with *Cardoza–Fonseca*. Of course, all these requirements must now be considered in light of the lower burden of proof which will be imposed on asylum applicants generally.

It must also be remembered that an alien who succeeds in establishing a well-founded fear of persecution will not necessarily be granted asylum. He must also show that the feared persecution would be on account of his race, religion, nationality, membership in a particular social group, or political opinion. Thus, for example, aliens fearing retribution over purely personal matters, or aliens fleeing general conditions of violence and upheaval in their countries, would not qualify for asylum. Such persons may have well-founded fears, but such fears would not be on account of their race, religion, nationality, membership in a particular social group, or political opinion. Finally, an applicant for asylum must also show that he merits the relief as a matter of discretion.

While under *Matter of Acosta* we were able to consider an application for asylum and withholding of deportation as, for most purposes, one, this approach requires some modification after *INS v. Cardoza–Fonseca*. Given that the core of evidence and testimony presented in support of the asylum and withholding applications will in almost every case be virtually the same, such evidence and testimony may still be presented in a single hearing. However, in actually adjudicating the applications, a clear delineation of the findings should be made as to each application. We anticipate that as a general rule the asylum application, with its lower burden of proof, will be adjudicated first. If the applicant is found eligible for asylum, and worthy of the relief as a matter of discretion, there may be no need to determine as well whether a clear probability of persecution exists.

We now turn to the application of these new standards to the case presently before us. The respondent fears persecution in Iran primarily because of an altercation he had with an official or agent of the regime of the Ayatollah Khomeini. The respondent testified and attested to the following facts regarding that incident. In February of 1981, while in the United States, the respondent went with an Iranian friend to the Iranian Interests Section at the Algerian Embassy. His purpose was to document his continuing student status, in order to enable him to continue receiving funds from relatives in Iran. To this end, he took with him photocopies of his passport and his Arrival–Departure Record (Form I–94). When he presented the photocopies to a student who was working at the Embassy, he was told that the originals were required. According to the respondent, he was informed that the originals were necessary because students who did not have them had probably submitted them to the Immigration and Naturalization Service in connection with asylum applications. The student-employee was insistent, and the respondent's friend asked to see the supervisor. The supervisor appeared, but further trouble ensued. The student apparently grabbed the respondent's friend's neck, but the supervisor separated them. The student then told the respondent's friend that he and "his kind had better keep their eyes and ears open because 'their day' would come soon." In response, the respondent told him that "he and his kind had robbed Iran of all that was worth living for and that they were nothing more than religious fascists stuffing their pockets with the nation's wealth." According to the respondent, the student then drew a gun, and he and his friend ran out the door. The respondent testified that there were cameras all around the room recording these events. A witness for the respondent testified at the hearing that he accompanied the respondent and his friend to the Algerian Embassy, although he waited in the car and did not go inside with them. This witness testified that, when the respondent and his friend returned to the car, they were nervous, and a couple of people were following them. It is the respondent's contention that he is now known to Khomeini officials and that as a result he has good reason to fear persecution if returned to Iran. The respondent also testified that he had participated in anti-Khomeini demonstrations in the United States.

After careful consideration of the entire record, we have concluded that a reasonable person in the respondent's circumstances would fear persecution if returned to Iran. We find the respondent's account of why he fears persecution based on his political opinions to be plausible, detailed, and coherent. The respondent's account of the incident at the Embassy appears to us to be credible, and there is nothing in the record to otherwise suggest that the respondent lacks credibility. The respondent clearly expressed his political views at the Iranian Interests Section and his opinions were extremely derogatory to the regime in power. The Service does not dispute that opponents of the Ayatollah Khomeini are often persecuted for their opposition. In this case, a reasonable person in the respondent's position would fear that his opposition to that regime has become known to those who are both in a position, and who have the inclination, to punish him for it. Under these circumstances, we find that the respondent has met his burden of showing a well-founded fear of persecution in Iran. Given the statements made to agents of the Khomeini regime by the respondent while in the Algerian Embassy, any persecution which might occur would be on account of political opinion.

There are no adverse factors of record in this case. We find no basis for considering a discretionary denial of relief. The application for asylum will accordingly be granted. We therefore find it unnecessary to decide whether the respondent has also established a clear probability of persecution for section 243(h) purposes. * * *.

* * *

As a concomitant to the sensible sequencing approach set out in the fourth from the last paragraph from *Mogharrabi* quoted above ("While under *Matter of Acosta* ...''), it is now well established in the case law that ''an alien who fails to satisfy the requirements for asylum * * * necessarily fails to meet the more stringent 'clear probability' standard required for withholding of deportation.'' *Angoucheva v. INS,* 106 F.3d 781, 788 (7th Cir. 1997).

The 1990 asylum regulations incorporated new substantive standards for establishing refugee status and thus meeting the threshold requirement for asylum under § 208, and the basic approach established there has been maintained in the regulations issued after the INA was amended in 1996. The regulations avoid use of the BIA's formulation asking whether a ''reasonable person in [the asylum applicant's] circumstances would fear persecution.'' Instead the regulations ask whether ''there is a reasonable possibility of suffering such persecution if he or she were to return to [the home] country.'' 8 C.F.R. § 208.13(b)(2).

## 3. INDIVIDUALIZED THREAT

Before *Stevic* and *Cardoza–Fonseca,* the Board routinely announced a requirement that the applicant for asylum ''must demonstrate a likelihood that he individually will be singled out and subjected to persecution.'' *Matter of Sibrun,* 18 I & N Dec. 354, 358 (BIA 1983). As part of discussing the level of risk, numerous court decisions—both before and after *Stevic* and *Cardoza–Fonseca*—have likewise employed the ''singling out'' formulation, or similar ones like ''a specific threat to the petitioner.'' *See, e.g., Carvajal–Munoz v. INS,* 743 F.2d 562, 573–74 (7th Cir. 1984); *Artiga Turcios v. INS,* 829 F.2d 720, 723 (9th Cir. 1987); *Cruz–Lopez v. INS,* 802 F.2d 1518, 1521 (4th Cir. 1986) (all three using the ''singled out'' language); *Ananeh–Firempong v. INS,* 766 F.2d 621, 627 (1st Cir. 1985) (''specific threat''). In *Ananeh–Firempong,* Judge (now Justice) Stephen Breyer explained the policy reasons underlying such requirements:

> [W]e recognize the need to require an alien * * * to offer reasonably specific information showing a real threat of individual persecution. Otherwise, given the unfortunately large number of repressive governments throughout the world, Congress's offer of haven to refugees present in the United States could severely weaken its more general legislative effort to impose overall limitations upon immigration.

*Id.* at 627 (applied specifically to withholding of removal, but the policy considerations are relevant also to § 208). The Seventh Circuit has also pursued this theme: ''the requirement that an asylum applicant demonstrate that he or she has a reasonable fear of being *singled out* for persecution 'is no doubt driven by Congress' concern that a more lenient and compassionate policy would qualify the entire population of many war torn nations for asylum.' '' *Milosevic v. INS,* 18 F.3d 366, 373–74 (7th Cir. 1994), quoting *Sivaainkaran v. INS,* 972 F.2d 161, 165 (7th Cir. 1992).

After *Cardoza–Fonseca,* it was unclear what level of individualized threat should be required. The asylum regulations now address this by stating that "the asylum officer or immigration judge shall not require the applicant to provide evidence that he or she would be singled out individually for persecution if" the applicant shows "a pattern or practice" in the home country of "persecution of a group of persons similarly situated to the applicant" and "establishes his own inclusion in and identification with such group of persons such that his or her fear of persecution upon return is reasonable." 8 C.F.R. § 208.13(b)(2)(iii). A similar caution about the "singling out" requirement applies to withholding of removal, although in the context of an overarching requirement that the applicant for withholding show that "it is more likely than not that he would be persecuted on account of race, religion, nationality, membership in a particular social group, or political opinion." 8 C.F.R. § 208.16(b)(2).

In *Yong Hao Chen v. INS,* 195 F.3d 198, 203–04 (4th Cir. 1999), Judge Motz reflected on the relationship between these different modes of proof:

> Individual targeting and systematic persecution do not necessarily constitute distinct theories. Rather, an applicant will typically demonstrate some combination of the two to establish a well-founded fear of persecution. *See, e.g., Angoucheva v. INS,* 106 F.3d 781, 789 (7th Cir. 1997) (Macedonian citizen of Bulgaria could establish well-founded fear by showing persecution of Macedonian community and her own visible role in Macedonian political advocacy group). "[T]he more egregious the showing of group persecution . . . the less evidence of individualized persecution must be adduced." *Kotasz v. INS,* 31 F.3d [847,] 853 [(9th Cir. 1994)]. Conversely, a stronger showing of individual targeting will be necessary where the underlying basis for the applicant's fear is membership in a diffuse class against whom actual persecution is haphazard and rare.

For a thorough consideration of these concerns, see Blum, *The Ninth Circuit, and the Protection of Asylum Seekers Since the Passage of the Refugee Act of 1980,* 23 San Diego L. Rev. 327, 343 (1986).

---

### Exercise

The readings above have covered a variety of formulations of the standard for claiming asylum-type protections under § 208 or § 241(b)(3). We have grouped the alternative interpretations below in two categories, first for *nonrefoulement* and second for asylum. Within each category, they range from the most demanding to the least.

1.  threat to life or freedom:

    A.  clear probability of persecution

      B.   persecution is more likely than not

   2.  well-founded fear of persecution:

      A.   realistic likelihood of persecution

      B.   reasonable possibility of persecution

      C.   good reason to fear persecution

      D.  a reasonable person in such circumstances would fear persecution upon return to the homeland.

Test your understanding of the various tests and their implications for concrete cases by applying them to the following hypotheticals, and keep them in mind as you consider the more detailed exploration of standards that follows these problems.

*Hypothetical A.* (1) A was a local leader in a teacher's organization that began a campaign of criticism against the authoritarian government in Ruritania and called for democratic reforms. The government has denounced the protests, but so far has done nothing further.

(2) Same facts, but now the Ruritanian government has shown some signs that it will crack down on opponents. So far, however, it has arrested only labor union leaders.

(3) Same facts, but Ruritania now branches out beyond labor leaders and seizes three top officials at the national level in the teacher's organization, holding them without charge for 10 days, then releasing them. Local leaders have not been bothered.

*Hypothetical B.* (1) Noncitizen B worked a two-acre farm in Montana province in Fredonia. That province has just come under the control of a local militia chief who has a reputation for ruling with an iron hand.

(2) Same facts, but now B adds that the bodies of two activists were found, decapitated, on the main street of the province's capital city shortly before he left for the United States.

(3) Same facts, but B adds that he attended an antigovernment demonstration three years ago at which the two activists gave a speech.

(4) Same facts, but B adds that he helped organize that demonstration, although he had been inactive since then.

(5) Same facts, but B adds that he was a lower-echelon leader in the organization to which the two activists belonged.

# SECTION C.   DISCRETION TO GRANT
# OR DENY PROTECTION

In distinguishing the different levels of risk required for *nonrefoulement* and asylum under U.S. law, the Supreme Court 1987 decision in *Cardoza–Fonseca* emphasized that although the 1980 Refugee Act changed *nonrefoulement* from discretionary to mandatory, the grant of asylum under INA § 208 is a discretionary decision.

The original text of the Refugee Act of 1980 specified:

> The Attorney General shall establish a procedure for an alien physically present in the United States or at a land border or port of entry, irrespective of such alien's status, to apply for asylum, and the alien may be granted asylum in the discretion of the Attorney General if the Attorney General determines that such alien is a refugee within the meaning of section 101(a)(42)(A).

Pub. L. 96–212, § 201(b), 94 Stat. 102, 105 (1980), adding INA § 208(a).

Although the words of this provision have been modified since 1980, the Attorney General's decision to grant or deny asylum remains a matter of discretion. The BIA has taken various approaches toward the exercise of such discretion, and its doctrines have met with a mixed reception in the courts of appeals. The first significant case was *Matter of Salim*, 18 I & N Dec. 311 (BIA 1982), which is cited in two decisions earlier in this chapter, *Matter of A–G–* and *INS v. Cardoza–Fonseca*. Salim was from Afghanistan, but he had spent some time in Pakistan and came to the United States on someone else's passport, which he had fraudulently purchased in order to obtain a visa as a nonimmigrant visitor for business. The Board found that he qualified for withholding, because of the persecution that threatened him in Afghanistan, and met the eligibility requirement for asylum under § 208. But emphasizing that asylum relief is a matter of discretion, the Board held:

> Attempting entry into the United States by way of fraudulently obtained documentation has consistently been considered a strong negative discretionary factor. * * * [T]he public interest requires that we do not condone this applicant's attempt to circumvent the orderly procedures that our government has provided for refugees to immigrate lawfully. The fraudulent passport was obtained after the applicant had escaped from Afghanistan, with the sole purpose of reaching this country ahead of all the other refugees awaiting their turn abroad. This is not the case where an alien was forced to resort to fraudulently obtained documentation in order to escape or prevent being returned to the country in which he fears persecution. *See Matter of Ng*, 17 I & N Dec. 536 (BIA 1980). This Board finds that the fraudulent avoidance of the orderly refugee procedures that this country has established is an extremely adverse factor

which can only be overcome with the most unusual showing of
countervailing equities. This case before us does not present
such equities. Consequently, the application for asylum relief
will be denied as a matter of discretion.

18 I & N Dec. at 315–16.

## Notes and Questions

1. According to this ruling, Salim could not obtain asylum status
(which would ultimately lead to permanent resident status in the United
States), but neither could he be returned to Afghanistan. As a practical
matter, this meant that the U.S. government would probably try to send him
back to Pakistan, where he had lived after leaving Afghanistan. This result
raises several questions. What should happen to Salim if Pakistan refused to
accept his return and no other country, save Afghanistan, would take him
in? The United States could not return him to Afghanistan, but could he be
held in detention in the United States indefinitely? Check Article 31 of the
1951 Convention to see if it provides assistance in answering these questions. (Chapter Nine will address detention more fully.)

2. Is "fraudulent avoidance of the orderly refugee procedures this
country has established" a valid reason to deny asylum? Was the possible
availability of a return to Pakistan here a better ground for denying Salim
asylum under § 208? For a critique of denying asylum to those who relied on
fraudulent documents, see Anker, *Discretionary Asylum: A Protection Remedy for Refugees Under the Refugee Act of 1980*, 28 Va. J. Int'l L. 1 (1987). *See
also* Fitzpatrick & Pauw, *Foreign Policy, Asylum and Discretion*, 28 Willamette L. Rev. 751 (1992).

3. The opinion's reliance on the "orderly procedures that our government has provided for refugees to immigrate lawfully" implies that Salim
jumped the queue because he was merely impatient. In light of the limited
number of refugees accepted by the overseas program for resettlement in the
United States, it is highly unlikely that Salim or any other individual refugee
could count on admission to the United States from a refugee camp on
another continent. Nonetheless, was the government's interest in maintaining orderly refugee processing overseas a sufficient reason to deny resettlement or asylum to Salim?

4. Several court cases, including *Hernandez–Ortiz v. INS*, 777 F.2d
509, 519 (9th Cir. 1985), took a view contrary to *Salim*:

We have not previously delineated the factors, or "legitimate
concerns" that the Board may consider when denying asylum to an
alien who has established refugee status. We note, however, that 8
C.F.R. § 208.8(f)(1) (1985) lists a small number of factors that
require the denial of relief, e.g., "the alien, having been convicted by
a final judgment of a particularly serious crime, constitutes a
danger to the community of the United States."[a] The regulation

---

**a.** When *Hernandez–Ortiz* and *Salim*
were decided, this regulation restated virtually word for word the exceptions to *nonrefoulement* protection set forth in the statutory withholding provision (you may wish
at this point to consult the current exceptions in INA § 241(b)(3)(B), which are virtually unchanged from the earlier statute).

also specifies one factor that would justify the discretionary denial of asylum: "there is an outstanding offer of resettlement by a third nation where the applicant will not be subject to persecution and the applicant's resettlement in a third nation is in the public interest." 8 C.F.R. § 208.8(f)(2) (1985). The factors mentioned in section 208.8 of the regulations are substantial factors involving the national interest or the welfare of the community, or they are factors relating to the existence of other means of ensuring the safety and security of the alien. Although we need not, at this time, define precisely the kinds of legitimate concerns that may serve as a basis for the Board's determinations, it would appear that, where the Board has not identified an alternative source of refuge, it can deny asylum only on the basis of genuine compelling factors— factors important enough to warrant returning a bona fide refugee to a country where he may face a threat of imminent danger to his life or liberty.

---

Recall that when the Supreme Court in *Stevic* and *Cardoza–Fonseca* addressed the degree of threat an applicant must face in her homeland to be eligible for *nonrefoulement* and asylum, the Court relied heavily on the discretionary nature of § 208 in explaining why Congress would provide a more generous standard as the test for that section's "greater form of relief." The Supreme Court queried why the Attorney General wished to confine to a narrow class of noncitizens his ability to exercise the discretion granted him by INA § 208. Sometimes officials prefer to have discretion, but other times it can be a burden to exercise that discretion and to gather relevant information. Administrators might prefer bright-line rules that make a difficult decision more straightforward as a matter of both substance and process.

Some observers worried that the Attorney General or the Board would respond to *Cardoza–Fonseca* by significantly tightening the standards for discretionary grants of asylum. *See* Anker & Blum, *New Trends in Asylum Jurisprudence: The Aftermath of the U.S. Supreme Court Decision* in *INS v. Cardoza–Fonseca*, 1 Int'l J. Refugee L. 67 (1989). Such an approach could result in large-scale deportation of persons found to meet the refugee definition but who failed to qualify for *nonrefoulement* under the withholding of removal provisions. Even those claimants who, despite a discretionary denial of asylum, did satisfy the withholding of removal standards would enjoy only limited benefits, falling far short of those that come with a grant of asylum. (See Chapter Two's discussion of the differences between asylum and *nonrefoulement*.)

Despite these worries of a restrictive response to *Cardoza–Fonseca*, the Board moved in the opposite direction.

The regulation also added two other factors mandating denial of asylum: (1) if the alien does not meet the refugee definition (an unnecessary provision, as he then would not qualify for asylum in any event), and (2) if the alien has been firmly resettled in a foreign country.—eds.

# MATTER OF PULA

Board of Immigration Appeals, 1987.
19 I & N Dec. 467.

\* \* \*

The applicant is a 26-year-old married male native of Albania and citizen of Yugoslavia. He arrived in the United States on June 5, 1986, and was placed in exclusion proceedings. The applicant does not contest on appeal his excludability under [the grounds for fraud or willful misrepresentation and failure to have valid travel documents]. \* \* \* The only issues to be decided by the present appeal are whether the immigration judge's denial of asylum and grant of withholding of deportation to Yugoslavia were proper.

The applicant testified that he was born in Albania and fled to Yugoslavia with his family as a refugee when he was 5 years old. He said that he left Yugoslavia in 1986 to avoid further encounters with police officials who, on numerous occasions since 1979, had detained, interrogated, and physically abused him for hours or days at a time. He stated that the police insisted that he was involved in the political activities of the Albanian minority in Yugoslavia, although he denied the accusation. He said that the police sought information from him about such matters as his contacts with his Albanian family and friends, Albanian anti-government demonstrations, and discussions among local Albanian university students. He also testified that one of the periods of detention occurred in 1982 after he approached Yugoslav authorities to request travel documents to visit his sister in the United States. The applicant explained that the police accused him of planning to go to the United States to participate in anti-Yugoslav demonstrations with Albanians here.

The applicant further advised that in 1985 Yugoslav authorities did issue him a titre de voyage[2] so he could travel out of the country, but the American Embassy denied his application for a visa. According to the applicant, he was told at the embassy that the titre de voyage did not guarantee his return to Yugoslavia. The applicant testified that he subsequently relinquished his refugee status and reluctantly accepted Yugoslav citizenship in order to qualify for a Yugoslav passport. He said that he left Yugoslavia on April 20, 1986, as soon as he managed to obtain the passport. He stated that he took a train to Brussels, Belgium, although he had made application to Yugoslav authorities only for permission to visit Turkey. He testified that he believed that the authorities would have denied him the passport if they had known that he intended to go to the United States. He also said that he was afraid to apply again for a visa at the American Embassy because most of the

---

2. A titre de voyage is a travel document issued in lieu of a passport under provisions of the United Nations Convention Relating to the Status of Refugees, July 28, 1951, 189 U.N.T.S. 150.

employees there were Yugoslav nationals who might be agents for the Government of Yugoslavia.

In addition, the applicant testified that he stayed in Brussels for 6 weeks with a man who had been a friend of his family in Albania and Yugoslavia. He said that his friend made a telephone call on his behalf to a refugee organization in Italy to inquire about whether he could obtain residency in an Italian refugee camp. According to the applicant, his friend was informed by the organization that citizens of Yugoslavia were not accepted as refugees in European states. The applicant also said that while he was in Brussels he applied for a tourist visa at the American Embassy, but his application was denied and he was told to go to Yugoslavia to apply for a visa. He testified that he did not ask for asylum at the American Embassy because he did not know that he could do so.

The applicant also stated that one day while he was discussing his situation in an Albanian coffee house in Belgium, a stranger there offered to sell him a titre de voyage for $1,000. He said that he gave the man his photograph and paid him the money 2 days later, when he returned with a titre de voyage issued by the Government of Belgium which had a tourist visa to the United States already entered. The applicant advised that the titre de voyage had been issued in the name of someone whom he did not know.

The applicant further testified that on June 5, 1986, he flew with his titre de voyage from Belgium to New York. He said that during a 2 to 3-hour stopover at the airport in Amsterdam, he mailed his Yugoslav passport to a cousin in the United States to avoid having it in his possession when he landed in New York. He explained that his inability to speak English made him concerned that immigration officials might discover the passport and put him on a plane to Yugoslavia before he could tell them about his desire for asylum. The applicant also stated that he did not dispose of the Yugoslav passport altogether because he planned to use it later to corroborate his account of events for his asylum request. In addition, the applicant advised that when he arrived in New York, language differences did in fact prevent him and the immigration officer from communicating and, as a result, he did not tell the officer anything or sign any statements.

The applicant also testified that he chose to flee to the United States because he had relatives here. He stated that he had a sister and two uncles who were lawful permanent residents of the United States, and cousins who were United States citizens. He further advised that his wife, who was still living in Yugoslavia with their daughter, also had an uncle and cousins in the United States. The record reflects that many of the applicant's relatives traveled from such places as upstate New York, Texas, and California on multiple occasions to attend the applicant's hearings in New York City.

* * * [The immigration judge] found that the applicant had established his eligibility for withholding of deportation to Yugoslavia and Albania. The immigration judge further found, however, that the appli-

cant was not eligible for asylum as a matter of discretion because the equity of his many relatives legally in the United States did not overcome the adverse factor of his having sought admission to the United States by use of a purchased travel document.

\* \* \*

We turn now to the issue of whether the applicant merits asylum in the exercise of discretion. In *Matter of Salim*, we denied asylum as a matter of discretion to an alien who was excludable [for fraud or misrepresentation] and who attempted to circumvent the orderly procedures provided for refugees to immigrate lawfully. We found the fraudulent avoidance of orderly refugee procedures to be an extremely adverse factor which could only be overcome with the most unusual showing of countervailing equities.

\* \* \*

[W]hile we find that an alien's manner of entry or attempted entry is a proper and relevant discretionary factor to consider in adjudicating asylum applications, we agree with the applicant that Matter of Salim places too much emphasis on the circumvention of orderly refugee procedures. This circumvention can be a serious adverse factor, but it should not be considered in such a way that the practical effect is to deny relief in virtually all cases. This factor is only one of a number of factors which should be balanced in exercising discretion, and the weight accorded to this factor may vary depending on the facts of a particular case. We therefore withdraw from *Matter of Salim* insofar as it suggests that the circumvention of orderly refugee procedures alone is sufficient to require the most unusual showing of countervailing equities.

Instead of focusing only on the circumvention of orderly refugee procedures, the totality of the circumstances and actions of an alien in his flight from the country where he fears persecution should be examined in determining whether a favorable exercise of discretion is warranted. Among those factors which should be considered are whether the alien passed through any other countries or arrived in the United States directly from his country, whether orderly refugee procedures were in fact available to help him in any country he passed through, and whether he made any attempts to seek asylum before coming to the United States. In addition, the length of time the alien remained in a third country, and his living conditions, safety, and potential for long-term residency there are also relevant. For example, an alien who is forced to remain in hiding to elude persecutors, or who faces imminent deportation back to the country where he fears persecution, may not have found a safe haven even though he has escaped to another country. Further, whether the alien has relatives legally in the United States or other personal ties to this country which motivated him to seek asylum here rather than elsewhere is another factor to consider. In this regard, the extent of the alien's ties to any other countries where he does not fear persecution should also be examined. Moreover, if the alien engaged in fraud to circumvent orderly refugee procedures, the seriousness of the fraud should be considered. The use of fraudulent documents to escape the country of persecution itself is not a significant adverse factor while, at the other extreme, entry under the assumed identity of a United States citizen with a United States passport, which was fraudulently obtained by the alien from the United States Government, is very serious fraud.

In addition to the circumstances and actions of the alien in his flight from the country where he fears persecution, general humanitarian considerations, such as an alien's tender age or poor health, may also be relevant in a discretionary determination. A situation of particular concern involves an alien who has established his statutory eligibility for asylum but cannot meet the higher burden required for withholding of deportation. Deportation to a country where the alien may be persecuted thus becomes a strong possibility. In such a case, the discretionary factors should be carefully evaluated in light of the unusually harsh consequences which may befall an alien who has established a well-founded fear of persecution; the danger of persecution should generally outweigh all but the most egregious of adverse factors.

Each of the factors mentioned above will not, of course, be found in every case. An applicant for asylum has the burden of establishing that the favorable exercise of discretion is warranted. Therefore, the alien should present evidence on any relevant factors which he believes support the favorable exercise of discretion in his case. In the absence of any adverse factors, however, asylum should be granted in the exercise of discretion.

In the case before us, the applicant attempted to enter the United States with a fraudulent document. Yet we note that the applicant had inquired about obtaining refugee status in Europe, only to be informed that the Yugoslav citizenship which he had recently accepted presented an obstacle to his being recognized by European countries as a refugee. Further, the record reflects that the applicant resorted to the purchase of the fraudulent document only after he was unsuccessful in several attempts at acquiring a visa to enter the United States legally to ask for asylum. We find no basis for doubting the applicant's testimony that he failed to request asylum at the American Embassy because he did not know that he could do so. In addition, the applicant remained in Belgium for only 6 weeks and was in the Netherlands for only a few hours; it does not appear that he was entitled to remain permanently in either country. Moreover, he decided to seek asylum in the United States because he had many relatives legally in the United States to whom he could turn for assistance. Although only the applicant's sister would typically be characterized as a "close" relative, the record reflects that many of his other relatives are also particularly supportive and concerned about him. We note that the applicant seems to have no significant ties to any other countries except for Albania and Yugoslavia, where he fears persecution.

Based on the foregoing factors, therefore, we find that asylum should be granted in the exercise of discretion. * * *

* * *

[The opinion of BOARD MEMBER HEILMAN, concurring in part and dissenting in part, is omitted.]

### Note

The Board strengthened the *Pula* approach to discretion in *Matter of Kasinga*, 21 I & N Dec. 357 (BIA 1996). Citing *Pula*, the Board explained:

> * * * The danger of persecution will outweigh all but the most egregious adverse factors. The type of persecution feared by the applicant is very severe.
>
> To the extent that the Immigration Judge suggested that the applicant had a legal obligation to seek refuge in Ghana or Germany, the record does not support such a conclusion. The applicant offered credible reasons for not seeking refuge in either of those countries in her particular circumstances.
>
> The applicant purchased someone else's passport and used it to come to the United States. However, upon arrival, she did not attempt to use the false passport to enter. She told the immigration inspector the truth.
>
> We have weighed the favorable and adverse factors and are satisfied that discretion should be exercised in favor of the applicant. Therefore, we will grant asylum to the applicant.

*Id.* at 367–68. After *Pula* and *Kasinga,* it became routine practice for discretion to be exercised in favor of granting asylum when the adjudicator found that the applicant had a well-founded fear of persecution. Discretionary denials still occurred in a small number of cases where the individual had engaged in serious misconduct (including fraud). But compare *Pula* with the following decision, which seems to reflect a more severe approach to discretion.

## MATTER OF A–H–
Attorney General of the United States, 2005.
23 I & N Dec. 774.

[ASHCROFT, ATTORNEY GENERAL:]

* * *

This matter was referred to the Attorney General by the Acting Commissioner of the Immigration and Naturalization Service ("INS" or "Service") from the decision of the Board of Immigration Appeals ("BIA" or "Board") granting respondent asylum. * * *

Respondent, an Algerian national, has been active in the Algerian Islamist movement for decades and is a self-proclaimed leader-in-exile of the Islamic Salvation Front of Algeria, known by its French acronym

"FIS." The FIS appeared to be on the verge of winning parliamentary elections in Algeria in 1992 when the elections were canceled by the Algerian Government. For some years thereafter, Algeria was wracked by internal conflict between security forces and armed Islamist groups bent on overthrowing the Government. * * *

Two of the most active and violent armed Islamist groups in Algeria were the Armed Islamic Group, or "GIA," and the Islamic Salvation Army, or "AIS." The AIS has been identified as the armed wing of the FIS. In May 1994, the GIA, the AIS, and other armed Islamist groups joined under one banner and became known collectively as the GIA. The record indicates that these armed groups engaged in terrorism and widespread persecution of civilians in Algeria. The Secretary of State has designated the GIA as a "foreign terrorist organization" for its activities during the mid-1990s. The State Department determined that these groups targeted journalists for assassination "because they are viewed as supportive of the Algerian government and antagonistic toward the goals of these militants" and murdered intellectuals who were deemed "unsympathetic to the Islamic cause as defined by Islamic militants." * * *

\* \* \*

The Attorney General may deny asylum in his discretion even where the applicant is otherwise eligible for asylum. * * * Contrary to the BIA's determination, I conclude that the record presented here makes it appropriate to deny respondent asylum in the exercise of my discretion, even if he would otherwise be eligible for asylum.

The INS introduced evidence below indicating that respondent, through his active leadership position in the FIS, had ties to the armed Islamist groups that committed acts of persecution and terrorism in Algeria in the mid-1990s. Respondent is an acknowledged leader and spokesman for the FIS, the principal Algerian Islamic opposition organization. There is evidence suggesting that the FIS was involved in the killing of civilians. See, e.g., Testimony of Professor Yonah Alexander, Director of the Terrorism Studies Program, George Washington University, testifying that "FIS and allied organizations such as the [GIA] have been waging a campaign of terrorism since 1992 against the Algerian government and secular persons and institutions," that FIS "engages in political assassination, attacks security forces and has murdered foreigners," and that FIS's targets "include journalists, physicians and other professionals" and "Western targets." Similarly, Amnesty International reported that the FIS "has repeatedly claimed that it has influence over the armed Islamist groups in Algeria." * * *

\* \* \*

The evidence suggests that respondent's statements purporting to justify terrorist activities by the armed Islamist groups in Algeria may have corresponded with an increase in the targeted killing of civilians. Human Rights Watch reported that "[s]ixteen journalists were assassinated in the first ten months of 1994." The February 1995 IC Publications[a] report estimated that 200 journalists had fled Algeria to France "after FIS threats began to translate into real acts."

Evidence also indicates that other leaders within the FIS believed respondent had "one foot in the GIA camp," and they associated him with the GIA's assassination of two FIS leaders in November 1995 because of his failure to condemn those assassinations. Finally, respondent testified below that after the GIA's murder of the FIS leaders, he "disassociated" himself from the GIA, which clearly implies that he was "associated" with the GIA up until at least November 1995.

I conclude that, taken together, the circumstances concerning respondent's links to the activities of the armed Islamist groups in Algeria, as outlined above, strongly weigh against a discretionary grant of asylum in this case, whether or not respondent has a well-founded fear of persecution if returned to Algeria. The United States has significant interests in combating violent acts of persecution and terrorism wherever they may occur, including in Algeria, and it is inconsistent with these interests to provide safe haven to individuals who have connections to such acts of violence. It is also in the national interest of the United States for Algeria to achieve a peaceful and stable resolution to the conflicts that have plagued that nation.

Moreover, certain additional factors weigh against asylum for respondent: Specifically, respondent testified that he received money from overseas for his political work, yet he never filed income tax returns in the United States and his children nevertheless received financial assistance from the Commonwealth of Virginia. Respondent's apparent tax violations and his abuse of a system designed to provide relief to the needy exhibit both a disrespect for the rule of law and a willingness to gain advantage at the expense of those who are more deserving. Although there are equities that weigh in respondent's favor—for example, his wife and children reside legally in the United States and three of his children are United States citizens—these equities do not outweigh the negative factors I have identified. My view, based on a thorough review of the record and considering the balance of factors discussed above, is that respondent is not entitled to become a lawful permanent resident of the United States. Therefore, I deny respondent's application for asylum in the exercise of my discretion.

[The Attorney General then remanded to the BIA to consider the respondent's eligibility for withholding or protection under the Convention Against Torture, including whether the respondent was ineligible for withholding because he had participated in the persecution of others or because he presented a danger to the security of the United States.]

### Notes and Questions

1. What factors influenced the outcomes in *Salim*, *Pula*, *Kasinga*, and *A–H–*? Can you fashion a coherent test to predict when discretion will be exercised to grant or deny asylum to an applicant who meets the basic test of a well-founded fear of persecution on account of one of the five enumerated grounds?

**a.** IC Publications is a news agency focusing on Africa and the Middle East.—eds.

2. Since *Pula* was decided, Congress has modified the asylum provision, expanding the list of factors that now call for mandatory denial of asylum—factors (such as firm resettlement or a growing list of criminal convictions) that formerly were simply matters to be taken into account in the exercise of discretion. Congress also imposed in 1996 a new one-year deadline (with limited exceptions) to apply for asylum, but that deadline does not apply to withholding. This change has significantly limited the ameliorative effect of *Pula*, because now a late filer can win protection only by showing that persecution is more likely than not. We will consider these mandatory bars to protection in Chapter Six, but let us pose this general question now: should certain conduct (fraud, passage through third countries, crimes, connections with terrorist organizations) be relevant to the discretionary aspect of granting or denying asylum on a case-by-case basis, or instead be laid out in the statute or regulations as general rules?

3. The issue of discretion has a special salience when eligibility for protection is based on a showing of past persecution. The next section of this chapter shows how past persecution and discretion are intertwined.

## SECTION D.   PAST PERSECUTION

The statutory definition of "refugee" in INA § 101(a)(42) refers to "persecution or a well-founded fear of persecution" as the basis for asylum. The second part of the phrase—"well-founded fear of persecution"—has been understood to refer to future persecution. The first part of this phrase—"persecution" (which has no counterpart in Article 1(A)(2) of the Convention definition)—has been understood to refer to persecution in the past. The following BIA decision analyzes the significance of past persecution under the statute and regulations. The decision is also a leading case for defining "particular social group"; here we omit that part of the decision but return to it in Chapter Four.

### 1.   THE SIGNIFICANCE OF PAST PERSECUTION

### MATTER OF H–

Board of Immigration Appeals, 1996.
21 I & N Dec. 337.

ROSENBERG, BOARD MEMBER:

\* \* \*

The decision of the Immigration Judge denying the applicant's request for relief rested on the conclusion that "there is no evidence there is a government in Somalia. A person is not entitled to political asylum in the United States because of clan warfare or because of civil warfare." \* \* \*

\* \* \* We find that the Immigration Judge erred as a matter of law in dismissing the factual and political context in which the claim arose, and in failing to give appropriate consideration to the claim of persecution on account of membership in a particular social group made by the applicant.

\* \* \*

III.   Law Governing the Applicant's Claim of Past Persecution

In the adjudication of an application for asylum or withholding of deportation, the first issue to be resolved is whether the applicant qualifies as a refugee. An applicant may so qualify based upon past persecution, a well-founded fear of persecution, or a clear probability of persecution, on account of a ground provided for by the Act. We limit our discussion here, given the facts of the case before us, to the adjudication of cases involving claims of past persecution.

\* \* \*

That past persecution can be the basis for a successful asylum claim is clear from the language of the statute. Section 208 of the Act provides that an alien may be granted asylum if he is found to be a "refugee" within the meaning of section 101(a)(42)(A) of the Act *"because of persecution."* (Emphasis added.)

\* \* \*

IV.   Evidence of Persecution Suffered by the Applicant

The applicant is a native of Somalia and an undisputed member of the Darood clan and the Marehan subclan, an entity which is identifiable by kinship ties and vocal inflection or accent. For 21 years Somalia had been ruled by Mohammed Siad Barre, a member of the Marehan subclan, which constitutes less than 1 percent of the population of Somalia. In December of 1990, an uprising was instituted by members of the other clans, which ultimately caused Mohammed Siad Barre to relinquish his power and to flee the capital city of Mogadishu on January 21, 1991.

As a result of favoritism that had been shown to members of the Marehan subclan during the course of Mohammed Siad Barre's often brutal regime, the clans which rebelled against his rule sought to retaliate against those who had benefited from the regime. The applicant's father, a businessman who had greatly benefited from his membership in the Marehan subclan, was murdered at his place of business in Mogadishu on January 12, 1991, by members of the opposition United Somali Congress, composed mostly of members of the Hawiye clan. The applicant's family home, located in the Marehan section of the city, was targeted 2 days later by the same group. During the course of that attack, the applicant's brother was shot. He was later murdered at the hospital to which he had been brought for the treatment of his injury.

On January 13, 1991, 1 day after the attack on the applicant's home, he fled Mogadishu with his step-mother and younger siblings to a smaller town, Kismayu, which was a stronghold of the Darood clan. Approximately 1 month later, that town was attacked by the United Somali Congress. As a result, the applicant, who was not with his family at the time, was rounded up and detained without charges along with many other Darood clan members. During the course of his 5-day detention, the applicant was badly beaten on his head, back, and forearm with a rifle butt and a bayonet, resulting in scars to his body which remain to the present. A maternal uncle of the applicant, who was a member of the United Somali Congress, recognized him and assisted in his escape, driving him approximately 40 kilometers in the direction of Kenya. The applicant traveled the rest of the way to Kenya, approximately 90 kilometers, by foot. He reunited with his family in the town of Leboi, Kenya, where they remained until April 1992, when they were transferred to a refugee camp elsewhere in Kenya. The applicant lived in that camp until August of 1994 when he was able to procure funds through a relative in Saudi Arabia which allowed him to travel to the United States.

\* \* \*

[The Board concluded that the applicant had been persecuted on account of membership in a "particular social group," namely his membership in his clan. Chapter Four will set out and examine this part of the decision.]

V.   Adjudication of Asylum Requests Involving Past Persecution

### A.   *Regulatory Presumption of the Well–Founded Fear of Future Persecution*

A finding of past persecution gives rise to a regulatory presumption that the applicant has a well-founded fear of future persecution. The regulations provide in pertinent part that an applicant who has established past persecution

> shall be presumed also to have a well-founded fear of persecution unless a preponderance of the evidence establishes that since the time the persecution occurred conditions . . . have changed to such an extent that the applicant no longer has a well-founded fear.

8 C.F.R. § 208.13(b)(1)(i). They further provide as follows:

> An application for asylum shall be denied if the applicant . . . is determined not also to have a well-founded fear of future persecution . . . unless it is determined that the applicant has demonstrated compelling reasons for being unwilling to return . . . arising out of the severity of the past persecution.

8 C.F.R. § 208.13(b)(1)(ii).

An alien who has demonstrated past persecution is not separately required by 8 C.F.R. § 208.13(b)(1)(ii) to demonstrate compelling reasons for being unwilling to return to his or her country of nationality or last habitual residence in order to be granted asylum. Rather, he or she is considered to have established eligibility for asylum both on account of the past persecution which has been demonstrated and the well-founded fear of future persecution which is presumed. The need to demonstrate compelling reasons for being unwilling to return resulting from the severity of the past persecution suffered by the applicant only arises if the presumption of a well-founded fear of future persecution is successfully rebutted.

To overcome the regulatory presumption, the record must reflect, by a preponderance of the evidence, that since the time the persecution occurred, conditions in the applicant's country of nationality or last habitual residence have changed to such an extent that the applicant no longer has a well-founded fear of being persecuted if he or she were to return to that country. 8 C.F.R. § 208.13(b)(1)(i). As a practical matter, it will be the Service's burden to rebut the presumption, whether by adducing additional evidence or resting upon evidence already in the record. We reiterate that notwithstanding such circumstances, for compelling reasons, an applicant may be afforded asylum even where the evidence establishes such a change in conditions that he or she may be found to no longer have a well-founded fear of persecution. Compelling reasons arising out of the severity of the past persecution suffered may be found on the basis of evidence already in the record or by presentation of additional evidence by the applicant.

### B. Exercise of Discretion

Statutory and regulatory eligibility for asylum, whether based on past persecution or a well-founded fear of future persecution, does not necessarily compel a grant of asylum. *INS v. Cardoza–Fonseca, supra.* An applicant for asylum has the burden of establishing that the favorable exercise of discretion is warranted. *Matter of Pula,* 19 I & N Dec. 467 (BIA 1987); *Matter of Shirdel,* 19 I & N Dec. 33 (BIA 1984). Factors which fall short of the grounds of mandatory denial may constitute discretionary considerations. In exercising discretion, the Board has considered it appropriate to examine the totality of the circumstances and actions of an alien in his or her flight from the country where persecution is feared. Once an applicant has established that he or she is a refugee on the basis of past persecution, a grant of asylum may, in select circumstances and as a matter of discretion, be founded solely on the basis of past persecution.

\* \* \*

Central to a discretionary finding in past persecution cases should be careful attention to compelling, humanitarian considerations that would be involved if the refugee were to be forced to return to a country where he or she was persecuted in the past. We note that the regulation follows the principle set forth by the Board in *Matter of Chen,* [20 I & N Dec. 16 (BIA 1989),] that, in certain instances, asylum should be granted in the exercise of discretion, even where there is little likelihood of future persecution, such as where the asylum applicant has suffered such severe persecution that he or she should not be expected to repatriate. *See also Matter of B–,* [21 I & N Dec. 66 (BIA 1995).]

Our caselaw also recognizes that general humanitarian reasons, independent of the circumstances that led to the applicant's refugee status, such as his or her age, health, or family ties, should also be considered in the exercise of discretion. *Matter of Pula, supra.* Although the totality of circumstances and actions of an alien in his or her flight from the country where persecution was suffered to the United States are to be considered, and may weigh against a favorable exercise of discretion, "the danger of persecution should generally outweigh all but the most egregious of adverse factors." *Matter of Pula, supra,* at 474.

\* \* \*

In the [proceedings on remand], we provide the Service, as well as the applicant, the opportunity to adduce evidence regarding current country conditions in Somalia. The parties will also have the opportunity to introduce any evidence or information relevant to the exercise of discretion. On remand the Immigration Judge should consider the following: the conditions that the applicant would face in Somalia; the possibility of future persecution; the degree of the persecution suffered by the applicant; and humanitarian considerations relevant to the applicant's case.

Insofar as the issue of this applicant's sojourn outside of Somalia may be relevant to the Immigration Judge's determination on remand, it would be appropriate for the Immigration Judge to consider the circumstances of the applicant's stay in Kenya based upon any information presented by the parties. Particular attention should be given to whether the applicant, while resident in a refugee camp in Kenya, was provided protection against *refoulement* consistent with the United States' commitment to *nonrefoulement* which is embodied in its ratification of the United Nations Protocol Relating to the Status of Refugees, Jan. 31, 1967, [1968] 19 U.S.T. 6223, T.I.A.S. No. 6577, 606 U.N.T.S. 267. Further, it may be relevant to address the issue of country-wide persecution and whether the applicant could avoid persecution anywhere in Somalia.[7]

## VI. Conclusion

This Board has found that the applicant in these proceedings suffered past persecution. It is now for the Immigration Judge to consider and rule upon any factors relevant to the ultimate disposition of the application for relief. We emphasize that by the remand of these proceedings, we in no way suggest a desired disposition before the Immigration Judge.

\* \* \*

**7.** This Board has found that it is appropriate to consider in the exercise of discretion whether an applicant, who is eligible for asylum based upon a well-founded fear of persecution, has the ability and can reasonably be expected to relocate in his or her home country. *Matter of R-*, 20 I & N Dec. 621 (BIA 1992). Where, as here, the well-founded fear is of a nongovernmental authority, the question arises as to whether that authority has the ability to persecute the applicant throughout the home country, and whether the applicant would have to pass through any unsafe part of Somalia. In particular, should the Service contend that the applicant would not face persecution throughout Somalia, the Service should clarify how it accomplishes the deportation of such individuals to a protected area.

[The dissenting opinion of BOARD MEMBER HEILMAN is omitted here but is set out in the edited version of *Matter of H–* that appears in Chapter Four].

## Notes and Questions

1.  Note that proof of past persecution plays two related but distinctly different roles—one evidentiary and one permitting discretionary relief for past victims even in the absence of future persecution. We focus first on the evidentiary use. According to the regulations, an asylum applicant who establishes past persecution "shall also be presumed to have a well-founded fear of persecution on the basis of the original claim." The government may rebut this presumption in limited ways, either (A) if there has been a fundamental change in circumstances such that the applicant no longer has a well-founded fear of persecution, or (B) the applicant could avoid future persecution by internal relocation when it would be reasonable to expect. *See* 8 C.F.R. § 208.13(b)(1)(i).

Why do the regulations set forth a formal evidentiary presumption? If there were no regulation on this particular question, what would be the evidentiary effect of an applicant's proof that he was persecuted in the past? Is the presumption approach too formalistic given the ways in which adjudicators are likely to approach the already difficult task of evaluating evidence in asylum cases? You may wish to keep this question in mind when we consider factfinding in greater detail in Chapter Eight.

2.  In *Matter of Chen*, 20 I & N Dec. 16 (BIA 1989), decided before any regulations addressed the past persecution issue, the Board ruled that past persecution established the rebuttable evidentiary presumption, and also held that discretion might appropriately be exercised to grant asylum, even if there were no risk of future persecution, to persons who had in the past "suffered under atrocious forms of persecution" (quoting from the UNHCR Handbook). Applying that principle, the Board granted asylum to Chen based on the treatment that he and his family suffered, because they were Christians, at the hands of the Red Guards during the Cultural Revolution in China. Though the Board found that Chen did not establish a well-founded fear of future persecution, the severity of Chen's mistreatment, which resulted in permanent injury and psychological trauma, made Chen statutorily eligible for asylum. This approach was later embodied in the regulations cited in the preceding opinion.

3.  Does *Matter of H–* dilute the *Chen* requirement and allow asylum in past persecution cases based on "general humanitarian reasons" rather than "atrocious" past persecution? Would such a dilution be sound policy? This consideration was especially important after the many striking changes of government that took place throughout the world in the late 1980s and early 1990s, as well as the settlement of the major conflicts in Central America around that time. Because a substantial number of U.S. asylum cases in that period turned on past persecution analysis, and because the INS was concerned that *Matter of H–* could be read to allow too much leeway for discretionary grants of asylum in the absence of a future risk, the INS pressed for new regulations on this point. They retain "compelling reasons" as the central factor permitting a grant of asylum based on past persecution

alone when the adjudicator decides that there is no well-founded fear of future persecution, but then go on to specify one further additional basis for a grant to a past victim in these circumstances: when there is a "reasonable possibility that he or she may suffer other serious harm upon removal to that country." 8 C.F.R. § 208.13(b)(1)(iii). The supplementary material published with the proposed rule, 63 Fed. Reg. 31945–50 (1998), suggests that this clause refers to harm as severe as persecution, but harm not inflicted on the basis of one of the five grounds. It does not include mere economic disadvantage or the inability to practice one's profession.

4.   U.S. law appears to be far more favorable toward claims based solely on past persecution than is the 1951 Convention. The INA definition recognizes refugee status when one is outside the country of origin "because of *persecution or* a well-founded fear of persecution." INA § 101(a)(42)(A) (emphasis added). Compare the analogous phrase in Article 1(A)(2) of the Convention definition: "owing to a well-founded fear of persecution." Does U.S. law then contravene the treaty? The treaty does treat some persons as refugees in the absence of a future risk, if there are compelling reasons, but it applies only to the narrow class identified in Article 1(A)(1). *See* the last sentence of Article 1(C). What is that class and why would the drafters have taken that approach?

5.   Consistent with the Convention, the central question in the asylum systems of most countries is essentially forward-looking, trying to determine what is likely to happen to the individual in the future if she returns to her home country. *See* J. Hathaway, The Law of Refugee Status 65–80 (1991). But consider this, from Judge Posner:

> If * * * the ultimate issue is what will happen to the alien when he is deported, one may wonder why past persecution figures at all in the decisional process. Why isn't the orientation of the inquiry entirely forward-looking? The answer is twofold. The past is sufficiently predictive of the future to warrant a shifting of the burden of production. But, as explained in *Chen*, the past has an additional significance, independent of prediction and therefore not necessarily affected by a demonstration that the alien is in no danger of being persecuted in the future. The experience of persecution may so sear a person with distressing associations with his native country that it would be inhumane to force him to return there, even though he is in no danger of further persecution. Very few of the surviving German Jews returned to Germany after the destruction of the Nazi regime, and it would have been cruel to force them to do so on the ground that bygones are bygones. In such cases the attempted rebuttal fails; in lesser cases of past persecution and perhaps even in the most serious cases if the persecuted group has become the ruling group, deportation may not be inhumane.

*Skalak v. INS*, 944 F.2d 364, 365 (7th Cir. 1991).

6.   Just what is "persecution" for purposes of the past persecution inquiry? Some courts have set very demanding standards. *See, e.g., Mikhael v. INS*, 115 F.3d 299, 304 (5th Cir. 1997) (no past persecution where applicant was briefly detained twice and had suffered the bombing of his home, his father was kidnapped and held three days, and a brother was

kidnapped and tortured for several days); *Prasad v. INS,* 47 F.3d 336 (9th Cir. 1995) (no past persecution where applicant was interrogated, beaten, and kicked while detained for six hours); *Ozdemir v. INS,* 46 F.3d 6, 7 (5th Cir. 1994) (no past persecution where applicant was detained three days and beaten on the soles of his feet); *Kapcia v. INS,* 944 F.2d 702, 705 (10th Cir. 1991) (no past persecution where applicants had been detained, beaten on occasion, fired from a job, and their houses were searched).

Other cases have seemingly gone to the opposite extreme, finding past threats or harassment, without physical harm, to be past persecution that shifts the burden of proof to the government. *See, e.g., Salazar–Paucar v. INS,* 281 F.3d 1069 (9th Cir.), *amended and rehearing denied,* 290 F.3d 964 (9th Cir. 2002) (threats to former barrio president by Shining Path guerrillas in Peru); *Vallecillo–Castillo v. INS,* 121 F.3d 1237, 1239 (9th Cir. 1996) (threats by Sandinista supporters in Nicaragua to person related to jailed Somoza supporters, accompanied by vandalism of his house). Compare the following ruling: "We have left open the possibility that threats of a most immediate and menacing nature might, in some circumstances, constitute past persecution. In the vast majority of cases, however, mere threats will not, in and of themselves, compel a finding of past persecution. Rather, unfulfilled threats will fall within that category of past experience more properly viewed as indicative of the danger of future persecution." *Boykov v. INS,* 109 F.3d 413, 416 (7th Cir. 1997).

What about the related argument that the effects of past persecution are such that past persecution constitutes a permanent and continuing act of persecution? Consider the next case, especially its reading and application of the governing regulation, 8 C.F.R. § 208.13(b)(1), an earlier version of which was the focus of the BIA's past persecution analysis in *Matter of H-.*

## 2. PAST PERSECUTION AS PERPETUAL PERSECUTION

### MATTER OF Y–T–L–

Board of Immigration Appeals, 2003, en banc.
23 I & N Dec. 601.

GRANT, BOARD MEMBER:

The respondent is a native and citizen of the People's Republic of China, who entered the United States in 1993 without valid entry documents. He is married and has three children. His family remains in China.

The respondent testified that the Chinese Government imposed a large fine after the birth of his second child and that he was only able to pay the fine with the assistance of his younger brother, who helped him borrow money. He indicated that his wife was forced to have an intra-uterine device ("IUD") inserted after the birth of their second child. However, she was simultaneously informed that she soon would have to undergo sterilization. In February 1985 they paid to have the IUD removed in secret, because they wanted additional children. The respondent's third child, a son, was born in December 1985. His wife was taken for sterilization in March 1986, and a substantial fine was imposed in April 1986.

Although the respondent and his wife were allowed to register their son in the household registry after the payment of the fine, they were not allowed to register him in school. He could attend school, but only with the payment of very high tuition. Their two daughters were suspended from school for one semester. The Government also confiscated land assigned to the family, from which they earned their livelihood by farming. They survived by borrowing money from friends and relatives to live and pay the fines, and eventually the respondent was employed in a relative's store.

\* \* \*

In his decision, the Immigration Judge accepted the respondent's testimony as credible, finding that he is married, that he and his wife have three children, and that his wife was subjected to involuntary sterilization pursuant to a coercive population control program. The Immigration Judge concluded that these facts established past persecution \* \* \*

The Immigration Judge noted, however, that \* \* \* the respondent remained in China for more than 7 years after his wife was sterilized, and he found no evidence that "anything significant has happened to either the respondent or his family in China" subsequent to his wife's sterilization and the payment of fines in 1986. He concluded that "with the passage of time and the lack of evidence of any further persecution," the Service met its burden of proving by a preponderance of the evidence that there had been a fundamental change in circumstances such that the respondent no longer has a well-founded fear of persecution. The Immigration Judge therefore denied the respondent's applications for asylum, withholding of removal, and relief under the Convention Against Torture.

\* \* \*

[Board Member Grant explained the 1996 amendment to INA § 101(a)(42) that overruled *Chang* with respect to coercive population control programs. See note 4 following *Chang*, earlier in this chapter at p. 99.]

\* \* \*

The [past persecution] regulation at issue \* \* \* was amended through the publication of a final rule, which became effective on January 5, 2001. The final rule amended 8 C.F.R. § 208.13(b)(1) to provide, in pertinent part, as follows:

> An applicant who has been found to have established such past persecution shall also be presumed to have a well-founded fear of persecution on the basis of the original claim. That presumption may be rebutted if an asylum officer or immigration judge makes one of the [following] findings. . . .

(i) Discretionary referral or denial. [A]n immigration judge, in the exercise of his or her discretion, shall deny the asylum application of an alien found to be a refugee on the basis of past persecution if any of the following is found by a preponderance of the evidence:

(A) There has been a fundamental change in circumstances such that the applicant no longer has a well-founded fear of persecution in the applicant's country of nationality, or if stateless, in the applicant's country of last habitual residence, on account of race, religion, nationality, membership in a particular social group, or political opinion....

(ii) Burden of proof. In cases in which an applicant has demonstrated past persecution under paragraph (b)(1) of this section, the Service shall bear the burden of establishing by a preponderance of the evidence the requirements of paragraphs (b)(1)(i)(A) or (B) of this section.

\* \* \*

We disagree with the Immigration Judge that the passage of time since the forced sterilization of the respondent's wife, coupled with the lack of enforcement of coercive family planning measures during that period, constitutes a "fundamental change" in the respondent's personal circumstances \* \* \*. The Immigration Judge's conclusion fails to take into account the continuing nature of the persecution inflicted on the respondent and his wife. Moreover, the principal reason that the respondent and his wife no longer fear a coerced sterilization or abortion, or future fines for "over-birth," is the fact that they have been rendered incapable of having children. Thus, the Immigration Judge's rationale could lead to the anomalous result that the act of persecution itself would also constitute the change in circumstances that would result in the denial of asylum to persons such as the respondent. It is highly unlikely that Congress contemplated such an interpretation when it deemed forced involuntary sterilization to be persecution on account of political opinion.

We recognize that the Immigration Judge premised his finding of changed circumstances primarily on the passage of time, and not on the act of sterilization itself. The logic of his analysis, which is amplified by the dissenting opinion of Board Member Filppu, is that persecution in this context must be addressed in a prospective fashion. As noted by the dissent, this prospective view is not only unobjectionable, but is a bedrock principle of refugee law, codified in the redrafted provisions of 8 C.F.R. § 208.13(b)(1). In this particular context, however, a purely prospective view, focusing on a well-founded fear of persecution in the future, would appear to limit relief under the amended refugee definition to those cases where involuntary sterilization has been threatened, but not carried out. While the dissent suggests that the finding of "changed circumstances" might not occur in cases where the involuntary sterilization has been carried out more recently, the fact remains that a completed sterilization removes any reasonable, objective basis on which to fear a future act of coerced abortion or sterilization. Fines for family planning violations could still be imposed, but our decisions in this area suggest that such fines rarely rise to the level of persecution.

To some extent, therefore, this case presents a dilemma. The respondent has, without question, sustained past persecution, which makes him eligible for asylum under the amended statute and our decisions * * *. On the other hand, the respondent has no reasonable basis to fear this form of persecution in the future, based on the very fact that he has already been persecuted. The keys to resolving this dilemma are to recognize the special nature of the persecution at issue here, and to give full force to the intent of Congress in extending asylum to those who have sustained such persecution. We consider these issues in reverse order.

First, * * * [i]t is manifestly clear that Congress intended to make eligible for asylum those who were victims of China's coercive family planning policy, not simply those who could be victims if returned to China. See, e.g., 142 Cong. Rec. H2629, H2633 (daily ed. Mar. 21, 1996) (statement of Rep. Christopher Smith). Our administrative decisions, and those of the various Immigration Courts, have granted asylum to significant numbers of persons who themselves, or whose spouses, have suffered involuntary sterilization within the meaning of the Act.

* * *

Second, in light of Congress's specific intent regarding the eligibility for asylum of past victims of coercive family planning practices, we cannot conclude that such an act of persecution can constitute a "change in circumstances" for purposes of the regulation. The act of forced sterilization should not be viewed as a discrete, onetime act, comparable to a term in prison, or an incident of severe beating or even torture. Coerced sterilization is better viewed as a permanent and continuing act of persecution that has deprived a couple of the natural fruits of conjugal life, and the society and comfort of the child or children that might eventually have been born to them. * * *

Finally, while this issue is not before us, it is fair to assume that if the respondent's spouse was subjected to a forced abortion, as opposed to a forced sterilization, the possibility of the spouse becoming pregnant and being subject to another forced abortion would preclude the argument that the forced abortion constitutes a "fundamental change" in circumstances for purposes of the regulation. We do not believe that it would be consistent with the intent of Congress for us to grant asylum to those subjected to a forced abortion, while denying relief to those subjected to a forced sterilization, simply because only the former act of persecution is one capable of repetition.

\* \* \*

In view of the foregoing, we find that the respondent has established statutory eligibility for asylum on account of past persecution and that the regulatory presumption of a well-founded fear of persecution arising from such past persecution has not been rebutted. Moreover, the facts cited are sufficient to support a conditional grant of asylum in the exercise of discretion. We further find that the respondent is eligible for withholding of removal. \* \* \*

\* \* \*

Dissenting opinion: LAURI STEVEN FILPPU, BOARD MEMBER, in which LORI L. SCIALABBA, CHAIRMAN, joined.

## I. INTRODUCTION

I respectfully dissent because I believe the majority misreads both the scope of the statute and the import of the regulation at issue here. The majority fails to recognize that this is a case of past harm, where an alien's eligibility for relief is governed by specific regulatory provisions focusing exclusively on either the "severity of the past persecution" or the "reasonable possibility" that the alien may suffer "other serious harm upon removal" that does not technically qualify as persecution. \* \* \*

Instead of following the regulatory tests governing relief when a well-founded fear of future persecution is absent, the majority construes the statute to preclude a denial of relief to the respondent. The majority, however, never actually focuses on the language of the statute in ruling that changed circumstances cannot exist for the spouse of a sterilization victim. Instead, it simply announces a new theory treating the respondent's past harm as a "permanent and continuing act of persecution." The majority's new perpetual persecution doctrine is not supported by our past case law, and it certainly is not reflected in the regulatory structure controlling asylum determinations.

The majority's ruling has the effect of preventing adjudicators from considering particular facts bearing on traditional refugee determinations, specifically, the effect of past sterilization on the risk of future harm or the severity of past harm. Not only is that ruling at odds with the existing regulatory structure, but it is inconsistent with basic precepts of refugee law. Those precepts involve protecting persons from future persecution and providing humanitarian relief to select individuals with severe past harm, even absent a risk of future persecution. The statute does not foreclose an application of the regulation in this case, and the majority's rationale turns our traditional asylum law on its head.

\* \* \*

I agree with both the Immigration Judge and the majority that the respondent has shown past persecution * * *.

As a result of this persecution, the respondent formed an intention to leave China in 1986 and succeeded in leaving in 1993, which was 7 years after his wife's sterilization and the imposition of the last fine. By that time, the fines had been paid and the relatives who loaned funds to pay the fines were evidently also repaid or had forgiven the debt. The respondent had found new employment and was able to make the tuition payments for his son. His wife had recovered from the infections she experienced after the sterilization. Further, at the time of the respondent's 2001 removal hearing, his family was continuing to live in China in the family home and his children were in school. His continuing concerns pertained to the tuition payments for his son and his son's ability to pursue a high school and college education.

The Immigration Judge found that there was "no evidence that since the sterilization and the payment of fines in 1986 that anything significant has happened to either the respondent or his family in China." The Immigration Judge also found that there had been no showing that the respondent was economically "worse off" by virtue of working at a relative's store in China in comparison to his prior employment as a farmer. Importantly, the Immigration Judge determined that the respondent had not been "persecuted" subsequent to his wife's 1986 sterilization, that there was no evidence that China would be inclined to harm the respondent or his wife today * * * particularly when his wife and children had remained in China "without incident" for 15 years following the sterilization.

Neither the respondent on appeal nor the majority seriously disputes any of the Immigration Judge's factual determinations. Neither makes any attempt to show how the respondent might actually experience any meaningful harm beyond that which has already occurred to him and his wife, and the majority acknowledges that "the respondent has no reasonable basis to fear . . . persecution in the future."

### III.　The Majority's Decision

The majority does not attack, as a matter of fact, the Immigration Judge's determination that there has been a "fundamental change in circumstances" within the meaning of 8 C.F.R. § 208.13(b)(1)(i)(A). Instead, the majority rules that such a finding cannot be made as a matter of law.

The majority reaches this conclusion for several reasons. It is concerned that a forced sterilization might never qualify an alien for relief and "could lead to the anomalous result that the act of persecution itself would also constitute the change in circumstances" eliminating the fear of future persecution.* * * Perhaps most significantly, the majority finds sterilization to be a "permanent and continuing act of persecution" that deprives a couple of future children, such that the statute itself actually "precludes the result urged by the Service." *Id.* at 607.

There is, no doubt, some uneasiness in accepting the notion that an act of persecution, here the sterilization of the respondent's wife, can be the primary basis for denying relief on grounds that future acts of persecution will not take place. But, except for its "continuing persecution" theory, neither the majority nor the respondent points to any meaningful new harm that might befall the respondent on return to China. So, as unsettling as the notion might seem initially, it is borne out to be factually accurate on this record.

But the evidence supporting a fundamental change in circumstances is not confined to the act of sterilization. After that sterilization and the contemporaneous fine, the respondent remained in China for 7 years, paying only tuition for his son and occasionally being pointed to as an example of past "bad" behavior. The same is true for the rest of his family, except that they have remained in China and have been free from harm constituting persecution for over 15 years.

We would not likely find a fundamental change in circumstances, despite the sterilization, had China periodically imposed meaningful imprisonment on the respondent for his past population control violations, instead of merely pointing to him as an example for others not to follow. The sterilization is obviously significant, but the case and the Immigration Judge's ruling are about much more than that one persecutory act.

Further, unless there is a bar to their consideration, the sterilization, the payment of all fines, and the subsequent treatment of the respondent and his family fit the literal "fundamental change in circumstances" language of the regulation. Under the governing regulations, this fundamental change, coupled with the absence of any reasonable fear of future persecution, means that we should assess the respondent's eligibility for relief on the strength of past persecution alone. * * *

## IV. The Statute

I agree with the majority that the statutory language reflects an intention to accord benefits to some persons who have been sterilized. As such, it would be inconsistent with the population control amendment to the definition of a "refugee" to construe the revised regulation in such a way as to categorically deny relief to everyone who has been forcibly sterilized. But that is not what the Immigration Judge held.

The statute is intended to accord refugee status each year to 1,000 victims of certain coercive population control practices, including "a person who has been forced to abort a pregnancy or to undergo involuntary sterilization, or who has been persecuted for failure or refusal to undergo such a procedure or for other resistance to a coercive population control program." Section 101(a)(42) of the Immigration and Nationality Act (defining "refugee"); see also section 207(a)(5) of the Act (limiting asylum grants and refugee admissions based on coercive population control methods to 1,000 each fiscal year).[a]

Persons who have themselves been forcibly sterilized fall directly under the terms of the statute. As to those actual victims of forced sterilization, I understand the statute to treat their level of persecution as sufficiently severe to be considered for inclusion among the 1,000 who may get asylum, even if based on that past harm alone. Thus "a person who has been forced ... to undergo involuntary sterilization" qualifies as a "refugee" and may well warrant, by virtue of the very nature of that past harm, one of the 1,000 refugee numbers, if available. Section 101(a)(42) of the Act.

\* \* \* [T]he actual victims of forced sterilizations may qualify for relief on the strength of their past persecution, particularly when they flee soon thereafter or continue to experience additional serious sanctions.\* \* \*

Relief, however, should not be automatic, even for the actual victims of forced sterilizations. Traditional asylum considerations are appropriate. There are differences between a person who departs immediately after a forced sterilization, while perhaps still facing significant unpaid fines, and one who remains for many years leading an otherwise normal life and whose eventual departure is motivated mainly by economic or family reunification concerns. Victims of other forms of severe persecution, who face little likelihood of future harm, are not guaranteed asylum when they have remained for decades in the country of persecution and have been able to enjoy generally normal lives after the events leading to the past persecution.

\* \* \*

The majority is correct that the statute equates persecution arising from a coercive population control program as being persecution "on account of political opinion." The statute, however, does not direct that persons suffering such persecution be exempt from the normal rules that apply to all persons who have suffered past persecution on account of political opinion but who lack a reasonable fear of future persecution. Instead, it is the majority that concocts a new theory of perpetual persecution to justify that exemption.

### V.   The Majority's New Theory

The majority's deviation from long-standing principles of asylum law, and from the analysis directed by the regulations, is most pronounced in its declaration that forced sterilization "is better viewed as a permanent and continuing act of persecution." \* \* \* The majority's perpetual persecution analysis is simply not consistent with either the case law or basic precepts of asylum law.

For example, in *Matter of Chen*, we accepted the alien's account that, because of his past experiences in China, he was "physically

**a.**  As explained earlier in the notes and questions following *Matter of Chang* in Section A of this chapter, page 106, this ceiling was repealed in 2005.—eds.

debilitated, must wear a hearing aid due to his head injury, [was] always anxious and fearful, and [was] often suicidal." We nonetheless found that Chen lacked a well-founded fear of future persecution, but granted relief because of the severity of the past persecution. Importantly, in doing so, we did not declare that Chen's ongoing physical disabilities and continuing psychological trauma amounted to "a permanent and continuing act of persecution," although the daily manifestations of his past persecution could easily have been so described.

I am also not aware that we find perpetual persecution from the death of a family member who was killed to inflict harm on the asylum applicant or even from permanent physical injuries to the applicant himself, such as loss of sight or loss of a limb. Certainly, severe injuries from persecution can give rise to relief for past persecution. The majority's perpetual persecution approach, however, would confine our traditional past persecution analysis to cases where the past injury had no lingering effect, or the majority will need to explain why a deprivation of the ability to procreate is to be given special treatment in comparison to other permanent injuries that can arise from acts of persecution.

Indeed, the majority's continuing or perpetual persecution concept would seem to override even the type of change in country conditions (such as an abandonment of population control measures by China) that we [have in the past] recognized as sufficient * * *.

\* \* \*

Asylum law is primarily about protecting people from future harm and, in select cases, providing humanitarian relief for severe past harm by itself. The goal of protection is not served by providing protection to someone who is not actually in need of protection. The goal of providing humanitarian relief in select cases is not served if the individual is not actually deserving of humanitarian relief.

As serious as forced sterilization is, the majority offers no sound reason to give it special treatment among the range of atrocities having permanent and ongoing consequences that victims of persecution may be forced to endure their entire lives. The continuing nature of past harm is certainly appropriate to weigh as a factor in a traditional *Chen*, past persecution assessment. The continuing nature of past harm, however, is not a basis for circumventing the regulations requiring a past persecution assessment when there is little or no likelihood of future persecution as a matter of fact.

\* \* \*

[The dissenting opinion of PAULEY, BOARD MEMBER, is omitted.]

### Notes and Questions

1.   Is the Board's ruling a sound reading of congressional intent? Of the Convention? Should it make any difference that in *Y–T–L–* it was the unsterilized husband, who had left China without his wife, who was applying for protection?

2. In *Qu v. Gonzales,* 399 F.3d 1195 (9th Cir. 2005), the Ninth Circuit expressed its agreement with *Y–T–L–,* including its conclusion that past persecution, as permanent and continuing persecution, can not only support eligibility for asylum but also guarantee *nonrefoulement.* According to *Qu,* "when an applicant suffers past persecution by means of an involuntary sterilization in accordance with a country's coercive population control policy, he is entitled by virtue of that fact alone to withholding of removal." *Id.* at 1203.

3. The Ninth Circuit also adopted the *Y–T–L–* approach in a case involving female genital cutting suffered by a young Somali woman.

> * * * [T]he extremely painful, physically invasive, psychologically damaging and permanently disfiguring process of genital mutilation undoubtedly rises to the level of persecution. * * * The [BIA] and the court [are] compelled to conclude that the government has failed to rebut the presumption of a well-founded fear of future persecution.
>
> The primary reason that such a conclusion is necessary is that persecution in the form of female genital mutilation is similar to forced sterilization and * * * must be considered a continuing harm that renders a petitioner eligible for asylum, without more.
>
> Like forced sterilization, genital mutilation permanently disfigures a woman, causes long term health problems, and deprives her of a normal and fulfilling sexual life. The World Health organization reports that even the least drastic form of female genital mutilation can cause a wide range of complications such as infection, hemorrhaging from the clitoral artery during childbirth, formation of abscesses, development of cysts and tumors, repeated urinary tract infections, and pseudo infibulation. * * * [I]n addition to the physical and psychological trauma that is common to many forms of persecution [female genital mutilation] involves drastic and emotionally painful consequences that are unending. Therefore, our precedent compels the conclusion that genital mutilation, like forced sterilization, is a "permanent and continuing" act of persecution, which cannot constitute a change in circumstances sufficient to rebut the presumption of a well-founded fear.
>
> Alternatively, even * * * [if] the presumption of a well-founded fear was rebuttable, the government might have some difficulty in establishing that Mohamed would not be subjected to further violence that is related to her past persecution, given the conditions in Somalia. * * * [There is] the possibility that on remand she could demonstrate that she is at risk for further genital mutilation, specifically infibulation, because she has engaged in extramarital sex.

*Mohammed v. Gonzales,* 400 F.3d 785, 799 (9th Cir. 2005).

4. What are the practical implications of *Y–T–L–* and *Mohammed*? Are they consistent with the regulation regarding past persecution? What would be the result if these cases had arisen in a haven country where protection decisions are governed solely by the standards of the Convention?

5. One can easily imagine continuing psychological harm based on many types of past persecution. Would that be sufficient, without more, to prevent the government from rebutting the presumption of future persecution? If not, what are the limiting principles? Is it persecution that alters a woman's reproductive rights? Is it persecution based on violations of bodily integrity? What then of someone who lost a limb as a result of past torture, but the torturing regime has been ousted?

6. Both the BIA in *Y–T–L–* and the Ninth Circuit in *Mohammed* imply there is something about the type of persecution—forced sterilization and forced genital mutilation—that render them a continuing harm. Both *Y–T–L–* and *Mohammed* further decide that these forms of suffering merit the grant of durable asylum in the United States even though there is no need for further protection from the original harm, and indeed even though their lives will include this continuing persecution even if they stay in the United States. Are these cases consistent with the underlying purposes of refugee protection as manifested in the Convention?

---

### Exercise

Victor seeks asylum in the United States based on what happened to him at a labor camp in his home country of Zarastan. At the labor camp, Victor was forced to do hard manual labor for ten hours every day, including cutting wood, hauling lumber and cooking for the entire camp. He was allowed only one meal a day. At the end of each day of work, Victor was forced to attend "reeducation" in an effort to compel him to accept the new Zarastanian government's religious teachings.

On one occasion, when Victor fell while carrying lumber, guards used the lumber to beat him on his face and hands. The guards broke both of Victor's arms, causing permanent muscle and nerve damage that leaves him unable to perform simple movements without rapid fatigue.

After Victor was released from the camp, he made his way to the United States. Since that time, "moderate" religious leaders have moved into the most powerful government posts in Zarastan and have dismantled the labor camps.

You are Victor's attorney. How would argue that his application for asylum should be granted?

Now assume that you are the attorney for the government in this case? How would you respond to the arguments by Victor's attorney?

# Chapter Four

# GROUNDS OF PERSECUTION

*On April 8 at about nine o'clock in the morning, I saw helicopters landing in the hamlets of Nixtamalapa and Papaturro. When I got home I heard a great noise of machine-gun fire directed against our own hamlet of Guadalupe. With my wife, Petrona, I took our children and started running toward the hill with the rest of the inhabitants.*

*The next day we stayed hidden, trying to make the children shut up and not make any noise. At about eleven o'clock I suddenly heard a voice shouting, "Nobody move!" and at the same time came a tremendous burst of machine-gun fire. We took the children and went running up the hill. We were still being machine-gunned, and they threw fire-bombs at us in order to set fire to the dry bush where the people were trying to hide. I saw my wife grab at a reed stem, with our eighteen-month son in her arms, and then both of them fell dead, hit by machine-gun bullets. At the same time my other three children were hit and fell. I took in my arms my only surviving child, Blanca, aged four, and followed the people in front of me. Running very hard, we managed to cross over the hill and reach a dry ravine.*

*After resting there for about an hour, we suddenly heard the soldiers approaching and realized we were surrounded. They aimed their guns at us, and the one who seemed to be command said: "Nobody move! Lay down your arms!" We weren't armed, so we answered: "As the Lord is with us, these are our arms," and we embraced the children and pointed to them.*

*The next day they took us to Santa Cruz Michapa, and on the way the soldiers destroyed the few maize plots that were left, and besides insulting us they were talking to each other so that we would hear, saying they wanted to drink blood and eat meat.*

*When we got to Santa Cruz Michapa they took us to the courthouse. We were assembled inside the building, and the captain told us: "I have brought you here together to tell you that nothing is going to happen to you. We are going to the Red*

*Cross. You must forget the subversives. You can go to San Salvador or back to where you lived before. But each and everyone of you is going to collaborate with us."*

—Campesino, El Salvador[1]

The 1951 Convention limits refugee status to those who have a "well founded fear of being persecuted *for reasons of* race, religion, nationality, membership of a particular social group or political opinion." U.S. legislation uses similar language: refugees are those who have "a well-founded fear of persecution *on account of* race, religion, nationality, membership in a particular social group, or political opinion," INA § 101(a)(42)(A). Withholding is available to those whose "life or freedom would be threatened * * * *because of* race, religion, nationality, membership in a particular social group, or political opinion." INA § 241(b)(3). All these formulations make clear that persecution itself is not sufficient to trigger refugee protection. Rather, individuals must prove that the persecution they fear is linked—in a certain way—to one of five grounds. Or, as much of the commentary frames it, there must be a connection, or a nexus, between the persecution and race, religion, nationality, membership in a particular social group, or political opinion.

On the face of it, this seems straightforward. All who fear persecution may desire protection, but refugee status is reserved for a subset of the persecuted. Persecution based solely on a personal grudge or persecution solely to secure financial gain will not result in refugee status. Some of this linkage between persecution and the five grounds is implicit in the very notion of "persecution," as indicated by the definitions in Chapter Three at pp. 97. That is, harsh sanctions do not usually amount to persecution unless they are inflicted on the basis of some characteristic that is thought not to justify such a response. A person imprisoned at hard labor after a valid conviction for armed robbery is not being persecuted.

Out of this seemingly clear-cut element of the refugee definition, however, the developing law has uncovered many complex questions. What are the outer limits of each of the five specified grounds? The statute explicitly calls for attention to these linkages, and the BIA sometimes requires close connection between the allegedly persecuting act and the precise basis or motive for the oppression before the threat can serve as a valid foundation for asylum. What if a persecutor incorrectly believes the victim to belong to a certain racial or religious or political group? Whose political opinion is relevant—the persecutor's or the victim's? What kind of connection must there be between the persecution and the ground? What if multiple factors are involved?

This chapter examines these questions, which are often difficult to separate neatly. We start our study of the law concerning the grounds of persecution by exploring what it means to be persecuted based on

1. C. Kismaric, Forced Out: The Agony
of the Refugee in Our Time 43–44 (1989).

political opinion. We begin there not only because political opinion is a concept that engendered vociferous debate in difficult cases involving civil war situations, but also because the approaches to political opinion that the federal courts and the Board of Immigration Appeals developed after the passage of the Refugee Act of 1980 laid the foundation for the prevailing approaches to all five grounds.

After political opinion, we look at cases that involve some combination of race, nationality, and religion to define groups that face persecution. We then turn to recent decisions on asylum claims involving allegations of persecution based on religious practices. Finally we survey the jurisprudence concerning persecution based on membership in a particular social group, a legal term that has presented a welter of conceptual difficulties.

## SECTION A.   POLITICAL OPINION

For many years the majority of asylum cases filed in the United States appeared to rely on fears of persecution based on political opinion. Many of these cases involved "classic" political opinion claims: the asylum seeker was a recognizable political dissident, the asylum seeker had participated in political demonstrations, and so on. The unfortunate growth of armed insurrections and civil wars in the late twentieth century generated new legal challenges in the asylum system as they spawned many claims of politically motivated persecution that did not fit within this paradigm. Two topics—neutrality and imputed political opinion—presented special difficulties, not only because each poses difficult questions individually, but also because they interact in complex ways.

Drawing by Amra, 12 years old, Croatian refugee. (Doctors
Without Borders/Médecins Sans Frontières)

## 1. NEUTRALITY

At one end of the spectrum, neutrality can be the result of apathy—of lack of any political opinion. At the other end, neutrality can be an articulated political view that expressly rejects the political aims of warring factions. In addition to the variety of thoughts, motives, and conduct that might be described as "neutrality," historical contexts vary. In revolutionary situations, such as the American colonial war against England, the warring factions often force the population to take sides. Those who proclaim themselves neutral are considered disloyal by both opponents. In other circumstances those proclaiming neutrality are left alone. The intersection of these issues came to the fore in the United States in a series of opinions reviewing asylum claims asserted by individuals from Central American societies riven by armed conflict. The next decision illustrates the BIA's approach.

## MATTER OF ACOSTA

Board of Immigration Appeals, 1985.
19 I & N Dec. 211.

* * * [T]he respondent testified, and attested in an affidavit attached to his asylum application, to the following facts. In 1976 he, along with several other taxi drivers, founded COTAXI, a cooperative organization of taxi drivers of about 150 members. COTAXI was designed to enable its members to contribute the money they earned toward the purchase of their taxis. It was one of five taxi cooperatives in the city of San Salvador and one of many taxi cooperatives throughout the country of El Salvador. Between 1978 and 1981, the respondent held three management positions with COTAXI, the duties of which he described in detail, and his last position with the cooperative was that of general manager. He held that position from 1979 through February or March of 1981. During the time he was the general manager of COTAXI, the respondent continued on the weekends to work as a taxi driver.

Starting around 1978, COTAXI and its drivers began receiving phone calls and notes requesting them to participate in work stoppages. The requests were anonymous but the respondent and the other members of COTAXI believed them to be from anti-government guerrillas who had targeted small businesses in the transportation industry for work stoppages, in hopes of damaging El Salvador's economy. COTAXI's board of directors refused to comply with the requests because its members wished to keep working, and as a result COTAXI received threats of retaliation. Over the course of several years, COTAXI was threatened about 15 times. The other taxi cooperatives in the city also received similar threats.

Beginning in about 1979, taxis were seized and burned, or used as barricades, and COTAXI drivers were assaulted or killed. Ultimately, five members of COTAXI were killed in their taxis by unknown persons.

Three of the COTAXI drivers who were killed were friends of the respondent and, like him, had been founders and officers of COTAXI. Each was killed after receiving an anonymous note threatening his life. One of these drivers, who died from injuries he sustained when he crashed his cab in order to avoid being shot by his passengers, told his friends before he died that three men identifying themselves as guerrillas had jumped into his taxi, demanded possession of his car, and announced they were going to kill him.

During January and February 1981, the respondent received three anonymous notes threatening his life. The first note, which was slipped through the window of his taxi and was addressed to the manager of COTAXI, stated: "Your turn has come, because you are a traitor." The second note, which was also put on the respondent's car, was directed to "the driver of Taxi No. 95," which was the car owned by the respondent, and warned: "You are on the black list." The third note was placed on the respondent's car in front of his home, was addressed to the manager of COTAXI, and stated: "We are going to execute you as a traitor." In February 1981, the respondent was beaten in his cab by three men who then warned him not to call the police and took his taxi. The respondent is of the opinion that the men who threatened his life and assaulted him were guerrillas who were seeking to disrupt transportation services in the city of San Salvador. He also has the impression, however, that COTAXI was not favored by some government officials because they viewed the cooperative as being too socialistic.

After being assaulted and receiving the three threatening notes, the respondent left El Salvador because he feared for his life. * * *

* * *

[The BIA analyzed whether the respondent feared "persecution on account of membership in a particular social group" and concluded that he did not. This part of *Acosta* is excerpted later in this chapter, in Section D.]

* * * [T]he respondent did not demonstrate that the persecution he fears is "on account of political opinion." The fact that the respondent was threatened by the guerrillas as part of a campaign to destabilize the government demonstrates that the guerrillas' actions were undertaken to further their political goals in the civil controversy in El Salvador. However, conduct undertaken to further the goals of one faction in a political controversy does not necessarily constitute persecution "on account of political opinion" so as to qualify an alien as a "refugee" within the meaning of the Act.

As we have previously discussed, the term "persecution" means the infliction of suffering or harm in order to punish an individual for possessing a particular belief or characteristic the persecutor seeks to overcome. It follows, therefore, that the requirement of "persecution on account of political opinion" means that the particular belief or characteristic a persecutor seeks to overcome in an individual must be his political opinion. Thus, the requirement of "persecution on account of political opinion" refers not to the ultimate political end that may be served by persecution, but to the belief held by an individual that causes him to be the object of the persecution. * * *

In the respondent's case there are no facts showing that the guerrillas were aware of or sought to punish the respondent for his political opinion; nor was there any showing that the respondent's refusal to participate in the work-stoppages was motivated by his political opinion. Absent such a showing the respondent failed to demonstrate that the particular belief the guerrillas sought to overcome in him was his political opinion. Therefore he does not come within this ground of persecution.

* * * [T]he respondent has not shown he is eligible either for asylum or withholding of deportation to El Salvador. Therefore, we shall dismiss his appeal.

---

The Ninth Circuit took a very different approach in the following decision soon after the enactment of the Refugee Act of 1980.

## BOLANOS–HERNANDEZ v. INS

United States Court of Appeals, Ninth Circuit, 1984.
767 F.2d 1277.

REINHARDT, CIRCUIT JUDGE.

* * *

Bolanos testified that for two years he had been a member of the Partido National de Reconciliation, a right-wing party in El Salvador. He had also been in the army and had been a member of Escolta Militia, a voluntary civilian police squad that guards against guerrilla infiltration for the government. According to Bolanos, the guerrillas believe that, because of his membership in these groups, he would be particularly useful to them in their plans to infiltrate the government. When he refused to join the guerrillas, they threatened him, telling him they would kill him if he did not join their forces or, alternatively, leave the country. Bolanos took this threat seriously because the guerillas had killed five of his friends and had used similar tactics to recruit his brother—whom he believes they may have subsequently killed. Bolanos left El Salvador eight days after the guerillas made their threat.

In addition to his own specific, individualized basis for fearing persecution, Bolanos testified about the great danger that male youths in general face in El Salvador. He also introduced newspaper articles attesting to the general conditions of violence, armed conflict, and guerrilla control in large portions of that country.

The government concedes that Bolanos has indicated his commitment not to be affiliated with either side in the political struggle—"his desire to remain neutral and not be affiliated with any political group." The Immigration Judge, however, determined that Bolanos had not shown that any danger he might be subject to would be because of his political opinion, and both the Immigration Judge and the Board of Immigration Appeals determined that Bolanos failed to show that he had a specific reason to fear persecution that distinguished his situation from that of other Salvadorans. We disagree.

\* \* \*

\* \* \* Bolanos did not present only general evidence of conditions that affect all Salvadorans equally or that merely raise a possibility that he, like almost all others, could be subject to the violent terror common in his homeland. Bolanos's general evidence, newspaper articles that demonstrate the political and social turmoil in El Salvador, was coupled with testimony about a specific threat to his life made by the guerrillas. Neither the Immigration Judge nor the Board of Immigration Appeals questioned Bolanos' credibility, or expressed any doubt about whether this threat had actually been made. But the Board concluded that the specific threat against Bolanos' life was merely "representative of the general conditions in El Salvador," while the Immigration Judge considered the specific, individualized evidence of the likelihood of persecution insufficient because not supported by "independent corroborative evidence." We disagree with both these views.

The Board's conclusion that the threat against Bolanos' life was insufficient simply because it was representative of the general level of violence in El Salvador constitutes a clear error of law. We are mystified by the Board's ability to turn logic on its head. While we have frequently held that general evidence of violence is insufficient to trigger [withholding of] deportation, not once have we considered a specific threat against a petitioner insufficient because it reflected a general level of violence. Even when the credibility of a petitioner's evidence has been questioned, we have rejected the categorization of evidence of specific threats as "general." It should be obvious that the significance of a specific threat to an individual's life or freedom is not lessened by the fact that the individual resides in a country where the lives and freedom of a large number of persons are threatened. If anything, as we point out *infra,* that fact may make the threat more serious or credible.

\* \* \*

Evaluating the seriousness of the threat to Bolanos' life involves a consideration of the past response of the guerrillas to those who politically oppose them or who do not join in their political struggle. Bolanos testified that five of his friends were killed because they refused to join the guerrillas' political cause. He also testified that his brother was pressed into the service of the guerrillas and may have been killed by them. The newspaper articles introduced by Bolanos note the violent retribution that may follow the expression of political views in El Salvador and the executions conducted in retaliation for refusals to join political guerrilla groups. This general documentary evidence supports Bolanos' contention that he would suffer political persecution if he returned to El Salvador.

Given the general climate of uncontrolled violence in El Salvador, it would be unreasonable to conclude that the threat to Bolanos' life or freedom was not a serious one. Because he refused to join their cause and infiltrate the government on their behalf, the guerrillas are likely to consider him a political opponent, just as they would if he had spoken out publicly in opposition to their cause or tactics. The evidence clearly shows that the guerrillas have the ability and the will to carry out their threats.

\* \* \*

The government concedes that Bolanos has consciously chosen not to join either of the contending forces in El Salvador because he wishes to remain neutral, yet it argues that any persecution Bolanos might suffer would not be because of his political opinion. We find it somewhat difficult to follow the government's argument. The government contends that Bolanos' decision to remain politically neutral is not a political choice. There is nothing in the record to support this contention. Presumably the government is suggesting either that neutrality is always apolitical or that an individual who chooses neutrality must establish that the choice was made for political reasons. We disagree with both of these contentions.

Choosing to remain neutral is no less a political decision than is choosing to affiliate with a particular political faction. Just as a nation's decision to remain neutral is a political one, *see, e.g.,* Neutrality Act of 1939, 22 U.S.C. §§ 441–465 (1982), so is an individual's. When a person is aware of contending political forces and affirmatively chooses not to join any faction, that choice *is* a political one. A rule that one must identify with one of two dominant warring political factions in order to possess a political opinion, when many persons may, in fact, be opposed to the views and policies of both, would frustrate one of the basic objectives of the Refugee Act of 1980—to provide protection to all victims of persecution regardless of ideology. Moreover, construing "political opinion" in so short-sighted and grudging a manner could result in limiting the benefits under the ameliorative provisions of our immigration laws to those who join one political extreme or another; moderates who choose to sit out a battle would not qualify.

The government's second suggestion is equally unconvincing. The motive underlying any political choice may, if examined closely, prove to be, in whole or in part, non-political. Certainly a political affiliation may be undertaken for non-political, as well as political, reasons. A decision to join a particular political party may, for example, be made to curry favor, gain social acceptability, advance one's career, or obtain access to money or positions of power. Similarly, a decision to remain neutral may be made, in whole or in part, for non-political reasons. However, the reasons underlying an individual's political choice are of no significance for purposes of sections 243(h) and 208(a) and the government may not inquire into them. Whatever the motivation, an individual's choice, once made, constitutes, for better or for worse, a manifestation of political opinion.

We have several reasons for reaching the conclusion that the government may not look behind the manifestation of an alien's political opinion and seek to determine why he made a particular political choice. First, it is simply improper for the government to inquire into the motives underlying an individual's political decisions. Second, the motives frequently will be both complex and difficult to ascertain; it may not be possible to separate the political from the non-political aspects. What standards would we use, for example, to determine whether a choice was sufficiently based on political principles or whether economic self-interest was the determinative factor? Third, and perhaps most important, it is irrelevant why the individual made his choice. It does not matter to the persecutors what the individual's motivation is. The guerrillas in El Salvador do not inquire into the reasoning process of those who insist on remaining neutral and refuse to join their cause. They are concerned only with an act that constitutes an overt manifestation of a political opinion. Persecution because of that overt manifestation is persecution because of a political opinion.

Here, Bolanos was quite aware of the political situation. He had severed his ties to the right-wing organizations with which he had been affiliated. However, he subsequently refused to join the guerrillas despite their threats to his life. By choosing neutrality and refusing to join a particular political faction, Bolanos expressed his opinion and took a political stance. That conduct is as much an affirmative expression of a political opinion as is joining a side, or speaking out for or against a side.

The evidence is uncontroverted that Bolanos is likely to be persecuted by a politically motivated group that frequently engages in terrorist tactics directed at those who refuse to join its armed political struggle. In light of Bolanos' refusal to join, and in light of the fact that his refusal represented a conscious political choice, the conclusion is inescapable that Bolanos' life is endangered because of his political opinion. Therefore, he may not be deported.

\* \* \* For the same reasons that we find that Bolanos has established that section 243(h) precludes his deportation, we find that he has demonstrated a well-founded fear of persecution. \* \* \*

\* \* \*

Reversed.

## Notes and Questions

1. Other courts disagreed with *Bolanos–Hernandez*. Recall *M.A. v. INS,* 899 F.2d 304, 315 (4th Cir. 1990) (en banc), discussed in the materials on

military conscription in Chapter Three, pp. 132–42. *M.A.* involved a Salvadoran who wished to avoid conscription into the national army because of its human rights violations in the course of fighting the civil war there. In a part of the decision not included in Chapter Three, the Fourth Circuit en banc majority stated :

> M.A. claims that he is "not ... strongly politically oriented" and does "not want to fight for either side in this civil war." His status as a political "neutral" is, however, irrelevant. It is unclear whether neutrality can be considered a "political opinion" within the meaning of the Refugee Act. The Ninth Circuit has ruled that it can in some circumstances, *see Bolanos–Hernandez,* and this circuit has declined either to accept or reject the position. However, even the Ninth Circuit requires that a person seeking to establish a "well-founded fear" on account of an opinion of neutrality must show that he has affirmatively made a decision to remain neutral, and has received some threat or could be singled out for persecution on account of the opinion of neutrality. M.A. has brought forward no evidence to show that the persecution he fears—if indeed the object of his fear can appropriately be called persecution, rather than random violence—has anything to do with his "neutral" political opinions.

The Eleventh Circuit in *Perlera-Escobar v. EOIR,* 894 F.2d 1292, 1298 (11th Cir. 1990), another Salvadoran case, took a similar position in endorsing what it read as the applicable BIA doctrine:

> In the context of a civil war, * * * the BIA has declined to apply the principle that a desire to remain neutral is an expression of a political opinion for purposes of asylum and withholding of deportation. The BIA's position is no doubt based upon the fact that adoption of such an interpretation would create a sinkhole that would swallow the rule.

In the Ninth Circuit itself, a separate opinion by Judge Sneed in *Mendoza Perez v. INS,* 902 F.2d 760, 767–68 (9th Cir. 1990), put a sharper edge on these points in criticizing earlier Ninth Circuit doctrine and comparing it to several other circuits:

> The Ninth Circuit has held that political neutrality is a political opinion for purposes of [the withholding provision]. This holding eviscerates the political opinion requirement of the statute. It means that a politically inactive alien, and perhaps most illegal aliens are, may now gain the protection of asylum. * * *

> \* \* \*

> This core idea of political activism underlies the concept of "refugee" status. * * * We distort the meaning of an important requirement for refugee status when we permit political aloofness to serve as an active "political opinion," that endangers its holder. It also demeans the true martyr for whom asylum was intended.

2. James Hathaway takes a strikingly different view in criticizing Canadian cases that ruled against the claimant because of "the objective

unimportance of the claimant's political acts, her own inability to characterize her actions as flowing from a particular political ideology, or even an explicit disavowal of the views ascribed to her by the state." J. Hathaway, The Law of Refugee Status 155–56 (1991). This focus is misguided, Hathaway argues, provided the proof of likely persecution is sufficient. The point of refugee law is to "establish a surrogate protection system for those whose membership in the national community has been fundamentally denied," and not simply "to protect persons on the basis of personal merit," such as the actual possession of some well-considered political opinion. *Id.* at 157.

3. Did Congress intend to protect only those who are targeted because of explicit political opinion they chose to adopt or express? If so, the Ninth Circuit's case law is wrong. Or do you think that a citizen's choice to remain neutral in the midst of a vicious civil war should be protected through *nonrefoulement* and asylum if he or she should flee to another country? In such a setting, a great contest is underway for the future of that country. Should citizens simply be expected to take a stand in the midst of such tragic circumstances, and abide any consequences?

Think about how you might have reacted to a stance of purported neutrality during the American Revolutionary War and Civil War. For an intriguing quasi-fictional treatment of these questions, see William Safire's novel, *Freedom* (1988), exploring the position of former U.S. Vice President and then-Senator John Breckenridge, who attempted after the firing on Fort Sumter to adhere to a kind of neutrality in favor of "the Union as it was" but ultimately became a Confederate general.

## 2. IMPUTED POLITICAL OPINION

Closely related to the question whether and when neutrality counts as political opinion is the topic of persecution based on characteristics that the persecutor imputes to the victim. Persecution on account of imputed political opinion is persecution on account of what the persecutor believes the victim's political opinion to be, regardless of the victim's actual political opinion. Imputed political opinion is closely related to the question of neutrality as political opinion. The connection is that whether or not neutrality is a form of traditional political opinion as "a conscious political choice" (to quote Judge Reinhardt's characterization of neutrality in *Bolanos–Hernandez*), neutrality still counts as political opinion if the persecutor imputes political opposition to anyone who remains neutral.

In *Hernandez–Ortiz v. INS,* 777 F.2d 509 (9th Cir. 1985), the Ninth Circuit addressed a set of facts similar to *Bolanos–Hernandez.* Suggesting a presumption that should operate in such circumstances, the court connected the concepts of neutrality and imputed political opinion. Because of the procedural posture of the case, the court assumed that the facts the applicant alleged were true. Under that account, in November 1980,

> Hernandez–Ortiz's brother—a teacher—and his wife were murdered in El Salvador by Salvadoran security forces. * * * [In] November 1982, Salvadoran soldiers entered her grandparents'

grocery store, threatened them with submachine guns, and robbed them of both goods and the store's gross receipts for the day. In June 1983, * * * her brother-in-law's wife was kidnapped late at night by members of the Salvadoran National Guard who beat her and threw salt and sand in her eyes. The Guardsmen returned to Hernandez–Ortiz's brother-in-law's house and threatened to kill both her brother-in-law and his wife.

777 F.2d, at 512.

The court addressed political opinion as follows:

The Board * * * concluded that neither Hernandez–Ortiz nor any of her relatives has ever been harmed "on account of race, religion, nationality, membership in a particular social group, or political opinion." A clear probability that an alien's life or freedom is threatened, without any indication of the basis for the threat, is generally insufficient to constitute "persecution" and thus to preclude the Attorney General from deporting the alien. There must also be some evidence that the threat is related to one of the [enumerated factors]. Although Hernandez–Ortiz opposes the current regime in El Salvador, the Board concluded that she failed to demonstrate that any threat to her life or freedom was related to her political opinion. The Board based this conclusion on the fact that Hernandez–Ortiz did not allege that she or any of her relatives was a member of any political groups or "had ever participated in the current conflict in El Salvador."

[The withholding statute] could be read as providing that only the alien's race, religion, nationality, membership in a particular social group, or political opinion, not the persecutor's, can be considered in determining whether oppressive conduct constitutes persecution. However, we do not believe the section may properly be given so restrictive or mechanical a construction. "Persecution" occurs only when there is a difference between the persecutor's views or status and that of the victim; it is oppression which is inflicted on groups or individuals because of a difference that the persecutor will not tolerate. For this reason, in determining whether threats or violence constitute political persecution, it is permissible to examine the motivation of the persecutor; we may look to the political views and actions of the entity or individual responsible for the threats or violence, as well as to the victim's, and we may examine the relationship between the two.

In this case it is the forces of the government that are inflicting the threats and violence. When a government exerts its military strength against an individual or a group within its population and there is no reason to believe that the individual or group has engaged in any criminal activity or other conduct that would provide a legitimate basis for governmental action, the most reasonable presumption is that the government's actions are politically motivated. Here, numerous incidents were all directed at members of the same family. Because the killings, kidnapping, beating, threats, robbery, and harassment were all inflicted by government forces, the inference that they were connected and politically motivated is an appropriate one.

A government does not under ordinary circumstances engage in political persecution of those who share its ideology, only of those whose views or philosophies differ, at least in the government's perception. It is irrelevant whether a victim's political view is neutrality, as in *Bolanos–Hernandez,* or disapproval of the acts or opinions of the government. Moreover, it is irrelevant whether a victim actually possesses any of these opinions as long as the government believes that he does. * * * [W]hen through legally cognizable inferences or otherwise, an alien establishes a *prima facie* case that he is likely to be persecuted because of the government's belief about his views or loyalties, his actual political conduct, be it silence or affirmative advocacy, and his actual political views, be they neutrality or partisanship, are irrelevant; whatever the circumstances, the persecution is properly categorized as being "on account of . . . political opinion."

777 F.2d, at 516–17.

---

*Hernandez–Ortiz* established a strong presumption that certain kinds of threats are to be treated as being "on account of" political opinion. Seven years later, the U.S. Supreme Court addressed imputed political opinion and several closely related issues in the following decision.

## INS v. ELIAS–ZACARIAS

Supreme Court of the United States, 1992.
502 U.S. 478, 112 S.Ct. 812, 117 L.Ed.2d 38.

Justice Scalia delivered the opinion of the Court.

The principal question presented by this case is whether a guerrilla organization's attempt to coerce a person into performing military service necessarily constitutes "persecution on account of . . . political opinion" under § 101(a)(42) of the Immigration and Nationality Act.

I

Respondent Elias–Zacarias, a native of Guatemala, was apprehended in July 1987 for entering the United States without inspection. In deportation proceedings brought by petitioner Immigration and Naturalization Service (INS), Elias–Zacarias conceded his deportability but requested asylum and withholding of deportation.

The Immigration Judge summarized Elias–Zacarias' testimony as follows:

> [A]round the end of January in 1987 [when Elias–Zacarias was 18], two armed, uniformed guerrillas with handkerchiefs covering part of their faces came to his home. Only he and his parents were there.... [T]he guerrillas asked his parents and himself to join with them, but they all refused. The guerrillas asked them why and told them that they would be back, and that they should think it over about joining them.
>
> [Elias–Zacarias] did not want to join the guerrillas because the guerrillas are against the government and he was afraid that the government would retaliate against him and his family if he did join the guerrillas. [H]e left Guatemala at the end of March [1987] ... because he was afraid that the guerrillas would return.

The Immigration Judge understood from this testimony that Elias–Zacarias' request for asylum and for withholding of deportation was "based on this one attempted recruitment by the guerrillas." She concluded that Elias–Zacarias had failed to demonstrate persecution or a well-founded fear of persecution on account of race, religion, nationality, membership in a particular social group, or political opinion, and was not eligible for asylum. She further concluded that he did not qualify for withholding of deportation.

The Board of Immigration Appeals (BIA) summarily dismissed Elias–Zacarias' appeal on procedural grounds. Elias–Zacarias then moved the BIA to reopen his deportation hearing so that he could submit new evidence that, following his departure from Guatemala, the guerrillas had twice returned to his family's home in continued efforts to recruit him. The BIA denied reopening on the ground that even with this new evidence Elias–Zacarias had failed to make a prima facie showing of eligibility for asylum and had failed to show that the results of his deportation hearing would be changed.

The Court of Appeals for the Ninth Circuit, treating the BIA's denial of the motion to reopen as an affirmance on the merits of the Immigration Judge's ruling, reversed. The court ruled that acts of conscription by a nongovernmental group constitute persecution on account of political opinion, and determined that Elias–Zacarias had a "well-founded fear" of such conscription. We granted certiorari.

## II

* * * The BIA's determination that Elias–Zacarias was not eligible for asylum must be upheld if "supported by reasonable, substantial, and probative evidence on the record considered as a whole." INA § 106(a)(4). It can be reversed only if the evidence presented by Elias–

Zacarias was such that a reasonable factfinder would have to conclude that the requisite fear of persecution existed.[1]

The Court of Appeals found reversal warranted. In its view, a guerrilla organization's attempt to conscript a person into its military forces necessarily constitutes "persecution on account of . . . political opinion," because "the person resisting forced recruitment is expressing a political opinion hostile to the persecutor and because the persecutor's motive in carrying out the kidnapping is political." The first half of this seems to us untrue, and the second half irrelevant.

Even a person who supports a guerrilla movement might resist recruitment for a variety of reasons—fear of combat, a desire to remain with one's family and friends, a desire to earn a better living in civilian life, to mention only a few. The record in the present case not only failed to show a political motive on Elias–Zacarias' part; it showed the opposite. He testified that he refused to join the guerrillas because he was afraid that the government would retaliate against him and his family if he did so. Nor is there any indication (assuming, *arguendo,* it would suffice) that the guerrillas erroneously *believed* that Elias–Zacarias' refusal was politically based.

As for the Court of Appeals' conclusion that the guerrillas' "motive in carrying out the kidnaping is political": It apparently meant by this that the guerrillas seek to fill their ranks in order to carry on their war against the government and pursue their political goals. But that does not render the forced recruitment "persecution on account of . . . political opinion." * * * The ordinary meaning of the phrase "persecution on account of . . . political opinion" in § 101(a)(42) is persecution on account of the victim's political opinion, not the persecutor's. If a Nazi regime persecutes Jews, it is not, within the ordinary meaning of language, engaging in persecution on account of political opinion; and if a fundamentalist Moslem regime persecutes democrats, it is not engaging in persecution on account of religion. Thus, the mere existence of a generalized "political" motive underlying the guerrillas' forced recruitment is inadequate to establish (and, indeed, goes far to refute) the proposition that Elias–Zacarias fears persecution on account of political opinion, as § 101(a)(42) requires.

Elias–Zacarias appears to argue that not taking sides with any political faction is itself the affirmative expression of a political opinion. That seems to us not ordinarily so, since we do not agree with the dissent that only a "narrow, grudging construction of the concept of 'political opinion' " would distinguish it from such quite different concepts as indifference, indecisiveness and risk-averseness. But we need

---

**1.** Quite beside the point, therefore, is the dissent's assertion that "the record in this case is more than adequate to *support the conclusion* that this respondent's refusal [to join the guerrillas] was a form of expressive conduct that constituted the statement of a 'political opinion,' "(emphasis added). To reverse the BIA finding we must find that the evidence not only supports that conclusion, but *compels* it—and also compels the further conclusion that Elias–Zacarias had a well-founded fear that the guerrillas would persecute him *because of* that political opinion.

not decide whether the evidence compels the conclusion that Elias–Zacarias held a political opinion. Even if it does, Elias–Zacarias still has to establish that the record also compels the conclusion that he has a "well-founded fear" that the guerrillas will persecute him because of that political opinion, rather than because of his refusal to fight with them. He has not done so with the degree of clarity necessary to permit reversal of a BIA finding to the contrary; indeed, he has not done so at all.[2]

Elias–Zacarias objects that he cannot be expected to provide direct proof of his persecutors' motives. We do not require that. But since the statute makes motive critical, he must provide some evidence of it, direct or circumstantial. And if he seeks to obtain judicial reversal of the BIA's determination, he must show that the evidence he presented was so compelling that no reasonable factfinder could fail to find the requisite fear of persecution. That he has not done.

The BIA's determination should therefore have been upheld in all respects, and we reverse the Court of Appeals' judgment to the contrary.

It is so ordered.

JUSTICE STEVENS, with whom JUSTICE BLACKMUN and JUSTICE O'CONNOR join, dissenting.

Respondent refused to join a guerrilla organization that engaged in forced recruitment in Guatemala. He fled the country because he was afraid the guerrillas would return and "take me and kill me." After his departure, armed guerrillas visited his family on two occasions searching for him. In testimony that the hearing officer credited, he stated that he is still afraid to return to Guatemala because "these people" can come back to "take me or kill me."

It is undisputed that respondent has a well-founded fear that he will be harmed, if not killed, if he returns to Guatemala. It is also undisputed that the cause of that harm, if it should occur, is the guerrilla organization's displeasure with his refusal to join them in their armed insurrection against the government. The question of law that the case presents is whether respondent's well-founded fear is a "fear of persecution on

---

**2.** The dissent misdescribes the record on this point in several respects. For example, it exaggerates the "well-foundedness" of whatever fear Elias–Zacarias possesses, by progressively transforming his testimony that he was afraid the guerrillas would " 'take me or kill me,' " into, first, "the guerrillas' *implied threat* to 'take' him or to 'kill' him," (emphasis added), and, then, into the flat assertion that the guerrillas "*responded by threatening* to 'take' or to 'kill' him" (emphasis added). The dissent also erroneously describes it as "undisputed" that the cause of the harm Elias–Zaca-rias fears, if that harm should occur, will be "the guerrilla organization's displeasure with his refusal to join them in their armed insurrection against the government." The record shows no such concession by the INS, and all Elias–Zacarias said on the point was that he feared being taken or killed by the guerrillas. It is quite plausible, indeed likely, that the taking would be engaged in by the guerrillas in order to augment their troops rather than show their displeasure; and the killing he feared might well be a killing in the course of resisting being taken.

account of . . . political opinion" within the meaning of § 101(a)(42) of the Immigration and Naturalization Act.

\* \* \*

Today the Court holds that respondent's fear of persecution is not "on account of . . . political opinion" for two reasons. First, he failed to prove that his refusal to join the guerrillas was politically motivated; indeed, he testified that he was at least in part motivated by a fear that government forces would retaliate against him or his family if he joined the guerrillas. Second, he failed to prove that his persecutors' motives were political. In particular, the Court holds that the persecutors' implicit threat to retaliate against respondent "because of his refusal to fight with them," is not persecution on account of political opinion. I disagree with both parts of the Court's reasoning.

I

A political opinion can be expressed negatively as well as affirmatively. A refusal to support a cause—by staying home on election day, by refusing to take an oath of allegiance, or by refusing to step forward at an induction center—can express a political opinion as effectively as an affirmative statement or affirmative conduct. Even if the refusal is motivated by nothing more than a simple desire to continue living an ordinary life with one's family, it is the kind of political expression that the asylum provisions of the statute were intended to protect.

As the Court of Appeals explained in *Bolanos–Hernandez v. INS,* 767 F.2d 1277 (9th Cir. 1985):

Choosing to remain neutral is no less a political decision than is choosing to affiliate with a particular political faction.
\* \* \*

*Id.,* at 1286.

The narrow, grudging construction of the concept of "political opinion" that the Court adopts today is inconsistent with the basic approach to this statute that the Court endorsed in *INS v. Cardoza–Fonseca.* In that case, relying heavily on the fact that an alien's status as a "refugee" merely makes him eligible for a discretionary grant of asylum—as contrasted with the entitlement to a withholding of deportation \* \* \*—the Court held that the alien's burden of proving a well-founded fear of persecution did not require proof that persecution was more likely than not to occur. \* \* \*

\* \* \*

Similar reasoning should resolve any doubts concerning the political character of an alien's refusal to take arms against a legitimate government in favor of the alien. In my opinion, the record in this case is more than adequate to support the conclusion that this respondent's refusal was a form of expressive conduct that constituted the statement of a "political opinion" within the meaning of § 208(a).[5]

## II

It follows as night follows day that the guerrillas' implied threat to "take" him or to "kill" him if he did not change his position constituted threatened persecution "on account of" that political opinion. As the Court of Appeals explained in *Bolanos–Hernandez, supra:*

> It does not matter to the persecutors what the individual's motivation is. The guerrillas in El Salvador do not inquire into the reasoning process of those who insist on remaining neutral and refuse to join their cause. They are concerned only with an act that constitutes an overt manifestation of a political opinion. Persecution because of that overt manifestation is persecution because of a political opinion.[6]

It is important to emphasize that the statute does not require that an applicant for asylum prove exactly why his persecutors would act against him; it only requires him to show that he has a "well-founded fear of persecution on account of . . . political opinion." As we recognized in *INS v. Cardoza Fonseca*, the applicant meets this burden if he shows that there is a " 'reasonable possibility' " that he will be persecuted on account of his political opinion (quoting *INS v. Stevic*). Because respondent expressed a political opinion by refusing to join the guerrillas, and they responded by threatening to "take" or to "kill" him if he did not change his mind, his fear that the guerrillas will persecute him on account of his political opinion is well founded.[7]

Accordingly, I would affirm the judgment of the Court of Appeals.

**5.** Here, respondent not only engaged in expressive conduct by refusing to join the guerrilla organization but also explained that he did so "[b]ecause they see very well, that if you join the guerrillas . . . then you are against the government. You are against the government and if you join them then it is to die there. And, then the government is against you and against your family." Respondent thus expressed the political view that he was for the government and against the guerrillas. The statute speaks simply in terms of a political opinion and does not require that the view be well developed or elegantly expressed.

**6.** The Government has argued that respondent's statement is analogous to that of a person who leaves a country to avoid being drafted into military service. The INS has long recognized, however, that the normal enforcement of selective service laws is not "persecution" within the meaning of the statute even if the draftee's motive is political. Thus, while holding that an Afghan soldier who refused to fight under Soviet command qualified as a political refugee, *Matter of Salim*, 18 I. & N. Dec. 311 (BIA 1982), the INS has adhered "to the long-accepted position that it is not persecution for a country to require military service of its citizens." *Matter of A–G–,* 19 I. & N. Dec. 502, 506 (BIA 1987); *cf.* United Nations High Commissioner for Refugees, Handbook on Procedures and Criteria for Determining Refugee Status ¶ 167 (1979) ("Fear of prosecution and punishment for desertion or draft-evasion does not in itself constitute well-founded fear of persecution under the [1967 United Nations Protocol Relating to the Status of Refugees]").

**7.** In response to this dissent, the Court suggests that respondent and I have exaggerated the "well-foundedness" of his fear. The Court's legal analysis, however, would produce precisely the same result no matter how unambiguous the guerrillas' threatened retaliation might have been. Moreover, any doubts concerning the sinister character of a suggestion to "think it over" delivered by two uniformed masked men carrying machine guns should be resolved in respondent's favor.

## Notes and Questions

1.    Should the Refugee Act be read to protect all those who have been or are likely to be targeted by politically motivated persecution, even if unfairly or even if only to make an example that might intimidate others? Consider the facts in *Matter of Juan* (BIA 1989), a nonprecedent decision reported in Refugee Reports, Nov. 17, 1989, at 13. The applicant was a fifteen-year-old Kanjobal Indian from Guatemala. Government soldiers appeared in his village with a list of names of people who allegedly had given corn to the guerrillas. Juan's father, whose name was on the list, was taken and found decapitated the next day. Shortly thereafter the guerrillas entered the village and abducted Juan's mother. She was found dead the next day. The immigration judge denied asylum, but the BIA, somewhat reluctantly, reversed, stating that it was bound in this case by Ninth Circuit precedents regarding "imputed political opinion."

Two members dissented, in an opinion by Board Member Heilman, arguing vigorously that asylum should not be granted. He wrote: "The only reason to speak in terms of imputed political opinion is to 'pigeon-hole' the case within one of the five categories set forth in the law for asylum. * * * It seems a bit absurd in these circumstances to try to divine some 'imputation' of opinion, as if the individual's political views would save or condemn him." He concluded that the government was more interested "in making examples and intimidating the population" than in inflicting persecution because of political opinion. *Id.* at 14.

This passage distills the essence of the debate over this issue and the Board's doctrine applying the "on account of" language in the definition. Looking at these materials on imputed political opinion as well as the preceding subsection 1 (on Neutrality), did Congress intend to protect only those who are targeted because of explicit political opinion they chose to adopt or express? Or should the Refugee Act be understood to protect all those who have been or are likely to be targeted by politically motivated persecution, even if unfairly or even if only to make an example that might intimidate others? What vision of the underlying purposes of, and policy constraints affecting, political asylum undergirds Heilman's position? What vision underlies the Ninth Circuit's position? Hathaway's? Yours?

2.    How much room does the Supreme Court in *Elias–Zacarias* leave for future asylum and withholding applicants to base their claims on persecution on account of imputed political opinion?

3.    In 1993, INS General Counsel Grover Joseph Rees issued a lengthy opinion that established the agency's position and led the way on future consideration of imputed political opinion claims. The validity of such claims was left open in *Elias–Zacarias*, he opined, because the Court "explicitly recognized" that the noncitizen in that case had not put that question in issue, citing this passage: "Nor is there any indication (assuming, *arguendo*, it would suffice) that the guerrillas erroneously *believed* that Elias–Zacarias' refusal was politically based." Rees then concluded that the imputed political opinion doctrine should be sustained because it serves the objectives of the

statute. He illustrated his point by an example based on the analogous notion of imputed religious belief:

> Thus [without some doctrine recognizing imputed characteristics], a Mr. Rosenberg whom the Nazi government of Germany had sentenced to the gas chamber because it erroneously believed him to be a Jew, but who had somehow made it to the United States to apply for asylum, would not qualify for asylum. No matter how clear it might be that the government was going to kill him upon his return, and that the killing would be specifically motivated by a desire to do unpleasant things to Jews, such persecution would not be "on account of ... religion" unless the government happened to be correct about Rosenberg's religion. This result is hardly compelled by the language of the statute; the most straightforward meaning of the words "persecution ... on account of ... religion" would appear to encompass a program specifically intended to stamp out Judaism even though implementation of the program should lead to some persecution of non-Jews. Nor does it seem appropriate to ascribe to Congress an unarticulated intention to generate such harsh results.
>
> Nevertheless, as the Court underscored in *Elias–Zacarias*, prosecution and punishment under a law of general applicability will not ordinarily constitute persecution "on account of" one of the five statutory grounds. The "imputed political opinion" exception to this rule arises only when there is evidence that the law and/or its enforcement are motivated in whole or in part by a desire to punish or deter one of the five characteristics protected by the asylum and refugee laws.
>
> Such evidence may be either direct or circumstantial. Direct evidence would consist of statements by the persecutor to the effect that violators of the law are to be regarded and punished not just as ordinary lawbreakers but as political enemies. * * * Circumstantial evidence has most commonly consisted of punishment so severe as to seem obviously directed at real or perceived enemies rather than at ordinary lawbreakers.

70 Interp. Rel. 498, 501–02 (1993).

4. The BIA clearly accepts the concept of imputed political opinion. *See, e.g., In re T–M–B–*, 21 I & N Dec. 775 (BIA 1997), as well as the next two decisions in this chapter, *Matter of R–*, 20 I & N Dec. 621 (BIA 1992), and *Matter of S–P–*, 21 I & N Dec. 486 (BIA 1996). And courts have also generally concluded that imputed political opinion remains a viable basis for an asylum claim after the Supreme Court's ruling. In addition to *Sangha v. INS*, 103 F.3d 1482 (9th Cir. 1997), which appears below, p. 217, *see, e.g., Zhou v. Gonzales*, 437 F.3d 860, 868–70 (9th Cir. 2006); *Najjar v. Ashcroft*, 257 F.3d 1262, 1289 (11th Cir. 2001); *Morales v. INS*, 208 F.3d 323, 331 (1st Cir. 2000), *Lwin v. INS*, 144 F.3d 505, 509 (7th Cir. 1998); *Cruz–Diaz v. INS*, 86 F.3d 330, 331–32 (4th Cir. 1996) (per curiam).

5. If the basic doctrine of imputed political opinion is relatively straightforward, the situation becomes much more complicated when the opinion imputed to the target of the persecutors is not necessarily an

articulated political vision, but rather the victim's desire to be neutral. These intertwined questions—when is neutrality a political opinion and when can it be imputed to someone—have posed challenges for asylum adjudicators. If, after *Elias–Zacarias*, INS, the BIA, and the courts have left room for applicants to show past or future persecution on account of *imputed* political opinion, have they necessarily left room for applicants to show past or future persecution on account of *neutrality as* political opinion, notwithstanding Justice Scalia's assertion that it "seems to us untrue" that "the person resisting forced recruitment is expressing a political opinion hostile to the persecutor"?

6.   Do *Elias–Zacarias* and the Rees opinion adequately explain why the conscription cases in Chapter Three, pp. 132–42, (and referred to footnote 6 in Justice Stevens' dissent) do not count as persecution on account of actual or imputed political opinion?

## 3.   APPLYING *ELIAS–ZACARIAS*

Asylum seekers frequently point to their fear of intimidation and violence at the hands of insurgent groups. In the next case, the BIA seemed to read *Elias–Zacarias* in a way that would disqualify a great many applicants coming from countries with internal strife or terrorist movements.

### MATTER OF R–

Board of Immigration Appeals, 1992.
20 I & N Dec. 621.

\* \* \*

\* \* \* [T]he applicant is a 21-year-old native and citizen of India, who raised a claim of past persecution, as well as a fear of future persecution in that country, on account of his religion and his actual or imputed political opinions. In particular, the applicant related that he was a Sikh from the Punjab region of India. He indicated that in January 1991, Sikh militants, apparently members of the All India Sikh Student Federation, came to his family home and demanded money to support their cause. In addition, the applicant stated that the militants sought to recruit him, although he rebuffed their efforts. He explained that while he favored an independent Sikh state, he rejected accomplishing this goal by violence. He also indicated that he did not want to cause problems for his father.

According to the applicant, his contact with these Sikhs was reported to the local police, who arrested him as a suspected militant. He testified that he was interrogated about the individuals who visited his house and subjected to brutal physical abuse by the police because they suspected him of being one of the militant Sikhs. The police ultimately released him without charging him or taking him before a judge after "good people in the area" went to the police station. He stated that upon his release, he returned to his family home, where he was again confronted by the Sikh militants. He testified that they beat him and told him that he must join their ranks. The applicant related that the militants threatened to kill him and a member of his family if he did not comply with their wishes. He indicated that, thereafter, both the police and the militants continued to seek him out. At one point during his testimony, the applicant stated that he was also beaten by the police on June 13, 1991, but the reasons or circumstances of this incident were not made clear. His testimony suggested that this beating occurred after another of his encounters with the militant Sikhs (whom the applicant referred to as "the boys"). He testified that, as a result, he went into hiding in June 1991 and departed India in September 1991. He indicated that he did not want to return to India because he feared the police and the militant Sikhs. He stated that the "Punjab police" are "very dirty" police who bring fake charges and kill people in false encounters.

\* \* \*

\* \* \* [W]e find that there is no persuasive evidence in the record to demonstrate that either the Sikh militants or the police who confronted the applicant sought to punish him on account of one of the grounds enumerated in the Act. As regards persecution on account of political opinion, we note the Supreme Court recently made clear in *INS v. Elias–Zacarias*, U.S., 112 S. Ct. 812, 816 (1992), that persecution must be on account of the victim's political opinion, not the persecutor's. The Court further held that an applicant for asylum must establish that the persecution or feared persecution is because of that political opinion, rather than a refusal to fight for a guerrilla group. Here, the record indicates that the Sikh militants were seeking operating resources from the applicant in the form of material assistance and manpower. The mere fact that the militants also may have had a generalized political agenda is inadequate to establish that the applicant fears persecution from them on account of political opinion. We find no persuasive evidence, direct or circumstantial, that the motives underlying the militants' conduct towards the applicant were tied to the applicant's actual or imputed political opinions, rather than to his refusal to assist them. In this regard, we note that the mere resistance of forced recruitment is not an "expression of political opinion hostile to the persecutor." *Id.* Here, in resisting recruitment, the applicant indicated that he told the militants that his father was an honest person and that "they" (apparently meaning the applicant and his father) believed in creating an independent Sikh state, but not through violent means. He stated that it was dangerous to tell the militants this because they had killed certain people who refused to join them. The militants then demanded money from the applicant's family and still wanted him to join their group. On another occasion, the militants returned and threatened to kill him and a family member if he would not join their cause. He testified that he was beaten by the militants on this occasion and told that he would not be beaten if he would join them. While the circumstances the applicant found himself in were terrible, there is no indication that the militants cared at all about the reasons for his refusal to join. They certainly did not cease to be interested in having him join their group because of his views. In fact, all of the evidence reflects (and the applicant seems to largely acknowledge on appeal) that the purpose of the threats and mistreatment by the militants was to coerce him into joining with them. The Supreme Court has held that persecution for this reason is not "because" of political opinion. *Id.* at 816.

Similarly, there is no indication that the police actions against the applicant extended beyond the investigation of and reaction against those thought—rightly or wrongly—to be militants seeking the violent overthrow of the government. Under the circumstances of this case, the police had reasons to investigate the extent of the applicant's knowledge of and involvement with Sikh militants. While the applicant states he was subjected to police brutality, which we certainly do not countenance, the record reflects that the purpose of the mistreatment was to extract information about Sikh militants, rather than to persecute the applicant "because" of his political opinions or the mere fact that he was a Sikh.[3] Accordingly, the applicant has not established his eligibility for either asylum or withholding of exclusion and deportation.

Concurring in part and dissenting in part: MARY MAGUIRE DUNNE, BOARD MEMBER:

\* \* \*

In regard to the underlying merits of the applicant's persecution claim concerning the Indian police, the majority finds that "the purpose of the mistreatment was to extract information about Sikh militants, rather than to persecute the applicant 'because' of his political opinions or the mere fact that he was a Sikh." In arriving at this conclusion, the majority has ignored relevant precedent of the United States Court of Appeals for the Ninth Circuit. As this case arises within the jurisdiction of that court, we are bound by its decisions. Specifically, the Ninth Circuit has ruled that while a government has the right to prosecute individuals accused of criminal activity, such as supporting a guerrilla faction, when violence or threats of violence usurp legal procedure, then persecution on the basis of political opinion exists.

In addition, the majority has ignored the principle enunciated in the Board's own precedent of *Matter of Fuentes*, 19 I & N Dec. 658, 662 (BIA 1988), that an alien does not bear the unreasonable burden of establishing the exact motivation of a persecutor where different grounds for actions are possible. In this light, I find improper the majority's confident conclusion that the persecution suffered by the applicant at the hands of the Indian police was not premised upon one of the protected grounds.

**3.** We certainly do not hold that there are no circumstances under which the motive for police abuses could be to persecute someone on account of a reason protected under the Act, but we find no direct or circumstantial evidence that such is the case here. There is no evidence that the police were concerned with anything other than the fact the applicant was thought to be involved with those engaged in a violent struggle against the government. There is nothing to indicate that, such being the case, the police cared what the applicant's individual political opinions may or may not have been or whether he was or was not a Sikh.

In reality, the majority employs a standard diametrically opposed to that set forth in *Matter of Fuentes*, by implicitly suggesting that an alien must prove a persecutorial motivation anchored upon one of the enumerated grounds to the exclusion of all other possible motivations. *Matter of Fuentes*, however, recognized that there can be more than one possible basis for a persecutor's actions. The task of the alien is simply to demonstrate the reasonableness of a motivation which is related to one of the enumerated grounds. Concomitantly, it is irrelevant whether the majority's interpretation of the events is reasonable; the proper focus is whether the applicant's interpretation is reasonable.

\* \* \*

Concurring opinion: MICHAEL J. HEILMAN, BOARD MEMBER:

\* \* \*

Unlike the dissenting opinion, I do not find all political opinion to be equal, or protected under the term "political opinion" as used in the Refugee Act of 1980. I am well aware, of course, that persecution is generally defined as the infliction of harm on account of a "differing" political opinion, one which the supposed agent of persecution finds "offensive." But this is a theory that is surely filled with dangerous pitfalls, if all opinions are treated as equal. If the political program of Sikh extremists includes the murder of policemen and government officials, as well as judges and political figures, is this not a program that one should differ with and try to overcome? Surely the opposite is not possible, that one should support it and grant asylum for it.

\* \* \*

We know that the Sikh extremists \* \* \* have a political program that, in their minds, justifies violence. What the Sikh extremists want and how they operate is no mystery to the Indian public, and most certainly not to the Indian police, who know how many policemen have been killed and the suffering that the extremists have caused. The police did not start this violence; the police did not one day decide to start killing Sikhs and drive them out of Punjab. How incredibly odd that the dissenting opinion assigns them the onus of "persecution." What a remarkable juxtaposition of victim and killer.

And here I will be as blunt as possible: Given the viciousness with which the extremists have murdered so many persons, among them many policemen and their families, would one realistically expect gentle treatment? It ill behooves us to label as agents of persecution the very people the Sikh extremists murder with abandon when they have the opportunity. \* \* \*

\* \* \*

Now compare the next BIA decision, which adopted a considerably different approach.

## MATTER OF S–P–

Board of Immigration Appeals, 1996.
21 I & N Dec. 486.

GUENDELSBERGER, BOARD MEMBER:

\* \* \*

The applicant is a 34-year-old Sri Lankan national of Tamil ethnici-ty. He was a welder by trade and had his own welding shop for several years. In November 1993, the applicant and his wife relocated to a Red Cross refugee camp near Elali in northern Sri Lanka. The Liberation Tigers of Tamil Eelam ("LTTE" or "Tigers") took the applicant from the refugee camp and forced him to work for them as a welder in one of their base camps near Elali. There were about 30 others in this camp who, like the applicant, were forced to work for the Tigers. These workers were taken to various work sites during the day and brought back to the Tigers' camp in the evening. The applicant testified that he was not mistreated by the Tigers, but that he was watched at all times and believed he would be severely punished were he to attempt an escape.

In March 1994, the applicant was in the Tigers' camp when it was raided by the Sri Lankan Army. The applicant hid in a bunker during the attack which lasted about 3 hours. When he emerged, he was surrounded by 50 to 60 Sri Lankan soldiers. The soldiers accused him of being a Tiger and took him and 12 other conscripted workers captured with him to the Sri Lankan Army camp in Elali. At that camp, he and the 12 other workers were kicked and beaten with plastic pipes and gun butts.

\* \* \*

The applicant was held by the Army in the Colombo prison for 6 months, from March 25 to September 18, 1994, during which time he was mistreated during at least eight sessions. On one occasion, he was placed in a room with burning chilies which caused choking and smoke inhalation. On other occasions, he was threatened with guns by drunken soldiers, tied up, and beaten. On four occasions the barrel of a gun was held to his head and he was told that if he did not tell the truth he would be killed. At various times, his head was repeatedly dunked in a bucket of water.

\* \* \*

On September 18, 1994, the applicant was released after his uncle paid a bribe to a guard. After his release, the applicant went to his uncle's house in Colombo, where he stayed for 8 days. During that 8 days, he only left his uncle's house two times to go to the temple.

On September 26, 1994, three policemen came looking for the applicant at his uncle's house. The applicant's uncle told the policemen that the applicant had returned to his own home. After this incident, the applicant moved to the house of a friend of his uncle, where he remained until leaving Sri Lanka on December 19, 1994. * * *

* * *

As noted above, it is often difficult to determine the exact motive or motives for which harm has been inflicted. There are at least two distinct areas of uncertainty in proving motive. First, in some cases, the events are such that no particular motive is readily ascertainable. For example, an unprovoked attack by unknown assailants may or may not have been for reasons protected by the Act. Without some evidence, either direct or circumstantial, of the reasons for the attack, the applicant will fail to prove eligibility for asylum.

A second area of uncertainty involves the question of motive in situations in which evidence arguably suggests multiple motives. For example, prosecution for an offense may be a pretext for punishing an individual for his political opinion. Similarly, in the instant case, the harm may have been inflicted for reasons related to government intelligence gathering, for political views imputed to the applicant, or for some combination of these reasons.

In adjudicating mixed motive cases, it is important to keep in mind the fundamental humanitarian concerns of asylum law. In enacting the Refugee Act of 1980, Congress sought to bring the Act's definition of "refugee" into conformity with the United Nations Convention and Protocol Relating to the Status of Refugees and, in so doing, give "statutory meaning to our national commitment to human rights and humanitarian concerns." See S. Rep. No. 256, 96th Cong., 2d Sess. 1, 4. Such an approach is designed to afford a generous standard for protection in cases of doubt.

It is also important to remember that a grant of political asylum is a benefit to an individual under asylum law, not a judgment against the country in question. * * * A decision to grant asylum is not an unfriendly act precisely because it is not a judgment about the country involved, but a judgment about the reasonableness of the applicant's belief that persecution was based on a protected ground. This distinction between the goals of refugee law (which protects individuals) and politics (which manages the relations between political bodies) should not be confused in charting an approach to determining motive. While it is prudent to exercise great caution before condemning acts of another state, this is not a reason for narrowly applying asylum law.

* * *

In applying asylum law in the context of the Sri Lankan conflict, it is not an easy task to evaluate an asylum applicant's claim that harm was inflicted because of imputed political views rather than a desire to obtain intelligence information. There may have been, in fact, a combination of these motives. The difficulty of determining motive in situations of general civil unrest should not, however, diminish the protections of asylum for persons who have been punished because of their actual or imputed political views, as opposed to their criminal or violent conduct. As the Court noted in *INS v. Cardoza–Fonseca*, "Congress has assigned to the Attorney General and his delegates the task of making these hard individualized decisions." That abuse occurred in the context of ongoing civil strife does not answer the question whether the abuse was on account of political opinion.

\* \* \*

In the instant case, there was no prosecution of the applicant. Therefore, the evidence must be evaluated in the context of the ongoing civil conflict to determine whether the motive for the abuse in the particular case was directed toward punishing or modifying perceived political views, as opposed to punishment for criminal acts; was part of the violence inherent in an armed conflict (i.e., lawful acts of war); or, was motivated by some other reason unrelated to asylum law. \* \* \* [T]he following elements, among others, may be considered in identifying motive:

    1.  Indications in the particular case that the abuse was directed toward modifying or punishing opinion rather than conduct (e.g., statements or actions by the perpetrators or abuse out of proportion to nonpolitical ends);

    2.  Treatment of others in the population who might be confronted by government agents in similar circumstances;

    3.  Conformity to procedures for criminal prosecution or military law including developing international norms regarding the law of war;

    4.  The extent to which antiterrorism laws are defined and applied to suppress political opinion as well as illegal conduct (e.g., an act may broadly prohibit "disruptive" activities to permit application to peaceful as well as violent expressions of views);

    5.  The extent to which suspected political opponents are subjected to arbitrary arrest, detention, and abuse.

This is certainly not an exhaustive list of factors to be taken into account in assessing motive. The list merely identifies some of the factors to be considered in the totality of the circumstances.

\* \* \* [I]n addition to establishing the fact that an applicant for asylum has a belief or characteristic offensive to the alleged persecutor, the applicant must prove that the alleged persecutor has the inclination and capacity to punish the alien for that belief or characteristic. Here we must examine the record for direct or circumstantial evidence from which it is reasonable to believe that those who harmed the applicant were in part motivated by an assumption that his political views were antithetical to those of the government.

\* \* \*

In presenting evidence related to the factors listed above, the alien "does not bear the unreasonable burden of establishing the exact motivation of a 'persecutor' where different reasons for actions are possible." *Matter of Fuentes*, [19 I & N Dec. 658], 662 [(BIA 1988)]. The task of the alien is "to demonstrate the reasonableness of a motivation which is related to one of the enumerated grounds." *Matter of R, supra*, at 629 (Dunne, concurring in part and dissenting in part). In some fact situations, the evidence may reasonably suggest mixed motives, at least one or more of which is related to a protected ground.

\* \* \*

Taking into account the context of the Sri Lankan conflict, the information in the State Department Country Reports, and the circumstances, duration and extent of the abuse inflicted, we find that the applicant has produced evidence from which it is reasonable to believe that those who harmed him were in part motivated by an assumption that his political views were antithetical to those of the Government. The record indicates that the applicant was detained and abused not only to obtain information about the identity of LTTE members and location of their camps but also because the capture of the applicant in an LTTE camp led Sri Lankan authorities to believe that the applicant was a political opponent. Thus, the applicant has met his burden of proving that he was subjected to past persecution in Sri Lanka.

\* \* \*

Having established past persecution, the applicant is presumed to have a well-founded fear of persecution unless a preponderance of the evidence establishes that since the time the persecution occurred, conditions in Sri Lanka have changed to such an extent that the applicant no longer has a well-founded fear of being persecuted were he to return. No such evidence of substantial changes in country conditions has been submitted in this case. Large-scale arrests of young Tamil males and abuse of detainees continue to occur.

There being no adverse factors of record, we will favorably exercise discretion in this case in order to grant the request for asylum. \* \* \*

\* \* \*

### Notes and Questions

1.  In granting asylum in *Matter of S–P–*, the BIA quoted favorably from Member Dunne's opinion in *Matter of R–*. Has the Board swung from one exaggerated view too far in the other direction? The standard articulated by the Board in *Matter of S–P–* is "direct or circumstantial evidence from which it is reasonable to believe that those who harmed the applicant were

in part motivated by an assumption that his political views were antithetical to those of the government" Is this standard consistent with *Elias–Zacarias*?

2.   Consider the majority's statement that: "A decision to grant asylum is not an unfriendly act precisely because it is not a judgment about the country involved, but a judgment about the reasonableness of the applicant's belief that persecution was based on a protected ground." Is this accurate? How can one judge the reasonableness of the applicant's belief without judging the actions of the government of the home country, or at least the conditions that obtain there?

3.   Are the analyses and outcomes in *Matter of R–* and *Matter of S–P–* consistent with the analyses and outcome in the prosecution vs. persecution materials in Chapter Three, pp. 113–17, especially the court decision in *Dwomoh* and the BIA decision in *Izatula*?

4.   For a critique of *Matter of R–*, see Blum, *License to Kill: Asylum Law and the Principle of Legitimate Governmental Authority to "Investigate its Enemies*," 28 Willamette L. Rev. 719 (1992).

---

The Ninth Circuit has had by far the largest quantity of cases basing an asylum claim on neutrality or imputed political opinion. As you read the following passages from an opinion that examines both issues in the context of forced recruitment, consider how its approach differs from the BIA's. Also ask yourself how accurately the following Ninth Circuit decision follows the Supreme Court's reasoning in *Elias–Zacarias*.

## SANGHA v. INS

United States Court of Appeals, Ninth Circuit, 1997.
103 F.3d 1482.

GOODWIN, CIRCUIT JUDGE.

\* \* \*

\* \* \* Baljinder Singh Sangha, then fifteen years old, lived with his father, mother, and older brother on a farm in Punjab, India. He attended school and helped his father on the farm.

In June, 1991, Sangha's father, Gursewak Singh, joined the Akali Dal Langowal party, and in July he assumed a local leadership role. The Akali Dal party criticized the militants and terrorists then operating in the Punjab, and it promoted peaceful solutions to political problems. In August, 1991, Sangha's father gave a speech criticizing the Bhindrawala Tiger Force (BTF) for promoting violence in the Punjab. The BTF was an organization dedicated to the creation of a separate Sikh homeland, commonly known as Khalistan. Sangha testified that he himself was never a member of the Akali Dal party, "didn't know anything," but "supported his father" in his activities.

In September, 1991, four armed men forced their way into the Sangha home. They beat up Sangha's father until Sangha and his brother came to protect him. The men identified themselves as members of the BTF. They demanded that Sangha's father cease his political activities, pay them 100,000 rupees, and give over Sangha and his brother. They said they wanted the two brothers to fight for Khalistan and they wanted to make the brothers unavailable to support the father. They gave Sangha's father three weeks to comply.

Early the next morning, Sangha's whole family left for the neighboring state of Uttar Pradesh to stay away until the terrorists left. A month or two later, however, Sangha's father returned to the farm only to receive a letter from the BTF. This letter reiterated the BTF's demands and threatened to kill the Sangha family. Sangha's father thereupon returned to Uttar Pradesh and arranged for his two sons to leave India.

* * *

* * * Under our case law, and unchanged by *Elias–Zacarias,* an applicant can establish his political opinion on the basis of his own affirmative political views, his political neutrality, or a political opinion imputed to him by his persecutors. * * *

* * *

In this case, Sangha did not establish that he held an affirmative political belief of his own. He testified that he was never a member of the Akali Dal Party, and he "didn't know anything." At the time of his persecution, he was living at home, going to school, and helping his father on the family farm. There is no evidence to show that Sangha had enunciated any affirmative political opinion or engaged in activities associated with affirmative political opinions. * * *

* * *

A second way an applicant can establish a "political opinion" under the Act is to show political neutrality in an environment in which political neutrality is fraught with hazard, from governmental or uncontrolled anti-governmental forces. We have held that political neutrality can be a political opinion under the Act. "Political neutrality" may include the absence of any political opinion. An applicant can establish his political neutrality by pronouncement, or by his actions.

We have held that an applicant's political neutrality must be the product of his conscious, deliberate choice. *Bolanos–Hernandez,* 767 F.2d at 1286. * * *

In a series of cases, we have held that an applicant can establish political neutrality by refusing in the face of threats to join guerilla or illegal government forces. This reasoning was questioned, but not overruled, in *Elias–Zacarias,* where the Court said it would distinguish political neutrality "from such quite different concepts as indifference, indecisiveness, and risk averseness." Recently, we have found political opinion based on neutrality when an applicant deserted from the military forces rather than be forced to shoot deserters illegally. *Ramos–Vasquez [v. INS],* 57 F.3d [857, 863 (9th Cir. 1995)].

In this case, Sangha has not argued, nor did the BIA have to believe, that he was politically neutral. There is no evidence that Sangha made a deliberate and conscious decision to be politically neutral in the Punjab strife. There is no evidence that Sangha ever articulated political neutrality. His only action which might evidence political neutrality was his refusal to join and fight with the BTF. Under *Elias–Zacarias,* accordingly, it is doubtful that this single refusal could establish political neutrality. A reluctance to leave the family farm and go fight a cause he knew nothing of proves nothing about political opinion.

Nonetheless, we do not decide whether Sangha was politically neutral under our case law. As discussed below, his case fails because he produced no evidence that the BTF persecuted Sangha "on account of" any political view he might have held. It was therefore irrelevant whether or not Sangha was politically neutral.

\* \* \*

The third way an applicant can establish a "political opinion" under the Act is to show an imputed political opinion. An imputed political opinion is a political opinion attributed to the applicant by his persecutors. In *Elias–Zacarias* the Supreme Court left open the possibility that an applicant could claim asylum based on persecution based solely on the prosecutor's erroneous beliefs. In *Canas–Segovia* we held that imputed political belief was still a viable form of relief after *Elias–Zacarias. Canas-Segovia v. INS,* 970 F.2d 599, 601–02 (9th Cir. 1992).

In establishing an imputed political opinion, the focus of inquiry turns away from the views of the victim to the views of the persecutor. We consider, however, not the persecutor's own political opinions, but rather the political views the persecutor rightly or in error attributes to his victims. If the persecutor attributed a political opinion to the victim, and acted upon the attribution, this imputed view becomes the applicant's political opinion as required under the Act.

To establish an imputed political opinion, the applicant must show that his persecutors actually imputed a political opinion to him. We have found an imputed political opinion in several different contexts. For example, one party to a conflict may insist to the victim that the victim is aligned with the other side. Or, the victim may have publicly expressed political views which could easily have been known to his persecutors. We have found imputed political neutrality where the applicant has refused to join a non-governmental guerilla group. We have also found imputed political opinion where the applicant is a member of a large, politically active family many of whom have already been persecuted for their political beliefs. In each of these situations, we have considered it likely that the persecutors will attribute the political views of others to the applicants.

In this petition, Sangha argues that he should fall under the doctrine of imputed political belief. Sangha argues, but without proof, that the BTF imputed to him his father's Akali Dal party views. Past persecution of family members is routinely considered as evidence of possible imputed political opinion. In considering such evidence, the trier of fact must examine how close a relationship exists between the persecution of family members and the situation of the applicant.

Because Sangha did not raise this argument before the BIA, we do not have its findings to review. Even if he did, however, there is little evidence in the record to support Sangha's argument. The BTF never expressly said that it was recruiting Sangha because of his father's views. The BTF claimed two different motivations. It claimed it was recruiting Sangha to help it gain Khalistan, and to deprive his father of his support. The BTF's actions do not suggest that the BTF imputed to Sangha his father's political views. Indeed, the BTF's actions suggest the contrary. When the BTF came to the Sangha house, it sought only Sangha's father and beat up only Sangha's father. If the BTF had imputed the Akali Dal political views to Sangha, it seems likely that the BTF would also have sought and beat up Sangha. The fact that the BTF ignored Sangha suggests that it did not believe that Sangha held his father's views.

Sangha argues that the BTF would impute his father's views to him because of their family relationship. Unlike the applicant in *Ramirez Rivas,* where we found an imputed political opinion based on family relationships, Sangha was not a member of a large, historically politically active family. Instead, the Sangha family numbered only four, and only one had just recently become politically active. * * *

* * *

Sangha must next show by direct or circumstantial evidence that his persecution occurred "on account of" his political beliefs. Before *Elias–Zacarias,* we held that where, as here, an applicant refused to fight with guerillas, that refusal in itself established that the persecutors were acting "on account of" the applicant's political views. In these cases, the victim was recruited by a political group. The victim refused, and the political group threatened death if he did not comply. We reasoned in those cases that the victim's refusal showed his political neutrality, which was the equivalent of a political opinion, and that the persecutor's threats were persecution on account of that political opinion.

In *Elias–Zacarias* the Supreme Court instructed us to change course. It held that an applicant's refusal to fight in the context of a forced recruitment is not enough by itself to show that the persecutor acted "on account of" his political views. The Supreme Court held that to qualify under the Act, the applicant must bring other evidence to show that the persecution was based on political opinion.

*Elias–Zacarias* left open, however, what type of direct or circumstantial evidence might suffice to show motivation. Since *Elias–Zacarias,* we have found persecution on account of political opinion when the persecutors say they are acting because of the victim's political beliefs. We have also found such persecution when there is no other logical reason for the persecution. We have also found persecution based on political opinion where a government persecutes a victim in the absence of any actual, legitimate criminal prosecution. When the victim claims persecution based on his own actual political opinion, we further require him to show that the persecutor was aware of those beliefs.

\* \* \*

As noted earlier, the BTF gave two reasons why it wanted to recruit Sangha. First, it wanted Sangha to help fight for Khalistan. This reason suggests that it was acting in furtherance of its own goals, rather than to persecute Sangha for any views he might hold. Second, the BTF wanted to make Sangha unavailable to support his father. This reason suggests that it wanted to punish Sangha's father, rather than to persecute Sangha for his political beliefs.

If the BTF imputed political neutrality to Sangha, there is no evidence that the BTF singled him out because he was neutral and sought to recruit him because of it. Similarly, if the BTF imputed the \* \* \* views of Sangha's father to Sangha, there is not evidence that it chose to recruit him especially because he had such views. To the contrary, it seems unlikely that the BTF would deliberately seek out those who opposed it in order to fill its ranks.

In this context, the \* \* \* proof tended to show that the BTF was not motivated by his political opinion. \* \* \* We agree that the BIA had ample reasons to believe that Sangha did not meet his burden of proof. Certainly, it was not compelled to find otherwise.

Petition denied.

### Notes and Questions

1. After *Elias–Zacarias* as interpreted by the Ninth Circuit in *Sangha*, what does it take to prove persecution "on account of political opinion" in the context of civil war?

2. In 2004–05, the House Judiciary Committee, and particularly its Chairman, James Sensenbrenner (R–Wisc.), voiced intense criticism of the doctrine of imputed political opinion, claiming that, particularly as construed by the Ninth Circuit, the doctrine makes it easy for terrorists to win asylum in the United States. See H.R. Rep. 108–724 (2004), Part 5 (text at notes 72–74). Is this criticism of imputed political opinion fair? What other safeguards against awarding asylum or other protection to terrorists or their supporters are available even while maintaining a robust doctrine of imputed political opinion? (Chapter Six explores how national security grounds (inc. terrorism) may preclude eligibility for asylum and withholding.)

### 4. MIXED MOTIVES

Cases like *Matter of R–*, *Matter of S–P–*, and *Sangha* suggest the difficulties of applying the refugee definition when the persecutor's motives are mixed. A guerrilla army may both want to augment its forces through coerced recruiting of any able-bodied male, but it may also express its rage at refusal in a way that reveals that it imputes a hostile political opinion to the refuser. Police officers may be enforcing normally acceptable provisions of the criminal law, but other features of their action suggest that the politics or the ethnic minority status of the accused played some role. How should the "on account of" test be applied to such circumstances? Judges on the Ninth Circuit took opposing views in the next case, in which mixed motives was the pivotal issue.

## GAFOOR v. INS

United States Court of Appeals, Ninth Circuit, 2002.
231 F.3d 645.

HAWKINS, CIRCUIT JUDGE.

This is the latest in a long line of immigration cases involving claims of racial and political persecution against people of Indian descent living on the South Pacific island of Fiji. Like those asylum-seekers before him, Abdul Gafoor claims he was persecuted by ethnic Fijians on account of his Indian background and that he and his family will be harmed if forced to return to Fiji. We have taken the claims of Indo–Fijians very seriously because of the severe mistreatment they have suffered in their adopted country. * * *

\* \* \*

Abdul Gafoor * * * was a police officer in Fiji with eighteen years experience. Born in Fiji to Indian parents, he was one of the few Indo–Fijians on the country's police force. One day in October 1987, he was on patrol when he heard screams in a nearby street and came upon a man in civilian clothing who was raping a 13-year-old girl. Gafoor arrested the man and escorted him to the police station, but his supervisor, an ethnic Fijian, explained that the man was a high-ranking army officer. The man was then released without being charged, and the supervisor warned Gafoor that his life was in danger.

The next night, the army officer he had arrested came to Gafoor's house with seven or eight other men, all dressed in army uniforms. They beat Gafoor in front of his wife and children and took him to an army camp in Nambala, where he was locked up for one week. During his captivity, several soldiers came to his cell and hit him in the stomach. They asked him why he had arrested an army officer, and they warned him not to tell anyone about the rape or his beating. They also accused him of opposing the army.

After he was released, Gafoor received treatment for his injuries and was transferred temporarily to a job as a court bailiff so that he could recover. Several nights later, he resumed his regular patrol duties and was walking down the street when a military van pulled up to the curb. The army had become involved in police work following the coups, and Gafoor thought the soldiers in the van had stopped to assist him. But when they stepped out of the van, he recognized the officer he had arrested among the group. The soldiers approached, beat him with their rifles, and threatened to kill him. They told him Fiji was their country and that he "should go back to India." Then, they left him in a water ditch, bleeding and unconscious. When he awoke the next morning, he was in a hospital, where he remained for nine days.

Gafoor feared the soldiers would return to kill him, so on November 15, 1987, he fled with his family to Canada. He stayed there until February 1991, when he entered the United States. The INS instituted deportation proceedings against Gafoor and his family in January 1993. He then applied for asylum and withholding of deportation. At his hearing before the Immigration Judge ("IJ"), Gafoor testified about the things that had happened to him. He also testified that ethnic Fijians had since taken over his house in Fiji and that he feared returning home.

\* \* \*

The BIA did not dispute that Gafoor was persecuted, and we think it clear he was. \* \* \*

The more pointed question is whether Gafoor was persecuted *on account of* his race, religion, nationality, membership in a particular social group, or political opinion. This question goes to the motives of his persecutors, and as we have long recognized, motives can be difficult to pin down. \* \* \*

Because it is so difficult to prove motives with any precision, the Supreme Court teaches that an applicant does not have to provide direct evidence that his persecutors were motivated by one of the protected grounds; instead, compelling circumstantial evidence is sufficient. *See Elias–Zacarias,* 502 U.S. at 483, 112 S.Ct. 812. In addition, in *Borja v. INS*, 175 F.3d 732, 736 (9th Cir. 1999) (en banc), we held that an applicant need not show that his persecutors were motivated solely by a protected ground. Nor does an applicant have to prove that the protected ground, by itself, would have led to the persecution. Rather, an applicant need only "produce evidence from which it is reasonable to believe that the harm was motivated, at least in part, by an actual or implied protected ground."

\* \* \*

\* \* \*In his testimony before the IJ, Gafoor stated that when he was locked up at Nambala, the soldiers asked him why he had arrested an army officer and accused him of opposing the army. Then, while they were beating him in the street, the soldiers told Gafoor that Fiji was their country and that he "should go back to India." Gafoor's testimony, which was accepted as true by the BIA, compels a conclusion that he was persecuted *not solely* because he arrested a high-ranking army officer, but also because of his race and the political opinion imputed to him by the soldiers. *See Sangha v. INS,* 103 F.3d 1482, 1489 (9th Cir. 1997) (holding that applicant may establish eligibility for asylum on basis of imputed political opinion).

\* \* \*

* * * The soldiers made clear to Gafoor that his race *and* imputed political opinion contributed to their hatred of him and provided them with additional motive for their actions.[3] That they did not tell him specifically that they were motivated by these factors is unimportant. As noted above, an applicant need not present direct evidence of a persecutor's motives if there is circumstantial evidence. *See Elias–Zacarias,* 502 U.S. at 483, 112 S.Ct. 812. And the soldiers' statements to Gafoor are unmistakable circumstantial evidence that they were motivated by his race and imputed political opinion.

The soldiers in this case were, to be sure, activated by the arrest of the army officer. They specifically questioned Gafoor about the arrest and warned him not to tell anyone about the rape. As we explained in *Borja* and have repeated in numerous cases, however, asylum may be granted if the persecution "was motivated, at least in part, by an actual or implied protected ground." *Borja,* 175 F.3d at 736; *see e.g., Hernandez–Montiel,* 225 F.3d at 1095–96; *Tarubac v. INS,* 182 F.3d 1114, 1119 (9th Cir.1999); *Singh,* 63 F.3d at 1509–10. The evidence presented by Gafoor leaves no doubt that the soldiers were motivated, at least in part, by his Indian background and by his purported opposition to the army. Their message to Gafoor was clear: he had, by simply doing his job as a police officer, challenged the notion that ethnic Fijians were above the law. The soldiers' statements were not "off-the-cuff" remarks or "vague accusation[s]" uttered incidentally. (Dissent at 658–59). They were pointed and specific statements made during two brutal beatings that reveal much about the motivation of those who made them, particularly when considered in the context in which they were made.

* * * But if we are to understand what motivated Gafoor's persecutors, we must consider the entire story. The soldiers were ethnic Fijians engaged in a military coup to depose an elected Indo–Fijian government, to subordinate Indo–Fijians politically and culturally, and to physically punish those perceived as standing in their way. When Gafoor arrested a high-ranking officer for raping a 13-year-old girl, they did not just warn him to mind his own business. * * * When the case is viewed in this context, a reasonable fact-finder could not conclude that Gafoor's persecution was motivated solely by a personal vendetta. The evidence compels a conclusion that he was persecuted, at least in part, on account of his race and an imputed political opinion.

* * *

Judge O'Scannlain argues that *Borja* does not relieve an applicant of the burden of proving that a protected ground "*actually* motivated" the

**3.** The dissent separates these two elements, as if there was no relation between the soldiers' hatred of Gafoor's race and the political opinion they imputed to him. Of course, the two are intimately connected. The 1987 coups were staged by the ethnic Fijian military to ensure the dominance of ethnic Fijians. To be Indo–Fijian was, by definition, to be opposed to this political coup. The dissent is therefore mistaken when it asserts that the soldiers' statement to Gafoor about his political opinion must be "taken alone." To the contrary, the statement must be taken together with the soldiers' statements about Gafoor's race.

persecution. In other words, he appears to argue, if there is evidence of two motives—one that is related to a protected ground and one that is not—the applicant must show persecution solely on the basis of the former motive. Judge O'Scannlain says the *Borja* court did not address this requirement, but that it did not matter anyway because the petitioner's political opinion was clearly "the sufficient and primary cause" of her persecution.

A careful reading of *Borja* undermines this argument. * * *

* * *

* * * *Borja* makes clear that an applicant need not show that a protected ground, standing alone, would have led to the persecution. The guerillas in *Borja* had two motives: they wanted money from the petitioner, and they wanted to punish her for a political opinion. But it was only when she could no longer afford to pay the tax that they persecuted her. Thus, the woman could not prove—and we did not require her to prove—that the guerillas would have persecuted her on the basis of her political beliefs alone. Instead, we simply required her to show that her persecutors were motivated, at least in part, by her political beliefs. It is only Judge O'Scannlain, here and in his *Borja* dissent, who would require more.

Judge O'Scannlain argues in essence that an action cannot be "on account of" some factor unless the factor, by itself, was sufficient to bring about the action. * * *

* * *

Petition granted. Remanded with instructions.

O'SCANNLAIN, CIRCUIT JUDGE, dissenting.

[The record] establishes fairly plainly that the army officer orchestrated the attacks on Gafoor purely as reprisals for his arrest and vivid warnings of what would befall Gafoor if he ever disclosed the facts surrounding it. * * *

* * * [Nonetheless,] the majority asserts that the vague accusation that Gafoor "oppos[ed] the army" and the slur to the effect that Gafoor "should go back to India" "compel[ ] a conclusion that he was persecuted *not solely* because he arrested a high-ranking army officer, but also because of his race and the political opinion imputed to him by the soldiers." Given that the evidence fails on the whole to do anything more than *suggest* that Gafoor's imputed political opinion and race actually animated his assailants' attacks, I think preposterous the majority's implicit contention that "a reasonable factfinder would *have to* conclude" that the evidence *established* as much. *Elias–Zacarias*, 502 U.S. at 481, 112 S.Ct. 812 (emphasis added).

* * *

* * * Taunting or degrading an opponent by referring to one or another of his traits hardly makes "clear" that the trait has any causal

significance—indeed, the trait may be wholly irrelevant to any actual difference of opinion. The majority cannot be serious in holding that the utterance of such a racial slur not only *suggests* that a contemporaneous assault is racially motivated but *compels that conclusion.*

\* \* \*

Reality is that policeman Gafoor was persecuted because he caught a powerful military figure *in flagrante delicto* and dared to arrest the officer whom he witnessed in the criminal act of attempting to rape a young girl. \* \* \*

\* \* \*

\* \* \* The fact that an act of abuse may be "motivated" by two or more distinct considerations does not dispense with the logical requirement that any single factor *actually* "motivated" the conduct.

This requirement, I would be the first to acknowledge, is not easily satisfied. Concluding that something actually "motivated" a human being to act is often not only speculative but conceptually challenging. Is a situational factor that makes a person's action more likely to occur than it otherwise would be a "motive"? What if only infinitesimally more likely? Is a factor a "motive" when it is sufficient to incite an action but does not make that action more likely to occur at all (because the action will certainly occur anyway)?

\* \* \*

Unlike the facts of *Borja*, the facts of this case plainly indicate that the petitioner would not have been persecuted absent a motive that is not enumerated in the Act—that is, Gafoor would never have been persecuted if he had not arrested the army officer. This case thus requires us to determine just how causally significant a factor must be for us to conclude that it is a "motive" for purposes of the Act. It is apparent that for the majority, a motivating factor need not have any causal significance at all. The majority claims that persecution may be "on account of" a protected ground even if the protected ground is neither a sufficient nor even a necessary cause of the persecution. The majority's definition of "motive" remains elusive, but it is apparent that it does not comprehend the concept of causation.

In dispensing with a causation requirement, the majority wilfully disregards the well-settled law of this court. We have regularly rejected the proposition that prosecutory conduct is "on account of" a statutorily protected characteristic just because the presence of that characteristic enhanced the probability that the persecutor conduct would occur.

\* \* \*

The BIA's dismissal of Gafoor's appeal was supported by substantial evidence and perfectly justified. Gafoor has endured dreadful misfortune, but he has not been persecuted on account of any statutorily enumerated ground. \* \* \*

I respectfully dissent.

## Notes and Questions

1. *Gafoor* involves not only mixed motives, but also a mixture of grounds of persecution—race or ethnicity combined with political opinion. We will examine persecution on account of a combination of race, nationality, and religion in the next section of this chapter.

2. If you were Gafoor's attorney, how could you more effectively frame Gafoor's political opinion argument that grows out of his act of arresting the military officer for rape, particularly in light of Judge O'Scannlain's (and apparently the BIA's) characterization of this act and the resulting retaliation as essentially a personal dispute?

3. The majority and the dissent in *Gafoor* battle over the meaning and application of the nexus requirement. How do they differ in their understanding that the feared persecution must be "on account of" a political opinion? Also, how do they differ in their understanding of the review standard that derives from *Elias–Zacarias*?

4. James Hathaway and other refugee law scholars have drawn up principles to assist in interpreting the Refugee Convention's reference to persecution for reasons of race, religion, nationality, political opinion, or membership in a particular social group. Hathaway, *Foreword: The Causal Nexus in International Refugee Law*, 23 Mich. J. Int'l L. 207 (2002). Known as the Michigan Guidelines on Nexus to a Convention Ground, they posit that "it is the applicant's predicament which must be causally linked to a Convention ground." *Id.* at 215. Rejecting causation standards from other bodies of law (in particular, the "but for" test from tort law), the guidelines further state:

> Standards of causation developed in other branches of international or domestic law ought not to be assumed to have relevance to the recognition of refugee status. Because refugee status determination is both protection-oriented and forward-looking, it is unlikely that pertinent guidance can be gleaned from standards of causation shaped by considerations relevant to the assessment of civil or criminal liability, or which are directed solely to the analysis of past events.

> The standard of causation must also take account of the practical realities of refugee status determination, in particular the complex combinations of circumstances which may give rise to the risk of being persecuted, the prevalence of evidentiary gaps, and the difficulty of eliciting evidence across linguistic and cultural divides.

> In view of the unique objects and purposes of refugee status determination, and taking account of the practical challenges of refugee status determination, the Convention ground need not be shown to be the sole, or even the dominant, cause of the risk of being persecuted. It need only be a contributing factor to the risk of being persecuted. If, however, the Convention ground is remote to the point of irrelevance, refugee status need not be recognized.

*Id.* at 217.

5. Stephen Legomsky proposes an elegant analysis of the nexus requirement. In summary, he argues that "on account of" means "because," and that the "but-for" test of causation in U.S. tort law provides a coherent framework for analyzing whether the feared persecution is on account of one of the specified grounds. He sketches a basic framework concerning causation and ties it to the policies underlying the U.S. asylum law. He addresses situations involving mixed motives and instances when two or more elements jointly define the persecuted group; in the latter case he asserts that each attribute that is a substantial factor in triggering the persecution should satisfy the nexus requirement. He offers this example:

> A despot singles out university students of Asian ancestry for persecution. The victims are not being persecuted *solely* on account of race; only the subset of Asians who are university students are being targeted. Does this mean the victims are not being persecuted on account of race? Of course not. The persecution would not have occurred but for their status as university students, but it also would not have occurred but for their race. There can be, and typically are, two or more elements that jointly define the persecuted group.

S. H. Legomsky, Immigration and Refugee Law and Policy 1038–39 (4th ed. 2005). Though Legomsky disagrees with the Michigan Guidelines' rejection of a "but-for" analysis in refugee law, he argues that his approach and the Michigan Guidelines are essentially consistent with each other.

## The REAL ID Act of 2005

Recall from the Notes and Questions following *Sangha v. INS,* earlier in this Section A, p. 217, that in 2004–05 the House Judiciary Committee, especially its chairman, Congressman James Sensenbrenner (R–Wisc.) strongly criticized the doctrine of imputed political opinion. An early version of amendments to asylum law that Rep. Sensenbrenner tried to attach to legislation implementing the recommendations of the 9/11 Commission would have provided: "the applicant must establish that [one of the five Convention grounds] was or will be *the central motive* for persecuting the applicant." H.R. 10, § 3007(a)(1), 108th Cong., 2d Sess. (2004) (as reported by the House Judiciary Committee) (emphasis added). The Committee report quoted extensively from Board Member Heilman's concurring opinion in *Matter of R–,* which was highly critical of the views ultimately adopted by the Board in *Matter of S–P–.* *See* H.R. Rep. 108–724 (2004), Part 5 (text at note 74).

This and related provisions touching on asylum provoked considerable opposition in Congress, and Sensenbrenner was ultimately persuaded to drop these provisions from the popular 9/11 Commission bill, in exchange for a promise of priority consideration in the following Congress. He cashed that promise by attaching what became the REAL ID Act to an emergency supplemental appropriations bill in May 2005. But negotiations had led to significant changes in the crucial language before enactment, as compared to the 2004 version of H.R. 10. In a section captioned "Preventing Terrorists From Obtaining Relief From Removal" the REAL ID Act added the following to INA § 208(b)(1):

> To establish that the applicant is a refugee * * * , the applicant must establish that race, religion, nationality, membership in a particular social group, or political opinion was or will be *at least one central reason* for persecuting the applicant.

Pub. L. 109–13, § 101(a), 119 Stat. 231, 303 (2005) (emphasis added).

This language obviously contemplates that persecutors may act with mixed motives, and it does not require the applicant to prove that a Convention ground is the dominant or sole motive. What makes a motive a "central reason" for persecution is left to be settled by case law. The Conference Committee report does state that the Ninth Circuit's decision in *Borja* and similar cases, discussed in the *Gafoor* excerpt, "have substantially undermined a proper analysis of mixed motive cases," but it does not elaborate on this charge. The report states: "with respect to so-called 'mixed motive' claims, under this amendment, asylum may be granted where there is more than one motive for mistreatment, as long as at least one central reason for the mistreatment is on account of race, religion, nationality, membership in a particular social group, or political opinion."

The Conference Committee Report, H.R. Rep. 109–72 (2005) (Section relating to Division B, Title I), explained that the REAL ID Act would overcome the Ninth Circuit imputed political opinion precedents that, according to the Conference Committee, made it too easy for terrorists to win asylum, because "an alien who is a terrorist could more easily fabricate a claim that his home government believes erroneously that he is a terrorist." *Id.* at 289. But does the language as enacted really work any change in imputed political opinion doctrine? Does it require changes in the Ninth Circuit's imputed political opinion and mixed motive rulings? In the BIA's approach as reflected in *Matter of S–P–*?

How do the Michigan Guidelines' "contributing factor" and Legomsky's "but-for" causation approach (see notes 3 and 4 in the immediately preceding set of Notes and Questions) interact with the REAL ID Act's new requirement in INA § 208(b)(1) that one of the five protected characteristics be "at least one central reason" for the threatened persecution? Can a peripheral reason be relevant? *Cf. Girma v. INS*, 283 F.3d 664, 668 (5th Cir. 2002), which held under pre-REAL ID law that "an applicant for asylum must present evidence sufficient for one to reasonably believe that the harm suffered was *motivated in meaningful part* by a protected ground" (emphasis added).

---

### Exercise

Before coming to the United States, where he has applied for asylum, Oleg worked as a tax auditor for the government of Ruritania, part of the former Soviet Union. During an audit of the Budro Corporation, Oleg uncovered an illegal tax-evasion scheme. Oleg discovered that Budro, founded by a high-ranking government official with close ties to the former communist leaders of Ruritania during Soviet days, had evaded the payment of automobile import duties. When Oleg reported his findings to officials at Budro, they tried to bribe him to change his report. Oleg refused the bribes and referred the matter to local prosecutors.

Oleg and his wife, Nicola, soon began receiving threats. Two men forcibly removed Nicola from a bus. Three days later, she suffered a miscarriage, which she attributed to this incident. Fearing for his safety, Oleg arranged for his cousin to drive him to work. While Oleg's cousin was driving alone in his car, equipped with tinted windows, he was shot. Oleg was supposed to be in the car but had cancelled at the last minute.

After Oleg and Nicola fled Ruritania for the United States, his apartment was vandalized, and some of Nicola's relatives were hurt in a suspicious car accident that Nicola suspects was caused by Budro officials.

You are the immigration judge in Oleg's case. How would you rule on his claim that he has a well-founded fear of persecution on account of political opinion if he is returned to Ruritania?

## SECTION B.   RACE, NATIONALITY, AND RELIGION

Nazi persecution of the Jews, the Roma, the Poles, and other groups was still fresh in the minds of the drafters of the 1951 Convention when they contemplated the need for protection from persecution. In specifying that protection should be available to those with a well-founded fear of persecution based on race, there is no evidence that they intended "race" to correspond to a scientific notion or category. Rather, race appeared to refer to ethnic groups identifiable by their shared culture as much as by any physical distinctiveness. When analyzing this type of persecution today, many look to the International Convention on the Elimination of All Forms of Racial Discrimination, G.A. res. 2106 (XX), Annex, 20 U.N. GAOR Supp. (No. 14) at 47, U.N. Doc. A/6014 (1966), 660 U.N.T.S. 195, *entered into force* Jan. 4, 1969, and its formulation that the term "race" includes "race, color, descent, or national or ethnic origin." Article 1(1).

Roma village.

With regard to the 1951 Convention's reference to persecution based on nationality, a similarly comprehensive approach prevails. For example, after national boundaries were drawn at the end of World War I and World War II, millions of ethnic Hungarians—people whose ancestors had spoken Hungarian for centuries and had pledged allegiance to the Kingdom of Hungary for generations—found themselves within the borders of Romania. Many deemed themselves Hungarian nationals subject to persecution by the tyrannical Ceausescu government, which was in power from 1965 to 1989. Nationality is frequently thus used to refer to those who have the same citizenship as the persecutors, but who belong to a different linguistic or political community.

Infamous persecutions of the past have often blurred the lines between race and nationality. Thousands of Ugandan citizens of Asian origin were expelled in 1972; multitudes of Vietnamese citizens of ethnic Chinese origin fled in 1975; the Tamils in Sri Lanka, the Tutsi in Rwanda; the Bosnians in the Balkans, and the Black Fulanis of Mauritania have all felt the sting of ethnic cleansing and persecution. The ethnic and political conflict in Fiji that led to the *Gafoor* decision (in the previous section of this chapter) shows how notions of race, nationality, and religion are often mixed with each other and with political opinion as persecution targets an identifiable group. Thus conflict between the Hindu and Muslim communities led to the partition of British India in 1947. And in Sri Lanka the conflict between the Tamil minority, largely Hindu, and the Singhalese majority, largely Buddhist, has led to years of bloodshed.

The next two decisions reflect contrasting approaches to similar situations involving civil disturbances and attacks on groups in Indonesia that are defined by a combination of ethnicity and religion. You will notice that these decisions also revisit and apply doctrines that Chapter Three explored with regard to the meaning of "persecution" and "well-founded fear,'' nongovernmental persecution, and the relevance of past persecution, as well as some of the basic approaches to asylum and withholding that the BIA and the courts worked out in the political opinion cases examined in the previous section of this chapter.

## LIE v. ASHCROFT

United States Court of Appeals, Third Circuit, 2005.
396 F.3d 530.

BECKER, CIRCUIT JUDGE.

* * * Both Lie and her husband are ethnically Chinese and are Christians. In the late 1990s, Indonesia's Chinese Christian population became the target of widespread attacks perpetrated by Muslim Indonesians. The 1999 United States State Department country report for Indonesia noted that "[i]nterreligious violence and violence against ethnic minorities continued. Attacks against houses of worship continued, and the lack of an effective government response to punish perpetrators and prevent further attacks led to allegations of official complicity in some incidents." U.S. Dep't of State, 1999 Country Reports on Human Rights Practices–Indonesia, Feb. 25, 2000 ("1999 Country Report"). In May 1998, there were "serious and widespread attacks" on Chinese-owned businesses and homes by Muslim Indonesians, which led to the deaths of over one thousand people. Thus, 1998 represented a period of significant violence and rioting against individuals of Chinese origin throughout Indonesia.

Lie alleges that at the start of this tumultuous period, in 1997, several native, Muslim Indonesians entered her husband's store, threatened him with a knife, called him a "Chinese pig," and then robbed him. Traumatized as a result of the robbery, her husband left for the United States in December 1997.

Lie further claims that in July 1998, two people knocked on the door of her home, called her a "Chinese pig," and demanded entry. They knocked down the door brandishing a knife, threatened to burn down her house, and demanded that she give them money. The intruders took some of Lie's money and jewelry and struck her in the left forearm with the knife when she tried to defend herself. When they left, Lie called the police, but claims that no one at the police station answered the phone. Lie received several stitches for the knife wound. However, for the next twenty-one months, Lie and her son continued to live in the same house without incident.

* * *

The IJ made credibility findings in Lie's favor, including that the IJ had "no reason to dispute the veracity of [the] claim that [Lie] and her husband are ethnically Chinese" and that Lie was in fact Catholic. The main issue addressed by the IJ was the motivation of the individuals who robbed Lie's husband and Lie. While finding that the attackers had some interest in simple robbery, the IJ concluded that, "taking into account the context in which the respondent's claim arises, it is reasonable to conclude that those who robbed the respondent and her husband were motivated at least in part by a desire to punish them because of their ethnicity." In addition to Lie's testimony about the incident, the IJ relied on evidence of the 1998 anti-Chinese riots and other violence directed against ethnic Chinese during this period documented in the 1999 Country Report. Therefore, the IJ found that Lie and her husband had suffered past persecution, and that the presumption of future persecution had not been rebutted by evidence of changed conditions in Indonesia.

The government appealed to the Board of Immigration Appeals (BIA), which overturned the IJ's grant of the Lies' asylum petition. The BIA found that "with regard to the single incident of abuse [Lie] has described, a robbery of her store, there was no evidence that it was motivated by her religion. As for her claim that the robbery was motivated by her Chinese ethnicity, the only evidence to support that claim was her testimony that her attackers said 'you Chinese pig, I want your money,'" which the BIA found to be insufficient.

The BIA further reasoned that even if the ethnic slur was sufficient to establish that the intruders were motivated by Lie's ethnicity or religion, the robbery incident did not constitute persecution. The BIA found significant that Lie's Chinese neighbors were not robbed, that Lie tried only once to contact the police, and that she lived for nearly two years after the attack without incident before fleeing to the United States. * * *

* * *

We agree with the BIA's conclusion and similarly hold that Lie has not established her claim of past persecution.

* * *

An asylum applicant must prove that she suffered past persecution or has a well-founded fear of future persecution "on account of" one of five enumerated grounds: "race, religion, nationality, membership in a particular social group, or political opinion." The Supreme Court, in *INS v. Elias–Zacarias,* [502 U.S. 478, 112 S.Ct. 812, 117 L.Ed.2d 38 (1992)], held that while an asylum-seeker would not "be expected to provide direct proof of his persecutors' motives," nevertheless, since the statute makes motive critical, he must provide *some* evidence of [motive], direct or circumstantial. And if he seeks to obtain judicial reversal of the BIA's determination, he must show that the evidence he presented was so compelling that no reasonable factfinder could fail to find the requisite fear of persecution.

We have recognized that "[a] persecutor may have multiple motivations for his or her conduct, but the persecutor must be motivated, at least in part, by one of the enumerated grounds." *Lukwago v. Ashcroft,* 329 F.3d 157, 170 (3d Cir. 2003).

\* \* \*

While the 1999 Country Report did provide evidence that there was widespread animus against ethnic Chinese, the BIA was nevertheless entitled to rely on the evidence that, in Lie's particular case, the robberies were motivated by money. We find that the evidence of general ethnic difficulties would not compel a reasonable factfinder to conclude that the intrusions were "on account of" Lie's ethnicity or religion. Therefore, the BIA's decision to deny Lie's claim on this basis was supported by substantial evidence in the record.

\* \* \*

The BIA also found that Lie failed to establish a well-founded fear of future persecution if she and her family were to return to Indonesia. To establish a well-founded fear of future persecution an applicant must first demonstrate a subjective fear of persecution through credible testimony that her fear is genuine. Second, the applicant must show, objectively, that "a reasonable person in the alien's circumstances would fear persecution if returned to the country in question." [*Zubeda v. Ashcroft,* 333 F.3d 463, 469 (3d Cir. 2003).] To satisfy the objective prong, a petitioner must show she would be individually singled out for persecution or demonstrate that "there is a pattern or practice in his or her country of nationality ... of persecution of a group of persons similarly situated to the applicant on account of race, religion, nationality, membership in a particular social group, or political opinion...." 8 C.F.R. § 208.13(b)(2)(iii)(A).[a]

It appears that the BIA denied Lie's well-founded fear claim primarily because Lie failed to establish that her fear of future persecution was genuine. \* \* \* [I]mportant to the BIA's finding that Lie lacked a subjective fear of returning to Indonesia was the fact that Lie did not leave Indonesia with her husband after the first robbery, and waited nearly two years after the subsequent robbery of her home to come to the United States because her son was still in school. \* \* \*

\* \* \*

Petitioners argue, with some force, that anti-Chinese violence persists, citing evidence in the record of widespread attacks on Chinese Christians in Indonesia, including press accounts of riots, vandalism, and robbery targeting Chinese Christians. Nevertheless, such violence does not appear to be sufficiently widespread as to constitute a pattern or practice. The 1999 Country Report on Indonesia indicated that there was a sharp decline in violence against Chinese Christians following the period of intense violence in 1998, and noted that the Indonesian government officially promotes religious and ethnic tolerance. Moreover, this violence seems to have been primarily wrought by fellow citizens

---

**a.** a The full text of this regulation is quoted in the next case, at p. 237 infra.

and not the result of governmental action or acquiescence. Given these considerations, we are not compelled to find that such attacks constitute a pattern or practice of persecution against Chinese Christians.

In sum, Lie has failed to demonstrate she has a subjective fear of persecution, which alone would be sufficient to foreclose her claim. Even if she could establish she subjectively fears persecution upon her return to Indonesia, Lie has not established the objective prong of the well-founded fear test because she has failed to establish an individualized risk of persecution or that there is pattern or practice of persecution of Chinese Christians in Indonesia. For the foregoing reasons, we will deny the petition for review.

---

The next case contrasts with *Lie* not only as to result, but also in that its facts reflect a stronger emphasis on religion as compared with nationality in defining the targeted ethnic group.

## EDUARD v. ASHCROFT

United States Court of Appeals, Fifth Circuit, 2004.
379 F.3d 182.

DeMoss, Circuit Judge.

\* \* \*

Petitioners Jopie Eduard ("Eduard") and his wife, Yuliana Pakkung ("Pakkung"), are natives and citizens of Indonesia. \* \* \*

\* \* \*

Eduard is a Christian of Manado ancestry; he asserts, however, that Indonesians presume he is Chinese because of his skin tone and the shape of his eyes. When Eduard lived in Indonesia, he was struck in the head with a rock while walking to church. Although Eduard was not able to identify the assailant, he nonetheless presumed that the assailant was a Muslim because the assault occurred just days after a large civil dispute between the Government and the Muslims. Eduard sustained cuts on his head and was given medication to stop the bleeding. Eduard also testified that he was taunted as a "pork eater" by a Muslim while he sat on a bus. Aside from the stone-throwing incident, Eduard was never physically punished or harmed in Indonesia because of his Christian faith or imputed Chinese ethnicity.

Pakkung is a Christian of Chinese ethnicity. She testified that she was taunted in school by Muslim students and that the bus of a fellow Christian was stoned in 1986. Pakkung, however, did not actually witness the stoning. Pakkung also stated that her grandparents tried to convert her to Islam when she was eight years old. She claimed that they "hit [her] and beat [her] up" when she refused to say Muslim prayers.

Pakkung, however, did not testify that she suffered any injuries or that she ever required medical treatment.

The IJ found that "the taunting described by [Eduard] and the general harassment does not rise to the level of a serious punishment or harm that would justify a grant of asylum." The IJ also concluded that "there is no evidence that [Pakkung] was ever targeted for any actual physical abuse in Indonesia."

The IJ's findings are supported by substantial evidence. Neither Eduard nor Pakkung were interrogated, detained, arrested, or convicted in Indonesia. The only violence suffered by either party, on account of either religion or ethnicity, was the injury to Eduard's head allegedly caused by a purported Muslim. The rest of the mistreatment recounted during the IJ hearing was composed of mere denigration, harassment, and threats. Neither discrimination nor harassment ordinarily amounts to persecution under the INA, even if the conduct amounts to "morally reprehensible" discrimination on the basis of race or religion. Thus, substantial evidence supports the IJ's finding that Petitioners failed to establish past persecution.

\* \* \*

Despite an adverse finding on their claims of past persecution, Petitioners can still establish their refugee status by demonstrating well-founded fears of persecution. \* \* \*

\* \* \*

Petitioners contend that the IJ applied erroneous law to conclude that Petitioners' feared persecution was not based on race or religion. The IJ concluded that Petitioners did not satisfy 8 C.F.R. § 208.13(b)(2)(i)(A), which requires that a fear of persecution be "on account of" a protected belief or characteristic. Although the IJ recognized that Petitioners' fears were partially due to their Christianity, the IJ held that such fear was not "on account of" their religion because Indonesia is rife with civil uprisings and violence which are not specific to Christian or Chinese inhabitants.

\* \* \*

These cases [cited by the immigration judge and the government on appeal] hold that an applicant's fear of persecution cannot be *based solely* on general violence and civil disorder. None of these cases, however, supports the IJ's proposition that fear based on a protected belief or characteristic is *negated* simply because of general violence and civil disorder. Congress no doubt anticipated that citizens of countries rife with general violence and civil disorder would seek asylum in the United States. If it had intended to deny refugee status to applicants from such countries, who also feared persecution based on one of the five statutorily protected beliefs and characteristics, it would have presumably stated so.

Upon review of the record, it is clear that Petitioners' fears of persecution were not based solely on the peripheries of civil violence and disorder. For example, Pakkung submitted in her application that she:

[I]s afraid to go back to Indonesia because Christians are being persecuted there by the Moslems and the Indonesian government cannot control them. Killings, bloodshed, burnings, persecutions of Christians are happening all over Indonesia in places like Jakarta, Bandung, Solo, Situbondo, Surabaya, Lombok, Bali, West Kalimantan, Ujung Pandang, Poso, Maluku Island and even in Irian Jaya.... When the Government catches the Moslem culprits, they pardon and release them.

She also testified that she feared being persecuted by the Laskar Jihad, a group which pressures Christians to convert to Islam.

Eduard testified that the Muslim majority presents a risk to Christians everywhere in Indonesia under present conditions. Eduard's siblings, who live in Indonesia, are afraid to attend church due to the violence. Another witness, Gideon Tandirerung, confirmed that Christians are pressured to convert to Islam and that churches are routinely burned. He also described the widespread influence of the Laskar Jihad, who are responsible for forced conversions and other physical violence against Christians.

A review of the record indicates that Petitioners' fears of persecution were based on their Christian faith in particular, and Indonesian civil strife in general. The IJ committed legal error by analyzing whether Petitioners' fear of persecution was "on account of" their race or religion using a standard not supported by case law or the regulations.

\* \* \*

Petitioners contend that the IJ erred by requiring them to prove that they "ha[d] been targeted for punishment or harm based on [a protected] belief or characteristic." The IJ held that Petitioners failed to meet this element: "Although a general climate of violence based, at least in part, on differences between Islam and Christianity and socio-economic tensions, as described by the United States State Department, which are exacerbated by Chinese ethnicity, exists in Indonesia, [Petitioners] have not been targeted for any of these reasons in the past in Indonesia."

The asylum regulations provide that:

In evaluating whether the applicant has sustained the burden of proving that he or she has a well-founded fear of persecution, the asylum officer or immigration judge *shall not require the applicant to provide evidence that there is a reasonable possibility he or she would be singled out individually for persecution* if:

(A) The applicant establishes that there is a pattern or practice in his or her country of ... persecution of a group of persons similarly situated to the applicant on account of race, religion, nationality, membership in a particular social group, or political opinion; and

(B) The applicant establishes his or her own inclusion in, and identification with, such group of persons such that his or her fear of persecution upon return is reasonable.

8 C.F.R. 208.13(b)(2)(iii) (emphasis added).

It is clear from the record, and the IJ's findings, that there was a pattern of persecution of Christians in Indonesia. Thus, Petitioners were not required to show that they would be singled out for persecution upon return to Indonesia. Moreover, requiring an applicant to prove past targeting to establish a well-founded fear would effectively replicate the past persecution inquiry. Thus, the IJ committed legal error by requiring that Petitioners prove they had been targeted in the past.

\* \* \*

Petitioners also contend that the IJ erred by requiring them to prove that "the persecutor is aware, or becomes aware, that the applicant possesses that belief or characteristic." It is well-settled that asylum applicants must only demonstrate that a feared persecutor "could easily become aware" of an applicant's protected beliefs or characteristics. \* \* \*

\* \* \*

Having carefully reviewed the record of this case, the parties' respective briefing and arguments, \* \* \* we hold \* \* \* [t]he IJ did not err by finding that Petitioners failed to establish past persecution. The IJ nonetheless erred by holding that Petitioners did not have a well-founded fear of persecution. In particular, the IJ applied erroneous law in concluding that: (1) Petitioners' fear was not based on race or religion, [and] (2) Petitioners' fear was unreasonable \* \* \*. Thus, the IJ's denial of Petitioners' applications for asylum [and] withholding of removal \* \* \* is reversed and remanded for further proceedings not inconsistent with this opinion.

\* \* \*

[The dissenting opinion of CIRCUIT JUDGE EMILIO M. GARZA is omitted.]

**Notes and Questions**

1. The Third Circuit concluded in *Lie* that being taunted as a "Chinese pig" during a robbery was insufficient basis for concluding a religious and ethnic motive for the robbery, whereas the Fifth Circuit concluded in *Eduard* that taunts of "pork eater" by a fellow bus passenger and being struck by a rock thrown by an unknown assailant several days after large civil disputes between the government and the Muslims constituted evidence of religious persecution. Do you agree? With both? With either? Are there other factors that might explain the different results?

2.   Both sets of asylum applicants had family members who continued to live in Indonesia without experiencing harm, though Pakkung's mother stated that she is afraid to go to church because of recent church bombings. The Third Circuit stated in *Lie*: "In this case, there is little evidence that Lie would face an individualized risk of persecution any more severe than that faced by her family members or other Chinese Christians in Indonesia." On the other hand, the Fifth Circuit said in *Eduard*: "It is clear * * * that there was a pattern of persecution of Christians in Indonesia." To what extent is information about the family members in Indonesia relevant?

Furthermore, what kind of pattern counts? Would such a pattern in Jakarta be relevant to an Indonesian Christian whose home is on the island of Borneo or Bali? How does the adjudicator determine whether the pattern is persecution of Christians instead of one aimed at Pentecostals or Catholics or church leaders or Christians who live in heavily Muslim communities? After *Eduard,* do all Indonesian Christians whose cases are heard by immigration judges within the jurisdiction of the Fifth Circuit have valid asylum claims? (The answers to such a question can be significant. In 2004–05, the Justice Department successfully prosecuted leaders of a major fraud ring that filed over 1,000 fraudulent applications on behalf of Indonesians in the United States. The central theme in the false stories used as the basis for asylum was persecution of Christians or ethnic Chinese by Muslims in Indonesia. *See* Markon, *26 Charged in Va. In Document Fraud,* Washington Post, Nov. 23, 2004, at A4; *11 Plead Guilty in Massive Asylum Fraud*, Inside ICE, Feb. 28, 2005, at 4.)

3.   One issue addressed by the Fifth Circuit in *Eduard* is the issue of persecution related in part to race and ethnicity in a setting beset by general violence and civil disorder. Can the Fifth Circuit's reasoning be reconciled with the approach taken in a somewhat similar setting by the Ninth Circuit majority in *Gafoor*, in Section A of this chapter, p. 222? Both cases involved an individual who suffers harm due in part to his ethnicity, yet the decisions took very different analytical paths. Why didn't ethnicity play a greater role in the reasoning in *Gafoor*?

## SECTION C.   RELIGIOUS PRACTICES AND BELIEFS

In the previous section of this chapter, race and nationality were intertwined with religion in that a persecuted group like Indonesia's Chinese–Christian minority was defined by others using a combination of all three elements. In such situations, the religious identification of a group by outsiders generally functions like a race or nationality distinction—because someone might be identified for persecution, e.g., as a Jew, even if in his own mind he is a nonbeliever. This section addresses a related but different set of situations—persecution that concerns religious practices and beliefs as opposed to external religious identification as part of defining a targeted group.

Before and after: Buddhas in Bamyan Valley, destroyed as
"idolatrous" by the Taliban, 2001. (Photos: Before ©
S.H.A.N.; After © UNESCO/Martin Hadlow)

In the first years after the Refugee Act of 1980, the case law
analyzing religious persecution was relatively sparse. This has begun to
change in recent years, perhaps sparked, in part, by a congressional
effort to give greater visibility to those suffering religious persecution. In
1998, the International Religious Freedom Act, Pub. L. 105–292, 112
Stat. 2787, established a new State Department Office on International
Religious Freedom and created a U.S. Commission on International
Religious Freedom to investigate and report on religious persecution
around the world. The legislation requires training for all U.S. officials
involved in refugee adjudication, and requires those who decide asylum
cases to refer to annual reports on international religious freedom.

Two recent cases concerning religious practice in China illustrate
some of the recurring issues that arise in religion-based asylum claims.

## TIAN-YONG CHEN v. INS

United States Court of Appeals, Second Circuit, 2004.
359 F.3d 121.

CABRANES, CIRCUIT JUDGE.

\* \* \*

Chen grew up in a Roman Catholic family in Changle county of the
Fujian province of China. In early 1994, his uncle led a campaign to
build, in Chen's home village, a Roman Catholic church that would be
loyal to the Vatican and the Pope, unlike the government-sanctioned

Patriotic Catholic Church that is by design and purpose independent of the Vatican. The uncle was guided in this effort by a Chinese Roman Catholic priest from overseas and a pro-Vatican retired priest of the Patriotic Catholic Church. Chen and a cousin solicited donations from neighbors to raise funds for the church. After a neighbor reported their activity to the local police, Chen and the cousin were arrested and detained for a week in March 1994.

According to Chen, the church was completed in early 1995, at which point he compiled a "simple[pamphlet about the life of Christ and the necessity to be loyal to the Pope" that he and his cousin distributed among Catholics in their village, including members of the Patriotic Catholic Church. Chen then learned of an investigation into the pamphlets, which led to a village meeting at which a police officer "encouraged villagers to turn the distributors in." Fearing danger, Chen and his cousin went into hiding in the uncle's house. Chen then learned that the police were looking for him and that his own house had been searched. At that point, Chen left China.

* * * Chen testified that he, along with his Roman Catholic family and approximately seventy to eighty other villagers, attended the local Patriotic Catholic Church. He stated that about forty of those members, like Chen's family, also subscribed to *Roman* Catholicism. Chen * * * described his arrest and detention in March 1994. Chen testified that, when he told the authorities that he had not done anything wrong, police officers "scolded" him and "then, they used their hands to beat [him] and [sic] as they were punishing [him.]."

Chen further testified that, upon his release, he continued to solicit donations for the church. He testified that the church was completed in 1995, and it was identified by a sign stating "Fin Chen Village Roman Catholic Church." * * *

* * *

At the hearing, the IJ received into evidence certain materials submitted by Chen, including a December 11, 1995 United States Department of State report on asylum entitled "China–Country Conditions and Comments on Asylum Applications" (the "Report"). * * *

* * * The Report explains that, in the 1950s, the Chinese government established an "official" Catholic Church—the Patriotic Catholic Church—to operate independently from the Vatican, and that no other Catholic establishment has authority to operate openly. The Report further explains that the Chinese government established the Patriotic Catholic Church and other Christian organizations "to curb perceived foreign domination of Christian groups," and it notes that "central policy is to cajole or force all groups to join official 'patriotic religious organizations' for control purposes."

The Report indicates that "[s]poradic repression in some areas has reflected official concern over the [g]overnment's inability to control the rapid growth of membership in [unsanctioned] Christian groups." It further states that "[i]n general, individual worshippers are not harassed by the regime" and that the regime "target[s] leaders," including priests, "particularly those who maintain connections with Rome." The Report also indicates that "authorities are sensitive to proselytizing," and that, "although some discreet proselytizing and distributing of religious texts outside official channels is tolerated," the government does "proscribe[ ] and sometimes punish[ ]" religious proselytizing.

The Report states that many Chinese are members of unsanctioned churches and that the number of unsanctioned-church members "clearly surpasses the number of members of 'sanctioned' churches." The Chinese government is reported to "generally tolerate ... the existence and activities of the unsanctioned churches, as long as services are small and there is no higher-level organizing." The Report refers to an October 3, 1995 article in *The New York Times* for a report of "relaxed restrictions on Christian worship in Changle county."

The Report also refers to the China chapter in the State Department's 1994 Country Reports for the observation that the official Christian churches and the unregistered "underground" churches enjoy a "murky relationship," which includes coexistence and even cooperation. The Country Reports' China chapter also provides further information on "detention of Christians, foreigners' unauthorized proselytizing, and closings of churches in some areas, noting ... that authorities elsewhere tolerate the existence of unofficial Catholic and Protestant churches as long as they remain small and discreet."

At the hearing's conclusion, the IJ rendered an oral decision denying Chen's application for asylum and withholding of deportation. The IJ summarized the events as Chen had described them in his application and testimony, including Chen's claim that he had been "interrogated about his activities" when he was detained in March 1994, but the IJ did not mention Chen's claim that he had been beaten. The IJ stated that Chen's "rendition of his situation in his native land failed to demonstrate any reasonable possibility that he would be harmed or threatened if returned to the People's Republic of China at this time." Concluding that Chen had not established past persecution or a well-founded fear of future persecution, the IJ denied Chen's application, while granting Chen's alternative request for voluntary departure.

On appeal by Chen, the BIA * * * concluded that Chen's arrest and detention were insufficient to constitute past persecution. In a footnote to its analysis of past persecution, the BIA remarked that "[a]lthough Chen's counsel in his brief states that [Chen] was beaten by Chinese officials during this detention, the record reflects that [Chen] did not testify that he was beaten, but did testify that he was interrogated." Proceeding from its determination on past persecution, the BIA further concluded that Chen failed to establish a well-founded fear of future persecution, finding insufficient evidence in the record "to demonstrate that anyone in China has the present inclination to persecute [Chen]." In support of this conclusion, the BIA cited the Report for its observations that the Chinese government "principally target[s] leaders" and "tolerates the existence and activities of the unsanctioned churches, as long as services are small and there is no higher-level organizing."

\* \* \*

What is troubling about this case is the undisputed failure by the IJ and the BIA (jointly and severally, the "immigration court") to acknowledge, much less evaluate, Chen's testimony that he had been beaten. At his deportation hearing, Chen specifically stated that the police "used their hands to beat [him]." A review of the BIA's decision reveals no consideration of that testimony. Indeed, not only did the BIA, in denying Chen's application, fail to mention Chen's testimony on being beaten, but the BIA also stated—explicitly but erroneously—that Chen had *not* testified to being beaten. \* \* \*

\* \* \*

Because the BIA did not consider Chen's testimony that he had been beaten, its decision is fatally flawed and we are unable adequately to consider whether substantial evidence supports the BIA's determination that Chen failed to establish either past persecution or a well-founded fear of future persecution.

\* \* \*

The immigration court on remand will be obligated to consider whether the *particular circumstances* asserted by Chen establish eligibility for asylum or withholding of deportation. We believe that, in considering those questions, the immigration court should be careful not to place excessive reliance on published reports of the Department of State such as the one received into evidence in the instant case. Such State Department reports are usually the result of estimable expertise and earnestness of purpose, and they often provide a useful and informative overview of conditions in the applicant's home country. But their observations do not automatically discredit contrary evidence presented by the applicant, and they are not binding on the immigration court. \* \* \*

In addition, the immigration court cannot assume that a report produced by the State Department—an agency of the Executive Branch of Government that is necessarily bound to be concerned to avoid abrading relations with other countries, especially other major world powers—presents the most accurate picture of human rights in the country at issue. We note the widely held view that the State Department's reports are sometimes skewed toward the governing administration's foreign-policy goals and concerns.

The Report received into evidence in this case suggests that the Chinese government, in its efforts to control religious practices in the mid-1990s, focused on "leaders" of unsanctioned churches. The Report, however, qualifies its observations by noting that this was the "general" approach of the Chinese government and that the government sometimes engaged in "[s]poradic repression in some areas," and the Report acknowledges that "the authorities are sensitive to proselytizing." Moreover, the observation that the government's control efforts were focused on church leaders does not undercut Chen's claims that he suffered past persecution and reasonably fears future persecution. Chen's testimony, if believed, establishes that he participated to a greater degree than an ordinary layperson by soliciting donations and distributing unauthorized religious pamphlets, and that the authorities targeted him for these activities. It is possible that someone in Chen's position is regarded as a "leader" in his effort freely to exercise his religious faith, especially in a country where high-level leaders of any church hierarchy—and particularly persons identified as leaders of the *Roman* Catholic Church— reportedly suffer serious adverse consequences and are often physically inaccessible to their congregations. Indeed, activities of the sort asserted by Chen may be more obvious to government authorities than those of high-level church leaders, whose roles may be intentionally concealed by the Vatican, for the protection of the leaders and their local churches. The Report's observations of religious persecution in China are only useful to the extent that they comment upon or are relevant to the highly specific question of whether *this individual* suffered persecution.

\* \* \*

\* \* \* [W]e grant Chen's petition for review, vacate the BIA's decision, and remand the case for further proceedings consistent with this opinion.

## XIADONG LI v. GONZALES

United States Court of Appeals, Fifth Circuit, 2005.
420 F.3d 500, vacated as moot, 429 F.3d 1153.

STEWART, CIRCUIT JUDGE.

\* \* \* Li grew up in Ningbo, China, and his parents continue to live there. Li was born into a Christian family, but the Chinese leadership, the Chinese Communist Party, suppressed religious activities, and his parents did not allow him to participate in the church.

Li's friend, Gao Ying, invited him to join a government church in November 1989, and Li signed up to be a member. In December 1989, the administrators of Li's school learned of his participation in the church and warned him against participating in a religion that did not support the Chinese Communist Party. The administrators threatened to discharge Li from school and to inform the police if he continued his participation. Li ended his participation in the government church.

Li then became involved in an underground church. He and his friend, Gao Ying, organized a group of six or seven members and held meetings at Li's home on Sundays. Li's parents did not approve of the meetings because they feared trouble if the police found out about them. During the meetings, the group studied the Bible and exchanged religious materials. The meetings began in December 1989, and continued through April 1995.

In December 1994, the police came to Li's house during a meeting, but found no religious materials and took no action. The police warned Li not to spread reactionary materials or religious materials. The group continued to have meetings, and the police returned in April 1995, at which time they found religious materials in Li's home. The police advised Li that he was holding an illegal gathering, and Li responded that the Constitution gave him the freedom to practice a religion. The police arrested Li for being a reactionary. He was the only participant arrested because he was recognized as the organizer of the gathering at his home.

Li was handcuffed and taken to the police station, where he was placed in a room and told to kneel. When he refused, the police beat him, kicking his leg in the back, hitting him in the head, and pulling his hair, forcing him to kneel. The police interrogated Li, seeking his admission that he was involved in an illegal gathering and had conducted an underground church, but Li refused to plead guilty. Li stated that there were two policemen in the room and one was holding a police bar, which he used to hit Li if the officer did not like Li's responses to the questions.

After two hours of questioning, Li signed a written confession, acknowledging that he was pleading guilty to conducting an illegal gathering against the government and organizing an underground church. Li was detained with a number of other prisoners under abusive conditions for five days, until he was bailed out by his uncle. Li lost his job and the police forced him to work in the streets cleaning public toilets, without pay. He continued doing this work until he left the country.

Li obtained a visa and a passport and left the country on November 4, 1995. After he had agreed to plead guilty, Li had been told that a hearing would be set in six months. He left the country before the hearing was conducted because he believed that he would have been sentenced to prison. Li testified that he did not believe that there was any part of China where he could practice his religion without harassment.

Li did not file an application for asylum until July 1999 because he had planned on returning to China. He testified that he had hoped that China's policy on religious practice would change, and he could return home without being subject to persecution. Li reported that he had sent religious materials back to China and that when the police discovered the materials, in March 1999, they interrogated his family members. The police warned his family to report to them if Li returned to China and warned them that if they did not the family members would be charged with an offense. After that incident, Li stated that he realized that China's policy had not changed toward underground churches and that conditions had worsened. He learned in May 1999 that his friend, Gao Ying, had been arrested and sentenced to prison for two years. Li testified that he believed that if he returned to China, he would face oppression, arrest, interrogation, jail time, and torture.

Li admitted on cross-examination that he had never registered his church and that it was an underground church. He explained that if he registered the church, the Government would use it for its own propaganda purposes. He agreed that it was against the law in China to have an underground church and that he had been arrested for a legal violation. Li also admitted that he had no problems with the church in the six years prior to the police visit in 1994. He stated that the bar used to beat him was an electric black wand and that the officer shocked him with the bar if the officer dislike[d] Li's responses. * * *

* * * Li applied for asylum in August 1999, after learning of his friend's imprisonment for religious activities, his family's interrogation in March, and that the police were looking for him because he had sent religious materials to China.

* * *

The IJ denied the application for asylum because Li failed to file it within one year of his arrival.[a] The IJ also determined that Li was not entitled to relief under [the Convention Against Torture]. Li has not challenged the IJ's ruling denying his application for asylum or the denial of relief under the CAT. However, the IJ granted Li withholding of removal and held that Li cannot be removed to China unless circumstances there change. * * * [T]he IJ found that Li was a credible witness with respect to his testimony about his personal experience in China. The IJ also determined that the testimony was consistent with the information provided by the United States State Department about the practices in China regarding underground religious organizations. The IJ recognized that unregistered religious activity in China is a punishable offense. The IJ further noted that the materials provided by the State Department showed that between 1994 and 1997, which included the time of Li's 1995 arrest, the police had stepped up a campaign against unregistered religious groups.

The IJ determined that the Chinese law against unregistered religious activities was an institutional form of persecution aimed at persons engaged in religious activities who cannot be controlled by the Government. The IJ found no evidence that the prohibition against unregistered religious groups is related to a legitimate attempt to stop terrorism or other legitimate interests in public order. The IJ concluded that if Li returned to China, it was more likely than not that he would be subject to persecution based on his religious activities in 1995.

The INS appealed the IJ's order granting withholding of removal. The BIA determined that Li was a credible witness but concluded that he had failed to show that it was more likely than not that he would be persecuted if he returns to China. The BIA averred that Li was punished for violating the law regarding unregistered churches and not because of

**a.** The one-year deadline for applying for asylum is discussed in Chapter Two, at p. 87 and in Chapter Six, at pp. 370–71.

his religion. The BIA further stated that the Chinese Government has a legitimate right to enforce the laws which it enacts and that Li's fears were of prosecution and not persecution. Finally, the BIA concluded that punishment by the Chinese government for violating its strict regulations of the amount of religious materials available to its citizens and the amount of materials brought into the country is also not a form of persecution. * * *

* * *

The Supreme Court has held that persecution is "on account of" one of the protected grounds if the persecutor's motivation to harm the victim is on account of the victim's possession of the characteristic at issue. *Elias–Zacarias,* 502 U.S. [478], 482, 112 S.Ct. 812[, 117 L.Ed.2d 38 (1992)]. The Court stated, as an example, that the Nazi regime's persecution of Jews was not persecution on account of political opinion. While, the Nazis' persecution was part of the pursuit of *their* political goals, the Nazis were not motivated by a desire to overcome a political opinion held by Jews; therefore, the persecution was not "on account of" political opinion. Likewise, the Court stated that "if a fundamentalist Moslem regime persecutes democrats, it is not engaging in persecution on account of religion." The federal courts and the BIA have also recognized that an alien may demonstrate that a persecutor's actions were on account of a protected characteristic even if a persecutor had mixed motivations; a persecutor does not have to be motivated solely by the victim's possession of a protected characteristic. *Girma v. INS,* 283 F.3d 664, 667–68 (5th Cir. 2002) (holding that the alien need not prove that the persecutor was motivated by a protected ground to the exclusion of all other motivations). The question thus becomes whether China was motivated, at least in part, by Li's religion in punishing Li.

The BIA held that Li did not establish that he would be persecuted if he was returned to China because Li did not prove that his punishment was on account of his religion. The BIA held that Li was punished for violating the law regarding unregistered churches and not because of his religion. The BIA noted that "China does not prohibit registered religions and its law is a legitimate sovereign right 'not institutional persecution.' "

We find it necessary at this point to examine China's regulation of religion in order to determine whether the Chinese government was punishing Li on account of his religion when it charged him with violating its religious regulations. The evidence in the record establishes the following: China recognizes five "official" religions: Catholicism, Protestantism, Buddhism, Islam and Taoism. Dep't of State, 106th Cong., Country Reports on Human Rights Practices for 1998 855 (Comm. Print 1999). Religious groups must be registered with the government's Religious Affairs Bureau (RAB). Government sanctioned "patriotic religious organizations" supervise religious groups and must in turn report to the RAB. Religious activity is permitted only at places of worship and by groups that are registered with the RAB and come under the supervision of the corresponding patriotic organization. For example, the government legally permits only Christian groups registered with the Catholic Patriotic Association or the (Protestant) Three–Self Patriotic Movement committee. Dep't of State, Bureau of Democracy, China: Profile of Asylum Claims and Country Conditions 6–7 (April 14, 1998). Since Li would be classified as a Protestant, his group would be supervised by the Three–Self Patriotic Movement committee. The Three–Self Patriotic Movement committee is a political organization established to oversee official Protestant church matters, promote patriotism and promote the three principles of self-administration, self-support, and self-propagation.

To become a registered religious group, the group must: possess an approved meeting place; contain citizens who are religious believers and who regularly take part in religious activity; have an organized governing board; have a minimum number of followers; have a set of operating rules; and have a legal source of income. Dep't of State, 106th Cong., Country Reports on Human Rights Practices for 1998 854. Li testified that other than the fact that his group had a regular meeting time and place, his group had no governing board or rules or other such formal structure. For this reason, Li's practice of meeting with seven other friends at his home to study the bible and sing hymns would not have been blessed with the government's approval and granted registration.

The Chinese government reported in 1997 that there are over 12,000 churches and 25,000 meeting places for the 10 to 15 million registered Protestant citizens; however, there are anywhere from 30 million to 80 million Chinese citizens who worship in house churches that are independent of government control like Li. Unofficial groups claim that government authorities often refuse them registration without explanation, but, it is not the case here that Li attempted to register his group but was refused. Religious activity that is not conducted by a group registered by the government at a place of worship sanctioned by the government is illegal. The State Department's country report in the record establishes that unregistered religious groups are the targets of harassment, detention, physical abuse, and interrogations.

* * *

* * * We agree that it is axiomatic that Li was punished because of religious activities, nonetheless, it does not necessarily follow that Li was punished because of his religion. With respect to the question of whether he was persecution [sic] based on his religion or whether he faces prosecution for his activities, albeit religious activities, it is a close question and Li's arguments have some force as shown by the IJ's decision, which found in his favor. Nevertheless, the BIA concluded that the record shows Li faces prosecution for illegal activities if returned to China, not persecution on account of religion. The standard of review confines us to grant a reversal only if the evidence presented is such that a reasonable factfinder would have to conclude that persecution existed. We must find that the evidence in the record *compels* reversal of the

BIA's conclusion. Having conducted an independent review of the record, we are unable to conclude that the record before us compels reversal. The record establishes that the Chinese government does permit millions of its citizens to practice Christianity without punishment as long as they are members of registered groups. The evidence suggests that the Chinese government condones, or rather tolerates, the Christian faith and seeks to punish only the unregistered aspect of Li's activities. There is therefore reasonable, substantial, and probative evidence to support the BIA's decision that Li's punishment was for his activities and not for his religion, and there is nothing in the record that mandates us to find otherwise. Thus, there is nothing in this record that compels us to find that it is more likely than not Li would be persecuted based on his religion if he was returned to China.[3]

Clearly, we are faced with a complicated issue in this case. The issue in this case is perplexing not only because it involves affairs of a foreign state that are contrary to our fundamental ideals but also because the line between religious belief and religious activity here is indeed a fine one and it is colored by sensitive political and religious concerns. However, while we may abhor China's practice of restricting its citizens from gathering in a private home to read the gospel and sing hymns, and abusing offenders, like Li, who commit such acts, that is a moral judgment not a legal one.[4] We are restricted by the confines of the withholding of removal standard and the record before us. Based on both, we cannot conclude that the BIA erred in denying Li withholding of removal.

* * *

For the foregoing reasons, we affirm the BIA's denial of Li's application for withholding of removal.

## Notes and Questions

1. After the Fifth Circuit's decision, the Department of Homeland Security filed a motion with the BIA to reopen the case and then withdrew

**3.** Li stated that he did not want to register his religious group because he did not agree with the Government's requirement that registered churches promote Communism and alter church teachings so as to not conflict with Socialist thought. Li also testified that the police accused him of being a reactionary against the government and he was arrested for, *inter alia,* conducting an illegal gathering against the government. The Government asserts that China regulates religion based on a concern that unregulated religious gatherings are a challenge to their authority and an alternative to Communist thought. Finally, the Three–Self Patriotic Movement committee that registered Protestant groups are supervised by is a "political" organization. Based on this record, perhaps it would have been more appropriate for Li to argue that he

was persecuted based on his political opinion.

**4.** [O]ne of the many probing questions that there is no definitive answer to is whether Chinese law makes a distinction between merely praying or discussing religious beliefs at home with family or friends, and organizing and operating an unregistered church. There is no definitive determination in the record as to how broadly Chinese law defines a "church" or a "religious group" (or whether Chinese law precludes a registered church from having a home location). We are not called upon to determine whether prosecution for merely saying a personal prayer in the presence of one or more others, or discussing religious beliefs at home in the presence of one or more others, is persecution on account of religion.

its appeal of the immigration judge's ruling in favor of Mr. Li. The unusual course of events is described in Nelson, *Shaking the Pillars: An Asylum Applicant Shakes Loose Some Unusual Relief,* 83 Interp. Rel. 1 (2006):

> Unlike many asylum denials, the Fifth Circuit's decision in *Li v. Gonzales* caused an uproar that extended beyond the insular community of professional human rights defenders. *Christianity Today* published an article that suggested that the *Li* decision may have essentially "removed religion as a basis of gaining asylum." Church groups and advocates of religious freedom made calls and wrote to their Congressional representatives; a religious freedom law firm volunteered to join Li's appellate team and filed a motion for rehearing *en banc*; religious organizations of all stripes teamed up with human rights groups to draft amicus briefs in support of the motion; and influential political players went behind the scenes in Washington to question how the government could have advocated for a position that seemed so hostile to religious freedom.

> The *coup de grace* in the campaign to overturn the decision in *Li v. Gonzales* came in the form of an unprecedented letter to the Attorney General from the United States Commission on International Religious Freedom ("USCIRF"). In the letter, the Chair of the USCIRF stated some of the concerns which members of the USCIRF had developed during their visit to China the previous month, including "specifically, efforts by the Chinese government to control and criminalize religious activities in violation of China's commitments under international law." Noting that "we have never before taken a position on a case involving an individual asylum claimant," the USCIRF informed Assistant Attorney General Keisler that "[g]iven the potential adverse impact which the decision in *Li*, as well as the arguments advanced by the Department of Justice, may have on both asylum adjudications and on U.S. efforts to promote international religious freedom, we now feel compelled to voice our concern."

83 Interp. Rel. at 2–3.

The BIA vacated its decision, and reinstated the immigration judge's decision granting Li withholding of removal. This led the Fifth Circuit to vacate its decision as moot. *Xiaodong Li v. Gonzales,* 429 F.3d 1153 (5th Cir. 2005). Despite the developments in this particular case, the issues addressed in *Li* recur in other cases involving religious persecution claims. For further comment on *Li*, see Martin, *Major Developments in Asylum Law Over the Past Year,* 83 Interp. Rel. 1889, 1896–97 (2006) ("Asylum is not reserved for protection of the kind of empty belief that never stimulates real-world behavior").

2. Footnote 3 suggests that Mr. Li should have alleged persecution based on political opinion, rather than on religion. Was the court serious in implying that protection should be withheld because the applicant incorrectly categorized his claim under the wrong ground? If so, does this mean that he should have made an argument closer to the arguments in *Lie* and *Eduard* that defined the persecuted group using multiple factors?

3. Does the court's decision in *Li* necessarily follow from the approach reflected in the BIA's decision in *Matter of Chang,* reprinted in Chapter Three, p. 99?

---

### Exercise

Garzeh testified at his asylum hearing that he fears re-turning to his country of Aridonia because the government there persecutes members of his church, the Jehovah's Witnesses. Garzeh presented evidence that Jehovah's Witnesses have been denied government jobs, housing assistance, and business licenses because they refuse on religious grounds to vote or participate in national service.

Garzeh further testified that he has been a Jehovah's Witness since 1984. He stated that Jehovah's Witnesses cannot participate in national service (which in Aridonia involves military service), because they "don't intend to kill anybody because we have to love each other." According to Garzeh, Jehovah's Witnesses were denied civil service positions and travel documents because they refused to participate in national service. Garzeh also testified that the Aridonian government arrested his brother for refusing to engage in national service. After a number of severe beatings in jail, Garzeh's brother was taken to a hospital where he eventually died.

Garzeh also said that he applied to the Aridonian govern-ment for a business license, but received a letter rejecting the application:

> You have applied for a business license to open a land irrigation consulting service. We have reviewed your application and found out that you are a follower of the Jehovah's Witnesses and have not registered or participated in the national service. We are obligated to follow the guidelines given to us by the government and have denied your application for the above reasons.

Has Garzeh met his burden of establishing a well-founded fear of persecution on account of religion?

---

Compare the religious practices and beliefs of the individuals seek-ing asylum in *Lie* and *Eduard* with the situation in the following case.

### MATTER OF S–A–

Board of Immigration Appeals, 2000.
22 I & N Dec. 1328.

\* \* \*

HURWITZ, BOARD MEMBER:

\* \* \*

The respondent is a native and citizen of Morocco, who is either 20 or 21 years old. She testified that she was schooled for 3 years and knows how to write her name, but she is otherwise illiterate.

The respondent claims that in Morocco she was a victim of her father's escalating physical and emotional abuse. According to the respondent, the abuse arose primarily out of religious differences between her and her father, i.e., the father's orthodox Muslim beliefs, particularly pertaining to women, and her liberal Muslim views. Her father beat her a minimum of once a week using his hands, his feet, or a belt. She notes that her father did not mistreat her two brothers.

The respondent related that when she was about 14 years old, her maternal aunt, who is a United States citizen and resides in this country, sent her a somewhat short skirt. On one occasion the respondent wore the skirt outside her home. Upon returning home, her father verbally reprimanded her, heated a straight razor, and burned those portions of her thighs that had been exposed while she was wearing the skirt. He told her that he was taking this action to scar her thighs so that, in the future, she would not be tempted to wear what he considered improper attire. The respondent stated that she and her mother were afraid to go to the hospital after the incident, so her mother went to the local pharmacy and procured an ointment to treat the burns.

On another occasion, the respondent went to a pay phone to call her aunt in the United States. She explained that family members used a pay phone located near her parents' home because the family did not receive telephone service. On her way to the telephone, a young man stopped the respondent to ask for directions and she engaged in a short dialogue with the man. Upon observing this interchange, her father came into the street, shouted at her and the individual with whom she was conversing, and beat both of them. He used a ring he was wearing to beat the respondent in the face, particularly her forehead, the area between her eyebrows, and the bridge and top of her nose. She testified that she bled from the beating. Thereafter, the respondent's father compelled her to remain in the house in order to prevent subsequent casual conversations with strangers. She was forbidden to attend school and was prohibited from other activities physically located outside her home. The respondent stated that her father believes that "a girl should stay at home and should be covered or veiled all the time."

One evening in 1997 the respondent sneaked out of the house to visit some girl friends. That night while she was asleep, her father entered her bedroom and asked whether she had gone out that day. Knowing that he had forbidden her to leave the house, the respondent lied about her outing. Her father showed her that, unbeknownst to her, he had been marking the soles of her shoes with chalk and was thereby monitoring her activities. He said that he knew she had left the house and had lied about it. He then slapped, punched, and kicked her and pulled her hair.

The respondent stated that she did not consider requesting police protection or seeking any other kind of governmental intervention because her mother's previous efforts in that regard had proven unproductive. According to the respondent, she twice attempted to commit suicide in Morocco, and on two other occasions she attempted to run away in an effort to escape her circumstances. After at least one of the suicide attempts, she had her stomach pumped in a hospital and was unconscious for 3 days.

\* \* \*

The respondent's maternal aunt testified on her behalf at the hearing. The aunt stated that she has weekly telephonic contact with her sister, the respondent's mother, and that she visits Morocco once a year. She testified that the respondent's father is

> very strict, he's Muslim . . . (and he) is very tough when it comes to the religion, so he wants (the respondent) to . . . wear . . . the long robe to cover her face with the veil and when she . . . doesn't listen to him, . . . he abuse her, he beat her up . . . because he said that his daughter, he want her to be Muslim girl, like to follow the Islam.

Claiming to have actually observed some of the beatings, the respondent's aunt stated that the respondent's father

> pull her hair, he kick her, sometime he punch her in the face, like for no excuse, just because she's like, she's putting lipstick or she's putting hair color in her hair or she's looking from the window or she's talking to any girls, he doesn't like her to talk to them or the way she dress.

According to the aunt, going to the police would have been futile, because under Muslim law, particularly in Morocco, a father's power over his daughter is unfettered. In conformity with his fundamentalist Muslim beliefs, the respondent's father severely limited her access to education and compelled her to stay in the home. Moreover, because the respondent left her country to come to the United States and traveled without the approval or supervision of a male family member, she violated the edicts of the father's orthodox Muslim beliefs and he would kill her if she were to be returned to Morocco.

\* \* \*

When adjudicating an alien's eligibility for relief, we are mindful of "the fundamental humanitarian concerns of asylum law." *Matter of S–P*, 21 I & N Dec. 486, 492 (BIA 1996); *see also Matter of Chen*, 20 I & N Dec. 16 (BIA 1989). \* \* \*

\* \* \*

In the instant case, the source of the respondent's repeated physical assaults, imposed isolation, and deprivation of education was not the government, but her own father. Although she did not request protection from the government, the evidence convinces us that even if the respondent had turned to the government for help, Moroccan authorities would have been unable or unwilling to control her father's conduct. The respondent would have been compelled to return to her domestic situation and her circumstances may well have worsened. *See, e.g. Matter of Chen, supra; Matter of D–V–,* [21 I & N Dec. 77 (BIA 1995)]. In view of these facts, we conclude that the respondent established that she suffered past persecution in Morocco at the hands of her father and could not rely on the authorities to protect her. The Service has made no showing that conditions in Morocco have materially changed such that, upon her return, the respondent could reasonably expect governmental protection from her persecutor.

\* \* \*

An alien may also establish eligibility for asylum by demonstrating that a reasonable person in his or her circumstances would fear persecution in the future on account of a protected ground. We find that the evidence of record convincingly establishes that, upon her return, the respondent would likely face severe, possibly fatal, persecution.

\* \* \*

We find that the persecution suffered by the respondent was on account of her religious beliefs, as they differed from those of her father concerning the proper role of women in Moroccan society. The record clearly establishes that, because of his orthodox Muslim beliefs regarding women and his daughter's refusal to share or submit to his religion-inspired restrictions and demands, the respondent's father treated her differently from her brothers. *See Fisher v. INS,* [79 F.3d 955, 961 (9th Cir. 1996)] (stating that Board decisions "define 'persecution' generally as 'the infliction of suffering or harm upon those who differ (in race, religion or political opinion) in a way regarded as offensive'" (quoting *Ghaly v. INS,* 58 F.3d 1425, 1431 (9th Cir. 1995))); *Hernandez–Ortiz v. INS,* 777 F.2d 509, 516 (9th Cir. 1985) (finding that an alien was a refugee where she had endured "oppression ... inflicted ... because of a difference that the persecutor [would] not tolerate").

Because the persecution suffered by the respondent was on account of her religious beliefs, we find this case distinguishable on the facts from circuit court decisions holding that persecution on account of gender alone does not constitute persecution on account of membership in a particular social group. *See, e.g., Gomez v. INS,* 947 F.2d 660 (2d Cir. 1991). We also find that because of the religious element in this case, the domestic abuse suffered by the respondent is different from that described in *Matter of R–A–,* Interim Decision 3403 (BIA 1999).

\* \* \*

Order: The respondent's appeal from the denial of her asylum application is sustained. The respondent is granted asylum and is admitted to the United States as an asylee.

### Notes and Questions

1.   Would the BIA have reached a different result if the father had justified his actions by "tradition" rather than by his religious beliefs?

2.   How if at all do religious practices play a different role in the facts of *Matter of S-A-* as compared to *Chen* and *Li*? Does it matter that the fervent religious believer is—or seems to be—the persecutor in *Matter of S–A–* and the persecuted in *Chen* and *Li*? Are the materials on neutrality and imputed political opinion in Section A, pp. 192–209, relevant in this regard?

3.   Near the end of its decision in *Matter of S–A–*, the BIA distinguishes *Matter of R–A–*, a significant case in which the BIA majority, over vigorous dissent, denied an asylum claim based on domestic abuse. Chapter Five (on Gender and Persecution) will devote considerable attention to the doctrinal complexities of *Matter of R–A–*, as well as the fact that it was subsequently vacated and therefore no longer serves as precedent. For now, it is worth asking: should the religious element in *Matter of S–A–* lead to an analysis or an outcome that differs from a domestic abuse situation without a religious element?

## SECTION D.   MEMBERSHIP IN A PARTICULAR SOCIAL GROUP

"Membership in a particular social group" may be the most elusive of the five factors listed in the Refugee Convention and in the U.S. statute. During the past decade the number of attempts to give meaning to this phrase seems to have increased geometrically.

### 1.   BASIC APPROACHES

A definition of particular social group that continues to be highly influential comes from *Matter of Acosta*, 19 I & N Dec. 211 (BIA 1985). Excerpts from that opinion setting forth the facts more fully and discussing the portion of the claim based on political opinion are reprinted in Section A of this chapter, p. 192.

## MATTER OF ACOSTA

Board of Immigration Appeals, 1985.
19 I & N Dec. 211.

* * * [T]he respondent testified, and attested in an affidavit attached to his asylum application, to the following facts. In 1976 he, along with several other taxi drivers, founded COTAXI, a cooperative organization of taxi drivers of about 150 members. COTAXI was designed to enable its members to contribute the money they earned toward the purchase of their taxis. It was one of five taxi cooperatives in the city of San Salvador and one of many taxi cooperatives throughout the country

of El Salvador. Between 1978 and 1981, the respondent held three management positions with COTAXI, the duties of which he described in detail, and his last position with the cooperative was that of general manager. He held that position from 1979 through February or March of 1981. During the time he was the general manager of COTAXI, the respondent continued on the weekends to work as a taxi driver.

[The Board summarized the respondent's testimony regarding threats received by COTAXI, other taxi cooperatives, and their members, including respondent. (This part of the decision is reprinted in Section A of this chapter, p. 192.) The Board then turned to the issue whether the respondent had a well-founded fear of persecution and then whether that persecution was on account of membership in a particular social group.]

\* \* \*

The requirement of persecution on account of "membership in a particular social group" comes directly from the Protocol and the U.N. Convention. Congress did not indicate what it understood this ground of persecution to mean, nor is its meaning clear in the Protocol. This ground was not included in the definition of a refugee proposed by the committee that drafted the U.N. Convention; rather it was added as an afterthought. International jurisprudence interpreting this ground of persecution is sparse. It has been suggested that the notion of a "social group" was considered to be of broader application than the combined notions of racial, ethnic, and religious groups and that in order to stop a possible gap in the coverage of the U.N. Convention, this ground was added to the definition of a refugee. A purely linguistic analysis of this ground of persecution suggests that it may encompass persecution seeking to punish either people in a certain relation, or having a certain degree of similarity, to one another or people of like class or kindred interests, such as shared ethnic, cultural, or linguistic origins, education, family background, or perhaps economic activity. The UNHCR has suggested that a "particular social group" connotes persons of similar background, habits, or social status and that a claim to fear persecution on this ground may frequently overlap with persecution on other grounds such as race, religion, or nationality.

We find the well-established doctrine of *ejusdem generis*, meaning literally, "of the same kind," to be most helpful in construing the phrase "membership in a particular social group." That doctrine holds that general words used in an enumeration with specific words should be construed in a manner consistent with the specific words. The other grounds of persecution in the Act and the Protocol listed in association with "membership in a particular social group" are persecution on account of "race," "religion," "nationality," and "political opinion." Each of these grounds describes persecution aimed at an immutable characteristic: a characteristic that either is beyond the power of an individual to change or is so fundamental to individual identity or conscience that it ought not be required to be changed. Thus, the other four grounds of persecution enumerated in the Act and the Protocol restrict refugee status to individuals who are either unable by their own actions, or as a matter of conscience should not be required, to avoid persecution.

Applying the doctrine of *ejusdem generis*, we interpret the phrase "persecution on account of membership in a particular social group" to mean persecution that is directed toward an individual who is a member of a group of persons all of whom share a common, immutable characteristic. The shared characteristic might be an innate one such as sex, color, or kinship ties, or in some circumstances it might be a shared past experience such as former military leadership or land ownership. The particular kind of group characteristic that will qualify under this construction remains to be determined on a case-by-case basis. However, whatever the common characteristic that defines the group, it must be one that the members of the group either cannot change, or should not be required to change because it is fundamental to their individual identities or consciences. Only when this is the case does the mere fact of group membership become something comparable to the other four grounds of persecution under the Act, namely, something that either is beyond the power of an individual to change or that is so fundamental to his identity or conscience that it ought not be required to be changed. By construing "persecution on account of membership in a particular social group" in this manner, we preserve the concept that refuge is restricted to individuals who are either unable by their own actions, or as a matter of conscience should not be required, to avoid persecution.

In the respondent's case, the facts demonstrate that the guerrillas sought to harm the members of COTAXI, along with members of other taxi cooperatives in the city of San Salvador, because they refused to participate in work stoppages in that city. The characteristics defining the group of which the respondent was a member and subjecting that group to punishment were being a taxi driver in San Salvador and refusing to participate in guerrilla-sponsored work stoppages. Neither of these characteristics is immutable because the members of the group could avoid the threats of the guerrillas either by changing jobs or by cooperating in work stoppages. It may be unfortunate that the respondent either would have had to change his means of earning a living or cooperate with the guerrillas in order to avoid their threats. However, the internationally accepted concept of a refugee simply does not guarantee an individual a right to work in the job of his choice. Therefore, because the respondent's membership in the group of taxi drivers was something he had the power to change, so that he was able by his own actions to avoid the persecution of the guerrillas, he has not shown that the conduct he feared was "persecution on account of membership in a particular social group" within our construction of the Act.

\* \* \*

\* \* \* [T]he respondent has not shown he is eligible either for asylum or withholding of deportation to El Salvador. Therefore, we shall dismiss his appeal.

## Notes

1. A different approach is evident in another leading precedent, the Ninth Circuit decision in *Sanchez–Trujillo v. INS*, 801 F.2d 1571 (9th Cir. 1986). In that case, petitioners argued that they feared persecution in El Salvador as members of the following group: "young, urban, working class males of military age who had never served in the military or otherwise expressed support for the government." *Id.* at 1573. (This was a common theme in many Salvadoran cases in the 1980s.) In rejecting this claim, the court reasoned:

> The statutory words "particular" and "social" which modify "group," indicate that the term does not encompass every broadly defined segment of a population, even if a certain demographic division does have some statistical relevance. Instead, the phrase "particular social group" implies a collection of people closely affiliated with each other, who are actuated by some common impulse or interest. Of central concern is the existence of a voluntary associational relationship among the purported members, which imparts some common characteristic that is fundamental to their identity as a member of that discrete social group.[7]

> Perhaps a prototypical example of a "particular social group" would consist of the immediate members of a certain family, the family being a focus of fundamental affiliational concerns and common interests for most people. In *Hernandez–Ortiz* [*v. INS*, 777 F.2d 509, 516 (9th Cir. 1985), excerpted in Section A of this chapter, p. 199—eds.], we regarded evidence of persecution directed against a family unit as relevant in determining refugee status, noting that a family was "a small, readily identifiable group." As a contrasting example, a statistical group of males taller than six feet would not constitute a "particular social group" under any reasonable construction of the statutory term, even if individuals with such characteristics could be shown to be at greater risk of persecution than the general population.

> Likewise, the class of young, working class, urban males of military age does not exemplify the type of "social group" for which the immigration laws provide protection from persecution. Individuals falling within the parameters of this sweeping demographic division naturally manifest a plethora of different lifestyles, varying interests, diverse cultures, and contrary political leanings. * * *

> In sum, such an all-encompassing grouping as the petitioners identify simply is not that type of cohesive, homogeneous group to which we believe the term "particular social group" was intended to apply. Major segments of the population of an embattled nation, even though undoubtedly at some risk from general political vio-

---

7. We do not mean to suggest that a persecutor's perception of a segment of a society as a "social group" will invariably be irrelevant to this analysis. But neither would such an outside characterization be conclusive. * * * [W]hat constitutes a "par-ticular social group," as opposed to a mere demographic division of the population, must be independently determined through the application of the statutory term in a particular context.

lence, will rarely, if ever, constitute a distinct "social group" for the purposes of establishing refugee status. To hold otherwise would be tantamount to extending refugee status to every alien displaced by general conditions of unrest or violence in his or her home country. Refugee status simply does not extend as far as the petitioners would contend.

*Id.* at 1576–77. *Cf. Li v. INS*, 92 F.3d 985, 987 (9th Cir. 1996) (persons of low economic status in China do not constitute a particular social group).

2.   Maryellen Fullerton provides the following analysis of two contrasting decisions of German courts that addressed the particular social group issue at around the same time as the BIA decision in *Acosta* and the Ninth Circuit decision in *Sanchez–Trujillo*.

* * * Two German courts * * * have attempted to articulate standards for evaluating social group claims. The Administrative Court of Hannover [Judgment of June 6, 1984, No. 1 OVGA 91/82 As, Verwaltungsgericht Hannover] reviewed an asylum claim submitted by a former government official from Ghana. The applicant admitted that he had illegally sold government-owned fertilizer to farmers at inflated prices and then fled Ghana after the leaders of a coup began investigating corruption by former officials. He claimed he would be persecuted in Ghana for his membership in the social group composed of corrupt officials. He bolstered his creative, perhaps brazen, claim by noting that the new government had selected a relatively harmless groups of offenders, denied them appropriate legal proceedings, subjected them to disproportionate penalties, and proclaimed a "holy war" against them. He argued that although the corrupt activity was illegal, those accused of non-violent, economic crimes were being scapegoated for political ends. He asserted that in this setting the relatively small group targeted constituted a particular social group.

While the court treated seriously the allegations of irregular legal proceedings and disproportionate penalties, the court did not agree that corrupt government officials formed a social group within the meaning of the Geneva Convention. The court focused on two elements: (1) was there a substantial degree of homogeneity among the individuals in the group? (2) was there some degree of inner structure in the group? The court concluded that individuals who did not necessarily even know each other, and whose only similarity to each other was that they had committed economic crimes, did not satisfy either of the requirements.

The Administrative Court of Wiesbaden [Judgment of April 26, 1983, No. IV/I E 06244/81, Verwaltungsgericht Wiesbaden] rejected the approach outlined by the Hannover court when it grappled with an asylum claim filed by a homosexual man from Iran. The asylum seeker had not suffered persecution in the past. Raised in Iran in the Islamic tradition, he had been allowed several times to depart freely from Iran and return at his convenience. The regime did not know his sexual orientation. He was concerned, nevertheless, that the Iranian government might learn about his homosexuality and imprison or even execute him for ignoring religious laws. The Federal Refugee Office in Germany rejected this asylum claim due to lack of persecution in the past and lack of evidence that the Iranian government was likely to learn of the asylum seeker's sexual orientation.

The Wiesbaden court reversed the agency's decision. After concluding that homosexuals are severely persecuted in Iran and that, consequently, the asylum seeker would likely face persecution there, the court examined whether homosexuals from Iran constitute a particular social group within the meaning of the Geneva Convention. The court expressly rejected the idea that group members must know one another or belong to an organization. Instead the court emphasized two issues: First, whether the general population views this collection of people as a group; second, whether an objective observer of society would say that the general population treats this group as undesirable. Looking at the prejudice expressed against homosexuals in Iran, the pejorative labels used to describe them, and the harsh treatment they suffer, the court found that Iranian society perceives homosexuals as a pariah group, and ruled that homosexuals in Iran constitute a particular social group within the meaning of the 1951 Geneva Convention.

In summary, the two German courts that attempted to define the social group term formulated two very different tests. The Hannover court focused on the internal structure of the putative group, whereas the Wiesbaden court focused on external perceptions—society's view of the group in question. Because the role of precedent is not significant in the German legal system, neither of the two trial courts attempted to explain why its approach and rationale differed greatly from that proffered by its sister court. Nor did the courts try to distinguish the facts of the cases in order to synthesize the legal standards they had articulated. Thus, the two different analytical approaches to the social group term in the refugee definition co-exist in German judicial jurisprudence.

Fullerton, *A Comparative Look at Refugee Status Based on Persecution due to Membership in a Particular Social Group*, 26 Corn. Int'l L.J. 505, 533–35 (1993).

## 2.   THE EVOLUTION OF THE CONCEPT

### a.   *Sexual Orientation*

Consider how the approaches set out in *Matter of Acosta* and *Sanchez–Trujillo* and the two German administrative courts might apply to cases involving claims of persecution on account of membership in a particular social group defined in part by sexual orientation.

# MATTER OF TOBOSO–ALFONSO

Board of Immigration Appeals, 1990.
20 I & N Dec. 819.

\* \* \*

The applicant is a 40-year-old native and citizen of Cuba who was paroled into the United States in June of 1980, as part of the Mariel boat lift.[a] In 1985 his parole was terminated [because he was convicted of possession of cocaine and he] applied for asylum and withholding of deportation to Cuba.

The immigration judge ultimately concluded that the applicant was statutorily eligible for asylum and withholding of deportation as a member of a particular social group who fears persecution by the Cuban Government. He denied the applicant's request for asylum in the exercise of discretion, but granted him withholding of deportation.

\* \* \*

In the instant case, the applicant asserts that he is a homosexual who has been persecuted in Cuba and would be persecuted again on account of that status should he return to his homeland. He submits that homosexuals form a particular social group in Cuba and suffer persecution by the government as a result of that status.

The applicant testified that there is a municipal office within the Cuban Government which registers and maintains files on all homosexuals. He stated that his file was opened in 1967, and every 2 or 3 months for 13 years he received a notice to appear for a hearing. The notice, the applicant explained, was a sheet of paper, "it says Fidel Armando Toboso, homosexual and the date I have to appear." Each hearing consisted of a physical examination followed by questions concerning the applicant's sex life and sexual partners. While he indicated the "examination" was "primarily a health examination," he stated that on many occasions he would be detained in the police station for 3 or 4 days without being charged, and for no apparent reason. He testified that it was a criminal offense in Cuba simply to be a homosexual. The government's actions against him were not in response to specific conduct on his part (e.g., for engaging in homosexual acts); rather, they resulted simply from his status as a homosexual. He further testified that on one occasion when he had missed work, he was sent to a forced labor camp for 60 days as punishment because he was a homosexual (i.e., had he not been a homosexual he would not have been so punished).

The applicant stated that at the time of the Mariel boat lift, the Union of Communist Youth received permission to hold a demonstration

---

**a.** The so-called Mariel boatlift in the spring and summer of 1980 brought approximately 125,000 asylum seekers from Cuba It began when the Cuban government opened the port of Mariel with an invitation to relatives in the United States to pick up their family members from Cuba. But Cuban officials also forced returning boats to carry thousands of others whom the the government wished to remove, a small but sizeable number of whom had criminal records in Cuba.—eds.

against homosexuals at the factory where he worked. Several of the members got on top of a table and screamed that all homosexuals should leave—should go to the United States. He testified that on that same day there was a sheet of paper tacked to the door of his home which stated that he should report to "the public order." The applicant presented himself at the police station in the town of "Guines" where he was informed by the chief of police that he could spend 4 years in the penitentiary for being a homosexual, or leave Cuba for the United States. He was given a week to decide and decided to leave rather than be jailed.

The applicant further testified that the day he left his town, the neighbors threw eggs and tomatoes at him. He claims that the situation was so grave that the authorities were forced to reschedule his departure time from the afternoon to 2:00 a.m., in order to quell the protesting residents.

In addition to the applicant's testimony, he supplemented the record with [reports, articles, and film concerning the treatment of homosexuals in Cuba.] * * *

The immigration judge found the "applicant's testimony to be credible and worthy of belief, and, if anything, perceive[d] that he was restrained in his testimony as to the difficulty of his life during the years that he lived in Cuba." The immigration judge further concluded that the applicant had been persecuted in Cuba and that he has a well-founded fear of continued persecution in that country. He found that this persecution resulted from the applicant's membership in a particular social group, namely homosexuals. The immigration judge denied the applicant's asylum application in the exercise of discretion because of the nature of the applicant's criminal record in the United States. However, as the immigration judge found that the applicant's crimes did not bring him within the scope of section 243(h)(2)(B) [the crime-based ineligibility ground, see Chapter Six—eds.], he granted his application for withholding of deportation to Cuba.

The Immigration and Naturalization Service appeals from the grant of withholding of deportation to Cuba to the applicant, arguing that homosexuals were not a particular social group contemplated under the Act, that the applicant has not presented adequate evidence to show either a well-founded fear or a clear probability of persecution, and that the applicant is ineligible for relief under [the withholding statute] because of his conviction for possession of cocaine.

We do not find that the Service has presented persuasive arguments on which to reverse the immigration judge's finding that the applicant established his membership in a particular social group in Cuba. The Service argues that "socially deviated behavior, i.e. homosexual activity is not a basis for finding a social group within the contemplation of the Act" and that such a conclusion "would be tantamount to awarding discretionary relief to those involved in behavior that is not only socially deviant in nature, but in violation of the laws or regulations of the country as well." The applicant's testimony and evidence, however, do not reflect that it was specific activity that resulted in the governmental actions against him in Cuba, it was his having the status of being a homosexual. Further, the immigration judge's initial finding that a particular social group existed in Cuba was not "tantamount to awarding discretionary relief" to that group. Individuals in a particular social group are not eligible for relief based on that fact alone, among other showings they must establish facts demonstrating that members of the group are persecuted, have a well-founded fear of persecution, or that their life or freedom would be threatened because of that status.

We principally note regarding this issue, however, that the Service has not challenged the immigration judge's finding that homosexuality is an "immutable" characteristic. Nor is there any evidence or argument that, once registered by the Cuban government as a homosexual, that [sic] that characterization is subject to change. This being the case, we do not find the Service's challenge to the immigration judge's finding that this applicant was a member of a particular social group in Cuba adequately supported by the arguments set forth on appeal.

The next issue is whether the immigration judge erred in finding that the applicant had established that his life or freedom would be threatened in Cuba. The immigration judge not only found the applicant's testimony regarding the events in Cuba credible, but concluded that, if anything, he was "restrained in his testimony as to the difficulty of his life during the years that he lived in Cuba." In this regard, he noted that the applicant simply took as a matter of course that he "would be frequently detained for days [by government officials] while being subjected to verbal and physical abusive treatment." The applicant's testimony that simply because of his status as a homosexual he was advised by his government to leave the country or face incarceration for a period of 4 years is not contested. There is no evidence or allegation that this "choice" he was given resulted from any specific acts on his part or that the government did not intend to jail him if he failed to leave. The record indicates that rather than a penalty for misconduct, this action resulted from the government's desire that all homosexuals be forced to leave their homeland. This is not simply a case involving the enforcement of laws against particular homosexual acts, nor is this simply a case of assertion of "gay rights." Particularly in view of the final governmental threat that precipitated the applicant's departure from Cuba, we agree with the immigration judge's finding that the applicant's freedom was and is threatened within the contemplation of section 243(h)(1).

\* \* \*

Order: The Service's appeal is dismissed.

Dissenting opinion: FRED W. VACCA, BOARD MEMBER [joined by MORRIS, BOARD MEMBER]

\* \* \*

I do not find this testimony regarding the circumstances of the applicant's previous experiences in Cuba as a known practicing homosexual to be such as to indicate a "clear probability" that his life or freedom would be threatened if he were to return to that country. There are apparently Cuban criminal laws regarding homosexuality. The applicant himself characterized his experiences with the authorities as part of either investigations or health examinations. He did not describe these incidents as his being "incarcerated" because he was a homosexual. The United States Supreme Court has in fact found that state criminal sodomy laws do not violate the fundamental rights of homosexuals. *Bowers v. Hardwick*, 478 U.S. 186 (1986).

\* \* \*

## Notes and Questions

1. The 1990 BIA ruling in *Toboso–Alfonso* was not published as a precedent decision until 1994, when Attorney General Reno ordered its publication "as precedent in all proceedings involving the same issue or issues." As a designated precedent decision, *Toboso–Alfonso* is binding on agency officials and immigration judges. *See* INA § 103(a)(1); 8 C.F.R. § 1003.1(g). The INS Asylum Office issued guidance for cases in which asylum is predicated on sexual orientation, based on a claim filed by a Mexican national. The INS memo stated that sexual orientation appears to meet the *Acosta* standards for a "particular social group," but it goes on to caution: "Our finding that 'particular social group' under the refugee definition can, under certain circumstances, be defined by homosexual orientation, does not imply a 'group,' blanket, or other generic determination regarding the asylum eligibility of Mexicans, homosexuals, or any other nationality or group. The [office's] decision does not obviate the need for individualized assessments under the entire refugee definition for all cases." 71 Interp. Rel. 652–53 (1994).

2. In *Lawrence v. Texas*, 539 U.S. 558, 123 S.Ct. 2472, 156 L.Ed.2d 508 (2003), the U.S. Supreme Court overruled *Bowers v. Hardwick*—cited by dissenting Board Member Vacca—and found that a state law punishing homosexual conduct unconstitutional as a violation of substantive due process. Is this relevant, given what the BIA said about the relevance of U.S. constitutional law in *Matter of Chang, see* Chapter Three, p. 103—that "the fact that a citizen of another country may not enjoy the same constitutional protections as a citizen of the United States does not mean that he is therefore persecuted on account of one of the five grounds"?

3. For a detailed account of a case in which the INS granted asylum to a gay Brazilian man who on several occasions had been sexually assaulted by military police officers, see 73 Interp. Rel. 1140 (1996). *See also Pitcherskaia v. INS*, 118 F.3d 641 (9th Cir. 1997), in the materials on the meaning of "persecution" in Chapter Three, p. 108.

4. In the *Law of Refugee Status*, James Hathaway argues that a "social group" must be connected to civil or political status:

> The notion of social group as an all-encompassing residual category is seductive from a humanitarian perspective, since it

largely eliminates the need to consider the issue of a linkage between fear of persecution and civil or political status. Yet this is precisely the reason that [this] analysis cannot stand. The drafters of the Convention did not wish to avoid drawing distinctions among various types of putative refugees, but rather intended to establish a demarcation between those whose fear was attributable to civil or political status (refugees) and those whose concern to flee was prompted by other concerns (not refugees). * * * [T]he Convention was designed simply as a means of identifying and protecting refugees from known forms of harm, not of anticipating future, distinct types of state abuse.

\* \* \*

This [*Acosta*] formulation includes within the notion of social group (1) groups defined by an innate, unalterable characteristic; (2) groups defined by their past temporary or voluntary status, since their history or experience is not within their current power to change; and (3) existing groups defined by volition, so long as the purpose of the association is so fundamental to their human dignity that they ought not to be required to abandon it. Excluded, therefore, are groups defined by a characteristic which is changeable or from which dissociation is possible, so long as neither option requires renunciation of basic human rights.

By basing the definition of "membership of a particular social group" on application of the *ejusdem generis* principle, we respect both the specific situation known to the drafters—concern for the plight of those whose social origins put them at comparable risk to those in the other enumerated categories—and the more general commitment to grounding refugee claims in civil or political status. Beyond that, the linkage between this standard and fundamental norms of human rights correlates well with the human rights-based definition of "persecution." Most important, the standard is sufficiently open-ended to allow for evolution in much the same way as has occurred with the four other grounds, but not so vague as to admit persons without a serious basis for claim to international protection.

J. Hathaway, The Law of Refugee Status 159–61 (1991).

---

In *Hernandez–Montiel v. INS*, 225 F.3d 1084 (9th Cir. 2000), the Ninth Circuit heard an appeal from a decision of the BIA that had denied asylum and withholding. Though the facts involved sexual orientation, the Ninth Circuit's decision addressed the definition of "particular social group" in general. Here is the court's summary of the facts:

Geovanni testified that, at the age of eight, he "realized that [he] was attracted to people of [his] same sex." At the age of 12, Geovanni began dressing and behaving as a woman.

He faced numerous reprimands from family and school officials because of his sexual orientation. His mother registered him in a state-run Mexican school and informed the school authorities about what she deemed to be his "problem," referring to his sexual orientation. School authorities directed Geovanni to stop socializing with two gay friends. The father of a schoolmate grabbed Geovanni by the arm and threatened to kill him for "perverting" his son. He was even prevented from attending a school dance because of the way he was dressed. Shortly after the dance, the school asked Geovanni's mother to consent to his expulsion because he was not acting appropriately. He could not enroll in another school because the school refused to transfer his paperwork until he agreed to change his sexual orientation. Geovanni's parents threw him out of their home the day after his expulsion.

Beyond his school and family, Geovanni also suffered harassment and persecution at the hands of Mexican police officers. On numerous occasions, the Mexican police detained and even strip-searched Geovanni because he was walking down the street or socializing with other boys also perceived to be gay. In 1992, the Mexican police twice arrested Geovanni and a friend. The police told them that it was illegal for homosexuals to walk down the street and for men to dress like women. The police, however, never charged Geovanni with any crime.

Police officers sexually assaulted Geovanni on two separate occasions. In November 1992, when Geovanni was 14 years old, a police officer grabbed him as he was walking down the street, threw him into the police car, and drove to an uninhabited area. The officer demanded that Geovanni take off his clothes. Threatening him with imprisonment if he did not comply, the officer forced Geovanni to perform oral sex on him. The officer also threatened to beat and imprison Geovanni if he ever told anyone about the incident.

Approximately two weeks later, when Geovanni was at a bus stop with a gay friend one evening, the same officer pulled up in a car, accompanied by a second officer. The officers forced both boys into their car and drove them to a remote area, where they forced the boys to strip naked and then separated them. One of the officers grabbed Geovanni by the hair and threatened to kill him. Holding a gun to his temple, the officer anally raped Geovanni. Geovanni believes that his friend was also raped, although his friend refused to talk about the incident. Even before the boys could get dressed, the police officers threatened to shoot if they did not start running. The boys were left stranded in an abandoned area.

A few months after the second assault, in February 1993, Geovanni was attacked with a knife by a group of young men who called him names relating to his sexual orientation. He was hospitalized for a week while recovering from the attack.

Geovanni fled to the United States in October 1993, when he was 15 years old. He was arrested within a few days of his October 1993 entry. When Geovanni returned to Mexico to live with his sister, she enrolled him in a counseling program, which ostensibly attempted to "cure" his sexual orientation by altering his female appearance. The program staff cut his hair and nails, and forced him to stop taking female hormones. Geovanni remained in the program from late January to late March 1994. Because his sister saw no changes in him, she brought Geovanni home to live with her. Soon thereafter, however, she forced Geovanni out of her house because he was not "cured" of his gay sexual orientation, despite his change in appearance. He again sought refuge in the United States.

225 F.3d at 1087–89.

Addressing the argument that Geovanni faced persecution on account of membership in a particular social group, the Ninth Circuit addressed its apparent requirement in *Sanchez–Trujillo*, 801 F.2d 1571 (9th Cir. 1986), that a particular social group be characterized by "a voluntary associational relationship among the purported members, which imparts some common characteristic that is fundamental to their identity as a member of that discrete social group." 801 F.2d at 1576. The court in *Hernandez–Montiel* explained:

> We are the only circuit to suggest a "voluntary associational relationship" requirement. The Seventh Circuit has noted that this requirement "read literally, conflicts with *Acosta*'s immutability requirement." *Lwin* [*v. INS*, 144 F.3d 505, 512 (7th Cir.1998)]. Moreover, in *Sanchez–Trujillo*, we recognized a group of family members as a "prototypical example" of a "particular social group." Yet, biological family relationships are far from "voluntary." We cannot, therefore, interpret *Sanchez–Trujillo*'s "central concern" of a voluntary associational relationship strictly as applying to every qualifying "particular social group." For, as *Sanchez–Trujillo* itself recognizes, in some particular social groups, members of the group are not voluntarily associated by choice.

> We thus hold that a "particular social group" is one united by a voluntary association, including a former association, *or* by an innate characteristic that is so fundamental to the identities or consciences of its members that members either cannot or should not be required to change it.

*Id.* at 1092–93. The court held that Geovanni had shown past persecution and a clear probability and well-founded fear of future persecution on account of membership in a particular social group "composed of gay men with female sexual identities in Mexico." *Id.* at 1094.

#### b. *Clan Warfare*

The next case is the BIA decision in *Matter of H-*, which appeared in Chapter Three, p. 171, edited there to highlight the issues of past persecution and discretion to grant or deny asylum. Here we focus on the decision's particular social group analysis.

## MATTER OF H–

Board of Immigration Appeals, 1996.
21 I & N Dec. 337.

Rosenberg, Board Member:

\* \* \*

The decision of the Immigration Judge denying the applicant's request for relief rested on the conclusion that "there is no evidence there is a government in Somalia. A person is not entitled to political asylum in the United States because of clan warfare or because of civil warfare." \* \* \*

\* \* \* We find that the Immigration Judge erred as a matter of law in dismissing the factual and political context in which the claim arose, and in failing to give appropriate consideration to the claim of persecution on account of membership in a particular social group made by the applicant.

\* \* \*

The applicant is a native of Somalia and an undisputed member of the Darood clan and the Marehan subclan, an entity which is identifiable by kinship ties and vocal inflection or accent. For 21 years Somalia had been ruled by Mohammed Siad Barre, a member of the Marehan subclan, which constitutes less than 1 percent of the population of Somalia. In December of 1990, an uprising was instituted by members of the other clans, which ultimately caused Mohammed Siad Barre to relinquish his power and to flee the capital city of Mogadishu on January 21, 1991.

As a result of favoritism that had been shown to members of the Marehan subclan during the course of Mohammed Siad Barre's often brutal regime, the clans which rebelled against his rule sought to retaliate against those who had benefited from the regime. The applicant's father, a businessman who had greatly benefited from his membership in the Marehan subclan, was murdered at his place of business in Mogadishu on January 12, 1991, by members of the opposition United Somali Congress, composed mostly of members of the Hawiye clan. The applicant's family home, located in the Marehan section of the city, was targeted 2 days later by the same group. During the course of that attack, the applicant's brother was shot. He was later murdered at the hospital to which he had been brought for the treatment of his injury.

On January 13, 1991, 1 day after the attack on the applicant's home, he fled Mogadishu with his step-mother and younger siblings to a smaller town, Kismayu, which was a stronghold of the Darood clan. Approximately 1 month later, that town was attacked by the United Somali Congress. As a result, the applicant, who was not with his family at the time, was rounded up and detained without charges along with many other Darood clan members. During the course of his 5-day detention, the applicant was badly beaten on his head, back, and forearm with a rifle butt and a bayonet, resulting in scars to his body which remain to the present. A maternal uncle of the applicant, who was a member of the United Somali Congress, recognized him and assisted in his escape, driving him approximately 40 kilometers in the direction of Kenya. The applicant traveled the rest of the way to Kenya, approximately 90 kilometers, by foot. He reunited with his family in the town of Leboi, Kenya, where they remained until April 1992, when they were transferred to a refugee camp elsewhere in Kenya. The applicant lived in that camp until August of 1994 when he was able to procure funds through a relative in Saudi Arabia which allowed him to travel to the United States.

* * *

This Board has interpreted the phrase "persecution on account of membership in a particular social group" to mean persecution that is directed toward an individual who is a member of a group of persons all of whom share a common, immutable characteristic. *Matter of Acosta*, 19 I & N Dec. 211 (BIA 1985); *Matter of Mogharrabi*, [19 I & N Dec. 439 (BIA 1987)]. In *Matter of Acosta*, *supra*, at 233–34, we set forth the following to develop what may constitute a "particular social group":

> The shared characteristic might be an innate one such as sex, color, or kinship ties, or in some circumstances it might be a shared past experience such as former military leadership or land ownership. The particular kind of group characteristic that will qualify under this construction remains to be determined on a case-by-case basis. However, whatever the common characteristic that defines the group, it must be one that the members of the group either cannot change, or should not be required to change because it is fundamental to their individual identities or consciences. Only when this is the case does the mere fact of group membership become something comparable to the other four grounds of persecution under the Act, namely, something that either is beyond the power of an individual to change or that is so fundamental to his identity or conscience that it ought not be required to be changed.

By construing "persecution on account of membership in a particular social group" in this manner, we preserve the concept that refugee status is restricted to individuals who possess a characteristic so fundamental to their identities or conscience that they are either unable to change by their own actions or that they should not be required to change in order to avoid persecution. *Id.*; accord *Fatin v. INS*, 12 F.3d 1233, 1240 (3d Cir. 1993).

* * * [I]nformation of record in the annual reports regarding human rights practices issued by the United States Department of State substantiates the presence of distinct and recognizable clans and sub-

clans in Somalia and the once-preferred position of the applicant's Marehan subclan. * * * The Country Reports on Human Rights Practices for 1991 noted that Siad was of the Marehan segment of the larger Darood clan and that the favoritism he showed toward his family and members of the Marehan clan, which resulted in their corrupt accumulation of wealth, was a common grievance among the clans which rebelled against his rule. The report characterized Siad's successors as being 10 or more clan-based factions, the 2 most powerful among them being the United Somali Congress, predominantly of the Hawiye clan, and the Somali National Movement, predominantly of the Isaak clan.

The respondent has demonstrated by credible evidence that he and his family are members of the Darood clan and the Marehan subclan. The record before us makes clear not only that the Marehan share ties of kinship, but that they are identifiable as a group based upon linguistic commonalities. We find, therefore, that, based upon the foregoing, the Marehan subclan can be characterized as a "particular social group" within Somalia, of which respondent is a member.

\* \* \*

The situation in Somalia since 1991 presents the question of whether the widespread chaos and violence caused by civil strife and the type of individualized harm which constitutes persecution on one of the five grounds protected under our asylum laws are necessarily mutually exclusive. This Board has acknowledged that persecution can and often does take place in the context of civil war. *Matter of Villalta*, 20 I & N Dec. 142 (BIA 1990) (finding a well-founded fear of harm from paramilitary groups on account of political affiliation). In the instant case, we observe that while interclan violence may fall within the general category of civil strife, that does not preclude certain acts from being persecutory and does not change the fact that certain types of harm may constitute persecution. Further, the fact that almost all Somalis can claim clan membership and that interclan conflict is prevalent should not create undue concern that virtually all Somalis would qualify for refugee status, as an applicant must establish he is being persecuted on account of that membership. Finally, we agree with the observation contained in [an INS General Counsel] Legal Opinion that "[p]ersecution may likewise occur in the rare instance illustrated by Somalia, where there is no national government in existence."

There is considerable evidence of record that there is substantial harm inflicted on individuals in Somalia, that such injury is inflicted by members of the United Somali Congress or Hawiye clan, and that it is inflicted on identifiable members of the Darood clan and the Marehan subclan. According to the 1991 Country Reports, during the January 1991 uprising, which produced thousands of casualties and violations of human rights, armed Hawiye gangs began attacking Darood neighborhoods in Mogadishu, resulting in the death or disappearance of hundreds of mostly Darood victims. The report further noted that "[s]ome disappearances occurred when groups resembling death squads attacked people because of their clan background and for the opportunity to loot their property." 1991 Country Reports, *supra*, at 345. The Country Reports on Human Rights Practices for 1992 presents an equally grim picture substantiating a pattern of anti-clan-motivated violence and persecution. * * *

* * *

The evidence contained in the Country Reports of repeated clan-motivated attacks by the Hawiye or United Somali Congress on the Marehan and Darood clans is consistent with the applicant's testimony that his father, a Marehan businessman, was murdered at his place of business in Mogadishu; that the family home in a Marehan neighborhood was targeted; and that his brother, also a Marehan, was murdered in a Mogadishu hospital to which he had been taken for treatment of injuries that he sustained when the family home was attacked. The applicant himself fled with his remaining family to Kismayu, where he was captured, detained, and beaten severely. The persecution suffered by the applicant also was at the hands of members of the United Somali Congress and occurred when the Hawiye stormed Kismayu, a location where many Darood were known to reside.

* * *

In light of the corroborative information of record provided by the Department of State and the Basic Law Manual, as well as the applicant's testimony, we find the applicant has met his burden and has set forth a persuasive account of the persecution that he suffered in Somalia. *Matter of Mogharrabi, supra,* (stating that evidence of treatment of persons similarly situated is persuasive of an applicant's claim of political persecution). One month prior to the persecution that the applicant suffered, his father and brother were murdered in separate incidents on the basis of their membership in the clan. Because of the applicant's clan membership he was detained and severely beaten; he bears scars from the beatings. That the applicant was persecuted in the context of clan warfare does not undermine his claim. The motivation of the persecutors reasonably appears to be, as the applicant contends, on account of his subclan affiliation. He presented an individualized claim which reflected that he became the object of harm and was physically abused simply because he was identified with the former ruling faction by being a member of the Marehan clan. Accordingly, we find that the applicant suffered persecution in Somalia on account of his membership in a particular social group, to wit, the Marehan clan.

[The Board found that the applicant suffered past persecution and remanded to the immigration judge to rule on factors relevant to discretion to grant or deny asylum. Those parts of the decision are set out in the edited version of *Matter of H–* that appears in Chapter Three, p. 171.]

* * *

Dissenting opinion, MICHAEL J. HEILMAN, BOARD MEMBER:

\* \* \*

With this decision, we have now joined the United States Court of Appeals for the Ninth Circuit in its quixotic attempt to right the wrongs of the world through the asylum process. For all intents and purposes, the majority has concluded that all persons who have been harmed or who fear harm due to civil war will be entitled to asylum in the United States. I see the situation differently, and do not understand the Refugee Act of 1980 to accord protection to members of warring clans in Somalia. Indeed, if one pursues the majority's logic, all warring sides persecute one another, and this means that all civil wars are nothing more than acts of persecution. The implications of such a sweeping conception of "persecution" should give us all pause.

### Notes and Questions

1.   What is your response to Board Member Heilman's argument?

2.   Is *Matter of H–* consistent with *Acosta*? With *Sanchez–Trujillo*? Is there something fundamentally different about clan-based civil war, such that it is more likely than politically based civil strife to give rise to persecution that fits the Convention definition?

### c.   *Landowners*

Compare *Matter of H–* with the following decision of the Court of Appeal in the United Kingdom.

## MONTOYA v. SECRETARY OF STATE FOR THE HOME DEPARTMENT

[2002] EWCA Civ 620.
Court of Appeal (Civil Division).
On Appeal from Immigration Appeal Tribunal.

LORD JUSTICE SCHIEMANN:

\* \* \*

2.   The appellant Mr Montoya is a Colombian who has sought refugee status here. The facts are not in dispute. He is accepted on all sides as being honest. He had threats in Colombia to the effect that if he did not pay 10,000,000 pesos per month to a marxist opposition group known as the EPL he would be murdered. His elder brother was murdered in Colombia in 1992 for political reasons. His uncle had received similar threats and had for a while made payments. He stopped paying and thereupon was murdered on 31.12.1995. The appellant had never been involved in politics but had refused to make any payments partly as a matter of principle and partly because they were beyond his means. He had a genuine fear of being killed and because of this had fled to this country in 1996. If he is returned to Colombia there is a reasonable likelihood that he will be murdered. The putative murderers

are the persons seeking to extort the money. The state authorities are not in a position to protect him. His claim to human sympathy is clearly strong. The Secretary of State has power to allow him to remain. Whether the Secretary of State should exercise this power rather than send him to a likely death is however not a question which the Court has jurisdiction to consider in these proceedings.

3.    The legal question which we have to determine is whether on those facts the IAT was entitled to come to the conclusion that the appellant did not fall within the definition of a refugee contained in the Geneva Convention relating to the status of refugees. * * *

* * *

5.    * * * The Immigration Appeal Tribunal * * * held that Mr Montoya's case was not covered by the Refugee Convention since (i) although he had a well-founded fear of being persecuted, the persecution in question was not for a Convention reason in that he was not a member of a particular social group as that phrase is used in the Convention nor was he threatened with persecution for his political opinion and (ii) even if he were to be regarded as a member of a particular social group, he had not shown that the threat to his life and property was the result of his being a member of such a group.

* * *

[The Court of Appeal then quoted the reasoning relied upon by the administrative body below.]

32.    We have no difficulty in accepting that for a number of purposes private landowners in Colombia are differentiated from other groups or categories. They are distinguished by the fact that they own land and that many of them work the land for profit. However, the question we have to ask is whether such a group constitutes a particular social group for Refugee Convention purposes.

33.    For reasons given earlier, as this appeal is primarily based on the risk of persecution feared at the hands of non-state agents, it is necessary to examine for what extent such a group is set apart from the rest of society not only by reference to the attitude of the State towards it but also to the attitude towards it of non-state actors, the EPL in particular. In current-day Colombia the position of landowners is nowhere near as distinct and demarcated as for example were landowners in pre-Revolutionary Russia. However, the Tribunal considers that it remains that such a group does have some significant internal characteristics. The only question is whether such characteristics are enough to constitute it a particular social group for Convention purposes.

34.    . . . .  We do accept that as a result of the common designation given to them of being "Maoist" it is reasonable to

infer that the EPL does view itself to some degree as involved in a class struggle and that it numbers among its class enemies those belonging to the landowners class.... It also seems to us evident enough that despite urbanisation Colombia remains a country dominated to a significant degree by the economics of its rural production. Historically the ruling classes have been the landowners ruling alongside or through major political parties representing their interests....

35. We would accept therefore that in such a society the status of being an owner of land that is worked for a profit is an ostensible and significant social identifier with historical overtones.

36. We would also accept that another characteristic which private landowners share is the fact that they are ineffectively protected ... accordingly the inability of the State to protect private landowners serves in this case to add an additional basis on which to recognise this group as a distinct entity.

37. However ... a further requirement must be met before the respondent can establish that he is a member of a particular social group composed of private landowners. That requirement is that such a group is one which shares an immutable characteristic.

38. * * * [S]uch a group clearly does not share an innate characteristic. * * * It would appear that in Colombia a person can divest himself of his status and identity of a land-owner by his voluntary action. It may not always be that easy for a person to do this in practice, but there are clearly no longer entirely rigid lines of social stratification such as would make it practically impossible for a person to change from being a landowner to some other status or position.

39. The * * * common non-innate characteristics of such a group is not one which falls within the requirement set out in *Re Acosta* [19 I & N Dec. 211 (BIA 1985)] * * * and other cases of being one that members of the group cannot change, or should not be required to change because it is fundamental to their individual identities or conscience. * * *

41. ... There was or is nothing to stop the respondent changing his perceived identity as a private land-owner.

43. We agree ... that there was some degree of interference in the respondent's and his family's civil and political rights. Their attempts at relocating to their family house in Balcazar did not solve their problems. The evidence was that the threats made to him as a result of his failure to pay extortion money on the coffee plantation in Risaralda continued there. Thus action on his part to continue as manager of the coffee plantation on behalf of his family had only been possible

at the expense of a considerable interference with his basic right to enjoy private and family life without threat or anxiety. That such interference would continue to be a real threat is strongly suggested by the evidence as to the current situation of the respondent's father.

44.  We also accept that the respondent did not and does not have opportunities available to him to preserve his personal freedom by reliance upon state protection. . . .

45.  However, these interferences in the respondent's and his family's civil and political rights have all occurred because of their status as private landowners. The latter is a status the respondent can change. He could change from being a land-owner without that having a fundamental impact on his identity or conscience.

47.  . . . Despite the very real respects in which the respondent and his family face interference in their civil and political rights, their membership of this group is not one which they are unable to change. The nature of present-day Colombian society would not prevent them from earning their livelihood in another way.

48.  It might be objected that whilst the respondent and his family might be able to change their status of land-owner to something else, the most likely result would be that they would remain a target for persecution by groups such as the EPL because of their continuing wealth. That may well be true, but it seems to us to demonstrate that in reality the only group of which they have membership is that of persons with wealth. But if it is wealth alone that makes them a target then such a group does not exist independently of their persecution.

\* \* \*

[The Court of Appeal then resumed its analysis.]

25.  The applicant here is, and is perceived as to be, a member of the rich land-owning class. The persecutors seek out members of that class and hunt them down in order to obtain their land or money. The essence of the Tribunal's decision is (1) that this class can not qualify as a PSG [particular social group] for the purposes of the Convention because each member of it can dispose of his land or wealth and (2) that in any event any persecution would not be because the immigrant is a member of the group but rather because the persecutors wished to have his money.

26.  A possible approach to the present case is to assume two matters in Mr Montoya's favour : 1. that he is a member of a PSG, and 2. that he has a well-founded fear of being persecuted.

27.  It is common ground that, even if those matters are assumed in his favour, he must still show that he has a well founded fear of being

persecuted for reasons of membership of a particular social group or political opinion. This brings us to the question whether the Tribunal was entitled on the evidence before it to conclude, as they did in paragraphs 12,13 and 50, that he was being persecuted not because he was a private landowner or because of his political beliefs, but because the persecutors wished to extract extortion money for their own use.

\* \* \*

30.   The Tribunal had a wealth of material before them, including some emanating from Mr Montoya, from the U.S. State Department Country Report for 1999 at page 11 and from the Home Office Country Report April 2000 paragraph 4.29, from which they were entitled to conclude that the motivation of his persecutors was financial. There is nothing before this court which would entitle it to upset the Tribunal's conclusion as to the motivation of the persecutors.

\* \* \*

32.   \* \* \* [H]ad Mr Montoya's family not been possessed of land they would not have been wealthy and thus would not have been the targets of persecution. Had the family not inherited or purchased the land they would not have been persecuted; had the family given all their land away they would not have been persecuted. There are a number of factors which have combined to produce the situation in which the family had at the relevant moment and apparently still has enough wealth to be a fruitful target for extortion. All this we would accept.

33.   The jurisdiction of this court is designed to enable it to set aside conclusions reached by the Tribunal which are erroneous in law— Immigration and Asylum Act 1999, Schedule 4, Paragraph 23. We see no legal error in the Tribunal's conclusion in the present case that Mr Montoya had a well-founded fear that he would be persecuted by reason of the fact that the persecutors wanted his money and that accordingly he would not be persecuted for a Convention reason.

\* \* \*

Order: Appeal dismissed; no order for costs; Application for permission to appeal to the House of Lords refused.

## Notes and Questions

1.   *Montoya* relies on the analysis of "particular social group" in *Matter of Acosta*, 19 I & N Dec. 211 (BIA 1985), as have many U.S. courts and by courts in other countries. *See, e.g. Ward v. Attorney General of Canada*, [1993] 2 S.C.R. 689, 103 D.L.R. 4th 1 (Canada); *Applicant A v. Minister for Immigration and Ethnic Affairs,* (1997) 190 CLR 225 (Australia); *Islam v. Secretary of State for the Home Dep't*, 2 A.C. 629 (House of Lords 1999) (United Kingdom).

2.   How is birth into a clan more immutable than birth into the landowning class? Even if being a member of the landowning family in an agricultural society is not immutable, why isn't this membership fundamen-

tal to one's identity? Is it likely that the framers of the 1951 Refugee Convention, familiar as they were with communist takeovers and property redistribution in Eastern Europe, intended to exclude landowners from protection as members of a particular social group? Did they intend to exclude people from protection because they could escape persecution by selling all they own and moving to another part of the country?

3.   In *Montoya*, the Court of Appeal quotes with approval this passage from paragraph 48 of the decision of the administrative body below: "if it is wealth alone that makes them a target then such a group does not exist independently of their persecution." A fuller explanation of the same idea appears in a one of the opinions in a leading decision from the United Kingdom's highest court, *Islam (A.P.) v. Secretary of State for the Home Dep't*, [1999] 2 A.C. 629 (House of Lords), which addressed the definition of particular social group in the context of asylum claims based on domestic abuse. (*Islam* is a principal decision in Chapter Five on Gender and Persecution, p. 351.) Relying on the reasoning of an Australian case defining particular social group, Lord Steyn's opinion in *Islam* explained:

> It is common ground that there is a general principle that there can only be a "particular social group" if the group exists independently of the persecution. In *Applicant A. v. Minister for Immigration and Ethnic Affairs* (1997) 71 A.L.J.R. 381, 401 McHugh J. neatly explained the point:
>
>> If it were otherwise, article 1(A)(2) [of the 1951 Convention, defining "refugee"] would be rendered illogical and nonsensical. It would mean that persons who had a well founded fear of persecution were members of a particular social group because they feared persecution. The only persecution that is relevant is persecution for reasons of membership of a group which means that the group must exist independently of, and not be defined by, the persecution.
>
> In other words relying on persecution to prove the existence of the group would involve circular reasoning. It is therefore unsurprising that counsel for the appellants and counsel for the United Nations High Commissioner for Refugees (U.N.H.C.R.) accept the general principle that there can only be a "particular social group" if it exists independently of the persecution.

*Islam*, 2 A.C. at 639–40. But should a group of individuals be denied protection because they did not place weight (or perhaps even see) what bound them together until they suffered persecution for that reason? Why can't a particular social group be defined by the persecution itself?

### d.   *Government Informants*

As background for the next decision, consider the following discussion of whether a group's visibility affects whether it is a "particular social group" for asylum or withholding purposes.

# T. ALEXANDER ALEINIKOFF,
# PROTECTED CHARACTERISTICS AND
# SOCIAL PERCEPTIONS: AN ANALYSIS
# OF THE MEANING OF "MEMBERSHIP
# IN A PARTICULAR SOCIAL GROUP"

Refugee Protection in International Law 285, 294–300.
(E. Feller, V. Türk, & F. Nicholson eds., 2003).

* * * The overriding concern expressed in the legal sources is that some limiting principle be identified to ensure that the "social group" ground not be all-encompassing. An overly broad interpretation is resisted for several reasons. First, it is stated that the Convention was not intended to provide protection to all victims of persecution—only to those who come within one of the five Convention grounds. Thus, to read the social group ground to include all other groups of persons who flee across borders or suffer human rights abuses would conflict with the structure of the Convention. Secondly, as a matter of legal logic, the social group cannot be read so broadly that it renders the other Convention grounds superfluous. Thirdly, it is argued that an overly broad definition of "particular social group" would undermine the balance between protection and limited State obligations implicit in the Convention.

* * *

[T]he development of the social group ground for refugee status in common law countries has occurred primarily—although not exclusively—through adoption and application of the protected characteristics approach. * * *

* * * [The protected characteristics approach] provides a limiting principle for interpretation of "particular social group" that resonates with a human rights perspective. That is, it might plausibly be argued—as the protected characteristics approach purports to do—that each of the first four Convention grounds are predicated on human rights conceptions, and thus the "particular social group" ground ought also to be limited to groups defined in human rights terms. A protected characteristics approach identifies groups that we might generally believe merit protection: those who would suffer significant harm if asked to give up their group affiliation, either because it would be virtually impossible to give up an "immutable" characteristic or because the basis of affiliation is the exercise of a fundamental human right. * * *

Balanced against these advantages, however, are disadvantages that need to be assessed. Significantly, the protected characteristics test is arguably in tension with a common sense meaning of the term "social group". Nothing in the refugee definition—and nothing in the *travaux préparatoires*—suggests that the immutability or fundamentality of characteristics is the key to understanding the Convention grounds. Furthermore, although the States Parties' jurisprudence displays a deep concern that the particular social group ground not be so broadly defined as to swallow up the other Convention grounds or to make all victims of persecution automatically refugees—a concern that is plainly consistent with the language, and purposes of the Convention—this consideration alone cannot support limitations that are not otherwise consistent with and reasonably inferable from the Convention.

The protected characteristics approach also appears to deny refugee protection to members of groups who may well be targets of persecution based on their associations that are widely recognized in society. Examples could include such groups as students, union members, professionals, refugee camp workers, or street children. * * *

* * *

An alternative reading of the Convention language is suggested by the majority opinions in the Australian High Court case of *Applicant A.* [*v. Minister for Immigration and Ethnic Affairs* (1997) 71 A.L.J.R. 381]. What constitutes a particular social group is "a common attribute and a societal perception that they stand apart". The attribute must not only be shared, it must unite the group as a matter of self-perception or societal perception. That is to say, the shared characteristic must make "those who share it a cognisable group within their society". * * *

* * *

* * * [T]he social perception analysis would appear to encompass the groups currently recognized under the protected characteristics approach. This is primarily due to the fact that groups recognized under the protected characteristics analysis are likely to be perceived as social groups. Why is this the case? It is so because persons in groups that are the subject of persecutory, discriminatory treatment will avoid the shared characteristic that defines the group if they are able to; but groups defined by immutable characteristics cannot do so, and groups defined by characteristics fundamental to human dignity often choose not to do so, nor should they be required to do so. Thus, such groups are likely to maintain their membership despite unfavorable treatment, and generally will be perceived as social groups—defined by the characteristic for which the abuse is imposed.* * *

While most "protected characteristics" groups are likely to be perceived as social groups, there may also be social groups perceived as such that are not based on protected characteristics. A social perception approach, therefore, moves beyond protected characteristics by recognizing that external factors can be important to a proper social group definition. Asking whether a group has been "marked as other" is not to collapse the social group and persecution issues, but rather to examine whether the group is a cognizable group in a particular cultural context.* * *

The social perception approach could also reach claims advanced by persons who believe in values at odds with the social mores of the societies in which they live. For example, women who object to FGM [female genital mutilation] or who refuse to wear traditional dress are likely to be perceived as constituting a social group because they have set themselves against the cultural, religious, or political practices of the society. By contrast, it may be more difficult to recognize some of these claims—for instance, one based on attire—under the protected characteristics approach.

\* \* \*

Another objection to the social perception test might be that it would appear to recognize groups no matter how trivial the shared characteristic is. Philatelists or roller-bladers, for example, might be understood as constituting "social groups" in particular countries. In contrast, the protected characteristics approach adopts a conceptual filter, ensuring that recognized groups be united by a truly important trait. In so doing, it preserves the powerful palliative of international protection for persons for whom it would be unfair to demand that they avoid or give up their unifying characteristic. \* \* \*

A response to this objection begins by noting that most trivial associations are not likely to attract persecutory acts; thus roller-bladers are quite unlikely to be recognized as refugees whether or not they constitute a "social group". If such groups were seen as groups in a society, however, and persons were subject to persecution on the basis of membership in the group, why should international protection be denied? Whatever we may think of philatelists or roller-bladers, clearly the persecutor sees them as a group that constitutes a threat and should be suppressed, and he or she is willing to inflict unjustifiable harm to accomplish the goal of suppression. The Convention is aimed at preventing the infliction of serious abuses based on group membership, not at preserving membership in groups that are deemed important or worthy. The triviality, or not, of the shared group characteristic therefore ought not to be relevant for Convention purposes. \* \* \* As human history makes clear, persecutors choose groups and victims for a variety of reasons, not simply based on the fundamentality of the trait that defines the group.

\* \* \*

A final concern with the social perception test might be that it creates too broad an interpretation of social group, opening the floodgates to any number of groups and claimants. Why might not the disabled, the poor, students, shopkeepers, athletes, or entertainers qualify under the test? Yet, as long as adjudicators observe the rule that the group must exist outside the persecution (properly understood), the social group category will be significantly limited. \* \* \*

Given the advantages and disadvantages of both the protected characteristics and social perception tests, which should the conscientious adjudicator adopt? \* \* \*

My proposal is that, rather than viewing the two approaches as inconsistent and competing analyses, one should conceptualize the protected characteristics approach as the core of the social perception analysis. That is, groups that qualify under the protected characteristics approach are virtually assured recognition under the social perception test as well. * * * That is, identification of a group under the protected characteristics approach would be sufficient, but not necessary, for Convention purposes.

---

On the occasion of the fiftieth anniversary of the 1951 Convention, the UNHCR convened a varied series of meetings over several months, involving expert roundtables, a conference of high-level government ministers, and special meetings of the UNHCR Executive Committee. Known as the Global Consultations, this initiative was intended to examine the current state of refugee law and practice, suggest future lines of development, and revitalize implementation. Drawing heavily on the Aleinikoff paper excerpted above, the UNHCR's Global Consultations suggested a careful expansion of the *Acosta* "protected characteristic" approach to include a "social perception" test in a new set of Guidelines, which plays a prominent role in the next decision.

## MATTER OF C–A–

Board of Immigration Appeals, 2006.
23 I & N Dec. 951.

HOLMES, BOARD MEMBER:

The respondents, a married couple and their two minor children, are natives and citizens of Colombia. * * *

* * *

The lead respondent * * * testified that he was born and raised in Cali, Colombia, the headquarters of the Cali drug cartel. He lived with his wife and two children in Cali, where he operated a bakery from 1990 to some time in 1995. During this time, he was an acquaintance of A–D–, a former policeman in the Cali Police Department who, after being fired for corruption, became the chief of security for the Cali cartel. The respondent was also a good friend of V–M–M–, the General Counsel for the city of Cali, who was responsible for investigating and prosecuting drug traffickers in Cali.

Between 1990 and 1994, A–D– would visit the respondent's bakery on weekends and talk openly about his involvement with the Cali cartel. A–D– identified people, places, and events related to the cartel's exportation of narcotics from Colombia to the United States and Europe. A–D– also informed the respondent of his close ties with the Rodriguez brothers and others involved in running the Cali drug cartel. The respondent passed the information he learned from A–D– along to V–M–M–. He told V–M–M– about A–D–'s statements that the Cali cartel had declared war against the Government of Colombia and that they would kill politicians who opposed the cartel. He also told V–M–M– what he had learned from A–D– about the location and size of Cali cartel assets, including banks, bank accounts, mansions, haciendas, villas, and other assets both within and outside of Colombia.

On May 15, 1995, the respondent was with his son, who was riding a bicycle, when a car suddenly blocked their path. Three men with pistols and an automatic weapon attempted to force the respondent into the car. When he resisted he was forced to the ground and beaten. The respondent's son screamed and one of the men hit him in the face with a pistol. The commotion brought people in the neighborhood out of their houses and the men fled in their car. As they departed, they warned the respondent that things would get worse for him and his family and that they would also get V–M–M–. The respondent took his son to a clinic where he underwent reconstructive surgery to repair his mouth and jaw.

After this attack, the respondents went to the lead respondent's parents' home in the northern section of Cali for the remainder of the month of May 1995. The respondent attempted to rent his bakery while he was away but the lessees were intimidated and some lessees were harmed for failing to disclose the whereabouts of the respondent. V–M– M– advised the respondent to go into hiding and eventually to leave Colombia. The respondent's parents relocated in Cali in attempts to evade persons looking for their son. After the respondent made two trips to the United States in 1995, the respondents entered this country in February 1996 as visitors for pleasure with authorization to remain until August, 8, 1996.

* * *

* * * Because we had not addressed whether noncriminal informants constitute a "particular social group" within the meaning of the Act, the [Eleventh Circuit] has now remanded that question for our consideration.

* * *

The United Nations High Commissioner for Refugees ("UNHCR") has recently adopted guidelines that combine elements of the *Acosta* immutable or fundamental characteristic approach, as well as the Second Circuit's "social perception" approach. The UNHCR *Guidelines* define a "particular social group" as

a group of persons who share a common characteristic other than their risk of being persecuted, or who are perceived as a group by society. The characteristic will often be one which is innate, unchangeable, or which is otherwise fundamental to identity, conscience or the exercise of one's human rights.

*Id.* at ¶ 11.

Having reviewed the range of approaches to defining particular social group, we continue to adhere to the *Acosta* formulation. Under *Acosta*, we do not require a "voluntary associational relationship" among group members. Nor do we require an element of "cohesiveness" or homogeneity among group members. As discussed below, we have considered as a relevant factor the extent to which members of a society perceive those with the characteristic in question as members of a social group.

\* \* \*

The Eleventh Circuit has directed us to consider whether "noncriminal informants" are a particular social group in the context of this case. We find that this group is too loosely defined to meet the requirement of particularity. The group of "noncriminal informants" could potentially include persons who passed along information concerning any of the numerous guerrilla factions or narco-trafficking cartels currently active in Colombia to the Government or to a competing faction or cartel. In considering whether informants are a particular social group, it is important to know the persons between whom the information is being provided, as well as the nature of the information passed along.

Although "noncriminal informants" do not constitute a particular social group, the respondent, in his initial appeal to the Board, referred to a subgroup of "former noncriminal government informants working against the Cali drug cartel." On remand, the respondent also refers to "noncriminal drug informants working against the Cali drug cartel." We understand the Eleventh Circuit's directive on remand to require consideration of these potentially narrower formulations of the particular social group within the larger group of noncriminal informants. We therefore examine whether "noncriminal drug informants working against the Cali drug cartel" constitute a particular social group.

\* \* \*

The respondent asserts that the historical fact of having informed on the Cali cartel is an immutable characteristic within the meaning of *Acosta*. A past experience is, by its very nature, immutable, as it has already occurred and cannot be undone. However, that does not mean that any past experience that may be shared by others suffices to define a particular social group for asylum purposes. For example, we do not afford protection based on social group membership to persons exposed to risks normally associated with employment in occupations such as the police or the military. In part, this is because persons accepting such employment are aware of the risks involved and undertake the risks in return for compensation. Similarly, a person who agrees to work as a government informant in return for compensation takes a calculated risk and is not in a position to claim refugee status should such risks materialize.

In *Matter of Fuentes*, [19 I & N Dec. 658 (BIA 1988)], we stated that, although a former member of the national police in El Salvador could not demonstrate persecution as a member of a social group based on attacks by guerrillas while performing his official duties as a police officer, his status as a former member of the national police was "an immutable characteristic, as it is one beyond the capacity of the respondent to change." *Id.* at 662. Were a situation to develop in which former police officers were targeted for persecution because of the fact of having served as police officers, a former police officer could conceivably demonstrate persecution based upon membership in a particular social group of former police officers. On the other hand, if a former police officer were singled out for reprisal, not because of his status as a former police officer, but because of his role in disrupting particular criminal activity, he would not be considered, without more, to have been targeted as a member of a particular social group.

The respondent emphasizes in his brief on remand that he informed on the Cali cartel, not for compensation or other quid pro quo, but out of a sense of civic duty and moral responsibility. The question in this case becomes whether the respondent's civic motives for working as a government informant distinguish his situation from that of informants employed by the government. We find that the fact that the respondent acted out of a sense of civic responsibility does not suffice to define a subgroup of uncompensated informants who would be considered to constitute a particular social group. Some persons employed as informants or otherwise receiving compensation as informants, including police officers, also act partly out of a sense of civic responsibility. Many such informants could plausibly claim that their primary motivation was a sense of civic duty and the compensation alone would not have provided sufficient incentive to undertake the risks involved. Therefore, the distinction between informants who are compensated and those who act out of civic motives is not particularly helpful in addressing the question of who is deserving of protection under the asylum law.

\* \* \*

Our decisions involving social groups have considered the recognizability, i.e., the social visibility, of the group in question. Social groups based on innate characteristics such as sex or family relationship are generally easily recognizable and understood by others to constitute social groups. In considering clan membership in *Matter of H–*, [21 I & N Dec. 337 (BIA 1996),] we did not rule categorically that membership in any clan would suffice. Rather, before concluding that membership in the Marehan subclan in Somalia constituted membership in a particular social group, we examined the extent to which members of the purported group would be recognizable to others in Somalia. We found evidence in the record of "the presence of distinct and recognizable clans and subclans in Somalia." *Id.* at 343. Significantly, we found that the various clans could be differentiated based on linguistic commonalities as well as kinship ties. We noted that the former Immigration and Naturalization Service's *Basic Law Manual* also recognized that "clan membership is a highly recognizable, immutable characteristic that is acquired at birth and is inextricably linked to family ties." *Id.* at 342.

\* \* \*

The recent *Guidelines* issued by the United Nations confirm that "visibility" is an important element in identifying the existence of a particular social group. The *Guidelines* explain that the social group category was not meant to be a "catch all" applicable to all persons fearing persecution. UNHCR *Guidelines, supra,* at ¶ 2. In this regard, the *Guidelines* state that "a social group cannot be defined *exclusively* by the fact that it is targeted for persecution." *Id.* However, "persecutory action toward a group may be a relevant factor in determining the *visibility* of a group in a particular society." *Id.* at ¶ 14 (emphasis added).

When considering the visibility of groups of confidential informants, the very nature of the conduct at issue is such that it is generally out of the public view. In the normal course of events, an informant against the Cali cartel intends to remain unknown and undiscovered. Recognizability or visibility is limited to those informants who are discovered because they appear as witnesses or otherwise come to the attention of cartel members.

The respondent's reliance on the distinction between informants who act out of a sense of civic responsibility, rather than for compensation to limit the membership in the relevant social group, would also tie group membership to a factor not "visible" to the Cali cartel or to other members of society. Notably, there has been no showing that whether an informant was compensated is of any relevance to the Cali cartel. Nor would members of society in general recognize a social group based on informants who act out of a sense of civic duty rather than for compensation.

The record in this case indicates that the Cali cartel and other drug cartels have directed harm against anyone and everyone perceived to have interfered with, or who might present a threat to, their criminal enterprises. In this sense, informants are not in a substantially different situation from anyone who has crossed the Cali cartel or who is perceived to be a threat to the cartel's interests. * * * While these respondents present very sympathetic personal circumstances, it is difficult to conclude that any "group," as actually perceived by the cartel, is much narrower than the general population of Colombia.

Given the voluntary nature of the decision to serve as a government informant, the lack of social visibility of the members of the purported social group, and the indications in the record that the Cali cartel retaliates against anyone perceived to have interfered with its operations, we find that the respondent has not demonstrated that noncriminal drug informants working against the Cali drug cartel constitute a "particular social group" as that term is used in the definition of a "refugee" in section 101(a)(42)(A) of the Act.

* * *

Order: The respondents' appeal is dismissed.

## Notes and Questions

1. The UNHCR Guidelines define a "particular social group" as "a group of persons who share a common characteristic other than their risk of being persecuted, *or* who are perceived as a group by society" (emphasis added). Has the BIA in *Matter of C–A–* turned the "or" into "and"? If so, is anything wrong with requiring social visibility in addition to an immutable common characteristic? What sorts of groups will be most affected by any such additional requirement?

2. Alex Aleinikoff writes, at the end of the excerpt above, "groups that qualify under the protected characteristics approach are virtually assured recognition under the social perception test as well." Is *Matter of C–A–* an exception? Should it be?

3. Recall these questions from note 3 on p. 277 following *Montoya* earlier in this chapter: should a group of individuals be denied protection because they did not place weight (or perhaps even see) what bound them together until they suffered persecution for that reason? Why can't a particular social group be defined by the persecution itself? To resume that line of inquiry in light of the Aleinikoff excerpt and *Matter of C–A–*: how would the social perception approach deal with cases where the group wasn't perceived as separate until the persecution started? Does this highlight a virtue of of social perception approach, or a problem with it?

4. On the issues raised in the previous note, useful analysis comes from *K v. Secretary of State for the Home Dep't,* [2006] UKHL 46 (House of Lords), a decision of the highest court in the United Kingdom, the Law Lords, a select group within the House of Lords. The decision unanimously reserved lower court denials of two separate asylum claims. One applicant, K–, was from Iran. Her husband had been arrested and imprisoned, and soon thereafter Revolutionary Guards searched her home and raped her there. Then they went to her seven-year-old son's school to ask about him a manner intended to intimidate her further. The other applicant, Fornah, had run away from her father's village in Sierra Leone to avoid female genital mutilation, but was captured by rebels and repeatedly raped by a rebel leader, by whom she became pregnant. Fornah based her asylum claim on her fear that, if returned to Sierra Leone, she would have nowhere to live but her father's village, where she would be at risk of FGM.

We will return to this decision later in this section and in Chapter Five, but for now compare Lord Bingham's treatment of the UNHCR Guidelines—in particular how he excerpts and comments on the Guidelines' treatment of the social perception of a "particular social group"—with the handling of the same document and issue by Board Member Holmes in *Matter of C–A–*:

> 15. Increased reliance on membership of a particular social group as a ground for claiming asylum prompted the UNHCR to convene an expert meeting at San Remo in September 2001, which was followed on 7 May 2002 by the issue of *Guidelines on International Protection* directed to clarifying this ground of claim. Having identified what it called the "protected characteristics" or "immutability" and "social perception" approaches, which it suggested would usually, but not always, converge, the UNHCR proposed:

B.  *UNHCR's Definition*

10.  Given the varying approaches, and the protection gaps which can result, UNHCR believes that the two approaches ought to be reconciled.

11.  The protected characteristics approach may be understood to identify a set of groups that constitute the core of the social perception analysis. Accordingly, it is appropriate to adopt a single standard that incorporates both dominant approaches:

> a particular social group is a group of persons who share a common characteristic other than their risk of being persecuted, or who are perceived as a group by society. The characteristic will often be one which is innate, unchangeable, or which is otherwise fundamental to identity, conscience or the exercise of one's human rights.

12.  This definition includes characteristics which are historical and therefore cannot be changed, and those which, though it is possible to change them, ought not to be required to be changed because they are so closely linked to the identity of the person or are an expression of fundamental human rights. It follows that sex can properly be within the ambit of the social group category, with women being a clear example of a social subset defined by innate and immutable characteristics, and who are frequently treated differently to men.

13.  If a claimant alleges a social group that is based on a characteristic determined to be neither unalterable or fundamental, further analysis should be undertaken to determine whether the group is nonetheless perceived as a cognizable group in that society. So, for example, if it were determined that owning a shop or participating in a certain occupation in a particular society is neither unchangeable nor a fundamental aspect of human identity, a shopkeeper or members of a particular profession might nonetheless constitute a particular social group if in the society they are recognized as a group which sets them apart.

The UNHCR accepted that a particular social group could not be defined exclusively by the persecution members suffer or fear, but also accepted the view advanced in *Applicant A* and accepted by some members of the House in [*Islam v. Secretary of State for the Home Dep't*, 2 A.C. 629 (House of Lords 1999), in Chapter Five, p. 351] that persecutory action towards a group may be a relevant factor in determining the visibility of a group in a particular society.

It appears to me that the *UNHCR Guidelines*, clearly based on a careful reading of the international authorities, provide a very accurate and helpful distillation of their effect.

*Id.* at ¶ 15.

5. For additional commentary on *Matter of C–A–*, see Martin, *supra*, 83 Interp. Rel. at 1893–94 (finding the BIA's focus on "desert, assumption of risk, and visibility" to be potentially useful in particular social group cases based on a person's past history, but raising questions about the application of those concepts in this case).

### e. *Families*

In *Thomas v. Gonzales*, 409 F.3d 1177 (9th Cir. 2005) (en banc), the Ninth Circuit reversed a BIA decision affirming an immigration judge's denial of asylum and withholding to Michelle Thomas, her husband David Thomas, and their two children, Shaldon and Tyneal, all citizens and natives of South Africa. The Ninth Circuit summarized the facts this way:

> The Thomases came to the United States to avoid threats of physical violence and intimidation to which they were subjected because of abuses committed by Michelle's father-in-law, "Boss Ronnie," who was a foreman at Strongshore Construction in Durban, South Africa. Boss Ronnie was and is a racist who abused his black workers both physically and verbally.
>
> At the hearing, Michelle testified about a number of events that support the Thomases' fears. The first took place in February 1996, when the family dog was poisoned. At that time they did not connect the incident with Boss Ronnie's abusive and racist conduct. The next month, their car was vandalized and its tires slashed, though nothing was taken out of the car. The police came, took fingerprints, and patrolled the area but did nothing else. The Thomases told Michelle's father-in-law about the incident. Boss Ronnie told them that he had just had a confrontation with his workers and that the family should buy a gun.
>
> In May 1996, human feces were thrown at the door of the Thomases' residence while they were at home. After hearing the noise, the Thomases saw people running away. Feces were also left outside their front and back gates at later times. The Thomases then had higher fencing installed and bars put on their windows; they got a guard dog and requested additional police patrols.
>
> In December 1996, Michelle's life was threatened by a person wearing overalls bearing a Strongshore logo. In her words,
>
> > I was sitting on the veranda the one evening with my children playing in the front yard and a Black man had come up to me and asked me if I knew Boss Ronnie

which was David's father and he said to me he'[d] come back and cut my throat. At that stage I'd taken the kids inside. The kids were very upset and I said to him we don't know him, he's just drunk. Let's go inside. At this stage I was really, really fearing for my life and I had told David on a number of occasions, please speak to his father which he did, but he was not interested in what we had to say.

In March 1997, Michelle was outside of her gate, on the way to the store, when four black men approached her and tried to take her daughter from her arms. As she testified, "[T]hey surrounded me and the next thing I knew is that they were trying to get Tyneal out [of] my arms. I held her tight and fell to the ground with her...." The men ran off after Michelle's neighbor came out of his house in response to Michelle's screaming. One of the men wore Strongshore overalls. After this incident Michelle was afraid that "they were going to come back and either kill one of us or take one of my children." It was at that point that Michelle decided that she needed to leave South Africa.

Michelle's brother-in-law had his house broken into and his car vandalized several times, and he and his family had received threats. Michelle believed that her family, rather than her father-in-law, had become the subject of attacks because her father-in-law owned weapons and lived in what was essentially a "fortress," so the attackers could not get to him. In addition to the evidence of particular attacks on their family, the Thomases also submitted evidence of the widespread crime problem in South Africa.

409 F.3d at 1180–81.

The Ninth Circuit discussed the Thomases' claim of persecution on account of membership in a particular social group of "persons related to Boss Ronnie." After discussing decisions issued by BIA, other federal appeals courts, and the Ninth Circuit, the court held that "a family may constitute a social group for the purposes of the refugee statutes." Turning to the facts of the case, the court concluded that "the Thomas family constitutes a particular social group * * * because the family demonstrated that the harm they suffered was solely a result of their common and immutable kinship ties with Boss Ronnie." Id. at 1187–88.

Four judges dissented. Pointing out that "[t]he BIA has never addressed whether a nuclear family is a 'particular social group,'" the dissenters urged remand to the BIA to decide if the Thomases were in fact a particular social group based on the evidence. 409 F.3d at 1192.

On review, the U.S. Supreme Court issued a summary reversal. It cast no doubt on the substantive ruling that a family can constitute a particular social group, but it held that a court of appeals, once it resolves an issue of doctrine in this manner, should remand an asylum case to the BIA for further factual inquiry. Here the Ninth Circuit made an "obvious" error in deciding the factual issue when the "agency has not yet considered whether Boss Ronnie's family presents the kind of 'kinship ties' that constitute a 'particular social group.' The matter requires determining the facts and deciding whether the facts as found fall within a statutory term." *Gonzales v. Thomas*, 547 U.S. ___, 126 S.Ct. 1613, 1615, 164 L.Ed.2d 358 (2006) (per curiam).

Assume that you are a member of the Board of Immigration Appeals. On the face of it, it seems plausible that a family may be a social group, but does this mean that all family members of targets of personal retaliation are now entitled to refugee status? Given all applicable precedents, how will you approach the issue? What will you decide?

On these questions, consider *K v. Secretary of State for the Home Dep't,* [2006] UKHL 46 (House of Lords). The opinion by Lord Bingham of Cornhill summarized the facts in one of the two asylum denials consolidated for decision and reversed:

> The first appellant [K] is an Iranian citizen. She is married to B with whom, and their child, she lived in Iran. In about April 2001 B disappeared. It appears he was arrested, and he has since been held in prison without, so far as the first appellant is aware, charge or trial. On her one visit to him in prison he appeared to her to show signs of ill-treatment. The grounds for his detention are not known. About two or three weeks after B's disappearance Revolutionary Guards, agents of the Islamic Iranian state, searched the first appellant's house and took away books and papers. About a week later the Revolutionary Guards again visited the first appellant's house: they searched the house further, and insulted and raped her. Following this incident the first appellant made herself scarce. She was not again approached by Revolutionary Guards and nor were members of her family. But the school year began on 23 September 2001 and on the following day the headmaster of the school attended by her son, then aged 7, told her that the Revolutionary Guard had been to the school to make enquiries about the boy. The Adjudicator found that the Revolutionary Guards had approached the school in an open manner knowing that this would come to the attention of the first appellant and that it would cause her great fear. She was indeed very frightened, and fled from Iran with her son. The Adjudicator accepted that in the then current situation in Iran the families of those of adverse interest to the authorities could well be targeted. The first appellant travelled via Turkey to the United Kingdom where, on 5 October 2001, the day after her arrival, she claimed asylum.

*Id.* at ¶ 2. Lord Hope of Craighead addressed the government's argument that K could not show that the persecution was on account of membership in her family as a particular social group without evidence—lacking in this case—that other members of her family were exposed to the same risk of persecution:

The reasoning [that all members of the group be susceptible to the persecution in question] requires more of an asylum seeker who claims that the particular social group of which he or she is a member is the family than is required of those who claim that the persecution of which they have a well-founded fear is for reasons of race, religion, nationality or political opinion. It is, of course, critical to identify what lies at the root of the threat of persecution. But it is not necessary to show that everyone else of the same race, for example, or every other member of the particular social group, is subject to the same threat. All that needs to be shown is that there is a causative link between his or her race or his or her membership of the particular social group and the threat of the persecution of which there is a well-founded fear. The fact that other members of the group are not under the same threat may be relevant to an assessment of the question whether the causative link has actually been established. Especially in a case such as the present, where it is not suggested that any other member of the family is at risk of being persecuted for reasons of membership of the family, the evidence of causation will need to be scrutinised very carefully. But the mere fact that no other member of the family is in that position is not determinative.

*Id.* at ¶ 47.

---

### Exercise: Drafting Guidelines

In December 2000 (the last full month of the Clinton Administration), the INS drafted guidelines for interpreting the meaning of "a particular social group" and issued them in the form of a Proposed Rule, but to date they have not been adopted. 65 Fed. Reg. 76588 (2000). They would revise section 208.15 of Title 8 of the Code of Federal Regulations to specify a non-exclusive list of factors to be considered in determining if a particular social group exists.

(3) Factors that may be considered * * * , but are not necessarily determinative, in deciding whether a particular social group exists include whether:

(i) The members of the group are closely affiliated with each other;

(ii) The members are driven by a common motive or interest;

(iii) A voluntary associational relationship exists among the members;

(iv) The group is recognized to be a societal faction or is otherwise a recognized segment of the population in the country in question;

(v) Members view themselves as members of the group; and

(vi) The society in which the group exists distinguishes members of the group for different treatment or status than is accorded to other members of the society.

*Id.* at 76,598.

Can you revise these guidelines so that they more completely capture the results in all of the cases in this Section D of this chapter on the meaning of "particular social group"? Can you revise these guidelines so they are more faithful to the Refugee Convention, or to your sense of the best approach to "particular social group"?

## SECTION E.   CONCLUDING THOUGHTS

### Rethinking the Nexus Requirement

Consider the following comments, taken from an article that analyzes *Matter of Chang* (reprinted in Chapter Three, p. 99) and many of the other cases in this section:

Courts and commentators tend to see the "persecution" issue primarily in terms of the level of harm imposed on an individual. The UNHCR *Handbook on Procedures and Criteria for Determining Refugee Status* is typical. In its brief discussion, it notes that

[t]here is no universally accepted definition of "persecution," and various attempts to formulate such a definition have met with little success. From Article 33 of the 1951 Convention, it may be inferred that a threat to life or freedom on account of race, religion, nationality, political opinion or membership in a particular social group is always persecution. Other serious violations of human rights—for the same reasons— would also constitute persecution.

Two considerations are at work in this paragraph: (1) the harm imposed must be of a serious nature; and (2) the harm must be imposed for one of the designated reasons for it to qualify as persecution within the terms of the Convention. The first point is sensible enough; surely neither international law nor the dramatic relief provided by U.S. asylum law need concern itself with minor inconveniences inflicted upon individuals, irrespective of the motive of the inflicter.

The second point, however, requires some further reflection. Why is the definition of persecution necessarily linked to the five specified grounds? My sense is that this gets at something other than just the level of harm—call it a "qualitative" or "normative" aspect of the definition of persecution. That is, persecution connotes unacceptable, unjustified, abhorrent infliction of harm, not simply a particular degree of harm. To see this, compare the case of an individual sentenced to life imprisonment for having committed murder with the case of a person sentenced to ten years in prison for having circulated a pamphlet opposing the government. The first case is unlikely to be seen as persecution; the second might well.

The *Handbook*'s use of the five grounds in its explication of "persecution," then, signals the unjustifiable, intolerable aspect of the infliction of harm. One's race or religion cannot provide an acceptable reason for the imposition of serious injury. But while one can understand how the existence of one of the five grounds might signal the qualitative aspect of the definition of persecution, it is not at all clear that persecution ought to be so limited—or, more importantly, that an applicant must be able to establish conclusively that one of the five grounds is at work in order to establish persecution. Persecution might well be given a "free-standing" meaning that requires judgments about both the degree of and justifications for the harm, but not one that necessarily invokes the five grounds as the test of the qualitative aspect.

\* \* \*

[T]he issue of persecution necessarily includes a normative, qualitative judgment about the degree of, and justification for, the harm imposed on an individual or group \* \* \*.

Aleinikoff, *The Meaning of "Persecution" in United States Asylum Law,* 3 Int'l J. Refugee L. 5, 12–13, 27 (1991).

Should the requirements for asylum and withholding be reoriented so that the inquiry focuses on the degree and nature of harm, and away from the current requirement that the harm be "on account of" one of the five enumerated grounds?

---

### Exercise

Alejandro is a young Guatemalan who entered the United States without inspection in 1994, at a time when Guatemala was in the midst of a bloody and bitter civil war. He is of Mayan Indian descent, and his family converted to the Pentecostal religion when he was 10 years old. Placed in removal proceedings 11 months after his entry, he requested asylum and withholding of deportation. During the merits hearing, his trial counsel described the asylum application as based on a political opinion imputed to him by Guatemalan guerrillas, but the asylum application form stated that he had been persecuted on account of a neutral political opinion.

Alejandro's application had been accompanied by an affidavit that he signed, plus two letters from a friend and a family member in Guatemala that indicated that he left Guatemala in search of a better life and future. At the hearing he testified that his youngest brother was forced into military service by the Guatemalan army, and that guerrillas molested and killed one of his sisters. According to his testimony, these guerrillas would come to his home town every Sunday and would go to each of the homes seeking food, clothing, or money. If the townspeople refused, they would be beaten or killed. He had personally witnessed such incidents, including one in which the guerrillas killed his grandfather while he watched, because his grandfather did not have money or food to give to them.

During one of these visits to Alejandro's hometown, the guerrillas noticed that he was old enough to join them. His father refused the guerrillas' request, whereupon they indicated that if Alejandro did not join them, they would kill him. According to Alejandro, it was common for the guerrillas to take people from the town, especially healthy young men, because the guerrillas wanted to increase their numbers.

After this threat was made, Alejandro would generally hide himself when the guerrillas came to town, but he was occasionally spotted. Alejandro asserted in his testimony that the guerrillas would accuse him of having the same mind set as his brother who was serving in the Guatemalan Army. He testified that they cursed him, threatened him, and hit him with their guns. Alejandro testified that he was beaten six times and that during his last beating the guerrillas threatened to kill him if he did not join them within three days. Alejandro left the next day and traveled to the United States.

The immigration judge denied asylum and withholding of deportation, noting that it was supported only by his "own unsubstantiated and conclusory statements." The guerrillas' actions toward him amounted only to an effort to coerce him into joining their ranks. The judge did not believe Alejandro's testimony that the guerrillas would attempt to induct him into their ranks at the same time that they attributed a pro-military opinion to him because of his brother's military service.

Assume that Alejandro presented these facts convincingly to the immigration judge, who found him credible but nonetheless denied asylum and withholding. You are an attorney hired by the applicant to handle the appeal to the BIA. Based on the factual statement above, prepare the best arguments you can on behalf of your client. Which of the five grounds might be relevant? Which provides the strongest basis for the claim? How can you best frame the nexus description to maximize the chances for your client? Which factual elements will you highlight? What are the most vulnerable points of the asylum claim or of your arguments?

Next, switch roles and assume that you are a member of the BIA. Review the facts proved in the immigration court hearing. Remember the statutory elements for asylum and for withholding. Analyze both potential remedies as you prepare your decision.

# Chapter Five

# GENDER AND PERSECUTION

---

*I personally belonged to a student group that favored the Shah. We refused to demonstrate with the students who favored Khomeni. I refused to wear a veil which was a sign or badge that I favor Khomeni.*

\* \* \*

*Q. [Why do you fear going back to Iran?]*

*A. Because of the government that is ruling the country. It is a strange government to me. It has different rules and regulation[s] th[a]n I have been used to \* \* \* [A]nybody who [has] been a Moslem\* \* \* [was required] to practice that religion [or] be punished in public or be jailed.*

*Q. [Would you wear a veil?]*

*A. I would have to, sir.*

*Q. And if you didn't?*

*A. I would be jailed or punished in public. Public mean by whipped or thrown stones and I would be going back to barbaric years. \* \* \**

*If I go back, I would try personally to avoid it [wearing a veil] as I could do\* \* \* I will start trying to avoid it as much as I could. \* \* \**

*As a feminist I mean that I believe in equal rights for women. I believe a woman as a human being can do and should be able to do what they want to do. And over there in \* \* \* Iran at the time being a woman is a second class citizen, doesn't have any right to herself \* \* \*.*

—Parastoo Fatin[1]

---

1. Fatin v. INS, 12 F.3d 1233, 1235–36 (3d Cir. 1993), reprinted later in this chapter.

Recent years have brought increasing attention to the impact of gender on refugee and asylum issues. As you have seen, the Refugee Convention does not specify sex or gender as one of the grounds of persecution that trigger international protection. That omission has led some to criticize the Convention definition. But others, for example Rodger Haines, assert that there is no need for an express reference to sex or gender; they argue that, so long as the Convention is interpreted without discrimination against women, the refugee definition provides ample protection:

> The failure of decision makers to recognize and respond appropriately to the experiences of women stems not from the fact that the 1951 Convention does not refer specifically to persecution on the basis of sex or gender, but rather because it has often been approached from a partial perspective and interpreted through a framework of male experiences. The main problem facing women as asylum seekers is the failure of decision makers to incorporate the gender-related claims of women into their interpretation of the existing enumerated grounds and their failure to recognize the political nature of seemingly private acts of harm to women.

Haines, *Gender-related Persecution*, in Refugee Protection in International Law 319, 323 (E. Feller, V. Türk, & F. Nicholson eds., 2003). *See also id.* at 327.

Because states are unlikely to modify the Refugee Convention to add an additional ground, the reality is that courts and agencies will grapple with gender issues within the framework of the current specified grounds of persecution: race, religion, nationality, membership in a particular social group, and political opinion.

Most, though not all, of the gender issues that arise in refugee and asylum claims concern women. This is not surprising for two reasons. First, according to the UNHCR, women and children comprise more than 80 percent of the world-wide refugee population. Second, in many societies women are powerless and vulnerable, which makes them easy targets for persecution and other harm and also makes their difficulties easy for societies and governments to overlook. In contrast to the refugee population in general, asylum seekers, those who manage to travel to industrialized countries where they seek lawful residence, are predominantly male. As a consequence, asylum procedures have sometimes developed in ways that implicitly respond to experiences more common to men. This has led to calls for more awareness in asylum adjudicators to the impact gender may have. At the same time, any less favorable treatment of women may not show up in statistics. Consider, for example, Thomas Spijkerboer's analysis of data from the Netherlands and Canada showing that women do better than men in the asylum application process, at least as a matter of the rate at which their asylum claims are approved. *See* T. Spijkerboer, Gender and Refugee Status 15–43 (2000).

Sudanese refugee women. (Photo: U.S. Gov't)

Gender in this context refers to social roles assigned to men and women, whereas sex refers to biological differences. *See* H. Crawley, Refugees and Gender: Law and Process (2001). Gender roles vary with societies and with historical periods, and they have important effects on an individual's identity, status, and responsibilities. The materials in this chapter highlight some of the situations in which decision-makers and advocates have begun to address the role of gender in refugee status determinations. They raise many complex legal issues, some of which we have touched upon in earlier chapters. For example, many of the administrative and judicial decisions explore whether women, or certain subsets of women, constitute a particular social group. Others examine the circumstances in which harm inflicted by private individuals— nongovernmental actors—counts as "persecution" within the meaning of the Refugee Convention. Still other decisions grapple with conceptually difficult notions of motive or nexus: whether persecution is "on account of" one of the five enumerated grounds. Imputed political opinion often arises in cases involving gender roles, and the line between prosecution and persecution is sometimes difficult to ascertain. This chapter provides an opportunity to revisit these issues and apply material from earlier chapters as they arise when gender is a central element of an asylum claim.

This chapter examines three different subsets of gender issues. We will look at instances in which the *form* of persecution is gender-specific, situations in which the *reason* for the persecution is related to gender, and *obstacles* that gender roles can cause in asylum procedures. Recognizing that these phenomena frequently overlap, we would like to distinguish between two terms. We will refer to forms of serious harm and persecution that occur specifically to women as gender-specific persecution. When persecution, which may not take a form that is specific to women, occurs because the individuals are women, we will refer to it as gender-related persecution.

## SECTION A.  GENDER-SPECIFIC PERSECUTION

### 1.  RAPE

During the past decade international law has expressly recognized sexual violence as a war crime and a crime against humanity. In particular, the international criminal tribunals set up in the wake of the genocidal conflicts in the former Yugoslavia and Rwanda have emphasized that rape may be an instrument of war, rather than just a by-product of the lawlessness that accompanies armed conflict. Women's reproductive capacity may make them a target by persecutors who want to change the ethnic composition of a society. In addition to the biological results of rape, there are social impacts:

> The violation of women's bodies acts as a symbol of the violation of the country (or * * * political, ethnic or national group). * * * During war, women's bodies become highly symbolic and the physical territory for a broader political struggle in which sexual violence including rape is used as a military strategy to humiliate and demoralize an opponent; women's bodies become the battleground for 'pay backs,' they symbolize the dominance of one group over another * * *.

H. Crawley, Refugees and Gender, *supra*, at 89–90.

Although the mass rapes in Yugoslavia and Rwanda in the early 1990s highlighted to the world the role of rape as persecution, this phenomenon has not been limited to those venues. In the United States asylum adjudicators grappled with these issues when a woman raped by soldiers in Haiti in 1992 claimed she had been persecuted and was entitled to asylum.

## MATTER OF D–V–

Board of Immigration Appeals, 1993.
21 I & N Dec. 77.

* * *

The applicant, a 27-year-old married female, is a native and citizen of Haiti who arrived in the United States on July 15, 1992. She bases her claim on brutal treatment that she suffered at the hands of soldiers because she was a supporter of former President Jean Bertrand Aristide. According to the applicant, she had worked for 6 months as a secretary for a government office under Aristide. She quit her job after she had problems with a co-worker, an Aristide opponent who repeatedly threatened her and told her that when Aristide fell she would pay. She had been an active member of a church group which was formed by and supported by Aristide. A brother of her co-worker also belonged to the group. The applicant and another member of the church committee were delegated to the larger group. The members collected money from the United States and forwarded it to the Aristide government. After the fall of Aristide, her coworker continued to threaten the applicant and other members of the church group. On one occasion the applicant's church was surrounded by government soldiers, whom the applicant referred to as chiefs. The soldiers took one member of the church group away, and the church members learned the next day that he had died.

The applicant stated that the soldiers subsequently came to her family home where they gang-raped and severely beat her. When the soldiers knocked on the gate to her house, they asked for her by her nickname. The soldiers entered the house after the applicant opened the door and her mother opened the outer gate. The applicant's husband was away on business at the time. The soldiers knew that she belonged to the church group. As they passed through the doorway, they said the other church group member had already been killed "so [she] was next, [she] was behind." The soldiers wore stockings on their heads and red scarves tied around their wrists. The scarves were like those worn by the Ton Ton Macoutes, which had signified blood and had meant that people and places would be ravaged. Although the applicant tried to tell the soldiers that the person they asked for was not at home, they identified her by the hair on her feet. One of the soldiers said to her, "[Y]ou're the one that supported a fanatic for Aristide." The soldiers then held a weapon next to the applicant's ear. Her mother gave them some money, pleading with them to spare the daughter's life. Three of the soldiers raped the applicant and beat her. The applicant's mother gave them a case with some American money to get them to leave. Before the soldiers went away, they warned the applicant that if she talked about them or reported them to the radio station they would be back. After the rape incident, the applicant went into hiding in different locations in Haiti until she was able to leave the country. While still in Haiti she was examined by a doctor, who told her that she would not be able to have children because she had sustained some type of internal shock. Since then, she has been pregnant but has miscarried after about 2 months.

In his decision, the Immigration Judge found the applicant credible. * * * Nevertheless, the Immigration Judge determined that the applicant had failed to demonstrate a well-founded fear of persecution on the basis of her political opinion because the evidence did not show her to be a prominent supporter of Aristide. According to the Immigration Judge, the applicant's fear of returning to Haiti was based on the general conditions of violence in that country, and it was pure speculation on her part that the same attackers would rape and beat her again or kill her.

Unlike the Immigration Judge, we find that the applicant has proven that she has a well-founded fear of persecution based on her political opinion and religion if she were returned to Haiti. The applicant's direct and uncontradicted testimony establishes that she has suffered grievous harm in direct retaliation for her support of and activities on behalf of Aristide. In the file is an advisory opinion from the United States Department of State's Bureau of Human Rights and Humanitarian Affairs (BHRHA) issued pursuant to 8 C.F.R. § 208.11 (1992). According to the BHRHA opinion dated November 20, 1992, "persons who were prominent supporters of President Aristide or are currently open and activist supporters of Aristide are likely to remain at risk, especially if they engage in public political activities." Clearly, the applicant was an active member of a church group, which provided funds for projects endorsed by Aristide. She thus could be considered one of Aristide's activist supporters. The evidence reflects that her attackers, who knew her by name and knew of her membership, targeted her previously because of her political and religious opinion and that they well might do so again if she were back in Haiti. There is apparently no significant adverse factor contravening a favorable exercise of discretion regarding her asylum application.

Accordingly, we will sustain the appeal and grant the applicant's asylum request. Inasmuch as the applicant's asylum application has been approved, we need not address the issue of her eligibility for withholding of deportation under the more stringent standard of section 243(h) of the Act.

\* \* \*

### Notes and Questions

1. Did this case involve gender-specific persecution, gender-related persecution, or both? To what extent, and if so why, was the BIA concerned about the social group(s) to which the asylum applicant belonged?

2. Although rape can be a form of persecution directed at men, *see, e.g., Hernandez–Montiel v. INS*, 225 F.3d 1084 (9th Cir. 2000), discussed in Chapter Four, p. 265, this occurs far less frequently. As the excerpts above suggest, the biological and symbolic impact of the widespread rape of the women of a particular community make it especially powerful when women are targeted. For further analyses of rape in the context of asylum claims, see H. Crawley, Refugees and Gender, *supra*; Anker, Kelly, and Willshire–Carrera, *Rape in the Community as a Basis for Asylum: The Treatment of Women Refugees' Claims to Protection in Canada and the United States*, 2 Bender's Immigr. Bull. 608 (1997).

### 2. FEMALE GENITAL MUTILATION

Rape is not the only form of sexual violence that is visited on women. Other forms of sexual abuse, sexual harassment, dowry-related violence, and so-called "honor killings" of women can also constitute persecution. In recent years there has been much attention to a form of gender-specific violence that generally targets young girls.

# MATTER OF KASINGA

Board of Immigration Appeals (en banc), 1996.
21 I & N Dec. 357.

SCHMIDT, CHAIRMAN:

* * * The Immigration Judge found the applicant excludable as an intending immigrant, denied her applications for asylum and withholding of deportation, and ordered her excluded and deported from the United States. Upon reviewing the appellate record anew ("de novo review"), we will sustain the applicant's appeal, grant asylum, and order her admitted to the United States as an asylee.

A fundamental issue before us is whether the practice of female genital mutilation ("FGM") can be the basis for a grant of asylum under section 208 of the Immigration and Nationality Act. On appeal, the parties agree that FGM can be the basis for a grant of asylum. We find that FGM can be a basis for asylum.

Nevertheless, the parties disagree about 1) the parameters of FGM as a ground for asylum in future cases, and 2) whether the applicant is entitled to asylum on the basis of the record before us. In deciding this case, we decline to speculate on, or establish rules for, cases that are not before us.

* * *

The applicant is a 19-year-old native and citizen of Togo. She attended 2 years of high school. She is a member of the Tchamba–Kunsuntu Tribe of northern Togo. She testified that young women of her tribe normally undergo FGM at age 15. However, she did not because she initially was protected from FGM by her influential, but now deceased, father.

The applicant stated that upon her father's death in 1993, under tribal custom her aunt, her father's sister, became the primary authority figure in the family. The applicant's mother was driven from the family home, left Togo, and went to live with her family in Benin. The applicant testified that she does not currently know her mother's exact whereabouts.

The applicant further testified that her aunt forced her into a polygamous marriage in October 1994, when she was 17. The husband selected by her aunt was 45 years old and had three other wives at the time of marriage. The applicant testified that, under tribal custom, her aunt and her husband planned to force her to submit to FGM before the marriage was consummated.

The applicant testified that she feared imminent mutilation. With the help of her older sister, she fled Togo for Ghana. However, she was afraid that her aunt and her husband would locate her there. Consequently, using money from her mother, the applicant embarked for Germany by airplane.

* * *

Upon arrival in Germany, the applicant testified that she was somewhat disoriented and spent several hours wandering around the airport looking for fellow Africans who might help her. Finally, she struck up a conversation, in English, with a German woman.

After hearing the applicant's story, the woman offered to give the applicant temporary shelter in her home until the applicant decided what to do next. For the next 2 months, the applicant slept in the woman's living room, while performing cooking and cleaning duties.

The applicant further stated that in December 1994, while on her way to a shopping center, she met a young Nigerian man. He was the first person from Africa she had spoken to since arriving in Germany. They struck up a conversation, during which the applicant told the man about her situation. He offered to sell the applicant his sister's British passport so that she could seek asylum in the United States, where she has an aunt, an uncle, and a cousin. The applicant followed the man's suggestion, purchasing the passport and the ticket with money given to her by her sister.

The applicant did not attempt a fraudulent entry into the United States. Rather, upon arrival at Newark International Airport on December 17, 1994, she immediately requested asylum. She remained in detention by the Immigration and Naturalization Service ("INS") until April 1996.

The applicant testified that the Togolese police and the Government of Togo were aware of FGM and would take no steps to protect her from the practice. She further testified that her aunt had reported her to the Togolese police. Upon return, she would be taken back to her husband by the police and forced to undergo FGM. She testified at several points that there would be nobody to protect her from FGM in Togo.

In her testimony, the applicant referred to letters in the record from her mother. Those letters confirmed that the Togolese police were looking for the applicant and that the applicant's father's family wanted her to undergo FGM.

The applicant testified that she could not find protection anywhere in Togo. She stated that Togo is a very small country and her husband and aunt, with the help of the police, could locate her anywhere she went. She also stated that her husband is well known in Togo and is a friend of the police. On cross-examination she stated that it would not be possible for her to live with another tribe in Togo.

The applicant also testified that the Togolese police could locate her in Ghana. She indicated that she did not seek asylum in Germany because she could not speak German and therefore could not continue her education there. She stated that she did not have relatives in Germany as she does in the United States.

\* \* \*

### 4. Description of FGM

According to the applicant's testimony, the FGM practiced by her tribe, the Tchamba–Kunsuntu, is of an extreme type involving cutting the genitalia with knives, extensive bleeding, and a 40-day recovery period. The background materials confirm that the FGM practiced in some African countries, such as Togo, is of an extreme nature causing permanent damage, and not just a minor form of genital ritual.

The record material establishes that FGM in its extreme forms is a practice in which portions of the female genitalia are cut away. In some cases, the vagina is sutured partially closed. This practice clearly inflicts harm or suffering upon the girl or woman who undergoes it.

FGM is extremely painful and at least temporarily incapacitating. It permanently disfigures the female genitalia. FGM exposes the girl or woman to the risk of serious, potentially life-threatening complications. These include, among others, bleeding, infection, urine retention, stress, shock, psychological trauma, and damage to the urethra and anus. It can result in permanent loss of genital sensation and can adversely affect sexual and erotic functions.

The FGM Alert, compiled and distributed by the INS Resource Information Center, notes that "few African countries have officially condemned female genital mutilation and still fewer have enacted legislation against the practice." Further, according to the FGM Alert, even in those few African countries where legislative efforts have been made, they are usually ineffective to protect women against FGM. The FGM Alert notes that "it remains practically true that [African] women have little legal recourse and may face threats to their freedom, threats or acts of physical violence, or social ostracization for refusing to undergo this harmful traditional practice or attempting to protect their female children." Togo is not listed in the FGM Alert as among the African countries that have made even minimal efforts to protect women from FGM.

The record also contains a May 26, 1995, memorandum from Phyllis Coven, Office of International Affairs, INS, which is addressed to all INS Asylum Officers and sets forth guidelines for adjudicating women's asylum claims. Coven, U.S. Dep't of Justice, Considerations For Asylum Officers Adjudicating Claims From Women (1995) [the INS Gender Guidelines]. Those guidelines state that "rape ..., sexual abuse and domestic violence, infanticide and genital mutilation are forms of mistreatment primarily directed at girls and women and they may serve as evidence of past persecution on account of one or more of the five grounds."

### 5. State Department Reports on Conditions in Togo

The record also contains two reports compiled by the United States Department of State. The first of these, dated January 31, 1994, 1) confirms that FGM is practiced by some ethnic groups in Togo; 2) notes that while some reports indicate that the practice may be diminishing, an expert indicates that as many as 50% of Togolese females may have been mutilated; and 3) notes that various acts of violence against women occur in Togo with little police intervention.

The second Department of State Report on Togo, prepared by the Bureau of Democracy, Human Rights and Labor, is dated April 1995. While not specifically addressing FGM, that report states that the President of Togo has a poor human rights record and confirms that the government's military and security forces have been involved in serious human rights abuses.

\* \* \*

[The INS had taken a different position on appeal than it had in immigration court, after a thorough headquarters review of the issues presented. Before the BIA it agreed that FGM could constitute persecution and urged the Board to clarify the doctrine on this matter. But noting that the immigration judge had found Kasinga to lack credibility, it urged remand for further factual inquiry under a proper understanding of the law. The Board rejected this request and found the applicant to be a credible witness.]

## II.   FGM As Persecution

For the purposes of this case, we adopt the description of FGM drawn from the record and summarized in Part I.B.4. of this opinion. We agree with the parties that this level of harm can constitute "persecution" within the meaning of section 101(a)(42)(A) of the Act.

While a number of descriptions of persecution have been formulated in our past decisions, we have recognized that persecution can consist of the infliction of harm or suffering by a government, or persons a government is unwilling or unable to control, to overcome a characteristic of the victim. *See Matter of Acosta*, 19 I & N Dec. 211, 222–23 (BIA 1985), *modified on other grounds*, *Matter of Mogharrabi*, 19 I & N Dec. 439 (BIA 1987). The "seeking to overcome" formulation has its antecedents in concepts of persecution that predate the Refugee Act of 1980.

As observed by the INS, many of our past cases involved actors who had a subjective intent to punish their victims. However, this subjective "punitive" or "malignant" intent is not required for harm to constitute persecution.

Our characterization of FGM as persecution is consistent with our past definitions of that term. We therefore reach the conclusion that FGM can be persecution without passing on the INS's proposed "shocks the conscience" test. We also agree with the parties that this case is not controlled by *Matter of Chang*, 20 I & N Dec. 38 (BIA 1989) (holding that China's population control policy is not persecution).

## III.   Social Group

To be a basis for a grant of asylum, persecution must relate to one of five categories described in section 101(a)(42)(A) of the Act. The parties agree that the relevant category in this case is "particular social group." Each party has advanced several formulations of the "particular social group" at issue in this case. However, each party urges the Board to adopt only that definition of social group necessary to decide this individual case.

In the context of this case, we find the particular social group to be the following: young women of the Tchamba–Kunsuntu Tribe who have not had FGM, as practiced by that tribe, and who oppose the practice. This is very similar to the formulations suggested by the parties.

The defined social group meets the test we set forth in *Matter of Acosta, supra. See also Matter of H–*, [21 I & N Dec. 337] (BIA 1996) (finding that identifiable shared ties of kinship warrant characterization as a social group). It also is consistent with the law of the United States Court of Appeals for the Third Circuit, where this case arose. *Fatin v. INS*, 12 F.3d 1233, 1241 (3d Cir. 1993) (stating that Iranian women who refuse to conform to the Iranian Government's gender-specific laws and social norms may well satisfy the *Acosta* definition).

In accordance with *Acosta*, the particular social group is defined by common characteristics that members of the group either cannot change, or should not be required to change because such characteristics are fundamental to their individual identities. The characteristics of being a "young woman" and a "member of the Tchamba–Kunsuntu Tribe" cannot be changed. The characteristic of having intact genitalia is one that is so fundamental to the individual identity of a young woman that she should not be required to change it.

\* \* \*

## V.  "ON ACCOUNT OF"

To be eligible for asylum, the applicant must establish that her well-founded fear of persecution is "on account of" one of the five grounds specified in the Act, here, her membership in a "particular social group." *See, e.g., Matter of H–, supra* (holding that harm or abuse because of clan membership constitutes persecution on account of social group).

Both parties have advanced, and the background materials support, the proposition that there is no legitimate reason for FGM. Group Exhibit 4 contains materials showing that the practice has been condemned by such groups as the United Nations, the International Federation of Gynecology and Obstetrics, the Council on Scientific Affairs, the World Health Organization, the International Medical Association, and the American Medical Association.

Record materials state that FGM "has been used to control woman's sexuality." It also is characterized as a form of "sexual oppression" that is "based on the manipulation of women's sexuality in order to assure male dominance and exploitation." During oral argument before us, the INS General Counsel agreed with the latter characterization. He also stated that the practice is a "severe bodily invasion" that should be regarded as meeting the asylum standard even if done with "subjectively benign intent."

We agree with the parties that, as described and documented in this record, FGM is practiced, at least in some significant part, to overcome sexual characteristics of young women of the tribe who have not been, and do not wish to be, subjected to FGM. We therefore find that the persecution the applicant fears in Togo is "on account of" her status as a member of the defined social group.

\* \* \*

We have weighed the favorable and adverse factors and are satisfied that discretion should be exercised in favor of the applicant. Therefore, we will grant asylum to the applicant.

\* \* \*

FILPPU, BOARD MEMBER, concurring:

\* \* \*

Despite the absence of any major dispute between the parties in this case, the Service requests that we adopt its broad "framework of analysis" for claims of this type. Its suggestion candidly is aimed at addressing issues it sees arising in relation to claims that may be made by women from other "parts of the world where FGM is practiced" and by those "who have been subjected to it in the past."

The Board engages in case adjudication. It decides those issues that lead to the resolution of the cases before it. Our published rulings act as precedent under the regulations, 8 C.F.R. § 3.1(g) (1995), and can affect many related cases. But the Board is not well positioned, in the context of a single disposition of a novel issue, to establish comprehensive rules or guidelines for the adjudication of all cases presenting variations on the case at hand. Yet, it is the cases that are not before us that seem to draw much of the Service's attention in its brief.

The Service points out that it is "estimated that over eighty million females have been subjected to FGM." It further notes that there is "no indication" that "Congress considered application of [the asylum laws] to broad cultural practices of the type involved here." The Service proceeds to argue that "the underlying purposes of the asylum system . . . are unavoidably in tension" in both providing protection for those seriously in jeopardy and in maintaining broad overall governmental control over immigration. The Service further argues that "the Board's interpretation in this case must assure protection for those most at risk of the harms covered by the statute, but it cannot simply grant asylum to all who might be subjected to a practice deemed objectionable or a violation of a person's human rights." It is from these underpinnings that the Service argues that the class of FGM victims who may be eligible for asylum "does not consist of all women who come from the parts of the world where FGM is practiced, nor of all who have been subjected to it in the past."

The Service then offers its "framework of analysis." That framework includes a new "shocks the conscience" test for persecution. The advantages seen by the Service of this test evidently include: 1) the ability to define FGM as "persecution" notwithstanding any lack of intent to "punish" FGM victims on the part of the victims' parents or tribe members who may well "believe that they are simply performing an important cultural rite that bonds the individual to the society"; 2) the ability to exclude other cultural practices, such as "body scarring," from the definition of persecution as these do not shock the conscience; and 3) the ability to exclude past victims of FGM from asylum eligibility if "they consented" to it or "at least acquiesced," as in the case of a woman who experienced FGM as "a small child," since FGM would not shock the conscience unless inflicted on "an unconsenting or resisting individual."

With respect to the past persecution question, the Service references 8 C.F.R. § 208.13(b)(1) (1995), and notes "that a woman once circumcised cannot ordinarily be subjected to FGM a second time." The regulation cited by the Service provides in part for a presumption of future persecution that arises from past persecution, and allows only one way of overcoming the presumption, namely, a change in country conditions. As conditions in countries where FGM is practiced may not have changed, it may be anomalous to have a binding presumption of future persecution where the act of persecution will never again take place for the individual past victim.

The Service's broad framework of analysis also seems to have led it to offer a social group definition that in one respect fits the test set forth in *Matter of Acosta*, 19 I & N Dec. 211 (BIA 1985), modified on other grounds, *Matter of Mogharrabi*, 19 I & N Dec. 439 (BIA 1987), yet is also defined largely by the harm sought to be included in the concept of persecution. For example, we simply do not know from this record whether the similar social groups proposed by the parties are recognized as groupings for any other purposes within Togolese society aside from the serious personal harm at issue here. The record does not disclose whether this group is seen as a distinct body within Togo or within the tribe both before and after the infliction of FGM on its members, or whether it is a group that exists exclusively in relation to the particular offensive practice at issue here. Because the social group definition has not been a real source of dispute between the parties, we are also not well informed as to the degree of affiliation between or the homogeneity among its members. See *Sanchez–Trujillo v. INS*, 801 F.2d 1571 (9th Cir. 1986).

The Service does not offer its new framework of analysis for our consideration as part of an effort to harmonize a line of past rulings, or otherwise to put some order into a series of decisions that have addressed FGM questions in a variety of contexts. Instead, the Service offers its new analysis in the context of a case of first impression for the Board. It sets out what appear to be a variety of policy considerations and potential areas of concern that might arise in related but nevertheless different cases. It then tries to develop a unifying theory or approach that would support grants of asylum to persons who may prospectively face FGM, but would not routinely make asylum available to persons who have simply previously suffered FGM.

It may be that the Board will end up with an analysis along the lines proposed by the Service as it confronts various issues involving asylum and FGM in the future. Then again the Board may settle upon a different view, which may be better or worse from the perspective of particular parties. But I am fully in agreement with the majority's decision not to attempt to set forth a comprehensive analytical framework in the context of this one case.

The Board certainly is not oblivious to immigration policy considerations in the disposition of cases falling within our jurisdiction. But we are not fundamentally a policy-making body. There may be some unsettling or unsatisfying aspects to the slower and less predictable development of legal guidelines that inures in the Board's case adjudication system. But there are alternatives if resort to the Board's issuance of precedent is not satisfactory in a particular context. The Service can seek to have the Attorney General issue regulations that comprehensively address competing concerns, or it can work within the Administration for appropriate legislative action by Congress. The Service should not, however, expect the Board to endorse a significant new framework for assessing asylum claims in the context of a single novel case, especially when that framework seems intended primarily to address cases that are not in fact before the Board yet.

ROSENBERG, BOARD MEMBER, concurring:

\* \* \*

First, this case involves the respondent's reasonable fear that she faces the possibility of harm or abuse, rising to the level of persecution, inflicted on account of her membership in a particular social group.

\* \* \*

In my view, there are three essential elements inherent in our definition of persecution, which, if established, constitute the basis for a discretionary grant of asylum, or a mandatory grant of withholding of deportation, or both. One is the factor of the applicant's genuine, subjective fear of persecution, which must be accompanied by objective evidence rendering the fear reasonable. The next is the factor of harm, abuse, or ill-treatment which rises to the level of, or amounts to, persecution and includes consideration of the applicant's attitude towards such treatment. The last is the reason for, or cause of, the infliction of persecution. This is known as the "on account of" factor, which includes consideration of the motives of the agent of persecution and requires a nexus between the infliction of harm which constitutes persecution and one of the five protected grounds or statuses, such as social group membership, set forth by the Act. In *Fatin v. INS*, 12 F.3d 1233, 1240 (3d Cir. 1993), the United States Court of Appeals for the

Third Circuit held that to prevail, an applicant claiming social group persecution must identify a cognizable social group, establish her membership in it, and show that persecution is based on that membership.

In this case, I conclude that the applicant's fear is of imminent female genital mutilation, related to being forced to enter an arranged marriage, documented in the record as constituting a mandatory tribal custom. The harm or abuse amounting to persecution is the genital mutilation opposed by the applicant. The reason the persecution would be inflicted, the "on account of" element, is because of the persecutor's intent to overcome her state of being non-mutilated and accordingly, free from male-dominated tribal control, including an arranged marriage.

I see no reason to depart from our existing jurisprudence in order to determine the claim set forth here. In my view, this issue is controlled by our precedent decisions, interpreting the statute and agency regulations, in which, only recently, we have recognized that government-tortured Sri Lankans; imprisoned and beaten Somalia tribesmen; persecuted Afghani Mujahedin fighters; and Haitian women, raped for political retribution, can set forth claims which deserve and warrant protection within our laws. *Matter of H–*, [21 I & N Dec. 337] (BIA 1996); *Matter of D–V–*, [21 I & N Dec. 77] (BIA 1993); *Matter of B–*, [21 I. & N. Dec. 66] (BIA 1995).

\* \* \*

Second, a social group definition that takes into account and differentiates the other component elements of the definition of persecution which warrant protection under United States law is critical.

There is nothing about a social group definition based upon gender that requires us to treat it as either an aberration, or as an unanticipated development requiring a new standard. While this is the first time that this Board has addressed the particular type of harm or abuse feared by the respondent—female genital mutilation—it is not the first time that the Board has addressed the "particular social group category," *see, e.g., Matter of Sanchez and Escobar*, 19 I & N Dec. 276 (BIA 1985); *Matter of Acosta*, 19 I & N Dec. 211 (BIA 1985). Indeed, this Board has specifically addressed the category of particular social group persecution in a recent decision. *Matter of H–*, [21 I & N Dec. 337] (BIA 1996) (holding that membership in an identifiable subclan of a Somalian tribe constitutes membership in a particular social group and that harm suffered on account of that membership constitutes persecution). \* \* \*

\* \* \*

Unlike requests for asylum premised upon political opinion, social group claims, like those involving race, ethnicity, or religion, are status based and do not necessarily require a showing of the presence of an individual's opinions or activities which spurs the persecutor's wrath or otherwise motivates the harm or persecution. *Matter of H–, supra.* Rather, such requests involve a determination of whether the shared characteristics are those which motivate an agent of persecution to seek to overcome or otherwise harm the individual. Consequently, while not inaccurate, it is surplusage to define the social group in this case by including as an element the applicant's opposition to the practice of female genital mutilation.

It may be true that sometimes an individual woman's political opinion may overlap or coexist with her membership in a group designated as a particular social group; however, that does not detract from the fact that social group membership is a status-based ground protected under the Act, just as is religion or ethnicity. While it is not impossible that a political or social opinion, either actual or imputed, may be shared by persons whom, as a result, we would characterize as constituting a particular social group within the meaning of the Act, that is not the case here. As I have stated, the applicant's political or social views—her attitude or intent—is not relevant to our definition of the social group to which she belongs, but rather to whether the harm or abuse she faces constitutes persecution.

In *Matter of H–,* this Board found, without difficulty or the need to qualify, that a man who was a member of a tribe in Somalia whose members were being systematically attacked by other tribes in retribution for the corruption and brutality of former ruler and tribe member, Siad Barre, had established persecution based on his clan membership alone. That his father and brother were killed and that he himself was brutally treated during detention was found to be persecution on account of his membership in a subclan in Somalia, a particular social group. His attitude towards that persecution was neither examined nor relevant.

The only distinguishing characteristic about this case that I can perceive to set it apart from others we already have decided is that it involves a woman. Reliance upon such a distinction to support a separate category for treatment of women's asylum claims, to my mind, would be impermissible. Here, the applicant is a member of a group: girls and women of a given tribe, some perhaps of marriageable age, whose members are routinely subjected to the harm which the majority finds to constitute persecution. The applicant's opposition (which happens to be present in this case) or the lack of it, is neither determinative, nor necessary to define the social group in accordance with the statutory language.

Third, it is the role of this Board to interpret and apply the statute in individual cases coming before us for the purpose of establishing a consistent framework for adjudication.

This Board has a significant history and an ongoing role in interpreting the statute and determining the law in cases involving immigrants and refugees. Under 8 C.F.R. § 3.1(g) (1995), our precedent decisions are to be binding on all subsequent adjudications involving the same issue or issues. As the designee of the Attorney General, we serve not only to adjudicate individual, unrelated cases on their facts, but also to give life to the provisions and terms of the law and establish agency policy through adjudication.

\* \* \*

VACCA, BOARD MEMBER, dissenting:

I respectfully dissent without opinion.

## Notes and Questions

1. Several months after the *Kasinga* decision, the New York Times and the Washington Post published articles that followed up with the people involved in the case. *See* Dugger, *A Refugee Escapes From Togo, Body Intact But Family Torn*, New York Times, Sept. 11, 1996, at A1, A8–9; Shiner, *Persecution by Circumcision; Woman Who Fled Togo Convinced U.S. Court But Not Town Elders,* Washington Post, July 3, 1996, at A1. The varied reactions of the relatives still in Togo to the worldwide attention the case had drawn are of particular interest. Some who initially favored the practice of female genital cutting reported changing their minds as a result of this experience. Ms. Kasinga (whose name is properly spelled Kassindja) also wrote a book recounting her experiences. F. Kassindja & L.M. Bashir, Do They Hear You When You Cry? (1998). Detailed back-story accounts of the *Kasinga* litigation and another highly publicized FGM case with surface similarities but belatedly revealed deep differences, *Abankwah v. INS,* 185 F.3d 18 (2d Cir. 1999), may be found in Martin, *Adelaide Abankwah, Fauziya Kasinga, and the Dilemmas of Political Asylum,* in Immigration Stories 245 (D. Martin & P. Schuck eds. 2005); and Kratz, *Circumcision Debates and Asylum Cases: Intersecting Arenas, Contested Values, and Tangled Webs,* in Engaging Cultural Differences: The Multicultural Challenge to Liberal Democracies 309 (R. Shweder, M. Minow, & H.R. Markus eds. 2002).

For reports on addressing FGM at the source including some successful efforts to persuade communities in Africa to cease the practice, see E. Gruenbaum, The Female Circumcision Controversy: An Anthropological Perspective 176–97 (2001); Walt, *Village by Village: Circumcising a Ritual*, Washington Post, June 7, 1998, at C1. For a comprehensive report on the practice of FGM, see U.N. Office for the Coordination of Humanitarian Affairs, Integrated Regional Information Networks (IRIN), Razor's Edge— The Controversy of Female Genital Mutilation (2005).

2. What is the particular social group to which Kasinga belongs? Board Member Rosenberg asserts that opposition to FGM is not an essential element of Kasinga's particular social group claim. Do you agree? In Rosenberg's view (agreeing with INS' argument on this point), opposition is relevant only to deciding whether the practice amounts to persecution in the particular case. Why is opposition relevant if a practice involves bodily invasion? Why does the majority's definition limit the group to those "who oppose the practice"?

Related questions about defining the particular social group arose in *K v. Secretary of State for the Home Dep't,* [2006] UKHL 46 (House of Lords), a Law Lords (U.K.) decision excerpted in Chapter Four, pp. 286, 290. The opinion by Lord Bingham of Cornhill summarized the facts of one of the two asylum denials that the Law Lords reversed:

4.  The second appellant [Fornah] was born in Sierra Leone on 23 May 1987. She arrived in the United Kingdom on 15 March 2003, aged 15, and claimed asylum. The basis of her claim was that, if returned to Sierra Leone, she would be at risk of subjection to female genital mutilation (FGM).

5.  In 1998 the second appellant and her mother were living in her father's family village to escape the civil war, and she overheard discussions of her undergoing FGM as part of her initiation into womanhood. In order to avoid this she ran away, but she was captured by rebels and repeatedly raped by a rebel leader, by whom she became pregnant. An uncle had arranged her departure from Sierra Leone to the United Kingdom. She resisted return on the ground that, if returned, she would have nowhere to live but her father's village, where she feared she would be subjected to FGM.

*Id.* at ¶ ¶ 4, 5.

Baroness Hale of Richmond addressed Fornah's claim of asylum based on membership in a particular social group:

109.  It cannot make any difference that the practice is widespread and widely accepted in Sierra Leonean society. As the UNHCR Guidelines remind us, in paragraph 5:

... harmful practices in breach of international human rights law and standards cannot be justified on the basis of historical, traditional, religious or cultural grounds.

There is no doubt that FGM is in breach of international human rights law and standards: indeed, the Secretary of State does not argue otherwise.

110.  It cannot make any difference that it is practised by women upon women and girls. Those who have already been persecuted are often expected to perpetuate the persecution of succeeding generations, as any reader of *Tom Brown's Schooldays* knows.

111.  Nor can it be seriously doubted that the persecution is visited upon its victims because they are members of a particular social group. It is only done to them because they are female members of the tribes within Sierra Leone which practise FGM. They share the immutable characteristics of being female, Sierra Leonean and members of the particular tribe to which they belong. They would share these characteristics even if FGM were not practised within their communities. Their social group exists completely independently of the initiation rites it chooses to practise.

112.  The stumbling block seems to have been the fact that FGM is a once and for all event. Once done, it can neither be undone nor repeated. Thus, it was argued, if many members of the group are no longer at risk, because they have already suffered, it can no longer constitute a group for this purpose. But if the group has to be defined only to include those at risk, it then looks as if the group is defined solely by the risk of persecution and nothing more.

113.   This is a peculiarly cruel version of Catch 22: if not all the group are at risk, then the persecution cannot be caused by their membership of the group; if the group is reduced to those who are at risk, it is then defined by the persecution alone. But the reasoning is fallacious at a number of levels. It is the persecution, not the fear, which has to be "by reason of" membership of the group. Even if the group is reduced to those who are currently intact, its members share many characteristics which are independent of the persecution—their gender, their nationality, their ethnicity. It is those characteristics which lead to the persecution, not the persecution itself which leads to those characteristics. But there is no need to reduce the group to those at risk. It is well settled that not all members of the group need be at risk. There is nothing in the Convention to say that all members have to be susceptible. It should not matter why they are not at risk. If the authorities of a particular State had a policy of mutilating all male members of a particular tribe or sect by cutting off their right hands, we would still say that the intact members of the tribe or sect faced persecution because of their membership of the tribe or sect rather than because of their intactness. To return to Professor Aleinikoff [*Protected characteristics and social perceptions: an analysis of the meaning of "membership of a particular social group,"* Refugee Protection in International Law 263 (E. Feller, V. Türk, & F. Nicholson eds., 2003), excerpted in Chapter Four, p. 278], at p 289:

> In sum, the definition of the class must describe a group
> that stands apart in society where the shared characteristic
> of the group reflects the reason for the persecution. This is
> importantly different from saying that a defined class must
> only include persons likely to be persecuted.

114.   For these reasons, the particular social group might best be defined as Sierra Leonean women belonging to those ethnic groups where FGM is practised: then it is quite clear that the reason for the persecution is the membership of that group. But it matters not whether the group is stated more widely, as all Sierra Leonean women, or more narrowly, as intact Sierra Leonean women from those ethnic groups. For all of them, the group has an existence independent of the persecution.

*Id.* at ¶ ¶ 109–114.

3.   Why is this "mandatory tribal custom" (as Board Member Rosenberg puts it) "persecution"? Is the intent behind the custom relevant? Is it persecution because of the links between the practice and male domination? What about the argument that it is not administered with malevolent intent to punish, and that it serves as cultural rite of passage into adulthood and full membership in the society? Is the INS' proposed "shocks the conscience" test—which specifically referred to western or American conscience—helpful in this regard? In connection with your answer, reconsider the quote from Richard Shweder in the Notes and Questions following *Pitcherskaia v. INS* in Chapter Three, at p. 112. Shweder argues that female genital alteration is cultural rite of passage which generally occurs with the

intent to admit the young woman into full membership in the community. Also consider this first-hand comment on the practice:

> It is difficult for me—considering the number of ceremonies I have observed, including my own—to accept that what appears to be expressions of joy and ecstatic celebrations of womanhood in actuality disguise hidden experiences of coercion and subjugation. Indeed, I offer that most Kono women [in Eastern Sierra Leone] who uphold these rituals do so because they *want* to—they relish the supernatural powers of their ritual leaders over against men in society, and they embrace the legitimacy of female authority and, particularly, the authority of their mothers and grandmothers.

Ahmadu, *Rites and Wrongs: An Insider/Outsider Reflects on Power and Excision*, in Female "Circumcision" in Africa: Culture, Controversy, and Change 283, 301 (B. Shell–Duncan & Y. Hernlund eds. (2000).

4.  Referring back to the discussion of "past persecution" in Chapter Three, pp. ___ how should this analysis apply in FGM cases, both for evidentiary purposes in proving a risk of future persecution and as laying the basis for a grant of humanitarian asylum even if there is no risk of similar harm in the future? Does *Kasinga* mean that any woman who has been subjected to FGM in the past now qualifies for asylum in the United States? The INS brief attempted to avoid this prospect by arguing that FGM is like other "bodily invasion," which, "even if severe," constitutes persecution "only when inflicted on an unconsenting or resisting individual. For example, surgery with consent is not persecution, even if it results in the amputation of a limb. For this reason, persons who were subjected to FGM in the past, at a time when they consented or at least acquiesced (as in the case of FGM practiced when the woman was a small child), have not experienced persecution and therefore cannot use that event as the foundation for a claim of past persecution." INS Brief, at 18. Alternatively, one who has been subjected to female genital cutting in the past, even if she resisted then, cannot ordinarily be cut again. Does that fact suffice to rebut the presumption of future persecution in these cases, thereby warranting a discretionary denial of asylum?

The Ninth Circuit has found the second argument unpersuasive. In a case brought by a Somali woman who had suffered one form of female genital mutilation. Relying on the BIA's decision in *Matter of Y–T–L–,* set forth in Chapter Three, p. 178, the court concluded that "persecution in the form of female genital mutilation is similar to forced sterilization and * * * must be considered a continuing harm that renders a petitioner eligible for asylum, without more." *Mohammed v. Gonzales*, 400 F.3d 785, 799 (9th Cir. 2005), discussed in the materials on past persecution in Chapter Three, p. 187. What does this ruling say about the underlying purposes of refugee law? If asylum is meant primarily to provide "surrogate protection" in another country against future persecution, what is the point of asylum when, by the court's theory, it will provide no abatement in the continuing harm?

5.  In the *Kasinga* case, the INS also asked the Board to pay more attention to what constitutes *forced* subjection to the practice, arguing that if the only sanction for failing to submit were reduced wages or social ostracism, then FGM is not forced. "If the individual has a choice, albeit a

burdensome one, that allows her to escape FGM, then she does not face the requisite risk of persecution—unless of course the other choices are themselves inherently persecutive." Do you agree? When, if ever, does ostracism amount to persecution? How such social pressures should be factored into asylum decisions has become important in many post-*Kasinga* FGM cases involving claims that the applicant's daughters will be subjected to the practice if the family is deported. *See, e.g., Nwaokolo v. INS,* 314 F.3d 303 (7th Cir. 2002). That is, the parent (often a single mother) opposes the practice, but fears her children will nonetheless be pressured, perhaps by relatives, into conforming. In that setting, to what extent should asylum law protect against social pressures (in the absence of physical compulsion)? Is it legitimate for proposed haven states to expect individuals simply to endure or resist such pressures, taking their own responsibility for resisting objectionable outcomes that might otherwise befall themselves or their children?

6.   The BIA majority asserts, without elaboration, "that this case is not controlled by *Matter of Chang.*" But is *Chang* (reprinted in Chapter Three, p. 99), distinguishable? After *Kasinga,* what is left of the approach to defining "persecution" that the BIA set out in *Matter of Chang*? (*Kasinga* was decided before the statutory amendment that superseded *Chang* in the context of coercive population control policies.)

7.   How would *Kasinga* apply to an asylum claim based on past subjection to, or future risk of, male circumcision? How would *Mohammed v. Gonzales?* Would the extent of surgical treatment be relevant? Statistics concerning likelihood of medical problems as a consequence? The age of the person to be circumcised? *See generally* Rodrick, *Unkindest Cut,* The New Republic, May 29, 1995, at 10 (reporting on U.S. organizations that denounce male circumcision and sought unsuccessfully to have Congress add a ban on that practice to a bill that made FGM a federal crime. *See* 18 U.S.C.A. § 116).

8.   The BIA rejected INS's proposed framework of analysis for cases of this type, because, in its view, a broad advisory opinion would be improper. Was the oft-cited ruling in *Matter of Acosta,* which set forth the immutable characteristics approach to "particular social group" claims, then also improper? Or should the BIA be expected to develop guidance in its precedent decisions that will help immigration judges and asylum officers assess a wide array of related cases likely to come before them? For judicial criticism that the BIA has provided too little doctrinal guidance in particular social group cases, see, e.g., *Ucelo–Gomez v. Gonzales,* 448 F.3d 180, 185–88 (2d Cir. 2006).

## SECTION B.   GENDER–RELATED PERSECUTION

As stated earlier, we use the term gender-related persecution to focus on situations in which individuals are targeted because they are women. The harm they face may be similar to that visited on other persecuted groups or it may be specific to women. Below we will review cases that have arisen when women transgress gender-related social norms and when they have been the victims of domestic abuse. Both these and other examples of gender-related persecution raise complex legal and policy questions. For an overview of related issues, *see* Neacsu, *Gender-based Persecution as a Basis for Asylum: An Annotated Bibliography 1993–2002*, 95 Law Lib. J. 191 (2003). We begin with a decision, authored by then-Judge (now Justice) Samuel Alito, from which the narrative that opens this chapter is taken.

Khorsand sisters, Mashad, Iran, 1977. (Photo: © Michael Ziegler)

## 1.   RESISTANCE TO SOCIAL NORMS

## FATIN v. INS

United States Court of Appeals, Third Circuit, 1993.
12 F.3d 1233.

Alito, Circuit Judge.

Parastoo Fatin has petitioned for review of an order of the Board of Immigration Appeals (the "Board" or "BIA") requiring her to depart or be deported from the United States. * * *

I.

The petitioner is a native and citizen of Iran. On December 31, 1978, approximately two weeks before the Shah left Iran, the petitioner entered the United States as a nonimmigrant student. She was then 18 years old. She attended high school in Philadelphia through May 1979, and the following September she enrolled in Spring Garden College, also in Philadelphia.

In May 1984, apparently while still attending college, she applied to the Immigration and Naturalization Service District Director for political asylum pursuant to Section 208(a) of the Immigration and Nationality

Act ("INA"), by submitting a completed INS Form I–589. In response to question 31 on this form, which asked what she thought would happen to her if she returned to Iran, she wrote: "I would be interrogated, and I would be forced to attend religious sessions against my will, and I would be publicly admonished and even jailed." In answer to question 34, which asked about any organization in Iran to which she or any immediate family member had ever belonged, she wrote:

> I personally belonged to a student group that favored the Shah. We refused to demonstrate with the students who favored Khomeni. I refused to wear a veil which was a sign or badge that I favor Khomeni. My cousin ... is now a refugee living in Paris France. He was formerly one of the guards for the Shah.

* * *

[In 1987, in proceedings before the immigration judge, she] reiterated and expanded upon the statements in her initial asylum application concerning the treatment of her relatives in Iran, adding that one of her cousins had subsequently been killed in a demonstration and that her brother was in hiding in order to avoid the draft. She also elaborated upon her political activities prior to coming to the United States, stating that she had been involved with a student political group and with a women's rights group associated with the Shah's sister.

When her attorney asked her why she feared going back to Iran, she responded: "Because of the government that is ruling the country. It is a strange government to me. It has different rules and regulation[s] th[a]n I have been used to." She stated that "anybody who [had] been a Moslem" was required "to practice that religion" or "be punished in public or be jailed," and she added that she had been "raised in a way that you don't have to practice if you don't want to." She subsequently stated that she would be required "to do things that [she] never had to do," such as wear a veil. When asked by her attorney whether she would wear a veil, she replied:

> A.  I would have to, sir.
>
> Q.  And if you didn't?
>
> A.  I would be jailed or punished in public. Public mean by whipped or thrown stones and I would be going back to barbaric years.

Later, when the immigration judge asked her whether she would wear a veil or submit to arrest and punishment, she stated:

> If I go back, I would try personally to avoid it as much as I could do.... I will start trying to avoid it as much as I could.

The petitioner also testified that she considered herself a "feminist" and explained:

> As a feminist I mean that I believe in equal rights for women. I believe a woman as a human being can do and should be able to do what they want to do. And over there in ... Iran

at the time being a woman is a second class citizen, doesn't have any right to herself. . . .

After the hearing, the immigration judge denied the petitioner's applications for withholding of deportation, asylum, and suspension of deportation. \* \* \*

Petitioner then appealed to the Board of Immigration Appeals. In her brief, she argued that she feared persecution "on account of her membership of a particular social group, and on the basis of her political opinion." Her brief identified her "particular social group" as "the social group of the upper class of Iranian women who supported the Shah of Iran, a group of educated Westernized free-thinking individuals." Her brief also stated that she had a "deep[ly] rooted belief in feminism" and in "equal rights for women, and the right to free choice of any expression and development of abilities, in the fields of education, work, home and family, and all other arenas of development." In addition, her brief observed that she would be forced upon return to Iran "to practice the Moslem religion." Her brief stated that "she would try to avoid practicing a religion as much as she could." Her brief added that she had "the personal desire to avoid as much practice as she could," but that she feared that "through religious ignorance and inexperience she would be unable to play the role of a religious Shi'ite woman." Her brief contained one passage concerning the requirement that women in Iran wear a veil in public:

> In April 1983, the government adopted a law imposing one year's imprisonment on any women caught in public without the traditional Islamic veil, the Chador. However, from reports, it is clear that in many instances the revolutionary guards . . . take the law into their own hands and abuse the transgressing women. . . .

Her brief did not discuss the question whether she would comply with the law regarding the wearing of a chador. Nor did her brief explain what effect submitting to that requirement would have upon her.

In the section of her brief devoted to political opinion, she mentioned her political activities while in Iran, as well as her current "deep-rooted beliefs in freedom of choice, freedom of expression [and] equality of opportunity for both sexes."

The Board of Immigration Appeals dismissed the petitioner's appeal. The Board noted that she had argued that she was entitled to relief "as a member of the social group composed of upper-class Iranian women" and as a person who "was educated in the western tradition." Rejecting this argument, the Board stated that there was no evidence that she would be "singled out" for persecution. Instead, the Board observed that she would be "subject to the same restrictions and requirements" as the rest of the population. The Board also noted that there had been "a considerable passage of time since [she] was in high school and participated in political activities." In addition, the Board stated that her claims were based on circumstances that had arisen since her entry into this country and that "[s]uch claims are dimly viewed."

After the Board issued its order requiring her voluntary departure or deportation, the petitioner filed the current petition for review.

## II.

* * *

Both courts and commentators have struggled to define "particular social group." Read in its broadest literal sense, the phrase is almost completely open-ended. Virtually any set including more than one person could be described as a "particular social group." Thus, the statutory language standing alone is not very instructive.

Nor is there any clear evidence of legislative intent. * * *

* * * When the Conference of Plenipotentiaries was considering the [UN Convention relating to the Status of Refugees] in 1951, the phrase "membership of a particular social group" was added to this definition as an "afterthought." The Swedish representative proposed this language, explaining only that it was needed because "experience had shown that certain refugees had been persecuted because they belonged to particular social groups," and the proposal was adopted. Conference of Plenipotentiaries on the Status of Refugees and Stateless Persons, Summary Rec. of the 3d Mtg., U.N. Doc. A/CONF.2/SR.3 at 14 (Nov. 19, 1951). Thus, neither the legislative history of the relevant United States statutes nor the negotiating history of the pertinent international agreements sheds much light on the meaning of the phrase "particular social group."

Our role in the process of interpreting this phrase, however, is quite limited. As the Supreme Court has explained, the Board of Immigration Appeals' interpretation of a provision of the Refugee Act is entitled to deference pursuant to the standards set out in *Chevron U.S.A., Inc. v. Natural Resources Defense Council, Inc.*, 467 U.S. 837, 104 S.Ct. 2778, 81 L.Ed.2d 694 (1984). Thus, in considering an interpretation adopted by the Board, we must ask "whether Congress has directly spoken to the precise question at issue." *Chevron*, 467 U.S. at 842, 104 S.Ct. at 2781. If it has not, we may not "simply impose [our] own construction on the statute." *Id.* at 843, 104 S.Ct. 2782. "Rather, if the statute is silent or ambiguous with respect to the specific issue, the question for the court is whether the agency's answer is based on a permissible construction of the statute." *Id.*

Here, the Board has interpreted the phrase "particular social group." In *Matter of Acosta*, 19 I. & N. Dec. 211, 233 (BIA 1985), the Board noted that the United Nations Protocol refers to race, religion, nationality, and political opinion, as well as membership in a particular social group. Employing the doctrine of *ejusdem generis*, the Board then reasoned that a particular social group refers to "a group of persons all of whom share a common, immutable characteristic." [Here the court quotes the key passage defining "particular social group" from *Matter of Acosta*, quoted in *Matter of H–*, in Chapter Four, p. 269]. We have no doubt that this is a permissible construction of the relevant statutes, and we are consequently bound to accept it.

With this understanding of the phrase "particular social group" in mind, we turn to the elements that an alien must establish in order to qualify for withholding of deportation or asylum based on membership in such a group. We believe that there are three such elements. The alien must (1) identify a group that constitutes a "particular social group" within the interpretation just discussed, (2) establish that he or she is a member of that group, and (3) show that he or she would be persecuted or has a well-founded fear of persecution based on that membership.

In the excerpt from *Acosta* quoted above, the Board specifically mentioned "sex" as an innate characteristic that could link the members of a "particular social group." Thus, to the extent that the petitioner in this case suggests that she would be persecuted or has a well-founded fear that she would be persecuted in Iran simply because she is a woman, she has satisfied the first of the three elements that we have noted. She has not, however, satisfied the third element; that is, she has not shown that she would suffer or that she has a well-founded fear of suffering "persecution" based solely on her gender.

In *Acosta*, the BIA discussed the meaning of the term "persecution," concluding that "the pre-Refugee Act construction" of that term should still be followed. Heeding this construction, the BIA interpreted "persecution" to include threats to life, confinement, torture, and economic restrictions so severe that they constitute a threat to life or freedom. By contrast, the BIA suggested that "[g]enerally harsh conditions shared by many other persons" do not amount to persecution. Among the pre-Refugee Act cases on which the BIA relied was *Blazina v. Bouchard*, 286 F.2d 507, 511 (3d Cir.), *cert. denied*, 366 U.S. 950, 81 S.Ct. 1904, 6 L.Ed.2d 1242 (1961), where our court noted that the mere "repugnance of ... a governmental policy to our own concepts of ... freedom" was not sufficient to justify labelling that policy as persecution. Thus, we interpret *Acosta* as recognizing that the concept of persecution does not encompass all treatment that our society regards as unfair, unjust, or even unlawful or unconstitutional. If persecution were defined that expansively, a significant percentage of the world's population would qualify for asylum in this country—and it seems most unlikely that Congress intended such a result.[10]

---

**10.** We are convinced that the BIA's interpretation of "persecution," like its interpretation of "particular social group," is permissible and thus must be followed. In ordinary usage, the term "persecution" denotes extreme conduct. For example, *The Random House Dictionary of the English Language* 1444 (2d ed. 1987) defines the term to mean "a program or campaign to exterminate, drive away, or subjugate a people because of their religion, race, or beliefs." We are aware of nothing indicating that Congress intended to depart from the ordinary meaning of the term "persecution." Moreover, authoritative interpretations of the United Nations Convention and Protocol also recognize that the concept of persecution refers to extreme conduct. *See, e.g.,* United Nations High Commissioner for

In this case, the evidence in the administrative record regarding the way in which women in Iran are generally treated is quite sparse. We certainly cannot say that "a reasonable factfinder would have to conclude," based on that record, that the petitioner, if returned to Iran, would face treatment amounting to "persecution" simply because she is a woman. *See INS v. Elias–Zacarias*, 502 U.S. 478, 481, 112 S.Ct. 812, 815, 117 L.Ed.2d 38 (1992). While the amici supporting the petitioner have called to our attention articles describing the harsh restrictions placed on all women in Iran, the facts asserted in these articles are not part of the administrative record. * * *

The petitioner's primary argument, in any event, is not that she faces persecution simply because she is a woman. Rather, she maintains that she faces persecution because she is a member of "a very visible and specific subgroup: Iranian women who *refuse to conform* to the government's gender-specific laws and social norms." This definition merits close consideration. It does not include all Iranian women who hold feminist views. Nor does it include all Iranian women who find the Iranian government's "gender-specific laws and repressive social norms" objectionable or offensive. Instead, it is limited to those Iranian women who find those laws so abhorrent that they "refuse to conform"—even though, according to the petitioner's brief, "the routine penalty" for noncompliance is "74 lashes, a year's imprisonment, and in many cases brutal rapes and death."

Limited in this way, the "particular social group" identified by the petitioner may well satisfy the BIA's definition of that concept, for if a woman's opposition to the Iranian laws in question is so profound that she would choose to suffer the severe consequences of noncompliance, her beliefs may well be characterized as "so fundamental to [her] identity or conscience that [they] ought not be required to be changed." *Acosta*. The petitioner's difficulty, however, is that the administrative record does not establish that she is a member of this tightly defined group, for there is no evidence in that record showing that her opposition to the Iranian laws at issue is of the depth and importance required.

The Iranian restriction discussed most prominently in the petitioner's testimony was the requirement that women wear the chador or traditional veil, but the most that the petitioner's testimony showed was that she would find that requirement objectionable and would seek to avoid compliance if possible. When asked whether she would prefer to comply with that law or suffer the consequences of noncompliance, she stated only that she "would try to avoid" wearing a chador as much as she could. Similarly, her brief to the BIA stated only that she would seek to avoid Islamic practices "as much as she could." She never testified that she would refuse to comply with the law regarding the chador or any of the other gender-specific laws or social norms. Nor did she testify that wearing the chador or complying with any of the other restrictions was so deeply abhorrent to her that it would be tantamount to persecu-

Refugees, *Handbook of Procedures*, §§ 51, 54, 55.

tion. Instead, the most that emerges from her testimony is that she would find these requirements objectionable and would not observe them if she could avoid doing so. This testimony does not bring her within the particular social group that she has defined—Iranian women who refuse to conform with those requirements even if the consequences may be severe.

The "particular social group" that her testimony places her within is, instead, the presumably larger group consisting of Iranian women who find their country's gender-specific laws offensive and do not wish to comply with them. But if the petitioner's "particular social group" is defined in this way, she cannot prevail because the administrative record does not satisfy the third element described above, i.e., it does not show that the consequences that would befall her as a member of that group would constitute "persecution." According to the petitioner, she would have two options if she returned to Iran: comply with the Iranian laws or suffer severe consequences. Thus, while we agree with the petitioner that the indicated consequences of noncompliance would constitute persecution, we must still inquire whether her other option—compliance— would also constitute persecution.

In considering whether the petitioner established that this option would constitute persecution, we will assume for the sake of argument that the concept of persecution is broad enough to include governmental measures that compel an individual to engage in conduct that is not physically painful or harmful but is abhorrent to that individual's deepest beliefs. An example of such conduct might be requiring a person to renounce his or her religious beliefs or to desecrate an object of religious importance. Such conduct might be regarded as a form of "torture" and thus as falling within the Board's description of persecution in *Acosta*. Such a requirement could constitute "torture" or persecution, however, only if directed against a person who actually possessed the religious beliefs or attached religious importance to the object in question. Requiring an adherent of an entirely different religion or a non-believer to engage in the same conduct would not constitute persecution.[11]

Here, while we assume for the sake of argument that requiring some women to wear chadors may be so abhorrent to them that it would be tantamount to persecution, this requirement clearly does not constitute persecution for all women. Presumably, there are devout Shi'ite women in Iran who find this requirement entirely appropriate. Presumably, there are other women in Iran who find it either inconvenient, irritating, mildly objectionable, or highly offensive, but for whom it falls short of constituting persecution. As we have previously noted, the petitioner's testimony in this case simply does not show that for her the requirement of wearing the chador or complying with Iran's other gender-specific

---

**11.** We do not suggest that an alien could establish that he or she would be persecuted or has a well-founded fear of persecution based solely on his or her sub- jective reactions. Presumably, conduct could not constitute persecution or "torture" within *Acosta* unless an objective require- ment is also satisfied.

laws would be so profoundly abhorrent that it could aptly be called persecution. Accordingly, we cannot hold that she is entitled to withholding of deportation or asylum based on her membership in a "particular social group."

The petitioner also argues that she is entitled to withholding of deportation or asylum based on her "political opinion," but her brief treats this argument as essentially the same as her argument regarding membership in a particular social group. * * * [W]e hold that the petitioner's argument regarding political opinion fails for reasons similar to those already discussed in relation to her argument based on group membership.

\* \* \*

* * * We therefore deny the petition for review.

### Notes and Questions

1. Writing for the court, Judge Alito rejected the asylum claim, largely because of the state of the record and the way in which petitioner chose to frame the "particular social group." The court examined various formulations that might describe the particular social group relevant to Fatin's asylum claim. Can you describe the different groups and identify the weaknesses the court ascribes to each? In light of this opinion, how should counsel in a similar case now define the particular social group?

2. Although much of the opinion focused on the particular social group issue, the court essentially concluded that wearing a chador did not rise to the level of persecution, at least not for Fatin. What proof could Fatin present to demonstrate that being forced, on pain of whipping and prison, to wear traditional clothes with religious and political symbolism constituted persecution for her? Under the court's reasoning, would Jews in Nazi Germany face persecution if they said they refused to wear yellow stars when they went out in public? Do the materials on internal flight in Chapter Three, pp. 119–31, provide any useful guidance on the question of what can be expected by way of mitigation by an individual who faces harm?

3. The *Fatin* court betrays concern about the numerical consequences of expansive doctrine governing claims like this one: "If persecution were defined that expansively, a significant percentage of the world's population would qualify for asylum in this country—and it seems most unlikely that Congress intended such a result." Are such consequentialist concerns a valid basis for interpretation? In any event, does the court's doctrine effectively guard against such an outcome? How difficult would it be for future applicants to allege more carefully that certain traditional practices are "abhorrent" or that their objections are "profound"? How should an asylum officer or immigration judge test such a claim?

4. A Ninth Circuit decision, *Fisher v. INS*, raised issues quite similar to those in *Fatin*. The applicant, Saideh Hasib–Tehrani, feared being subjected to Iran's "moral codes" governing attire and other behavior for women, and in fact had been punished in the past for violations. A panel of the Ninth Circuit originally reversed the BIA, finding that the enforcement of the codes

was an attempt to suppress her beliefs. 61 F.3d 1366 (9th Cir. 1994) (amended opinion). But the full court, sua sponte, took the case for en banc reconsideration and eventually reached the opposite result, finding that Fisher "received routine punishment for violating generally applicable laws." 79 F.3d 955, 964 (9th Cir. 1996) (en banc). She failed to show selective enforcement or that the laws were a pretext enabling the government of Iran to persecute her for her beliefs. Persecution "does not include mere discrimination, as offensive as it may be." *Id.* at 962. Nor was there evidence that if she returned to Iran, she would not conform with the codes. The court went on to say: "Persecution on account of sex is not included as a category allowing relief under section 101(a)(42)(A) of the Act." *Id.* at 963. Two concurring judges stated emphatically that the last statement quoted was dictum, because Fisher's attorney disavowed reliance on persecution based on gender. *Id.* at 965.

In dissent, Judge Noonan echoed concerns similar to those raised in *Kasinga* by Board Member Rosenberg. Noonan argued that the focus in the case should not be on the applicant's personal beliefs. Instead he emphasized imputed religious and political grounds:

> [W]hat befell Saidel Hassib–Tehrani was not because she had demonstrated a sympathy for feminism or voiced a more tolerant interpretation of Islam than the Ayatollah's or expressed in Iran any dissent from the rigorist regime. The arrests and search occurred because the regime perceived her as a religious nonconformist. The way in which she led her daily life was enough to invite repression. It was on account of her religious opinion, as perceived by the regime viewing her unconventional routine behaviors, that she was arrested * * *. As Iran is a theocracy, the religious beliefs imputed to her by the regime were also political opinions, and the persecution she fears from the regime would also be "on account of" those imputed political opinions.

*Id.* at 970. Is Judge Noonan's reliance on "persecution on account of religion" consistent with the cases on religious beliefs and practices—*Chen* and *Li*—in Chapter Four, pp. 244, 240? *See also Safaie v. INS*, 25 F.3d 636 (8th Cir. 1994) (ruling against applicant on similar facts); *Sharif v. INS*, 87 F.3d 932, 936 (7th Cir. 1996) (rejecting Iranian woman's asylum application based on claim that she will be persecuted because of her family and her status as a "westernized woman"); *Yadegar–Sargis v. INS*, 297 F.3d 596 (7th Cir. 2002) (opposition of an Iranian Christian woman to the wearing of Islamic garb was not sufficiently fundamental to her identity or conscience to make out a claim based on membership in a particular social group).

5.  The *Fisher* majority's reference to "generally applicable laws" prompts a comparison of the *Fisher* and *Fatin* decisions with the population control policy in *Matter of Chang*, in Chapter Three, p. 99. Is *Fatin* consistent with *Chang*? Put differently, should prevailing social norms in a given country be viewed, for asylum and *nonrefoulement* purposes, as a "uniform national policy"? Why or why not?

6.  Recall *Matter of S–A–*, 22 I & N Dec. 1328 (BIA 2000), discussed in the materials on religious beliefs and practices in Chapter Four, pp. 251. If *Matter of S–A–* is viewed as a case involving religious persecution of a

woman who did not subscribe to a strict interpretation of Islam, wouldn't that perspective also apply to Parastoo Fatin? On the other hand, what factors might differentiate that case from this one?

## 2. FORCED MARRIAGE

In a recent case the Second Circuit faced an asylum claim based on another social custom that falls heavily on women in many societies. The court analyzed whether forced marriages constitute persecution based on membership in a particular social group.

### GAO v. GONZALES

United States Court of Appeals, Second Circuit, 2006.
440 F.3d 62.

STRAUB, CIRCUIT JUDGE.

* * * Gao, who was twenty years old when she left China, grew up in a rural village in the Fujian Province. In this region of China, parents routinely sell their daughters into marriage, and this practice is sanctioned by society and by the local authorities.

When Gao was nineteen years old, her parents, through a broker, sold Gao to a man named Chen Zhi; in return for an up-front payment of 18,800 RBM, Gao's parents promised that Gao would marry Zhi when she turned twenty-one. Gao's parents used this money to pay off previous debts. At first, Gao acquiesced in the arrangement under pressure from her parents. However, because Zhi soon proved to be bad-tempered, and gambled, and beat her when she refused to give him money, Gao decided that she did not want to marry Zhi. When Gao tried to break their engagement, Zhi threatened her. He also threatened that, if she refused to marry him, his uncle, a powerful local official, would arrest her. Gao had heard that Zhi's uncle had arrested other individuals for personal reasons, and so she was afraid the same would happen to her.

To escape Zhi, Gao moved an hour away by boat and took a job in the Mawei district of Fuchou. Zhi continued to visit Gao's family and demand that she marry him, and when her parents refused to tell him where she had moved, he vandalized their home. Zhi also figured out that Gao was living in Mawei by following her to her boat one night when she was returning from a visit with her family. About half a year later, Gao fled to the United States out of fear that, if she remained in China, she would be forced to marry Zhi. Since Gao left, Zhi and his cohorts have continued to harass her family, to the point where the family has had to move repeatedly.

* * *

* * * The IJ found Gao credible, but concluded that Gao had not made out a claim for asylum or withholding of removal. Specifically, the IJ found that Gao's predicament did not arise from a protected ground such as membership in a particular social group, but was simply "a dispute between two families." * * * The BIA summarily affirmed.

A.  PARTICULAR SOCIAL GROUP

* * * Of the various categories, "particular social group" is the least well-defined on its face, and the diplomatic and legislative histories shed no light on how it was understood by the parties to the Protocol or by Congress. There is, fortunately, a substantial body of case law, although its value as precedent is somewhat limited by the fact-specific nature of asylum cases.

* * *

[The]   Courts of Appeals have deferred to *Matter of Acosta*'s broad interpretation of "particular social group" as encompassing any group, however populous, persecuted because of shared characteristics that are either immutable or fundamental. * * *

* * *

* * * [T]he proper balance to strike is to interpret "particular social group" broadly (requiring only one or more shared characteristics that are either immutable or fundamental) while interpreting "on account of" strictly (such that an applicant must prove that these characteristics are a central reason why she has been, or may be, targeted for persecution). As the Tenth Circuit explained in *Niang v. Gonzales*, "the focus with respect to [gender-related] claims should be not on whether either gender constitutes a social group (which both certainly do) but on whether the members of that group are sufficiently likely to be persecuted that one could say that they are persecuted 'on account of' their membership." 422 F.3d 1187, 1199–1200 (10th Cir. 2005) (quoting INA § 101(a) 42(A)).

* * *

The general law in our own Circuit on particular social groups is less clear. In *Gomez v. INS*, we denied the petition of a woman whose asylum claim was based on the fact that she had been raped and beaten by guerilla forces on five different occasions between the ages of twelve and fourteen. * * * [W]e wrote that "[p]ossession of broadly-based characteristics such as youth and gender will not by itself endow individuals with membership in a particular group."

* * *

We need not decide the exact scope of *Gomez* here because Gao belongs to a particular social group that shares more than a common gender. Gao's social group consists of women who have been sold into marriage (whether or not that marriage has yet taken place) and who live in a part of China where forced marriages are considered valid and enforceable. Clearly, these common characteristics satisfy the *Matter of Acosta* test. Moreover, Gao's testimony, which the IJ credited, also establishes that she might well be persecuted in China—in the form of lifelong, involuntary marriage—"on account of" her membership in this group.

The IJ's reasons for reaching the opposite conclusion are unclear. * * * The IJ appears to have concluded that Gao did not face persecution on account of an immutable characteristic because her situation arose from "a dispute between two families," but the logical connection between the IJ's premise and conclusion is not evident, nor is it explained in the IJ's opinion. The IJ also wrote that "[t]he other reason that [Gao] does not establish that she is a member of a particularly persecuted social group of female [sic] is because her mother violated the oral [marriage] contract that she had with this go-between, and that is what caused the anger by the boyfriend in this situation. . . ." To the extent the IJ might have reasoned that the financial arrangement between the families somehow precluded a finding that Zhi's motive in targeting Gao was discriminatory, we reject this logic as antithetical to the very notion of individual rights on which asylum law is based. While Zhi may have a legitimate financial claim against Gao's parents, the possibility remains that if they continue to be unable to repay his money, Zhi will force Gao to marry him.

* * *

For the reasons stated above, we hold that Gao has established a nexus between the persecution she fears and the "particular social group" to which she belongs. * * *

[The court also vacated the immigration judge's findings that Gao had not met her burden of establishing that the Chinese government would not protect her, and that Gao could have relocated within China.]

For the foregoing reasons the petition for review is granted, the decision of the BIA is vacated, and the case is remanded to the BIA for further proceedings consistent with this opinion.

### Notes and Questions

1.   The court found that the particular social group was defined by two factors: having been sold into marriage and living in a part of China where forced marriages are considered valid and enforceable. But the court also subscribes to *Acosta's* requirement that PSGs be based on immutable characteristics. How can the second factor be considered immutable?

2.   One of the notes following *Fatin*, earlier in this section of this chapter, asked whether *Fatin* is consistent with *Chang*. The premise of the question was that prevailing social norms in a given country might be viewed, for asylum and *nonrefoulement* purposes, as a "uniform national policy," enforcement of which would not count as persecution. In this respect, is the practice involved in *Gao* different from the social norms involved in *Fatin*?

3.   Is the Second Circuit's analysis in *Gao* consistent with the BIA's analysis of female genital mutilation in *Kasinga*?

## 3.   DOMESTIC ABUSE

A study conducted by the World Health Organization (WHO) and published in the medical journal *The Lancet* in October 2006 estimated the extent of physical and sexual intimate partner violence against women in 15 sites in ten countries: Bangladesh, Brazil, Ethiopia, Japan, Namibia, Peru, Samoa, Serbia and Montenegro, Thailand, and the United Republic of Tanzania. Based on interviews with nearly 25,000 women, the study found that the reported lifetime prevalence of physical or sexual partner violence, or both, varied from a low of 15 percent in Yokohama, Japan, to a high of 71 percent in rural Ethiopia. Violence against women by their live-in spouses or partners, according to the study, is a widespread phenomenon, both in the developed and developing world, as well as in rural and urban areas. *See* Garcia–Moreno *et al.*, *Prevalence of Intimate Partner Violence: Findings From the WHO Multicountry Study on Women's Health and Domestic Violence*, 368 The Lancet 1260 (2006); Rosenthal, *Women Face Greatest Threat of Violence at Home, Study Finds*, New York Times, Oct. 6, 2006, at A7.

Over the past decade a growing number of women have filed asylum claims based on domestic violence. Typically, they fear persecution at the hands of their male partner, who may not articulate a reason for his actions and may not act in this manner toward anyone else. These cases raise multiple legal questions, many of which we examined in Chapters Three and Four. Does violence by individuals, as opposed to organized groups, constitute persecution? To what extent does the government acquiesce in the nongovernmental actor's conduct? What alternatives within her home country are available to the claimant? Is the violence "on account of" one of the specified Refugee Convention grounds? Are victims of domestic abuse a particular social group? Although these issues are not unique to gender-related asylum cases, they pose particularly difficult conceptual puzzles in this developing area of the law.

Many cases outside the gender context have cast a skeptical eye on asylum claims founded on a risk of violence growing out of a private dispute, even when there was some political or governmental involvement. The decisions form part of the body of law on mixed motives that we examined in Chapter Four, pp. 221–30. For example, in *Kozulin v. INS*, 218 F.3d 1112 (9th Cir. 2000), the court denied asylum to a sailor in Russia's merchant marine who was beaten by unidentified men after sending a letter to authorities complaining of his captain's stealing of supplies; he believed the men had been sent by the captain. To satisfy the nexus requirement, the court held, a claimant "must prove something more than violence plus disparity of views" (quoting *Sangha v. INS*, 103 F.3d 1482, 1487 (9th Cir. 1997), which is included in Chapter Four, p. 217). For similar results, see *Zayas–Marini v. INS*, 785 F.2d 801 (9th Cir. 1986) (asylum denied because threats deriving from charges and countercharges of corruption among prominent families and officials in Paraguay under the Stroessner dictatorship arose from a private dispute), and *Molina–Morales v. INS*, 237 F.3d 1048 (9th Cir. 2001) (asylum denied despite past beatings of applicant when he tried to report the rape of his aunt by a prominent Salvadoran businessman and politician).

*Lazo–Majano v. INS*, 813 F.2d 1432 (9th Cir. 1987), appeared as an early exception to this pattern, in the specific setting of severe domestic abuse. Olimpia Lazo–Majano was a domestic servant who had been raped and battered by her employer, a sergeant in the Salvadoran army who coerced her into remaining with him. Focusing largely on the sergeant's threatening accusations that Lazo–Majano was a "subversive," the court held that Lazo–Majano had established persecution on account of political opinion. But at about the same time, another court gave short shrift to an asylum claim filed by a Salvadoran woman who had been raped and threatened by masked gunmen during that country's civil war. *See Campos–Guardado v. INS*, 809 F.2d 285, 290 (5th Cir. 1987) ("we can infer that Congress did not intend to confer eligibility for asylum on all persons who suffer harm from civil disturbances—conditions that necessarily have political implications"). Other cases were similarly unreceptive to claims of this general type. *See, e.g., Gomez v. INS*, 947 F.2d 660 (2d Cir. 1991) (rejecting "social group" claim characterized as "women who have been previously battered and raped by Salvadoran guerrillas").

Nonetheless, similar claims began to appear more often, and some decisionmakers showed greater acceptance. For example, in *Matter of D–V–*, 21 I & N Dec. 77 (BIA 1993), which appears in Section A of this chapter, p. 299, the BIA granted asylum to a Haitian woman who had been gang-raped and beaten by members of the Haitian military. *See also Angoucheva v. INS,* 106 F.3d 781 (7th Cir. 1997) (reversing and remanding to the BIA for more complete consideration of the claim that an interrupted sexual assault committed by a Bulgarian security officer during interrogation amounted to persecution on account of a protected ground).

Against this background, the BIA considered the next case in 1999.

## MATTER OF R–A–

Board of Immigration Appeals, 1999.
22 I & N Dec. 906.
Vacated by the Attorney General pending further action, 2001.

FILPPU, BOARD MEMBER:

\* \* \*

The question before us is whether the respondent qualifies as a "refugee" as a result of the heinous abuse she suffered and still fears from her husband in Guatemala. Specifically, we address whether the repeated spouse abuse inflicted on the respondent makes her eligible for asylum as an alien who has been persecuted on account of her membership in a particular social group or her political opinion. We find that the group identified by the Immigration Judge has not adequately been shown to be a "particular social group" for asylum purposes. We further find that the respondent has failed to show that her husband was motivated to harm her, even in part, because of her membership in a particular social group or because of an actual or imputed political opinion. * * *

* * *

The respondent is a native and citizen of Guatemala. She married at age 16. Her husband was then 21 years old. He currently resides in Guatemala, as do their two children. Immediately after their marriage, the respondent and her husband moved to Guatemala City. From the beginning of the marriage, her husband engaged in acts of physical and sexual abuse against the respondent. He was domineering and violent. The respondent testified that her husband "always mistreated me from the moment we were married, he was always . . . aggressive."

* * * As their marriage proceeded, the level and frequency of his rage increased concomitantly with the seeming senselessness and irrationality of his motives. He dislocated the respondent's jaw bone when her menstrual period was 15 days late. When she refused to abort her 3- to 4-month-old fetus, he kicked her violently in her spine. He would hit or kick the respondent "whenever he felt like it, wherever he happened to be: in the house, on the street, on the bus." The respondent stated that "(a)s time went on, he hit me for no reason at all."

The respondent's husband raped her repeatedly. He would beat her before and during the unwanted sex. When the respondent resisted, he would accuse her of seeing other men and threaten her with death. The rapes occurred "almost daily," and they caused her severe pain. He passed on a sexually transmitted disease to the respondent from his sexual relations outside their marriage. Once, he kicked the respondent in her genitalia, apparently for no reason, causing the respondent to bleed severely for 8 days. The respondent suffered the most severe pain when he forcefully sodomized her. When she protested, he responded, as he often did, "You're my woman, you do what I say."

* * *

When asked on cross-examination, the respondent at first indicated that she had no opinion of why her husband acted the way he did. She supposed, however, that it was because he had been mistreated when he was in the army and, as he had told her, he treated her the way he had been treated. The respondent believed he would abuse any woman who was his wife. She testified that he "was a repugnant man without any education," and that he saw her "as something that belonged to him and he could do anything he wanted" with her.

The respondent's pleas to Guatemalan police did not gain her protection. On three occasions, the police issued summons for her husband to appear, but he ignored them, and the police did not take further action. Twice, the respondent called the police, but they never responded. When the respondent appeared before a judge, he told her that he would not interfere in domestic disputes. Her husband told the respondent that, because of his former military service, calling the police would be futile as he was familiar with law enforcement officials. The respondent knew of no shelters or other organizations in Guatemala that could protect her. The abuse began "from the moment (they) were married," and continued until the respondent fled Guatemala in May 1995. One morning in May 1995, the respondent decided to leave permanently. With help, the respondent was able to flee Guatemala, and she arrived in Brownsville, Texas, 2 days later.

A witness, testifying for the respondent, stated that she learned through the respondent's sister that the respondent's husband was "going to hunt her down and kill her if she comes back to Guatemala."

We struggle to describe how deplorable we find the husband's conduct to have been.

\* \* \*

Dr. Doris Bersing testified that spouse abuse is common in Latin American countries and that she was not aware of social or legal resources for battered women in Guatemala. Women in Guatemala, according to Dr. Bersing, have other problems related to general conditions in that country, and she suggested that such women could leave abusive partners but that they would face other problems such as poverty. Dr. Bersing further testified that the respondent was different from other battered women she had seen in that the respondent possessed an extraordinary fear of her husband and her abuse had been extremely severe.

Dr. Bersing noted that spouse abuse was a problem in many countries throughout the world, but she said it was a particular problem in Latin America, especially in Guatemala and Nicaragua. As we understand her testimony, its roots lie in such things as the Latin American patriarchal culture, the militaristic and violent nature of societies undergoing civil war, alcoholism, and sexual abuse in general. Nevertheless, she testified that husbands are supposed to honor, respect, and take care of their wives, and that spouse abuse is something that is present "underground" or "underneath in the culture." But if a woman chooses the wrong husband her options are few in countries such as Guatemala, which lack effective methods for dealing with the problem.

The Department of State issued an advisory opinion as to the respondent's asylum request. The opinion states that the respondent's alleged mistreatment could have occurred given its understanding of country conditions in Guatemala. The opinion further indicates:

> [S]pousal abuse complaints by husbands have increased from 30 to 120 a month due to increased nationwide educational programs, which have encouraged women to seek assistance. Family court judges may issue injunctions against abusive spouses, which police are charged with enforcing. The (Human Rights Ombudsman) women's rights department and various non-governmental organizations provide medical and legal assistance.

The respondent has submitted numerous articles and reports regarding violence against women in Guatemala and other Latin American countries. * * *

[The immigration judge found the applicant credible and granted asylum. The Guatemalan government was either unable or unwilling to control the husband's violence, and the respondent's harm was on account of a protected ground. She was persecuted because of membership in the particular social group made up of "Guatemalan women who have been involved intimately with Guatemalan male companions, who believe that women are to live under male domination." Further, she was persecuted because her husband imputed to her a political opinion, based on her resistance to his violence, that women should not be dominated by men.]

### VI.  ANALYSIS

* * * [W]e agree with the Immigration Judge that the severe injuries sustained by the respondent rise to the level of harm sufficient (and more than sufficient) to constitute "persecution." We also credit the respondent's testimony in general and specifically her account of being unsuccessful in obtaining meaningful assistance from the authorities in Guatemala. Accordingly, we find that she has adequately established on this record that she was unable to avail herself of the protection of the Government of Guatemala in connection with the abuse inflicted by her husband. The determinative issue, as correctly identified by the Immigration Judge, is whether the harm experienced by the respondent was, or in the future may be, inflicted "on account of" a statutorily protected ground.

It is not possible to review this record without having great sympathy for the respondent and extreme contempt for the actions of her husband. The questions before us, however, are not whether some equitable or prosecutorial authority ought to be invoked to prevent the respondent's deportation to Guatemala. Indeed, the Service has adequate authority in the form of "deferred action" to accomplish that result if it deems it appropriate. Rather, the questions before us concern the respondent's eligibility for relief under our refugee and asylum laws. And, as explained below, we do not agree with the Immigration Judge that the respondent was harmed on account of either actual or imputed political opinion or membership in a particular social group.

### A.  *Imputed Political Opinion*

The record indicates that the respondent's husband harmed the respondent regardless of what she actually believed or what he thought she believed. * * *

* * *

[U]nder *Elias–Zacarias*, [502 U.S. 478, 112 S.Ct. 812, 117 L.Ed.2d 38, reprinted in Chapter Four, p. 201] the victim also must offer some evidence, direct or circumstantial, that it was the victim's political opinion that motivated the persecutor. The respondent's husband, it seems, must have had some reason or reasons for treating the respondent as he did. And it is possible that his own view of men and women played a role in his brutality, as may have been the case with the brutality that he himself experienced and witnessed. What we find lacking in this respondent's showing, however, is any meaningful evidence that her husband's behavior was influenced at all by his perception of the respondent's opinion.

The respondent argues that, given the nature of domestic violence and sexual assaults, her husband necessarily imputed to her the view that she believed women should not be controlled and dominated by men. Even accepting the premise that he might have believed that the respondent disagreed with his views of women, it does not necessarily follow that he harmed the respondent because of those beliefs, rather than because of his own personal or psychological makeup coupled with his troubled perception of her actions at times. *See id.* at 482; *Sangha v. INS*, 103 F.3d 1482, 1487 (9th Cir. 1997) ("(T)he petitioner must prove something more than violence plus disparity of views.").

The Immigration Judge found, and the respondent argues, that her husband imputed a hostile opinion to her from her acts of resistance to his violence, and that he then punished her for that hostile opinion. The Court's ruling in *Elias–Zacarias,* however, establishes that the existence of a political opinion held by a persecutor, and actions by a victim that conflict with the demands of the persecutor, are not sufficient to require a conclusion that the persecutor seeks to harm the victim because of a contrary political opinion attributed to the victim. Both the respondent's argument and the "male domination" reasoning of *Lazo–Majano [v. INS*, 813 F.2d 1432 (9th Cir. 1987)] seem to us to be akin to the analysis which the Supreme Court later did not accept as conclusive of political opinion persecution.

As we understand the respondent's rationale, it would seem that virtually any victim of repeated violence who offers some resistance could qualify for asylum, particularly where the government did not control the assailant. Under this approach, the perpetrator is presumed to impute to the victim a political opinion, in opposition to the perpetrator's authority, stemming simply from an act of resistance. Then, notwithstanding any other motivation for the original violence, the imputed political opinion becomes the assumed basis for the infliction of more harm.

It is certainly logical and only human to presume that no victim of violence desires to be such a victim and will resist in some manner. But it is another matter to presume that the perpetrator of the violence inflicts it because the perpetrator believes the victim opposes either the abuse or the authority of the abuser. We do not find that the second proposition necessarily follows from the first. Moreover, it seems to us that this approach ignores the question of what motivated the abuse at the outset, and it necessarily assumes that the original motivation is no longer the basis, at least not by itself, for the subsequent harm. We are unwilling to accept a string of presumptions or assumptions as a substitute for our own assessment of the evidence in this record, particularly when the reliability of these presumptions as genuine reflections of human behavior has not been established.

As for the record here, there has been no showing that the respondent's husband targeted any other women in Guatemala, even though we may reasonably presume that they, too, did not all share his view of male domination. * * *

### B. *Particular Social Group*

#### 1. *Cognizableness*

Initially, we find that "Guatemalan women who have been involved intimately with Guatemalan male companions, who believe that women are to live under male domination" is not a particular social group. Absent from this group's makeup is "a voluntary associational relationship" that is of "central concern" in the Ninth Circuit [citing *Sanchez–Trujillo v. INS* [801 F.2d 1571 (9th Cir. 1986), excerpted in Chapter Four, p. 258] and related cases].

Moreover, regardless of Ninth Circuit law, we find that the respondent's claimed social group fails under our own independent assessment of what constitutes a qualifying social group. We find it questionable that the social group adopted by the Immigration Judge appears to have been defined principally, if not exclusively, for purposes of this asylum case, and without regard to the question of whether anyone in Guatemala perceives this group to exist in any form whatsoever. The respondent fits within the proposed group. But the group is defined largely in the abstract. It seems to bear little or no relation to the way in which Guatemalans might identify subdivisions within their own society or otherwise might perceive individuals either to possess or to lack an important characteristic or trait. The proposed group may satisfy the basic requirement of containing an immutable or fundamental individual characteristic. But, for the group to be viable for asylum purposes, we believe there must also be some showing of how the characteristic is understood in the alien's society, such that we in turn may understand that the potential persecutors in fact see persons sharing the characteristic as warranting suppression or the infliction of harm.

Our administrative precedents do not require a voluntary associational relationship as a social group attribute. But we have ruled that the term "particular social group" is to be construed in keeping with the other four statutory characteristics that are the focus of persecution: race, religion, nationality, and political opinion. *Matter of Acosta* [19 I & N Dec. 211 (BIA 1985), reprinted pp. 192, 255]. These other four characteristics are ones that typically separate various factions within countries. They frequently are recognized groupings in a particular society. The members of the group generally understand their own affiliation with the grouping, as do other persons in the particular society.

In the present case, the respondent has shown that women living with abusive partners face a variety of legal and practical problems in obtaining protection or in leaving the abusive relationship. But the respondent has not shown that "Guatemalan women who have been involved intimately with Guatemalan male companions, who believe that women are to live under male domination" is a group that is recognized and understood to be a societal faction, or is otherwise a recognized segment of the population, within Guatemala. The respondent has shown neither that the victims of spouse abuse view themselves as members of this group, nor, most importantly, that their male oppressors see their victimized companions as part of this group.

The lack of a showing in this respect makes it much less likely that we will recognize the alleged group as a particular social group for asylum purposes, or that the respondent will be able to establish that it was her group characteristic which motivated her abuser's actions. Indeed, if the alleged persecutor is not even aware of the group's existence, it becomes harder to understand how the persecutor may have been motivated by the victim's "membership" in the group to inflict the harm on the victim.

The respondent's showing fails in another respect, one that is noteworthy in terms of our ruling in *Matter of Kasinga* [21 I & N Dec. 357 (BIA en banc 1996)]. She has not shown that spouse abuse is itself an important societal attribute, or, in other words, that the characteristic of being abused is one that is important within Guatemalan society. The respondent has shown official tolerance of her husband's cruelty toward her. But, for "social group" purposes, she has not shown that women are expected by society to be abused, or that there are any adverse societal consequences to women or their husbands if the women are not abused. While not determinative, the prominence or importance of a characteristic within a society is another factor bearing on whether we will recognize that factor as part of a "particular social group" under our refugee provisions. If a characteristic is important in a given society, it is more likely that distinctions will be drawn within that society between those who share and those who do not share the characteristic.

Here, the respondent has proposed a social group definition that may amount to a legally crafted description of some attributes of her tragic personal circumstances. It may also be true that this description fits many other victims of spouse abuse.

In our opinion, however, the mere existence of shared descriptive characteristics is insufficient to qualify those possessing the common characteristics as members of a particular social group. The existence of shared attributes is certainly relevant, and indeed important, to a "social group" assessment. Our past case law points out the critical role that is played in "social group" analysis by common characteristics which potential persecutors identify as a basis for the infliction of harm. *Matter of Kasinga, Matter of H–* [21 I & N Dec. 337 (BIA 1996), reprinted in Chapters Three and Four, pp. 171, 268]. But the social group concept would virtually swallow the entire refugee definition if common characteristics, coupled with a meaningful level of harm, were all that need be shown.

The starting point for "social group" analysis remains the existence of an immutable or fundamental individual characteristic in accordance with *Matter of Acosta, supra.* We never declared, however, that the starting point for assessing social group claims articulated in *Acosta* was also the ending point. The factors we look to in this case, beyond *Acosta's* "immutableness" test, are not prerequisites, and we do not rule out the use of additional considerations that may properly bear on whether a social group should be recognized in an individual case. But these factors are consistent with the operation of the other four grounds for asylum and are therefore appropriate, in our judgment, for consideration in the "particular social group" context.

On the record before us, we find that the respondent has not adequately established that we should recognize, under our law, the particular social group identified by the Immigration Judge.

*2. Nexus*

\* \* \*

In this case, even if we were to accept as a particular social group "Guatemalan women who have been involved intimately with Guatemalan male companions, who believe that women are to live under male domination," the respondent has not established that her husband has targeted and harmed the respondent because he perceived her to be a member of this particular social group. The record indicates that he has targeted only the respondent. The respondent's husband has not shown an interest in any member of this group other than the respondent herself. The respondent fails to show how other members of the group may be at risk of harm from him. If group membership were the motivation behind his abuse, one would expect to see some evidence of it manifested in actions toward other members of the same group.

\* \* \*

The Immigration Judge nevertheless found, and the respondent argues on appeal, that her various possible group memberships account for her plight, in large measure because the social climate and the Government of Guatemala afford her no protection from her husband's abuse. Societal attitudes and the concomitant effectiveness (or lack thereof) of governmental intervention very well may have contributed to the ability of the respondent's husband to carry out his abusive actions over a period of many years. But this argument takes us away from looking at the motivation of the husband and focuses instead on the failure of the government to offer protection.

Focusing on societal attitudes and a particular government's response to the infliction of injury is frequently appropriate in the adjudication of asylum cases. It is most warranted when the harm is being inflicted by elements within the government or by private organizations that target minority factions within a society. But governmental inaction is not a reliable indicator of the motivations behind the actions of private parties. And this is not a case in which it has been shown that the Government of Guatemala encourages its male citizens to abuse its female citizens, nor in which the Government has suddenly and unreasonably withdrawn protection from a segment of the population in the expectation that a third party will inflict harm and thereby indirectly achieve a governmental objective.

The record in this case reflects that the views of society and of many governmental institutions in Guatemala can result in the tolerance of spouse abuse at levels we find appalling. But the record also shows that abusive marriages are not viewed as desirable, that spouse abuse is recognized as a problem, and that some measures have been pursued in an attempt to respond to this acknowledged problem. In this context, we are not convinced that the absence of an effective governmental reaction to the respondent's abuse translates into a finding that her husband inflicted the abuse because she was a member of a particular social group. * * *

* * *

The adequacy of state protection is obviously an essential inquiry in asylum cases. But its bearing on the "on account of" test for refugee status depends on the facts of the case and the context in which it arises. In this case, the independent actions of the respondent's husband may have been tolerated. But, as previously explained, this record does not show that his actions represent desired behavior within Guatemala or that the Guatemalan Government encourages domestic abuse.

Importantly, construing private acts of violence to be qualifying governmental persecution, by virtue of the inadequacy of protection, would obviate, perhaps entirely, the "on account of" requirement in the statute. We understand the "on account of" test to direct an inquiry into the motives of the entity actually inflicting the harm. *See INS v. Elias–Zacarias*. Further, the adoption of such an approach would represent a fundamental change in the analysis of refugee claims. We see no principled basis for restricting such an approach to cases involving violence against women. The absence of adequate governmental protection, it would seem, should equally translate into refugee status for other categories of persons unable to protect themselves.

A focus on the adequacy of governmental protection would also shift the analysis in cases of refugee claims arising from civil war, as well as any other circumstance in which a government lacked the ability effectively to police all segments of society. This is not to say that the outcome of such an analysis would necessarily yield different results. The point, however, is that the existing statutory formula for assessing refugee claims would be altered. Instead of assessing the motivation of the actual persecutor, we might, for example, be focusing on the motivation or justification of the government for not intervening and affording real protection.

We reject the approach advocated by the respondent in view of the existing statutory language and the body of case law construing it. Consequently, the respondent must show more than a lack of protection or the existence of societal attitudes favoring male domination. She must make a showing from which it is reasonable to conclude that her husband was motivated to harm her, at least in part, by her asserted group membership.

\* \* \*

### 3. The Kasinga Decision

Our decision in *Matter of Kasinga, supra*, does not prescribe a different result. \* \* \*

In contrast to our ruling in *Matter of Kasinga*, the Immigration Judge in the instant case has not articulated a viable social group. The common characteristic of not having undergone FGM was one that was identified by Kasinga's tribe, and motivated both her family and the tribe to enforce the practice on Kasinga and other young women. Indeed, the tribe expected or required FGM of women prior to marriage, signifying the importance of the practice within that tribal society. The record in Kasinga indicated that African women faced threats or acts of violence or social ostracization for either refusing the practice or attempting to protect female children from FGM. Moreover, although the source of Kasinga's fear of physical harm was limited to her aunt and husband, she established that FGM was so pervasive that her tribal society targeted "young women of the Tchamba–Kunsuntu Tribe who have not had FGM, as practiced by that tribe, and who oppose the practice."

The respondent in this case has not demonstrated that domestic violence is as pervasive in Guatemala as FGM is among the Tchamba–Kunsuntu Tribe, or, more importantly, that domestic violence is a practice encouraged and viewed as societally important in Guatemala. She has not shown that women are expected to undergo abuse from their husbands, or that husbands who do not abuse their wives, or the nonabused wives themselves, face social ostracization or other threats to make them conform to a societal expectation of abuse. While the respondent here found no source of official protection in Guatemala, the young woman in Kasinga testified that the police in Togo were looking for her and would return her to her family to undergo FGM.

We recognize that the respondent's situation is similar to that in *Kasinga*, in part, because the person actually inflicting the harm or feared harm is a family member of the victim. While the cases bear some similarities in this regard, we do not find this to be a factor that *supports* the claim of group recognition. Rather, it is a factor to be overcome if the group is to be accepted. * * *

* * *

*4.   The Dissent*

* * *

[T]he dissent's arguments for a political or social group motivation seem artificial. In our judgment, asylum law is not simply about the construction of various presumptions and inferences for bringing inarguably atrocious human action within one of the five grounds for which relief may be granted, particularly when those presumed or inferred motivations are undetected by both the abuser and the victim. For example, the perpetrators and victims of persecution because of race, religion, and political opinion typically understand and can explain the societal hatreds that lead to the harm or feared harm. We find it very difficult to accept the proposition that a persecutor targets persons who qualify as refugees for reasons that neither the persecutor nor the victims have been shown to understand as playing any role in the persecution.

In *Matter of S–P–* [21 I & N Dec. 486 (BIA 1996), reprinted in Chapter Four, p. 213], for example, we found that it was reasonable to believe that imputed political opinion played a role in the harm suffered by a person captured during a military operation and suspected of being a member of an armed opposition force in a civil war context. The political aspects of the conflict itself were readily apparent, and the participants on both sides well understood the conflict to have a significant political dimension. We were not required to presume the existence of a motivating factor that escaped recognition by any of the parties to the civil war. Our inquiry was simply to determine whether it was reasonable to believe that a known motivating factor in the existing conflict had actually contributed to the particular prisoner's torture.

In the case now before us, it simply has not been shown that political opinion or social group membership can reasonably be understood as the motivation behind the spouse abuse.* * *

The dissent also relies on the impunity with which the respondent's husband acted as support for its "on account of" conclusions. In this regard, it draws on the opinion of Lord Hoffman in *Islam (A.P.) v. Secretary of State for the Home Dep't,* [[1999] 2 A.C. 629 (House of Lords), discussed in the notes following this case], which argues that a Jewish businessman attacked by an Aryan competitor in Nazi Germany would be a victim of persecution on account of race because of the failure of the authorities to provide protection, even though the competitor was personally motivated only by business rivalry. But the very point of this example was to shift the focus away from the motivation of the entity causing the harm and to focus instead on governmental discrimination as satisfying the causation or nexus element for refugee status. Indeed, it does not appear that Lord Hoffman's nexus argument would be any different if the business competitor inflicting the harm had also been Jewish. The dissent's argument, consequently, is a variant of the respondent's claim that she should be accorded refugee status simply because she was not adequately protected by her government. We are not persuaded by this argument in the context of this case for the reasons we set forth earlier in addressing the respondent's contention.

We do agree with the dissent that the reasons set forth by the respondent's husband obviously do not in any way justify the abuse. But we find the lack of legitimate motives, an unconscionable level of harm, the escalation of the harm over time, and even the very incomprehensibleness of the abuse to be an inadequate basis from which to infer a statutorily qualifying motive. It is the respondent who bears the burden of proof. The dissent's approach, however, would seem effectively to shift the burden to the Service, as it would presume the existence of a qualifying case arising from serious harm and the absence of any apparently legitimate motive. * * *

\* \* \*

The respondent in this case has been terribly abused and has a genuine and reasonable fear of returning to Guatemala. Whether the district director may, at his discretion, grant the respondent relief upon humanitarian grounds—relief beyond the jurisdiction of the Immigration Judge and this Board—is a matter the parties can explore outside the present proceedings. We further note that Congress has legislated various forms of relief for abused spouses and children. The issue of whether our asylum laws (or some other legislative provision) should be amended to include additional protection for abused women, such as this respondent, is a matter to be addressed by Congress. In our judgment, however, Congress did not intend the "social group" category to be an all-encompassing residual category for persons facing genuine social ills that governments do not remedy. The solution to the respondent's plight does not lie in our asylum laws as they are currently formulated.

\* \* \*

Accordingly, the appeal will be sustained, and the respondent will be granted voluntary departure.

\* \* \*

GUENDELSBERGER, BOARD MEMBER, dissenting [joined by four other Board Members]:

I respectfully dissent. I agree with the thorough and well-reasoned decision of the Immigration Judge that the respondent has demonstrated past persecution and a well-founded fear of future persecution based on her membership in a particular social group and upon her express and imputed political opinion.

\* \* \*

The harm to the respondent occurred in the context of egregious governmental acquiescence. When the respondent sought the aid and assistance of government officials and institutions, she was told that they could do nothing for her. This is not a case in which the government tried, but failed, to afford protection. Here the government made no effort and showed no interest in protecting the respondent from her abusive spouse. Thus, when the respondent went to the police or to the court to seek relief from threats, physical violence, broken bones, rape, and sodomy inflicted by her husband, Guatemalan police officials and the judge refused to intervene.

The record confirms the Immigration Judge's finding that in Guatemala there are "institutional biases against women that prevent female victims of domestic violence from receiving protection from their male companions or spouses." The Immigration Judge found that these institutional biases "appear to stem from a pervasive belief, common in patriarchal societies, that a man should be able to control a wife or female companion by any means he sees fit: including rape, torture, and beatings." Because of the principle that men should control women with whom they are intimately involved and the belief that domestic abuse is a family matter in which others must not intervene, women are not protected when they complain of domestic violence, and men who inflict such violence are not prosecuted. The respondent's husband told her that because of his connections to the military, the police and courts would not support her against him, and consistent with his threats, when she sought governmental intervention, her pleas fell on deaf ears and she was told she could not divorce him because her husband's consent was needed. No one, neither society nor the government, was able or willing to protect the respondent from her husband.

* * *

### III.   PERSECUTION ON ACCOUNT OF MEMBERSHIP IN A PARTICULAR SOCIAL GROUP

The respondent has been harmed in the past and possesses a well-founded fear of harm in the future "on account of . . . membership in a particular social group." The majority proposes a laundry list of hurdles to be cleared before she may demonstrate membership in a particular social group. This stringent approach to asylum law disregards decisions of tribunals, both domestic and foreign, which extend asylum protection to women who flee human rights abuses within their own homes. * * *

#### A.   The Immigration Judge's Finding of a Particular Social Group is Consistent With Board Precedent

The Immigration Judge found that the respondent was a member of a social group comprised of "Guatemalan women, who have been involved intimately with Guatemalan male companions, who believe that women are to live under male domination." In so finding, she carefully analyzed the facts of the case and correctly applied the law as set forth in *Matter of Acosta*, and, most recently, in *Matter of Kasinga.*

\* \* \*

Under *Acosta,* \* \* \* immutability is of the essence. In a number of decisions, we have applied the *Acosta* immutability standard to recognize particular social groups. In each case, we recognized an immutable trait or past experience shared by the members of the social group. The shared past experience of former members of the national police force in El Salvador, for example, has been recognized as an immutable characteristic which makes such individuals members of a particular social group for asylum purposes. *Matter of Fuentes*, 19 I & N Dec. 658 (BIA 1988). Similarly, gay men and lesbians in Cuba have been found to constitute a particular social group. *Matter of Toboso–Alfonso*, 20 I & N Dec. 819 (BIA 1990). Members of the Darood clan and Marehan subclan in Somalia have been found to share immutable characteristics required for social group recognition, *Matter of H–*, 22 I & N Dec. 337 (BIA 1996) \* \* \*.

\* \* \*

The Immigration Judge decided the case before her consistent with our precedent decision in *Kasinga*. In both cases, the social group was defined by reference to gender in combination with one or more additional factors. In *Kasinga,* the social group was defined by gender, ethnic affiliation, and opposition to female genital mutilation ("FGM"). In the instant case, the social group is based on gender, relationship to an abusive partner, and opposition to domestic violence. As the Immigration Judge below correctly observed, the respondent's relationship to, and association with, her husband is something she cannot change. It is an immutable characteristic under the *Acosta* guidelines, which we affirmed in *Kasinga. Id.* at 366.

\* \* \*

In attempting to distinguish this case from *Kasinga*, the majority contends that domestic violence in Guatemala, unlike FGM in Togo, is not so pervasive or "societally important" that the respondent will face "social ostracization" for refusing to submit to the harm. The majority's distinction is flawed. The facts of *Kasinga* did not suggest that Kasinga would face severe social ostracization for her refusal to submit to FGM; rather, as a member of a social group defined by her unique circumstances, she faced harm only because she lost the protection of her father. In *Kasinga*, a family member, Kasinga's aunt, targeted her after the death of her father who, as the primary authority figure in her family, had previously protected her from FGM. In other words, the practice was not so pervasive in Togo that her father, also a member of the ethnic group which had targeted her, had been unable to identify the practice as harmful. Some persons within Togo viewed FGM as an acceptable practice; other persons, even those within the same ethnic group (such as Kasinga's father, mother, and sister), did not. We extended asylum protection to Kasinga not because she faced societal ostracization, but because she demonstrated a well-founded fear of harm on account of her membership in a group composed of persons sharing her specific circumstances.

In the end, there are no meaningful distinctions that justify recognizing the social group claim in *Kasinga* while refusing to recognize such a social group claim in the instant case. The gender-based characteristics shared by the members of each group are immutable, the form of abuse resisted in both cases was considered culturally normative and was broadly sanctioned by the community, and the persecution imposed occurred without possibility of state protection.

\* \* \*

### C. Gender–Related Social Group Claims, Like Those Involving Race, Religion, Nationality, and Political Opinion, Implicate Fundamental Human Rights

The international community has recognized that gender-based violence, such as domestic violence, is not merely a random crime or a private matter; rather, such violence is a violation of fundamental human rights. In recognition of the special issues confronting female victims of violence, international bodies have responded accordingly.

\* \* \*

More recently, in conjoined appeals involving women seeking asylum protection in the United Kingdom for domestic violence in Pakistan, the House of Lords found "women in Pakistan" to constitute a particular social group under the Convention's refugee definition, *Islam (A.P.) v. Secretary of State for the Home Dep't, supra*. Lord Steyn found "women in Pakistan" to be a "logical application of the seminal reasoning" of *Acosta*. Lord Hoffman recognized the importance of context in deciding whether a social group has been identified: "While persecutory conduct cannot define the social group, the actions of the persecutors may serve to identify or even cause the creation of a particular social group." *Id*. Citing the example of a Jew whose business was destroyed by a competitor in Nazi Germany, Lord Hoffman recognized that a persecutor's knowledge that he could act with impunity "for reasons of" (i.e., "on account of") his victim's religion went to the heart of the analysis of why the harm occurred. *Id*.

### D. The Respondent Was Harmed and Has a Well–Founded Fear of Harm on Account of Membership in a Particular Social Group

Once a particular social group has been recognized, the asylum applicant must present at least "some evidence" of motive on the part of the persecutor, either direct or circumstantial, from which it is reasonable to believe that the harm was motivated, at least in part, by an actual or imputed protected ground. \* \* \*

First, to assess motivation, it is appropriate to consider the factual circumstances surrounding the violence. The factual record reflects quite clearly that the severe beatings were directed at the respondent by her husband to dominate and subdue her, precisely because of her gender, as he inflicted his harm directly on her vagina, sought to abort her pregnancy, and raped her.

Second, the very incomprehensibleness of the husband's motives supports the respondent's claim that the harm is "on account of" a protected ground. This is not a case of simple assault. * * * Under these circumstances, to place undue emphasis on the respondent's explanations for her husband's motives misses the obvious point that no good reason could exist for such behavior.

Illegitimate motives can give rise to an inference that the harm has occurred on account of a statutorily protected characteristic which, in this case, is the respondent's membership in a particular social group and her actual or imputed political opinion. * * *

Third, we should attempt to identify why such horrific violence occurs at all. In *Kasinga*, we determined that FGM exists as a means of controlling women's sexuality. So too does domestic violence exist as a means by which men may systematically destroy the power of women, a form of violence rooted in the economic, social, and cultural subordination of women. * * * Moreover, it is well established in the record before us that Guatemalan society is especially oppressive of women generally. The materials submitted reveal that extreme patriarchal notions are firmly entrenched in Guatemalan society.

Finally, as has been advanced by the House of Lords in *Islam (A.P.) v. Secretary of State for the Home Dep't, supra*, the level of impunity with which a persecutor acts is relevant to an "on account of" determination. Like the persecutor who targets the Jewish shopkeeper because he knows he can act with impunity owing to his victim's religion, the respondent's husband knows he can commit his atrocities with impunity because of the respondent's gender and their relationship. The respondent testified that her husband repeatedly expressed that it would be "useless" for her to contact the authorities, especially given his connections with members of the police. The respondent's husband was not a simple criminal, acting outside societal norms; rather, he knew that, as a woman subject to his subordination, the respondent would receive no protection from the authorities if she resisted his abuse and persecution.

It is reasonable to believe, on the basis of the record before us, that the husband was motivated, at least in part, "on account of" the respondent's membership in a particular social group that is defined by her gender, her relationship to him, and her opposition to domestic violence.

IV.   Persecution on Account of Actual or Imputed Opinion
Opposing Domestic Abuse and Violence Against Women

* * *

The notion that the "heinous abuse" suffered by the respondent, who opposed her husband's abuse, challenged his dominance, attempted to leave him, and sought relief from the government, was only personal and does not constitute anything more than illegitimate criminal conduct unprotected under the Act is unacceptable. This type of differentiation between the supposedly more private forms of persecution, typically suffered by women, and the more public forms of persecution, typically suffered by men, is exactly the type of outdated and improper distinction that the DOJ Guidelines were intended to overcome.

\* \* \*

The majority insists that the respondent's husband persecuted her regardless of what she believed or what he thought she believed, claiming that the record does not reflect he was motivated by gender animus generally. The majority contends that the abuser was not, even in part, motivated by the respondent's resistance to his domination, even though he had told her he viewed women as property to be treated brutally in order to sustain his domination. This is contrary to fact, law, and logic. To reach such a conclusion, the majority must ignore entirely the mixed motive doctrine, which not only constitutes a well-established basis for asylum in cases arising before the Ninth Circuit, but also constitutes a basis for asylum in claims made before this Board. Furthermore, as we stated in conjunction with our consideration of the respondent as a member of a particular social group, illegitimate motives triggering persecution raise an inference that the harm has occurred on account of a statutorily enumerated ground.

\* \* \*

\* \* \* Had the respondent been subjected to such heinous abuse due to political opposition to communism, imputed as a result of her family's economic class or political activities, the majority would recognize her situation as one of persecution on account of political opinion. She is not less eligible or entitled to protection on account of her political opinion opposing male domination expressed through the abuse of women by their husbands, or the political opinion attributed to her, than were the comparably qualifying applicants to whom we have granted asylum.

\* \* \*

### Notes and Questions

1.   Consider this passage from *Matter of S–A–,* 22 I & N Dec. 1328 (BIA 2000), discussed in the materials on religious beliefs and practices in Chapter Four, p. 251:

Because the persecution suffered by the respondent was on account of her religious beliefs, we find this case distinguishable on the facts from circuit court decisions holding that persecution on account of gender alone does not constitute persecution on account of membership in a particular social group. *See, e.g., Gomez v. INS,* 947 F.2d 660 (2d Cir. 1991). We also find that because of the religious element in this case, the domestic abuse suffered by the respondent is different from that described in *Matter of R–A–*, [22 I & N Dec. 906] (BIA 1999).

22 I & N Dec. at 1337.

Can *Matter of R–A–* be reconciled with *Matter of S–A–*?

2. Perhaps the distinction between *Matter of S–A–* and *Matter of R–A–* turns on the familial roles. Reading these decisions together, do they imply that the BIA thinks that young women cannot realistically protect themselves or leave their father's homes, but that wives can? Or do consequentialist concerns explain the distinction—that is, is parental abuse considered less likely to create a wave of asylum seekers because fewer parents severely abuse their daughters than husbands abuse their wives—or perhaps that fewer children will be able to escape and travel to a distant country to claim protection? Are consequentialist concerns in this context cynical? Illegitimate?

3. At the INS' urging, *Matter of S–A–* was designated for publication as a precedent in June 2000, while the Justice Department wrestled with its ultimate response to *Matter of R–A–*. In December 2000, the Department published proposed amendments to the asylum regulations, including new definitions of "persecution," "on account of," and "membership in a particular social group." 65 Fed. Reg. 76588–98 (2000). The changes were intended, in major part, to make the doctrine more amenable to domestic violence claims, although the proposed rules show signs of internal departmental differences over how to handle such matters. The next month, in one of her last acts in office, Attorney General Janet Reno vacated the BIA decision in *Matter of R–A–*, and remanded the case to the BIA. Reno directed the Board to wait until the new asylum regulations were final and then to reconsider the case in light of those regulations. *See* 78 Interp. Rel. 256, 335 (2001); Musalo & Knight, *Steps Forward and Steps Back: Uneven Progress in the Law of Social Group and Gender–Based Claims in the United States*, 13 Int'l J. Refugee L. 51 (2001).

After the change in administration, Attorney General John Ashcroft "recertified" the case to himself in February 2003. The Department of Homeland Security, which had absorbed the INS in the government reorganization, filed a brief urging the Attorney General to grant asylum to R–A–. *See* 81 Interp. Rel. 245 (2004). The DHS brief disagreed with earlier proposals as to how the particular social group should be understood. Instead it offered this description: "married women in Guatemala who are unable to leave the relationship." In DHS's view, the husband inflicted harm because of R–A–'s membership in that group. Hence the nexus requirement was satisfied without looking to the precise reasons why state protection was unavailable in Guatemala. Ashcroft evidently found the issues in *Matter of R–A–* to be more complicated than originally anticipated, however. After waiting two years without taking action, he followed his predecessor's lead by remanding the case to the BIA with instructions to decide the case in accordance with final asylum regulations that were to be issued on the basis of the December 2000 notice of proposed rulemaking. *Matter of R–A–*, 23 I & N Dec. 694 (AG 2005). As of this writing in October 2006, the final regulations still have not appeared, and thus the BIA has not reconsidered R–A–'s case.

4. In the meantime, despite the vacating of the Board's ruling in *Matter of R–A–*, which means that it cannot serve as a precedent, asylum officers and immigration judges of course must continue to decide claims based on the threat of domestic abuse. It appears that most such decisions reflect doctrine that is far more generous to such claims than the approach of the BIA majority in *Matter of R–A–*. *See* Knight, *Seeking Asylum from Gender Persecution: Progress Amid Uncertainty*, 79 Interp. Rel. 689 (2002).

5. For a broader perspective on gender-related claims, consider this comment on the relationship between domestic abuse and FGM:

> * * * These two categories [gender and sexual orientation] have been central to the progressive agenda of refugee law at least since the early 1990s. It is hardly mere coincidence that the paradigm of the persecutor shifted from strong to weak states roughly at the same time. The discourse on gender and refugee protection pivoted on the opposition of the enlightened female individual with an alien and premodern culture, which the state of origin was unable or unwilling to control. The cultural element was apparently important to sever those cases which would be clearly worthy of refugee protection from those whose worth would be not so clear. Female genital mutilation (FGM) is not practiced by majority populations of states in the North. Therefore, it is comparatively easy to include the suppression of FGM amongst the positive obligations which a state has under international human rights law, in particular the right not to be treated inhumanely. There is hardly a risk that a state in the North will default on this particular obligation, so the grant of asylum or alternative forms of protection to a person at risk of being subjected to FGM upon return comes at no risk to the self-perception of the host state.

> The converse is true for the case of domestic violence. At face value, domestic violence is as much borne out by a societal culture as female genital mutilation. Conceptually, it would not be a problem to subsume the latter under the former, and it is striking and illustrative that the two forms of harm have been put into separate boxes by the discourse on gender and persecution. However, the issue of violence against women in the privacy of family and partnership relations is a problem that is not particular to the South, but also haunts states in the North, many of which have proven unable to effectively counter their own cultures in this area. Here, the grant of protection would come at a considerable price. From the perspective of the restrictive governments in the North, the group of potential beneficiaries appears excessively large. And legally, the grant of asylum would imply that the protection of women from domestic violence is part of the positive obligations under human rights law which states in the North must also honor. Indeed, it is part of a core obligation—an obligation strong enough to come within the ambit of the persecution concept. Culturally, the difference between the enlightened urban North and the premodern

rural South would break down, and the asylum procedure could no longer reproduce the identity of the host state. Therefore, applicants may be referred back to the protection of the institutions of her country of origin in cases of domestic violence. In doing so, the positive obligation has been displaced from the state to the individual. It is for the individual to ensure that the state protects her human rights, rather than for the state to ensure that the individual's human rights are respected by other individuals. The outcome is manifestly absurd. Under the logic of human rights law, it makes no sense to "oblige" an individual to protect herself.

This selectivity—female genital mutilation tends to be included, while domestic violence tends to be excluded—would not have been possible without the malleability of the concept of being persecuted and the shifting of positive obligations under human rights law.
* * *

Noll, *Asylum Claims and the Translation of Culture Into Politics*, 41 Texas Int'l L.J. 491, 495–96 (2006).

———————

In most asylum cases the agent of persecution is either the state or a state-like organization that uses force in its efforts to control territory and to gain political power. Domestic abuse cases are configured differently, as *Matter of R–A–* illustrates. Typically, the persecution is carried out by one individual and the state's role is not immediately visible. Further, the motive for the abuse is often unarticulated. The following excerpt explores these issues and proposes a bifurcated approach to analyzing the bases of persecution.

## T. ALEXANDER ALEINIKOFF, PROTECTED CHARACTERISTICS AND SOCIAL PERCEPTIONS: AN ANALYSIS OF THE MEANING OF "MEMBERSHIP IN A PARTICULAR SOCIAL GROUP"

Refugee Protection in International Law 301–02.
(E. Feller, V. Türk, & F. Nicholson eds., 2003).

*The "nexus" requirement and non-State actors*

In many social group cases, the difficult issue for the adjudicator may not be the definition of the group so much as the "nexus" requirement, that is, the persecution be *for reasons of* membership in the group. * * * [S]everal discrete issues need to be considered * * * [in] the situation where the agent of persecution is not the State.

Examples may be drawn from the cases: (i) a woman is abused by her spouse in a State that takes no action against such abuse; (ii) a woman is threatened with FGM by her tribal group in a State that prohibits, but cannot stop, the practice; (iii) a criminal enterprise threatens the family of someone who owes it money. Difficulties arise in such cases in deciding whether the conduct of the persecutor and/or the failure of State protection is "for reasons of" the victim's membership of a social group. For instance, in *Matter of R.A.*, the BIA concluded that the applicant—who had suffered very severe abuse—could not satisfy the nexus requirement because she could not show that group membership was the motivation behind the abuse by her husband. This was so, according to the majority, because there was no evidence that the husband had or would target other members of the group. They found: "On the basis of this record, we perceive that the husband's focus was on the respondent because she was *his* wife, not because she was a member of some broader collection of women, however defined, whom he believed warranted the infliction of harm."

The specific reasoning in *R.A.* is open to serious question. Indeed, the proposed INS rules—formulated to provide "clarification" of the Board's reasoning—in fact implicitly disapprove of the Board's "nexus" analysis. Whether or not the persecutor has acted against others in a similar situation may be probative, but it surely cannot be a required element of the case, any more than a person who claims race discrimination must show that the perpetrator has also discriminated against others on the basis of race. The Convention requires a showing that *her* fear of persecution is for reasons of a characteristic *she* possesses. * * *

Even where it cannot be shown that the persecutor has acted "for reasons of" one of the Convention grounds, there are circumstances in which a refugee claim might be recognized. [In another chapter in this volume, Rodger] Haines * * * [emphasizes that] "persecution" is a construct of two separate but essential elements, namely the risk of serious harm and failure of protection.

In other words, the claimant must show that the feared persecution is "for reasons of one" of the Convention grounds and that the State does not afford protection. The Convention ground may be supplied either by the non-State persecutor (coupled with a State that is unable or unwilling to afford protection) or by the State (when it is unwilling to afford protection for one of the Convention reasons).

This bifurcated analysis means that a social group claim may require separate analyses of both the conduct of the non-State actor and the State to see if either is acting for reasons of the claimant's membership of a particular social group. Consider again the example of an abusive husband. A social group claim may be established either by showing (i) that the man's actions are predicated on his spouse's gender and the State is unable (or unwilling) to provide protection against such conduct; or (ii) that, whatever the reasons for the husband's actions, the State is unwilling to protect the spouse because of her gender.

Importantly, this analysis does not suggest that every case of domestic abuse establishes a refugee claim. First, the State may have an adequate legal process for sanctioning abusers; thus the applicant would be unable to establish a lack of State protection. Secondly, even where a particular applicant had been unable to secure police protection, it might be * * * that the failure was atypical, due to the attitude or ineptitude of a particular police officer, based on police inefficiency, or based on police reluctance to become involved in domestic disputes. The claimant would have to show "something more"—a requirement that "would be satisfied at least by a sustained or systemic absence of state protection for members of a particular social group attributable to a perception of them by the state as not deserving equal protection under the law with other members of the society". [Quoting the Australian decision in *Minister of Immigration and Multicultural Affairs v. Khawar*, [2000] FCA 1130, 23 Aug. 2000, para. 160].

———

Compare *Matter of R–A–* with the following decision from the Law Lords in the United Kingdom. This decision wrestled in particular with the issues of whether the victim of domestic abuse is a member of a particular social group and whether her membership has triggered her persecution. Both the majority and the dissent in *Matter of R–A–* refer to this decision, which found for the asylum seekers by a vote of 4–to–1.

## ISLAM v. SECRETARY OF STATE FOR THE HOME DEPARTMENT

House of Lords.
[1999] 2 A.C. 629.

[The opinion of LORD STEYN is omitted.]

LORD HOFFMAN:

\* \* \*

These appeals concern two women who became victims of domestic violence in Pakistan, came to the United Kingdom and claimed asylum as refugees. Shahanna Islam is a graduate school teacher from Karachi. In 1990 she became involved in a playground dispute between rival gangs of politically motivated boys. Those supporting the Mohaijur Quami Movement or "MQM" told her husband, who belonged to the same party, that she had been unfaithful to him. As a result he gave her severe beatings which eventually drove her out of the house. The other woman, Syeda Shah is simple and uneducated. She was frequently beaten by her husband and eventually, when pregnant, turned out of the house. She too came to the United Kingdom, where her child was born.

\* \* \*

Domestic violence such as was suffered by Mrs. Islam and Mrs. Shah in Pakistan is regrettably by no means unknown in the United Kingdom. It would not however be regarded as persecution within the meaning of the Convention. This is because the victims of violence would be entitled to the protection of the state. The perpetrators could be prosecuted in the criminal courts and the women could obtain orders restraining further molestation or excluding their husbands from the home under the Domestic Violence and Matrimonial Proceedings Act 1976. What makes it persecution in Pakistan is the fact that according to evidence which was accepted by the special adjudicator in Mrs. Islam's case and formed the basis of findings which have not been challenged, the state was unwilling or unable to offer her any protection. The adjudicator found it was useless for Mrs. Islam, as a woman, to complain to the police or the courts about her husband's conduct. On the contrary, the police were likely to accept her husband's allegations of infidelity and arrest her instead. The evidence of men was always deemed more credible than that of women. If she was convicted of infidelity, the penalties could be severe. Even if she was not prosecuted, as a woman separated from her husband she would be socially ostracised and vulnerable to attack, even murder, at the instigation of her husband or his political associates. * * *

* * *

The question in both cases was therefore whether the women had a well founded fear of persecution within the meaning of the Convention and, critically, whether such persecution was for one of the five enumerated reasons, namely, "race, religion, nationality, membership of a particular social group or political opinion." Of these, the only serious candidate for consideration was that they feared persecution because they were members of a "particular social group." * * *

The problem for both women was to specify the "social group" of which they claimed their membership had given rise to persecution. Mrs Shah's counsel seems to have tried to persuade the special adjudicator that "women who had suffered domestic violence" were a social group. * * *

* * *

Mrs Islam also argued before the special adjudicator that she feared persecution because she belonged to a social group defined as "Pakistani women subject to domestic violence, namely wife abuse."

* * *

By th[e] time [of appeal], the definition of the social group had been greatly elaborated * * * as "Pakistani women ... accused of transgressing social mores (in the instant case, adultery, disobedience to husbands) ... who are unprotected by their husbands or other male relatives."

* * *

The notion that the Convention is concerned with discrimination on grounds inconsistent with principles of human rights is reflected in the influential decision of the U.S. Board of Immigration Appeals in *In re Acosta* (1985) 19 I. & N. 211 where it was said that a social group for the purposes of the Convention was one distinguished by:

> an immutable characteristic ... [a characteristic] that either is
> beyond the power of an individual to change or that is so

fundamental to his identity or conscience that it ought not to be
required to be changed.

This was true of the other four grounds enumerated in the Convention.
It is because they are either immutable or part of an individual's
fundamental right to choose for himself that discrimination on such
grounds is contrary to principles of human rights.

It follows that I cannot accept that the term "particular social
group" implies an additional element of cohesiveness, co-operation or
interdependence. The fact that members of a group may or may not have
some form of organisation or interdependence seems to me irrelevant to
the question of whether it would be contrary to principles of human
rights to discriminate against its members. Among the other four categories, "race" and "nationality" do not imply any idea of co-operation;
"religion" and "political opinion" might, although it could be minimal.
* * *

* * *

To what social group, if any, did the appellants belong? To identify a
social group, one must first identify the society of which it forms a part.
In this case, the society is plainly that of Pakistan. Within that society, it
seems to me that women form a social group of the kind contemplated by
the Convention. Discrimination against women in matters of fundamental human rights on the ground that they are women is plainly in pari
materiae with discrimination on grounds of race. It offends against their
rights as human beings to equal treatment and respect. It may seem
strange that sex (or gender) was not specifically enumerated in the
Convention when it is mentioned in article 2 of the Universal Declaration of Human Rights. But the Convention was originally limited to
persons who had become refugees as a result of events occurring before 1
January 1951. One can only suppose that the delegates could not think
of cases before that date in which women had been persecuted because
they were women. But the time limit was removed by the 1967 New
York Protocol and the concept of a social group is in my view perfectly
adequate to accommodate women as a group in a society that discriminates on grounds of sex, that is to say, that perceives women as not
being entitled to the same fundamental rights as men. As we have seen,
La Forest J. in [*Attorney–General of Canada v. Ward* [1993] 2 S.C.R.
689] had no difficulty in saying that persecution on grounds of gender
would be persecution on account of membership of a social group. I
therefore think that women in Pakistan are a social group.

As we have seen, however, the appellants in the Court of Appeal did
not say that they feared persecution simply on the ground that they were
women. They produced a much more restricted and complicated definition of the social group to which they claimed to belong and membership
of which was said to be the ground for their persecution. * * *

* * *

The reason why the appellants chose to put forward this restricted and artificial definition of their social group was to pre-empt the question of whether their feared persecution was "for reasons of" their membership of the wider group of women. It was argued for the Secretary of State that they could not fear persecution simply for the reason that they were women. The vast majority of women in Pakistan conformed to the customs of their society, did not chafe against discrimination or have bullying husbands, and were not persecuted. Being a woman could not therefore be a reason for persecution. The question is essentially one of causation. Being a woman does not necessarily result in persecution and therefore cannot be the reason for those cases in which women are persecuted. The appellants' argument in the Court of Appeal accepted this reasoning and tried to confess and avoid by opting for a sub-category of women.

\* \* \*

I turn, therefore, to the question of causation. What is the reason for the persecution which the appellants fear? Here it is important to notice that it is made up of two elements. First, there is the threat of violence to Mrs Islam by her husband and his political friends and to Mrs Shah by her husband. This is a personal affair, directed against them as individuals. Secondly, there is the inability or unwillingness of the State to do anything to protect them. There is nothing personal about this. The evidence was that the State would not assist them because they were women. It denied them a protection against violence which it would have given to men. These two elements have to be combined to constitute persecution within the meaning of the Convention. As the Gender Guidelines for the Determination of Asylum Claims in the U.K. (published by the Refugee Women's Legal Group in July 1998) succinctly puts it (at p. 5): "Persecution = Serious Harm + The Failure of State Protection."

Answers to questions about causation will often differ according to the context in which the question is asked. \* \* \* Suppose oneself in Germany in 1935. There is discrimination against Jews in general, but not all Jews are persecuted. Those who conform to the discriminatory laws, wear yellow stars out of doors and so forth can go about their ordinary business. But those who contravene the racial laws are persecuted. Are they being persecuted on grounds of race? In my opinion, they plainly are. It is therefore a fallacy to say that because not all members of a class are being persecuted, it follows that persecution of a few cannot be on grounds of membership of that class. Or to come nearer to the facts of the present case, suppose that the Nazi government in those early days did not actively organise violence against Jews, but pursued a policy of not giving any protection to Jews subjected to violence by neighbours. A Jewish shopkeeper is attacked by a gang organised by an Aryan competitor who smash his shop, beat him up and threaten to do it again if he remains in business. The competitor and his gang are motivated by business rivalry and a desire to settle old personal scores, but they would not have done what they did unless they knew that the authorities would allow them to act with impunity. And the ground upon which they enjoyed impunity was that the victim was a Jew. Is he being persecuted on grounds of race? Again, in my opinion, he is. An essential element in the persecution, the failure of the authorities to provide protection, is based upon race. It is true that one answer to the question "Why was he attacked?" would be "because a competitor wanted to drive him out of business." But another answer, and in my view the right answer in the context of the Convention, would be "he was attacked by a competitor who knew that he would receive no protection because he was a Jew."

In the case of Mrs Islam, the legal and social conditions which according to the evidence existed in Pakistan and which left her unprotected against violence by men were discriminatory against women. For the purposes of the Convention, this discrimination was the critical element in the persecution. In my opinion, this means that she feared persecution because she was a woman. There was no need to construct a more restricted social group simply for the purpose of satisfying the causal connection which the Convention requires.

\* \* \*

LORD HOPE OF CRAIGHEAD:

\* \* \*

The issue which is common to these appeals is whether the appellants, who are both married women of Pakistani nationality, are members of a "particular social group." The "particular social group" to which they claim to belong is said to comprise women in Pakistan accused of transgressing social mores who are unprotected by their husbands or other male relatives.

\* \* \*

[W]hile the risk of discrimination by society is common to all five of the Convention reasons, the persecution which is feared cannot be used to define a particular social group. The rule is that the Convention reasons must exist independently of, and not be defined by, the persecution. To define the social group by reference to the fear of being persecuted would be to resort to circular reasoning \* \* \*.

I turn now to the phrase "particular social group." As a general rule it is desirable that international treaties should be interpreted by the courts of all the states parties uniformly. So, if it could be said that a uniform interpretation of this phrase was to be found in the authorities, I would regard it as appropriate that we should follow it. But, as my noble and learned friend Lord Steyn has demonstrated in his review of the United States, Australian and Canadian case law, no uniform interpretation of it has emerged. The only clear rule which can be said to have been generally recognised is that the persecution must exist independently of, and not be used to define, the social group. I agree that the traveaux [sic] préparatoires of the Convention are uninformative. But it is more important to have regard to the evolutionary approach which must be taken to international agreements of this kind. This enables account to be taken of changes in society and of discriminatory circumstances which may not have been obvious to the delegates when the Convention was being framed.

In general terms a social group may be said to exist when a group of people with a particular characteristic is recognised as a distinct group by society. The concept of a group means that we [are] dealing here with people who are grouped together because they share a characteristic not shared by others, not with individuals. The word "social" means that we are being asked to identify a group of people which is recognised as a particular group by society. As social customs and social attitudes differ from one country to another, the context for this inquiry is the country of the person's nationality. The phrase can thus accommodate particular social groups which may be recognisable as such in one country but not in others or which, in any given country, have not previously been recognised.

* * *

The unchallenged evidence in this case shows that women are discriminated against in Pakistan. I think that the nature and scale of the discrimination is such that it can properly be said the women in Pakistan are discriminated against by the society in which they live. The reason why the appellants fear persecution is not just because they are women. It is because they are women in a society which discriminates against women. In the context of that society I would regard women as a particular social group within the meaning of article 1A(2) of the Convention.

* * *

[The opinion of LORD HUTTON is omitted.]

LORD MILLETT:

* * *

The appellants are women from Pakistan who claim to have a well founded fear of persecution by reason of their membership of a particular social group. They identify the particular social group to which they belong as consisting of (i) women in Pakistan (ii) accused of transgressing social norms (in the present case by adultery and disobedience to their husbands) and (iii) who are in consequence unprotected by their husbands or other male relatives. Both appellants have satisfied the authorities that they have a fear of persecution and that this fear is well founded. * * *

Persecution may be indiscriminate. It may be for any reason or none. It is not, however, enough for an applicant for asylum to show that he or she has a well founded fear of persecution. The persecution must be discriminatory and for a Convention reason. By limiting the persecution in this way, the Convention contemplates the possibility that there may be victims of persecution who do not qualify for refugee status. Furthermore, if the reason relied upon is membership of a particular social group, it is not enough that the applicant is a member of a particular social group and has a well founded fear of persecution. The applicant must be liable to persecution because he or she is a member of the social group in question.

* * *

The denial of human rights, however, is not the same as persecution, which involves the infliction of serious harm. The 1951 Convention was concerned to afford refuge to the victims of certain kinds of discriminatory persecution, but it was not directed to prohibit discrimination as such nor to grant refuge to the victims of discrimination. * * * The inclusion of sex as a basis of discrimination in the Universal Declaration and the failure to include it as a ground of persecution in the 1951 Convention is noteworthy. It may be due to the fact that, while sexual discrimination was widely practised in 1951, and women are condemned to a subordinate and inferior status in many societies even today, it is difficult to imagine a society in which women are actually subjected to serious harm simply because they are women. * * *

* * *

It is in my opinion essential to bear in mind at all times that it is not enough for the applicant for asylum to establish that he or she is a member of a particular social group and is liable to persecution. The applicant must also establish that he or she is liable to persecution *because* he or she is a member of the group. The applicant must be the subject of attack, not for himself or herself alone, but because he or she is one of those jointly condemned in the eyes of their persecutors for possession of the characteristic which is common to the group.

* * * I turn to consider the social group to which the present appellants claim to belong and for membership of which they fear persecution. As formulated by the appellants it consists of women in Pakistan who have been or who are liable to be accused of adultery or other conduct transgressing social norms and who are unprotected by their husbands or other male relatives. It is a subset of the set "women" (and of the subset "married women"). The third qualifying condition can be disposed of at once. The fact that the appellants have no one to protect them helps to show that their fear of persecution is well founded. But it does not help to define the social group to which they belong. I am content to assume that the appellants would not be persecuted if they had someone to protect them from attack. But they are not persecuted because they have no one to protect them; that is not the ground of persecution. The "but for" test of causation, which is always necessary but rarely sufficient, is beguilingly misleading in this context.

This qualifying condition was no doubt included because of an erroneous belief that all the members of the group must be equally liable to persecution. That is not the case. It is no answer to a claim for asylum that some members of the group may be able to escape persecution, either because they have powerful protectors or for geographical or other reasons. Such factors do not narrow the membership of the group, but go to the question whether the applicant's fear of persecution is well founded. * * *

Whether the social group is taken to be that contended for by the appellants, however, or the wider one of Pakistani women who are perceived to have transgressed social norms, the result is the same. No cognisable social group exists independently of the social conditions on which the persecution is founded. The social group which the appellants identify is defined by the persecution, or more accurately (but just as fatally) by the discrimination which founds the persecution. It is an artificial construct called into being to meet the exigencies of the case.

The appellants contended for the subset because they recognised that the head set of "women" or "married women" would not do. Officially, I understand, Sharia law regards women as "separate but equal," a description which, I observe, was also applied, with scant regard for the truth, to apartheid in South Africa. The evidence clearly establishes that women in Pakistan are treated as inferior to men and subordinate to their husbands and that, by international standards, they are subject to serious and quite unacceptable discrimination on account of their sex. But persecution is not merely an aggravated form of discrimination; and even if women (or married women) constitute a particular social group it is not accurate to say that those women in Pakistan who are persecuted are persecuted because they are members of it. They are persecuted because they are thought to have transgressed social norms, not because they are women. There is no evidence that men who transgress the different social norms which apply to them are treated more favourably.

In the course of argument an illuminating instance was put forward. Suppose, in the early years of the Third Reich, Jews in Nazi Germany were required to wear a yellow star on pain of being sent to a concentration camp and murdered if they did not. Would they have failed to qualify as refugees on the ground that they were not liable to persecution on racial grounds, but because they were defying the law? Of course we know now that they should not have failed to qualify, because the law was not merely discriminatory but a necessary part of the intended persecution. Jews were required to wear a distinguishing badge in order to mark them out for persecution. At the time this would have been a matter of evidence; but given the absence of any other rational explanation for the law, the virulence of the state-inspired racial propaganda which formed the background against which it was enacted, and the wholly disproportionate penalty for disobedience, there should have been no difficulty in satisfying the requirements of the Convention even in the absence of other evidence of persecution (of which there was an abundance). I find the example instructive precisely because of the differences between it and the present case rather than the similarities.

I am accordingly not willing to accept, as a general proposition, the submission that those who are persecuted because they refuse to conform to discriminatory laws to which, as members a particular social group, they are subject, thereby qualify for refugee status. Such persons are discriminated against because they are members of the social group in question; but they are persecuted because they refuse to conform, not because they are members of the social group. * * *

\* \* \*

Such questions will depend on the evidence. The evidence in the present case is that the widespread discrimination against women in Pakistan is based on religious law, and the persecution of those who refuse to conform to social and religious norms, while in no sense required by religious law, is sanctioned or at least tolerated by the authorities. But these norms are not a pretext for persecution nor have they been recently imposed. They are deeply embedded in the society in which the appellants have been brought up and in which they live. Women who are perceived to have transgressed them are treated badly, particularly by their husbands, and the authorities do little to protect them. But this is not because they are women. They are persecuted as individuals for what each of them has done or is thought to have done. They are not jointly condemned as females or persecuted for what they are. The appellants need to establish that the reason that they are left unprotected by the authorities and are liable to be persecuted by their husbands is that they are women. In my opinion they have not done so.

I would dismiss the appeals.

### Notes and Questions

1. Under Lord Hoffman's approach, would all women from Pakistan qualify for asylum in the United Kingdom? Why or why not?

2. The UNHCR Guidelines on Gender-Related Persecution, adopted in 2002, take an approach similar to that suggested by Lord Hoffman:

> In cases where there is a risk of being persecuted at the hands of a non-State actor (e.g., husband, partner or other non-State actor) for reasons which are related to one of the Convention grounds, the causal link is established, whether or not the absence of State protection is Convention-related. Alternatively, where the risk of persecution at the hands of a non-State actor is unrelated to a Convention ground, but the inability or unwillingness of the State to offer protection is for reasons of a Convention ground, the causal link is also established.

U.N. Doc. HCR/GIP/02/01, at para. 21.

Is this position a correct interpretation of the law? Does it matter that the framers of the 1951 Convention did not contemplate coverage of these forms of private persecution? Given that domestic abuse is a major problem in a great many countries, can the political asylum system sustain the additional numbers of potential victims of private harm that may be covered under such doctrine? Are such consequentialist considerations legitimate in shaping doctrine? If domestic abuse is generally not to be covered by the refugee definition, how should the immigration system provide for women who face grave risks of this type if returned to their home countries? (Note the suggestions made by the majority in *Matter of R–A–*.)

---

Compare the focus on particular social group in the BIA decision in *Matter of R–A–* and the Law Lords' decision in *Islam* with the very different approach taken by the Ninth Circuit in *Aguirre-Cervantes v. INS*, 242 F.3d 1169 (9th Cir. 2001). The court granted asylum to a young Mexican woman who, along with all of her siblings and her mother, had been subjected to severe, repeated physical abuse by her father. The court first held that the woman's family qualified as a particular social group:

> Consistent with decisions from our circuit, our sister circuits and the BIA, we hold that a family group may qualify as a particular social group * * *. This is not to say, however, that every family group will qualify. Qualification will depend upon the circumstances of each case. The factors which lead us to conclude that the petitioner's family group qualifies as a "particular social group" are that the petitioner's family members are part of an immediate, as opposed to an extended, family unit; they now live or have lived together and are otherwise readily identifiable as a discrete unit; and they share the common experience of all having suffered persecution at the hands of the petitioner's father.

*Id.* at 1176. The court then held that the persecution in this case was on account of membership in this particular social group:

> The undisputed evidence demonstrates that Mr. Aguirre's goal was to dominate and persecute members of his immediate family. He abused his wife and all of his children to whom he had access. There is no evidence that he ever acted violently toward any non-family member. The petitioner was most severely attacked by her father when she tried to defend her mother against abuse, particularly when her mother was pregnant. The petitioner's uncle also testified that two of the petitioner's brothers, who now live in the United States, fled Mexico because of frequent abuse by their father. It was the immediate family that was the target of Mr. Aguirre's assaults. It was established by abundant evidence—and undisputed—that it was the petitioner's status as a member of that family that prompted her beatings. The conclusion is inescapable that she suffered those beatings on account of her family membership.

*Id.* at 1178.

The Ninth Circuit granted rehearing en banc, vacating the panel decision. Six weeks later, however, the court remanded the case to the

BIA by stipulation of the parties after the applicant's father was shot to death. *See* Hoppin, *Murder Moots Key Abuse Asylum Case: Father's Death Muddles a Groundbreaking Ruling*, Nat'l L.J., Dec. 24–31, 2001. Hence the panel opinion has no precedential force. The case was administratively closed in December 2005 for unspecified reasons.

Is the approach in *Aguirre–Cervantes v. INS*, in particular its focus on the family as a particular social group, an approach to domestic violence that is more analytically sound, or more faithful to the statute and Convention, or preferable for other reasons to the way the issues were framed and the particular social group defined in *Matter of R–A–* or in *Islam*? Does it give you pause that in this approach, the persecutor and his victims are members of the same social group?

The government's motion for rehearing en banc in *Aguirre–Cervantes* raised deference and exhaustion issues in these terms:

> Whether Congress in its legislation implementing the U.N. Refugee Protocol intended to protect members of a "particular social group" that consists of the immediate family of a domestic violence victim is a question that implicates the expertise of the Executive Branch charged with interpreting and applying the asylum statute. Indeed, the question ultimately at issue in this case—whether, and to what extent, the victims of domestic violence should be eligible for asylum in the United States—involves policy judgments of the most sensitive nature that must be resolved in the first instance by the Executive Branch. Judgments in the areas of domestic violence asylum and "gender asylum" claims begin with questions about what types of treatment of women or children in other cultures—ranging from different codes of dress or conduct for women to sanctioned violence against them—warrant protection under the United States' asylum laws. This question necessary [sic] implicates additional judgments about the nature and causes of domestic violence in other countries and, because asylum is not granted to protect the victims of private crimes, about the role of the foreign government in either perpetuating or trying to limit domestic violence. Domestic violence and discrimination against women occur in many—perhaps all—countries. Even our own country is not free from these problems. These considerations indicate both that the number of potential asylum applicants who may bring claims based upon domestic violence is very large, and that the judgment as to which victims of domestic violence are "refugees" within the meaning of the asylum statute is one of great delicacy. The Attorney General is charged with responsibility for making this judgment in the first instance, and if the INA's definition of "refugee" is indeed to be interpreted to include the victims of domestic violence, then it is critically important that the interpretation of the term in this new context be developed, in the first instance, by the

Executive Branch bodies to which Congress has entrusted the interpretation and application of the asylum laws.

INS Petition for Rehearing en banc, *Aguirre–Cervantes v. INS*, No. 97–70861, at 10–11, quoted and discussed in Knight, *Seeking Asylum From Gender Persecution: Progress Amid Uncertainty*, 79 Interp. Rel. 689, 694–95 (2002).

What is your response? How if at all should the factors mentioned in the government's brief be considered in asylum decisionmaking? What doctrine regarding particular social group, nexus, and persecutor motivation versus failure of state protection should govern domestic abuse cases?

## SECTION C.  PROCEDURAL OBSTACLES IN GENDER–SENSITIVE CASES

Persecution against women can obviously take many forms that are not gender-specific and can be motivated by race, religion, nationality, political opinion, ethnic background, social class, linguistic community, or other non-gender-related attributes. Within the context of claims that are based on or related to gender, though, many cases feature experiences that are humiliating and that have extremely negative social consequences if they are made public. These factors mean that asylum seekers raising gender issues may face serious obstacles in conveying the details of their claims in interviews and hearings.

As gender-related asylum claims have drawn increasing attention in recent years, there have been international and national efforts to heighten awareness of the impact of gender in asylum cases. These efforts have resulted in a series of gender guidelines for adjudicators. Generally, the guidelines address both substantive and procedural issues that arise in the context of gender cases, and they often review the national jurisprudence. The UNHCR issued gender guidelines in 1991, which led to similar guidelines in the United States, Canada, and the United Kingdom, excerpted in this section, as well as guidelines issued by the Australian Department of Immigration and Multicultural Affairs, July 1996. A decade later, the UNHCR gave major attention to gender-related cases as part of its Worldwide Consultations undertaken in connection with the fiftieth anniversary of the adoption of the 1951 Convention, and new UNHCR Guidelines resulted from that process. Guidelines on International Protection: Gender Related Persecution within the Context of Article 1A(2) of the 1951 Convention and/or its 1967 Protocol relating to the Status of Refugees; U.N. Doc. HCR/GIP/02/01 (7 May 2002).

In the United States, the INS asylum office issued a set of gender guidelines in 1995. *See* Considerations for Asylum Officers Adjudicating Asylum Claims from Women, 72 Interp. Rel. 771, 781 (1995). These guidelines have effectively been replaced by a chapter in the Asylum Officers Training Manual, which the Asylum Office uses and treats as guidance even though it remains officially in draft form. One section of these materials explains considerations related to gender and culture:

> Cultural factors, such as the expected role of a woman in her society, may significantly affect an applicant's testimony. In order to properly elicit and evaluate testimony, the asylum officer must be aware of such factors when eliciting testimony at the interview.

> 1.   Cultural norms may exacerbate reluctance to relate sensitive information

> Due to strict cultural norms in many countries, asylum applicants may be reluctant to disclose experiences of sexual violence. This may be especially true for women from societies that place extreme importance on preserving a woman's virginity. In many societies, sexual assault is seen as a violation of community or family morality, for which the victim herself is held responsible. The combination of shame, feelings of responsibility and blame for having been victimized in this way can seriously limit a woman's ability to discuss or even to mention such experiences.

> 2.   Cultural norms may limit an applicant's knowledge of other family members' activities

> In some cultures, men normally do not share the details of their political, military or even social activities with spouses, sisters, daughters or mothers. Women from such cultures may be able to present only vague testimony about experiences of male relatives, even husbands. Some women may not be able to explain which male relatives were politically active or, if they are aware of the relative's political activity, may be unable to provide any details about it.

> 3.   Presence of relatives may inhibit testimony

> For a variety of reasons, the presence of relatives, particularly a husband or father, may impede an asylum applicant's willingness to discuss gender-related persecutory acts or fears. For example:

>> a.   The applicant's relatives may not be aware of the harm experienced by the applicant. She may wish that the relative remain unaware of her experiences, or she may be ashamed to say what she has experienced or fears in front of a relative.

>> b.   The applicant's claim may be based, in part, on fear of the male relative who is present.

>> c.   In some cases, a woman may be accustomed to having a male relative speak for her and may try to defer to that male relative in the interview, or the male relative may insist on speaking for the applicant.

While the presence of a male relative may inhibit testimony, as described above, in other cases a woman may be more comfortable testifying with the presence of a relative, male or female. Therefore, to the extent possible, the choice of whether to be interviewed alone or with a relative present should be left to the applicant. She should be asked her preference, when possible, prior to the interview.

If the applicant elects for the relative to be present at the interview, the asylum officer should exercise sound judgment during the interview; determining whether the presence of the relative is impeding communication. If, it appears that relative's presence is interfering with open communication, the relative should be asked to wait in the waiting room.

4.   Interpreters may inhibit testimony

Testimony on sensitive issues such as sexual abuse may be diluted when received through the filter of an interpreter. The applicant may not feel comfortable discussing gender issues with an interpreter of the opposite sex. The same holds true for the interpreter; even if the applicant feels comfortable using a particular interpreter, the interpreter may be inhibited about discussing gender-related issues or using certain terms. For example, the interpreter may substitute the word "harm" for "rape," because the interpreter is not comfortable discussing rape or because of cultural taboos.

Asylum Officer Basic Training Course: Female Asylum Applicants and Gender–Related Claims 15–17 (Jan. 27, 2006).

Several other countries have adopted guidelines that address a similar array of topics. For example, the U.K. Gender Guidelines list some of the sensitive matters that arise in gender-related asylum cases:

Gender-specific harm may include but is not limited to sexual violence and abuse, female genital mutilation, marriage-related harm, violence within the family, forced sterilisation and forced abortion. * * *

Sexual violence can include, but is not limited to, rape; enforced nakedness; mechanical or manual stimulation of the erogenous zones; the insertion of objects into the body openings; the forced witnessing or commission of sexual acts; forced masturbation; fellatio and oral coitus, a general atmosphere of sexual aggression, the loss of the ability to reproduce plus threats of the above: sexual violence is a form of aggression.

United Kingdom Immigration Appellate Authority, Asylum Gender Guidelines 14–15 (2000).

In addition to difficulties inherent in discussing humiliating experiences, women from certain societies are not accustomed to speaking in public or to men who are not members of their family. These cultural constraints may also lead to gender biases in asylum interviews. In response to these concerns, some governments have begun to train asylum interviewers concerning the impact of gender on testimony and to have female interviewers available for sensitive cases. The U.S. Guidelines include a section on Suggested Interview Techniques:

In all cases, the asylum officer must use his or her utmost care to assure that the interview is conducted in a non-adversarial and open atmosphere that allows for the discussion of past experiences and fears of future harm and its ramifications.

Some techniques that may be employed (discussed in greater detail in the lessons on interviewing) include the following:

1.    Begin with easy topics to establish rapport and give the applicant time to become accustomed to the interview.

2.    If the applicant becomes upset, pause to allow the applicant to regain her composure.

3.    Acknowledge how difficult it may be for the applicant to answer certain questions by assuring the applicant that it is all right to let the asylum officer know when something is difficult to discuss in detail.

Note: An asylum officer should require a certain level of detail in order to establish credibility. The applicant may be able to provide sufficient detail about certain parts of the claim to establish credibility, without providing minute detail on particularly sensitive topics. Example: Applicant provides detail about circumstances of arrest and conditions of detention, but finds it extremely painful to provide detailed description of certain torture she endured during detention. The asylum officer does not need to press for detail about the torture if the applicant's testimony about the arrest and the general conditions of detention is credible.

4.    Temporarily switch from the sensitive topic to something less sensitive, remembering to return to the sensitive topic later if more information is required.

5.    Approach the issue from a different angle. For example, ask about events that led up to the traumatic experience and how the applicant felt after the experience, instead of asking about the specifics of the traumatic incident.

6.    Switch the focus to another victim the applicant has testified about and then return to the applicant's experience.

7.    Emphasize the confidential nature of the interview.

8. Remind the applicant that, for the asylum officer to evaluate eligibility for asylum, the asylum officer
needs to understand the applicant's history, including
the harm she may have experienced.

The Canadian Gender Guidelines similarly highlight different cultural norms and psychological syndromes related to gender that might
exacerbate the difficulties inherent in refugee status hearings:

Women refugee claimants face special problems in demonstrating that their claims are credible and trustworthy. Some of
the difficulties may arise because of cross-cultural misunderstandings. For example:

\* \* \*

3. Women refugee claimants who have suffered
sexual violence may exhibit a pattern of symptoms
referred to as Rape Trauma Syndrome, and may require extremely sensitive handling. Similarly, women
who have suffered domestic violence may also be reluctant to testify. In some cases it will be appropriate to
consider whether claimants should be allowed to have
the option of providing their testimony outside the
hearing room by affidavit or by video tape, or in front
of members and refugee hearing officers specifically
trained in dealing with violence against women. \* \* \*

Immigration and Refugee Board, Women Refugee Claimants Fearing
Gender–Related Persecution Guidelines Issued by the Chairperson Pursuant to Section 65(3) of the Immigration Act (1993; updated 1996;
<http://www.irb-cisr.gc.ca/en/references/policy/guidelines/women_e.
htm>)

Another procedural hurdle arises on occasion when women seek
asylum as part of a family unit. In these instances the claims of female
asylum seekers may be perceived as derivative of those raised by their
male relatives. The women may be interviewed cursorily or mainly to
corroborate their husband's experiences. This approach can lead to
several different problems that are addressed in the guidelines excerpted
in this section. Sometimes the women have substantial fears of persecution, but their male relatives may not raise them because they are not
aware of the details or are ashamed to mention them. This allows
asylum claims to be overlooked. Other times, women are asked to
corroborate their male relatives' claims. Women from cultures in which
men do not share information with females will find it difficult to
respond.

## Concluding Question

Think back to the opening of this chapter and in particular to the quote from Rodger Haines, who observed:

> The failure of decision makers to recognize and respond appropriately to the experiences of women stems not from the fact that the 1951 Convention does not refer specifically to persecution on the basis of sex or gender, but rather because it has often been approached from a partial perspective and interpreted through a framework of male experiences. The main problem facing women as asylum seekers is the failure of decision makers to incorporate the gender-related claims of women into their interpretation of the existing enumerated grounds and their failure to recognize the political nature of seemingly private acts of harm to women.

Haines, *Gender-related Persecution*, in Refugee Protection in International Law 319, 323 (E. Feller, V. Türk, & F. Nicholson eds., 2003).

Is he right? How many of the cases in this chapter would have come out differently if gender were a sixth ground in the definition of refugee?

# Chapter Six

# LIMITATIONS ON PROTECTION: EXCLUSION AND CESSATION

---

*My first memory of the civil war was fighting I heard was taking place in Monrovia in about 1989. There are a number of parties involved in the fighting, among them a group led by Prince Johnson, the [N]ational Patriotic Front of Liberia (NPFL) led by Charles Taylor, and a party called ULIMO. They were fighting primarily amongst themselves and also against the government troops. Around this time peacekeeping forces from neighbouring African countries arrived in Liberia but had little effect on the fighting.*

*The first time the war came to my village was in about [deleted] when Charles Taylor's group, the NPLF, came to [my village]. They said they had heard that a lot of people from the Prince Johnson group were hiding in the village and they came to find and kill them. They found about 40 people living in [my village] who we knew to be members or supporters of Prince Johnson. It was early in the morning, around 4:00 am, and these 40 or so men were taken from their houses and shot, without having had a chance to escape. The rest of the village watched on and some of the younger men, including myself and my brother, decided that we had to try and get away. We had heard that Charles Taylor was forcibly recruiting young men into his "army" and we knew we would be prime targets. These young men are trained to kill and I did not want to be put in the position where I would have to kill someone or be killed. If you refused to take part, then of course the NPLF would have no need for you and you would be killed.*

*My brother and I * * * were intercepted before we could get away * * *.*

*Another 10 or so young men from our village were also recruited and all of us were taken by truck to their training camp* *which was in [deleted] * * *. The camp itself was just a large open space with a number of shelters and I believe there were about 400 men there. Charles Taylor also had a house in the camp although this was some way from where we were to live. Although there were no fences the camp was heavily guarded by NPLF forces who all carried guns.*

\* \* \*

*About six weeks after I arrived I was told that soon I would be sent on a "riot" which is what Charles Taylor called the occasions when he would go out to fight Prince Johnson forces, which at that time were his most bitter enemies\* \* \*. I took part in about 6 of these riots and although I did not wish to kill anybody I knew either I had to shoot them or I would be shot. However, I always avoided shooting anyone in the head or chest because I knew that would mean instant death for them, instead aiming only at their legs or arms \* \* \*.*

\* \* \*

*After about three months in the camp I was accused by a member of the group of trying to [assassinate] Charles Taylor, which was totally untrue. However, as the accusation had been made I was now to be locked up in one of the many guard rooms around the camp until a "hearing" of the charge could be arranged. I was locked into a guard room with about 8 other men.*

*On about the fifth day of my imprisonment one of the eight men died. We told the guards and eventually it was decided that four of us would be made to dig a grave for this man and bury him \* \* \*. Because the body had started to smell the guards who had accompanied us to the grave site stood some way from us. When the guards turned away we all took the opportunity to escape \* \* \*.*

—asylum seeker in Australia[1]

In the past few chapters we have examined some of the conceptual and practical difficulties of establishing a well-founded fear of persecution based on one of the reasons specified in the 1951 Refugee Convention and in U.S. statutes. Individuals who overcome these hurdles and present convincing proof of a fear of persecution have taken only the first step in obtaining protection, however. The government can deny asylum as matter of discretion, as discussed in Chapter Three. In addition, U.S. law imposes further restrictions on individuals who seek asylum. Those who have a well-founded fear of persecution, but have

**1.** Refugee Review Tribunal (Australia) Reference: N96/12101 (25 Nov. 1996), ex-　cerpted in Section B, below.

secured a safe and lawful residence elsewhere will not qualify for protection in the United States. Those who wait too long after arriving in the United States to apply for asylum will not qualify. Those who committed serious crimes before they arrived in the United States or pose a security risk also will not qualify.

Some individuals arrive in the United States with a well-founded fear of persecution and are not subject to these exclusions from protection, but find that the situation in their homeland improves dramatically. If this occurs before their asylum application has been decided, they will face questions about whether their fear is still well-founded. If it occurs after they have received asylum, the government has the power to terminate their protection in the United States. We will explore both exclusion from protection and cessation, or termination, of protection in this chapter. In addition, because the 1951 Refugee Convention addresses both issues, we will also refer to some of the international practice regarding exclusion and termination.

## SECTION A.    EXCLUSION FROM PROTECTION: TIMING AND TRANSIT

### 1.   FILING DEADLINE

Asylum applicants must file their claims within one year of their arrival in the United States. INA § 208(a)(2)(B). Applications may be filed later only if there are changed circumstances that materially affect the asylum seeker's eligibility for asylum or if there are extraordinary circumstances that are related to the delay. INA § 208(a)(2)(D). The regulations spell out more detailed standards. 8 C.F.R. §§ 208.4(a)(4),(5); 1208.4(a)(5) (2006). They provide that physical and mental conditions may constitute "extraordinary circumstances" if they are "directly related to the failure to meet the 1-year deadline." Certain legal obstacles, such as ineffective assistance of counsel, or the possession of another temporary legal status until a reasonable period before filing, may satisfy the "extraordinary circumstances" exception. *Id.* There is no judicial review of an administrative decision that the filing fails to comply with the statutory filing provisions, INA § 208(a)(3), but a person denied by an asylum officer because of the deadline can get de novo consideration of that issue before the immigration judge, and can then appeal a deadline ruling to the BIA. Importantly, withholding of removal is not subject to any deadline requirement.

The administrative agencies appear to construe the deadline exceptions in a reasonably liberal manner. INS and DHS data for 1998 to 2004 (covering non-Mexican asylum applicants) show that asylum officers found that late filers qualified for an exception between 33 percent (2003) and 63 percent(1998) of the time. In a precedent decision, the BIA overruled an immigration judge's rejection of a late filing by a 16-year-old unaccompanied minor. The Board found that the applicant was under a legal disability (minority) during the first year of his time in the United States and acted in a timely fashion by attempting to file his claim five months after release by the INS into the custody of his uncle, thus meeting the "extraordinary circumstances" exception. *Matter of Y–C–*, 23 I & N Dec. 286 (BIA 2002).

The filing deadline has been heavily criticized in the United States since its adoption in 1996. Many refugees appear to delay filing for asylum in the hope that things will improve at home before too long and they will be able to return. Some have suffered traumatic experiences that effectively disable them. For many, the difficulty of obtaining legal assistance dissuades them from acting. The impediments of a foreign language and different cultural expectations compound the other difficulties. *See,* e.g., Pistone, *Asylum Filing Deadlines: Unfair and Unnecessary*, 10 Geo. Imm. L. J. 95 (1996), Schrag & Pistone, *The 1996 Immigration Act: Asylum Application Deadlines and Expedited Removal—What the INS Should Do*, 73 Interp. Rel. 1565 (1996). Proponents of a deadline often point to Article 31 of the 1951 Convention in support of the requirement. Does the language of that article support their case?

It is fair to note, however, that other countries have short filing deadlines. In Spain, for example, asylum seekers must file their applications within one month of entering the country. Art. 7, Implementing Decree of Law 5/1984 Regulating Refugee Status and the Right to Asylum, as Amended by Law 9/1994. In Portugal asylum seekers must apply within eight days. Art. 11 (1), Asylum Law 15/1998. The laws imposing short deadlines generally allow late applications if there are extenuating circumstances.

## 2. TRANSIT THROUGH THIRD COUNTRIES

In many instances an individual passes through intermediate countries on the way to the United States—countries to which he or she might have applied for asylum, or from which he or she might have applied for resettlement in the United States as a refugee under INA § 207. Should this be a factor in deciding whether they are eligible for protection in the United States?

Various countries in Europe have enacted provisions, frequently referred to as "safe third country" laws, that bar asylum based on proof that the applicant could have applied for asylum in another country en route. This concept has now been codified for all European Union countries under Council Directive 2005/85/EC on minimum standards on procedures in Member States for granting and withdrawing refugee status (Procedures Directive), [2005] OJ L326/13. The Procedures Directive allows EU states to refuse to examine the merits of an asylum application and instead to return the asylum seeker to the "safe" country that she traveled through before she reached the EU state where she filed her asylum application. Art. 25. The Procedures Directive sets forth preconditions that must be satisfied before a nation can be considered as a safe third country. Art. 27. For example, the safe third country must respect the *nonrefoulement* obligation of the 1951 Convention, Art. 27(1)(b), and allow the asylum seeker access to the refugee status procedure, Art. 27(1)(d). Further, there must be an individual examination of whether the third country is safe for the particular asylum seeker, Art. 27(2)(b), and there must be sufficient connection between the asylum seeker and the third country that it would be reasonable for the asylum seeker to go there, Art. 27(2)(a).

The United States enacted a limited safe third country provision in 1996. Individuals are not eligible even to apply for asylum if they "may be removed, *pursuant to a bilateral or multilateral agreement*," to a country where there is no threat to life or freedom on the protected grounds and where "the alien would have access to a full and fair procedure for determining a claim to asylum or equivalent temporary protection." INA § 208(a)(2) (emphasis added). By placing this language in § 208(a)(2), which limits those eligible to apply for asylum, Congress contemplated pretermitting the asylum claim at the earliest possible stage, if the person is covered by the specified kind of international agreement. Judicial review is precluded. INA § 208(a)(3).

After many years of on-again, off-again negotiations, the United States entered into its first such agreement with Canada in December 2002. The text of the agreement can be found at 79 Interp.Rel. 1431 (2002) and the implementing regulations were published (with an explanatory statement) at 69 Fed. Reg. 69479 (2004). Under this agreement, those who apply for asylum at a land border port of entry (not at an airport) will have their claims determined by the country in which the person was physically present immediately before claiming refugee status. In other words, those seeking asylum as they enter Canada from the United States will fall under the jurisdiction of the U.S. asylum laws, and vice versa. There are exceptions for unaccompanied minors, travelers in certain visa categories, and travelers with certain family members in the other country. Most significantly, if Canada returns an asylum applicant to the United States, the United States may not return the individual to another country which he or she had entered prior to the United States. Rather, the United States must decide the merits of the asylum claim. (The same applies in reverse if the U.S. returns an asylum applicant to Canada.)

The safe third country concept raises important policy considerations. Should the asylum seeker have the discretion to choose a country in which he or she will be able to speak the language, employ his or her skills, resettle within a familiar ethnic or linguistic community, join family members? Or should the law require an individual to seek asylum in the first country in which it is theoretically possible to do so? Is there some middle ground?

Destination countries emphasize the need to avoid forum-shopping among asylum countries, and this can be a legitimate objective. Refugee advocates emphasize the practical realities. Sometimes they question the safety—in practice, not in theory—of a country that the asylum seeker passed through. They note the ease with which a chain deportation can occur with unacceptable threats to life and freedom, if every country along the route simply returns asylum seekers to the prior stop, and the country that borders the persecuting state does not adhere in practice to the international *nonrefoulement* norms. Other times the desire to return asylum seekers to intermediate countries results in the "refugee in orbit" phenomenon: countries refuse to accept responsibility for deciding the merits of the claim and send the asylum seekers back and forth between ports of entry.

The excerpt below describes the increasing attention paid to countries that asylum seekers pass through before they apply for asylum. It outlines some of the legal and practical issues connected with this phenomenon, and argues that issues of transit through countries overlap substantially with issues of firm resettlement.

## STEPHEN H. LEGOMSKY, SECONDARY REFUGEE MOVEMENTS AND THE RETURN OF ASYLUM SEEKERS TO THIRD COUNTRIES: THE MEANING OF EFFECTIVE PROTECTION

15 Int'l. J. Ref. Law 567, 568–572 (2003).

[T]he shortest distance between a persecutor and a permanent safe haven is seldom a straight line. Perhaps it was never unusual for refugees to travel circuitous routes through several countries before reaching their intended final stops. It is certainly not unusual today.

A refugee's presence in one of these "third countries" might be a matter of hours or a matter of years. It might be legally sanctioned or irregular. The person might or might not formally request protection in the third country. If protection is requested, it might or might not be granted. If granted, protection might take any of several forms, ranging from some type of de facto stopgap protection to formal long-term residence. The person might or might not receive identity papers, or immigration papers, or travel documents. The person might be under the care of the government of the host state, or UNHCR, or an NGO, or some combination of the above, or the person might not be under anyone's care. The person might possess a single, continuing legal status or might change status along the way. He or she might enter with any number of intentions and might alter those intentions any number of times. The person might be part of a mass refugee influx or might be alone or part of a small group.

Under any of these scenarios, refugees often decide to leave the third countries and seek protection in more favorable places. Why do they do so?

In the case of people who never sought any protection from the third country, the question is often asked: "Well, why didn't they seek protection there?". There are a number of possible reasons. It might have been obvious that the other country would not grant protection. Conditions in that country might not have been hospitable or even acceptable. Possibly the person had always regarded that country as nothing more than a temporary stop or even just a point of transit, and the person had intended all along to seek protection in the ultimate destination country. Or, perhaps, the refugee recognition rates or reception arrangements or integration conditions were more favorable in the destination country.

Even when the third country actually granted some form of temporary protection, people might move on for any number of reasons. Some move for the same reasons that inspire voluntary migrants—better life opportunities for themselves and their families, including educational or employment opportunities. Or the person might have family members in the destination country, or at least an existing enclave from the person's country of origin or a community of people with similar ethnic, religious, or cultural backgrounds. Sometimes the person's status in the third country was always meant to be temporary, and the person is eager to start rebuilding his or her life in a more durable environment. In many cases, the decisions as to itinerary are in the hands of professional smugglers or traffickers, and the refugees themselves have little or no say in the matter. And, as noted below, the third countries are often developing states in which the living conditions, personal freedoms, or physical safety levels fall far short of acceptable international standards or even basic subsistence.

* * *

The premise * * * of third country restrictions is that, under certain circumstances, an asylum seeker should be somebody else's responsibility. Immigration or refugee officials in the destination country are instructed to refuse to decide such cases in substance and, instead, to return the applicants to the relevant third countries.

These cases * * * have traditionally been grouped under two headings. [Under] the so-called "safe third country" concept * * * the state rejects asylum applications filed by individuals who have traveled through countries that are generally thought to be safe and where, it is felt, the person should have requested protection. * * * The other heading, which covers people who in fact received some kind of protection in a third country, is termed "first country of asylum". The precise requirements vary.

In theory, the two concepts are quite distinct; one is for the person who merely "should" have requested protection elsewhere, while the other applies when the person "actually received" protection. A basic thesis of this article, however, is that in actual practice the two strategies occupy two points on the same continuum. * * * [T]he difference between first countries of asylum and safe third countries can best be envisioned as one of degree. In each case, the person spent some amount of time in a third country before arriving in the country where the asylum application was filed. The longer, the more meaningful, the more formal, and the more secure the person's stay in the third country, the more likely it is that the country will be described as a "first country of asylum" rather than a "safe third country".

\* \* \*

Destination countries that adopt third country return practices clearly have legitimate interests in reducing irregular migration and also in assuring that their asylum determination systems function smoothly and efficiently. The difficulty is that the returns can give rise to a host of other serious problems. Most are concerns for the asylum seekers. \* \* \*

There is, first, the problem of "orbit"—refugees who have escaped from persecution or from other trauma, only to be shuttled consecutively from one country to another. There is the more serious problem of "chain" refoulement, in which the third country in turn refoules the person to his or her persecutors in the country of origin. The third country might not have a fair refugee status determination procedure in place. The third country might not be a party to the 1951 Refugee Convention. The third country might not provide formal refugee or other lawful status or might not provide the kind of documentation that the person needs to procure the necessities of life or to travel. The protection afforded by the third country might not be durable. The third country might be unable to protect the person from discrimination, or persecution, or other human rights violations; indeed, the government of the third country might engage in those practices itself. There might be threats to the applicant's physical security or basic subsistence. The third country might practice indiscriminate or long-term detention or might otherwise inhibit essential freedom of movement. One recurring problem has been the return of asylum seekers to third countries to which they have no links or connections. There might be serious deficiencies in the procedures by which the destination country itself decides whether return is appropriate in a particular case. Finally, some of the more common destination state practices have the effect of distributing the responsibility for refugee protection inequitably, so that the obligations fall disproportionately on developing countries and on countries whose frontiers are geographically the most accessible.

\* \* \*

## Notes and Questions

1. Legomsky's article convincingly identifies deficiencies endemic in many first-asylum countries, such as refusal to supply birth certificates for refugee children, lack of educational opportunities, detention of refugees, gender discrimination, that impel some refugees to continue their journey onward. Legomsky discusses solutions to reduce both primary migration and secondary irregular migration, and he proposes a three-part plan that might induce destination countries and transit countries to work together to share responsibilities for refugees. *Id.* at 610–611. Ultimately, though, he acknowledges that there will always be efforts to return asylum seekers to other countries and he argues forcefully for a complicity principle: any state that returns a refugee to a state that violates the refugee's rights under interna-

tional law will be complicit in—and liable for—that violation of international law, so long as the returning country has knowledge of the circumstances creating the legal wrong. *Id.* at 621. Legomsky further sets forth minimum legal requirements for returning an asylum seeker to a third country. They include an express agreement that the third state will readmit the asylum seeker and provide a fair refugee status determination procedure or provide effective protection without requiring a procedure; a finding that the third country is willing and able to provide effective protection for as long as the refugee needs it; a prohibition on return if this would violate the applicant's right to family unity; and an individualized application of the standards. *Id.* at 673. Is Legomsky's prescription too idealistic? Do you think states will agree to invest so much time and energy on individual asylum seekers who stopped in other countries en route? Or do you think that the opposite might occur: will Legomsky's scheme have the effect of encouraging states to accept asylum seekers into their procedure rather than engaging in a complicated analysis of whether there is a safe third country for each particular asylum seeker?

2. The U.S. statute requires a pre-existing agreement with a country that will allow a full and fair asylum procedure. The U.S.–Canada Agreement forbids the country exercising jurisdiction over the claim from returning the applicant to another country to decide the asylum application. These elements go somewhat beyond the protections ordinarily accorded in other countries when they rely on the "safe third country" principle. Would the U.S. protections be sufficient under Legomsky's view? If not, what additional protections would make this third-country restriction sound?

3. Refugee advocates on both sides of the border have generally been highly critical of the U.S.–Canada agreement. *See* Macklin, *Disappearing Refugees: Reflections on the Canada–U.S. Safe Third Country Agreement*, 36 Colum. Hum. Rts. L. Rev. 101 (2005); Frelick, *North America Considers Agreement to Deflect Asylum Seekers*, 7 Bender Immigration Bulletin 1404 (2002); 79 Interp.Rel. 1077, 1431, 1570 (2002); Cutler, *The U.S.-Canada Safe Third Country Agreement: Slamming the Door on Refugees*, 11 I.L.S.A. J, Int'l & Comp L. 121 (2004). *See also* 82 Interp.Rel. 229 (discusses and reproduces Chief Immigration Judge Creppy's memorandum explaining how to adjudicate cases governed by the agreement).

4. Contrasting assessments of the European arrangements that pioneered the safe third country principle can be found in Hurwitz, *The 1990 Dublin Convention: A Comprehensive Assessment*, 11 Int'l J. Refugee L. 646 (1999); Hathaway, *Harmonizing for Whom? The Devaluation of Refugee Protection in the Era of European Economic Integration*, 26 Cornell Int'l L.J. 719 (1993); Neuman, *Buffer Zones Against Refugees: Dublin, Schengen, and The German Asylum Amendment,* 33 Va.J.Int'l L. 503 (1993); Hailbronner, *Perspectives of a Harmonization of the Law of Asylum after the Maastricht Summit,* 29 Common Mkt.L.Rev. 917 (1992). Additional commentary on related European developments can be found in Byrne & Shacknove, *The Safe Country Notion in European Asylum Law*, 9 Harv. H. Rts. J. 195 (1996) and in New Asylum Countries? Migration Control and Refugee Protection in an Enlarged European Union (R. Byrne, G. Noll, and J. Vested–Hansen eds., 2002).

5. The EU Procedures Directive mentioned at the beginning of this section refers to both safe third countries and first countries of asylum, Art. 25(2), and permits states to reject applicants for either of these reasons. Rejection based on first country of asylum grounds can only occur if the "first country" has recognized the individual as a refugee or "otherwise [provides] sufficient protection," including *nonrefoulement*. Art. 26.

## 3. FIRM RESETTLEMENT

Those who are firmly resettled in another country are excluded from protection in the United States. This applies both to those who apply for asylum in the United States and those who apply overseas for the U.S. refugee resettlement program that will be discussed in Chapter Ten. Initially a factor bearing on the exercise of asylum discretion, *see generally Rosenberg v. Yee Chien Woo*, 402 U.S. 49, 91 S.Ct. 1312, 28 L.Ed.2d 592 (1971), firm resettlement became a mandatory ground for denial of asylum under regulations adopted in 1990. The 1996 Act then incorporated the preclusion directly into the statute. Persons who have been firmly resettled are now flatly ineligible for asylum. INA § 208(b)(2)(A)(vi). Withholding is not barred in the case of firm resettlement, but recall that withholding is country-specific. A grant of withholding would not prevent sending the asylum seeker back to the third country—if that country will still accept her. If not, she is likely to remain in the United States, but withholding generally results only in limited status protections. As you may remember from Chapter Two, Section B, withholding allows work authorization and access to some public assistance programs, but no family reunification rights and no clear path to LPR status, no matter how long she remains here.

The concept of firm resettlement is defined in 8 C.F.R. § 208.15:

> An alien is considered to be firmly resettled if, prior to arrival in the United States, he or she entered into another nation with, or while in that nation received, an offer of permanent resident status, citizenship, or some other type of permanent resettlement * * *.

But the regulation goes on to provide that a finding of firm resettlement can be overcome if the applicant shows either that "entry into that nation was a necessary consequence of his or her flight from persecution, that he or she remained in that nation only as long as was necessary to arrange onward travel, and that he or she did not establish significant ties in that nation;" or that "the conditions of his or her residence in that nation were so substantially and consciously restricted by the authority of the country of refuge that he or she was not in fact resettled." The regulation then lists factors to consider in making the second determination.

The BIA opinion below interpreted the firm resettlement concept in 1989, when this doctrine was still a discretionary factor in the asylum decision. It provides a useful glimpse into evaluations concerning temporary residence and significant ties in other countries.

# MATTER OF SOLEIMANI

Board of Immigration Appeals, 1989.
20 I & N Dec. 99.

MILHOLLAN, CHAIRMAN:

The respondent is a 34-year-old native and citizen of Iran. Evidence included in the record establishes that she is Jewish. In various affidavits and statements, as well as her testimony at her deportation hearing, she related that she fled Iran on October 23, 1981, with her mother and brother, traveling over the mountains to Pakistan without a visa, where they later obtained a visa to remain in Pakistan temporarily until November 4, 1981. According to the respondent, after staying 5 days in Pakistan, she and her family flew to Athens, Greece, without visas and, being unsuccessful in obtaining visas there, subsequently flew to Rome, Italy, again without visas. From there, after 2 or 3 days, they flew to Israel without visas in November 1981, where she remained until September 15, 1982. The record also includes the respondent's Iranian passport but does not document the type of visa or status the respondent had during her stay in Israel.

According to the respondent, she obtained a visa as a visitor for pleasure while in Israel, initially intending to remain with her family in Israel only until the situation in Iran improved. In her affidavits, statements, and hearing testimony, she related that she never worked or owned property in Israel and was never directly offered Israeli citizenship, permanent resettlement, or resident status in Israel. She also reported that she had developed pneumonia during her travels and was sick and under a physician's care for months of her stay in Israel. The respondent was hospitalized there due to her illness. She reportedly lived with her grandmother while in Israel, apparently paying rent. Observing that she had visited Israel seven different times in the past, she related that she had gone to school to study Hebrew during her last stay in Israel but had never received any financial assistance for any reason from the Israeli Government, as she had relied on her brothers and her own funds for support.

While in Israel, the respondent was issued a nonimmigrant visitor for pleasure visa by the American consulate on June 10, 1982, with which she entered the United States on September 16, 1982, with her Iranian passport. She was authorized to remain until December 16, 1982, and on November 22, 1982, applied for asylum with the district director. The district director denied the application on November 1, 1984. Deportation proceedings were instituted on March 1, 1985.

The respondent has reported that she initially obtained the nonimmigrant visitor's visa and came to the United States in order to attend a family wedding and to visit her three brothers. According to the respondent, she remained in the United States for several months visiting family and friends and then filed her application for asylum, as she was still unable to return safely to Iran and had no other home. She observed that she had not expected the regime in Iran to remain in power as long as it had and, for this reason, had also not sought asylum in Israel previously. The respondent related that her three brothers, her mother, her sister, and a nephew were in the United States, and that her only remaining family in Israel was her grandmother. According to the respondent's asylum application, one brother was a student, while her other brothers, as well as her mother and sister, were also asylum applicants.

In conjunction with the respondent's initial asylum application, the district director requested and obtained an advisory opinion from the United States Department of State's Bureau of Human Rights and Humanitarian Affairs ("BHRHA"). In the advisory opinion, dated October 26, 1984, the BHRHA expressed its view that the respondent, if a member of the Jewish faith, had a well-founded fear of persecution if returned to Iran. However, it also concluded that in view of Israel's Law of Return, which entitled the respondent as a member of the Jewish faith to reside permanently and enjoy the rights of citizenship in Israel, it was probable that she was offered resident status, citizenship, or some other type of permanent resettlement. It appeared to the BHRHA that the respondent had become firmly resettled in Israel and was therefore ineligible for asylum * * *.

Following the deportation hearing, the immigration judge concluded in his decision that the respondent, as an Iranian Jew, would be persecuted if returned to her native country, and he accordingly granted her application for withholding of deportation to Iran. However, he also denied her asylum application, concluding that she was ineligible due to her firm resettlement in Israel, in that she could have become a resident of Israel and by her own choosing decided not to do so. The respondent contends on appeal that she had not become firmly resettled in Israel.

* * *

* * * [T]he immigration judge concluded that the respondent had been "offered" permanent resettlement under Israel's Law of Return, and that her choosing not to become a resident did not obviate the fact of her firm resettlement. However, there is nothing in the record, beyond the BHRHA's perfunctory reference to its existence, documenting the nature and purpose of Israel's Law of Return or the specific provisions of that law. Absent any such documentation, the Board cannot find that the respondent had been offered permanent resettlement in Israel within the meaning of the firm resettlement concept. There exists no evidence that the respondent would be eligible for an offer of resettlement under any such law and no evidence regarding the extent of any restrictions or conditions that may be placed on offers of resettlement, under that law. Foreign law is a matter to be proven by the party seeking to rely on it, and the Immigration and Naturalization Service has submitted nothing of record regarding Israel's Law of Return.

Moreover, whether or not an outstanding offer of permanent residence or citizenship to all Jews who arrive in Israel constitutes a specific offer of permanent resettlement to the respondent herself, the pertinent regulations and the Board's prior decisions cannot be read so restrictively that the respondent's circumstances in Israel become irrelevant. An alien will not be found to be firmly resettled elsewhere if it is shown that his physical presence in the United States is a consequence of his flight in search of refuge, and that his physical presence is reasonably proximate to the flight and not one following a flight remote in point of time or interrupted by an intervening residence in a third country reasonably constituting a termination of the original flight in search of refuge. The question of resettlement is not always limited solely to the inquiry of how much time has elapsed between the alien's flight and the asylum application. Other factors germane to the question of whether the alien has firmly resettled include family ties, intent, business or property connections, and other matters.

As a preliminary matter, the Board concludes that, at the time the respondent first arrived in Israel in November 1981, she was then fleeing persecution, having escaped Iran by fleeing over the mountains into Pakistan. The respondent herself has stated that she and her family had left Iran due to the political situation there. The fact that she may have had some hope that circumstances there would improve so as to allow her to return does not change the fact that she had fled on account of persecution or a fear of persecution.

However, the record demonstrates that her intervening residence in Israel before applying for asylum in the United States did not reasonably constitute a termination of her original flight in search of refuge. Her later physical presence in the United States remained reasonably proximate to her flight. In this regard, the Board points out that the respondent took no active steps demonstrating that she had firmly resettled in Israel or had an intent to do so. She remained there only 10 months, and during this time lived with her grandmother, recuperating from her illness and attending school in order to study Hebrew. Her attending school in itself does not demonstrate firm resettlement. Additionally, she neither worked nor sought employment in Israel. She did not seek any financial or other benefits from the Israeli authorities. The respondent has also testified, and the Service has not contested, that she only received a nonimmigrant visitor's visa in Israel and never sought a more permanent status or the benefits accruing from a more permanent status during her stay in Israel. Although she does have permanent family in that country, this consists solely of her grandmother, while the remainder of her family lives in the United States. Given these circumstances, the Board concludes that the respondent had not firmly resettled in Israel or any other country prior to her application for asylum in the United States.

\* \* \*

[The BIA granted the asylum application in the exercise of discretion.]

### Notes and Questions

1. Look back at the regulation that precedes the *Soleimani* opinion to ascertain whether the mere offer of resettlement, without more, is sufficient to conclude that an individual is firmly resettled. How did the Board in this case assess the offer of resettlement available to Soleimani?

2. One could characterize *Soleimani* as a case in which the government lacked sufficient proof of another country's law and practice. What more evidence did the Board think was necessary? If in future cases the government introduces proof that Israeli law offers permanent resettlement to all Jews, does this mean that any Jew who passes through Israel en route to the United States will be statutorily ineligible for asylum? Would such a conclusion be objectionable? Why should the United States provide asylum to someone who had full access to citizenship (as appears to be the case under Israel's Law of Return) in a democratic country and who actually lived there for 10 months before ever coming to the United States? Does the Convention provide a free choice of asylum location for those who meet the refugee definition? Should it?

3. Should the focus of the firm resettlement exclusion be on the termination of the asylum seeker's flight at an earlier time or on the legal protections afforded the asylum seeker? Which does the BIA emphasize? Are they inconsistent rationales?

4. In examining what policy underlies the wording of the firm resettlement regulation, it may be helpful to look to an analogous provision in the 1951 Convention. Article 1(E) excludes from refugee status those resettled in another country if the government authorities grant them "the rights and obligations which are attached to the possession of the nationality of that country." Is U.S. law consistent with this exclusion?

5. For additional decisions evaluating the firm resettlement exclusion, *compare Abdille v. Ashcroft*, 242 F.3d 477 (3d Cir.2001) (INS must establish an offer of permanent resettlement) *with Cheo v. INS*, 162 F.3d 1227 (9th Cir.1998) (three years of peaceful residence in Malaysia supports a rebuttable presumption of firm resettlement).

## SECTION B.   EXCLUSION FROM PROTECTION: PERSECUTORS, SERIOUS CRIMINALS, AND SECURITY DANGERS

The U.S. statute contains several broad exceptions or preclusions to asylum and withholding because of serious criminal behavior by the applicant—exceptions that would override a grant of protection even if she proves a risk of persecution that otherwise meets the standards. When Congress adopted the first list of exceptions in the Refugee Act of 1980, the legislative history signaled that these were to be interpreted consistently with exceptions that apply under the refugee treaties. Nonetheless, the language of the statutory exclusions sometimes departs markedly from the Convention. Moreover, Congress has seen fit to expand the list of exclusions to asylum on several occasions over the past twenty years. Some factors that used to be simply negative considerations in the exercise of discretion under § 208 have now been made firm statutory bars to protection.

U.S. practice usually treats these statutory exclusions as a threshold issue when they arise in immigration court. If an exclusion applies, the immigration judge generally will not schedule a hearing on the merits of the claim. If the case can be resolved by reviewing a certified copy of a criminal conviction serious enough to bar asylum and withholding, for example, there will be no need to prolong the matter and receive extensive evidence on the threatened persecution. Accordingly, efficiency supports addressing criminal conduct and other matters that preclude asylum and withholding first.

As we will see below, however, the UNHCR and a number of commentators have maintained that the exclusions based on criminal conduct require a balancing test, weighing the seriousness of the crime against the gravity of the persecution that the individual would face on return. This, of course, would required a full evidentiary hearing on the persecution issue in every case. The United States has resisted this approach. Currently, though, the practical implications of categorizing the exclusions as a threshold issue have diminished. Immigration judges now review together an applicant's claim for protection under asylum, withholding, and the Convention Against Torture, and criminal conduct does not constitute an exclusion from CAT.

## 1. PERSECUTORS

The U.S. statute defining a refugee includes an express bar of "any person who ordered, incited, assisted, or otherwise participated in the persecution of any person on account of race, religion, nationality, membership in a particular social group, or political opinion." INA § 101(a)(42). Because this provision is included in the refugee definition, it applies to those seeking resettlement through the overseas refugee program and to those within the United States seeking asylum or withholding, both of which are predicated on satisfying the refugee definition. Congress apparently did not want there to be any ambiguity, and added statutory provisions specifying that persons who assisted in persecuting others must be excluded from asylum, INA § 208(b)(2)(A)(i), and withholding of removal. INA § 241(b)(3)(B)(i).

The exclusion of persons who participated or assisted in persecution is written in very broad terms. This reflects its provenance, for the language mirrors the language of former § 241(a)(19), now § 237(a)(4)(D), a particularly strict provision directed at those who aided Nazi persecution in Germany in the 1930s and 1940s. As those provisions have been interpreted by the BIA, they provide for the removal of such persons, even if they assisted the persecution involuntarily or under duress. *See Matter of Fedorenko,* 19 I & N Dec. 57 (BIA 1984); *Matter of*

Laipenieks, *18 I & N Dec. 433 (BIA 1983).* Cf. *Fedorenko v. United States, 449 U.S. 490, 101 S.Ct. 737, 66 L.Ed.2d 686 (1981) (denaturalization case). But the Board's holding in* Laipenieks *was reversed, based on a holding that "active personal involvement in persecutorial acts needs to be demonstrated" for a finding of deportability under this provision.* Laipenieks v. INS, *750 F.2d 1427 (9th Cir.1985).* See generally *Creppy, Nazi War Criminals in Immigration Law, 12 Geo. Immigr. L.J. 443 (1998).*

Some have questioned whether the BIA's harsh construction, however appropriate it might have been for those who collaborated with the Nazis 65 years ago, should continue to govern the persecutor exception to asylum and withholding of removal. The BIA faced this question in a case that arose in the civil war in El Salvador.

## MATTER OF RODRIGUEZ–MAJANO

Board of Immigration Appeals, 1988.
19 I & N Dec. 811.

MILHOLLAN, CHAIRMAN:

* * *

The respondent is a 23-year-old native and citizen of El Salvador who * * * has conceded deportability. * * * The immigration judge found that the respondent was ineligible for [asylum and withholding of deportation] because he had engaged in the persecution of others. * * * The respondent contends that his activities did not constitute persecution or assistance in persecution * * *.

The respondent testified that he worked for his father, a cattle businessman, in 1983 in San Miguel, El Salvador. He drove a truck from San Miguel to his father's store in Santa Inez a short distance away. He reported that he was stopped many times by guerrillas on the road. They demanded that he carry merchandise for them in order to be allowed to pass. In this way he became acquainted with the guerrillas in his area. At about the same time, the respondent's uncle and his cousin were kidnapped from their homes in San Miguel by armed men and were killed along with five other men in the town. It was reported they were killed by army security forces because they were guerrillas.

The respondent stated that he was seized in May 1983 by the police and questioned about collaborating with the guerrillas. The chief of police released him because he knew the respondent's father, but he told the respondent to report to the police on the guerrillas' whereabouts. In June 1983, the guerrillas commandeered the respondent and several of his father's trucks, and he drove supplies to San Miguel for a battle with the government forces which lasted a day and a half. He also transported the guerrillas out of the city. The respondent was stopped at a roadblock on his return and was questioned about his activities by the military. He admitted to them he had been forced to help the guerrillas. He was released but he was threatened with death if he helped the guerrillas again. In September, the respondent was taken from his home by the guerrillas, who had acquired a new leader. He alleges he was forced to join them. He was taken to their training camp where he was given military training. He accompanied guerrillas on propaganda trips and once covered them with his weapon while they burned cars.

The respondent reported that he deserted the guerrillas after 2 months.

\* \* \*

The respondent argues \* \* \* that the immigration judge incorrectly found that the respondent had engaged in the persecution of others rendering him ineligible for asylum and prohibited from obtaining withholding of deportation. \* \* \* In particular, the respondent argues that, where there is open combat, acts of warfare taken in furtherance of political goals are not persecutory acts. Further, the respondent argues he was never an established member of the guerrilla organization, and, therefore, cannot be held accountable for the actions of the organization. The Service agreed at oral argument that the respondent's actions do not constitute participation in persecution so as to disqualify him from relief. However, the Service argued that the immigration judge, in effect, found that the respondent lacked credibility \* \* \*.

The participation or assistance of an alien in persecution need not be of his own volition to bar him from relief. See *Fedorenko v. United States*, 449 U.S. 490 (1981). However, mere membership in an organization, even one which engages in persecution, is not sufficient to bar one from relief, but only if one's action or inaction furthers that persecution in some way. It is the objective effect of an alien's actions which is controlling. *Laipenieks v. INS*, 750 F.2d 1427, 1435 (9th Cir. 1985) \* \* \*.

\* \* \* We find that the immigration judge in this case gave too expansive a definition to the statutory term "persecution." \* \* \*

The argument was made by respondent's counsel that activities directly related to a civil war are not persecution. We agree. By this statement we mean that harm which may result incidentally from behavior directed at another goal, the overthrow of a government or, alternatively, the defense of that government against an opponent, is not persecution. In analyzing a claim of persecution in the context of a civil war, one must examine the motivation of the group threatening harm. \* \* \* Thus, the drafting of youths as soldiers, the unofficial recruiting of soldiers by force, the disciplining of members of a rebel group, or the prosecution of draft dodgers are necessary means of achieving a political goal, but they are not forms of persecution directed at someone on account of one of the five categories enumerated in section 101(a)(42)(A) of the Act. See e.g., *Rodriguez–Rivera v. United States*, INS, No. 87–7140 (9th Cir. June 7, 1988) \* \* \*. We would include in this list the engaging in military actions, the attacking of garrisons, the burning of cars, and the destruction of other property as actions outside the limits of the term "persecution."

\* \* \*

Were we to hold that practices such as attacking military bases, destroying property, or forcible recruiting constitute persecution, members of armed opposition groups throughout the world would be barred from seeking haven in this country. As the concept of what constitutes persecution expands, the group which is barred from seeking haven in this country also expands, so that eventually all resistance fighters would be excluded from relief. We do not believe Congress intended to restrict asylum and withholding only to those who had taken no part in armed conflict. Regardless of whether the respondent aided the guerrillas voluntarily or not, the only harm or injury he may have inflicted arose as the natural consequence of civil strife. Harm resulting from generalized civil strife is not persecution.

\* \* \*

[The BIA remanded for consideration of the availability of protection under the asylum statute and the withholding provision.]

### Notes and Questions

1. The Board adopted much of the strong doctrine of the Nazi cases, but did not consider Rodriguez–Majano a persecutor precluded from asylum. What was the BIA's rationale? What impact is this approach likely to have on future case law interpreting the statutory bars against persecutors?

2. In *Ofosu v. McElroy,* 933 F.Supp. 237, 239 (S.D.N.Y.1995), the alien had been a senior official in the Committee for the Defense of the Revolution (CDR), an elite security force in Ghana under the Rawlings regime. He participated for years in spying and numerous arrests, with knowledge that many thus arrested were then imprisoned and even tortured, without trial. He claimed that he eventually became disillusioned with the CDR and the regime, disobeyed orders to arrest certain demonstrators, and then left the country. The district court upheld the BIA's finding that he was personally and actively involved in persecution and therefore precluded from asylum and withholding. "The petitioner, after some years of employment as a persecutor, now abjures that career choice. However commendable his conversion, Congress did not enact an exception \* \* \* which absolves a persecutor of his past on account of a belated crisis of conscience." The court of appeals was not so sure. Ruling on a preliminary stay motion, the court thought the BIA's holding debatable. "[I]n none of the cases relating to involvement in persecution did it appear that one who assisted or participated in any degree ultimately rejected the repressive activities in which he was involved, or put himself at risk in order to protect those who were persecuted." 98 F.3d 694, 701 (2d Cir.1996). The opinion did not reach the merits. Should the clause prohibiting asylum for those who assisted in persecution be read to allow asylum for Ofosu? (Later proceedings in the *Ofosu* case, if any, are not reported.) How do you compare *Rodriguez–Majano* with *Ofosu*? With *Dwomoh v. Sava,* discussed in Chapter Three, Section A, which

awarded asylum to an asylum seeker who fled Ghana after a failed coup attempt against the Rawlings government which itself came to power in a coup?

3.   Conscription often poses difficult issues about the nature of persecution and the need for protection. How does *Rodriguez–Majano* compare with the conscientious objection cases in Chapter Three, Section A? If Rodriguez–Majano had escaped from El Salvador before the guerrillas forced him to accompany them, had reached the United States and claimed fear of persecution by the guerrillas (or the army), would he have been eligible for asylum and/or withholding?

4.   In *Miranda Alvarado v. Gonzales*, 449 F.3d 915 (9th Cir. 2006), *cert. denied*, 127 S.Ct. 505 (2006), the Ninth Circuit sustained the exclusion from protection of a Peruvian who fled death threats from the Shining Path. Miranda had joined the Civil Guard at age 19 and served as an interpreter during interrogations of Shining Path guerrillas. He conceded that he had been present during the questioning, which included electric shock torture, but stated he had never participated in the torture and had frequently asked the interrogators to stop. The court distinguished *Rodriguez–Majano*, saying that Miranda had not established that the interrogations involving torture were in direct response to terrorist acts or civil strife. Because Miranda was not in a position of authority and used no force during the interrogations, the court considered him "at the margin of the culpability required under the statute" but concluded that his actions as an interpreter were crucial to the interrogations and were sufficient evidence that he had assisted in the persecution of others.

5.   How would Rodriguez–Majano fare in the post-September 11 United States? After the terrorist attacks on that day, Congress adopted changes to the exclusion provisions that, as construed by the executive branch, apply a sweeping exclusion to virtually anyone who has provided "material support" to terrorist activity (which itself is very broadly defined). We will consider these new provisions later in this section.

## A Comparative Perspective

Other nations often expressly rely on Article 1(F) of the 1951 Convention when assessing applicants who admit they participated in the persecution of others. Before you read the following Australian case, look at the U.S. statutory provisions that exclude individuals, including those with a well-founded fear of persecution, from asylum based on their prior conduct, INA § 208 (b)(2)(A)(i–vi), and compare them with the exclusions contained in Article 1(F):

> The provisions of this Convention shall not apply to any person with respect to whom there are serious reasons for considering that:
>
> (a) he has committed a crime against peace, a war crime, or a crime against humanity, as defined in the international instruments drawn up to make provision in respect of such crimes;

(b) he has committed a serious nonpolitical crime outside the country of refuge prior to his admission to that country as a refugee;

(c) he has been guilty of acts contrary to the purposes and principles of the United Nations.

## REFUGEE REVIEW TRIBUNAL REFERENCE N96/12101

Sydney, Australia, 25 November 1996.

LAYTON, TRIBUNAL MEMBER:

[The tribunal's opinion included the personal statement of the applicant, a young man forcibly recruited by one of the warring factions in Liberia. The key excerpt is set forth at the beginning of this chapter.]

\* \* \*

The Applicant was a member of the NPFL [National Patriotic Front of Liberia—eds.], which is a rebel group operating in Liberia. There was 'flagrant disregard for human rights by the 40,000 to 60,000 fighters in the major factions' and 'high levels of atrocities' committed by the rebel groups, including the NPFL, in Liberia. In the course of a raid on his village, he was forcibly conscripted into, and kept in, the NPFL; while a member of the group, before he was able to escape, he went on about six raids to villages. These raids were essentially against civilians, albeit the NPFL accused some of supporting a rival rebel group. In the course of these raids, and, as part of the NPLF, he shot at people's legs and hands, rather than, as others did, aiming to kill. Accordingly, his participation in the group raises the question of whether he is excluded from claiming protection under the Convention under Article 1F.

\* \* \*

ARTICLE 1F(a)

\* \* \*

[The court quoted Guy Goodwin–Gill, The Refugee in International Law 98–99 (2d ed. 1996)]:

Just as the International Military Tribunal succeeded to an existing body of law, so Article 1F(a) today must be interpreted in the light of more recent developments, and the "relevant international instruments" referred to have been considerably supplemented since 1951. The principles of the IMT Charter have been strengthened by the 1949 Geneva Conventions and the 1977 Additional Protocols. "War crimes" are thus considered to include "grave breaches" of the Geneva Conventions, summarized to include any of the following acts: wilful killing; torture [or] inhuman treatment, including biological experiments; wilfully causing great suffering or serious injury to body or health; extensive destruction and appropriation of property, not justified by military necessity and carried out unlawfully and wantonly; compelling a prisoner of war or a civilian to serve in the forces of a hostile power; wilfully depriving a prisoner of war or a civilian or [sic] the rights of fair and regular trial; unlawful deportation or transfer or unlawful confinement of a civilian; and taking civilians as hostages.

Additional Protocol I also includes attack on or indiscriminate attack affecting the civilian population; attack on those known to be hors de combat; population transfers; practices of apartheid and other inhuman and degrading practices involving outrages on personal dignity based on racial discrimination; and attacking non-defended localities and demilitarized zones * * *.

Crimes against humanity * * * are akin to war crimes, save on a larger scale * * *. The Statutes for the tribunals on Yugoslavia and Rwanda each provide for jurisdiction with respect to crimes against humanity, defined to include murder, extermination, enslavement, deportation, imprisonment, torture, rape, persecutions on political, racial and religious grounds, and other inhumane acts.

\* \* \*

### ARTICLE 1F(b)

In relation to 'serious non-political crime,' Goodwin–Gill states that,

The standard finally to be applied is an international standard * * *. Each case will require examination on its merits, with regard paid to both mitigating and aggravating factors, and to the level of individual responsibility * * *. A person with a well-founded fear of very severe persecution, such as would endanger life or freedom, should only be excluded for the most serious reasons * * *.

With a view to promoting consistent decisions, UNHCR proposed that, in the absence of any political factors, a presumption of serious crime might be considered as raised by evidence of commission of any of the following offences: homicide, rape, child molesting, wounding, arson, drugs trafficking, and armed robbery. However, that presumption should be capable of rebuttal by evidence of mitigating factors * * * [including] [that the–eds.] offender was merely an accomplice; other circumstances surrounding commission of the offence (for example, provocation and self-defence).

\* \* \*

### ARTICLE 1F(c)

Goodwin–Gill * * * states,

In summary, article 1F(c) will generally exclude high officials of State responsible for the implementation of policies that violate human rights or are otherwise contrary to the purposes and principles of the United Nations. In appropriate circumstances, however, it also applies to individuals at some remove from political responsibility, who are party to human rights violations, either individually, or as members of organizations engaged in such activities. * * *

\* \* \*

### TRIBUNAL'S CONCLUSION AS TO WHETHER THE APPLICANT IS EXCLUDED UNDER ARTICLE 1F

In summary, the act of shooting, as part of an attack by a rebel group on a civilian village may exclude an applicant under all three clauses in Article 1F.

Liberia is in a state of civil war. There are various rebel factions, including the NPFL which engage in crimes against humanity and crimes against the principles and purposes of the United Nations.

Attacking a civilian village, albeit that some of the targets in the village are alleged to be supporters of rival factions, can be termed not only a crime against humanity, but also a 'serious non-political crime' and an act contrary to the purposes and principles of the United Nations. After considering the material above, the Tribunal finds that shooting civilians, even if not to kill, as part of a rebel group, could fall within the ambits of any of the categories of Article 1F.

### RESPONSIBILITY AND DEFENCES

Exclusion under Article 1F must be considered in the light of all the circumstances, including the purposes of the Refugees' Convention. In this case, the Applicant was himself a victim of a crime against humanity, in that he was a civilian in a village attacked by rebels, was forcibly conscripted by the rebels, and was incarcerated by them without fair trial on the charge of attempting to kill their leader. The Applicant alleged that he was present at NPFL raids where people were killed, but that he himself shot not to kill. He was a member of the NPFL not because of his political beliefs, but rather, because he and his brother were forcibly made to join the NPFL in the course of a raid on their village, in which, it was clear from the shooting of others, resistance would be fatal. The Applicant shot at people, because his alternative was to be shot by other NPFL members. He was not in a position of authority in the NPFL. He escaped the NPFL when he had the opportunity to do so. He attempted to lessen the impact of the orders to kill by shooting in a manner to avoid killing anyone. The Tribunal has found his claims plausible and credible.

\* \* \*

### RESPONSIBILITY AND DEFENCES—THE TRIBUNAL'S CONCLUSIONS:

After applying that law to the facts, the Tribunal finds that the acts charged were done to avoid an immediate danger both serious and irreparable, the Applicant had no other means of escape, the remedy (shooting not to kill) was not disproportionate to the evil (being killed by leaders of the group for not participating). Therefore the defence of duress is made out, and the Applicant is not excluded under Article 1F(a) due to commission of a crime against humanity.

The Tribunal finds that the defence of duress is equally applicable to the question of responsibility for a serious non-political crime and acts contrary to the purposes and principles of the United Nations. The Tribunal applies the same reasoning as set out above, and finds that the Applicant has a defence of duress to Article 1F(b) and Article 1F(c) of the Convention as well.

After consideration of all the facts, including the forced conscription of the Applicant, the likely consequences to the Applicant if he had shown resistance to NPL [sic] orders, and his attempts to at least lessen the harm the Applicant caused to others, the Tribunal finds that the Applicant is not excluded, under Article 1F, from seeking the protection of the Convention.

[The tribunal ruled that the 1951 Convention obliged Australia to afford protection to the applicant.]

### Notes and Questions

1. According to the Australian tribunal, what specific acts constituted a serious nonpolitical crime? The UNHCR Handbook on Procedures and Criteria for Determining Refugee Status suggests that a serious nonpolitical crime must be a capital crime or a very grave offense. ¶ 155. In addition, the Handbook proposes a balancing test: "If a person has well-founded fear of very severe persecution, e.g., persecution endangering his life or freedom, a crime must be very grave in order to exclude him." *Id.* Does the text of the Exclusion Clause support such a balancing test? Did this tribunal effectively employ a balancing test? If not, how would you characterize the tribunal's approach?

2. Under the reasoning of the Australian tribunal, are there organizations in which membership alone is sufficient to invoke the exclusion clauses? The SS in Nazi Germany? The Khmer Rouge in Cambodia? For an opinion ruling that membership in the Chilean Department of Clandestine Operations in the 1970s was sufficient to lead to exclusion, see *Naredo v. Canada (Minister of Citizenship and Immigration)*, 192 D.L.R. 4th 373 (2000).

3. The extended civil war in El Salvador during the 1980s and 1990s gave rise to asylum claims by participants on both sides of the conflict and to charges that atrocities committed by both sides excluded the soldiers from protection. In *Moreno v. Canada (Minister of Employment & Immigration)*, 107 D.L.R. 4th 424 (1993), a Canadian court considered whether a 16 year old army conscript was excluded from refugee status due to his membership in military forces that treated civilians inhumanely and due to his participation as a guard in the torture of a prisoner. The court ruled that mere membership in an organization involved in war crimes is an insufficient basis for triggering the exclusion clause and that passive acquiescence in torture is also insufficient.

In contrast, the court in *Ramirez v. Canada (Minister of Employment and Immigration)*, 89 D.L.R. 4th 173 (1992) concluded that a 17 year old Salvadoran who enlisted in the army and re-enlisted for a second term was excluded from protection. In the latter case the asylum applicant had deserted after 33 months, and had witnessed multiple tortures, executions, and military engagements.

4.  On a related note, news headlines about the presence of armed combatants in refugee camps in Central and West Africa in the 1990s highlighted the grave practical problems involved when human rights abusers are not excluded from refugee protection. A report on UNHCR attempts to establish exclusion procedures during these crises concluded that the outcome was a failure: despite major UNHCR efforts to establish procedures and exclude human rights violators, "the results were insignificant, and the decision to exclude was taken in only a handful of cases." Lawyers Committee for Human Rights, Refugees, Rebels and the Quest for Justice 48 (2002). This compounded the refugee crisis as *génocidaires* then were able to rely on the food and shelter of the refugee camps and coerce bona fide refugees into supporting them. *Id.* at 3. Ultimately, the report concluded that screening refugees for possible exclusion, especially in situations of mass influx, requires

> a huge increase in dedicated resources, including trained interviewers and investigators, forensic capacity, access to country information, witness protection programs, competent interpreters, and professionals able to advise refugees of their rights * * *. Unless this kind of infrastructure is built, the effort to distinguish genuine refugees from those who are undeserving of protection is likely to degenerate into a witch-hunt, a further spectacle of impunity, or a pretext to restrict access to refugees and diminish the protection they so desperately need.

*Id.* at 49.

5.  Although many refer to article 1(F) as "the" Exclusion Clause, the 1951 Convention contains two additional provisions that exclude certain categories of individuals who otherwise satisfy the definition from protection. Article 1(D) specifies that the Convention does not apply to refugees if they are already receiving protection or assistance from other United Nations' agencies. In essence, this means that Palestinian refugees who are aided by UNRWA, the United Nations Relief Works Agency, are ineligible for refugee status. Article 1(E) excludes from refugee status those accorded citizenship rights by the authorities of the country in which they reside. In contrast to Articles 1(D) and 1(E), in which the individuals are excluded from refugee status based on the availability to them of an alternate avenue of protection, the bar to refugee status found in Article 1(F) corresponds to a sense that certain people are not worthy of protection as refugees due to their past reprehensible conduct. In addition, as we discuss below, Article 33(2) excludes from *nonrefoulement*, the Convention's central protection, those refugees "whom there are reasonable grounds for regarding as a danger to the security of the [haven] country" or who have been convicted of particularly serious crimes.

6. For a thorough treatment of the international law and practice governing these matters, see *Exclusion from Protection*, 12 Int'l J. Refugee L., supplement 1 (special issue) (July 2000). *See also* The European Council on Refugees and Exiles, *Position on Exclusion from Refugee Status*, 16 Int'l J. Refugee Law 257; UNHCR, *Background Note on the Application of the Exclusion Clauses*, 15 Int'l J Refugee Law 502 (2003).

## 2. CHILD SOLDIERS

Child soldiers in Sierra Leone. (Photo: Sebastian Bolesch/DFA/Still Pictures)

A series of brutal insurgencies and civil wars in the last decades of the twentieth century were marked by large-scale conscription of children by warlords and rebel groups. These gave rise to a growing number of asylum claims filed by former child soldiers, who frequently recounted harrowing tales of persecution and torture they endured, as well as persecution and torture they were forced to inflict on others. Below is a chilling account of the forced recruitment of a six year old child.

## DON STEINBERG, HIS LIVING NIGHTMARE

The Philadelphia Inquirer, Aug. 4, 2006, at A 1.

It is impossible to imagine the nightmares that burn in the mind of 27-year-old Kassim Ouma, memories that smolder and crackle like hot coals, forever threatening to burst into flames. The fact that he will fight a must-win boxing match tomorrow night at Madison Square Garden against a dangerous, undefeated opponent has nothing to do with it. The fight is almost a welcome distraction from thoughts of the childhood in Africa that he escaped.

\* \* \*

In the weeks before a fight, Ouma doesn't like to talk about his past, his manager Tom Moran says quietly away from the ring. It upsets him too much. He loses sleep, loses focus, his training suffers.

"It was 1984, when they kidnapped him, so that would have made him 6 years old," Moran says. In Kiboga, Uganda, a village outside of Kampala, armed soldiers of Yoweri Museveni's rebel army took Ouma and his classmates from their school. The rebels put the children into a garbage truck and hauled them away, then enslaved them as soldiers in a bloody civil war.

The first day, Ouma has told Moran, the captors told the children, " 'There's no mommies and there's no daddies now,' " Moran said. "They said, 'If you cry, something's going to happen to you.' He woke up the next morning to see many of his classmates dead."

A United Nations special adviser has called the abduction, enslavement and torture of thousands of children in Uganda "the world's most neglected humanitarian crisis." Over the last two decades, the violent leaders there have changed, but the tactics have not.

Ouma was made a child soldier, or *kadogo* ("little one" in Swahili), by Museveni's National Resistance Army. Museveni deposed president Milton Obote in 1985, and Kassim became a member of the national army, eventually escaping. During the last 19 years, a group called the Lord's Resistance Army has waged an insurgent campaign to oust Museveni, also abusing children in horrific ways, according to many reports.

The 2006 documentary *Uganda Rising* illuminates how abductors expose abducted children to violent death immediately to terrify and desensitize them. In the film, a 17-year-old escapee named Charles tells that newly abducted boys were given instructions on handling rifles.

"After that," Charles says in the film, "they said we should start shooting at one another. They lined us up 10 people on one side and 10 on the other side * * *. After the shooting, sometimes four people would die on this side and five people would die on the other side."

Under threat of death or mutilation, children have been forced to execute unspeakable acts. A boy in the documentary tells of being ordered to take babies from captured women and smash them against trees. Another says he was ordered to beat civilians to death with a tree branch, then lick the blood.

Ouma has said he was given an AK–47 before he was big enough to carry it. "He had to shoot a kid because he lost three bullets," Moran says, as Ouma poses in the ring. "A friend of his. He won't talk about that now. He doesn't want to remember it."

Ouma joined the Ugandan army boxing team, and when the team received visas to compete in the World Military Boxing Championship in San Antonio, Texas, in 1998, he was able to get his passport, which the government was holding. He fled by himself, first to Kenya, then on a flight to the United States.

* * *

Although the ranks of child soldiers seem to be swelling, the law concerning the exclusion of child soldiers from refugee protection is under-developed. As an example, the Australian opinion excerpted above acknowledged that the asylum seeker was young, but the tribunal's analysis of the crimes alleged and the duress defense did not expressly take into account the applicant's age or maturity. A lengthy survey of current legal issues surrounding the Exclusion Clauses of the 1951 Refugee Convention devoted solely this one paragraph to the application of these provisions to minors.

> There is no internationally accepted minimum age of criminal responsibility. Equally, there is no equivalent to Article 1F in Article 22 of the Convention on the Rights of the Child. The Rome Statute eschews jurisdiction over 'any person who was under the age of 18 at the time of the alleged commission of a crime'. Nevertheless, it would be possible to exclude [from refugee protection] applicants who were under that age when they acted contrary to Article 1F. Child soldiers could be excluded for their participation in genocide, war crimes or crimes against humanity unless one could show a lack of *mens rea*. However, UNHCR has argued that, even if one applies Article 1F to a child, he or she should still be protected from *refoulement*, partly because 'the fact that a child has been a combatant may enhance the likelihood and aggravate the degree of persecution he or she may face upon return'. Responses to child applicants who would be excludable under Article 1F need to be age-sensitive. It is not for UNHCR to devise mechanisms and processes to meet the needs of children who may well have committed heinous offences, and States should not contribute to the traumatization of the child by washing their hands of them through the process of exclusion from refugee status.

Gilbert, *Current Issues in the Application of the Exclusion Clauses*, in Refugee Protection in International Law 473 (E. Feller, V. Türk, and F. Nicholson eds., 2003).

### Notes

1. A study prepared by the Lawyers Committee for Human Rights analyzing the application of the exclusion clauses in the refugee crises in Central and West Africa in the 1990s, came to similar conclusions regarding child soldiers:

> It is highly unlikely that exclusion from international refugee protection will ever be in conformity with the best interests of the

child, the guiding principle in all actions concerning children. A child's best interests may be protected in other ways, particularly through support programs aimed at their rehabilitation and education. In exceptional circumstances where exclusion is considered for older children, due consideration should be given to any extenuating circumstances * * *. Although few, if any, legal systems preclude criminal liability for minors in absolute terms, in no event should a child under the age of 16 be subject to exclusion.

With respect to crimes committed during war, the duress and coercion present in the experience of child soldiers reinforces the presumption against criminal responsibility for minors. [Extreme caution should be exercised] in examining whether minors had sufficient maturity and mental capacity to understand the nature of their acts and whether they had a moral choice.

Lawyers Committee for Human Rights, *Refugees, Rebels and the Quest for Justice* 169–170 (2002).

2. For further commentary on exclusion of minors, *see* Gallagher, *Soldier Boy Bad: Child Soldiers, Culture and Bars to Asylum*, 13 Int'l J. Refugee Law 310 (2001).

### 3. SERIOUS CRIMES PRIOR TO ARRIVAL

In addition to denying protection to those who persecuted others, the asylum statute and the withholding statute expressly prohibit relief to (1) those who committed a serious nonpolitical crime outside the United States prior to arrival, INA §§ 208(a)(2)(A)(iii); 241(b)(3)(B)(iii) (wording slightly different in § 241), and to (2) those who have been convicted of a particularly serious crime in the United States. INA §§ 208(a)(2)(A)(ii); 241(b)(3)(B)(ii). The former tracks the exclusion clause contained in Article 1(F)(b) of the 1951 Convention; the latter incorporates the exception to *nonrefoulement* contained in Article 33(2). We will consider them in that order.

It is easy to confuse these statutory terms: what is a "serious nonpolitical crime" and how is it different from a "particularly serious crime"? Highlighting the location and the time when the criminal activity occurred makes it clear which statute applies. The first exclusion focuses on criminal conduct committed outside the United States before the asylum seeker arrived. In recognition that governments frequently label their dissidents as criminals, the statute does not bar all criminals from protection; rather it denies protection to those involved in serious nonpolitical crimes. Indeed, many of the difficult challenges in analyzing this barrier to protection is determining whether certain criminal conduct should be characterized as political or nonpolitical.

In 1999 one of these challenges reached the Supreme Court. The BIA had ruled an applicant ineligible for withholding because he had committed a serious nonpolitical crime in Guatemala before he arrived in the United States. The Ninth Circuit reversed the BIA on three grounds. First, relying on the UNHCR Handbook, it held that the BIA was required to balance the seriousness of the offense against the gravity of the persecution risked upon return. Second, the BIA had not sufficiently considered whether Aguirre's acts were of an "atrocious" nature. And, finally, the BIA "should have considered the political necessity and success of Aguirre's methods."

## INS v. AGUIRRE–AGUIRRE

United States Supreme Court, 1999.
526 U.S. 415, 119 S.Ct. 1439, 143 L.Ed.2d 590.

JUSTICE KENNEDY delivered the opinion of the Court.

We granted certiorari to consider the analysis employed by the Court of Appeals in setting aside a determination of the Board of Immigration Appeals (BIA). The BIA ruled that respondent, a native and citizen of Guatemala, was not entitled to withholding of deportation based on his expressed fear of persecution for earlier political activities in Guatemala. The issue in the case is not whether the persecution is likely to occur, but whether, even assuming it is, respondent is ineligible for withholding because he "committed a serious nonpolitical crime" before his entry into the United States. The beginning point for the BIA's analysis was its determination that respondent, to protest certain governmental policies in Guatemala, had burned buses, assaulted passengers, and vandalized and destroyed property in private shops, after forcing customers out. These actions, the BIA concluded, were serious nonpolitical crimes. * * * On appeal, the Court of Appeals for the Ninth Circuit concluded the BIA had applied an incorrect interpretation of the serious nonpolitical crime provision, and it remanded for further proceedings. * * *

* * *

According to the official hearing record, respondent testified that he and his fellow members would "strike" [in support of their political objectives in Guatemala] by "burning buses, breaking windows or just attacking the police, police cars." Respondent estimated that he participated in setting about 10 buses on fire, after dousing them with gasoline. Before setting fire to the buses, he and his group would order passengers to leave the bus. Passengers who refused were stoned, hit with sticks, or bound with ropes. In addition, respondent testified that he and his group "would break the windows of . . . stores," "t[ake] the people out of the stores that were there," and "throw everything on the floor."

* * *

In addressing the definition of a serious nonpolitical crime, the BIA applied the interpretation it first set forth in *Matter of McMullen*, 19 I. & N. Dec. [90, 97–98 (BIA 1984)]: "In evaluating the political nature of a crime, we consider it important that the political aspect of the offense outweigh its common-law character. This would not be the case if the crime is grossly out of proportion to the political objective or if it involves acts of an atrocious nature." In the instant case, the BIA found, "the criminal nature of the respondent's acts outweigh their political nature." The BIA acknowledged respondent's dissatisfaction with the Guatemalan government's "seeming inaction in the investigation of student deaths and in its raising of student bus fares." It said, however: "The ire of the ES [Aguirre's student organization] manifested itself disproportionately in the destruction of property and assaults on civilians. Although the ES had a political agenda, those goals were outweighed by their criminal strategy of strikes.... " The BIA further concluded respondent should not be granted discretionary asylum relief in light of "the nature of his acts against innocent Guatemalans."

\* \* \*

Because the Court of Appeals confronted questions implicating "an agency's construction of the statute which it administers," the court should have applied the principles of deference described in *Chevron U.S.A., Inc. v. Natural Resources Defense Council, Inc.*, 467 U.S. 837, 842, 104 S.Ct. 2778, 81 L.Ed.2d 694 (1984). \* \* \*

\* \* \* [W]e have recognized that judicial deference to the Executive Branch is especially appropriate in the immigration context where officials "exercise especially sensitive political functions that implicate questions of foreign relations." *INS v. Abudu*, 485 U.S. 94, 110, 108 S.Ct. 904, 99 L.Ed.2d 90 (1988). A decision by the Attorney General to deem certain violent offenses committed in another country as political in nature, and to allow the perpetrators to remain in the United States, may affect our relations with that country or its neighbors. The judiciary is not well positioned to shoulder primary responsibility for assessing the likelihood and importance of such diplomatic repercussions.

\* \* \*

The Court of Appeals' error is clearest with respect to its holding that the BIA was required to balance respondent's criminal acts against the risk of persecution he would face if returned to Guatemala. \* \* \* As a matter of plain language, it is not obvious that an already-completed crime is somehow rendered less serious by considering the further circumstance that the alien may be subject to persecution if returned to his home country.\* \* \*

\* \* \* The BIA, in effect, found respondent ineligible for withholding even on the assumption he could establish a threat of persecution. This approach is consistent with the language and purposes of the statute.

In reaching the contrary conclusion and ruling that the risk of persecution should be balanced against the alien's criminal acts, the Court of Appeals relied on a passage from the Office of the United Nations High Commissioner for Refugees, Handbook on Procedures and Criteria for Determining Refugee Status (Geneva, 1979) (U.N. Handbook). \* \* \*

The U.N. Handbook may be a useful interpretative aid, but it is not binding on the Attorney General, the BIA, or United States courts.

"Indeed, the Handbook itself disclaims such force, explaining that 'the determination of refugee status under the 1951 Convention and the 1967 Protocol is incumbent upon the Contracting State in whose territory the refugee finds himself.' " * * *

Also relying on the U.N. Handbook, the Court of Appeals held that the BIA "should have considered whether the acts committed were 'grossly out of proportion to the alleged objective.' * * * The political nature of the offenses would be 'more difficult to accept' if they involved 'acts of an atrocious nature.' " * * *

We do not understand the BIA to dispute that these considerations—gross disproportionality, atrociousness, and comparisons with previous decided cases—may be important in applying the serious nonpolitical crime exception. In fact, by the terms of the BIA's test (which is similar to the language quoted by the Court of Appeals from the U.N. Handbook), gross disproportion and atrociousness are relevant in the determination. * * * Our decision takes into account that the BIA's test identifies a general standard (whether the political aspect of an offense outweighs its common-law character) and then provides two more specific inquiries that may be used in applying the rule: whether there is a gross disproportion between means and ends, and whether atrocious acts are involved. Under this approach, atrocious acts provide a clear indication that an alien's offense is a serious nonpolitical crime. In the BIA's judgment, where an alien has sought to advance his agenda by atrocious means, the political aspect of his offense may not fairly be said to predominate over its criminal character. Commission of the acts, therefore, will result in a denial of withholding. The criminal element of an offense may outweigh its political aspect even if none of the acts are deemed atrocious, however. For this reason, the BIA need not give express consideration to the atrociousness of the alien's acts in every case before determining that an alien has committed a serious nonpolitical crime.

The BIA's approach is consistent with the statute, which does not equate every serious nonpolitical crime with atrocious acts. * * *

[The Court reversed the Ninth Circuit and remanded for further proceedings.]

## Notes and Questions

1. The Supreme Court unanimously concluded that all three rulings by the Ninth Circuit were erroneous. The excerpt addresses the first two issues: whether the seriousness of the offense should be balanced against the gravity of persecution risked upon return, and whether the atrocious nature of the acts was properly considered. As to the third issue, the Supreme Court upheld the BIA's determination that the exception clause applied because of the lack of proportion between his criminal acts and his political objectives. The BIA was not required to investigate further the "necessity" or "success" of the conduct.

2.   The Supreme Court emphasized the *Chevron* doctrine, discussed in Chapter Two, Section C, and the particular deference that courts should give to the BIA's statutory interpretation. It did not address the *Charming Betsy* canon of statutory construction that U.S. legislation should be reconciled with international law when possible (also discussed in Chapter Two, Section B). In fact, the Supreme Court noted that the Ninth Circuit paid heed to international sources, but rejected the appellate court's reliance on the UNHCR Handbook. Does the Supreme Court reject the significance of international law in interpreting U.S. statutes? Does it cast doubt on the UNHCR Handbook as an authoritative source of international law? What source(s) of international law would be more authoritative? Does the text of the treaty itself, Article 1(F), support the use of a balancing test in these circumstances?

3.   Compare the Supreme Court's approach to that adopted in the Australian decision, RRT Reference N96/12101, included earlier in this section. Does the Australian case treat the UNHCR Handbook as binding? Does the Australian tribunal balance the applicant's criminal acts against the risk of persecution he would face if returned to his homeland? Against another factor?

## 4.   EXTRADITION AND SERIOUS NONPOLITICAL CRIMES

The issue of extradition sometimes arises when an asylum seeker has been accused of committing serious nonpolitical crimes in another country before arriving in the United States. One scholar explained the intersection of the law of extradition and the law of asylum as follows:

> The [serious nonpolitical crime] exclusion disallows the claims of persons who are liable to sanctions in another state for having committed a genuine serious crime, and who seek to escape legitimate criminal liability by claiming refugee status. This exclusion clause is not a means of bypassing ordinary criminal due process for acts committed in a state of refuge, nor a pretext for ignoring the protection needs of those whose transgressions abroad are of a comparatively minor nature. Rather, it is simply a means of bring refugee law into line with the basic principles of extradition law, by ensuring that important fugitives from justice are not able to avoid the jurisdiction of a state in which they may lawfully face punishment * * *.

James C. Hathaway, The Law of Refugee Status (1991), at 221.

When the country requesting extradition is the same one in which the asylum seeker claims a well-founded fear of persecution, the United States must examine both the evidence of criminal activity and the likelihood of persecution. The law of asylum and withholding will protect the asylum seeker who is likely to be persecuted on account of one of the statutory grounds—unless the extraditable crimes constitute conduct that preclude the grant of asylum or withholding. In other words, if there are substantial reasons to believe the asylum seeker committed a serious nonpolitical crime outside the United States, he or she is not eligible for protection in the United States and will likely be extradited.

Analyzing whether the criminal conduct in question is serious and nonpolitical thus becomes the central issue for an asylum seeker who is resisting extradition. Simultaneously, the central inquiry in the parallel extradition proceeding typically is whether the crime can be characterized as a political offense, which most extradition agreements treat as a bar to extradition. Though the terms and the case law are not identical, they can seem like opposite sides of the same coin: individuals accused of political crimes will not be extradited; individuals credibly accused of serious nonpolitical crimes will be denied protection in the United States.

The Ninth Circuit considered the relationship between political offenses and serious nonpolitical crimes when it analyzed whether a former member of the Provisional Irish Republican Army whose extradition was sought by the United Kingdom was ineligible for protection in the United States based on his prior criminal acts in Northern Ireland and on his persecution of others. As recounted in the opinion below, McMullen entered the United States on a false visa and filed an asylum application as a defense to deportation. When the United Kingdom sought to extradite him, the INS suspended his deportation during the extradition proceedings.

A U.S. magistrate ruled that McMullen had committed a political offense and could not be extradited to England based on the provisions of the Extradition Treaty then in force between the United States and the United Kingdom (The treaty was later amended to cover a broader range of crimes, Supplementary Treaty to the Extradition Treaty of June 8, 1972, with annex, signed 25 June 1985, entered into force 23 December 1986, 1556 U.N.T.S. 369, T.I.A.S. 12050.) Under U.S. law, the government may not appeal an unfavorable ruling by a magistrate in this kind of extradition proceeding. In principle, the government can bring a second extradition proceeding and perhaps have the same issues considered by a different judge, *see Matter of Mackin*, 668 F.2d 122 (2d Cir. 1981); Van Cleave, *The Role of the United States Federal Courts in Extradition Matters*, 13 Temple Int'l & Comp. L. J. 27 (1999), but the government did not institute a second extradition proceeding in McMullen's case.

When the deportation proceeding resumed, the INS argued that the U.S. could deport McMullen to the United Kingdom even though it could not extradite him there. The court then grappled with whether the same conduct could constitute a serious nonpolitical crime that precluded protection in the United States.

## McMULLEN v. INS

United States Court of Appeals, Ninth Circuit, 1986.
788 F.2d 591.

WALLACE, CIRCUIT JUDGE.

\* \* \*

### I

In January 1972, McMullen deserted the British Army and joined the Provisional Irish Republican Army (the PIRA), an offshoot of the paramilitary Irish Republican Army. He participated in a bombing by the PIRA of the Palace Barracks, where he had been stationed. * * * McMullen participated actively in the PIRA from 1972 to 1974, [when] he formally resigned from the PIRA because he, as he stated, felt that the group had become extremist, employed too much terrorist violence and did not represent the Irish populace. On November 23, 1974, the Republic of Ireland police (Garda) arrested McMullen. The government charged him with membership in the PIRA, sedition (incitement to riot), and possession of a gun. After conviction on these charges, he was imprisoned for three years at Portalaise Prison. * * *

In March 1977, the government released McMullen from Portalaise. * * * After several instances of PIRA intimidation, McMullen again began to participate in PIRA activities.* * *

[After he refused to obey a PIRA order, he fled to the U.S. where he hoped to obtain asylum in exchange for knowledge about PIRA activities.]

In July of 1978, the United Kingdom sought McMullen's extradition to face criminal charges stemming from the 1974 Claro Barracks bombing in England. His deportation was held in abeyance during the extradition proceedings. * * * At his subsequent deportation hearing, McMullen testified that the PIRA was aware of his cooperation with the authorities in the United States and that he was considered a traitor who should be killed. In support of his position, he submitted over 100 pages of exhibits documenting PIRA terrorist activities.

* * *

## II

We first consider whether the BIA's finding that McMullen was ineligible for withholding of deportation under section 243(h)(2)(C) on the basis of "serious reasons for considering that [McMullen] has committed a serious nonpolitical crime" is supported by substantial evidence. * * *

* * *

[T]he only clear signal that can be gleaned from the legislative history is that Congress intended the nonpolitical crimes exception to withholding of deportation to be consistent with the Convention and Protocol * * *.  * * *

Under this standard, a "serious non-political crime" is a crime that was not committed out of "genuine political motives," was not directed toward the "modification of the political organization or . . . structure of the state," and in which there is no direct, "causal link between the crime committed and its alleged political purpose and object." In addition, even if the preceding standards are met, a crime should be considered a serious nonpolitical crime if the act is disproportionate to the objective, or if it is "of an atrocious or barbarous nature."

We have found little assistance from prior cases to help us in the application of this standard. The nearest analogy to this principle appears to be the "political offense" exception to extradition. Under this doctrine, the application of which usually turns on the precise language of the extradition treaty, a person may not be extradited to face prosecution for crimes committed in furtherance of a political uprising, movement or rebellion in the country in which such occurrences are taking place. * * *

The BIA found that McMullen's alleged participation in PIRA activities directed at civilians, and his other actions, including the training of others for terrorist operations and his own participation in coordinating arms shipments and bombings, were not within the political offense exception:

> [McMullen's] involvement in the terrorist use of explosives and his participation in the PIRA's campaign of violence randomly directed against civilians represent acts of an atrocious nature out of proportion to the political goal of achieving a unified Ireland and are not, therefore, within the political offense exception.

McMullen argues that the BIA's weighing of the nature of his alleged offenses against the political ends he sought to obtain is impermissible under the political offense doctrine as it has been developed in extradition cases. See *Quinn* [*v. Robinson*, 783 F. 2d 776 (9th Cir. 1986)] at 805, 817 (dicta) He argues that the same standard for determining whether a particular act, normally a common law crime, is a political offense in extradition cases should be applied when determining whether withholding of deportation is mandated under section 243(h)(2)(C). Under his proposed standard [drawn from the Ninth Circuit's ruling in *Quinn*], an act would be considered a political offense when (1) there was an insurrection or rebellion at the time the criminal acts were committed, and (2) the criminal acts were incident to or in furtherance of that insurrection or rebellion. This formulation is consistent with the traditional definition of a political offense for extradition purposes.* * *

We conclude that McMullen's analysis puts too much weight on the definition of political offenses in extradition cases because, although it may serve as a guide, the definition does not control our analysis of political offenses under section 243(h)(2)(C). When extradition is the issue, the attempt to remove an individual from the requested country is initiated at the specific request of another sovereign, whom the individual contends is seeking to extradite him solely in order to prosecute him for his political beliefs. Thus, the analysis in an extradition case turns on the language of the particular treaty, while the political offense analysis in withholding of deportation cases turns on a single standard—the Convention and Protocol.

In addition, in contrast to extradition, deportation is a matter solely between the United States government and the individual seeking withholding of deportation. No other sovereign is involved. The question, therefore, is whether the individual has committed a criminal act that puts him outside the statutory provisions for withholding of deportation under section 243, an act which Congress has determined makes the individual an "undesirable" in the eyes of the law. Moreover, the individual need not be deported to any country specifically seeking to extradite him; all the United States seeks is to expel him from its *own* borders. * * * When we *deport* an individual we are not "interfering with any *internal* struggle" of another nation.

It appears to us that the BIA's interpretation of the statute is consistent with the Convention, and thus consistent with congressional intent. A balancing approach including consideration of the offense's "proportionality" to its objective and its degree of atrocity makes good sense. *See* G. Goodwin–Gill, [The Refugee in International Law (1983)], at 61. Moreover, this approach better recognizes the type of crime involved in this and most such cases. There is a distinction between "pure" political crimes, such as sedition, treason, and espionage, and "relative" political crimes, crimes that have both common law criminal aspects and political aspects. *See Eain* [*v. Wilkes*, 641 F. 2d 504 (7th Cir.)], at 512. An approach that considers the proportionality and atrocity of a particular course of conduct is better suited to the analysis of "relative" political offenses under the Convention and Protocol.

\* \* \*

Thus, we conclude that * * * the denial of his asylum petition was not an abuse of discretion.

[The concurring opinion of Judge Goodwin is omitted.]

### Notes and Questions

1.   After affirming the BIA's interpretation of "serious nonpolitical crime," the Ninth Circuit ruled that, though McMullen's PIRA activity was part of a political movement to expel the British from Northern Ireland, it was so atrocious and disproportionate to the political objectives that it was a serious nonpolitical crime. *Id.* at 598. Do you find this logic convincing? If not, is everyone who commits crimes with an ultimate political goal in mind guaranteed protection in the U.S. if he can demonstrate a fear of persecution by his political opponents?

2.   What about the court's distinctions between deportation and extradition? As most extradition treaties contain an exception for political offenses and there is ample jurisprudence on the political offense doctrine, why is it relevant that each extradition case turns on the language of a particular treaty? Is there truly a significant difference between extraditing an individual and deporting him?

3.   You may have noticed that the Supreme Court in *Aguirre–Aguirre*, excerpted earlier in this Section, referred to the definition of serious nonpolitical crimes set forth by the BIA in *Matter of McMullen,* 19 I & N Dec. 90

(BIA 1984). The 1984 BIA decision was an earlier phase of the case reviewed by the Ninth Circuit in the opinion above. The BIA ruled that McMullen was excluded from protection in the United States on two grounds: (1) he had assisted in the persecution of others in Ireland and (2) he had committed serious nonpolitical crimes. The Ninth Circuit majority opinion in *McMullen* concluded that he was barred based on serious nonpolitical crimes, and declined to address the issue of persecuting others. The concurrence, however, concluded that the evidence was overwhelming that McMullen had assisted in the persecution of others, but thought it was insufficient to show his acts had been nonpolitical.

4.  In *McMullen*, the Ninth Circuit made reference to an expansive approach to the political offense definition, for purposes of extradition, that had been articulated in *Quinn v. Robinson*, 783 F.2d 776 (9th Cir. 1986). That decision concluded that the objectives of the uprising and the means employed, even if they involve harm to civilians, are irrelevant so long as the offense was committed in furtherance of a political uprising. (The *Quinn* court permitted extradition, but only because the alleged murder on which the extradition request was based took place in England. The uprising rule, in its view, applies solely to violence committed in the state where the uprising occurs; here the uprising was occurring in Northern Ireland, not in England.) Other courts have been less willing to include revolutionary violence against civilians within the political offense concept. *See, e.g., Ahmad v. Wigen*, 910 F.2d 1063 (2d Cir. 1990) (attack on commercial bus carrying civilians not a political offense; acts inconsistent with the law of armed conflict do not come within the political offense exception).

5.  There is a rich literature on the political offense doctrine in extradition. *See, e.g.,* Bassiouni, *The "Political Offense Exception" Revisited: Extradition Between the U.S. and the U.K.—A Choice Between Friendly Cooperation Among Allies and Sound Law and Policy*, 15 Denv. J. Int'l L. & Pol'y 255 (1987); Smith, *America Tries to Come to Terms With Terrorism: the United States Anti-Terrorism and Effective Death Penalty Act of 1996 v. British Anti-Terrorism Law and International Response*, 5 Cardozo J. Int'l & Comp. L. 249 (1997); Lubet, *Extradition Reform: Executive Discretion and Judicial Participation in the Extradition of Political Terrorists*, 15 Cornell Int'l L.J. 247 (1982); Epps, *The Validity of the Political Offender Exception in Extradition Treaties in Anglo-American Jurisprudence*, 20 Harv. Int'l L. J. 61 (1979); A look at the interplay between asylum, extradition, and rendition procedures can be found in Fitzpatrick, *The Post-Exclusion Phase: Extradition, Prosecution and Expulsion*, 12 Int'l J. Refugee Law (special issue) 272 (2000).

## 5.  PARTICULARLY SERIOUS CRIMES WITHIN THE UNITED STATES

The Refugee Act of 1980 barred those convicted of a particularly serious crime in the United States from withholding. Although the statute did not exclude these individuals from asylum, the government could use discretion to deny asylum for individuals who had been convicted of these types of crimes. Eventually, the regulations mandated a negative exercise of discretion in such circumstances.

In the mid-1980s the BIA examined the meaning of "particularly serious crime" and adopted a case by case approach. In *Matter of Frentescu*, 18 I & N Dec. 244, 247 (BIA 1982), the Board held that burglary with intent to commit theft did not constitute a "particularly serious crime." It noted: "[A] 'particularly serious crime' is more serious than a 'serious nonpolitical crime,' although many crimes may be classified [as] both * * *.   * * * Crimes against persons are more likely to be categorized as 'particularly serious' * * * [yet] there may be instances where crimes * * * against property will be considered as such crimes."

Another issue led to litigation concerning the statutory bars based on crimes within the United States. The legislative text, based on Article 33(2) of the 1951 Convention, has varied slightly over time, but the most common version refers to a noncitizen who, "having been convicted by a final judgment of a particularly serious crime, constitutes a danger to the community of the United States," INA § 208(a)(2)(A)(ii). This gave rise to arguments that the statute required asylum adjudicators to make two separate findings: (1) a prior conviction of a particularly serious crime, and (2) a present danger to the community. The BIA addressed this issue in the opinion below.

## MATTER OF CARBALLE

Board of Immigration Appeals, 1986.
19 I & N Dec. 357.

Milhollan, Chairman:

* * *

The applicant is a 22-year-old native and citizen of Cuba. After departing Cuba and arriving at Key West, Florida, in April 1980 as part of the Mariel boatlift, the applicant was paroled into the United States.

On February 18, 1983, in the Circuit Court for Dade County, Florida, the applicant was convicted, on his plea of guilty, of (1) robbery with a firearm, to wit, a pistol (two counts), (2) attempted robbery with a firearm, to wit, a pistol (two counts), (3) grand theft second degree, and (4) accessory after the fact * * *. The applicant was sentenced to terms of 15 years each on the robbery and attempted robbery counts with the sentences to run concurrently. He also was sentenced to terms of 5 years each on the grand theft and accessory counts with the sentences to run concurrently with the robbery counts. * * *

At his [immigration] hearing, the applicant * * * requested asylum and withholding of deportation. The applicant submitted that he would be imprisoned and singled out for disparate treatment by Cuban authorities because he was one of the first Cubans to enter the Peruvian Embassy in Havana in 1980 [in an incident that embarrassed the Cuban government and eventually led to the Mariel boatlift]. The record includes a "Safe Conduct Definitive," issued by the Cuban Government, which essentially authorized the applicant's safe conduct from the Peruvian Embassy to any country that offered him a visa. Also, the applicant stated that he would be persecuted in Cuba because of his robbery convictions in the United States.

* * * [T]he immigration judge found that the applicant was ineligible for relief under section 243(h) of the Act as one who had been convicted of a particularly serious crime and constituted a danger to the community of the United States. For the same reason, the immigration judge denied asylum.

* * *

On appeal, the applicant contends that the immigration judge erred * * *. Through counsel, he submits that section 243(h)(2)(B) requires two separate factual findings. First, it must be determined that an applicant has committed a particularly serious crime. Then, there must be a second, distinct finding that the applicant constitutes a danger to the community of the United States. The applicant submits that "the use of the present tense verb 'constitutes' in section 243(h)(2)(B) indicates that this second question should be appraised in light of present circumstances and the record should therefore be carefully scrutinized for evidence of rehabilitation or other factors indicating that [the] applicant may not now be a danger to the community."

The Service, however, argues that both the language of section 243(h)(2)(B) of the Act and its legislative history make clear that only one test is required. It is submitted that section 243(h)(2)(B) "establishes a cause and effect relationship between the two clauses." If Congress had "intended to establish two separate criteria," the Service argues, "it could have easily done so by its use of the conjunction 'and.' Instead, the grammatical structure shows that a conviction for a particularly serious crime is the sole factor which Congress has made determinative of whether the alien constitutes a danger to the community."

The Service contends that the legislative history of this statutory provision supports the contention that only one finding is required. The present provisions of section 243(h) of the Act were enacted as part of the Refugee Act of 1980. The House Judiciary Committee Report, in reviewing the provisions of section 243(h), noted that an exception to eligibility for such relief included "aliens ... who have been convicted of particularly serious crimes which make them a danger to the community of the United States." (Emphasis added.) The Service submits that this language reflects the congressional understanding of how section 243(h)(2)(B) is properly read. The phrase "danger to the community" is an aid to defining a "particularly serious crime," not a mandate that administrative agencies or the courts determine whether an alien will become a recidivist.

We find section 243(h)(2)(B) of the Act does not require that two separate and distinct factual findings be made in order to render an alien ineligible for withholding of deportation. It must be determined that an applicant for relief constitutes a danger to the community of the United

States to come within the purview of section 243(h)(2)(B). However, the statute provides the key for determining whether an alien constitutes such a danger. That is, those aliens who have been finally convicted of particularly serious crimes are presumptively dangers to this country's community. The clauses of section 243(h)(2)(B), nevertheless, are inextricably related. * * * The focus here is on the crime that was committed. If it is determined that the crime was a "particularly serious" one, the question of whether the alien is a danger to the community * * * is answered in the affirmative. * * *

\* \* \*

It is evident, based on the applicant's convictions for armed robbery and attempted armed robbery, that asylum would be denied as a matter of discretion. * * * Accordingly, the appeal will be dismissed.

———

Since this relatively early BIA decision, Congress has amended the statutes in order to expand the application of the criminal exception clauses and has increasingly legislated bright-line rules. The 1990 Act added language to the withholding provision providing that an aggravated felony, as defined in INA § 101(a)(43), is to be considered *per se* a "particularly serious crime." It also barred asylum for anyone convicted of an aggravated felony. The 1996 Act greatly expanded § 101(a)(43) by adding new offenses to the list and by reducing the minimum sentence necessary for many crimes already on the list to be considered aggravated felonies. For example, theft offenses formerly required a five-year sentence to be counted as an aggravated felony. Now a one-year sentence will suffice.

Asylum remains barred for all aggravated felonies. INA § 208(b)(2)(B)(i). The Attorney General is expressly authorized to consider other offenses as well to be particularly serious crimes. INA § 208(b)(2)(B)(ii). With regard to withholding of removal, in apparent recognition that a complete ban on withholding of removal for this wider class might violate the Convention—or at least that it might be overly harsh—the 1996 Act provided in INA § 241(b)(3)(B) a threshold of a five-year aggregate sentence for automatic preclusion of withholding of removal.

> For purposes of [the clause excluding those convicted of particularly serious crimes], an alien who has been convicted of an aggravated felony (or felonies) for which the alien has been sentenced to an aggregate term of imprisonment of at least 5 years shall be considered to have committed a particularly serious crime. The previous sentence shall not preclude the Attorney General from determining that, notwithstanding the length of sentence imposed, an alien has been convicted of a particularly serious crime.

INA 241 (b)(3)(B).

Litigation arose involving individuals convicted of aggravated felonies but sentenced to less than five years in prison. The BIA confronted this issue in two separate withholding cases involving Laotian nationals, *Matter of L–S–,* 22 I & N Dec. 645 (BIA 1999) (noncitizen convicted of bringing an undocumented alien into the U.S. and sentenced to 3½ months, held not barred from withholding); *Matter of S–S–,* 22 I & N Dec. 458 (BIA 1999) (noncitizen convicted of robbery in the first degree while armed with a handgun and sentenced to 55 months in prison, held barred). The BIA held that if the sentence falls below that threshold, there is no presumption that the crime is particularly serious, even if it fits the definition of an aggravated felony. Instead, the BIA ruled that a careful case-by-case inquiry into the facts and circumstances of the offense must be undertaken.

Attorney General Ashcroft overruled at least parts of the BIA's approach when he took three similar cases on referral from the BIA in 2002. (See Chapter Two, Section C concerning the Attorney General's power to reverse BIA decisions.) The three applicants for withholding had each been convicted of a drug trafficking offense, and had been sentenced to confinement of a year and a day, 24 months, and 25 months, respectively. The BIA found them eligible for withholding, but the Attorney General reversed the decision.

### MATTER OF Y–L–

Attorney General, 2002.
23 I & N Dec. 270.

[ASHCROFT, ATTORNEY GENERAL:]

\* \* \*

According to the BIA, the 1996 INA amendments—which eliminated a provision declaring that *all* aggravated felonies are "particularly serious crimes"—reflected Congress' desire to replace classifications based on the "category or type of crime that resulted in the conviction" with classifications "based on the length of sentence imposed." *See In re S–S–, supra.* I do not concur. The BIA's interpretation of these amendments places far too much weight on the first sentence of section 241(b)(3)'s final clause (the mandatory designation) and far too little weight on the final clause's second sentence (the grant of discretionary authority to the Attorney General). The fact that Congress designated as *per se* "particularly serious" every aggravated felony resulting in a term of incarceration of at least five years hardly reflects an intent to subordinate the nefarious or harmful *character* of a crime to mere secondary consideration, let alone remove it from the equation. While the imposition of certain harsh sentences may obviate the need to probe the underlying circumstances of a particular crime, the discretionary authority reserved to the Attorney General with respect to offenses from which less severe sentences flow is clearly intended to enable him to emphasize factors *other than* length of sentence.

\* \* \*

[After discussing the seriously negative effects of the drug trade, the Attorney General went on:] I might be well within my discretion to conclude that all drug trafficking offenses are *per se* "particularly serious crimes" under the INA. I do not consider it necessary, however, to exclude entirely the possibility of the very rare case where an alien may be able to demonstrate extraordinary and compelling circumstances that justify treating a particular drug trafficking crime as falling short of that standard. While this opinion does not afford the occasion to define the precise boundaries of what those unusual circumstances would be, they would need to include, at a *minimum*: (1) a very small quantity of controlled substance; (2) a very modest amount of money paid for the drugs in the offending transaction; (3) merely peripheral involvement by the alien in the criminal activity, transaction, or conspiracy; (4) the absence of any violence or threat of violence, implicit or otherwise, associated with the offense; (5) the absence of any organized crime or terrorist organization involvement, direct or indirect, in relation to the offending activity; and (6) the absence of any adverse or harmful effect of the activity or transaction on juveniles. Only if *all* of these criteria were demonstrated by an alien would it be appropriate to consider whether other, more unusual circumstances (e.g., the prospective distribution was solely for social purposes, rather than for profit) might justify departure from the default interpretation that drug trafficking felonies are "particularly serious crimes." I emphasize here that such commonplace circumstances as cooperation with law enforcement authorities, limited criminal histories, downward departures at sentencing, and post-arrest (let alone post-conviction) claims of contrition or innocence do not justify such a deviation. (Emphasis in original).

\* \* \*

[The Attorney General reversed the BIA and ruled that none of the applicants was entitled to relief.]

## Notes and Questions

1. Around the same time, Attorney General Ashcroft handed down another decision greatly restricting the favorable exercise of discretion over asylum and related waivers. *Matter of Jean*, 23 I & N Dec. 373 (AG 2002), excerpted below in Section C of this chapter. After refusing to exercise his discretion in favor of a mother of five who had been convicted of manslaughter, the Attorney General added: "I am highly disinclined to exercise my discretion—except \* \* \* in extraordinary circumstances, such as those involving national security or foreign policy considerations, or cases in which an alien clearly demonstrates that the denial of relief would result in exceptional and extremely unusual hardship—on behalf of dangerous or violent felons seeking asylum." *Id.* at 385.

2. Because asylum is a discretionary matter under U.S. law, it is hard to dispute on legal grounds the view that criminal conduct warrants the negative exercise of discretion except in very narrow circumstances. But what about withholding, which is non-discretionary? The 1951 Convention excludes individuals convicted of particularly serious crimes from protection

against *nonrefoulement*, but it does not permit the exclusion of refugees who have committed lesser criminal offenses. Can every conviction that receives a five-year sentence and falls within the broad aggravated felony classification truly be considered a particularly serious crime? Read the second paragraph of Article 33 and compare it with the parallel U.S. statute, which lists four exceptions to *nonrefoulement*. § INA 241(b)(3)(B)(i–iv).

3. Although Article 33(2) removes a state's *nonrefoulement* obligation for those convicted of a particularly serious crime, the Convention itself does not define a "particularly serious crime," nor does the UNHCR Handbook that provides guidance for interpreting Convention terms. Commentators agree that a "particularly serious crime" refers to more heinous conduct than a "serious crime," and the UNHCR Handbook concludes that a "serious crime" refers to "a capital crime or a very grave punishable act," UNHCR Handbook, ¶ 155. Under this reasoning, a "particularly serious crime" would refer to the very worst conduct criminalized. *See, e.g.*, Hathaway, The Law of Refugee Status, at 224.

4. Prominent scholars also suggest that the Article 33 *nonrefoulement* exception implies a balancing test:

> [T]he application of article 33(2) ought always to involve the question of proportionality, with account taken of the nature of the consequences likely to befall the refugee on return. The offence in question and the perceived threat to the community would need to be extremely grave if danger to the life of the refugee were to be disregarded, although a less serious offence and a lesser threat might justify the return of an individual likely to face only some harassment or discrimination.

G. Goodwin–Gill, The Refugee in International Law (2d ed.), at 140.

In addition, scholars have concluded that the particularly serious crime exception of Article 33(2) requires two findings: (1) the crime was "particularly serious" and (2) the refugee who committed the crime constitutes a danger to the community. Hathaway, The Law of Refugee Status, at 226. Under this view, a conviction of a particularly serious crime in the distant past or a recent conviction that involved mitigating circumstances might pose no current danger to the community. Lauterpacht and Bethlehem, *The Scope and Content of the Principle of Non-refoulement*, in Refugee Protection in International Law 87 (E. Feller, V. Türk, and F. Nicholson eds., 2003).

5. Does the language of the treaty support the use of a balancing test in the *nonrefoulement* setting? The use of a test that requires both proof of the conviction and proof of dangerousness to the community? What are the advantages and disadvantages of using the Board's more categorical approach? If there is a conviction of a serious crime that precludes protection, doesn't it make sense to address that first, without beginning to review evidence on the merits of the persecution claim?

**Exercise**

As you consider these scenarios, you should have a copy of the relevant legislation at hand so that you identify the specific statutory section that applies and the precise statutory language that is relevant.

A.  Crimes Outside the United States

1.   Suppose your client, an asylum seeker, was convicted of extortion and murder in Freedonia, which caused her to flee to the United States to seek protection. She has convincing proof that she is a member of an ethnic group that the Freedonian government has traditionally persecuted. Is she eligible for asylum or withholding? What additional facts would you need to learn to assess the bars to protection she might face?

2.   Same facts as above, except your client fled as soon as she learned that criminal charges had been filed against her and she has not been convicted of any crimes.

3.   Same facts as scenario 2, and your client has proof that she is a prominent member of the pro-democracy opposition to the military government.

4.   Same facts as scenario 2, but your client admits she and her colleagues collected a monthly "tax" from villagers in order to raise funds for the pro-democracy movement.

5.   Same facts as scenario 4, and your client says the murder charge arose when she shot her former boyfriend, a police officer, to stop him from beating her.

B.  Crimes Within the United States

1.   Suppose your client, an asylum seeker, has been convicted of extortion in the United States and sentenced to three years in prison. Nonetheless, she has strong proof that she would likely be persecuted if returned to her home country of Ruritania. She acknowledged that her erratic behavior was a result of substance abuse, and she entered a rehabilitation program. She has now been sober for two years, and her psychiatrist will testify that a relapse is extremely unlikely.

2.   Same facts as the above scenario, but she was not convicted of any crime.

8.   Same facts as the scenario in B.1, but she was sentenced to 5 years in prison.

## 6.  SECURITY DANGERS AND TERRORIST ACTIVITY

In addition to the exclusions based on serious crimes, Congress has stated that withholding is not available when "there are reasonable grounds for regarding the alien as a danger to the security of the United States." INA § 241(b)(3)(B)(iv). The statute also prohibits asylum for those considered security dangers. INA § 208(b)(2)(A)(iv). These exclusions are based on Article 33(2) of the 1951 Convention.

Congress has also added a provision to the withholding statute that equates engaging in terrorist activity (and certain other connections with terrorism) with posing a security danger to the United States, INA § 241(b)(3)(B)(last sentence), and has added an explicit ban on asylum for those involved in terrorist activity, INA § 208(b)(2)(A)(v). These provisions employ intricate cross-references to various portions of a highly complex inadmissibility ground, INA § 212(a)(3)(B). Although the underlying decision to bar terrorists from protection in the United States is not surprising, the broad impact of these statutory provisions has become highly controversial. The problem is that Congress has amended the legislation repeatedly in recent years, each time expanding the circumstances in which individuals can be considered to have engaged in terrorist activity or to have a disqualifying connection to terrorism. Often the congressional debate focused on the inadmissibility ground, without attention to the impact of the changes, by means of arcane cross-references, on refugees. As a consequence, many applicants who genuinely fear persecution are barred from asylum and withholding. The following exercise should help you become acquainted with this complex statutory scheme.

---

### Exercise

Sandor Dempsky is a member of the Transylvania Society of Free Democrats, a political party that espouses reunification of Transylvania, a mountainous area that lies within the borders of present-day Romania, with Hungary. There have been charges that the Transylvania Society of Free Democrats is allied with the Transylvania Liberation Army (TLA). The TLA espouses immediate secession from Romania and either independence or reunification with Hungary. Armed TLA groups have attacked Romanian government outposts; two Romanian border control officers were killed in the attacks. There is no evidence that Dempsky has harmed anyone or has ever been a member of TLA.

Suppose you are an attorney for the U. S. government. You have been asked to consider the applicability of INA § 212(a)(3)(B) to Mr. Dempsky's application for asylum and withholding. Please list each portion of this statutory provision that may apply to Mr. Dempsky.

Are there further facts that you must know in order to analyze Dempsky's case under § 212(a)(3)(B)? Be specific about

> the information you need to know and the reason you need to know it.

Some of the litigation involving bars based on terrorist activity has involved fairly well known armed groups and assassinations of political opponents. For example, a member of the Irish National Liberation Army (INLA) was denied asylum and withholding based on several crimes involving firearms and a conspiracy to kill a Royal Ulster Constabulary officer, crimes for which he had been convicted and imprisoned in Northern Ireland. The BIA and the federal court concluded that he had engaged in terrorist activity, which constitutes reasonable grounds for being regarded a danger to the security of the United States. Consequently, he was ineligible for asylum and withholding. *McAllister v. Attorney General*, 444 F.3d 178 (3d Cir. 2006).

But the definition of engaging in terrorist activities goes far beyond explicit commission of violent terrorist acts. It includes providing any type of material support "to any individual the actor knows, or reasonably should know, has committed or plans to commit a terrorist activity," or to terrorist organizations, as that term is broadly defined. INA § 212(a)(3)(B)(iv)(VI). DHS and the Department of Justice have construed this provision very broadly, to include even minimal support given under duress, a stance that has provoked heated debate. Critics have pointed out that the broad reach of this interpretation leads to perverse consequences. For example, refugees who had been extorted to provide food and drink to armed groups, and then fled precisely to avoid future such exactions, are precluded from protection under this reading of U.S. law.

The material support provision has also blocked decisions to include a significant number of refugee groups overseas who are otherwise considered good candidates for resettlement in the United States. As a consequence, refugees from areas where many in the population responded to pressure for support exerted by guerrilla organizations seem doubly cursed. *See* Benesch and Chafee, *The Ever-Expanding Material Support Bar: An Unjust Obstacle for Refugees and Asylum Seekers*, 83 Interp. Rel. 465 (2006). We will consider the material support issue as it affects the resettlement of refugees in the United States in more detail in Chapter Ten.

Overseas refugee admissions are discretionary under international law, but *nonrefoulement* protection for persons already in the United States is not, if they meet the provisions of the 1951 Convention. The BIA and the courts are only beginning to consider the legal questions raised by the executive branch's interpretation of the material support provision, particularly in cases involving support that was negligible or provided at the point of a gun. The statute does not expressly provide for a duress defense or a *de minimis* exception, and courts to date have not been eager to read these defenses into the statutory scheme. In 2004 the Third Circuit addressed the *de minimis* issue, as the majority and dissent debated the amount of assistance necessary to constitute material support.

## SINGH–KAUR v. ASHCROFT

United States Court of Appeals, Third Circuit, 2004.
385 F.3d 293.

ALDISERT, CIRCUIT JUDGE.

Charangeet Singh–Kaur, a native and citizen of India, petitions this Court to review an order of the Board of Immigration Appeals ("BIA") that Singh be deported from the United States to India. This appeal requires us to determine whether providing food and setting up shelter for people engaged in terrorist activities constitutes affording "material support" within the meaning of the Immigration and Nationality Act ("INA") § 212(a)(3)(B)(iv)(VI) (2002). * * *

* * *

* * * Singh submitted an application for asylum, asserting that if he returned to India he would be arrested and persecuted. He claimed membership in the "Babbar Khalsa Group," whose purpose, he said, was "to protect and promote the Sikh faith," and the "Sant Jarnail Sing Bhindrawala Militant Group," whose purpose was "to fight for and protect the religious and political cause of Sikh community." Singh stated that he had participated in demonstrations and other activities of these two groups. He further claimed to be "on the military and police wanted list because of known and suspected activities against the government" of India.

In an affidavit supporting his asylum application, Singh stated that after the Indian military attacked a Sikh holy site called the Golden Temple in 1984, he "together with many other young men in our village formally took the vows to join and follow the militant section of Sant Jarnail, known as Babbar Khalsa." He said that he participated in "planning meetings" and "became involved in assisting the freedom fighters in the movement of weapons through my village and other villages, as well as giving shelter to militants who were involved in the transportation of weapons." Subsumed in all of this is a statement of military activity against the government of India.

Singh submitted additional materials supporting his application for asylum, including evidence of active membership in the International Sikh Youth Federation and a statement by the Khalistan Commando Force that Singh had taken an oath to participate with the Force.

* * *

The State Department * * * commented:

The applicant * * * admits to membership in the International Sikh Youth Federation, a radical offshoot of the AISSF, as well as the Khalistan Commando Force, a notorious terrorist group responsible for a grisly April 1985 random killing in a Punjab village, and the equally notorious Babbar Khalsa, an even more fundamentalist terrorist group with a reputation for its use of explosives. Many of the bombings resulting in the murder of innocent persons in recent years are attributed to the latter group.

* * *

Singh then submitted an affidavit purporting to clarify statements in his asylum application. He asserted that he had never been involved in or supported violent activities against Indian government officials. He stated that the Indian police and military merely presumed that he, as a Sikh, opposed the government. He said that he had undergone an induction ceremony known as "Amrit Chakna," in which he committed to remain faithful to his religion, to wear a turban and to keep his hair and beard long. He stated that he was enrolled as a member of Babbar Khalsa at the time of this ceremony.

He further stated that, having participated in Amrit Chakna, he was expected to make charitable contributions to the community, including "provision of food and assistance to the poor." * * *

* * *

At a hearing on January 22, 1997, Singh told the IJ that he assisted with meetings of Sant Jarnail Singh followers:

We—I used to help by putting that tent and organize the mondo [sic] or the tent. . . . I never kept any weapons. Those Sikhs who were baptized, they used to come and they knew that I am also baptized and I just help them with the—giving them food.

* * *

* * * [O]ur task tracks the narrow compass of determining whether Singh's conduct in providing food and setting up tents constituted "material support" either "for the commission of terrorist activity" or "to any individual who the actor knows, or reasonably should know, has committed or plans to commit a terrorist activity." * * *

* * *

In response to questioning from the IJ at a hearing on January 22, 1997, Singh described his role in meetings of Sant Jarnail Singh followers:

Q.   Well, but in this statement, sir, that I just read to you, you say there were known activities that you took against the Indian government. What were those activities?

A.   Sant Jarnail Singh organized meetings in different villages to propagate religion.

Q.   So, in other words you're telling me that you attended these meetings, correct?

A.   Yes. We used to have those people to arrange our tents and put some—some sort of—arrange preparation of the food and also arrange to bring people to these gatherings and then take them back to their places.

Later in the same hearing, Singh responded to questions from the INS attorney:

Q.   So, in other words, you were helping the militants who were involved in terrorist activities? Isn't that true?

A.   When we came from far away to this (indiscernible) congregation, then we may have some contact. We never help in any other way than giving them food. Yes.

Taking Singh's statement of minimal participation, it is beyond cavil that Singh furnished food and shelter to Sant Jarnail Singh followers participating in meetings. The sole remaining issue is whether the individuals to whom Singh provided food and shelter come within the rubric of INA section 212(a)(3)(B)(iv).

\* \* \*

\* \* \* The evidence is clear that at the time of Singh's participation with them, the members of the various militant Sikh organizations opposed to the Indian government had committed or planned to commit terrorist activity.

Although Singh stated that the purpose of the meetings at which he provided food and shelter was to propagate the teachings of Sant Jarnail Singh, he did not elaborate at the January 22, 1997 hearing on the content of those teachings. In his first affidavit, however, Singh stated: "Sant Jarnail Singh Bhindrawala was never inclined to be militant. However, after his death his group became militant because of the violence perpetrated upon him and his and his [sic] followers by the Indian Military."

A 1985 Amnesty International Report submitted by Singh as part of his asylum application related a June 5, 1984 battle, where "heavy fighting ensued between the army and the followers of Sant Jarnail Singh Bhindranwale, the Sikh fundamentalist leader who had taken refuge in the temple and who the government blamed for directing much of the violence in the Punjab in recent years."

\* \* \*

Even in light of the recantations made in his second affidavit, Singh's self-described activities in conjunction with his membership in various militant Sikh organizations consisted of: (1) providing food to militant Sikhs who had committed or planned to commit terrorist activity; and (2) setting up tents for meetings of militants who had committed or planned to commit terrorist activity.

Although Singh himself denied participating directly in any violence, substantial evidence supports the BIA's determination that he knew or should have known the militant Sikhs to whom he provided food and shelter had committed or planned to commit terrorist activities within the meaning of the statute. * * * The petition for review will be denied.

FISHER, CIRCUIT JUDGE, dissenting.

Finding that Singh–Kaur helped members of Sikh militant groups "by giving them food and helping to set up tents," the Board of Immigration Appeals ("BIA") held that Singh–Kaur "engaged in terrorist activities." However, Singh–Kaur testified that the meetings were for religious purposes, and the BIA did not find Singh–Kaur's testimony to lack credibility. The issue here is therefore straightforward—whether providing food and tents for such meetings, without more, constitutes "engag[ing] in terrorist activity" through provision of "material support." The acts here are not of the degree and kind contemplated by the "material support" provision—*material* acts in support of terrorism. Because the majority's holding ignores the plain language of the statute by reading "material" out of "material support," I respectfully dissent.

* * *

It must be further noted that Singh–Kaur testified that the food and tents were set up for religious meetings. Neither the IJ nor the BIA made an adverse credibility finding. * * * Therefore, we must assume Singh–Kaur's testimony before the IJ to be true.

* * * [T]he BIA's holding rests solely on the narrow ground that the provision of food and tents prior to 1989 to unnamed members of the Babbar Khalsa and Sant Jarnail organizations was the provision of "material support . . . to any individual the actor knows, or reasonably should know, has committed or plans to commit a terrorist activity." However, the record does not contain any evidence as to what terrorist acts, if any, these unnamed individuals committed or planned to commit.

* * *

Examining the statute's plain language and employing the "normal tools of statutory construction," I conclude that Congress did not intend "material support" to embrace acts that are not of importance or relevance to terrorism. To hold otherwise reads "material" out of "material support" and treats half of the statutory term as surplusage. Such a result is inconsistent with the plain language of the statute and with the normal tools of statutory construction.

* * *

* * * I have no doubt that the term "support," in isolation, could embrace food and tents. As noted by the majority, support is defined as: "Sustenance or maintenance; esp., articles such as food and clothing that

allow one to live in the degree of comfort to which one is accustomed." *Id.* (quoting Black's Law Dictionary 1453 (7th ed.1999)). Had the statute referred to mere "support," I might concur with my colleagues, as substantial evidence shows that "support" was afforded.

But the analysis does not end there because "material" qualifies "support." The majority correctly notes two meanings for "material" in this context—"[h]aving some logical connection with the consequential facts," and "significant" or "essential." * * * Even a cursory examination of the "material support" provision makes it clear that both meanings of "material"—relevance and importance—are embraced by the statute. * * *

Therefore, even under the broadest possible reading, "material" in this context must mean both "important" and "relevant" to terrorism. "Material support," by its plain language, means that the *act affording support must be of a kind and degree that has relevance and importance to terrorist activity, terrorists, or terrorist organizations.* Put another way, an act "affording material support" must move the ball down the field for terrorism. This is not to say that under certain circumstances, food and shelter could not be "material support." But as these are normal types of "support," the facts must show that they are more than *mere* support—i.e., they must be of relevance and importance to terrorism.

* * *

Applying the facts to the law, substantial evidence does not support the BIA's finding that Singh–Kaur provided "material support." Nothing in the record shows how the food and tents were important and relevant to terrorism, and indeed, Singh–Kaur testified that they were provided for religious meetings. The majority therefore relies on speculation by concluding that mere support to unnamed persons who may or may not have engaged in unknown terrorist activities constitutes "material support." This conclusion substitutes conjecture for proof and reads "material" out of "material support."

* * *

* * * There is no dispute that Singh–Kaur supplied food and tents prior to 1989 to unnamed members of at least one of these organizations. But the administrative record contains nothing about whether the individuals at issue had engaged in terrorist acts or planned to do so. Indeed, the record is to the contrary—Singh–Kaur testified that the meetings were for religious purposes. * * *

* * *

A review of [his] testimony makes it clear that Singh–Kaur disclaimed any connection to violence. It also shows that the meetings at question were "to propagate religion." It further shows that the tents and food were supplied to members of Sant Jarnail. Nothing in the testimony reflects that the purpose or subject of the meetings was to facilitate terrorism.

\* \* \*

[T]he majority hold[s] that Singh–Kaur supplied "material support" to \* \* \* an "individual who the actor knows, or reasonably should know, has committed or plans to commit a terrorist activity." But the record is devoid of any evidence of who these individuals were, what terrorist activities they had done, or what terrorist acts they planned to commit. There is also no evidence of what Singh–Kaur knew or should have known regarding these unknown activities. The only evidence that the BIA and majority appear to latch upon in this regard is the following exchange at the end of the government's questioning of Singh–Kaur:

> Q:  So, in other words, you were helping the militants who were involved in the terrorist activities. Isn't that true?
>
> A:  When we came from far away to this (indiscernible) congregation, then we may have some contact. We never help in any other way than giving them food. Yes.

\* \* \*

The majority's reliance on this passage is questionable at best. Although admissions may certainly be based on leading questions, it is difficult to know whether or not Singh–Kaur was agreeing to the words put into his mouth by the government lawyer and transmitted through the translator, or what he meant by the response relayed back through the translator. Indeed, moments before, Singh–Kaur had adamantly *denied* that the persons he helped were "militants." Further, in the context of this appeal, the term "terrorist activity" has a specified legal definition, whereas we have no idea what Singh–Kaur understood the term to mean. At the very least the passage is ambiguous, and at the worst, reliance on the passage fails the substantial evidence test because it requires us to speculate as to what Singh–Kaur was saying "Yes" to.

Despite these concerns, the case need not turn on this issue, because even if we were to assume that Singh–Kaur admitted that the unnamed "militants" had engaged in unspecified "terrorist activity," the BIA still has not established that the food or the tents were material in any way. Nothing in the record shows the type of terrorist activities committed or planned by these unnamed individuals, and nothing shows how the food and tents were relevant and important to these unnamed persons engaging in unknown terrorist activities. Under such circumstances, finding mere support to be "material" support reads "material" out of the statute. \* \* \*

\* \* \*

\* \* \* I have no doubt that under the right facts, the provision of a single glass of water to a terrorist could be material support. If bin Laden were dying of thirst and asked for a cup of water to permit him to walk another half mile and detonate a weapon of mass destruction, such support would be "material" to terrorism. But those facts are not before us, and permitting a mere cup of water, without more, to be "material support" reads "material" out of the statute.

\* \* \*

A more recent BIA decision evaluates whether $685 donated over the course of a year amounts to material support and whether supporting the democratic opposition to a military autocracy constitutes terrorist activity.

## MATTER OF S–K–

Board of Immigration Appeals, 2006.
23 I & N Dec. 936.

PAULEY, BOARD MEMBER:

\* \* \*

The respondent, a native and citizen of Burma, is a Christian and an ethnic Chin. According to the respondent, she faces persecution and/or torture if returned to Burma because the Government, currently a military dictatorship ruled by the majority Burman ethnic group, regularly commits human rights abuses against ethnic and religious minorities and, in fact, arrested and detained both the respondent's brother and fiancé, the latter ultimately being killed by the military.

In 2001, the respondent became acquainted with an undercover agent for the Chin National Front ("CNF") who was a friend of her deceased fiancé. She became sympathetic to the CNF's goal of securing freedom for ethnic Chin people and donated money to the organization for approximately 11 months. In addition, she attempted to donate some other goods, such as a camera and binoculars, to the CNF, but they were confiscated after she had given them to the undercover agent. The agent informed the respondent that she should flee Burma because the Burmese military, known to torture anyone affiliated with the CNF, had seen a letter written by the respondent to the CNF; the military knew that the respondent was the person who had attempted to provide the material goods. The respondent was actually residing in Singapore at the time, but since her temporary work visa was about to expire and she could not return to Burma, she fled to the United States in order to request asylum.

Although the Immigration Judge found that the respondent had established a well-founded fear of persecution in order to qualify for asylum, he denied her application for relief because, by providing money and other support to the CNF, an organization which uses land mines and engages in armed conflict with the Burmese Government, the respondent provided material support to an organization or group of individuals who she knew, or had reason to know, uses firearms and explosives to endanger the safety of others or to cause substantial property damage. Therefore, she was statutorily barred from asylum and from withholding of removal * * *.

## II. ANALYSIS

### A. TERRORIST ORGANIZATION

During oral argument and on appeal, the respondent argued that the Burmese Government is not legitimate because the military junta rules the country under martial law and crushes any attempts at democratic reform. According to the respondent, the United States does not recognize the Burmese Government's legislative acts, and therefore the CNF's actions are not unlawful under Burmese law. Rather, she asserts, the organization's actions are similar to those of forces fighting the Taliban in Afghanistan or forces rebelling against Saddam Hussein in Iraq, which are supported by the United States. Its goals are democracy and it uses force only in self-defense. Moreover, the CNF is allied with the National League of Democracy, which the United States has recognized as a legitimate representative of the Burmese people and is recognized by the United Nations. Therefore, the respondent contends that the Immigration Judge erred in concluding that the CNF is a terrorist organization.* * *

Whether the CNF's actions are lawful in Burma is a question of foreign law and is a factual issue on which the respondent bears the burden of proof, inasmuch as the "evidence indicates" that the terrorism bar to asylum may apply. * * * During oral argument, the respondent pointed to testimony from the Assistant Secretary of State describing the Burmese military as a "group of thugs," as well as to the fact that the United States Government has passed the Burmese Freedom and Democracy Act of 2003, acknowledging that the National League of Democracy is the legitimate representative of the Burmese people. * * *

* * *

Although the respondent urges us to determine that the Burmese Government is illegitimate and argues that we have such authority, we are unable to agree with the respondent's argument. While there may have been cases in which we determined that certain acts by foreign governments were unlawful in terms of harming individuals who sought asylum here, we have not gone so far as to determine that a foreign sovereignty would not be recognized by the United States Government. Such a determination is beyond our delegated authority and is a matter left to elected and other high-level officials in this country.

Furthermore, the respondent cites to past case law interpreting asylum applicants' claims and granting relief where aliens have attempted to overthrow governments that do not allow citizens to change the political structure and therefore exercise illegitimate power when prosecuting such individuals. In other words, she asserts that the motivation of the group seeking to effect change in a country must be analyzed in order to determine whether the harm produced is persecution or, as claimed in this case, terrorist activity. See *Matter of Izatula*, 20 I & N Dec. 149 (BIA 1990) (holding, in a case involving an alien who actively assisted the mujahedin in Afghanistan, that the general rule that prosecution for an attempt to overthrow a lawfully constituted government does not constitute persecution is inapplicable in countries where a coup is the only means of effectuating political change); *Matter of Rodriguez–Majano*, 19 I & N Dec. 811 (BIA 1988) (holding that an alien who had involuntarily helped the guerrillas in El Salvador was not barred from asylum for having participated in the persecution of others, because harm that may result incidentally from behavior aimed at another goal, e.g., the overthrow of a government or the defense of a government against an opponent, particularly in the context of civil war, is not directed at overcoming a belief or characteristic of those persecuted). During oral argument, counsel for the respondent acknowledged that by utilizing such factors to determine whether an organization falls within section 212(a)(3) of the Act, he was advocating that we apply a "totality of the circumstances" test.

We are unable to find any support for the respondent's assertion that such a test should be utilized. Our past case law is not inconsistent with some of the respondent's arguments. However, that case law does not address the bar to relief in section 212(a)(3)(B)(i)(I) of the Act. In this case, we are dealing with specific statutory language, which we read as applying to the respondent.

As noted by the DHS during oral argument, the fact that Congress included exceptions elsewhere in the Act for serious nonpolitical offenses and aliens who have persecuted others, even where persecuted themselves, and that it has not done so in section 212(a)(3)(B), indicates that the omission of an exception for justifiable force was intentional. In fact, having reviewed the statutory sections, we find that Congress intentionally drafted the terrorist bars to relief very broadly, to include even those people described as "freedom fighters," and it did not intend to give us discretion to create exceptions for members of organizations to which our Government might be sympathetic. Rather, Congress attempted to balance the harsh provisions set forth in the Act with a waiver [in INA § 212(d)(3)(B)], but it only granted the power to make exemptions to the Attorney General and the Secretaries of State and Homeland Security, who have not delegated such power to the Immigration Judges or the Board of Immigration Appeals.

* * * [T]here is no exception in the Act to the bar to relief in cases involving the use of justifiable force to repel attacks by forces of an illegitimate regime. As noted by the Immigration Judge, there was sufficient evidence in the record to conclude that the CNF uses firearms and/or explosives to engage in combat with the Burmese military, and the respondent has not provided evidence that would rebut this conclusion or lead us to interpret the Act differently. Moreover, the record shows that the respondent knew or should have known of the CNF's use

of arms. Thus, assuming the respondent provided material support to the CNF, her sole remedy to extricate herself from the statutory bar appears to lie in the waiver afforded by Congress for this purpose, for which the DHS stated at oral argument she is eligible to apply. * * *

### B.   Materiality of Support Provided

The respondent also argues that the type and amount of support which she provided to the CNF was not material. * * * Since no evidence was submitted to support a conclusion that the respondent's contributions were relevant to a specific terrorist goal, the respondent asserts that finding that her contributions were material goes against the congressional intent to tie materiality to terrorist activity. In support of her argument, the respondent has attached an advisory opinion from the United Nations High Commissioner for Refugees ("UNHCR") to her counsel, which indicates that materiality must be assessed in conjunction with the alien's claim of persecution and the question whether or not the alien presents a present or future danger to the security of the United States.[7]

* * * The UNHCR advisory opinion correctly asserts that the term "material support" is not completely defined and that while the list of examples following the term provides some clarification regarding its scope, its meaning remains somewhat ambiguous. The advisory opinion goes on to state that when assessing the scope of the term, one must look at the regularity and amount of funds or goods/services provided and determine whether they are sufficiently serious to warrant exclusion. It concludes that denial of relief is only warranted where the alien constitutes a present or future danger to the security of the United States.

We are unaware of any legislative history which indicates a limitation on the definition of the term "material support." * * * Rather, the statute is clearly drafted in this respect to require only that the provider afford material support to a terrorist organization, with the sole exception being a showing by clear and convincing evidence that the actor did

---

**7.** Implicit in the UNHCR's advisory opinion is the assertion that our holding, which would (apart from the possibility of a waiver) bar asylum to this alien and possibly future aliens who have been or will be persecuted, conflicts with international law, which must be interpreted alongside and consistently, where possible, with our domestic laws. It is also well established that Congress may enact statutes that conflict with international law. However, we are not convinced that it was the intent of Congress to do so here. While it is clear that our government leaders have taken a strict approach to dealing with suspected terrorists and have attempted to make it more difficult for those involved in terrorism to gain relief of any kind, they also have expressly provided a waiver that may be exercised in cases where the result reached under the terrorist bars to relief would not be consistent with our international treaty obligations or where, as a matter of discretion, the Secretary of State or the Secretary of Homeland Security determines that the facts of a specific case warrant such relief. [INA § 212(d)(3)(B).] Accordingly, while the Immigration Judges and the Board do not have the authority to grant the respondent or similarly situated aliens a discretionary waiver, other officials, including the Secretary of State, prior to the instigation of removal proceedings, or the Secretary of Homeland Security, at any time upon consultation with other agency officials, have been granted this power. We find no reason to assume they will not act consistently with our international treaty obligations in exercising their power to grant such a waiver.

not know, and should not reasonably have known, that the organization was of that character. Section 212(a)(3)(B)(iv)(VI)(dd) of the Act. We thus reject the respondent's assertion that there must be a link between the provision of material support to a terrorist organization and the intended use by that recipient organization of the assistance to further a terrorist activity. Especially where assistance as fungible as money is concerned, such a link would not be in keeping with the purpose of the material support provision, as it would enable a terrorist organization to solicit funds for an ostensibly benign purpose, and then transfer other equivalent funds in its possession to promote its terrorist activities.

We turn then to the respondent's claim that the statute's requirement of material support means that trivial or unsubstantial amounts of assistance, such as she allegedly provided, are not within the statutory bar. In *Singh–Kaur v. Ashcroft, supra,* the Third Circuit found that the provision of very modest amounts of food and shelter to individuals who the alien reasonably should have known had committed or planned to commit terrorist activity did constitute material support. * * *

* * *

As the DHS contends, it is certainly plausible * * * that the list in section 212(a)(3)(B) was intended to have an expanded reach and cover virtually all forms of assistance, even small monetary contributions. Congress has not expressly indicated its intent to provide an exception for contributions which are de minimis. Thus the DHS asserts that the term "material support" is effectively a term of art and that all of the listed types of assistance are covered, irrespective of any showing that they are independently "material."

On the other hand, the respondent's contrary argument that "material" should be given independent content is by no means frivolous. However, we find it unnecessary to resolve this issue now, inasmuch as we agree with the DHS that based on the amount of money the respondent provided, her donations of S$1100 (Singapore dollars) constituted material support.[13] Specifically, the respondent testified that she contributed approximately S$100 per month over an 11-month period, representing approximately one-eighth of her monthly income. This was sufficiently substantial by itself to have some effect on the ability of the CNF to accomplish its goals, whether in the form of purchasing weaponry or providing routine supplies to its forces, for example. We therefore agree with the Immigration Judge that the respondent provided material support to the CNF.

## III.  CONCLUSION

Based on the foregoing, we agree with the Immigration Judge's decision that the respondent is statutorily ineligible for asylum and withholding of removal for having provided material support to a terror-

---

**13.** We take administrative notice that this corresponded at the time to approximately US$685. * * * By contrast, the av-erage annual per capita income in Burma was approximately US$225. * * *

ist organization. The respondent's appeal will therefore be dismissed in part regarding her applications for that relief. However, during oral argument, the DHS conceded that the respondent is eligible for deferral of removal under the Convention Against Torture. We agree and will therefore sustain the respondent's appeal and vacate the Immigration Judge's decision in that regard. * * *

OSUNA, ACTING VICE CHAIRMAN, concurring:

I join the majority's decision. I agree with the majority that the Immigration Judge properly denied the respondent's applications for asylum and withholding of removal, as this result is compelled by the specific language of the statute. I write separately because I have considerable doubts that this result is what Congress had in mind when it enacted the "material support" bar to asylum.

We are finding that a Christian member of the ethnic Chin minority in Burma, who clearly has a well-founded fear of being persecuted by one of the more repressive governments in the world, one that the United States Government views as illegitimate, is ineligible to avail herself of asylum in the United States despite posing no threat to the security of this country. It may be, as the majority states, that Congress intended the material support bar to apply very broadly. However, when the bar is applied to cases such as this, it is difficult to conclude that this is what Congress intended.

* * *

* * * The organization that the respondent provided support to, the Chin National Front ("CNF"), has an armed wing that is resisting the Government of Burma. The CNF is allied with the National League of Democracy, which is recognized by the United States as a legitimate representative of the Burmese people.

In enacting the material support bar, Congress was rightly concerned with preventing terrorists and their supporters from exploiting this country's asylum laws. It is unclear, however, how barring this respondent from asylum furthers those goals. The respondent provided funds and some equipment to a member of the CNF, an organization that has not been designated by the Department of State as a terrorist organization under section 212(a)(3)(B)(vi) of the Act. The available information in the record indicates that the CNF engages in violence primarily as a means of self-defense against the Burmese Government, a known human rights abuser that has engaged in systematic persecution of Burmese ethnic minorities, including the Chin Christians. * * *

* * *

The broad reach of the material support bar becomes even starker when viewed in light of the nature of the Burmese regime, and how it is regarded by the United States Government. In 2003, Congress passed the Burmese Freedom and Democracy Act of 2003, which, among other things, imposes sanctions on the Burmese Government as a result of its deplorable human rights record. The Secretary of State has designated Burma as one of a handful of "countries of particular concern" in light of this record, including its treatment of ethnic and religious minorities. In particular, the Burmese Government has engaged in arrests of Christian clergy, destruction of churches, prohibition of religious services and proselytizing by Christians, and forced conversions of Christians. These efforts are part of a larger effort to "Burmanize" the Chin ethnic minority.* * *

\* \* \*

In sum, what we have in this case is an individual who provided a relatively small amount of support to an organization that opposes one of the most repressive governments in the world, a government that is not recognized by the United States as legitimate and that has engaged in a brutal campaign against ethnic minorities. It is clear that the respondent poses no danger whatsoever to the national security of the United States. Indeed, by supporting the CNF in its resistance to the Burmese junta, it is arguable that the respondent actually acted in a manner consistent with United States foreign policy. And yet we cannot ignore the clear language that Congress chose in the material support provisions; the statute that we are required to apply mandates that we find the respondent ineligible for asylum for having provided material support to a terrorist organization.

\* \* \*

### Notes and Questions

1. *Matter of S–K–* and *Singh–Kaur* provide a telling contrast in political settings. The former arises in the context of groups espousing democracy against a military regime that refuses to allow elections and is a pariah to most of the world, the latter in the context of separatist conflict in a multiparty democracy. Is the BIA correct that Congress does not want any distinction to be drawn between the situations? If Congress believes there should be no distinction, is that good policy?

2. Why didn't Osuna dissent in *Matter of S–K–*? How would you change his opinion to turn it into a dissent?

3. In *Matter of S–K–*, the BIA took administrative notice that $1100 Singapore dollars corresponded to $685 in U.S. currency, and that this amount was triple the average annual income in Burma. In addition, the BIA stressed that contributing $100 Singapore dollars per month constituted one-eighth of the applicant's monthly income. Should the focus be on the percentage of income? Is the average income relevant? What other measures of "materiality" should be considered?

4. Whether calculated in Singapore or U.S. dollars, the amount in *Matter of S–K–* appeared to be substantially more than the support given in *Singh–Kaur*. In the *Singh–Kaur* majority's view, why did the food and

shelter supplied by the applicant constitute material support? Was it the number of people involved, the amount of food and shelter offered, the sense that it was a recurrent situation? Would offering a single bowl of rice to a relative who attended the meeting have been sufficient?

5. Does the apparent change in Singh–Kaur's account of his activities between the first filing of his application and his later clarifications have any bearing on the court's conclusion? Should it?

6. If S–K–receives no waiver under INA § 212(d)(3)(B) and then petitions in federal court for review of the denial of asylum and withholding, how should the court construe "material support"? Consider in this connection the provisions of the 1951 Convention that underlie the exclusion grounds in U.S. law. Would S–K–be excluded under these provisions? Isn't it reasonable to consider that providing a modest amount of aid to a violent organization constitutes "reasonable grounds for regarding" a person to be a "danger" to security?

In light of the reality that haven state officials will not have ready access to proof about all donations to violent organizations, how much of a showing should be required for concluding that reasonable grounds exist? How clear and present must the danger be? Does the Convention allow a state party to give the benefit of the doubt to the safety of its citizens?

Would you reach the same conclusion in a case where, rather than focusing on the amount, there was plausible evidence that the applicant had provided support under duress? In its footnote, the BIA seems to acknowledge that international law may require a different application of exclusion grounds from the one it reaches here (though it assumes that executive waiver will satisfy international law). Recall Chief Justice Marshall's rule of interpretation in *Murray v. The Charming Betsy*, 6 U.S. (2 Cranch) 64, 118, 2 L.Ed. 208 (1804): "an act of Congress ought never to be construed to violate the law of nations if any other possible construction remains." How does this rule of construction fit with the deference to administrative interpretation required by *Chevron* (discussed in Chapter Two, Section C above)?

7. Some members of Congress have proposed to amend the INA to reduce the impact of the "material support" provision on refugees, but without undermining its use (and that of a related criminal provision, 18 U.S.C. § 2339A) to deal with real supporters of dangerous terrorist organizations or activities. See, e.g., 83 Interp. Rel. 1046, 1047–48 (2006)(describing an unsuccessful amendment to this provision offered by Senator Leahy and several cosponsors). What are the key issues that such legislation should address? How would you change the statute to provide a more targeted exclusion provision?

8. At the time of this writing, we are unaware of any asylum case in which a waiver under § 212(d)(3)(B) has been granted, although there are reports that several dozen asylum cases involving the material support issue have been held for many months while final policy guidance on the waiver is developed. What is apparently the first use of that waiver power did occur, however, in May 2006, to enable a specific group of more than 9,000 Burmese refugees to be considered for resettlement in the United States

under the overseas refugee provisions of INA § 207. 83 Interp. Rel. 930 (2006). For more on the overseas refugee process, see Chapter Ten.

9. The statutory provisions applicable when Singh–Kaur was decided in 2004 had become more severe by 2006, when the BIA decided *Matter of S–K–*. The ever-increasing expansion of the terrorist activity bar can be traced through the statutory amendments in the 1996 Act, Pub. L. No. 104–208, 110 Stat. 3009, the 1996 Anti–Terrorism and Effective Death Penalty Act (AEDPA), Pub. L. No. 104–132, 110 Stat. 1214, the 2001 USA PATRIOT Act, Pub. L. No. 107–56, 115 Stat. 272, and the 2005 REAL ID Act, Pub. L. No. 109–13, 119 Stat. 231. For further commentary on the material support provision, *see* Lombardo, Buwalda, and Lyman, *Terrorism, Material Support, the Inherent Right to Self-Defense, and the U.S. Obligation to Protect Legitimate Asylum Seekers in a Post-9/11, Post-Patriot Act, Post-Real ID Act World*, 4 Regent J. Int'l L 237 (2006); Townley, *The Hydraulics of Fighting Terrorism*, 29 Hamline L.Rev. 65 (2006); Cole, *Enemy Aliens,* 54 Stan.L.Rev. 953 (2002).

### A Comparative Perspective

Article 33(2) provides an exception to the *nonrefoulement* obligation when there are reasonable grounds for regarding a refugee as a danger to the security of the country. In the wake of the terrorist attacks that occurred on September 11, 2001, we have begun to see more reliance on this clause. A Canadian court considering the deportation of a refugee from Sri Lanka based on his membership in the Liberation Tigers of Tamil Eelam (LTTE), commented: "[W]e believe courts may now conclude that the support of terrorism abroad raises a possibility of adverse repercussions on Canada's security * * *. It may once have made sense to suggest that terrorism in one country did not necessarily implicate other countries. But after the year 2001, that approach is no longer valid." *Suresh v. Canada (Minister of Citizenship and Immigration),* [2002] 1 S.C.R. 3, 2002 SCC 1, discussed at greater length in Chapter Seven.

In *Secretary of State for the Home Department v. Rehman,* 2001 UKHL 47 (2001), the highest court in the United Kingdom rejected a challenge to the government's decision to deport a Pakistani national on grounds of national security. Although the case did not concern an asylum seeker or applicant for refugee status, the deference paid by the Law Lords to the executive's deportation decision, which was based on confidential sources, was instructive. Lord Hoffman's concluding comment captured the tone:

> I wrote this speech some three months before the recent events in New York and Washington. They are a reminder that in matters of national security, the cost of failure can be high. This seems to me to underline the need for the judicial arm of government to respect the decisions of ministers of the Crown on the question of whether support for terrorist activities in a foreign country constitutes a threat to national security. It is not only that the executive has access to special information and

expertise in these matters. It is also that such decisions, with serious potential results for the community, require a legitimacy which can be conferred only by entrusting them to persons responsible to the community through the democratic process. If the people are to accept the consequences of such decisions, they must be made by persons whom the people have elected and whom they can remove.

---

### Exercise

Suppose your client, an asylum seeker in the United States, is a Tamil who had grown up in Sri Lanka. She has strong evidence that she would be persecuted if returned to her home country. The majority-Tamil area where she lived has been occupied for many years by the national army, made up primarily of ethnic Sinhalese, the majority group in Sri Lanka. In each scenario below, the question is whether she is barred from receiving protection in the United States.

1. In response to the occupation and in order to receive protection against marauding soldiers, she joined the Liberation Tigers of Tamil Elam (LTTE), a group accused of committing terrorist attacks in Sri Lanka and listed by the U.S. State Department as a terrorist organization. She did nothing to support the LTTE other than sign a membership card.

2. Same as scenario 1, but your client has convincing evidence that she is no longer a member of LTTE and has not been for the past five years.

3. Your client has never been a member of the LTTE, but did allow her brother, an active LTTE member, to stay at her house for one week. What if he stayed only one day?

4. Suppose your client had never been a member of the LTTE or knowingly helped anyone who was a member. After several people from her village were found decapitated, however, she gave the equivalent of $20 to two young women in her village in Sri Lanka whom she thought might be preparing a suicide bombing targeted against the occupying Sinhalese military forces.

---

## SECTION C. CESSATION OF PROTECTION

Thus far, Chapter Six has explored circumstances in which individuals who fear persecution are nonetheless barred from obtaining protection in the United States. We turn now to examine those who may have faced serious threats of persecution in the past but who no longer do so. In what situations can they be denied asylum or other protection in the

United States on the theory that they no longer need it? We will first look at cases involving individuals to whom government authorities have formally granted permission to remain in the United States based on their fear of persecution. Subsequently, we will address a different, but related situation: what should happen when an individual who had a genuine fear of persecution when she applied for asylum finds that the need for protection may have ceased while her application for asylum and withholding was pending.

## 1. TERMINATING PROTECTION

U.S. legislation states explicitly that the grant of asylum "does not convey a right to remain permanently in the United States." INA § 208 (c)(2). The Attorney General may terminate asylum in the following circumstances:

- the asylee no longer needs protection due to a fundamental change in circumstances;

- the asylee has voluntarily obtained the protection of his or her homeland by returning to the homeland with permanent resident status or the reasonable possibility of obtaining such status;

- the asylee has acquired a new nationality and has obtained the protection of the country of new nationality;

- the asylee may be removed pursuant to a bilateral or multilateral agreement to a third country where he or she would be eligible for asylum or equivalent temporary protection;

- the asylee has committed the wrongful conduct discussed in the prior section of this chapter that renders applicants ineligible for asylum.

INA § 208 (c)(2)(A–E).

In addition, the implementing regulations specify that asylum may also be terminated if there was fraud in the asylum application that rendered the applicant ineligible for asylum at the time it was granted, 8 C.F.R. § 208.24 (a)(1). The regulations also establish the termination procedure:

> Prior to the termination of a grant of asylum or withholding of deportation or removal, the alien shall be given notice of intent to terminate, with the reasons therefor, at least 30 days prior to the interview * * * before an asylum officer. The alien shall be provided the opportunity to present evidence showing that he or she is still eligible for asylum or withholding * * *. If the asylum officer determines that the alien is no longer eligible * * *, the alien shall be given written notice that asylum status or withholding * * * and any employment authorization * * * are terminated.

8 C.F.R. § 208.24(c).

Under the regulations, an immigration judge or the BIA can also terminate a grant of asylum or withholding in conjunction with a removal proceeding, provided that the individual has received a notice of intent to terminate and the government establishes by a preponderance of the evidence the grounds for termination delineated in the statute and the regulations. *Id.* at § 208.24(f).

In reality, the termination provisions are rarely invoked. Immigration courts frequently consider statutory grounds that might justify termination—changed political conditions, protection afforded by another country, past wrongdoing, and so on—but generally these issues do not arise after asylum has been granted. Rather they are addressed during the asylum procedure itself, and they affect whether the judge grants asylum in the first place. Sometimes, however, individuals granted protection in the United States are later convicted of crimes. Several recent cases explore the circumstances in which the United States can remove refugees due to their U.S. criminal convictions.

The cases below concern individuals admitted through the overseas refugee resettlement process, which will be discussed in Chapter Ten, rather than individuals who received asylum or withholding after arriving in the United States and then filing asylum applications. The core issue, however, is the same: when can the U.S. terminate protection of those acknowledged to have a well-founded fear of persecution?

The procedural setting of the cases involves applications for permanent resident status in the United States, a process that generally occurs after refugees have lived in the United States for one year. In the first case, the refugee from Haiti had not yet changed from refugee status to permanent resident status when she was convicted of her crime.

## MATTER OF JEAN

Attorney General, 2002.
23 I & N Dec. 373.

[ASHCROFT, ATTORNEY GENERAL:]

\* \* \*

Respondent Melanie Beaucejour Jean is a forty-five-year-old foreign national from Plaisance, Haiti. Accompanied by her husband and five children, she was conditionally admitted into the United States as a refugee in November 1994.

\* \* \*

In August 1995, the respondent pled guilty \* \* \* to one count of second-degree manslaughter in connection with the March 30, 1995 death of nineteen-month-old R–J–. \* \* \* R–J– had been left in her care that day by the boy's mother \* \* \*.

[After Jean completed her sentence, the INS began removal proceedings. The immigration judge denied all relief. The BIA reversed. The Attorney General overrode the BIA.]

### A.   Adjustment of Refugee Status

\* \* \* Section 209(a) provides that a refugee who has been physically present in the United States for at least one year and whose conditional admission status has not been previously terminated must return (or be returned) to INS custody for inspection and examination to determine eligibility for lawful permanent residency. If, after conducting this examination, an immigration officer concludes that the alien seeking permanent residency "is not clearly and beyond a doubt entitled to be admitted," he or she must be detained for a removal proceeding. \* \* \*

In the case at bar, the INS charged the respondent with being inadmissible by virtue of her conviction for a crime involving moral turpitude. She \* \* \* conceded her statutory inadmissibility. [Nevertheless, she] sought a waiver pursuant to INA § 209(c), a provision empowering the Attorney General to waive most disqualifying barriers to an alien refugee's admissibility under INA § 212(a) "for humanitarian purposes, to assure family unity, or when it is otherwise in the public interest."

\* \* \*

The Board's analysis, which makes no attempt to balance claims of hardship to the respondent's family against the gravity of her criminal offense, is grossly deficient. The opinion marginalizes the depravity of her crime, stating simply that the panel had "weighed the equities in this case against the respondent's criminal conviction" and concluded that discretionary relief was warranted. Little or no significance appears to have been attached to the fact that the respondent confessed to beating and shaking a nineteen-month-old child to death, or that her confession was corroborated by a coroner's report documenting a wide-ranging collection of extraordinarily severe injuries.

To be sure, the respondent's removal will undoubtedly impose a strain on her family.\* \* \* Administrative evaluations of requests for waivers of inadmissibility under INA § 209(c) cannot, however, focus solely on family hardships, but must consider the nature of the criminal offense that rendered an alien inadmissible in the first place.

In my judgment, that balance will nearly always require the denial of a request for discretionary relief from removal where an alien's criminal conduct is as serious as that of the respondent. \* \* \* It would not be a prudent exercise of the discretion afforded to me by this provision to grant favorable adjustments of status to violent or dangerous individuals except in extraordinary circumstances, such as those involving national security or foreign policy considerations, or cases in which an alien clearly demonstrates that the denial of status adjustment would result in exceptional and extremely unusual hardship. Moreover, depending on the gravity of the alien's underlying criminal offense, such a showing might still be insufficient. From its inception, the United States has always been a nation of immigrants; it is one of our greatest strengths. But aliens arriving at our shores must understand that residency in the United States is a *privilege*, not a *right*. For those aliens, like the respondent, who engage in violent criminal acts during their stay here, this country will not offer its embrace. The BIA's grant of lawful permanent residency is reversed.

### B. Asylum

The respondent also sought asylum pursuant to INA § 208. * * *

Establishing "refugee" status is not the only hurdle an alien seeking asylum must clear in order to be considered eligible for such relief. Indeed, there are a series of exceptions outlined in INA § 208(b)(2) under which all aliens—including "refugees"—are statutorily barred from asylum. As relevant here, an alien convicted of a "particularly serious crime," defined for these purposes as any "aggravated felony," may not be granted asylum under any circumstances. Furthermore, even if asylum eligibility is established, the decision whether to grant an application is committed to the Attorney General's discretion.

* * *

Ultimately, however, it is unnecessary for me to resolve whether the respondent's conviction constitutes a "crime of violence" or whether she has otherwise satisfied the eligibility standards for asylum. Even assuming that the respondent not only qualifies as a "refugee," but that her criminal conviction does not preclude her eligibility, she is manifestly unfit for a *discretionary* grant of relief. For the same reasons articulated in the earlier discussion of the respondent's application for adjustment of status, I am highly disinclined to exercise my discretion—except, again, in extraordinary circumstances * * *.

### C. Withholding of Removal

Finally, the respondent asserts that she is legally entitled to withholding of removal * * *.

* * *

Once again, however, it is unnecessary for me to address the proper characterization of the respondent's criminal offense because there are other, clearer grounds for the denial of her claim for relief. In particular, she has failed to prove that her life or freedom would be threatened in Haiti on the basis of race, religion, nationality, membership in a particular social group, or political opinion.

* * *

The respondent maintains that she is likely to be persecuted by members of the former Haitian Army as well as the Ton Ton Macoutes, a private Haitian death squad first organized by former President Francois Duvalier. To support this claim, the respondent and her husband testified at the removal hearing that the husband was assaulted and nearly killed in the early 1990s as a result of his work with the Fanmi Lavalas, a political party headed by then-opposition leader Jean-Bertrand Aristide. They further alleged that Haitian soldiers burned the home shared by the respondent and her husband, as well as the homes of many of their relatives. The soldiers also purportedly killed the father and two cousins of the respondent's husband.

Although clearly tragic, these events do not demonstrate that any past persecution was directed at the respondent. As the immigration judge correctly noted, the attacks described at the hearing were all targeted at the respondent's *husband*, not at the respondent *herself*. Respondent did testify that she was a member of "Committee 1991 Haiti," a social group supposedly regarded by the Haitian Army as an opposition political faction. Yet, she offered no evidence that this affiliation would have been sufficient to make her an independent target of either the Haitian Army or the Ton Ton Macoutes.

Furthermore, even assuming that the respondent could establish a presumption of future persecution based on the events detailed above, she still would be entitled to no relief here. The political climate in Haiti has changed dramatically since the respondent left in 1994, and it is no longer likely that her life or freedom would be threatened there. * * *

\* \* \*

The State Department's most recent country report also fails to bolster the respondent's claim. [It] points out that members of the former opposition party to which the respondent's husband belonged now occupy most key government positions, including the national law enforcement institutions. Moreover, Aristide was elected to a second term as President in February 2001, and the Fanmi Lavales [sic] maintained control of the Haitian Senate in the 2000 elections. In short, the record simply does not support the respondent's claim that her life or freedom would be threatened if she were returned to Haiti. Accordingly, her application for withholding of removal is denied.

\* \* \*

In *Matter of Jean* the immigration judge had ruled against Jean twice and had been reversed both times by the BIA. In its second opinion, the BIA maintained that Jean's second-degree manslaughter conviction did not constitute a crime of violence and that Jean's application for a waiver of inadmissibility should be granted due to the equities in favor of Jean, a mother of five and a refugee from Haiti. The Attorney General directed the BIA to refer the case to him for review; he designated his opinion, with its ferocious criticism of the BIA's ruling, as a precedent. The Fifth Circuit affirmed. *Jean v. Gonzales*, 452 F.3d 392 (5th Cir. 2006).

In the next case, a refugee from Bosnia–Herzegovina had adjusted his status from refugee to lawful permanent resident before his convictions.

# MATTER OF SMRIKO

Board of Immigration Appeals, 2005.
23 I & N Dec. 836.

HOLMES, BOARD MEMBER:

* * *

The respondent was admitted to the United States as a refugee [from Bosnia and Herzegovena] on October 20, 1994* * *. In May 1996, his status was adjusted to that of a lawful permanent resident pursuant to section 209 of the Act. Following his convictions for theft offenses in December 1996 and April 1999, the respondent was placed in removal proceedings and was charged with having been convicted of crimes involving moral turpitude.

* * *

The respondent relies on section 207(c)(4) of the Act for the proposition that he remains a refugee under section 207 and is therefore immune from removal proceedings until his refugee status is terminated. Section 207(c)(4) provides as follows:

> The refugee status of an alien (and of the spouse or child of the alien) may be terminated by the Attorney General pursuant to such regulations as the Attorney General may prescribe if the Attorney General determines that the alien was not in fact a refugee within the meaning of section 101(a)(42) at the time of the alien's admission.

The respondent asserts that he cannot be removed from the United States based on his criminal convictions because his refugee status was not terminated pursuant to section 207(c)(4), and there is no other provision in the Act or the regulations that provides for termination or cancellation of refugee status.

* * *

The provisions governing refugee admissions provide support for the view that Congress did not intend to immunize aliens admitted as refugees from placement in removal proceedings. Section 207 of the Act outlines the process for admission of refugees * * *. For aliens admitted as refugees under section 207, section 209 of the Act provides [a] framework for eventual adjustment of status to lawful permanent resident * * *.

Under this provision, a refugee whose admission has not been terminated by the Attorney General is to be inspected and examined for admission as an immigrant within the general framework for removal proceedings. * * *

* * *

\* \* \* [T]he refugee adjustment process indicates that a refugee, although conditionally admitted to the United States, may be placed in removal proceedings without regard to whether refugee status has been terminated pursuant to section 207(c)(4). The respondent's argument that the Attorney General's termination of refugee status is a precondition to removal is directly refuted by the statute, the promulgating regulation, and the Attorney General's explanation of the refugee adjustment process in *Matter of Jean, supra.* \* \* \*

If conditional admission as a refugee does not immunize an alien from the general grounds of admissibility, it follows that a refugee admitted as a lawful permanent resident, such as the respondent, is not immunized from the grounds for removal that are applicable to all other aliens. Otherwise, a refugee convicted of a removable offense prior to adjustment of status could be placed in removal proceedings, while a refugee who, like the respondent, was convicted after adjustment of status for the same offense would be immune from removal. We find no logical basis, and no support in the statutory or regulatory framework, for drawing such a distinction based on whether the conviction occurred before or after adjustment of status. \* \* \*

Under the respondent's view, an alien admitted as a refugee who subsequently adjusted status could commit crimes with impunity, or even engage in terrorist activity and remain exempt from removal from the United States, without regard to whether he or she had a continuing need for protection from persecution in the country of origin, so long as refugee status was not terminated by the Attorney General. Given that the Attorney General is authorized to terminate refugee status only when it is determined that the alien was not, in fact, a refugee at the time of his or her initial admission as a refugee, the vast majority of aliens admitted as refugees would be immune from removal without regard to conduct after admission. It is difficult to imagine that Congress intended such a result.

\* \* \*

The respondent argues that his removal would violate the United Nations Convention Relating to the Status of Refugees \* \* \*. This argument fails to take into account the protections included in the context of removal proceedings, which implement the provisions of the Convention and the Protocol. These protections are afforded to all aliens, not just to those admitted as refugees. Most importantly, section 241(b)(3) of the Act generally precludes the return of any alien to a country where the alien's life or freedom would be threatened because of race, religion, nationality, membership in a particular social group, or political opinion. Additionally, the provisions of the asylum law in section 208 of the Act afford relief from removal to aliens who continue to meet the definition of a "refugee" \* \* \*.

In this regard, the Convention provides that its refugee protections cease to apply in situations in which "the circumstances in connexion with which [refugee status was recognized] have ceased to exist." Convention, art. 1C(5). The respondent was afforded the opportunity to pursue a claim to asylum or withholding of removal in the proceedings below. He ultimately declined to seek such relief after acknowledging that he no longer faces a threat to his life or freedom and no longer has a well-founded fear of persecution in Bosnia and Herzegovina. We therefore find little force to the respondent's contentions that the statutory framework under which he was found removable violates provisions of the Convention or the Protocol.

* * *

[The BIA dismissed the appeal and ordered Smriko removed to Bosnia and Herzegovina.]

### Notes and Questions

1.   These opinions outline the basic statutory framework: certain criminal conduct is the basis for removing non-citizens, including permanent residents, from the United States. Non-citizens can contest these charges in immigration court; those deemed removable can seek asylum or withholding. The immigration court then must provide them with a full hearing on their current eligibility for protection.

When Jean and Smriko were admitted as refugees, they established that they had a well-founded fear of persecution. Later, as part of the removal proceedings, both had the opportunity to present evidence showing that they still had a well-founded fear of persecution. At first blush, it seems curious and redundant: refugees, admitted because they feared persecution, have to establish a second time that they fear persecution and therefore are eligible for asylum, or—more realistically—withholding. Two factors have changed, however, since they were admitted as refugees: (1) time has passed and (2) they have been convicted of crimes. Consequently, the removal proceedings transform the matter into a forward-looking inquiry. They will only be able to stave off removal if they can show a well-founded fear of persecution in the future.

2.   The thrust of Smriko's argument is that removing a refugee from the U.S. requires two steps: (1) terminating refugee status, and (2) applying the basic removal procedures. The BIA concluded that Congress did not intend to provide a two-part process. Putting aside the congressional intent, can you think of policy reasons that support Smriko's viewpoint? Does the 1951 Refugee Convention support Smriko? For an argument that international law requires the explicit termination of refugee status before removal from the country, see Huber (Note), *Refugees in the U.S.: Protected from Persecution or Vulnerable to Unjust Removal?*, 20 St. John's J. L. Comm. 199 (2005). What about the BIA's conclusion that this would grant refugees impunity for future wrongdoing?

3.   In addition to refugees resettled from overseas, those granted asylum can apply to adjust their status to permanent resident. They must wait one year after being granted asylum, show their continuing eligibility for asylum, and demonstrate they are admissible to the U.S. When granted, their lawful permanent residence dates back one year prior to approval of their application. INA § 209 (b)(2). Originally, the statute imposed a limit on

the number of asylees who could be granted permanent residence each year, which created great backlogs, but, as noted in Chapter Two, Section B, the annual quotas were eliminated by legislation in 2005.

## 2. CHANGED CIRCUMSTANCES

Political and social conditions are dynamic. Many times the situation that impelled people to flee their homeland changes. Sometimes it changes for the better, sometimes for the worse. In those fortunate scenarios when things improve, many people return to their country of origin. Should they be forced to return? Or, more precisely, do the countries that gave them shelter have the right to send them away? As noted above, the statute provides that asylum can be terminated when a fundamental change in circumstances removes the fear of persecution that an asylee once had.

Although the statute provides for this possibility, which reflects international norms that will be discussed below, the United States has not made a practice of revoking asylum when conditions in the homeland improve. Wars have ended, dictators have been overthrown, and other less dramatic improvements have occurred in countries from which U.S. asylees fled, but there are no reported decisions of U.S. authorities seeking to revoke asylum based on these changes in circumstances.

Evidence of changed circumstances does play a frequent role in asylum adjudication, however, in the context of applicants proving their asylum claim. Changes in circumstances can become relevant when the situation in the country of origin improves during the interim between the asylum seeker's departure and the filing of the asylum application, or when the improvement occurs while the asylum adjudication is ongoing. The regulations establish a presumption of future persecution if the applicant proves past persecution on a Convention ground, which shifts the burden of proof to the government. One basis for government rebuttal is a showing that there has been a "fundamental change in circumstances such that the applicant no longer has a well-founded fear of persecution" in the home country. 8 C.F.R. § 208.13(b)(1). A similar presumption applies to withholding of removal, which is worded somewhat differently to reflect the different risk standard applicable to withholding. 8 C.F.R. § 208.16(b)(1). The Second Circuit recently engaged in a searching analysis of the proof relevant to establishing change in circumstances. You may wish to refer to the text of the regulations as you consider this case.

## TAMBADOU v. GONZALES

United States Court of Appeals, Second Circuit, 2006.
446 F.3d 298.

PARKER, CIRCUIT JUDGE.

The petitioner, Cheikh Tambadou, a thirty-one-year-old Muslim native of Mauritania, seeks review of an order of the Board of Immigration Appeals dismissing his appeal from the denial for his application for asylum. * * * [T]he BIA concluded that the claim for asylum failed because Petitioner "no longer has an objectively reasonable fear of future persecution" in Mauritania due to a "fundamental change in circumstances" there.

* * *

Tambadou was born in the town of Jowel, Mauritania and raised in a family of farmers. His ethnic background is Soninke, a small minority group in Mauritania. The Maurs, the dominant ethnic group in Mauritania, controlled the government and, as Tambadou testified, "have a deep hatred for the Soninke because [of] the color of our skin and our ethnic background." Tambadou supported, but was not a member of, the Liberation Front of Africans in Mauritania ("FLAM"), an organization whose main objective is "equality among all the groups, white and black." According to the United Nations High Commissioner for Refugees ("UNHCR"), the Mauritanian government considers FLAM a threat to its control of the country.

Tambadou further testified that, at age 15, while preparing to work in the field with his brother and father, a military vehicle with six officers inside stopped at the field. When the officers got out of the truck, Petitioner saw that there were a number of people detained in the truck. The officers asked for their identification cards. When his father protested and inquired, the officers stated that they "heard [they] were not Mauritanians, [that they were] from Senegal." Tambadou and his brother were too young to have identification cards, but did have birth certificates. His father returned to the house, retrieved family identification papers, and presented them to the officers, who cursorily examined them, tore them up, and, again, accused them of not being native Mauritanians. Tambadou testified that when he protested, the officers grabbed and beat him, threw him into the truck, and took him to prison where he remained for two months. Tambadou testified that while in jail he received little food and frequent beatings and was housed in a crowded cell where the prisoners slept in shifts due to a lack of space. The guards repeatedly asked Tambadou and the other prisoners to confess that they were Sengalese [sic] and not Mauritanian. For over two months, Tambadou maintained that he was Mauritanian, but he and other prisoners eventually acquiesced and told their jailers that they were Senegalese.

At that point, in February 1990, the officers, at gunpoint, escorted him with fifteen other detainees by truck to a river bank where they were told to cross the river or be shot. Tambadou and the others entered the river by canoe while the officers fired at them. When one of the shots pierced the canoe, Tambadou hit his head on a metal object and the canoe overturned. He and the others were then picked up in a second canoe by the International Red Cross.

* * * Tambadou was then taken, unconscious, to a hospital in Matam, Senegal where he remained for over two months. In May, 1990,

the Red Cross representatives transferred him to a refugee camp where he was reunited with his family. At the hearing, Tambadou introduced into evidence his identification card from the camp.

Tambadou testified that he left the camp in November 1995 because the Red Cross was not providing adequate food and went to Dakar where he found work as a porter in a store. His family remained at the camp. In January 1996, Tambadou left Dakar and traveled to the United States by ship* * *.

In September 1997, Tambadou applied for political asylum, withholding of removal, and voluntary departure. The IJ denied the application. * * *

The BIA denied Tambadou's appeal, * * * finding "a fundamental change in circumstances in Mauritania such that [Tambadou] no longer has an objectively reasonable fear of future persecution there." In reaching this conclusion, the BIA relied almost exclusively on a State Department Report published in 1997, which reported that the Mauritanian government was cooperating with humanitarian groups "to assist returnees from the refugee camps in Senegal" who were expelled between 1989 and 1991. The BIA found that, because Petitioner did not offer contradictory evidence, the State Department profile was entitled to deference. * * *

* * *

We have provided guidance on how State Department country reports should be utilized, emphasizing that "the immigration court should be careful not to place excessive reliance" on them. *Tian-Yong Chen* [*v. INS*, 359 F.3d 121 (2d Cir. 2004)] at 130. Specifically, we have explained:

> Such State Department reports are usually the result of estimable expertise and earnestness of purpose, and they often provide a useful and informative overview of conditions in the applicant's home country. But their observations do not automatically discredit contrary evidence presented by the applicant, and they are not binding on the immigration court. Thus, where a report suggests that, *in general*, an individual in the applicant's circumstances would not suffer or reasonably fear persecution in a particular country, the immigration court may consider that evidence, but it is obligated to consider also any contrary or countervailing evidence with which it is presented, as well as the particular circumstances of the applicant's case demonstrated by testimony and other evidence.

> In addition, the immigration court cannot assume that a report produced by the State Department—an agency of the Executive Branch of Government that is necessarily bound to be concerned to avoid abrading relations with other countries, especially other major world powers—presents the most accurate picture of human rights in the country at issue. We note the

widely held view that the State Department's reports are some-times skewed toward the governing administration's foreign-policy goals and concerns.

*Id.* (internal citations omitted).

The BIA, in an abbreviated (three paragraph) opinion, found that the Report established that Mauritanians expelled in 1989–1991 were being repatriated without persecution and then concluded that Tamba-dou had failed to present evidence to the contrary. To support its finding, the BIA relied almost exclusively on its own case, Matter of T–M–B, for the proposition that where an asylum applicant offers no contradictory evidence to a State Department report, the BIA defers to the report. 21 I. & N. Dec. 775, 779 (BIA 1997), rev'd by *Borja v. INS*, 175 F.3d 732 (9th Cir. 1999) (en banc). Here, not only was there contradictory testimony that the BIA ignored, but it failed to use the information in the Report in a case-specific manner and supplement it with further analysis. Moreover, Matter of T–M–B, had been reversed by the Ninth Circuit en banc, before the BIA decided this case. The Ninth Circuit found that the BIA erred as a matter of law because it failed to conduct an "individualized analysis of how changed conditions [would] affect the specific petitioner's situation." *Borja*, 175 F.3d at 738 (internal quotation marks omitted).* * * The BIA generally stated that refugees were reportedly being repatriated over a number of years, and concluded that this analysis was sufficient to deny asylum. For several reasons, we do not agree.

To begin, the Report catalogues conditions as they existed in Mauri-tania in 1996. When the BIA considered this appeal in 2002, it is difficult to see how the Report could be said to describe "current" conditions. See *Tian-Yong Chen*, 359 F.3d at 131–132. Also, in his appeal to the BIA, the Petitioner cited the Report and explained that it did not "indicate any significant changes in the human rights conditions of black ethnic people in Mauritania." Citing his testimony before the IJ, Tambadou asserted that for him "to return to a country where, according to the State Department, slavery in the form of unofficial, forced or involuntary servitude exists, will undoubtedly subject him to continued persecution by the very government which ousted him from Mauritania." In addi-tion, he testified that the "prevailing Mauritanian governmental attitude also allows the Mauritanian government to continue to practice human rights abuses because the victims who are part of the Mauritanian status quo have no recourse against this atrocious treatment." Moreover, during cross-examination, the government asked whether Tambadou was aware that, "according to the Department of State that of the approximately 70,000 Afro–Mauritanians who were expelled from Mauri-tania and fled to Senegal during [1989–1991], that it's estimated that 30,000 to 35,000 have returned?" Petitioner answered: "I heard that people went back. What I hear right now that those who went back, many of them were killed. I am concerned about myself. Others, what they do, I'm not concerned about it but I do know that some of them went back and they were killed." Petitioner also testified that, "They do not want us physically in there because they don't like us and they will kill us."

Thus, the record does not support the BIA's conclusion that Petitioner presented no evidence in response to the "changed conditions" described by the Report. On the contrary, the BIA deferred to the Report in a casual, conclusory fashion, ignored the contradictory information that Tambadou presented, and then failed to make the required individualized analysis.

The BIA also ignored significant information favorable to Tambadou in the Report. * * * Specifically, the Report identifies abuses of returned refugees in communities along the Senegal River, noting only that the "extent of the abuses [had] declined." The BIA apparently did not fully perceive the significant distinction between a drop in abuses and an end to abuses.

The Report does not support the BIA's conclusion that conditions have so improved such that the Soninke are no longer persecuted* * *. * * * [T]he Report notes that many members of certain ethnic groups, including the Soninke, feel excluded from political representation and that "some hostility and bitterness persist[s] between ethnic groups." In addition, the Report notes widespread distrust of the judicial system and a belief that security officials are "not subject to legal restraints," in part due to a failure to "bring to justice officials who commit abuses and fail to observe legal procedures."

In sum, the BIA used an outdated report that may not have accurately reflected the current conditions in Mauritania, accepted general statements in this outdated Report as fact, ignored the complexities of the reported information, did not make an individualized assessment of Tambadou's situation, and failed to consider his evidence which contradicted the changed conditions described in the Report. See *Tian-Yong Chen*, 359 F.3d 121 at 131–32. Moreover, the Board did not engage in an individualized analysis beyond its general conclusions based on its over-simplified reading of a complex document. Thus, the BIA's changed circumstances determination, its sole basis for denying the appeal, was not supported by "reasonable, substantial, and probative evidence in the record when considered as a whole." *Secaida–Rosales* [*v. INS*, 331 F.3d 297 (2d Cir. 2003)] at 307 (internal quotation omitted). Consequently, we vacate the BIA's decision and remand.

\* \* \*

### Notes and Questions

1. Sixteen years had passed between Tambadou's departure from Mauritania and the Second Circuit's opinion. The court acknowledged that there had been a significant improvement in the conditions in Mauritania, but criticized the BIA for its reliance on outdated materials and for its failure to make an individualized assessment of how the general changes would affect Tambadou. Is this a reasonable burden to impose on the government? What

kind of evidence would be sufficiently detailed to satisfy the court? How hard would it be to obtain that evidence?

2. Even if there had been current information that was relevant to Tambadou's personal situation, how would the court know whether the changes that had occurred were "fundamental," as the statute requires? In this context, does fundamental mean widespread? Long-lasting? Democratic?

3. If Tambadou had been granted asylum and the U.S. had sought to terminate protection due to a fundamental change in circumstances, INA § 208(c)(2)(A), which party would bear the burden of proof? Generally, the asylum seeker has the burden of proving eligibility for asylum. INA § 208 (b)(1)(B); 8 C.F.R. § 208.13(a). Should the burden of proof shift to the government when it seeks to withdraw protection from an individual previously granted asylum or recognized as a refugee? Who should bear the burden of proving changed circumstances when the asylum seeker has not yet been recognized as a refugee? U.S. regulations require the government to prove a fundamental change in circumstances when trying to rebut eligibility for asylum once the individual has successfully shown past persecution, 8 C.F.R. § 208.13(b)(1)(ii), but what about changes in circumstances that might affect an applicant who had not suffered past persecution? Consider the regulations on both termination and past persecution in connection with your answer: 8 C.F.R. §§ 208.13(b), 208.16(b), 208.24.

### An International Perspective

The 1951 Convention views refugee status as a temporary phenomenon. The first portion of Article 1 defines those who qualify as a refugee, and the very next clause specifies that the treaty shall cease to apply to refugees in certain circumstances. As you read the terms of Article 1(C), often referred to as the Cessation Clause, you should compare them to the U.S. legislative provisions described at the beginning of this section. INA § 208(c)(2), 8 C.F.R. § 208.24(a),(b). Article 1(C) provides that protection shall cease to apply to the following persons:

- the refugee has voluntarily re-availed herself of the protection of her country of nationality;

- the refugee, having lost her nationality, has voluntarily reacquired it;

- the refugee has acquired a new nationality and enjoys the protection of the country of new nationality;

- the refugee has voluntarily re-established herself in the country of persecution;

- the refugee can no longer refuse to avail herself of the protection of the country of nationality because the circumstances in connection with her recognition as a refugee have ceased to exist;

- the refugee, though stateless, can return to her country of long-term residence because the circumstances in connection with her recognition as a refugee have ceased to exist.

You can see that the first four provisions of Article I (C) focus on changes in the personal situation of the individual refugee, whereas the others focus on changes in the country conditions that triggered the need for protection. Common to all of the provisions is the belief that it is legitimate to terminate refugee status when the refugee no longer fears persecution, either because she has found permanent protection elsewhere or because she can reclaim the protection of her homeland.

There is relatively little commentary concerning the Cessation Clause, although it has begun to draw attention lately. It appears that states rarely, if ever, invoke these provisions as a basis for terminating refugee status. The UNHCR, however, has garnered some experience in this area. The UNHCR has reviewed the refugee populations receiving UNHCR assistance and questioned whether improvements in the conditions in the countries of origin would justify ending some of the assistance programs. This has not happened frequently; over the past 25 years the UNHCR has only identified 21 situations in which it applied the "ceased circumstances" clause, and many of these were the result of the end of the Cold War. Fitzpatrick and Bonoan, *Cessation of Refugee Protection*, in Refugee Protection in International Law (E. Feller, V. Türk, and F. Nicholson eds., 2003), at 501. Nonetheless, there is a growing interest in the applicability of the cessation provisions of the 1951 Refugee Convention, and a recent study analyzes many of the relevant issues.

## JOAN FITZPATRICK AND RAFAEL BONOAN, CESSATION OF REFUGEE PROTECTION

Refuge Protection in International Law
(E. Feller, V. Türk, and F. Nicholson eds., 2003).
491, 494–96, 501, 512–13, 530–31, 539.

The experience of being a refugee can be a defining moment in a person's life, but refugee status is not necessarily intended to be permanent. The cessation of refugee protection poses policy and administrative challenges for States and the Office of the United Nations High Commissioner for Refugees (UNHCR), as well as risks for refugees.

\* \* \*

The *Handbook* articulates a concept of 'fundamental changes in the country [of origin], which can be assumed to remove the basis of the fear of persecution'.

\* \* \*

A fundamental change in circumstances has typically involved developments in governance and human rights that result in a complete political transformation of a country of origin. Evidence of such a transformation may include 'significant reforms altering the basic legal or social structure of the State \* \* \* [or] democratic elections, declarations of amnesties, repeal of oppressive laws and dismantling of former security services'. In addition, the 'annulment of judgments against political opponents and, generally, the re-establishment of legal protections and guarantees offering security against the reoccurrence of the discriminatory actions which had caused the refugees to leave' may also be considered. Changes in these areas must also be 'effective' in the sense that they 'remove the basis of the fear of persecution'. It is therefore necessary to assess these developments 'in light of the particular cause of fear'.

\* \* \*

Large-scale successful voluntary repatriation may also provide evidence of a fundamental change in circumstances. The repatriation and reintegration of refugees can promote the consolidation of such developments. However, refugees may choose to return to their country of origin well before fundamental and durable changes have occurred. Therefore, voluntary repatriation may be considered in an evaluation of conditions in the country of origin, but it cannot be taken as evidence that changes of a fundamental nature have occurred.

\* \* \*

Despite receiving regular consideration within the organization, the ceased circumstances provisions have only been applied by UNHCR to refugee populations under its mandate on twenty-one occasions during the period from 1973 to 1999. According to UNHCR, the cessation clauses have not been used extensively for two reasons. First, the availability of alternative solutions, such as voluntary repatriation, has usually obviated the need to invoke the cessation clauses. Secondly, it has often been difficult to determine whether developments in a country of origin warranted the application of the cessation clauses. Rather, UNHCR has issued declarations of cessation mainly to 'provide a legal framework for the discontinuation of UNHCR's protection and material assistance to refugees and to promote with States of asylum concerned the provision of an alternative residence status to the former refugees'.

The cases in which UNHCR has ultimately invoked Article 1C(5) and (6) on a group basis can be organized according to the kind of change that has occurred in the country of origin. Three basic types of change in circumstances can be identified: (i) accession to independent statehood; (ii) achievement of a successful transition to democracy; and (iii) resolution of a civil conflict.

\* \* \*

Although frequently considered by UNHCR, the ceased circumstances cessation clauses are 'little used' by States. The reasons vary, but they include the administrative costs of terminating individual grants of refugee status based upon a review of general human rights conditions in the State of origin, the recognition that termination of refugee status may not result in repatriation where the refugee is eligible to remain with another legal status, and State facilitation of naturalization pursuant to Article 34 of the 1951 Convention. In the case of group-based refugee protection, States of refuge may hesitate to declare cessation because of the instability of conditions in the State of origin and because assistance from the international community may be adversely affected.

\* \* \*

Article 1C has been incorporated into some national asylum laws, especially those enacted within the past decade. Unfortunately, these statutes sometimes combine cessation provisions with others concerning revocation (cancellation) of refugee status on grounds of fraudulent procurement, exclusion under Article 1F, and expulsion under Article 33(2). Similar confusion characterizes statutes in some African States implementing Article 1.4 of the OAU Refugee Convention. The better practice is to treat cessation separately, and not to combine it with provisions concerning persons undeserving of protection. Distinct treatment of cessation in national law facilitates careful attention to procedural fairness and to compelling circumstances that justify non-return.

Ceased circumstances cessation poses serious difficulties for States Parties, particularly in regard to: (i) assessment of fundamental, durable, and effective change in the State of origin; (ii) fair process; and (iii) provision for exceptions to cessation or to return.

\* \* \*

Serious confusion may arise where elements usually associated with cessation figure during refugee status determination. In some asylum States that generally do not impose cessation on recognized refugees, the volume of recent cases involving changed circumstances between flight and initial adjudication is extensive. \* \* \* '[R]efugee status determination and cessation procedures should be seen as separate and distinct processes'.

\* \* \*

The differences between cessation proper and denial of refugee status because post-flight developments have undermined an asylum claim should be emphasized. The tendency of asylum States to apply cessation concepts during initial status determination creates confusion that may undermine the development of clear and fair substantive and procedural standards for cessation.

\* \* \*

### Notes and Questions

1.    Fitzpatrick and Bonoan worry that some national legislation mixes together issues of cessation, revocation, exclusion, expulsion, and initial refugee status determination. Can you articulate what each term means and how each differs from the others? What are the advantages of treating these

issues together? Of treating them separately? How does the U.S. asylum law deal with these issues?

2.    In another portion of the article, the authors emphasize the need for procedural fairness in applying the cessation provisions. At a minimum they specify the need for (1) a notice to appear (and notice of intent to terminate protection) in a language the refugee understands, (2) a neutral decision maker, (3) a hearing where the refugee can produce a wide range of evidence and rebut the state's evidence, (4) an individualized analysis of the impact of the changed conditions on the refugee's personal situation; (5) an interpreter for the hearing, if necessary, (6) an opportunity to apply for another lawful status or to seek other relief if there are compelling reasons to avoid repatriation, (7) burden of proof on the state; (8) a delay in order to assess the permanence of the change; and (9) a possibility of appeal. *Id*. at 515, 538. How do the U.S. termination procedures fare under these guidelines?

3.    The authors also examine the four cessation clauses relating to change in the personal circumstances of refugees, such as voluntarily reavailing themselves of the protection of their homeland or voluntarily re-establishing themselves there. They stress that the voluntariness of the refugees' actions, the refugees' actual intent, and the ability of the homelands to provide effective protection are critical. *Id*. at 523–529.

4.    Although the 1951 Refugee Convention requires voluntary conduct by the refugee before states can withdraw refugee status based on individual actions taken by refugees, does the Convention implicitly require voluntary return before states can withdraw refugee status based on changed circumstances? In a provocative article, James Hathaway argues that states have the right to repatriate refugees involuntarily so long as there has been a fundamental and enduring change in circumstances in the country of origin that has removed the reasons for flight. He distinguishes the UNHCR emphasis on voluntary repatriation after circumstances have changed, a sensible approach for an agency dealing with complex emergency situations involving many states, from the normative framework that applies to asylum states after the underlying conflict ceases in the refugees' homelands. Hathaway, *The Right of States to Repatriate Former Refugees*, 20 Ohio State J. on Disp. Res. 175 (2005). *See* also Zieck, *Vanishing Points of the Refugee Law Regime: Response to James Hathaway*, 20 Ohio St. J. on Disp. Res. 217 (2005).

5.    The UNHCR has provided guidance on Cessation Clause issues in UNHCR, Guidelines on International Protection: Cessation of Refugee Status under Article 1C(5) and (6) of the 1951 Convention, HCR/GIP/03/03, 10 Feb. 2003; UNHCR, The Cessation Clauses: Guidelines on their Application, Apr. 1999; UNHCR, Note on the Cessation Clauses, UN doc. EC/47/SC/CRP.30, 30 May 1997. For additional commentary, *see* Tarwater, *Analysis and Case Studies of the "Ceased Circumstances" Cessation Clause of the 1951 Refugee Convention*, 15 Geo. Imm. Law J. 563 (2001); Cheng, *Emigres of the Killing Fields: The Deportation of Cambodian Refugees as a Violation of International Human Rights*, 25 B.C. Third World L.J. 221 (2005). Analysis of relevant Australian jurisprudence can be found in O'Sullivan, *Before the High Court: Minister for Immigration v. QAAH: Cessation of Refugee Status*, 28 Sydney L. Rev. 359 (2006).

# Chapter Seven

# THE CONVENTION AGAINST TORTURE

---

*When I was fourteen and graduated from primary school, my whole class joined or went to the military school or boot camp.* * * * *In my case, I dreaded the thought of working by the machete—working on my family's parcel of land. It was too hard and too much suffering and poverty. I would do anything to avoid that.*

\* \* \*

*After six months of training, we were divided up. About two hundred of us were sent to paratroopers school. We learned parachuting, self-defense, torture, and how to kill using a bayonet.* * * *

*The purpose of the torture and bayonet killing was to be able to kill and not leave traces that the military had done the killing. We learned how to break bones, puncture lungs, which made bodies inflate, rupture or sever blood vessels so they would bleed to death. We learned how to electrocute using two needles and an outlet. We used this especially against professors and students.*

*\* \* \* Our first assignment was to kill 1,500 campesinos from different zones in the area. We were given a list of names and told that these campesinos were buying and selling their produce through cooperatives, that they had refused to sell to the government corporation, ENDECA, from which the government made a lot of money. The other reason was simply that the campesinos were sitting on good land that either a military officer or a millionaire or the government wanted.*

\* \* \*

> —*Ex-Army sergeant,*
> *Guatemala*[1]

---

**1.** C. Kismaric, Forced Out: The Agony of the Refugee in Our Time 56 (1989).

Suppose that your client has been convicted of extortion or another aggravated felony and sentenced to more than five years imprisonment, but that you have what you regard as powerful, well-corroborated evidence that she would be tortured if returned to her home country. She has no recourse under §§ 208 or 241(b)(3) because of the exclusion provisions discussed in Chapter Six. Must—or may—the United States return her to the hands of torturers?

At the end of the twentieth century, the international community developed a treaty to address this problem, and the United States became a party to that treaty. Consequently, we must examine both statutory and treaty provisions to determine what protection your client may claim under the United Nations Convention Against Torture and Other Cruel, Inhuman, and Degrading Treatment (CAT), UNGA Res. 39/46, 39 U.N. GAOR Supp. No. 51, at 197, U.N.Doc. A/RES/39/708 (1984).

## SECTION A.  *NONREFOULEMENT* AND THE CONVENTION AGAINST TORTURE

The centerpiece of the United Nations Convention Against Torture is the agreement that torture is illegitimate. Furthermore, the Convention not only forbids torture, but it also forbids governments from returning individuals to countries where they will face torture. The *nonrefoulement* obligation appears in Article 3 of the CAT:

> No State Party shall expel, return (*"refouler"*) or extradite a person to another State where there are substantial grounds for believing that he would be in danger of being subjected to torture.

Because disagreements can arise as to what constitutes torture, the Convention sets forth a detailed definition of torture:

> any act by which severe pain or suffering, whether physical or mental, is intentionally inflicted on a person for such purposes as obtaining from him or a third person information or a confession, punishing him for an act he or a third person has committed or is suspected of having committed, or intimidating or coercing him or a third person, or for any reason based on discrimination of any kind when such pain and suffering is inflicted by or at the instigation of or with the consent or acquiescence of a public official or other person acting in an official capacity. It does not include pain or suffering arising only from, inherent in or incidental to lawful sanctions.

Art. 1, CAT.

Abu Ghraib (Photo: AP)

Under this definition, many acts that constitute torture give rise to a well-founded fear of persecution. Accordingly, the asylum and *nonrefoulement* protection that arises under the U.S. statutes and the 1951 Refugee Convention usually overlaps with the *nonrefoulement* protection afforded by the CAT. As a consequence, the asylum and withholding machinery we have examined in prior chapters ordinarily suffices to honor Article 3 of the CAT in practice. But in certain circumstances the protections do not coincide. For example, torture routinely meted out as part of the punishment of common criminals would not be inflicted *on account of* one of the five grounds specified in the refugee treaties. Thus, it would not trigger protection under asylum or withholding, but it would implicate the *nonrefoulement* obligations of the CAT. Moreover, as the discussion in Chapter Six emphasized, certain conduct disqualifies those who have a well-founded fear of persecution from asylum and even disqualifies those who face a probability of persecution from withholding. The Torture Convention does not include a similar disqualification. Accordingly, persecutors, serious criminals, and security dangers can seek CAT protection, assuming they can show they are likely to face torture if removed from the United States.

The following excerpt provides a succinct account of the relationship between CAT protection and the more traditional forms of refugee protection.

> * * * The petitioner, Navaratwam Kamalthas, a 25-year-old Sri Lankan national, claims that as a Tamil male, he would face a substantial risk of torture if he were sent back to Sri Lanka. The BIA, which had previously found Kamalthas's account of past persecution to lack credibility in the context of his asylum application, [ruled] that Kamalthas submitted no new evidence to rebut the prior credibility determination, and that he thereby failed to present a prima facie case for relief under the [Torture] Convention.

> * * * [T]he BIA impermissibly conflated the standards for granting relief in asylum and Convention cases. In particular, * * * the BIA abused its discretion in failing to recognize that country conditions alone can play a decisive role in granting relief under the Convention * * *.

> * * *

> * * * [C]laims for relief under the Convention are analytically separate from claims for asylum under INA § 208 and for withholding of removal under INA § 241(b)(3). Put another way, a claim under the Convention is not merely a subset of claims for either asylum or withholding of removal. * * * [T]o be eligible for relief under the Convention, a petitioner must show "that it is more likely than not that he or she would be tortured if removed to the proposed country of removal." In an important sense, then, the Convention's reach is both broader and narrower than that of a claim for asylum or withholding of deportation: coverage is broader because a petitioner need not show that he or she would be tortured "on account of" a protected ground; it is narrower, however, because the petitioner must show that it is "more likely than not" that he or she will be tortured, and not simply persecuted upon removal to a given country.

*Kamalthas v. INS*, 251 F.3d 1279 (9th Cir. 2001).

Despite the conceptual differences, torture, in the modern world, is most commonly administered in a campaign against political opponents or to target disfavored groups on account of race or religion. Therefore, potential victims of torture frequently are eligible to seek asylum. Those who qualify for both protection under CAT and asylum under INA § 208 would prefer the latter because CAT protection does not by itself bring any status benefits equivalent to asylum, and a grant of asylum assures U.S. compliance with the CAT. Hence the Torture Convention is likely to apply most importantly to those excluded from the normal asylum or withholding protections by the exception clauses.

## SECTION B.  U.S. IMPLEMENTATION OF THE CONVENTION AGAINST TORTURE

The United Nations adopted the Convention Against Torture in 1984, and four years later President Reagan signed it and submitted it to the Senate for approval. The United States became a party to the treaty in 1994, after the Senate's resolution of advice and consent, 136 Cong. Rec. 36198–99 (1990). The Senate's ratifying resolution, meant to clarify the obligations and guide implementation, focused on the treaty's definition of torture, Art. 1.

The Senate's advice and consent is subject to the following understandings, which shall apply to the obligations of the United States under this Convention:

(1)(a) * * * [I]n order to constitute torture, an act must be specifically intended to inflict severe physical or mental pain or suffering and that mental pain or suffering refers to prolonged mental harm caused by or resulting from: (1) the intentional infliction or threatened infliction of severe physical pain or suffering; (2) the administration or application, or threatened administration or application, of mind altering substances or other procedures calculated to disrupt profoundly the senses or the personality; (3) the threat of imminent death; or (4) the threat that another person will imminently be subjected to death, severe physical pain or suffering, or the administration or application of mind altering substances or other procedures calculated to disrupt profoundly the senses or personality.

* * *

(d) * * * [T]he term "acquiescence" requires that the public official, prior to the activity constituting torture, have awareness of such activity and thereafter breach his legal responsibility to intervene to prevent such activity.

* * *

(2) * * * [T]he United States understands the phrase, "where there are substantial grounds for believing that he would be in danger of being subjected to torture," as used in article 3 of the Convention, to mean "if it is more likely than not that he would be tortured."

* * *

## Notes and Questions

1. Look at the CAT definition of torture in Article 1. Many potentially difficult questions are raised. For example, "lawful sanctions" generally will not constitute torture. Does this mean that a nation may avoid having any of its cruelties called torture simply by authorizing them in a statute? Does the Senate's Understanding (1)(a) provide any interpretive assistance in answering this question? What evidence of the intent or purpose of the person who inflicts the pain is required by the definition? Could a uniform government policy, such as that examined in the context of asylum and withholding in the *Chang* case in Section A of Chapter Three, ever constitute torture?

2. When a state attaches unilateral statements, such as an "understanding" or a "reservation," to its ratification of a treaty, it can give rise to complicated issues of international law. This is particularly true with multilateral treaties, such as the CAT, because many states have agreed to be bound by the text of the treaty, and the text of the treaties has often been reached after intense negotiations. If one state publicly modifies the text, what impact does this have on the other parties to the treaty? The Vienna Convention on the Law of Treaties, May 23, 1969, 1155 U.N.T.S., provides rules regarding the meaning and effect of reservations, Art. 19–23, and defines a reservation as a unilateral statement, however phrased or titled, made by a state ratifying a treaty that purports to modify the legal effects of a provision of the treaty as it applies to that state. Art. 2(d). Sometimes a state attaches an understanding or a declaration to its ratification of a treaty, with the intent to influence the domestic interpretation or enforcement of the treaty. Drawing the line between statements made for domestic political considerations and statements made to influence the relations between states can be difficult. *See generally* Mark W. Janis, An Introduction to International Law 23–26 (4th ed. 2003). Could you argue that at least some of the Senate's understandings regarding the CAT are, in reality, reservations to the treaty?

3. In a notorious memorandum dated August 1, 2002 the Office of Legal Counsel of the U.S. Justice Department defined torture as physical pain "of an intensity akin to that which accompanies serious physical injury such as death or organ failure," and stated that national security concerns could justify the use of torture in some interrogations in the war on Al Qaeda and its allies. Memorandum for Alberto R. Gonzales, Counsel to the President, from Jay S. Bybee, Assistant Attorney General (Aug. 1, 2002) (reprinted in The Torture Papers: The Road to Abu Ghraib 172 (K. Greenberg & J. Dratel, eds., 2005)). How does the memorandum's definition of torture compare with that in the Torture Convention? On December 30, 2004, the U.S. Justice Department rescinded the earlier memo and proffered a broader definition of torture: conduct specifically intended to inflict severe physical or mental pain or suffering, including circumstances when severe physical suffering does not involve severe physical pain. Memorandum for James B. Comey, Deputy Attorney General, from Daniel Levin, Acting Assistant Attorney General (Dec. 30 2004), <http://www.usdoj.gov/olc/dagmemo.pdf>. How does this view compare with the Torture Convention provision?

## 1. APPLICATIONS FOR PROTECTION

Once the Senate ratified the Torture Convention, the United States was bound to enforce its provisions, but there was no implementing legislation for a number of years. As a consequence, INS initially made informal arrangements for honoring CAT's *nonrefoulement* requirements. *See* Rosati, *The United Nations Convention Against Torture: A Viable Alternative for Asylum Seekers*, 74 Interp. Rel. 1773 (1997). Four years after ratification, Congress enacted the Foreign Affairs Reform and Restructuring Act of 1998 (FARRA), Div. G., Pub. L. 105–277, 112 Stat. 2681, which provided implementing legislation for Article 3 of the CAT with respect to both removal and extradition; it also mandated that the affected agencies issue implementing regulations within 120 days. *Id.,* § 2242. The INS published regulations, 64 Fed. Reg. 8478 (1999) which can be found primarily in 8 C.F.R. §§ 208.16–.18 and 208.30–.31.

Under the regulations published by INS, immigration judges must consider the applicability of the Torture Convention when they determine requests for protection in the United States. In fact, applicants for protection under the CAT file their claims using the I–589 form, the same form used for asylum claims. The immigration judge then can examine all the requests for protection together and decide whether to grant asylum, withholding of removal under § 241(b)(3), or withholding of removal under the CAT. Generally, the immigration judge will determine the applicability of protection under the Torture Convention only if the person fails to qualify for asylum or regular withholding.

The expedited removal procedure, which we will discuss in greater detail in Chapter Nine, also incorporates consideration of torture claims into the credible fear determinations. A noncitizen found there to have a credible fear of torture will ordinarily be placed in full removal proceedings before an immigration judge to have the CAT claim determined. 8 C.F.R. § 235.3(b)(4).

Those who have a well-founded fear of persecution but are ineligible for asylum or withholding of removal due to prior criminal conduct, persecution of others, or national security may be eligible for protection under the CAT. If so, they are awarded "deferral of removal" status, which can be terminated more easily than asylum or "withholding of removal" status in the event that conditions change that might permit lawful deportation either to the country of origin or to a third country. *Cf.* 8 C.F.R. § 208.17(d) and § 208.24(f).

Those denied protection under the CAT can appeal to the BIA. In limited circumstances, which will be discussed later in this section, they can appeal from BIA decisions denying CAT claims to the federal courts.

## 2. CRIMINAL CONDUCT

One of the controversies that has arisen under the Torture Convention is the extent to which its protection is available to persons who themselves are guilty of heinous conduct. At the time the Senate ratified the treaty, it is unlikely that it fully understood the way the treaty might benefit persons convicted of serious crimes. By 1998, when it passed the implementing legislation, Congress had become more aware of the potential impact of the CAT on removal of persons otherwise precluded from Refugee Convention coverage. Consequently, it provided in the implementing legislation that noncitizens who are covered by a bar in INA § 241(b)(3)(B) should be excluded from the protections to be set forth in the new regulations "[t]o the maximum extent consistent with the obligations of the United States under the Convention." As explained in the last chapter, INA § 241(b)(3)(B) prohibits the application of withholding of removal to serious criminals, persons who have assisted in the persecution of others, and those viewed as security threats to the United States.

INS determined, however, that the protection of the CAT is absolute for those who show the requisite risk of torture, whatever threats they pose or bad acts they may have committed. Nonetheless, the regulations found a different way to honor the congressional mandate. They provide that anyone subject to the mandatory preclusions of INA § 241(b)(3)(B) but entitled to CAT protection will receive only "deferral of removal," as mentioned earlier. 8 C.F.R. § 208.17. Furthermore, the regulations contemplate that such persons can be held in detention, even if given deferral of removal. *Id.* at § 208.17(c). Perhaps because of the emphasis placed on criminal removals over the last decade and the far-reaching preclusions on asylum and withholding for persons with criminal records enacted in 1996, CAT claims have become a significant issue in immigration court proceedings. The U.S. Department of Justice reports that over 33,000 cases in FY 2005 presented a CAT issue, and a significant body of case law is developing. (Grant rates, when the CAT issue was actually reached, have run at approximately two percent.)

## 3. GOVERNMENT INVOLVEMENT OR ACQUIESCENCE

The Convention against Torture prohibits torture, but by its terms it only applies to torture when there is government involvement. As a result, torture by private individuals is beyond its purview. This is in marked contrast to the approach taken under the 1951 Refugee Convention. As you may recall from Chapter Three, Section A, in claims for asylum and *nonrefoulement* based on fear of persecution, U.S. law grants protection if the agents of persecution are private groups that the government is "unwilling or unable" to control.

If you look back to the CAT definition of torture at the beginning of this chapter, you will see that torture means acts that inflict severe pain or suffering, but only "when such pain or suffering is inflicted by or at the instigation of or with the consent or acquiescence of a public official or other person acting in an official capacity." The meaning of this portion of Article 1 has generated many published opinions focusing on the question of governmental involvement or acquiescence in the threatened mistreatment. The BIA's first precedent decision applying the CAT offered the following views on the acquiescence requirement.

# MATTER OF S–V–

Board of Immigration Appeals, 2000.
22 I & N Dec. 1306.

HEILMAN, BOARD MEMBER:

\* \* \*

\* \* \* [T]he respondent is a native and citizen of Colombia. He was admitted to the United States on or about February 7, 1981, as a lawful permanent resident. On February 4, 1998, the respondent was convicted \* \* \* of grand theft, resisting arrest without violence, and driving while his license was suspended [and] robbery and was sentenced to 4 years' imprisonment \* \* \*.

\* \* \* [He] argues that he would be in danger from nongovernmental guerrilla, narcotrafficking, and paramilitary groups in Colombia. The respondent contends \* \* \* that the guerrillas finance their operations through kidnaping. According to the respondent, ever since the Government of Colombia gave the guerrillas land as an element of peace negotiations, authorities are no longer able to control the kidnaping that occurs nationwide. The respondent contends that individuals who are kidnaped suffer subhuman conditions at the hands of their captors, and he asserts that he would be a target for kidnapers because he has family in the United States and is unable to speak Spanish correctly.

[The BIA ruled that his criminal conviction and sentence made him ineligible for withholding of removal, and then proceeded to consider his claim for relief under the CAT.]

A public official's acquiescence to torture "requires that the public official, prior to the activity constituting torture, have awareness of such activity and thereafter breach his or her legal responsibility to intervene to prevent such activity." In its resolution of advice and consent to the Convention Against Torture, the United States Senate included an understanding replacing the word "knowledge" in this definition of acquiescence with the word "awareness," indicating that actual knowledge of activity constituting torture is not required. This revision is also reflected in the regulations. The Senate Committee on Foreign Relations clarified the point by stating that "(t)he purpose of this condition is to make it clear that both actual knowledge and 'willful blindness' fall within the definition of the term 'acquiescence.'" Consequently, the definition of "torture" "includes only acts that occur in the context of governmental authority."

\* \* \* To demonstrate "acquiescence" by Colombian Government officials, the respondent must do more than show that the officials are aware of the activity constituting torture but are powerless to stop it. He must demonstrate that Colombian officials are willfully accepting of the guerrillas' torturous activities. To interpret the term otherwise would be to misconstrue the meaning of "acquiescence," the dictionary definition of which is "silent or passive assent." The Oxford Universal Dictionary 17 (3d ed. 1955). Accordingly, we consider that a government's inability to control a group ought not lead to the conclusion that the government acquiesced to the group's activities.

We note that we have granted asylum to applicants who feared persecution at the hands of nongovernmental entities where the applicant demonstrated that government authorities were unable to provide protection from the would-be persecutors. However, Article 3 of the Convention Against Torture does not extend protection to persons fearing entities that a government is unable to control. In fact, the United Nations Committee Against Torture has stated that Article 3 does not provide protection in cases where pain or suffering is inflicted by a nongovernmental entity that is not acting by or at the instigation, consent, or acquiescence of a public official.

\* \* \*

[The Board ruled that the respondent was not entitled to protection under CAT.]

[The concurring and dissenting opinions are omitted.]

---

Several years after *Matter of S–V–*, Attorney General Ashcroft issued the following opinion as a major precedent to guide future application of the CAT. The decision applies the acquiescence requirement of the Torture Convention to three individuals who had been convicted of drug trafficking and so were precluded from withholding of removal under INA § 241(b)(3). *Matter of Y–L–* originated when three individuals appeared in separate proceedings before different immigration judges; in two of the three cases the immigration judge denied relief and ordered removal from the United States. The BIA considered the three appeals separately, but ruled in all three cases that the drug trafficking conviction at issue did not constitute a particularly serious crime and that the applicants were entitled to withholding of removal. Attorney General Ashcroft directed the BIA to refer all three cases to him. He concluded that drug trafficking, even when followed by a short sentence, constitutes a particularly serious crime in almost all circumstances. (The portion of the opinion excluding the individuals from withholding appears in Chapter Six, Section B.) He then turned to the issue of acquiescence.

## MATTER OF Y–L–

Attorney General, 2002.
23 I & N Dec. 270.

[ASHCROFT, ATTORNEY GENERAL:]

\* \* \*

Although the respondents are statutorily ineligible for *withholding* of removal by virtue of their convictions for "particularly serious crimes," the regulations implementing the Convention Against Torture allow them to obtain a *deferral* of removal notwithstanding the prior criminal offenses if they can establish that they are "entitled to protection" under the Convention. *See* 8 C.F.R. § 208.17(a). To secure such relief, the respondents must demonstrate that, if removed to their country of origin, *it is more likely than not* they would be tortured by, or with the acquiescence of, government officials acting under color of law. None of the respondents has come close to making such a showing.

### A.   Y–L–

Y–L–, who was paroled into the United States in 1979, maintains that he will be killed if sent back to his native Haiti. He testified at his removal hearing that two months prior to his arrival in America, members of the Ton Ton Macoutes—a private army of Haitian death squads organized by former president Francois Duvalier and nurtured by his successor, Jean Claude Duvalier—murdered his father and aunt, and broke his cousin's leg as retribution for his father's unspecified criticism of the Duvalier government. Y–L– further insisted that the same group of people responsible for the death of his father killed his cousin in 1998, approximately twenty years after Y–L– initially left the country.

Y–L–'s claim for relief under the Convention Against Torture fails on at least two different levels. First, as the immigration judge correctly found, Y–L– produced no reliable evidence that he would likely be subjected to torture if returned to Haiti. While voluntarily visiting Haiti on two prior occasions, he was never personally harmed or threatened. Although he suggested that his cousin was murdered by the same faction that purportedly killed his father nearly twenty years earlier, the immigration judge found this testimony speculative and unconvincing. Meanwhile, the Department of State's authoritative asylum profile on Haiti, which was introduced at the removal hearing, reveals that the political climate has improved substantially in recent years, and that charges of politically-motivated persecution against individuals who fled during the Duvalier reign have proven to be frequently untrue or grossly exaggerated.

Second, even assuming Y–L–'s various allegations have some basis in fact, and even if his own alleged fears of torture are genuine, he is not entitled to deferral of removal under the Convention Against Torture because he has not established that *current government officials acting in an official capacity* would be responsible for such abuse. The regulations implementing the Convention allow for relief only if torture would be "inflicted by or at the instigation of or with the consent or acquiescence of *a public official or other person acting in an official capacity*." 8 C.F.R. § 208.18(a)(1) (emphasis added). Violence committed by individuals over whom the government has no reasonable control does not implicate the treaty. *See In re S–V–*, 22 I & N Dec. 1306, 1312 (BIA 2000) ("To demonstrate 'acquiescence' by [foreign] Government officials, the respondent must do more than show that the officials are aware of the activity constituting torture but are powerless to stop it. He must demonstrate that [the foreign] officials are willfully accepting of the . . . torturous activities.''). The State Department's asylum profile on Haiti underscores that the Ton Ton Macoutes have effectively disbanded and neither play a role in, nor enjoy the tacit support of, the current Haitian government. Both Y–L– and his counsel conceded this point. If, by some chance—which has certainly not been proven to be more likely than not—former Ton Ton Macoute elements seek revenge on Y–L– because of his relationship to his father, there is no competent evidence in the record indicating that the current Haitian administration would either participate in, or turn a blind eye to, such violence. In short, Y–L– has failed to sustain his burden of establishing entitlement to deferral of removal.

## B.   A–G–

The evidence advanced by A–G– similarly falls far short of what is required to obtain relief under the Convention Against Torture. At some point following his entry into the United States, A–G– decided to supplement his income as a maintenance worker by trafficking in illegal narcotics. His supplier was his long-time friend and roommate, K–C–, who had a drug-dealing base in Jamaica. As so often happens to those in the drug trade, A–G– was ultimately arrested by the FBI, charged with unlawful distribution of cocaine, and convicted on multiple counts of cocaine trafficking. To minimize his exposure to prison, he agreed to assist federal law enforcement officials by participating in a number of controlled drug purchases designed to implicate K–C–.

During a period in which both K–C–and A–G– were temporarily incarcerated at the same facility, K–C– allegedly delivered a message to A–G– that he would be killed if he returned to Jamaica. In addition, according to A–G–'s brothers and sisters, two or three men came to the family residence in Jamaica in either 1998, 1999, or 2000—the dates and other key particulars diverged sharply among these witnesses—and inquired as to A–G–'s whereabouts. At least one sibling claimed that these men were armed and made threats that A–G– would be murdered by K–C– or others if he returned to Jamaica.

Citing these apparent threats to his life, A–G– seeks to avoid removal pursuant to the Convention Against Torture. The main problem with his claim is that the record is devoid of credible evidence suggesting that the Jamaican government would bear any responsibility—either direct or through passive acquiescence—for physical harm visited upon A–G–. In fact, several of the witnesses candidly acknowledged at the hearing that no one in the family even reported the alleged threats to Jamaican authorities.

In finding some government role in the alleged torture, the presiding immigration judge speculated that the Jamaican ''government cannot or will not control those who wish to persecute the respondent.'' The judge's reasoning proceeded as follows: (i) there are major problems with corruption in Jamaica, (ii) local police routinely beat detainees, (iii) major drug traffickers operate in Jamaica with impunity and are cozy with corrupt law enforcement officials, and (iv) as a result of (i)–(iii), drug trade associates of K–C– may well either attack A–G– themselves or arrange for A–G– to be arrested on bogus charges and then encourage the corrupt local police to beat him.[16] Incredibly, the BIA found this reasoning both "thorough" and correct. I do not agree. To the contrary, the immigration judge's factual findings are clearly erroneous.

Although there are indications that corruption and brutality affect some elements of Jamaican law enforcement, the national government has undertaken substantial efforts at reform. *See* Office of Asylum Affairs, Dep't of State, *Country Reports on Human Rights Practices—Jamaica* 1 (Feb. 2001) ("Country Report"). For example, the Jamaican Parliament passed a major anti-corruption bill in December 2000, and recently ratified the Inter-American Convention Against Corruption. It also bolstered the national anti-money laundering laws. Notwithstanding the allegations of A–G– and his family to the contrary, the U.S. State Department has found that the policy of the Jamaican government is to investigate all credible reports of police corruption. The State Department has further reported that the Jamaican government does not encourage or facilitate the illicit production or distribution of narcotics. While acknowledging that abuses by some members of the security forces occasionally occur, the State Department's 2000 Country Report for Jamaica makes clear that "[c]ivilian authorities generally maintain effective control of the security forces," and "[t]he Government generally respect[s] the human rights of its citizens." To be sure, there is room for improvement. But the record does not support the extreme, uncorroborated claims made on behalf of A–G– with respect to knowing government acquiescence in prospective acts of torture.

Ultimately, of course, it is impossible to say with certainty whether A–G– will be exposed to torture by particular individuals upon his return to Jamaica. Those who engage in the illegal drug trade quite commonly expose themselves to the risk of violence; it is an occupational hazard. The relevant inquiry under the Convention Against Torture, however, is whether governmental authorities would approve or "willfully accept" atrocities committed against persons in the respondent's position. *See* Matter of S–V–, *supra*. To suggest that this standard can be met by evidence of isolated rogue agents engaging in extrajudicial acts of brutality, which are not only in contravention of the jurisdiction's laws and policies, but are committed despite authorities' best efforts to root out such misconduct, is to empty the Convention's volitional requirement of all rational meaning. As the courts have clearly recognized, relief is

---

**16.** The immigration judge explained his determination by stating: "[I]t seems that we have a situation where the drug lords may act on their own and simply pay the police to look the other way or the drug lords may actually get the police involved . . . so that they do the dirty work for them on the basis of a trumped up case. . . . We do not know which it is but one of the two is more likely than not."

available only if the torture would "occur[] in the context of governmental authority," not "as a wholly private act." *Ali v. Reno*, 237 F.3d 591, 597 (6th Cir.2001). There being no such credible evidence in the case at bar, A–G–'s request for deferral must be denied.

### C.  R–S–R–

Turning to R–S–R–, a foreign national from the Dominican Republic who has resided in Puerto Rico continuously since his arrival there in 1985, it is clear that his application for relief under the Convention Against Torture suffers from largely the same maladies as those of the other two respondents.

Beginning no later than March 1997, R–S–R– entered into an elaborate "conspiracy to produce multi-kilogram quantities of cocaine in Puerto Rico which would then be transported to New York, where the cocaine would be sold." * * *

Invoking the Convention Against Torture, R–S–R– now seeks deferral of removal on the grounds that he will be subjected to physical cruelties by individuals in the Dominican Republic—including two of his co-defendants who he maintains are corrupt law enforcement agents— angered by his decision to cooperate with authorities. * * *

* * *

[E]ven if all of R–S–R–'s testimony was credited as true, he still would not be eligible for deferral of removal because he has not established the requisite governmental involvement in the prospective torture he portrayed. The scope of the Convention is confined to torture that is inflicted under color of law. It extends to neither wholly private acts nor acts inflicted or approved in other than "an official capacity." *Ali*, 237 F.3d at 597; 8 C.F.R. § 208.18(a)(1). While R–S–R– offered colorful testimony describing forms of torture that he "think[s] would happen to cooperating witnesses when they are deported," his testimony and evidence failed to provide a plausible basis for concluding that such practices would be inflicted upon *him* with the consent or approval of *authoritative government officials acting in an official capacity*. If anything, his testimony indicates merely that two corrupt, low-level agents may seek to exact personal vengeance on him for personal reasons. Such private conduct falls far short of what is required to demonstrate the probability of government-sanctioned atrocities under the Convention Against Torture. Accordingly, R–S–R– is not entitled to relief.

### Notes and Questions

1.  Accepting the importance of showing government involvement in torture, should the actions of "isolated rogue [police] agents" be dismissed as a "wholly private act"? Wouldn't it be accurate to say the agents were acting under color of law? Should that be the test?

2.  On the other hand, if the authorities really are applying "their best efforts to root out [corrupt law enforcement] conduct," should the harm be seen as state action? Or is this mixing two separate issues: (1) government

involvement and (2) likelihood of risk? Would evidence of such best efforts more appropriately be considered in making the factual determination of whether torture is more likely than not?

———————

Despite Attorney General Ashcroft's explicit intention of expounding precedential guidance concerning Torture Convention protection, the federal courts have not all agreed with his view. In particular, the Ninth Circuit has examined claims for protection under CAT and has expressly disapproved the "willful acceptance" interpretation of the concept of acquiescence, as propounded in *Matter of S–V–* and *Matter of Y–L–*.

## ZHENG v. ASHCROFT

United States Court of Appeals, Ninth Circuit, 2003.
332 F.3d 1186.

Pregerson, Circuit Judge.

[According to his testimony] Li Chen Zheng ("Zheng"), a Chinese native and citizen, * * * left China because he "was in a very low position." His parents had violated China's birth control policy. Under China's policy, if the "first born is a boy, you cannot have a second child"; Zheng's parents had two daughters after Zheng was born.

Human smugglers who transport Chinese immigrants from China to the United States and other countries—known as "snakeheads" or "seaman"—brought Zheng, along with approximately one-hundred and fifty Chinese nationals, into the United States on a large boat. On or about April 23, 1999, Zheng was apprehended seeking to enter Guam. In the custody of the United States Marshal, Zheng lived on Tinian Island until June 1999.

While on Tinian Island, Zheng was a material witness in a criminal proceeding against the smugglers and "reported all the names of the seamen and said that they tortured me, tortured us." The same evening that Zheng reported the names of his smugglers, a snakehead nicknamed Lu Son approached Zheng as he waited for the restroom. Zheng testified that the snakehead told him "you be careful, you [will] be dead for sure." Zheng thought that the snakehead was going to "beat me." But a "police officer using [a] flashlight" came by and the snakehead left. Zheng told "an adult" about the snake head's death threat. The adult told Zheng "this is not a big problem. Since we are here in the United States the American Government will protect us. We become their witnesses and they will be responsible for us." Zheng stated that "[a]fter I heard this, I did not report" the snakehead's threat.

* * *

* * * When asked why he was afraid of being sent back to China, Zheng stated that "[t]he snakehead will kill me ... [b]ecause I am a witness for the American Government against them.... I reported all

the names of the seaman and said that they tortured me, tortured us. . . . I am afraid that the snakehead will kill me." * * *

Zheng testified that there was "[n]o way" the Chinese government would protect him from the snakeheads "[b]ecause snakeheads are connected with the Chinese government officials." As an example of the collusion between the government officials and the snakeheads, Zheng testified that he saw the snakeheads give three cartons of cigarettes to the police at the harbor before they were allowed to board the boat.

* * *

The State Department Country Report for China states that "China appears to be taking active measures to target people smugglers and stop illegal departures by economic migrants. Several scores of people smugglers and Fujian officials reportedly have been convicted, fired from jobs, or expelled from the Communist Party." Zheng argued * * * that this report indicated that there was official participation in alien smuggling in Fujian, the province Zheng is from.

In passing the [Trafficking Victim Protection Act], Congress found, in relevant part, that "[t]rafficking often is aided by official corruption in countries of origin[;] . . . enforcement against traffickers is also hindered by official indifference, by corruption, and sometimes even by active official participation in trafficking." * * *

* * *

[Relying on *Matter of S–V–*, excerpted above], the BIA stated that "[w]hen the alien alleges a likelihood of torture from non-governmental sources, he or she must demonstrate that government officials 'are willfully accepting of' the non-governmental source's 'torturous activities.'" The BIA found that, even assuming Chinese government officials knew about the smuggling operations and failed to stop them, Zheng did not show that government officials would acquiesce in harm that rises to the level of torture. * * *

[The court reviewed the history of the adoption of the Convention Against Torture.]

On December 10, 1984, the United Nations General Assembly adopted the Convention by unanimous agreement. President Reagan signed the Convention on April 18, 1988. One month later, the President transmitted to the Senate the Convention for approval with nineteen proposed United States conditions, many of which concerned the human rights community, American Bar Association, and other groups. One of those conditions was an understanding that the United States interpreted the term *acquiescence* to "require[ ] that the public official, prior to the activity constituting torture, have *knowledge* of such activity." According to the Senate Foreign Relations Committee, "[t]hose conditions, in number and substance, created the impression that the United States was not serious in its commitment to end torture worldwide." In January 1990, the Bush administration submitted a revised and reduced list of proposed United States conditions on the Convention: "the conditions proposed . . . in large measure eliminate[d] th[e] problem" that the United States appeared insincere in its commitment to end torture worldwide. Under one of the new proposed understandings, the United States no longer required a public official to have "knowledge of [torture]" to acquiesce to torture; rather the public official need only an "awareness" of torture. The Committee stated that the purpose of requiring awareness, and not knowledge, "is to make it clear that both actual knowledge and 'willful blindness' fall within the definition of the term 'acquiescence.' " In recommending ratification of the Convention with the new conditions, including the understanding that acquiescence required only awareness and not actual knowledge, the Committee found that "[r]atification is a natural follow-on to the active role that the United States played in the negotiating process for the Convention and is consistent with longstanding U.S. efforts to promote and protect basic human rights and fundamental freedoms throughout the world." * * *

* * * [T]he Foreign Affairs Reform and Restructuring Act of 1998, * * * implementing Article 3 of the Convention Against Torture,* * * states that it is "the policy of the United States not to expel, extradite, or otherwise effect the involuntary return of any person to a country in which there are substantial grounds for believing the person would be in danger of being subjected to torture." FARRA instructed "heads of the appropriate agencies [to] prescribe regulations to implement the obligations of the United States under Article 3 of the [Convention], subject to any reservations, understandings, declarations, and provisos contained in the United States Senate resolution of ratification of the Convention."

* * *

* * *To qualify for relief under the Convention Against Torture, Zheng must establish that it is more likely than not that if removed to China, the snakeheads would torture him and that the torture would be inflicted with the *acquiescence* of Chinese government officials. The Convention does not require, as the INS purports, the government to "*knowingly* acquiesce" to such torture. And contrary to the BIA's ruling, the Convention does not require that Zheng prove that Chinese government officials would be "willfully accepting of" the torture inflicted on Zheng by the smugglers. As explained below, Congress made its intent clear that actual knowledge, or willful acceptance, is not required for a government to "acquiesce" to the torture of its citizens. Rather, subject to the understanding contained in the Senate's ratification of the Convention, "[a]cquiescence of a public official requires that the public official, prior to the activity constituting torture, have *awareness* of such activity and thereafter breach his or her legal responsibility to intervene to prevent such activity." We conclude that the BIA's interpretation of the term *acquiescence* to require that Zheng must prove that the government is "willfully accepting of" torture, instead of proving that public

officials are aware of the torture, impermissibly narrows Congress' clear intent in implementing relief under the Convention Against Torture.

\* \* \*

Thus, to qualify for relief under the Convention, Zheng has to prove that the torture inflicted by the snakeheads would be carried out with the awareness of the Chinese government officials. That awareness includes "both actual knowledge and 'willful blindness.'" The Senate did not in its understandings to the Convention modify the terms awareness and acquiescence with the adjective "knowing" as the INS does in their briefs to the BIA and this court. Nor did the Senate require willful acceptance. Rather, the Senate ratified a version of the Convention that eliminated an understanding that acquiescence required a public official's *knowledge* and replaced it with an understanding that acquiescence required only a public official's *awareness*. The Senate Committee on Foreign Relations expressly stated that the purpose of requiring awareness, and not knowledge, "is to make it clear that both actual knowledge and 'willful blindness' fall within the definition of the term 'acquiescence.'"

The BIA in Zheng's case, however, required Zheng to prove more than awareness of torture by public officials. Instead, the BIA required that "[w]hen the alien alleges a likelihood of torture from non-governmental sources, he or she must demonstrate that government officials *'are willfully accepting of'* the non-governmental source's torturous activities."

In *Matter of S–V–*, the BIA en banc \* \* \* "interpreted the regulation at 8 C.F.R. § 208.18(a) [defining acquiescence] to be limiting"— more limiting than the Senate's just quoted intent to require awareness and not actual knowledge. *Id.* Creating a standard more stringent than Congress clearly intended, the BIA held that to demonstrate acquiescence "the respondent *must do more than show that the officials are aware* of the activity constituting torture but are powerless to stop it. He must demonstrate that the Colombian officials are *willfully accepting of* the guerillas' torturous activities." (emphases added). \* \* \*

To interpret the term acquiescence as the BIA did, however, misconstrues and ignores the clear Congressional intent quoted by the BIA merely a paragraph above its restrictive holding. The BIA's interpretation and application of acquiescence impermissibly requires more than awareness and instead requires that a government be willfully accepting of a third party's tortuous [sic] activities. There is nothing in the understandings to the Convention approved by the Senate, or the INS's regulations implementing the Convention, to suggest that anything more than awareness is required. Yet, the BIA ignored the Senate's clear intent and constructed its own interpretation of acquiescence, an interpretation that requires more than awareness, includes "willfully accepting of," and seemingly excludes "willful blindness." Under this narrowed interpretation of acquiescence, the BIA stated that "[t]he relevant inquiry under the Convention Against Torture ... is whether governmental authorities would ... 'willfully accept' atrocities committed against persons in the respondent's position." The correct inquiry as intended by the Senate is whether a respondent can show that public officials demonstrate "willful blindness" to the torture of their citizens by third parties, or as stated by the Fifth Circuit, whether public officials "would turn a blind eye to torture."

* * * [T]he INS argues that "[t]he definition of torture has been properly left to INS." * * * The INS, however, is wrong. The definition of torture has been properly left, not to the INS, but to Congress, who instructed the INS to "prescribe regulations to implement the obligations of the United States under Article 3 of the [Convention], *subject to any* reservations, *understandings,* declarations, and provisos contained in the United States Senate resolution of ratification of the Convention." FARRA § 2242(b) (emphasis added). One of the "understandings" in the Senate resolution of ratification of the Convention Against Torture was that acquiescence of a public official requires "awareness" and not "knowledge" or "willful[ ] accept[ance]." Because "the intent of Congress is clear, that is the end of the matter; for th[is] court, as well as the agency, must give effect to the unambiguously expressed intent of Congress."

To the extent that decisions such as *Matter of S–V–* and *Matter of Y– L, A–G, R–S–R–,* require actual knowledge and "willful[ ] accept[ance]"—contrary to clear congressional intent to require only awareness—we disapprove of those decisions. We note that "we have taken care not to exceed our authority, and not to second-guess the BIA. Our decision[ ] simply give[s] effect to the will of Congress" that the BIA adhere to the definition of acquiescence intended by Congress when it ratified the Convention Against Torture and created legislation implementing Article 3 of the Convention Against Torture; the BIA may not construe its own, more limited definition of acquiescence.

\* \* \*

[The court vacated the BIA's decision and remanded the case for further proceedings.]

### Notes and Questions

1. In *Zheng, Matter of S–V–,* and *Matter of Y–L–*, the applicants for protection under the Torture Convention had all been involved in criminal activity, and all said they feared torture by members of criminal organizations if returned to their homelands. Nonetheless, there were significant differences in their prior relationships with the feared torturers. Further, although they all alleged that the governments in their respective countries were aware of and acquiesced in the torture likely to be administered by the criminal gangs, there were significant differences in their allegations of government collusion. With regard to analyzing the allegation of government acquiescence, what details do you think are salient in each of the above cases?

The Ninth Circuit agreed with the applicant in *Zheng,* ruling that it was unnecessary to show that the government condoned the activity. Is the Ninth Circuit view persuasive? Generally, does awareness of activity constitute acquiescence in it? How much impact did Zheng's personal situation have? Although he had hired criminals to smuggle him to the United States, he was not part of a criminal gang and, in fact, he had testified against the smugglers in a criminal proceeding. In contrast, S–V– had been convicted of unrelated crimes in the United States and he argued that he would be a target for guerrilla groups that the Colombian government is genuinely unable to control. Should these factors make a difference?

2.   As noted in *Matter of S–V–*, the regulation concerning acquiescence refers to both awareness of the torture and "thereafter breach of [the public official's] legal responsibility to intervene to prevent such activity." 8 C.F.R. § 208.18(a)(7). In this context, what evidence would be relevant to breach of responsibility? Would news accounts of flourishing criminal gang activity be sufficient? Would the applicant for protection need to show complaints had been made, but that the police had not opened an investigation? Would lackluster police investigations be relevant? How would an individual obtain such information?

---

### Exercise

The CAT defines torture as severe pain or suffering inflicted for improper purposes "at the instigation of or with the consent or acquiescence of a public official or a person acting in an official capacity." In interpreting the reach of the statute, the BIA, the Attorney General, and the Ninth Circuit have discussed different degrees of involvement by government officials: actual knowledge, willful blindness, willful acceptance, or awareness. Under the opinions you have read, which of the following situations would fall within the statutory requirement?

A.   Torture in the presence of a government official:

1.   Torture by a private person and the police chief says nothing.

2.   Torture by a private person and the police chief protests, but initiates no investigation or prosecution.

B.   Torture outside the presence of a government official:

1.   The police chief learns that torture might occur and takes no action to prevent it.

2.   The police chief learns that torture has occurred and says nothing.

3.   The police chief learns that torture has occurred and expresses disapproval, but takes no action because he believes the government is unable to control the torturer.

4.   The police chief hears rumors that torture might have occurred, but considers the rumors unreliable and does nothing.

C.   Would any of your answers change if the government official involved were a low-level police officer rather than a police chief? Several low-level police officers?

## 4.   BURDEN OF PROOF AND LEVEL OF RISK

The text of Article 3 of the Torture Convention forbids governments to return individuals if there are "substantial grounds" for believing they will face torture. As noted at the beginning of this chapter, the U.S. Senate's ratification of the Torture Convention specified that the Senate understood "substantial grounds" to mean that torture is "more likely than not" to occur. The subsequent regulations reiterate this standard, set forth the burden of proof, and acknowledge the importance of uncorroborated evidence in some cases.

> The burden of proof is on the applicant for withholding of removal under this paragraph to establish that it is more likely than not that he or she would be tortured if removed to the proposed country of removal. The testimony of the applicant, if credible, may be sufficient to sustain the burden of proof without corroboration.

8 C.F.R. § 208.16(c)(2).

Not long after the regulations became effective, the BIA examined these issues in the following case.

## MATTER OF M–B–A–

Board of Immigration Appeals, 2002.
23 I & N Dec. 474.

HOLMES, BOARD MEMBER:

* * *

The respondent is a 40-year-old native and citizen of Nigeria who [was convicted] of importation of a controlled substance and possession of heroin with intent to distribute * * *. She was initially sentenced to 121 months' imprisonment, but her sentence was later reduced to 78 months as a result of her assistance to Government controlled substances investigations.

* * * The Immigration Judge concluded that the respondent's conviction and sentence precluded her from establishing eligibility for any relief other than deferral of removal under Article 3 of the Convention Against Torture * * *.

In her application for protection under the Convention Against Torture, the respondent stated that if she is returned to Nigeria she would be imprisoned and tortured as a result of her drug conviction in this country. In support of this claim, the respondent submitted a detailed affidavit, evidence of country conditions in Nigeria, and a copy of a 1990 Nigerian federal military government decree which, in part, criminalized the conduct of Nigerians who are convicted of narcotic drug offenses in a foreign country and bring the name of Nigeria into disrepute, or who are detected carrying a narcotic drug into a foreign country after a journey originating from Nigeria. *See* National Drug Law Enforcement Agency (Amendment) Decree 1990, Decree No. 33 (Oct. 10, 1990) ("Decree No. 33").

During proceedings before the Immigration Judge on December 14, 1999, the respondent testified that she had traveled to Nigeria in 1993 to meet her then-fiancé's family and had been unwillingly involved in drug trafficking by his relatives and associates when she traveled back to the United States. She testified that because of this conviction she would be immediately turned over to drug enforcement authorities and imprisoned if she is returned to Nigeria, that she would be in jail for years before she would be able to see a judge, that she was subject to a mandatory 5-year term of imprisonment, and that she would be subjected to torture while jailed.

When asked how she knew that this would occur, the respondent referred to Decree No. 33 and also testified that some years before she had communicated with an unnamed Nigerian friend who had been convicted of a drug offense in this country and then returned to Nigeria. The respondent indicated that she spoke by telephone to her friend and her friend's parents in 1995. She was told that her friend had been detained upon her return to Nigeria in 1995, that her family had had to bring food and medication to the jail and pay money for her protection, that she slept on the floor, and that "you probably get raped and beat down" by the guards because they have authority to do "whatever they can do." Her friend remained in jail for 2 months until her family paid a bribe to get her released. The respondent did not know whether her friend had gone before a judge before being incarcerated or whether she had been raped in prison.\* \* \*

The respondent further testified that there was no one to help her in Nigeria if she were jailed. Her father had died and her mother was "presently" living in England with her mother's sister. However, the respondent's mother was not a citizen or resident of the United Kingdom and the respondent did not know how long she would be staying in England. The respondent testified that all of her brothers and sisters were in the United States and that her only relations in Nigeria were an uncle and his children, but that they would not assist her and she would not even want her uncle to know that she was in Nigeria because he had sexually abused her as a child. The respondent did not present any testimony from her siblings in this country or otherwise testify regarding her relationship with them or their individual circumstances.

The respondent testified, and provided supporting medical evidence, that she suffers from depression, a chronic ulcer, and asthma. She stated that she had no one to rely on to supply her with medicine if she were jailed in Nigeria. In addition, the respondent testified that she would probably be beaten and raped by prison guards. She stated that most women are subjected to such treatment in prison and that the government does not have the ability to protect them. She also claimed that she would be particularly vulnerable because her ex-fiancé would pay prison guards to harm her because of her cooperation with drug enforcement authorities in this country. The respondent indicated that her ex-fiancé was now in Nigeria, but she did not testify to any communications from or about him, or otherwise identify a specific basis for her claim that he had the ability and intent to cause her harm if she were detained in Nigeria.

\* \* \*

In order to establish eligibility for deferral of removal, the respondent must show that it is more likely than not that she will be subject to torture by a public official, or at the instigation or with the acquiescence of such an official. \* \* \*

\* \* \*

The actual status of Decree No. 33 is not entirely clear on the record before us, but we will assume that it has not been repealed and is enforceable. However, even assuming that such is the case, there is little evidence of record on which to base any meaningful conclusion regarding the extent to which this provision is presently enforced, and how and against whom it is enforced. The fact that the decree is written in mandatory terms is not in itself determinative because it is common to couch criminal provisions in such terms. \* \* \*

The respondent's own evidence concerning the present manner of enforcement of Decree No. 33 does not go much beyond conjecture, and her reference to the circumstances that were related to her by her friend and her friend's parents in 1995 involved one individual some 7 years ago under a different regime in Nigeria. \* \* \* The respondent has been represented in these proceedings since 1999, and the importance of providing evidence on the issue of the likelihood of her detention has been emphasized. On the record before us, we are not satisfied that she has met her burden of providing adequate evidence to establish that it is more likely than not that her return to Nigeria would result in her detention or imprisonment.

In this regard, we do not find it sufficient for the respondent simply to cite the existence of Decree No. 33 and her unnamed friend's experiences in 1995. The respondent must provide some current evidence, or at least more meaningful historical evidence, regarding the manner of enforcement of the provisions of Decree No. 33 on individuals similarly situated to herself.\* \* \*

The respondent's eligibility for deferral of removal rests upon a finding that it is more likely than not that she will be identified as a convicted drug trafficker upon her return to Nigeria; that, as a result, she will be detained on arrival; that, when detained, she will be held in detention without access to bail or judicial oversight; that she will be detained for a significant period of time; and that, as a result of this detention, she will suffer mistreatment that rises to the level of torture at the hands of prison guards or authorities. Given the evidence of harsh and life-threatening prison conditions in Nigeria and the serious drug trafficking problems that Nigerian authorities are attempting to address, the respondent's fear of return to her home country is understandable. On the record before us, however, we find that the respondent's case is based on a chain of assumptions and a fear of what might happen, rather than evidence that meets her burden of demonstrating that it is *more likely than not* that she will be subjected to torture by, or with the acquiescence of, a public official or other person acting in an official capacity if she is returned to her home country.

\* \* \*

[The BIA dismissed the appeal.]

Rosenberg, Board Member, concurring and dissenting:

\* \* \*

## II. Likelihood of Torture Based on Evidence in the Record

The majority's analysis turns on the evidence in the record, finding it to be insufficient to satisfy the respondent's burden of proof under the "more likely than not" standard provided in 8 C.F.R. § 208.16(c)(2) (2002). According to the majority's reasoning, the respondent's claim that it is more likely than not that she will be identified, imprisoned, and subjected to torture upon her return to Nigeria is little more than a product of her speculation. I disagree.

\* \* \*

Although the majority opinion acknowledges the existence of Decree No. 33, the majority rejects the likelihood that it will be enforced and the respondent will be imprisoned.\* \* \* [D]espite conceding that Decree No. 33 continues in force, the majority asserts that the record lacks sufficient evidence to indicate how it is enforced or that it would be enforced against the respondent. \* \* \*

However, notwithstanding the majority's protestations, we may take administrative notice of the fact that international journalists continue to report the aggressive enforcement of Decree No. 33. *See Matter of S– M–J–*, 21 I & N Dec. 722, 728 n.2 (BIA 1997); *Matter of R–R–*, 20 I & N Dec. 547, 551 n.3 (BIA 1992), and cases cited therein (stating that it is well established that administrative agencies may take administrative notice of commonly known facts). First, a recent news report indicates that, as a result of a Nigerian Federal High Court ruling that the

"Decree does not portend double jeopardy," the constitutionality of Decree No. 33 has been affirmed.* * *

Second, recent news reports confirm that enforcement is even greater under the present Obasanjo regime.* * *

Third, women are not exempt from being targeted and punished as drug smugglers.* * * These news articles reflect that the decree exists, that it is actively enforced by the Obasanjo government, and that it is enforced against women.

* * *

### C.　Adjudication Under the "More Likely Than Not" Standard

* * *

In my view, the majority imposes a standard far beyond that required to qualify for relief under the statutory and regulatory provisions of the Convention Against Torture. The majority dismisses proof of Decree No. 33, the respondent's status as a convicted drug trafficker, her forcible return to Nigeria, and evidence of the mistreatment of a similarly situated friend some years earlier, and it demands either more "current evidence" or "meaningful historical evidence" before the respondent can establish that it is more likely than not that she will be identified, imprisoned, and tortured. If we actually quantify and apply the standard imposed by the majority, we must conclude that the respondent is charged with establishing the likelihood of torture *beyond a reasonable doubt*. However repugnant noncitizens convicted of criminal offenses may be, that is not the proper standard.

It is critical to recognize that we do not have the benefit of an accomplished act to examine.* * * Accordingly, in assessing whether it is more likely than not that the respondent will face torture in a Nigerian prison once returned to Nigeria, it is necessary to draw inferences about what may happen in the future and the reasons it may occur.

* * *

The significant factors that should be measured to determine whether it is more likely than not the respondent will be tortured if removed to Nigeria are (1) that the respondent was convicted of drug trafficking; (2) that under current Nigerian law, which is actively enforced, a person convicted of a drug offense is subject to imprisonment for a period of 5 years; (3) that medications are withheld as a means of punishment in Nigerian jails; (4) that the respondent has asthma and, if imprisoned, has no family to provide such medication or any other form of sustenance; (5) that the respondent has a former fiancé who has reason to seek retribution against her; and (6) that rape and other assaults of female inmates are prevalent in Nigerian jails. The respondent may satisfy her burden of proof that it is more likely than not she will be tortured based on the reasonable inferences that can be drawn from these facts in the record.

The evidence presented by the respondent is not merely based on her own fear and speculation, but on solid, uncontradicted evidence of enforcement efforts against smugglers, who are subjected to horrific prison conditions, including denial of medication, assault, and rape by prison guards, all committed by Nigerian Government officials with impunity. The majority's rejection of the respondent's evidence as no more than a "chain of assumptions," reveals its imposition of an improper standard, leading it to erroneously reject evidence that establishes it is more likely than not the respondent will be tortured if returned to Nigeria.

SCHMIDT, BOARD MEMBER, dissenting [joined by four other Board Members]:

I respectfully dissent.

I agree with Board Member Rosenberg's conclusion that the respondent has shown that it is more likely than not that she will be imprisoned under Decree No. 33 upon return to Nigeria.* * * I write separately to address the question the majority avoids: whether the respondent more likely than not will be tortured while in prison. I find that she will be tortured.

* * *

### B.  Prison Conditions as Torture

In *Matter of J–E–* [23 I & N Dec. 291 (BIA)], we effectively established a presumption that mistreatment in prison is not torture under the Convention Against Torture, but merely "cruel, inhuman or degrading treatment"—reprehensible, worthy of condemnation, but not a basis for relief.

To rebut this presumption, a respondent who is likely to be imprisoned upon removal must show that: (1) "torture" exists in the foreign prison system; and either (2) it is probable that any prisoner detained in the system will be tortured, or (3) he or she possesses individual characteristics making it more likely than not he or she will be tortured.

* * *

### III.  ANALYSIS

### A.  Torture Exists in the Nigerian Prison System

The most recent Department of State country report on Nigeria describes the abuses that are rampant in the Nigerian prison system. Bureau of Democracy, Human Rights, and Labor, U.S. Dep't of State, *Nigeria Country Reports on Human Rights Practices—2001* (Mar. 2002), *available at http://www.state.gov/g/drl/rls/hrrpt/2001/af/8397.htm ("Country Reports")*. At least one aspect of that abuse, intentional withholding of needed medical treatment for improper purposes, which is relevant to this respondent's situation, constitutes "torture" under the test set forth in *Matter of J–E–, supra.*

The respondent is a chronic asthmatic with no family in Nigeria who could provide food or proper medical treatment while she is in jail. *The Country Reports* state that "[p]rison officials, police, and security forces *often denied inmates food and medical treatment as a form of punishment or to extort money from them.*" *Country Reports, supra*, at 6 (emphasis added).

That report goes on to state the following:

> Harsh conditions and *denial of proper medical treatment* contributed to the *deaths* of *numerous* prisoners. A reputable human rights organization estimated in 1999 that at least *one inmate died per day* in the Kiri Kiri prison in Lagos *alone.* According to the Prisoners Rehabilitation and Welfare Action (PRAWA), a nongovernmental organization (NGO), dead inmates promptly are buried on the prison compounds, usually without notifying their families. A nationwide estimate of the number of inmates who *die daily* in the country's prisons is *difficult to obtain* because of poor record keeping by prison officials. PRAWA and other NGO's alleged that prison conditions were worse in rural areas than in urban districts.

*Id.* (emphasis added).

Clearly, death caused at least in part by intentional withholding of medical treatment for improper purposes is common in the Nigerian prison system. The extent of the problem probably is understated because of the difficulty in obtaining accurate documentation from the Nigerian system.

\* \* \*

### B. Respondent's Personal Characteristics Make Torture Likely

The respondent is a woman, suffering from chronic asthma, without family to support and assist her in Nigeria, returning from the United States with a drug conviction. Decree No. 33, discussed by the majority, shows, at a minimum, that the Nigerian Government has a particular interest in those returning with foreign drug convictions.

The respondent's combination of personal traits places her in a particularly high-risk category to suffer torture through the intentional denial of medical treatment for her chronic asthma by Nigerian prison officials bent upon improperly punishing or extorting her.\* \* \* Consequently, I find that the respondent more likely than not will be tortured if imprisoned in Nigeria.

\* \* \*

The legal standards that apply in cases filed under the Torture Convention continue to pose challenges to judges. In 2006, the Attorney General issued an opinion reversing the BIA and criticizing an immigration judge for the way the CAT claim was developed and resolved, in a case involving a convicted rapist with a history of mental illness.

## MATTER OF J–F–F–

Attorney General, 2006.
23 I & N Dec. 912.

[GONZALES, ATTORNEY GENERAL:]

Respondent, a native and a citizen of the Dominican Republic and a permanent resident of the United States, was convicted of rape by force and found removable because his rape conviction qualifies as an aggravated felony under section 101(a)(43)(A) of the Immigration and Nationality Act. The Immigration Judge concluded, however, that it was more likely than not that respondent would be tortured if returned to the Dominican Republic and therefore granted a deferral of removal under the Convention Against Torture * * *.

In a brief order, the Board of Immigration Appeals affirmed. On February 10, 2006, pursuant to my authority under 8 C.F.R. 1003.1(h), I directed the Board to refer to me for review its decision in this matter and stayed the decision pending my review. * * *

\* \* \*

Between March 23 and June 3, 2004, respondent appeared before the Immigration Judge for five hearings in his removal proceedings. In these proceedings, respondent admitted the allegations and the charge of removability; he confirmed that he was a native and citizen of the Dominican Republic and admitted that he had been convicted of rape by force. * * * Acting sua sponte, the Immigration Judge then dismissed the case without prejudice on the ground that this and other behavior showed that respondent was incompetent.

The Board reversed the Immigration Judge's termination of proceedings. It first noted that the psychiatric evaluation of respondent in the record and respondent's testimony before the Immigration Judge suggested that respondent was fit for trial. It pointed out that at the Immigration Judge's request, the Government had introduced a psychiatric evaluation, dated February 19, 2004, in which the psychiatrist "cleared [respondent] to stand trial," although this report stated that respondent had schizoaffective and bipolar disorders and observed that respondent had been admitted to various hospitals as a result of his mental illness. It also noted respondent's hearing testimony confirming the psychiatrist's assessment that he fully understood the proceedings and wanted to proceed. * * * [T]he Board reminded the Immigration Judge that regulations provide for removal proceedings against incompetent aliens, with others being allowed to appear on the alien's behalf, *see* section 240(b)(3) of the Act, 8 C.F.R. § 1240.4 (2006), and remanded to the Immigration Judge for further proceedings consistent with its opinion.

On remand, the Immigration Judge introduced the prospect of CAT relief, questioned respondent on the subject until he decided to make the claim, and ultimately granted CAT relief on grounds respondent had not mentioned in his application. When the Immigration Judge first asked respondent whether he was "afraid of being persecuted or tortured in the Dominican Republic," he responded, "Uh, no, ma'am." Respondent said he was aware that his admission required that the Immigration Judge order him removed and deported to the Dominican Republic. After asking a series of questions to which respondent gave answers that did not support deferral of removal under the CAT, the Immigration Judge asked, "So, what do you wish to do?" He replied, "The reason that I don't wanna get deported [is] because I have nobody in [the] Dominican Republic. All my family's in the United States." The Immigration Judge then presented respondent with his choices: "[T]he Board of Immigration Appeals has determined that you do not qualify for the [212(c)] waiver, sir. So, the only option I have left is whether or not you can prove that you would be tortured in the Dominican Republic." Respondent replied, "There's no civil war going on in [the] Dominican Republic. There's a slight disturbance." Trying again, the Immigration Judge asked, "Sir, do you fear returning to the Dominican Republic?" When respondent answered, "Yes, ma'am," she asked, "Do you wish to apply for protection under the Torture Convention?" Respondent said, "Yes."

Respondent then submitted the Form I–589 (Application for Asylum and Withholding of Removal) necessary to apply for deferral of removal under the Convention Against Torture. Respondent's application for CAT relief did not mention fear of police brutality, nor did his initial testimony at the 1-day hearing. In answer to the Form I–589 question, "Why [do] you believe you would or could be harmed or mistreated," respondent wrote, "They might try to kill me. Communists might try to kill me. They might know me." In answer to the form question, "Why [are] you . . . afraid and describe the nature of the torture you fear, by whom, and why it would be inflicted," he wrote, "They was after the family who work for the government to kill us." At the hearing, respondent maintained that he feared harm or mistreatment on return to the Dominican Republic at the hands of "[f]ormer people that used to be under the Communists" or "criminals" who "would use a machete to kill people to rob them." The Immigration Judge asked whether he thought the police would "bother" him in the Dominican Republic. Without specifying whether he feared Communists, criminals, the police, or other actors, he agreed that there is "torture in [the] Dominican Republic, they mistreat people over there very bad, especially if you [are] a stranger."

In response to questioning by the Immigration Judge about his mental condition, respondent testified that he takes the medication Xyprexa once a day, which he buys with the aid of state benefits. He admitted that there have been a few times when he has stopped taking his medication—on occasion simply "[t]o see what would happen"—and that when he did stop "[n]othing happened." He said that he had been "perfectly fine" without his medication when he spent 8 months in a county jail. When asked whether "anything happen[s]" when "you're not in jail, and you don't take your medication," he responded, "No." Specifically, the Immigration Judge asked whether respondent was "not taking medication," when he committed the rape. He responded that he was "[t]aking medication" at the time.

The Immigration Judge then asked respondent whether he thought he needed his medication. After stating that "nothing happened" when he was not medicated and agreeing that he was "perfectly fine" without it, respondent finally agreed that he needed his medication to "keep [him] in balance" because without medication he got "a little rowdy." The Immigration Judge asked him whether it was under these circumstances that "the police arrest you," to which he responded, "Yeah." According to respondent, the medication that he took is "unavailable in the Dominican Republic" because "they don't have no hospital like they have in United States." He conceded, though, that his basis for this supposition was weak because he did not "know much about [the] Dominican Republic, how they run the government, how they run the social department."

On the basis of this testimony, and the State Department's Country Report on the Dominican Republic, discussed below, the Immigration Judge granted respondent's application for deferral of removal.

* * *

In granting respondent deferral of removal under the Convention Against Torture, the Immigration Judge strung together a series of suppositions: that respondent needs medication in order to behave within the bounds of the law; that such medication is not available in the Dominican Republic; that as a result respondent would fail to control himself and become "rowdy"; that this behavior would lead the police to incarcerate him; and that the police would torture him while he was incarcerated. The evidence does not establish that any step in this hypothetical chain of events is more likely than not to happen, let alone that the entire chain will come together to result in the probability of torture of respondent.

First, respondent gave contradictory testimony about his behavior when unmedicated. * * *

Second, based on respondent's admittedly uninformed guess that he could not procure his medication in the Dominican Republic, and a single sentence about the general shortage there of mental health resources from the State Department's Country Report, the Immigration Judge presumed that respondent would not receive medication while in the Dominican Republic. This is a far cry from proving the point. * * * [T]he Immigration Judge concluded that in the absence of evidence that he *could* get his medication, she would presume otherwise. This conclusion flips the burden on its head, inappropriately relieving respondent of his responsibility to prove his case. *See* 8 C.F.R. § 1208.16(c)(2). If one cannot know from the evidence whether he will have access to medication, then respondent has by definition failed to show he is more likely than not to be denied access.* * *

Third, in concluding that these first two points would lead to respondent's arrest in the Dominican Republic, the Immigration Judge relied on her belief—contrary to respondent's testimony—that respondent "without his medication, has found himself in the hands of the police in this country." * * * Again, the evidence presented by respondent is contradictory; he does not show that it is likely—with or without medication—that he would attract the attention of the Dominican police, and therefore cannot show that torture by the police is more likely than not.

Next, there is the central question how police in the Dominican Republic would treat respondent if they had cause to interact with him. Respondent has admitted that the Dominican Government has never tortured either him or, to his knowledge, anyone in his family. Putting aside whether he is more likely than not to find himself in police custody, respondent did not present any direct evidence that the police would more likely than not torture someone in his position. * * * Only after his primary testimony had ended, and after hearing the Immigration Judge's explanation of her tentative decision to the Government's lawyer, did respondent point to evidence to support the Immigration Judge's theory. He did so solely by reading a few passages from the Department of State Country Report on the Dominican Republic, and not from personal knowledge.

\* \* \*

At the Immigration Judge's urging, respondent has speculated that he may lack access to appropriate psychiatric medication in the Dominican Republic, that the lack of medication may affect his behavior, that his behavior may cause him to be arrested, and that once arrested he may face mistreatment at the hands of criminals or lower-level police officers. Taken together these speculations do not amount to a likelihood of torture. Because respondent has failed to carry his burden, I disapprove the Board's decision, deny the respondent's application for deferral of removal, and affirm the Immigration Judge's February 3, 2005 order of removal and deportation to the Dominican Republic.

\* \* \*

### Notes and Questions

1.  In its Understanding 2, printed at the beginning of this chapter, the Senate made a point of expressly adopting the *Stevic* standard—the harm is more likely than not—for assessing the threat level that triggers protection. Recall that the *Stevic* standard, discussed in Chapter Three, Section B, is

more difficult to satisfy than the well-founded fear standard applied in the asylum determination. Thus, in terms of standards of risk as well as potential benefits, the Senate is aligning protection under the CAT with the lesser protection available under withholding of removal rather than with asylum status.

2. What is the heart of the dispute between the majority and the dissents in *Matter of M–B–A–*? Does the majority believe that it is unlikely that the woman in question will be jailed in Nigeria or is the majority simply agnostic as to the likelihood of detention? What evidence could sway the majority on this point? In contrast, the dissents believe it is more likely than not that this Nigerian woman will be jailed and will have her asthma medication withheld. But the Country Reports state that this often occurs; does "often" equate to "more likely than not"?

3. As *Matter of J–F–F–* and *Matter of M–B–A–* suggest, many CAT cases involve individuals convicted of crimes in the United States who are concerned they will be jailed when they are removed. Consequently, prison conditions in the country to which the applicants will be removed often become a focal point of the CAT litigation. As the Schmidt dissent in *Matter of M–B–A–* noted, the BIA has effectively established a rebuttable presumption that mistreatment in prison is not torture. *See Matter of J–E–*, 23 I & N Dec. 291 (BIA 2002).

4. In his opinion, the Attorney General strongly criticized the immigration judge for her conduct in *Matter of J–F–F–*:

> It is appropriate for Immigration Judges to aid in the development of the record, and directly question witnesses, particularly where an alien appears pro se and may be unschooled in the deportation process, but the Immigration Judge must not take on the role of advocate. *See* section 240(b)(1) of the Act (providing that Immigration Judges shall "interrogate, examine, and cross-examine the alien and any witnesses"); 8 C.F.R. § 1240.11(a)(2) (2006) ("The immigration judge shall inform the alien of his or her apparent eligibility to apply for any of the benefits enumerated in this chapter and shall afford the alien an opportunity to make application during the hearing."); *see also Agyeman v. INS*, 296 F.3d 871, 884 (9th Cir. 2002) (stating that "the IJ has a duty to fully develop the record when an alien proceeds pro se"). * * * [T]he Immigration Judge's conduct at the original hearing * * * went well beyond her obligations, even bearing in mind that respondent was proceeding pro se. Therefore if respondent does move to reopen and the Board grants the motion, I am directing that the case be assigned to another randomly selected Immigration Judge for decision.

23 I & N Dec. at 922.

Do you think that the judge stepped over the line between aiding in the development of the record and serving as the advocate for the applicant? How relevant is it that the applicant was unrepresented and had a history of mental illness? That the psychiatric evaluation indicated that the applicant was fit for trial?

5. As you know from the discussion in Chapter Two, Section C, decisions issued by immigration judges in removal proceedings can be appealed by either side to the BIA, and BIA decisions (but only those that go against the individual) can be appealed to the federal appellate courts. Although infrequently used, there is also authority for the Attorney General to review BIA decisions before judicial review in three instances: when the Attorney General directs referral, when the BIA chairman or a majority of the BIA orders referral, or when the Secretary of Homeland Security requests referral. 8 C.F.R. § 1003.1(h). In his *Matter of J–F–F–* opinion, the Attorney General spelled out his power over individual cases:

> I review de novo all aspects of the Board's and Immigration Judge's decisions in this case. * * * The Executive Office for Immigration Review, which includes the Board and Immigration Judges, is subject to the direction and regulation of the Attorney General. While Attorneys General have delegated their authority to the Board and Immigration Judges in the first instance, I retain the power to exercise full decisionmaking upon review.

23 I & N Dec. at 913.

## 5.  JUDICIAL REVIEW

In addition to establishing a higher standard concerning the risk that torture will occur, the implementing legislation, FARRA § 2242(d), limits judicial review of challenges under the Convention Against Torture. It provides that courts can review CAT claims only "as part of the review of a final order of removal pursuant to INA § 242." Cf. INA § 242(a)(4)(added in 2005). Essentially, the petition for review procedure discussed in Section C of Chapter Two is the only avenue for judicial review of CAT claims. Moreover, it is crucial to note that Congress has limited judicial review in many instances when removal is based on criminal offenses, INA § 242(a)(2)(C), although in those instances it has preserved judicial review insofar as the challenge raises constitutional claims or questions of law. INA § 242 (a)(2)(D).

Nonetheless, challenges to denials of Torture Convention protection have begun to make their way to the federal judiciary. As the following Sixth and Seventh Circuit opinions indicate, some courts are insisting that the immigration judges and the BIA provide thorough and careful analyses of the claims and the available evidence.

### TRAN v. GONZALES

United States Court of Appeals, Sixth Circuit, 2006.
447 F.3d 937.

GUY, CIRCUIT JUDGE.

\* \* \*

Tran was born in South Vietnam to Chinese parents who had immigrated to Vietnam during French colonization. The family never assimilated into Vietnamese culture, and Tran does not speak Vietnamese. In 1978, Tran's family fled Vietnam to Hong Kong. Tran and his family entered the United States in 1980 as refugees and later adjusted their status to lawful permanent residents. Several of his immediate family members became United States citizens.

Tran was charged in Ohio state court in 1987 of aggravated murder and robbery. A jury found Tran guilty and, in May 1988, during the appeals process, he entered into a plea agreement in which he agreed to plead guilty to the charged crimes and serve a term of 20 years in exchange for the prosecution dropping its request for the death penalty. At the hearing on the plea agreement, the trial court asked the defense counsel if Tran had been advised of the immigration consequences of his plea. Tran's counsel responded that Tran had been advised that the INS's practice was not to deport people to Vietnam because there were no diplomatic relations between the two countries. The trial court approved the plea agreement in May 1988. INS officials visited Tran in prison shortly after he began serving his sentence and asked him to sign a paper agreeing to his deportation. Tran refused.

[The court first reviewed whether Congress intended that legislative changes concerning the aggravated felony provision should apply retroactively to Tran's conviction, and concluded that they should.]

Tran's second appeal concerns the BIA's rejection of his claim for protection under the CAT. To obtain relief under the CAT, the applicant bears the burden of establishing that "it is more likely than not that he or she would be tortured if removed to the proposed country of removal." 8 C.F.R. § 208.16(c)(2). A court is instructed to look at all relevant evidence relating to the possibility of future torture, including: (1) evidence of past torture inflicted on the applicant; (2) evidence that the applicant could relocate to a part of the country where he is likely not to be tortured; (3) evidence of gross, flagrant, or mass violations of human rights within the country to which the applicant will be removed; and, (4) other relevant information about the country to which the applicant will be removed. 8 C.F.R. § 208.16(c)(3).

Tran presented the following evidence to show the probability that he would face torture upon return to Vietnam. He testified that following the Vietnam war, in which his eldest brother served as an informant for the United States Army, the communists captured his brother and repeatedly tortured him in prison camps. Specifically, they beat Tran's brother with an AK–47 gun, cut him severely enough to leave many scars, starved him, put a gun to his head acting as if they would shoot him, hung him by his feet while interrogating him, and put him in a hole in the ground with rats. Tran's father and another brother were imprisoned, beaten, and put in "re-education camps" because they fought in the war. The communists knew that Tran's family had served in the South Vietnamese Army because they had acquired the salary records of the soldiers. The communists confiscated the property of Tran's family. Shortly before fleeing Vietnam in 1979, Tran received a draft order for service in the Vietnamese military, but he refused to serve. His family paid money to flee Vietnam without proper documentation or approval of local authorities, who would have killed Tran and his family if they had known. Tran testified that he believes the communists will detain him at the airport if he is forced to return to Vietnam because (1) the communists would know that he is ethnic Chinese because he does not speak Vietnamese and has Chinese physical features, (2) the communists would know that his father and brother served in the South Vietnamese Army because they still have the service records, and (3) he has no family living in Vietnam. Tran believes he will be tortured once detained by the communists.

Dr. Alain Marsot, who testified for Tran as an expert on Vietnam, stated that the Vietnamese have a deep and long-held hatred of the Chinese. When the communists took control of Vietnam in 1975, they tried to drive the Chinese out by imposing severe political and economic restrictions against the Chinese and Chinese property. They also expelled whole groups of Chinese. Many Chinese decided to flee Vietnam on boats to other countries as refugees. Marsot also explained that Vietnam is a dictatorial government with no independent judiciary. There is no freedom of speech or freedom of religion. Marsot predicted that if Tran were forcibly returned to Vietnam, he would be detained at the airport and subjected to abuse. The federal officers escorting Tran would be an indication to the communists that Tran was being deported for a criminal offense. Tran would face torture and execution for having been convicted of a serious crime. Vietnam is a poor country and does not want American criminals. Second, the communists would be immediately suspicious of anyone returning from a foreign country, and Tran would face more than a 50% risk of being tortured so that they could determine whether he works for a foreign organization. Third, the communists would torture him because he is of Chinese origin. Consequently, Marsot testified that Tran faced a greater than 50% chance of torture if returned to Vietnam * * *. Marsot stated that he was not aware of any Vietnamese citizen who fled the communist regime and then returned to Vietnam to live.

Tran presented documentary evidence showing the following: (1) Vietnamese officials torture people in detention or during interrogation, including beating, kicking, and shocking with electric batons; (2) there is no access to detainees in the early stages of detention, "allowing situations to arise where torture and cruel, inhuman or degrading treatment can easily take place"; (3) innocent people in Vietnam are tortured because of their ethnicity or pro-democracy beliefs; and (4) Vietnam does not allow international groups such as the Red Cross or the United Nations Human Rights Commission to monitor human rights conditions.

* * * [Because Tran was convicted of an aggravated felony], our review of Tran's CAT claim is limited to questions of law or constitutional issues. Therefore, our jurisdiction is limited to the legal issues Tran presents—whether the BIA used the correct standard in reviewing the IJ's decision and whether it assigned to him the correct burden of proof.

The BIA reviews an IJ's findings of fact for clear error. "The Board will not engage in *de novo* review of findings of fact determined by an immigration judge. Facts determined by the immigration judge, including findings as to the credibility of testimony, shall be reviewed only to determine whether the findings of the immigration judge are clearly erroneous." 8 C.F.R. 1003.1(d)(3)(i). \* \* \*

"A finding is clearly erroneous when the reviewing court on the entire evidence is left with the definite and firm conviction that a mistake has been committed." [citation omitted] The BIA's decision never stated the standard of review that it employed in reaching its conclusion, and the words "clear error" do not appear. The BIA's opinion was based on the conclusion that there were several deficiencies in the evidence. First, the BIA noted, there was no evidence of any mistreatment against returnees to Vietnam, let alone returnees who had committed serious crimes in other countries or returnees whose families had opposed the communist regime. Second, the Board observed that "although the documentary evidence shows that longstanding societal discrimination against ethnic minorities is widespread, the documentary evidence does not report that ethnic Chinese face harm that rises to the level of torture." Third, the Board found Tran's expert's opinion as to the likelihood of Tran facing torture if returned "too speculative," because it was not based on any objective evidence of the treatment of returnees.

In addition to challenging whether the BIA reviewed his CAT claim for clear error, Tran also raises the issue of whether the BIA applied the correct burden of proof. Tran contends that the BIA improperly elevated Tran's burden of proof beyond the "more likely than not" standard by disaggregating his proffered bases for torture, effectively requiring that he establish a greater than 50% likelihood of being tortured on each individual basis. Tran contends that, instead, the BIA should have considered the proffered bases in combination, looking to the likelihood that Tran would be tortured because of his status as a Chinese returnee with a serious criminal record and no family or friends in Vietnam, who has been in the United States for an extended period of time, and whose family members opposed the communist regime. Finally, Tran argues that the BIA placed an impossible burden on him—a burden to prove that other returnees faced torture when, in fact, Vietnam does not accept returnees.

The BIA opinion's lack of reference to any standard of review and its treatment of Tran's claims does not make it evident to this Court what standard of review the BIA employed. The standard of review is particularly significant in Tran's case because the IJ granted withholding of removal under the CAT, and Tran presented unrebutted expert testimony as to his likely treatment in Vietnam. Because BIA review under an incorrect standard of review implicates Tran's due process rights, we conclude that remand to the BIA is appropriate for its consideration of Tran's CAT claim under the correct standard of review and burden of proof.

[The court remanded the case to the BIA for further proceedings.]

## Notes and Questions

1.   Would the court in *Tran* have reached a different decision if the BIA had added one sentence stating that it was applying the clearly erroneous standard of review? Will the addition of a boiler-plate sentence about the standard of review protect future BIA decisions in the Sixth Circuit?

2.   Or did *Tran* demonstrate the importance of having legal representation, presenting documentary evidence about country conditions, and hiring expert witnesses? Though the BIA dismissed the expert testimony as speculative, the court emphasized that it was unrebutted; it is infrequent that the government will introduce its own experts to challenge the applicant's case.

## TUNIS v. GONZALES

United States Court of Appeals, Seventh Circuit, 2006.
447 F.3d 547.

POSNER, CIRCUIT JUDGE.

Badiatu Tunis, a native of Sierra Leone who became a permanent resident of the United States, was ordered removed (deported) on the basis of her conviction in a Wisconsin state court of two counts of selling a small amount of cocaine (less than a gram). These were felonies for which the court sentenced her to two years in prison plus two years of "extended supervision" but suspended all but seven months of the prison term. Were it not for the classification by the immigration judge, seconded by the Board of Immigration Appeals, of her offense as a "particularly serious crime," she would be eligible for asylum and alternatively for withholding of removal. She challenges the classification, together with the denial of relief under the Convention Against Torture.

[The court rejected the challenge concerning classification as a particularly serious crime.]

* * * Her [Torture Convention] claim is based on the procedure (really procedures—and that will become important in our analysis but can be ignored for the moment) that used to be called "female circumcision" or "clitoridectomy and infibulation" but is now more commonly referred to, in places where it is not an acceptable practice, as "female genital mutilation" (FGM). It is well-nigh universal in Sierra Leone, where it is not illegal, and is performed not by doctors but by members of women's secret societies. Tunis underwent it when she was 10 years old, but later, when she first had sexual intercourse, her sexual partner complained that she was only a "half-woman," which was taken to mean that the procedure had been somehow incomplete. Tunis fears that if she is returned to Sierra Leone she will be forced to undergo the procedure again. She claims without contradiction that she does not want this to happen, and we have held that forcibly subjecting a girl or woman to the procedure is torture.

The government argues that Tunis's fears are chimerical. It points out that most females in Sierra Leone are subjected only to clitoridectomy—more precisely, to "excision," which is "the removal 'of the clitoris together with part or all of the labia minora,' " *Abay v. Ashcroft*, 368 F. 3d 634, 638 n.1 (6th Cir. 2004) (quoting a Department of State study)— and not to infibulation as well, which is "stitching or narrowing [as by rings] of the vaginal opening, leaving a very small opening, about the size of a matchstick, to allow for the flow of urine and menstrual blood." *Id.* So even if Tunis just underwent excision the first time, she need have little fear of being forced to undergo infibulation. But this misses the point. As far as the record reveals, she had a botched procedure when she was 10 years old, as a result of which her excision was only partial. This exposes her to the risk of being forced (should she be returned to Sierra Leone) to repeat the excision, and we have held that involuntary excision, even if unaccompanied by infibulation, is torture.

At argument, the government's lawyer pointed out that notes of a pelvic exam of Tunis imply that she is infibulated. This seems mistaken, since the notes include a hand-drawn picture of her pelvic area that clearly shows an entirely open vagina. More important, the statement in the notes that mentions infibulation supports the hypothesis of an incomplete excision: "Clitoris—absent. s/p anterior infibulation.... Labia—*present* posteriorly, absent anteriorly" (emphasis added). That is, Tunis's labia have not been entirely removed, and the labia that remain may have been what gave rise to the "half-woman" comment.

The examining doctor may have thought infibulation a generic term for clitoridectomy and infibulation—as did the immigration judge, who said "there is one procedure I believe and the one procedure involves infibulation, I believe that's the term, for everything. *It is infibulation where all of the female genitalia is removed*. But that's only 15 percent of [women in Sierra Leone]" (emphasis added).

Infibulation is neither here nor there, as far as the present case is concerned. Tunis's argument is that the excision, a separate procedure, was incomplete.

Besides assuming that Tunis had undergone a complete excision and that the "half-woman" comment, if it had been made at all, was a reference to her not having undergone infibulation as well, the immigration judge refused to credit the comment, on the ground that it was "quadruple hearsay." Tunis, he said, had "testified in a general manner that a male friend had related this to her sister who related this to her mother who related this to" Tunis. What Tunis actually testified was that people from the village had taunted her about the incomplete procedure; that a member of the secret society had told her mother that the members realized they'd "never finished what they did" and would have "to complete what they started"; and that the "half-woman" comment had been made directly to her. *That* testimony was not hearsay; she was testifying to what she had heard, not to the truth of the statement. Likewise her testimony about taunts made to her. And although the statement by her mother was hearsay, immigration judges, like other administrative adjudicators, are not bound by the rules of evidence.

The judge also ruled that the government of Sierra Leone does not direct or acquiesce in female circumcision, and without such acquiescence the Convention Against Torture cannot provide any protection to Tunis. The procedure is performed by the secret societies, which are private groups, and the judge said that "the government is not responsible for individuals whom it is unable to control." True, but irrelevant: Female circumcision is legal in Sierra Leone, obviously well known to the government, and, considering the strong international condemnation of the practice, condoned and thus acquiesced in by the government, therefore entitling Tunis to the Convention's protection.

The determination that Tunis is unlikely to be subjected to government-condoned torture if she is returned to her village cannot stand, given the errors committed by the immigration judge and left uncorrected by the Board of Immigration Appeals. * * * [T]he immigration judge's opinion is not reasoned, and its defects were not repaired by the Board's perfunctory discussion of the torture issue in its opinion affirming the immigration judge. The petition for review is therefore granted (though only with respect to the issue of torture) and the case returned to the Board for further proceedings consistent with this opinion.

## Notes and Questions

1.   Judge Posner, who wrote the *Tunis* opinion, is a well-known and vocal critic of adjudication in the immigration courts and BIA. (See his remarks in Section C of Chapter Eight.) Did he limit his review to the legal and constitutional claims raised by Tunis, or did he reassess the factual determinations made by the immigration judge?

2.   In comparing the cases decided by the BIA and the Attorney General to those decided by the courts in *Tran* and *Tunis*, how much depends on the countries to which the individual is being returned (Nigeria, the Dominican Republic, Vietnam, Sierra Leone), how much depends on the type of torture alleged, and how much depends on other factors?

3.   The formal U.S. understanding on the issue of official acquiescence to torture requires both an official's awareness of the activity constituting torture and a "breach [of the official's] legal responsibility to intervene to prevent such activity." Has the court misapplied that doctrine here? What is the source of a legal responsibility to intervene if female circumcision is legal in Sierra Leone?

## Exercise

The opinions in this chapter have expressed the U. S. government's resolve to prevent members of criminal enterprises from obtaining CAT protection based on reprisals they may face from other criminals. They have also demonstrated the government's reluctance to equate terrible prison conditions with torture. In light of these concerns, how would you represent a client with a criminal conviction in the following situations.

1.　Suppose your client, a refugee who arrived from Cambodia 30 years ago at the age of two, was convicted in the United States of involuntary manslaughter and sentenced to seven years in prison. After release from prison, he faces removal to Cambodia, where he has no relatives or friends and does not speak the language. He fears the Cambodian authorities will imprison him because the person he killed was a prominent Cambodian businessman, and he fears he will be tortured in a Cambodian prison. What evidence do you need to obtain to show that your client is eligible for protection under CAT?

2.　Same as above, but your client in the above circumstances has submitted a report from a reputable human rights organization that contained eyewitness accounts of systematic beatings in Cambodian jails. The report indicates that the prisoners, not the jailers, generally administer the beatings. The accounts of beatings are so widespread that it appears likely the jailers are aware that they occur. Is your client eligible for protection under CAT?

3.　Same as in scenario 1, but there is evidence that prison officials use dogs to control the prisoners and the prison inmate population has a high incidence of injuries from dog attacks?

## SECTION C.　NATIONAL SECURITY AND THE CONVENTION AGAINST TORTURE

In the post-September 11th world, terrorism and national security have become high profile concerns. Not surprisingly, they have sometimes been raised in the context of applications for protection under the Torture Convention. As we saw earlier in Section B.2.a., the U.S. implementing legislation for the Convention Against Torture directed the exclusion of certain individuals from CAT protection "[t]o the maximum extent consistent with the obligations of the United States under the Convention." Among those Congress desired to exclude were individuals "for whom there are reasonable grounds to believe that the alien is a danger to the security of the United States." INA § 241(b)(3)(B)(iv). We also saw that the INS concluded that the Torture Convention protects all who can show they face a substantial risk (defined by the Senate's ratifying resolution as one more likely than not to occur), no matter what the applicant's conduct.

Other nations have also grappled with the impact of the Convention Against Torture on those accused of supporting terrorism and threatening national security. In the opinion below the Supreme Court of Canada adopted a less categorical approach than the United States.

# SURESH v. CANADA (MINISTER OF CITIZENSHIP & IMMIGRATION)

Supreme Court of Canada, 2002.
[2002] 1 S.C.R. 3, 2002 SCC 1.

PER CURIAM:

\* \* \*

### I.   FACTS AND JUDICIAL PROCEEDINGS

7.   The appellant, Manickavasagam Suresh, was born in 1955. He is a Sri Lankan citizen of Tamil descent. Suresh entered Canada in October 1990, and was recognized as a Convention refugee by the Refugee Division of the Immigration and Refugee Board in April 1991. Recognition as a Convention refugee has a number of legal consequences; the one most directly relevant to this appeal is that, under s. 53(1) of the *Immigration Act*, generally the government may not return (*"refouler"*) a Convention refugee "to a country where the person's life or freedom would be threatened for reasons of race, religion, nationality, membership in a particular social group or political opinion."

8.   \* \* \* [I]n late 1995, the Solicitor General of Canada and the Minister of Citizenship and Immigration commenced proceedings to deport Suresh to Sri Lanka on security grounds.

9.   The first step in the procedure was a certificate under s. 40.1 of the *Immigration Act*, alleging that Suresh was inadmissible to Canada on security grounds. The Solicitor General and the Minister filed the certificate with the Federal Court of Canada on October 17, 1995, and Suresh was detained the following day.

10.   The [decision] was based on the opinion of the Canadian Security Intelligence Service (CSIS) that Suresh is a member of the LTTE, an organization that, according to CSIS, is engaged in terrorist activity in Sri Lanka and functions in Canada under the auspices of the World Tamil Movement (WTM). LTTE supports the cause of Tamils in the ongoing Sri Lankan civil war. The struggle is a protracted and bitter one. The Tamils are in rebellion against the democratically elected government of Sri Lanka. Their grievances are deep-rooted, and atrocities appear to be commonplace on both sides. The conflict has its roots in measures taken by a past government which, in the view of the Tamil minority, deprived it of basic linguistic, cultural and political rights. Subsequent governments have made attempts to accommodate these grievances, find a political solution, and re-establish civilian controls on the security and defence establishments, but a solution has yet to be found.

11. Human rights reporting on the practices of the Sri Lanka security forces indicates that the use of torture is widespread, particularly against persons suspected of membership in the LTTE. * * *

\* \* \*

14. * * * The adjudicator [at the deportation hearing] found no reasonable grounds to conclude Suresh was directly engaged in terrorism under s. 19(1)(f)(ii), but held that he should be deported on grounds of membership in a terrorist organization under ss. 19(1)(f)(iii)(B) and 19(1)(e)(iv)(C).

\* \* \*

16. Donald Gautier, an immigration officer for Citizenship and Immigration Canada, considered the submissions and recommended that the Minister issue an opinion under s. 53(1)(b) that Suresh constituted a danger to the security of Canada. Noting Suresh's links to LTTE, he stated that "[t]o allow Mr. Suresh to remain in this country and continue his activities runs counter to Canada's international commitments in the fight against terrorism." At the same time, Mr. Gautier acknowledged that "... Mr. Suresh is not known to have personally committed any acts of violence either in Canada or Sri Lanka" and that his activities on Canadian soil were "non-violent" in nature. Gautier found that Suresh faced a risk on returning to Sri Lanka, but this was difficult to assess; might be tempered by his high profile; and was counterbalanced by Suresh's terrorist activities in Canada. He concluded that, "on balance, there are insufficient humanitarian and compassionate considerations present to warrant extraordinary consideration." Accordingly, on January 6, 1998, the Minister issued an opinion that Suresh constituted a danger to the security of Canada and should be deported pursuant to s. 53(1)(b). Suresh was not provided with a copy of Mr. Gautier's memorandum, nor was he provided an opportunity to respond to it orally or in writing. No reasons are required under s. 53(1)(b) of the *Immigration Act* and none was given.

17. Suresh applied to the Federal Court for judicial review, alleging that the Minister's decision was unreasonable * * *.

18. * * * McKeown J. found that the Minister, weighing the risk of exposing Suresh to torture against the danger that Suresh posed to the security of Canada, had satisfied the requirements of fundamental justice. * * *

\* \* \*

20. Suresh appealed to the Federal Court of Appeal. It too dismissed his application. Robertson J.A., for the court, held that the right under international law to be free from torture was limited by a country's right to expel those who pose a security risk. * * *

\* \* \*

IV. ANALYSIS

1. *Standard of Review*

\* \* \*

39.   This brings us to the question of the standard of review of the Minister's decision on whether the refugee faces a substantial risk of torture upon deportation. * * * [W]hether there is a substantial risk of torture if Suresh is deported is a threshold question. The threshold question here is in large part a fact-driven inquiry. It requires consideration of the human rights record of the home state, the personal risk faced by the claimant, any assurances that the claimant will not be tortured and their worth and, in that respect, the ability of the home state to control its own security forces, and more. It may also involve a reassessment of the refugee's initial claim and a determination of whether a third country is willing to accept the refugee. Such issues are largely outside the realm of expertise of reviewing courts and possess a negligible legal dimension. We are accordingly of the view that the threshold finding of whether Suresh faces a substantial risk of torture, as an aspect of the larger s. 53(1)(b) opinion, attracts deference by the reviewing court to the Minister's decision. The court may not reweigh the factors considered by the Minister, but may intervene if the decision is not supported by the evidence or fails to consider the appropriate factors. It must be recognized that the nature of the evidence required may be limited by the nature of the inquiry. * * *

* * *

## 2.   Are the Conditions for Deportation in the Immigration Act Constitutional?

* * *

45.   The principles of fundamental justice are to be found in "the basic tenets of our legal system". * * * The approach is essentially one of balancing. * * * Deportation to torture, for example, requires us to consider a variety of factors, including the circumstances or conditions of the potential deportee, the danger that the deportee presents to Canadians or the country's security, and the threat of terrorism to Canada. In contexts in which the most significant considerations are general ones, it is likely that the balance will be struck the same way in most cases. It would be impossible to say in advance, however, that the balance will necessarily be struck the same way in every case.

* * *

47.   Determining whether deportation to torture violates the principles of fundamental justice requires us to balance Canada's interest in combatting terrorism and the Convention refugee's interest in not being deported to torture. Canada has a legitimate and compelling interest in combatting terrorism. But it is also committed to fundamental justice. The notion of proportionality is fundamental to our constitutional system. Thus we must ask whether the government's proposed response is reasonable in relation to the threat. * * * We must ask whether deporting a refugee to torture would be such a response.

48. With these thoughts in mind, we turn to the question of whether the government may, consistent with the principles of fundamental justice, expel a suspected terrorist to face torture elsewhere: first from the Canadian perspective, then from the perspective of the international norms * * *.

(i) *The Canadian Perspective*

* * *

58. Canadian jurisprudence does not suggest that Canada may never deport a person to face treatment elsewhere that would be unconstitutional if imposed by Canada directly, on Canadian soil. To repeat, the appropriate approach is essentially one of balancing. The outcome will depend not only on considerations inherent in the general context but also on considerations related to the circumstances and condition of the particular person whom the government seeks to expel. On the one hand stands the state's genuine interest in combatting terrorism, preventing Canada from becoming a safe haven for terrorists, and protecting public security. On the other hand stands Canada's constitutional commitment to liberty and fair process. This said, Canadian jurisprudence suggests that this balance will usually come down against expelling a person to face torture elsewhere.

(ii) *The International Perspective*

* * *

66. Deportation to torture is prohibited by both the ICCPR [International Covenant on Civil and Political Rights], which Canada ratified in 1976, and the CAT, which Canada ratified in 1987. * * *

* * *

75. We conclude that the better view is that international law rejects deportation to torture, even where national security interests are at stake. * * *

*(iii) Application to s. 53(1)(b) of the Immigration Act*

76. The Canadian rejection of torture is reflected in the international conventions to which Canada is a party. The Canadian and international perspectives in turn inform our constitutional norms. The rejection of state action leading to torture generally, and deportation to torture specifically, is virtually categoric. Indeed, both domestic and international jurisprudence suggest that torture is so abhorrent that it will almost always be disproportionate to interests on the other side of the balance, even security interests. This suggests that, barring extraordinary circumstances, deportation to torture will generally violate the principles of fundamental justice * * *.

* * *

78. We do not exclude the possibility that in exceptional circumstances, deportation to face torture might be justified * * *. Insofar as

Canada is unable to deport a person where there are substantial grounds to believe he or she would be tortured on return, this is not because Art. 3 of the CAT directly constrains the actions of the Canadian government, but because the fundamental justice balance under s. 7 of the *Charter* generally precludes deportation to torture when applied on a case-by-case basis. We may predict that it will rarely be struck in favour of expulsion where there is a serious risk of torture. However, as the matter is one of balance, precise prediction is elusive. The ambit of an exceptional discretion to deport to torture, if any, must await future cases.

\* \* \*

(b) *Are the terms "danger to the security of Canada" and "terrorism" unconstitutionally vague?*

(i) *"Danger to the Security of Canada"*

\* \* \*

85.   \* \* \* [W]e accept that a fair, large and liberal interpretation in accordance with international norms must be accorded to "danger to the security of Canada" in deportation legislation. We recognize that "danger to the security of Canada" is difficult to define. We also accept that the determination of what constitutes a "danger to the security of Canada" is highly fact-based and political in a general sense. All this suggests a broad and flexible approach to national security and, as discussed above, a deferential standard of judicial review. Provided the Minister is able to show evidence that reasonably supports a finding of danger to the security of Canada, courts should not interfere with the Minister's decision.

\* \* \*

87.   \* \* \* [W]e believe courts may now conclude that the support of terrorism abroad raises a possibility of adverse repercussions on Canada's security. \* \* \* It may once have made sense to suggest that terrorism in one country did not necessarily implicate other countries. But after the year 2001, that approach is no longer valid.

88.   First, the global transport and money networks that feed terrorism abroad have the potential to touch all countries, including Canada, and to thus implicate them in the terrorist activity. Second, terrorism itself is a world-wide phenomenon. The terrorist cause may focus on a distant locale, but the violent acts that support it may be close at hand. Third, preventive or precautionary state action may be justified; not only an immediate threat but also possible future risks must be considered. Fourth, Canada's national security may be promoted by reciprocal cooperation between Canada and other states in combating international terrorism. These considerations lead us to conclude that to insist on direct proof of a specific threat to Canada as the test for "danger to the security of Canada" is to set the bar too high. There must be a real and serious possibility of adverse effect to Canada. But the

threat need not be direct; rather, it may be grounded in distant events that indirectly have a real possibility of harming Canadian security.

89. While the phrase "danger to the security of Canada" must be interpreted flexibly, and while courts need not insist on direct proof that the danger targets Canada specifically, the fact remains that to refoule a refugee under s. 53(1)(b) to torture requires evidence of a serious threat to national security. * * *

90. These considerations lead us to conclude that a person constitutes a "danger to the security of Canada" if he or she poses a serious threat to the security of Canada, whether direct or indirect, and bearing in mind the fact that the security of one country is often dependent on the security of other nations. The threat must be "serious," in the sense that it must be grounded on objectively reasonable suspicion based on evidence and in the sense that the threatened harm must be substantial rather than negligible.

\* \* \*

*(c) Does deportation for membership in a terrorist organization unjustifiably violate the Charter guarantees of freedom of expression and freedom of association?*

\* \* \*

109. Suresh argues that s. 19 is so broadly drafted that it has the potential to catch persons who are members of or participate in the activities of a terrorist organization in ignorance of its terrorist activities. He points out that many organizations alleged to support terrorism also support humanitarian aid both in Canada and abroad. Indeed, he argues that this is so of the LTTE, the association to which he is alleged to belong. While it seems clear on the evidence that Suresh was not ignorant of the LTTE's terrorist activities, he argues that it may be otherwise for others who were members or contributed to its activities. * * *

110. We believe that it was not the intention of Parliament to include in the s. 19 class of suspect persons those who innocently contribute to or become members of terrorist organizations.* * * This permits a refugee to establish that the alleged association with the terrorist group was innocent. In such case, the Minister, exercising her discretion constitutionally, would find that the refugee does not fall within the targeted s. 19 class of persons eligible for deportation on national security grounds.

\* \* \*

### 3. Are the Procedures for Deportation Set Out in the Immigration Act Constitutionally Valid?

\* \* \*

122.   We find that a person facing deportation to torture under s. 53(1)(b) must be informed of the case to be met. Subject to privilege or similar valid reasons for reduced disclosure, such as safeguarding confidential public security documents, this means that the material on which the Minister is basing her decision must be provided to the individual, including memoranda such as Mr. Gautier's recommendation to the Minister. Furthermore, fundamental justice requires that an opportunity be provided to respond to the case presented to the Minister. While the Minister accepted written submissions from the appellant in this case, in the absence of access to the materials she was receiving from her staff and on which she based much of her decision, Suresh and his counsel had no knowledge of which factors they specifically needed to address, nor any chance to correct any factual inaccuracies or mischaracterizations. Fundamental justice requires that written submissions be accepted from the subject of the order *after* the subject has been provided with an opportunity to examine the material being used against him or her. The Minister must then consider these submissions along with the submissions made by the Minister's staff.

123.   Not only must the refugee be informed of the case to be met, the refugee must also be given an opportunity to challenge the information of the Minister where issues as to its validity arise. Thus, the refugee should be permitted to present evidence pursuant to s. 19 of the Act showing that his or her continued presence in Canada will not be detrimental to Canada, notwithstanding evidence of association with a terrorist organization. The same applies to the risk of torture on return. Where the Minister is relying on written assurances from a foreign government that a person would not be tortured, the refugee must be given an opportunity to present evidence and make submissions as to the value of such assurances.

* * *

126.   The Minister must provide written reasons for her decision. These reasons must articulate and rationally sustain a finding that there are no substantial grounds to believe that the individual who is the subject of a s. 53(1)(b) declaration will be subjected to torture, execution or other cruel or unusual treatment, so long as the person under consideration has raised those arguments. The reasons must also articulate why, subject to privilege or valid legal reasons for not disclosing detailed information, the Minister believes the individual to be a danger to the security of Canada as required by the Act. In addition, the reasons must also emanate from the person making the decision, in this case the Minister, rather than take the form of advice or suggestion, such as the memorandum of Mr. Gautier. Mr. Gautier's report, explaining to the Minister the position of Citizenship and Immigration Canada, is more like a prosecutor's brief than a statement of reasons for a decision.

127.   These procedural protections need not be invoked in every case, as not every case of deportation of a Convention refugee under s. 53(1)(b) will involve risk to an individual's fundamental right to be

protected from torture or similar abuses. It is for the refugee to establish a threshold showing that a risk of torture or similar abuse exists before the Minister is obliged to consider fully the possibility. This showing need not be *proof* of the risk of torture to that person, but the individual must make out a *prima facie* case that there *may* be a risk of torture upon deportation. If the refugee establishes that torture is a real possibility, the Minister must provide the refugee with all the relevant information and advice she intends to rely on, provide the refugee an opportunity to address that evidence in writing, and after considering all the relevant information, issue responsive written reasons. This is the minimum required to meet the duty of fairness and fulfill the requirements of fundamental justice under s. 7 of the *Charter*.

\* \* \*

[The court remanded the case to the Minister for reconsideration in accordance with the procedures set forth in the opinion.]

### Notes and Questions

1. The Canadian Supreme Court addressed many issues in *Suresh*, including the "fundamental justice" standard of Canadian Constitutional Law, the international law obligations, the meaning of danger to national security, and the procedural protections necessary when deportation may result in a risk of torture. Does the Court conclude that the national law of Canada trumps the international law embodied in the Torture Convention? Does the Court conclude that Canadian constitutional law and the Torture Convention will always lead to the same result?

2. In paragraph 39, the *Suresh* Court considered the appropriate standard of review of the government's decision on a highly charged political question. How similar is the analysis in *Suresh* to that required by INA § 242(b)(4)(B) (administrative findings of fact are conclusive unless any reasonable adjudicator would be compelled to conclude to the contrary)? See Chapter Two, Section C concerning judicial review of orders removing noncitizens from the United States.

3. The *Suresh* opinion echoes concerns about threats to national security that also arise in the context of applicants for asylum. As we saw in Chapter Six, Section B, those posing security threats to the United States, as well as those who have been persecutors or have committed criminal acts, are excluded from both asylum and withholding of removal. INA § 241 (b)(3)(B). For example, *Matter of S–K–* denied asylum and withholding to a woman who supported a Burmese group that the Burmese government deemed terrorist. Nonetheless, the U.S. conceded that S–K– was eligible under CAT for deferred removal despite her support for terrorist activity. *Matter of S–K–*, 23 I & N Dec. 936, 946 (BIA 2006).

Although the case did not involve the CAT, the Law Lords in the U.K. examined the issue of security dangers posed by support for insurrectionary groups abroad in *Secretary of State for the Home Department v. Rehman*,

2001 UKHL 47 (2001), noted in Chapter Six, Section B. Like the Canadian Supreme Court, the Law Lords adopted an expansive view of conduct that constitutes a security danger and concluded that executive decisions concerning terrorism and security are entitled to great deference.

4. In Chapter Six, we explored issues involved in the termination of asylum or refugee status and the exclusion of certain individuals from protection as refugees. *Suresh* faced both termination of his refugee status in Canada and deportation to Sri Lanka, where there was a substantial risk he would face torture. The Court ruled that such a momentous decision required greater procedural protections and remanded it for a new hearing. What safeguards did the Court specify for the rehearing? Is every applicant for CAT protection guaranteed this type of hearing? Does U.S. law provide similar safeguards to those seeking protection under the Torture Convention?

5. The Hong Kong Court of Final Appeal addressed similar procedural concerns in the case of a Tamil fisherman apprehended in Hong Kong while en route to Canada and convicted of traveling on a forged Canadian passport. Because the 1951 Refugee Convention does not apply to Hong Kong, he sought protection against deportation to Sri Lanka under the Torture Convention. The Court stated:

> 51. In considering the potential deportee's torture claim, the necessary high standards of fairness should be approached as follows: (1) The potential deportee, who has the burden of establishing that he would be in danger of being subjected to torture if deported to the country concerned, should be given every reasonable opportunity to establish his claim. (2) The claim must be properly assessed by the Secretary [of Security]. * * * (3) Where the claim is rejected, reasons should be given by the Secretary. The reasons need not be elaborate but must be sufficient to enable the potential deportee to consider the possibilities of administrative review and judicial review.
>
> \* \* \*
>
> 53. It is for the Secretary to comply with the high standards of fairness when considering individual cases. The following observations may, however, be of assistance. First, the difficulties of proof faced by persons in this situation should be appreciated. The person concerned may have fled from the country concerned with few belongings and documents and his level of education may be relatively low. * * *
>
> 54. Secondly, it would not be appropriate for the Secretary to adopt an attitude of sitting back and putting the person concerned to strict proof of his claim. It may be appropriate for the Secretary to draw attention to matters that obviously require clarification or elaboration so that they can be addressed by the person concerned. * * *

*Secretary for Security v. Sakthevel Prabakar*, [2005] 1 HKLRD 289; (2004) 7 HKCFAR 187 (Hong Kong Court of Final Appeal, 2004).

6. In a highly publicized case involving rendition, the process by which a government delivers an individual in its custody to another government in

the absence of extradition proceedings or any judicial review, U.S. officials received information from the Canadian government that Maher Arar, a dual citizen of Canada and Syria, was involved with terrorist organizations. U.S. officials stopped Arar in September 2002 as he passed through JFK Airport in New York en route home to Canada, and sent him to Jordan, which then sent him to Syria, where he was imprisoned and tortured for a year and then released without any charges. Arar returned to Canada in October 2003 and reported these events, which led the Canadian government to establish a commission of inquiry. Led by Justice Dennis O'Connor, the commission issued a 1,200 page report in September 2006, which exonerated Arar of any ties to terrorism and criticized Canadian and U.S. government officials for relying on inaccurate information and inadequate procedures. Commission of Inquiry into the Actions of Canadian Officials in Relation to Maher Arar, Report of the Events Relating to Maher Arar: Analysis and Recommendations, Sept. 18, 2006, at 1–376, <http://www.ararcommission. ca/eng/AR_English.pdf>. The head of the Royal Canadian Mounted Police publicly apologized to Arar for the faulty procedures that allowed false information to be entered into his file and shared with other governments. CBC News, RCMP Chief Apologizes to Arar for "Terrible Injustices," Sept. 28, 2006, <http://www.cbc.ca/canada/story/2006/09/28/zaccardelliappearance. html>. As you read the next decision, consider the responsibility of Canada, the United States, Jordan, and Syria under the Convention Against Torture in the Arar rendition.

## SECTION D. THE COMMITTEE AGAINST TORTURE

Article 17 of the Convention Against Torture creates a Committee Against Torture to monitor compliance and requires states that have ratified the Convention to submit regular reports on measures they have taken to give effect to the Convention's provisions. If the Committee receives "reliable information" indicating systematic torture, the Committee "shall invite" the state in question to examine and respond to the information, and may ultimately assign a Committee member to make a confidential investigation, Art. 20. States that have ratified the Convention have the option of consenting to the Committee's jurisdiction to review complaints alleging violations of the Torture Convention filed by other state parties, Art. 21, or by individuals, Art. 22. The United States has not consented. More than 50 states have, though, and individual complaints have been filed against Australia, Canada, the Netherlands, Spain, Sweden, and Switzerland, affording the Committee Against Torture the opportunity to begin to develop a body of decisional law. UNHCHR, Statistical Survey of Individual Complaints, <http://www. unhchr.ch/html/menu2/8/stat3.htm>.

The Committee Against Torture has issued more than 150 decisions. Roughly 80 percent of the Committee's decisions have involved petitions filed by rejected asylum seekers who allege they will face torture if forced to return to their country of origin. *See, e.g.*, University of Minnesota Human Rights Library, <http://www1.umn.edu/humanrts/cat/decisions/ cat-decisions.html>. Some cases, such as the one below which involves an asylum seeker rejected on national security grounds after the Swedish police warranted he was a high-level terrorist, have been filed after the applicants have been forcibly sent back to their homeland.

## DECISION OF THE COMMITTEE AGAINST TORTURE OF 24 MAY 2005

CAT/C/34/D/233/2003.

1.1   The complainant is Ahmed Hussein Mustafa Kamil Agiza, an Egyptian national born on 8 November 1962, detained in Egypt at the time of submission of the complaint. He claims that his removal by Sweden to Egypt on 18 December 2001 violated article 3 of the Convention. He is represented by counsel, who provides as authority to act a letter of authority issued by the complainant's father. The complainant himself, detained, is allegedly not allowed to sign any documents for external purposes without special permission from the Egyptian State prosecutor, and according to counsel such a permit cannot be expected.

### THE FACTS AS PRESENTED

2.1   In 1982, the complainant was arrested on account of his family connection to his cousin, who had been arrested for suspected involvement in the assassination of the former Egyptian President, Anwar Sadat. Before his release in March 1983, he was allegedly subjected to torture. The complainant, active at university in the Islamic movement, completed his studies in 1986 and married Ms. Hannan Attia. He avoided various police searches, but encountered difficulties, such as the arrest of his attorney, when he brought a civil claim in 1991 against the Ministry of Home Affairs, for suffering during his time in prison.

2.2   In 1991, the complainant left Egypt for Saudi Arabia on security grounds, and thereafter to Pakistan, where his wife and children joined him. After the Egyptian embassy in Pakistan refused to renew their passports, the family left in July 1995 for Syria under assumed Sudanese identities, in order to continue to Europe. This plan failed and the family moved to Iran, where the complainant was granted a university scholarship.

2.3   In 1998, the complainant was tried in Egypt for terrorist activity directed against the State before a "Superior Court Martial" in absentia, along with over one hundred other accused. He was found guilty of belonging to the terrorist group "Al Gihad", and was sentenced, without possibility of appeal, to 25 years' imprisonment. In 2000, concerned that improving relations between Egypt and Iran would result in his being returned to Egypt, the complainant and his family bought air tickets, under Saudi Arabian identities, to Canada, and claimed asylum during a transit stop in Stockholm, Sweden, on 23 September 2000.

2.4   In his asylum application, the complainant claimed that he had been sentenced to "penal servitude for life" in absentia on account of terrorism linked to Islamic fundamentalism, and that, if returned, he would be executed as other accused in the same proceedings allegedly had been. His wife contended that, if returned, she would be detained for many years, as the complainant's wife. On 23 May 2001, the Migration Board sought the opinion of the Swedish Security Police on the case. On 14 September 2001, the Migration Board held a "major enquiry" with the complainant, with a further enquiry following on 3 October 2001. During of the same month, the Security Police questioned the complainant. On 30 October 2001, the Security Police advised the Migration Board that the complainant held a leading position in an organisation guilty of terrorist acts and was responsible for the activities of the organisation. The Migration Board thus forwarded the complainant's case, on 12 November 2001, to the Government for a strength of the decision under chapter 7, section 11(2)(2), of the Aliens Act. In the Board's view, on the information before it, the complainant could be considered entitled to claim refugee status; however, the Security Police's assessment, which the Board saw no reason to question, pointed in a different direction. The balancing of the complainant's possible need for protection against the Security Police's assessment, thus had to be made by the Government. On 13 November 2001, the Aliens Appeals Board, whose view the Government had sought, shared the Migration Board's assessment of the merits and also considered that the Government should decide the matter. In a statement, the complainant denied belonging to the organisation referred to in the Security Police statement, arguing that one of the designated organisations was not a political organisation but an Arab-language publication. He also claimed that he had criticised Usama Bin Laden and the Afghan Taliban in a letter to a newspaper.

2.5  On 18 December 2001, the Government rejected the asylum applications of the complainant and of his wife. * * * On 18 December 2001, the complainant was deported, while his wife went into hiding to avoid police custody.

2.6  On 23 January 2002, the Swedish Ambassador to Egypt met the complainant at Mazraat Tora prison outside Cairo. The same day, the complainant's parents visited him for the first time. They allege that they [sic] when they met him in the warden's office, he was supported by an officer and near breakdown, hardly able to shake his mother's hand, pale and in shock. His face, particularly the eyes, and his feet were swollen, with his cheeks and bloodied nose seemingly thicker than usual. The complainant allegedly said to his mother that he had been treated brutally upon arrest by the Swedish authorities. During the eight hour flight to Egypt, in Egyptian custody, he allegedly was bound by hands and foot. Upon arrival, he was allegedly subjected to "advanced interrogation methods" at the hand of Egyptian state security officers, who told him the guarantees provided by the Egyptian Government concerning him were useless. The complainant told his mother that a special electric device with electrodes connected to his body was utilized, and that electric shocks were utilized if he did not respond properly to orders.

2.7   On 11 February 2002, a correspondent for Swedish radio visited the complainant in prison. According to him, the complainant walked with difficulty but he could not see any sign of torture. In response to a question by counsel, the correspondent stated that he had explicitly asked the complainant if he had been tortured, and that he had replied that he could not comment. After the initial visit, the Ambassador or other Swedish diplomats were permitted to visit the complainant on a number of occasions. Counsel states that what can be understood from the diplomatic dispatches up to March 2003, is that the complainant had been treated "relatively well", and that he had not been subjected to torture even if the prison conditions were harsh.

2.8   On 16 April 2002, the complainant's parents again visited him. He allegedly told his mother that after the January visit further electric shocks had been applied, and that for the last ten days he had been held in solitary confinement. His hands and legs had been tied, and he had not been allowed to visit a toilet. At a following visit, he told his parents that he was still in solitary confinement but no longer bound. He was allowed to visit a toilet once a day, and the cell was cold and dark. With reference to a security officer, he was said to have asked his mother, "do you know what he does to me during the nights?" He had also been told that his wife would soon be returned to Egypt and that she and his mother would be sexually assaulted in his presence. Thereafter, the complainant's parents visited him once a month until July 2002 and then every fortnight. According to counsel, the information available is that he is held in a two square metre cell, which is artificially cooled, dark and without a mattress to sleep on. His toilet visits are said to be restricted.

2.9   In December 2002, the complainant's Egyptian lawyer, Mr. Hafeez Abu Saada, the head of an Egyptian human rights organization with knowledge of local conditions of detention and interrogation methods, met in Cairo with Mr. Thomas Hammarberg, head of the Olaf Palme International Centre. Mr. Abu Saada expressed his belief that the complainant had been subjected to torture.

2.10   On 5 March 2003, the Swedish Ambassador met the complainant with a human rights envoy from the Swedish Ministry of Foreign Affairs. The complainant allegedly stated for the first time that he had been subjected to torture. In response to the question as to why he had not mentioned this before, he allegedly responded, "It does no longer matter what I say, I will nevertheless be treated the same way".

### THE COMPLAINT

3.1   Counsel claims that the reason that he lodged the complaint over one and a half years after the complainant's removal was that for a long period it was uncertain who was able to represent him. * * *

3.2   As to the merits, counsel argues that the complainant's removal to Egypt by Sweden violated his right under article 3 of the Convention. He bases this proposition both on what was known at the time the complainant was expelled, as viewed in the light of subsequent events. He contends that it has been satisfactorily established that the complainant was in fact subjected to torture after his return.

3.3 Counsel argues that torture is a frequently used method of interrogation and punishment in Egypt, particularly in connection with political and security matters, and that accordingly the complainant, accused of serious political acts, was at substantial risk of torture. In counsel's view, the State party must have been aware of this risk and as a result sought to obtain a guarantee [from the Egyptian government] that his human rights would be respected. Counsel emphasizes, however, that no arrangements had been made prior to expulsion as to how the guarantees in question would be implemented after the complainant's return to Egypt. * * *

3.4 Subsequent events are said to bear out this view. Firstly, Amnesty International expressed concerns about the complainant's situation in communiqués dated 19 and 20 December 2001, 10, 22 January, and 1 February 2002. Secondly, the conclusions drawn by the State party as a result of its visits should be discounted because they took place in circumstances which were deficient. In particular, the visits were short, took place in a prison which is not the one where the complainant was actually detained, were not conducted in private and without the presence of any medical practitioners or experts. Thirdly, independent evidence tends to corroborate that torture did occur. Weight should be attached to the complainant's parents' testimony as, although supervised, not every word was recorded as it was with the official visits and there was opportunity for him to share sensitive information, especially when bidding his mother farewell. In the course of these visits, supervision lessened, with persons entering and leaving the room. Counsel argues it would not be in the parents' or the complainant's interests for them to have overrepresented the situation, as this would needlessly put him at risk of prejudicial treatment as well as distress the complainant's family still in Sweden. In addition, the parents, elderly persons without political motivation, would thereby be placing themselves at risk of reprisal.

3.5 Furthermore, the complainant's Egyptian lawyer is well qualified to reach his conclusion, after meeting with the complainant, that he had been tortured. Mr. Hammarberg, for his part, considers this testimony reliable. In advice dated 28 January 2003 provided by Mr. Hammarberg to counsel, the former considered that there was prima facie evidence of torture. He was also of the view that there were deficiencies in the monitoring arrangements implemented by the Swedish authorities, given that during the first weeks after return there were no meetings, while subsequent meeting [sic] were neither in private nor with medical examinations undertaken.

3.6 For counsel, the only independent evidence on the question, that of the radio correspondent's visit, confirms the above conclusions, as the complainant declined to answer a direct question as to whether he had been tortured. He would not have done this had he not feared further reprisals. The complainant also informed the Swedish Ambassador directly on 5 March 2003 that he had been subjected to torture, having by that point allegedly given up any hope that the situation would change.

3.7 Counsel concludes that the complainant's ability to prove torture has been very limited, though he has done his best to inform on his experiences in prison. He has been unable to present a full statement of his experiences or corroborative evidence such as medical reports.

THE STATE PARTY'S SUBMISSIONS ON THE ADMISSIBILITY
AND MERITS OF THE COMPLAINT

4.1 By submission of 5 December 2003, the State party contests both the admissibility and the merits of the complaint. It regards complaint [sic] as inadmissible (i) for the time elapsed since the exhaustion of domestic remedies, (ii) as an abuse of process, and (iii) as manifestly ill-founded.

\* \* \*

4.8 An alien otherwise in need of protection on account of a well-founded fear of persecution at the hand of the authorities of another State on account of a reason listed in the Convention on the Status of Refugees (under chapter 3, section 2, of the Swedish Aliens Act of 1989) may however be denied a residence permit in certain exceptional cases, following an assessment of that alien's previous activities and requirements of the country's security (chapter 3, section 4 of the Act). However, no person at risk of torture may be refused a residence permit (chapter 3, section 3 of the Act). In addition, if a person has been refused a residence permit and has had an expulsion decision issued against him or her, an assessment of the situation at the enforcement stage must be made to avoid that an individual is expelled to face, inter alia, torture or other cruel, inhuman or degrading treatment or punishment.

4.9 The State party recalls UN Security Council Resolution 1373 of 28 September 2001, which enjoins all UN Member States to deny safe haven to those who finance, plan, support or commit terrorist acts, or themselves provide safe haven. The Council called on Member States to take appropriate measures, consistent with international human rights and refugee law, to ensure asylum seekers have not planned, facilitated, or participated in, terrorist acts. It also called upon Member States to ensure, in accordance with international law, that the institution of refugee status is not abused by perpetrators, organizers or facilitators of terrorist acts.\* \* \*

\* \* \*

4.11 As to the facts of the present case, the State party details the information obtained by its Security Police, which led it to regard the complainant as a serious security threat. At the State party's request, this information, while transmitted to counsel for the complainant in the context of the confidential proceedings under article 22 of the Convention, is not set out in the Committee's public decision on the present complaint.

4.12   The State party observes that on 12 December 2001, after referral of the case from the Migration and Aliens Appeals Boards, a state secretary of its Ministry of Foreign Affairs met with a representative of the Egyptian government in Cairo. At the State party's request and with the Committee's agreement, details of the identity of the interlocutor are deleted from the text of the decision. As the State party was considering to exclude the complainant from protection under the Refugee Convention, the purpose of the visit was to determine the possibility, without violating Sweden's international obligations, including those arising under the Convention, of returning the complainant and his family to Egypt. After careful consideration of the option to obtain assurances from the Egyptian authorities with respect to future treatment, the State party's government concluded it was both possible and meaningful to inquire whether guarantees could be obtained to the effect that the complainant and his family would be treated in accordance with international law upon return to Egypt. Without such guarantees, return to Egypt would not be an alternative. On 13 December 2002, requisite guarantees were provided.

4.13   The State party then sets outs in detail its reasons for refusing, on 18 December 2001, the asylum claims of the complainant and his wife. These reasons are omitted from the text of this decision at the State party's request and with the agreement of the Committee.

4.14   The State party advises that the complainant's current legal status is, according to the Egyptian Ministries of Justice and Interior, that he presently serves a sentence for his conviction, in absentia, by a military court for, among other crimes, murder and terrorist activities. His family provided him with legal representation, and in February 2002, a petition for review of the case was filed with the President. By October 2002, this had been dealt with by the Ministry of Defence and would soon be handed to the President's office for decision. Turning to the monitoring of the complainant's situation after his expulsion, the State party advises that his situation has been monitored by the Swedish embassy in Cairo, mainly by visits approximately once every month. As of the date of submission, there had been seventeen visits. On most occasions, visitors have included the Swedish Ambassador, and several on [sic] other visits a senior official from the Ministry of Foreign Affairs.

4.15   According to the embassy, these visits have over time developed into routine, taking place in the prison superintendent's office and lasting an average 45 minutes. At no time has the complainant been restrained in any fashion. The atmosphere has been relaxed and friendly, with the visitors and the complainant being offered soft drinks. At the end of the June 2002 visit, embassy staff observed the complainant in seemingly relaxed conversation with several prison guards, awaiting return to detention. At all times he has been dressed in clean civilian clothes, with well-trimmed beard and hair. He appeared to be well-nourished and not to have lost weight between visits. At none of the visits did he show signs of physical abuse or maltreatment, and he was able to move around without difficulty. At the request of the Ambassador, in March 2002, he removed his shirt and undershirt and turned around, disclosing no sign of torture.

4.16    In the embassy's report of the first (January 2002) visit, the complainant did not seem to hesitate to speak freely, and told the Ambassador that he had no complaints as to his treatment in prison. Asked whether he had been subjected to any kind of systematic abuse, he made no claim to such effect. When asked during the April 2002 visit whether he had been in any way maltreated, he noted that he had not been physically abused or otherwise maltreated. During most visits he had complaints concerning his general health, concerning a bad back, gastric ulcer, kidney infection and thyroid gland, causing inter alia sleeping problems. He had seen a variety of internal and external medical specialists, and had had an MRI spinal examination, physiotherapy for his back and an X-ray thyroid gland examination. The X-ray revealed a small tumour for which he will undergo further tests. In August 2003, he expressed to the Ambassador, as he had done before, his satisfaction with the medical care received. At the November 2003 visit, he advised that a neurologist had recommended a back operation. He has received regular medication for various health problems.

4.17    During the May and November 2002 visits, the complainant remarked adversely about the general conditions of detention. He referred to the absence of beds or toilets in the cell, and that he was being held in a part of the prison for unconvicted persons. According to him, this generally improved after December 2002, when he was no longer kept apart from other prisoners and could walk in the courtyard. In January 2003, he was moved on health grounds to a part of the prison with a hospital ward. In March 2003, in response to a question, he said he was treated neither better nor worse than other prisoners; general prison conditions applied. At no subsequent visits did he make such complaints.

4.18    On 10 February 2002, that is at an early stage of detention, the Swedish national radio reported on a visit by one of its correspondents with the complainant in the office of a senior prison official. He was dressed in dark-blue jacket and trousers, and showed no external signs of recent physical abuse, at least on his hands or face. He did have some problems moving around, which he ascribed to a long-term back problem. He complained about not being allowed to read and about lack of a radio, as well as lack of permission to exercise.

4.19    Further issues that have been brought up regularly between the complainant and embassy staff are visits from family and lawyers. Following the June 2002 visit, a routine of fortnightly family visits appeared to have been established. At the time of submission this routine continued, though visits in May and June 2003 were restricted for security reasons. The complainant remarked that he had only received two visits from his lawyer, in February and March 2002. He had not requested to see his lawyer as he considered it meaningless. This issue was raised in the embassy's follow-up meetings with Egyptian government officials, who affirmed that the complainant's lawyer is free to visit and that no restrictions apply.

4.20    As the complainant on several occasions and in reply to direct questions, stated he had not suffered abuse, the Ambassador concluded after the November 2002 visit that, although the detention was mentally trying, there was no indication that the Egyptian authorities had breached the guarantees provided.

\* \* \*

4.24    \* \* \* The guarantees were issued by a senior representative of the Egyptian government. The State party points out that if assurances are to have effect, they must be issued by someone who can be expected to be able to ensure their effectiveness, as, in the State party's view, was presently the case in light of the Egyptian representative's senior position. In addition, during the December 2001 meeting between the Swedish state secretary and the Egyptian official, it was made clear to the latter what was at stake for Sweden: as article 3 of the Convention is of absolute character, the need for effective guarantees was explained at length. The state secretary reaffirmed the importance for Sweden to abide by its international obligations, including the Convention, and that as a result specific conditions would have to be fulfilled in order to make the complainant's expulsion possible. \* \* \*

\* \* \*

9.4    The Committee noted that Egypt has not made the declaration provided for under article 22 recognizing the Committee's competence to consider individual complaints against that State party. The Committee observed, however, that a finding, as requested by the complainant, that torture had in fact occurred following the complainant's removal to Egypt, would amount to a conclusion that Egypt, a State party to the Convention, had breached its obligations under the Convention without it having had an opportunity to present its position. This separate claim against Egypt was thus inadmissible *ratione personae*.

\* \* \*

10.4    On 15 June 2004, the Aliens Appeals Board granted the complainant's wife and her five children permanent resident status in Sweden on humanitarian grounds. Later in June, the Egyptian Government through prerogative of mercy reduced the complainant's twenty-five year sentence to fifteen years' of imprisonment. According to counsel for the complainant, the complainant last met Swedish representatives in July 2004. For the first time, the meeting was wholly private. After the meeting, he met his mother and told her that prior to the meeting he had been instructed to be careful and to watch his tongue, receiving from an officer the warning "don't think that we don't hear, we have ears and eyes."

\* \* \*

ISSUES AND PROCEEDINGS BEFORE THE COMMITTEE

### Consideration of the Merits

13.1   The Committee has considered the merits of the complaint, in the light of all information presented to it by the parties, pursuant to article 22, paragraph 4, of the Convention. The Committee acknowledges that measures taken to fight terrorism, including denial of safe haven, deriving from binding Security Council Resolutions are both legitimate and important. Their execution, however, must be carried out with full respect to the applicable rules of international law, including the provisions of the Convention, as affirmed repeatedly by the Security Council.

### Substantive Assessment Under Article 3

13.2   The issue before the Committee is whether removal of the complainant to Egypt violated the State party's obligation under article 3 of the Convention not to expel or to return a person to another State where there are substantial grounds for believing that he or she would be in danger of being subjected by the Egyptian authorities to torture. The Committee observes that this issue must be decided in the light of the information that was known, or ought to have been known, to the State party's authorities at the time of the removal. Subsequent events are relevant to the assessment of the State party's knowledge, actual or constructive, at the time of removal.

13.3   The Committee must evaluate whether there were substantial grounds for believing that the complainant would be personally in danger of being subjected to torture upon return to Egypt. The Committee recalls that the aim of the determination is to establish whether the individual concerned was personally at risk of being subjected to torture in the country to which he was returned. It follows that the existence of a consistent pattern of gross, flagrant or mass violations of human rights in a country does not as such constitute a sufficient ground for determining that a particular person was in danger of being subjected to torture upon his return to that country; additional grounds must exist to show that the individual concerned was personally at risk. Similarly, the absence of a consistent pattern of gross violations of human rights does not mean that a person could not be considered to be in danger of being subjected to torture in his or her specific circumstances.

13.4   The Committee considers at the outset that it was known, or should have been known, to the State party's authorities at the time of the complainant's removal that Egypt resorted to consistent and widespread use of torture against detainees, and that the risk of such treatment was particularly high in the case of detainees held for political and security reasons. The State party was also aware that its own security intelligence services regarded the complainant as implicated in terrorist activities and a threat to its national security, and for these reasons its ordinary tribunals referred the case to the Government for a decision at the highest executive level, from which no appeal was possible. The State party was also aware of the interest in the complainant by the intelligence services of two other States: according to the facts submitted by the State party to the Committee, the first foreign State offered through its intelligence service an aircraft to transport the complainant to the second State, Egypt, where to the State party's knowledge, he had been sentenced in absentia and was wanted for alleged involvement in terrorist activities. In the Committee's view, the natural conclusion from these combined elements, that is, that the complainant was at a real risk of torture in Egypt in the event of expulsion, was confirmed when, immediately preceding expulsion, the complainant was subjected on the State party's territory to treatment in breach of, at least, article 16 of the Convention [which bars cruel, inhuman, and degrading treatment] by foreign agents but with the acquiescence of the State party's police. It follows that the State party's expulsion of the complainant was in breach of article 3 of the Convention. The procurement of diplomatic assurances, which, moreover, provided no mechanism for their enforcement, did not suffice to protect against this manifest risk.

\* \* \*

### Procedural Assessment Under Article 3

13.6   The Committee observes that the right to an effective remedy for a breach of the Convention underpins the entire Convention, for otherwise the protections afforded by the Convention would be rendered largely illusory. \* \* \* In the Committee's view, in order to reinforce the protection of the norm in question and understanding the Convention consistently, the prohibition on refoulement contained in article 3 should be interpreted the same way to encompass a remedy for its breach, even though it may not contain on its face such a right to remedy for a breach thereof.

13.7   The Committee observes that in the case of an allegation of torture or cruel, inhuman or degrading treatment having occurred, the right to remedy requires, after the event, an effective, independent and impartial investigation of such allegations. The nature of refoulement is such, however, that an allegation of breach of that article relates to a future expulsion or removal; accordingly, the right to an effective remedy contained in article 3 requires, in this context, an opportunity for effective, independent and impartial review of the decision to expel or remove, once that decision is made, when there is a plausible allegation that article 3 issues arise. The Committee's previous jurisprudence has been consistent with this view of the requirements of article 3, having found an inability to contest an expulsion decision before an independent authority, in that case the courts, to be relevant to a finding of a violation of article 3.

13.8   The Committee observes that, in the normal course of events, the State party provides, through the operation of the Migration Board and the Aliens Appeals Board, for review of a decision to expel satisfying the requirements of article 3 of an effective, independent and impartial review of a decision to expel. In the present case, however, due to the presence of national security concerns, these tribunals relinquished the complainant's case to the Government, which took the first and at once final decision to expel him. The Committee emphasizes that there was no possibility for review of any kind of this decision. The Committee recalls that the Convention's protections are absolute, even in the context of national security concerns, and that such considerations emphasise the importance of appropriate review mechanisms. While national security concerns might justify some adjustments to be made to the particular process of review, the mechanism chosen must continue to satisfy article 3's requirements of effective, independent and impartial review. In the present case, therefore, on the strength of the information before it, the Committee concludes that the absence of any avenue of judicial or independent administrative review of the Government's decision to expel the complainant does not meet the procedural obligation to provide for effective, independent and impartial review required by article 3 of the Convention.

### Frustration of Right Under Article 22 to Exercise Complaint to the Committee

13.9   The Committee observes, moreover, that by making the declaration under article 22 of the Convention, the State party undertook to confer upon persons within its jurisdiction the right to invoke the complaints jurisdiction of the Committee. That jurisdiction included the power to indicate interim measures, if necessary, to stay the removal and preserve the subject matter of the case pending final decision. In order for this exercise of the right of complaint to be meaningful rather than illusory, however, an individual must have a reasonable period of time before execution of a final decision to consider whether, and if so to in fact, seize the Committee under its article 22 jurisdiction. In the present case, however, the Committee observes that the complainant was arrested and removed by the State party immediately upon the Government's decision of expulsion being taken; indeed, the formal notice of decision was only served upon the complainant's counsel the following day. As a result, it was impossible for the complainant to consider the possibility of invoking article 22, let alone seize the Committee. As a result, the Committee concludes that the State party was in breach of its obligations under article 22 of the Convention to respect the effective right of individual communication conferred thereunder.

### The State Party's Failure to Co-operate Fully with the Committee

13.10   Having addressed the merits of the complaint, the Committee must address the failure of the State party to co-operate fully with the Committee in the resolution of the current complaint. The Committee observes that, by making the declaration provided for in article 22 extending to individual complainants the right to complain to the Committee alleging a breach of a State party's obligations under the Convention, a State party assumes an obligation to co-operate fully with the Committee, through the procedures set forth in article 22 and in the Committee's Rules of Procedure. In particular, article 22, paragraph 4, requires a State party to make available to the Committee all information relevant and necessary for the Committee appropriately to resolve the complaint presented to it. The Committee observes that its procedures are sufficiently flexible and its powers sufficiently broad to prevent an abuse of process in a particular case. It follows that the State party committed a breach of its obligations under article 22 of the Convention by neither disclosing to the Committee relevant information, nor presenting its concerns to the Committee for an appropriate procedural decision.

14. The Committee against Torture, acting under article 22, paragraph 7, of the Convention against Torture and Other Cruel, Inhuman or Degrading Treatment or Punishment, decides that the facts before it constitute breaches by the State party of articles 3 and 22 of the Convention.

15. In pursuance of rule 112, paragraph 5, of its rules of procedure, the Committee requests the State party to inform it, within 90 days from the date of the transmittal of this decision, of the steps it has taken in response to the Views expressed above. The State party is also under an obligation to prevent similar violations in the future.

[The opinion by Committee Member Yakovlev, dissenting in part, is omitted.]

### Notes and Questions

1. Both Sweden and Egypt are parties to the Convention Against Torture, and this decision concludes that Egyptian officials tortured Mr. Agiza. Why is Sweden the focus of this decision and what precisely does the Committee say Swedish officials did that violated their obligations under the Torture Convention?

2. The Convention Against Torture precludes returning an individual to a state where there is a serious risk the individual will face torture. Sweden recognized this obligation and sought assurances from Egypt that Mr. Agiza would not be tortured. The Committee considered these assurances insufficient, ¶ 3.14. What would have made them effective? For a discussion of diplomatic assurances, *see* Jones, *Lies, Damned Lies and Diplomatic Assurances: the Misuse of Diplomatic Assurances in Removal Proceedings*, 8 Eur. J. of Migration and Law 9 (2006).

3. In the United States the Attorney General, in consultation with the Secretary of State, may consider diplomatic assurances from the government of the country to which the person would be returned. 8 C.F.R. § 208.18(c). The Attorney General must assess "whether the assurances are sufficiently reliable to allow the alien's removal to that country consistent with Article

3'' of the CAT. Only a limited list of high-level officials of Cabinet or immediate sub-Cabinet rank are authorized to make this assessment. *Id.*

4.   In light of the Committee's decision, what must a state party do if it concludes that an asylum seeker is a member of a terrorist organization that has committed violent acts in another country, but will face a serious risk of torture or inhuman and degrading treatment if returned to his country? Must a state grant that individual asylum? Must a state allow that individual to remain indefinitely? It is possible that the alleged terrorist activities occurred outside the criminal jurisdiction of the state with custody of the asylum seeker. What if the state can neither prosecute the individual nor send him back to his country of origin? May a state detain such an individual indefinitely without a trial if it concludes that deportation will lead to a serious risk of torture, but that release poses a risk that the individual will commit or facilitate future violent acts?

5.   Around the same time that the Committee Against Torture decided the complaint filed by Mr. Agiza, the Committee issued a report on Canada. The Committee commented on the *Suresh* case included in the previous section of this chapter, and took strong objection to the Canadian Supreme Court's suggestion that deportation to torture might be legitimate in exceptional circumstances:

> The Committee expresses its concern at:

> (a) The failure of the Supreme Court of Canada, in *Suresh v. Minister of Citizenship and Immigration*, to recognize at the level of domestic law the absolute nature of the protection of article 3 of the Convention, which is not subject to any exception whatsoever.

<http://www.unhchr.ch/tbs/doc.nsf/0/3cb671dd5759dc86c125704300482db6?Opendocument>.

6.   Article 30.1 of the Convention Against Torture provides that state parties that disagree about the interpretation or application of the provisions should resolve their dispute by negotiation. If that fails, any of the parties to the dispute can refer this matter to arbitration. If after six months they cannot agree on the format for the arbitration, any party to the dispute can refer the matter to the International Court of Justice. Article 30.2 allows state parties to opt out of this dispute resolution mechanism. The United States has opted out.

# Chapter Eight

# THE FACTFINDING CHALLENGE

---

*I told [the legal assistant I first met that] I was Kenyan and had applied through another law firm for permission to stay in Britain but had been refused. I said I had been told he could help.*

*He told me to forget I was Kenyan and that he was going to introduce me to a member of staff who could help me. He introduced me to another assistant, Beatrice Angira, telling her: "Now, she is from Rwanda. As far as I am concerned, she left Rwanda yesterday. Take and teach her everything that she needs to know."*

*\* \* \* Ms. Angira said she would create a fictitious file for me, giving me a new identity and a story of how I came to be in Britain. She told me, however, that I would have to read the file and learn the stories as if they were my own. She told me she would have to go to Amnesty International to collect press cuttings, and names of people who had been murdered in the Rwandan genocide.*

*\* \* \* Later [after I paid 40 pounds in cash] she gave me the statement that had been promised at the first interview. She had told me my new Rwandan name was to be Yvonne Mukangezi, a Tutsi refugee. We went through the documents together, dealing first with the questions I may be asked at the Home Office and my new story, which was already typed out as a Malik Law Associates document. All I had to do was sign.*

*My story was a harrowing account of a Tutsi refugee. It said: "I was leaving [sic] in a village that was a stone's throw from a Hutu village. There was constant fighting and killings between the two tribes. My father was killed in the process.*

*"I was raped on several occasion and I even got pregnant but I miscarriages [sic] because of the torture that I went through. I experienced both physical and psychological anguish and I even attempted suicide at one time. I also witnessed my mother being raped and my dad being beaten to death."*

*Another section detailed an attack by rebel forces burning the village. "My brothers and I decided to flee but as made [sic]*

**511**

*our way through the forest we [sic] attacked by some Tutsi boys. My two younger brothers were killed and so I was left all alone. I will never forget that day. I was engulfed with a deep feeling of loneliness and sorrow.''*

*The story said I hitchhiked to Tanzania, where I met an agent who helped me get to Britain and who deserted me at Heathrow. The last line read: ''I would rather die than go back home and face persecution''.*

—Yvonne Ndege, reporter[1]

This journalist's undercover investigation of a high-volume immigration law firm in London (later closed down) revealed a more sinister side to some refugee claims. In prior chapters we have been assuming that we had an accurate account of the facts. We have focused primarily on legal questions and on making sense of how the legal standards apply in different scenarios. But such an assumption glosses over one of the major difficulties in asylum cases—accurate factfinding. Asylum and withholding cases may present some of the greatest factfinding challenges known to administrative law, and this chapter will examine some of the recurring factfinding issues that arise.

The reality of refugee suffering properly evokes genuine sympathy and determination to help. The possibility of privileges resulting from refugee status, especially a potential right to resettle indefinitely, evokes suspicion that the unworthy may claim that status. In addition to the exposé that appeared in British newspapers, there have been some dramatic instances of fraudulent asylum applications in the United States. For example, the claimant in *Abankwah v. INS*, 185 F.3d 18 (2d Cir.1999), drew wide publicity and the support of many celebrities when the BIA denied asylum. She had claimed that, if returned to Ghana, she faced female genital mutilation because she had engaged in premarital sex. The court of appeals reversed the BIA's denial, in an opinion that was critical of the Board's demanding requirements for corroboration and of INS' assertions that there were gaps or other credibility problems with her story. But a combination of journalistic and government investigations eventually revealed that the claimant had stolen another woman's identity and concocted her story about the tribal practices she said she feared. Ultimately she was tried and convicted of perjury. A thorough account of all the proceedings in the Abankwah case and the later discovery of the fraud appears in Martin, *Adelaide Abankwah, Fauziya Kasinga and the Dilemmas of Political Asylum*, Immigration Stories 245 (D. Martin & P. Schuck eds. 2005). Martin's account also provides a detailed sense of how asylum cases are handled, from the first master calendar hearing, through efforts to obtain counsel, the filing of the

**1.** Ndege, *Investigation: Harrowing Tale I Learnt to Tell as a Bogus 'Refugee,'* The Independent (London), Jan. 13, 2000, at 13.

application with accompanying affidavits, courtroom proceedings, BIA appeal, and on to appellate court review.

Another asylum seeker from Nigeria was profiled in a highly sympathetic front-page story in the New York Times. Dugger, *After a 'Kafka-esque' Ordeal, Seeker of Asylum Presses Case*, New York Times, Apr. 1, 1997, at A1. But when that story was printed, others who knew first-hand of some of the events described contacted the *Times*, sometimes calling from overseas, to point out certain falsehoods. Eventually a story ran on page 24 discounting much of the earlier information. Dugger, *Doubts Cast on Identity of Nigerian Who Says He's a Political Refugee*, New York Times, May 24, 1997, at 24. In both instances the very notoriety of the case led to the unveiling of the falsehoods, because it triggered investigations by journalists in the country of origin—something that government attorneys, faced with tens of thousands of asylum cases annually, can almost never undertake. Putting aside questions of the logistics of investigations overseas and the resources that they would demand, governmental inquiries in the country of origin also would raise significant problems, because they might endanger friends or family of genuine asylum seekers. *See also United States v. Chen*, 324 F.3d 1103 (9th Cir.2003) (prosecution for perjury in an asylum application).

Episodes involving fraudulent asylum claims have caused some government officials to call for rethinking the international protection regime. Jack Straw, then-British Home Secretary, commented at a European asylum conference in June 2000 that the 1951 Convention, "although designed to give effect to the principle of the rule of law," instead "operates to undermine other aspects of the rule of law, and in some circumstances, and inadvertently, positively to feed serious criminality." Quoted in Fitzpatrick, *Taking Stock: The Refugee Convention at 50,* in U.S. Committee for Refugees, World Refugee Survey 2001, at 23. Then-UN High Commissioner for Refugees, Ruud Lubbers, noted regretfully in March 2001: "Today, refugees and economic migrants—along with a criminal element—have become seriously confused—even assimilated—in the public mind. Extremist politicians have been quick to exploit public fears * * *." *Id.*

Although it is unfair to conclude from a few notorious examples that most asylum claims are unfounded, it is important to recognize that an inherent tension runs through all political and legal decisionmaking on refugee and asylum questions. The tug between sympathy and skepticism is strong. Compounding the policy difficulties is the imprecision of the governing legal standard for deciding just who is a refugee. Under the usual legal definitions, a refugee is someone who demonstrates "a well-founded fear of persecution" in his or her homeland, based on race, religion, nationality, membership in a particular social group, or political opinion. But when is a fear well-founded? What is persecution? When is the feared harm sufficiently linked to one of the five listed grounds? What kind of evidence is necessary to prove the needed facts? As the numbers of asylum applications in the United States mushroomed in the 1980s and early 1990s, this built-in tension in American asylum law became more glaringly apparent.

Other stable and wealthy countries, including Canada, Australia, and much of Europe, have wrestled with the same dilemmas, and controversies over asylum seekers have often played central roles in the national politics of receiving states. Charges of "bogus" refugees and "manifestly unfounded" claims have entered the political discourse in many industrialized countries. The excerpt below explores the impact that oversimplification—bona fide refugee versus economic migrant, for example—has on policy decisions and asylum adjudication.

## DAVID A. MARTIN, REFORMING ASYLUM ADJUDICATION: ON NAVIGATING THE COAST OF BOHEMIA

138 U.Pa.L.Rev. 1247, 1270, 1273–75, 1277–79 (1990).

\* \* \*

Although Americans (along with most of the Western world) are virtually united in a commitment to protect refugees, they are far from united in a common conception of "refugee." Everyday parlance tends to treat anyone fleeing life-threatening conditions as a refugee, whether the source of the threat be natural disaster, foreign invasion, civil unrest, or deliberate persecution. The legal framework of course employs a narrower concept than this journalistic usage, and the 1951 Convention definition might be expected to provide the basis for a unified common understanding, built around the phrase "well-founded fear of persecution." But this phrase too can also take on a variety of shapes, from highly expansive to narrowly crabbed, often depending, it seems, on whether the speaker wishes to include or exclude a particular group of claimants.

\* \* \*

Compounding [the problem of agreed interpretation] are the images we (both citizens and government officials) bring to judgments about asylum policy. [Under the case law, the] legal standard looks, in most cases, toward a finely calibrated individualized judgment of the risk of persecution the applicant would face in the homeland. The judgment must be based, to some extent, on general information about human rights conditions in the home country. But the primary reliance will fall, most of the time, on information specific to that individual.

Public debate on asylum policy, however, proceeds in cruder terms. Partisans are often ready to make sweeping judgments, by nationality, about the merit of large groups of asylum seekers. \* \* \*

*a. The essential problem.* This kind of stereotyping or oversimplification is unfortunately commonplace—and to a significant extent inevitable—in public debate and policy decisions. In a classic work, Walter Lippmann explored comprehensively the influence on policy of these "pictures in our heads."[81] In explaining how easily policymakers can err by relying on their own misconceptions about foreign lands, he wrote:

> [T]he real environment is altogether too big, too complex, and too fleeting for direct acquaintance. We are not equipped to deal with so much subtlety, so much variety, so many permutations and combinations. And although we have to act in that environment, we have to reconstruct it on a simpler model before we can manage with it. To traverse the world men must have maps of the world. Their persistent difficulty is to secure maps on which their own need, or someone else's need, has not sketched the coast of Bohemia.[82]

The "coast of Bohemia" problem bedevils both public debate and adjudication in the asylum field. But perhaps the image for our purposes should be shifted from the littoral to the physiographical. Few nations enjoy a political geography characterized by a reliably fertile plain of steady human rights observance. Outcroppings of abuses appear, sometimes intermittent hills, sometimes whole mountain ranges of severe persecution. The partisans in refugee debates—as well as adjudicators and judges under the current system—are too often inclined, in looking at nations to which they are favorably disposed, to mistake mountains for hills—or plains. The same people, in looking at nations to which they are hostile or for whose exiles they have (understandably) developed sympathy, often picture mountains where they should see hills, and then rush to the conclusion that that nation's exiles are refugees. Whatever the actual geography, it is also easy to forget that many people in those distant nations continue to inhabit the valleys even when the mountains loom large and forbidding.

*b. Boxes vs. spectrums.* A related and persistent misunderstanding compounds the difficulties in achieving a sensible and widely supported asylum policy, and it also occasionally complicates adjudication. Much of the debate proceeds as though there are two sharply different categories of persons who find their way into the asylum adjudication system in this country: refugees, on the one hand, and economic migrants (or simply "illegal aliens") on the other. A recent book on U.S. refugee policy (in other respects quite thorough and insightful) reflects this attitude:

> Refugees are neither immigrants nor illegal migrants, although, like immigrants, they have forsaken their homelands for new

**81.** W. Lippmann, Public Opinion 3 (1960).

**82.** *Id.* at 16. [Lippman alludes to Shakespeare's setting of Act 3, Scene 3 of The Winter's Tale in "Bohemia: A desert country near the sea." The scholarly consensus is that Shakespeare's "mistake" was intentional: he needed a shipwreck to drive the plot, so he brought the sea to Bohemia, the play's setting. Thus, dramatic needs led to a reconstructed—and distorted—map.—eds.]

countries and, like illegal migrants, they may enter those new countries without permission. But a refugee is, in the end, *unlike either*. Both the immigrant and the illegal migrant are drawn to a country. *The refugee is not drawn but driven;* he seeks not to better his life but to rebuild it, to regain some part of what he has lost.[84]

Even if this sharply dichotomous view might, at one time, have captured the realities of refugee flows, it does not offer a helpful way to approach today's asylum caseload. Today's dilemma is both tragic and surpassingly difficult precisely because, among current asylum applicants, refugees are so much like illegal migrants. Only an indistinct and difficult line separates those who should succeed on their asylum applications from those who should not. That is, most of those applying in the United States today were both drawn and driven, and they chose to come in response to a complex mix of political and economic considerations. Asylum seekers are not so different from the rest of us. We have a hard time deciding, particularly when we make difficult, life-altering decisions, and when we finally do choose a course of action, we act from a mix of motives.

\* \* \*

\* \* \* [In judging an asylum claim under definitions derived from the UN Convention, we do not need to assess the applicant's] primary motivation \* \* \*, nor the immediately precipitating event. The best way to understand asylum adjudication is to focus on the degree of risk [the applicant] would face when she returns. If the risk of persecution is sufficiently substantial, her fear is well-founded, even if it was her need for funds to feed her children that sent her on the particular \* \* \* trip at the particular time. \* \* \*

\* \* \*

The 1951 Convention definition best translates into workable adjudicative guidance only in this light. It does not ask how much of a role economics played in the decision to leave; it asks about risk levels upon return. The economic migrant/political refugee distinction, however phrased, is misleading and unnecessary.

If all asylum applicants did fit neatly into one of two boxes—refugee or economic migrant—the adjudicative task would certainly be simplified. The job would simply be to unmask the impostors, those economic migrants who are base enough to pose as something they are not. Unfortunately some people with authority over asylum decisions in Western countries sometimes speak of adjudications as though they did present such a morality play. They hasten to label as abusive, frivolous, or lawless those claims that simply fall short of the necessary showing.

---

**84.** [N.L. Zucker & N.F. Zucker, The Guarded Gate: The Reality of American     Refugee Policy] xiv (emphasis added).

But the world is not that simple. Asylum adjudication, it must be recognized, is at best a crude and incomplete way to respond to the complex realities that the world presents. Our legal structure, for ultimately sound reasons, demands a simple yes or no answer to the asylum claim. But the dichotomous character of the results should not obscure the complexity onto which that yes-or-no grid is forced. Asylum seekers present a spectrum of situations, with only subtle shadings distinguishing the risk levels they face. Adjudication must draw a line at some point on that spectrum. And it must do so with care, so that it protects those whose risks exceed the threshold, even if they happen to have joined a migration stream made up principally of those less severely threatened, who therefore lack, in this technical sense, a well-founded fear of persecution.

\*    \*    \*

## Notes and Questions

1. In addition to Martin's article, which provides a history of U.S. asylum procedures and prescriptions for reform, other examinations of the U.S. asylum system can be found in Palmer, Yale–Loehr, and Cronin, *Why Are So Many People Challenging Board of Immigration Appeals Decisions in Federal Court? An Empirical Analysis of the Recent Surge in Petitions for Review*, 20 Geo. Immigr. L.J. 1 (2005); Schrag, A Well-Founded Fear: The Congressional Battle to Save Asylum in America (2000); Legomsky, *An Asylum Seeker's Bill of Rights for a Non-Utropian World*, 14 Georgetown Immigr. L.J. 619 (2000); and Deborah E. Anker, Law of Asylum in the United States (3d ed. 1999).

2. For commentary on developments affecting asylum seekers in other industrialized countries, *see* Kjaerum, *Refugee Protection between State Interests and Human Rights: Where is Europe Heading?*, 24 Human Rts. Q. 513 (2002); New Asylum Countries? Migration Control and Refugee Protection in an Enlarged European Union (R. Byrne, G. Noll, & J. Vedsted–Hansen eds., 2002); Fullerton, *Inadmissible in Iberia: The Fate of Asylum Seekers in Spain and Portugal*, 17 Int'l J. Refugee Law 659 (2005); Fullerton, *Failing the Test: Germany Leads Europe in Dismantling Refugee Protection,* 36 Tex. Int'l L.J. 231 (2001); Hansen, *Asylum Policy in the European Union*, 14 Geo. Immigr. L.J. 779 (2000); Rey Koslowski, Migrants and Citizens: Demographic Change in the European State System (2000); Mary Crock, Immigration and Refugee Law in Australia (1998); Refugee Rights and Realities: Evolving International Concepts and Regimes (F. Nicholson & P. Twomey eds., 1999) (Part 4: The European Regime).

---

It is deceptively easy to talk about complex situations that impel people to leave their homelands in simple terms. It is also deceptively easy to describe the legal standards in the asylum procedure in simple terms. Understanding and applying the law in a consistent fashion to infinitely varying situations that involve human suffering is exceedingly difficult, however.

Just as asylum seekers present a spectrum of situations, the factfinding challenges posed by asylum cases involve a wide spectrum of issues. Asylum adjudication everywhere places great weight on the credibility of the asylum seeker; indeed, the credibility assessment is generally the key factor in determining which individuals need protection. But asylum seekers are, usually, from another culture and they often speak a different language. Thus, there may be multiple barriers to basic communication and ultimately to reliable credibility assessments.

We will begin by raising some of the framework issues that affect factfinding in asylum cases. To what extent do language, culture, class, and similar matters impinge on reliable factfinding? Are there unspoken assumptions and unconscious biases that skew the process? If so, how can they be ameliorated? After we explore these points, we will look at issues on another portion of the factfinding spectrum: what legal standards and evidentiary requirements must asylum seekers satisfy to demonstrate their need for protection in the United States?

# SECTION A.   COMMUNICATION CHALLENGES

Many say that asylum cases are particularly difficult to prepare and resolve. They point to the often insuperable obstacle of obtaining reliable evidence from abroad, and they note the challenges that arise when the sole testimony is that of the asylum seeker. How different is this from other areas of the law? Don't many criminal law matters revolve around the word of one witness? In the globalized economy, aren't there many disputes that rely on evidence from faraway places? A European scholar, Gregor Noll, articulates some of the elements that make asylum procedures unique—and uniquely difficult.

### GREGOR NOLL, INTRODUCTION: RE-MAPPING EVIDENTIARY ASSESSMENT IN ASYLUM PROCEDURES
Proof, Evidentiary Assessment and Credibility in
Asylum Procedures 1–5 (G. Noll ed., 2005).

#### 1.1.   WHAT MAKES ASYLUM ADJUDICATION SPECIAL?

The law is expected to treat like cases alike. In asylum law, this poses veritable challenges. Today, an important fraction of applications are arguably decided on the basis of evidentiary assessment rather than on legal issues. In particular, the credibility of the applicant's account plays a central role. This moves decisions into a domain characterised by the discretion of the person who assesses the accounts, and raises the issue where its limits are—or ought to be.

\* \* \*

Now, one could argue, such concerns are familiar to the legal profession at large. After all, areas of law other than asylum pivot on evidentiary issues, criminal law being only the tip of the iceberg. Why should we accept asylum law as being so extraordinary, worthy of our heightened attention? Because the distribution of roles, the production of proof, the assessment of credibility and the weighing of evidence in asylum cases raises a cluster of very specific issues and concerns * * *. * * * [T]he issues related to evidentiary assessment in asylum cases are exposed to a higher degree of fragmentation and indeterminacy than [in] other areas of adjudication * * *.

### 1.2.  DETERMINING MEMBERSHIP IN HYBRID PROCEDURES

Asylum adjudication is about membership in a protective community. It is located at the threshold of, rather than within, the domestic legal system. This sets it out from other areas of law, which are typically dealing with intra-community claims * * *.  * * *

The special nature of the membership claim might explain why the asylum procedure is a double hybrid. First, its design incorporates traits from both inquisitorial and adversarial models. Second, it feature elements and concepts derived from administrative and penal procedure. * * * [A]sylum procedures [are] a *sui generis* phenomenon * * *.

* * *

### 1.3.  COMMUNICATING AND PROCEDURALIZING EVIL

Asylum procedures are both marked by paucity and richness at the same time. Their paucity is due to the predominant role of a single means of proof, namely the applicant's account. In this account, however, an overwhelming richness may be embedded. In quite a number of cases, the adjudicator is asked to give credence to the incredibility of evil, which poses challenges in its own right. There are others, easier to rationalize perhaps: the account of the applicant emerges from a foreign context, is told in a foreign language and accompanied by demeanour and other cultural attributes which are not familiar to the adjudicator. In some cases, the effects of trauma, depression or other medical impairments need to be added to the list of impediments. The adjudicator must feel compelled to reduce this richness and complexity by resorting to stereotyping, presumptions, eventually reducing the monstrosity of the account.

What else is there to counter the applicant's narrative? The growing body of information on countries of origin introduces a second, far more general account. A database versus a personal testimony—these are the poles between which the adjudicator finds himself in most cases. Unlike in other cross-border legal relations, the authorities of the country of origin cannot be involved, given that they might indeed be persecutors. Moreover, in contrast to intra-community claims, witnesses and case-specific documents are rarely available. Where the applicant indeed introduces documents into the procedure, the assessment of their authenticity and significance might prove more difficult than they would be in the domestic domain. At times, expert testimonials in medical or linguistic issues or embassy reports on the existence of specific risks add further elements.

This cluster of communicative challenges will put significant obstacles between applicant and adjudicator, with the latter not always fully conscious of their existence. Translators, interpreters, medical and other experts acquire critical importance as mediators, while the quality of their work is usually beyond the scope of review mechanisms. The bridging of the distance between applicant and adjudicator and the overcoming nature of the enumerated obstacles requires effort and expertise beyond what is demanded in adjudication exclusively turning on domestic claims. Simultaneously, decision-takers build up their horizon of expectations along domestic analogies ('what would a reasonable person do?'). This might imply that they use standards of what is deemed credible, plausible and probable which are inappropriate in the alienated setting of asylum adjudication.

These obstructions are amplified by others, and brought about by the legal system itself. As a rule, access to the territory of putative asylum countries is unavailable by legal means. Most applicants have used the services of a human smuggler, who might have advised clients to destroy travel and identity documents, to use forgeries and to give a prefabricated and standardized account of persecution. It is laborious for decision-takers to reach beyond this veil of misinformation. Additionally, the elapsing of time brought about by the asylum procedure itself wears down the memory of crucial events in the narrative of the applicant. In both types of cases, adjudicators often find altered stories to lack credibility. Ultimately, the design of migration and asylum law distorts the production and availability of proof and could, in extreme cases, produce rejections by design.

\* \* \*

## 1. Language

Asylum seekers frequently complain that the asylum officers and immigration judges did not understand them. Sometimes the asylum applicants mean this literally: the factfinder did not speak the asylum seeker's language. Sometimes the asylum seekers mean that the factfinder did not understand the context in which the events that triggered a fear of persecution occurred. Both types of interpretation challenges are subsets of the difficulties inherent in asylum adjudication: the difficulties of communications across cultures.

Courts have insisted that procedural due process applies to noncitizens facing removal from the United States, *Reno v. Flores*, 507 U.S. 292, 113 S. Ct. 1439, 123 L. Ed. 2d 1 (1993), *Landon v. Plasencia*, 459 U.S. 21, 103 S. Ct. 321, 74 L. Ed. 2d 21 (1982), and that asylum seekers must have an opportunity to present evidence on their behalf and to rebut evidence presented by the government or considered by the judge. *See, e.g., Circu v. Gonzales*, 450 F.3d 990 (9th Cir. 2006) (due process violated when IJ took administrative notice of country report without providing opportunity for asylum seeker to rebut); *Nazarova v. INS*, 171 F.3d 478 (7th Cir. 1999) (lack of interpreter prevented asylum seeker from meaningful opportunity to be heard and constituted exceptional circumstances that justified her failure to appear). But how can asylum seekers receive adequate notice and respond in a meaningful manner if they do not speak or read the language of the proceedings?

The regulations provide that non-English-speaking individuals who file an affirmative application for asylum, discussed in Chapter Two, Section C, must provide, at their own expense, a competent interpreter fluent in both English and a language the applicant understands. 8 C.F.R. § 208.9(g). Attorneys for the asylum seekers and witnesses at the hearings may not serve as an interpreter. *Id*. Non-English speakers who arrive without an interpreter can be considered to have failed to appear, which can result in the dismissal of the application. *Id*..; 8 C.F.R. § 208.10.

USCIS has been considering reforms that would result in a government-provided interpreter at asylum office interviews. Some of the impetus for this proposal stems from concern that smugglers in fraudulent asylum schemes may provide an interpreter to ensure that the English version of the applicant's answer at the interview does not vary from the false story set forth in the application.

The situation is different in immigration court. Neither the statute nor the regulations provide the right to an interpreter, but, in practice, the immigration court furnishes interpreters for non-English-speakers. The BIA has held that the applicant's testimony must be translated. *Matter of Tomas*, 19 I & N Dec. 464 (BIA 1987); *Matter of Exilus*, 18 I & N Dec. 276 (BIA 1982).

Even when interpreters are present, many difficulties can arise. A sample of the exchange between an immigration judge and an asylum seeker whose mother tongue is Wolof illustrates some of the impediments. The immigration judge clearly became impatient with the language obstacles, and the Third Circuit severely criticized him for the disrespect he displayed (and reversed his decision). Even a patient judge, though, might have found the testimony confusing, particularly if it were part of what appeared to be many inconsistencies about basic facts within the personal knowledge of the witness.

## CHAM v. ATTORNEY GENERAL

United States Court of Appeals, Third Circuit, 2006.
445 F.3d 683.

BARRY, CIRCUIT JUDGE.

\* \* \*

\* \* \* At the very outset of the [immigration] hearing, petitioner Abou Cham [an asylum seeker from The Gambia] said, in English, that he was born in 1978.

JUDGE TO MR. CHAM

Q.   All right. Remember what I told you, Mr. Cham? Mr. Cham, these instructions are not really earth shattering. They're not that complicated. We are going to stay totally in the Wolof language, now. All right?

A.   Okay.

Q.   Just, just answer in the Wolof language. It's rather simple. All right. What's your full date of birth, sir?

A.   1979.

Q.   All right. Did you not just tell me 1978?

A.   '78.

Q.   Mr. Cham—

MS. DUSSEK TO MS. IBRAHIM[4]. It's going to be a long day.

JUDGE TO MR. CHAM

Q.   Mr. Cham, the question is a rather basic question. When were you born? You said in English, 1978. You said to interpreter in the Wolof language, 1979, or at least that was interpreted as 1979. I just brought that to your attention. Now, we're back to 1978. When were you born, Mr. Cham? Give me your date of birth?

A.   I, I cannot count it in Wolof. That's the reason why I'm a little confused.

Q.   I want to know the date you were born, sir.

A.   1978.

Q.   What date? Give me a month.

A.   September. September 28.

Q.   And, please—

A.   I'm sorry, sir. I'm sorry.

Q.   Would you, please, remain in the Wolof language. I don't know why you're doing this. I'm giving you instructions to speak only in Wolof and you keep intermingling English and Wolof. So, what's your date of birth, now? Sir, the questions are going to get progressively more difficult. We're two minutes into the hearing and already you're having difficulty with a simple question. When were you born?

A.   When it come to counting, Your Honor, I am, I'm not very, very good at it in Wolof. I am better at counting in English than I am in Wolof. I'm very sorry.

Q.   I'm not asking you to count. I'm asking you to give me a month. Give me a month that you were born.

**4.**   Ms. Dussek was government counsel and Ms. Ibrahim was Cham's counsel.

A.   Okay. I would like to know, Your Honor, if I can say the month in English?

JUDGE TO [INTERPRETER]

Mr. Interpreter, in the Wolof language, are the months January, February, March—are there 12 months?

[INTERPRETER]   TO JUDGE

Yes, there are, there are 12 months but they use the [A]rabic [names for the] month . . .

JUDGE TO [INTERPRETER]

All right. Well, you'll know that. You'll know the months—don't you?

[INTERPRETER]   TO JUDGE

Your Honor, personally, I know few of them. I don't know all of them . . . I use the French or the English . . .

JUDGE TO MR. CHAM

Q.   Okay. What's the—give me your date in English, date of birth in English.

Q.   September 28, 1978.

And just moments later:

JUDGE TO MR. CHAM

Q.   Mr. Cham, do you have a problem following directions?

A.   I'm sorry, sir. I'm sorry.

Q.   Well, I'm, I'm tired. I'm sorry. And I'm tired of hearing you say I'm sorry. I don't want you speaking English.

A.   Okay.

Q.   Don't you understand the problem? Don't you understand this premise?

A.   Okay.

Q.   I don't want you speaking English. I gave you the opportunity and you flubbed the opportunity. You were tripping all over the words in English. Your English is not that good. I thought it was better. Now, instead of using your native language with the interpreter that I've provided at some cost to the Government, you want to impress me with your English. Stay in that Wolof language.

A.   Okay, sir.

Q.   You're just delaying everything here.

[The court vacated the BIA order, remanded the case to the BIA, and recommended that the matter be assigned to a different immigration judge for further proceedings.]

Many scholars and courts have referred to the importance of adequate interpreters and translators in asylum cases, but there has been little sustained research and analysis of the roles these individuals perform and the impact they have. One experienced observer had this to say:

> Language barriers * * * impair the immigration judge's ability to assess accurately an asylum applicant's credibility. * * * [T]he manner of speech, including fluency and tone, influence credibility determinations. Clearly, neither fluency nor verbal nuances can reflect veracity when the speaker is struggling with a second language or speaking through an interpreter. Nor can the immigration judge simultaneously associate the asylum-seeker's non-verbal behavior with her words when the judge conducts the hearing through an interpreter. Although some interpreters may enhance the asylum-seeker's ability to communicate with the judge, interpreter credentials are not regulated for asylum hearings, and the quality of translation varies widely from interpreter to interpreter. Misunderstandings due to faulty translations, both of the applicant's responses and the immigration judge's questions, may engender seemingly inconsistent, implausible or confusing accounts which lead to adverse credibility findings.

Ruppel, *The Need for a Benefit of the Doubt Standard in Credibility Evaluation of Asylum Applicants*, 23 Colum. Hum. Rts. L. Rev. 1, 18–19 (1992).

A recent study of the use of interpreters in the asylum process in the United Kingdom focused on the significance of interpreters in establishing credible accounts of fear of persecution. It further identified two distinct concepts of interpretation relevant in the asylum setting: "linguistic interpreting" and "community interpreting," each with different implications for the selection and training of interpreters, as well as for their performance. The study reported the importance of "cultural advocacy" as well as linguistic knowledge to many asylum applicants and their representatives. M. Inghilleri, Translation, Interpretation and Asylum Adjudication (Economic and Social Research Council, London, 2004). It is to the cultural component that we will now turn.

## 2. Cultural Context

In addition to needing interpretation from one language to another, factfinders often need interpretation of the cultural context of the asylum seeker's testimony. As decisionmakers assess the probative value of evidence submitted by applicants and witnesses, they must try to understand what is normal and plausible in another society. They must be aware that their views of the relevance of details and narrative coherence are culturally contingent. Yet, at the same time, they know that they cannot simply believe everyone and everything. The two articles excerpted below discuss some of the distortions and unconscious assumptions that bedevil attempts to understand and evaluate testimony in asylum hearings. The first article examines specific categories of obstacles that interfere with communication between asylum seekers and government officials.

## WALTER KÄLIN, TROUBLED COMMUNICATIONS: CROSS-CULTURAL MISUNDERSTANDINGS IN THE ASYLUM HEARING

20 Int'l Migration Rev. 230 (1986).

This article demonstrates how misunderstandings rooted in the differences between the asylum-seeker's and the official's cultural background can seriously distort the process of communication during the asylum-hearing and thus impair the ability of refugees from Third World countries to make their asylum-claims credible.[a]

\* \* \*

Since few asylum-seekers are able to prove their claims through written evidence such as decisions of courts, warrants of arrest or press reports of their arrest, many countries rely primarily upon an in-person interrogation or a hearing to establish the facts and to examine the credibility of the applicant. In the absence of written evidence, the interrogation or hearing, and thus the communication between asylum-seeker and official, becomes crucial to the decision on political asylum applications. This is especially true if the competent authorities tend to substantiate negative decisions primarily with factual arguments, i.e. if they try to show that due to contradictory and implausible statements or apparent lies the applicant has not been able to prove his or her claim as a genuine refugee.

This article identifies five (partially overlapping) obstacles to an undistorted interaction between asylum-seeker and official. These include a) the manner in which the asylum-seeker expresses him-or herself; b) the interpreter; c) the cultural relativity of notions and concepts; d) different perceptions of time; and e) the cultural relativity of the concepts of "lie" and "truth". Although this list is far from exhaustive, it elaborates factors which not only have been repeatedly observed by the author in his capacity as a lawyer advising and representing asylum-seekers, but also have been identified by anthropologists and sociologists as generally (i.e. outside the asylum context) characteristic either of legal procedures or of cross-cultural communication.

\* \* \*

**a.** Kälin's numerous references to psychological and sociological studies have been omitted.—eds.

### Manner of Expression

The credibility of a person's statements depends not only on their content but also on how they are expressed. There is ample evidence that the manner of speaking affects the credibility of persons involved in legal procedures. It has been noted, for example, that "defendants who were more polite and spoke in more grammatically complete sentence tended more often to be acquitted" * * *. * * * [T]he trustworthiness of a witness depends, as has been experimentally shown, to a considerable extent on the individual's ability to render his or her statement in a "narrative" and coherent as opposed to a "fragmented" manner.

Although the ability to express oneself well depends, at least partly, on personality and on the educational background of the speaker, even well-educated refugees with strong personalities may be unable to present their claims forcefully for reasons specific to asylum-seekers. Many of them are victims of * * * the "bewildering, confusing, depressing, anxiety-provoking, humiliating, embarrassing and generally stressful" situation of persons who move from one culture to another. Especially in the case of refugees from Third World countries, the experience of culture shock obviously can gravely impair the applicant's ability to make a forceful statement: Such an asylum-seeker may speak in a confused, nervous, fragmented and unconvincing manner not because he or she is lying but because of the anxiety and insecurity caused by the difficulties of life in an entirely new social and cultural environment.

The concept of subculture is useful in identifying an additional source of credibility problems relevant for certain groups of asylum-seekers. For example, former members of political parties and groups which were illegal in their home countries have deeply internalized the values of secrecy and suspicion toward outsiders; they were part of a social network largely founded on these values which were crucial for the success of the organization and the freedom and even survival of its members. Such persons have difficulty in communicating openly and revealing themselves, their feelings, beliefs and experiences to everyone not belonging to their group because by doing so they violate basic norms of their subculture. If, in the course of the asylum hearing, they perceive the interrogating official as not sharing their own ideology and political views, they are likely to be reserved and hesitant in the manner in which they express themselves and thus to present a fragmented and confusing story.

Finally, the ability to speak forcefully can, however unintentionally, be curtailed by the official and the manner in which he or she attempts to structure and direct the interaction with the asylum-seeker. Several authors have observed that in certain non-Western societies it is important to let persons involved in legal procedures speak freely about issues which appear to be not directly relevant to the topic of the procedure. In Switzerland (as well as in other Western countries) the asylum-hearing is structured in a different way: Officials often tell the applicants to answer only questions asked and they intervene if the asylum-seeker starts to explain something which he or she feels is important, but is perceived as irrelevant by the official. This may lead to a situation in which "both speakers utterly fail in their efforts to negotiate a common frame in terms of which to decide on what is being focused on and where the argument is going at any one time" and where they are "on parallel tracks which don't meet."

INTERPRETER

Interpreters not only make communication between persons who do not share a common language possible, they also act "as mediators between cultures". Because of the close links between language and culture, however, even excellent translators fulfill this task only when they attempt to communicate in their translations the cultural context of words and concepts. Interpreters used in the asylum procedure often not only lack this sophistication; sometimes they are also not qualified or they make mistakes because of fatigue resulting from a lengthy hearing. All this may distort the communication between asylum-seeker and refugee. Of special importance is a structural problem created by the necessity of using interpreters. At least in Switzerland, interpreters are often of the same nationality as the asylum-seeker because Swiss interpreters are not available. In these cases asylum-seekers regularly suspect the interpreter of being a collaborator with the embassy of their country, capable of passing information to the persecuting government. As a consequence, asylum-seekers may be intimidated, restrict their statements to a minimum of critical information or even withhold facts which would be crucial for obtaining asylum. The * * * Swiss Asylum Act * * * provides that the asylum-seeker can use an interpreter of his or her own choice * * *. This provision, however, only partially solves the problem; it often shifts to the official the suspicion of bias in interpretation. Such interpreters are often friends of the asylum-seeker or persons who share his or her political commitments. The official, therefore, might suspect them of not merely translating but instead interpreting and improving upon the statements of the applicant. This becomes a particular problem where, as is often the case, the interpreter comments upon and expresses open support for the asylum seeker's claims during the hearing.

THE CULTURAL RELATIVITY OF NOTIONS AND CONCEPTS

* * * The cultural relativity of words, notions and concepts, and even more importantly, the lack of consciousness of these differences in perception, are major sources of misunderstandings in cross-cultural communication. The problem certainly affects the asylum procedure: Too often officials assume that the way they think is also the way the asylum seeker thinks. * * * This may result in serious misunderstandings and even contribute to the denial of asylum for genuine refugees who, while doing their best to give all the requested information, fail because their counterpart misinterprets their statements.

\* \* \* Words like "me", "self", "country" or "politics", for instance, embody completely different concepts and significations for such diverse groups as American and Iranian students and the terms "brother" or "cousin" covers for many Africans not only very close relatives but all members of his or her tribe. If the official e.g. does not know this use of "brother" he or she will probably reject the statement of an African asylum-seeker as implausible that, for example, he was helped to leave his country by his brothers working in the jail, the passport-office and the airport. A similar misunderstanding occurred in a Swiss case in which the application of a Turkish asylum-seeker was rejected; among other reasons the decision stated that the applicant's claim to have escaped arrest by hiding in the mountains near his hometown could not be true because the town in question was not surrounded by mountains. In reality, the particular town is situated amid hills. A Swiss makes a sharp distinction between a "mountain" which is a steep and rocky elevation rising higher than timber-line, and a "hill". The official presumably reached his incorrect conclusion because he did not know that, in contrast to the Swiss usage, in Turkish the term "mountain" also applies to hilly regions. Cross-cultural misunderstandings also can be caused by the official's unintentional bias in interpreting the statements in the light of his own legal concepts. This happened in another Swiss decision which rejected the application of a young Turkish worker for lack of credibility due to contradictions in his statement; the argument was made that the applicant in his written request for asylum had declared himself to be a former member of an illegal political party whereas he had admitted during the hearing that he was only a supporter of the party who had distributed propaganda materials.

The official's legal distinction between "members" and "supporters" of a political party makes perfect sense for parties in Switzerland but is not a meaningful one for analyzing membership in such illegal, underground organizations which rest on a structure of small "cells" with a carefully selected membership and are essentially dependent on a large number of supporters to do propaganda work; these supporters are not peripheral to the organization nor are they considered so by the authorities; they have to face similar kinds of persecution as members of the "cells" in case of arrest. \* \* \*

* * *

### DIFFERENT PERCEPTIONS OF TIME

Many asylum applications are rejected due to contradictory statements concerning the time and duration of specific events. Time related contradictions can result from a variety of causes and are, therefore, not necessarily a proof that the asylum-seeker has lied. They may e.g, be due to a fading memory during the sometimes more than a year long period between the flight and the asylum-hearing or the asylum-seeker uses, in his daily life, a non-Western (e.g. Muslim) calendar and makes a mistake in converting to analogous Western dates. Moreover, time is not universally perceived, but members of different cultures have varying conceptions of time and its relevance. Balinese time-reckoning, for example "is clearly not durational but punctual . . . it is not used . . . to measure the rate at which time passes, [or] the amount which has passed since the occurrence of some event". In Africa, members of tribes like the Nuer, "think much more easily in terms of activities and of successions of activities and in terms of social structure and of structural difference than in pure units of time", and many Latin Americans or Middle Easterners adhere to time patterns which are directly opposed to the emphasis of Europeans and North Americans on schedules, promptness and segmentation of time units.

Given the fact, then, that some asylum-seekers of non-Western origin perceive time in a different way, the insistence of most officials on exact dates and consistency of statements on the temporal setting of events raises a serious problem. An asylum-seeker who, as a result of his or her cultural origin, has difficulties in clearly remembering all the relevant dates is confronted with a dilemma: Either he or she admits being unable to answer or tries to meet the expectations of the official and guesses at dates which might not be accurate. In both cases the applicant risks being found lacking credibility. Since the official normally is unaware of this dilemma and its cultural basis, he or she will be inclined to reject the application of an asylum-seeker who gives contradicting statements about the time and duration of events. Thus cross-cultural differences of time-perception can seriously hinder the accurate assessment of credibility during the asylum-hearing.

Officials conducting the asylum-hearing must be knowledgeable not only of the relevant legal provision but also of the specific problems of cross-cultural communication and the particular cultural background of the asylum-seekers whose cases they have to decide. This requires not only adequate training but also an organizational scheme which permits officials to deal with asylum-seekers from only one or a few culturally similar countries. It is important to avoid an atmosphere of intimidation during the hearing which makes the already confused and anxious asylum-seeker even more nervous and unconvincing and to use an interrogation technique which lets the asylum-seeker determine what he or she regards as relevant statements. The official's questions should not be framed in a way directly reflecting his or her legal concepts and cultural values. * * *

\* \* \*

No matter how well-intentioned the factfinder, nor how conscientious, assumptions at the subconscious level continue to operate. The author of the following essay reflects on the factfinding challenges she faced as a refugee law judge in Canada and the difficulties that arose when she lacked a shared culture with the asylum seeker.

## AUDREY MACKLIN, TRUTH OR CONSEQUENCES: CREDIBILITY DETERMINATIONS IN THE REFUGEE CONTEXT

International Association of Refugee Law Judges.
October 14–16, 1998, Ottawa, Canada.

When I became a Member of the Refugee Division of Immigration and Refugee Board in 1994 * * * I quickly realized that relatively few of the cases coming before me would raise the kind of legal questions that pre-occupied me as a scholar * * *.

Instead, the vast majority of my time would be spent on credibility determination—did I believe the claimant's story or, more precisely, did I believe enough of the story to render a positive decision? Ultimately I found this to be the most challenging aspect of the job * * *.

* * * Our goal? To "search for truth". If we just ask enough questions, get enough evidence, observe the claimant closely enough, we will be able to determine what really happened or, at least, what didn't really happen. * * *

But we never have all the information. In my experience, we rarely have even as much information as I would consider necessary to choose a new appliance, much less make a decision about a person's future. Nevertheless, we do formulate theories about what happened, or didn't happen, and these often take shape in accordance with inchoate ideas about the truth-telling quality of the claimant before us.

Credibility determination is hard. It is frequently difficult to articulate in rational terms why one does, or does not, believe another. Decision makers may put a lot of faith in their "gut feelings" about credibility, but recognize that "gut feeling" does not amount to a legally defensible basis for a decision. * * * [T]here is a temptation to avoid basing negative decisions on credibility, even though that is the real reason for the rejection. This avoidance usually manifests in a reliance on some other ground for turning down the application, such as the availability of state protection, or an internal resettlement option * * *.

* * *

[T]here are the various factors influencing what and how the claimant relates to the decision-maker. She may have every reason not to trust anyone in authority. Experience may have taught her that the key to survival is telling the person in authority whatever he or she wants to hear. She may have been threatened by her smuggler not to disclose the actual means by which she arrived in her country. She may recite a story that did not happen to her because she was assured that it was a "winning script", and because she has no story of her own or doubts that her own story will be taken seriously.

The tools we use to attribute meaning to all of this are usually the following: consistency, plausibility and demeanour. I'll begin with the last, which is in some sense the easiest. Examining demeanour for clues to credibility presupposes that we know what truth-telling looks like, and that it looks the same on everybody. The stereotype goes something like this: truth-tellers look us in the eye, answer the questions put to them in a straightforward manner, do not hesitate, show an "appropriate" amount of emotion, and are neither too laconic, nor too verbose. Liars do not look us in the eye (out of embarrassment or shame), do not answer the questions put to them (are evasive), say too little (because there is nothing to say—the story is invented), say too much (because they are trying to distract you), are neither too demonstrative (melodramatic) nor lacking in affect (betraying the fact that nothing happened). Yet, as we all know (or should know), culture, gender, class, education, trauma, nervousness and simple variation among humans can all affect how people express themselves. It is dangerous at best, and misleading at worst, to rely on a uniform set of cues as demonstrative of credibility, or lack thereof.

That is not to say that demeanour conveys nothing. It is, rather, to suggest that the messages conveyed by demeanour are indeterminate and contingent. Speaking personally, I became very wary of relying on demeanour, and did so infrequently.

Plausibility usually refers to the relationship between what the claimant describes and what we think we "know" about how the external world works. Consistency examines the relationship between different statements made by the claimant and searches for contradiction. Plausibility and consistency are sometimes assumed to be equivalent to the truth. They are not. They are, rather, proxies or substitutes for truth. Claimants may tell stories that are perfectly plausible and entirely consistent, yet wholly fabricated. The converse is also true.

In my case, I recall one claimant whose story struck me and my colleague as consistent and plausible. His demeanour was confident, his testimony was straightforward, and he held up fine under questioning. The only problem was that his written story happened to be plagiarized word for word from that of a claimant I had heard a few months earlier.

In another case related to me by a former colleague, the claimant insisted that she arrived in Canada in late November by jumping ship in Halifax. Literally. From a height of about four stories, into the freezing and thoroughly unwholesome ocean waters of Halifax Harbour. I would have had no hesitation in agreeing with my colleague that the scenario was wholly implausible—if not for the fact that the event was photographed by local newspapers.

One particular case haunts me to this day, because it exposes how culturally contingent the qualities of consistency can be. I once heard a refugee claimant testify about the reasons he fled his country. The claimant was an elite athlete and escaped his country against the orders of his trainers, who were connected to government. He feared that if returned, he would be subject to persecution by authorities. Over the course of the hearing, the claimant provided three different versions of his escape. The accounts were contradictory regarding certain significant details. The claimant's demeanour was earnest, polite, co-operative and unsophisticated. He just could not keep his story straight. When confronted with the inconsistencies, he would either stick with his most recent version, or change the story yet again. His manner was entirely guileless and for that reason, disconcerting. Most claimants understand that it is bad to be caught in a contradiction, and if confronted with an apparent inconsistency, they will attempt to deny it, explain it, or reconcile it. Yet this claimant simply did not "get it". It seemed rather that he was intent on pleasing us, and if his first version seemed to cause us consternation, he would change it in an effort to find a story we liked better. In addition, the claimant was simply not able to explain why authorities would want to punish him so severely should he return, given that he was the top—and world class—athlete in his sport in the whole country.

The next day, the counsel for the claimant produced a Canadian witness, a coach who had significant experience with the system of elite sports in claimant's country of origin. He was able to corroborate certain aspects of the claimant's story and, most importantly, confirm the fate of an athlete who leaves the country without permission. He also explained how a person in the claimant's position would be targeted for very harsh treatment in order to make an example of him to other athletes who might consider leaving their country for the more promising (and lucrative) future abroad. At that point, we had the requisite information, and were able to accept the claimant*. Without the benefit of a Canadian witness—someone who provided the answers using a shared "cultural" language—I cannot say what our decision would have been. Why the claimant could not or did not provide us with a single, consistent account of his escape I do not know, yet I am as confident about the ultimate decision as I am about any others I have rendered. I know that this progressive mutation of a story under questioning is a phenomenon I have noticed among other claimants from the same country of origin as this claimant. In many of those cases, it led to negative decisions because of serious inconsistencies in the claimant's story. Is this a problem of cultural difference? If so, whose culture is the problem?

\* \* \*

## Notes and Questions

1. "Credibility", a British parliamentarian has noted, "is a way by which the interviewer is able to express his ignorance of the world. What he finds incredible is what surprises him." Thomas, *Assessing the Credibility of Asylum Claims: EU and UK Approaches Examined*, 8 Eur. J. Migration & Law 79, 84 (2006). There is a kernel of truth, at least, in this caustic remark, but do you think that the requirement of credible evidence should be eliminated? In the same vein, a judge on the British Asylum and Immigra-

---

\* I omit here other aspects of the claimant's story which were important to establishing the elements of the claim.

tion Tribunal noted that "[w]hat may be plausible for a person in a Western environment may be completely implausible for some one in a non-Western environment. * * * Adjudicators must take great care in not allowing their own perceptions and values to influence that judgment." *Ibrahim Ali v. Secretary of State for the Home Department* [2002] UKIAT [U.K. Immigration Appeal Tribunal] 07001, para. 3.

2.   Asylum officers now receive training on the pitfalls of cross-cultural misunderstandings and ways to approach traumatic topics. See Schmitt, *Asylum Agents Learn to Assess Tales of Torture*, N.Y. Times, Dec. 21, 1997, at 5 (describing a program to train asylum officers on interview techniques needed to elicit information delicately "without touching off an onslaught of traumatic memories for the refugee" and also how to sort truth from lying in these sensitive cases).

3.   The scholarly literature on credibility assessments in asylum cases is growing. See, e.g., Gregor Noll (ed.), Proof, Evidentiary Assessment and Credibility in Asylum Procedures (2005); Kagan, *Is Truth in the Eye of the Beholder? Objective Credibility Assessment in Refugee Status Determination*, 17 Geo. Immigr. L.J. 367 (2003); Cohen, *Questions of Credibility: Omissions, Discrepancies and Errors of Recall in the Testimony of Asylum Seekers*, 13 Int'l J. Refugee L. 293 (2001); Kneebone, *The Refugee Review Tribunal and the Assessment of Credibility: An Inquisitorial Role?*, 5 Austl. J. Admin. L. 78 (1998); Pfeiffer, *Credibility Findings in INS Asylum Adjudications: A Realistic Assessment,* 23 Tex. Int'l L.J. 139 (1988). The Canadian government has issued guidelines regarding credibility findings, Immigration and Refugee Board, Assessment of Credibility in Claims for Refugee Protection (2002).

4.   For a seminal work on interpreters in U.S. asylum procedures, see Anker & Rubin, *The Right to Adequate Translation in Asylum Proceedings*, 9 Immigr.J. 10 (1986).

---

In the case below the Third Circuit refused to credit the immigration judge's conclusion that a Chinese asylum seeker lacked credibility. The court ruled that the immigration judge's lines of questioning were both hostile and irrelevant to the legal issues, thus tainting the factfinding. As you read the opinion, consider the extent to which cultural differences played a role in the immigration judge's assessment of the asylum application.

## WANG v. ATTORNEY GENERAL

United States Court of Appeals, Third Circuit, 2005.
423 F.3d 260.

FUENTES, CIRCUIT JUDGE.

* * *

Wang is a 34-year-old native and citizen of the People's Republic of China. He alleges that an intrauterine device (IUD) was forcibly inserted into his wife by government officials after she gave birth to their first daughter in November 1998. Wang claims that because the daughter was born with a disability, and because he and his wife wanted a son, they asked the local authorities for permission to have a second child. Their request was denied pursuant to Fujian Province Family Planning Regulations, under which those with an agricultural registration, including Wang's wife, are not permitted to have more than one child. Wang alleges that his wife had the IUD removed by a private doctor and she became pregnant again in December 1999. Wang's wife hid at her parents' house until she gave birth to a second daughter. Because she did not wish to burden her ill and aging parents, and because she did not desire to remain in hiding forever, Wang's wife returned home one month after the birth of her second daughter, in October 2000. Shortly thereafter, Wang alleges that a local birth control cadre came into their home and dragged his wife to a family planning center where she was involuntarily sterilized. Wang submitted into evidence the 1989 Fujian Province Family Planning Regulations that prescribe such measures. The officials also allegedly fined Wang 12,000 RMB (or "Renminbi"), and upon his refusal to pay, began deducting a penalty from Wang's parents' retirement pension.

\* \* \* Wang ultimately left China for the United States through a smuggler whom he paid approximately $60,000 in borrowed funds [and sought asylum].

\* \* \*

[At Wang's hearing before Immigration Judge Garcy] counsel and the IJ took Wang through a recital of his basic factual allegations, [and] they reached his claim that his parents' pension was being withheld as a penalty for his violation of birth control policy. The IJ questioned Wang as to why he had not paid the fine he was issued as a result of that violation, in order to restore his parents' pension:

JUDGE TO MR. WANG:

Q. Well, why don't you just pay the fine and solve your parents [sic] problem. I don't understand why you haven't paid it.

A. I do not have the money to pay.

Q. Oh come on. You're here in the United States of America after having paid a smuggler to get here. And a lawyer's working on your case and you're dressed in a suit and tie and you want me to believe that you can't pay $1,500.

A. The money I pay to the snake head [smuggler] I have to borrow money in order to pay the snake head.

Q. So you choose to pay the smuggler instead of paying the fine and protecting your parents [sic] pension. What sympathy do you want from me about that?

A. Not that I do not want to protect my parents. If I will stay in China no one will lend me money to pay the fine.

Q.  You're not in China, you're in the United States and you're making money when you work.

A.  Yes, I do.

Q.  So why do you expect sympathy from me that you choose to pay money to a smuggler instead of protecting your parents [sic] pension? You must be out of your mind if you think I have sympathy for that.

A.  First of all, I believe when government impose fine against my family it's outrageous. Secondly, I owe a lot of money to different sources and I have to pay them back. They force me to. Certainly I do regularly send money back to support my parents.

Q.  All these sources that you're describing are a bunch of illegal people who conspired with you for you to be smuggled into the United States. Are those the sources that you're describing to me?

A.  Yes, my trip was arranged by snake head.

Q.  Well understand clearly, I have no sympathy with your problem about that.

[After further questioning, the judge asked why the applicant's wife had not come to the U.S. to seek asylum instead of the applicant.]

A.  Because while my wife was there my handicapped child was there as well.

Q.  Well, wherever your wife goes the child with the disability goes, right?

A.  Yes, yes.

Q.  And let's talk about her. Have you ever had medical records about your darling first child Ming Wang brought to the United States of America? Yes or no. I want a short answer, yes or no. Do you have her medical records here, yes or no?

A.  Only photos.

Q.  Okay. Well why haven't you ever, ever gone to a doctor in the United States with medical records about your first born child to see whether there's a better treatment for her here in this country?

A.  I did produce my daughter's old x-ray film to my cousin and my cousin helped me to inquire doctors and we were told that in America she might need operation.

Q.  Well why don't you have any medical records here to prove to me that you care enough about your daughter to have asked the doctor here about her welfare?

A.  I really indeed care my daughter, but I just was not aware that I need such document be produced into the Court.

Q.  Well you care about your daughter, that's interesting because all you write about in your application here is how you want to try to have your wife come here because you're upset about his fine and you're upset about how you can't produce a son. Why is it in all these pages you've never once made any effort to try to find out whether medical care would be available to your child here potentially even on a visa for her to travel to this country?

A.  Indeed I am a father of a child. I really care for my kids especially my daughter and I just did not, I was just not aware that I need to produce such a particular document to this Court.

* * *

The IJ's oral opinion was consistent in tone and substance with her comments during the preceding hearing. "[E]mbarass[ed]" to have Wang in her court room, in her oral opinion, she described Wang as "obsessed" with having a son and maligned him for "ignor[ing]" his daughter. She reiterated her horror that Wang was interested only in "his wife's ability to reproduce . . . instead of taking responsibility for the child that is in existence at the present time. That is an outrageous thing." She observed that she was "comfortable denying asylum to the respondent as a matter of discretion because he's a horrible father as far as the Court's concerned because he pays no attention to his daughter except to the extent that a picture of her arm might win the heart of the undersigned so as to have the respondent granted asylum in this Court." She indicated that she was not bothered "about the respondent's plight."

The IJ found Wang's wife's statement of events incredible in part because she too failed to exhibit the sentiments the IJ was looking for. The IJ explained that "[b]oth the respondent and his wife, shocking to the conscious [sic] of the undersigned, make absolutely no comments about how they wish that they could come to the United States for careful medical treatment of their first born daughter who apparently has limited physical mobility in her arms." She concluded from this that "the wife's statement was obviously designed for her to sign" and untruthful. In her disdain for the Wangs, the IJ seriously considered the possibility that Wang's wife was sterilized after Wang arrived in the United States, perhaps to aid his asylum application.

In her opinion, the IJ affirmed her earlier characterization of Wang as selfish for refusing to pay the fine for his second child: "That's just so horrible that the respondent would allow his parents to have their pension taken away because the respondent egotistically doesn't want to pay a fine that's imposed upon him and his family." The IJ later continued: "In other words, he thinks it's more ethical to make his wife and his parents suffer than it is to pay smugglers."

Finding it ridiculous that Wang had not made headway on the fine while working in the United States, the IJ warned Wang: "If the respondent thinks that this Court is going to be sympathetic to the fact that he owes smugglers and he's worried about his welfare here, the respondent is sadly mistaken. There is absolutely nothing noble, not even for 10 seconds in paying a smuggler even one cent of money when the respondent is here in the federal building that houses the United States Attorney's office" and could file a statement against the smuggler. Based on this reading of the situation, the IJ found "that the respondent's problem with the fee is self imposed because the respondent has chosen to pay a smuggler instead of paying off a fee."

In the course of her opinion, the IJ focused repeatedly on Wang's actions towards his elder daughter and parents. The IJ found "infuriating" and "beyond comprehension" that Wang "never even one time did anything honest" on behalf of his disabled daughter, i.e., he allegedly failed to pursue free medical treatment for his elder daughter in the United States. Accordingly, the IJ chose to humiliate Wang, observing that:

> [Wang] [s]pends a lot of time talking about how he can get his wife's sterilization reversed so that he could have more kids and doesn't spend one line talking about what he might do for his child that he actually has. For the child that is alive. For the child that should matter. For the child who apparently can't even feed herself and dress herself. That's a situation that the respondent has crafted that obviously is troubling to the Court because it certainly does reveal somebody who acts with selfishness and who acts with complete disdain for honesty with regard to an application for a non-immigrant visa, and frankly, with complete lack of concern about somebody who he has created.

\* \* \*

In light of the clear standards governing immigration proceedings \* \* \* we are sorely disappointed that the IJ here chose to attack Wang's moral character rather than conduct a fair and impartial inquiry into his asylum claims. The tone, the tenor, the disparagement, and the sarcasm of the IJ seem more appropriate to a court television show than a federal court proceeding. But we hasten to emphasize that our concerns about the IJ's opinion are not limited to her choice of words. Substantively, many of the issues addressed by the IJ at length, and to which she gave substantial weight, were irrelevant to Wang's asylum, withholding, and CAT claims. The factual issue before the IJ was whether Wang's wife had been forcibly sterilized and whether, if he returned to China, the Chinese government would inflict improper punishment on him for leaving the country. The IJ was not called upon to determine whether Wang was a good father and son.

While the IJ explicitly deemed her broad character judgments relevant to her decision, they were not. "The personal choices that an asylum applicant has made concerning marriage, children, and living arrangement should not be used to evaluate the applicant's credibility concerning his claims of persecution, unless they reflect some inconsistency in a relevant portion of the applicant's testimony."

\* \* \*

\* \* \* [T]he IJ's conduct so tainted the proceedings below that we cannot be confident that Wang was afforded the opportunity fully to develop the factual predicates of his claim. We stress that we have only considered the IJ's findings to the extent that the BIA relied upon them. Based on this review, we conclude that we cannot credit the IJ's conclusions as to Wang's credibility and find that her denial of Wang's claims was unsupported by substantial evidence.

\* \* \* [W]e will grant the petition for review. In doing so, we note that, "while we recognize that assignment of an IJ is within the province of the Attorney General, if on remand an IJ's services are needed, we believe the parties would be far better served by the assignment [of] [these] proceedings [to] a different IJ."

### Notes and Questions

1.   The immigration judge's comments in this case displayed a lack of judicial temperament, at the very least. But do they suggest cross-cultural communication problems as well? On the first score, the Third Circuit strongly criticized the tone and tenor of the immigration judge's comments during the hearing, although it "hastened to add" that the judge made substantive errors by relying on irrelevant factors. Was the hostile and sarcastic tone in itself sufficient to support a reversal? What if the judge had not used an aggressive tone, but had said more or less the same things?

2.   To the extent possible, concentrate solely on the immigration judge's adverse credibility finding. The IJ refused to credit the testimony submitted by the applicant's wife because the judge thought the document had likely been prepared to bolster Wang's case. Is it likely that the document had been prepared in anticipation of the asylum hearing? Can the content (or lack of content) of a document, without more, be a sufficient basis for concluding that the document is not credible?

## SECTION B.   EVIDENTIARY REQUIREMENTS

The applicant has the burden of proving he or she is eligible for asylum or withholding of removal. This requires the applicant both to produce evidence that demonstrates eligibility and to persuade the decisionmaker to conclude from the evidence that the applicant will face a substantial risk of persecution if returned. Prior chapters have outlined the legal elements of asylum and withholding claims. Although individual cases vary, the law requires every applicant to present evidence concerning a risk of persecution in the future and evidence that persecution is on account of one of the five Convention grounds.

In general, applicants may submit any probative evidence in order to prove the elements of their claims. Most applicants rely on their own testimony. Some applicants also present testimony from other individuals, including expert witnesses. In addition, applicants sometimes present documentary evidence, some of which may pertain particularly to them and some of which may refer more generally to conditions in their homeland. Although testimonial and documentary evidence are staples of the U.S. legal system, asylum and withholding claims present especially difficult challenges for decisionmakers because the sources of relevant information are often inaccessible or in faraway locations and because they require a prediction about the likelihood of future conduct in another cultural and political system.

Before we highlight some of the evidentiary issues that are unique in asylum adjudication, we think it is helpful to identify the different layers of factfinding involved in every asylum case. In contrast to the retrospective factfinding process that occurs in much litigation in the United States, asylum claims involve both predictions of the future and evidence about the past. Furthermore, asylum cases involve both proof of general situations and evidence of events specific to an individual. To understand the daunting factfinding process that occurs in every asylum case, it is helpful to break the factual determination down into three parts, each of which presents its own challenges. First, the trier of fact must make broad determinations about conditions in the country of origin, including the practices of the government or other alleged persecutors in the home country. These are properly deemed legislative facts, in the terminology developed by Professor Kenneth Culp Davis, *see* 3 K. Davis, Administrative Law Treatise, ch. 15 (2d ed. 1980). Second, the trier of fact must decide about past events specific to the claimant. These are adjudicative facts, in Professor Davis's framework, the classic retrospective factfinding of most litigation. Third, the trier of fact must make an informed prediction, perhaps not truly a finding, about the degree and type of danger the applicant is likely to face upon return. The third element is actually a prediction based on a combination of the first two elements.

Do not assume that these are three separate steps performed sequentially. They are closely interwoven; acquaintance with the general conditions is especially helpful in assessing the threats to the individual. In addition, the findings of fact, both legislative and adjudicative, will provide the basis for the third component, which requires an assessment of past threats or abuse against the backdrop of information about country conditions, the nature of the risk asserted, and the extent to which any threat is focused or targeted on the applicant or others similarly situated. The cases usually have not carefully separated these elements. The following materials explore some of the central factfinding issues.

## 1.  LEGISLATIVE FACTS

The term "legislative facts" refers in asylum cases to findings concerning the way the government and other social organizations operate in the asylum seeker's homeland. The focus is not on what has happened to the applicant, but rather on what happens more generally in the country. These important factual questions are frequently referred to in shorthand as country conditions. In the opinion that follows, the BIA relied heavily on the applicant's failure to introduce evidence of country conditions.

## MATTER OF DASS

Board of Immigration Appeals, 1989.
20 I & N Dec. 120.

\* \* \*

The respondent's persecution claim is based upon his claimed membership in a political party known as the "Dal Khalsa." \* \* \* The objective of the party was to obtain independence for the State of Punjab in India. The respondent testified that the party did not advocate violence and that he and other party members were not involved in violent demonstrations. \* \* \*

\* \* \*

The immigration judge concluded that the respondent had not met his burden of proof \* \* \*.

The respondent appealed, challenging the denial of his applications for asylum and withholding in very general terms, and submitting that the immigration judge "erroneously ignored my testimony that the lives of Dal Khalsa's are in danger only because I could not provide government publications." \* \* \*

\* \* \*

[I]n determining whether an asylum applicant has met his burden of proof, we have recognized the difficulties that may be faced by aliens in obtaining documentary or other corroborative evidence to support their claims of persecution. \* \* \* If an intelligent assessment is to be made of an asylum application, there must be sufficient information in the record to judge the plausibility and accuracy of the applicant's claim. Without background information against which to judge the alien's testimony, it may well be difficult to evaluate the credibility of the testimony. We note that this problem is addressed in the Office of the United Nations High Commissioner for Refugees, Handbook on Procedures and Criteria for Determining Refugee Status under the 1951 Convention and the 1967 Protocol Relating to the Status of Refugees para. 42 (Geneva, 1979) ("Handbook"), which includes the following observations:

> The applicant's statements cannot, however, be considered in the abstract, and must be viewed in the context of the relevant background situation. A knowledge of conditions in the applicant's country of origin—while not a primary objective—is an important element in assessing the applicant's credibility. \* \* \*

Particularly when the basis of an asylum claim becomes less focused on specific events involving the respondent personally and instead is more directed to broad allegations regarding general conditions in the respondent's country of origin, corroborative background evidence that establishes a plausible context for the persecution claim (or an explanation for the absence of such evidence) may well be essential. The more sweeping and general a claim, the clearer the need for an asylum applicant to introduce supporting evidence or to explain its absence. Furthermore, there is a greater likelihood that corroborative evidence will be available if the claim is of longstanding, widespread persecution.

In addressing this respondent's appeal from the denial of his application for asylum, we note that there are two aspects to his testimony. First, he testified to factual matters involving himself personally (e.g., his activities and his arrest). Secondly, he testified in a far more general and conclusory manner regarding the situation, or his views of the general situation, concerning Dal Khalsa/Akali Dal members in India. As noted by the immigration judge, no supporting documentation or evidence of any kind was introduced in support of the claim.

The respondent clearly failed to establish a well-founded fear of persecution based on the evidence regarding his own circumstances. His testimony in this regard reflects that he was a member of the Dal Khalsa from the age of 17 until he left India in 1982. He was active in giving speeches and encouraging party membership. Over the entire period of his activities in India, the only incident with the police in which he was involved arose when he was accused of advocating violence along with 10 others, was detained overnight, and was released when the authorities were satisfied that he had not done anything wrong. Six months to a year later, he left India with nothing having occurred to him in the interim. * * *

We do not find this application enhanced by the respondent's general allegations regarding conditions in India. He has not provided background evidence of any kind to corroborate his sweeping claim that the Government of India persecutes members of the Dal Khalsa or Akali Dal. This is, in fact, the sort of factual claim, which, if true, one would expect could be supported by corroborative evidence. The unexplained absence of such information may well indicate an exaggerated or unfounded claim. Moreover, we do not find any credible explanation for the absence of such supporting evidence in this case. The respondent states in his appeal statement that he could not get corroborating evidence, which includes, by his description, "widely known" government publications, because he was detained. Respondent's counsel, however, entered an appearance in his case on October 14, 1983. The initial hearing was conducted on November 17, 1983, during which a continuance was granted to permit the filing of an application for asylum. The hearing on the merits was not conducted until January 17, 1984. Not only does the record not include any "widely known" supporting evidence, it does not reflect that any effort was ever made to obtain such information. Moreover, the information provided by the Department of State indicates to the contrary that members of the Dal Khalsa are punished only for criminal conduct and that this is done in accordance with the constitutional protections of the Indian system of criminal justice.

We conclude that the respondent has failed to establish a well-founded fear of persecution on account of his alleged political activities, and, therefore, that he has not established eligibility for asylum under section 208 of the Act. We find further that in view of his failure to satisfy that burden of proof with respect to asylum, he also has failed to satisfy the higher burden of proof for withholding of deportation under section 243(h) of the Act.

\* \* \*

The appeal is dismissed.

---

In the next case the First Circuit criticizes the BIA for inferences it drew from a report on general country conditions. This opinion, as well as the prior one, shows the interaction between evidence of general country conditions and evidence focused on the individual asylum seeker.

## ZAROUITE v. GONZALES

United States Court of Appeals, First Circuit, 2005.
424 F.3d 60.

BOUDIN, CIRCUIT JUDGE.

\* \* \*

\* \* \* [Abdelhafid] Zarouite was born and raised in Casablanca, Morocco, attended university there, and lived in the city until 1996. In that year—according to Zarouite—he and his parents were forced by the Moroccan government to move to the territory of Western Sahara. Morocco currently occupies much of the area; the remaining parts of the territory are apparently controlled by an independence movement, the Polisario Front. In the 1990s Morocco and the Polisario Front negotiated, under United Nations auspices, a possible referendum to determine the territory's status.

A dispute existed as to whether all residents would be permitted to vote in the referendum, or only those (mainly ethnic Sahrawis) who resided in Western Sahara prior to 1975. Zarouite claimed that he and his parents, of Sahrawi descent, were compelled to move to Western Sahara in 1996 because the Moroccan government wanted more votes against independence. Zarouite contends that for three years after his arrival in Western Sahara, he suffered beatings and attacks at the hands of the Polisario Front, which wanted him to leave.

In 1999, Zarouite returned to Casablanca where he said he was imprisoned by the Moroccan government and given the choice between returning to Western Sahara or remaining in jail. After several months he returned to Western Sahara where, he says, he again suffered harassment from the Polisario Front. In June 2000 he left, entered the United States unlawfully through Canada, and was apprehended by American authorities.

After a hearing, the immigration judge denied the request for asylum and withholding of removal * * *. * * * [The BIA] issued a two-paragraph affirmance. The BIA said that * * * "the record ... reveals fundamental changes in Morocco since [Zarouite's] departure such that his fear of returning is no longer well-founded."

For this last proposition, the BIA cited only a State Department "country report" on Morocco dated March 4, 2002. The BIA summarized the report by saying that it showed that, despite some past abuses, today "the Moroccan government generally respects the rights of its citizens and that Sahrawis who have departed to Morocco are encouraged to return provided they recognize Morocco's sovereignty over the Western Sahara." This was the sole support offered to show that Zarouite's assumed fear was unfounded.

* * *

In this case, says the Attorney General, the substantial evidence standard applies and the BIA's decision should be upheld unless the record "compels" the opposite result. Compare *Aguilar–Solis v. INS*, 168 F.3d 565, 569 (1st Cir.1999). Admittedly, the record does not "compel" the conclusion that the Moroccan government will repeat the alleged behavior that Zarouite attributes to it, but the problem here is that the country report does not directly address such behavior at all, so the rationality of the inference is open to question.

The most pertinent sentences in the report are as follows:

> The Government also encouraged the return of Sahrawis who have departed Morocco due to the conflict in the Western Sahara, provided that they recognize the Government's claim to the region. The Government did not permit Western Saharan nationalists who have been released from prison to live in the disputed territory.

Zarouite's testimony, if believed, suggests that the Moroccan government once had a policy of requiring some Moroccans to move to Western Sahara in order to bolster a vote in Morocco's favor in an anticipated referendum. It would hardly make sense for the Moroccan government to make one family alone move back. If Morocco once had such a policy, abandonment of the policy would defeat the basis for Zarouite's claim. But the quoted language from the country report neither concedes such a policy nor suggests that, if it once existed, it has now been discontinued.

The BIA paraphrased the report in another, far more general, respect. It said that the Moroccan government generally respects the rights of its citizens. Inferences can be drawn from the general to the particular; conceivably, a country report could reflect such a firm present adherence by a government to high human-rights standards, across a range of activities, that forced relocation of population for political purposes would be implausible and defeat any well-founded fear of repetition of past abuses.

It is enough to say in summary that the country report says that the human rights record in Morocco, once discouraging, is now improving, but this is far from the kind of blanket endorsement just posited. Indeed, a pertinent excerpt from the report reads: "The Government generally respected the rights of citizens in most areas; however, the Government's record was generally poor in a few areas." Thus, it is difficult to understand why the BIA thinks that the country report makes Zarouite's assumed fear of future repetition unreasonable.

Notably, the government's brief makes no developed argument to show that the report rebuts Zarouite's fear of future persecution; it merely asserts this proposition in conclusory terms and passes on with suspicious swiftness. * * *

Nothing in the brief shows that the country report "disproves" Zarouite's fear, nor does the report itself do so when read in full. Thus there was no need for Zarouite to "discount" the country report since it does not contradict the thrust of his testimony. The inference that the BIA seeks to draw from the report is not rational, or if it could be rationally explained, the government has failed to do so.

* * *

[The court vacated the order and remanded it to the BIA.]

---

In the excerpted article below, the author explicitly addresses two different ways in which legislative facts can be crucial to assessing an asylum claim.

### David A. Martin, Reforming Asylum Adjudication: On Navigating the Coast of Bohemia
138 U.Pa.L.Rev. 1247, 1282–1285 (1990).

* * *

The second critical element of factfinding requires determinations about broader patterns of governmental behavior in the home country. For example, the asylum applicant may prove to the factfinder's satisfaction, through his own detailed testimony, that he was active as a union organizer for two years before leaving for the United States and that he heard stories of arrests of organizers in nearby towns before he left. But in order to assess the risk that the individual would face on return, the adjudicator must also learn from some source about relevant legislative facts. Does the government regard union organizers as opponents, subject to suppression? If so, what forms does the suppression take? Loss of a job or limitation of schooling options for organizers' children might not amount to persecution (even though it would constitute a human rights violation), but beatings, jailings, or killings in reprisal for peaceful union activity certainly would. If there have been some reports of such violence, how widespread are the abuses? Were they based on the victim's union affiliation or on some other characteristic? In other words, is the current applicant relevantly similar to other persecution victims? And has there been a material change in the country since those events, such as a complete revamping of the police forces responsible for the earlier abuses, including reliable disciplining of the violators?

\* \* \*

Legislative facts should not be regarded, however, as simply something the adjudicator looks up or examines after he has completed the proceedings addressed to finding the adjudicative facts, even though much of his knowledge about country conditions will doubtless come from documentary sources rather than live testimony. Knowledge of political developments and patterns of persecution contributes toward making the final predictive judgment about risks faced if the individual returns home, but perhaps more importantly, such knowledge can also play a useful role in developing and assessing the adjudicative facts themselves.

This second use of knowledge about country conditions is often overlooked, but it remains crucial. An adjudicator thus equipped can better pick out those parts of the applicant's story that are most relevant, and can ask specific questions that will flesh out the testimony in the most helpful fashion. Such expert questioning can also help expose inconsistencies and falsehoods more effectively. Since there are so few other checks on the asylum seeker's story (given that he is likely to be the only available witness to the key events), the system badly needs to make use of whatever other tools might be available for such assessment.

\* \* \*

### Notes and Questions

1. In *Dass*, has the BIA placed an appropriate requirement on an individual applicant, in view of the relative capacities of the applicant and the government to provide information on country conditions as opposed to adjudicative facts specific to the individual? In *Matter of S–M–J–*, 21 I & N Dec. 722 (BIA 1997), the Board seemed to retreat some from *Dass* and mark out more extensive responsibilities for the Service and the immigration judge in developing the record regarding country conditions. The Board stated that "while the burden of proof in principle rests on the applicant, the duty to ascertain and evaluate all the relevant facts is shared between the applicant and the examiner." *Id.* at 729. In asylum cases, "a cooperative approach in Immigration Court is particularly appropriate," and it is the immigration judge's role to ensure "that the applicant presents his case as fully as possible and with all available evidence." *Id.* at 724, 729.

2.  Can the BIA's approach in *Zarouite* be viewed as a return to the *Dass* standard? In *Zarouite*, the immigration judge ruled that Zarouite was not credible and had not experienced persecution, but the BIA assumed for purposes of the appeal that past persecution had occurred and, relying on a U.S. State Department country report, concluded that conditions had changed. Without the presumption based on past persecution, Zarouite's evidence was thin. Perhaps the BIA thought that Zarouite's claim was deficient because he failed to introduce evidence about the current Moroccan policy regarding the return of Moroccan citizens from the Western Sahara territory. Would such a conclusion be justifiable? Does the outcome of this appeal depend on the evidentiary presumptions arising from a finding of past persecution, discussed in Chapter Three, Section D?

3.  The government can draw upon the Resource Information Center associated with the headquarters asylum office, which compiles extensive information about source countries, from both governmental and nongovernmental sources. The State Department has also traditionally been a key resource for information needed in asylum decisionmaking, albeit often a controversial one, owing to concern that its advice might be skewed by the needs of diplomacy. *See, e.g, Zamora v. INS*, 534 F.2d 1055, 1064–65 (2d Cir.1976); *Matter of Exilus*, 18 I & N Dec. 276 (BIA 1982). On this point, the Second Circuit recently stated: "[T]he immigration court cannot assume that a report produced by the State Department—an agency of the Executive Branch of Government that is necessarily bound to be concerned to avoid abrading relations with other countries, especially other major world powers—presents the most accurate picture of human rights in the country at issue." *Tambadou v. Gonzales,* 446 F.3d 298, 302 (2nd Cir. 2006) (excerpted in Chapter Six, Section C).

4.  Before the creation of the specialist asylum officer corps, the State Department was asked to comment specifically on each case. Today, a copy of all application forms is sent promptly to State, but individualized comments are rare. Instead, asylum officers are more likely to consult the State Department's Country Reports on Human Rights Practices, published annually under statutory mandate, which cover virtually every country in the world. These reports are now available on line, <http://www.state.gov/g/drl/hr/c1470.htm>. The discussion in each country report is broken down by topic, for example, torture and other cruel or inhuman treatment, arbitrary arrests and detentions, civil and political rights, economic conditions, and the treatment of women's rights. Although human rights organizations have criticized some of the reports for underreporting serious abuses committed by countries viewed as allies of the United States, both asylum applicants and government officials frequently consult the annual reports. The State Department also often supplements these reports with generic fact sheets sent to the USCIS Asylum Division, covering more specific developments, such as the treatment of a particular ethnic or religious group, that may have a bearing on a significant number of asylum cases.

## 2.  ADJUDICATIVE FACTS

We next turn to "adjudicative facts." In asylum cases, determining adjudicative facts means deciding what actually happened to this individual, his family, friends, and associates. Was he in fact, as he claims, beaten by the police shortly before he left the home country? Were his student group's leaders rounded up during a demonstration? Was he really held for the ten days he asserts? The central source of information on these matters in nearly all cases consists solely of the testimony of the asylum seeker, perhaps coupled with that of family members or friends who happen to be in this country. This feature presents difficulties, for both government and claimant. The asylum applicant obviously may have reasons to embellish or wholly falsify an account, given that a successful claim can mean the difference between swift deportation and lawful residence in a wealthy country and that the government will rarely have its own witnesses to the critical events, which occurred far away.

On the other hand, asylum seekers who have been tortured or traumatized may be unable to testify easily or convincingly before strangers or to convey the full range of their suffering. And they too will often lack other witnesses who can help bolster their account. Close questioning of the applicant, probing the detail, consistency, and coherence of the account, is probably the best way to test the credibility of the testimony—but if the applicant has truly been a victim, overly tough questioning might make it more difficult to elicit crucial information.

The BIA and the courts have taken highly varied and sometimes rapidly changing approaches toward adjudicative facts. These conflicts and tensions in the case law testify to the difficulties of performing adequate factfinding in asylum cases. We will focus on two extremely important issues: credibility and corroboration. For ease of discussion, we will examine them separately, but you should remember that they often go hand in hand in the courtroom.

### a.  Credibility

In 2005 Congress enacted the REAL ID Act, Pub. L. No. 109–13, § 101(a)(3), 119 Stat. 231, 302, which included the following standard for assessing credibility in asylum cases:

> Considering the totality of the circumstances, and all relevant factors, a trier of fact may base a credibility determination on the demeanor, candor, or responsiveness of the applicant or witness, the inherent plausibility of the applicant's or witness's account, the consistency between the applicant's or witness's written and oral statements * * *, the internal consistency of each such statement, the consistency of such statements with other evidence of record (including the reports of the Department of State on country conditions), and any inaccuracies or falsehoods in such statements, without regard to whether an inconsistency, inaccuracy, or falsehood goes to the heart of the applicant's claim, or any other relevant factor.

INA § 208 (b)(1)(B)(iii). This provision applies only to applications filed after the effective date of the REAL ID Act, May 11, 2005.

Prior to this statute, the BIA had ruled that credibility involves deciding whether the "testimony is believable, consistent, and sufficiently detailed to provide a plausible and coherent account of the basis for his fear." *Matter of Mogharrabi*, 19 I & N Dec. 439, 445 (BIA 1987). Take a moment and compare this formulation with the statutory provision just above. To what extent has Congress changed the template for determining a witness's credibility? Picture the situation of an asylum seeker, the main witness to the relevant adjudicative facts, on the witness stand in immigration court. How would you as a DHS trial attorney go about testing the applicant's credibility? What sorts of questions would you pose? On what issues would you focus? How might you inform yourself in order to perform this task effectively? Is your job simply to break down the story? Or do you bear some affirmative obligation to help round out a complete picture of the applicant's past treatment, even if his attorney has left gaps (or in cases where he is unrepresented)?

Now picture yourself as the immigration judge. What would you look for in trying to assess credibility? What is your role with regard to gaining a full understanding of the applicant's claim? How can you move beyond your personal sympathy or skepticism and decide if someone is believable? In the excerpt below, a factfinder gives us a first-hand report. This former asylum officer, whose responsibilities included reviewing affirmative asylum applications, describes in Chapter Two, Section C, vividly describes the testimony that she and her colleagues found credible.

## SHOSHANNA MALETT, AFFIRMATIVE ASYLUM CLAIMS FROM CHINA BASED ON COERCIVE FAMILY PLANNING

Immigr. Briefings 7–9, June 2006.

\* \* \*

\* \* \* [I]t is imperative that your client present credible testimony at the interview. This sounds so simple; yet you would be surprised to discover how many applicants fail to explain what happened to them in a coherent and understandable manner. You may also be surprised to learn how many applicants change their stories from one minute to the next. \* \* \* Legally, Asylum Officers are looking for credible testimony, testimony which is detailed, consistent, and plausible. Practically, Asylum Officers are listening for the facts of a story told by the person who was there, to whom the events actually occurred. Your client must be able to bring the events to life, inserting details that only he or she would know because he or she was there. Does your client recall that the smell of tea was strong the morning the cadres came into the kitchen and dragged his wife to the waiting van? Did the baby cry when the new mother was taken for a tubal ligation? With whom did your client leave his newborn if he followed his wife and the cadres to the hospital and how, exactly, did that work? The details. The small and specific details that make the story rich, that make the story your client's.

\* \* \*

\* \* \* Many Officers like to ask open-ended questions to allow applicants to provide the rich detail so necessary to paint a vivid picture. At times I would find myself actually asking an applicant to "put me into a situation"—to explain it to me so that I could see the event for myself. If the applicant could not provide me with that level of detail, with that texture necessary so that I could experience what happened to that person, I often found myself having a problem with that applicant's credibility.

Consistency is the next piece of the credibility equation. If the event occurred, the client should be able to tell and retell the story in the same manner no matter how many times an Officer asks him or her to explain a particular event. The rendition of that event should be consistent regardless of where in the chronology of events the Officer asks the question. In other words, if an applicant testifies that their first child was born in 1999 at the beginning of the interview, and an Officer asks the same question at the end of the interview, your client had better answer 1999. In fact, if your client testified that their first child was born on 10/3/1999, that answer should remain 10/3/1999 however many times the Officer asks it no matter when he or she asks it during the interview.

\* \* \*

With the understanding that the detail your client gives the Officer is paramount, and knowing that your client must be consistent within his/her testimony and with other evidence submitted, the final thing you must keep in mind is that your client's testimony must be plausible.

\* \* \*

### Notes and Questions

1. "Consistency, plausibility, and detail" are the credibility mantra. But recent work on memory suggests that the memories of traumatic events are much more fragmentary than non-traumatic memories. Furthermore, over time the peripheral details of the trauma, which for many asylum seekers included dates, were more likely to change than the central details. And the longer the time between hearings, the more the details changed for asylum seekers with post-traumatic stress disorder. These findings suggest that, ironically, the most traumatized asylum seekers are likely to provide inconsistent testimony. Herlihy, *Evidentiary Assessment and Psychological Difficulties*, in Proof, Evidentiary Assessment and Credibility in Asylum Procedures 123–137 (Gregor Noll ed., 2005). Is the statutory emphasis on consistency misplaced, at least for those suffering from post-traumatic stress disorder?

2. The U. S. statute expressly permits factfinders to base credibility determinations on "demeanor, candor, or responsiveness." INA § 208

(b)(1)(B)(iii). With that in mind, consider the following comment by an author of an empirical study of Dutch asylum hearings:

> * * *Literature on non-verbal communication acknowledges that there are very few objective cues for truth and deception. People generally assume that eye contact, physical movement and facial expression reveal hidden motives underlying the content of the conversation. However, since these cues have different meanings in different cultures, they can easily be misjudged in intercultural interview settings. Moreover, people are able to control their movements and expressions to a certain extent. Deception is therefore more likely to manifest itself in a lack of movements. There are many lay misconceptions about the nature of truthful communication. Liars and the people who want to expose them are easily caught up in a play in which they try to restrain or reveal *perceived* suspicious behaviour. In an experimental study, researchers showed [Dutch immigration] officers video fragments of an actor playing an asylum seeker. They asked the officers to assess his reliability on the basis of body language. The findings showed that officers were neither uniform nor consistent in their assessment. Immigration officers stressed that they were reluctant to draw any firm conclusions based on non-verbal behaviour.
>
> The present study [finds] that emotions, whether expressed verbally or non-verbally by asylum applicants, do play a role in the assessment of credibility. In some cases, the [Dutch immigration] officers considered the applicant's emotional reactions to be a sign of veracity, whereas in other cases in which officers expected emotions to appear, they perceived the *absence* of emotions as a sign of incredibility.

Doornbos, *On Being Heard in Asylum Cases: Evidentiary Assessment Through Asylum Interviews*, in Proof, Evidentiary Assessment and Credibility in Asylum Procedures 103, 106–107 (Gregor Noll ed., 2005).

3.  Courts in other countries have grappled with the importance of oral testimony in making credibility determinations, and the European Court of Human Rights (ECHR) confronted this issued directly in *N v. Finland*, App. No. 38885/02 (2005), <http://echr.coe/int.eng>. A Congolese asylum seeker challenged Finland's denial of protection, arguing that returning him to the Democratic Republic of the Congo would violate Article 3 of the European Convention of Human Rights, which forbids exposing individuals to inhuman or degrading treatment or torture. Because the central issue was whether the inconsistencies in the Congolese asylum seeker's testimony supported the Finnish determination that he was not credible, the European Court of Human Rights appointed two of its members as delegates to take oral testimony from the asylum seeker. In this regard the Court said:

> 160.  The Court's examination of the existence of a risk of ill-treatment in breach of Article 3 must necessarily be a thorough one in view of the absolute character of this provision and the fact that it enshrines one of the fundamental values of the democratic societies making up the Council of Europe. In determining whether substantial grounds have been shown for believing that a real risk

of treatment contrary to Article 3 exists, the Court will assess the issue in the light of all the material placed before it and, if necessary, material obtained of its own motion. The assessment of the existence of the risk must be made on the basis of information concerning the conditions prevailing at the time of the Court's consideration of the case, the historical position being of interest in so far as it may shed light on the present situation and its likely evolution.

The Court noted that its members had been able to interview a corroborating witness whose testimony had not been available during the Finnish proceedings. The ECHR concluded, by a vote of 6–1, that the Congolese asylum seeker was credible and would risk serious persecution if returned to the Democratic Republic of the Congo.

_____

As outlined in Chapter Two, Section C, if an asylum officer concludes that an asylum seeker is not credible and does not grant asylum, the applicant can renew the request for asylum and withholding before an immigration judge. An applicant can appeal a negative ruling by an immigration judge to the BIA. In earlier days the BIA had authority to review IJ factual findings de novo, including affirmative or negative credibility determinations. Under regulations adopted by the Attorney General in 2002, the BIA has a much more limited role. The BIA now may reverse credibility and other findings only upon a determination that they are "clearly erroneous." See 8 C.F.R. § 1003.1(d)(3)(i) (2003). Furthermore, when federal courts review BIA decisions they apply deferential standards. They review the record to see if substantial evidence supports the decision below, and they overturn administrative factfindings only if the evidence compels the contrary conclusion. INA § 242 (b)(4)(B).

Nonetheless, credibility findings remain subject to both administrative and judicial review, and an extensive body of case law has developed. Courts have taken strikingly diverse stances in carrying out judicial review of administrative determinations of credibility. Many circuits are deferential, but other circuit decisions impose a more demanding standard of review. The following case sets forth the Ninth Circuit standards concerning both credibility determinations and the significance of corroborative evidence (we omit here most of the abundant citations to circuit precedent). There follows a vigorous statement of objections to the doctrine, voiced by Judge Kozinski in dissenting from the court's refusal to rehear the case _en banc_. It is important to note that this case was decided before Congress enacted the more specific credibility provisions set forth at the beginning of the discussion of adjudicative facts above.

## ABOVIAN v. INS

United States Court of Appeals, Ninth Circuit, 2006.
219 F.3d 972 (9th Cir. 2000), as amended, 228 F.3d 1127, 234 F.3d 492 (9th Cir. 2000), rehearing and rehearing en banc denied, 257 F.3d 971 (9th Cir.2001).

PREGERSON, Circuit Judge.

Soghomon Abovian, his wife Iskoui Abovian, and their twenty-three-year-old daughter Lousine are natives and citizens of Armenia. They petition for review of the Board of Immigration Appeal's ("BIA's") de novo decision denying their requests for asylum and withholding of deportation. * * *

* * * Abovian * * * refuse[d] to work for and adopt the ideology of the KGB and its successor the National Security Council ("NSC"). The root of Abovian's intense opposition to communism and the KGB was his father's zealous endorsement of both. * * *

[Despite attempting to escape his father's legacy, Abovian was periodically harassed and abused for the next 26 years. Even after the fall of the Soviety Union and democratic elections in Armenia, the] KGB/NSC in Armenia took Abovian in for questioning on numerous occasions. He was ridiculed and threatened for not becoming a member of the KGB like his father. * * * In 1991, Abovian was interrogated by the KGB about his membership in an informal social group promoting "real independence" for Armenia. Abovian told them that he would never work for the KGB/NSC or spread their "pro-Russia" ideology.

Not long after this interrogation, Abovian and his family began receiving threatening telephone calls. * * * [In June 1993] Abovian's then-seventeen-year-old daughter, Lousine, was hit by a car while sitting on a bench outside their apartment building in Armenia. * * * Abovian believed that the driver was associated with Ter–Petrosyan, the President of Armenia at the time and the leader of the KGB/NSC. * * *

[In August 1993] someone kidnapped Abovian's daughter * * *. Abovian met with Ter–Petrosyan and was told that he was "playing with our honor" by refusing to work for them as his father had. * * * They, in essence, gave him an ultimatum: work for us or leave Armenia. * * *

\* \* \*

We review the BIA's determination that an alien has not established eligibility for asylum or withholding deportation under the substantial evidence standard. Substantial evidence can be found lacking only if the applicant shows that the evidence which he presented "was so compelling that no reasonable factfinder could fail to find the requisite fear of persecution." *INS v. Elias–Zacarias.*

"We review de novo claims of due process violations in deportation proceedings." *Perez–Lastor v. INS*, 208 F.3d 773, 778 (9th Cir.2000).

### A.   DUE PROCESS VIOLATION

When the BIA decides an asylum case "based on an independent, adverse, credibility determination, contrary to that reached by the IJ, it must give the petitioner an opportunity to explain any alleged inconsistencies that it raises for the first time." To do otherwise, violates the petitioner's due process rights. Here, the IJ did not make a credibility finding. Where the IJ makes no credibility finding, the petitioner's credibility is assumed. The IJ's decision therefore did not put the

Abovians on "notice that [their] credibility was questioned" or that they should provide the BIA with " 'explanations for alleged discrepancies' "in their testimony. As a result, the BIA violated the Abovians' rights to due process. We must therefore remand this matter to the BIA so that Abovians will have that opportunity.

Even assuming no due process violation, the BIA's credibility finding is not supported by substantial evidence. To deny asylum on credibility grounds, the BIA must have a "legitimate articulable basis to question the petitioner's credibility, and must offer a specific, cogent reason for any stated disbelief." The BIA found Abovian's testimony to be "disjointed, incoherent, and implausible."

This circuit has consistently held that an "immigration judge is in the best position to make credibility findings because he sees the witness as the testimony is given." The BIA does have "the power to conduct a de novo review of the record, to make its own findings, and independently to determine the legal sufficiency of the evidence."[a] But the "special deference" accorded to an IJ's credibility determination that is based on firsthand observations of the alien's demeanor and assessments of the tone and tenor of the alien's testimony does not apply to the BIA's independent, adverse credibility determination. " 'Rather, we examine the record to see whether substantial evidence supports that conclusion and determine whether the reasoning employed by the [BIA] is fatally flawed.' " Any reasons put forth in support of an adverse credibility finding " 'must be substantial and bear a legitimate nexus to the [credibility] finding.' "

As one of two reasons for its adverse credibility finding, the BIA stated that Abovian "did not support his claims with documentary proof or adequately explain his failure to do so." It is well settled in this circuit that independent corroborative evidence is not required from asylum applicants where their testimony is unrefuted. Here, there is no evidence refuting or in any way contradicting Abovian's testimony. A lack of corroborating evidence is certainly not substantial evidence supporting an adverse credibility finding.

The second reason the BIA gave in support of its adverse credibility finding was an alleged inconsistency in Abovian's testimony. Specifically, the BIA noted that "when pressed to testify about specific abuses inflicted by the KGB, the respondent testified that 'there have been physical abuses in my life but I cannot say it's the KGB or not and I don't want to lie'." That particular exchange, however, relates to events in 1974. In later testimony, Abovian consistently stated that, beginning in 1988, he received threatening phone calls from the KGB/NSC and its affiliates, demanding that he work for them as a translator in Turkey, otherwise he would be unable to obtain "a job or a house." It is well established that "inconsistencies of less than substantial importance for which a plausible explanation is offered" cannot form the sole basis for an adverse credibility finding. What happened to Abovian in 1974 is

**a.** This decision predates the 2002 regulations removing this BIA authority.—eds.

certainly less important than what has happened to him since 1988, leading up to his departure from Armenia.

The BIA did not find that Abovian lied or misrepresented the facts in his application or testimony. Nor did the BIA point to specific and direct evidence in the record that contradicted Abovian's testimony. Under such circumstances, this court has rejected an adverse credibility finding as unsupported by substantial evidence. Here, * * * there is "a 'total absence of contradictory evidence' in the record as a whole that potentially undermines [the petitioner's] credibility." The BIA's decision to reject Abovian's assertions as "implausible" appears to be solely a matter of conjecture. *See Lopez–Reyes v. INS,* 79 F.3d 908, 912 (9th Cir.1996) (stating that "conjecture is not a substitute for substantial evidence"). Without stating "cogent" reasons why it did not believe Abovian, the BIA simply characterized Abovian's claims as "dramatic" and "implausible." "Non-evidence based assumptions about conduct in the context of other cultures must be closely scrutinized.... 'As a general rule, in considering claims of persecution ... it [is] highly advisable to avoid assumptions regarding the way other societies operate.' "

Additionally, the record suggests that the purported "disjointed [ness]" and "incoherence" in Abovian's testimony " 'were possibly the result of mistranslation or miscommunication' [which is] not a sufficient basis for an adverse credibility finding." * * *

In sum, the BIA did not give a "legitimate articulable basis to question the petitioner's credibility" or a "specific, cogent reason for [the] stated disbelief."

\* \* \*

The petition for review is GRANTED, the BIA's decision is vacated, and the case is REMANDED to the BIA for further proceedings consistent with this opinion.

[The dissenting opinion by Judge Wallace is omitted.]

KOZINSKI, Circuit Judge [joined by seven other judges], dissenting from the order denying the petition for rehearing en banc:

The majority overthrows a perfectly reasonable BIA decision by invoking novel rules divorced from administrative law, Supreme Court precedent and common sense. While this is a particularly egregious case, it is not the first one where we have whittled away the authority and discretion of immigration judges and the BIA, imposing ever more stringent standards on how these adjudicatory officers must perform their functions. What the majority does here is the antithesis of administrative deference.

The majority doesn't defer to the Supreme Court either. While reciting that we may only reverse the BIA if petitioner has presented evidence "so compelling that no reasonable factfinder could fail to find the requisite fear of persecution," the majority reverses based on a story so wild, implausible and uncorroborated that no reasonable factfinder could believe it. The majority effectively inverts the standard by saddling the BIA with the burden of proving that petitioner is not entitled to relief.

Abovian testified that Levon Ter–Petrosyan, who then was the President of Armenia, had met with him in a hotel more than fifteen times to recruit him for service in the KGB. He made no mention of such extraordinary interviews in his written asylum application. Nor did he try to reconcile his story with our State Department's Country Report for Armenia, which observes that Ter–Petrosyan led his country to independence from the Soviet Union and is a political adversary of the Communists. Although Abovian testified that "everybody knows" that independence is a fiction and that Ter–Petrosyan works for the Russians, he presented no affidavits, letters or articles in support. In fact, Abovian presented nothing but his own testimony to document this fantastic claim. His wife and daughter testified, yet neither corroborated his story.

\* \* \*

\* \* \* [The majority] chooses to ignore well-established principles of judicial restraint and holds that Abovian's hearing was fundamentally unfair, because the BIA decided to disbelieve his testimony, without first giving him a chance to explain away inconsistencies and supplement the record.

This constitutional rule exists nowhere outside the Ninth Circuit. The majority contends that the BIA violated Abovian's right to a fair hearing, but what kind of unfairness can there be when the BIA uses the petitioner's own words against him? A petitioner who testifies, like any other witness, puts his credibility at issue. \* \* \*

\* \* \*

The majority's second reason for reversing the BIA also has no support in the immigration laws and pushes our court even further adrift from the law of other circuits [with regard to corroboration requirements]. \* \* \*

\* \* \*

While our past cases put us on the wrong side of this circuit conflict, the majority takes our law one step farther and holds that the BIA can't consider the fact that petitioner has failed to present corroborating evidence even in deciding whether to believe him. Abovian claimed that everyone in Armenia knew the president was a KGB stooge, yet he didn't present a single newspaper article or human rights report that supported that claim. Although Abovian testified that "every Armenian you ask, they'll say the same thing," his own wife and daughter did not corroborate this "fact." Surely, there are other Armenian immigrants in this country, yet Abovian didn't call any of them to testify, nor did he present any affidavits. Abovian testified that his daughter was hospitalized for twenty days after being hit by a KGB car, yet he offered no hospital records. * * *

* * *

The majority holds that the total absence of corroborating evidence is irrelevant to whether petitioner's story is believable. The only time the BIA may fault a petitioner for the absence of corroboration is where the INS already has "evidence refuting or in any way contradicting [his] testimony." The majority's rule relieves petitioner of any burden of proving his story and saddles the INS with the burden of *dis*proof. * * *

[This] puts the INS in an impossible position. The specific facts supporting a petitioner's asylum claim—when, where, why and by whom he was allegedly persecuted—are peculiarly within the petitioner's grasp. By definition, they will have happened at some time in the past—often many years ago—in a foreign country. In order for the INS to present evidence "refuting or in any way contradicting" petitioner's testimony, it would have to conduct a costly and often fruitless investigation abroad, trying to prove a negative—that the incidents petitioner alleges did not happen. The task is made even more difficult if (as we have held) the INS is barred from casting doubt on petitioner's story because it is inconsistent with the State Department Country Report, or if (as we have also held) petitioner is free to present significant facts at the asylum hearing that were not alluded to in his application. I find it hard to accept that, in passing the asylum statute, Congress meant for the BIA to believe every applicant's story, no matter how wild and implausible, unless the INS chases all over the world and finds contrary evidence.

The majority opinion eliminates all incentive for a petitioner in our circuit to present corroboration, because anything he presents in addition to his own testimony could give the INS grounds for disbelieving him. Far better for him to present nothing but his own testimony. So long as he can craft a story, plausible or not, the BIA will be barred from holding it against him that he did not present witnesses, documents or other corroborating evidence, even where such evidence should be readily available to him. * * *

While, with the corroboration rule, the majority prohibits the BIA from faulting petitioner for what he does not present, with its third rule, it blocks the BIA from faulting him for what he does present. Under this rule, the BIA may not doubt a petitioner on the basis of inconsistencies that concern matters of "less than substantial" importance. As we have said in the past, "[m]inor inconsistencies in the record such as discrepancies in dates which reveal nothing about an asylum applicant's fear for his safety are not an adequate basis for an adverse credibility finding." Like the rule about corroborating evidence, this is another evidentiary rule that has no ready analogue outside the immigration context.

We have justified our materiality requirement on the ground that minor inconsistencies raise no suspicions because there is no reason a petitioner " 'would intentionally have provided incorrect information on such trivial points.' '' But the trier of fact doesn't deny relief because it believes the petitioner made up only the minor details. Rather, inadvertent contradictions as to details can give rise to the suspicion that the petitioner made up the whole story, and the minor inconsistencies reflect the difficulty in telling a good lie.

Details are the stuff of effective cross-examination. After a petitioner testifies on direct, opposing counsel tries to shake his story by asking him to recall specifics. Petitioner's counsel can't object to such questions as irrelevant. That's because cross-examining a witness on the finer details is a time-honored way of testing the veracity of the critical points of his testimony. While anyone can invent a story to support an asylum claim, cross-examination forces the witness to describe small details that someone would know right away from being there, but that a liar might stumble over when put on the spot.

Because a witness will never testify exactly the same way twice, certain inconsistencies may reveal merely the limits of memory. In immigration cases, inconsistencies might also arise because the petitioner had trouble understanding English or because the translator made a mistake. But while such inconsistencies may be innocent, they may also signal that the petitioner is telling a tale. When a petitioner fails to recall how he was tortured, when he mixes up the chronology of events, or when he embellishes his story with new details, the trier of fact may reasonably infer that the petitioner is fibbing. Ultimately, it falls to immigration judges and the BIA to sort out whether those inconsistencies are innocent or not; our job does not include making credibility judgments.

Our opinions make liberal use of this materiality requirement to upset credibility determinations with which we disagree. In numerous cases, we have applied this rule to substitute our own reading of the facts for those of the BIA [list of cases and descriptions omitted here].[9]

\* \* \*

Lastly, the majority concludes that the plausibility of Abovian's tale has no bearing on the BIA's evaluation of his credibility. In the majority's view, the BIA cannot count the implausibility of Abovian's story against him, because such a judgment is "solely a matter of conjecture." What the majority calls "conjecture," others would call common sense. Whether to credit the testimony of a witness always involves some uncertainty, yet we must constantly make decisions without full information. We often rely on common sense—our understanding of how the world works—to fill the gap. When you meet a man on the Brooklyn

---

**9.** These cases are but the tip of the iceberg, as we have set aside credibility judgments in dozens of others. Moreover, we are the only circuit to do so routinely, which makes life very difficult for the INS because we hear considerably more than our share of asylum appeals. A Westlaw search of immigration cases decided since January 1, 1998, turns up forty-three cases where we have reversed adverse credibility determinations, roughly twenty-three percent of the cases where credibility was at issue. Over that same period, all the other circuits combined have set aside credibility judgments in only four cases, for a reversal rate of about six percent. \* \* \*

Bridge, you are much more likely to believe that he owns the clothes on his back than the bridge on which you are standing. The majority bars the BIA from drawing precisely this kind of inference when a petitioner testifies that the elected president of a foreign country is, in fact, a spy for the Russians.

\* \* \*

When taken together, these four rules take the asylum decision from the BIA and put it in the hands of our court. Except in the rare case where the petitioner breaks down under cross-examination and admits that his story is fabricated, there will be nothing the BIA or the IJ can do to insulate its exercise of discretion from reversal by our court. The petitioner will be entitled to spin a tale that bears no resemblance to reality, and his most implausible explanations have to be accepted. If the IJ does not believe petitioner's story, the judge must give cogent reasons, which cannot include internal inconsistencies, lack of corroboration, his failure to raise important points in his petition, the fact that his story contradicts the State Department Country Report or that it is otherwise wholly implausible. One might wonder what those cogent reasons might possibly be that the IJ can offer for disbelieving a petitioner's story.

\* \* \*

\* \* \* I emphatically dissent.

### Notes and Questions

1. Most circuits take a more deferential approach than *Abovian. See, e.g., Chun v. INS*, 40 F.3d 76, 78 (5th Cir.1994) ("We will not review decisions turning purely on the immigration judge's assessment of the alien petitioner's credibility." (internal quotation marks omitted)); *Ghasemimehr v. INS*, 7 F.3d 1389, 1391 (8th Cir.1993) (per curiam) ("We defer to an IJ's finding that an alien's testimony is not credible as long as the finding is supported by a specific, cogent reason for disbelief"; a determination that the testimony was general and speculative, and that corroboration was missing, constitutes such a reason). Which approach is more consistent with the standard of review Congress placed in the statute in 1996, INA § 242(a)(4)(B)?

2. The REAL ID Act specifies that "any inaccuracies or falsehoods in [the applicant's or witness's] statements, without regard to whether an inconsistency, inaccuracy, or falsehood goes to the heart of the applicant's claim" are relevant to credibility. INA § 208(b)(1)(B)(iii). Would this standard have had any impact on the review of the adverse credibility finding in the *Abovian* case? Would it have had an impact in *Aguilera–Cota v. United States INS,* 914 F.2d 1375 (9th Cir.1990), which stated that the immigration judge "must not only articulate the basis for a negative credibility finding, but those reasons must be substantial and must bear a legitimate nexus to the finding" and noted that "a petitioner's admission that he lied to the INS about his citizenship does not support a negative credibility finding"? *Id.* at 1381–82 & n. 7.

3. Although the REAL ID Act lists a wider range of factors on which a negative credibility finding can be based, it does favor applicants in certain situations. After listing the factors, the new credibility section continues: "There is no presumption of credibility, however, if no adverse credibility determination is explicitly made, the applicant or witness shall have a rebuttable presumption of credibility on appeal." INA § 208(b)(1)(B)(iii).

4. In A*bovian* the immigration judge did not make a finding on the applicant's credibility. In such a situation, the BIA generally presumes the applicant's testimony was credible. Based on the arguments advanced in the majority and dissenting opinions, why do you think the BIA departed from this approach and made its own credibility finding? Is it legitimate for the BIA, which does not see the applicants in person, to make adverse credibility findings? The current regulations do permit the BIA to reverse clearly erroneous credibility findings. *See Matter of S–H–*, 23 I & N Dec. 462 (BIA 2002) (remanding a cursory decision and emphasizing the need for clear and complete factual findings by immigration judges). Can one argue that the BIA's review of the record only warrants reversals of negative credibility findings, and that the BIA's lack of first-hand evaluation of the applicant precludes it from reversing positive credibility determinations?

5. Much of Judge Kozinski's dissent in *Abovian* focuses on lack of corroborative evidence, which we will discuss in the next section. In addition, Judge Kozinski argues that the claim is incredible because it is implausible. How does the majority respond to this argument? Under the majority's view, are there any types of claims that, without more, are too implausible to support a claim for asylum in the United States?

### b.   Corroboration

The importance of corroborative evidence has been a recurring issue in asylum adjudication. In early cases decided under the Refugee Act of 1980, the Board and several courts appeared ready to impose a stringent requirement that the noncitizen's statements be corroborated by "objective evidence," which were contrasted with "the alien's own speculations and conclusional statements." *Matter of Sibrun*, 18 I & N Dec. 354, 358 (BIA 1983). *See also, e.g., Dally v. INS*, 744 F.2d 1191, 1195–96 (6th Cir.1984). Beginning at least with *Matter of Acosta*, 19 I & N Dec. 211 (BIA 1985), and *Matter of Mogharrabi*, 19 I & N Dec. 439 (BIA 1987), however, the Board began to show much more understanding of the dilemma faced by bona fide asylum seekers, many of whom have little direct evidence beyond their own statements to support the specific facts that underlie their claims. Under those two cases, the applicant's own uncorroborated testimony was no longer so readily dismissed as self-serving. It can be sufficient, the Board held, to justify a favorable ruling, without specific corroboration, provided that the "testimony is believable, consistent, and sufficiently detailed to provide a plausible and coherent account of the basis for his fear." *Mogharrabi*, 19 I & N Dec. at 445. The regulations incorporate this view. 8 C.F.R. §§ 208.13(a), 208.16(b).

A related issue involves the type of evidence that the asylum applicant should be expected to provide. In earlier decisions the BIA had recognized that the applicant's testimony will usually play a central role and may suffice by itself to carry her burden of proof, but required the applicant to testify under oath at the hearing to be available to respond to questions that the immigration judge might wish to ask. *Matter of Fefe*, 20 I & N Dec. 116 (BIA 1989). In 1997 the BIA ruled that both the INS and the immigration judge share in the responsibility for developing an adequate record in order to assure fulfillment of U.S. obligations under international refugee law, and stated that "[w]here the record contains general country condition information, and an applicant's claim relies primarily on personal experiences not reasonably subject to verification, corroborating documentary evidence of the asylum applicant's particular experience is not required." *Matter of S–M–J–*, 21 I & N Dec. 722, 725 (BIA 1997).

The following year, however, the Board issued a decision ostensibly tightening up the standards and imposing a stronger, though not absolute, corroboration requirement. The case that ushered in this new doctrine, *Matter of M–D–*, follows. It has had a significant impact on asylum practice. Ever since *M–D–*, attorneys for applicants have needed to pay close attention to which elements of their client's story might be seen as subject to corroboration, and then to develop any additional available information.

## MATTER OF M–D–

Board of Immigration Appeals, 1998.
21 I & N Dec. 1180.

HURWITZ, BOARD MEMBER:

\* \* \*

The respondent testified that he is a half-black Mauritanian national who is a member of the Peurh ethnic group. \* \* \* According to the respondent's testimony, a group of five white and two black Maurs [the dominant ethnic group in Mauritania—eds.] from the military came to the respondent's house [and] accused the respondent and his family of being Senegalese. They demanded to see the respondent's identity documents, which the Maurs destroyed. \* \* \* His family members were arrested and forced to cross the river into neighboring Senegal, but the respondent was beaten, blindfolded, thrown into a car, and taken to the village of M'Bagne, where he was imprisoned. \* \* \*

[After 18 months of beatings and hard labor in prison, he was released from prison with two other prisoners and forced] into the river at gunpoint and ordered \* \* \* to swim to the other side. They screamed to get the attention of a passing Senegalese fisherman, who transported them to Senegal. \* \* \* [He] walked 4 hours to the refugee camp in Horefode, where he joined his family. He testified that he remained at the camp for 11 months. Concerned by rumors that Mauritanians in the camp would be sent back to Mauritania, the respondent fled to the city of Dakar in November 1993, leaving his wife and family behind in the refugee camp, where they remain to this day. In Dakar, he earned money working at the harbor. On January 15, 1994, he paid the equivalent of $60 to travel by boat from Dakar to the United States and landed in Miami on February 20, 1994.

\* \* \*

In the case at bar, we find that the respondent has not provided sufficient evidence to meet his burden of proof. We acknowledge that the respondent has submitted numerous articles and reports regarding general country conditions in Mauritania and the oppression of black Mauritanians on account of their race. Furthermore, the record contains a country profile prepared by the Department of State. Bureau of Democracy, Human Rights, and Labor, U.S. Dep't of State, Mauritania— Profile of Asylum Claims & Country Conditions (July 1995) (hereinafter Profile). However, we note the conspicuous lack of documentary evidence corroborating the specifics of the respondent's testimony.

As an initial matter, there is no evidence to confirm the respondent's purported Mauritanian nationality, a central element in his claim. No passport, birth certificate, or identification card has been submitted by the respondent, although we note that the respondent testified that his identity documents were destroyed by the Maurs upon his arrest. It would be reasonable to expect the respondent to attempt to obtain some identity documentation or to adequately explain why replacement documentation was not available. However, even were we to excuse the production of identity documents in this case, we note that the respondent often communicates with his sister who lives in Senegal, outside the refugee camp. We do not find it unreasonable to expect some type of corroboration from the sister in the form of a letter or affidavit, especially given her frequent contact with the respondent. We further note that while he communicates with his sister primarily by telephone, the respondent testified to having received at least one letter from his sister. Neither this letter, nor any other correspondence or affidavits substantiating the respondent's testimony, has been submitted into the record. *See Matter of S–M–J–,* [21 I & N Dec. 722, 725 (BIA 1997)] (stating that an applicant should provide "documentary support for material facts which are central to his or her claim and easily subject to verification").
\* \* \*

Likewise, the respondent has submitted no supporting evidence from his family, despite the fact that his sister maintains regular contact with them in the refugee camp. We find it reasonable to expect some corroboration of the respondent's identity, arrest, and detention, or at least of the family's forcible expulsion from Mauritania.

Finally, the respondent has provided no evidence of his former presence at the refugee camp in Senegal, where he claims to have lived for 11 months. He admits that he and his family were issued refugee cards by the United Nations, but claims that he lost his refugee card.

Significantly, even after the Immigration Judge granted the respondent a 7-week continuance in which to obtain official verification from the United Nations High Commissioner for Refugees ("UNHCR") of his presence at the camp, he was unable to do so. The respondent was also unable to offer evidence confirming his family's presence in the camp, despite the fact that his family has been living there for the past 7 years and continues to reside in the camp.

Given the complete lack of evidence corroborating the specifics of the respondent's asylum claim, we agree with the Immigration Judge that the respondent has failed to sustain his burden of proof. We find it reasonable in this case to expect basic documentation of nationality and identity, as well as confirmation of his or his family's presence at the refugee camp. These are "material facts which are central to (the respondent's) claim" and which are "reasonably subject to verification." Furthermore, we find significant the lack of any explanation for the respondent's inability to obtain such verification. Due to the respondent's failure to produce such evidence or to satisfactorily explain its absence, we conclude that the respondent has failed to meet his burden of proof in establishing his claim to asylum or withholding of deportation under sections 208 and 243(h) of the Act. Accordingly, we will dismiss the respondent's appeal.

[The separate dissenting opinions of Chairman Schmidt and Board Member Rosenberg are omitted.]

---

On review of the *M–D–* decision, the Second Circuit accepted the basic corroboration standards set out by the BIA, but took the Board to task for incorrectly applying them.

## DIALLO v. INS

United States Court of Appeals, Second Circuit, 2000.
232 F.3d 279.

WALKER, CIRCUIT JUDGE.

\* \* \*

\* \* \* [Moussa Diallo] applied for asylum and withholding of deportation \* \* \* based on his past persecution and fear of future race-based persecution in his native country of Mauritania. \* \* \*

At his June 1996 deportation hearing, Diallo put before the IJ materials from various sources, including the State Department. According to these materials, the white-dominated government of Mauritania engaged in massive human rights abuses against its black citizens between 1989 and 1992. The government expelled about 70,000 blacks from the country—claiming in many cases that they were Senegalese—and forced many of them into refugee camps in neighboring Senegal.

Frequently, the deportations were preceded by destruction of proof of citizenship and expropriation of property, and often accompanied by mass arrests, torture, and executions.

In addition to introducing the above materials in support of his applications, Diallo testified at the hearing. He described the conditions in Mauritania and his own experience in considerable detail. * * *

* * *

In its decision, the BIA articulated the following standard concerning the need for corroboration in asylum and withholding of deportation cases:

> [W]here an alien's testimony is the only evidence available, it can suffice where [it] is believable, consistent, and sufficiently detailed to provide a plausible and coherent account of the basis of the alien's alleged fear. However, ... the introduction of [supporting] evidence is not purely an option with the asylum applicant; rather, corroborating evidence should be presented where available.
>
> ... [W]here the record contains general country information, and an applicant's claim relies primarily on personal experiences not reasonably subject to verification, corroborative documentary evidence of the asylum applicant's particular experience is not required. However, ... where it is reasonable to expect corroborating evidence for certain alleged facts pertaining to the specifics of an applicant's claim, such evidence should be provided or an explanation should be given as to why such information was not presented. The absence of such corroboration can lead to a finding that an applicant has failed to meet his burden of proof.

This is an accurate statement of the standard the BIA has developed in recent decisions upon which the BIA has announced its intent to rely. * * *

* * * In our view, the standard developed and applied by the BIA in its recent cases, including the case below, is consistent with INS regulations, international legal standards, and our precedent and therefore is entitled to deference from this court.

* * *

Nevertheless, several fatal flaws in the BIA's application of this standard to the facts of this case undermine its ultimate decision and require vacatur and remand.

We review the factual findings underlying the BIA's determination that an alien has failed to sustain his or her burden of proof to qualify for asylum or withholding of deportation under the substantial evidence standard. Such findings must be upheld if they are "supported by reasonable, substantial, and probative evidence on the record considered as a whole." We reverse only if no reasonable fact-finder could have failed to find the past persecution or fear of future persecution necessary to sustain the petitioner's burden.

\* \* \*

We see no reason to question any of the BIA's factual determinations here. Upon *de novo* review of the BIA's application of its corroboration standard in this case, however, we conclude that its decision cannot be sustained because the BIA failed to: (1) rule explicitly on the credibility of Diallo's testimony; (2) explain why it was reasonable in this case to expect additional corroboration; or (3) assess the sufficiency of Diallo's explanations for the absence of corroborating evidence.\* \* \*

\* \* \*

\* \* \* On the record before us, we think the IJ was plainly in error to find that Diallo failed to provide "specific, credible detail" in his testimony. Moreover, we agree with the petitioner that it is inappropriate to base a credibility determination solely on the failure to provide corroborative evidence. The presence or absence of corroboration may properly be considered in determining credibility. However, corroboration cannot be the only factor taken into account because this would effectively require corroboration in all cases, contrary to explicit provisions in the law that applicants may be able to rely exclusively on their testimony. \* \* \*

\* \* \*

Second, we are not convinced that, under the BIA's own precedent, it was reasonable to expect additional corroboration beyond the materials supplied by Diallo. Corroboration in this context typically includes both evidence of general country conditions and evidence that substantiates the applicant's particular claims. The BIA has repeatedly emphasized the importance of providing background evidence concerning general country conditions, especially where it tends to confirm the specific details of the applicant's personal experience. In this case, as the BIA acknowledged, Diallo provided such evidence: he "submitted numerous articles and reports regarding general country conditions in Mauritania and the oppression of black Mauritanians on account of their race." Moreover, Diallo's description of his personal experiences closely parallels the patterns of persecution in Mauritania chronicled in these sources, which included reports prepared by the State Department, Amnesty International, and Human Rights Watch.

Corroboration of the specifics of an applicant's personal experiences may also be reasonably expected, but only under certain circumstances. According to the BIA, specific documentary corroboration is required only for

> material facts which are central to [the applicant's] claim and easily subject to verification, such as evidence of his or her place of birth, media accounts of large demonstrations, evidence of a publicly held office, or documentation of medical treatment. If

the applicant does not provide such information, an explanation should be given * * *.

* * * Given these standards, it is unclear to us why Diallo's claim failed for lack of specific corroboration.

As an initial matter, Diallo plainly provided substantial corroboration of the specifics of his story. Although Diallo was functionally illiterate, on cross-examination he was able to describe the Mauritanian flag accurately and indicate basic knowledge of ethnic groups and tensions in Mauritania, thereby corroborating his claim of Mauritanian citizenship. He also displayed the scars he allegedly received at the hands of prison guards.

Nevertheless, the BIA listed four forms of additional corroboration that, in its view, Diallo should reasonably have been able to provide * * *.

But the BIA did not explain why it was reasonable to expect provision of such materials under its own standards. Most importantly, we do not see how these materials were easily accessible to Diallo, given his functional illiteracy, [and] the circumstances of his departure—which were not conducive to the calm assembly and preservation of documents to be used in future asylum proceedings * * *.

Third, the BIA did not assess Diallo's explanations for his failure to produce the requested corroborative evidence, but limited its analysis simply to the fact that the failure had occurred. Accordingly, we do not know whether the BIA (or the IJ) credited Diallo's explanations, which, at least facially, appear reasonable. * * *

* * * The BIA's failure to address Diallo's explanations violates both the letter and spirit of its own standard, which specifically provides that, even under circumstances where corroboration may reasonably be expected, petitioners may meet their burden of proof by offering a believable and sufficient explanation as to why such corroborating evidence was not presented.

* * *

[The court granted the petition for review and remanded the case to the BIA.]

### Notes and Questions

1. In this case Diallo had argued that the BIA's doctrine requiring corroboration was fundamentally inconsistent with treaty standards and the governing regulations. The regulations provide: "The testimony of the applicant, if credible, may be sufficient to sustain the burden of proof without corroboration." 8 C.F.R. §§ 208.13(a), 208.16(b). The Second Circuit disagreed with this part of Diallo's argument and concluded that the BIA's basic rule requiring either corroboration where it can be reasonably expected, or else an explanation for why corroboration cannot be provided, is entirely consistent with the governing regulations and with international standards, as reflected in the UNHCR Handbook. The court explicitly

rejected the contrary rule in the Ninth Circuit, which it described as "a blanket holding that credible testimony is automatically sufficient and renders corroborating evidence unnecessary," citing *Cordon–Garcia v. INS*, 204 F.3d 985, 992 (9th Cir.2000).

2. The Ninth Circuit reaffirmed and elaborated its credibility doctrine in *Ladha v. INS*, 215 F.3d 889 (9th Cir.2000). In that case the INS had defended the *M–D–* approach and had relied on earlier circuit cases indicating that credible testimony alone would be sufficient if corroborative evidence is unavailable. The *Ladha* decision rejected such an interpretation of its earlier rulings; "this circuit assumes evidence corroborating testimony found to be credible is 'unavailable' if not presented." *Id.* at 900. A footnote, however, appeared to limit the full impact of this doctrine: "We do not address if or when it is proper to consider the 'availability' of corroborating evidence as a basis for an adverse credibility finding; we are concerned only with the body of cases addressing corroboration after a finding that an applicant is credible." *Id.* at 900 n.11. In *Sidhu v. INS*, 220 F.3d 1085, 1090 n. 2 (9th Cir.2000), the court applied this doctrine in affirming the BIA's authority to make an adverse credibility finding when the applicant failed to produce his father to corroborate his story. The father lived in a nearby suburb in the United States and had been a witness to the central events in India. Nonetheless, later Ninth Circuit cases returned to a stronger version of the rule that the BIA generally may not insist on corroboration. *See, e.g., Kataria v. INS*, 232 F.3d 1107, 1114 (9th Cir.2000), and *Abovian v. INS*, excerpted above.

3. The corroboration requirement, as restated and implemented in *M–D–*, has been quite important in immigration court practice, even though the courts have sometimes taken a dim view of BIA implementation of this doctrine. For example, *see Lin v. Gonzales*, 445 F.3d 127 (2nd Cir. 2006) (factfinder explained neither why corroboration was reasonable to expect nor why explanations of its absence were unsatisfactory); *Diallo v. Gonzales*, 439 F.3d 764 (7th Cir. 2006) (factfinder did not adequately explain reasons for requiring corroboration); *Abdulai v. Ashcroft*, 239 F.3d 542 (3d Cir.2001) (similarly approving the BIA's general corroboration requirement but finding its application too severe in the particular case). *But see Obale v. Attorney General*, 453 F.3d 151 (3rd Cir. 2006) (factfinder correctly applied BIA's corroboration requirement).

---

In 2005, Congress enacted the REAL ID Act, Pub. L. No. 109–13, § 101(a)(3), 119 Stat. 231, 302, and elaborated on the need for corroboration in asylum and withholding cases. It reiterated the basic proposition that corroborating evidence is not necessary in every case, but it heightened the importance of corroboration:

> The testimony of the applicant may be sufficient * * * without corroboration, but only if the applicant satisfies the trier of fact that the applicant's testimony is credible, is persuasive, and refers to specific facts sufficient to demonstrate that the applicant is a refugee. * * * Where the trier of fact deter-

mines that the applicant should provide evidence that corroborates otherwise credible testimony, such evidence must be provided unless the applicant does not have the evidence and cannot reasonably obtain the evidence.

INA § 208 (b)(1)(B)(ii).

Congress further specified:

No court shall reverse a determination made by a trier of fact with respect to the availability of corroborating evidence * * * unless the court finds * * * that a reasonable trier of fact is compelled to conclude that such corroborating evidence is unavailable.

INA 242 § (b)(4).

These provisions apply only to applications filed after May 11, 2005. As a consequence, no significant case law interpreting the new legislation has yet developed. What impact do you think it would have had on the *Diallo* decision? On *Abovian* and the other Ninth Circuit cases discussed in Note 2 above?

## SECTION C.   ASYLUM ADJUDICATION SYSTEM UNDER FIRE

In recent years there have been mounting criticisms of the quality of the asylum decisions by immigration judges and the BIA. Judge Posner of the Seventh Circuit cataloged the following "disturbing features" of immigration cases that he had reviewed: 1) a lack of familiarity with foreign cultures; 2) an overly generous expectation of how many details people know about their religion; 3) a highly optimistic view of the availability of documentary evidence from the country of origin; 4) insensitivity to the misunderstandings caused by the use of interpreters and translators of other languages; 5) a lack of appreciation for the difficulty evaluating the demeanor of a person from a remote culture; 6) an unwillingness to specify the reason for concluding the asylum seeker has not sustained the burden of proof; and 7) BIA affirmances with no opinion or with short boilerplate rationales. *Iao v. Gonzales*, 400 F.3d 530, 533–535 (7th Cir. 2005). This list of deficiencies reflects many of the cross-cultural communication obstacles identified above.

Judge Posner noted that "[t]he cases that we see are not a random sample of all asylum cases, and the problems that the cases raise may not be representative," but added: "Even if they are representative, given caseload pressures and, what is the other side of that coin, resource constraints, it is possible that nothing better can realistically be expected than what we are seeing in this and like cases. But we are not authorized to affirm unreasoned decisions even when we understand why they are unreasoned." *Id.* at 535. Not long after, Judge Posner offered a quantitative assessment:

In the year ending on the date of the argument, different panels of this court reversed the Board of Immigration Appeals in whole or part in a staggering 40 percent of the 136 petitions to review the Board that were resolved on the merits. The corresponding figure, for the 82 civil cases during this period in which the United States was the appellee, was 18 percent. Our criticisms of the Board and of the immigration judges have frequently been severe. Other circuits have been as critical.

This tension between judicial and administrative adjudicators is not due to judicial hostility to the nation's immigration policies or to a misconception of the proper standard of judicial review of administrative decisions. It is due to the fact that the adjudication of these cases at the administrative level has fallen below the minimum standards of legal justice. Whether this is due to resource constraints or to other circumstances beyond the Board's and the Immigration Court's control, we do not know, though we note that the problem is not of recent origin.

*Benslimane v. Gonzales*, 430 F.3d 828, 829–830 (7th Cir. 2005) (citations omitted).

A news article examining the Immigration Court in New York used statistics to give a vivid picture of the heavy caseloads that many immigration judges handle. It also remarked on the patience and politeness displayed by some of the judges, attributes that rarely draw headlines.

New York Immigration Court, 26 Federal Plaza. (Photo: © Joshua Kleinman, 2007)

## NINA BERNSTEIN, NEW YORK'S IMMIGRATION COURTS LURCH UNDER A GROWING BURDEN

The New York Times, October 8, 2006.

\* \* \*

It is always judgment day in the windowless courtrooms where immigrants plead to stay in the United States. But these days, as never before, the nation's 218 immigration judges are also being judged, even as they struggle to complete 350,000 cases a year amid an immigration debate that promises to send them many more.

Appeals courts criticize some judges by name, citing abusive behavior and bad decisions. Studies highlight stark disparities in judgment, like 90 percent of asylum cases granted by one judge and 9 percent down the hall. Faced with mounting criticism, Attorney General Alberto R. Gonzales vowed to introduce yearly performance evaluations of the judges, who are Justice Department employees. The Harvard Law Review urged a campaign to turn the five worst judges into "media villains" to motivate reform.

Yet a more complicated picture emerges in the federal building in Lower Manhattan. There \* \* \* 27 immigration judges [are] searching for ways to handle 20,000 cases a year, driven as much by scarce resources and escalating demands as by quirks of personality and power.

In asylum cases, the wrong decision can be a death sentence. In others, banishment hangs in the balance, with the prospect of families split up or swept into harm's way. But before they can consider the merits of a case, judges must cope with an intricate web of laws, changing conditions in distant lands, and a mix of false and truthful testimony in 227 tongues vulnerable to an interpreter's mistake as small as pronouncing "rebels" like "robbers."

As the caseload has grown, spurred in part by stepped-up enforcement, so has the pace demanded by "case completion goals" set in Washington. To stay afloat, New York judges schedule 30 to 70 cases at a time, hold 4 contested hearings a day and decide more than 15 cases a week, all without law clerks, bailiffs, stenographers or enough competent lawyers.

"The court is a stepchild of the whole immigration system," said Sandra Coleman, who spent years on the immigration bench in Miami. "They want to make the judges the villains, and there are judges who are villains, I don't deny that. But the problem is the system."

Many federal judges agree. "I fail to see how immigration judges can be expected to make thorough and competent findings of fact and conclusions of law under these circumstances," John M. Walker Jr., chief judge of the United States Court of Appeals for the Second Circuit, told the Senate Judiciary Committee in April, urging that the number of immigration judges be doubled.

With one of the largest caseloads among the nation's 53 immigration courts, and with nearly half its cases concerning asylum, New York illustrates the crunch that judges face in many big cities where complicated matters crowd the docket.

Caseloads exploded in the 1990's. In 2000, an unpublished report by a Justice Department evaluation team warned that New York judges were "reaching the point of exhaustion and burnout." The report urged a slower pace and an increase in the staff-judge ratio to three to one from two to one. Instead, an evaluation last year found that the ratio had slipped even lower.

Justice Department rules do not allow immigration judges to speak to reporters. But weeks of observation, court records and interviews with lawyers, clerks, interpreters and immigrants show that the judges are coping in very different ways, with far-reaching consequences.

Patricia Rohan, who keeps a twinkling Statue of Liberty lamp in her chambers, is recognized after 24 years on the bench as a model of soft-spoken fairness and efficiency. On a recent weekday, with 575 cases pending, she patiently took notes as a man who shells fish explained why deportation to Gambia would put his Bronx-born daughters at risk of genital mutilation. She gently questioned an Ecuadorean cleaning woman of 55 who avowed that love, not a green card, had prompted her marriage to an American 15 years after she immigrated illegally. Teasing out supporting evidence in both cases, Judge Rohan dictated favorable decisions into an aging tape recorder.

Other judges have a different approach. Sandy K. Hom, appointed in 1993, is also invariably polite, but so quick and predictable in his denials of asylum—91 percent in recent years, compared with Judge Rohan's 25 percent—that lawyers regularly advise people assigned to him to move to another state. Given his speed, he has the fewest pending cases, about 345. But many of his decisions have been rejected on appeal, including one in which he denied asylum to a widowed Armenian Christian and her children and ordered them deported to Iraq, arguing that since Saddam Hussein's ouster, they had no reason to fear religious persecution.

\* \* \*

Down the hall and at the other end of the spectrum, Margaret McManus grants asylum at the highest rate in the country—90 percent—but at the price of what Kevin Kerr, president of the clerks' and interpreters' union local, complains is a chaotic calendar with 931 pending cases. She typically reschedules cases until petitioners can secure supporting documents, pursue other avenues or find lawyers.

A judge's fact-finding is much harder without a lawyer to speak for those facing deportation, who are not entitled to court-appointed counsel. Many get what the 2000 Justice Department report called "the high-volume, low-margin, piecework approach" practiced by "an unsavory subculture" of "travel agency" lawyers. Nor do government lawyers know each case.

\* \* \*

Many of the critiques of asylum adjudication came on the heels of the streamlining that occurred at the BIA in 2002 and the large increase in appeals of BIA decisions, which resulted in a dramatic surge of immigration cases at the federal courts of appeals (described in Chapter Two, Section C). The higher incidence of judicial review and the publication of federal appellate decisions such as *Wang v. Attorney General* and *Cham v. Attorney General* that forcefully criticized the reasoning and the tone of immigration court opinions focused public attention on the problems in asylum adjudication. In response, in early 2006 Attorney

General Gonzales ordered a comprehensive review of the competence and civility of immigration judges:

> I have watched with concern the reports of immigration judges who fail to treat aliens appearing before them with appropriate respect and consideration and who fail to produce the quality of work that I expect from employees of the Department of Justice. While I remain convinced that most immigration judges ably and professionally discharge their difficult duties, I believe there are some whose conduct can aptly be described as intemperate or even abusive and whose work must improve.

Memorandum from Attorney Gen. Alberto Gonzales to Immigration Judges (Jan. 9, 2006), <http://humanrightsfirst.info/pdf/06202–asy-ag-memo-ijs.pdf>.

While the Justice Department investigation was ongoing, an empirical study offered further support to the view that asylum adjudicators act inconsistently and unfairly. The Transactional Records Access Clearinghouse (TRAC), a research organization affiliated with Syracuse University, analyzed close to 300,000 asylum cases decided between 1994 and 2004 and reported great disparities between immigration judges in their rejection rates of asylum claims. For example, ten percent of the 208 immigration judges denied asylum in 86% of their cases, while ten percent denied asylum in only 34% of their cases. The typical denial rate was 65%, with eight judges denying 90% of the claims before them, and two denying 10% of the claims they heard. The extreme variations persisted even when the data were restricted to judges in the same immigration court and to asylum seekers from the same country of origin. TRAC Immigration Judges Report, <http://trac.syr.edu/immigration/reports/160/>. This report highlights the "coast of Bohemia problem" discussed in the Martin article excerpted at the opening of this chapter.

Two weeks after the TRAC report, Attorney General Gonzales announced a series of reforms to improve the immigration courts and the BIA. The proposed reforms include performance evaluations, a competency exam in immigration law, additional members for the BIA, improving the BIA "streamlining" efforts by increasing the number of written and reasoned opinions, and devoting greater resources to the immigration adjudication system. Attorney General Alberto R. Gonzales Outlines Reforms for Immigration Courts and Board of Immigration Appeals (06–520) Press Release, <http://www.usdoj.gov/opa/pr/2006/August/06_ag_520.html>. Notably, the Attorney General specifically called for improvements in the selection, screening, and hiring of interpreters. He also proposed improved training of immigration judges and up-to-date reference materials.

Various individuals and groups, including the immigration judges' association, voiced immediate critiques of some of the proposed reforms. Whether these proposals will be fully implemented and whether they will prove effective in remedying the problems canvassed in this chapter remains to be seen.

## SECTION D.   ASYLUM APPLICATION AND HEARING

We close this chapter by asking you to consider the factfinding challenges posed by the asylum claim of Luz Marina Silva, which was reported as *Silva v. Attorney General*, 448 F.3d 1229 (11th Cir. 2006). Luz Marina Silva came to the United States from Colombia in early 2000 and she filed an affirmative asylum application in March 2001. Ms. Silva represented herself in immigration court. Later, on appeal, she had counsel. Although the information disclosed in asylum applications is confidential, in this case the court reprinted portions of Ms. Silva's application as Appendix A and reprinted the hearing transcript as Appendix B. We include both appendices here: the grammar, spelling, deletions, and bracketed material are all as they appear in the judicial opinion.

We begin by reprinting the published excerpts of her asylum application. You will recognize the questions on the I–589. As you read her responses to each question, consider any ambiguities that you would like to have resolved. What further types of information, if any, would you like to see addressed in the application? Immediately after the application, we have reprinted the actual transcript of her asylum hearing. You will want to keep in mind the contents of the application as you read the hearing transcript, as well as ambiguities in the evidence, prior and current inconsistencies, and additional information that one might have expected.

## 1.   ASYLUM APPLICATION

The relevant part of Ms. Silva's asylum application (the items in bold type are the questions printed on the I-589 form) appears below.

### Application for Asylum or Withholding of Removal

**1.   Why are you seeking asylum? Explain in detail what the basis is for your claim.**

I am seeking political asylum in the United States, because my life is at risk in my country Colombia because of death treats by F.A.R.C.

I come from a family traditionally linked to the Conservative Party and very involved in politics. For our family it was very natural to actively participate with our party on different campaigns and on different positions in the government. On question no. I mentioned some of the names of my closed relatives that have had important political positions in my country. In 1994 I became involved with the Movimiento Civico Independiente Visionario, but for the mayoral position only, and this is because of the person who was running for this position.

I am very closed to my cousin Alicia Eugenia Silva, current general secretary of the Mayoralty in Bogota. Presided by Mayor Mockus. Together we participated on Mayor Mockuses political campaign. We believed on him even though he does not belong to the Conservative Party. He is from the "Partido Civico Independiente" party, so anyone from any of the two traditional parties can vote for him. This is his second period as Bogota's mayor, he was the Mayor of Bogota in 1994. He resigned from his first period in order to postulate himself for the Presidency in 1997, for the 1998 presidential elections. He lost the presidential elections but run for the mayoralty campaign, and was elected as Mayor again, on October 2000.

I worked very hard on both of Mayor's Mockus campaigns because he is a very honest and hard working man, who is wanting to take the challenge of being the mayor of one of the most dangerous capitals of the world and works very hard to change and improve its image, even though I believe now that it is very difficult if not impossible, given the overwhelmed internal violence of my country.

I worked very actively for the 1994 mayor's campaign, which fortunately we won. I started working for Antanas Mockus again in 1997 when he was running for President, which after a lot of efforts and worked, he lost. In August of 1999, after I came back from the United States I got involved again for his new postulation as mayor. I worked very actively in August, September and October when I had to leave the country because of the death threats against my life.

I began my political participation on this last campaign in August of 1999, after I went back to Bogota from my trip to the United States. I began working for the mayoralty campaign. I used to go to the party's meeting at the headquarters every week, where we planned the different strategies that we were going to follow in order to pursue our goals. In there, we also organized the health campaigns that were going to take place in the different marginal neighborhoods. I also did this campaigns when I worked for the Conservative Party, and was aware of its procedures. Through these campaigns we helped the people and at the same time we got new adepts for the party.

My problems started around the third week of September of 1999, while I was in the "Santa Fe" neighborhood talking to the people about getting an education to get ahead in life and in order to help Colombia to overcome the difficult situation that it is currently involved in. After I finished talking a lady came to me and handed me an envelope which I kept in my pocket and thanked the lady. That evening in my house when I opened the envelope I realized that it was a suffrage with my name on it and the words: May Luz Marina Silva rest in peace, because she was doing what she was not suppose to in the wrong neighborhood. It was signed by FARC. Known the country's situation, I got scared but promise myself not to let these subversive intimidate me and continued with my political and social involvement.

From that moment on the phone calls from FARC started almost daily at my house and at my restaurant "Tomillo Laurel y Pimienta", they were wanting me to stop with my visits to these neighborhoods and to my surprise they also knew all my family background and my family political participation. They mentioned that to kill me was a nice way to take revenge of my all my political relatives that were taking advantage of the Colombians who did not know the evil underneath my family that we were on looking for our welfare not for the welfare of the working class.

On October 9, 1999, (a day that I will never forget). When I was going back home from my restaurant, in my car I was followed by 2 men on a motorcycle, that shoot at my car hitting the left rear window, missing me by very little. I accelerated and I don't even know how I got home. From that moment on, I stopped all my activities and decided to leave the country which I did on March 8, 00, very sad and upset because I don't know when I will be able to see my family and go back to my country.

FARC continued calling me at my house until the same day that I left the country. On the last call, I was told that I was missed on October 9, but that it was not going to happen again. For all these reasons I am seeking political asylum in this country. I know that if I go back to my country I will be kill.

**2.  Have you or any member of your family ever belonged to or been associated with any organization or groups in your home country, such as, but not limited to, a political party, student group, labor union, religious organization, military or paramilitary group, civil patrol, guerrilla organization, ethnic group, human rights group, or the press or media?**

Yes.

\* \* \*

Traditionally, I and the rest of my family are of the Colombia Conservative Party.

To the Colombian Chamber of Commerce.

Alfonso Valdivieso, former Secretary of Justice in Colombia (Conservative Party). Cousin. He now is the Colombian Ambassador at the United Nations.

Humberto Silva Valdivieso, Governor of Santander, Colombia and Ambassador in Montevideo, Uruguay. Uncle.

Enrique Silva Valdivieso, Councilman of the Republic, in Bogota, Colombia. Uncle.

Alicia Eugenia Silva, Cousin, Former Secretary of Government, and current General Secretary to the Mayoralty with Mayor Mockus.

**3.  Have you or any member of your family ever been mistreated or threatened by the authorities of your home country or any other county or by a group or groups that are controlled by the government, or that the government of the country is unable or unwilling to control?**

Yes.

**If YES, was it because of** ... **Political Opinion**?

[Yes]    * * *

I was threatened to death by the FARC's urban militias. Because of my family background and my political participation, many in my family have been threatened to death by the guerrilla but most of them are protected by bodyguards.

**4.  Have you or any member of your family ever been accused, charged, arrested, detained, interrogated, convicted and sentenced, or imprisoned in your country or any other country, including the United States?**

No. * * *

**5.  Do you fear being subjected to torture (severe physical or mental pain or suffering, including rape or other sexual abuse) in your home country or any other country if you return?**

Yes.

I was already psychologically tortured by FARC when I found out that they declared me a military objective, I was shot at on October 9, 1999. I know that if I go back to Colombia the psychological torture will start all over again, knowing that they will find me sooner or later, to be tortured and killed and FARC always does.

See Addendum. [Response to Question 1]

**6.  What do you think would happen to you if you returned to the country from which you claim you would be subjected to persecution? Explain in detail and provide information or documentation to support your statement, if available.**

I would be killed as FARC sentenced me. See Addendum. [Response to Question 1]

**7.  Describe in detail your trip to the United States from your home country. After leaving the country from which you are claiming asylum, did you or your spouse or child(ren), who are now in the United States, travel through or reside in any other country before entering the United States?**

No. * * *

## 2. HEARING TRANSCRIPT

Before PEDRO MIRANDA, Immigration Judge

For the Immigration and Naturalization Service: Gail Schwartz

For the Respondent: Pro se

JUDGE FOR THE RECORD

December 13, 2002, Miami, Florida. I am Judge Pedro Miranda. These are removal proceedings in the case of Luz Marina Silva, 79 344 105. Present is the respondent, pro se; the Service represented by trial attorney Gail Schwartz (phonetic sp.) in the proceedings in the Spanish language through Court interpreter Ms. Lanell Haza (phonetic sp.). We're here for a hearing in the respondent's application for asylum withholding of removal, relief under the torture convention.

JUDGE TO MS. SILVA

Ma'am, we're here today for a hearing on your asylum case, are you ready to proceed?

MS. SILVA TO JUDGE

Yes.

JUDGE TO MS. SILVA

Did you try to get an attorney, ma'am?

MS. SILVA TO JUDGE

Yes.

JUDGE TO MS. SILVA

Do you have an attorney?

MS. SILVA TO JUDGE

No.

JUDGE TO MS. SILVA

Why not?

MS. SILVA TO JUDGE

I contacted several of the attorneys around the list, the Service's list, and they couldn't take my case because they were too busy. Then I contacted other attorneys and these attorneys were charging me too much money. I have here a copy of the letters from the people who sent me answers about my request. I don't know if you need to see that.

JUDGE TO MS. SILVA

Well, I don't need to see them, you have a right to an attorney, I can't give you one. I can only give you time to get one if you want. If, you know, but if you don't have an attorney then you will have to represent yourself. What do you want to do? Are you ready to represent yourself today?

MS. SILVA TO JUDGE

Yes.

JUDGE TO MS. SILVA

Okay, so you don't want to get an attorney?

MS. SILVA TO JUDGE

No.

JUDGE TO MS. SILVA

Okay. Please stand and raise your right hand. Do you swear to tell the truth, the whole truth, and nothing but the truth, so help you God?

MS. SILVA TO JUDGE

Yes, I swear.

JUDGE TO MS. SILVA

Sit down. Now, I told you at previous hearings that if you represented yourself you have the right to present witnesses and documents in your case. Do you have any documents that you want the Court to look at?

MS. SILVA TO JUDGE

No.

JUDGE TO MS. SILVA

Okay. You can sit right there and testify from there, all right.

MS. HAZA TO JUDGE

I requested for her to get closer to the interpreter, Your Honor, thank you.

JUDGE TO MS. SILVA

Q. Now, your name is Luz Marina Silva?

A. Yes.

Q. You are Colombian? You have to use your voice, ma'am.

A. Yes.

Q. How old are you?

A. I'm 48.

Q. Are you married or single?

A. Single.

Q. Do you have any children?

A. No.

Q. Now, when did you come to the United States?

A. The last time I came into the United States was March 8, 2000.

Q. Had you been to the United States previous to that?

A. Yes.

Q. How many times?

A. Twice.

Q. When was the first time?

A. June 10, '99.

Q.   Why did you come here on June 10, '99?

A.   As a tourist.

Q.   How long did you stay?

A.   One month.

Q.   Then you went back to Colombia?

A.   Um-hum, yes.

Q.   And when did you come back?

A.   November 21, '99.

Q.   What was the purpose of that visit?

A.   Because I had an attempt in Colombia from the FARC (phonetic sp.).

Q.   So why did you come here?

A.   Because if I had stayed in my country probably something would have happened to me, and it was the easiest and fastest way to come to this country.

Q.   Did you come with a tourist visa?

A.   Yes.

Q.   How long did you stay?

A.   A little over a month.

Q.   Who did you stay with when you came that time?

A.   The second time?

Q.   Yes.

A.   I was in an apartment in Miami Beach.

Q.   Did you rent the apartment?

A.   Yes.

Q.   So why did you only stay a month and a half if you had had a problem in Colombia?

A.   Well I started watching off already that things had already been over with, I have spent Christmas and New Year's here, I felt anguish. I had an aunt back in Balta who was gravely ill and I thought enough time had elapsed and that I could go back, that things might be different.

Q.   And where did you live in Colombia, Balta?

A.   Yes.

Q.   How long had you lived in Balta?

A.   My whole life.

Q.   Did you belong to any, any groups or organizations in Colombia?

A.   Yes, always.

Q.   What?

A.  Yes, I belonged to the conservative group. My family had always belonged to the conservative group, and lately I was working with Antanna Mockus.

Q.  Who is Antanna Mockus?

A.  At this moment he is the mayor of the city of Bogota.

Q.  What do you mean you worked for him?

A.  For his party, visionary party. I did politics for him.

Q.  Since when did you do politics for him?

A.  More or less since '94.

Q.  How long has he been the mayor of Bogota?

A.  At this moment two years.

Q.  Was he running for mayor in '94?

A.  Yes.

Q.  Did he win?

A.  Yes, he won in '95.

Q.  So how long has he been the mayor of Bogota?

A.  No, he was the mayor from '95 to '97, and then he resigned before '97 because he was running for the presidency of the republic.

Q.  He ran for the presidency of Colombia?

A.  Yes

Q.  On behalf of what party?

A.  Visionary.

Q.  So were you a member of that party?

A.  Yes.

Q.  I thought you were a member of the conservative party?

A.  Always.

Q.  Both then?

A.  Yes, always but people who belong to the visionary party can be, can be from either party, the two stronger parties of Colombia, the liberal party and the conservative party. They can belong to the visionary party and be with both groups.

Q.  So how many times has Mr. Mockus run for public office?

A.  Twice for the mayor's office and one for the presidency.

Q.  And did you help him out in all three of these campaigns?

A.  Yes, always.

Q.  What was your job in the campaign?

A.  Well, organize the help brigade, talk to people so they would vote for the party, go to the headquarters and listen to the party's platform.

Q.   Did you occupy any particular position with a title in any of the campaigns?

A.   No, no.

Q.   Were you in charge of people?

A.   No. Only corporation.

Q.   Did you speak publicly?

A.   With the people around me to be in front of an audience using a microphone, no, but only the people around me.

Q.   Did you have a paying job in Bogota?

A.   A restaurant.

Q.   You owned a restaurant?

A.   Yes.

Q.   What was the name of the restaurant?

A.   Tol Medrial Mebianta (phonetic sp.)

Q.   Were you a sole owner?

A.   Yes.

Q.   And this restaurant is in Bogota?

A.   Yes.

Q.   When did you open it?

A.   More or less around 1991.

Q.   Okay. Is it still open?

A.   Yes, my mother has it.

Q.   Do you still own it?

A.   Yes.

Q.   Why did you come to the United States, why are you seeking asylum, ma'am?

A.   Because I had an attempt against my life, the FARC tried to kill me before I came over here.

Q.   That was before you came in November of '99?

A.   Yes.

Q.   When was this attempt, when?

A.   It happened October 9, 1999.

Q.   What happened?

A.   I was leaving my restaurant, the restaurant is in my house, in my mother's house on the first floor.

Q.   Okay.

A.   I was on my way to my apartment from the restaurant, two men arrived in a motorcycle, two people, and these people, these two men came close to my car and they shot into the car. The bullet did not hit me because it went in to the back window. And that is why I am here asking for political asylum.

Q.  Who were these two people, do you know?

A.  No.

Q.  Why did they shoot you, shoot at you, do you know?

A.  I have no idea but days before I was receiving—they were calling me anonymous phone calls.

Q.  Who was calling you?

A.  Different people always. In one of the neighborhoods where we were doing the help brigade I received a condolence note.

Q.  When did you receive a condolence note?

A.  Around three weeks before the attempt.

Q.  What did the note say?

A.  Luz Marina Silva rest in peace for doing what she shouldn't be doing in the wrong place and the FARC signed it.

Q.  Do you have that condolence letter?

A.  No.

Q.  Where is it?

A.  I lost it, it disappeared. To tell you the truth I never thought that I was going to be the victim of an attempt. And one never things that.

Q.  Okay, did you report this, any of these calls, the note or the shooting to the police?

A.  No.

Q.  Why not?

A.  Because on the day of the attempt on that evening at 7 p.m., 7 in the evening, they called me at my apartment and they told me don't you dare even think about making a report. That is a well known fact in Colombia.

Q.  Who called you?

A.  One man.

Q.  Identified?

A.  No, no, never in any of them.

Q.  So you were too scared to go to the police?

A.  Yes.

Q.  So what you did was you came to the United States the next month?

A.  Yes, in November.

Q.  Between that—up to November of 1999 had you had any other problems?

A.   No, no, no.

Q.   So you returned to Bogota when, in January of 2000?

A.   Yes.

Q.   Okay, and did you have any further problems after you returned to Bogota?

A.   Yes.

Q.   What happened?

A.   I began to receive once again telephone calls from the urban group.

Q.   Before the calls previous had been anonymous. Were these calls identified?

A.   No. The same way, anonymous.

Q.   What did they say?

A.   We missed already once, don't provoke us again. We missed on the 9th, we are not going to miss a second time, we're going to kill you. A very rude, very obscene.

Q.   Did you—what did they mean, don't provoke us again?

A.   To provoke means—not to provoke them means not to be there, if I had already come here not to return.

Q.   After you returned in January of 2000 how many threatening calls did you receive until you left two months later?

A.   They were always daily, all the time.

Q.   Always anonymous?

A.   Yes.

Q.   Aside from calls did you have any other problems during this time?

A.   No.

Q.   When was the last time that you were involved in politics?

A.   Before the attempt.

Q.   That's a long—that could be any time, when? When was the last time you participated?

A.   A few days before the attempt in October, since I arrived, since I returned in the United States, August, September, October, more or less.

Q.   Did anybody else working with you have problems?

A.   No, none.

Q.   You were the only one?

A.   Yes, but what it is is that my family has always been involved in politics.

Q.   So, so have many other families in Colombia. Why would you be singled out?

A.   Well, I have a cousin, Alicia Alhanio Silva (phonetic sp.) and she's completely immersed in the visionary party, and I have always helped her. Currently she is the secretary for the mayor of office, for Mockus right now at this time. In one of the telephone calls, the anonymous telephone calls that I received I was told that my family had always exploited the Colombian people. And supposedly I was the one who suffered the attempt that the did this to me because it was easier to get to me than to get to members of my family that have bodyguards.

Q.   How do you know all this, how do you know this? Is this something that you're speculating on, or how do you know this?

A.   That's why—that's the way that they had to take revenge on my family. The one phone call they said, they said, during one of those phone calls is that this is a way that they found to take revenge on my family because they have bodyguards.

Q.   Is that your family on your father's side or your mother's side?

A.   My father's.

Q.   When did this phone call explaining all this occur?

A.   Before the attempt, they would say some things.

Q.   This cousin of yours who is now the secretary of the mayor of Bogota, has she had any problems?

A.   They have always received anonymous phone calls, always. In Bogota in the whole Colombia they are always calling and sending letters to terrorize people.

Q.   So a lot of people get letters and phone calls?

A.   Yes. If the person that's involved in some political group or is the first time doing something that they are not in—that they don't want this person to do for whatever reasons.

Q.   Apart from all that you stated today, did anything else happen to you in Colombia?

A.   No.

Q.   What do you think would happen to you if you went back to Colombia?

A.   I'd be killed. They already warned me when I returned in January.

Q.   Did you tell the police about these latest phone calls?

A.   No.

Q.   Why not?

A.   Because that is just not done. People cannot go make a report in Colombia.

Q.   Ma'am, the government of Colombia is in an all out war with the guerrillas. The president of Colombia, Mr. Orebet (phonetic sp.) apparently has a very effective campaign. Well, I—I mean, how are they going to help if people don't file—don't tell them what's happening?

A.  Because when one is called on the phone and one is told do not make a report, do not do this, do not do that, one doesn't do it because people are afraid, people are afraid in Colombia.

Q.  Anything else that you want to say?

A.  No.

JUDGE TO MS. SCHWARTZ

Ms. Schwartz?

MS. SCHWARTZ TO JUDGE

Yes, Your Honor, a few questions for her, thank you.

MS. SCHWARTZ TO MS. SILVA

Q.  Ma'am, when did you buy your apartment in Miami Beach? Or when did you rent an apartment in Miami Beach?

A.  I did not buy one. In November when I arrived. And also the first time that I came over. It's an apartment in a hotel. It's a room with a kitchen and bath.

Q.  And how long was the lease for?

A.  No, monthly.

Q.  Okay, and at any time did anybody call you and ask you for money?

JUDGE TO MS. SCHWARTZ

In Colombia you mean?

MS. SCHWARTZ TO JUDGE

Q.  In Colombia.

A.  No.

Q.  Did anybody ever call you in Colombia and ask you to collaborate with them?

A.  No.

Q.  Does your mother still live in her home above the restaurant?

A.  Yes.

Q.  And the restaurant is still open for business?

A.  Yes.

Q.  Is that a family restaurant?

A.  I don't understand.

Q.  Does your family run it?

A.  My mother does. And my family is supported by the earnings of that restaurant, my siblings.

JUDGE TO MS. SILVA

Wait, your brothers, male brothers?

MS. SILVA TO JUDGE

Four.

JUDGE TO MS. SCHWARTZ

Okay.

MS. SCHWARTZ TO MS. SILVA

Q. Do you all four of your brothers currently live in Colombia?

A. Yes.

Q. And do you have any sisters?

A. No.

Q. And your father, is he still in Colombia?

A. No.

Q. Where is your father?

A. He died.

JUDGE TO MS. SILVA

Q. What do your brothers do in Colombia?

A. Well, they don't do much, truly.

Q. What does that mean?

A. One doesn't work, the other one has a temporary job and they all live in my mother's house with her.

Q. Have they had any problems with the FARC or anybody?

A. No, none of them.

Q. Go—I mean, if this was a family thing why wouldn't they come after your brothers?

A. They were not involved in politics.

Q. You said that your whole family was perceived as being members of the conservative party and because you are part of that family they wanted to get you.

A. Yes.

Q. What about your brothers?

A. No, my brothers have never been involved in politics. When I say my family I meant uncles, cousins, my father's cousins. My father's side of the family. My brothers have never been involved in politics.

MS. SCHWARTZ TO JUDGE

I just have one or two more questions, Your Honor.

MS. SCHWARTZ TO MS. SILVA

Q. On the day of October 9, 1999 you were followed from your restaurant, correct?

A. Yes, I suppose.

Q. Okay, and has this, the restaurant or your mother's house ever been targeted by the FARC?

A. No, never.

MS. SCHWARTZ TO JUDGE

Okay, I have nothing further.

JUDGE TO MS. SILVA

Anything else that you want to say, ma'am?

MS. SILVA TO JUDGE

No.

## Notes and Questions

1. Suppose you had to decide this case. Based on reading the testimony Luz Marina Silva gave in the courtroom and the information she provided in her asylum application, could you in good conscience rule on this application for asylum and withholding? In other words, do you think it would be important—perhaps critical—for you to observe the applicant in person? To observe the interpreter? If you were restricted to the record that you have just read, could you determine whether Ms. Silva was a credible witness?

2. To the best of your ability, put yourself in the shoes of Immigration Judge Pedro Miranda. Based on your knowledge of the applicable legal standards and your awareness of the factfinding challenges involved in assessing the evidence, write a draft opinion. Be sure to provide the basis for each of the findings that justify your ultimate conclusion on Ms. Silva's requests for protection.

3. Now try to draft an opinion reaching the opposite result. Since the law remains the same, you will need to assess the facts differently. Which facts presented in the application and at trial are capable of yielding opposing inferences? What was the weakest point in the first opinion you drafted and how would you address that point here?

4. If you had been assigned as Ms. Silva's lawyer prior to the immigration court hearing, what steps would you have taken to help her present a stronger claim for protection? What additional facts would you have tried to develop? Are there additional legal arguments you would try to make?

5. You can find the immigration judge's decision and the Eleventh Circuit's review of this case at *Silva v. Attorney General*, 448 F.3d 1229 (11th Cir. 2006). The opinions raise many of the issues examined in Chapter Four, Section A, concerning political violence in civil wars and polarized societies.

# Chapter Nine

# DETENTION, DETERRENCE, AND RESTRICTIONS ON ACCESS TO THE ASYLUM PROCEDURE

*When I set foot on American soil, I had finally reached the land of liberty, the land of peace, and I had a strong feeling of gratitude toward the Most High who had allowed me to escape death and to reach a life of freedom. \* \* \* After completing my statement [at the airport,] \* \* \* [an] officer arrived with hand-cuffs. Then he handcuffed my wrists, but I sincerely thought this was a case of mistaken identity. Later on he explained to me that this was the established procedure. We left for [a county] prison. They put me in a cell where it was really cold, and I had no blanket with me. The idea of a land of liberty was beginning to be cast into serious doubt in my mind.*

*After spending two days in this prison, I was transferred to another prison, and before leaving they not only handcuffed my wrists but also put shackles on my feet. Then they brought me to [an immigration] Detention Center, where I am presently detained. My hope of a land of liberty has been transformed into a nightmare. To this is added moral suffering due to detention, for I do not know how long I will spend in this detention center. It is as if I am living through a bad dream, and soon will wake and finally reach this land of freedom that I still seek.*

—Rwandan refugee,
detained several months
before receiving asylum[1]

*My wife and parents, you know, in Africa, they understand this a different way. I have never been in prison before, I have*

---

**1.** Human Rights First, In Liberty's Shadow: U.S. Detention of Asylum Seekers in the Era of Homeland Security 1 (2004).

*never committed any kind of crime—they don't understand what I have done to deserve this.*

*We need natural lighting. \* \* \* When I came in, I could read and see letters from a distance, but now I tend to lose focus, because of the constant [fluorescent] light in the dorm. \* \* \* Even outdoors here is not outside.\* \* \* If at least in a month, they could give people one chance to go outside, it would help to breathe fresh air. It would also bring down the stress that we are feeling. \* \* \* Keeping people indoors all the time, with the light coming only from above, just like a chicken. \* \* \* Even criminals in federal prisons get natural light, they get to go outdoors. \* \* \* And these people have done crimes, great crimes—but asking for asylum is something so simple, I don't think people should be penalized for it to that extent. \* \* \**

> —Ugandan pastor, detained
> while seeking asylum in the
> United States[2]

Nations have long desired to exercise control over those who enter their territory—an objective that is in obvious tension with the refugee protection system that has developed since World War II. As numbers of asylum seekers increased, sometimes quite dramatically, in the wealthier countries of the global North in the 1980s and 1990s, those states began to tighten traditional control devices, such as visa requirements, and also to deploy new measures, such as interdiction of boats on the high seas. They also began to alter the treatment of those who still made it to the national territory, in an effort to deter future arrivals. European states often required asylum seekers to live in specifically assigned government accommodations, prohibited them from working, required that asylum claims be filed within very limited periods, and restricted their movements within national territory. The United States denied public assistance and expanded the use of detention for at least certain categories of asylum seekers pending resolution of their claims—the practice described in the first-hand accounts reprinted above.

James Hathaway and Alexander Neve provide a useful summary of these developments, which they label "*non-entrée* practices":

[In recent years,] Northern states have sought to avoid the arrival of refugees by adopting policies of external deterrence. Because developed states have the logistical capacity to prevent the arrival of many, and sometimes most, refugees, they have been able to implement *non-entrée* practices that prevent refugees from even reaching their frontiers. Since legal duties arise only once refugees successfully access a state's jurisdiction, *non-entrée* practices are a relatively invisible, and hence politically

2. *Id.* at 36.

expedient, means to ensure that refugees are never in a position to assert their legal right to protection.

Specifically, most Northern states impose a visa requirement on the nationals of refugee-producing states, and penalize airlines and other transportation companies for bringing unauthorized refugees into their territories. By refusing to grant visas for the purpose of making a claim to asylum, Northern countries have been able to insulate themselves from many potential claimants of refugee status. The United Nations High Commissioner for Refugees (UNHCR) has expressed concern that visas are a serious obstacle to the admission to protection of refugees, and may in some instances put refugees at serious risk of *refoulement*, that is, of return to the country in which they assert they will be at risk of grave harm.

Multilateral burden-shifting arrangements and bilateral readmission treaties have also proved popular with Northern states. These arrangements deny entry to asylum-seekers who have not arrived by direct transportation, and authorize their summary removal to so-called "safe third countries" to pursue their claims. In Europe, refugees are thus removed from Northern and Western Europe to the transit states of Southern, Central, and Eastern Europe. The governments of Canada and the United States have similarly explored the possibility of an arrangement with Mexico that would authorize the return to that country of Central and South American asylum-seekers. These procedures are premised neither on substantive nor procedural harmonization of refugee determination at a level that ensures meaningful protection. Because the largely uncoordinated system of international refugee protection is incapable of delivering consistent results from state to state, burden-shifting arrangements can deprive persons who are genuine refugees of internationally guaranteed rights, including the right to protection against *refoulement*.

Even when refugees are able to navigate the course of visas, interdiction, and burden-shifting arrangements, they often remain at risk of *refoulement*. Developed states that wish to avoid receiving refugees adopt restrictive interpretations of the Convention refugee definition as a means of influencing refugees' choice of a destination state. The result is a downward spiral of protection toward the lowest common denominator, and a failure to recognize the claims of persons who are entitled to international protection. * * *

More dramatically, Northern states are beginning to adopt summary exclusion procedures and to interdict refugees at frontiers and in international waters. France, for example, detains asylum-seekers in artificially designated "international zones" of its airports, in which it has claimed to be free from the constraints of either domestic or international law. The interdiction at sea of Haitian refugees by the United States is another example. The U.S. Coast Guard forced asylum-seekers onto its vessels, destroyed their boats, and returned them to Haiti where many suffered further human rights abuse. The U.S. Supreme Court condoned this policy. In addition, recent legislation adopted in the United States allows for the quick turnaround of refugees at border points. Refugees who rely on false documentation to avoid visa controls will now be subject to a summary removal process after no more than a rudimentary examination of their need for protection. European governments have similarly approved expedited exclusion procedures for a wide-ranging category of asylum-seekers, including those whose claims are deemed (without a hearing on the merits) "inconsistent, contradictory or fundamentally improbable." Because both the American and European procedures authorize the removal of asylum-seekers whose claims to refugee status have not been seriously considered, they raise the specter of *refoulement*. * * *

Hathaway & Neve, *Making International Refugee Law Relevant Again: a Proposal for Collectivized and Solution-oriented Protection,* 10 Harv. Hum. Rts. J. 115, 119–23 (1997).

This Chapter examines in more detail three of these practices: interdiction, detention, and summary procedures (the U.S. version is known as "expedited removal"). They raise many questions, both empirical and conceptual. For example, what impact do they have on asylum seekers? Is the impact different for persons who have truly suffered persecution or serious threats as opposed to those with marginal or spurious claims? Can improper effects be minimized by more modest changes in the practices (e.g., shifting from jail-like detention to a less restrictive regime housing persons in government barracks)? Or should all such practices be abandoned?

On a conceptual level, these developments pose fundamental questions about the purposes (both actual and ideal) of the global refugee protection regime. Deterrence and *non-entrée* practices are certainly in tension with the system's humanitarian or protective premises—but are these the only premises of the system we have? Of the system we should have? As we have seen, the drafters of the 1951 Convention manifested caution in shaping the treaty's obligations—most clearly in limiting the initial definition of refugee to persons displaced as a result of events occurring before 1951. Even when that dateline was eliminated by the 1967 Protocol, the adopting states acted within a context that presupposed solid state controls on most migration, through systems that included visa requirements and border guards. To what extent should or must the latter yield as the protection regime is implemented and elaborated? Whatever the assumptions of the drafters, have law and practice evolved to the point of requiring access to haven state territory?

If not, are there better ways to strike an appropriate balance between migration control and protection?

We begin with practices that largely occur outside the borders of the potential state of refuge—visa regimes and equivalent measures, plus interdiction of asylum seekers. These have taken several forms, and they have resulted in significant (and controversial) decisions by high courts in several countries. The opinions from some of those decisions help lay the groundwork for evaluating other deterrent measures as well.

## SECTION A.  VISA REQUIREMENTS AND INTERDICTION

### 1.  HISTORICAL CONTEXT: VISAS AND CARRIER SANCTIONS

The United States adopted an extensive visa regime in the 1920s, not long after the world community, stimulated by the turmoil and security concerns deriving from World War I, began making much more systematic use of border controls and passport requirements. A passport is usually issued by the country of nationality, and generally serves to vouch for the identity and nationality of the individual, as well as to assure receiving states that the issuing country will accept return of the person once the sojourn has been completed. A visa, in contrast, is issued by officials of the destination country, usually its consular officers posted abroad, after an examination of the admissibility of the applicant, often including a personal interview. A visa typically does not guarantee admission to the country that issues it. It is more in the nature of permission to board a carrier and then apply for admission at the port of entry of the destination country. In the vast majority of cases, those who have a duly issued visa are admitted, but border inspectors retain the authority to determine that the person is ineligible, despite possession of such a document, and to refuse admission.

The crucial impact of a visa system is that a person usually cannot even embark on international travel unless the visa requirements of the destination country have been satisfied. Carriers—initially steamship companies and now primarily airlines—play a vital role in assuring that these requirements are honored. Carriers are not supposed to permit a noncitizen who lacks a passport or visa to board a vessel or plane bound for the United States (unless the visa requirement is inapplicable), and they are subject to significant fines if they fail in this duty. See INA § 273. Carrier staff are not expected to be expert in the receiving state's immigration law—that is the job of the consular officer. In principle, the staff at the ticket counter simply checks to see whether the person presents the proper documents.

For the last 20 years, the United States has waived the visa requirement for short-term visitors from approximately 25 specifically named countries, mostly in Europe, with low rates of visa abuse. *See* INA § 217. (Most other countries had adopted a similar practice many years earlier.) These waivers apply by nationality, so that carrier personnel generally need only to check the ticket holders' passports to see whether they qualify, rather than making any other more complicated determinations. A wish to apply for asylum, or even a solid showing of likely persecution, has never been the basis for the carrier to allow boarding by those who lack a required document.

This basic U.S. visa system grew up for reasons having nothing to do with asylum—and indeed in an era when there were very few protection obligations under international or domestic law. The traditional pattern has been to require visas of nearly anyone who wishes to travel to the United States, because performing the primary screening of potential immigrants and visitors while they are overseas, before they ever reach U.S. shores, carries many advantages, for both the state and (in the ordinary case) the individual. See T.A. Aleinikoff, D. Martin, & H. Motomura, *Immigration and Citizenship: Process and Policy* 489–91, 497–500 (5th ed. 2003).

Satisfying the refugee definition is not a basis for receiving a U.S. visa, although it can provide a basis, in certain highly specific circumstances, for the issuance of other papers that will ultimately lead to admission under the overseas refugee program (discussed in Chapter Ten). Furthermore, a consular officer's judgment that the visa applicant may be interested in asylum in the United States could even lead to the refusal of a temporary-visit visa for which the applicant seems otherwise qualified. This is because U.S. law bars the issuance of a nonimmigrant visa in the most widely used categories, such as a student or tourist, if there are indications that the person intends, for any reason, to abandon his or her foreign residence. *See, e.g.,* INA § 101(a)(15)(B), (F). Ironically, then, an apparent need for asylum may actually make it harder to get a U.S. visa, if the consular officer applies these provisions with technical strictness. Finally, the United States has reached agreements with a handful of other countries permitting the stationing of U.S. inspectors at a foreign airport for purposes of verifying travel documents or even conducting the actual U.S. admission screening before the passengers board the plane. Occasionally someone with a valid visa is denied boarding as a result of that pre-inspection process.

European countries had traditionally applied far less rigorous or extensive visa regimes than had the United States, placing greater reliance instead on screening by inspectors at the border. But when the numbers of asylum seekers rose significantly in many European states in the 1980s and 1990s, triggering political backlash, several countries moved much closer to the U.S. model. They imposed visa requirements on additional countries, particularly those that were the source of significant asylum pressures. And they began to impose more precise duties on carriers to help implement this system, with new or augmented fines for those that brought persons without proper visas. These changes evoked considerable criticism from refugee advocates in Europe, where such visa practices were far less familiar than in the United States. Nonetheless, the visa system has been progressively strengthened, and remains a key component of the harmonization of migration controls being developed by the European Union for its member countries. *See* Juss, *The Decline and Decay of European Refugee Policy*, 25 Oxford J. Legal Stud. 749, 766–69 (2005); Gilbert, *Is Europe Living Up to Its Obligations to Refugees?*, 15 European J. Intl. L. 963, 971 (2004).

The combination of a visa requirement and sanctions on carriers that transport unauthorized individuals means that, as a practical matter, most asylum seekers cannot use the normal migration procedures to reach U.S. or European soil and apply for asylum. Their only access to an asylum procedure, if any is available at all, will then be in the country where they are currently located, which they may judge inadequate for a variety of reasons. (We saw some indication of the impact of this system in *Matter of Salim,* 18 I & N Dec. 311 (BIA 1982), described in Chapter Three, Section C, pp. 161–62, *supra.*) As a result, it is not surprising that asylum seekers would seek means other than travel aboard a standard international carrier to get to the United States or to Europe. In the U.S. context, significant migration by small craft from Haiti (and under certain conditions from Cuba) led the United States to implement maritime interdiction and other deterrent measures. Europe and Australia later adopted some roughly similar measures, to be explored below.

## 2.  U.S. COAST GUARD INTERDICTION

In October 1981 the Reagan administration commenced a program of Coast Guard interdiction of boats in the waters between Haiti and the United States, clearly meant to cut down on the number of asylum seekers. The program began pursuant to an agreement with the Haitian government and a proclamation in which President Reagan characterized "the continuing illegal migration by sea of large numbers of undocumented aliens into the southeastern United States" as "a serious national problem detrimental to the interests of the United States." The documents establishing the program carefully stated that no genuine refugees were to be returned to Haiti, *see* Proclamation 4865, 46 Fed. Reg. 48107 (1981); Executive Order 12324, 46 Fed.Reg. 48109 (1981), and INS agents were stationed aboard Coast Guard cutters in order to interview the passengers of any interdicted boats. Up until the Haitian coup of September 1991, 22,716 Haitians had been stopped and interviewed in this fashion. Only 28 were allowed to proceed to the United States for further pursuit of an asylum claim. Refugee Reports, Feb. 28, 1994, at 13.

A Coast Guard launch ferries interdicted Haitians from
sailboat to the cutter. (Photo: U.S. Coast Guard)

Critics voiced strong objections to the interdiction program:

Interdiction represents a radical departure from normal
inspection and inquiry procedures which afford an alien the
opportunity to present his or her case, through counsel, to an
immigration judge. As to refugees, interdiction runs afoul of the
obligations under the domestic withholding provision and its
international law correlative—Article 33 of the Protocol relating
to the Status of Refugees—to refrain from refoulement. * * *

A refugee who would otherwise undergo persecution might
be returned upon interdiction without any recourse simply
because of an inability to articulate the reasons feared, or to
persuade an on-ship inspector that the fear is well-founded, or
simply because he or she is afraid to speak to authorities. This
is particularly so since there would be no access to counsel
under these circumstances.

A refugee fleeing persecution after a stressful and surreptitious journey often lacks the documentary resources, the psychological reserve, and even perhaps the willingness to persuade
someone of the integrity of his or her asylum claim. Indeed, the
*Handbook on Procedures and Criteria for Determining Refugee
Status* of the United Nations High Commissioner for Refugees,
used by the United States in the analysis of asylum claims,
emphasizes the difficulties experienced by aliens in pursuing

asylum at a national border: "[The applicant for refugee status] finds himself in an alien environment and may experience serious difficulties, technical and psychological, in submitting his case to the authorities of a foreign country, often in language not his own." The *Handbook* recommends taking special care in processing such applications.

Helton, *Political Asylum Under the 1980 Refugee Act: An Unfulfilled Promise,* 17 U.Mich.J.L.Ref. 243, 255–56 (1984). *Cf.* Motomura, *Haitian Asylum Seekers: Interdiction and Immigrants' Rights,* 26 Cornell Int'l L.J. 695, 709–14 (1993) (suggesting that interdicted noncitizens should be treated as having reached the "functional equivalent of the border"). *See also* Legomsky, *The Haitian Interdiction Programme, Human Rights, and the Role of Judicial Protection,* Int'l. J. Refugee L. 181 (Special Issue, Sept. 1990).

The Reagan interdiction program withstood a court challenge alleging that it violated statutes, treaties, and the Constitution. *Haitian Refugee Center, Inc. v. Gracey,* 600 F.Supp. 1396 (D.D.C.1985), *affirmed on other grounds,* 809 F.2d 794 (D.C.Cir.1987) (lack of standing). Ten years after the interdiction program began, INS announced new procedures to assure more careful and thorough questioning of interdicted noncitizens aboard the vessel that picked them up, in order to determine whether they had a "credible fear" of persecution, a considerably lower threshold than "well-founded fear." *See INS Revises Policy for Screening Haitians Interdicted at Sea,* 68 Interp.Rel. 793 (1991); Alvarez, *Haitians Get Longer Hearings at Sea,* Miami Herald, March 16, 1991, at Bl.

But these innovations were quickly overtaken by major political changes inside Haiti. Boat departures had nearly disappeared after Jean–Bertrand Aristide, widely popular among Haiti's poor, was elected President early in 1991. When a military coup ousted Aristide in September, the Organization of American States imposed an embargo on Haiti, which was followed by United Nations-imposed global sanctions against the regime. In the wake of the coup and the deprivations imposed by the sanctions, thousands more Haitians took to the seas in search of refuge elsewhere. The interdiction controversy became a major public issue. As the numbers outran the capacity of shipboard processing, the U.S. government initially began taking the Haitians to the U.S. naval base at Guantánamo, Cuba (about 100 miles across the Windward Passage from Haiti) for INS screening. Roughly one-third of those interviewed were found to have a credible fear of persecution—about 10,000 applicants—and so were approved for onward travel to the mainland United States, where full adjudication of the application could occur.

Litigation challenging several aspects of the screening and interdiction process was unsuccessful at the appellate level, *see, e.g., Haitian Refugee Center, Inc. v. Baker,* 949 F.2d 1109 (11th Cir.1991); 953 F.2d 1498 (11th Cir.1992), *cert. denied,* 502 U.S. 1122, 112 S.Ct. 1245, 117 L.Ed.2d 477 (1992) (challenges included failure to provide access to counsel or opportunity for judicial review). When temporary court stays were ultimately lifted, the Coast Guard resumed returning "screened-out" applicants to Haiti in March 1992. The outflow declined temporarily, but then large-scale boat traffic reappeared in May, and the George H.W. Bush administration decided that the Guantánamo process was no longer feasible. The President authorized direct return of interdicted individuals to Haiti, without any screening. Haitians who believed they were threatened in their home country were invited to apply at the U.S. embassy in Port-au-Prince for in-country screening and possible inclusion in a U.S. refugee program for direct departures.

The new Executive Order was ruled unlawful in *Haitian Centers Council, Inc. v. McNary*, 969 F.2d 1350 (2d Cir.1992), on the basis that it was inconsistent with INA § 243(h) (at the time, the provision for withholding of removal). The Supreme Court stayed the injunction, however, and set an expedited schedule for its review. In the meantime, President Clinton, who had harshly criticized the Bush policy during the 1992 presidential campaign, surprisingly announced just before his inauguration that he would continue the interdiction—apparently to avoid a sudden outflow of Haitian boats built in anticipation of his taking office. This was the setting in which the Supreme Court heard oral argument and issued its opinion on the U.S. interdiction policy.

## SALE v. HAITIAN CENTERS COUNCIL

Supreme Court of the United States, 1993.
509 U.S. 155, 113 S.Ct. 2549, 125 L.Ed.2d 128.

JUSTICE STEVENS delivered the opinion of the Court.

The President has directed the Coast Guard to intercept vessels illegally transporting passengers from Haiti to the United States and to return those passengers to Haiti without first determining whether they may qualify as refugees. The question presented in this case is whether such forced repatriation, "authorized to be undertaken only beyond the territorial sea of the United States," violates [the law]. We hold that neither § 243(h) nor Article 33 of the United Nations Protocol Relating to the Status of Refugees applies to action taken by the Coast Guard on the high seas.

\* \* \*

On September 30, 1991, a group of military leaders displaced the government of Jean Bertrand Aristide, the first democratically elected president in Haitian history. As the District Court stated in an uncontested finding of fact, since the military coup "hundreds of Haitians have been killed, tortured, detained without a warrant, or subjected to violence and the destruction of their property because of their political beliefs. Thousands have been forced into hiding." Following the coup the Coast Guard suspended repatriations for a period of several weeks, and the United States imposed economic sanctions on Haiti.

On November 18, 1991, the Coast Guard announced that it would resume the program of interdiction and forced repatriation. The following day, the Haitian Refugee Center, Inc., representing a class of interdicted Haitians, filed a complaint in the United States District Court for the Southern District of Florida alleging that the Government had failed to establish and implement adequate procedures to protect Haitians who qualified for asylum. * * *

In the meantime the Haitian exodus expanded dramatically. During the six months after October 1991, the Coast Guard interdicted over 34,000 Haitians. Because so many interdicted Haitians could not be safely processed on Coast Guard cutters, the Department of Defense established temporary facilities at the United States Naval Base in Guantanamo, Cuba, to accommodate them during the screening process. Those temporary facilities, however, had a capacity of only about 12,500 persons. In the first three weeks of May 1992, the Coast Guard intercepted 127 vessels (many of which were considered unseaworthy, overcrowded, and unsafe); those vessels carried 10,497 undocumented aliens. On May 22, 1992, the United States Navy determined that no additional migrants could safely be accommodated at Guantanamo.

With both the facilities at Guantanamo and available Coast Guard cutters saturated, and with the number of Haitian emigrants in unseaworthy craft increasing (many had drowned as they attempted the trip to Florida), the Government could no longer both protect our borders *and* offer the Haitians even a modified screening process. It had to choose between allowing Haitians into the United States for the screening process or repatriating them without giving them any opportunity to establish their qualifications as refugees. In the judgment of the President's advisers, the first choice not only would have defeated the original purpose of the program (controlling illegal immigration), but also would have impeded diplomatic efforts to restore democratic government in Haiti and would have posed a life-threatening danger to thousands of persons embarking on long voyages in dangerous craft. The second choice would have advanced those policies but deprived the fleeing Haitians of any screening process at a time when a significant minority of them were being screened in.

On May 23, 1992, President Bush adopted the second choice. After assuming office, President Clinton decided not to modify that order; it remains in effect today. The wisdom of the policy choices made by Presidents Reagan, Bush, and Clinton is not a matter for our consideration. We must decide only whether Executive Order No. 12807, 57 Fed.Reg. 23133 (1992), which reflects and implements those choices, is consistent with § 243(h) of the INA.

* * *

### III

Both parties argue that the plain language of § 243(h)(1) is dispositive. It reads as follows:

The Attorney General shall not deport or return any alien (other than an alien described in [a section relating to persons involved in Nazi persecution or genocide]) to a country if the Attorney General determines that such alien's life or freedom would be threatened in such country on account of race, religion, nationality, membership in a particular social group, or political opinion.

Respondents emphasize the words "any alien" and "return"; neither term is limited to aliens within the United States. Respondents also contend that [a]1980 amendment deleting the words "within the United States" from the prior text of § 243(h), obviously gave the statute an extraterritorial effect. This change, they further argue, was required in order to conform the statute to the text of Article 33.1 of the Convention, which they find as unambiguous as the present statutory text. Petitioners' response is that a fair reading of the INA as a whole demonstrates that § 243(h) does not apply to actions taken by the President or Coast Guard outside the United States; that the legislative history of the 1980 amendment supports their reading; and that both the text and the negotiating history of Article 33 of the Convention indicate that it was not intended to have any extraterritorial effect.

We shall first review the text and structure of the statute and its 1980 amendment, and then consider the text and negotiating history of the Convention.

### A.   The Text and Structure of the INA

Although § 243(h)(1) refers only to the Attorney General, the Court of Appeals found it "difficult to believe that the proscription of § 243(h)(1)—returning an alien to his persecutors—was forbidden if done by the attorney general but permitted if done by some other arm of the executive branch." Congress "understood" that the Attorney General is the "President's agent for dealing with immigration matters," and would intend any reference to her to restrict similar actions of any Government official. As evidence of this understanding, the court cited § 103(a). That section, however, conveys to us a different message. It provides, in part:

The Attorney General shall be charged with the administration and enforcement of this chapter and all other laws relating to the immigration and naturalization of aliens, *except insofar as this chapter or such laws relate to the powers, functions, and duties conferred upon the President, the Secretary of State, the officers of the Department of State, or diplomatic or consular officers* . . . . (Emphasis added.)

Other provisions of the Act expressly confer certain responsibilities on the Secretary of State, the President, and, indeed, on certain other officers as well. The 1981 and 1992 Executive Orders expressly relied on statutory provisions that confer authority on the President to suspend the entry of "any class of aliens" or to "impose on the entry of aliens any restrictions he may deem to be appropriate." [INA § 212(f).] We cannot say that the interdiction program created by the President, which the Coast Guard was ordered to enforce, usurped authority that Congress had delegated to, or implicated responsibilities that it had imposed on, the Attorney General alone.

The reference to the Attorney General in the statutory text is significant not only because that term cannot reasonably be construed to describe either the President or the Coast Guard, but also because it suggests that it applies only to the Attorney General's normal responsibilities under the INA. The most relevant of those responsibilities for our purposes is her conduct of the deportation and exclusion hearings in which requests for asylum or for withholding of deportation under § 243(h) are ordinarily advanced. Since there is no provision in the statute for the conduct of such proceedings outside the United States, and since Part V and other provisions of the INA obviously contemplate that such proceedings would be held in the country, we cannot reasonably construe § 243(h) to limit the Attorney General's actions in geographic areas where she has not been authorized to conduct such proceedings. Part V of the INA contains no reference to a possible extraterritorial application.

Even if Part V of the Act were not limited to strictly domestic procedures, the presumption that Acts of Congress do not ordinarily apply outside our borders would support an interpretation of § 243(h) as applying only within United States territory. The Court of Appeals held that the presumption against extraterritoriality had "no relevance in the present context" because there was no risk that § 243(h), which can be enforced only in United States courts against the United States Attorney General, would conflict with the laws of other nations. We have recently held, however, that the presumption has a foundation broader than the desire to avoid conflict with the laws of other nations. *Smith v. United States*, 507 U.S. 197, 206–207 n. 5, 113 S.Ct. 1178, 1183 n. 122 L.Ed.2d 548 (1993). * * *

### B. The History of the Refugee Act of 1980

As enacted in 1952, § 243(h) authorized the Attorney General to withhold deportation of aliens "within the United States." Six years later we considered the question whether it applied to an alien who had been paroled into the country while her admissibility was being determined. We held that even though she was physically present within our borders, she was not "within the United States" as those words were used in § 243(h). *Leng May Ma v. Barber*, 357 U.S. 185, 186, 78 S.Ct. 1072, 1073, 2 L.Ed.2d 1246 (1958). We explained the important distinction between "deportation" or "expulsion," on the one hand, and "exclusion," on the other. * * * Under the INA, both then and now, those seeking "admission" and trying to avoid "exclusion" were already within our territory (or at its border), but the law treated them as though they had never entered the United States at all; they were within United States territory but not "within the United States." Those who had been admitted (or found their way in) but sought to avoid "expulsion" had the added benefit of "deportation proceedings"; they were both within United States territory *and* "within the United States." Although the phrase "within the United States" presumed the alien's actual presence in the United States, it had more to do with an alien's legal status than with his location.

The 1980 amendment erased the long-maintained distinction between deportable and excludable aliens for purposes of § 243(h). By adding the word "return" and removing the words "within the United States" from § 243(h), Congress extended the statute's protection to both types of aliens, but did nothing to change the presumption that both types of aliens would continue to be found only with United States territory. The removal of the phrase "within the United States" cured the most obvious drawback of § 243(h): as interpreted in *Leng May Ma*, its protection was available only to aliens subject to deportation proceedings. * * *

In sum, all available evidence about the meaning of § 243(h)—the government official at whom it is directed, its location in the Act, its failure to suggest any extraterritorial application, the 1980 amendment that gave it a dual reference to "deport or return," and the relevance of that dual structure to immigration law in general—leads unerringly to the conclusion that it applies in only one context: the domestic procedures by which the Attorney General determines whether deportable and excludable aliens may remain in the United States.

### IV

* * * Both Congress and the Executive Branch gave extensive consideration to the Protocol before ratifying it in 1968; in all of their published consideration of it there appears no mention of the possibility that the United States was assuming any extraterritorial obligations. Nevertheless, because the history of the 1980 Act does disclose a general intent to conform our law to Article 33 of the Convention, it might be argued that the extraterritorial obligations imposed by Article 33 were so clear that Congress, in acceding to the Protocol, and then in amending the statute to harmonize the two, meant to give the latter a correspondingly extraterritorial effect. Or, just as the statute might have imposed an extraterritorial obligation that the Convention does not (the argument we have just rejected), the Convention might have established an extraterritorial obligation which the statute does not; under the Supremacy Clause, that broader treaty obligation might then provide the controlling rule of law. With those possibilities in mind we shall consider both the text and negotiating history of the Convention itself.

Like the text and the history of § 243(h), the text and negotiating history of Article 33 of the United Nations Convention are both completely silent with respect to the Article's possible application to actions taken by a country outside its own borders. Respondents argue that the Protocol's broad remedial goals require that a nation be prevented from repatriating refugees to their potential oppressors whether or not the refugees are within that nation's borders. In spite of the moral weight of that argument, both the text and negotiating history of Article 33 affirmatively indicate that it was not intended to have extraterritorial effect.

### A.    The Text of the Convention

* * *

The full text of Article 33 reads as follows:

"*Article 33.—Prohibition of Expulsion or Return ('refoulement')*"

"1. No Contracting State shall expel or return (*'refouler'*) a refugee in any manner whatsoever to the frontiers of territories where his life or freedom would be threatened on account of his race, religion, nationality, membership of a particular social group or political opinion.

"2. The benefit of the present provision may not, however, be claimed by a refugee whom there are reasonable grounds for regarding as a danger to the security of *the country in which he is*, or who, having been convicted by a final judgment of a particularly serious crime, constitutes a danger to the community of that country." Convention Relating to the Status of Refugees, July 28, 1951 (emphasis added).

Under the second paragraph of Article 33 an alien may not claim the benefit of the first paragraph if he poses a danger to the country in which he is located. If the first paragraph did apply on the high seas, no nation could invoke the second paragraph's exception with respect to an alien there: An alien intercepted on the high seas is in no country at all. If Article 33.1 applied extraterritorially, therefore, Article 33.2 would create an absurd anomaly: Dangerous aliens on the high seas would be entitled to the benefits of 33.1 while those residing in the country that sought to expel them would not. It is more reasonable to assume that the coverage of 33.2 was limited to those already in the country because it was understood that 33.1 obligated the signatory state only with respect to aliens within its territory.

Article 33.1 uses the words "expel or return ('refouler')" as an obvious parallel to the words "deport or return" in § 243(h)(1). There is no dispute that "expel" has the same meaning as "deport"; it refers to the deportation or expulsion of an alien who is already present in the host country. The dual reference identified and explained in our opinion in *Leng May Ma v. Barber* suggests that the term "return ('refouler')" refers to the exclusion of aliens who are merely " 'on the threshold of initial entry.' "

This suggestion—that "return" has a legal meaning narrower than its common meaning—is reinforced by the parenthetical reference to "*refouler,*" a French word that is *not* an exact synonym for the English word "return." Indeed, neither of two respected English–French dictionaries mentions *"refouler"*as one of many possible French translations of "return." Conversely, the English translations of *"refouler"* do not include the word "return." They do, however, include words like "repulse," "repel," "drive back," and even "expel." To the extent that they are relevant, these translations imply that "return" means a defensive act of resistance or exclusion at a border rather than an act of transporting someone to a particular destination. In the context of the Convention, to "return" means to "repulse" rather than to "reinstate."

The text of Article 33 thus fits with Judge Edwards' understanding [expressed in his concurring opinion in the 1987 ruling that upheld the initial interdiction program adopted by the Reagan Administration] that " 'expulsion' would refer to a 'refugee already admitted into a country' and that 'return' would refer to a 'refugee already within the territory but not yet resident there.' Thus, the Protocol was not intended to govern parties' conduct outside of their national borders." *Haitian Refugee Center v. Gracey,* 257 U.S.App.D.C., at 413, 809 F.2d, at 840 (footnotes omitted). From the time of the Convention, commentators have consistently agreed with this view.[40]

The drafters of the Convention and the parties to the Protocol—like the drafters of § 243(h)—may not have contemplated that any nation would gather fleeing refugees and return them to the one country they had desperately sought to escape; such actions may even violate the spirit of Article 33; but a treaty cannot impose uncontemplated extraterritorial obligations on those who ratify it through no more than its general humanitarian intent. Because the text of Article 33 cannot reasonably be read to say anything at all about a nation's actions toward aliens outside its own territory, it does not prohibit such actions.

### B.   The Negotiating History of the Convention

* * * At a negotiating conference of plenipotentiaries held in Geneva, Switzerland, on July 11, 1951, the Swiss delegate explained his understanding that the words "expel" and "return" covered only refugees who had entered the host country. He stated:

> "In the Swiss Government's view, the term 'expulsion' applied to a refugee who had already been admitted to the territory of a country. The term *'refoulement'* on the other hand, had a vaguer meaning; *it could not, however, be applied to a refugee who had not yet entered the territory of a country.* The word 'return', used in the English text, gave that idea exactly.
> * * * [T]he States represented at the Conference should take a

---

**40.** See, *e.g.,* * * * 2 A. Grahl–Madsen, The Status of Refugees in International Law 94 (1972) ("[*Non-refoulement*] may only be invoked in respect of persons who are already present—lawfully or unlawfully—in the territory of a Contracting State. Article 33 only prohibits the expulsion or return (*refoulement*) of refugees to territories where they are likely to suffer persecution; it does not obligate the Contracting State to admit any person who has not already set foot on their respective territories"). * * *

definite position with regard to the meaning to be attached to the word 'return'. The Swiss Government considered that in the present instance *the word applied solely to refugees who had already entered a country, but were not yet resident there.* According to that interpretation, States were not compelled to allow large groups of persons claiming refugee status to cross its frontiers. * * * ''(Emphases added).

No one expressed disagreement with the position of the Swiss delegate on that day or at the session two weeks later when Article 28 [the *nonrefoulement* provision in that draft] was again discussed. At that session, the delegate of the Netherlands recalled the Swiss delegate's earlier position:

" * * * According to that interpretation, article 28 would not have involved any obligations in the possible case of mass migrations across frontiers or of attempted mass migrations.

"He wished to revert to that point, because the Netherlands Government attached very great importance to the scope of the provision now contained in article 33. The Netherlands could not accept any legal obligations in respect of large groups of refugees seeking access to its territory. * * *

"In order to dispel any possible ambiguity and to reassure his Government, he wished to have it placed on record that the Conference was in agreement with the interpretation that the possibility of mass migrations across frontiers or of attempted mass migrations was not covered by article 33.

"There being no objection, the PRESIDENT *ruled* that the interpretation given by the Netherlands representative should be placed on record. * * * ''

Although the significance of the President's comment that the remarks should be "placed on record" is not entirely clear, this much cannot be denied: At one time there was a "general consensus," and in July of 1951 several delegates understood the right of *non-refoulement* to apply only to aliens physically present in the host country. There is no record of any later disagreement with that position. * * *

* * * The negotiating history, which suggests that the Convention's limited reach resulted from a deliberate bargain, is not dispositive, but it solidly supports our reluctance to interpret Article 33 to impose obligations on the contracting parties that are broader than the text commands. We do not read that text to apply to aliens interdicted on the high seas.

V

Respondents contend that the dangers faced by Haitians who are unwillingly repatriated demonstrate that the judgment of the Court of Appeals fulfilled the central purpose of the Convention and the Refugee Act of 1980. While we must, of course, be guided by the high purpose of both the treaty and the statute, we are not persuaded that either one places any limit on the President's authority to repatriate aliens interdicted beyond the territorial seas of the United States.

\* \* \* We therefore find ourselves in agreement with the conclusion expressed in Judge Edwards' concurring opinion in *Gracey*, 257 U.S.App. D.C., at 414, 809 F.2d, at 841:

> This case presents a painfully common situation in which desperate people, convinced that they can no longer remain in their homeland, take desperate measures to escape. Although the human crisis is compelling, there is no solution to be found in a judicial remedy.

The judgment of the Court of Appeals is reversed.

JUSTICE BLACKMUN, dissenting.

When, in 1968, the United States acceded to the United Nations Protocol Relating to the Status of Refugees, it pledged not to "return (*'refouler'*) a refugee in any manner whatsoever" to a place where he would face political persecution. In 1980, Congress amended our immigration law to reflect the Protocol's directives. Today's majority nevertheless decides that the forced repatriation of the Haitian refugees is perfectly legal, because the word "return" does not mean return, because the opposite of "within the United States" is not outside the United States, and because the official charged with controlling immigration has no role in enforcing an order to control immigration.

I believe that the duty of nonreturn expressed in both the Protocol and the statute is clear. The majority finds it "extraordinary" that Congress would have intended the ban on returning "any alien" to apply to aliens at sea. That Congress would have meant what it said is not remarkable. What is extraordinary in this case is that the Executive, in disregard of the law, would take to the seas to intercept fleeing refugees and force them back to their persecutors—and that the Court would strain to sanction that conduct.

### I

I begin with the Convention, for it is undisputed that the Refugee Act of 1980 was passed to conform our law to Article 33, and that "the nondiscretionary duty imposed by § 243(h) parallels the United States' mandatory *nonrefoulement* obligations under Article 33.1...." \* \* \*

### A

Article 33.1 of the Convention states categorically and without geographical limitation:

> No Contracting State shall expel or return (*'refouler'*) a refugee in any manner whatsoever to the frontiers of territories where his life or freedom would be threatened on account of his race, religion, nationality, membership of a particular social group or political opinion.

The terms are unambiguous. Vulnerable refugees shall not be returned. The language is clear, and the command is straightforward; that should be the end of the inquiry. Indeed, until litigation ensued, see *Haitian Refugee Center v. Gracey*, 257 U.S.App.D.C. 367, 809 F.2d 794 (1987), the Government consistently acknowledged that the Convention applied on the high seas.

The majority, however, has difficulty with the treaty's use of the term "return (*'refouler'*)." "Return," it claims, does not mean return, but instead has a distinctive legal meaning. * * *

The ordinary meaning of "return" is "to bring, send, or put (a person or thing) back to or in a former position." Webster's Third New International Dictionary 1941 (1986). That describes precisely what petitioners are doing to the Haitians. * * *

The straightforward interpretation of the duty of nonreturn is strongly reinforced by the Convention's use of the French term *"refouler."* The ordinary meaning of *"refouler,"* as the majority concedes, is "[t]o repulse, . . . ; to drive back, to repel." Larousse Modern French–English Dictionary 631 (1981). Thus construed, Article 33.1 of the Convention reads: "No contracting state shall expel or [repulse, drive back, or repel] a refugee in any manner whatsoever to the frontiers of territories where his life or freedom would be threatened. . . ." That, of course, is exactly what the Government is doing. It thus is no surprise that when the French press has described the very policy challenged here, the term it has used is *"refouler."* See, *e.g., Le bourbier haïtien*, Le Monde, May 31–June 1, 1992 ("[L]es Etats–Unis ont décidé de refouler directement les réfugiés recueillis par la garde cotiére." (The United States has decided [de refouler] directly the refugees picked up by the Coast Guard)).

And yet the majority insists that what has occurred is not, in fact, *"refoulement."* It reaches this conclusion in a peculiar fashion. After acknowledging that the ordinary meaning of *"refouler "*is "repulse," "repel," and "drive back," the majority without elaboration declares: "To the extent that they are relevant, these translations imply that 'return' means a defensive act of resistance or exclusion at a border. . . ." I am at a loss to find the narrow notion of "exclusion at a border" in broad terms like "repulse," "repel," and "drive back." Gage was repulsed (initially) at Bunker Hill. Lee was repelled at Gettysburg. Rommel was driven back across North Africa. The majority's puzzling progression (*"refouler "*means repel or drive back; therefore "return" means only exclude at a border; therefore the treaty does not apply) hardly justifies a departure from the path of ordinary meaning. The text of Article 33.1 is clear, and whether the operative term is "return" or *"refouler, "*it prohibits the Government's actions.

Article 33.1 is clear not only in what it says, but also in what it does not say: It does not include any geographical limitation. It limits only where a refugee may be sent "to," not where he may be sent from. This is not surprising, given that the aim of the provision is to protect refugees against persecution.

Article 33.2, by contrast, *does* contain a geographical reference, and the majority seizes upon this as evidence that the section as a whole applies only within a signatory's borders. That inference is flawed. Article 33.2 states that the benefit of Article 33.1

> may not . . . be claimed by a refugee whom there are reasonable grounds for regarding as a danger to the security of the country in which he is, or who, having been convicted by a final judgment of a particularly serious crime, constitutes a danger to the community of that country.

The signatories' understandable decision to allow nations to deport criminal aliens who have entered their territory hardly suggests an intent to permit the apprehension and return of noncriminal aliens who have not entered their territory, and who may have no desire ever to enter it. One wonders what the majority would make of an exception that removed from the Article's protection all refugees who "constitute a danger to their families." By the majority's logic, the inclusion of such an exception presumably would render Article 33.1 applicable only to refugees with families.

* * *

## II

### A

Like the treaty whose dictates it embodies, § 243(h) of the Immigration and Nationality Act of 1952 (INA) is unambiguous. * * * "With regard to this very statutory scheme, we have considered ourselves bound to assume that the legislative purpose is expressed by the ordinary meaning of the words used." *Cardoza–Fonseca*, 480 U.S., at 431, 107 S.Ct., at 1213 (internal quotation marks omitted). Ordinary, but not literal. The statement that "the Attorney General shall not deport or return any alien" obviously does not mean simply that the person who is the Attorney General at the moment is forbidden personally to deport or return any alien, but rather that her agents may not do so. In the present case the Coast Guard without question is acting as the agent of the Attorney General. "The officers of the Coast Guard insofar as they are engaged . . . in enforcing any law of the United States shall . . . be deemed to be acting as agents of the particular executive department . . . charged with the administration of the particular law . . . and . . . be subject to all the rules and regulations promulgated by such department . . . with respect to the enforcement of that law." 14 U.S.C. § 89(b). The Coast Guard is engaged in enforcing the immigration laws. * * *

* * *

C

That the clarity of the text and the implausibility of its theories do not give the majority more pause is due, I think, to the majority's heavy reliance on the presumption against extraterritoriality. * * *

* * *

In this case we deal with a statute that regulates a distinctively international subject matter: immigration, nationalities, and refugees. Whatever force the presumption may have with regard to a primarily domestic statute evaporates in this context. There is no danger that the Congress that enacted the Refugee Act was blind to the fact that the laws it was crafting had implications beyond this Nation's borders. The "commonsense notion" that Congress was looking inwards—perfectly valid in a case involving the Federal Tort Claims Act, such as *Smith* [*v. United States*, 507 U.S. 197 (1993)]—cannot be reasonably applied to the Refugee Act of 1980. * * *

* * *

III

The Convention that the Refugee Act embodies was enacted largely in response to the experience of Jewish refugees in Europe during the period of World War II. The tragic consequences of the world's indifference at that time are well known. The resulting ban on *refoulement*, as broad as the humanitarian purpose that inspired it, is easily applicable here, the Court's protestations of impotence and regret notwithstanding.

The refugees attempting to escape from Haiti do not claim a right of admission to this country. They do not even argue that the Government has no right to intercept their boats. They demand only that the United States, land of refugees and guardian of freedom, cease forcibly driving them back to detention, abuse, and death. That is a modest plea, vindicated by the treaty and the statute. We should not close our ears to it.

I dissent.

## Notes and Questions

1. In *Sale,* the majority of the Supreme Court focused on the drafting history and on early commentators like Atle Grahl–Madsen and Paul Weis (nongovernmental figures who were clearly sympathetic to the protection of refugees). All of these sources, the Court found, suggested that the understanding in 1951 was that *nonrefoulement* did not include nonrejection at the frontiers. But most academic commentators in the 1990s sharply criticized the *Sale* decision's interpretation of Article 33 of the 1951 Refugee Convention. In addition, the UNHCR, acknowledged by the Supreme Court in *INS v. Cardoza–Fonseca*, 480 U.S. 421, 439 n.22, 107 S.Ct. 1207, 94 L.Ed.2d 434 (1987), as a source of guidance in interpreting the treaty's terms, strongly rejected the territorial limitation imposed on Article 33 by the *Sale* majority:

UNHCR considers the Court's decision a setback to modern international refugee law which has been developing for more than forty years, since the end of World War II. It renders the work of the Office of the High Commissioner in its global refugee protection role more difficult and sets a very unfortunate example.

*UN High Commissioner for Refugees Responds to U.S. Supreme Court Decision in Sale v. Haitian Centers Council,* 32 I.L.M. 1215 (1993).

Is this UNHCR statement an implicit concession that the original Convention did not bar such measures but that "modern international refugee law" does so, owing to later developments? Can the meaning of a treaty change over time? If so, what developments would be relevant in showing such evolution—state practice, scholarly writings, additional experience forcing government officials and international actors to elaborate the full implications and meaning of the treaty provisions, other human rights developments? On the other hand, what practices or understandings might undercut such a conclusion? Should the Supreme Court have shown greater deference to the views of international bodies in construing international obligations? (UNHCR had filed an amicus curiae brief in *Sale.*) Keep these questions in mind as we consider related court decisions in other countries (below).

2. Later the Haitian Center for Human Rights filed a challenge to the U.S. interdiction policy with the Inter–American Commission on Human Rights. In 1997 the Commission ruled that the U.S. interdiction and repatriation of certain Haitian asylum seekers constituted violations of the American Declaration of Human Rights, specifically the rights to life, liberty, security of the person, equality before the law, resort to the courts, and the right to seek and receive asylum. The Commission specifically noted its disagreement with the *Sale* decision, but did not provide an extensive discussion of its reasons for doing so. It also recommended that the United States provide adequate compensation to the victims of these violations. The Haitian Center for Human Rights v. United States, Decision of the Commission, Report No. 51/96, Inter–Am.C.H.R., OEA/Ser.L/V/II.95 Doc.7 rev. at 550 (1997).

3. For a vivid chronicle of the litigation that led to *Sale v. Haitian Centers Council,* see Brandt Goldstein, Storming the Court: How a Band of Yale Law Students Sued the President—and Won (2005). *See also* Koh, *Reflections on* Refoulement *and* Haitian Centers Council, 35 Harv. Int'l L.J. 1 (1994); Koh, *The Human Face of the Interdiction Program,* 33 Va. J. Int'l L. 483 (1993); Note, *Litigating as Law Students: An Inside Look at* Haitian Centers Council, 103 Yale L.J. 2337 (1994). Additional insights can be found in Legomsky, *An Asylum Seeker's Bill of Rights in a Non-Utopian World,* 14 Geo. Immigr. L.J. 619, 626–27 (1998); Frelick, *Haitian Boat Interdiction and Return: First Asylum and First Principles of Refugee Protection,* 26 Cornell Int'l L.J. 675 (1993).

4. Legislation to alter the U.S. interdiction policy was proposed, but was not successful. See 69 Interp.Rel. 149, 213, 249, 672 (1992); Refugee Reports, June 19, 1992, at 11; *id.,* Jan. 29, 1993, at 1; *id.,* June 30, 1993, at 1. We will examine some of the offshore processing that resulted from the continued Coast Guard interdiction program in Chapter Eleven.

### 3. DEVELOPMENTS AFTER *SALE v. HAITIAN CENTERS COUNCIL*

President Clinton had justified his continuation in 1993 of the Haitian interdiction program in part by emphasizing the new diplomatic steps his Administration was taking to force the junta to leave power and restore the elected President Aristide. For a while after Supreme Court's ruling in *Sale*, this new activity seemed to bear fruit, as the generals agreed in July 1993 to a gradual process for the transfer of power. But little real progress took place. In April 1994, Randall Robinson, an activist who had been instrumental in the effort to end apartheid in South Africa, announced a hunger strike until Haitian interdiction ended. President Clinton decided to make a significant change in policy the following month. Interdicted Haitians would not be immediately returned, but instead would be taken to a large U.S. ship anchored in Jamaica for full refugee screening (not simply a determination of "credible fear" that would require further adjudication in the United States). Those found to have a well-founded fear of persecution were to be brought to the United States in full refugee status, under INA § 207, the provision that governs resettlement as part of overseas refugee programs (to be discussed in Chapter Ten). The rest would be repatriated.

These arrangements proceeded for a few weeks, but the numbers began to overwhelm the processing capacity. Once again the U.S. naval facility at Guantánamo was opened as an interviewing and temporary lodging site. When the outflow reached as high as 3000 per day, however, the Administration announced another change of course. On July 5, 1994, the President stated that Haitians would no longer be allowed to resettle in the United States, but instead would be taken to "safe havens" in the region. Guantánamo would be the first of such sites—and as it turned out, the only one needed for Haitians. Refugee screening was ended; any who wished to stay in Guantánamo would be allowed to (save for some residual efforts to remove persons with criminal records).

The effect on the outflow from Haiti was dramatic. Within two weeks the rate fell below 200 a week. Meantime, many Haitians chose to repatriate rather than remain in the bleak tent cities of Guantánamo. Then on September 19, U.S. military forces entered Haiti under UN authority, and by October 15, Aristide was back in the Presidential Palace in Port-au-Prince. Clearly the ongoing flow of asylum seekers from Haiti—and governmental discomfort at ongoing unscreened returns, despite the Supreme Court's legal ruling—had played a significant role in sustaining U.S. interest in a military intervention in order to solve the problem at the source. Thereafter the large majority of Haitians on Guantánamo repatriated voluntarily, some after the offer of cash and job-training incentives. Over 3,500 refused to volunteer, but were eventually sent home anyway. (We will discuss the use of offshore safe havens more extensively in Chapter Eleven.)

U.S. troops deploy in the Haitian countryside during
the 1994 UN-authorized intervention.

Coast Guard interdiction of boats possibly containing asylum seek-ers remains an active part of U.S. migration control. For a comprehen-sive description of these operations, written by a Coast Guard captain and professor at the Coast Guard Academy, see Palmer, *Guarding the Coast: Alien Migrant Interdiction Operations at Sea,* 29 Conn. L.Rev. 1565 (1997). After 1994, the practice generally reverted to the pre-1992 pattern, incorporating some form of shipboard screening, usually using a "credible fear" threshold. Those who pass the screening are brought to the United States for full consideration of asylum. When renewed instability and political violence in Haiti in 2004 led to the forced departure of President Aristide, President George W. Bush ordered increased U.S. Coast Guard controls off the coast of Haiti. Over 900 persons were returned at a time of great uncertainty about governmen-tal authority within Haiti; none among the interdicted were found to meet the screening standard allowing them to travel to the United States. Press accounts raised doubt about the seriousness of any effort to identify potential returnees who might have a credible fear of persecu-tion, and President Bush even stated that he had made it "abundantly clear to the Coast Guard that we will turn back any refugee [sic] that attempts to reach our shore." *See* Frelick, *"Abundantly Clear": Refoule-ment,* 19 Geo. Immigr. L.J. 245, 245–47 (2005).

Thus U.S. practice has mixed interdiction with a wide variety of screening and adjudication measures:

(1) Threshold screening (usually employing a "credible fear" standard, though apparently interpreted more stringently in some

specific interdiction efforts than in others), which leads to full adjudication of asylum claims in the United States for those screened in. This has been the most common form of interdiction, but it produced discomfort in the early 1990s because the U.S. adjudications proceeded slowly and returns of rejected asylum seekers seemed unlikely.

(2) No screening, returning all interdicted passengers to the country of origin—the practice at issue in *Sale*.

(3) Full offshore adjudication of the persecution claim, aboard ship or at Guantánamo, leading to U.S. admission in full refugee status under INA § 207 for those whose claims are found valid. This was used by the Clinton administration for a short period in 1994, but the boat outflow from Haiti outpaced the adjudication capacity.

(4) Some type of screening but with protection provided to the screened-in only in offshore safe havens or in countries other than the United States—policy for Cubans for a short while in the mid-1990s (discussed further in Chapter Eleven, Section C).

(5) No screening but with the same limited non-U.S. venues for protection for those who chose to remain—the pattern for Haitians in late 1994, with haven only at Guantánamo.

(6) Maritime pickup with protection generously available in the United States after only minimal review to screen out those with criminal or terrorist records. This has sometimes been the approach with Cubans "rescued" at sea aboard small craft or homemade rafts (also discussed in Chapter Eleven, Section C).

Which of these approaches are most consistent with the premises of the international refugee regime? Which, if any, would make for the best U.S. policy? Which best balance political constraints with genuine protection?

From 1982 through 2006, the U.S. Coast Guard interdicted over 215,000 individuals. Over half have come from Haiti, 60,000 from Cuba, and 30,000 from the Dominican Republic. Yearly totals varied widely—as high as 40,627 in fiscal year 1994 and 64,443 in 1996, sandwiched around 10,584 in 1995, then declining to a low of 2,194 in 1997. Recent years have seen 10,899 individuals interdicted in fiscal 2004, 9,455 in 2005, and 6,796 in 2006. U.S. Coast Guard, Alien Migrant Interdictions, Migrant Statistics, available at <http://www.uscg.mil/hq/g-cp/comrel/factfile/>.

## 4. COMPARATIVE PERSPECTIVES

### a. *Australia*

Other countries facing the arrival of increasing numbers of asylum seekers have sometimes adopted policies similar to the U.S. interdiction program. In a widely publicized incident that began in August 2001, Australia refused landing to the *M/V Tampa*, a Norwegian vessel that had picked up over 400 asylum seekers, mostly from Afghanistan, from a foundering vessel near Australian waters. Irregular boat arrivals had been increasing in Australia, and the government had already adopted severe measures meant to discourage such attempts, although it had not sent its ships to sea to turn away approaching boats. After a standoff that lasted several weeks, including stays resulting from litigation in Australia's courts that ultimately upheld the government's action, Australia made arrangements for most of the *Tampa* asylum seekers to be taken to the small island nation of Nauru for refugee screening. New Zealand also accepted 150 of them for processing, and for resettlement if they qualified as refugees.

Australia guaranteed that Nauru would not be left with any who proved their refugee status (which it honored, but generally without accepting the refugees in Australia), and it agreed to pay all costs associated with the process, including for the construction of camps and facilities. Nauru accepted some additional asylum seekers from a few later boats on the same terms, but thereafter Australia made similar arrangements with Papua New Guinea, which then became the main site for such processing. Fewer than 70 from the *Tampa* were found to be refugees. The boat flow receded, and the Australian government's actions were seen as highly beneficial to the incumbent government in elections that followed in November 2001. *See* Kirtley, Note, *The Tampa Incident: The Legality of* Ruddock v. Vardalis *under International Law and the Implications of Australia's New Asylum Policy*, 41 Colum. J. Transnat'l L. 251, 253–56, 281, 289–90 (2002).

Most of the commentary has been harshly critical of Australia's actions, especially on the grounds that it did not honor the "right to seek and enjoy asylum from persecution" set forth in Article 14 of the Universal Declaration of Human Rights. See, e.g., Bostock, *The International Legal Obligations Owed to the Asylum Seekers on the MV Tampa*, 14 Int'l J. Refugee L. 279 (2002); Crock, *In the Wake of the Tampa: Conflicting Visions of International Refugee Law in the Management of Refugee Flows*, 12 Pac. Rim L. & Pol'y J. 49 (2003); Peyser, *"Pacific Solution"?: The Sinking Right to Seek Asylum in Australia*, 11 Pac. Rim L. & Pol'y J. 431 (2002). As one writer said:

> The assumption underlying Australia's adoption of the practice of interdiction—that extraterritorial interception (or, in the case of the *Tampa*, interception *within* the territorial sea) of asylum seekers is permissible—is generally not accepted. Article 33 of the Refugee Convention expressly refers to *refoulement* "in any manner whatsoever." Chain *refoulement* by causing a person to return to another place from which *refoulement* occurs is prohibited. Rejection of asylum seekers at the frontier is also prohibited by this phrase and agreement as to the interpretation of the Convention on this point is reflected in numerous conclusions of the Executive Committee of the UNHCR. Article 3(1) of the General Assembly's Declaration on Territorial Asylum also recognizes the principle of nonrejection at the frontier.

Just as other human rights obligations cannot be avoided by extraterritorial exercises of jurisdiction, so the obligation not to reject refugees and asylum seekers at the frontier cannot be avoided by the exercise of extraterritorial jurisdiction by a state that luxuriates in the absence of land borders.

Ultimately, the legality of the interdiction program depends on the risks of *refoulement*. No asylum seeker has been returned directly to a place of persecution. On the other hand, Australia has not put in place satisfactory safeguards against chain *refoulement*. Several vessels have now been escorted back to Indonesian waters, and the Australian government clearly wants boats to return to Indonesia in the future. Indonesia is not a party to the Refugee Convention.

Mathew, *Australian Refugee Protection in the Wake of the Tampa*, 96 Am.J. Int'l L. 661, 666–67 (2002).

Another writer reached a more positive judgment, finding that Australia had complied with the principle of *nonrefoulement*:

Abuse of the asylum status determination system erodes the perceived validity of asylum procedures in general, wastes resources that could be better spent protecting "true" refugees, and contributes to the overburdening of the system. Despite its many failings, [Australia's agreement with Nauru and New Zealand for offshore screening does] send a clear message to illegal immigrants that they may end up in a safe country, but one with fewer economic opportunities available than Australia and other Western nations. For refugees who are genuinely fleeing persecution or torture, temporary protection in a country like Nauru can provide respite from the persecution that induced their flight. For economic migrants posing as refugees, however, offshore temporary protection regimes send the clear message that they may end up in a safe territory, but one where their economic opportunities will not necessarily be greater than in their country of origin. * * *

Australia's new refugee policy is also beneficial insofar as it removes incentives for economic migrants to pose as refugees, while deterring people-traffickers from illegally and hazardously transporting asylum seekers to Australia via Indonesia. Finally, the agreement is salutary, because it encourages international burden-sharing *vis-à-vis* refugees, while vividly highlighting the need for UNHCR to facilitate the creation of a more effective burden-sharing regime. * * * [S]uch regimes should be tolerated by the international community, if not actively encouraged.

Kirtley, *supra*, 14 Colum. J. Transnat'l L., at 293, 298–99.

### b. United Kingdom

In 2001, the same year that the Australian government refused to allow the *Tampa* to bring asylum seekers to shore, British officials took offshore action against asylum seekers arriving by air, not by sea. They stationed British immigration officers at the Prague airport to inspect the travel documents of passengers, to question them as deemed necessary, and to refuse boarding on planes bound for the United Kingdom if the person appeared unqualified. The clear objective was to respond to a recent surge in asylum applications regarded as marginal or frivolous filed by Czech citizens, mostly from the Roma minority. The UK might have achieved a similar result by imposing a visa requirement, but it evidently regarded that step as an unwelcome inconvenience if applied to all Czech citizens.

The British pre-inspection effort did limit the number of travelers from Prague who applied for asylum in the UK, but it was challenged as discriminating against the Roma and inconsistent with the 1951 Convention. In 2002 a British court upheld the program, reasoning that the pre-inspection procedure was no different from a visa control system, and that there was no requirement that the United Kingdom admit to its territory all individuals wishing to seek asylum. The case was appealed to the House of Lords, which issued its ruling in 2004, after the inspectors had been removed from Prague. The House of Lords concluded that the pre-inspection screening at the Prague airport had discriminated against the Roma, but ruled that the refusal to allow Czech nationals to travel to the UK did not violate international law, in part because the travelers were not prohibited from going to another country to claim asylum. The court emphasized its view that international law requires a state to protect those within its territory, not individuals trying to leave another territory to travel to the UK. *Regina (European Roma Rights) v. Immigration Officer at Prague Airport*, [2005] 2 A.C. 1 (H.L. 2004).

The heart of the ruling on the application of the 1951 Convention was set forth in the opinion of Lord Bingham of Cornhill (four of the five Law Lords hearing the case expressly supported this reasoning):

> [A]ttention must be drawn to certain features of the Convention. First, it was (like its predecessor) a convention relating to the status of refugees. The focus of the Convention was on the treatment of refugees within the receiving state. Secondly, and like most international conventions, it represented a compromise between competing interests, in this case between the need to ensure humane treatment of the victims of oppression on the one hand and the wish of sovereign states to maintain control over those seeking entry to their territory on the other. Thirdly, the Convention was exclusively directed to those who are "outside the country" of their nationality or, in the case of stateless persons, "outside the country" of their former habitual residence. It is only to persons meeting that definition, expressed in article 1A(2) of the Convention, that the Convention applies at all, unless they have been considered to be refugees under earlier arrangements. Fourthly, the Convention is directed towards those who are within the receiving state. Fifthly, the

French verb *refouler* and the French noun *refoulement* are, in article 33, the subject of a stipulative definition: they must be understood as having the meaning of the English verb and noun "return".* * *

In his work *Convention Relating to the Status of Refugees* (Institute of Jewish Affairs, 1953), Nehemiah Robinson wrote:

> Article 33 concerns refugees who have gained entry into the territory of a Contracting State, legally or illegally, but not to refugees who seek entrance into this territory. In other words, Article 33 lays down the principle that once a refugee has gained asylum (legally or illegally) from persecution, he cannot be deprived of it by ordering him to leave for, or forcibly returning him to, the place where he was threatened with persecution, or by sending him to another place where that threat exists, but that no Contracting State is prevented from refusing entry in this territory to refugees at the frontier. In other words, if a refugee has succeeded in eluding the frontier guards, he is safe; if he has not, it is his hard luck.

This opinion was endorsed by Weis ["The United Nations Declaration on Territorial Asylum" (1969) CYIL 92, 123–124] and Grahl–Madsen [*The Status of Refugees in International Law*, vol. 2, at 94 (1972)]. It was upheld by a majority of the United States Supreme Court in *Sale*. It has been upheld by the High Court of Australia in *Minister for Immigration and Multicultural Affairs v. Ibrahim*, [(2000)] 204 CLR 1, para 136, and *Minister for Immigration and Multicultural Affairs v. Khawar* (2002) 210 CLR 1, para 42. * * *

The House was referred to no judicial authority to contrary effect. * * * In 1967 the United Nations adopted a Declaration on Territorial Asylum which provided, in article 3, that no person entitled to invoke article 14 of the Universal Declaration of Human Rights should be subjected to measures such as rejection at the frontier, but a conference held in 1977 to embody this and other provisions in a revised convention ended in failure. As Gummow J put it in *Ibrahim* 204 CLR 1, para 142, in his judgment given in October 2000, "there have been attempts which it is unnecessary to recount here to broaden the scope of the Convention itself by a Draft United Nations Convention on Territorial Asylum but these collapsed more than twenty years ago."

* * * [T]he Vienna Convention on the Law of Treaties * * *, reflecting principles of customary international law, requires a treaty to be interpreted in the light of its object and purpose. But I would make an important caveat. However generous and purposive its approach to interpretation, the

court's task remains one of interpreting the written document to which the contracting states have committed themselves. It must interpret what they have agreed. It has no warrant to give effect to what they might, or in an ideal world would, have agreed. * * * It is also noteworthy that article 31(4) of the Vienna Convention requires a special meaning to be given to a term if it is established that the parties so intended. That rule is pertinent, first, because the Convention gives a special, defined, meaning to "refugee" and, secondly, because the parties have made plain that "refouler", whatever its wider dictionary definition, is in this context to be understood as meaning "return". It is in principle possible for a court to imply terms even into an international convention. But this calls for great circumspection since, as was said in *Brown v Stott* [2003] 1 AC 681, 703, "it is generally to be assumed that the parties have included the terms which they wished to include and on which they were able to agree, omitting other terms which they did not wish to include or on which they were not able to agree," and caution is needed "if the risk is to be averted that the contracting parties may, by judicial interpretation, become bound by obligations which they did not expressly accept and might not have been willing to accept." * * *

[2005] 2 A.C. at 29–31.

Lord Hope of Craighead added the following:

* * * What the Convention does is assure refugees of the rights and freedoms set out in Chapters I to V when they are in countries that are not their own. It does not require the state to abstain from controlling the movements of people outside its borders who wish to travel to it in order to claim asylum. It lacks any provisions designed to meet the additional burdens which would follow if a prohibition to that effect had been agreed to. The conclusion must be that steps which are taken to control the movements of such people who have not yet reached the state's frontier are not incompatible with the acceptance of the obligations which arise when refugees have arrived in its territory. To argue that such steps are incompatible with the principle of good faith as they defeat the object and purpose of the treaty is to argue for the enlargement of the obligations which are to be found in the Convention. * * * I am not persuaded that this is the way in which the principle of good faith can operate.

*Id.* at 52–53.

## Notes and Questions

1.  Other European countries have also seen major increases in the arrival of asylum seekers by small boat, especially to enclaves or islands that are Spanish territory but are located on or close to the African continent.

The first such surge went to Ceuta and Melilla, small Spanish outposts on Morocco's north coast, but Spain responded with enhanced fencing. Summer 2006 then brought a major jump in arrivals in the Canary Islands, some 75 miles out into the Atlantic from southwestern Morocco. As of early September 2006, over 20,000 Africans had been intercepted in the Canary Islands that year, as compared to 4,751 for all of 2005. Roman, *A New Record for Africans Risking Boat Route to Europe,* Wash. Post, Sept. 4, 2006, at A14. Italy and Malta have also received waterborne asylum seekers across the Mediterranean. These European countries, with some help from the EU, have responded with enhanced naval patrols, high fences and other physical barriers, and cooperative efforts undertaken with North African countries to prevent departures. (Most of these boat arrivals have been nationals of sub-Saharan Africa, rather than nationals of the countries from which the boats depart.) *See* Brand, *Spain Appeals for EU Help on Migrants*, Wash. Post, Sept. 21, 2006; Leidel, *Tighter EU Borders Forcing Refugees to Take Bigger Risks*, Deutsche Welle, March 23, 2006 (available at <http://www.dw-world.de/dw/article/0,2144,1941393,00.html>).

Migrants challenge razor wire and double fencing, trying to cross from Morocco into the Spanish enclave of Melilla, August 2006 (Photo: UK Indymedia)

2.   In support of an evolutionary understanding of the requirements of the UN treaties, some have pointed (as Lord Bingham acknowledged) to Article 3 of the 1967 United Nations Declaration on Territorial Asylum, GA Res. 2312 (XXII), 22 U.N. GAOR Supp. (No. 16) at 81, U.N. Doc. A/6716 (1967), adopted by the UN General Assembly, which does call for states to apply *nonrefoulement* so as to include nonrejection at the frontier. (Mathew also refers to this Declaration in her criticism of Australian policy, excerpted above.) But the full text of that article of the Declaration, adopted in the same year as the 1967 Protocol, contains a significant (and perhaps surprising) qualification. It provides in relevant part:

1.  No person * * * shall be subjected to measures such as rejection at the frontier or, if he has already entered the territory in which he seeks asylum, expulsion or compulsory return to a State where he may be subjected to persecution.

2.  Exception may be made to the foregoing principle only for overriding reasons of national security or in order to safeguard the population, as in the case of a mass influx. * * *

What is the significance of the exception, particularly in the way it is linked to mass influx? How far does the exception extend? Does it apply even to *refoulement* of persons who have entered national territory? Would it justify the Haitian interdiction upheld in *Sale*? Australia's refusal to let the *Tampa* reach Australian shores? The British response to a sharp increase in asylum applications in the late 1990s? The response of Spain, Italy, and Malta to the increase in boat arrivals from Africa?

### c.  *Further Issues Raised by a Comparative Review of Interdiction*

The most obvious reason for questioning the judicial conclusions regarding U.S. and Australian interdiction, as well as the dictum in the *Prague Airport* case construing the Convention, is the logic underlying refugee protection to begin with. What good are the rights guaranteed in the Convention if people cannot access them? Thus the "object and purpose" of the Convention—traditional elements of treaty interpretation—seem to point strongly in the direction of permitting access. The governments' counterargument says in essence that the treaties have more complex objectives and purposes than pure refugee protection. The contracting governments meant to provide protection, but without greatly undercutting their traditional sovereign rights to control migration. A rough—very rough—balance was maintained, in this view, by leaving in government hands certain crude tools to meter their obligations or make them politically manageable. Preventing the arrival of asylum seekers was not rendered unlawful, at least in times of threats to the "national security" or prospective "mass influx." Without this crude reassurance, states might never have entered into the treaty commitments in the first place.

If one rejects this tacit argument on behalf of the governments, the opposing position still leaves further questions about the outer boundaries of the resulting doctrine. Under this more explicitly humanitarian view, governments are obligated not to impede arrival of potential asylum seekers. Does this mean that visa systems are invalid, or at least invalid if they lack (as most do) an exception mandating issuance of a visa to a person who makes a threshold showing (perhaps a "credible fear of persecution") to the consular officer—or even to the airline official controlling boarding? The House of Lords, in a portion of the *Prague Airport* opinion (para. 16) not reprinted above, found that the treaty did not cast doubt on visa systems, largely because the refugee definition explicitly covers only persons outside their country of nationality, whereas nearly all applicants apply for their visas in the country of nationality. But if one is relying primarily on the treaty's object and purpose (or on evolving humanitarian understandings) in order to reject unduly restrictive interpretations, giving such weight to the "outside the country" limitation seems equally artificial and sharply out of keeping with the refugee protection object of the Convention. Under this perspective, the central concern of the treaty is clearly the threat of persecution. The requirement for being outside the country of origin is a logistical detail, and obviously would be satisfied quickly if only the threatened person were given a visa, allowed to board the aircraft, and thereby escape to the territory of the visa-granting country.

Consider further implications, suggested in part by the arguments of Andrew Shacknove in his article, *Who is a Refugee?*, 95 Ethics 274 (1985), excerpted in Chapter One. Shacknove rejects the "alienage" requirement of the traditional definition—the requirement that a person be outside the country of origin in order to be counted as a refugee—and argues instead that the central notion underlying that provision is being "so situated that international assistance is possible." Those outside their country of origin simply constitute one subset of the class of persons within reach of international assistance. Moreover, the demonstrated repertoire of potential international responses has certainly expanded in the two decades since Shacknove wrote—to include not only aid in place provided by the international community despite the home country's objection or resistance, but also humanitarian military intervention (under UN auspices or by NATO or another coalition of the willing) to end the persecution. International action could also take the form of affirmative rescue, stationing boats or aircraft in temporarily secured areas to facilitate escape—doubtless a less daunting task than full-scale humanitarian intervention to oust the abusing regime and help develop a functioning rights-observing government in its place. With this wider repertoire, the class of refugees or potential refugees to whom the international community owes concerted action is presumably quite broad.

### Questions

1. Why should the obligation of a state party to the Convention reach only so far as avoiding measures (like visas and interdiction) that *impede* the asylum seeker's travel? Should it carry more affirmative duties to *facilitate* the relocation of threatened persons, including proactive rescue efforts, if we are really to serve the core object and purpose of the Convention?

2. If that conclusion seems too extreme, why is that the case? Without such extension, isn't the Convention then simply a "clean hands" document—merely barring states from anything too overt or obvious that implicates them in persecution carried out elsewhere—rather than a framework for a real commitment to address the broad the problem of global persecution? Or are there other reasons why the Convention pulls up short of these conclusions, instead serving a more modest, but still important, "palliative" role—to use Professor Hathaway's term (*see* Hathaway & Neve, *Making International Refugee Law Relevant Again: a Proposal for Collectivized and*

*Solution-oriented Protection,* 10 Harv. Hum. Rts. J. 115, 140 (1997))—in those (frequent) circumstances where the international community is unable or unwilling to take more costly actions to end persecution at the source? Nonetheless, accepting a mere palliative role is to concede that the Convention's protective object and purpose are indeed often bounded by practical considerations. Is that what the three high courts (U.S., UK, and Australia) relied on in sustaining the *non-entree* devices examined in this Section?

## SECTION B.   EXPEDITED REMOVAL

In 1996 Congress enacted an expedited removal procedure that generally applies to arriving aliens who seek admission to the United States but have no documents, have fraudulent or invalid documents, or have committed immigration fraud in the past. INA § 235(b)(1) (applying expedited removal to arriving aliens covered by the inadmissibility grounds set forth in § 212(a)(6)(C) or (7)). Mandatory detention during the initial portion of the procedure, possibly followed by detention as a matter of discretion during later stages, constitutes an important component of the process. The House Report that accompanied this legislation explained:

> One urgent problem in recent years has been the arrival at U.S. airports of smuggled aliens who possess fraudulent or otherwise invalid travel documents, or who have destroyed their documents en route, and who make claim to asylum in order to be able to remain in the U.S. Because of delays in the asylum system, hearings were often scheduled for months later. If not detained, the aliens would most often disappear and become long-term illegal residents.

H.R.Rep. No. 104–879, 104th Cong., 2d Sess. 107 (1997).

Another part of the motivation for developing this system derived from a wish to create an alternative or supplement to interdiction to cope with mass influxes. Though the Supreme Court in *Sale* had found no legal obstacle to returning interdicted individuals without refugee screening, discomfort with such a process as a matter of policy lingered. Some technique that might permit more thorough or effective screening on dry land in the United States, while still preventing access to a lengthy asylum procedure unless the person passed a reasonable and speedily applied threshold test, appeared to hold some promise. In fact, the major legislative debate over expedited removal in 1996 pitted a proposal that would have authorized expedited removal only for use in time of declared immigration emergency against one which applied the procedure to all persons fitting certain initial criteria. Congress chose the latter model.

## 1.   AT PORTS OF ENTRY

The law applies expedited removal at all times to "arriving aliens," defined in the regulations to mean aliens seeking admission at ports of entry and also aliens interdicted at sea and brought to U.S. territory for processing. 8 C.F.R. § 1.1(q). Such persons are subject to expedited removal if they are judged inadmissible under INA § 212(a)(6)(C) (relating to past or present attempts to obtain admission or other immigration benefits through fraud or misrepresentation), or § 212(a)(7) (lack of a valid passport, visa, or other required document).[2] The statute also gives the Secretary of Homeland Security (formerly the Attorney General) discretion to apply such a procedure to anyone who entered without inspection and has been present in the United States for less than two years. We will consider the exercise of that authority in Section B3 below.

The expedited removal statute authorizes an immigration officer who finds a noncitizen inadmissible on the specified grounds to order him removed "without further hearing or review unless the alien indicates either an intention to apply for asylum under section 208 or a fear of persecution." INA § 235(b)(1)(A)(i). Under the regulations and operating manuals, such an order may be issued only after an extended interview in secondary inspection, followed by supervisory review of the officer's conclusion that the person meets the criteria for expedited removal. *See* 8 C.F.R. § 235.3. If the person claims asylum or asserts a fear of return, however, the inspector may not issue a removal order. Instead, after completing the interview and making a summary record of the results, she arranges for the noncitizen to be sent to a detention facility where he will be interviewed by a specially trained asylum officer no sooner than 48 hours later. 8 C.F.R. § 208.30. By statute, the noncitizen may consult with anyone of his choosing after secondary inspection and before this interview, but at no expense to the government and without causing "unreasonable delay." The asylum officer's duty is to determine whether the individual has a "credible fear of persecution," a term initially developed for use in interdiction. But in the expedited removal setting, it is specifically defined in the statute, INA § 235(b)(1)(B)(v), as follows:

> a significant possibility, taking into account the credibility of the statements made by the alien in support of the alien's claim and such other facts as are known to the officer, that the alien could establish eligibility for asylum under section 208.

If upon interview the asylum officer does not find a credible fear, he or she issues an expedited removal order, but the noncitizen may secure one additional review of the credible fear issue, before an immigration judge in a special procedure that must be completed within seven days. If unsuccessful there, he is subject to immediate removal on the basis of the order previously issued. If either the asylum officer or the immigration judge finds a credible fear, however, the person is scheduled for a full merits hearing in immigration court, and may be released on parole while his case is pending. Thus the immigration officer doing the first interview finally disposes of the case only if there is no request for

---

**2.** An obscurely worded exception exempts Cubans arriving by air from the coverage of expedited removal. INA § 235(b)(1)(F).

asylum or other expression of fear. Otherwise the case goes on to an asylum officer to apply a threshold screening standard. If that decision is negative, the person has another chance to tell her story to an immigration judge, in order to secure a full hearing.

There is one other avenue toward expanded review of the initial determination by the inspector. Persons who claim under oath to be U.S. citizens or to be returning to the United States after previous admission as a refugee, asylee, or lawful permanent resident are entitled to pursue that claim before an immigration judge. Such "status claimants" may also obtain a limited form of individual judicial review in habeas corpus, whereas individualized court access is essentially denied to others in expedited removal, even those who claim asylum but fail to prove a credible fear. INA § 242(e).

Departure under an expedited removal order carries the same consequences as that based on an order issued by an immigration judge. In particular, when issued to an arriving alien, the order makes the person inadmissible for five years, subject to a limited waiver. *See* INA § 212(a)(9)(A)(i). But immigration officers interviewing persons who initially seem subject to expedited removal have discretion to allow them to withdraw their applications for admission. *See* INA § 235(a)(4), 8 C.F.R. § 235.4(a). The individual has no absolute right to withdraw the application; withdrawal must be approved by the inspector. The stakes are high in this decision, because withdrawal, though it ordinarily entails immediate return to the country of departure, is not considered removal under a formal order. Thus the person incurs no bar to reapplying for admission later—for example, after returning home and correcting any technical problem with the visa they initially presented. About 70 percent of noncitizens potentially subject to expedited removal in fiscal year 2004 (a total of 184,000) were permitted to withdraw their applications for admission. The remaining 55,000 were placed in expedited removal proceedings, where 7,900 expressed a fear of return and so were referred to an asylum officer. About 94 percent of that group were found to have a credible fear and so were taken out of the expedited removal process and scheduled for a full hearing before an immigration judge. DHS Office of Immigration Statistics, Immigration Enforcement Actions: 2004, at 6 (Nov. 2005). Expedited removal (usually involving people who express no fear of return) now accounts for a high proportion of annual removals under formal orders, as shown in Table 9.1. *See* Martin, *Two Cheers for Expedited Removal in the New Immigration Laws,* 40 Va. J.Int'l L.673, 682–88 (2000).

A research team based at the University of California, Hastings College of Law, undertook its own Expedited Removal Study by analyzing INS data for FY 1997–99. The study found that during this time Mexican nationals accounted for 86 percent of expedited removals. The overwhelming majority of expedited removals took place at land ports of entry. In fact, the top ten land ports of entry accounted for about 81 percent of all expedited removals. The referral rate for a credible fear

**Table 9.1**
**Total and Expedited Removals: 1994–2004**

| Fiscal year | Total removals* | Expedited removals |
|---|---|---|
| 2004 | 202,842 | 41,752 |
| 2003 | 189,368 | 43,758 |
| 2002 | 150,542 | 34,536 |
| 2001 | 178,026 | 69,841 |
| 2000 | 186,222 | 85,926 |
| 1999 | 181,072 | 89,170 |
| 1998 | 173,146 | 76,078 |
| 1997 | 114,432 | 23,242 |
| 1996 | 69,680 | N/A |
| 1995 | 50,924 | N/A |
| 1994 | 45,674 | N/A |

\* Counts only departures under formal orders of removal.

Source: DHS Office of Immigration Statistics, Immigration Enforcement Actions: 2004, Table 2 (Nov. 2005)

interview was much higher at airports than at land border ports of entry. Women were removed through expedited removal at a higher rate than men from the same country. For example, the percentage of women from China, Guatemala, Haiti, Nigeria and the Philippines who were removed through expedited removal was 25 to 30 percent higher than the percentage of men from those countries whose removals were expedited. *See* Musalo, *et. al., The Expedited Removal Study: Report on the First Three Years of Implementation of Expedited Removal,* 15 Notre Dame J.L. Ethics & Pub. Pol'y, 1, 42–70 (2001).

## 2. POINTS OF CONTROVERSY

In the view of its proponents, the expedited removal system provides a focused and discriminate deterrent by providing for removal within a few hours or days of those who lack proper documents or commit fraud, while still allowing a full hearing for genuine asylum seekers. Its critics have argued that it is inappropriate and unnecessary, that it is applied inconsistently, that genuine asylum seekers could find it hard to initiate a claim in this setting or to have it heard fairly, and that the detention features of the system are especially onerous. We consider the debate in more detail here, subdivided to address the separate parts of the process that have come under challenge. At various points we will refer to a 2005 report by the U.S. Commission on International Religious Freedom (CIRF), a bipartisan independent governmental body created in 1998 by the International Religious Freedom Act, Pub. L. 105–292, 112 Stat. 2787 (1998). The Commission was specifically mandated by statute to undertake a study in order to assess various concerns about implementation of expedited removal. CIRF, Report on Asylum Seekers in Expedited Removal (2005).[3]

### a. Identifying Asylum Seekers

An early concern was that persons wishing to claim asylum would not find their way into the credible fear procedure. They might be too intimidated in the setting of the inspection office at the port of entry, where the initial questioning occurs, and so might not even voice a fear of return before being hurried back across the border or onto a return flight. Or expressions of such fear might be ignored or overridden. Or the noncitizens might not realize that that interview would be their only opportunity to request protection.

INS tried to address some of these concerns in its regulations, 8 C.F.R. § 235.3, by requiring a fairly extensive initial interview by the inspector in every expedited removal case (whether or not asylum was requested), usually taking an hour or more and always resulting in a sworn statement. The individual is to initial each page of the statement and to sign the document at the end. That statement, written out by the inspector (in English) as the interview proceeds, summarizes the person's story but is not a verbatim transcript. The regulations require an extended interview in order both to gain full information that will foster an accurate decision by the officer on whether the stated inadmissibility grounds apply and to provide an opportunity for the person to request asylum. The regulations also mandate review of the file by a high-ranking supervisor before an expedited removal order is issued.

Further, INS designed the form that structures the inspector's interview so as to assure the conveyance of certain key information and the posing of specific questions about fears of return. Record of Sworn Statement in Proceedings under Section 235(b)(1) of the Act, Form I–867A/B. In an expedited removal case, the examining officer in secondary inspection must read the following, early in the interview, in a language that the noncitizen can understand:

> U.S. law provides protection to certain persons who face persecution, harm or torture upon return to their home country. If you fear or have a concern about being removed from the United States or about being sent home, you should tell me so during the interview because you will not have another chance. You will have the opportunity to speak privately and confidentially to another officer about your fear and concern. That officer will determine if you should remain in the United States and not be removed because of that fear.

Toward the end of the interview, the officer must pose the following questions, spelled out on the Form I 867A/B, and record the individual's answers:

**3.** Volume I contains the Commission's Findings and Recommendations, and Volume II reprints a series of expert studies and statistical compilations chartered by the Commission. The report (vol. 1, p. 29) contains a helpful flow chart mapping the intricately complex steps involved in the expedited removal process.

Q.   Why did you leave your home country or country of last residence?

A.

Q.   Do you have any fear or concern about being returned to your home country or being removed from the United States?

A.

Q.   Would you be harmed if you are returned to your home country or country of last residence?

A.

Q.   Do you have any questions or is there anything you would like to add?

A.

Inclusion of these required advisories and questions alleviated some of the initial concerns, but problems persist. For example:

> With regard to secondary inspections, there have been some accounts of aliens being forced to wait for hours before an inspector can examine them. Some aliens have reported being shackled to a bench for more than 12 hours—often without food. * * * In a few cases, the responsible INS detention or deportation officer has neglected to notify the appropriate asylum office that an alien needs a credible fear interview, thus leaving the individual waiting in detention for days or even weeks.

Osuna & Mariani, *Expedited Removal: Authorities, Implementation, and Ongoing Policy and Practice Issues*, 97–11 Imm. Briefings 10, 10–11 (1997).

The study by the Commission on International Religious Freedom identified potentially more disturbing problems. The Commission did detailed analysis of data from 2001 and 2003, examined closely the files involved in a random sample of 855 cases, and also sent observers to a total of 79 proceedings. Although it generally accepted that policies and procedures governing the interview were sound, it identified significant deficiencies in implementation. Officers often did not read the full set of questions required on the I–867A/B form, though in 95 percent of observed cases they read at least one of the key queries. Further, 15% of noncitizens who expressed fear of return in the observed proceedings were removed without access to asylum officers for credible fear interviews, based on the inspector's judgment that the expression of fear did not qualify. "The 12 cases that were not referred included expressions of economic fear, but also fear related to political, religious, or ethnic persecution, as well as unspecified fear, fear of spouse abuse, and fear of smugglers. Under DHS regulations, all of these aliens should have been referred for a credible fear interview." I CIRF Report 54. The Commission recommended the development of clearer guidance to govern this part of the process, structural changes to accomplish better coordination among the governmental agencies involved, and enhanced quality assurance measures, including expanded use of videotapes of the secondary inspection interviews. *Id.* at 8–9.

#### b.  *The Credible Fear Interview*

After the expedited removal provision was enacted, critics voiced concerns that asylum seekers would not have a fair opportunity to tell their stories during the credible fear process, owing to fatigue after a long journey or predictable reticence deriving from the fact of detention or from interrogation by officials in a wholly unfamiliar setting. Further, the limited statutory opportunity for consultation with others, especially since it must not cause undue delay or be at the expense of the government, would preclude a minimally adequate role for counsel.

INS responded in its initial design of the detailed procedures by setting a guideline (though not one included in the regulations themselves) that the credible fear interview would not take place earlier than 48 hours after the person's arrival in a detention center following referral from secondary inspection. *See* 62 Fed.Reg. 10,312, 10,320 (1997) (descriptive statement accompanying the expedited removal regulations). Most interviews are held 2–14 days after arrival. I CIRF Report 29. This timing was also meant to afford additional time and a setting for consultation, which could include consultation with counsel. In some detention facilities, arrangements have been made with nongovernmental organizations (NGOs) to facilitate meetings with attorneys or accredited NGO representatives before the asylum officer interview. But the CIRF Report found that many of the over 180 different detention facilities housing persons involved in expedited removal lack any such arrangements. I CIRF Report 59, 70–71. Furthermore, the Commission found that, of those represented by counsel, 25% were granted asylum in immigration court, whereas only 2% of those appearing without legal representation were successful. (This statistic really goes more to the role of counsel in regular immigration court asylum proceedings than to any issue unique to expedited removal.)

The credible fear process since the beginning has resulted in a very high approval rate. The Commission determined that asylum officers found credible fear in over 90 percent of cases in which they conducted an interview, and therefore referred the case onward for full proceedings before an immigration judge. Only one percent resulted in a negative credible fear determination. *Id.* at 4. (In the rest, apparently the request was abandoned or the person's status was otherwise resolved.) This high referral rate has muted some of the early criticism of procedural difficulties, including concerns about the adequacy of translation in these interviews. *See* Osuna & Mariani, *supra,* at 10–11. But the Commission, somewhat surprisingly, hinted that the approval rate may be too high. It added the following to its recommendations (I CIRF Report, at 76):

> The credible fear determination by an asylum officer, which—by law—is reviewable by an immigration judge, has proven success-

ful at ensuring that bona fide asylum seekers referred from the port of entry will not be removed without a full asylum hearing. The credible fear process fails, however, at making asylum more efficient by failing to screen out invalid claims and thus putting more strain on detention and immigration court resources. With a screen-in rate consistently exceeding 90 percent, and a negative determination rate of approximately 1 percent, some view the credible fear process itself as somewhat lacking in credibility. The Asylum Division subjects negative determinations to a much more intensive quality assurance process than positive determinations. * * * We would suggest that this bias in favor of positive credible fear determinations be addressed by subjecting them to similar quality assurance procedures * * * .

### c.   *Detention*

A recurrent criticism of expedited removal has focused on its mandatory detention provisions. *See generally* Taylor, *The 1996 Immigration Act: Detention and Related Issues,* 74 Interp.Rel. 209, 212–13 (1997). The expedited removal statute and regulations require detention, with very limited exceptions (for medical emergency or "legitimate law enforcement reasons"), throughout the initial stages of consideration by the inspector and the asylum officer. 8 C.F.R. § 235.3(b)(2)(iii). Release on parole is permitted, however, for those who pass the credible fear test, in the discretion of the director of the appropriate DHS field office. *See* 62 Fed.Reg. 10312, 10320 (1997) (supplemental information accompanying the main 1996 Act rulemaking). That decision is supposed to be guided by the usual release criteria, focusing on whether the person is likely to abscond or would be a danger to the community. Official policy states that release is a "viable option" once there has been a positive credible fear finding. Actual practice, however, has varied widely. I CIRF Report 2, 60–62. The Commission found that some districts regularly release those who have passed credible fear while a few rarely do. Release rates varied from 0.5 percent in New Orleans and 3.8 percent in Newark to 94 percent in San Antonio and 97.6 percent in Harlingen, Texas (2003 data). *Id.* at 33.

The Commission included the following in its recommendations (*id.* at 67–68):

> The INS established criteria for the release of asylum seekers (i.e. credible fear, community ties, establishment of identity, and not a suspected security risk) and these criteria continue, in theory, to be in effect at DHS. The Study, however, found that rates of release vary dramatically in different parts of the country and there is no evidence that these criteria are being applied consistently. Codification of the parole criteria into regulations will help ensure that DHS consistently detains those aliens who do not meet the criteria and releases those who do. * * *

In addition to codifying its criteria in formal regulations, DHS should create standardized forms and review procedures to address inconsistent application of its release criteria for asylum seekers. In trying to understand the wide variations in release rates, the Study found no evidence of quality assurance procedures to ensure that these criteria are being followed. Nor do DHS files usually include the information or forms necessary to ascertain whether or not the criteria are being applied. [DHS] should develop a form, * * * as well as associated national review procedures, to assess consistent application of the parole criteria.

Other Commission criticisms and recommendations addressed the conditions of detention for asylum seekers. These are considered in section C below.

### d. *Administrative and Judicial Review*

Critics have charged that the expedited removal procedures provide inadequate checks against erroneous decisions. Orders issued by inspectors without referral for a credible fear interview are not appealable, by statute. Negative credible fear determinations may be reviewed by an immigration judge, but in an oral procedure that the statute says is ordinarily to be completed within 24 hours, and in all cases in no longer than seven days. INA § 235(b)(1)(B)(iii)(III). Judicial review is available, through habeas corpus, only in extremely limited circumstances. A person subject to an expedited removal may go to court with an identity challenge—i.e., the petitioner alleges that she is not the person named in the expedited removal order, a highly unlikely eventuality. Status claimants (persons who claim they are U.S. citizens, lawful permanent residents, or previously admitted asylees or refugees) may also secure court review of that particular allegation after exhausting administrative review. But asylum seekers in expedited removal may not access the courts for consideration of any merits-related issue. *See* INA § 242(e)(2), (5). (All who pass credible fear screening, however, and are thus referred for full hearing of the asylum claim in immigration court, do have full access to the BIA and federal court for review if asylum is denied in those forums.)

The statute also provides for expedited hearing of challenges to "the validity of the system." INA § 242(e)(3). Such a case, however, must be filed within 60 days of the implementation of the challenged regulation, procedure, or policy, and venue lies only in the district court for the District of Columbia. It is is evident from the disposition of the primary case so far considered under this provision—a broad challenge to the overall system filed shortly after its effective date—that standing and other jurisdictional obstacles are considerable. *See American Immigration Lawyers Assn. v. Reno,* 18 F.Supp.2d 38 (D.D.C. 1998), *aff'd,* 199 F.3d 1352 (D.C.Cir.2000). The plaintiffs in that case raised several claims: that the INS failed to follow its own regulations, that the regulations governing secondary inspection were inconsistent with the statute (by limiting an arriving alien's communications with family and friends, providing inadequate language interpretation, and providing inadequate access to counsel), and that Congress did not intend expedited removal to apply to arriving aliens with facially valid visas. After rejecting these statute- and regulation-based claims, the court turned to the plaintiffs' constitutional due process challenges, namely that the expedited removal system "creates an unreasonably high danger that [those] entitled to enter the United States ... will be erroneously removed." 18 F.Supp. 3d at 58 (quoting the complaint). But it did not reach the question of what process is due in these circumstances, because it ruled that under long-standing Supreme Court and circuit precedent, "[w]hatever the procedure authorized by Congress is, it is due process as far as an alien denied entry is concerned." *United States ex rel. Knauff v. Shaughnessy,* 338 U.S. 537, 544, 70 S.Ct. 309, 94 L.Ed. 317 (1950). Accordingly, aliens have "no constitutional right[s] with respect to their applications for admission," citing *Landon v. Plasencia,* 459 U.S. 21, 32, 103 S.Ct. 321, 74 L.Ed.2d 21 (1982). Id. at 58–59 (internal quotation marks omitted).

### Notes and Questions

1.   What is your assessment of the expedited removal system? Are there sufficient safeguards for asylum seekers? In design? In practice? The CIRF Report found significant implementation deficiencies by DHS field offices (such as failures to provide all required advisories or to refer cases where the person mentioned a fear of return). If expedited removal were abolished, would this eliminate the risk that field office deficiencies could effectively undercut an arriving alien's right to apply for asylum? CIRF offered several recommendations intended to assure more consistent implementation and to facilitate monitoring by managers so as to detect and speedily correct departures from policy. Would sufficient safeguards exist in the current expedited removal system if the CIRF recommendations were adopted?

2.   The procedures require the secondary inspector to provide certain advisories and pose specific questions, but these do not include asking the noncitizen directly if he wishes to "apply for asylum." Some have argued that this specific question about asylum should be posed. See Schrag & Pistone, *The New Asylum Rule: Not Yet a Model of Fair Procedure,* 11 Geo. Immig. L.J. 267, 286 (1997). Should it be required?

3.   The congressionally chartered blue-ribbon Commission on Immigration Reform issued wide-ranging recommendations in the late 1990s on our overall immigration system, after a multi-year study and nationwide hearings. It concluded that expedited removal should apply only during migration emergencies, as had been proposed in some earlier versions of the 1996 legislation, and urged Congress to amend the law accordingly. Credible fear screening, the Commission asserted, is not an appropriate standard for deciding who will have access to the full procedure, except in migration emergencies, when an overloaded system might need some way to do preliminary sorting. It concluded, however, that the current credible fear procedure could appropriately function to decide which asylum seekers should be released during the pendency of full-fledged immigration court

proceedings. Continued confinement of those who could not satisfy the credible fear standard would provide a justifiable deterrent against future abuse of the asylum system. U.S. Commission on Immigration Reform, U.S. Refugee Policy: Taking Leadership 30–32 (1998).

Do you agree? The CIRF Report noted that only about one percent of asylum seekers who are referred to asylum officers are found to lack a credible fear, and it was mildly critical of that outcome. Would such a screening mechanism be workable in a migration emergency? Should the standard, at least in a migration emergency, be tightened? How would you do so?

4.  Accelerated asylum procedures occur at the border in France, Spain, the United Kingdom, Switzerland, and many more countries. *See* Hélène Lambert, Seeking Asylum: Comparative Law and Practice in Selected European Countries 20–41 (1994). Asylum seekers are generally detained in locked areas of the airport during these expedited proceedings. In France the average detention of asylum seekers during the accelerated procedure at the airport increased to seven days in the late 1990s. European Council on Refugees and Exiles, *European Asylum Systems: Legal and Social Conditions for Asylum Seekers and Refugees in Western Europe: France*, 2003, *available at* <http://www.ecre.org/conditions/2003/france2003.pdf> [series hereafter referred to as *ECRE Country Report*]. In Spain the asylum seeker must be admitted into the country if the decision has not been reached within six days. *ECRE Country Report: Spain,* 2003, *available at* <http://www.ecre.org/conditions/2003/spain2003final.pdf>; Fullerton, *Inadmissible in Iberia: The Fate of Asylum Seekers in Spain and Portugal*, 17 Int'l J. Refugee L. 659, 672–673 (2005). In the United Kingdom, asylum seekers at the airport can seek bail after seven days of detention. *ECRE Country Report: United Kingdom*, 2000, *available at* <http://www.ecre.org/conditions/2000/unitedkingdom.pdf>. In Switzerland, the maximum detention of asylum applicants at an airport facility cannot exceed 22 days. *ECRE Country Report: Switzerland,* 2003, *available at* <http://www.ecre.org/conditions/2003/switzerland2003.pdf>.

5.  The Office of the UNHCR has generally been critical of the U.S. expedited removal procedure. The Executive Committee of the UN High Commissioner's Programme, however, has adopted a formal resolution, known as Conclusion No. 30, that countenances special procedures "for dealing in an expeditious manner with applications which are considered to be so obviously without foundation as not to merit full examination at every level of the procedure." UNHCR, Exec. Comm. Conclusion No. 30 (XXXIV), *The Problem of Manifestly Unfounded or Abusive Applications for Refugee or Asylum,* ¶ 97.2, U.N. Doc. A/AC. 96/631 (1983). It went on: "Such applications have been termed either 'clearly abusive' or 'manifestly unfounded' and are to be defined as those which are clearly fraudulent or not related to the criteria for the granting of refugee status laid down in the 1951 United Nations Convention relating to the Status of Refugees nor to any other criteria justifying the granting of asylum." The Executive Committee also "[r]ecognized the substantive character of a decision that an application for refugee status is manifestly unfounded or abusive, [and] the grave consequences of an erroneous determination for the applicant." In that light it went on to specify standards for such a procedure:

(i) as in the case of all requests for the determination of refugee status or the grant of asylum, the applicant should be given a complete personal interview by a fully qualified official and, whenever possible, by an official of the authority competent to determine refugee status;

(ii) the manifestly unfounded or abusive character of an application should be established by the authority normally competent to determine refugee status;

(iii) an unsuccessful applicant should be enabled to have a negative decision reviewed before rejection at the frontier or forcible removal from the territory. Where arrangements for such a review do not exist, governments should give favourable consideration to their establishment. This review possibility can be more simplified than that available in the case of rejected applications which are not considered manifestly unfounded or abusive.

How does the U.S. expedited removal procedure measure up against these standards? How do the European procedures? Is judicial review required? Could the procedure remain truly expedited if judicial review were involved? For a generally favorable assessment of the U.S. procedure in light of the Conclusion's standards, see Martin, *Two Cheers for Expedited Removal, supra,* 40 Va. J. Int'l L. at 692–94.

## 3. EXPANSION BEYOND PORTS OF ENTRY

Expedited removal automatically applies by statute to all arriving aliens. What about aliens who enter surreptitiously across other parts of the border? As to this second group, the statute gives the Attorney General the "sole and unreviewable discretion" to designate for expedited removal aliens who have not been admitted or paroled into the United States, if they do not affirmatively show, to the satisfaction of an immigration officer, that they have been continuously present in the United States for the preceding two years. INA § 235(b)(1)(A)(iii), 8 C.F.R. § 235.3(b)(1). (Upon the creation of the Department of Homeland Security, this authority was transferred to the Secretary of Homeland Security.) This means that expedited removal can, but need not, be applied to all noncitizens who entered the United States without inspection and have been present less than two years.

The first use of this authority was precipitated by the landing of a boat full of Haitian asylum seekers on the beach at Key Biscayne, Florida, in October 2002, apparently after evading the normal Coast Guard interdiction. In order to be sure that such cases could be handled in summary fashion in the future, Attorney General Ashcroft designated for expedited removal "aliens who arrive in the United States by sea, either by boat or other means, who are not admitted or paroled, and who have not been physically present in the United States continuously for the two-year period prior to the determination of inadmissibility." Cuban nationals are excluded from the designation. 67 Fed. Reg. 68924 (2002). A central motivation for this designation may have been its effect in assuring that such persons would be subject to the stricter detention rules that apply in expedited removal. *See* INA § 235(b)(1)(B)(iii)(IV). We will consider that element further in Section C below.

In 2004 the Department of Homeland Security announced another major expansion of the expedited removal program. It applies to noncitizens who entered without inspection and who are stopped within 100 miles of the U.S.–Mexico border or the U.S.–Canada border, unless they can show that they have been continuously present in the United States for more than 14 days. 69 Fed. Reg. 48877 (2004). The published notice explained:

> DHS has a pressing need to improve the security and safety of the nation's land borders, and expanding expedited removal between ports of entry will provide DHS officers with a valuable tool to meet that objective. Presently DHS officers cannot apply expedited removal procedures to the nearly 1 million aliens who are apprehended each year in close proximity to the borders after illegal entry. It is not logistically possible for DHS to initiate formal removal proceedings against all such aliens. * * *

> Without limiting its ability to exercise its discretion in the event of a national emergency, other unforeseen events, or change in circumstances, DHS plans under this designation as a matter of prosecutorial discretion to apply expedited removal only to (1) third country nationals and (2) to Mexican and Canadian nationals with histories of criminal or immigration violations, such as smugglers or aliens who have made numerous illegal entries. * * *

> It is anticipated under this designation that expedited removal will be employed against those aliens who are apprehended immediately proximate to the land border and have negligible ties or equities in the U.S. Nevertheless, this designation extends to a 100-mile operational range because many aliens will arrive in vehicles that speedily depart the border area, and because other recent arrivals will find their way to near-border locales seeking transportation to other locations within the interior of the U.S.

*Id.* at 48878–79. The notice made it clear that such individuals would be subject to the same procedures for asylum claims and credible fear screening that apply to arriving aliens in expedited removal.

### Questions

What is your assessment of these expansions of expedited removal? Is there a stronger case for applying summary procedures to persons who attempt to enter clandestinely than to arriving aliens—i.e., persons who apply for admission in the regular course to inspectors at a port of entry? What additional risks of misapplication arise when expedited removal is expanded beyond ports of entry? Beyond the immediate vicinity of the border?

## SECTION C.    DETERRENCE AND DETENTION

The preceding sections have considered mechanisms states have used to control access either to their territory or to the full asylum adjudication procedure. Knowing that such control can never be fully effective, states have also adopted a number of measures to deter persons who might claim asylum in their territory. Usually states avoid describing their aims as including deterrence of asylum seekers. They instead portray the affected population as illegal migrants, speak of preventing dangerous journeys, or emphasize national security imperatives. (All of these characterizations may carry some genuine explanatory truth, though they usually do not tell the whole story.)

Most of this section will address detention regimes, but deterrence has also provided some of the motivation for recurrent proposals to establish either processing centers away from wealthy destination countries or offshore safe havens (discussed in Chapter Eleven) as ultimate places for protection (or both)—so that prospective asylum seekers would have no assurance of gaining residence rights in a country they deemed desirable. For example, in 2003 the government of the United Kingdom proposed that the European Union establish "transit processing camps" outside EU territory for asylum seekers who wanted to enter the European Union. The next year Germany and Italy recommended establishing transit camps in Libya to forestall thousands of forced migrants from making perilous journeys across the Mediterranean Sea into Europe. (As noted in Section A3 of this chapter, such boat arrivals from Africa have recently risen sharply in Spain, Italy, and Malta.) *See* Junker, Note, *Burden Sharing or Burden Shifting?: Asylum and Expansion in the European Union*, 20 Geo. Immig. L.J. 293, 316–18 (2006). We will consider certain initial questions in light of both these types of practices or proposals.

## 1.    IS DETERRENCE LEGITIMATE?

A preliminary question is whether deterrence of asylum seekers is legitimate at all—or perhaps legitimate only under certain limited circumstances. UNHCR, particularly in commenting on detention of asylum seekers, has been sharply critical of such an aim. As early as 1984, the UNHCR stated in a formal document regularly prepared for the Executive Committee:

> It has become evident that in certain countries the practice of detaining asylum-seekers is part of a clearly perceptible policy of discouraging the arrival of further asylum-seekers. In these countries refugees are frequently confined in prison or detained under prison-like conditions for prolonged periods of time in accordance with a policy of so-called "humane deterrence". *Needless to say practices of this kind—given their underlying motivation—are at variance with the principles of international protection.*

Note on International Protection (submitted by the High Commissioner), para. 29, UN Doc. A/AC.96/643 (1984) (emphasis added). And the latest UNHCR guidelines on detention state:

> Detention of asylum seekers * * * *as part of a policy to deter future asylum seekers*, or to dissuade those who have commenced their claims from pursuing them, is contrary to the norms of refugee law.

UNHCR Revised Guidelines on Applicable Criteria and Standards relating to the Detention of Asylum Seekers, (Feb. 1999), *available at* <http://www.unhcr.ch/> (emphasis added).

Beyond this, a group of experts, gathered by UNHCR in Geneva as part of the extensive Global Consultations on International Protection convened in connection with the fiftieth anniversary of the 1951 Convention, included the following in its Summary Conclusions on Article 31:

> Refugees and asylum seekers should not be detained on the ground of their national, ethnic, racial, or religious origins, or for the purposes of deterrence.

Refugee Protection in International Law: UNHCR's Global Consultations on International Protection, Chapter 3.2, para. 11(c) (E. Feller, V. Türk & F. Nicholson, eds. 2003). *See also* Helton, *Detention of Refugees and Asylum Seekers: A Misguided Threat to Refugee Protection,* Refugees and International Relations 135 (G. Loescher & L. Monahan eds. 1989); Aust, *Fifty Years Later: Examining Expedited Removal And The Detention Of Asylum Seekers Through The Lens Of The Universal Declaration Of Human Rights,* 20 Hamline J. Pub. L. & Pol'y 107, 133–34 (1998).

In contrast, support for deterrent measures, even in the context of detention, has sometimes found support from unexpected quarters. For example, the Select Commission on Immigration and Refugee Policy, chartered by Congress in 1978, was chaired by Father Theodore Hesburgh, President of the University of Notre Dame and a former chair of the U.S. Commission on Civil Rights. It also included other members with strong civil liberties or humanitarian credentials among its members. Nonetheless, deeply affected by the disorderly Mariel boatlift from Cuba in 1980, which brought 125,000 Cuban asylum seekers to Florida within a few months and which occurred as this body was wrapping up its deliberations, the Commission included focused support for deterrent measures in the section of its Final Report that follows.

## SELECT COMMISSION ON IMMIGRATION AND REFUGEE POLICY, FINAL REPORT
### Pp. 165–68 (1981).

Considering the possible recurrence of mass first asylum situations and the exponential growth in new asylum applicants other than Cubans and Haitians, the Select Commission has made a series of recommendations as to how the United States should attempt to manage such emergencies. These recommendations stem from the view of most Commissioners that:

• The United States, in keeping with the Refugee Act of 1980, will remain a country of asylum for those fleeing oppression.

• The United States should adopt policies and procedures which will deter the illegal migration of those who are not likely to meet the criteria for acceptance as asylees. Therefore, asylee policy and programs must be formulated to prevent the use of asylum petitions for "backdoor immigration."

• The United States must process asylum claims on an individual basis as expeditiously as possible and not hesitate to deport those persons who come to U.S. shores—even when they come in large numbers—who do not meet the established criteria for asylees.

\* \* \*

The Select Commission [recommends that an interagency planning body] develop contingency plans for opening and managing federal asylum processing centers, where asylum applicants would stay while their applications were processed quickly and uniformly. Although some Commissioners who voted against this proposal believe that the existence of such centers could act as an incentive to those using asylum claims as a means of gaining entry to the United States, the Commission majority holds that these centers could provide a number of important benefits:

• Large numbers of asylum applications could be processed quickly. No delays would result because addresses were unknown or because of the time required to travel to an examination site;

• Staff whose training and experience make them uniquely qualified to deal with mass asylum situations could be provided;

• Applicants could be centrally housed, fed and given medical aid;

• Law enforcement problems, which might arise as a result of a sudden influx of potential asylees, could be minimized;

• Resettlement of those applicants who, for a variety of reasons, were not accepted by the United States would be facilitated by providing a setting for the involvement of the U.N. High Commissioner for Refugees and the regional mechanism the Commission has proposed to deal with migration issues;

• Ineligible asylum applicants would not be released into communities where they might later evade U.S. efforts to deport them or create costs for local governments; and

• A deterrent would be provided for those who might see an asylum claim as a means of circumventing U.S. immigration law. Applicants would not be able to join their families or obtain work while at the processing center.

\* \* \*

### Note

The U.S. Commission on Immigration Reform, chartered in 1990, offered many similar recommendations for dealing with "mass migration emergencies." U.S. Commission on Immigration Reform, U.S. Refugee Policy: Taking Leadership 20–28 (1997). The latter Commission placed a major emphasis, however, on the creation of regional temporary protection sites at various locations in the hemisphere, funded by the United States, where most of those screened in would find temporary protection that would last for the duration of the crisis.

———————

Professor James Hathaway, a consistent and forceful advocate of the rights of refugees and asylum seekers and one of the world's leading scholars on refugees, also elaborated, in cooperation with his colleague Alexander Neve, an innovative proposal for a significant shift in the way the world approaches refugee protection. It seeks to permit states to satisfy their migration control imperatives but without resorting to *non-entrée* practices or refugee warehousing (the authors' summary of such objectionable practices appears in the introduction to this chapter). Under this proposal, built on a novel way to take advantage of nascent interest convergence among a diverse range of states, participating states (from both the global North and the global South) would agree on collective responsibility for providing protection, in a system that allows for different states to make different types of contributions—processing locations, sites for temporary protection, financial contributions, etc. (We will consider more closely the burden-sharing elements of this plan—and of a similar plan offered by Professor Peter Schuck—in Chapter Ten.)

Under the Hathaway proposal, protection would normally be temporary (although this could last for a considerable period), but it would be provided in a way that is "solution-oriented," effectively preparing refugees for successful return when conditions permit, thus boosting the chances for eventual transition of the home country to a functioning, rights-protecting state. Most pertinent for present purposes would be arrangements whereby asylum seekers would not necessarily obtain refuge—temporary or permanent—in the country where they initially present the claim. Note, as you read the following excerpt, the nuanced role that deterrence plays in this plan.

### JAMES C. HATHAWAY & R. ALEXANDER NEVE, MAKING INTERNATIONAL REFUGEE LAW RELEVANT AGAIN: A PROPOSAL FOR COLLECTIVIZED AND SOLUTION–ORIENTED PROTECTION

10 Harv. Hum. Rts. J. 115, 117–18, 145–50 (1997).

The critical right of at-risk people to seek asylum will survive only if the mechanisms of international refugee protection can be reconceived to minimize conflict with the legitimate migration control objectives of states, and dependably and equitably to share responsibilities and burdens. In the analysis that follows, we argue for a shift to a solution-oriented temporary protection of refugees, conceived within a framework of common but differentiated responsibility among states. * * *

A system of collectivized responsibility would respond to the desire of Northern states to avoid the fraudulent claims resulting from the individuated duty to admit every asylum-seeker into their territories until the claim to refugee status is denied. To the extent that developed states commit themselves to membership in refugee protection interest-convergence groups, they would secure access to a legitimate means by which to dissociate the site of arrival from the place of asylum. * * * Governments are legally entitled to allocate the responsibility to protect refugees, so long as the assignment of protective responsibility is the result of common agreement among the states concerned, and poses no risk to the refugee's right to protection against *refoulement*, and to enjoy other basic human rights.

With agreements in place that authorize the asylum-seeker to be sent to a safe country in his or her region of origin for refugee status determination, there would be no incentive to make a fraudulent claim in a country outside the region. As a result, Northern governments would be able to preserve their migration control objectives without blocking access to asylum-seekers by resorting to deflection and other *non-entrée* mechanisms. The problems of wasted resources and diminished support for refugee protection that confront Northern countries could therefore be addressed without constraining access to first asylum in any way.

The result of this trade-off would clearly be an increase in the number of refugees protected in the South. But, because eighty percent of the world's refugee population is already protected in the less developed world, even an agreement to assign the entire refugee population of the North to protection in the South * * * would increase the refugee population in the less developed world only marginally. The resulting system, however, could address the growing concerns of Southern governments regarding fairness and sustainability in meeting the needs of the bulk of the refugee population [and help assure funding from the Northern states]. * * *

* * *

[There are] three ways in which collectivized protection would also benefit the vast majority of the world's refugees. First and foremost, access to asylum would be promoted. Because the arrival of refugees would no longer pose the risk of either unfair or unsustainable obligations, states within the region of origin could remain open to the provision of asylum. Access to asylum would also be improved for the minority of refugees who need to flee to a state outside their own region. Many such refugees are presently deflected by visa control and other blunt responses to the problem of fraudulent claims. Collectivized responsibility, in contrast, would allow governments to deter unfounded asylum claims without closing extraregional escape routes.

Second, the dismantling of *non-entrée* systems would free up substantial sums of money presently spent to enforce *non-entrée* and to process fraudulent claims. Re-channelling funds presently wasted on the processing of non-genuine claims in the North would ensure a more adequate funding base to address the needs of the majority of the refugee population that is already protected within the regions of origin.

Third, collectivized responsibility should result in firm guarantees of access to extraregional resettlement in special needs cases, and in cases where safe repatriation remains impossible after a reasonable period of temporary protection. Whereas the present system allocates protection outside the region largely on the basis of the relative wealth and mobility of particular asylum-seekers, a more structured sharing regime would allow these decisions to be made on the basis of relative need.

\* \* \*

### Note

Hathaway and Neve include a 1991 estimate of the cost of administering asylum procedures and providing social welfare benefits to refugee claimants in 13 of the major industrialized states, which placed that cost at $7 billion. *Id.* at 153 n. 155. They point out that if only 20 percent of claimants are "non-genuine," then the sum spent on their claims exceeds $1 billion. *Id.* at 142. Other estimates of annual overall expenditures in Europe for these purposes have run as high as $11.5 billion. *See* Michael Jandl, Structure and Costs of the Asylum Systems in Seven Countries (International Center for Migration Policy Development, 1995); Junker, *supra,* 20 Geo. Immig. L.J. at 320 (2006) (reporting an estimate by an intergovernmental body that processing and caring for 400–500,000 applicants in the EU each year would cost $10 billion, or $20,000 per person). If appropriate deterrent measures greatly reduced the cost of those systems, could the money be more effectively spent to address persecution at its source? Is that politically feasible? How exactly would you use those resources for that end?

———

The following reading considers circumstances in which deterrence might be a valid goal and explores alternatives to detention in serving that goal.

## DAVID A. MARTIN, REFORMING ASYLUM ADJUDICATION: ON NAVIGATING THE COAST OF BOHEMIA

138 U.Pa.L.Rev. 1247, 1288–92 (1990).

In other adjudication processes, such as those governing disability claims or public welfare or licensing, the applicant ordinarily does not enjoy the benefit sought until there has been a determination on the merits that he fully qualifies. Nothing in the application and waiting process itself tempts the unqualified to clog the system. With political asylum, in contrast, the simple act of applying has usually brought important benefits [work authorization and free movement within the country] that magnify the attractions, whatever the ultimate determination on the merits. * * * These two features comprise the bulk of the main benefits expected from asylum itself, particularly for those who know they have weak claims.

* * * [S]peedier final decisions are not the only way to eliminate the artificial attractions of the asylum-seeker stage. One could simply end the provision of free movement and work authorization during this period. Many Western countries have been moving in this direction, imposing a variety of restrictions and deterrents that have raised the concern of UNHCR and provoked harsh condemnation from the nongovernmental organizations (NGOs) that support asylum seekers and advocate refugee causes. These restrictive practices include denials of work authorization, enforced housing in austere communal facilities, other limits on freedom of movement, and sometimes full-scale detention in jail-like facilities.

Considerable misunderstanding has arisen regarding the use of deterrent measures and restrictive practices. NGOs sometimes act as though any deterrent steps are illegitimate—sheer vindictiveness visited upon innocents, many of whom may prove to be bona fide refugees. Some perspective is needed. Designing policy to discourage the unqualified from even applying for a benefit is a perfectly legitimate policy objective, particularly when existing statistics demonstrate that a high percentage of applications lack merit. To the extent that current measures are meant to encourage self-selection, so that only those with strong cases bother to leave their home countries, they address an unimpeachable administrative aim. In design, at least, these restrictive practices are meant to send a "general deterrence" message to persons still in the home country.

The message grows more complex in practice. At this preliminary stage, deterrent measures almost inevitably apply to all asylum applicants, whatever the strength or weakness of their claims. (To sort the strong from the weak at this stage—save for screening out wholly frivolous applications—would simply be too cumbersome, because of all the factual difficulties.[d]) Thus, the burdens of these measures often fall on genuine refugees. It is not wholly surprising, then, that some judges might view these measures as penalties for filing an asylum claim, or as coercion meant to force current applicants to withdraw their applications and return home, rather than as deterrents addressed to those still in the home country, designed to convince them (if they are not substantially threatened) to decide against coming to the United States. If they

**d**  Further discussion of factfinding challenges may be found in Chapter Eight—eds.

see such measures this way, courts are likely to declare the deterrents invalid for conflicting with the statutory right to apply for asylum.

The basic problem is that these deterrent measures and restrictive practices are indiscriminate in their impact. By their very nature, they fall equally on deserving refugees and the most flagrant abusers during the asylum application stage. A case could even be made that they fall with more debilitating effect on true refugees, because lengthy uncertainty over their ultimate fate, coupled with enforced idleness and perhaps prison-like detention, will carry the most severe psychological impact for those who know with substantial assurance that persecution awaits them at home. (It may be even more devastating for those who have already been tortured or severely mistreated.) For these reasons, such deterrents plainly should be avoided if workable alternatives are available. * * *

We need instead a discriminate deterrent, more precisely focused on the marginal cases, and one that takes away the artificial attractions of the asylum applicant stage of the proceedings. Such a deterrent is available, *if* we can change the adjudication system to achieve one crucial result: the prompt reappearance in the home village of applicants whose cases were at best marginal. Such an event makes apparent to others similarly situated that such a trip is not worthwhile; they will not be able to work long enough even to repay the "travel agent's" fee. Speedy finality is the essential precondition of this deterrent. The message is lost if two or three years pass between departure and return, particularly if the applicant has been working while the application was pending.

How much speed is necessary? We lack empirical data to calculate the outside limits with any kind of accuracy (and anyway the calculations would vary by country and by travel agent). But if all but the most complicated cases could reach finality within six to nine months, including all the stages of consideration and review, little in the application process would add artificially to the attractions of the asylum system.

* * *

## Note

In the decade and a half since Martin wrote, major changes have been made in the U.S. asylum system. It is now much more capable of reaching final decisions within a matter of months. Yet U.S. practice still makes extensive use of detention in prison-type facilities. Why would that be so? *See* Martin, *Two Cheers for Expedited Removal, supra,* 40 Va. J. Int'l L. at 701–03 (suggesting that the devotion to detention on the part of key immigration officials derives from the system's lingering inability to carry out removal orders successfully, even if the adjudication is resolved promptly). What further changes might be necessary or useful to create the political climate that would enable a reduction in reliance on detention?

## 2.  DETENTION

### a.  *U.S. Practices*

Detention is employed in all migration control systems, and it has been a regular feature of U.S. immigration law. Concerns about immigration control have led to the increasing funding for, and use of, detention in recent years. As of 2006, DHS has access to over 21,000 detention bed spaces in federal detention facilities, facilities run by private contractors, and state and local jails. Asylum seekers, particularly those who are arriving aliens, are often detained.

The INA provides that arriving aliens "shall be detained," INA § 235(b)(2), but this provision does not prevent release while removal proceedings are pending, under the parole power of INA § 212(d)(5). The immigration agencies have promulgated regulations governing such parole, which include a broad provision authorizing release of aliens "whose continued detention is not in the public interest." 8 C.F.R. § 212.5. DHS field office directors usually make such decisions, and may condition release on other requirements, such as the posting of a bond. Immigration judges lack jurisdiction to review release decisions affecting arriving aliens. 8 C.F.R. §§ 236.1(c)(11); 1003.19(h)(2)(i)(B).

For aliens other than arriving aliens, both those who have been admitted and those who have entered without inspection, different rules apply. The INA authorizes release during the pendency of removal proceedings, either on the individual's own recognizance or on bond (minimum $1500). INA § 236(a); 8 C.F.R. § 236.1(c). DHS directors make the initial decision on terms of release, but in this setting the noncitizen may seek what is called "bond redetermination" before an immigration judge, and may appeal that ruling to the BIA. The immigration judge may reduce the bond or decide that release without bond is appropriate. 8 C.F.R. § 1003.19(b). In all settings, the key determinations are whether the person is likely to appear for future proceedings or might be a danger to others if released. Key factors to be considered in the bond hearing include the person's employment history, length of residence in the community, family ties, and record of appearance or nonappearance at court proceedings. *See Matter of Sugay,* 17 I & N Dec. 637, 638–39 (BIA 1981). Different rules apply to juveniles, and certain categories of noncitizens, particularly those with criminal convictions or in the early stages of expedited removal, are subject to mandatory detention. For more on the overall detention system, see Taylor, *Symbolic Detention,* 20 In Defense of the Alien 153 (1997); Schuck, *INS Detention and Removal: A White Paper,* 11 Geo, Immig. L.J. 667 (1997); Legomsky, *The Detention of Aliens: Theories, Rules, and Discretion,* 30 U. Miami Inter–Am. L.Rev. 531 (1999); Hutchins, *Detention of Aliens: An Overview of Current Law,* 03–4 Imm. Briefings (2003).

In the 1980s, faced with rising numbers of asylum seekers, the Reagan administration changed a previous operating presumption of release for persons in exclusion proceedings (now known as arriving aliens), and the change led to more extensive detention of asylum seekers. Challenges to this changed policy raised claims based on regulations, statutes, constitutional provisions, and international treaties. In general, courts upheld detention of excludable noncitizens who were applying for asylum. The excerpt below focuses on both the Refugee Act of 1980 and on Article 31 of the 1951 Refugee Convention.

## SINGH v. NELSON

United States District Court for the Southern District of New York, 1985.
623 F.Supp. 545.

[The 28] petitioners are refugees from Afghanistan held in detention in the custody of the Immigration and Naturalization Service * * * pending the completion of exclusion proceedings to determine their admissibility to the United States. * * * According to petitioners, they are opponents of the Soviet-backed regime governing Afghanistan. They have actively assisted the Mujahedeen or "freedom fighters" who are resisting the Soviets and the Afghan government. Many were imprisoned and tortured because of their opposition. They fled Afghanistan fearing further persecution. Initially some travelled to Pakistan, then continued to India. In Pakistan and India they were threatened and attacked by agents of the Afghan government and Pakistani Communists. Those who applied * * * for asylum and refugee status at United States embassies in India and Pakistan in order to gain admission to the United States were unsuccessful in such efforts, apparently because they did not have sufficiently close ties to the United States. * * * In desperation they purchased plane tickets and travel documents from people in Pakistan and India and made their way to the United States. At various times from July 10, 1984 to March 20, 1985, petitioners arrived in the United States at John F. Kennedy International Airport from England, Holland, Romania, Pakistan and India. Some had travelled through several countries after leaving Afghanistan.

* * *

[When they arrived in the United States, they lacked valid travel documents, and U.S. immigration inspectors concluded that they were not entitled to enter the country. They were detained pending exclusion hearings. They applied for asylum, which ultimately was denied as a matter of discretion, but they were granted withholding of removal. They remained in detention throughout the procedure, which took more than a year in some cases, and began a hunger strike to protest their continued detention. The district court reviewed the evolving detention policy and then examined its legitimacy under U.S. and international law.]

As the result of changed circumstances during the intervening twenty-five-year period, the Service's parole policy has become far more restrictive. The purpose behind this policy change is to deter persons from attempting to enter the United States illegally. 47 Fed.Reg. 30,044 (1982). The restrictions imposed on parole eligibility for undocumented excludable aliens such as petitioners is related to the Service's attempt to stem the flow of undocumented aliens arriving in the United States by airplane or ship. By refusing to parole undocumented excludable aliens, the Service is attempting to discourage people from entering the United States without permission and serves notice that aliens will not be able to circumvent the procedures governing lawful immigration to this country. This goal provides a rational basis for distinguishing among categories of illegal aliens. * * *

Petitioners next argue that the detention regulations frustrate the purpose of the Refugee Act of 1980 * * * Petitioners contend that by creating a fear of detention the INS hopes to deter undocumented aliens from coming to the United States to seek asylum. * * * It is argued that the length of time it takes to process an asylum application penalizes detained asylum applicants. Indeed, the lengthy proceedings and prolonged periods of imprisonment have induced several petitioners to withdraw their claims for admission in order to become eligible for parole. Petitioners argue that the burden the regulations place on detained asylum applicants demonstrates that the detention regulations are at odds with purpose of the Refugee Act. * * *

The Service argues that the primary purpose of the regulations is not to deter aliens from lawfully emigrating but to assist the Service in upholding its obligations to enforce the immigration laws. In addition, the regulations are consistent with Congressional intent to eliminate use of the parole statute as a means of granting refuge and to replace it with a uniform asylum application process. * * *

The petitioners in this case have had their asylum applications considered by immigration judges. They also have had the opportunity to avail themselves of the subsequent procedural rights that are afforded to all other asylum applicants. The fact that they are detained while such procedural steps are taken does not negate those facts. In addition, according to the legislative history, Congress contemplated that asylum applicants would be detained while their applications were pending.

* * * [I]t is this Court's determination that petitioners have been afforded the same procedural opportunities regarding their asylum applications that are available to all other asylum applicants. Although the lengthy process of pursuing an asylum application may present petitioners with the discouraging prospect of prolonged incarceration, such detention is not inconsistent with the right to apply for asylum created by the Refugee Act. * * *

Next, petitioners allege that the regulations violate Article 31 of the United Nations Convention Relating to the Status of Refugees, which is incorporated by the United Nations Protocol Relating to the Status of Refugees. Petitioners claim that Article 31 is a self-executing treaty provision and therefore has the same authority as federal statutes under United States law. They contend that the lengthy periods of detention they have had to endure amount to a penalty under Article 31(1), which forbids the imposition of penalties on refugees by reason of their illegal entry. Furthermore, because there has been no showing that they will abscond or pose a threat to society, the detention policy imposes an unnecessary restriction on their movement in violation of Article 31(2).

The Service argues that the Protocol and the Convention do not grant any rights or privileges not provided for in the Immigration Act or the Refugee Act of 1980. More persuasive, however, is the Service's contention that petitioners may not invoke Article 31 of the Protocol because it applies only to "refugees who[ ] com[e] directly from a territory where their life or freedom was threatened." In this case, all petitioners came to the United States from various countries. Not one came directly from Afghanistan.

The Service has argued correctly that the language of Article 31 must be taken literally. The debates at the United Nations General Assembly Conference on the Status of Refugees and Stateless Persons that drafted the Convention indicate that exemption from the consequences of an illegal entry should be considered only in the case of the first receiving country. * * *

The Conference debates also make it plain that the word "penalties" in ¶ 1 of Article 31 referred to "penalties imposable for the unlawful crossing of a frontier. . . . The government concerned would nevertheless retain its right to expel an alien who had entered its territory illegally." U.N. Refugee Conference, Summary Record of the Thirteenth Meeting, at 14 (July 10, 1951) (Remarks of Mr. Herment) (U.N. Doc. A/Conf.2/SR.13). Article 31 was not intended to "prevent a government detaining a person who entered the country illegally, pending a decision whether that person was to be regarded as a bona fide refugee. It would merely prevent his being punished for such illegal entry if the decision went in his favor." U.N. Refugee Conference, Summary Record of the Thirty-Fifth Meeting, at 12 (July 25, 1951) (Remarks of Mr. van Heuven Goedhart [U.N. High Commissioner for Refugees] ) (U.N.Doc. A/ Conf.2/SR.35). It was also contemplated that in aid of its efforts to investigate the circumstances in which a refugee had entered a country, the government could detain and keep him in custody. U.N. Refugee Conference, Summary Record of the Fourteenth Meeting, at 15 (July 10, 1951) (Remarks of Mr. Larsen) (U.N. Doc. A/Conf.2/SR.14); Summary Record of the Thirty-Fifth Meeting, at 12–13 (July 25, 1951) (U.N. Doc. A/Conf.2/SR.35). * * *

This review of the "legislative history" of the Convention indicates that the Protocol and the Convention do not apply to petitioners under the circumstances of this case.

### Notes and Questions

1. *Amanullah v. Nelson,* 811 F.2d 1 (1st Cir.1987) also sustained the detention of other Afghan asylum seekers. The court included these comments (*id.* at 14–15):

The appellants argue at length that the INS, whatever its stated reasons for detaining asylum applicants, is in reality employing quarantine as a form of coercion in an impermissible attempt to force asylum seekers to abandon the prosecution of their applications. In their view, such coercion countermands the aims and entitlements of the Refugee Act, is punitive in its essence, and is fundamentally unfair to boot. But, this argument topples of its own weight. As we have mentioned repeatedly, the intention of the government is to protect our shores against a wave of itinerant asylum seekers bent on circumventing the coherent scheme of the Refugee Act, not to punish aliens for seeking asylum. These cases testify eloquently to the core element of the problem. After all, these four petitioners were detained *before* they became applicants for asylum. * * * Just as the disability of pretrial detention does not amount to "punishment" in the constitutional sense, neither does the disability incident to the justifiable temporary detention of excludable aliens.

How can the court be so sure of the government's intention in these circumstances?

2.   Do these court decisions shed light on whether deterrence of asylum seekers is a valid goal of public policy? When should detention be employed for deterrent purposes? Does detention overdeter—that is, close down the prospect of asylum for people the United States should be trying to protect, or induce people already here to withdraw meritorious applications? Could a more precise and discriminating deterrent be devised? What sort of detention system should be implemented? *See* Pistone, *Justice Delayed is Justice Denied: A Proposal for Ending the Unnecessary Detention of Asylum Seekers*, 12 Harvard Human Rights J. 197 (1999) (arguing for rules modeled on those for pre-trial detention in criminal cases).

3.   Article 26 of the 1951 Refugee Convention requires member states to "accord to refugees lawfully within its territory the right to choose their place of residence and to move freely within its territory." Article 31 forbids the imposition of penalties on refugees due to their illegal entry if they have come directly from a territory where their lives or freedom were threatened and "present themselves without delay to the authorities and show good cause for their illegal entry or presence." It also provides that states "shall not apply to the movements of such refugees restrictions other than those which are necessary * * *." Is the U.S. practice at issues in *Singh* and *Amanullah* consistent with Arts. 26 and 31 of the Convention, as applied to asylum seekers who otherwise lack legal status? *See generally* Legomsky, *supra*, 30 U. Miami Inter–Am. L. Rev. 531. If the petitioners in *Singh* had come directly from Afghanistan to the United States, the court could not have found that the key provisions of Article 31 were inapplicable. How should it then rule? When is a restriction on movement "necessary"?

### b.   *Post-September 11 Developments in the United States*

Since September 11, 2001, U.S. government reliance on interdiction, expedited removal, and detention has intensified. The George W. Bush administration has expanded the use of detention, with an especially strong focus on Haitian asylum seekers. The first precipitating event was the December 2001 interdiction by the Coast Guard of a rickety vessel still offshore near Biscayne National Park holding 167 Haitians. The passengers were processed using expedited removal procedures.

Shortly thereafter, INS promulgated a new policy reversing, for Haitian nationals arriving in south Florida, what was characterized as a general presumption of release for asylum seekers who pass credible-fear screening in expedited removal. The new policy provided that release of such Haitians required approval of INS headquarters, and such approval was sparingly given. Some of the vessel's passengers who were thereby subjected to lengthy detention challenged the policy in court. The judge sustained the policy and its application against arguments based on statute, regulation, treaty, and the equal protection and due process clauses. *Jeanty v. Bulger*, 204 F.Supp.2d 1366 (S.D.Fla.2002), *affirmed sub nom. Moise v. Bulger*, 321 F.3d 1336 (11th Cir.2003). Congressional hearings, however, provided a forum for critics of the policy, some of whom focused their objections on the singling out of Haitians for these measures. *See* 79 Interp.Rel.1500 (2002).

In October 2002, 216 Haitians evaded interdiction and made it to land near Biscayne Bay before being apprehended. They asked for asylum. They were not subject to expedited removal under then-existing rules because they were not arriving aliens, having already made an entry. For the same reason, the INS decisions on detention and the terms of release became subject to review by immigration judges in bond redetermination proceedings. Immigration judges and the BIA, applying the usual individualized criteria of flight risk and dangerousness, ordered release of many of the Haitians. Key players in the Justice Department, however, were determined to assure that most of this group would remain in detention pending final decisions on their asylum claims—explicitly in order to deter future Haitian boat arrivals. In *Matter of D–J–*, 23 I & N Dec. 572 (AG 2003), Attorney General Ashcroft took referral of one of these detention cases after the BIA had ruled. (Referral is a discretionary procedure which makes the Attorney General the highest administrative tribunal for a particular case; Attorney General rulings after referral become precedents binding on administrative officers, unless overruled by a federal court.) Ashcroft issued a broadly worded precedent decision requiring detention in these circumstances:

> I conclude that releasing respondent, or similarly situated undocumented seagoing migrants, on bond would give rise to adverse consequences for national security and sound immigration policy. As demonstrated by the declarations of the concerned national security agencies submitted by INS, there is a substantial prospect that the release of such aliens into the United States would come to the attention of others in Haiti and encourage future surges in illegal migration by sea. Encouraging such unlawful mass migrations is inconsistent with sound immigration policy and important national security interests. As substantiated by the government declarations, surges in such illegal migration by sea injure national security by diverting valuable Coast Guard and DOD [Department of Defense] re-

sources from counterterrorism and homeland security responsibilities. * * * The persistent history of mass migration from Haiti, in the face of concerted statutory and regulatory measures to curtail it, confirms that even sporadic successful entries fuel further attempts. * * *

Even if the respondent *were* entitled to an individualized hearing, * * * such a conclusion would not support a contention that this respondent's request for release on bond must be determined exclusively on the basis of his individual situation, rather than on the basis of general considerations applicable to a category of migrants, as a matter of constitutional due process. The mere fact that general considerations [of national security and deterrence] are introduced does not negate the individual nature of the hearing.

*Id.* at 579–80, 583.

Among the declarations describing national security threats that were part of the record, the Attorney General singled out a State Department declaration stating that it had "noticed an increase in third country nationals (Pakistanis, Palestinians, etc.) using Haiti as a staging point for attempted migration to the United States. This increases the national security interest in curbing this migration route." *Id.* at 579. Later in the opinion, the Attorney General responded briefly to a contention that such a ruling would be inconsistent with the internationally recognized right to seek asylum: "The national security interests invoked in this opinion are directed at unlawful and dangerous mass migrations by sea, not the right to seek asylum. Aliens who do arrive in the United States, including the respondent himself, are afforded the right to apply for asylum and have those applications duly considered." *Id.* at 584.

In order to avoid further release proceedings of this kind in the future, in November 2002, months before the *D–J–* decision, the Department published a notice expanding for the first time the application of expedited removal beyond its statutory application to arriving aliens. See INA § 235(b)(1)(A)(iii), allowing application of expedited removal to certain entrants without inspection, discussed in section B above. Henceforth expedited removal applies to EWIs, with the exception of Cubans, who "arrive in the United States by sea, either by boat or other means" and who cannot show that they have been continuously present in the United States for the preceding two years. The notice specified that this change specifically makes such noncitizens subject to the more restrictive detention regime associated with expedited removal—which does not allow bond redetermination by immigration judges. 67 Fed.Reg. 68924–26 (2002).

### Notes and Questions

1. Are such measures targeted at Haitians consistent with the equal protection and due process guarantees of the Constitution? With the nondiscrimination provision in the 1951 Convention (Article 3)?

2. Is the invocation of national security concerns to justify detention consistent with the Convention? Consider in this regard Conclusion 44 of the UNHCR Executive Committee, discussed in the next subsection. Is national security plausibly applied here?

### c. *International Standards*

Articles 26 and 31(2) of the 1951 Convention are potentially relevant to issues of detention, though the first applies, by its terms, only to refugees lawfully in the territory. Article 31 applies to all refugees, but allows movement restrictions "which are necessary." It does not further explain that standard. The Executive Committee of the UN High Commissioner's Programme, which is made up of government representatives from over 40 nations that are party to the UN Convention or Protocol, adopted a lengthy resolution in 1986, known as Conclusion 44, addressing the appropriate circumstances for detention of asylum seekers. After expressing concern about excessive use of detention, the Conclusion states:

> If necessary, detention may be resorted to only on grounds prescribed by law to verify identity; to determine the elements on which the claim to refugee status or asylum is based; to deal with cases where refugees or asylum-seekers have destroyed their travel and/or identity documents or have used fraudulent documents in order to mislead authorities of the State in which they intend to claim asylum; or to protect national security or public order.

Executive Committee Conclusion on International Protection, No. 44, *Detention of Refugees and Asylum Seekers*, UNHCR (1986), at para. b. Is U.S. practice consistent with these provisions?

The Office of the High Commissioner has spoken out more strongly against the use of detention for deterrent purposes.

> The detention of asylum seekers is in the view of UNHCR inherently undesirable. * * *

> Detention of asylum seekers may exceptionally be resorted to for the reasons set forth [in Conclusion 44] as long as this is clearly prescribed by a national law which is in conformity with general norms and principles of international human rights law.* * *

> There should be a presumption against detention. Where there are monitoring mechanisms which can be employed as viable alternatives to detention (such as reporting obligations or guarantor requirements * * *), these should be applied first unless there is evidence to suggest that such an alternative will not be effective in the individual case. * * *

> Detention of asylum seekers which is applied for purposes other than those listed above, for example, as part of a policy to deter future asylum seekers, or to dissuade those who have

commenced their claims from pursuing them, is contrary to the norms of refugee law.

UNHCR Revised Guidelines on Applicable Criteria and Standards relating to the Detention of Asylum Seekers (Feb. 1999).

The UNHCR Guidelines set forth specific alternatives to detention that should be considered based on an individual assessment of the asylum seeker and of the current conditions in the receiving country. The non-exhaustive list suggests periodic reporting requirements, required residency at a specified location, providing a guarantor, release on bail, or assignment to a specific reception center which would allow asylum seekers to leave during stipulated times.

Further, the UNHCR Guidelines set forth minimal procedural safeguards if detention is ordered:

(i) to receive prompt and full communication of any order of detention, together with the reasons for the order, and the rights in connection with the order, in a language and in terms they understand.

(ii) to be informed of the right to legal counsel. Where possible, they should receive free legal assistance.

(iii) to have the decision subjected to an automatic review before a judicial or administrative body independent of the detaining authorities. This should be followed by regular periodic reviews of the necessity for the continuance of detention, which the asylum seeker or his representative would have the right to attend.

(iv) either personally or through a representative to challenge the necessity of the deprivation of liberty at the review hearing * * *.

(v) to contact and be contacted by the local UNHCR Office, available national refugee bodies or other agencies and an advocate. * * *

*Id.* Not surprisingly, UNHCR has criticized recent U.S. detention practices. *See* 79 Interp.Rel. 620 (2002) (UNHCR advisory opinion criticizing U.S. detention policy).

### Notes and Questions

1.   Could the U.S. government make a case for the consistency of its detention practices with Articles 26 and 31(2)? With Conclusion 44? What does it mean to use detention "to determine the elements on which the claim to refugee status or asylum is based"?

2.   What is the status of Conclusions of the UNHCR Executive Committee or of Guidelines promulgated by the Office of the UNHCR? Check the text of the Convention and Protocol to see what authority they give to either of these bodies to provide authoritative interpretations of the treaties or of other international law relating to refugees. *See generally* Jerzy Sztucki, *The Conclusions on the International Protection of Refugees Adopted by the*

Executive Committee of the High Commissioner's Programme, *1 Int'l J. Refugee L. 285, 308 (1989); James C. Hathaway, The Rights of Refugees under International Law 112–14 (2005). Professor Hathaway has been moderately critical of guideline documents issued by UNHCR staff, because they may diverge from what can honestly be understood as international law requirements, as demonstrated through state practice, including judicial rulings. He wrote:*

> [T]he recent proliferation of various forms of UNHCR position papers on the interpretation of refugee law has made it increasingly difficult for even state parties committed to a strong UNHCR voice to discern the precise agency position on many key protection issues. * * *

> The critical role of UNHCR in providing Art. 35 guidance to state parties is compromised not only by the sheer volume of less-than-fully-consistent advice * * *, but more fundamentally by recent efforts to draft institutional positions at such a highly detailed level that they simply cannot be reconciled with the binding jurisprudence of state parties.

*Id.* at 116–118 (2005).

3. The United States is not the only country to employ detention as part of a policy meant to deter the arrival of asylum seekers. Australia, in particular, adopted a far more rigorous policy in the 1990s that calls for detention, usually in a remote location, of virtually all irregularly arriving asylum seekers throughout the time while their claims are being considered. Australia's policy has been popular with its electorate. For a critique, *see, e.g.,* Schloenhardt, *To Deter, Detain and Deny: Protection of Onshore Asylum Seekers in Australia*, 14 Int'l J. Refugee L. 302 (2002).

4. Within Europe, and even within a single country, the detention policies concerning asylum seekers vary widely. In Spain, for example, all undocumented asylum seekers who appear at an airport or a seaport are detained during the seven days of the expedited proceeding, but those who enter without being stopped at the border phone for an asylum interview, surrender their travel documents, and receive a permit allowing them to remain in Spain for 60 days while their application is reviewed. They are neither detained nor provided accommodations during this phase of the asylum procedure. Undocumented migrants who land in the Canary Islands and other Spanish coastal areas via the small unscheduled craft known as *pateras* are frequently detained for illegal entry. They can apply for asylum from detention, which is limited to 40 days. At the end of that time, those who have not been returned to their homeland or to the countries through which they traveled must be released. *See* Fullerton, *Inadmissible in Iberia: The Fate of Asylum Seekers in Spain and Portugal*, 18 Intl. J. Refugee Law 659 (2005). What kind of deterrent effect is a 40-day limit on detention likely to have on asylum seekers and other migrants?

5. In most European countries asylum seekers are generally not detained while they pursue their claims through the ordinary asylum procedure. In some countries they survive on their own; in some the states provide accommodations. Spain, for example, provides housing for only a small percent, the most vulnerable of the asylum seekers. *ECRE Country*

*Report: Spain*, 2003, *available at* <http://www.ecre.org/conditions/2003/spain 2003final.pdf>. Germany takes a different approach, assigning all asylum seekers to reception centers where they live in dormitories or apartment buildings and receive their meals and some basic social services; they generally may leave these centers during the day. *See* Fullerton, *Failing the Test: Germany Leads Europe in Dismantling Refugee Protection*, 36 Texas Intl. L. J. 231 (2001); *ECRE Country Report: Germany*, 2000, *available at* <http://www.ecre.org/conditions/2000/germany.pdf>. In contrast to most other European Union states, the United Kingdom frequently detains asylum seekers, and the law does not place explicit limits on the length of detention. Nonetheless, the U.K. detains far fewer asylum seekers than the United States. In 2000 the U.K. opened a new immigration detention center; the number detained hovered just below 1,000. *ECRE Country Report: United Kingdom*, 2000, *available at* <http://www.ecre.org/conditions/2000/unitedkingdom.pdf>.

### d.  Conditions of Confinement

Objections to the U.S. use of detention often go beyond the fact of detention to address as well the conditions of confinement. It is not just that asylum seekers are detained, but that they are detained in prison-style facilities, even though the detention is not punitive in intent and is considered civil in character. The quotations from detained individuals that begin this Chapter give some sense of life in most such facilities. Although detailed immigration detention standards, developed in the 1990s in a cooperative process that involved the American Bar Association and other NGOs, have brought some standardization and improvements, they do not alleviate the effects that a prison-type regimen can have on asylum seekers. In fact, the DHS standards frequently use as a point of reference the standards of the American Correctional Association, which is an accrediting body for criminal justice prison facilities. (The DHS standards, several hundred pages in length, constitute the DHS Detention Operations Manual, *available at* <http://www.ice.gov/partners/dro/opsmanual/index.htm>.) Arriving detainees are classified according to their perceived level of dangerousness, and generally are required to wear color-coded jumpsuits based on the classification. Privacy is minimal. Most detention takes place in dormitories, and detainees may have to change clothes, shower, and use the bathroom in full view of other inmates and of guards.

The literature contains extensive criticism of U.S. immigration detention practices, particularly as applied to asylum seekers. *See, e.g.,* Human Rights First, in Liberty's Shadow—U.S. Detention of Asylum Seekers in the Era of Homeland Security (2004); Physicians for Human Rights, From Persecution to Prison: The Health Consequences of Detention for Asylum Seekers (2003); Rizza, *INS Detention: The Impact on Asylum Seekers*, 17 Refugee Reports No. 8, at 2 (Aug. 30, 1996); Taylor, *Detained Aliens Challenging Conditions of Confinement and the Porous Border of the Plenary Power Doctrine*, 22 Hastings Const. L.Q. 1087, 1158 (1995). Some have criticized the even more deleterious effect detention tends to have on vulnerable populations. *See, e.g.,* Women's Commission for Refugee Women and Children, Liberty Denied: Women

Seeking Asylum Imprisoned in the United States (April 1997); Women's Commission for Refugee Women and Children, An Uncertain Future, A Cruel Present: Women in INS Detention (1996), reviewed in 73 Interp. Rel. 371 (1996).

The Commission on International Religious Freedom took a close look at conditions in detention facilities, as part of its congressionally chartered study of expedited removal. It offered these suggestions:

> [Recommendation 3.3:] When non-criminal asylum seekers in Expedited Removal are detained, they should not be held in prison-like facilities, with the exception of those specific cases in which DHS has reason to believe that the alien may pose a danger to others. Rather, noncriminal asylum seekers should be detained in "non-jail-like" facilities such as the model developed by DHS and INS in Broward County, Florida. DHS should formulate and implement nationwide detention standards created specifically for asylum seekers. The standards should be developed under the supervision of the proposed Office of the Refugee Coordinator, and should be implemented by an office dedicated to the detention of non-criminal asylum seekers, developing a small number of centrally managed facilities specific to and appropriate for, asylum seekers. The current DHS standards—based entirely on a penal model—are inappropriate.

> [Further comments:] * * * We have found that detained asylum seekers in Expedited Removal are subjected to conditions of confinement that are virtually identical to those in prisons or jails. These conditions create a serious risk of institutionalization and other forms of psychological harm. They are inappropriate, particularly for an already traumatized population of asylum seekers, and unnecessary. ICE's own "non-jail-like detention" model in Broward County, Florida has demonstrated that asylum seekers may be securely detained in an environment which does not resemble a jail and which is no more expensive than more secure facilities. Broward is, however, the only such non-jail-like detention facility among the 185 jails, prisons, and detention centers where ICE detains asylum seekers.

> The Study concurs with the UNHCR Executive Committee that asylum seekers have different issues and needs than those faced by prisoners or even other aliens, and standards should be developed in recognition of this important distinction.

I CIRF Report, *supra*, at 68.

The CIRF Report contains few additional details about the Broward County facility, but it allows individuals to retain their own clothing, affords greater privacy, imposes less regimentation on freedom of movement on facility grounds, offers educational programs and counseling, and permits expanded contact with family and others outside. Note also that other countries, as described above, have employed models that may impose some restrictions on asylum seekers but do not amount to prison-style detention. Germany, for example, assigns asylum seekers to communal housing facilities but allows free movement within the municipality during the day. Some of these are family facilities, keeping family units together.

## Questions

Would the use of these less restrictive forms of restraint—either the Broward County or German model—address the underlying concerns that UNHCR and many NGOs have about detention? What other governmental concerns (about liability, safety, or enforcement imperatives) may cause resistance in DHS toward adopting such an approach?

# Chapter Ten

# RESETTLEMENT AND OTHER DURABLE SOLUTIONS

---

*I was born in Southern Sudan in the Upper Nile, in Bor.
\* \* \* [C]ivil war broke out in 1983. This civil war intensified
and spread in the whole Sudan. It was marked by unreasonable
looting of properties, demolition of shelters, abduction of children, and later on when all the livelihood was swept away,
deliberate killings were launched on us—the southerners. We
were attacked both aerially through bombing, and on the ground
through shooting. Thousands of lives were lost. It was a genocide. Life became valueless and meaningless. I lost almost a half
decade of my life. I lost my father and many relatives. That was
1986. \* \* \**

*I was separated from my brothers, mum, sister, and rela-
tives. I found myself among the mass of people, mainly children,
heading to an unknown destination. We wandered in despair
and agony in the Sudan, looking for peace. The only relative who
was with me during those doom days was my uncle's son. He
used to carry me on his shoulder some distance, and I walked
the rest on my own. We headed eastward of the Sudan. On our
way, we were bothered by mosquitoes and terrified by wild
animals. We experienced a burning thirst in some distances,
and, of course, starvation.*

\* \* \*

*After two and a half months, we found ourselves along a
fast running river. \* \* \* That was the Ethiopia and Sudan
border. \* \* \* Our fellow friends, the Ethiopians, came to our
rescue.*

\* \* \*

*What was our refugee life like in Ethiopia? It was a chance
for independent and reliable thoughts and work. I had not
known how to cook my own food, how to thatch my hut, how to*

live in the bush, but adversity had taught me how to do these things. Four years of refugee life in Ethiopia was actually a rehearsal for the suffering we had to bear.

*When the Mengistu regime was toppled [1991], we were expelled from the camp by the new government. Our exodus from Ethiopia back to Sudan was a curse to bear.*

\* \* \*

*[After an arduous journey we were eventually sent to a camp] in the interior of the northern part of Kenya in Turkana district—to a placed called Kakuma. \* \* \* I was physically and mentally demoralized, upset with my own life. Kakuma was like a pool without an outlet. Year after year, the refugee numbers increased.*

*The camp was composed of different refugees from different nationalities, within Africa. The obvious ones were Somalis, Ethiopians, Congolese, Burundians, and of course the Sudanese, who were predominant. In fact, Kakuma was a multinational, multiethnic, multicultural, and multireligious camp. That huge number of people were confined in the camp. As the number grew larger and larger, the shortages of food, water, and living space and all the health problems became major crises.*

*We were asked to queue up to meet every one of our needs. There was frequent fighting in food distribution centers—barbed wires and razor wires nearly tore everyone during struggles for food. That food was not enough. However, it made the difference between little and none. Either an adult or a child was given the same ration. Two cups of maize, a quarter cup of beans, and a jerry can top full of oil were given to every individual for a fortnight. Firewood was a source of death—ladies were raped by the local people when found astray in search of firewood. Fetching firewood or kindling was an unforgivable crime. Therefore, we had to give them a portion of our ration in exchange for firewood and kindling. The local people killed many because firewood and kindling were taken without permission. We cried for help, but the government turned deaf ears to us. The local people almost became wild because of hardship on their own land. They begged that they could get a share of the ration provided to us by the UN They started an open robbery. I wished I could leave the camp, but there was no safe place that I knew of. We had to live like prisoners.*

*Recently, in August 2000, I was called to the UNHCR compound for the U.S. resettlement interview. I emotionally prayed to God that I would get an outlet from the camp. My petition was only to leave the cruel life of the camp, not to come to the U.S. I knew of nothing good in my world even in the U.S. In October 2000, I was summoned to the UN compound for the*

*JVA [joint voluntary agency] interview for resettlement. To my astonishment, I was given an approval letter by the INS [Immigration and Naturalization Service]. I had to leave within no time.*

*On February 26, 2001, my name appeared on the top of the list of forty-five children scheduled for the February 27, 2001 flight. It was unbelievable to me until I stood the following day by the plane's door among the forty-five on board. I was the first to be called in. At the door, I stood motionless. I had nothing with me except my IOM [International Organization for Migration] bag. The dream had come true. The waving hands of my fellow friends brought tears to my eyes. My heart pumped as if it would burst open. The bitter image of my ten years reappeared vividly in my mind during those seconds of standing. I did not dare to wave goodbye in return. Then I got onto the plane. I left the savage life of the concentration camp in Kakuma, Kenya.*

*My first plane journey was not simple. I felt nervous because that was my first time flying in the air like a bird. The plane swayed from side to side, bumped up and down. The lack of oxygen and the motor sound of an airplane were all troubling to me. "No journey is easy," I concluded.*

*The rest of the journey from Nairobi to Washington, D.C. was better. My arrival to the city was crowned with mixed moods and feelings. The flickering, glimmering lights, the roads upon roads, the endless queue of fast running vehicles, and the magnificent sights I saw and heard were all new and strange. Totally fantastic! "Yesterday in the darkness, today in the light," I remarked.*

*My departure from Africa, the third world continent, and arrival in the heart of the advanced world in Houston, Texas was a remarkable turning point in my life. The horrible images of the bitter fourteen years of refugee life in Africa and the strangeness of the new way of life in Houston are the greatest rivals in the small brain of this one Sudanese Lost Boy.*

—William Majak Deng, Sudan[1]

Earlier chapters have focused primarily on detailed legal consideration of claims to refugee status or other recognized protection founded in statute or treaty. But most of the world's displaced do not go through such a process. They may find haven, but usually it is based on a far rougher process of accommodation on the part of the host state or the nearby population, often spurred by international pressure and assistance, much of it transmitted or provided by the Office of the UN High Commissioner for Refugees. Once immediate safety (more or less) has

**1.** U.S. Committee for Refugees, World Refugee Survey 2001, at 108–11.

been accomplished, attention turns to ultimate resolution, through what are conventionally called "durable solutions."

Sudanese refugees arrive at Pittsburgh airport in 2001 wearing U.S. Refugee Program sweatshirts and toting IOM bags. (Photo: Copyright, Pittsburgh Post-Gazette, 2001, all rights reserved. Reprinted with permission.)

This Chapter will take a brief look at the range of durable solutions and then give extended attention to one of them, resettlement, which has played a major role in the history of U.S. responses to refugee situations. (Resettlement is also sometimes known, in the U.S. context, as the overseas refugee program, or, particularly in Europe, as the quota refugee program.) It is useful to keep in mind that global response to forced migration rarely involves a single form of solution, but instead usually reflects a mix of approaches. And solutions inevitably have to be quite case-specific, depending heavily on diplomatic, political, and financial factors unique to each such situation. U.S. resettlement is based primarily on discretionary choices about which refugee populations to include. But it operates within a specific legal framework that also requires officers of the U.S. government to apply the 1951 Convention refugee definition in many (but not all) circumstances before an individual receives final approval to resettle. We will examine the legal and institutional underpinnings of U.S. resettlement, recount their historical evolution, and explore selected legal and policy questions posed by that history and by today's needs for durable solutions.

## SECTION A.  THE DURABLE SOLUTION FRAMEWORK

### UNHCR, RETHINKING DURABLE SOLUTIONS

The State of the World's Refugees 2006: Human Displacement in the New Millennium. Chapter 6, pp. 129–30 (2006).

It is not acceptable, former High Commissioner Ruud Lubbers said in 2001, that refugees spend years of their lives in confined areas. Yet the political failure to find durable solutions for refugees leads to precisely the kinds of protracted situations that degrade the displaced. Unable to return to their homeland, settle permanently in their country of first asylum or move to a third state, many refugees find themselves confined indefinitely to camps or holding areas, often in volatile border zones. Such restrictive conditions are a denial of rights under the 1951 UN Refugee Convention and a waste of human talent. Furthermore, the prevalence in prolonged refugee situations of idleness, aid-dependency, a legacy of conflict and weak rule of law can induce fresh cycles of violence, threatening human security. With more than 6 million refugees stranded in a 'long-lasting and intractable state of limbo' at the end of 2004, it is imperative that the search for durable solutions be intensified.

Three durable solutions—voluntary repatriation, local integration in the country of first asylum or resettlement in a third country—are the options available for the permanent resolution of the 'refugee cycle'. All three are regarded as durable because they promise an end to refugees' suffering and their need for international protection and dependence on humanitarian assistance. The search for durable solutions has been a central part of UNHCR's mandate since its inception. The organization's statute commands the High Commissioner to seek 'permanent solutions for the problem of refugees by assisting Governments ... to facilitate the voluntary repatriation of such refugees, or their assimilation within new national communities'. However, the role of the three durable solutions and the relative priority accorded to each has changed with time.

\* \* \*

During the Cold War and the national-liberation struggles of the 1960s and 1970s, those who fled communist regimes and colonial oppression were granted refugee status on the assumption that repatriation was not an option. Resettlement and local integration were generally regarded as the most viable and strategically desirable durable solutions. With the demise of communism and colonialism, however, repatriation became more realistic and attractive for states. Furthermore, the increase since the 1980s in migration from poor to rich countries and the growing association of refugees with migrants fleeing poverty have added to the reluctance of wealthy nations to offer resettlement. As for southern states, in the aftermath of economic adjustment and democratization most of them have been less willing to support local integration. This is in contrast to the situation in the 1960s and 1970s when, in Africa, for instance, rural refugees were allowed a high level of de facto local integration.

Consequently, repatriation is now often regarded as the most desirable durable solution—provided that return is genuinely voluntary and sustainable. The 1990s became the decade of repatriation: more than 9 million refugees returned home between 1991 and 1996. However, returns under pressure from host governments—particularly the 1996 return of Rwandan refugees hosted by Zaire (now the Democratic Republic of Congo, or DRC) and Tanzania—have raised fresh questions about the degree of voluntariness and the role of compulsion in 'imposed return'. Moreover, arguably premature repatriations to the former Yugoslav republics and Afghanistan in the early 2000s have renewed debate on sustainable reintegration and its relationship to post-conflict reconstruction.

The recognition, on the one hand, that voluntary repatriation is not always possible and, on the other, that indefinite encampment is unacceptable has led to a profound review of the three durable solutions and how they relate to one another. The need to avoid human degradation while simultaneously safeguarding voluntariness has spurred the development of new methods and approaches. The period covered in this book saw the culmination of a cycle of reflection within UNHCR on the use of durable solutions, with the debate reinvigorated by new initiatives. The Global Consultations on International Protection with states, academics, NGOs and refugees resulted in the publication of an Agenda for Protection which stressed the need to redouble the search for durable solutions. To further these aspirations, UNHCR and partner states published a Framework for Durable Solutions for Refugees and Persons of Concern * * *. This elaborated the '4Rs': Repatriation, Reintegration, Rehabilitation and Reconstruction, as a process that would bridge the gap between relief and development. It also emphasized the two related concepts of Development Assistance for Refugees and Development through Local Integration.

\* \* \*

## UNHCR, 2005 GLOBAL REFUGEE TRENDS

Introduction, pp. 4–5 (9 June 2006).[a]

### Refugee Arrivals

Refugees escaping war often move in large groups and flee the same conditions during the same time frame. By being part of the same group, these persons are often accorded refugee status as a group, i.e. on a *prima facie* basis. During 2005, a total of 136,000 *prima facie* refugee

---

**a.** Paragraph numbers omitted—eds.

arrivals were reported by 19 asylum countries. The level of new outflows in 2005, however, was the lowest since 1976 when 113,700 persons fled their country in a mass outflow. As such, the 2005 level was also significantly lower compared to 2004 ($-46\%$) and 2003 ($-59\%$).

Ten asylum countries reported the arrival of more than 1,000 *prima facie* refugees during 2005, including Chad (32,400), Benin (25,500), Uganda (24,000), Ghana (13,600) and Yemen (13,200).

There were six countries of origin which produced more than 10,000 *prima facie* refugees in 2005: Togo (39,100), Sudan (34,500), the Democratic Republic of the Congo (15,600), Somalia (13,600), the Central African Republic (11,500) and Iraq (10,500).

### Voluntary Repatriation

Based on consolidated reports from countries of asylum (departure) and origin (arrival), it is estimated that some 1.1 million refugees repatriated voluntarily to their country of origin during 2005. In all, there were a total of 15 voluntary repatriation movements involving more than 1,000 refugees.

The main countries of origin to which refugees returned during 2005 included Afghanistan (752,100), Liberia (70,300), Burundi (68,300), Iraq (56,200) and Angola (53,800).

The past four years saw an almost unprecedented level of voluntary repatriation, mainly due to the return of more than 4.6 million Afghans from Pakistan and the Islamic Republic of Iran. Globally, more than six million refugees were able to return home during 2002–2005, of which 4.6 million with UNHCR assistance.

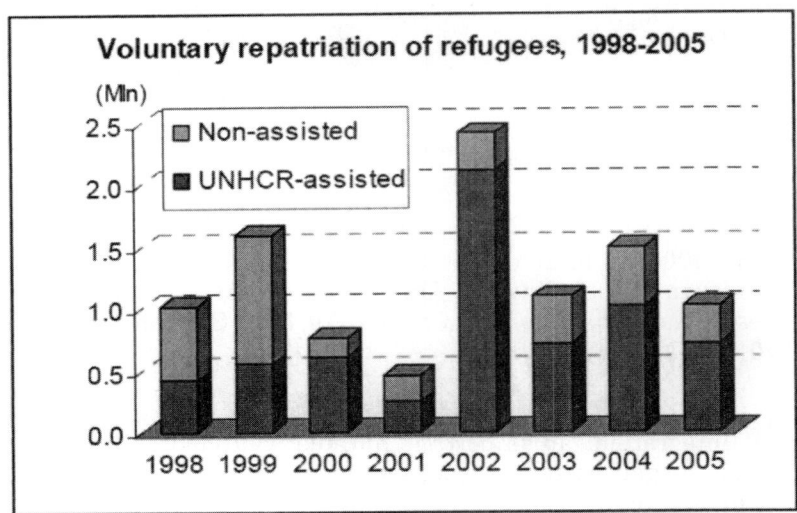

For statistical purposes, only refugees who have repatriated during the calendar year are included in the population of concern to UNHCR. In practice, however, operations may assist returnees for longer periods.

This is for instance the case for Angola where, since the signing of the peace accord in 2002, more than 364,000 Angolan refugees have returned home, many of them benefiting from UNHCR reintegration activities.

RESETTLEMENT

In 2005, some 30,500 refugees were resettled from their previous asylum countries with UNHCR assistance, virtually the same level as during 2004. The main nationalities benefiting from UNHCR-facilitated resettlement were refugees from Somalia (5,900), Liberia (4,700), Sudan (3,200), Afghanistan (3,200) and Myanmar (2,900).

Some 83 UNHCR country offices were engaged in facilitating resettlement departures during 2005, fifteen more than in 2004. The largest number of refugees resettled with UNHCR assistance departed from Kenya (6,800), Thailand (2,500), Guinea (1,900), Ghana (1,800) and Egypt (1,300).

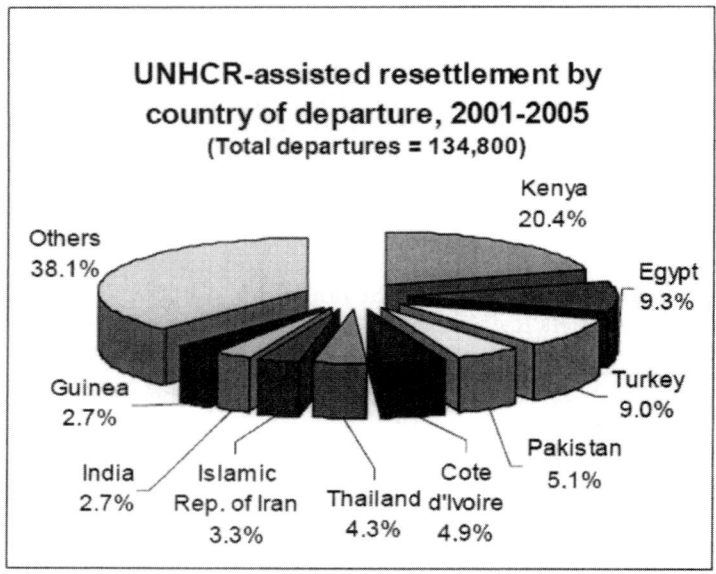

During 2005, a total of 16 countries reported the admission of resettled refugees, including the United States (53,800 during the US Fiscal Year), Australia (11,700), Canada (10,400), Sweden (1,300), Finland (770) and Norway (750).

LOCAL INTEGRATION

Local integration, an important durable solution to the plight of refugees, is a legal, economic, socio-economic and political process. In some countries, refugees have the opportunity to integrate locally because the host country has provided them with access to land or the labour market, while in others they remain confined to camps where they depend on assistance from the international community. Using UNHCR beneficiary statistics, it is possible to determine the degree to which refugees depend on the international community for their survival. Industrialized countries, where assistance is usually provided by the host country, are generally not included in these statistics.

By the end of 2005, 69 per cent of the estimated 6.1 million refugees hosted by developing countries had access to assistance provided by or through UNHCR. On a global scale, the proportion has remained fairly stable over the past five years ranging from 66 to 72 per cent. However, the proportion of refugees benefiting from international assistance varies greatly from one country to another, reflecting the different opportunities provided to refugees by the host country for local integration and self-reliance. Major asylum countries where less than 75 per cent of the refugee population depends on international aid include the United Republic of Tanzania (64%), Sudan (51%), Zambia (48%), the Democratic Republic of the Congo (8%), India (8%) and Armenia (5%).

Acquiring the citizenship of the country of asylum is the final and crucial step towards obtaining the full protection of the host country. However, national laws do not always permit refugees to get naturalized. Moreover, statistical data on the provision of citizenship to refugees is available on a limited scale only, and is thus under-reported. During 2005, UNHCR was informed about significant numbers of refugees being granted citizenship by the host country in the United States (58,900; during January–September 2005 only), Kyrgyzstan (3,400), Armenia (2,300), Belgium (2,300), Mexico (1,200) and Ireland (580).

### Notes

1. The 1951 Convention and the UNHCR Statute (the UN General Assembly Resolution that initially established the powers and duties of the office) generally point toward a highly individualized determination of whether an individual comes within the UNHCR's mandate or the Convention's protection, according to the familiar "well-founded fear of persecution" definition. Nonetheless, UNHCR early discovered a need to act with greater dispatch in many situations involving mass influx, and so helped develop the practice referred to at the beginning of the second reading above:

> Group determination on a *prima facie* basis means in essence the recognition by a State of refugee status on the basis of the readily apparent, objective circumstances in the country of origin giving rise to the exodus. Its purpose is to ensure admission to safety, protection from *refoulement* and basic humanitarian treatment to those patently in need of it. * * * It is widely applied in Africa and in Latin America, and has in effect been practised in relation to large-scale flows in countries, such as those in South Asia, that have no legal framework for dealing with refugees. * * * Under this practice, the objective evidence available on the situation or event prompting the exodus is used to determine that members of the group are at risk for refugee reasons.

UNHCR, Protection of Refugees in Mass Influx Situations: Overall Protection Framework, Background Paper prepared for the Global Consultation on International Protection, UN Doc. EC/GC/01/4, para. 6–7 (Feb. 19, 2001).

For more on the evolution of UNHCR's role and of its legal authorities, see Martin, *Refugees and Migration,* in 1 United Nations Legal Order 391 (O. Schachter & C. Joyner eds. 1995).

2. Review carefully Chapter One, section A3, for a more complete picture, including statistics, of the range of possible long-term solutions to refugee crises and the relative use of these measures in recent years. That Chapter also portrays the situation of the many millions who have not found a durable solution but who remain in camps or in an otherwise tenuous existence in a host state.

3. As those passages from Chapter One indicate, and as the reading from *State of the World's Refugees* (particularly the final paragraph) also suggests, a major obstacle to durable solutions can be the resistance of host populations. Sometimes they simply resent the new arrivals, fearing competition for jobs or living space, and so press their governments to confine the refugees to a camp, deny them any role in the local economy, or perhaps force them away. That resentment takes on a different form, particularly in developing countries, if the international community rallies to provide support for the refugees, thereby giving them opportunities not available to the local population. UNHCR and donor governments have therefore tried in recent years to include more provision for ancillary assistance to local populations whenever the international community undertakes a major effort to assist a refugee population. *See* Rowley, Burnham & Drabe, *Protracted Refugee Situations: Parallel Health Systems and Planning for Integration of Services,* 19 J. Refugee Studies 158 (2006); Posner, et al., *Differences in Welfare and Access to Care among Internally Displaced and Local Women: Seven Years after Relocation in Azerbaijan,* 15 *id.* 296 (2002); Whitaker, *Refugees in Western Tanzania: The Distributions of Burdens and Benefits among Local Hosts,* 15 *id.* 339 (2002).

---

### Exercise: Refugees in Tanzania

As you consider the legal and policy issues involved in devising durable solutions for refugees, it is useful to have in mind a particular refugee situation in need of durable solutions. Here we will focus your attention on the current status of refugees in the East African country of Tanzania. Think about the best ways to respond, given the general dimensions of the situation. We also want you to think more broadly about unintended negative consequences of international intervention or assistance and how best to avoid them. We provide below a factual description about this refugee situation, as well as a list of additional resources for developing more information about refugees in Tanzania and elsewhere, and about possible policy responses.

We start with some questions that you should have in mind as you evaluate the report about the refugee situation in Tanzania.

**1. Durable solutions in general:** What are the elements that must go into a decision as to which durable solutions are promising? What tools are available to help achieve any particular solution? What political, diplomatic, and logistical obstacles stand in the way?

**2. Resettlement in particular:** When might a major resettlement program, to the United States or elsewhere, be appropriate? What are the disadvantages? How could they be minimized? Might resettlement actually draw more people in to the haven state from surrounding countries? What problems might develop with fraud or manipulation? What specific strategies would you develop to counter these potential problems? What camp management practices might facilitate sound decisions on durable solutions? When might resettlement be impossible? Why? In that case, what other durable solutions would be appropriate and feasible?

**3. Refugee camp management:** What camp management practices might deter fraud or manipulation? How might camp management practices facilitate decisions on durable solutions and increase the odds that such solutions will actually succeed? What practices are best for the welfare of the refugees?

**4. Access to information:** What further information, beyond what is available in the reading, you would need in order to make sound decisions on these matters?

**5. Perspective:** How might your approach and perspective differ if you are (a) a UNHCR officer, (b) a U.S. diplomat, (c) a high official in the U.S. Department of Homeland Security, (d) a European Union diplomat, (e) a high government official of the host country, (f) an official of the source country, or (g) an official of other states in the region.

## U.S. COMMITTEE FOR REFUGEES AND IMMIGRANTS, WORLD REFUGEE SURVEY 2006

Country Update: Tanzania, pp. 95–97.

[Tanzania hosts approximately 550,000 refugees and asylum seekers from nearby countries in east Africa. They come primarily from Burundi (390,000), which has been the site of vicious interethnic battles between Hutu and Tutsi, occasionally producing widespread massacres over the past several decades, and from the Democratic Republic of Congo, which has experienced a lengthy civil war in which millions have died from brutal treatment, war injuries, or widespread illness untreated because of the war-induced chaos. Both source countries have seen some improvements in recent years, but progress remains tenuous. Some of the refugees in Tanzania have been present since the 1970s. Tanzania has a total population of 36.5 million and a gross national income per capita of $320 annually.]

*Refoulement*/**Physical Protection.** Tanzania continued to *refoule* large numbers of asylum seekers * * *.

Early in the year, the Government closed all the refugee reception centers in northwestern Tanzania [the main area accessible to Burundians, Rwandans, and Congolese]. The Government ceased allowing Rwandan asylum seekers to apply for asylum but, after UNHCR intervened, it reviewed the process and began screening them again. In December, Kibondo's District Commissioner ordered all adult Burundian refugees to produce letters explaining why they did not want to return and threatened to close two of the three camps in the area saying, "I used to be a harmless barking dog, now I bark and I bite."

Nearly 62,000 Burundian refugees repatriated during the year, as compared with 83,000 the year before. The repatriations were nominally voluntary but the pervasive threat of *refoulement*, oppressive restrictions on movement and livelihoods, and reports of sexual exploitation by police in camps made claims of voluntary repatriation questionable.

* * * Normally, the National Eligibility Committee (NEC) decided asylum claims but local authorities began unilaterally screening new arrivals from Burundi and Congo–Kinshasa without allowing UNHCR to monitor. After UNHCR objected, the Government established ad hoc committees of local immigration and Ministry of Home Affairs (MHA) officials to screen them. The final authority to determine refugee status remained with the MHA, which could accept or reject the decisions of the NEC or the ad hoc committees. The MHA rejected far more Burundian than Congolese cases. * * * The various decision making bodies together only granted asylum to a small number of applicants.

* * *

**Freedom of Movement and Residence.** The Government generally forbade refugees from leaving the camps in the country's western region but did allow them to gather firewood within about 2.5 miles (4 km) of the camps. With the approach of general elections in the fall, the Kibondo District Commissioner announced that refugees could not even do that, citing concerns that refugees would attempt to vote illegally. While local authorities did not enforce the prohibition on gathering firewood, those who did venture within the 2.5-mile limit, generally women and children, were subject to robbery, physical abuse, and rape. * * *

The Government vigorously enforced the general movement restriction and, in many cases, violators remained incarcerated for six months because they could not pay the $43 (50,000 Shillings) fine or a bribe. The Government could also prosecute violators for unlawful presence under the Immigration Act, which provided for immediate deportation or two years imprisonment followed by deportation.

The Government granted a few refugees the right to reside outside the camps for educational, medical, or security reasons.

**Right to Earn a Livelihood.** The Government severely restricted refugee trade activity by keeping several camp markets closed. In December, the Kibondo District Commissioner announced a ban on all income-generating activities, even inside the camps, in order to dissuade refugees from remaining in Tanzania. In August, police destroyed refugee-owned shops in camps.

Local authorities allowed only Tanzanian nationals with special permission to trade in camp markets. Refugees in camps trained in weaving, carpentry, bread-making, shoe-making, woodcarving, and other trades that generated limited income but gave refugees a skill they could apply after repatriating. The movement restrictions prevented refugees from selling goods in towns and made it infeasible to obtain wood or other raw materials.

\* \* \* Women and children in the camps sometimes resorted to prostitution.

The [National Refugee Policy] prohibited refugees from owning land, but allocated 38-by-38 yard plots to each household for shelter and "kitchen gardening" within the camps. The Government continued to forbid refugees from occupying and farming plots of land left vacant by other refugees who had repatriated. The Government allowed refugees to own businesses and transfer capital. The 1998 Refugees Act required refugees to turn over all personal property to the Government at the time of repatriation for fair compensation.

\* \* \*

**Public Relief and Education.** Persistent shortfalls in funding forced the World Food Programme to keep rations at only 78 percent of acceptable standards for caloric intake, which was 60 percent of previous levels. Several times, it had to suspend rations altogether. A survey completed in September showed that malnutrition and anemia among children had increased compared to previous years, but overall health status was acceptable by World Health Organization standards.

UNHCR and its implementing partners provided free primary education to all refugee children in all the camps. \* \* \*

Refugees received free medical services and other supplies. Tanzanian nationals also received services at camp hospitals and clinics, although this reportedly did little to stem local resentment of the burden that they perceived the camps placed on them.

--------

1.   Based on what you have read, sketch out the solutions you recommend for the refugee situation in Tanzania.

2.   What problems or obstacles do you think pose the greatest concern?

3.   What recommendations do you have to help minimize the potential problems?

4.   No single reading can provide a comprehensive picture, and refugee situations are always in flux. Therefore, we have identified additional resources that you may wish to consult in thinking about durable solutions for refugees in Tanzania (or indeed regarding other refugee situations). Our highly selective listing includes:

UNHCR website,

UNHCR, State of the World's Refugees (volumes published in 1993, 1995, 1998, 2000, 2006)

Refugees (UNHCR's quarterly magazine)

U.S. State Department human rights country reports, <www.state.gov/g/drl/hr/>

Information on refugees from the State Department's Bureau of Population, Refugees, and Migration (PRM), <www.state.gov/g/prm/refadm/rls/>

Report to Congress on Proposed Refugee Admissions (annual; includes summary descriptions of specific refugee situations), available on the PRM website

US Committee for Refugees and Immigrants website <www.refugees.org>, including the organization's annual World Refugee Survey and the periodical *Refugee Reports*

The International Journal of Refugee Law

The Journal of Refugee Studies

Center for International and European Law on Immigration and Asylum, University of Konstanz,

## SECTION B.   RESETTLEMENT

Resettlement has figured prominently in the history of U.S. responses to refugees, even though it provides a durable solution to a relatively small percentage of the world's displaced populations. Only a few countries routinely provide resettlement in significant numbers, though global interest in resettlement has grown in recent years, and UNHCR has taken modest steps to expand the use of this particular durable solution.

A small number of states have major annual resettlement programs; a few other states agree to resettle refugees on an ad hoc basis. In absolute numbers, the largest annual resettlement programs are those of the United States, Australia, and Canada, all of which have powerful identities as societies founded by immigrants. During 2005 the resettlement programs of these three states admitted 53,813, 11,654, and 10,400 refugees, respectively, combining for 75,867 of the 80,796 global resettlements for that year. (This number is considerably larger than that reported in the *Global Refugee Trends* excerpt above, because that study counted only resettlement assisted by UNHCR.) The Nordic states, the Netherlands, and New Zealand also contributed several hundred spaces. UNHCR, Refugees by Numbers 17 (2006 edition). (See also Chapter One, p. 24, Table 1.4, for complete UN statistics.) Each state chooses its own selection criteria and the numerical limits on its involvement (hence the frequently applied term "quota refugees"). Some that provide a relatively limited number of spaces essentially compensate by taking hard-to-resettle cases, such as individuals with handicaps or other extensive medical needs. A few states delegate to UNHCR the task of applying their criteria and actually interviewing and choosing the refugees, subject only to a dossier review by state officials. The United States, Canadian, and Australian refugee programs all select refugees after having their own officers interview them in foreign countries, and then fly them to the resettlement country, where they provide the newly arrived refugees with financial and social support. *See generally* J. van Selm, T. Woroby, E. Patrick & M. Matts, Feasibility of Resettlement in the European Union (Migration Policy Institute 2003); J. Frederiksson & C. Mougne, Resettlement in the 1990s: A Review of Policy and Practice (UNHCR Evaluation Report, Dec. 1994).

## 1. THE U.S. REFUGEE RESETTLEMENT PROGRAM: HISTORY AND LEGAL FRAMEWORK

We now examine in more detail what has regularly been the worlds' largest refugee resettlement program, that of the United States. It is a system that has fallen on difficult times in recent years, dropping from resettlement numbers that regularly exceeded 100,000 in the early 1990s to a level of roughly 50,000 today (and far lower totals in 2002 and 2003). Use these initial readings to make your own judgments on why that has happened, whether it is a reasonable or desirable trend, and if not, what can be done to reverse it. Also, any resettlement system is selective. Consider what grounds have been used for U.S. selection and whether changes are in order. Has U.S. selection been too much influenced by political ideology rather than humanitarian need? Too little? Should the statute governing this kind of discretionary selection be so closely tied to the Convention refugee definition? In what ways has U.S.

selection already departed from the Convention refugee definition? Were those departures justified? Answering those questions requires attention not just to the U.S. decisionmaking system, but also to global developments. The readings in the remainder of this Chapter provide various perspectives on these issues.

We begin by locating refugee provisions within the broad outline of U.S. immigration law, bearing in mind that this structure is not representative of immigration laws around the world. The United States, a large and wealthy country proud of its immigration history, provides multiple avenues that allow hundreds of thousands of noncitizens to gain permanent residence each year. But because demand far exceeds the congressionally established supply of immigration spaces, only persons meeting specific criteria are eligible. In broad sweep, permanent immigration to the United States (as distinguished from temporary permission granted to nonimmigrants) is based on one of three elements: family ties to citizens or lawful permanent residents (LPRs) already present, occupational links, or humanitarian grounds. (*See* T.A. Aleinikoff, D. Martin & H. Motomura, Immigration and Citizenship: Process and Policy 265, 274–90 (5th ed. 2003) for a more complete description of the general U.S. admission system.)

The humanitarian category is primarily for refugees, but in this context "refugee" can have numerous specific and subtly different meanings. It is vital to be clear about the meaning for a specific context. Most importantly, a noncitizen's successful claim that she is a refugee may lead to permanent residence in the United States through two quite different paths, each with its own distinctive set of procedures, constraints, and legal and policy dilemmas. Preceding chapters of this book have looked closely at one of these paths, political asylum (and related protections). In that setting, noncitizens who make their own way to the border or the interior of the country, even illegally, may be able to defeat expulsion (and eventually gain LPR status) by proving that they satisfy the refugee definition. The refugee claim there serves essentially as a basis for relief from removal, a trump that overrides deportability.

Historically, however, U.S. practice tended to think of refugees not in that context but as persons selected overseas and brought in from abroad as part of a deliberate (but focused and selective) rescue effort. In this latter setting, known as resettlement or refugee admissions or overseas refugee programs, refugee status serves more as a basis for admission, akin to an immigrant visa issued (after consular screening) on the basis of family or occupational ties. Refugees in the resettlement context, however, are usually screened by DHS officers rather than consular officials, and the travel documents they receive are not visas, though they serve similar functions. Occupational skills and preexisting family ties in the United States are usually not relevant, though U.S. law allows for close family members to enter with the principal refugee or to follow later in order to join a relative previously resettled.

There was little attention in the United States to admission programs for refugees prior to the end of World War II. In fact, post-war decisions to resettle refugees derived in part from a recognition that pre-war efforts, especially on behalf of Jewish refugees, had been appallingly insufficient. *See generally* J. Simpson, The Refugee Problem (1939); D. Wyman, Paper Walls: America and the Refugee Crisis, 1938–1941 (1968); H. Feingold, The Politics of Rescue: The Roosevelt Administration and The Holocaust, 1938–1945 (1970). Shortly after World War II ended, President Truman issued a directive that ordered priority use of regular immigration quota numbers for the admission of some of the millions of displaced persons left stranded by the war.

A few years later, Congress passed the first significant refugee legislation in American history in order to meet the same problem. The Displaced Persons Act of 1948, Ch. 647, 62 Stat. 1009, provided a temporary program for the admission of over 200,000 people from the categories specified in the legislation (the ceiling was raised to 400,000 in later legislation). Throughout the next decade, Congress enacted other statutes providing specific numbers of admission spaces for designated groups of refugees. Nearly all of these measures were conceived as a one-time response to known problems and did not set up an ongoing statutory mechanism to treat future episodes. Nonetheless, under these provisions, a network of processing centers came into being in western Europe, usually involving refugee assistance NGOs who would help the arriving "escapees" and prepare their cases for consideration to be resettled in the United States. *See, e.g.,* Refugee Relief Act of 1953, Ch. 336, 67 Stat. 400; Act of Sept. 11, 1957, Pub.L. No. 85–316, § 15, 71 Stat. 639, 643–44; Refugee Fair Share Law, Pub.L. No. 86–648, 74 Stat. 504 (1960). *See generally* N.L. Zucker & N.F. Zucker, The Guarded Gate: The Reality of American Refugee Policy (1987); G. Loescher & J. Scanlan, Calculated Kindness: Refugees and America's Half-Open Door, 1945–Present (1986); Congressional Research Service, 96th Cong., 2d Sess., Review of U.S. Refugee Resettlement Programs and Policies (Comm.Print, Senate Comm. on the Judiciary, 1980).

When the Soviet Union put down the Hungarian revolution in 1956, its action sent hundreds of thousands across the borders, mainly to Austria, and generated pressure for a quick United States response. But adequate admission provisions were unavailable to offer resettlement and thereby assist the overburdened first-asylum countries. The Eisenhower Administration finally decided to act anyway, and it chose to bring more than 30,000 Hungarian refugees to the United States using the administrative procedure known as "parole." Parole is technically not an admission of the noncitizen. A parolee remains constructively at the border and was traditionally subject to exclusion rather than deportation proceedings if the government later chose to remove the individual—even years later. Parolees also enjoy more limited statutory and constitutional rights. (After the 1996 reforms, a parolee in these circumstances will generally be treated as an arriving alien, the least favored category, if parole is revoked. The current parole provision appears at INA § 212(d)(5).)

After Fidel Castro came to power in Cuba, parole was used increasingly to grant thousands of Cubans refuge in the United States. From the executive branch's standpoint, the parole power was outstandingly convenient. It allowed for flexible response to developing crises without the need for new legislation. But its use carried certain disadvantages for the individuals, as noted above. Furthermore, when the Hungarian and Cuban programs began, there was no direct way to adjust the status of a parolee to permanent resident status, even though both refugee programs clearly were intended to bring the refugees here for a permanent stay and the beginning of a new life in a new country. Congress eventually cured this problem by special statutes authorizing adjustment of status for Hungarians and Cubans after two years' presence. Act of July 25, 1958, Pub.L. No. 85–559, 72 Stat. 419; Act of Nov. 2, 1966, Pub.L. No. 89–732, 80 Stat. 1161. But many members of Congress asserted that the parole power was being misused to bring in large groups of refugees without direct legislative approval.

The Hungarian and Cuban programs also taught an additional lesson. These two episodes disabused Americans of any notion that refugee problems would disappear once World War II's displaced persons had all found new homes. Some permanent provision for refugee programs, available to meet new crises, would have to be made.

Congress enacted landmark immigration legislation in 1965 that replaced the national origins quota system with one that allotted admission primarily on the basis of family and occupational preference categories. As part of this bill, Congress adopted a new "seventh preference" designed to make permanent provision for overseas refugee resettlement programs. It made available for refugees up to six percent of the annual numerically limited immigration numbers, but the provision applied only to refugees as precisely defined therein. A person could qualify for this program only by establishing that he had "fled" persecution in a "Communist or Communist-dominated country" or a "country within the general area of the Middle East." Immigration and Nationality Act Amendments of 1965, Pub.L. No. 89–236, § 3, 79 Stat. 911, 913, amending § 203(a)(7) of the INA. (This section also authorized admission of "persons uprooted by catastrophic natural calamity", but that provision was never used. *See generally* Parker, *Victims of Natural Disasters in United States Refugee Law and Policy,* Transnational Legal Problems of Refugees, 1982 Mich. Y.B. Int'l L. 137.) The seventh preference provision was often called "conditional entry," because its beneficiaries did not come in on immigrant visas. They entered in a somewhat more tenuous status known as "conditional entrant," which in most respects was identical to parole. But importantly, the 1965 law provided for fairly routine adjustment out of conditional entrant status to permanent resident status two years after arrival.

Congressional committee reports accompanying the 1965 amendments stated that parole was not to be used in the future for large groups of refugees, now that permanent provision for such admissions had been made through the seventh preference. This legislative history, however, had stunningly little effect. President Johnson announced a major new parole program for Cubans during the very ceremony, held at the base of the Statue of Liberty, in which he signed the 1965 Act into law. That program came to be known as the Freedom Flights, because the Administration had negotiated arrangements with the Cuban government allowing direct air travel from Havana to Florida. By the time Cuba halted the program in 1973, over 700,000 Cubans had immigrated to the United States since Fidel Castro's rise to power. When the Freedom Flights ended, the controversy over the use of parole for refugees diminished for awhile. But in 1975 the Administration used its parole power to bring in over 100,000 Vietnamese who fled upon the fall of the South Vietnamese regime, which the United States had supported during the years of America's costly involvement in Vietnam. After a lull in 1976 and 1977, the exodus from Vietnam and neighboring countries picked up again and reached enormous proportions in the late 1970s. The United States responded with large new refugee paroles. (The legal and logistical adjustments made to cope with the Southeast Asian refugee exodus, which continued for two decades, have played a major role in shaping the U.S. resettlement system. The final reading in this Chapter provides additional information about that effort as well as the global response.)

The permanent seventh preference provision, which by 1978 allowed the admission of 17,400 people a year, was plainly not adequate to meet the high numerical demand experienced in refugee emergencies like the one that occurred in Southeast Asia. Moreover, by this time the United States had established other, but much smaller, refugee resettlement programs for persons not from Communist countries or from the Middle East—such as modest programs for former political prisoners from Argentina and Chile. The evident inadequacy of the seventh preference, coupled with lingering doubts about the legitimacy of using the parole power for refugees, convinced Congress and the executive branch of the need for new legislation. Their combined efforts led to the Refugee Act of 1980, Pub.L. 96–212, 94 Stat. 102 (1980), which establishes the current framework for refugee admissions.

## 2. THE REFUGEE ACT OF 1980 AND THE CURRENT SYSTEM

The Refugee Act of 1980 repealed the old, numerically limited, seventh preference in its entirety. Its limitation to refugees from Communist countries and the Middle East had come under wide criticism as "ideological and geographic discrimination." In place of that specification, Congress essentially adopted the refugee definition from the Convention and Protocol relating to the Status of Refugees, albeit with slight variations that can be important in some contexts. Furthermore, it had become apparent that a single fixed ceiling, applicable every year, simply would not fit the variable needs created by the rise and fall of refugee flows. But congressional drafters of the Refugee Act were unwilling to leave refugee admissions totally to the executive, ungoverned by numerical limits fixed in some systematic fashion. The Refugee Act therefore established a novel decisionmaking structure that results in a specific ceiling on refugee admissions set early each fiscal year, accompanied by a broad allocation of those numbers among the regions of the world. *See* Martin, *The Refugee Act of 1980: Its Past and Future*, 1982 Mich. Y.B.Int'l L. Stud. 91.

Before we examine this system in detail, you should review the current statutory framework governing overseas refugee programs, INA §§ 101(a)(42), 207 and 209—provisions added by the Refugee Act. Note also that Congress sought to close in 1980 what it regarded as a parole loophole, by adding subparagraph (B) to INA § 212(d)(5). It forbids the parole of a refugee unless it is determined "that compelling reasons in the public interest with respect to that particular alien require that the alien be paroled" rather than admitted under the normal refugee provisions of § 207.

Once the numbers and allocations are established by the President, sometime around October 1 each year, the Secretary of Homeland Security has authority under INA § 207(c) to admit persons who meet the refugee definition and the further criteria adopted administratively to govern inclusion in a particular resettlement initiative. Usually a U.S. resettlement initiative is not open to all who believe they are refugees in a particular country, but only to those who meet more detailed access criteria specific to that initiative. Those criteria, in essence, define which refugees are "of special humanitarian concern to the United States," in the terminology of the Refugee Act—a term of art allowing selectivity. INA § 207(a)(3), (c)(1). The United States could therefore decide to take only those refugees, for example, who came from a named region of the source country, belong to a specific ethnic group, arrived in the camp before a stated date, or already have a particular type of connection to the United States (e.g., past employment with a U.S. company or distant relatives here). Officers of the Department of Homeland Security (DHS), now usually part of a professional Refugee Corps in the Department, travel to processing sites to interview applicants who have passed through preliminary access screening, although there are a few more permanent sites where DHS has a regularly staffed office. These officers judge whether applicants meet the refugee definition and assure that they are not covered by other specific disqualifications (for example because of involvement in the drug trade or terrorism).

An elaborate public-private partnership, involving refugee NGOs, UNHCR, the International Organization for Migration (IOM), and the U.S. government, works together to provide screening, health services, cultural orientation, transportation, and—importantly—assured sponsorship by an established voluntary agency (volag) with experience in refugee resettlement. In most processing locations, one of the volags or the IOM works under contract with the State Department to do preliminary interviews of potential applicants and complete a file with a photo, biometrics, and extensive information developed during those interviews regarding the person's or family's history and persecution claim. The purpose is to prepare the case so that DHS officers can efficiently conduct the official interview when they arrive at the site, in order to make a final decision on qualifications. The organization that performs these functions is known as an Overseas Processing Entity (OPE).

An OPE staff member interviews a Somali Bantu family in Kenya, preparing a detailed file for the DHS officer's use. (Photo: Staff of the Refugee Processing Center)

Volags also play a vital role in providing assured sponsorship for all refugees (usually grouped by family) before they embark for the United States. Sponsorship responsibilities are divided up case by case in weekly meetings of national volag representatives. The allocation takes account of medical needs and resources to meet them, the location of any family of the refugee already in the United States, and other factors. As a result, a local affiliate of the assigned volag meets the refugees at the airport serving the destination community, and then helps them with housing, job placement and training, and other elements of a successful transition to their new homeland. A detailed description of all the steps in this complicated and impressive system, with a flow chart, may be found in D. Martin, The United States Refugee Admissions Program: Reforms for a New Era of Refugee Resettlement 67–78 (2005) (hereafter referred to as Martin, Admissions Program).

Some of the dynamics of the sponsorship process, as well as some constraints that affect the refugees' transition to life in the United States, are evident from the following reading.

## SARA LIPKA, UNSETTLED IN AMERICA

The Chronicle of Higher Education, August 11, 2006, p. A32.

\* \* \*

When the State Department grants refugee status to a person, it sends his or her name and biographical information to a group of 10 agencies that coordinate the resettlement process. The U.S. Conference of Catholic Bishops and the Lutheran Immigration and Refugee Service are the largest of those groups, followed by other religiously affiliated and secular organizations.

Representatives of those agencies meet weekly, in Rosslyn, Va., to decide where to settle each new group of refugees. Arrivals with relatives in the United States are permitted to join them. Many others are placed in existing ethnic communities—Iraqis in Detroit, for example, and Burmese in Indianapolis.

For most refugees, however, the luck of the draw determines where they will live. "It's basically like a draft," says Terry Abeles, director of program development at the Lutheran group.

Regional branches of those organizations lead refugees through a "reception and placement" process, which includes a whirl of applications for jobs, Social Security, and apartment leases. For their first four to eight months, refugees are eligible for modest stipends from the states where they are placed. \* \* \* [R]efugees in Washington, for example, say they each received $140 per month for four months.

The problem for prospective students is that the resettlement process was designed to make refugees economically self-sufficient—not to help them get an education. In many states, refugees who enroll as full-time students automatically lose their eligibility for the monthly stipends, even if they are also employed.

Some coordinators of state refugee programs say they typically discourage newcomers from going to college. One reason: The programs' federal funds are designated for employment services only. The federal Office of Refugee Resettlement, in the Department of Health and Human Services, checks up regularly on how many refugees the state programs place in jobs within the first six months of their arrival.

"There is a lot of pressure on the system to get that person to go to work," says Bill Sperling, dean of learning services at Everett Community College, in Washington State. "If we can pry a year of ESL [training in English as a Second Language] and a couple of quarters of job training, that's usually the maximum the system will support."

Most refugees cannot afford to pay for college on their own. Those who are dependents may qualify for student aid, but single heads of household \* \* \* are often ineligible for federal and state grants. In the 2007–8 academic year, a single head of household with no dependents and no savings would qualify for a Pell Grant only if he made less than $17,000 annually.

Where a refugee happens to settle may also affect how accessible college is to him or her. Those who live in cities or towns with a strong refugee-support network or a community-college outreach program have a better shot at an education than those who move to places without such resources.

\* \* \*

A beneficiary of the overseas refugee program, once selected and given the necessary documents for travel to the United States, enters in a specific immigration status, created by the Refugee Act of 1980 and known as "refugee" status. (It bears some similarities to, but is definitely distinct from, the "asylee" status established by INA § 208 and described in more detail in Chapter Two above.) The first year of admission could be considered a kind of probationary period; refugee status can be terminated if it is discovered that the individual was not in fact a refugee, as defined in § 101(a)(42), at the time of admission. But this is a narrow standard, and termination is rare. Changes in the home country after admission that end the risk of persecution are not relevant (this feature also distinguishes the treatment of resettled refugees from asylees). As a result, virtually all persons admitted as refugees under INA § 207, barring criminal convictions since admission, may adjust routinely to LPR or green-card status one year later. INA § 209(a). This adjustment of status is retroactive in effect, so that the clock starts running toward qualification for U.S. citizenship from the initial date of arrival in the United States. INA § 209(a)(2).

The 1980 legislation made persons who enter as part of overseas refugee programs eligible for a broad range of federal assistance and retraining programs provided under INA §§ 411–414 (added by the Refugee Act). *See generally Chu Drua Cha v. Noot,* 696 F.2d 594 (8th Cir.1982); *Nguyen v. U.S. Catholic Conference,* 548 F.Supp. 1333 (W.D.Pa.1982), *affirmed,* 719 F.2d 52 (3d Cir.1983). Refugees are also exempt, for the first five years of their residence, from most of the restrictions on access to welfare imposed on permanent resident aliens by the 1996 welfare reforms.

We now consider in greater detail the quantitative and qualitative limits on overseas refugee admissions established by the Refugee Act and implementing regulations and directives, along with several policy questions that those provisions raise.

### 3. NUMERICAL LIMITS

Annually, before the beginning of the federal fiscal year, which starts October 1, the President is required to consult with the Judiciary Committees of the Congress on the executive branch's plans for refugee admissions. The Refugee Act lays out in some detail the procedures to be observed in this consultation process, and it specifies a variety of reports and data to be presented to Congress. INA § 207 (d), (e). This information is provided in an annual consultation document compiled by the Departments of State, Homeland Security, and Health and Human Services. Following consultation, the President issues a formal Presidential Determination that sets a total numerical ceiling applicable for the next fiscal year, *id.* at § 207(a)(1), and also specifies allocation of those admission spaces by geographical region.

The statute is designed and administered so that not all who might meet the statutory definition of "refugee" in INA § 101(a)(42) are equally eligible to apply to a DHS officer seeking to migrate to the United States. Some groups, though clearly meeting the definition, can be refused an allocation of numbers altogether—based on a judgment, for example, that conditions may soon settle down in the home country allowing voluntary repatriation, that local integration in the first asylum country is preferable to distant resettlement, that this group has sufficient opportunities to resettle in distant lands other than the United States, that the host government is uncooperative, that conditions are too insecure for U.S. officers to do the necessary processing in the country of first asylum, or that foreign policy objectives call for such a stance. The statute permits this selectivity through its specification that admissions are to go to refugees "of special humanitarian concern to the United States," but it provides no more precise standard to guide these allocations. INA § 207(a)(3), (c)(1). (According to some of the Act's proponents, however, this phrasing was intended to emphasize that humanitarian considerations, rather than politics or ideology, were to play a primary role in selections. *See* Anker & Posner, *The Forty Year Crisis: A Legislative History of the Refugee Act of 1980*, 19 San Diego L.Rev. 9 (1981).)

Refugee emergencies, of course, might also spring up anew in the middle of a fiscal year. The Refugee Act makes provision for "unforeseen emergency refugee situations" by authorizing a new round of consultations followed by a new Presidential Determination in such circumstances. INA § 207(b). That new Determination may add further admission numbers, but in the succeeding fiscal year (which begins the following October), admission spaces to meet that particular crisis are supposed to be worked into the regular consultation process and the standard Presidential Determination. As indicated in Table 10.1 below, that emergency power has been deployed three times to date.

The most recent Presidential Determination follows. Later Determinations will be included in successive Statutory Supplements and are always printed in the Federal Register around the beginning of the fiscal year.

# PRESIDENTIAL DETERMINATION ON FY 2007 REFUGEE ADMISSIONS NUMBERS AND AUTHORIZATIONS OF IN-COUNTRY REFUGEE STATUS

Presidential Determination No. 2007–1, 71 Fed.Reg. 64435 (Oct. 11, 2006).

MEMORANDUM FOR THE SECRETARY OF STATE

In accordance with section 207 of the Immigration and Nationality Act (the "Act") (8 U.S.C. 1157), as amended, and after appropriate consultations with the Congress, I hereby make the following determinations and authorize the following actions:

The admission of up to 70,000 refugees to the United States during FY 2007 is justified by humanitarian concerns or is otherwise in the national interest * * * . This ceiling shall be construed as a maximum not to be exceeded, and not as a minimum to be achieved.

The 70,000 admissions numbers shall be allocated among refugees of special humanitarian concern to the United States in accordance with the following regional allocations; provided, however, * * * that the number allocated to the former Soviet Union shall include persons admitted who were nationals of the former Soviet Union, or in the case of persons having no nationality, who were habitual residents of the former Soviet Union, prior to September 2, 1991:

| | |
|---|---:|
| Africa | 22,000 |
| East Asia | 11,000 |
| Europe and CentralAsia | 6,500 |
| Latin America/Caribbean | 5,000 |
| Near East/South Asia | 5,500 |
| Unallocated Reserve | 20,000 |

The 20,000 unallocated refugee admissions shall be allocated to regional ceilings as needed. Upon providing notification to the Judiciary Committees of the Congress, you are hereby authorized to use unallocated numbers in regions where the need for additional numbers arises.

Additionally, upon notification to the Judiciary Committees of the Congress, you are further authorized to transfer unused numbers allocated to a particular region to one or more other regions, if there is a need for greater admissions for the region or regions to which the admissions are being transferred. Consistent with section 2(b)(2) of the Migration and Refugee Assistance Act of 1962, as amended, I hereby determine that assistance to or on behalf of persons applying for admission to the United States as part of the overseas refugee admissions program will contribute to the foreign policy interests of the United States and designate such persons for this purpose.

Consistent with section 101(a)(42) of the Act (8 U.S.C. 1101(a)(42)) and after appropriate consultation with the Congress, I also specify that, for FY 2007, the following persons may, if otherwise qualified, be considered refugees for the purpose of admission to the United States within their countries of nationality or habitual residence:

a.   Persons in Vietnam

b.   Persons in Cuba

c.   Persons in the former Soviet Union

d.   In exceptional circumstances, persons identified by a U.S. Embassy in any location

You are authorized and directed to report this determination to the Congress immediately and to publish it in the Federal Register.

George W. Bush

———————

Refugee admissions exceeded 200,000 in 1980, the height of the Vietnamese exodus, then dropped below 100,000 two years later. After several years of admissions between 60,000 and 80,000, the totals rose well above 100,000 in 1989 and stayed there for six years, as the globe came to terms with the end of the Cold War and also responded to refugees from the conflicts in the former Yugoslavia.

Refugee admissions since adoption of the Refugee Act are shown in Table 10.1. Note that 70,000 has been a popular number in recent Presidential Determinations, and also note that many times the actual admissions are well below the ceiling established at the beginning of the fiscal year. What factors might cause the agencies involved to fall short of using all the numbers made available by the President? Should that number be understood as a ceiling or a target?

The steep reduction in actual admissions beginning with FY 2002 deserves some further comment. Initially, the refugee resettlement system was a major casualty of the government's urgent review of immigration systems in the wake of the terrorist attacks on September 11, 2001. The entire resettlement program was halted for two months, and the President's FY 2002 Determination setting refugee admissions numbers appeared a full six weeks after the start of the fiscal year. Refugees were subjected to new security screening, and even those refugees previously approved for admission and ready to travel in early September 2001 had to wait while these new steps were completed. The security review often took many months and often required more than a year, creating a ripple effect of other logistical problems. Other potentially eligible refugees were stranded because INS officers cut back on their circuit rides to refugee interview sites until adequate security could be assured there. And at about this time, INS and the State Department also introduced new review procedures to detect and deter fraud in certain categories of admissions. These reviews also slowed down the process considerably. *See* Martin, Refugee Admissions, *supra*, at 49–51, 71–72, 89–90.

The net result was a significant immediate shortfall in refugee admissions, to fewer than 28,000 in FY 2002, as against a ceiling of 70,000—by far the lowest admission totals since the enactment of the Refugee Act. The new screening procedures had become more routine

## Table 10.1
## Refugee Admissions and Ceilings, FY 1980–2006

| FY | Actual Admissions | Original Ceiling | Revised Ceiling | % |
|---|---|---|---|---|
| **1980** | 207,116 | 231,700 | | 89% |
| **1981** | 159,252 | 217,000 | | 73% |
| **1982** | 98,096 | 140,000 | | 70% |
| **1983** | 61,218 | 90,000 | | 68% |
| **1984** | 70,393 | 72,000 | | 98% |
| **1985** | 67,704 | 70,000 | | 97% |
| **1986** | 62,146 | 67,000 | | 93% |
| **1987** | 64,528 | 70,000 | | 92% |
| **1988** | 76,483 | 72,500 | 87,500 | 87% |
| **1989** | 107,070 | 94,000 | 116,500 | 92% |
| **1990** | 122,066 | 125,000 | | 98% |
| **1991** | 113,389 | 131,000 | | 87% |
| **1992** | 132,531 | 142,000 | | 93% |
| **1993** | 119,448 | 132,000 | | 90% |
| **1994** | 112,981 | 121,000 | | 93% |
| **1995** | 99,974 | 112,000 | | 89% |
| **1996** | 76,403 | 90,000 | | 85% |
| **1997** | 70,488 | 78,000 | | 90% |
| **1998** | 77,080 | 83,000 | | 93% |
| **1999** | 85,525 | 78,000 | 91,000 | 94% |
| **2000** | 73,147 | 90,000 | | 81% |
| **2001** | 69,304 | 80,000 | | 87% |
| **2002** | 27,110 | 70,000 | | 39% |
| **2003** | 28,422 | 70,000 | | 41% |
| **2004** | 52,868 | 70,000 | | 76% |
| **2005** | 53,813 | 70,000 | | 77% |
| **2006\*** | 41,500 | 70,000 | | 59% |
| **Total\*\*** | 2,330,055 | | 2,786,700 | 84% |

\*   2006 admissions projected.
\*\* Ceiling total includes final ceilings for each year, after revision where applicable.

Source: Bureau of Population, Refugees, and Migration, June 2004; Proposed Refugee Admission for Fiscal Year 2007: Report to Congress, Table I (2006).

nature of refugee flows and host state responses, to be considered in sections B4a and B5 below.

Some NGOs and members of Congress have been quite critical of the low admissions numbers and have pressed the Department of State to spare no effort to restore historic admissions levels. They point to the continued existence of over nine million refugees around the world and to a promise by key State Department officials in August 2001 that refugee admissions would be brought back up to the level of 90,000 annually. Others defend the current situation and suggest that with the end of the Cold War and the conclusion of the Indochinese resettlement, the era of large refugee programs has passed. Because global refugee totals have declined considerably over the last decade, reduced admissions should be expected, they say, with a narrower focus on especially vulnerable individuals and small groups, or perhaps only those groups whose admission would further other U.S. foreign or domestic policy objectives. *See* 79 Interp.Rel 1467 (2002); Refugee Reports, Jan./Feb. 2002, at 1–9, *id.*, Sept./Oct. 2002, at 1–6; Martin, Refugee Admissions, *supra*, at 9–14.

### Notes and Questions

1. Work through the Presidential Determination reprinted above and satisfy yourself as to the significance of each provision. Consider especially the paragraph relating to persons still "within their countries of nationality or habitual residence."

2. In 1995 the bipartisan U.S. Commission on Immigration Reform, charged by Congress to evaluate the implementation and impact of U.S. immigration policy, recommended that after a transition period the number of refugees admitted annually from overseas should be set at 50,000 as a general rule. It further recommended that this cap be exceeded only in emergency situations and only with more direct and affirmative participation by Congress than occurs in the current process. The Commission explained the proposed reduction from the then-recent historical average of 120,000 admissions by noting that 80 percent of those admissions came from Southeast Asian and Soviet refugee initiatives that were winding down. *See* U.S. Commission on Immigration Reform, Legal Immigration: Setting Priorities 121–59 (1995).

In 1997, the Commission issued a report devoted solely to refugees. In contrast to its position in 1995, this time the Commission adopted a noticeably different emphasis:

> The Commission is opposed to establishing a statutory level of admissions that can be exceeded only by special legislation. Such a provision could impede U.S. flexibility to respond to humanitarian emergencies requiring higher admissions. The Commission remains concerned, however, that resettlement could drop to unacceptably low levels as the need for the two principal resettlement efforts of the 1980s and early 1990s—for refugees from Southeast Asia and the former Soviet Union—declines. Hence, we believe that to pre-

clude a steady erosion of admissions, it is necessary to establish a minimum target or goal for post-Cold War refugee admissions.

U.S. Commission on Immigration Reform, U.S. Refugee Policy: Taking Leadership 46–47 (1997).

3. The Commission did not state what its target would be. Should there be a minimum target under the conditions of the early twenty-first century? How does the President or Congress or anyone arrive at a particular number? Should the consistent willingness of Presidents to authorize at least 70,000 admissions, plus Congress' willingness to fund at that level, be considered a humanitarian resource that the State Department should be sure to employ every year, even in the absence of programs like the former Indochinese or Soviet resettlement programs that were seen to mesh closely with foreign policy objectives? Or should the end of those large programs be the occasion for a significant reduction in admissions? Does the overall decline in the number of refugees in the world, as counted by UNHCR (*see* Chapter One, Table 1.1, first column), justify a reduction in U.S. admissions?

## 4. SELECTION PRIORITIES AND ACCESS CRITERIA

### a. *Background*

Once the annual Presidential Determination has set the broad framework for resettlement numbers, who actually gets to use them? Early activity under the Refugee Act was dominated by resettlement from Southeast Asia in the aftermath of the Vietnam war and from the Soviet Union. Recent years, however, have seen a trend toward a far more diverse set of source countries for those resettled in the United States, including much higher admissions from Africa. An initial sense of the evolution of the resettlement program can be derived from reviewing Table 10.1 above (gross admission totals) and Table 10.2, which shows the geographic allocations over time and reflects the changing patterns.

But changing allocations among these continental categories do not tell the full story. There has also been a significant evolution in the way that access to particular resettlement initiatives is structured. Today much more of the caseload is made up of (1) individual cases or specific groups referred by UNHCR, and (2) priority groups selected by the United States but defined in highly specific ways. For example, a 2003 initiative provided access for Hmong refugees in Thailand. (The Hmong ethnic group had been particularly supportive of the United States during the Vietnam war, and some of its members were still in refugee camps or precarious settlements.) But the opening was not for all Hmong refugees in Thailand, but instead for a specific group (estimated at 15,000 people) in the Wat Tham Krabok refugee camp. *See Resettlement of Hmong Lao Continues; No New Program Planned,* 3 U.S. Refugee Program News, Issue 4 (May 2005).

Table 10.2

**Allocations of Refugee Admissions and Actual Admissions, Selected Fiscal Years, 1980-2006[a]**

| Fiscal year | 1980 | 1985 | 1990 | 1995 | 2000 | 2001 | 2002 | 2003 | 2004 | 2005[c] | 2006[c] |
|---|---|---|---|---|---|---|---|---|---|---|---|
| Africa (admissions) | 955 | 1,953 | 3,494 | 4,779 | 17,549 | 18,979 | 2,548 | 10,717 | 29,125 | 20,749 | 17,200 |
| Africa (allocation) | 1,500 | 3,000 | 3,500 | 7,000 | 18,000 | 21,000 | 22,000 | 20,000 | 30,000 | 21,000 | 20,000 |
| East Asia (admissions) | 163,799 | 49,970 | 51,611 | 36,296 | 4,561 | 3,725 | 3,525 | 1,724 | 8,079 | 12,071 | 5,800 |
| East Asia (allocation) | 169,200 | 50,000 | 51,800 | 40,000 | 8,000 | 6,000 | 4,000 | 4,000 | 8,500 | 13,000 | 15,000 |
| Eastern Europe (Europe and Central Asia since 2003)[b] (admissions) | 5,025 | 9,350 | 6,196 | 9,987 | 22,551 | 15,776 | 5,439 | 11,269 | 9,254 | 11,316 | 11,500 |
| Eastern Europe (allocation) | 5,000 | | | | 27,000 | 20,000 | 9,000 | 16,500 | 13,000 | 15,500 | 15,000 |
| USSR/Former USSR (admissions) | 28,444 | 640 | 50,716 | 35,716 | 14,542 | 14,888 | 9,963 | | | | |
| USSR/Former USSR (allocation) | 33,000 | 10,000 | 58,300 | 48,000 | 20,000 | 17,000 | 17,000 | | | | |
| Latin America/Caribbean (admissions) | 6,662 | 138 | 2,309 | 7,618 | 3,233 | 2,972 | 1,933 | 452 | 3,556 | 6,700 | 3,000 |
| Latin America/Caribbean (allocation) | 20,500 | 3,000 | 2,400 | 8,000 | 3,000 | 3,500 | 3,000 | 2,500 | 3,500 | 7,000 | 5,000 |
| Near East/South Asia (admissions) | 2,231 | 5,994 | 4,991 | 4,464 | 10,079 | 12,086 | 3,702 | 4,260 | 2,854 | 2,977 | 4,000 |
| Near East/South Asia (allocation) | 2,500 | 6,000 | 5,000 | 5,000 | 8,000 | 12,500 | 15,000 | 7,000 | 3,000 | 3,500 | 5,000 |
| Unallocated | | | | 2,000 | 6,000 | | | 20,000 | 12,000 | 10,000 | 10,000 |
| Privately Funded (Unallocated) | | | 3,009 | 2,000 | | | | | | | |
| Privately Funded (allocation) | | | 4,000 | 2,000 | | | | | | | |
| Total (admissions) | 207,116 | 68,045 | 122,326 | 99,490 | 72,515 | 68,426 | 27,110 | 28,422 | 52,868 | 53,813 | 41,500 |
| Total (allocation) | 231,700 | 70,000 | 125,000 | 112,000 | 90,000 | 80,000 | 70,000 | 70,000 | 70,000 | 70,000 | 70,000 |

[a] This Table reflects regional allocations in the Presidential Determination, as adjusted (in limited instances) after mid-year congressional consultations. Specific regional admissions exceeded the regional allocations in a few cases, but overall admissions have always remained within the global ceiling for the year.

[b] In FY 1985, 1990, and 1995, the Eastern Europe allocation ceiling was combined with the ceiling for the USSR, but admission totals were reported separately. In FY 2004-06, this regional category was relabeled as Europe and Central Asia, and thereafter incorporated with Eastern Europe all the countries that devolved from the former Soviet Union, without separate reporting of ceilings or admissions.

[c] Admission numbers for FY 2005 are preliminary and those for FY 2006 are estimates.

Sources: Refugee Reports, Dec. 12, 1990, at 9, for FY 1980 and 1985; id., Dec. 31, 2002, at 9, for FY 1990; id., Feb. 2006, at 15, for FY 1995-2004 (with slight corrections based on Proposed Refugee Admissions for Fiscal Year 2006: Report to Congress 6, Table I (2005)); Proposed Refugee Admissions for Fiscal Year 2007: Report to Congress 5, Table I (2006), for FY 2005-06.

Consider this explanation (offered by one of this book's coauthors) for some of the changes in the admissions picture, excerpted from the report of a lengthy study chartered by the State Department in 2003.

## DAVID A. MARTIN, THE UNITED STATES REFUGEE ADMISSIONS PROGRAM: REFORMS FOR A NEW ERA OF REFUGEE RESETTLEMENT

Pp. 1–4 (Migration Policy Institute 2005).

* * * FY 2002 brought the United States to the end of several familiar elements of past refugee programs, placing us into a significantly new context for US refugee resettlement—a difficult transition whose dimensions were obscured by the September 11 responses. Largely gone are the massive, steady, and more predictably manageable programs that had dominated US admissions since the passage of the Refugee Act of 1980—the Indochinese and Soviet programs, followed for a few years by programs for those fleeing the former Yugoslavia. We are in a distinctively new era for refugee resettlement, and we need to recognize the true dimensions of the change. The new era brings both disadvantages and important new opportunities for the program to reflect on its core objectives and to respond to a wider range of genuine refugee needs.

* * *

Decisions to resettle have political impact, arousing political support and political resistance, both domestic and international, that must be worked through before deciding whether, and if so exactly whom, to resettle. A key feature is this: The refugee populations that make up the generally used estimate of twelve to fourteen million refugees worldwide are not a static pool that can simply be dipped into to ladle out however many the United States or other resettlement countries might want to admit. The act of resettling, even the act of openly discussing a major resettlement program, affects both future migration and the attitudes and actions of existing camp populations. It can affect the politics in the country of origin as well as the country of asylum, and it can have unintended consequences in discouraging other—and sometimes superior—durable solutions. * * *

Refugees are not a breed apart. Nearly all have had prior settled lives, often thriving existences—as farmers, merchants, herders, teachers, businesspeople, students, government officials. They are not just the passive objects of domestic or international policy—the helpless or inert victims—often portrayed in the media. They are subjects, persons with objectives and life-plans and the capacity to take action to better their own lot if given a reasonable chance. Most never expected to find themselves tagged with the label of refugee, and most find the restrictions and boredom that are characteristic even of a well-run refugee camp stifling and diminishing.

Although we often speak of refugees as having been driven from their homes, in fact the exit decision is rarely so stark. Short of truly desperate emergency evacuations, refugees exercise choice over whether and when to leave and, to some extent, where to go. Moreover, the escalation of dangers is often gradual. Conditions deteriorate in the home country, economically, politically, militarily, or a combination. * * *

Where refugees go and when they leave their country of origin is influenced by their understanding of what awaits them in the destination, measured against the dangers if they remain at home. This dynamic is the source of one of the major complications in resettlement decisions. Dangers in the home country are always matters of degree. Many choose to stay in familiar territory and cope with risks, even severe risks—particularly if life across the border appears to offer little prospect for a meaningful existence for oneself and one's children. But if that cross-border picture changes because the chance for resettlement out of the camps to a prosperous and stable country is introduced, the dynamic is altered. If the resettlement offer is perceived as open-ended, then the potential refugee's calculus for departure can be significantly influenced. Resettlement offers therefore can create a magnet effect— what the Office of the UN High Commissioner for Refugees (UNHCR) often calls a "pull factor." Carelessly managed resettlement, even on a large scale, may actually wind up increasing the size of camp populations in the first-asylum country, if out-migration fails to keep pace with new arrivals drawn largely by chances for resettlement. To say this is not to disparage the real dangers that propel refugee movements. It is simply to recognize that human beings often choose to put up with dangers. Refugee flight is rarely a clear-cut decision, and refugees consider more than just the condition of their home territory when deciding to leave.

Host countries are certainly aware of these effects. They, or at least certain key factions within the host government, such as the military, may resist the beginnings of a US resettlement program from their country, precisely because of fears about the potential for new migration—migration that otherwise would be deterred by knowledge of the conditions of camp life. (Host countries sometimes keep camp conditions stark in order to discourage additional movements.) * * *

In the large refugee programs of the past, for reasons specific to each, the magnet effect was of more limited concern, at least during crucial stages. In Indochina, the United States felt a sufficient historical responsibility for the persons fleeing Vietnam that early moves (from 1975 through the mid-1980s) were essentially premised on the idea that this country and its international partners would find room for all who escaped. * * * With the Soviet program, a similar Cold War dynamic undergirded a broad welcome for virtually all who could manage to leave. Significantly, in that context, any magnet effect was counterbalanced by the continuing presence of Soviet exit controls, which in fact generally kept outmigration to levels that the US and other transit or resettlement countries considered manageable.

* * *

[Under today's conditions,] several deliberate tools can be used to minimize the magnet effect. Prominently mentioned during project interviews was a strategy of focusing resettlement initiatives on well-defined groups whose boundaries are clearly marked—so that persons contemplating new cross-border migration understand that they simply will not qualify. * * * The wave of the resettlement future is probably what some persons interviewed for this project called "finite groups."

\* \* \*

#### b.　The Priority System

Access to the U.S. resettlement program is structured by a system of priority categories plus designations, within that system, of specific groups or individual characteristics that will make a person eligible. (In addition, as a practical reality, choices about where to establish refugee processing sites, permanent or temporary, also play a role in determining who may succeed in applying for U.S. resettlement.) These elements are described in the annual documents sent to Congress as part of the consultation process. The latest such document explains: "These processing priorities are distinct from the issues of whether an applicant is legally admissible to the United States or meets the statutory 'refugee' definition. A determination that a person falls within a particular processing priority only permits access to apply to the admissions program and does not entitle that person to admission to the United States." Proposed Refugee Admissions for Fiscal Year 2007: Report to the Congress 8 (2006).

The refugee processing priorities have changed over time. In the early years of the Refugee Act, the numbers were high (exceeding 200,000 in 1980), and the program to resettle refugees from Indochina claimed by far the largest share of attention, resources, and resettlement spaces. The program for refugees from the Soviet Union and eastern Europe accounted for most of the remaining admissions, although a few thousand refugees from Latin America, Africa, the Near East, and South Asia were resettled each year. Through 1994, the State Department used a priority system for distributing approved admission spaces that reflected the primacy of the needs of refugees from these two major source regions, particularly from Indochina. The first priority was reserved for those in immediate danger of loss of life and certain others such as political prisoners. Only a tiny fraction of annual admissions fell within this category. The next four priority groups all required some kind of earlier tie to the United States or U.S. companies or residents, by family, education, or employment. The final priority, known as P–6, potentially covered all others found to meet the refugee definition. In most regions of the world, P–6 processing was unavailable; only the first five priorities (sometimes only the first four) were deemed eligible for the U.S. refugee program.

By the mid-1990s, the Indochina program was beginning to wind down, and the State Department launched a new refugee priority system in September 1994. See Martin, Refugee Admissions, supra, 37–58. It redefined Priority One (P–1) to cover cases referred by a U.S. embassy or by UNHCR, including persons in immediate danger of armed attack or *refoulement,* former political prisoners, women at risk, torture survivors, and those from UNHCR's list of persons for whom other durable solutions are unavailable and whose first asylum situation is not feasible for the long term. The second priority (P–2) focuses on precisely defined groups of refugees of special concern to the United States, established as needed by nationality or national subgroup. For FY 1995 those groups were specified categories from Bosnia, Burma, Cuba, Haiti, Iran, Laos, Vietnam, and the former Soviet Union. Refugee Reports, Oct. 27, 1994, at 8; *id.,* Dec. 31, 1994, at 6–7. By FY 2003, the list had shrunk to cover the three groups eligible for selection while still in their countries of origin, as set forth in the Presidential Determination (Cuba, Vietnam, and the Former Soviet Union), plus three other small categories: Somali Bantu in refugee camps in Kenya, Baku Armenians in Russia, and Iranian religious minorities, primarily processed in Austria. The consultation document for FY 2007, Proposed Refugee Admissions for FY 2007, *supra,* at 10, describes an expanded list, in addition to the three in-country programs:

> The admissions program will continue to process several Priority 2 groups outside their countries of origin, including Burmese in Tham Hin Refugee Camp, Iranian religious minorities (primarily in Austria), certain Burundi refugees in Tanzania, Kunama in Ethiopia, Tibetans in Nepal, and Congolese Banyamulenge in Burundi. The program will continue to expand and include new Priority 2 groups during FY 2007. These groups may include Bhutanese in Nepal and, subject to interagency consultations and further consideration of the use of the material support inapplicability authority where necessary and appropriate, Burmese at other camps in Thailand.

P–3, the only other category in current use, now covers spouses, unmarried minor children, and parents of persons initially admitted to the United States as refugees or asylees. To be admitted in this refugee category, all of them have to meet the refugee definition by showing their own risk of persecution. This processing priority is not made available worldwide; the government lists the specific source countries for whose nationals it will be available, based on an assessment about which countries have enough such refugees to make processing feasible. (Some critics charge that the list was kept short because concerns about fraud had led the government to disfavor P–3 admissions.) At the beginning of FY 2003, only four nationalities were on the P–3 list, but for FY 2007 the list is back up to 17. *Id.* at 10–11. The anchor relative refugee already in the United States initiates the P–3 process by filing an "affidavit of relationship," which is first reviewed by USCIS.

It is important to note, however, that P–3 is not the only provision available for family reunification within the overseas refugee processing system. The statute allows spouses and minor unmarried children to "follow to join" the principal refugee, and these family members, unlike

P–3 refugees, do not have to prove that they individually meet the refugee definition. They obtain their status derivatively from the principal, who successfully established his or her persecution claim. INA § 207(c)(2). This process, sometimes known as "Visas 93," is available worldwide, for refugees of all nationalities. The refugee already admitted to the United States initiates the process by filing a Form I–730 with USCIS. Under current rules he or she must file within two years of admission. For a more complete description of P–3 and Visas 93, plus an account of systems implemented over the last few years to catch fraudulent P–3 applications (which had become a significant issue in some locations, as camp organizers pressured approved refugees to claim phantom family members), see Martin, Refugee Admissions, *supra*, at 46–51.

Although refugee advocates and assistance organizations initially welcomed the change in the priority system in 1994, by the end of the decade they were raising questions about its design. For example, P–1, although properly focusing on rescue of individuals in greatest danger, requires a referral from UNHCR or a U.S. embassy. In many locations, critics claimed, neither office was equipped for these duties. The State Department responded to this criticism in 2005 by permitting designated refugee NGOs to provide referrals under certain circumstances. Other critics suggested a separate priority for women and children at risk (currently simply one of the grounds for a possible P–1 referral). Further criticisms focused on the limited use that the State Department was making of P–2 group designations. *See generally* Frelick, *Rethinking U.S. Refugee Admissions: Quantity and Quality,* in U.S. Committee for Refugees, World Refugee Survey 2002, at 28; Martin, Refugee Admissions, *supra*, at 37–58.

### Notes and Questions

1.  How would you design a priority system for current conditions? That is, what *should* be the basis for refugee selections? How should the State Department decide which refugees are of "special humanitarian concern"? If you were setting refugee resettlement priorities, what regions, countries, groups, and individuals would you emphasize, and what subsidiary screening criteria would you use? Would you incorporate any of those criteria in statute, or would you leave them to Presidential Determinations and State Department priority categories and access guidance?

2.  To focus your thinking about answers to the questions in the previous note, consider the situation in Africa, which according to one respected estimate, has over three million refugees, as well as over 10 million internally displaced persons. US Committee on Refugees and Immigrants, World Refugee Survey 2006, at 4, 9. Should the United States move toward raising the 22,000 admissions allocated to Africa for FY 2007? If so, how would you select those who should come? Remember that under the African Union's refugee treaty, many persons counted as refugees in Africa were uprooted by conflict rather than targeted persecution, and so might not qualify under INA § 207. What impact should that factor have on plans for U.S. resettlement initiatives in Africa?

3. What if UNHCR asks the U.S. government *not* to initiate a resettlement program for certain nationalities because the program might interfere with that organization's efforts to initiate large-scale voluntary repatriation? Because it might make the initial receiving countries less willing to allow local integration? How long should the United States wait for such efforts to succeed? Should the United States defer to UNHCR on these questions? For accounts of UNHCR's priorities for resettlement, reflecting its sometimes ambivalent attitudes toward this solution, as compared with voluntary repatriation and local settlement in the asylum country, see Troeller, *UNHCR Resettlement as an Instrument of International Protection,* 3 Int'l J. Refugee L. 564 (1991); Troeller, *UNHCR Resettlement: Evolution and Future Direction*, 14 Int'l J. Refugee L. 85 (2002).

4. How could admissions priorities be designed so as not to create exaggerated expectations of future U.S. resettlement opportunities among those not selected? So as to avoid a "pull factor" inducing more people from the source country to come to first-asylum countries? So as to avoid a brain drain of the most educated or entrepreneurial among those in the camps? Are such considerations validly taken into account in a humanitarian program of this kind?

## 5. INDIVIDUAL ELIGIBILITY

As the State Department regularly warns, inclusion in one of the priority categories does not guarantee admission to the United States as part of the resettlement program. It only provides access, permitting the individual to be interviewed by a DHS officer. The main qualitative requirements imposed by statute that must be satisfied by individual applicants to the program are threefold (see INA § 207(c)(1)): (1) they must meet the basic admissibility requirements that apply to other U.S. immigrants, except as those are waived or modified under § 207(c)(3); (2) they must not be "firmly resettled in any foreign country"; and (3) they must satisfy the refugee definition of INA § 101(a)(42).

### a. Admissibility, Including "Material Support" for Terrorism

INA § 212(a) contains a wide range of inadmissibility grounds, including health conditions, past criminal convictions, involvement in terrorist activities, past fraud or other immigration violations, and polygamy. These apply to all persons coming to the United States on either a temporary or permanent basis, although waivers are available for some of the grounds under intricate and complex rules. The statute exempts all refugees from some of these inadmissibility grounds, notably the grounds based on a lack of required documents (passport and visa) and on likelihood of becoming a public charge. (By the very nature of refugee flight, most refugees would fail those tests.) The Secretary of Homeland Security has the discretionary authority, in individual cases, to waive most of the other inadmissibility grounds "for humanitarian purposes, to assure family unity, or when it is otherwise in the public interest." INA § 207(c)(3). Inadmissibility based on drug trafficking and most parts of the lengthy ground covering inadmissibility for involvement in terrorism are not waivable. Since September 11, DHS interviewing and additional computerized security checks assure close scrutiny of applicants' qualifications on these grounds.

The expansion of the terrorism ground of inadmissibility in the USA PATRIOT Act of 2001 and the REAL ID Act of 2005 has posed significant problems for the refugee admissions program. The law bars persons who provide "material support" for terrorist activity or terrorist organizations. This bar is certainly not surprising in its general concept, but the recent amendments brand as terrorist organizations any "group of two or more individuals," even if not specifically designated by the State Department or the Department of Homeland Security, if they have committed terrorist activities, which includes virtually all uses of violence "other than for mere personal monetary gain." *See* INA § 212(a)(3)(B)(iii)(V), (iv)(VI), (vi)(III). The definition is clearly broad enough to cover support for armed organizations opposing governments (like the Burmese regime) that the United States has condemned, or even for insurgents that the United States actively aids. The executive branch has also construed the bar to cover all forms of support, no matter how minor, and to allow of no exception for support provided under duress. Under this interpretation, persons who provided rice at gunpoint to a guerrilla organization that had seized control of their village are excluded from the U.S. program. (This inadmissibility ground is treated in more detail in Chapter Six, Section B6, pp. 411–28, above.)

The problem for the refugee program is not only that individuals at real risk of persecution, perhaps from the very organization that extorted the support, may be excluded upon interview, but also that the "material support" provision is now severely hampering the designation of new P–2 groups from conflict areas. This issue played a significant role in causing the decline in refugee admissions from 2005 to 2006. Several thousand Burmese refugees awaiting resettlement, as well as refugees from Vietnam, Somalia, Liberia, and Cuba, have been stranded by this provision. *See* Swarns, *Provision of Antiterror Law Delays Entry of Refugees*, N.Y. Times (Mar. 8, 2006).

The material support statute does provide that executive branch officials, after consultations among the Secretary of State, Secretary of Homeland Security, and Attorney General, can specify certain circumstances in which the material support prohibition is waived (or technically, considered inapplicable). INA § 212(d)(3)(B). As of late 2006, no guidelines had been issued concerning the use of this power, but Secretary of State Rice employed it for the first time in May 2006, to allow ethnic Karen refugees from Burma, housed in a specific camp in Thailand, to be considered for resettlement despite having provided material support to the Karen National Union, the *de facto* government in the areas where many Karen resided. The State Department distinguished between those who provided material support to the KNU and those who are members of the KNU and its armed wing, the Karen National Liberation Army (KNLA). Only the former (nonmember supporters) were eligible for the waiver. About 9,000 persons were made eligible by this decision, and approximately 2,700 from that group were individually approved for inclusion in the resettlement program. In late August 2006, the waiver was expanded to cover Burmese refugees in a wider array of camps throughout Thailand. 83 Interp. Rel. 930 (2006); Department of State Press Releases (May 5, 2006, Aug. 30, 2006).

### Questions

Critics have called for changes in the interpretation of the material support statute, wider use of the waiver, and for statutory amendments. *See* Refugee Council USA, Application and Interpretation of "Material Support" Admissions Bar (Oct. 25, 2006); Hearings Before the Subcommittee on Immigration, Border Security and Citizenship, Senate Comm. on the Judiciary, Sept. 27, 2006. How would you change the statute to (a) bar only those who supported armed groups that favored the wrong (or more abusive) side in a conflict, (b) effectively distinguish negligible or extorted support from the kind of willing aid that would suggest that a person's admission could truly be dangerous?

———————

The health grounds of inadmissibility could also be a problem in refugee admissions, given conditions in many refugee settlements. No refugee is finally approved to travel to the United States until there has been a thorough health screening by a doctor approved by the U.S. Public Health Service. In many settings this screening is performed by physicians of the International Organization for Migration (IOM) under cooperative arrangements with the U.S. government. But those arrangements also ordinarily include provision for IOM-managed treatment or therapy so as to overcome identified health problems and permit the person to remain in the processing pipeline, even if some additional time is required. *See* IOM, Migration Health Services, Annual Report 2002, at 5–30 (2003). Waivers are also possible, even for persons who have serious illness, including HIV/AIDS, but those cases are specially flagged so that the sponsoring volag that ultimately helps the person to settle in at the U.S. destination can make special advance arrangements for the additional medical needs.

### b. *Firm Resettlement*

Refugees "firmly resettled" in a third country are ineligible for the refugee admissions program. This requirement reserves U.S. refugee program spaces for those who have not already received and pursued resettlement offers elsewhere. In 1971 the Supreme Court approved INS's application of a "firmly resettled" bar even though the statutes at the time did not explicitly disqualify firmly resettled refugees. The refugee from mainland China had lived in Hong Kong for several years before entering the United States, and the Supreme Court noted that the "central theme of U.S. refugee legislation" has been "the creation of a haven for the world's *homeless* people," not simply the maintenance of a preference for people who at one time had to flee persecution. *Rosenberg v. Yee Chien Woo,* 402 U.S. 49, 55, 91 S.Ct. 1312, 1315, 28 L.Ed.2d 592 (1971) (emphasis added). Congress restored the "firmly resettled" language to the text of the INA when it passed the Refugee Act, *see* INA § 207(c)(1), and regulations have clarified the application of the concept. 8 C.F.R. §§ 207.1(b), (c) (overseas refugee programs); 208.15 (asylum). Firm resettlement is considered more closely in Chapter Six, Section A3, pp. 377–81, above.

### c. *The Refugee Definition and Its Variations*

INA § 207 clearly requires that an applicant for refugee resettlement in the United States must satisfy the statutory refugee definition, set forth in INA § 101(a)(42). That definition, as we have seen, is based on, but is not wholly identical to, Article 1 of the 1951 Convention, as modified by the 1967 Protocol. There was wide support in Congress for this more universal definition at the time when the Refugee Act was under consideration—especially in comparison to the old limitations that applied to the seventh preference (restricted to persons fleeing Communist countries or the Middle East). Nonetheless, some observers have questioned whether overseas refugee programs should be limited in this manner, particularly given that armed conflict, rather than targeted persecution, provides the root cause of many large forced migration flows in the world of the 21st century. Nothing in the Convention or Protocol obligates a country to use this definition in its *admission* decisions. The Convention is largely devoted to obligations and requirements that arise with respect to persons *already physically present* in the territory of a contracting state, if they are determined to be refugees. For this reason, the Refugee Act made the definition in § 101(a)(42)(A) the central qualification for asylum under INA § 208. In earlier chapters, we have seen how that language has usually been construed with a fair degree of strictness in the asylum setting. The question is whether the same strictness is appropriate in overseas refugee admissions, where the physical setting assures that the resettling state can set deliberate limits on its numerical exposure, whatever definition it employs.

The Convention and Protocol, by their terms, do not require adhering states to admit anyone. But equally, they were not meant to narrow the discretion of states to choose to admit persons based on other humanitarian considerations. A few other industrialized nations that are parties to the Convention and Protocol have had statutory provisions expressly allowing the admission, as part of quota refugee programs, of needy people who may not technically meet the UN definition of refugee. *See, e.g.,* Canadian Immigration Act, 1976, 25–26 Eliz. II, Ch. 52, § 6(2) (providing for admission, without regard to other regulations under the Act, of Convention refugees and also of groups "designated by the Governor in Council as a class, the admission of members of which would be in accordance with Canada's humanitarian tradition with respect to the displaced and the persecuted"); M. Crock, Immigration and Refugee Law in Australia 124–25 (1998) (describing Australia's comparable practice). *See generally* Hathaway, *Selective Concern: An*

*Overview of Refugee Law in Canada,* 33 McGill L.J. 676 (1988); Meissner, *Class II Refugees: An Answer to a Growing Need,* World Refugee Survey: 1986 in Review, at 22 (1987) (proposing a system similar to Canada's designated classes for U.S. overseas refugee admissions). Canada's current legislation permits resettlement of Convention refugees as well as a "country of asylum" class, which includes persons "seriously and personally affected by civil war and armed conflict." *See* Refugee Resettlement Division, Refugee Branch, Citizenship and Immigration Canada, Canada's Refugee Resettlement and Humanitarian Program 5 (Nov. 8, 2002) (paper prepared for Geneva Workshop on Resettlement of the Intergovernmental Consultations).

Using the Convention refugee definition to govern most parts of overseas refugee processing carries certain practical drawbacks:

> Under current law, even with regard to persons who have spent many years in a bleak refugee camp and have been given access to the application process because of a P–2 group designation, DHS officers are now obligated to spend interview time exploring the individualized risk of persecution that the applicant would face. Some officers with whom I spoke [during interviews for this State Department study] expressed a concern that applicants in this setting often have difficulty articulating an individualized basis for a fear of persecution, precisely because it has been so many years since they lived in the country of origin. In the interview, they tend to want to speak of the miseries of life in the refugee camp, not realizing that US law makes risks in the home country the crucial factor. Much interview time is then diverted to drawing out the details of their distant experience in the home country, slowing overall processing and taking time away from questions addressed to identity and possible grounds of inadmissibility. * * * [I]t would be more straightforward to recognize directly that the US has made a policy decision at the highest levels to respond to the needs of this camp population through resettlement, based on a broader judgment that the risks in the home country preclude any reasonable prospect of safe return. If the law were changed to empower the President to designate groups for admission in the refugee program, he could, for example, designate all individuals on a verified UNHCR registration list in camp X who arrived there before date Y (say, 5 years before the designation). The DHS officer could then swiftly decide whether the person meets these objective qualifications, and could devote the balance of the interview to a closer inquiry into identity and any inadmissibility grounds (such as possible drug use or security risks).

Martin, Refugee Admissions, *supra*, at 113 (the author goes on to provide suggested language for a redrafted § 207 embodying this approach).

### i. In-Country Refugees

Rather late in its deliberations on the Refugee Act in 1980, Congress did add a clause (B) to the refugee definition in § 101(a)(42), which permits a clear departure from the 1951 Convention definition for purposes of admissions under INA § 207:

> [I]n such special circumstances as the President after appropriate consultation [with Congress] may specify, [the refugee definition includes] any person who is within the country of such person's nationality * * * and who is persecuted or who has a well-founded fear of persecution on account of race, religion, nationality, membership in a particular social group, or political opinion.

Though this clause requires a special certification in the annual Presidential Determination, when it is triggered it overcomes one significant limitation of the Convention definition, the requirement that a refugee be outside the country of origin. Congress added that language in 1980 because of its awareness that some important earlier initiatives, especially the Freedom Flights from Havana, involved individuals not yet outside their countries of origin when they were approved for the refugee admission program. But this congressional modification still left intact the central Convention requirement, that the person show current persecution or a well-founded fear of future persecution. *See* Martin, *The Refugee Act of 1980: Its Past and Future,* 1982 Mich. Y.B. Int'l L. Stud. 101, 111–14.

Should Congress provide a general method for easing that persecution requirement as well (either to reach out to long-warehoused refugees who fled primarily from a civil war, or to simplify processing once a group is included in a P–2 designation)? Or would such a change make it too easy to distort admission decisions in order to serve foreign policy goals or to placate domestic constituencies rather than to fulfill humanitarian objectives? Congress has in fact provided one such mechanism, known as the Lautenberg Amendment, that eases the persecution requirement, but only for certain groups specified in the statute. That method for easing the persecution requirement, including the tangled history that led to its adoption, merits a closer look.

### ii. The Lautenberg Amendment

Historically, INS and DHS officers conducting overseas refugee interviews have generally applied a generous understanding of the refugee definition. This approach has facilitated relatively swift processing of caseloads already identified through the allocation process as priorities for U.S. resettlement. Nonetheless, the fact that the statute applies the same refugee definition to both asylum applicants and refugee admissions applicants has sometimes resulted in sudden problems, when individual officers or high officials familiar with the strict application of the definition in the asylum setting raised questions about the variation. A new INS district director in Bangkok in 1981, for example, on his own initiative, directed strict application of the definition at a crucial phase in the Vietnamese resettlement program, causing high rejection rates, major diplomatic difficulties, and a hectic scramble in headquarters to respond. The response eventually resulted in the issuance of "Worldwide Guidelines for Overseas Refugee Processing" in August 1983 that restored much of the earlier approach. *See* Refugee Reports, Sept. 7, 1984, at 1–3.

A similar episode arose in the processing of refugees from the Soviet Union. That refugee flow dropped off in the early 1980s, as the Soviets cut back sharply on exit visas, particularly for Soviet Jews, in order to express displeasure with the new Reagan administration. After Mikhail Gorbachev came to power, however, relations thawed and approved exits increased. But the expansion stimulated a new look at the program in the Justice Department. In August 1988, Attorney General Edwin Meese wrote to White House National Security Advisor Colin Powell: "Changes must be made in our Soviet refugee admissions program. * * * Current practices * * * appear not to conform with the requirements" of the Refugee Act of 1980. He directed a transition to "the proper statutory processing of Soviets," meaning careful case-by-case evaluation of the persecution claims of each individual applicant. Refugee Reports, April 28, 1989, at 1. This memorandum marked the beginning of a systematic INS effort to apply the "worldwide refugee definition," as its proponents called it, consistently in all settings, whether involving asylum or overseas processing. The change therefore also resulted in higher denial rates for Vietnamese, Cambodians, and Laotians.

The transition to this new approach did not go smoothly. Hundreds of Soviet Jews in Rome (then a primary location for U.S. processing) suddenly found their applications denied. The Italian government, having admitted them in anticipation of onward movement to the United States, was not pleased. Likewise, many applicants being processed in Moscow were turned down, even though, having previously secured exit documents from Soviet authorities, they had already given up their jobs and apartments in the expectation of resettlement. The NGOs assisting these groups protested vigorously, emphasizing the hardships visited on people who had relied on an implicit American promise of resettlement. Some members of Congress joined the protest, particularly because of the Administration's failure to consult before changing the de facto processing standards. The executive branch's initial response to these hardships and complaints was an offer to parole into the United States, at the rate of 2,000 per month, any Soviet applicant whose refugee claim was denied. But because parolees were ineligible for the federal funding the Refugee Act authorizes for persons admitted as refugees, and because they could not easily adjust status from parolee to lawful permanent resident, criticism persisted. *See* 65 Interp.Rel. 1286 (1988); Refugee Reports, April 28, 1989, at 1.

Eventually Congress adopted the Lautenberg Amendment, in 1989, to address the problems caused by the executive decision to apply a worldwide refugee definition. Foreign Operations, Export Financing, and

Related Programs Appropriations Act for 1990, Pub.L. 101–167, § 599D, 103 Stat. 1195, 1261 (1989), 8 U.S.C.A. § 1157 Note. But instead of changing the standard for all persons in the overseas refugee program or, more cautiously, using the model of § 101(a)(42)(B) (the in-country provision) to give the President targeted flexibility on these matters, Congress chose instead to specify particular groups in the statute who could qualify as refugees based on a reduced showing regarding the risk of persecution. Under the amendment, the executive branch was to designate "categories of aliens" from the Soviet Union, Vietnam, Laos, or Cambodia "who share common characteristics that identify them as targets of persecution" in the country of origin. The statute also specifically provided that Jews and Evangelical Christians in the Soviet Union, active members of the Ukrainian Catholic Church or the Ukrainian Orthodox Church, and all those in Southeast Asia covered by the 1983 INS Worldwide Guidelines were to count as such categories. The key operative language then provided:

> In the case of an alien who is within a category of aliens established [through the process described above], the alien may establish, for purposes of admission as a refugee under section 207, * * * that the alien has a well-founded fear of persecution on account of race, religion, nationality, membership in a particular social group, or political opinion by asserting such a fear and asserting a credible basis for concern about the possibility of such persecution.

As the quoted language indicates, the relaxed standard applies only for purposes of overseas refugee admissions, not to asylum decisions under INA § 208. The bill was enacted as a temporary measure effective only through September 1990, but successive Congresses have extended it, with only modest substantive changes, in one or two year increments ever since. There was one significant expansion, however. In January 2004, Congress added Iranian religious minorities to the list of groups for whom the State Department is to develop categories showing "common characteristics that identify them as targets of persecution." This change derived from congressional displeasure with what key members regarded as an unreasonably high rejection rate of Iranian applicants in Vienna, where most such applicants were being processed. (The latest version of the Lautenberg Amendment is printed in the Statutory Supplement.)

## Notes and Questions

1. Look closely at the language of the Lautenberg Amendment. How does it differ from the "designated class" approach, formerly used by Canada and described in the introduction to section B5c above? Should more—or less—discretion be given to the executive branch? Should there be a general provision in U.S. law permitting inclusion in the overseas refugee program of persons displaced by armed conflict, on the model of the more recent Canadian legislation described in the same paragraph? What would be the advantages and disadvantages?

2.  Why did Congress apparently find it so important to bring the persons from the Soviet Union whose rejections led to the Lautenberg amendment under the specific umbrella of the "refugee" label, rather than supporting their continued admission as parolees or carving out some other special category? Is it more important than Congress recognized to preserve the integrity of the refugee category, by insisting on consistent application of a "worldwide refugee definition" without presumptions? Which approach, Congress's Lautenberg approach or the Reagan administration's use of parole, is more subject to political manipulation? Which better promotes candor about the true grounds for admission decisions? Are there reasons why it be more appropriate (and politically feasible) to ease the standards for the resettlement program while still insisting on fairly strict application of the refugee definition in adjudicating requests for political asylum? *See* Martin, Refugee Admissions, *supra*, at 61–62, 111–15. Or is any formal expansion in refugee criteria politically vulnerable?

3.  The Soviet Union has been gone from the map since 1991, and the governments of the successor nations generally owe their positions to elections. Nonetheless, Congress has regularly extended the Lautenberg Amendment since these changes—and the former Soviet Union continued to claim a major allocation of refugee admissions through the first few years of the 21st century, with a high percentage of these beneficiaries approved via in-country processing in Moscow. Those who support continuing refugee admissions from the former Soviet Union usually point to the persistence of nationalist extremists in Russia, the risk of a resurgence in anti-Semitism, and indications of backsliding on democratic reforms. These risks are real, but do they adequately distinguish the case from current victims such as Sudanese from the Darfur region who have fled to Chad, or Colombians in Venezuela?

4.  The immigration subcommittee of the Senate Judiciary Committee held hearings on February 12, 2002, in which many Senators expressed concerns about the steep fall-off in refugee admissions over the preceding several months. Several NGO representatives testified about the need to revive the program and suggested additional refugee populations that should be included in the priority system. Bill Frelick, then Director of Policy for the U.S. Committee for Refugees, and a prolific author on refugee issues, proposed a detailed alternative priority system. (He elaborated on this proposal in Frelick, *Rethinking U.S. Refugee Admissions: Quantity and Quality,* 2002 World Refugee Survey 28.) In the colloquy after the prepared statements were delivered, the following dialogue occurred:

[SENATOR] BROWNBACK: Do we need to go more of the Lautenberg approach then to change this [decline in admissions] and put in statute certain groups to drive this process, to move it on forward.

* * *

FRELICK: I would hope not because, in part, what that tends to do is to calcify a situation, and we have got a changing refugee world out there. * * *

BROWNBACK: I look at a calcified approach as going the wrong way.

*Empty Seats in a Lifeboat: Are There Problems with the U.S. Refugee Program?,* Hearing Before the Subcomm. on Immigration, S. Comm. on the Judiciary, 107th Cong., 2d Sess., at 59 (2002). What is the problem Frelick describes as calcification? Is the current system subject to it?

5. Turning to pragmatic concerns, how should a member of one of the Lautenberg-specified groups establish "a credible basis for concern about the possibility of such persecution"? How far into the future (or the past) does this formulation reach?

## 6. THE ROLE OF IDEOLOGY AND FOREIGN POLICY IN OVERSEAS REFUGEE ADMISSIONS

The preceding materials demonstrate that refugee admissions to the United States began in earnest with one of the signal events of the Cold War, the 1956 Hungarian revolt against the Communist government. The United States then gave refuge to hundreds of thousands of Cubans who fled after Fidel Castro rose to power and declared himself a Marxist–Leninist. The first permanent overseas refugee resettlement program was statutorily limited to those fleeing persecution from Communist countries or from the Middle East. The parole power was not so limited, but one study found that from 1968 to 1980, parole was used to admit 7,150 persons from non-Communist countries and 608,365 persons from Communist countries. Helton, *Political Asylum Under the 1980 Refugee Act: An Unfulfilled Promise,* 17 U. Mich. J.L. Ref. 243, 248 (1984). Even after the law was changed in the Refugee Act of 1980, with much talk of ending the "ideological and geographic discrimination" of the seventh preference, admissions still went overwhelmingly to refugees from Vietnam and the Soviet Union. Without question, politics and ideology, rather than a pure and neutral humanitarian impulse, have shaped U.S. refugee admissions from overseas. Is that shaping role appropriate? The following readings provide perspective on that question.

The late Arthur Helton, a refugee activist and scholar, was highly critical of this situation: "Eight years after the passage of the Refugee Act of 1980, its mandate that uniform and neutral standards be utilized in conferring refugee protection remains unfulfilled. Rather, the Act's mandate is subservient to foreign and domestic policy considerations which continue to dominate protection determinations." Helton, *New Asylum Rules: The Need for Reform in Asylum and Refugee Protection in the United States,* 11 In Defense of the Alien 115, 115 (1989). Other seasoned observers commented: "At no time have the refugee admissions numbers reflected the actual worldwide distribution of refugees. * * * The overseas refugee admissions program often seems to function more as a family-based immigration category and a device for increasing or relieving pressures on foreign governments than a means of rescuing persons from persecution. * * * Congress [has failed] to insure that the admissions program created under section 207 was not heavily infected with foreign policy objectives * * *." Fitzpatrick & Pauw, *Foreign Policy, Asylum and Discretion,* 28 Willamette L.Rev. 751, 762–64 (1992). But

Congressman Bruce Morrison (D–Conn.), who once chaired the House immigration subcommittee, has observed: "The people who can come here are a trickle [compared to those who want to come]. Therefore, there is an impossible picking and choosing. By the very nature of things, there has to be a reason for why we take a particular person. And that gives rise to politics, not in a corrupt sense, but in a sense of identifying American interests." Quoted in Biskupic, *Sweeping Changes Abroad Confound U.S. Policy*, 1990 Cong. Q. Weekly Rep. 592, 594.

Consider also the perspective in the following reading from philosopher and political theorist Michael Walzer—clearly not a Cold Warrior himself. He treats some of these issues at length in his book *Spheres of Justice: A Defense of Pluralism and Equality* (1983). He addresses the practical limitations of neutrality and examines the quandaries of preferences and priorities. After acknowledging that refugee dilemmas often simply have no satisfactory answers, he goes on:

Toward some refugees, we may well have obligations of the same sort that we have toward fellow nationals. This is obviously the case with regard to any group of people whom we have helped turn into refugees. The injury we have done them makes for an affinity between us: thus Vietnamese refugees had, in a moral sense, been effectively Americanized even before they arrived on these shores. But we can also be bound to help men and women persecuted or oppressed by someone else—if they are persecuted or oppressed because they are like us. Ideological as well as ethnic affinity can generate bonds across political lines, especially, for example, when we claim to embody certain principles in our communal life and encourage men and women elsewhere to defend those principles. * * * [C]onsider the thousands of men and women who fled Hungary after the failed revolution of 1956. It is hard to deny them a similar recognition [as a kind of kin], given the structure of the Cold War, the character of Western propaganda, the sympathy already expressed with East European "freedom fighters." These refugees probably had to be taken in by countries like Britain and the United States. The repression of political comrades, like the persecution of co-religionists, seems to generate an obligation to help, at least to provide a refuge for the most exposed and endangered people. Perhaps every victim of authoritarianism and bigotry is the moral comrade of a liberal citizen: that is an argument I would like to make. But that would press affinity too hard, and it is in any case unnecessary. * * * [W]hen the number increases, and we are forced to choose among the victims, we will look, rightfully, for some more direct connection with our own way of life. * * * Once again, communities must have boundaries; and however these are determined with regard to territory and resources, they depend with regard to population on a sense of relatedness and mutuality. Refugees must appeal to that sense. One wishes them success; but in particular cases, with reference to a particular state, they may well have no right to be successful.

*Id.* at 49–50.

Consider certain other effects of ideology on refugee policy. The political commentator and author James Fallows, after traveling through Southeast Asia for several months in the early 1980s, at a high point of the Vietnamese refugee flows and of international sympathy for the "boat people," reflected on the dynamics of the Indochinese refugee migration and on the assumptions that underlay the world's efforts to provide resettlement:

> What kind of deplorable country must they be running if everyone wants to leave? In the case of Cambodia under Pol Pot, using refugees to draw dire conclusions about the regime was clearly justified. But after seeing Burma and Vietnam back to back, my idea about the meaning of the Vietnamese boat people has changed. * * *

> [B]ad treatment does not automatically make people into refugees. To say this the other way around, the people who do leave by boat are not necessarily the ones who have suffered most. They may simply be the ones for whom this gamble makes the most practical sense * * *. Life in Vietnam, though terrible, may not be that much worse than life in many other countries. The rewards for leaving may simply be better.

> From what I could see, life in Burma is, for most people, fully as hopeless as life in Vietnam. Burma does not have enormous re-education camps, but then most Vietnamese are not in the camps either. For many Filipinos, life is worse than it is for nearly all Vietnamese. China is both poor and repressive. Bangladesh has every problem a country can have. But Vietnam, Cambodia, and Laos are the only Asian countries from which hundreds of thousands flee. Why? The basic reason, I think, is that if Burmese or Filipinos leave, they're sent back home. They're not presumed to be political refugees, they're not processed for resettlement in the West. For them, becoming a refugee is pointless; for a Vietnamese, it is a risky but sensible step to take.

Fallows, *No Hard Feelings?*, The Atlantic Monthly, Dec. 1988, at 71, 77–78.

Other studies also support a finding that high expectations about resettlement played a major role in stimulating the outflow from Vietnam in the 1970s and 1980s (without necessarily negating that a significant proportion of the flow qualified as genuine refugees). *See* Robinson, *Sins of Omission: The New Vietnamese Refugee Crisis,* World Refugee Survey—1988 in Review 5, 8 (1989); Suhrke, *Indochinese Refugees: The Law and Politics of First Asylum,* 467 The Annals 102 (1983). Those advocating refugee resettlement policies must ask whether it is desirable—and possible, humanely—to break through this cycle of expectation.

A related, but different, question is what impact refugee resettlement has on those left behind. In 1989, Doris Meissner, then Senior Associate at the Carnegie Endowment and later Commissioner of the INS from 1993 to 2000, made the point sharply, in reflecting on the hundreds of thousands of Cubans and Vietnamese admitted to the United States:

> The fact that Cuba and Vietnam have been among the slowest nations in the communist world to change is not unrelated to this exodus. Unwittingly, and with the best intentions, our refugee policy has provided a means for these nations to export the critical mass of people most likely to challenge the system from within and spark political and economic reform.

Meissner, *Let the Contras Find a Haven Rebuilding Peace in Nicaragua, Not Living in the U.S.,* Los Angeles Times, Sept. 11, 1989, § 2, at 5, col. 2.

### Notes and Questions

1. What role, if any, should ideology and foreign policy play in selecting the groups that will benefit from U.S. resettlement?

2. What exactly would a neutral refugee resettlement policy look like? What standards or benchmarks would you use to judge whether humanitarian criteria play the leading role in selection? Should U.S. refugee admissions mirror the profile of refugee populations around the world? Would delegating resettlement allocation decisions to UNHCR assure neutrality? If you were a UNHCR officer, on what would you base resettlement selections?

## SECTION C. REFORM PROPOSALS

The overall global protection system has provided durable solutions to millions in the post-World War II era. Nonetheless, it is complex, messy, and unsatisfactory on many fronts. It combines detailed and expensive legal and factual inquiry, which can lead, for those who navigate the system, to full residence rights in a wealthy country, with rough-hewn temporary haven elsewhere in refugee camps, which themselves range from well-run to squalid. The system is vulnerable to fraud and, because it impinges on jealously guarded sovereign rights, to political backlash in receiving states, sometimes resulting in overreaction, harsh treatment, and deterrent measures. Even so, some states that use deterrents with one hand reach out with the other to resettle thousands in quota resettlement programs.

This contradictory picture has prompted many to think about better ways to structure the global protection system. We present one ambitious reform proposal here, in a lengthy excerpt from a 1997 article by Professor Peter Schuck. The excerpt also contains a broad description of how the world coped with the massive exodus from Vietnam, Cambodia and Laos from 1978 to the mid-1990s. The world's response included the 1989 Comprehensive Plan of Action (CPA), which Schuck uses as a model for parts of his proposal. That description is also useful for deepening one's understanding of the U.S. resettlement system as we have examined it above, because the United States refugee system was profoundly shaped by the Vietnamese refugee experience, given this country's historical involvement in the Vietnam war and the fact that many of those fleeing were at risk because they had supported America and its ally, the defeated South Vietnamese government. The United States played a lead role in many of the developments Schuck describes in that part of his article

## PETER H. SCHUCK, REFUGEE BURDEN–SHARING: A MODEST PROPOSAL

22 Yale J. Int'l L. 243 (1997).

The world is awash in refugees. According to the most recent estimates, more than fifteen million individuals are already outside their countries and in need of international protection and assistance. This population, already immense, is growing steadily and remorselessly with the proliferation of refugee-producing and migration-facilitating conditions: political repression, armed conflict, civil strife, environmental disaster, famine, social and economic disintegration, wretched governmental policies, and improvements in communications and transportation opportunities. Refugee emergencies have become so endemic that the rhetoric of crisis today is as likely to numb as it is to energize.

The current legal and political arrangements for managing refugee flows were established to manage European cross-border refugee flows during the post-World War II era. The cause of these flows became much more varied as time went on, their locus shifted during the 1960s, 1970s, and 1980s to other regions, notably Africa, south and southeast Asia, the Middle East, and the Caribbean, and internally displaced individuals became more numerous than the border-crossing refugees. By the 1980s, Europe had come to think of the refugee burden as more of a problem for the Third World and the United States than for itself. Protected from large-scale refugee movements by an impregnable Iron Curtain in the east, Europe seemed relatively immune to the threat.

It is no longer possible to entertain this comforting illusion. With the dissolution of the Soviet Union, Germany's reunification, the militarization of bitter ethnic conflicts in the Balkans, and the failure of many former European colonies to establish viable political and economic systems, refugees are once again pouring into the very heart of Europe. Moreover, new migration routes, facilitated by cheap transportation and intricate social networks, are bringing migrants to Europe (and thence to the United States) from Asia, Africa, and the Pacific archipelago. Although few of these migrants are likely to meet the legal qualifications for Convention refugee status, many of them nevertheless seek some form of temporary or permanent protection and must be processed in one or another European state until their status can be determined—with the attendant fiscal, social, and political burdens on the receiving state that such processing ordinarily entails. Europe thus joins the Third World, North America (the United States and Canada), and the other traditional receiving regions in facing the prospect of additional flows of migrants claiming protection through the international refugee system, broadly defined.

\* \* \*

Rather than focus on the suffering that refugees endure or the root causes of their flight, I take these remorseless facts as tragically given. I emphasize instead the burdens that the sudden, massive refugee flows that are now endemic impose on states. I do so not because these burdens are more than the international order, taken as a whole, can or should bear (they are not) but because I am convinced of the following three propositions. First, the emerging state responses to these burdens are seriously jeopardizing the viability of any meaningful regime of international human rights protection. Second, any realistic solution to this problem must somehow forestall these responses by easing these burdens in exchange for a set of obligations that states are more willing to accept and implement. Third, this can only be accomplished by distributing obligations more widely and fairly among states over time.

Doubtless, my effort to salvage a meaningful human rights regime from the carcass of state sovereignty will seem rather odd to many well-informed commentators on refugee law and policy in the academy and in the field. They often maintain that state sovereignty constitutes perhaps the chief threat and impediment to the fulfillment of human rights goals. To them, state sovereignty is the problem, not the solution.

\* \* \*

This line of argument is true as far as it goes, but it does not go nearly far enough. For it is also true that for the foreseeable future, genuine human rights protections—particularly the protection of refugees—can only be enforced and implemented by sovereign states or by other entities such as supranational agencies and nongovernmental organizations (NGOs) working with their assistance or sufferance. This is a brutal reality of which any practicable, meaningful reform proposal must take full account. To ignore or deny it is to engage in a dangerous fatuity.

But the link between sovereignty and protection is more than a regrettable necessity. \* \* \* The mature nation-state is a unique formation conceived through communal imagination, cemented by history, fueled by political ideology, and equilibrated by institutions. Its combination of scale, power, predictability, and normativity enable it to generate levels of self-sacrifice and coordinated action in the common interest of which other groupings, whether larger or smaller, seem incapable.

\* \* \* My premise is that the current refugee regime is ''broke''—in the limited but important sense that it fails to afford adequate protection to the enormous and growing number of people fleeing from what seem to be, and often are, intolerable conditions—and that it needs fixing. This is not to deny the many important and often heroic responses that the international community has mounted to address human rights emergencies. Indeed, I describe one such response, the Comprehensive Plan of Action and Orderly Departure Program in Southeast Asia (CPA), in some detail. It is simply to say that much more needs to be done as these emergencies continue to proliferate.

* * *

I wish to emphasize one systemic, institutional failure that I believe contributes substantially to all of the others: the failure of refugee burden-sharing among states. If meaningful reform of the refugee protection system is to occur, it must start here.

The problem is simpler to state than to solve. Although the entire international community ought to shoulder the burdens of dealing with massive refugee flows, only a relatively small number of nations and regions actually do so. Some of those least capable of bearing these burdens have in fact carried a disproportionately large share of them. This is most strikingly true of some African states that often serve as countries of first asylum for many of the most wretched refugees. Conversely, some of the states that are most capable of incurring refugee burdens have stood on the sidelines watching.

No strong norm of refugee burden-sharing currently exists in international law or practice. This is not to say that the appeal of such a norm has gone unremarked. In recent years, a number of commentators have called for the creation or recognition by the international community of a norm of equitable burden-sharing. Some have inferred a principle of international solidarity from more abstract principles of justice or have discerned such a principle from existing international instruments from which the norm of equitable burden-sharing of refugees might be derived as a logical and normatively desirable corollary. Such inferences, however, are more in the nature of moral exhortation and prudential argument than expositions of authoritative legal principles. In practice, there have been very few instances of large-scale burden-sharing arrangements designed to expand rather than restrict refugee protection. The most important example is the CPA.

THE COMPREHENSIVE PLAN OF ACTION

The CPA resettlement program provides a useful study of the conditions under which burden-sharing can succeed. They developed and were refined over an extended period of time, and involved intensive bilateral and multilateral negotiations conducted in a crisis atmosphere in which national self-interest was the main driving force and jerry-built, practical solutions were the principal desiderata.

After the sweep of communist victories in southeast Asia in 1975, well over two million people fled Vietnam, Cambodia, and Laos for "first asylum'' in neighboring countries. Before 1979, these people received relatively little international assistance, and refugee camps were poorly organized. A coordinated international response began in July 1979, when the United Nations convened an international conference in Geneva to seek solutions to the burgeoning refugee crisis. Conference participants were attentive to the differing abilities of countries to assist the refugees. In its report on the conference, UNHCR noted that ''[s]ince the countries of first asylum were developing countries confronted with serious economic and social constraints, it was essential that countries outside the area assumed the principal responsibility for resettlement.''

The sixty-five governments attending the Geneva conference agreed to three principal commitments: (1) countries in the region would provide at least temporary asylum; (2) the international community would offer resettlement places for those who had already fled; and (3) the countries of origin would discourage hazardous departures and would cooperate with the United Nations and other countries to promote direct outflows through an Orderly Departure Program (ODP).

The 1979 accord reflected the national self-interest of the conference participants. Resettlement countries wanted to preserve the precarious temporary refuge policies of first-asylum countries, which were not signatories to the 1951 Refugee Convention or to its 1967 Protocol. The United States in particular was committed to protecting its wartime allies, and to providing ''a noncommunist alternative to the peoples of Indochina.'' In addition to providing humanitarian assistance, the U.S. interest was served by a system that accorded presumptive refugee status to all those fleeing the southeast Asian communist regimes. The resettlement program also supported the conventional immigration policy goals of resettlement countries.

First-asylum countries in southeast Asia, burdened by the expense and political difficulties of providing refuge, hoped to stem the tide of refugees and spread the costs of assistance. As one observer noted, these countries were persuaded to provide first asylum by the ''assurance that the international community will effectively take care of the refugees, and the smooth operation of a resettlement programme aiming at an equitable sharing of the burden imposed on the southeast Asian countries.'' The cooperation of the first-asylum countries was also bolstered by Vietnam's agreement to reduce the outflows by resuming its dubious policy of prohibiting illegal departures and by creating an in-country Orderly Departure Program (ODP). Finally, the costs to first-asylum countries were reduced by agreements to place some first-asylum camps under UNHCR auspices and to have UNHCR cover the direct costs of their operation.

The Geneva conference produced immediate results. In 1979, thirty-eight countries accepted Indochinese refugees for resettlement. Vietnam clamped down on smuggling operations, causing an immediate decline in refugee outflows. Resettlement rates increased, causing the population of boat people in the region to decline from 205,000 in mid-1979 to 40,000 three years later. From 1979 until 1989, over 1.7 million Indochinese refugees were resettled under the framework laid out at the 1979 conference, and over 150,000 left through the ODP.

In addition to the confluence of national self-interests, the Indochinese resettlement program demonstrates three points about burden-sharing. First, full-scale international cooperation was implemented under the leadership of the United States and UNHCR. UNHCR coordinated international discussions, established refugee camps and holding centers, channeled funds to care for the refugees, and monitored the implementation of the resettlement programs. The United States, the largest resettlement country, shouldered a significant share of the costs. The sheer number of cooperating countries reflected, at least in part, U.S. leadership. Had the United States and UNHCR not borne the brunt of the resettlement and organizational burdens, the international consensus might have unraveled.

Second, the program's success depended upon the full cooperation of all countries involved; any shirking of one country's responsibilities could upset the precarious international balance. Several incidents illustrate this point. In May 1989, Malaysia instituted a policy of turning back boatloads of Vietnamese refugees and migrants, likely causing some neighboring countries to experience a drastic increase in boat arrivals. In Indonesia, for instance, 3787 Vietnamese arrived in May alone—the highest figure since the beginning of the outflow. Another such example occurred in 1986, when Vietnam suspended interviews of ODP applicants for U.S. departures. As a result, illegal departures from Vietnam surged, along with the number of arrivals in first-asylum countries. The neighboring countries responded by refusing asylum to the new arrivals. Thailand, for example, began sending back boats and denied those migrants who were admitted an opportunity to seek resettlement. Similar reactions occurred in Indonesia and Hong Kong. In sum, one country's defection triggered exclusionary reactions in others; interlocking interests contributed not only to the implementation of burden-sharing programs, but also to their effective maintenance.

Third, effective burden-sharing requires efforts to reduce the burdens on all countries and spread them over time. As the Indochinese resettlement program progressed, countries began worrying that it caused a "pull effect" by encouraging people to flee their countries in search of resettlement in the West. As the number of boat arrivals increased and the average stay in the refugee camps lengthened in the late 1980s, first-asylum countries began taking unilateral and sometimes inhumane measures to deter further arrivals and to reduce camp populations.

In response to these concerns, the resettlement program was refined in 1989 at a second Geneva conference on Indochinese refugees. The conference participants adopted a new program, the Comprehensive Plan of Action (CPA), to address the Vietnamese and Lao refugee problems. The CPA, which was scheduled to expire on June 30, 1996, preserved the basic framework of the earlier resettlement program, with one modification. Under the CPA, refugee status was no longer conferred automatically on all those who arrived in first-asylum countries; instead, arrivals were subject to refugee screening by local immigration officials. Those screened in were eligible to seek resettlement in a third country, while those screened out remained in holding centers and faced eventual repatriation. To balance concerns over national sovereignty and human rights, conference participants agreed to establish a "region-wide refugee status-determination process . . . in accordance with national legislation and internationally accepted practice," including UNHCR training and oversight. To secure the support of first-asylum countries, resettlement countries committed to expedited resettlement of all refugees who arrived prior to the cut-off date set by the CPA. The CPA also called for additional countries to join the resettlement effort.

At the time of the sixth follow-up meeting of the Steering Committee of the International Conference on Indochinese Refugees in March 1995, there remained 36,339 screened-out Vietnamese and 2048 with refugee status in first-asylum countries. Although the Steering Committee called for the completion of all repatriation and resettlement by the end of 1995, the process was delayed both because a number of screened-out Vietnamese refused to be repatriated at all costs, and because the United States [as a result of a surprise floor amendment adopted on short notice by the U.S. House of Representatives] proposed to offer screened-out boat people a second chance to apply for refugee status according to U.S., not CPA, refugee criteria. Word of the U.S. proposal caused "violent anti-repatriation protests" in the camps and impeded the repatriation and resettlement under the CPA In early 1996, the Vietnamese government and the United States agreed to procedures whereby "[p]otential returnees would register for a U.S. interview before departing the camps. Upon return to Vietnam, they would go back to their areas of origin to await their interview. Those accepted would be processed for U.S. resettlement." UNHCR announced that the CPA would formally end on June 30, 1996.

\* \* \*

[The Proposal]

[We now provide Schuck's summary of his proposal for a new system—paragraphs relocated from Part I of the article—followed by excerpts presenting a portion of his more detailed description and argument.]

In Part IV [of this article], I consider four broad strategies for improving refugee protection. In the order of their abstract desirability, they are: (1) eliminating the root causes of refugee flows; (2) prompt repatriation of refugees; (3) temporary protection of refugees; and (4) permanent resettlement of refugees in third countries. I conclude (with virtually all other commentators) that each of these is problematic and that the practical realities of refugee crises and international refugee politics often require resort to the strategies of temporary protection and permanent resettlement because the more desirable ones are simply not available.

In Part V, I describe my proposal, which is intended to ameliorate some, but certainly not all, of the most important inadequacies in the current system. Details aside, the proposal consists of two main elements. First, a group of states would agree to observe a strong norm of proportional burden-sharing for refugees, would seek to induce other states to join the group, and would arrange for an existing or newly-established international agency to assign to each participating state a refugee protection quota. A state's quota would commit it to assure temporary protection or permanent resettlement for a certain number of refugees over a certain time period. Second, the participating states would then be permitted to trade their quotas by paying others to fulfill their obligations. As noted immediately below, states would participate in the quota-cum-market system voluntarily, albeit under the influence of their more powerful neighbors. Accordingly, the system should require only limited regulation by the agency. * * * [The agency's] chief responsibilities would be to administer the system, including the quotas and the flow of information about refugees, and to ascertain whether the requisite protection is actually being delivered.

I propose that this scheme be entirely consensual on the part of the participating states and that it be established on a regional or even a subregional basis, rather than on a global one. These states would define the refugees who might look to them for protection according to agreed-upon criteria. For example, the criteria might prefer refugees from countries of origin located in the region, refugees in first-asylum states located there, or refugees from countries with historical ties to participating states.

A regionally-structured system would possess several important advantages over a more global one. It could exploit a tradition of regional responsibility for localized refugee flows and solutions, the greater commonality of interests and values that regions tend to share, and the more intense patterns of interaction that they exhibit. It would minimize the psychological, fiscal, and other costs of having to relocate refugees over long distances and of locating them farther from their homes. Its limited size and consensual character would also make it administratively more manageable. As with other groups seeking gains from trade, however, participating states would have an incentive to expand the membership over time if the scheme proved successful.

I also discuss in Part V why this unusual burden-sharing scheme might actually be politically acceptable and practically workable. Such a happy outcome, however, is far from clear. Under the existing regime, after all, states that are not states of origin or of first asylum are entirely free to join in, or refrain from, refugee protection efforts, as their interests dictate. Why then would they choose to surrender that freedom of action and accept a burden-sharing obligation that is likely to be costly, risk domestic political tensions, and probably ratchet upwards over time?

Some states will probably reject such an obligation out of hand; they will point out that they neither generate refugee flows nor are likely to receive them. They may also point to the fact that the kind of massive refugee flows that have occurred in Rwanda and the former Yugoslavia are the exception, not the rule. The larger, wealthier, and more stable states can often absorb smaller, more gradual refugee movements without resorting to extraordinary measures.

Even these states, however, might be attracted to burden-sharing for the same reason that many individuals are attracted to catastrophic health insurance: States may rationally prefer to incur a small and predictable protection burden now in order to avoid bearing large, sudden, unpredictable, unwanted, and unstoppable refugee inflows in the future. They might prefer a system that created strong incentives for more states to support temporary protection of refugees, largely in the Third World, over the current one, which generates strong pressures for an even more dreaded (from their perspective) form of relief: permanent resettlement.

As the world grows smaller and more interconnected, and as an increasing number of refugees can more easily reach more places and claim protection there, such "refugee crisis insurance" might well be a "good buy"—perhaps even for relatively insular states. By introducing a market in quota obligations, the scheme would permit even greater flexibility. For many states, then, this burden-sharing scheme would be fairer and more rational than the status quo—especially if, as I propose, it were established on a regional basis. So, at least, I shall argue.

Part V concludes by discussing how such a scheme would be enforced. Briefly, I suggest that while the scheme would be administered and to some extent enforced by an international agency, it is the states with the greatest interest in a better refugee protection system—those in North America and Western Europe—that would have the strongest incentives to deploy the various carrots and sticks of international diplomacy at their disposal (trade benefits, other forms of assistance, security guarantees, etc.) in order to secure both initial agreement and subsequent compliance.

The United States has compelling reasons to seize the initiative on this issue. As the only remaining superpower and the leading funder of the existing international refugee system, it has the greatest stake in assuring a just and stable world order. The Bosnian tragedy revealed a vacuum of leadership in European refugee crises that only the United States can fill. Finally, the United States continues to be vulnerable to its own sudden refugee flows from the Caribbean, which it has experienced from time to time since 1980.

\* \* \* [This proposal's] quotas feature seeks to build on the embryonic burden-sharing norm that the CPA experience \* \* \* exemplified. Because the proposal will certainly be controversial in the refugee-policy community, Part VI defends it against a variety of anticipated objections, particularly to its market element, which is bound to arouse the most opposition. At the outset, however, I wish to emphasize a point that should inform one's reaction to the entire analysis. Although the proposal entails many problems, virtually all of those problems already exist, sometimes to an even greater degree, in the current system. For this reason, I urge the reader to keep the "compared to what" question firmly in mind as she ponders these problems.

\* \* \*

The system should maximize the total resources available for the genuine protection of refugees. I view this as the paramount objective; its primacy justifies compromising, where necessary, other important but less central goals. Protection resources can be maximized in two ways: by drawing new resources into the system and by better utilizing whatever resources exist. Thus, as many states as possible should participate in the protective system, not just those that possess a particular resource (such as cash, space, or ethnic diversity) or that happen to abut a refugee-producing area. In addition, the system should create incentives to use those resources most effectively. Specifically, it should encourage each state to allocate whatever resources it possesses or can mobilize to the refugee-protection strategy or strategies—root cause, temporary protection-cum-repatriation, and resettlement—that can be achieved to the greatest extent at the least cost.

\* \* \*

The proposal consists of five main structural elements: (1) agreement by states in a region on a strong norm that all ought to bear a share of temporary protection and permanent resettlement needs proportionate to their burden-bearing capacity; (2) a process for determining the number of those who need such protection; (3) a set of criteria for allocating this burden among states in the form of quotas; (4) a market in which states can purchase and sell quota compliance obligations; and (5) an international authority to administer the quota system and regulate this market. I shall discuss each of these elements and then identify some of the implementation and enforcement issues that would need to be resolved for the system to work.

\* \* \*

[We now continue with the author's elaboration of a few of these elements:]

### THE PRINCIPLE OF BURDEN SHARING

\* \* \*

The [burden sharing] norm should express a principle of fairness in the distribution of refugee protection burdens. Specifically, it should satisfy three criteria of fairness: consent, broad participation, and proportionality.

Consent is essential. No state should be obliged to participate in the burden-sharing scheme unless it voluntarily undertakes to do so. This is a concession not only to practical politics but also to a concern that states both feel a genuine commitment to the enterprise and take responsibility for its success or failure. As the discussion immediately above suggests, a state may consent for a variety of reasons. Its consent is not ordinarily vitiated by the fact that it feels constrained to participate because of pressures exerted by other, more powerful states. States in the international system routinely deploy carrots and sticks in order to influence the decisions of other states and actors; only in the most extreme case would such inducements amount to duress negating consent.

\* \* \*

The proportionality principle is both a norm of fairness and a constraint dictated by political prudence. It demands that a state's share of the burden be limited to its burden-bearing capacity relative to that of all other states in the international community. Rough proportionality is probably essential to both consent and broad participation. Taken together, these three values imply a norm that all states in a region must shoulder some of the burden but that none must shoulder a burden that it cannot in fairness bear.

THE NEEDS ASSESSMENT PROCESS

In order to allocate the burden of refugee protection, we must first consider how the overall burden is to be defined, determined, and used as the basis for assigning quotas.

The overall burden is defined as the number of refugees who need to be offered protection—either temporary refuge or permanent resettlement—during a given time period. This number would be calculated by an international agency to be described below, and would be adjusted as unanticipated refugee emergencies occurred. Suffice it to say here that the agency must be equipped to conduct the necessary investigations, make the requisite factual findings, administer and enforce the quotas, and regulate the quotas market with due regard to changing circumstances.

Two difficult, inevitably controversial issues are embedded in this definition: the number of people seeking protection who are to be treated as refugees, and the number of those refugees who need either temporary protection or permanent resettlement (rather than immediate repatriation). Both issues, however, already arise under the current system and can be resolved, as they are now, through a combination of factual analysis, calculated conceptual ambiguity, and old-fashioned negotiation. As a formal matter, the first issue—refugee status—is a legal one requiring application of the refugee definition under the Convention or its domestic law equivalent. To varying extents in different states, asylum adjudications exhibit such formalism. In contrast, decisions about which individuals are to be temporarily or permanently protected are relatively ad hoc; they focus less on the legal refugee definition than on the number of people that the protecting state can handle and, in the case of resettlement, on the putative refugee's social and political acceptability to the receiving state. Accordingly, many of those selected for temporary or permanent protection would probably fail to qualify as refugees in the more legalistic setting of asylum adjudication. This practice suggests that the international agency can resolve the issue of refugee status for purposes of this scheme through the relatively informal, low-cost modalities that UNHCR, the first-asylum states, and other states (often with the assistance of NGOs) now use to make protection decisions.

The agency must then calculate a world-wide total of refugees who need temporary protection and a total of those who need permanent resettlement, and then allocate those totals among participating states by assigning a quota to each. The notion of "need" that must inform such a calculation is bound to be controversial. To some extent, need is in the eye of the beholder, as evidenced by the frequent disagreements that now arise over this issue between (and within) UNHCR, potential protecting states, and NGOs. Under the current system, UNHCR determines how many slots are needed and proceeds to solicit offers from states that it thinks can be persuaded to offer protection. In resisting these entreaties, states may dispute UNHCR's assessment of need, as well as assert their inability to accept more refugees. If further negotiations ensue, the parties may articulate competing conceptions of need; hopefully, some agreement on numbers (if not on the underlying conceptions) may be reached. Under the proposal, the agency would proceed in a similar fashion.

\* \* \*

THE CRITERIA FOR ALLOCATING THE PROTECTION BURDEN

\* \* \*

The attractiveness of national wealth as the sole criterion for assigning refugee protection quotas is especially great in a system like the one I propose here, which would allow a state to pay other states to provide those protection services that it cannot or will not provide on its own territory. For this reason, a state's wealth should probably trump other objective factors such as population density and land mass. Although these factors may well affect the ease with which a state can protect or resettle refugees on its own territory, these factors are probably best taken into account as they are reflected in the prices that states are willing to pay to transfer their burden to other states. For example, Malaysia and Singapore are countries of relatively great wealth but with high population densities, small land mass, and severe ethnic tensions that refugees might further inflame. These countries would be assigned large quotas but would probably offer a high price to shift the protection burden elsewhere.

Two exemptions from the quota system should be provided, and neither is likely to be controversial in practice. First, no quota should be assigned to a state that engages in systematic violations of human rights, nor should such states be permitted to purchase other states' quotas. * * * The second exception should be for states whose wealth falls below some minimal level, as determined by international agencies.

\* \* \*

### A MARKET IN REFUGEE PROTECTION QUOTAS

Would states be interested in paying others to protect refugees? The short answer is that they already are doing so. In some refugee crises like Rwanda, some relatively wealthy states contribute funds to the first-asylum state to support its protection efforts *in situ*. Although these delegations of protection resources and responsibilities are certainly better than nothing, they suffer from a number of limitations. The delegation transactions are inevitably ad hoc, with each transaction having to be organized and coordinated by UNHCR, a dedicated but sluggish and highly politicized bureaucracy. They invite strategic behavior by states with conflicting interests hoping to free ride on the efforts of others.

A market system cannot eliminate these conditions, but it can hope to leverage certain constraints on refugee protection into an improved system. Just as increasing refugee flows, by exposing even traditionally insular states to the risk of sudden influxes, might encourage them to participate in the system of refugee protection, a market system might transform two other real-world constraints into important refugee policy virtues. First, state actors are motivated largely by their perceptions of national self-interest, broadly defined; they are unlikely to adopt humanitarian policies that are inconsistent with those perceptions. Second, states vary enormously in both the attitudes and the resources that they bring to refugee policy. A few states willingly devote substantial resources to refugee protection while other states do little but pass the buck.

Although reformers cannot count on changing either states' motivations or states' heterogeneity, they can devise mechanisms to guide states' self-interest into channels conducive to humanitarian goals. These mechanisms can encourage states to exploit their heterogeneity through exchanges that serve both their self-interest and the public interest in refugee protection. A properly regulated market in refugee protection quotas promises to accomplish both of these ends.

\* \* \*

In effect, the transferor state would pay the transferee state, which might not be a member of the regional burden-sharing system. The transferor state would be purchasing a discharge of its obligation from the transferee. The payment presumably would take the form of cash, but it could, in principle, be any resources that the transferee values enough to accept: credit, commodities, development assistance, technical advice, weapons, political support, or some combination of these assets.

\* \* \*

By facilitating voluntary trades, moreover, the quota market could reduce the overall cost of the refugee protection system, giving it more "bang for the buck." First, it would tend to move protection programs from higher-cost states to lower-cost ones, enabling more refugees to be protected for any given resource level than under the existing system. Second, by increasing the number of states in a region that participate in the refugee protection system (as either buyers or sellers of discharge quotas), the system would reflect in the quota's market price the costs of shifting refugees from the state of first asylum to another place; hence, those costs would be minimized. In this way, high-quota states would seek to discharge their quotas by paying states of first asylum or neighbors of such states to protect those refugees where they are already located. Third, the quota price would reflect the risk that protection, initially meant to be temporary, will evolve into the more costly situations of long-term custody and permanent resettlement. Thus, transferor states, wishing to minimize the price they must pay to induce transferees to assume their burden, would have an interest in maintaining the integrity of temporary protection, which in turn is essential to the viability of any voluntary refugee protection system, including the current one.

\* \* \*

## Notes and Questions

1. A similar system was proposed, in the same year that Schuck wrote, by James Hathaway and Alexander Neve. A portion of their discussion was presented in Chapter Nine. They did not include a component permitting market trades of refugee quotas, however. They also discussed at greater length the impact such a system might have in deterring fraudulent claims, because asylum seekers could not be sure that they would obtain either temporary or permanent protection in a destination state they prefer. Partly because of this latter factor, they argued, such a system would provide an incentive for states to dismantle *non-entrée* measures (interdiction and other deterrent practices such as extensive detention). Hathaway & Neve, *Making International Refugee Law Relevant Again: a Proposal for Collectivized and Solution-Oriented Protection*, 10 Harv. Hum. Rts. J. 115 (1997). *See also* Helton, The Price of Indifference: Refugees and Humanitarian Action in the New Century (2002). The principal proposals were sharply criticized in D. Anker, J. Fitzpatrick, and A. Shacknove, *Crisis and Cure: A Reply to Hathaway/Neve and Schuck,* 11 Harv. Hum. Rts. J. 295 (1998). *See also* Schuck, *A Response to the Critics,* 12 Harv. Hum.Rts.J. 385 (1999).

2. Schuck uses the 1989 Comprehensive Plan of Action (for Indochinese refugees) as a partial model for his proposal, but what problems do you see in the system set up by the CPA? What incentives did it create for the nearby refugee-receiving states (for either temporary or permanent resi-

dence)? What disadvantages might derive from the world community's efforts to persuade a refugee-producing state to adopt an orderly departure program? For more on the CPA, see Symposium, *Focus on the Comprehensive Plan of Action,* 5 Int'l J. Refugee L. 507 (1993) (key documents relevant to the CPA appear at *id.* 617–46); Bari, *Refugee Status Determination under the Comprehensive Plan of Action (CPA): A Personal Assessment,* 4 Int'l J. Refugee L. 487 (1992); Le, Note, *ROVR: Resettlement Opportunities for Vietnamese Returnees or Refoulement of Vietnamese Refugees,* 12 Geo. Immigr. L.J. 125, 130–31 (1997).

3.   What problems do you see with the Schuck proposal? What advantages would it bring? Why has there been no progress on developing such a system in the decade since this proposal and that of Hathaway and Neve were presented? What changes could be introduced to make these proposals more attractive to government leaders? Are there other ways that resettlement offers could be leveraged to improve the overall protection system? *See* Strategic Use of Resettlement: A Discussion Paper Prepared by the Working Group on Resettlement [for UNHCR's Global Consultations], UN Doc. WGR/03/04.Rev3 (2003).

4.   For a broad and highly useful overview of the evolving world refugee situation and the world's responses, see UNHCR, The State of the World's Refugees, a series of well-written and thoughtful volumes published under this general title every few years since 1993. The most recent edition, the fifth, is subtitled Human Displacement in the New Millennium (2006).

# Chapter Eleven

# BEYOND ASYLUM: OTHER FORMS OF PROTECTION FOR FORCED MIGRANTS

*I remember the dawn of July 17, when we heard the cry, "Run, the soldiers are coming!" The children began to cry, terrorized, but after we started walking they calmed down some. Each person carried his belongings, his poncho, some tortillas, corn meal, or whatever he could find. Each child who could walk also carried something.*

*The people of three villages came together in one place. We were resting when we again heard shots nearby. Once again we fled. Finally we came to another place farther away, where we found more people from other villages. There we rested again and shared what we had. We ran out of water and ate dry corn meal. We became nauseated from lack of water. There were too many of us, so we decided to divide up into smaller groups. But in all this activity, families got divided up. In my group there was a child carrying his mother's clothes and a poncho, while his mother went off in a second group carrying their tortillas. Her oldest child was in a third group, and the father, with the rest of the ponchos, went with yet a fourth group. I saw a little girl about five years old who had lost her parents. But there we were!*

*We found a little orange tree loaded with oranges. We piked them all. They were very acidic, but they helped a lot. After a long walk—all day long—we came to another place about 9 PM and slept there. At this place they gave us hot tortillas, water, and a little salt.*

*On July 18 at 5 AM, we were all up and ready to go. We washed with the dew from the plants. We found yucca and some other food, and we each ate a little. We were busy doing all this when we heard shots. We had to run again. Minutes later we saw the soldiers come running down a road. What hurt me most was seeing the old people with their canes, but thank God we managed to get away. From a distance, we saw the village burn.*

—Regina Hernandez,
*campesina,* Guatemala[1]

Throughout this book we have emphasized that refugees are only one of the many groups of forced migrants in the world. Refugee status is restricted to those who cross international frontiers, have a well founded fear of persecution if they return, have not been convicted of serious crimes, and do not pose threats to order and security in the receiving country. In this Chapter we will examine alternative avenues of protection for forced migrants who cannot satisfy the requirements set forth in the international and national laws relating to refugees.

Many persons are forced to leave their homes for compelling reasons other than specific persecution directed at them. They may be fleeing generalized conditions of violence or social disorder, or a natural disaster such as a hurricane, tsunami or earthquake. Some individuals clearly face persecution, but the persecution is not triggered by one of the five enumerated grounds discussed in Chapter Four. Other individuals are at risk of suffering serious harm that does not rise to the level of persecution. Some individuals face persecution on account of one of the specified grounds, but have criminal convictions that preclude refugee status. See Chapter Six, Section B. Over the years governments have developed a variety of legal mechanisms to respond to individuals such as these who do not meet one or more of the technical elements of the refugee definition but nonetheless seem to merit some form of humanitarian assistance. Sometimes legislation authorizes protection beyond that afforded by refugee status; sometimes administrative discretion leads to new protection policies. In general, the solutions have tended to be pragmatic and somewhat ad hoc. We will divide these approaches into two categories, although the distinction is not always a clear one. We begin by considering forms of protection provided on an individual basis. We then move to group-based protection, normally adopted by states as responses to mass flows of persons in refugee-like situations.

## SECTION A.   INDIVIDUALS NOT GRANTED REFUGEE STATUS

During the past few decades many industrialized countries have developed laws to protect those who do not fall within the terms of the refugee definition, but who would nonetheless face serious harm if returned to their country of origin. Called humanitarian protection, or "B-status," or "exceptional leave to remain," or "stay of deportation," these policies have extended legal protection to a larger subset of forced migrants than those who could prove persecution. Some of these policies developed in Europe to allow Americans who resisted military conscription during the unpopular Vietnam war to find haven. Other measures

---

**1.**   Carole Kismaric, Forced Out: The Agony of the Refugee in Our Time 76–78 (1989).

developed in order to shield those who were at risk of torture if returned to their home countries, but who could not show nexus to a Convention ground—persons whose *refoulement* is now prohibited by the Convention Against Torture. Sometimes protection was granted in civil war situations when the conditions in the home country were precarious for almost everyone. Other situations justified extending some form of protection. Consider, for example, the case of a woman seriously victimized in a domestic relationship where the persecutor is not a state actor nor may a state be implicated in the failure to protect the woman. Or recall the *Montoya case*, discussed in Chapter Four. There the British judges concluded that there was a reasonable likelihood that the Colombian landowner would be murdered if he returned to his homeland, but denied him asylum in the U.K. Though not a refugee, "[h]is claim to human sympathy is clearly strong. The Secretary of State has power to allow him to remain," they said. *Montoya,* in Chapter Four at 272–76.

Under U.S. law, persons denied asylum status or withholding of removal may be eligible for other forms of relief from removal that focus on the individual's situation. These include protection under the Convention Against Torture (discussed in Chapter Seven), cancellation of removal under § 240A of the Immigration and Nationality Act, and protection offered for certain victims of trafficking and criminal abuse under nonimmigrant visas in the T and U categories. *See* INA §§ 101(a)(15)(U), (V); 214(o), (p). Less formal forms of relief are also available, such as parole and "deferred action status" (in this context, an administrative actions akin to an exercise of prosecutorial decision not to seek removal of a noncitizen from the U.S.).

Other countries have similar statutes and administrative practices that prevent the removal of persons denied asylum but whose return would cause severe hardships. Canadian law recognizes relief for persons "if the Minister is of the opinion that it is justified on humanitarian and compassionate considerations relating to them." Immigration and Refugee Protection Act, S.C., ch. 27, § 25(1) (2001). Persons denied refugee protection by the Immigration and Refugee Board may apply for such relief. Canadian law also provides for a pre-removal risk assessment (PRRA) to provide protection not only for people whose removal is prohibited by Article 3 of the Convention Against Torture, but also for those whose removal "would subject them personally * * * to a risk to their life or to a risk of cruel and unusual treatment or punishment." Id., §§ 97, 112–113. A more complete description is available at http://www.cic.gc.ca/english/refugees/asylum–4.html.

The next sections will discuss forms of relief in Europe for forced migrants other than refugee status.

## 1.   THE EUROPEAN CONVENTION ON HUMAN RIGHTS

More than 40 European countries, including all the EU states, have ratified the European Convention for the Protection of Human Rights and Fundamental Freedoms (ECHR), 213 U.N.T.S. 222, European T.S. No. 5, which since its inception in 1950 has prohibited torture and inhuman or degrading treatment or punishment. There are no exceptions or qualifications to Article 3, which states: "No one shall be subjected to torture or to inhuman or degrading treatment or punishment." As these states have also ratified the Convention Against Torture, they have overlapping obligations and parallel enforcement mechanisms: the European Court of Human Rights and the Committee Against Torture, respectively. The European Convention, which entered into force three decades earlier than the Convention Against Torture, has a substantially more extensive jurisprudence interpreting the provisions outlawing torture and inhuman and degrading treatment.

The European Court of Human Rights has interpreted Article 3's prohibition to include an obligation not to return persons who face a "real risk" of torture or inhuman treatment in the country of origin. *See* N. Mole, Asylum and the European Convention on Human Rights 9–22 (2000). The path-breaking case for the Court was *Soering v. United Kingdom*, 161 Eur. Ct. H. R. (ser. A) (1989), which held that Article 3 prohibited the United Kingdom from extraditing Soering to the United States where he faced the risk of a prolonged period on "death row" in Virginia—treatment that would be inhuman or degrading within the terms of the Convention. *See* Dugard and van den Wyngaert, *Reconciling Extradition with Human Rights*, 92 Am. J. Int'l.L. 187, 191–93 (1998). The Court has also held that it would violate Article 3 to expel a Sikh separatist (even on national security grounds) if he faced a real risk of torture or inhuman treatment in India. *Chahal v. United Kingdom*, App. No. 22414/93, 23 Eur. H.R. Rep. 413 (1997). Similarly, it would violate Article 3 to deport an individual convicted of serious criminal offenses if he faced a serious risk of inhuman or degrading treatment from non-government forces upon his return to Somalia. *Ahmed v. Austria*, App. No. 25964/94, 24 Eur. H.R. Rep. 278 (1997). And the Court has gone so far as to rule that it would violate Article 3 to deport an individual in the advanced stages of AIDS to his or her homeland if he or she has inadequate access to the medical system there. *B.B. v. France,* App. No. 39030/96, 1998–VI Eur. Ct. H.R. 2595; *D. v. United Kingdom*, App. No. 30240/96, 24 Eur. H.R. Rep. 423 (1997).

Relying on the growing body of Article 3 case law, asylum seekers whose claims for refugee status have been rejected by a European state can file a complaint with the European Court of Human Rights to seek protection against *refoulement* if they would risk torture or inhuman treatment in their country of origin.

In addition to the substantive law developed under the European Human Rights Convention, a powerful procedural protection is sometimes available. The Rules of the European Court of Human Rights provide that the Court can enter provisional orders, which are binding on the states. *Mamatkulov and Askarov v. Turkey*, App. No. 46827/99, 41 E.H.R.R. 25 (2005) (interpreting Rule 39). Accordingly, an asylum seeker whose application has been denied by a European state may file a complaint with the Court and simultaneously seek an order preventing expulsion while the case proceeds.

An example of the Court's analysis of Article 3 follows.

# HILAL v. UNITED KINGDOM

App. No. 45276/99, 33 Eur. H.R. Rep. 2 (2001).

59. The Court recalls at the outset that Contracting States have the right, as a matter of well-established international law and subject to their treaty obligations including the Convention, to control the entry, residence and expulsion of aliens. However, in exercising their right to expel such aliens, Contracting States must have regard to Article 3 of the Convention which enshrines one of the fundamental values of democratic societies. The expulsion of an alien may give rise to an issue under this provision where substantial grounds have been shown for believing that the person in question, if expelled, would face a real risk of being subjected to treatment contrary to Article 3 in the receiving country. In such circumstances, Article 3 implies an obligation not to expel the individual to that country.

60. In determining whether it has been shown that the applicant runs a real risk, if deported to Tanzania, of suffering treatment proscribed by Article 3, the Court will assess the issue in the light of all the material placed before it, or, if necessary, material obtained *proprio motu*. Ill-treatment must also attain a minimum level of severity if it is to fall within the scope of Article 3, which assessment is relative, depending on all the circumstances of the case.

61. The Court recalls that the applicant arrived in the United Kingdom from Tanzania on 9 February 1995, where he claimed asylum. In the domestic procedures concerning his asylum application, his claim was based on his membership of the CUF, an opposition party in Tanzania, and the fact that he had been detained and tortured in Zanzibar prior to his departure. He also claimed that his brother had been detained and had died due to ill-treatment and that the authorities were accusing him of tarnishing Tanzania's good name, increasing the risk that he would be detained and ill-treated on his return.

62. The Government have urged the Court to be cautious in taking a different view of the applicant's claims than the special adjudicator who heard him give evidence and found him lacking in credibility. The Court notes however that the special adjudicator's decision relied, inter alia, on a lack of substantiating evidence. Since that decision, the applicant has produced further documentation. Furthermore, while this material was looked at by the Secretary of State and by the courts in the judicial review proceedings, they did not reach any findings of fact in that regard but arrived at their decisions on a different basis—namely, that even if the allegations were true, the applicant could live safely in mainland Tanzania (the "internal flight" solution).

63. The Court has examined the materials provided by the applicant and the assessment of them by the various domestic authorities. It finds no basis to reject them as forged or fabricated. The applicant has provided an opinion from the professor of social anthropology at All Souls College, Oxford, that they are genuine. Though the Government have expressed doubts on the authenticity of the medical report, they have not provided any evidence to substantiate these doubts or to contradict the opinion provided by the applicant. Nor did they provide an opportunity for the report and the way in which the applicant obtained it to be tested in a procedure before the special adjudicator.

64. The Court accepts that the applicant was arrested and detained because he was a member of the CUF opposition party and had provided them with financial support. It also finds that he was ill-treated during that detention by, inter alia, being suspended upside down, which caused him severe haemorrhaging through the nose. In the light of the medical record of the hospital which treated him, the apparent failure of the applicant to mention torture at his first immigration interview becomes less significant and his explanation to the special adjudicator—that he did not think he had to give all the details until the full interview a month later—becomes far less incredible. While it is correct that the medical notes and death certificate of his brother do not indicate that torture or ill-treatment was a contributory factor in his death, they did give further corroboration to the applicant's account which the special adjudicator had found so lacking in substantiation. They showed that his brother, who was also a CUF supporter, had been detained in prison and that he had been taken from the prison to hospital, where he died. This is not inconsistent with the applicant's allegation that his brother had been ill-treated in prison.

65. The question remains whether, having sought asylum abroad, the applicant is at risk of ill-treatment if he returns home. The Government have queried the authenticity of the police summons, pointing out that it was dated 25 November 1995, while the package to his parents intercepted by the authorities was sent on 27 November 1995. It may be observed however that the special adjudicator's summary of the applicant's evidence referred to his claim that his parents had not been receiving any of his letters. Nevertheless, his only proof of postage related to a registered package with money concerning which he had entered into correspondence with the Royal Mail. He provided this correspondence to prove that his mail had been interfered with; it does not appear from the documents that he claimed that it was from interception of this particular item that the police first knew that he was in the United Kingdom. His account is therefore not inconsistent on this point.

66. The Court recalls that the applicant's wife, who has now also claimed asylum in the United Kingdom, informed the immigration officer in her interview that the police came to her house on a number of occasions looking for her husband and making threats. This is consistent with the information provided about the situation in Pemba and Zanzibar, where CUF members have in the past suffered serious harassment,

arbitrary detention, torture and ill-treatment by the authorities. This involves ordinary members of the CUF and not only its leaders or high-profile activists. The situation has improved to some extent, but the latest reports cast doubt on the seriousness of reform efforts and refer to continued problems faced by CUF members. The Court concludes that the applicant would be at risk of being arrested and detained, and of suffering a recurrence of ill-treatment if returned to Zanzibar.

67. The Government relied on the "internal flight" option, arguing that even assuming that the applicant was at risk in Zanzibar, the situation in mainland Tanzania was more secure. The documents provided by the parties indicate that human rights infringements were more prevalent in Zanzibar and that CUF members there suffered more serious persecution. It nonetheless appears that the situation in mainland Tanzania is far from satisfactory and discloses a long-term, endemic situation of human rights problems. Reports refer in general terms to police in Tanzania ill-treating and beating detainees and to members of the Zanzibari CCM visiting the mainland to harass CUF supporters sheltering there. Conditions in the prisons on the mainland are described as inhuman and degrading, with inadequate food and medical treatment leading to life-threatening conditions. The police in mainland Tanzania may be regarded as linked institutionally to the police in Zanzibar as part of the Union and cannot be relied on as a safeguard against arbitrary action There is also the possibility of extradition between Tanzania and Zanzibar.

68. The Court is not persuaded, therefore, that the "internal flight" option offers a reliable guarantee against the risk of ill-treatment. It concludes that the applicant's deportation to Tanzania would breach Article 3 as he would face a serious risk of being subjected to torture or inhuman or degrading treatment there.

## Notes and Questions

1. The drafters of the European Convention in 1950 decided to omit any reference to a right of asylum, and no later Protocol (there have been many) addressed this issue. Was it then appropriate for the European Court of Human Rights to find a *nonrefoulement* protection in Article 3? When the adopting states promised not to inflict torture or CIDT, were they also guaranteeing to shield on their soil anyone anywhere in the world who is at risk of such practices when inflicted by another government? How far should or must this extraterritorial protection extend? Would it violate article 3 to deny a visa to someone in his country of nationality who claims that he will suffer CIDT unless allowed to leave?

2. If the European Convention's bans on torture and CIDT are understood to include the protection of *nonrefoulement*, is the Convention on Torture's explicit ban on return necessary? Note that Article 3 of CAT mandates *nonrefoulement* only where there are substantial grounds for believing that a person would be in danger of being subjected to torture; that is, it does not expressly provide such protection to those who face a real risk of CIDT.

## 2. SUBSIDIARY PROTECTION

In 2004 the European Union created a uniform humanitarian protection policy, called "subsidiary protection," for all 25 member states. Council Directive 2004/83, 2004 O.J. (L 304) 12 (EC) (on minimum standards for the qualification and status of third country nationals or stateless persons as refugees or as persons who otherwise need international protection and the content of the protection granted).

Known as the Qualifications Directive, it requires member states to provide refugee status to those who satisfy the 1951 Convention requirements and also to provide "subsidiary protection" to those for whom there are "substantial grounds" to believe that they would face "a real risk of serious harm" if turned away from the EU. Articles 15–18. Serious harm includes the following:

- death penalty or execution; or

- torture or inhuman or degrading treatment or punishment of an applicant in the country of origin; or

- serious and individual threat to a civilian's life or person by reason of indiscriminate violence in situations of international or internal armed conflict.

Art. 15.

Those entitled to subsidiary protection must be granted a renewable residence permit valid for at least one year, travel documents, access to education, social welfare, health care, and accommodation, Art. 24–29, 31, and they must be granted freedom of movement within the state. In contrast, refugees are granted renewable residence permits valid for at least three years. Furthermore, refugees have few or no conditions placed on their rights within the EU country, but states may condition the employment of those granted subsidiary protection on the labor market situation and may limit social welfare and health care to "core benefits." *Id.*

EU member states were to have brought their laws into compliance with this Council Directive by October 2006. To the extent that compliance with the measure merely harmonizes the different humanitarian protection policies already in place, the effect may be small. The requirement that states provide protection to individuals threatened by the indiscriminate violence that accompanies armed conflict, though, covers many people in a broad array of countries. On its face, this appears to be a substantial expansion of international protection. The manner in which it will be applied remains to be seen.

### Notes and Questions

1. Does the EU definition of serious harm essentially guarantee protection to much of the population in countries experiencing armed conflict? For example, in light of the unrelenting violence and massive civilian casualties

in Iraq since 2004, are most Iraqis eligible for subsidiary protection in Europe?

2. For commentary on the EU approach, *see, e.g., Subsidiary Protection of Refugees in the European Union: Complementing the Geneva Convention?* (D. Bouteillet–Paquet ed. 2002); McAdam, *The European Union Qualification Directive: The Creation of a Subsidiary Protection Regime,* 17 Int'l J. Ref. L. 461 (2005).

## SECTION B.　PROTECTION FOR GROUPS OF FORCED MIGRANTS NOT RECOGNIZED AS REFUGEES

### 1. EXTENDED VOLUNTARY DEPARTURE

For many decades, U.S. practice has found ways to provide a form of humanitarian protection or safe haven, usually designed to be temporary, for selected groups who faced serious threats in their countries of origin. Safe haven has been a supplement to asylum and withholding, covering a wider range of threatened individuals. But sometimes it has also served as an intermediate response to the uncertainties caused by civil war or a regime change—a substitute for asylum until matters clarify in the home country. That is, in the fluid circumstances of civil war or changes of government, it may not be clear just who faces a threat of persecution or how severe the threat may be. Further, although a grant of safe haven normally does not prevent its beneficiaries from proceeding with an asylum application, they may prefer not to do so, hoping for a swift end to the war that would permit them to return home.

Between 1960 and 1990, most humanitarian protection was provided under the awkward label of "extended voluntary departure" (EVD), which was essentially an exercise of prosecutorial discretion. When the Attorney General decided, usually on the advice of the State Department, to grant blanket EVD to nationals of a certain country, this decision meant that INS would take no action to force departure for as long as the policy remained in effect. But EVD also often meant that INS took note of the probable illegality of the noncitizen's presence. (If the noncitizen could qualify for other, less tenuous, categories—for example through asylum or through marriage to an American citizen—he or she would have every incentive to claim the conventional immigration status.) EVD beneficiaries received work authorization, but no routine mechanism existed for eventual adjustment from EVD to lawful permanent resident status. EVD was largely equivalent to parole—a discretionary arrangement meant to cut through other technical requirements and to be granted and terminated with relative ease. Because of the intricacies associated with the entry doctrine as it existed under pre-1996 law, however, parole could not be given to people who had already entered the country. And most of the people for whom safe haven has been a significant issue have already made an entry, either as nonimmigrants or as surreptitious entrants.

The earliest use of EVD may have been for Cubans already present in the United States at the time of Fidel Castro's revolution. Thereafter, to take a few examples from the 1970s and early 1980s, the State Department recommended, and the Attorney General approved, EVD for Ethiopians in 1977 during the period of the Red Terror of the Mengistu regime, Ugandans in 1978 who had fled Idi Amin, Iranians after the Shah was overthrown in 1979, Nicaraguans for a brief period after the 1979 ouster of Somoza, nationals of Afghanistan after the 1980 Soviet invasion, and Poles after the 1981 crackdown on the Solidarity union movement.

As civil war deepened in several countries in Central America in the mid-1980s, executive branch resistance to further uses of EVD began to build—not only because of the proliferating number of countries that seemed to be encountering civil war or generalized oppression, but also because of worries that few covered people left when the EVD period ended. At the same time, many in Congress felt that it was appropriate to grant EVD to nationals of El Salvador, where a particularly intense civil war was going on, and from which well over 100,000 citizens had migrated to the United States by the end of the decade. Legislation was proposed on many occasions, unsuccessfully, to provide safe haven in some form to Salvadorans. While that legislative dispute simmered, other members of Congress sought to provide a better overall statutory framework than the misnamed EVD for what they expected would remain discretionary executive-branch decisions to grant temporary safe haven. *See generally* Note, *Temporary Safe Haven for De Facto Refugees from War, Violence, and Disasters,* 28 Va.J.Int'l.L. 509 (1988).

## 2. TEMPORARY PROTECTED STATUS IN THE UNITED STATES

In the Immigration Act of 1990, Congress added what is now § 244 to the INA. It authorizes the Attorney General (now the Secretary of Homeland Security) to grant "temporary protected status" (TPS) to nationals of foreign states in which armed conflict, natural disaster, or other circumstances pose a serious threat to personal safety or the ability of the state to handle the return of the individuals covered by the decision. INA § 244(b)(1). Designations are not subject to judicial review, but decisions as to whether a particular individual falls within a designated group may be. The statute sets forth in detail the procedures that apply, and it provides for the waiver of certain inadmissibility grounds. It also requires regular reporting to Congress on the number of people protected and the reasons for designations. TPS may be granted for no more than 18 months, but may be extended if the Attorney General finds that the reasons for the initial granting of the status continue. (TPS is typically granted in one-year increments.) Beneficiaries are entitled to work authorization. The 1990 law also specified that Salvadorans would be considered a designated group, valid through June 1992 and subject to renewal.

TPS under section 244 is now the principal vehicle for safe haven for individuals fleeing civil war or other broad threats to safety in their countries of origin. But it is not the exclusive basis for such protection, even though § 244(g) would seem to say that Congress intended for that to be the case. Presidents have sometimes also decreed "deferred enforced departure" (DED) for specified groups, including Chinese at the time of the Tiananmen Square massacre in 1989 (before TPS was enacted), Salvadorans in 1994, and Haitians in 1997. DED is functionally equivalent to TPS for most purposes (it clearly includes work authorization), but it is not statutorily based and hence could cover situations that do not fit the criteria of § 244. DED also is not subject to the congressional reporting requirements of INA § 244(i). See 69 Interp.Rel. 600 (1992).

### a. TPS in Practice

In February 1991, the Department of Justice announced the first designations for temporary protected status under the new TPS provision (in addition to the Salvadorans automatically included through the 1990 legislation). They covered noncitizens in the United States from Kuwait, Lebanon and Liberia. 56 Fed.Reg. 12745 (1991); 68 Interp.Rel. 214 (1991). TPS for Kuwait was allowed to lapse in 1992, over a year after Kuwait was liberated from the Iraqi invasion, and that for Lebanon ended in April 1993. 70 Interp.Rel. 175, 215, 1063 (1993). In later years Somalia, Bosnia, Rwanda, Burundi, Sierra Leone, Sudan, Guinea–Bissau, and Angola were added to the list; TPS for several of them has been allowed to end. Persons from the Kosovo province of Yugoslavia received TPS in June 1998, and the class was redesignated and expanded in June 1999, effective until December 8, 2000. 77 Interp. Rel. 696 (2000). Owing to the success of the NATO intervention there, TPS for Kosovars was not further extended.

In August 1997 the Attorney General used for the first time the provision of INA § 244(b)(1)(B), relating to "environmental disaster," when she designated the small island of Montserrat, the site of a devastating active volcano. 62 Fed.Reg. 45685 (1997). Other environmental disasters soon followed. The Attorney General provided TPS for nationals of Nicaragua and Honduras in January 1999, based on the destruction caused by Hurricane Mitch, and for Salvadorans in March 2001, in the wake of a massive earthquake in that country. TPS was terminated for citizens of Montserrat in 2005, giving rise to the difficult situation described in the news article excerpted below.

The process by which TPS is granted or extended is somewhat mysterious, lacking in transparency and subject to political pressures. See Fitzpatrick, *The End of Protection: Legal Standards for Cessation of Refugee Status and Withdrawal of Temporary Protection*, 13 Geo. Immig. L.J. 343, 373 (1999). Though a significant number of nations have been embroiled in crises and civil strife since the advent of TPS (and would thus meet the Act's criteria), the fact that only a handful of nations have received TPS status suggests that designations are influenced by foreign policy and domestic politics. *See* Martin, Schoenholtz & Meyers, *Temporary Protection: Towards a New Regional and Domestic Framework*, 12 Geo. Immig. L.J. 543, 568–69 (1998).

### b. *Policy Issues*

Two issues continue to complicate safe haven decisions. First, there is concern that granting such a status will create a "magnet effect." If mere arrival in the United States from a strife-torn country (plus the absence of a criminal record) suffices to gain a residence status of sorts, including work authorization, then perhaps many thousands of additional persons will be tempted to make the journey. The TPS statute addresses this concern in a way that places practical limits on the magnet effect but is conceptually unsatisfying. Under § 244(c)(1), as it has been interpreted, TPS designations can shield only persons already in the United States as of the date of designation (or, if the government chooses, a stated earlier date). Persons arriving thereafter are not entitled to TPS. But this is anomalous from the standpoint of the humanitarian concerns that trigger TPS, if the war or other threat continues undiminished in the country at issue. Later arrivals will be just as much endangered if they are forcibly returned.

The statute does allow one avenue for helping such later-arriving individuals, although successive administrations have often been reluctant to use it. An *extension* of TPS (*e.g.,* for an additional 12 months) at the expiration of an initial designation period merely allows the original group of beneficiaries, already present in the United States as of the original cut-off date, to stay for the added period. But if the Secretary of Homeland Security instead *redesignates* the nationality group, the cut-off date can be advanced—potentially shielding all nationals of the stated country who are present as of the redesignation.

It was the situation of Liberians in the United States that led the Department of Justice to use redesignation. Liberia was one of the first countries whose nationals were designated for TPS protection after the TPS provision was enacted in 1990. As of 1997, successive extensions had allowed some 4,000 Liberians from the original group to remain in the country. But an estimated 5,000 more had arrived, and the bloody civil war that had devastated that country had not been resolved. Attorney General Reno broke new ground when she issued the first redesignation under the statute, establishing a new cutoff date, April 7, 1997. The notice candidly referred to concern about the magnet effect that might be triggered by redesignation (because Liberians outside the United States might expect another such redesignation later), but it maintained that such a concern is merely one factor for the Attorney General to consider in exercising her discretion under § 244. 62 Fed.Reg. 16608 (1997). Here that concern was outweighed by evidence of renewed conflict in Liberia. Liberians were later redesignated twice more, with an intervening period of simple DED during a stage where the violence temporarily subsided in Liberia. Thus Liberians arriving up until August 25, 2004 were eligible to register for TPS. (As of this writing, TPS is slated to terminate on October 1, 2007, based on the conclusion of Department of Homeland Security that the conditions have improved following the end of armed conflict. *See* http://www.uscis.gov/graphics/ publicaffairs/questsans/Liberia_20se06.pdf.) The former resistance to re-designation has largely subsided, as a number of countries have enjoyed new, later cut-off dates as a result of redesignation.

The second issue that complicates the use of TPS and other forms of safe haven has been the concern over whether such protection can truly remain temporary. By the time conditions calm down in the home country, the beneficiaries of safe haven have often lived in the United States for many years and established substantial ties here. Moreover, the new governments that have come to power at the end of a civil war or after the overthrow of a tyrant have often requested that the United States not end safe haven—because their populations had come to rely on remittances sent home from family members in the United States and because they feared that massive returns would hamper their efforts to rebuild their countries. Historically, even when an end to safe haven has been decreed, the United States has not been very successful in securing the return of many of the beneficiaries. There are therefore good reasons why safe haven should perhaps be transformed into permanent status, at least for those who have spent many years in TPS status. On the other hand, the fear that TPS is never truly temporary has been a powerful argument wielded against new grants of the status. Opponents of TPS have sometimes seized on this history to resist new proposals to extend safe haven, even in the face of strong humanitarian need. (We discuss proposals for changing the TPS system below, pp. 741–49.)

## NINA BERNSTEIN, CHASED FROM ISLAND BY VOLCANO AND FROM U.S. BY HOMELAND SECURITY

The New York Times, Mar. 2. 2005, at B8.

For months, the Montserratians of New York have agonized over their unwanted choices: to return to their island in the Caribbean, a British colony that has been devastated by an active volcano; to start from scratch in Britain; or to become outlaws, defying an order by the Department of Homeland Security to leave the United States by the end of February [2005].

Time ran out this week * * * * Everson Farrell, who had sold all his furniture in preparation of a move to Montserrat last Sunday, postponed his flight at the last minute after a long goodbye visit with his four young children, who will remain in the Bronx.

Mr. Farrell, an auto mechanic who separated a year ago from the children's mother, a permanent resident, said he would leave later this week after repairing a leak in the children's bathroom. But after seven years here, where he has a thriving auto-repair business in the Bronx, he made no secret of his reluctance.

"I'm going back home to zero," he said of his native island, much of it uninhabitable because of volcanic ash, toxic gas, and the threat of new eruptions.

Homeland Security officials do not argue that it is safe to go back to Montserrat, but say rather that it is not going to be safe anytime soon. Since the disaster is no longer temporary, they ruled last June, the 292 Montserratians in the United States are no longer eligible for the "temporary protected status" that had allowed them to stay and work legally.

About a third managed to gain legal status in other ways. The government's advice to the rest: move to Britain, where Montserrat natives have a right to citizenship.

British citizenship doesn't benefit me, "one woman protested late last week * * * * I still have to take my children and move. How do I pay their passages? When I get to the airport, where do I go?"

———————

Beneficiaries of safe haven have sometimes succeeded in obtaining statutory avenues toward permanent resident status. The complex and patchwork forms of relief reflect interest-group lobbying more than a considered set of humanitarian decisions. For example, in 1987, Congress enacted a special law authorizing LPR status for persons who had been covered by EVD grants over the preceding five years. Pub.L. 100–204, § 902, 101 Stat. 1331 (1987). The main impetus for this measure came from Sen. Jesse Helms, who introduced the measure in a form that would have benefited only Polish nationals—during a critical stage of the late Cold War. (It was later expanded to provide the wider coverage.)

The main such example in recent years is the Nicaraguan Adjustment and Central American Relief Act (NACARA), enacted in late 1997. Pub.L. 105–100, 111 Stat. 2160 (1997). Section 203 of NACARA provided benefits to Salvadorans who had enjoyed both TPS and later DED in the early 1990s, as well as Guatemalans who were similarly covered by the settlement of the class-action lawsuit in *American Baptist Churches v. Thornburgh,* 760 F.Supp. 796 (N.D.Cal.1991) (challenging the government's treatment of Central American asylum-seekers), and so had enjoyed the functional equivalent of a form of safe haven, though never actually given TPS. Section 203 allowed these groups to receive LPR status through generous suspension-of-deportation rules that were barred to nearly everyone else by the 1996 Act. (The Clinton administration adopted special regulations that established a strong presumption that ex-TPS beneficiaries and *ABC* class members qualified for the benefit, and so made LPR status nearly automatic. 64 Fed. Reg. 27856–82 (1999).) Lobbying during the consideration of this bill also expanded the coverage of the suspension measure to include persons in the United States before 1991 from the former Soviet bloc countries. And lobbying also resulted in a far more generous provision for Nicaraguans. Merely showing that they had been present in the United States since 1995 and had no serious criminal record could result in an immediate grant of LPR status. NACARA § 202. Nicaraguans had not officially enjoyed

TPS, but a special administrative program had given them what amounted to a form of safe haven.

A year later, under strong urging from the Clinton administration, Congress provided a generous program for adjustment to LPR status, much like the one for Nicaraguans, to Haitians who had been in the asylum system since 1995. Haitian Refugee Immigration Fairness Act of 1998, Pub.L. 105–277, Div. A., Title IX, 112 Stat. 2681. *See* Silverman & Joaquin, *NACARA for Guatemalans, Salvadorans and Former Soviet Bloc Nationals: An Update*, 76 Interp.Rel. 1141 (1999); Jacklin, *The Haitian Refugee Immigration Fairness Act ("HRIFA")*, 99–09 Immig. Briefings (1999).

### Notes and Questions

1.   Is fear of a magnet effect a valid basis to deny a relatively secure status to persons who have fled a strife-torn nation? Are there better ways of dealing with the potential magnet effect of TPS?

2.   Do the ad hoc legislative responses providing permanent status to some who entered the United States under temporary protection programs undercut the TPS statutory scheme? Or are they, instead, a welcome safety net that assist many, though not all, individuals who have become part of the fabric of American life?

3.   Although most commentary has focused on TPS as a response to recent disasters or conflict, there have also been calls to apply TPS to the longstanding Palestinian situation. See Akram & Rempel, *Temporary Protection as an Instrument for Implementing the Right of Return for Palestinian Refugees*, 22 Boston U. Intl. L J. 1 (2004).

4.   Advocates for victims of Colombian civil strife have lobbied for TPS for Colombians living in the United States. They have been joined by the Colombian government, UNHCR, and several members of Congress. *See* Bauer, Note, *They Beg for Our Protection and We Refuse: U.S. Asylum Law's Failure to Protect Many of Today's Refugees*, 79 Notre Dame L. Rev. 1081, 1111 (2004). These efforts have led to proposed legislation that would grant TPS to Colombians. *See, e.g.*, Colombian Temporary Protected Status Act of 2006, H.R. 4886, 109th Cong. (2006). Would you support such legislation? What facts and considerations would be important to you in reaching a judgment?

———————

### c.   *TPS Statistics*

### Table 11.1
### Temporary Protected Status

Eligible Groups and Registration Dates as of October 2006

|  | *Entered U.S. by* | *Current TPS Expiration* |
|---|---|---|
| Burundi | 11–09–99 | 11–02–07 |
| El Salvador | 03–09–01 | 09–09–07 |
| Honduras | 01–05–99 | 07–05–07 |
| Liberia | 08–25–04 | 10–01–07 |
| Nicaragua | 01–05–99 | 07–05–07 |
| Somalia | 09–04–01 | 03–17–08 |
| Sudan | 10–07–04 | 05–02–07 |

Source: Bureau of Citizen and Immigration Services, Temporary Protected Status website http://www.uscis.gov/graphics/services/tps_inter.htm

### 4.　TEMPORARY PROTECTION IN THE EUROPEAN UNION

As the United States enacted TPS legislation in the early 1990s, European countries faced similar dilemmas about providing temporary protection to those fleeing civil strife. The war in the Balkans triggered the flight of hundreds of thousands of Bosnians, together with smaller numbers of Croats and Serbs. Germany provided temporary legal status to about 345,000 Bosnians displaced by the war, while all other European Union countries combined hosted around 247,000. United Nations High Commissioner for Refugees, The State of the World's Refugees 1997: A Humanitarian Agenda ch. 5, fig. 5.6 (1997). Hungary, at that time not yet an EU state, and other countries neighboring Yugoslavia also provided refuge to substantial numbers. Those nations hosting the largest populations of displaced persons called for "burden sharing" by their sister states within the European Union, but no effective program developed to respond to the ad hoc and unequal situation. *See generally* Fitzpatrick, *Temporary Protection of Refugees: Elements of a Formalized Regime*, 94 Am. J. Int'l L. 279, 289–91 (2000) (discussing responsibility sharing).

After the Dayton Accords ended the fighting in Bosnia in 1995, Germany terminated the temporary protection and exhorted all those displaced by the war to return home. It forcibly repatriated several hundred Bosnians who refused to return because they said it was unsafe. In 1999, Germany reported that more than two-thirds of the Bosnians had left Germany, although the data did not show whether they had returned to Bosnia or gone elsewhere. The German government currently states that "[t]he return of 345,00 Bosnian refugees admitted to Germany can generally ... be considered as concluded."[2] In contrast,

**2.**　http://www.bmi.bund.de/cln_028/nn_148248/Internet/Content/Themen/Auslaender_Fluechtlinge_Asyl_Zuwanderung/　Einzelseiten/Readmission_agreements_Id_57694_en.html.

many other European countries—with smaller groups of displaced Bosnians—allowed the Bosnians to assume a more permanent status and did not attempt to repatriate them. *See* Koser, *Germany: Protection for Refugees or Protection from Refugees?* in Kosovo's Refugees in the European Union (J. van Selm ed. 2000).

Starting in the mid 1990s, the Kosovo crisis led more than 100,000 Kosovar Albanians to seek asylum in EU states. This forced migration was dwarfed by the war that broke out in 1999, when 900,000 fled Kosovo in several months. The 15 EU countries maintained that collectively they could accept only 100,000 of the million war refugees, and they called on Albania, Macedonia, and other states neighboring Kosovo to allow international organizations to establish temporary camps to house the others displaced by the attacks and the NATO bombing. Germany, mindful of its recent experience with forced migrants from Bosnia, agreed to accept a quota of 10,000 Kosovars, but only after invoking recent legislation that limited "war refugees" to a three-month stay in Germany. The war refugees were accepted as a group, without the need of proving individual risk, their freedom of movement within Germany was limited and they were not eligible to apply for refugee status. Koser, pp. 30–32. Ultimately, Germany accepted close to 15,000 war refugees. The other 14 EU states accepted a total of 38,000 Kosovars, while more than 800,000 remained in Albania, Macedonia, and Montenegro. Hundreds of thousands more were displaced within Kosovo and Serbia. Van Selm, Appendix 2.

These forced migrations on its doorstep led the European Union to issue a mandate on temporary protection. The title of Council Directive 2001/55/EC, 2001 O.J. (L 212) 12 (EC), describes its scope and purpose: "minimum standards for giving temporary protection in the event of a mass influx of displaced persons and on measures promoting a balance of efforts between member states in receiving such persons and bearing the consequences thereof." Temporary protection is defined as follows:

> a procedure of exceptional character to provide, in the event of a mass influx or imminent mass influx of displaced persons from third countries who are unable to return to their country of origin, immediate and temporary protection to such persons, in particular if there is also a risk that the asylum system will be unable to process this influx without adverse effects for its efficient operation, in the interests of the persons concerned and other persons requesting protection.

Art. 2(a).

Under this mandate, a member state or the EU Commission may propose that the temporary protection procedure be activated for a specified group, noting the date when it should take effect and a prediction of the number of displaced persons who will take advantage of it. If the governing body, the EU Council, votes to approve the proposal, temporary protection shall be activated for the defined group for one year. Art. 4–5. It may be extended by six month intervals for a maximum of one more year. Art. 4 (1). It may be terminated sooner if the EU Council decides that a "safe and durable return" is possible. Art. 6.

Those provided temporary protection receive the following benefits:

- residence permit
- work authorization (subject to labor market conditions)
- housing
- social welfare
- medical care

Art. 12–13.

Persons granted temporary protection may not be prohibited from seeking refugee status. Art. 3. Individuals who have committed serious non-political crimes, crimes against peace, war crimes, crimes against humanity, or acts contrary to the purposes and principles of the UN may be excluded from temporary protection. Art. 28.

The temporary protection directive entered into force in 2001, but member states were given several years in which to adopt measures to comply with the directive. Note that the directive embraces a "minimum standards" approach. Member states are free to provide temporary protection to more people and to guarantee them more legal protection than that specified in the directive.

Malta, one of the states that joined the EU in 2004, has reportedly received 5000 asylum seekers and other migrants in the past four years. Jordan, *An Island Engulfed by Migrants: Tiny Malta Struggles to Absorb Boatloads of Desperate Africans,* Wash. Post, June 4, 2006, at A14. A small island state, Malta is less than 200 miles from the coast of Libya, where authorities say there are more than 1.5 million sub-Saharan African asylum seekers, many fleeing persecution in the Darfur region of Sudan and in Somalia. Malta has responded to the surge of forced migrants by detaining all asylum seekers, and has requested urgent assistance from other EU states. Biletsky, *Malta fears sinking under migrants*, Int'l Herald Tribune, June 7, 2006. The EU has shown no inclination to invoke either temporary protection or burden sharing mechanisms, although there have been discussions of what assistance might be offered to Malta. *Migration News Sheet*, Sept. 2005, at 10–12. Thus far, no other EU state has proposed invoking the directive's temporary protection measures.

### Notes and Questions

1. How workable is the EU approach? Since the temporary protection mechanism can only be triggered by a majority vote of the EU Council, member states may vote not to invoke temporary protection measures if those fleeing harm are concentrated in a few of the EU countries. Are refugee crises generally localized?

2. How similar is the EU approach to TPS in the United States? Is it more or less likely to create a magnet effect or to prevent permanent relocation? Does it favor a group determination? Which approach leaves more to ad hoc policy decisions, rather than proceeding by means of fixed legal requirements? What are the advantages and disadvantages of the more flexible approach? Consider this issue from the perspective of (1) persons seeking protection, (2) executive branch officials, (3) judges, (4) the political impact on the citizenry of receiving states.

3.  For commentary on the EU temporary protection regime, see Gibney, *Between Control and Humanitarianism: Temporary Protection in Contemporary Europe*, 14 Geo. Immig. L.J. 689 (2000); Sopf, *Temporary Protection in Europe after 1990: The Right to Remain of Genuine Convention Refugees*, 6 Wash. U. J. L. & Policy 109 (2001); van Selm, *Return Seen from a European Perspective: An Impossible Dream, An Improbable Reality, or An Obstruction to Refugee Policy?*, 28 Fordham Int'l L.J. 1504 (2005).

# SECTION C.   DETERRENCE OF MASS FLOWS

## 1.  OFFSHORE SAFE HAVENS

### a.  *Haitian Asylum Seekers*

Chapter Nine, Section A2, discussed the interdiction program used in various forms since 1981 to prevent Haitian asylum seekers from reaching the United States—usually, but not always, employing some form of refugee screening before Haitians were returned. Exact U.S. practices changed in light of changing political and military developments inside Haiti and of ebbs and flows in the migration stream. One significant phase, however, involved the use of offshore safe haven as part of the program.

President Clinton, despite campaign criticisms of the first Bush administration's use of a form of interdiction that returned Haitians without refugee screening, decided to continue that program when he took office. His administration then won a Supreme Court ruling, in *Sale v. Haitian Centers Council,* 509 U.S. 155 (1993), finding no legal fault with that policy. Nonetheless sharp criticism continued, particularly as international pressures through 1993 and early 1994 made little headway in forcing the Haitian generals who had overthrown the democratically elected Aristide government to cede power. Finally in May 1994 President Clinton changed policy. He ordered that interdicted Haitians were to be taken to a large U.S. ship anchored near Jamaica for full refugee screening (not a mere threshold determination that would lead to further proceedings in the United States). Those found to have a well-founded fear of persecution were to be brought to the United States in full refugee status, under INA § 207, the provision that governs overseas refugee programs. The rest would be repatriated.

These arrangements proceeded for a few weeks, but the numbers soon overwhelmed the processing capacity. Many of the migrants were therefore taken to the U.S. naval facility at Guantánamo, on the island of Cuba, for interviews and temporary lodging. When the outflow reached as high as 3000 per day, however, the Administration announced a significant change of course. On July 5, 1994, the President stated that Haitians would no longer be screened (except minimally for criminal background), but at the same time, no more would be allowed to resettle in the United States. Instead any who still wished to come would be taken to "safe havens" in the region, beginning with a safe haven site at Guantánamo. This change had a dramatic impact on the outflow from Haiti, which fell to below 200 a week. Meantime, many Haitians chose to repatriate rather than remain in the bleak tent cities of Guantánamo.

Then on September 19, U.S. military forces entered Haiti under UN authority, and by October 15, Aristide was back in the Presidential Palace in Port-au-Prince. By December 1, as a result of voluntary repatriations, the Haitian population at Guantánamo was reduced to 4,600. In late December, the U.S. government announced that conditions in Haiti were generally safe for return, and it offered cash and job-training incentives to those who repatriated voluntarily by January 5, 1995. Nearly 700 accepted. The remaining 3,900 were screened and then were involuntarily returned unless they showed substantial reasons for believing that they would face "serious harm not arising out of a personal dispute" if returned to Haiti. UNHCR objected to what it regarded as a cursory screening process and the use of a standard not known to international law—and so refused involvement in the repatriation. By March, fewer than 100 Haitians remained behind, pending further investigation of their serious harm assertions. *See* Refugee Reports, Jan. 31, 1995, at 5–7; Suro, *U.S. Policy Changed with Guantánamo Safe Havens,* Washington Post, Feb. 5, 1995, at A24.

### Notes and Questions

1. Does the standard adopted by the United States to decide on repatriations after the UN intervention in Haiti, "serious harm not arising out of a personal dispute," include all Convention refugees? If not, was the UNHCR's objection valid?

2. Humanitarian intervention in the source country could perhaps also be considered a way of providing an offshore safe haven. For more on humanitarian intervention, including the role that refugee or asylum seeker flows can play in stimulating such action, *see, e.g.,* Humanitarian Intervention: Ethical, Legal and Political Dilemmas (J. L. Holzgrefe, R. Keohane eds. 2003); Enforcing Restraint: Collective Intervention in Internal Conflicts (L. Damrosch ed. 1993); To Loose the Bands of Wickedness: International Intervention in Defense of Human Rights (N. Rodley ed. 1992); Martin, *Strategies for a Resistant World: Human Rights Initiatives and the Need for Alternatives to Refugee Interdiction,* 26 Cornell Int'l L.J. 753 (1993).

### b. *Cuban Asylum Seekers*

One of the most troubling points of the Haitian interdiction program, since its inception in 1981, had always been the sharp contrast between the treatment of Haitians and the boat people from the next island over, Cuba. During much of the time that the U.S. Coast Guard was interdicting Haitians and returning some or all of them in the early 1990s, other Coast Guard cutters were patrolling nearby waters to pick up Cubans who had slipped past government guards and managed to get their rafts to the high seas outside Cuba's twelve-mile limit. Until summer 1994, Cuban rafters picked up this way were taken to Florida, where they were warmly greeted and put on a fast-track toward permanent residency, without having to demonstrate a well-founded fear of persecution.

This grand-daddy of all safe haven programs dates back to the early years of Castro's revolution, when the U.S. government essentially decided to allow all Cubans to enter and to stay as long as was necessary. Many were paroled in; those who had already made an entry became some of the first beneficiaries of EVD. When it became apparent that the Castro government would not quickly fade away, Congress enacted the Cuban Adjustment Act of 1966, Pub.L. 89–732, 80 Stat. 1161. It provides that the status of Cubans who have been "inspected and admitted or paroled into the United States subsequent to January 1, 1959, * * * may be adjusted by the Attorney General, in his discretion and under such regulations as he may prescribe, to that of an alien lawfully admitted for permanent residence" after one years' physical presence in the United States (originally two years). This was taken by generations of Cuban–Americans and many politicians to be an open-ended entitlement to LPR status for virtually all Cubans who could make it to U.S. soil.

In 1980, Fidel Castro found himself in an embarrassing dispute with the Peruvian government over an issue of diplomatic asylum at the Peruvian Embassy in Havana. He responded by removing guards from the perimeter of that facility; in short order, some 10,000 Cubans descended on the embassy, hoping that they would thereby secure an exit from Cuba. When this unexpected development soured Cuba's relations with much of Latin America, Castro effectively changed the subject. He promptly announced that he was opening the northern port of Mariel so that Cuban–Americans could come and pick up the embassy contingent as well as other relatives. The resulting Mariel boatlift brought some 125,000 Cubans directly to the United States in the span of a few weeks before U.S. policy effectively responded to stem the southward boat flow. This massive and disorderly flow sorely tested the limits of U.S. (and Florida) hospitality.

The 1966 Act remained unchanged, however, perhaps because after 1980 the flow had remained low as Cuba reinstated close enforcement of its exit controls. Then in August 1994 Fidel Castro responded to internal unrest—as he had often done before—by trying to create a new migration crisis for the United States. Guards stopped patrolling the beaches of northern Cuba, and eager rafters by the thousands set off for the high seas in flimsy home-made craft. Governor Chiles of Florida, in the middle of a hard-fought election campaign, declared a state of emergency and pushed the federal government to act to reduce the influx.

The Clinton administration responded fairly quickly, setting in motion a chain of events that basically ended the open-door policy for Cubans. Instead of bringing the Cubans to the United States, the administration opted to use the model of offshore safe haven that had recently proven so effective in discouraging further departures from Haiti. (The Cuban crisis began about five weeks after Clinton announced that departing Haitians would receive only temporary safe haven in Guantánamo.) Rescued Cuban rafters were taken to a separate camp in Guantánamo, and later some were moved to a safe-haven camp in Panama paid for and operated by the U.S. government. Initially this change in policy seemed to have little effect on departures from Cuba, but after about 10 days the numbers began to decline. Before the dissuasive effect was fully tested, however, Cuba and the United States reached a migration agreement on September 9, 1994. Cuba agreed to end departures "using mainly persuasive means," and the United States agreed to take a minimum of 20,000 Cubans for permanent, orderly migration each year, after advance screening and selection in Havana, most of them by use of the parole power. *See* 71 Interp.Rel. 1091, 1213, 1236–37 (reprinting the agreement), 1409, 1474 (1994). Administration officials asserted that these unprecedented arrangements were the price that had to be paid to bring an end to 35 years of inequitable policy and the expectations that had been generated. *See generally* Aleinikoff, *Safe Haven: Pragmatics and Prospects*, 35 Va.J. Int'l L. 71 (1994); Fitzpatrick, *Flight from Asylum: Trends Toward Temporary "Refuge" and Local Responses to Forced Migrations, id.* at 13.

Departures from Cuba slowed to a trickle after the September agreement, but there remained the knotty issue of what to do with the roughly 20,000 Cubans still at Guantánamo. In May 1995, after dealing with considerable tension in the camp, the Clinton Administration announced that most of the Cubans at Guantánamo would be allowed into the United States, at the rate of about 500 per week. Moreover, they would be counted as part of the 20,000 Cubans to be admitted annually under the September 1994 agreement. At the same time, to minimize the risk of triggering a new raft flow, the Administration announced another major change in policy: any Cubans interdicted on the high seas thereafter would be returned to Cuba, rather than taken to safe havens. Generally, any Cubans so returned to Cuba could come to the United States only by applying for admission after return, under the terms of the September 1994 agreement. New interdiction program guidelines did provide for shipboard interviews to determine whether any interdicted Cuban had a "credible fear of persecution," but this determination was supposed to take into account the availability of the in-country refugee processing. *See* 72 Interp.Rel. 623, 1407 (1995). From May 1995 through January 1997, 656 Cubans were interdicted by the U.S. Coast Guard; 86 percent were returned directly to Cuba, some after further interviews at Guantánamo. Fifteen were taken to the United States, and the rest went to various third countries.

By the end of the summer of 1994, then, and for the next few years, far greater parity had been brought to the treatment of Cubans and Haitians—and a democratically elected President had been returned to Haiti as a result of armed U.S. intervention. Two agonizing immigration crises had been mastered fairly speedily, as these things go, through the use of offshore safe haven. Some officials waxed enthusiastic about this practice. The May 1995 decision permitting parole of the Cuban safe haven population had allowed an orderly and gradual movement of 20,000 Cubans to the United States, minimizing the political fallout and allowing the United States to avoid confronting the repatriation issue on a mass scale. By March 1996, Guantánamo had resumed its normal functions.

Some Cuban boats continue to come today, and this basic interdiction policy continues. But that policy, when combined with the continued vitality of the Cuban Adjustment Act, has given rise to a rather curious set of ground rules known in shorthand as "wet foot–dry foot." Those who get far enough to set foot on dry land in the United States are usually allowed to remain and eventually obtain full residence status under the Act. Those caught before landing, even close to shore in U.S. territorial waters, are sent back to Cuba, after a special form of credible-fear screening. Today, Guantánamo is used to temporarily house those Cubans deemed ineligible to be returned to Cuba due to such a fear of persecution. See Sartori, *The Cuban Migration Dilemma: An Examination of the United States' Policy of Temporary Protection in Offshore Safe Havens*, 15 Geo. Immig. L.J. 319, 352–55 (2001). (Guantánamo of course also serves as a detention and interrogation center for persons captured in the war against terror.)

The post-9/11 era has further diminished Cubans' hopes and chances of migrating to the United States. First, the Bush administration has continued and expanded the United States' interdiction policy through Operation Distant Shore, which coordinates a number of different federal, state, and local agencies to stop and return any boats from any Caribbean nation, including Cuba. Second, in 2003, in response to a threat issued by Fidel Castro to release a mass of Cuban refugees, the United States took the position that it would consider a general exodus as an act of aggression. Castro has not acted on his threat. *See* Ackerman, UNHCR Emergency & Security Services, Cuba: Potential Refugee Crisis? An Assessment 9, 10 (June 2006).[3] Political instability in Cuba may well be in the offing, given Castro's illness and temporary relinquishment of day-to-day governing responsibilities in September 2006. The migration implications of a post-Castro Cuba remain unknown, but potentially quite significant.

## 2. OFFSHORE PROCESSING AND SAFE HAVEN

### a. *Australian Practice*

As noted in Chapter Nine, in 2001 Australia refused to allow the Norwegian ship *MV Tampa* to land the 433 asylum seekers it had rescued nearby. Instead, Australia turned to the small island nation of Nauru located nearly 2500 miles from Australia in the South Pacific. Australia promised to pay for camps, processing centers, and other facilities where refugee screening could be done. Two hundred and eighty-three of the *Tampa* asylum-seekers were taken to Nauru. In addition, 150 were processed in New Zealand. Australia subsequently entered into an agreement with Papua New Guinea for the housing and processing of asylum-seekers. Over the past five years, more than 1500 persons have been taken to processing centers in Nauru and Papua New

---

**3.** http://www.unhcr.org/home/RSDCOI/
44eb2fd44.pdf.

Guinea; the centers are run by the International Organization for Migration. About half have been determined to be refugees, and 380 of them have been brought to Australia. The others have been resettled in other countries. Many asylum-seekers waited months in the offshore processing centers months for processing and for eventual resettlement. *See* Taylor, *The Pacific Solution or a Pacific Nightmare?: The Difference between Burden Shifting and Responsibility Sharing,* 6 Asian–Pacific L. & Pol'y J. 1 (2005). Symposium, *Australia's Tampa Incident: The Convergence of International and Domestic Refugee and Maritime Law in the Pacific Rim,* 12 Pac. Rim L. & Pol'y J. 1 (2003).

### b. European Proposals

Although no European countries have established offshore processing centers or safe havens, there have been recurrent discussions of the possibility of creating "transit processing centers" outside EU territory, possibly in Albania, Russia or Ukraine, where all asylum seekers would be sent until their claims are decided. In 2003 the British made such a proposal, which echoed similar ideas that the Danish and the Dutch governments had raised in earlier years. The U.K. proposed sending asylum seekers who arrived in the EU to extraterritorial transit processing centers for screening. Those who qualified for refugee or subsidiary protection status would be resettled in EU states according to a burden-sharing formula, while those determined not to need protection would be repatriated directly to their countries of origin. The British acknowledged that it might not be possible to return all rejected applicants to their homelands immediately; accordingly, they proposed establishing offshore safe havens known as "regional protection areas" where those denied refugee status but unable to return home safely could stay temporarily. These regional protection areas would be outside the EU, in the regions where the asylum seekers originated. For a thorough analysis of the UK proposal, see Amnesty International, *Unlawful and Unworkable: Proposals for Extraterritorial Processing of Asylum Claims,* at 6–10, June 23, 2003.

Some EU states, such as Austria, expressed interest in exploring the U.K. proposal, while the governments in Germany and Sweden strongly criticized it. UNHCR responded that it was willing at least to explore these ideas with the EU. *See Unlawful and Unworkable, supra;* Alan Travis, *Blunkett Proposes Asylum Claims Assessed Outside EU,* The Guardian, April 3, 2003, at 10; Philip Johnston, *News—Blunkett's "Safe Havens" Refugee Plan is Censured,* The Daily Telegraph, March 28, 2003, at 14. At the moment the British government has withdrawn its proposal, but the idea of diverting asylum seekers to safe areas outside the EU will likely resurface in political discussions concerning forced migrants.

The current state of off-shore processing centers in Europe is described in a recent UNHCR publication:

While Denmark, the Netherlands, Italy and Spain were outspoken supporters of the idea, a number of member states, including Sweden, Germany and France, were clearly opposed. By mid-2003 it had emerged that the United Kingdom could not muster enough support for a radical reformulation of the protection system.

Nonetheless, a number of experimental pilot projects with a regional protection component were launched in collaboration with the European Union, interested member states and UNHCR. In 2004, the German government changed its earlier stance * * *. Later that same year Italy deported boat arrivals from the island of Lampedusa to Libya, which is not a signatory to the 1951 UN Refugee Convention. It seemed as if a crude version of the British government's "vision" was being implemented, with Italy taking the lead. "Outsourcing" had clearly grasped the imagination of the European Commission, which decided to sketch plans for "Regional Protection Programmes." However, unlike the United Kingdom's plan, the programmes would include the transformation of third countries to safe ones.

Outsourcing refugee protection: extraterritorial processing and the future of the refugee regime, UNHCR, The State of the World's Refugees 2006: Human Displacement in the New Millennium 38.

## 3. REFORM OF THE TEMPORARY PROTECTION SYSTEM

### SUSAN MARTIN, ANDREW SCHOENHOLTZ, DEBORAH MEYERS, TEMPORARY PROTECTION: TOWARDS A NEW REGIONAL AND DOMESTIC FRAMEWORK

12 Geo. Immig. L. J. 543 (1998).

During the past thirty-five years, the United States has seen the direct influx of thousands of individuals leaving politically unstable countries. While some seeking entry have proved themselves to be refugees and obtained permanent protection in the United States, far more, including a large number of people fleeing civil war, natural disasters, or comparable forms of upheaval in their home countries, have failed to demonstrate that they would be targets of persecution. Yet, their return to their home countries has been complicated by the very circumstances that led to their flight: conflict, violence, and repression. Over time, the United States developed a series of ad hoc responses that protected such individuals, culminating in the Immigration Act of 1990 which provided legislative authority for Temporary Protected Status ("TPS"). Nevertheless, * * * many problems remain in the application of the law.

* * *

Current policies fail on two accounts. First, the temporary protection provision in the law generally has failed to protect the vast majority of those in danger as a crisis develops and unfolds. Second, current policies regarding protection in the United States do not provide the control mechanisms to ensure that protection is not abused and that return, when appropriate, is effected.

\* \* \*

## IV.  TOWARDS A NEW TEMPORARY PROTECTION REGIME

An effective temporary protection regime must \* \* \* ensure \* \* \* that migrants will not be returned to places where they face potential loss of life or liberty. The regime must work for the individual protection seeker as well as for those fleeing en masse during a migration emergency. \* \* \* [T]emporary protection \* \* \* should not be seen as a substitute for a fair and effective asylum system.

Temporary protection should also not be seen as an avenue towards long-term admission. An effective capacity to repatriate those granted temporary protection when conditions permit would greatly enhance the willingness of nations to provide safe haven when needed. However, [i]n some circumstances \* \* \* the grant of protection will continue for so long that return may not be feasible. Hence, a temporary protection regime must plan for the eventual end-game, whether repatriation, settlement in the country providing safe haven, or resettlement in a third country.

Below, we outline the framework for a new temporary protection regime. First, we detail the elements of a regional protection system. Then, we outline a new set of temporary protection policies for the United States.

### A.  *Regional Temporary Protection*

\* \* \*

### 3.  Responsibility-sharing

[One] aspect of regional safe haven is responsibility-sharing during a mass migration. Under such responsibility-sharing, the United States would receive assistance from other Western Hemisphere countries when migrants are heading toward the United States and would assist these other countries should the situation be reversed. Such responsibility-sharing is viable only if the United States assumes significant leadership and shares part of the burden, both in terms of monetary contributions and program initiatives. \* \* \*

\* \* \*

The Inter-governmental Consultations on Asylum, Refugee, and Migration Policies have often been mentioned as an example of successful ongoing multilateral discussions and could be a model for regional cooperation on migration issues. The Puebla Process, through which the United States, Canada, Mexico and the Central American countries discuss common immigration interests, could also be expanded to include discussion of regional safe haven mechanisms.

Perhaps the most fitting forum for these discussions is the Organization of American States. * * *

* * *

4.  Operational Issues

Identifying sites to house those granted temporary protection is the key operational issue to be resolved in negotiating a regional agreement. Various sites may be needed depending on the size of the movements, their proximity to the source country, and geopolitical sensitivities regarding a particular emergency. To the extent possible, the migrants would be released into local communities and be provided employment opportunities while awaiting return to their home countries. When the size of the protected group, their impact on the local population, or other factors make release impossible, camps may be a necessary alternative. The negotiations on establishing the regional protection system should address minimum requirements in terms of overall conditions, access to medical and other services, presence of nongovernmental organizations, specific policies related to unaccompanied minors and women at risk, and other similar issues.

The negotiations should also set criteria for use of safe haven sites within the country of origin. These should be used only as a last resort when all else has proven ineffective in responding to the humanitarian emergency. The risks to life for both protected and protectors have so often outweighed the potential benefits of such in-country protection that only in the most extraordinary circumstances can they be justified.

There is little disagreement that the United States military is best able to establish safe haven camps during an emergency, whether they are located on a military base, such as Guantánamo, or inside another country, such as the safe area in northern Iraq. In addition, there is little disagreement, even within the military, that management of the camps should be turned over to civilians as quickly as possible. There is also little disagreement that a military base is far from an ideal site for temporary protection.

* * *

5.  Durable Solutions

* * *

What are the alternatives for those unable to return after a significant period of time? One option is to maintain them in a safe haven indefinitely, not a particularly attractive solution, although one encountered in many refugee situations internationally. An option more in keeping with the humanitarian nature of this proposal is coordinated action to find durable solutions aside from repatriation. Local integration and third country resettlement should be considered for individuals whose continued presence in protection sites cannot be sustained.

Under some circumstances, a regional framework for protection can serve as an impetus for safe return. Certainly, the decision to provide safe haven to Haitian boat people bolstered the United States and regional resolve to restore President Aristide to Haiti. The military intervention then provided the security necessary for return.

Even without such intervention, regional and international cooperation on the return of refugees and displaced persons can help create favorable conditions for repatriation.

\* \* \*

The Concerted Plan of Action adopted by the International Conference on Central American Refugees ("CIREFCA") is another potential model for coordinated regional action. The CIREFCA plan is particularly relevant because it involved many countries in the Americas and succeeded in managing the return of Salvadorans, Nicaraguans, and Guatemalans from camps in the region. While the Central American peace process began prior to the conference, CIREFCA helped institutionalize the political and economic developments in the region that supported an end to the civil conflicts. \* \* \*

\* \* \*

### B.   Protection in the United States

A regional temporary protection regime does not obviate the need for the United States to have credible temporary protection policies of its own. If the United States is to take leadership in negotiating a regional agreement, our own policies should set an example for others. Even when the regional regime is established and triggered, some migrants are likely to reach United States shores. Their treatment in the United States should be in accordance with the principles of protection discussed above. Moreover, the United States will continue to receive individual applicants who do not meet the criteria for asylum but have a well-founded fear for their lives if returned prematurely to their home countries.

\* \* \*

In our view, a case-by-case determination process that screens applicants for both asylum and temporary protection best serves the humanitarian and immigration control interests. Although there remains a role for group designations, particularly at the start of an emergency when the personnel may not be in place for individual screening of claims, a case-by-case procedure more effectively addresses the weaknesses in current temporary protection policies.

1.   Eligibility Determination

\* \* \*

One reason that the group designation is rarely used for nationals fleeing from nearby countries \* \* \* is the magnet concern. A group designation may draw out people who are not, in fact, in danger in their home countries. Even countries with civil wars have safe zones in which citizens live in safety. Experience teaches that people will take great risks, including the dangers of small boat voyages, if there is any possibility for permanent residence in an economically more advantaged country. To the extent that temporary protection is seen as an avenue towards such permanent residence, there remains a serious reason to be concerned about the magnet effects of this designation.

In order to address [these] concerns * * * we propose that TPS be granted on a case-by-case basis. Under this proposal, an alien could apply for asylum and temporary protected status at the same time. If the individual failed to meet the refugee standard, but met the TPS standard (i.e., the individual's country of origin was in the midst of civil war or other circumstances that would make return dangerous), he or she would be granted TPS for a specified time. This process could be implemented within the regional protection system, if appropriate, or on a unilateral basis. If implemented as part of the regional system, those granted TPS may be permitted to remain in the United States or sent to a regional site, depending on numbers, likelihood of magnet effects if permitted to remain in the United States, and other similar factors.

This proposal provides greater flexibility in determining the appropriate status for an individual. It permits protection of those who truly fear return not only because of persecution, but also because of civil wars and other extreme violence. It does not require the Executive Branch to designate all members or even a subpart of a particular national group for TPS. Instead, case-by-case determinations would be made against agreed-upon criteria. For example, individuals from certain geographic areas might be safely returned to a country with a civil war while others would face grave danger. Thus, the temporary protection seeker would be required to establish two primary elements: (1) a civil war, natural disaster, or comparable form of upheaval has occurred in the home country and its effects are ongoing; and (2) requiring the return of this individual to that country would pose a serious threat to his or her personal safety. If the determination system were implemented well, a case-by-case system could separate those in genuine need of protection from those who could be immediately returned.

The timing of such a process must balance the importance of providing protection seekers a fair opportunity with the significance of quickly sending a message to those who do not deserve protection that only the bona fide need apply. The evidence to date of the streamlined affirmative asylum process suggests that such balances can be made in setting up the process. * * *

An individualized determination system also would reduce the political and foreign policy pressures on determining what nationalities would be eligible and how long temporary protection is needed. It could be both generous and credible. * * *

4. Detention/Release

Given the degree of illegal migration into the United States, fairly quick reception into the community may act as a magnet for those who are not fleeing dangerous conditions but simply are seeking a better economic life. From an immigration control point of view, it may be necessary to detain those who receive temporary protection for the duration of protection, that is, until conditions in the home country permit return. Such controls would be needed to lessen any magnet effect by helping to ensure that those who do not deserve protection do not come. Support for this line of reasoning comes from the rapid reduction in boat departures from Haiti and Cuba when the United States offered protection in Guantánamo but no entry into the United States. Initial detention would also help ensure that disruptions of local communities are minimized when large numbers of migrants enter in a short period.

Currently, there is insufficient capacity to hold significant numbers of people seeking temporary protection in the United States, even if the detention were limited to the initial determination phase. Possible holding facilities include closed military bases, where barracks still stand or other forms of shelter could be raised quickly. If the flow of those seeking temporary protection is concentrated in significant numbers, immediate response teams may need to include the military in order to establish the infrastructure for holding centers.

From the humanitarian point of view, detention unfairly punishes those who genuinely need protection. Other forms of control over the protected population can be devised. In several European countries, open camps are used that do not restrict the movement of those provided protection, but restrict their access to work and other benefits. * * *

A middle ground would be a system of reporting to a third party so that the whereabouts of those provided temporary protection is always known. In the early 1980s, certain Haitian migrants who were initially detained were ultimately released into the community under an arrangement whereby they regularly reported to voluntary agencies that forwarded such information through Fordham University to the INS. Reportedly, the compliance rate was very high. * * *

What is clear is that a single detention/release policy is unlikely to fit for all temporary protection situations. The federal government should have the flexibility to base release decisions on specific criteria—the number of applications, their geographic concentration, and the likely duration of the crisis causing the flight, among others. In the final analysis, protection must be the guiding determinant. Although seldom desirable, detention will be preferable to return to life-threatening situations.

5. Work Authorization/Eligibility for Public Benefits

Another major issue regarding the rights of those temporarily protected in the United States concerns authorization to work and eligibility for public benefits.

Work authorization has been favored over public financing in the United States, and recent laws have sought to grant work authorizations in a manner that does not create a magnet for those who do not deserve an immigration benefit. Now, the asylum system generally authorizes work only for those granted asylum, a process that takes several months, whereas in the past, that benefit attached to the asylum seeker during the application process. If policymakers continue to favor employment authorization over public funding, they will need to determine when work would be permitted based on a number of questions:

1) How soon might the conflict in the home country end and repatriation be safe?

2) Should work authorization be delayed for some period (six months, for example) to discourage individuals not deserving of protection from taking advantage of a humanitarian program?

3) How many workers within a specified period of time can enter the local workforce without causing serious adverse consequences to the already-resident workers?

\* \* \*

6.   The End Game

The upheavals that cause people to flee their homelands are varied and often complex. Conditions must improve to the point that people can safely return home before temporary protection is no longer needed. What happens when temporary protection ends is key to the credibility of protection policies in the United States. Until we are able to be firm when firmness is possible, we will not be able to be generous in providing protection inside this country.

If conditions improve within a reasonable period of time, most people will be able to return home. If conditions do not improve within such a period, questions will arise as to the continued viability of a temporary protection regime. \* \* \*

i.   Return

Return of those granted temporary protection could be accomplished in a number of ways. Removal under our existing immigration laws could be used. Once temporary protection status is ended, those who remain in the country would be here illegally. Notices to appear would be issued against such over-stayers, initiating the removal process. If deportation is carried out, it removes the concern some have of providing protection at all. On the other hand, carrying out deportations in large numbers may create destabilizing conditions in the home country. Moreover, deportation is a costly process, requiring INS officers and Immigration Judges to handle large numbers of cases. Some believe that it is simply wrong to return forcibly those who have fled civil wars and other emergencies that significantly damage a country, noting that the humanitarian impulse that justified temporary protection needs to be matched by a humanitarian return approach.

A more fitting end game is to plan for return as a part of the larger political and economic reconstruction processes in the home country. Return of those granted temporary protection could be accomplished by voluntary means with a combination of individual financial and home country development aid incentives. * * *

Under an option emphasizing humanitarian return, people would be assisted in returning voluntarily. Such assistance could include direct financial assistance targeted to communities to which people return * * *. The International Organization for Migration runs a number of programs assisting individual returnees going from developed back to developing countries. Under some of these programs, IOM helps returnees find employment in their home countries and pays the differential in salary for a limited time. Several Western European countries have negotiated return agreements with Eastern European nations that provide assistance for the reintegration of returnees.

Funding any return policy is critical. Financial assistance from taxpayers requires sufficient public support for the policy. Another option would be to set aside Social Security payments made by those temporarily protected in a special fund to be distributed only upon return. The employee Social Security contributions would go directly to the individual, while the employer contributions could be targeted to the communities to which nationals are returning.

Providing financial incentives and aid to returnees and local communities may encourage the return of a good number of people. However, it is difficult to assist the home country communities enough to ensure that returnees will not be simply added to high unemployment rates and subject to rising crime rates where a civil war or other emergency has just ended. If people believe that conditions at home will not allow them to provide food, shelter, and clothing for their families, they will opt to stay illegally in the United States. Our reform proposal, therefore, combines voluntary and mandatory elements. Return of those granted temporary protection could be accomplished first through voluntary means with assistance; but, if that does not work, removal under existing immigration laws would proceed. Under this proposal, people would be given a period of time to avail themselves of repatriation benefits, such as those described above. Those who do not opt for that form of return during the period when it is offered would be subject to removal as well as to possible penalties regarding future immigration to the United States.

* * *

### iii. Cancellation of Removal and Adjustment of Status

When the United States permits certain individuals or groups to enter or remain in the United States in emergency circumstances, that permission is generally intended to be a temporary one. The United States expects forced migrants to return home when circumstances improve and the emergency ends. But emergencies do not always end before such individuals become part of the United States community.

Under current policy, those who enter the United States when fleeing dangerous conditions at home enjoy varying benefits regarding if, and when, they can become permanent residents. * * *

* * *

We propose a more consistent approach that would provide for automatic adjustment to permanent residence, regardless of nationality, if the grant of temporary protection continues for a very lengthy period. The potential for return diminishes over time and the United States should recognize this fact in its policies. Rather than require statutory authority or a lengthy judicial process to address the inevitable problems in returning people so long after they left their home countries, this approach enables a more streamlined administrative process. If the federal government determines that the conditions for return have not been met within the specified period (e.g., seven years), recipients of TPS would be eligible to become legal immigrants unless they failed to meet the usual tests regarding public charge, criminal behavior, and related grounds of inadmissibility.

### Notes and Questions

1. Note that the authors begin by arguing that regional cooperation will be crucial in developing an effective temporary protection program. For other regional protection proposals—generally directed at persons who qualify under the refugee definition—see Schuck at pp. 703–15, *supra;* Hathaway and Neve, *Making International Refugee Law Relevant Again: A Proposal for Collectivized and Solution-Oriented Protection*, 10 Harv. Hum. Rts. J. 115 (1997).

2. Would the authors' suggestion that work authorization be denied for an initial six-month period sufficiently counter the potential magnet effect they acknowledge? What effect would the suggested seven-year waiting period for permanent status have?

3. Although the prevailing view is that safe haven is a discretionary political decision, some scholars have argued that international humanitarian or human rights law or other aspects of customary international law forbid nations to return persons to countries beset by war or civil strife. *See, e.g.,* G. Goodwin–Gill, The Refugee in International Law 97–100 (1996); Perluss & Hartman, *Temporary Refuge: Emergence of a Customary Norm*, 26 Va.J.Int'l L. 551 (1986). Some of these views were challenged in Hailbronner, Non-Refoulement *and "Humanitarian" Refugees: Customary International Law or Wishful Legal Thinking?*, 26 Va.J.Int'l L. 857 (1986); Martin, *Effects of International Law on Migration Policy and Practice: The Uses of Hypocrisy*, 23 Int'l Migration Rev. 547, 564–68 (1989). The BIA rejected the claim that international law prohibited return to countries involved in civil war in *Matter of Medina,* 19 I & N Dec. 734 (BIA 1988). Courts reached

conclusions similar to the Board's in *Echeverria-Hernandez v. INS,* 923 F.2d 688 (9th Cir.1991), and *American Baptist Churches v. Meese,* 712 F.Supp. 756, 769–71 (N.D.Cal.1989). *See also Bradvica v. I.N.S.,* 128 F.3d 1009 (7th Cir. 1997) (deferring to BIA holding that it lacked jurisdiction to hear the customary international law claim and expressing doubts on the merits of such a claim).

---

### Exercise: Temporary Protection Role Play

This role-playing exercise, developed by Professor Philip Schrag of Georgetown University Law Center, asks you to consider multiple issues involved in temporary protection. Each participant in the exercise will play the part of a U.S. government official who will meet with other U.S. government officials to develop a new U.S. policy. Participants will be given secret role instructions that pertain to the role they are playing.

First, study the Memorandum (set out below) from the White House Chief of Staff. Then study your own role. Start with your secret role instructions, but also think in more basic terms about how your character would approach the issues. Do not share your secret instructions with others or discuss the exercise with other students before the exercise begins.

When the role-playing session begins, the student(s) playing the representative(s) of the National Security Advisor will convene the interagency meeting. (We suggest that the meeting last approximately one hour.) The role instructions for the student(s) representing the National Security Council include a direction to press for decisions to be made before the end of the time designated for the meeting.

The memo from the White House Chief of Staff follows.


**MEMORANDUM**

**TO:** Attorney General

Secretary of Homeland Security

Secretary of State

Secretary of Labor

Secretary of Health and Human Services

National Security Advisor

Director for Congressional Relations (Executive Office of the President)

Director of the Office of Intergovernmental Relations (Executive Office of the President)

**FROM:** White House Chief of Staff

**RE:** Possible temporary protection for refugees who are not fleeing from persecution on one of the grounds that qualify under current refugee and asylum law.

The President desires that you establish an inter-agency task force to consider whether the Administration should recommend new legislation to provide temporary protection for people who flee other nations but do not qualify for asylum because they do not face possible persecution on one of the five grounds specified in the definition of a "refugee" in the Immigration and Nationality Act. At present, U.S. law provides for a very limited kind of temporary protection, called "temporary protected status" (TPS). A major criticism of TPS is that it is too limited: it only affects those from countries designated by the Secretary of Homeland Security, and it covers only nationals from those countries who are already in the United States at the time crises arose in their home countries.

(Under the statute, INA § 244, the Attorney General appears to have this designation authority, but the Homeland Security Act of 2002, Public Law 107–296, transferred the authority to designate a country (or part thereof) for TPS, and to extend and terminate TPS designations, from the Attorney General to the Secretary of Homeland Security. At the same time, responsibility for administering the TPS program shifted from the former Immigration and Naturalization Service to U.S. Citizenship and Immigration Services (USCIS), a component of the Department of Homeland Security.)

Examples of situations (past and current) for which a new, broader type of protection might be considered are:

1. anarchy and economic collapse in Haiti in the mid-1990s, and possibly again today;

2. civil war in Liberia, Sierra Leone;

3. the genocide in Darfur;

4. devastation caused by a hurricane in Honduras;

5. economic collapse and civil strife in Somalia;

6. widespread devastation caused by a tsunami in Southeast and South Asia.

The White House has no preconceptions of whether any new legislation should be proposed, or, if so, what it should provide. Your task force should start with a blank slate. However, please keep in mind that the German government agreed to give six months' temporary shelter (with social services, but no prospect of permanent resettlement) to 345,000 people who fled from the civil war in

Bosnia in the early 1990s. Some remained far longer than that, but even so Germany was the subject of much international criticism for forcibly deporting thousands of them. The criticism was based on risks deriving from ongoing ethnic discord, even though all significant combat had ended with the Dayton Accords.

As you know, interagency task forces make decisions by discussion and consensus. If consensus is not possible at the "working level" of government (the people each of you designate for the first round of discussions), meetings of more senior officials become necessary to resolve disputes. Because those more senior meetings are often difficult to arrange (officials at the Assistant Secretary level and above have many issues to juggle), and because the working level generally understands the issues better than the managers anyway, consensus at the working level is highly desirable.

If the working level meeting concludes that the President should propose new legislation, it should make decisions about as many of the following issues as possible:

• who should qualify for this status?

• should any new legislation apply only to people from North America and the Caribbean?

• what procedures should be used to decide on qualifications (e.g., group admissions or individualized determinations, and by whom)?

• what rights should the beneficiaries enjoy? (Should they be housed on U.S. military bases or perhaps at Guantánamo ? Detained in jails? Or allowed to move freely? If allowed to move freely, should they be given welfare benefits, allowed to work, or afforded neither source of income? Should they be allowed any rights of family unification? Should their children receive an education? Should they have the right to travel abroad on US documentation?)

• should they have, or be denied, the right to seek durable asylum under INA § 208?

• under what conditions and through what procedures should they be returned involuntarily (as necessary) when the U.S. deems their countries safe for return?

Any new legislation must be revenue-neutral: if new expenditures are contemplated, there must be corresponding reductions in other immigration-related activities, which the task force should identify.

As usual, discussions of interagency task force meetings are not formally classified but are completely confidential.

The task force will be chaired by the representative(s) of the National Security Advisor and will include representatives of these other offices, unless a representative is unavoidably absent:

Department of State, Bureau of Population, Refugees and Migration

Department of State, Bureau of Democracy, Human Rights, and Labor

Department of Health and Human Services

Department of Labor

Department of Justice, Executive Office for Immigration Review

Department of Justice, Federal Bureau of Investigation

Department of Justice, Office of Immigration Litigation

Department of Homeland Security, Office of the General Counsel

Department of Homeland Security, Office of Immigration and Customs Enforcement

Department of Homeland Security, Asylum Division, US Citizenship and Immigration Services

Executive Office of the President, Office of Congressional Relations

Executive Office of the President, Office of Intergovernmental Relations

## SECTION D.  PROTECTION OF INTERNALLY DISPLACED PERSONS

Individuals who flee persecution but stay within their own country fall outside the international and regional refugee definitions. Though they have not crossed an international boundary, their flight is often impelled by the same risks that make refugees flee and their desperate need is often similar to that experienced by asylum seekers. For decades their geographical location in their homeland put them beyond the scope of the international community and the U.N. institutions. This began to change in the 1990s, and, as discussed briefly in Chapter One, the United Nations named a Special Rapporteur to examine the applicability of refugee law and international human rights and humanitarian law to the protection of internally displaced persons (IDPs).

The investigation led by Special Rapporteur Francis Deng resulted in the articulation of a set of principles that should apply to the treatment of internally displaced persons. The article below describes the growth of the internal displacement phenomenon, the genesis of the

Deng report, and the decision to recommend new international standards.

## ROBERTA COHEN, THE GUIDING PRINCIPLES ON INTERNAL DISPLACEMENT: AN INNOVATION IN INTERNATIONAL STANDARD SETTING

10 Global Governance 459–67 (2004).

The need for international standards for internally displaced persons first became apparent in the 1990s when the number of persons uprooted within their own countries by armed conflict, ethnic strife, and human rights abuse began to soar. When first counted in 1982, only 1.2 million people could be found forcibly displaced in eleven countries. By 1995, there were an estimated 20 to 25 million in more than forty countries, almost twice as many as refugees. Many were separated from their families or communities, trapped in the midst of conflicts, and often deprived of food, medicine, and shelter. They were also easy targets for physical violence.

When relief organizations in the field began to try to help IDPs, they found that they had no clear rules for doing so. Indeed, the UNHCR, the UN Children's Fund (UNICEF), and NGOs began to appeal for a document they could turn to that would define IDPs and their entitlements.

For many at the UN, the problem was not only a humanitarian emergency but also a potential political and security crisis. If left unaddressed, conflict and displacement in one country could disrupt national stability and also create political and economic turmoil throughout geographic regions. Whether in the Great Lakes region of Africa, the former Yugoslavia, or West Africa, conflict and displacement in one country could be seen spilling over borders, overwhelming neighboring countries with refugees, and helping to ignite regional wars.

The end of the Cold War helped bring the plight of internally displaced populations to the fore. As superpower competition waned, possibilities opened up for crossing borders and for reaching people in need, reinforced by changing notions of sovereignty. The view that people at risk inside their own countries should be a legitimate concern of the international community had long been championed by the human rights movement. Now, humanitarian organizations began to demand international access to people whose survival was at stake. In 1989, the UN aggressively pressed the Khartoum government to accept Operation Lifeline Sudan to bring in food and supplies to starving Sudanese under both government and insurgent rule. Two years later, in Iraq, with hundreds of thousands of Kurds stranded at the Turkish border in the wake of the Gulf War, a U.S.-led coalition carved out a security zone in the north, and the Security Council demanded "immediate access" for humanitarian organizations so that they could reach people *inside*. Subsequent UN resolutions also insisted on "unimpeded access" to persons displaced internally, whether in Somalia, Bosnia, Rwanda, or East Timor. In some instances, the UN authorized the use of force to ensure the delivery of relief and to provide protection for IDPs.

But no coherent institutional approach was developed to deal with internally displaced persons. Neither an institution nor a convention existed that was applicable to IDPs. As UNICEF's former executive director, James Grant, observed, "The world has established a minimum safety net for refugees. Whenever people are forced into exile ... refugees can expect UNHCR to be on the scene in a matter of days or on the outside, a matter of weeks. This is not yet the case with respect to internally displaced populations."

* * * A [U.N. Human Rights Commission] resolution in 1992 called on the secretary-general to appoint a representative on IDPs and asked the representative, as one of his first assignments, to examine the applicability of international human rights and humanitarian and refugee law to the protection of IDPs. Francis M. Deng, a distinguished scholar and diplomat from Sudan who was chosen to be the representative, immediately set about to identify persons and institutions to provide him with legal guidance and also donors to underwrite the process.

* * *

Overall, the legal team found that IDPs receive a good deal of coverage under existing international human rights and humanitarian law and analogous refugee law. However, IDPs are not explicitly mentioned in that law, and there are significant areas in which the law fails to provide adequate protection. Indeed, the *Compilation and Analysis* identified seventeen areas of insufficient protection, owing to inexplicit articulation of the law, and eight areas of clear gaps in the law. In the case of inexplicit articulation, the lawyers found that, although a general norm might exist in the law, a more specific articulation of that norm was needed to make it relevant to the needs of the internally displaced. For example, although there may be a general norm prohibiting cruel and inhuman treatment, there is no explicit prohibition against the forcible return of IDPs to places of danger. Or, although there may be a general norm covering essential medical care, the special needs of internally displaced women in the areas of reproductive and psychological health care would need to be spelled out. As for clear gaps in the law, the legal team found that in a number of instances the law is silent. For example, there exists no explicit norm on the restitution of property lost as a consequence of displacement during conflict or on the need for personal identification and documentation [of IDPs]. In such cases, the team pointed out, rights would have to be inferred from other provisions of law.

* * *

There were three main reasons for the decision to develop the Guiding Principles. First, there was no support from governments for a convention. The subject of internal displacement was still too sensitive. * * *

Second, time was a factor. Treaty making could take decades, whereas there was urgent need for a document *now* to address the emergency needs of IDPs. It bears underscoring that humanitarian organizations in the field that had increasingly become involved in helping IDPs needed a clear and concise document to guide their work.

Third, sufficient international law applicable to internally displaced persons already existed. What was required was to bring together the myriad of provisions now dispersed in a large number of instruments and to tailor them to the specific needs of the internally displaced.

*Development and Content of the Principles*

* * *

The principles, thirty in number, provide guidance to all actors that deal with the internally displaced, whether governments, insurgent groups, international organizations, or NGOs. They apply to all phases of displacement. They offer standards for protection *against* arbitrary displacement, innovatively enunciating a right *not* to be arbitrarily displaced. They set forth standards for protection during displacement, tailoring the full range of civil, political, economic, social, and cultural rights to the specific needs of IDPs. Finally, they offer standards for protection during return, resettlement, and reintegration. In short, they provide a comprehensive international minimum standard for the treatment of IDPs. The principles define IDPs as:

> Persons who have been forced or obliged to flee or to leave their homes or places of habitual residence in particular as a result of, or in order to avoid the effects of, armed conflict, situations of generalized violence, violations of human rights or natural or human-made disasters, and who have not crossed an internationally recognized state border.

The two crucial features are: being coerced to move and remaining within one's national borders. Economic migrants were not included because the element of coercion was not considered to be so clear. However, those uprooted by floods, earthquakes, famine, or nuclear plant eruptions, or forced by development projects to relocate, were included in addition to the more traditionally accepted IDPs—those uprooted by conflict and human rights violations. Not all humanitarian or human rights groups wanted to include these other groups, preferring to limit the IDP definition to those subject to persecution or who would be considered refugees if they crossed a border. But the overriding opinion was that persons uprooted by natural and human-made disasters or development projects are also displaced and in need of attention; moreover, they can be neglected or discriminated against by their governments on political or ethnic grounds or have their human rights violated in other ways.

If there can be said to be a philosophical foundation behind the principles, it is the concept of sovereignty as a form of responsibility, developed by Deng and other scholars. Besides positing primary responsibility for the welfare and safety of IDPs with their governments, the concept also considers it an obligation of the international community to provide humanitarian assistance and protection to IDPs when the governments concerned are unable to fulfill their responsibilities. In such an instance, governments are supposed to request and accept outside offers of aid. If they refuse or deliberately obstruct access and put large numbers of persons at risk, the international community, under this concept, has a right—and even a responsibility—to step in and assert its concern.

\* \* \*

## Notes and Questions

1.  The Guiding Principles have no enforcement provisions. How will they be effective? Do the Guiding Principles provide a tool that the displaced themselves can use? Will they be able to make their claims to courts? To international agencies? To the press?

A recent report of UNHCR explains some uses to which the Guiding Principles have been put:

> Over the past five years, governments have begun to make the Guiding Principles a basis for their policies and laws on internal displacement. Angola based its 2001 law relating to the resettlement of displaced persons on the principles, and Peru used them when developing its 2004 law providing benefits to the internally displaced. Colombia's Constitutional Court based three decisions in support of aid to the displaced on the principles, and Georgia amended its laws and improved its practices on the voting rights of internally displaced persons to conform to them. Burundi, the Philippines, Sri Lanka and Uganda have also based national policies on the principles, and Liberia's president has announced his government's adoption of them.
>
> Regional inter-governmental bodies use the Guiding Principles as a monitoring tool when measuring conditions on the ground and as a framework for their programmes and activities. UN agencies and NGOs provide training in the principles, while local groups in different countries have produced handbooks and illustrated materials to adapt them to conditions on the ground. In Sri Lanka, the Consortium of Humanitarian Agencies published a *Toolkit* based on the principles in three national languages, while lawyers in the South Caucasus and the Russian Federation have evaluated the laws of their countries in terms of the principles. To date, the Guiding Principles have been translated into more than 40 languages.

Applying the Guiding Principles, UNHCR, The State of the World's Refugees 2006: Human Displacement in the New Millennium 165.

2. To the extent that UN and regional agencies may attempt to monitor compliance with the Guiding Principles, what obstacles may they face in gaining access to the groups and in their ability to investigate their treatment?

3. For further discussions of international efforts to establish a firmer legal foundation for assistance to growing numbers of individuals displaced within their own countries by armed conflict or natural disaster, *see* Walter Kälin, Guiding Principles on Internal Displacement: Annotations (2000); R. Cohen & F. Deng, Masses in Flight: The Global Crises of Internal Displacement (1998); Plender, *The Legal Basis of International Jurisdiction to Act with Regard to the Internally Displaced*, 6 Int'l J.Ref.L. 345 (1994); *Comprehensive study on the human rights issues related to internally displaced persons,* UN Doc. E/CN.4/1993/35 (1993).

---

The publication of the Guiding Principles on Internal Displacement in 1998 did not end the discussion. Vigorous debate ensued within the international community about the legitimacy of the principles, their non-binding nature, their intrusion into state sovereignty. There was also a debate about the operational realities, with Ambassador Richard C. Holbrooke, U.S. Representative to the United Nations, strongly voicing the belief that refugees and internally displaced persons should receive equal treatment as forced migrants from an expanded UNHCR. We excerpt his speech to the U.N. Security Council in January 2000 and then provide an alternative view from a leading refugee law scholar.

* * * [T]wo-thirds of the refugees in the world do not fall under the official purview of the UNHCR. We call them IDPs. In our Mission, across the street, we have tried to figure out ways to abolish this odious terminology. The very use of initials to refer to people is not, in itself, healthy. * * * [T]hese are people, and to a person who has been driven from his or her home by conflict, there is no difference between being a refugee or an IDP. In terms of what has happened to them, they are equally victims but they are treated differently.

Now I recognize that the distinction raises complex legal issues of international sovereignty; it raises enormous questions of resource allocation; and it has far-ranging bureaucratic implications as well. * * * But let us remember that individual lives are at stake. What is an IDP? What is a refugee? They do not care. They are all homeless, and we must address this problem. We need to acknowledge, frankly, that there is no real difference to the victims involved and then we need to call upon the world body and all its specialized agencies and its Member States to figure out what to do with the problem that was not fully foreseen when the *Charter of the UN* was formed and when the UNHCR drew its mandate.

For example, Francis Deng is responsible to the Human Rights Commission in Geneva. I applaud the Human Rights

Commission, but in my view he should be working directly with and for the UNHCR * * * * I think that responsibility for IDPs should be fixed in a single bureaucratic entity.

When my colleagues and I were in Angola last month, we saw that 90 percent of refugees were classified as IDPs and that, for the most part, they were out of the reach of the international community's assistance. To the extent they had support, it tended to be from * * * the World Food Program. The WFP is a fine organization, but the best organization operating in the world, the best one with the longest track record and the best infrastructure is the UNHCR.

Some of the NGOs in the room have told me how sometimes the UNHCR does not support efforts even when it has surplus capacity of motor vehicles or personnel either because of bureaucratic restrictions, restrictions of the host government, and occasionally, I regret to say, inadequate relationships between the agencies involved. The * * * UNHCR [is] our last, best hope for dealing with these problems. * * *

Amb. Richard C. Holbrooke, Statement in the Security Council on Promoting Peace and Security: Humanitarian Assistance to Refugees in Africa (January 13, 2000), available at http://www.un.int/usa/00_006.htm.

## GUY GOODWIN GILL, UNHCR AND INTERNAL DISPLACEMENT: STEPPING INTO A LEGAL AND POLITICAL MINEFIELD

2000 World Refugee Survey, pp. 26–31.

* * *

[T]here are practical, political, and principled reasons for distancing UNHCR from the problems of the internally displaced. * * * It is the very status of the refugee as refugee in international law that opens the statutory, legal door to the protection of his or her rights. In a society of independent, sovereign nation states, internationally relevant judicial facts, such as cross-border movement, still retain their importance. * * *

And other consequences will likely flow. For one, the distinctive quality enjoyed by the refugee as a subject entitled to international protection will be erased. Rights, duties, and responsibilities will be eradicated, and the refugee left, once more, unprotected in an era of uncontrolled and uncontrollable discretion.

* * *

Although the protection of the internally displaced has often been highlighted as a major aspect of UNHCR's work in recent years, its overall success in this area is highly doubtful. UNHCR has no legal basis to protect internally displaced people, but must * * * proceed by consent of the sovereign state and any *de facto* fighting force exercising control over the territory in question. And negotiating is frequently equivalent to "negotiating away," whether it be 20 percent of relief supplies so that the warring parties can continue the conflict, or a 30 percent tax on the wages of local humanitarian workers. And consent given can easily be withdrawn.

As soon as UNHCR steps outside its recognized legal role, as soon as it accepts mandates from others, such as the UN secretary-general, it abandons any claim to autonomy. It steps into the political minefield, replete with conflicts of interest, and must pay the political price; so too, unfortunately, must its principal constituency.

UNHCR has considerable skills and experience in the international protection of refugees, but these cannot be automatically transferred to the internally displaced. The language of similar experience is misleading, and should not disguise essential differences, namely:

- Internal displacement is still a phenomenon occurring within the territorial jurisdiction of a sovereign state, and states still assert their sovereignty.

- External displacement is, by definition, international; it steps at once beyond the limiting and restrictive lines of sovereignty and consent, and into the domain of international law.

- The domain of international law contains, in regard to refugees,

    —clear rules,

    —a functional protection agency,

    —a regime, and

    —a framework of individual rights.

This is not to say that the internally displaced have no call on the international community; only that this should not be met at the price of the international protection of refugees. After all, there is enough to be done there.

\* \* \*

Ironically, the provision of relief is quite likely to be more effective, more efficient, if left primarily in the hands of those who do not have a potentially incompatible client-specific mandate.

Perhaps something can be learned from the experiences of the International Committee of the Red Cross (ICRC) during the Second World War. Should it have spoken out about the conditions in the concentration camps, and about the treatment of the Jews? In his 1988 work, *Une mission impossible?*, Jean Claude Favez tries to understand the lamentably inadequate response of this great humanitarian organization to the most terrible challenge in its history.

He notes the legal constraints afflicting the ICRC at the time, that the Jews of Europe were not among the class of protected persons within the mandate of the Red Cross, whose primary concern was with the war wounded and with prisoners of war. To this were added "national constraints," and the fact that the ICRC had to rely on a national Red

Cross organization effectively taken over by the SS. Finally, there were practical constraints, among them what he characterizes as the rule—the "golden rule"—that priority should be given everywhere to immediate relief rather than the formulation of general principles.

\* \* \*

Of course, there were exceptions, and many thousands of Jews owed their survival to the ICRC and to the tireless efforts of many individual delegates throughout Europe. But the institutional lessons are compelling; translating them to the UNHCR context, they might be framed as follows:

- Excessive donor "dependency" can be as debilitating as totalitarianism.

- A clear mandate gives strength.

- For an agency charged with protection, principles have their place.

\* \* \*

UNHCR's "interest" in the internally displaced should only be functional at most, incidental to programs for its primary constituency, refugees. In principle, the protection of the internally displaced, while still the responsibility of the territorial state, should be entrusted, as is now often the case, to the International Committee of the Red Cross, complemented as appropriate by the distinctive role of the United Nations High Commissioner for Human Rights, and/or by a competent regional organization such as the Organization for Security and Cooperation in Europe; the necessary human and financial resources will need to be provided.

### Notes and Questions

1. Which argument do you find more persuasive? Should the legal distinctions between internally displaced persons and refugees be erased? Should there be one international agency that is in charge of them all?

2. Various relief, assistance and humanitarian organizations within the UN system—including UNHCR, WHO, UNICEF, UNDP, WFP—have begun to work together, along with some NGOs, on internal displacement situations. They have established a collaborative response, piloting this "clusters" approach to bring assistance and protection to IDPs in certain countries. A recent UNHCR paper describes and assesses the refugee agency's role in these efforts:

> During the 36th meeting of the Standing Committee from 26–28 June 2006, member States reaffirmed their strong support for UNHCR's expanded role in support of the interagency response to internal displacement situations. They encouraged the Office to continue to strengthen its leadership role for IDPs in conflict situations in the areas of protection, camp coordination/camp man-

agement, and emergency shelter. Member States recognized however, that UNHCR needed to invest additional resources and time to fulfil these new responsibilities.

They pledged their support both politically and financially as witnessed by the much appreciated sizeable cash contributions both to the Global Cluster Appeal as well as to the country operations.

Recognizing the greater responsibility associated with this new role and the time required to be fully operational on these new responsibilities, member States requested UNHCR to set a road map with clear objectives, tangible activities and impact indicators that would be used in the coming months and years to measure UNHCR's performance in this field. Some countries also noted that an institutional shift in focus and skill set would be required to successfully fulfil this responsibility, and requested information about plans to mainstream the IDP leadership role in programming and training. Other Members requested information on UNHCR's activities to expand its operational capacity, including the development of emergency rosters. Finally, recognizing the need to maintain the dialogue between member States and the Office on progress made on this expanded role, the Standing Committee requested frequent updates on the successes and challenges of UNHCR's IDP operations in both the cluster pilot countries and in its other IDP operations.

\* \* \*

Generally speaking UNHCR is successfully assuming its leadership role under the cluster approach in the four pilot countries, and most recently in Lebanon and Côte d'Ivoire. However, to judge its performance more systematically, the Office will need to use measurable impact and performance indicators which would be agreed upon with the country operations. \* \* \*

UNHCR's success in IDP operations depends on its ability to develop strong links and partnerships with many humanitarian actors. Admittedly, there have and continue to be challenges as the organization adapts towards developing more strategic partnerships which involve greater consultation and defining realistically UNHCR's added value and capacity to deliver. Even so, stronger relationships with other protection partners are increasingly operational at both headquarters and field levels. In both cluster and non-cluster pilot countries, UNHCR is working collaboratively with governments, NGOs, the Red Cross/Red Crescent Movement, and UN agencies. UNHCR's expertise in protection (particularly with regard to protection monitoring and return planning), emergency shelter, and camp coordination/camp management greatly contribute to the overall strategic humanitarian action plans and relief efforts that benefit hundreds of thousands of IDPs. However, UNHCR must continue to identify and build relationships with partners with implementing capacity to maximize the impact of UNHCR's contributions.

UNHCR's Expanded Role in Support of the Inter-agency Response to Internal Displacement Situations (UNHCR Informal Consultative Meeting, Sept. 12, 2006).

## SECTION E.  A CONCLUDING COMMENT
## ON FORCED MIGRATION

Let us define a (hypothetical) Principle on Forced Migration:

No person should be compelled to leave his or her place of habitual residence. Any person so compelled who can not avail him or herself of the protection and assistance of his or her state of habitual residence should receive international protection and assistance. This principle applies whether or not the person is outside his or her state of habitual residence.

To what extent does the Principle describe current domestic and international legal norms or current domestic or international practices? To what extent does the Principle reach beyond protection afforded to "refugees"? Is such a Principle practical? Are there mechanisms—extant or imaginable—for its effective implementation? If you think the hypothetical principle is too broad, can you propose an alternative Principle on Forced Migration?

Do existing legal norms and state practices implicitly define a "law of forced migration"?

*

# Index

†